A Dictionary of
Marxist Thought

SECOND EDITION

A Dictionary of
Marxist Thought

SECOND EDITION

Edited by

Tom Bottomore

Editorial Board

Laurence Harris
V. G. Kiernan
Ralph Miliband

Blackwell
Publishing

BLACKWELL PUBLISHING
350 Main Street, Malden, MA 02148-5020, USA
108 Cowley Road, Oxford OX4 1JF, UK
550 Swanston Street, Carlton, Victoria 3053, Australia

First published 1983
First published in paperback 1985
Second revised edition 1991
Reprinted in paperback 1994, 1995, 1996, 1997, 1998, 1999, 2001 (twice), 2003, 2005

Library of Congress Cataloging-in-Publication Data

A Dictionary of Marxist thought/edited by Tom Bottomore—2nd ed.
Includes bibliographical references and index.
ISBN 0–631–16481–2 — ISBN 0–631–18082–6 (pbk)
1. Communism–Dictionaries. 2. Socialism–Dictionaries.
I. Bottomore, T. B.
HX17.D5   1991
91–17658   335.4′03—dc20
                                            CIP

A catalogue record for this title is available from the British Library.

Set in 8 on 10 pt Sabon
by Hope Services (Abingdon) Ltd
Printed and bound in the United Kingdom
by MPG Books Ltd, Bodmin, Cornwall

The publisher's policy is to use permanent paper from mills that operate a sustainable
forestry policy, and which has been manufactured from pulp processed using
acid-free and elementary chlorine-free practices. Furthermore, the publisher ensures
that the text paper and cover board used have met acceptable environmental
accreditation standards.

For further information on
Blackwell Publishing, visit our website:
www.blackwellpublishing.com

Contents

Preface

We wish to thank the contributors old and new for the care and thought which they have devoted to their entries, and for their responsiveness to editorial suggestions. We should also like to thank the staff of Blackwell Publishers for their very efficient organization and valuable advice during the preparation of this work. In the early stages of planning the dictionary we were also greatly helped by Leszek Kolakowski.

Since the first edition of this Dictionary was published several of those who wrote entries for it have died, and we should like to pay tribute here to the very great contribution they made, including in some cases substantial revision of their existing entries and preparing new ones: Tamara Deutscher, Stanley Diamond, Moses Finley, Eleanor Burke Leacock, Geoffrey Ostergaard, Eugene Schulkind.

The Editors

Entries New to the Second Edition

agrarian question
analytical Marxism
Annales school
British Marxist historians
Capital
cinema and television
collectivization
colonial liberation movements
Communist Manifesto
Condition of the Working Class in England
crisis in socialist society
De Leon, Daniel
democratic centralism
dependency theory
Dietzgen, Joseph
Economic and Philosophical Manuscripts
economic planning
Eisenstein, Sergei
Finance Capital
Fromm, Erich
gender
German Ideology
Grundrisse
Habermas, Jürgen

History and Class Consciousness
justice
Kalecki, Michał
Lange, Oskar
liberation theology
long waves
market socialism
Marxism in Africa
Marxism in India
Marxism in Latin America
modernism and postmodernism
Morris, William
Origin of the Family, Private Property and the State
peasantry
petty commodity production
Poulantzas, Nicos
Prison Notebooks
regulation
Revolution Betrayed, The
Robinson, Joan
rural class structure
State and Revolution
Veblen, Thorstein
Williams, Raymond
world-system

Contributors

Hamza Alavi
University of Manchester

Andrew Arato
*New School for Social Research,
New York*

Christopher J. Arthur
Brighton

Michèle Barrett
City University, London

Lee Baxandall
Oshkosh, Wisconsin

Ted Benton
University of Essex

Henry Bernstein
*Institute for Development Policy
and Management,
University of Manchester*

Roy Bhaskar
Linacre College, Oxford

Michael Billig
University of Loughborough

Tom Bottomore
*Professor Emeritus,
University of Sussex*

Chris Bramall
Sidney Sussex College, Cambridge

W. Brus
St Antony's College, Oxford

Peter Burke
Emmanuel College, Cambridge

T. J. Byres
*School of Oriental and African Studies,
University of London*

Julius Carlebach
*Hochschule für Jüdische Studien,
Heidelberg*

Terrell Carver
University of Bristol

David Coates
University of Leeds

Ian Cummins
Monash University

Basil Davidson
*Centre of West African Studies,
University of Birmingham*

R. W. Davies
University of Birmingham

Meghnad Desai
London School of Economics

Tamara Deutscher

Pat Devine
University of Manchester

Stanley Diamond

Elizabeth Dore
Portsmouth Polytechnic

Gary A. Dymski
University of California, Riverside

Roy Edgley
Brighton

Ferenc Fehér
New School for Social Research,
New York

Zsuzsa Ferge
Institute of Sociology and
Social Policy,
Eötvos Loránd University, Budapest

Iring Fetscher
University of Frankfurt

Ben Fine
Birkbeck College, University of
London

Moses Finley

Milton Fisk
Indiana University

Duncan Foley
Barnard College, Columbia
University

Norman Geras
University of Manchester

Israel Getzler
Hebrew University of Jerusalem

Paolo Giussani
Milan

Patrick Goode
Thames Polytechnic, London

David Greenberg
New York University

G. C. Harcourt
Jesus College, Cambridge

Neil Harding
University College of Swansea

Laurence Harris
School of Oriental and African Studies,
University of London

David Harvey
St Peter's College, Oxford

András Hegedüs
Budapest

David Held
Open University

Björn Hettne
Peace and Development
Research Institute,
University of Gothenburg

R. H. Hilton
University of Birmingham

Susan Himmelweit
Open University

Robert J. Holton
Flinders University of South Australia

Richard Hyman
University of Warwick

Russell Jacoby
Los Angeles

Jeremy Jennings
University College of Swansea

Bob Jessop
Univerity of Lancaster

Monty Johnstone
London

Eugene Kamenka
Australian National University

Naomi Katz
San Francisco State University

Cristóbal Kay
Institute of Social Studies,
The Hague

Harvey J. Kaye
University of Wisconsin-Green Bay

János Kelemen
Accademia d'Ungheria, Rome

David Kemnitzer
San Francisco State University

V. G. Kiernan
Professor Emeritus,
University of Edinburgh

Gavin Kitching
University of New South Wales

Philip L. Kohl
Wellesley College, Massachusetts

Tadeusz Kowalik
Polish Academy of Science, Warsaw

David Lane
Emmanuel College, Cambridge

Jorge Larrain
University of Birmingham

Eleanor Burke Leacock

Alain Lipietz
Centre d'Études Prospectives
d'Économie Mathématique
Appliquées à la Planification, Paris

Steven Lukes
European University Institute,
Florence

Frank McHugh
Christian Social Ethics Research Unit,
St John's Seminary, Guildford

Stuart Macintyre
University of Melbourne

David McLellan
University of Kent

Ernest Mandel
Vrije Universiteit Brussel

Mihailo Marković
University of Belgrade

István Mészáros
London

Ralph Miliband
London and Graduate School, City
University of New York

Simon Mohun
Queen Mary and Westfield College,
University of London

Geoffrey Nowell-Smith
London

G. Ostergaard

William Outhwaite
University of Sussex

Prabhat Patnaik
Jawaharlal Nehru University,
New Delhi

Brian Pearce
New Barnet, Herts.

Gajo Petrović
University of Zagreb

Tony Pinkney
University of Lancaster

Katalin Radics
Institute of Linguistics, Hungarian
Academy of Sciences

John Rex
University of Warwick

Julian Roberts
Architectural Association School of
Architecture

George Ross
Harvard University

Anne Showstack Sassoon
Kingston Polytechnic, Surrey

Stuart R. Schram
Fairbank Center for East Asian
Research, Harvard University

Eugene Schulkind

Anwar Shaikh
New School for Social Research,
New York

William H. Shaw
Tennessee State University

Roger Simon
Richmond, Surrey

Gareth Stedman Jones
King's College, Cambridge

Paul Sweezy
New York

John G. Taylor
South Bank Polytechnic, London

Richard Taylor
University College of Swansea

Jan Toporowski
South Bank Polytechnic, London

Bryan S. Turner
University of Essex

Immanuel Wallerstein
*State University of New York,
Binghamton*

John Weeks
*Centre for Development Studies,
School of Oriental and African
Studies, University of London*

Janet Wolff
University of Leeds

Stephen Yeo
Ruskin College, Oxford

Robert M. Young
London

Editors' Introduction

A hundred years after Marx's death the ideas which he launched upon the world have come to constitute one of the most lively and influential currents of modern thought, acquaintance with which is indispensable for all who work in the social sciences or are engaged in political movements. Yet it is equally clear that these ideas have acquired none of the fixity of a closed and completed system, but are still actively evolving; and in the course of this century they have assumed a great variety of forms. This has occurred not only by extension into new fields of enquiry, but also through an internal differentiation, in response on one side to critical judgements and new intellectual movements, and on the other to changing social and political circumstances.

In the period since the publication of the first edition, Marxist ideas have perhaps been more diversely interpreted and more widely challenged than at any time since the great controversies of the early part of the century. In this new edition we have taken account of these changes by including many new entries, and substantial additions to, or revisions of, existing entries, in which our contributors reconsider the Marxist theory of history, the post-war development of capitalism, the problems that have beset socialist societies, and in particular such contentious issues as economic planning and market socialism.

This new edition therefore provides a still more comprehensive and up-to-date guide to the basic concepts of Marxism, taking account of different interpretations and criticisms, and to the individuals and schools of thought whose work has contributed to forming the body of Marxist ideas since Marx's day. It is designed to be of use to the many students and teachers in higher education who encounter Marxist conceptions in the course of their own studies, and also to the large number of general readers who want to be informed about a theory and doctrine that has played, and continues to play, a major part in shaping institutions and modes of action in the present-day world. The entries are presented in such a manner as to be accessible to the non-specialist reader, so far as the nature of the various subjects allows; but there are some cases, more particularly in economics and philosophy, where technical terms are unavoidable and some previous knowledge is assumed.

Each entry is intended to be complete in itself, but where it is desirable, for a fuller understanding of a particular concept, problem or interpretation, to consult other entries, cross-references to these entries are printed in small capitals in the text. In this new edition some major Marxist texts now have separate entries devoted to them; these texts are indicated in the list of new entries. There is also a general index at the end of the volume through which the reader will be able to trace all references to a specific individual or subject. Each entry is followed by suggestions for further reading, and all works referred to there, as well as in the text, are listed with full publication details in the general bibliography which has itself been fully updated and revised. There is also a separate bibliography of the writings of Marx and Engels mentioned in the text (where they are usually cited by a short title), and this includes, in addition to full publication details of individual works, information about collected editions of their works.

Tom Bottomore   *V. G. Kiernan*

Laurence Harris   *Ralph Miliband*

A

abstract labour   Since a COMMODITY is both a USE VALUE and a VALUE, the labour which produces the commodity has a dual character. First, any act of labouring is 'productive activity of a definite kind, carried on with a definite aim' (*Capital* I, ch. 1); so considered, it is 'useful labour' or 'concrete labour', and its product is a use value. This aspect of labouring activity 'is a condition of human existence which is independent of all forms of society; it is an eternal natural necessity which mediates the metabolism between man and nature, and therefore human life itself' (ibid.). Secondly, any act of labouring can be considered apart from its specific characteristics, as purely the expenditure of human LABOUR POWER, 'human labour pure and simple, the expenditure of human labour in general' (ibid.). The expenditure of human labour considered in this aspect creates value, and is called 'abstract labour'. Concrete labour and abstract labour are not different activities, they are the same activity considered in its different aspects. Marx summarizes as follows:

> On the one hand, all labour is an expenditure of human labour-power, in the physiological sense, and it is in this quality of being equal, or abstract, human labour that it forms the value of commodities. On the other hand, all labour is an expenditure of human labour-power in a particular form and with a definite aim, and it is in this quality of being concrete useful labour that it produces use-values. (Ibid.)

And he emphasizes that 'this point is crucial to an understanding of political economy' which he was the first to elucidate and elaborate (ibid.).

However, there is considerable controversy within Marxism concerning the process of abstraction whereby Marx arrives at the nature of value-creating labour. While Marx talks of the physiological expenditure of 'human brains, muscles, nerves, hands etc.' (ibid.), whose

measurement in units of time suggests that value can be interpreted as an embodied labour coefficient, he also insists that 'not an atom of matter enters into the objectivity of commodities as values' and emphasizes that 'commodities possess an objective character as values only in so far as they are all expressions of an identical social substance, human labour . . . their objective character as values is therefore purely social' (ibid.).

What Marx means here is that it is *only* through the exchange of commodities that the private labour which produced them is rendered social (this is one of the peculiarities of the equivalent form of value); the equalization of labour as abstract labour *only* occurs through the exchange of the products of that labour. On the face of it, these two views are not readily compatible.

Consider first the 'physiological' interpretation. With a series of quotations from Marx to support his view, Steedman writes:

> It being understood then that the object of discussion is a capitalist, commodity producing economy, 'co-ordinated' through money flows in markets, and that only socially-necessary, *abstract social* labour, of average skill and intensity is referred to, it may be said that the 'magnitude of value' is a quantity of embodied labour time. That this statement acccurately reflects Marx's position cannot be altered by pointing to the fact that Marx was much concerned with the 'form of value', with the nature of 'abstract social' labour and with the 'universal equivalent'. (1977, p. 211)

Shaikh's argument is of the same genus. He argues that the concept of abstract labour is not a mental generalization, but the reflection in thought of a real social process: the LABOUR PROCESS, which in capitalism is permeated throughout by commodity relations. Since 'abstract labour is the property acquired by human labour when it is directed towards the production of commodities' (Shaikh 1981, p. 273), then labour in commodity production 'is both concrete and abstract from the very outset' (ibid. p. 274). Again, the implication is that embodied-labour coefficients can be calculated from examination of the capitalist production process alone and that this is what is meant by value. Further, Shaikh distinguishes the actual total labour time expended under given production conditions, which defines the total value of the product, the unit social value of the commodity, and hence its regulating price; and the total labour time that is required to satisfy expressed social need, which specifies the relationship between the regulating price and the market (ibid. pp. 276–8; see also SOCIALLY NECESSARY LABOUR).

Critics of this position argue that it has more in common with Ricardo's labour theory of value than with Marx's (see RICARDO AND MARX.) To consider value simply as embodied labour certainly renders heterogeneous labour commensurable, and hence can be used as a means of aggregation, but there is then nothing to restrict the use of the value category to capitalist society. Marx comments: 'If we say that, as values, commodities are simply congealed quantities of human labour, our analysis reduces them, it is true, to the level of abstract value, but does not give them a form of value distinct from their natural forms' (*Capital* I, ch. 1).

The abstraction which renders embodied labour abstract labour is a social abstraction, a real social process quite specific to capitalism. Abstract labour is not a way of reducing heterogeneous labours to the common dimension of time, via the commodity relations of the labour process, but has a real existence in the reality of EXCHANGE. Rubin (*1973*, ch. 14) argues that exchange here must be considered not in its specific meaning as a particular phase of the reproductive circuit of capital, but more generally as a form of the production process itself. And it is only in the exchange process that heterogeneous concrete labours are rendered abstract and homogeneous, that private labour is revealed as social labour. It is the market which does this; and so there can be no *a priori* determination of abstract labour. Colletti goes further and argues that not only does the abstraction emerge out of the reality of exchange, but also that abstract labour is alienated labour: exchange provides the moment of social unity in the form of an abstract equalization or reification of labour power in which human subjectivity is expropriated. (Colletti 1972, p. 87. For a dissenting view see Arthur 1979.)

The debate over the nature of abstract labour is at the heart of most of the controversies in Marxist economics (Himmelweit and Mohun 1981). In general, the embodied labour school focuses on the derivation of prices from labour times, and tends to see emphasis on dialectics and method as misplaced and metaphysical. The abstract labour school tends to focus on the ways in which Marx used the results of his confrontation with Hegel to break with Ricardian political economy and to determine a dialectical resolution of the difficulties in a formal logic approach to the derivation of prices. (See also HEGEL AND MARX; PRICE OF PRODUCTION AND THE TRANSFORMATION PROBLEM.)

Reading

Arthur, Chris 1979: 'Dialectics and Labour'. In John Mepham and David-Hillel Ruben, eds *Issues in Marxist Philosophy*, vol. 1.

Colletti, Lucio 1972: *From Rousseau to Lenin*.

Elson, Diane 1979: 'The Value Theory of Labour'. In *Value: The Representation of Labour in Capitalism*.

Himmelweit, Susan and Mohun, Simon 1981: 'Real Abstraction and Anomalous Assumptions'. In Ian Steedman *et al. The Value Controversy*.

Rubin, I. I. 1928 (*1973*): *Essays on Marx's Theory of Value*.

Shaikh, Anwar 1981: 'The Poverty of Algebra'. In Ian Steedman *et al. The Value Controversy*.

Steedman, Ian 1977: *Marx After Sraffa*.

Weeks, John 1981: *Capital and Exploitation*.

SIMON MOHUN

accumulation 'Accumulate, accumulate! That is Moses and the prophets!' (*Capital* I, ch. 24, sect. 3). With these words Marx reveals what in his analysis is the most important imperative or driving force of bourgeois society. Despite the religious metaphor Marx does not see accumulation as the result of a rising Protestant ethic of thrift, as is suggested by Weber. Nor is accumulation the result of abstinence on the part of individuals seeking to satisfy a subjective preference for future CONSUMPTION at the expense of consumption in the present, as is argued by neoclassical bourgeois economics based on utility theory. For Marx, it is of the essence of CAPITAL that it must be accumulated, independent of the subjective preferences or religious beliefs of individual capitalists.

The coercion on *individual* capitalists to accumulate operates through the mechanism of COMPETITION. Because capital is self-expanding VALUE, its value must at least be preserved. Because of competition the mere preservation of capital is impossible unless it is, in addition, expanded. At different stages of development of capitalist production, the mechanism of competition operates in different ways. Initially, accumulation takes place through the transformation of the relations of production (see PRIMITIVE ACCUMULATION) to create wage labour with methods of production remaining the same. For underdeveloped methods of production, inherited and adapted from precapitalist societies, accumulation is necessary to guarantee an expansion of the workforce, to provide it with raw materials and allow for economies of scale in the supervision of labour. For MANUFACTURE, accumulation is necessary to permit the employment of labour in the appropriate proportions in the COOPERATION and DIVISION OF LABOUR. For MACHINERY AND MACHINOFACTURE, accumulation provides for the necessary fixed capital and expanded use of raw materials and labour associated with it.

Accumulation is not, however, simply a relationship between the production and capitalization of SURPLUS VALUE. It is also a relationship of reproduction. For the CIRCULATION of capital, this is examined by Marx in *Capital* II, and to a lesser extent in *Capital* I. Reproduction is examined as embodying simple reproduction in which value and surplus value relations remain unchanged, as the basis for reproduction on an expanded scale for which the ORGANIC COMPOSITION OF CAPITAL may or may not rise. In each case, a definite proportion must be established in value and in USE VALUE terms between sectors of the economy and this is examined in the REPRODUCTION SCHEMA.

In *Capital* III, Marx analyses accumulation from the perspective of the DISTRIBUTION (and redistribution) of surplus value and capital. For early stages of development, the basis for accumulation is in the concentration of capital. At later stages of development, centralization (see CENTRALIZATION AND CONCENTRATION OF CAPITAL) is the dominant method by which the use of ever-increasing sizes of capital is organized. This presupposes an advanced CREDIT system. While the object of accumulation is productivity increase, the mechanism of achieving it is through access to credit. Consequently a divergence between the accumulation of capital in production and of capital in the financial system is created. This is the basis of fictitious capital and can lead to the intensification of ECONOMIC CRISES when accumulation fails to overcome the obstacles confronting the continuing expansion of the production of surplus value. In addition, the centralization of capital and the uneven pace of accumulation itself is to be associated with UNEVEN DEVELOPMENT of economies and societies. Accordingly the accumulation process is never simply an economic process but also involves the general development of social relations including, for example, COLONIALISM, IMPERIALISM, and changing roles for the state, as has always been stressed within the Marxist tradition.

For Marx, the accumulation process would never be a smooth, harmonious or simple expansion. At times it would be interrupted by crises and recessions. But the barriers to capital accumulation are never absolute but are contingent upon the intensification of the contradictions of capitalism which may be temporarily resolved to allow a new phase of expansion. The analysis of the development of such an intensification of contradictions is studied at the economic level by Marx in terms of the law of the tendency of the FALLING RATE OF PROFIT; this is itself associated with the law as such (based on the rising organic composition of capital) in contradiction with its counteracting influences. Here Marx distinguishes himself from Ricardo for whom a falling profitability depends upon declining productivity in agriculture, and from Smith for whom a limited extent of the market is crucial.

Marx devotes a considerable part of his economic analysis to the effects and forms of the accumulation process, drawing upon logical and empirical study. He develops laws for the LABOUR PROCESS itself, distinguishing between different stages of development of the methods of production. He also examines the effects of accumulation upon the working class. With machinery and machinofacture, other methods of production are coerced into extreme forms of EXPLOITATION to remain competitive. Machinery and machinofacture itself creates a RESERVE ARMY OF LABOUR and with it, the General Law of Capitalist Accumulation; namely, that a section of its stagnant layer increases in size as the officially pauperized. Otherwise the working class is subject to deskilling and the dictates of machinery even as it is increasingly organized in strength to resist accumulation through the formation of trade unions.

In the Marxist tradition the necessity of capital accumulation has been stressed by those who, like Lenin, argue that monopoly is the intensification of and not the negation of competition. Otherwise, writers have tended to emphasize one or more aspects of the accumulation process at the expense of a complex totality. Underconsumptionists stress a tendency to stagnation and have seen monopoly as displacing competition and the coercion to invest. Accordingly, deficiencies in market levels of demand become the focus of attention (as is the case for Keynesian theory). Luxemburg is most frequently cited in this context although she also emphasized the role of militarism. Baran and Sweezy are more recent representatives of this line of thought. Others in the neo-Ricardian or Sraffian tradition follow Marx by taking accumulation as axiomatic, but have left this unexplained by neglecting to incorporate a compulsion to accumulate within their analysis. Competition merely serves to equalize rates of profit and wages. Wages are then taken as the focus in determining the pace of accumulation which is threatened when wages rise and reduce profitability in the absence of productivity increase.

BEN FINE

Adler, Max Born 15 January 1873, Vienna; died 28 June 1937, Vienna. After studying jurisprudence at the University of Vienna Adler became a lawyer, but devoted most of his time to philosophical and sociological studies, later

teaching in extra-mural and university courses, and to his activities in the Austrian Social Democratic Party (SPÖ). In 1903, with Karl Renner and Rudolf Hilferding, he established a workers' school in Vienna; and in 1904, with Hilferding, he founded the *Marx-Studien*. From the time of the first world war he associated himself with the left wing of the SPÖ, strongly supported the workers' COUNCILS movement, and was a frequent contributor to *Der Klassenkampf* (the journal of the left wing of the German Social Democratic Party) from its first publication in 1927. Adler's principal contribution to Austro-Marxism was his attempt to establish the epistemological foundations of Marxism as a sociological theory, in which he was strongly influenced by neo-Kantian ideas in the philosophy of science, and by the positivism of Ernst Mach. But he also wrote widely on other subjects, and published interesting studies on revolution, the changes in the working class after the first world war, intellectuals, and law and the state (criticizing Kelsen's 'pure theory of law'). (See also AUSTRO-MARXISM.)

Reading
Adler, Max 1904: *Kausalität und Teleologie im Streite um die Wissenschaft.*
— 1914: *Der soziologische Sinn der Lehre von Karl Marx.*
— 1922: *Die Staatsauffassung des Marxismus. Ein Beitrag zur Unterscheidung von soziologischer und juristischer Methode.*
— 1930, 1932 (1964): *Soziologie des Marxismus,* vols. I and 2.
Bourdet, Yvon 1967: Introduction to Max Adler: *Démocratie et conseils ouvriers.*
Heintel, Peter 1967: *System und Ideologie. Der Austromarxismus im Spiegel der Philosophie Max Adlers.*
TOM BOTTOMORE

Adorno, Theodor Born 11 September 1903, Frankfurt; died 6 August 1969, Visp, Switzerland. From secondary school onwards Adorno developed interests in both philosophy and music. After receiving his doctorate in 1924 for a work on Husserl he studied composition and piano with Alban Berg and Eduard Steuermann in Vienna. In 1931 he began teaching philosophy at the University of Frankfurt, but with the advent of National Socialism he left Germany for England. Four years later he moved to the USA where he joined the Institute of Social Research (see FRANKFURT SCHOOL). In 1950 he returned with the Institute to Frankfurt, received a professorship and became a director of the Institute. While Adorno was one of the most prominent representatives of the Frankfurt School, his work was in a great many respects unique. At first glance some of his views on contemporary society seem bizarre. He suggested that we live in a world completely caught in a web spun by bureaucracy, administration and technocracy. The individual is a thing of the past: the age of concentrated capital, planning and mass culture has destroyed personal freedom. The capacity for critical thinking is dead and gone. Society and consciousness are 'totally reified': they appear to have the qualities of natural objects – to possess the status of given and unchanging forms (see REIFICATION).

But Adorno's thought cannot be fully comprehended if content is considered at the expense of form. Through 'provocative formulation', 'startling exaggeration' and 'dramatic emphasis', Adorno hoped to undermine ideologies and to create conditions through which the social world could once more become visible. His extensive use of the forms of essay and aphorism (best seen in *Minima Moralia*) reflects directly his concern to undermine what he saw as closed systems of thought (Hegelian idealism, for example, or orthodox Marxism) and to prevent an unreflected affirmation of society. He presented his ideas in ways which demand from the reader not mere contemplation but a critical effort of original reconstruction. He wanted to sustain and create capacities for independent criticism, and receptivity to the possibility of radical social change.

The scope of Adorno's work is astonishing. His collected works (now being published in a standard edition) amount to twenty-three large volumes (1970–). They include writings within, and across the boundaries of, philosophy, sociology, psychology, musicology and cultural criticism. Among his achievements are a provocative critique of all philosophical first principles and the development of a unique materialist and dialectical approach (1966), a major analysis (with Max Horkheimer) of the origin and nature of instrumental reason (1947), a philosophy of aesthetics (1970), and many original studies of culture, including analyses of such figures as Schönberg and Mahler (1949) and discussions of the modern entertainment industry (1964).

Reading
Adorno, Theodor 1949 (*1973*): *Philosophy of Modern Music.*
— 1951 (*1974*): *Minima Moralia.*
— 1955 (*1967*): *Prisms.*
— 1955 (*1967, 1968*): 'Sociology and Psychology'.
— 1964 (*1975*): 'Culture Industry Reconsidered'.
— 1966 (*1973*): *Negative Dialectics.*
— 1970–: *Gesammelte Schriften,* twenty-three vols.
Adorno, Theodor and Horkheimer, Max 1947 (*1972*): *Dialectic of Enlightenment.*
Adorno, Theodor *et al.* 1950: *The Authoritarian Personality.*
Buck-Morss, Susan 1977: *The Origin of Negative Dialectics.*
Habermas, Jürgen 1971: *Philosophisch-politische Profile.*
Rose, Gillian 1978: *The Melancholy Science.*

DAVID HELD

aesthetics There is no systematic theory of art to be found in the writings of Marx and Engels. Both writers had an early, and lifelong, interest in aesthetics and the arts, however, and their various brief discussions of such questions have formed the basis for numerous attempts, particularly in the last few decades, to produce a specifically Marxist aesthetics. The scattered statements of Marx and Engels on the arts have been collected in recently edited volumes, and referred to in books surveying the development of Marxist thought on aesthetics (Arvon 1973; Laing 1978). Not surprisingly, the fragmentary nature of these comments has produced a variety of emphases and positions in the work of later writers. This entry begins by briefly identifying some of these starting-points in the work of Marx and Engels and the way in which they have proved suggestive for various authors. It then looks at some central themes in the history of Marxist aesthetics and in recent work in this field.

Aesthetics in the work of Marx and Engels

A humanist aesthetics has been constructed from Marx's comments on the nature of art as creative labour, no different in quality from other (non-alienated) labour (Vázquez 1973). When Marx talks (*Capital* I, ch. 5, sect. 1) about the essentially human character of labour, comparing the architect and the bee, it is significant that the architect is invoked merely as an example of a human worker and not as a privileged category of artist. The notion that *all* non-alienated labour is creative, and hence intrinsically the same as artistic labour, provides the basis for a humanist aesthetics which successfully demystifies art by encouraging us to look at its historical development and separation from other activities (see ALIENATION).

A corollary of this view is the recognition that under capitalism art, like other forms of labour, increasingly becomes *alienated labour*. Art itself becomes a commodity, and the relations of artistic production reduce the position of the artist to one of an exploited labourer, producing surplus value. As Marx says (*Theories of Surplus Value*, pt. I, Appendix on 'Productive and Unproductive Labour') 'capitalist production is hostile to certain branches of spiritual production, for example, art and poetry'. He goes on to clarify the transformation of artistic labour under capitalism:

> Milton, who did the *Paradise Lost* for five pounds, was an *unproductive labourer*. On the other hand, the writer who turns out stuff for his publisher in factory style, is a *productive labourer*. . . . The literary proletarian of Leipzig, who fabricates books . . . under the direction of his publisher, is a *productive labourer*; for his product is from the outset subsumed under capital, and comes into being only for the purpose of increasing that capital. A singer who sells her song for her own account is an *unproductive labourer*. But the same singer commissioned by an entrepreneur to sing in order to make money for him is a *productive labourer*; for she produces capital.

This analysis of the distortion of artistic labour and of cultural products under capitalism is the premiss of later critiques of the 'culture industry' (for example by Adorno and Horkheimer) in which regulation by the law of value and the transformation of cultural products into commodities are said to reduce culture and the arts to the status of conformist,

repetitive, worthless things, whose function is to ensure political quietude. From Marx's general theory of commodity fetishism, the Marxist aesthetician, Lukács, developed a theory of art. In his major philosophical work, *History and Class Consciousness*, Lukács described the reified and fragmented nature of human life and experience under capitalism, analysing the impact of commodity fetishism on consciousness. Reified thought fails to perceive the totality of social and economic relations. The whole of the rest of Lukács's life was devoted to work on literature and aesthetics, in which the concept of 'totality' remains central. In Lukács's view, great literature is that which manages to penetrate beyond surface appearances, to perceive and expose the social totality, with all its contradictions.

Related to this is the theory of realism in art. In Lukács's opinion, good 'realist' literature portrays the totality through the use of 'typical' characters. This notion of realism receives support from other writings by the founders of Marxism, and in particular from two important letters written by Engels in the 1880s to aspiring women novelists. In these letters Engels firmly rejects so called 'tendency-literature' – literature which carries an explicit political message – in favour of the 'realist' text, out of which a correct political analysis may still emerge. 'The more the opinions of the author remain hidden, the better for the work of art. The realism I allude to may crop out even in spite of the author's opinions' (letter to Margaret Harkness, April 1888, in Marx and Engels *On Literature and Art* (1973), p. 116). He goes on to give the example of Balzac, who presents 'a most wonderfully realistic history of French "Society" ', despite the fact that he is a legitimist, whose 'sympathies are all with the class doomed to extinction'. The notion of realism, as the accurate portrayal of a society and its structural (class) conflicts, through the use of 'types', has been a central one in Marxist aesthetics.

More broadly, theories of the relationship between art or literature and the society in which it arises are indebted to Marx's formulation, in the 1859 Preface to the *Contribution to the Critique of Political Economy*, of the metaphor of base and superstructure, in which the aesthetic is explicitly cited as part of the superstructure, and as one of the 'ideological forms' in which class conflict is carried out. An early formulation of this view of art as the ideological expression of its age is found in the work of Plekhanov, for whom 'literature and art are the mirror of social life' (Arvon 1973, p. 12). At its crudest, such an account reduces art to nothing more than a reflection of social relations and class structure, automatically produced out of these material features. More complex accounts of art as ideology can be found in the work of more recent writers, for example, Goldmann.

Lastly, a rather different tradition in Marxist aesthetics emphasizes the revolutionary potential of art, and the question of commitment for the artist. As Engels's comments on realism make clear, he himself placed more importance on objective description than on overt partisanship. Nevertheless, Marxists have extracted a theory of radicalism in the arts from the writings of Marx and Engels. Lenin recommended that the writer should put his art at the service of the party (1905 (1970) pp. 22–7). (Those who have used this as evidence of his philistinism, however, ignore his other essays on art and literature, in particular his studies of Tolstoy (ibid. pp. 48–62).) From the Marxist notion that 'men make their own history', and that consciousness plays a crucial role in political transformation, aestheticians and artists from Mayakovsky, Brecht and Benjamin to present-day film-makers such as Godard and Pasolini have drawn a programme for revolutionary aesthetic practice.

Major themes in Marxist aesthetics

The concept of *realism* has remained central for a good deal of Marxist aesthetics, including its variants of socialist realism (whether official Soviet or Chinese versions, or those of Western Marxism; see Laing 1978 and Arvon 1973). It has also been the focus of two kinds of attack. The first goes back to an early debate between Lukács and Brecht (Bloch 1977; see Arvon 1973), in which Brecht argues that classical nineteenth-century realist literature is no longer appropriate for twentieth-century readers or audiences, and in particular that it has no power to radicalize. Clearly, the issue now becomes one of the evaluation of art or literature either in terms of its accurate, and critical, portrayal of society, or

primarily in terms of its revolutionary potential. The present-day version of this debate counterposes the avant-garde and the formally innovative to the more traditional narrative forms in art, literature and drama, proponents of the former arguing that the latter encourage passive and uncritical viewing, however radical the content of the work. The second attack on realism is related to this argument. It maintains that traditional realism, based as it is on a unified and coherent narrative, obscures real contradictions and oppositions in what it reflects, and projects an artificial unity in its representation of the world. The modernist text, on the other hand, is able to capture the contradictory, and to allow the hidden and the silenced to speak, by techniques of textual fragmentation and interruption. This tendency has been influenced by the work of Pierre Macherey, a collaborator of Althusser, and also by French semiologists such as Roland Barthes and Julia Kristeva.

The theory of *art as ideology* has been greatly refined and modified in recent work, particularly in Western Marxism, but also in East Germany and the USSR. Art, though still understood as ideological in an important sense, is not dismissed as mere reflection of social life, but is seen as expressing ideology in mediated form. In particular, the forms and codes of representation have been given their due, as central processes and conventions through which ideology is produced in literary and artistic form. The influence of STRUCTURALISM and semiotics has been important, as has the revival of interest in the work of the Russian Formalists (Bennett 1979). The institutions and practices of the arts are similarly increasingly regarded as essential to an understanding of the production and nature of texts – for example, the role of mediators such as publishers, galleries, critics, and so on. The latter, however, have so far only been taken seriously by a few writers, many of them Marxist sociologists of the arts or the media. Last, the role of audiences and readers has been recognized as partly constitutive of the work of art itself, often by authors citing in support Marx's comment in the introduction to the *Grundrisse* that 'consumption produces production'. Hermeneutic theory, semiotics, and reception-aesthetics – most of them not themselves within the Marxist tradition – have provided insights and tools for the analysis of the active role of recipients in producing cultural works and their meanings. That is to say, the 'meaning' of a work is no longer regarded as fixed, but is seen as dependent on its audience.

The question of *aesthetics and politics* continues to be central to contemporary Marxist aesthetics (Baxandall 1972). It is linked to the debates about realism discussed above. A revival of interest in the work of Benjamin has given rise to a focus on the possibility of revolutionizing the means of artistic production as a political act and strategy, rather than concentrating entirely on questions of radical content or even the form of cultural products. Another aspect of the present-day debate is an examination, for example by socialist playwrights, of the question whether radical ideas are most usefully expressed on television, with its potential mass audience as well as its scope for technical innovation and 'Brechtian' devices, or in the theatre, with its relative freedom from structural, professional, and, in the case of community or street theatre, ideological constraints, but its far smaller audiences. Finally, concomitant with the development of a feminist critique of Marxism itself (see FEMINISM), there has recently grown up a socialist-feminist cultural practice and theory, in which patriarchal themes in the arts and patriarchal relations in the theatre and other cultural institutions are subjected to criticism and reversal, in conjunction with a central emphasis on questions of class and ideology.

Last, the development of a Marxist aesthetics has thrown into question the notion of *aesthetic value*. The recognition that not only the arts themselves, but also the practices and institutions of art criticism, must be construed as ideological and interest-related, exposes the relative and arbitrary nature of the conferral of value on works of art. Until recently this was not thought by Marxist aestheticians to be a problem, and writers such as Lukács managed to preserve a 'great tradition' in literature, perhaps surprisingly close to the great tradition of mainstream bourgeois criticism, by invoking certain political-aesthetic criteria. The question of the relation between 'high' and popular art, like that of the partial perspective of the critic, was rarely addressed. The problem of value is

currently confronted by Marxists in a number of ways, ranging from a willing acceptance of the relativist implications of the critique of ideology to an attempt to reassert absolute standards of beauty and value on the basis of supposed human universals of an anthropological or psychological kind (see also ART; CULTURE; LITERATURE).

Reading

Arvon, Henri 1973: *Marxist Esthetics.*

Baxandall, Lee (ed.) 1972: *Radical Perspectives in the Arts.*

Bennett, Tony 1979: *Formalism and Marxism.*

Bloch, Ernst et al. 1977: *Aesthetics and Politics.*

Laing, David 1978: *The Marxist Theory of Art.*

Lenin, V. I. 1905 (1967): *On Literature and Art.*

Vázquez, Adolfo Sanches 1973: *Art and Society. Essays in Marxist Aesthetics.*

Williams, Raymond 1977: *Marxism and Literature.*

JANET WOLFF

agnosticism   Laborious efforts to disprove the existence of God Engels seems to find not only unconvincing, but a waste of time (*Anti-Dühring*, pt. 1, ch. 4). To him and Marx religion, except as a historical and social phenomenon, was not much better than an old wives' tale; and the agnostic's position, of keeping an open mind on the subject, or admitting God as an unproved possibility, was not one which they were likely to take seriously. They looked upon the Reformation as 'revolutionary' because it represented the challenge of a new class to feudalism, and also, in the longer run, because the overthrow of the old Church opened the way to a gradual secularization of thought among the literate classes, with religion coming to be viewed more and more as a purely private concern.

From the Reformation onwards, Marx wrote in 1854 in an essay on 'The Decay of Religious Authority', the literate 'began to unfasten themselves individually from all religious belief'; in France as well as the Protestant countries by the eighteenth century, when philosophy held sway in its plàce. Deism was in Marx's eyes much the same as agnosticism, a convenient way of jettisoning outworn dogmas. By alarming the upper classes the French Revolution had brought about a big but superficial change, an outward alliance between them and the Churches, which the troubles of 1848 revived; but this was precarious now, and governments acknowledged ecclesiastical authority only so far as was convenient. Marx illustrated this situation by pointing out that in the Crimean War, which broke out in 1854 with Britain and France on the side of Turkey, Protestant and Catholic clergy were being obliged to pray for infidel victory over fellow Christians; this he thought would make the clergy still more the creatures of the politicians in the future.

Educated foreigners settling in England in mid century were astonished, according to Engels, at the religious solemnity they found among the middle classes; but now cosmopolitan influences were coming in and having what he called a civilizing effect (*On Historical Materialism*). The decay of faith which poets like Tennyson and Arnold lamented in pathetic accents struck him in a comic light. Agnosticism was now nearly as respectable as the Church of England, he wrote in 1892, and a good deal more so than the Salvation Army; it was really, to use a Lancashire term, 'shamefaced' materialism (Introduction to *Socialism: Utopian and Scientific*). Engels went on to discuss agnosticism in its philosophical sense of uncertainty about the reality of matter, or causation; and it is in this way that the term has most often been used by later Marxists. Lenin in particular, in his polemic against empirio-criticism (1908), was at great pains to maintain that the novel ideas of Mach and his positivist school were really no different from the old ideas stemming from Hume, which Engels had attacked as harmful agnosticism. To admit that our sensations have a physical origin, but to treat it as an open question whether they give us correct information about the physical universe, is in Lenin's view mere playing with words (op. cit. ch. 2, sect. 2). (See also PHILOSOPHY.)

Reading

Lenin, V.I. 1908 (1962): *Materialism and Empirio-Criticism.*

V. G. KIERNAN

agrarian question The notion of the 'agrarian question' has acquired different layers of meaning since it was first identified by Marxists in the late nineteenth century. Each connotation continues to be an important part of present-day Marxist discourse. Each relates to economic backwardness.

An unresolved agrarian question is a central characteristic of economic backwardness. In its broadest meaning, the agrarian question may be defined as the continuing existence in the countryside of a poor country of substantive obstacles to an unleashing of the forces capable of generating economic development, both inside and outside agriculture. Originally formulated with respect to incomplete *capitalist* transition, and certain political consequences of that incompleteness, the agrarian question is now part, also, of the debate on possible *socialist* transition in poor countries.

In the late nineteenth century, the notion of an agrarian question bore a particular connotation. It is from that initial rendering that our present broader usage has developed. Three distinct senses of the agrarian question may be distinguished: (a) the Engels sense, (b) the Kautsky-Lenin sense, and (c) the Preobrazhensky sense.

The initial formulation derived from an explicitly political concern: how to capture political power in European countries where capitalism was developing but had not yet replaced pre-capitalist social relations as the overwhelming agrarian reality, with the expected stark opposition of capitalist farmer and wage labour. Had capitalism done its work, a strategy similar to that pursued in urban areas, and geared to the rural proletariat, would have been suggested. There was, then, an 'agrarian question'. This was the sense in which Engels viewed the matter in his 'The Peasant Question in France and Germany', written in 1894 and first published in 1894–5. For Engels, and other Marxists of his time, the 'agrarian question' was the 'peasant question': the continuing existence throughout Europe of large peasantries. Central to that 'peasant question', and its accompanying political difficulties, were peasantries which were differentiated, and subject to forces that were hastening differentiation (see PEASANTRY and RURAL CLASS STRUCTURE). The agrarian/peasant question, then, became one of deciding which sections or strata of the peasantry could be won over. That was a critical matter for immediate, careful analysis and was a subject of intense political debate (Hussain and Tribe 1981, vol. 1). It continues to be a critical issue in present-day poor countries. The ultimate resolution of the agrarian question, however, was seen in the development and dominance of capitalist agriculture, and its accompanying fully developed capitalist relations of production, with a rural proletariat free in Marx's double sense – free of the means of production and free to sell its labour power.

In 1899, there appeared two full-scale and remarkable Marxist analyses of the agrarian question: Kautsky's *The Agrarian Question* and Lenin's *Development of Capitalism in Russia*. With Kautsky and Lenin we see the agrarian question break into its component parts, which was to bring a shift of meaning as one of the component parts became the clear focus of attention. The concern becomes the extent to which capitalism has developed in the countryside, the forms that it takes and the barriers which may impede it. This rendering of the agrarian question is now detached from the more explicitly political sense used by Engels, and becomes central. It is the one most widely accepted today. But, as with Engels, the agrarian question was the peasant question. The fact of a differentiated and differentiating peasantry was crucial. It looms large in Kautsky. It lies at the very heart of Lenin's treatment. For Lenin, it is the key to understanding the nature of the agrarian question in Russia. The agrarian question in this sense is a matter of great concern and prolonged debate in today's poor countries: see, for example, on the Indian debate, Patnaik 1990; on Latin America, de Janvry 1981; on Africa, Mamdani 1987.

Lenin distinguished two broad paths of agrarian capitalism: capitalism from above (the Prussian path), where the class of capitalist farmers emerges from the feudal landlord class; and capitalism from below (the American path), where the source is a differentiated peasantry. The historical diversity of such agrarian capitalism has, in fact, been considerable, and has taken some surprising forms (Byres 1991).

The third sense derived from the socialist experience. In the Soviet Union, in the aftermath of the Revolution, the essence of the agrarian question continued to be a differentiated and differentiating peasantry, with attention directed towards the possibly disruptive role of the kulak (the rich peasantry). This had important political implications: an Engels sense of the agrarian question in the socialist context. The agrarian question also had a Kautsky-Lenin reading: the manner and forms of, and the obstacles to, the development of socialism in the countryside. But it was not limited specifically to the development of socialism in agriculture. This new preoccupation derived from the needs of *overall* socialist transformation: needs dictated by difficulties in securing accumulation outside of agriculture. In particular, this related to the accumulation required by socialist industrialization. The countryside was cast as an essential source of the necessary surplus. The agrarian question became, in part, a question of the degree to which agriculture could supply that surplus, the means by which the fledgling socialist state might appropriate such surplus, and the speed and smoothness of transfer. The most cogent and sophisticated exponent of this position was Preobrazhensky, whose celebrated work, *The New Economics*, appeared in 1926. This new layer of meaning is now a central part of discourse on the agrarian question and the transition to socialism. But it has also broadened, fruitfully, the notion of the agrarian question as that relates to capitalism. In the socialist case, COLLECTIVIZATION has been seen as a way of resolving the agrarian question in each of the three indicated senses (on socialist transition see Saith 1985, especially Saith's own excellent essay).

The *broad* sense of the agrarian question, then, in both the capitalist and the socialist cases, encompasses urban/industrial as well as rural/agricultural transformation. By an agrarian transition thus broadly construed one envisages those changes in the countryside of a poor country necessary to the *overall* development of either capitalism or socialism and the ultimate dominance of either of those modes of production in a particular national social formation. This is not to abandon either the Engels or the Kautsky-Lenin renderings. On the contrary, it remains essential to explore, with the greatest care, the agrarian question in each of these senses. But we should note the important possibility that, in the capitalist case, the agrarian question in this broad sense may be partly, and even fully, resolved without the dominance of capitalist relations of production in the countryside (on the remarkable absence of wage labour in North American and Japanese agriculture, for example, and the staying power of the peasantry in France, see Byres 1991). There are also those who currently argue that socialism is possible without collective agriculture: for instance, that the agrarian question in the broad sense may be resolved without socialist relations of production in the countryside (see, for example, Nolan 1988).

Reading

Byres, T. J. 1986: 'The Agrarian Question and Differentiation of the Peasantry'. In Atiur Rahman, *Peasants and Classes: A Study in Differentiation in Bangladesh.*

— 1991: 'The Agrarian Question and Differing Forms of Capitalist Agrarian Transition: An Essay with Reference to Asia'. In J. C. Breman and S. Mundle, eds. *Rural Transformation in Asia.*

de Janvry, Alain 1981: *The Agrarian Question and Reformism in Latin America.*

Hussain, Athar and Tribe, Keith 1981: *Marxism and the Agrarian Question.* Vol. 1: *German Social Democracy and the Peasantry 1890–1907*; vol. 2: *Russian Marxism and the Peasantry 1861–1930.*

Kautsky, Karl 1899 (*1988*): *The Agrarian Question*, trans. Pete Burgess.

Lenin, V. I. 1899 (*1960*): *The Development of Capitalism in Russia.*

Mamdani, Mahmood 1987: 'Extreme but not Exceptional: Towards an Analysis of the Agrarian Question in Uganda'.

Nolan, Peter 1988: *The Political Economy of Collective Farms.*

Patnaik, Utsa ed. 1990: *Agrarian Relations and Accumulation: The 'Mode of Production Debate' in India.*

Preobrazhensky, E. 1926 (*1965*): *The New Economics*, trans. Brian Pearce.

Saith, Ashwani ed. 1985: *The Agrarian Question in Socialist Transitions.*

                                          T. J. BYRES

alienation In Marx's sense an action through which (or a state in which) a person, a group, an institution, or a society becomes (or remains) alien (1) to the results or products of its own activity (and to the activity itself), and/or (2) to the nature in which it lives, and/or (3) to other human beings, and – in addition and through any or all of (1) to (3) – also (4) to itself (to its own historically created human possibilities).

Thus conceived, alienation is always self-alienation, i.e. the alienation of man (of his self) from himself (from his human possibilities) through himself (through his own activity). And self-alienation is not just one among the forms of alienation, but the very essence and basic structure of alienation. On the other hand 'self-alienation' is not merely a (descriptive) concept; it is also an appeal, or a call for a revolutionary change of the world (de-alienation).

The concept of alienation, regarded today as one of the central concepts of Marxism, and widely used by both Marxists and non-Marxists, entered the dictionaries of philosophy only in the second half of the twentieth century. However, before it was recognized as an important philosophical term it was widely used outside philosophy: in everyday life, in the sense of turning or keeping away from former friends or associates; in economy and law, as a term for the transfer of property from one person to another (buying and selling, stealing, making a gift); in medicine and psychiatry, as a name for deviation from normality, insanity. And before it was developed as a metaphilosophical (revolutionary) 'concept' in Marx, it was developed as a philosophical concept by Hegel and Feuerbach. In his elaboration of alienation Hegel in turn had a number of precursors. Some of them used the term without coming close to its Hegelian (or Marxian) meaning, some anticipated the idea without using the term, and in some cases there was even a kind of meeting between the idea and the term.

The Christian doctrine of original sin and redemption has been regarded by many as one of the first versions of the story of man's alienation and de-alienation. Some have insisted that the concept of alienation found its first expression in Western thought in the Old Testament concept of idolatry. The relationship of human beings to *logos* in Heraclitus can also be analysed in terms of alienation. And some have maintained that the source of Hegel's view of nature as a self-alienated form of the Absolute Spirit can be found in Plato's view of the natural world as an imperfect picture of the noble world of Ideas. In modern times the terminology and problematic of alienation can be found especially in the social theorists. Thus Hugo Grotius used alienation as a name for transfer of sovereign authority over oneself to another person.

But regardless of whether they use the term (like Grotius) or not (like Hobbes and Locke), the very idea of the social contract can be interpreted as an attempt at making progress in de-alienation (achieving more freedom, or at least security) through a deliberate partial alienation. This list of precursors could easily be enlarged. But probably no thinker before Hegel could be read and understood in terms of alienation and de-alienation better than Rousseau. To mention just two among the many relevant points, the contrast Rousseau draws between the natural man (*l'homme de la nature, l'homme naturel, le sauvage*) and the social man (*l'homme policé, l'homme civil, l'homme social*) could be compared with the contrast between the non-alienated and the self-alienated man; and his project of overcoming the contradiction between the *volonté générale* and the *volonté particulière* could be regarded as a programme for abolishing self-alienation. However, despite all precursors, including Rousseau, the true philosophical history of alienation begins with Hegel.

Although the idea of alienation (under the name of *Positivität* (positivity)) appears in the early writings of Hegel, its explicit elaboration as a philosophical term begins with his *Phenomenology of Mind*. And although the discussion of alienation is most direct and concentrated in the section entitled 'Mind alienated from itself; Culture', it is really the central concept and the leading idea of the whole book. In the same way, although there is no concentrated, explicit discussion of alienation in his later works, the whole philosophical system of Hegel, as it is briefly presented in his *Encyclopaedia of the Philosophical Sciences in Outline*, and more extensively in all of his later works and lectures, was constructed with the help of ideas of alienation and de-alienation.

In one basic sense the concept of self-alienation is applied in Hegel to the Absolute. The Absolute Idea (Absolute Mind), which is the only reality for Hegel, is a dynamic Self engaged in a circular process of alienation and de-alienation. It becomes alienated from itself in nature (which is the self-alienated form of the Absolute Idea) and returns from its self-alienation in the Finite Mind, man (who is the Absolute in the process of de-alienation). Self-alienation and de-alienation are in this way the form of Being of the Absolute.

In another basic sense (which follows directly from the first) self-alienation can be applied to the Finite Mind, or man. In so far as he is a natural being, man is a self-alienated spirit. But in so far as he is a historical being, able to achieve an adequate knowledge of the Absolute (which means also of nature and of oneself), he is able to become a de-alienated being, the Finite Mind fulfilling its vocation to accomplish the construction of the Absolute. Thus the basic structure of man can also be described as self-alienation and de-alienation.

There is a further sense in which alienation can be attributed to man. It is an essential characteristic of finite mind (man) to produce things, to express itself in objects, to objectify itself in physical things, social institutions and cultural products; and every objectification is of necessity an instance of alienation: the produced objects become alien to the producer. Alienation in this sense can be overcome only in the sense of being adequately known.

A number of further senses of alienation have been discovered in Hegel, for example by Schacht who has concluded that Hegel uses the term in two quite different senses: 'alienation₁' which means 'a separation or discordant relation, such as might obtain between the individual and the social substance, or (as "self-alienation") between one's actual condition and essential nature', and 'alienation₂' which means 'a surrender or sacrifice of particularity and wilfulness, in connection with the overcoming of alienation₁ and the reattainment of unity' (Schacht 1970, p. 35).

In his 'Contribution to the Critique of Hegel's Philosophy' (1839), and in further writings (such as *The Essence of Christianity* (1841), and *The Principles of the Philosophy of the Future* (1843)) Feuerbach criticized Hegel's view that nature is a self-alienated form of Absolute Mind and that man is Absolute Mind in the process of de-alienation. For Feuerbach man is not a self-alienated God, but God is self-alienated man – he is merely man's essence abstracted, absolutized and estranged from man. Thus man is alienated from himself when he creates, and puts above himself, an imagined alien higher being and bows before him as a slave. The de-alienation of man consists in the abolition of that estranged picture of man which is God.

Feuerbach's concept of alienation was first

criticized and extended by Moses Hess, but a criticism along the same lines was carried out more fully and deeply by Hess's younger friend (of that time), Marx (especially in the *Economic and Philosophical Manuscripts*). Marx praised Hegel for having grasped 'the self-creation of man as a process, objectification as loss of the object, as alienation and transcendence of this alienation . . .' (3rd Manuscript). But he criticized Hegel for having identified objectification with alienation, and for having regarded man as self-consciousness, and the alienation of man as the alienation of his consciousness: 'For Hegel, *human life, man* is equivalent to *self-consciousness*. All alienation of human life is therefore *nothing* but *alienation of self-consciousness*. . . . All re-appropriation of alienated objective life appears therefore as an incorporation in self-consciousness' (ibid.).

Marx agreed with Feuerbach's criticism of religious alienation, but he stressed that religious alienation is only one among the many forms of human self-alienation. Man not only alienates a part of himself in the form of God; he also alienates other products of his spiritual activity in the form of philosophy, common sense, art, morals; he alienates products of his economic activity in the form of the commodity, money, capital; he alienates products of his social activity in the form of the state, law, social institutions. There are many forms in which man alienates the products of his activity from himself and makes of them a separate, independent and powerful world of objects to which he is related as a slave, powerless and dependent. However, he not only alienates his own products from himself, he also alienates himself from the very activity through which these products are produced, from the nature in which he lives and from other men. All these kinds of alienation are in the last analysis one; they are different aspects or forms of man's self-alienation, different forms of the alienation of man from his human 'essence' or 'nature', from his humanity.

Since alienated labour: (1) alienates nature from man, and (2) alienates man from himself, from his own active function, his life activity; so it alienates him from the species. . . . (3) . . . It alienates from man his own body, external nature, his mental life and his *human* life. . . .

(4) A direct consequence of the alienation of man from the product of his labour, from his life activity and from his species life is that *man* is *alienated* from other *men*. . . . In general, the statement that man is alienated from his species life means that each man is alienated from others and that each of the others is likewise alienated from human life. . . . Every self-alienation of man, from himself and from nature, appears in the relation which he postulates between other men and himself and nature. (*Economic and Philosophical Manuscripts*, 1st Manuscript)

The criticism (unmasking) of alienation was not an end in itself for Marx. His aim was to pave the way for a radical revolution and for the realization of communism understood as 'the reintegration of man, his return to himself, the supersession of man's self-alienation', as 'the *positive* abolition of *private property*, of *human self-alienation*, and thus the real appropriation of *human* nature through and for man' (ibid. 3rd Manuscript). Although the terms alienation and de-alienation are not very much used in Marx's later writings, all of them, including *Capital*, present a criticism of the existing alienated man and society and a call for de-alienation. And there is at least one great work of the later Marx, the *Grundrisse*, in which the terminology of alienation is widely used.

The *Economic and Philosophical Manuscripts* were first published in 1932, and the *Grundrisse* (first published in 1939) became accessible in practice only after their re-publication in 1953. These may have been among the main 'theoretical' reasons (there have been practical reasons too) for the neglect of the concepts of alienation and de-alienation in all interpretations of Marx (and in philosophical discussion in general) in the nineteenth century and in the first decades of the twentieth. Some important aspects of alienation were discussed for the first time in Lukács's *History and Class Consciousness* under the term REIFICATION, but there is no general and explicit discussion of alienation in the book. Thus the discussion only began after the publication of the *Economic and Philosophical Manuscripts* in 1932. Marcuse (1932) was among the first to stress the importance of the *Manuscripts* and to draw attention to the concept of alienation in them, A. Cornu (1934) was one of the first to study the 'young Marx' more carefully, and H. Lefebvre (1939) was perhaps the first who tried to introduce the concept of alienation into the then established interpretation of Marxism.

A more widespread and intense discussion of alienation began after the second world war. Those who have taken part in it include not only Marxists but also existentialists and personalists, and not only philosophers but also psychologists (especially psychoanalysts), sociologists, literary critics, writers. Among non-Marxists it was especially Heidegger who gave an important impulse to the discussion of alienation. In *Being and Time* (1967) he used *Entfremdung* to describe one of the basic traits of the inauthentic mode of man's Being, and in 1947 he stressed the importance of alienation. In *Being and Time* (1967) he used the concept *Heimatlosigkeit*. Others too have found an analogy between Marx's self-alienation and Heidegger's *Seinsvergessenheit* and also between revolution and Heidegger's *Kehre*. Further important impulses came from Sartre, who used 'alienation' in both his existentialist and his Marxist phase; P. Tillich, in whose combination of Protestant theology, existential philosophy and Marxism the concept of alienation plays a prominent role; A. Kojève, who interpreted Hegel with the help of insights from the young Marx; J. Hyppolite, who discussed alienation (and especially the relationship between alienation and objectification) in Hegel and Marx; J. Y. Calvez, whose criticism of Marx from a Christian standpoint was based on an interpretation of the whole of Marx's thought as a criticism of different forms of alienation; and H. Barth whose analysis of truth and ideology included a detailed discussion of alienation.

Among the Marxists, Lukács studied alienation in Hegel (especially the young Hegel) and Marx, and tried to specify his own concept of alienation (and its relationship to reification); Bloch, who used the concept without a special insistence on it, tried to draw a clear distinction between *Entfremdung* and *Verfremdung*; and E. Fromm not only carefully studied the concept of alienation in Marx, but made it a key tool of analysis in his sociological, psychological and philosophical studies.

Those Marxists who tried to revive and develop Marx's theory of alienation in the 1950s and 1960s have been heavily criticized for idealism and Hegelianism, on one side by the representatives of the established (Stalinist) interpretation of Marx, and on the other by the so called structuralist Marxists (e.g. Althusser). Such opponents of the theory of alienation have insisted that what was called alienation in the early Marx was much more adequately described in later works by scientific terms such as private property, class domination, exploitation, division of labour, etc. But it has been argued in reply that the concepts of alienation and de-alienation cannot be fully reduced to any (or all) of the concepts which have been offered as replacements, and that for a truly revolutionary interpretation of Marx the concept of alienation is indispensable. As a result of these debates the number of Marxists who still oppose any use of alienation has considerably declined.

Many who were ready to accept Marx's concept of alienation did not accept that of self-alienation, which seemed to them unhistorical, because it implied that there is a fixed and unchangeable human essence or nature (SEE HUMAN NATURE). Against such a view it has been argued that alienation from oneself should be understood not as alienation from a factual or ideal ('normative') human nature, but as alienation from historically created human possibilities, especially from the human capacity for freedom and creativity. Thus instead of supporting a static or unhistorical view of man the idea of self-alienation is a call for a constant renewal and development of man. This point has been strongly argued by Kangrga: to be self-alienated means 'to be self-alienated from oneself as one's own deed (*Werk*), self-activity, self-production, self-creation; to be alienated from history as human praxis and a human product' (1967, p. 27). Thus 'a man is alienated or self-alienated, when he is not becoming man', and this occurs when 'that which is and was, is taken as the authentic and only truth', or when one operates 'inside a ready-made world, and is not active practically-critically (in a revolutionary way)' (ibid.).

A further controversial point is whether alienation applies in the first place to individuals, or to society as a whole. According to some of those who see it as applying in the first place to individuals, the non-adjustment of the individual to the society in which he lives is a sign of his alienation. Others (e.g. Fromm in *The*

Sane Society) have argued that a society can also be sick or alienated, so that an individual who is not adapted to the existing society is not himself necessarily 'alienated'. Many of those who regard alienation as applicable only to individuals make it even narrower by conceiving of it as a purely psychological concept referring to a feeling or state of mind. Thus according to Eric and Mary Josephson alienation is 'an individual feeling or state of dissociation from self, from others, and from the world at large' (Josephson and Josephson 1962, p. 191). Others have insisted that alienation is not simply a feeling, but in the first place an objective fact, a way of being. Thus A. P. Ogurtsov in the Soviet *Encyclopaedia of Philosophy* defines alienation as 'the philosophical and sociological category expressing the objective transformation of the activity of man and of its results into an independent force, dominating him and inimical to him, and also the corresponding transformation of man from an active subject to an object of social process'.

Some of those who characterize 'alienation' as a state of mind regard it as a fact or concept of psychopathology; others insist that, although alienation is not 'good' or desirable, it is not strictly pathological. They often add that one should distinguish alienation from two related but not identical concepts, anomie and personal disorganization. 'Alienation refers to a psychological state of an individual characterized by feelings of estrangement, while anomie refers to a relative normlessness of a social system. Personal disorganization refers to disordered behaviour arising from internal conflict within the individual' (M. Levin in Josephson and Josephson 1962, p. 228).

Most of the theorists of alienation have made a distinction between different forms of alienation. For example, Schaff (1980) finds two basic forms: objective alienation (or simply alienation), and subjective alienation (or self-alienation); E. Schachtel four (the alienation of men from nature, from their fellow men, from the work of their hands and minds, from themselves); M. Seeman five (powerlessness, meaninglessness, social isolation, normlessness and self-estrangement). Each of these classifications has merits and demerits. Thus instead of trying to compile a full list of such forms, some have tried to clarify the basic criteria according to which such classifications should be (or actually have been) made.

A question which has been particularly widely discussed is whether self-alienation is an essential, imperishable property of man as man, or is characteristic only of one historical stage in human development. Some philosophers (especially existentialists) have maintained that alienation is a permanent structural moment of human existence. Besides his authentic existence, man also leads a non-authentic one, and it is illusory to expect that he will one day live only authentically. The opposed view is that the originally non-self-alienated human being, in the course of development, alienated himself from himself, but will in the future return to himself. This view is to be found in Engels and in many present-day Marxists; Marx himself seems to have thought that man had always been self-alienated thus far, but that he nonetheless could and should come into his own.

Among those who have accepted the view of communism as de-alienation there have been different opinions about the possibilities, limits and forms of de-alienation. Thus according to one answer, an absolute de-alienation is possible; all alienation – social and individual – can be once and for all abolished. The most radical representatives of such an optimistic viewpoint have even maintained that all self-alienation has already been eliminated in principle in socialist countries; that it exists there only in the form of individual insanity or as an insignificant 'remnant of capitalism'. It is not difficult to see the problems with such a view. Absolute de-alienation would be possible only if humanity were something given once and for all, and unchangeable. And from a factual standpoint, it is easy to see that in what is called 'socialism' not only 'old', but also many 'new' forms of alienation exist. Thus against the advocates of absolute de-alienation it has been maintained that only a relative de-alienation is possible. According to this view it is not possible to eliminate all alienation, but it is possible to create a basically non-alienated society that would stimulate the development of non-self-alienated, really human individuals.

Depending on the view of the essence of self-alienation, the means recommended for overcoming alienation have also differed. Those who regard self-alienation as a 'psychological' fact dispute the importance or even relevance of any external change in 'circumstances' and suggest that the individual's moral effort, 'a revolution within the self', is the only cure. And those who regard self-alienation as a neurotic phenomenon are quite consistent in offering a psychoanalytical treatment for it. At the other pole stand those philosophers and sociologists who, basing themselves on a degenerate variant of Marxism called 'economic determinism', regard individuals as passive products of social (and especially economic) organization. For such Marxists the problem of de-alienation is reduced to the problem of social transformation, and the problem of social transformation to the problem of the abolition of private property.

As against both the above-mentioned views a third conception has been proposed according to which de-alienation of society and of individuals are closely connected, so that neither can be carried out without the other, nor can one be reduced to the other. It is possible to create a social system that would be favourable to the development of de-alienated individuals, but it is not possible to organize a society which would automatically produce such individuals. An individual can become a non-alienated, free and creative being only through his own activity. But not only can de-alienation not be reduced to de-alienation of society; the de-alienation of society in its turn cannot be conceived simply as a change in the organization of the economy that will be followed automatically by a change in all other spheres or aspects of human life. Far from being an eternal fact of social life, the division of society into mutually independent and conflicting spheres (economy, politics, law, arts, morals, religion, etc.), and the predominance of the economic sphere, are according to Marx characteristics of a self-alienated society. The de-alienation of society is therefore impossible without the abolition of the alienation of the different human activities from each other.

Equally, the problem of de-alienation of economic life cannot be solved by the mere abolition of private property. The transformation of private property into state property does not introduce an essential change in the situation of the worker, or the producer. The de-alienation of economic life also requires the abolition of state property, its transformation into real social property, and this cannot be achieved without organizing the whole of social life on the basis of the self-management of the immediate producers. But if the self-management of producers is a necessary condition of the de-alienation of the economic life, it is not of itself a sufficient condition. It does not solve automatically the problem of de-alienation in distribution and consumption, and is not by itself sufficient even for the de-alienation of production. Some forms of alienation in production have their roots in the nature of present-day means of production, so that they cannot be eliminated by a mere change in the form of managing production.

Reading

Fromm, Erich 1961: *Marx's Concept of Man*.

Israel, Joachim 1972: *Der Begriff Entfremdung*.

Josephson, Eric and Mary eds. 1962: *Man Alone: Alienation in Modern Society*.

Kangrga, Milan 1967: 'Das Problem der Entfremdung in Marx' Werk'.

Mészáros, István 1970: *Marx's Theory of Alienation*.

Ollman, Bertell 1971 (1976): *Alienation: Marx's Conception of Man in Capitalist Society*.

Petrović, Gajo 1967: *Marx in the Mid-Twentieth Century*.

Schacht, Richard 1970: *Alienation*.

Schaff, Adam 1980: *Alienation as a Social Phenomenon*.

Vranicki, Predrag 1965: 'Socialism and the Problem of Alienation'. In Erich Fromm ed. *Socialist Humanism*.

GAJO PETROVIĆ

Althusser, Louis   Born 16 October 1918, Birmandreïs, Algeria; died 22 October 1990, in La Verrière, Yvelines. In the early 1960s Louis Althusser, French communist and philosopher, put forward a view of Marx's work that soon became widely influential. With *For Marx* and *Reading 'Capital'* it won an international audience. It originated as a challenge to humanist and Hegelian themes then much current in discussion of Marx and inspired by his early writings, and it proffered a novel conception of Marxist philosophy.

Althusser sought to impugn the pre-eminent status accorded by many to these early writings, arguing that whatever the superficial similarities between them and Marx's mature work, here were two radically distinct modes of thought. The problematic of each – that is, the theoretical framework or system determining the significance of each particular concept, the questions posed, central propositions and omissions – was fundamentally different: in the young Marx, an ideological drama of human alienation and self-realization, with humanity the author of its unfolding destiny much in the manner of the world spirit according to Hegel; thereafter, however, a science, historical materialism, theory of social formations and their history; and its concepts of structural explanation: the forces and relations of production, determination by the economy, superstructure, state, ideology. The two systems of thought were separated by an *epistemological break* (in which a new science emerges from its ideological pre-history), and that break was disclosed, according to Althusser, by a critical reading of Marx's work, able to discern in his discourse, in its sounds and in its silences alike, the symptoms of its underlying problematic.

The notions deployed in this periodization of Marx's thought – the problematic and the epistemological break, the idea of a so-called *symptomatic reading* – were proposed by Althusser as themselves belonging to the revolutionary new philosophy inaugurated by Marx. This philosophy, dialectical materialism, was implicit in the foundation of the science, historical materialism – though, because only implicit, in need of articulation and development – and was in the first instance epistemology, a theory of knowledge or science. Its chief target was empiricism, a view of cognition in which the knowing subject confronts the real object and uncovers its essence by abstraction; and which seeks, from this assumption of thought's direct encounter with reality, of the subject's unmediated vision of the object, for external guarantees of knowledge's truth. To the conception of knowledge as vision dialectical materialism opposed a conception of it as production, as theoretical practice; and was itself, therefore, said to be the *theory of theoretical practice* (see KNOWLEDGE, THEORY OF).

This practice, Althusser maintained, takes place entirely within thought. It works upon a theoretical object, never coming face to face with the real object as such, though that is what it aims to know, but having to do rather with

what he called *Generalities I, II* and *III* respectively: a theoretical raw material of ideas and abstractions; conceptual means of production (the problematic aforesaid) brought to bear upon these; and the product of this process, a transformed theoretical entity, knowledge. Theoretical practice needs no external guarantees of the latter's validity, since every science possesses internal modes of proof with which to validate its own products. Governed by the interior requirements of knowledge, not by extra-theoretical exigencies, interests of society or class; autonomous therefore, not part of the superstructure, but following its own developmental course some way removed from the vicissitudes of social history; theoretical or scientific practice is distinct from ideological practice, distinct too from political practice and economic practice. These are all, nevertheless, equally practices, types of production. They share a common formal structure, each with its own raw material, means of production, production process and product. That is the way the world is. Epistemology in the first place, dialectical materialism contains also its ontology, theory of the ultimate nature and constituents of being.

Reality, Althusser insisted, is irreducibly complex and manifold, subject to multiple causation, in a word *overdetermined*, and the scientific, Marxist concept of social totality is not to be confused, consequently, with the Hegelian, whose complexity is merely apparent. The different features of a historical epoch, Hegel thought – its economy, polity, art, religion – are all expressions of a single essence, itself only a stage in the development of the world spirit. With each successive totality conceived as *expressive* in this way, explanation of history becomes reductionist, simplifying towards a unique central origin. Even Marxism has been thus vitiated in some of its deviant forms: such as ECONOMISM, in which the elements of the superstructure are seen as but passive effects of the economic base's pervasive determinism; and such as HISTORICISM, whose special fault is that, assimilating all practices within a common historical present, it relativizes knowledge, deprives science of its autonomy and treats Marxism itself, not as an objective science, but as the self-expression of the contemporary world, class consciousness or view point of the proletariat. Correctly understood, however, a social formation has no essence or centre; is said, therefore, to be *decentred*. It is a hierarchy of practices or structures, genuinely distinct one from another, and although, amongst them, the economic is causally primary, the others are relatively autonomous, possessing a *specific effectivity* of their own and, in some degree, independent histories. In certain circumstances they can even play the dominant role. The economic level is only determining in the last instance.

All this – vital to Marxist politics: that society be grasped, and each historical conjuncture analysed, in its full complexity – Althusser encapsulated in terming the social formation a *structure in dominance*. Its causality, dubbed by him *structural*, governs historical development (see STRUCTURALISM). Human beings are not the authors or subjects of this process which, decentred, has no motive subject. They are supports, effects, of the structures and relations of the social formation. Marx, according to Althusser, rejected the idea of a universal human essence or nature. He espoused thereby a theoretical antihumanism.

Althusser's work has provoked strong reactions, both partisan and hostile. Calm judgement will be more balanced. Though couched at times in an overblown, pretentious rhetoric, some of what he said was important, especially when he said it. A new theory does emerge in Marx's writings from 1845 and this, the materialist conception of history, is superior, cognitively and politically, to his early work. To have insisted upon it, and in an anti-reductionist form; and on the relative autonomy of science; and that Marx himself believed in the possibility of objective scientific knowledge – which he unquestionably did, aspiring to contribute to the sum of it – these were merits. However, the problematic and related notions also had less salutary results. Apart from its theoretical absurdity, the claim, for example, that Marx rejected *all* concepts of human nature is textually insupportable. The same with Althusser's argument that even a communist society will have its ideology, imaginary representation of the real: rightly or wrongly, in maturity as in youth, Marx reckoned here on a society transparent to its members (see FETISHISM). Althusser, of course, was not obliged to agree with him about this or anything else. But to pretend to have read *in* Marx the opposite of

what is there is a form of obscurantism.

The Althusserian system, moreover, for all its emphasis on materialist science, displayed many of the features of an idealism. It attenuated the relationship borne by Marxism, as a developing theory, to the contemporary history of class struggles. In the name of rejecting empiricism, it cloistered knowledge within a wholly circular, self-validating conceptual realm. Shut off from direct access to what is given in reality, theory was allowed, nevertheless, a more mysterious correspondence with it, whose secret, at least as regards social reality, was nothing other than the *unique common essence* shared by theory and the other social practices as, ultimately, modes of production. The analogy with material production enabled Althusser to make important points about the conditions of theoretical knowledge. Legislating, however, that all levels of social reality are intrinsically so structured created a metaphysic of dubious value: in the case of politics, for example, it was a mere assertion, yielding no comparable elaboration or insight. Partly to remedy some of these weaknesses, Althusser subsequently offered a new definition of philosophy, but this was no advance. Whatever its defects, his original definition had both substance and clarity. The new one was vacuous. Previously theory of theoretical practice, philosophy was now said to have no object: not to be a theory at all, and yet to represent theory, and be a theoretical intervention, within politics; and not to be politics (the class struggle), yet to represent politics, and be a political intervention, within theory. Philosophy was, in other words, nothing in its own right and, at the same time, practically everything.

It has to be said, finally, that the ideas he proposed as the basis for complex, concrete historical analysis were remarkably barren in that role in Althusser's own hands, one measure of this being that on Stalinism, by his own account of things a key issue, he had nothing worthwhile to say: on the one hand, declarations unargued and cryptic, smacking of evasion or apologia; on the other, an astonishingly trivializing explanation of it in terms of economism – and of humanism to boot.

Reading

Althusser, Louis 1965 (1969): *For Marx*.

— 1971: *Lenin and Philosophy and other Essays*.

— 1976: *Essays in Self-Criticism*.

Althusser, Louis and Balibar, Étienne 1970: *Reading 'Capital'*.

Anderson, Perry 1976: *Considerations on Western Marxism*.

— 1980: *Arguments Within English Marxism*.

Callinicos, Alex 1976: *Althusser's Marxism*.

Elliot, Gregory 1987: *Althusser: The Detour of Theory*.

Geras, Norman 1972: 'Althusser's Marxism: An Account and Assessment'.

Gerratana, Valentino 1977: 'Althusser and Stalinism'.

Glucksmann, André 1972: 'A Ventriloquist Structuralism'.

Thompson, E. P. 1978: *The Poverty of Theory*.

NORMAN GERAS

analytical Marxism A term given to theoretical approaches which use contemporary methodologies of philosophy and social science to reconsider Marxist propositions about society. In contrast to theories such as Althusser's, analytical Marxism denies that Marxism is defined by its distinctive method. Its practitioners' central interest is to determine whether substantive Marxist claims hold in the precise languages of modern methodologies and models, including methodologies and models developed by non-Marxist scholars. The term sometimes refers more narrowly to the approaches of specific analytical Marxists, particularly G. A. Cohen and John Roemer.

Analytical Marxism as broadly defined above is not new. Its roots lie in the debate between Böhm-Bawerk and HILFERDING about the logical consistency of labour values and prices of production. A milestone was Sraffa's application of linear algebra to this problem. Sraffa's model was subsequently generalized by Morishima and others, using the general equilibrium model of economics. These theorists found that while the labour theory of value does not hold in most general equilibria, the 'Fundamental Marxian Theorem' does. This theorem demonstrates that profits can be positive if and only if the rate of surplus value is positive.

Analytical Marxism received renewed impetus in the 1970s when several philosophers revitalized Marxism as a topic of philosophical inquiry by systematically restating the theory of historical materialism in the syntax of analytical philosophy. Particularly noteworthy were the writings of Wood (1972, 1981) and G. A. Cohen (1978). Both authors interpreted historical materialism as a theory of how changes in the forces of production are the source of changes in all other social relations. Both argued that this theory of history, the core of Marx's theory, retains explanatory power only if its argument is carefully and narrowly defined, and its logic consistently applied. For Cohen, a Marxist analysis can account for phenomena at the level of social relations of production or of the 'superstructure' (see BASE AND SUPERSTRUCTURE) only by showing that they are structurally compatible with – that is, *functional* for – the forces of production. For Wood, a Marxist theory must accept the idea that productive forces impose constraints on production relations. In these functionalist approaches to Marxist theory, the behaviour and motives of individuals play no role.

In the 1980s, this interest in modern analytical approaches was taken up by a number of Marxist social scientists, who applied mathematical methods widely used in neo-classical economics – such as game theory, optimization theory, and general equilibrium theory – to Marxist topics. In general, these methods rely on individualist explanations: to explain any social phenomenon is to demonstrate that goal-seeking individuals would freely choose to behave in ways which would produce that phenomenon. Jon Elster (1985) presents the most thorough exploration of Marxist methodology from an individualist perspective. In contrast to functionalist explanation, which treats individual actions as bounded by structures, Elster asserts that in individualist explanation, collective action has to be interpreted as aggregated individual actions. By implication, classes as behavioural entities are themselves unimportant in social explanation (Elster 1985, 1986). By further implication, the notion of dialectic can be consistently defined (in lieu of its Hegelian interpretation) only as a social fallacy of composition wherein individuals intending one result instead achieve another.

The most provocative works reinterpreting Marxist substantive propositions with individualist methodology are those of John

Roemer (1982, 1988). Roemer has insisted that Marxist claims, if they are to qualify as truly 'general', must hold in a Walrasian general equilibrium. The Walrasian equilibrium is an artificial setting in which market allocation works perfectly because agents are able to make uncoerced choices with perfect information, and all transactions are costless and coordinated in advance so that supply always equals demand. Roemer argued that this equilibrium represented capitalism in its purest form, which was Marx's central concern in his economic theory.

Roemer has demonstrated that when agents with different initial amounts of productive assets interact in a Walrasian equilibrium, a number of 'Marxist' features follow – specifically, the Fundamental Marxian Theorem obtains, exploitation exists and classes emerge. All behaviour by agents in this setting derives from these agents' maximization of their utility given their initial endowments of assets. Further, these Marxian results obtain whether the rich hire the poor in a labour market or lend out their assets in a credit market. When differential ownership of productive assets (DOPA) is absent and all agents optimize, these Marxian features are not to be found. Initially, Roemer (1982) concluded that Marxian theory was concerned with a basic social inequality, which was equally revealed by examining who owned what or who worked for whom. However, Roemer later (1988) asserted that DOPA is the core analytical concern of Marxism, not exploitation. If all agents do not seek maximum income, he argued, an anomalous case emerges: a rich agent might be 'hired' to work with a poor agent's assets. In this case, Marxian exploitation (who hires whom) is a misleading criterion of social injustice; only an analysis using DOPA reaches the correct ethical conclusion that the poor are disadvantaged.

Roemer has drawn a number of conclusions from these results. First, classes are the simple product of agents' individual optimizing choices; they are not pre-given social entities. This is termed the capital–exploitation correspondence principle: some agents optimize by selling (buying) labour power; these agents are exploited (exploiters) from the perspective of the transfer of surplus labour. Second, the existence of exploitation requires no direct relationship between capital and labour; exploitation is a characteristic of an economy as a whole, not a specific relationships among agents in that economy. Third, because exploitation is at best redundant and at worst ethically misleading, DOPA and not exploitation should be the fundamental concern of Marxist theory. Finally, because these results obtain in the abstract setting of a Walrasian equilibrium, they are 'general' – that is, they should guide the development of Marxist economics as a whole.

Roemer's conclusions, and the entire edifice of results based on individualist models of rational choice, are controversial. Counterarguments to both the method and the substantive assertions of analytical Marxists have been developed. Both Wood (1981) and Lebowitz (1988) have questioned the appropriateness of methodological individualism as a means of conducting Marxist inquiry. For Lebowitz, Marxist theory is inseparable from the notion that epistemological priority must be assigned to the structures within which individuals act, and in turn to the historical and other determinants of those structures. Wood has mounted a similar methodological critique, centred on the notion of the dialectic. In Wood's view, Marx's vision takes the form of a Hegelian dialectic, wherein the true metric of society lies in a simple approximation embodying its essential nature. Wood's methodological critique leads to a critique of Roemer's claim about the immorality of DOPA: as a materialist perspective, he argues, Marxism can pose no moral critique of capitalism; events and ideologies in capitalism must be understood as predetermined by economic structure.

Other Marxist social scientists have applied models incorporating individualism and contemporary analytical tools to Marxist topics, but have arrived at very different conclusions than has Roemer. One important alternative to Roemer's work is the 'contested exchange' approach of Bowles and Gintis (1990). These authors argue that the Walrasian equilibrium does not represent the purest form of the capitalist economy, because capitalist labour markets are 'incomplete'. That is, the exchange of labour power for a wage does not guarantee the amount of labour which will actually be performed; indeed, the labourer would prefer less effort, the capitalist more. Thus, conflict exists at the root of the exchange between capitalist and labourer, which is therefore 'contested'.

This contested exchange is not settled by market relations, and is settled instead through non-market means such as political power. Bowles and Gintis's model combines optimization techniques with the theory of private information to provide a behavioural basis for a conflict theory of the capitalist economy. This model clearly falls within analytical Marxism, since it uses the modern tools of neo-classical economics to reach its conclusions. At the same time, it contrasts profoundly with Roemer's model: it rejects the Walrasian general equilibrium as a useful characterization of the capitalist economy; it regards the labour market and labour process as essential to Marxist theory; and it views some agents' (labourers') decisions as being coerced, not free.

In sum, contemporary work in analytical Marxism has deepened controversies among philosophers and social scientists over what Marxism is and what it claims. Even in the realm of methodology, some analytical Marxists have denied that Marxist theory has a distinct method, while others have asserted that Marxism is defined by its method. A useful collection of essays exploring these controversies is Ware and Neilsen (1989); Ware's introductory essay includes a comprehensive bibliography.

Reading

Bowles, Samuel, and Gintis, Herbert 1990: 'Contested Exchange: New Microfoundations for the Political Economy of Capitalism'.

Cohen, G. A. 1978: *Marx's Theory of History: A Defence.*

Elster, Jon 1985: *Making Sense of Marx.*

— 1986: 'Three Challenges to Class'. In John Roemer, *Analytical Marxism.*

Lebowitz, Michael 1988: 'Is "Analytical Marxism" Marxism?'

Roemer, John 1982: *A General Theory of Exploitation and Class.*

— ed. 1986: *Analytical Marxism.*

— 1988: *Free to Lose.*

Ware, Robert, and Neilsen, Kai, eds. 1989: 'Analyzing Marxism'.

Wood, Allen 1972: 'The Marxian Critique of Justice'.

— 1981: *Karl Marx.*

GARY A. DYMSKI

anarchism The doctrine and movement which rejects the principle of political authority and maintains that social order is possible and desirable without such authority. Its central negative thrust is directed against the core elements that make up the modern state: its territoriality with the accompanying notion of frontiers; its sovereignty, implying exclusive jurisdiction over all people and property within its frontiers; its monopoly of the major means of physical coercion by which it seeks to uphold that sovereignty, both internally and externally; its system of positive law which claims to override all other laws and customs; and the idea of the nation as the paramount political community. The positive thrust of anarchism is directed towards the vindication of 'natural society', i.e. a self-regulated society of individuals and freely-formed groups.

Although anarchism rests on liberal intellectual foundations, notably the distinction between state and society, the protean character of the doctrine makes it difficult to distinguish clearly different schools of anarchist thought. But one important distinction is between individualist anarchism and socialist anarchism. The former emphasizes individual liberty, the sovereignty of the individual, the importance of private property or possession, and the iniquity of all monopolies. It may be seen as liberalism taken to an extreme conclusion. 'Anarcho-capitalism' is a contemporary variant of this school (see Pennock and Chapman 1978, chs. 12–14). Socialist anarchism, in contrast, rejects private property along with the state as a major source of social inequality. Insisting on social equality as a necessary condition for the maximum individual liberty of all, its ideal may be characterized as 'individuality in community'. It represents a fusion of liberalism with socialism: libertarian socialism.

The first systematic exposition of anarchism was made by William Godwin (1756–1836), some of whose ideas may have influenced the Owenite cooperative socialists. However, classical anarchism as an integral, albeit contentious, part of the wider socialist movement was originally inspired by the mutualist and federalist ideas of PROUDHON. Proudhon adopted an essentially cooperative approach to socialism, but he insisted that the power of capital and the power of the state were synonymous and that the proletariat could not emancipate itself through the use of state power. The latter ideas were vigorously propagated by BAKUNIN under whose leadership anarchism developed in the late 1860s as the most serious rival of Marxist socialism at the international level. Unlike Proudhon, however, Bakunin advocated the violent and revolutionary expropriation of capitalist and landed property, leading to a form of collectivism. Bakunin's successor, Peter Kropotkin (1842–1921), emphasized the importance of mutual aid as a factor in social evolution; he was mainly responsible for developing the theory of anarchist communism, according to which 'everything belongs to everyone' and distribution is based exclusively on needs; and in his essay, 'The State: its historic role', he provided a perceptive analysis of the anarchists' *bête noire*.

Bakunin's strategy envisaged spontaneous uprisings of the oppressed classes, peasants as well as industrial workers, in widespread insurrections in the course of which the state would be abolished and replaced by autonomous communes, federally linked at regional, national and international levels. The PARIS COMMUNE of 1871 – hailed by Bakunin as 'a bold and outspoken negation of the state' – approximated to this anarchist model of revolution. In the period following its crushing – a consequence, in Engels's view, of its lack of centralization and authority and the failure to use its coercive authority freely enough – the tendency towards state socialism of both the Marxist and reformist varieties gained ground. Some anarchists then adopted the tactic of 'propaganda by the deed' – acts of assassination of political leaders and terrorism of the bourgeoisie – intended to encourage popular insurrections. The consequent repression of the movement led other anarchists to develop an alternative strategy associated with SYNDICALISM. The idea was to turn labour unions into revolutionary instruments of the proletariat in its struggle against the bourgeoisie, and to make unions, rather than communes, the basic units of a socialist order. The revolution, it was envisaged, would take the form of a General Strike in the course of which the workers would take over the means of production, distribution and exchange, and abolish the state. It was through syndicalism that anarchism in the period 1895–1920 exer-

cised its greatest influence on labour and socialist movements. The influence lasted longer in Spain where, during the Civil War (1936–39), the anarcho-syndicalists attempted to carry through their conception of revolution. Since the decline of syndicalism, anarchism has exercised only a limited influence on socialist movements, but there was a notable revival of anarchist ideas and tendencies (not always recognized as such) in the New Left movements of the 1960s. Currently, anarcho-pacifism, drawing on a tradition of Christian anarchism but inspired more by the non-violent direct action techniques popularized by M. K. Gandhi (1869–1948), is a significant tendency within Western peace movements.

Both individualist and socialist anarchism, as expressed by Max Stirner (1805–56), Proudhon and Bakunin, were deemed sufficiently important to merit the extensive criticisms of Marx and Engels (see Thomas 1980). In general, they saw anarchism as a petty bourgeois phenomenon, allied, in Bakunin's case, with the adventurism and revolutionary phrase-mongering characteristic of de-classed intellectuals and the LUMPENPROLETARIAT. As an out-moded 'sectarian' tendency within the socialist movement, it reflected the protest of the petty bourgeoisie against the development of large-scale capitalism and of the centralizing state which safeguards the interests of the bourgeoisie. The protest took the form of a denial, not of any actual state but of 'an abstract State, the State as such, a State that nowhere exists' (*The Alliance of Socialist Democracy and the International Working Men's Association*, 1873, s. II). More importantly, anarchism denied what was essential in the struggle for the emancipation of the working class: political action by an independent working-class party leading to the conquest, not the immediate destruction, of political power. 'For communists', as Engels explained, 'abolition of the state makes sense only as the necessary result of the abolition of classes, with whose disappearance the need for organized power of one class for the purpose of holding down the other classes will automatically disappear' (Marx, Engels, Lenin 1972, p. 27).

Anarchism survived such criticisms and remains a major source for the critique of Marxist theory and, particularly, of Marxist practice. The commonly-held view that Marxists and anarchist communists agree about the end (a classless, stateless society) but differ about the means to that end appears to be inadequate. At a deeper level, the disagreement is about the nature of the state, its relationship to society and to capital, and how politics as a form of alienation may be transcended.

Reading

Apter, David and Joll, James eds. 1971: *Anarchism Today.*

Corder, Alan B. 1988: *Marx: A Radical Critique.*

Guérin, Daniel 1970: *Anarchism*

Kropotkin, P. A. 1970: *Selected Writings on Anarchism and Revolution.*

Marx, Engels, Lenin 1972: *Anarchism and Anarcho-Syndicalism.*

Miller, David 1984: *Anarchism.*

Pennock, J. R. and Chapman, J. W. eds. 1978: *Anarchism.*

Thomas, Paul 1980: *Karl Marx and the Anarchists.*

Woodcock, George 1986: *Anarchism.* 2nd edn.

GEOFFREY OSTERGAARD

ancient society Marxism has introduced a wholly new dimension into the traditional periodization of history because the grounds for periodization and the explanation of the succession of periods are integral to the general theory of historical development (see STAGES OF DEVELOPMENT). It is therefore a not insignificant verbal symbol that Marxists prefer to speak of ancient society rather than of the ancient *world*. The classic statement appears in the preface to Marx's *Critique of Political Economy* (1859):

> In the social production which men carry on they enter into definite relations that are indispensable and independent of their will; these relations of production correspond to a definite stage of development of their material powers of production. . . . At a certain stage of their development, the material forces of production come in conflict with the existing relations of production, or – what is but a legal expression for the same thing – with the property relations within which they had been at work before. . . . Then comes the period of social revolution. . . . In broad outline we can designate the Asiatic, the ancient, the feudal and the modern

bourgeois modes of production as so many epochs in the progress of the economic formation of society.

Marx's list of historical epochs may have been 'repeatedly revised by his most devoted followers' (Hobsbawm 1964, p. 19), but for a century a simplified, 'vulgar' version in fact became virtually canonical. ASIATIC SOCIETY disappeared, to be replaced by a pre-class epoch of PRIMITIVE COMMUNISM; the word 'progress' was taken to refer to a unilinear evolution, a chronological succession of epochs; and 'social revolution' was understood literally, as the overthrow of one system by a class exploited within the old system. Unfortunately for both the simplistic dogma and its many later interpreters and commentators, Marx had himself undermined central points in a bulky set of notebooks he composed during the years 1857–58 in preparation for writing the *Critique* and its sequel, *Capital.* Entitled *Grundrisse der Kritik der politischen Ökonomie (Foundations of the Critique of Political Economy)*, this work was a kind of thinking aloud, written by Marx for himself, not for publication. It was finally published in Moscow (1939–41) but was hardly noticed until the Berlin publication in 1952 and 1953. Reference here is made to the excellent English translation by Martin Nicolaus (1973), but the one section directly relevant to ancient society (pp. 471–514), headed by Marx 'Forms which precede capitalist production', has been separately available in English since 1964.

In that section of the *Grundrisse* one learns – though it is written on a high level of abstraction and often elliptically – that Marx identified Germanic, ancient and Slavonic forms of property and production as other routes out of primitive communism alternative to the Asiatic; that both slavery and serfdom were 'always secondary, derived, never original, although a necessary and logical result of property founded on the community and labour in the community' (p. 496). It follows that the various forms did not historically succeed each other in a unilinear evolution, that, in particular, Asiatic society did not create within itself the seeds of its own destruction.

Why after 1859 Marx and Engels (and their immediate successors) appear to have abandoned the more complex scheme of the *Grund-*

risse, thus opening the way for the simpler unilinear evolution that became canonical, is outside the scope of this brief essay. It may just be pointed out, however, that their interest in pre-capitalist formations was subordinate to their concern with the theory of historical development, and did not demand either the intensive research or the sophisticated nuancing that were required for their overriding concern, the analysis and understanding of capitalist society. As Hobsbawm (1964) pointed out, Marx himself did not discuss 'the internal dynamics of pre-capitalist systems except in so far as they explain the preconditions of capitalism', or 'the actual economic contradictions of a slave economy', or 'why in antiquity it was slavery rather than serfdom which developed', or why and how the ancient mode was replaced by feudalism. Nor did the major theorists in more recent times, whether Lenin or Gramsci or Althusser, for example, and for the same reasons: their energies were taken up either with the contemporary world and its politics or with theory, philosophy, in its most abstract, general form (or with both together, e.g. Lukács). The occasional exception in recent years, such as Hindess and Hirst (1975), has foundered on inadequate knowledge of ancient society.

In the end it has been left to Marxist historians of antiquity to find their own way in filling that gap in Marxist literature. One need go back no further than the first full-scale post-*Grundrisse* inquiry, that by Welskopf (1957), which remains the safest guide to the ideas on the subject of Marx, Engels, Lenin and Stalin, quite apart from her own analysis. The complexity and magnitude of the problems cannot be overstated. The ancient (Graeco-Roman) world became a political unity under the Roman Empire. At its greatest extent, in the early second century AD, that empire included western Asia, the whole of northern Africa from Egypt to Morocco, and most of Europe, including Britain but not the northern regions of the continent, a territory of perhaps 1,750,000 square miles with a population of the order of 60,000,000. Barring marginal regions on the edges of that huge territory, there is no question about the firmness of the control by the centre, or about the systematic exploitation through taxes, tribute and (during periods of war and conquest) booty. Otherwise, however, the empire was a mosaic of heterogeneous societies which retained their essential distinctness despite the migration of tens of thousands of Italians to the provinces, the rise of local elites who served the central Roman administration and acquired Roman citizenship and even senatorial rank, the founding of Graeco-Roman-style cities in areas that had never known them before, notably on the northern frontiers and in Western Europe, or the extensive transfer of goods over considerable distances. In other words, there was no movement towards an empire-wide dependency system as has occurred in modern imperialism. Such a development was neither possible nor necessary. The way in which the Roman ruling class exploited the provinces required no fundamental interference in or transformation of the property regime or of the social relations of production within the regions they conquered and incorporated. Not surprisingly, therefore, efforts to define an ancient or a slave mode of production (whether they were considered to be the same or two different modes) have run into seemingly insurmountable difficulties.

An important step forward has been the shift in stress from MODE OF PRODUCTION to SOCIAL FORMATION, defined as a 'concrete combination of modes of production organized under the dominance of one of them' (Anderson 1974, p. 22, n.6). That shift was necessary to register the reality, to quote Anderson again, of a 'plurality and *heterogeneity* of possible modes of production within any given historical and social totality'. This removes the difficulty that in Roman Italy, in particular, during the centuries in which slavery on the land reached a magnitude and an importance beyond anything known before, a free landowning PEASANTRY remained numerically significant. But there are still serious problems in other periods and places of the ancient world. Classical Greece of the fifth and fourth centuries BC, for instance, was a 'totality' only culturally. There were city-states, such as Athens, in which the slave mode of production was dominant, but there were also many, perhaps the majority, in which it clearly was not: Sparta, for example, with its helots, or the large 'backward' regions, such as Thessaly and Aetolia or Illyria and Macedonia on the fringes. In what meaningful sense, then, can Greece be called *a* social formation?

Then, after Alexander the Great conquered the Persian empire, an invading Graeco-Macedonian ruling class established a Greek-style urban civilization in the newly acquired eastern territories, from Egypt to Bactria, but the underlying peasant populations were neither free in the old Greek (or Roman) sense nor chattel slaves, and the characteristic political structure was not the city-state but absolute monarchy. Marxist historians have in the past neglected this period, now conventionally known as Hellenistic, but a very recent major study has shown that the eastern, far the most important, regions should be classed as an Asiatic social formation, whereas the original Greek component of that world retained the ancient mode (Kreissig 1982). Again we are dealing with only a cultural 'totality', and a weak one at that, until the whole of the territory was incorporated into the Roman Empire, where the slave mode of production was dominant only in the attenuated sense that the Roman ruling class continued to draw its wealth directly (as distinguished from exploitation of the provinces) from slave labour in Italy and Sicily. As the ruling class became geographically diversified, furthermore, to the point, beginning in the second century AD, when Spain, Gaul, North Africa or Syria were providing most emperors, it became increasingly untrue that this class rested on exploitation of the slave mode of production.

The unanswered questions reflect the lack of consensus and the uncertainties that characterize current Marxist historiography. Probably no one would disagree that private property in land and a measure of commodity production were necessary conditions for the establishment of ancient society, or that the city-state, the community of citizens, was its appropriate political form. Beyond that, most major questions remain a continuing subject for debate, notably two. The first is the nature and role of SLAVERY (best discussed in that context); the second is the periodization of the history of ancient society (analogous to the far better understood PERIODIZATION OF CAPITALISM), which lasted more than a thousand years. At one extreme, all difficulties are put aside by retention of the over-simplified, unilinear view, recently defended at great length by an eccentric, Procrustean definition of the essential Marxist categories (de Ste Croix 1981). The other extreme is marked by

the decision that Marxists should abandon the category of antiquity altogether as having no more validity than 'Africa since the era of da Gama' (Hindess and Hirst 1977, p. 41).

Neither extreme is likely to command much support: to evade the difficulties is not to resolve them. Probably the most serious arise from the search for the dialectical process through which new relations of production emerged and eventually became dominant. The word crisis recurs regularly, but there is no agreement either about its specific characteristics or even about its date. The difficulties become most acute with the Roman Empire and the transition from ancient society to feudalism (see FEUDAL SOCIETY). Firstly, as we have already seen, the slave mode of production was then dominant only in a peculiar sense. Secondly, the eastern and western halves of the Empire developed differently: only in the latter did feudalism finally replace the ancient social formation. No one now believes in a revolutionary overthrow of ancient society, a notion that never had any foundation except in dogma (Staerman and Heinen, in Heinen 1980). But the east–west divide requires explanation, which must lie in the distinction between the Asiatic and the ancient formations that had been brought together under one political system, and in the introduction into the western Empire of the Germanic mode (Anderson 1974). Thirdly, now that historians, Marxist and non-Marxist, are largely agreed that the feudal system is to be dated much later than used to be thought, leaving a 'transition period' of perhaps six centuries, serious consideration must be given to the suggestion that we must find 'a late-ancient social and economic formation' (Giardina 1982), though surely something better than 'impérial-esclavagiste' (Favory 1981). The whole question of periodization of ancient society has become an open one, with basic implications for the very account of ancient society.

Reading

Anderson, P. 1974: *Passages from Antiquity to Feudalism.*

Capogrossi, L. *et al.* eds. 1978: *Analisi marxista e società antiche.*

de Ste. Croix, G. E. M. 1981: *The Class Struggle in the Ancient Greek World.*

Favory, F. 1981: 'Validité des concepts marxistes pour

une théorie des sociétés de l'Antiquité: Le modèle impérial romain'.

Giardina, A. 1981: 'Lavoro e storia sociale: antagonismi e alleanze dall'ellenismo al tardoantico'.

Heinen, H. ed. 1980: *Die Geschichte des Altertums im Spiegel der sowjetischen Forschung.*

Hindess, B. and Hirst, P. Q. 1975: *Pre-capitalist Modes of Production.*

— 1977: *Mode of Production and Social Formation. An Auto-critique.*

Hobsbawm, E. 1964b: Introduction to Marx, *Pre-Capitalist Economic Formations.*

Kreissig, H. 1982: *Geschichte des Hellenismus.*

Welskopf, E. C. 1957: *Die Produktionsverhältnisse im alten Orient und in der griechisch-römischen Antike.*

MOSES FINLEY

Annales school Why should one discuss the *Annales* school in a dictionary of Marxist thought? None of the great names of this school – Lucien Febvre, Marc Bloch, Fernand Braudel – considered himself a Marxist. And many a Marxist has denounced the *Annales* school as anti-Marxist. And yet it does seem appropriate. For just as there are many rooms in the house of Marx, so are there many in the *Annales* tradition, and there are points of significant convergence and overlap.

If one can trace Marxist thought back to the 1840s, one can trace an *Annales* tradition back to circa 1900 with Henri Beer and his *Revue de synthèse historique.* From 1900 to the end of the second world war there was virtually no direct intellectual link, certainly no organizational link, between the Marxist and the *Annales* schools of thought. For one thing, at that time, Marxist thought had virtually no entry into the world of academia; its locus was in the movement, or rather the movements, which proclaimed themselves Marxist. The *Annales* school was, by contrast, pre-eminently an intellectual thrust within academia, especially of course in France. The two currents did not cross; one may wonder how much the intellectuals associated with the one read or knew of the other current.

Still they pursued parallel paths in regard to certain key issues. They both shared the view that beneath the immediate public interplay of political forces, there were deeper, underlying long-term economic and social forces, whose mode of functioning could be analysed and

whose elucidation was essential to rational action. They both shared a holistic epistemology which resisted simultaneously an empiricist, idiographic approach to knowledge and a trans-historical universalizing nomothetic approach. In that sense they both advocated a 'middle path'. And they both shared a sense that they were rebels against the intellectual Establishments of the modern world.

Whereas, up to the second world war, they were as ships passing in the night, in the immediate post-war period they were both turned into direct antagonists and paradoxically pushed together for the first time. In the atmosphere of the early Cold War, where everyone had to choose sides, *Annales* historiography was roundly denounced by communist historians in the USSR and in the West. (This was, of course, particularly true in France and Italy where both the *Annales* school and Communist parties were strong. For the different reaction of British communist historians, see Hobsbawm 1978.) Conversely, however, the *Annales* historians were more restrained. Fernand Braudel said that *Annales* 'did not hold [Marxism] at a distance' (1978). It was precisely because French intellectuals were resisting being overwhelmed by Cold War exigencies that *Annales* insisted on a balanced view. (For an elaboration of this complex process, see Wallerstein 1982.)

And it was in the period after 1968, less marked by the Cold War, that the two schools seemed to draw apart again. On the one hand, Marxism became less identified with one particular dogmatic version. We had entered the era of a thousand Marxisms, and many of these found enormous profit in the work of *Annales* historians. On the other hand, many of the *Annales* historians were entering into a 'post-Marxist' mood. This involved a turning away from or minimizing of economic history and a renewed emphasis on mentalities or representations which linked up with a similar turn to the symbolic sphere among anthropologists and among those interested in political culture. In an empirical sense, while the writings of many Marxists were becoming more 'global', the writings of many of those identified with the so-called 'third generation' of the *Annales* were becoming more 'local'.

Given the fast-moving pace today of intellectual rethinking, this may not be the end of the story. If 'Marxism' and 'Annales historiography' continue to be identifiable currents of thought in the decades ahead, their paths may come closer once again, given their past history.

Reading

Braudel, Fernand 1978: 'En guise de conclusion'.

Hobsbawm, Eric 1978: 'Comments'.

Wallerstein, I. 1982: 'Fernand Braudel, Historian, *homme de la conjuncture*'.

I. WALLERSTEIN

anthropology The interest of Marx and Engels in anthropology was aroused primarily by the publication of L. H. Morgan's *Ancient Society* (1877). In the years 1879–82 Marx made copious notes on Morgan's book, as well as on the works of Maine, Lubbock, Kovalevsky and other students of early societies (see Krader 1972; Harstick 1977); and Engels's *Origin of the Family* was, as he noted in the preface, 'in a sense, the execution of a bequest', the accomplishment of the task which Marx had set himself, but had been unable to carry out, of assessing Morgan's researches in the light of the materialist conception of history. From this standpoint Marx and Engels opposed 'the doctrine of general evolutionary progress then advanced by ethnologists' (Krader, op. cit., p. 2), and concentrated instead upon the specific 'empirically observable mechanisms' by which human societies advanced from lower to higher stages; a process summed up by Engels (op. cit.) as the development of labour productivity, private property and exchange, the breakdown of the old society founded on kinship groups, and the emergence of classes, class struggles and the state.

But these studies by Marx and Engels did not give rise to any systematic Marxist anthropological research; and when modern anthropology was being created in the first few decades of the twentieth century by Boas (1858–1942), Malinowski (1884–1942) and Radcliffe-Brown (1881–1951) the Marxist influence upon it was negligible. The principal Marxist contribution, in this period, to the study of early societies came from an archaeologist, Gordon Childe (see ARCHAEOLOGY AND PREHISTORY). A major survey of anthropology (Kroeber 1953) contained only the most cursory (and inaccurate) references to Marxism, and Firth (1972) noted that 'general works by anthropologists have cheerfully dispensed with all but minimal use of Marx's ideas on the dynamics of society' (p. 6), being much more strongly influenced by the tradition stemming from Durkheim. But the situation has altered profoundly in recent years, and in Firth's words 'new issues have been raised [closer to Marxist concerns] as social anthropologists have been confronted with societies in conditions of radical change' (p. 7).

Since the early 1960s in fact there has been a notable development of Marxist anthropology (see Copans and Seddon 1978 for an informative general survey), which has taken two principal forms. In North America there has emerged a radical 'dialectical anthropology' which rejects the distinction made between 'primitive' and 'civilized' in terms of inferior and superior, conceives anthropology as a search for the 'natural' human being, and assigns to the anthropologist the role of 'a relentless critic of his own civilization' (Diamond 1972). From this perspective Marxism is a 'philosophical anthropology', first formulated in Marx's early writings (notably in the *Economic and Philosophical Manuscripts*), and closely related to Rousseau's critique of modern civilization. Diamond argues further that Marx's and Engels's increasing preoccupation, from the 1870s onwards, with primitive and early forms of society was in part an expression of 'growing hatred and contempt for capitalist society' (cited from Hobsbawm 1964, p. 50) but that their commitment to a nineteenth-century conception of progress 'inhibited them from further inquiry into the actual conditions of primitive culture' (Diamond op. cit. p. 419). Thus Engels, in *Origin of the Family*, expounds what he regards as a necessary (and generally progressive) process of development while making occasional references to the 'simple moral greatness of the old gentile society'. In similar vein Marx had praised the societies of classical antiquity 'in which the human being . . . always appears as the aim of production', and observed that 'from one aspect, therefore, the childlike world of antiquity seems loftier . . . whereas the modern world . . . is *base* and *vulgar*' (*Grundrisse*, pp. 487–8).

Two related themes in this radical anthropology are: (i) a sustained criticism of the historical connection between traditional anthropology and imperialism, a connection which was most obvious at the time when anthropology was regarded as making an important contribution to the training of colonial administrators; and (ii) a critical view of Soviet ethnology which, it is argued, neglects the study of present-day primitive societies and concentrates instead upon 'early' societies (using the data of archaeology and prehistory) in order to uphold 'the five-stage theory of evolutionary, and progressivist, determinism' (Diamond ed. 1979, pp. 5–10; but see also in the same volume, Yu. V. Bromley, 'Problems of Primitive Society in Soviet Ethnology', pp. 201–13, which outlines the Soviet approach).

The second main form of recent Marxist anthropology, which has had a profound and widespread influence (see Bloch 1975 for its impact on British anthropology), is that of the French structuralists, whose ideas have been shaped partly by the structuralist anthropology of Lévi-Strauss, partly by the methodological writings of Althusser (see STRUCTURALISM). The most prominent contributors to this current of thought – Godelier, Meillassoux and Terray – apply the concepts of historical materialism to primitive societies in order to achieve a theoretical analysis of 'primitive modes of production' as part of a general theory of modes of production. The central problem in this analysis is to determine the role of kinship in primitive societies (its place in the mode of production), and here several different conceptions have emerged (Copans and Seddon, op. cit., pp. 36–8). Godelier (1966, pp. 93–5) argues that kinship relations *function* as relations of production, but also as political and ideological relations, so that kinship is both base and superstructure; and in a later work (1973, p. 35) he poses as 'the major problem in the social sciences today' the question as to why a particular social factor (e.g. kinship) becomes dominant and assumes the function of 'integrating' all other social relations. Terray (1969), however, adopts a more reductionist approach in proposing that kinship relations are the product of a triple determination ('overdetermination' in Althusser's terminology) acting upon a given substratum (p. 143), as does Meillassoux (1960, 1964) who regards kinship relations as an 'expression' of the relations of production.

This kind of analysis has also had an impact upon other fields of inquiry. For example, Godelier (1973, pt. IV) examines the contribution that Lévi-Strauss's analyses of the logic of myths have made to a theory of ideological superstructures, and undertakes an interpretation of the ideological consequences of the changes in relations of production brought about by the Inca conquest of Andean tribal communities. More generally, there has been a revival of interest in Marxist studies of myth and ritual. The study of tribal societies and kinship relations from the perspective of primitive modes of production has also led to a wider concern with pre-capitalist modes of production and the problem of evolutionary sequences (particularly with regard to ASIATIC SOCIETY; see Godelier 1966), with peasant societies (Meillassoux 1960), and with current issues of 'underdevelopment' (Taylor 1979).

Finally, the structuralist approach has raised important methodological questions. Godelier (1973, ch. 1) distinguishes between functionalist, structuralist and Marxist methods; then criticizes (i) functionalism for its empiricism (its confusion of social structure with visible social relations), its notion of functional interdependence which excludes problems of causality (the 'specific efficacity' of each function), and its conception of equilibrium which disregards the existence of 'contradictions', and (ii) the structuralism of Lévi-Strauss for its conception of history as a 'a mere succession of accidental events' (p. 47). In contrast, Marxist structuralism, which also recognizes the existence of real (though hidden) structures beneath the surface pattern of social relations, propounds in addition 'the thesis of the law of order in social structures and their changes' (ibid.).

These two versions of recent Marxist anthropology differ profoundly. The first gives an entirely new orientation to anthropology by conceiving it as a humanist philosophy, the principal aim of which is to criticize modern civilization. In this respect it has obvious affinities with the cultural critique practised by the Frankfurt School. But the materials for its criticism are still drawn from the traditional field of study of anthropology, and according to Diamond (1972, p. 424) the specific claim it makes is that 'our sense of primitive communal societies is the archetype for socialism'. The second current of thought reconstructs anthropology as a science, by establishing a new theoretical scheme in which the essential concepts are those of mode of production and socio-economic formation (conceived as a structured whole). In this form anthropology has a close affinity with sociology (in so far as the latter is also treated as a theoretical science), and can indeed be regarded as the sociology of primitive and early societies, continuous with the study of other types of society. Marxist anthropology today thus displays in quintessential form the division in Marxist thought between 'humanists' and 'scientists'.

Reading

Bloch, Maurice 1975: *Marxist Analyses and Social Anthropology*.

Copans, Jean and Seddon, David 1978: 'Marxism and Anthropology: A Preliminary Survey'. In David Seddon ed. *Relations of Production: Marxist Approaches to Economic Anthropology*.

Diamond, Stanley 1972: 'Anthropology in Question'. In Dell Hymes ed. *Reinventing Anthropology*.

— ed. 1979: *Toward a Marxist Anthropology*.

Firth, Raymond 1972: *The Sceptical Anthropologist: Social Anthropology and Marxist Views on Society*.

Godelier, Maurice 1966 (1972): *Rationality and Irrationality in Economics*.

— 1973 (1977): *Perspectives in Marxist Anthropology*.

Harstick, Hans-Peter ed. 1977: *Karl Marx über Formen vorkapitalischer Produktion*.

Krader, Lawrence ed. 1972: *The Ethnological Notebooks of Karl Marx*.

Meillassoux, Claude 1960 (1978): '"The Economy" in Agricultural Self-Sustaining Societies: A Preliminary Analysis'. In David Seddon ed. *Relations of Production*.

— 1964: *Anthropologic économique des Gouro de Côte d'Ivoire: de l'économie d'autosubsistance à l'agriculture commerciale*.

Terray, Emmanuel 1969 (1972): *Marxism and 'Primitive Societies'*.

TOM BOTTOMORE

archaeology and prehistory Marx's famous analysis of the labour process and production of use values emphasizes the importance of archaeological materials (*Capital* I, pt. III, sect. 1):

Relics of by-gone instruments of labour possess the same importance for the investigation of extinct economical forms of society, as do fossil bones for the determination of extinct species of animals. It is not the articles made, but how they are made, and by what instruments, that enables us to distinguish different economical epochs. Instruments of labour not only supply a standard of the degree of development to which human labour has attained, but they are also indicators of the social conditions under which that labour is carried on.

This passage, quoted by Stalin in *Dialectical and Historical Materialism*, profoundly influenced the application of historical materialism to archaeological research in the Soviet Union (Artsikhovskii 1973) and was incorporated into the seminal prehistoric syntheses of V. Gordon Childe in Western archaeology (1947, pp. 70–71; 1951, pp. 18, 26–7). Ironically, however, Marx's and Engels's knowledge of archaeology and prehistory was thin and consisted of little more than general awareness that stone implements had been found in caves (Marx, ibid.) and that ruins had been excavated in barren regions of the Near East which documented the importance of irrigation systems in Asiatic societies (Engels to Marx, 6 June 1853; see ASIATIC SOCIETY). Marx was aware that the Scandinavians were pioneers in archaeological research (Marx to Engels, 14 March 1868) and realized that prehistoric discoveries and recently defined periods, such as the Palaeolithic, could be interpreted in a manner consistent with the stages of social evolution advanced by Morgan (cf. Marx's bibliographic notes in Krader 1972, p. 425).

Yet within the Marxist tradition ethnological accounts of primitive peoples and the ancient history of Greece and Rome remained the basic sources for reconstructing primitive society and the origin of the state well into the twentieth century. For example, in Plekhanov's essay, *The Materialist Conception of History*, references to archaeological discoveries are almost non-existent and used only to support the unilinear evolutionary concept that all peoples passed through similar stages of social development (see STAGES OF DEVELOPMENT). Plekhanov writes: 'our ideas of "primitive man" are merely conjectures' since 'men who inhabit the earth today . . . are found . . . already quite a long way removed from the moment when man ceased to live a purely animal life.' Such a statement implies that archaeological data are essentially incapable of reconstructing earlier forms of society and recalls Johnson's famous dictum, written a ~entury earlier, that prehistory was 'all conjecture about a thing useless'. Social evolution, of course, formed a major topic of early Marxist writings, particularly Engels's *Origin of the Family*, but careful reading shows that prehistory was reconstructed almost entirely from ethnographic and historical studies (Engels's note to the 1888 English edition of the *Communist Manifesto* where the opening phrase is emended to read: 'The *written* history of all hitherto existing society . . .').

It is incorrect and insufficient to explain this dismissal of archaeological evidence simply on the grounds that major archaeological discoveries, such as Evans's exposure of Bronze Age palaces on Crete, were made only after the turn of the century. Hieroglyphic and cuneiform writing had been deciphered and Egyptian and Mesopotamian sites excavated during Marx's and Engels's lifetime but did not attract their attention for sociological reasons relating to the practice and structure of early archaeology. The study of archaeological remains did not form part of the classical education of the day, and nineteenth-century archaeologists essentially were not concerned with the problems of social evolution that interested the founders of historical materialism. A major stimulus for archaeological research in Europe was the growth of nationalism (Kristiansen 1981, p. 21), while work in the Near East was inspired largely by the desire to verify the historical accuracy of the Bible. Interest in human evolution was stimulated by Darwin, but early Palaeolithic archaeologists, such as G. de Mortillet, were trained in the natural sciences, particularly geology, and expected prehistory to unfold as a natural, not social, process in a series of successive epochs comparable to those that defined the history of the earth. Archaeology had a romantic appeal that attracted members of the leisured class (e.g. Daniel 1976, p. 113), and antiquities were accessible to and discovered by peoples living in the countryside, not urban areas. Thus, *contra* Godelier's (1978) imaginative explanation for the apparent rigidity of Marx's stages of socio-economic formations, the wide gulf between archaeological practice and early Marxist praxis makes it doubtful whether knowledge of later archaeolo-

gical discoveries would have significantly modified Engels's discussion of the emergence of class society or altered early debates on the nature and universality of the Asiatic mode of production.

Archaeology was first incorporated into the Marxist tradition in the Soviet Union after the Russian revolution. In 1919 Lenin created the Academy of the History of Material Culture, which became the country's leading archaeological research institution, and in the late twenties young archaeologists, such as A. V. Artsikhovskii in Moscow and V. I. Ravdonikas in Leningrad, began to apply systematically the principles of historical materialism to archaeological data, insisting upon both the possibility and necessity of reconstructing earlier forms of society upon its basis (Masson 1980). In the 1930s Soviet archaeologists, such as P. P. Efimenko, abandoned the Three Age (Stone, Bronze, and Iron) system and classified prehistoric societies into pre-clan (*dorodovoe obshchestvo*), gentile (*rodovoe*), and class formations, a scheme subsequently criticized by Childe (1951, p. 39) and repudiated in its dogmatic form of a theory of stages by Soviet archaeologists in the early 1950s (Klein 1977, pp. 12–14). In the People's Republic of China such stages are still important and focus research interests, though there is no consensus on questions such as when China passed from a slave to a feudal society (Chang 1980, p. 501). In China archaeological research projects formulated from strictly scholarly considerations are relatively rare compared with public or salvage archaeological programs. The major research institution, the Institute of Archaeology of the Chinese Academy of Social Sciences (CASS), was patterned on the Soviet model and founded in 1950, though interestingly, Palaeolithic archaeology was kept separate and today forms a research section of the Institute of Vertebrate Paleontology and Paleoanthropology of the Chinese Academy of Sciences (CAS).

Western archaeology continued to develop outside the Marxist tradition. Nationalistic and even racist interpretations of prehistory characterized a substantial proportion of the work conducted in Europe in the early twentieth century, and prior to the first world war most major excavations in foreign countries were funded by private sources and museums which were interested in recovering fine works of art. In the Near East, for example, large public buildings – temples and palaces – in the centres of the largest urban sites were excavated almost exclusively and provided little information on the social infrastructure that supported and built such monuments. Settlement pattern studies or analyses of the distribution of different types of settlements – villages, fortresses, special production sites, etc. – which were conducted for the purpose of discerning how the entire society functioned were introduced as an archaeological procedure in Western archaeology by G. Willey in the early 1950s, nearly fifteen years after such methods were employed by S. P. Tolstov in Soviet Central Asia.

The Australian-British prehistorian V. Gordon Childe (1892–1957) was the major scholar in the West who attempted to integrate Marxist concepts with archaeological materials. Childe strongly combated racist abuses of archaeological data and tried to correlate forms of society with technological innovations. He realized that technological developments or advances in the forces of production did not automatically occasion social change and correctly felt that the archaeological record, despite its imperfections, constituted the primary source for documenting social evolution, preferable to speculations based on general principles or analogies drawn from ethnography:

> Human needs are not rigid and innate in man since his emergence from the prehuman; they have evolved . . . as much as everything else. Their evolution has to be treated by comparative and historical methods just like that of other aspects of the process. . . . Hence, the rank of any technical device or process in the evolutionary hierarchy cannot be deduced from any general principle, but must be inferred from archaeological data. The sole advantage of technological over political or ethical criteria is that they are more likely to be recognizable in the archaeological record. (1951, p. 21)

Despite this empirical bias, Childe wrote imaginatively of prehistoric transformations of society, coining the commonly accepted terms – *neolithic* and *urban revolutions*. His writings, however, can be criticized not just for their focus on technology, but for their descriptive emph-

asis on defining discrete stages in prehistory rather than explaining the processes by which societies evolved or devolved from one level to another. Unfortunately, this concern with the static description of abstract stages still dominates archaeological research which defines itself explicitly as Marxist in some countries, particularly in Latin America (for a harsh critique cf. Lorenzo 1981, p. 204).

While Western archaeology largely developed apart from the Marxist tradition, prehistoric discoveries – primarily transmitted through the syntheses of Childe – strongly influenced Marxist discussions of social evolution by the second half of the twentieth century. For example, debates on stages in social development (e.g. *Marxism Today* 1962) frequently referred to archaeological work that modified or altered the traditionally accepted sequence of socio-economic formations and refined the concept of primitive communism. Prehistoric discoveries greatly extended the timespan of human existence, opening vistas not contemplated by the founders of historical materialism. Following Childe, Europe was seen to have existed throughout most of its history on the barbarian fringe of the Near East and to have benefited from this relationship since it was unfettered by the stagnant, absolute form of government characteristic of the ancient Near East (Hobsbawm in ibid. p. 254). Perhaps more importantly, Marxists became aware that class society first arose during prehistoric times, a realization forcing, in other words, a second emendation to the opening sentence of the *Communist Manifesto*. Dissolution of kin-based society, the beginnings of social inequality, and the origin of the state were problems that had now to be approached by reference to archaeological data.

At the same time, a resurgence of evolutionary thought and reconsideration of materialist/ecological explanations of cultural phenomena in Western anthropology (see ANTHROPOLOGY) strongly influenced archaeology. In the United States archaeologists, such as Taylor, attempted to 'discover the Indian behind the artefact' (i.e. to reconstruct the society of 'context' in which the remains had been fashioned), and in the 1960s a 'new archaeology' attempted to formulate archaeological criteria for recognizing stages of socio-political complexity, such as bands or chiefdoms. Some archaeologists influenced by these developments, particularly R. McC. Adams (1966), became interested in comparing evolutionary sequences from different areas and implicitly acknowledged a debt to the Marxist tradition. Most, however, remained unaware of Marxism and independently reached conclusions on the ultimate goals of archaeological research that were broadly similar – though based on a more positivistic and sophisticated view of science – to those advocated by Soviet archaeologists in the late 1920s (Masson 1980, p. 20; Klejn 1977, p. 13).

Reconstruction of past forms of society and explanations as to how they evolve and transform themselves are goals that almost universally guide contemporary archaeological research. Recent advances in archaeological methods, such as the introduction of chronometric dating techniques, the broad utilization of physical-chemical analyses for determining artefactual provenance, the standard recovery of floral and faunal materials directly documenting past subsistence activities, and the focus on regional settlement pattern determination – make possible the fulfilment of these goals in a manner never conceived by Childe. Today, some Western archaeologists, such as A. Gilman (1981), creatively utilize Marxist concepts in interpreting their data, but most present materialist accounts of change that minimize social conflict and treat human prehistory as a form of adaptation to a particular environmental setting or as a mere extension of natural history. The potential for reconstructing past social forms, or archaeological optimism, implicit in Marx's discussion of early tools is generally accepted, though scarcely realized, by contemporary archaeologists. A credible synthesis of prehistory emphasizing past social formations and their relations of production remains to be written.

Reading

Adams, R. McC. 1966: *Evolution of Urban Society*.

Chang, K. C. 1980: 'Archaeology'. In L. A. Orleans ed. *Science in Contemporary China*.

Childe, V. G. 1947: *History*.

— 1951: *Social Evolution*.

Gilman, A. 1981: 'The Development of Social Stratification in Bronze Age Europe'.

Godelier, M. 1978: 'The Concept of the "Asiatic Mode of Production" and Marxist Models of Social Evolu-

tion'. In David Seddon ed. *Relations of Production: Marxist Approaches to Economic Anthropology*.

Green, S. 1981: *Prehistorian: A Biography of V. Gordon Childe*.

Klejn, L. S. 1977: 'A Panorama of Theoretical Archaeology'.

Kristiansen, K. 1981: 'A Social History of Danish Archaeology (1805–1975)'. In G. Daniel ed. *Towards a History of Archaeology*.

Lorenzo, J. L. 1981: 'Archaeology South of the Rio Grande'.

Trigger, B. G. 1980: *Gordon Childe: Revolutions in Archaeology*.

PHILIP L. KOHL

aristocracy Since Marx first put forward his theory of the RULING CLASS, its conflict with other classes and the modes by which it maintains its HEGEMONY, many historians have utilized it to analyse particular societies in the past, from ancient Greece and Rome (Finley 1973), and the old regimes of pre-industrial Europe (Kula 1962), to the industrial societies of the nineteenth century (Hobsbawm 1968). The history of Japan has also been viewed in these terms (Honjo 1935).

The value of this approach has been to encourage a more analytical social history and to show the relationship between the economic, social and political behaviour of social groups. Its influence (combined with that of Pareto, Veblen, Weber and others), can be seen on historians of aristocracies who are non-Marxist (Stone 1965), or even anti-Marxist (Hexter 1961). However, the analysis has run into problems.

Historians began by seizing on particular societies (Rome in the first century BC, Florence in the thirteenth century, France in the seventeenth and eighteenth centuries, and so on), as examples of the decline of a 'feudal' aristocracy and the rise of a 'bourgeoisie', representing a new epoch. It later turned out, in these and other instances, to be difficult, if not impossible, to distinguish the two groups at any point, whether in terms of their investments or their ideology. Hence the Soviet historian Boris Porshnev came to speak of the 'feudalization' of the French bourgeoisie in the seventeenth century, while Hobsbawm (1968), wrote of the British aristocracy of the nineteenth century that it was, 'by continental standards, almost a bourgeoisie'. A way out of this sort of difficulty has been shown by Brady (1978), who has described the patriciate of sixteenth-century Strasbourg as 'a complex social class composed of two fractions, one rentier and the other mercantile', and studied how they were in practice integrated.

The latent ambiguities in Marx's concept of CLASS have also become apparent. A powerful attack on the use of the term to describe groups in pre-industrial societies has been launched by the French historian Roland Mousnier (1973), who prefers the contemporary word 'estate'. The most effective replies to this sort of criticism have come from historians and sociologists who have admitted the value of the contemporary concept, but argue that analysis must work with 'estate' and 'class' categories simultaneously (Ossowski 1957).

Reading

Bottomore, Tom 1966: *Elites and Society.*

Brady, Tom 1978: *Ruling Class, Regime and Reformation in Strasbourg, 1520–1555.*

Finley, Moses 1973: *The Ancient Economy.*

Hexter, J. H. 1961: 'A New Framework for Social History'. In *Reappraisals in History.*

Hobsbawm, Eric 1968: *Industry and Empire.*

Honio, Eijiro 1935 (1965): *The Social and Economic History of Japan.*

Kula, Witold 1962: *Economic Theory of the Feudal System.*

Mousnier, Roland 1969 (1973): *Social Hierarchies.*

Stone, Lawrence 1965: *The Crisis of the Aristocracy.*

PETER BURKE

art   Marx and Engels propounded no general aesthetic theory, nor did they undertake any systematic studies of art and literature. Marx's *obiter dicta* on the subject have given rise to controversy rather than providing a reliable canon of interpretation. In an oft-quoted passage in the *Grundrisse* (Introduction) Marx observes that 'it is well known that some golden ages of art are quite disproportionate to the general development of society, hence also to the material foundation', and goes on to say that in the case of Greek art, although it is bound up with specific forms of social development, it nevertheless remains for us, in certain respects, 'a norm and an unattainable ideal' and exercises an 'eternal charm'. This suggests that some kinds of art have, for whatever reason (and Marx here adumbrates a psychological explanation), a universal, transhistorical value, which is not rigorously determined by the material base of society. Elsewhere (*Theories of Surplus Value*, ch. IV, sect. 16) Marx derides 'the illusion of the French in the eighteenth century satirised by Lessing. Because we are further ahead than the ancients in mechanics, etc., why shouldn't we be able to make an epic too?' Such views may attribute to art 'a special status within the ideological superstructure' (Laing 1978, p. 10), but they also conform with the more general qualification of the relation between BASE AND SUPERSTRUCTURE indicated by Engels in several letters of the 1890s (to C. Schmidt, 5 August and 27 October 1890; to J. Bloch, 21 September 1890; to F. Mehring, 14 July 1893; to W. Borgius, 25 January 1894).

On the other side, in a criticism of Stirner's conception of the 'unique individual' in relation to the place of the artist in society (*German Ideolology*, vol. I, pt. III, sect. III 2), Marx argues that 'the exclusive concentration of artistic talent in particular individuals and its related suppression among the mass of people is a consequence of the division of labour . . . In a communist society there are no painters, but at most people who among other things also paint'. Here the very existence of art as a specialized activity is questioned, in terms which follow from Marx's general view of the importance of overcoming the division of labour (ibid. pt. I, sect. Al): 'In communist society, where nobody has one exclusive sphere of activity but each can become accomplished in any branch he wishes, production as a whole is regulated by society, thus making it possible for me to do one thing today and another tomorrow, to hunt in the morning, fish in the afternoon, rear cattle in the evening, criticize after dinner, without ever becoming hunter, fisherman, herdsman or critic.' This idea is both speculative, verging upon the concoction of 'recipes for the cookshops of the future', and in its literal sense quite unrealistic in relation to any complex and technologically developed society, especially with regard to artistic creation, but it expresses an important conception of the nature of human beings which runs through Marx's early writings in particular (see HUMAN NATURE; PRAXIS). From this standpoint art, or a developed aesthetic sense, is seen as being, like language, a universal and distinctive human capacity; and just as Gramsci observed that all human beings are intellectuals, though only some of them have the social function of intellectuals, so it could be said that they are all artists.

The pioneering works of Marxist aesthetics were those of Mehring (1893) and Plekhanov (1912), the former being concerned primarily with LITERATURE rather than the visual arts or music. Plekhanov aimed to develop a strictly deterministic theory, saying that 'the art of any people has always, in my opinion, an intimate causal connection with their economy' (p. 57). From this standpoint he analysed dance in primitive society as a re-experiencing of the pleasure of labour (e.g. a hunt), and music as an aid to work (through rhythm); but in discussing the general relation between labour, play and art he argued that while art has a utilitarian origin in the needs of material life, aesthetic enjoyment becomes a pleasure in its own right. Beyond the primitive level, according to Plekhanov, art is determined only indirectly by the economy, through the mediating influence of class divisions and class domination. Thus in his account of French drama and painting in the eighteenth century he argued that it represented the triumph of the 'refinement of aristocratic taste', but later in the century, when the rule of the aristocracy was challenged by the bourgeoisie, the art of Boucher and Greuze 'was eclipsed by the revolutionary painting of David and his school' (p. 157).

The October Revolution in Russia and the revolutionary movements in Central Europe brought into the forefront of debate two themes which were in some respects antithetical: revolutionary art and proletarian art. In Russia, Lunacharsky, Commissar for Education and the Arts from 1917 to 1929, 'had few inhibitions about bringing in the avant-garde' (Willett 1978, p. 34); thus he encouraged the Vitebsk art school, of which Chagall was appointed head, as well as re-establishing the Moscow art studios, where Kandinsky, Pevsner and others taught, which became the cradle of 'Constructivism' (ibid. pp. 38–9). In Germany, the workers' council movement also supported the avant-garde in the arts, and notwithstanding the political defeat of the movement some of its achievements (e.g. Gropius's Bauhaus) survived until the triumph of fascism. During the early 1920s there was also a lively interaction between the representatives of revolutionary art in Russia and Germany.

The idea of proletarian art (or culture), on the other hand, was criticized by some leading Bolsheviks (among them Trotsky), and the Proletkult organization came to be seen as a rival to the party and potentially counter-revolutionary. But in the longer term the idea that the proletariat needed a class-art of its own, and that the artist should above all be 'partisan', acquired great influence, and entered as an important element into the official Soviet aesthetic doctrine of 'Socialist Realism', enforced by Stalin and Zhdanov. Under this regime there could be no question of radical experimentation or avant-garde movements in art, and a dreary mediocrity prevailed. But the situation did not wholly exclude fresh thought about art, and Lifshitz (with whom Lukács worked in the Marx-Engels Institute in Moscow) besides editing the first selection of Marx's and Engels's comments on art (1937) published an interesting study of Marxist aesthetic theory (1933) based largely upon Marx's notebooks and early writings.

In the 1930s and subsequently, however, the principal contributions to a Marxist theory of art were made in the West. Brecht (1938 (1977)) opposed to socialist realism his own conception of the 'epic theatre', and commented on Lukács and his associates in Moscow that 'they are, to put it bluntly, enemies of production . . . they themselves don't want to produce [but] to play the apparatchik and exercise control over other people' (Bloch et al. 1977, p. 97). Brecht's ideas profoundly influenced the aesthetic theory of Benjamin, who took the epic theatre as a model of how the forms and instruments of artistic production could be transformed in a socialist direction (Benjamin 1968). The conflict between Brecht and Lukács was part of a wider controversy between the advocates of 'socialist realism' (i.e. the bourgeois realism of the nineteenth century with a new content) and the supporters of 'modernism' (particularly German Expressionism, but also Cubism and Surrealism), who included, besides Brecht and Benjamin, Bloch and Adorno (see Bloch et al. 1977; Willett 1978).

Another major contribution of the 1930s,

which has only recently become widely known, is Raphael's volume (1933), comprising three studies in the sociology of art. One study, on the Marxist theory of art, sets out from a detailed analysis of Marx's text in the *Grundrisse* (Introduction) to construct a sociology of art that would overcome the existing weaknesses of dialectical materialism, which 'has not been able to undertake more than fitful, fragmentary investigations into specific artistic problems' (p. 76). Raphael emphasizes the importance of Marx's conception of Greek mythology as the intermediary between the economic base and Greek art, and raises a series of new questions about the general relation between mythology and art. He then considers various problems connected with the 'disproportionate development' of material production and art, and finally criticizes Marx's explanation of the 'eternal charm' of Greek art, which he regards as 'essentially incompatible with historical materialism' (p. 105). Raphael's own explanation of the 'normative value' of Greek art in certain periods of European history is that 'revivals of antiquity' occurred whenever the total culture underwent a crisis as a result of economic and social changes. In the third of these studies, Raphael analyses the art of Picasso as the most typical example of modernism and relates it to the transition from free-enterprise capitalism to monopoly capitalism.

In the past two decades Marxist writing on art has been predominantly methodological (concerned with the abstract formulation of an adequate Marxist *concept* of art) and few substantive studies have been undertaken. One notable exception, from a somewhat earlier period but recently republished, is Klingender's excellent study of art in the industrial revolution (1947), which deals particularly with interaction between art and technology, and with the effects upon art of the rise to power of 'new-fangled men'. Another is Willett's detailed account (1978) of the modernist movement in painting, architecture and music in Weimar Germany. The recent theoretical discussions deal with two themes which have preoccupied Marxist thinkers from the outset and have their source in Marx's own diverse reflections on art: (i) art as ideology; and (ii) art as one of the principal manifestations of human creativity.

An analysis of art as ideology has to show, on one side, the specific place that a style of art (both form and content) occupies in the whole body of ideas and images of a dominant class during a particular historical phase of its existence. This involves (as Goldmann (1956) argued with respect to literary works) first establishing the immanent structure of meaning of an art work or style, and then situating it in the broader structure of class relations in a given mode of production. Both Plekhanov and Raphael attempted to do this in the studies mentioned earlier. On the other side, some kinds of art may be regarded as ideological weapons of a subordinate class in its struggle for emancipation, and the dispute over realism and modernism was very largely concerned with the proper characterization and analysis of 'revolutionary art'. One significant feature of recent Marxist thought about art as ideology is the growing interest in popular art and the 'culture industry' (see CULTURE), notably in the work of some members of the Frankfurt School (Adorno, Marcuse). From their standpoint, art in the era of advanced capitalism is not only degraded as a result of mechanical reproduction and wide diffusion, but also acquires a greater power of pacifying and integrating dissident classes and groups; while at the same time the ideological effectiveness of any revolutionary art is diminished because radical innovations are easily assimilated into the body of dominant images. Benjamin, however, took an opposite view; for him the principal effect of mechanical reproduction was to destroy the elitist 'aura' of art, bring about 'a tremendous shattering of tradition' (1968, p. 223), and create a bond between the proletariat and the new cultural forms (e.g. film; see CINEMA AND TELEVISION).

The theme of art as creative expression poses very complex problems in the analysis of aesthetic value (see AESTHETICS) and of human nature (see also PSYCHOLOGY). In these two spheres, not only have Marxist ideas remained relatively undeveloped until quite recently, but the growing body of work in the past two decades has revealed profound disagreements among Marxist thinkers. At the level of social practice, however, the notion of art as an expression of a universal human creativity, and as a liberating force (however this notion may eventually be formulated in theoretical terms) suggests two elements of a Marxist approach to art in a socialist society. The first is that art (like intellectual life in general) should develop freely, enabling 'a hundred flowers to bloom', and should certainly not be required to conform with some artistic dogma, least of all one imposed by a political authority. The second, conforming broadly with the idea expressed by Marx in the *German Ideology* (see above), is that alongside the development of 'high art' by exceptionally gifted individuals, artistic creativity should be widely fostered and encouraged as a universal human need and source of enjoyment.

Reading

Benjamin, Walter 1968: 'The Work of Art in the Age of Mechanical Reproduction'. In *Illuminations*.

Bloch, Ernst *et al.* 1977: *Aesthetics and Politics*.

Klien, Manfred ed. 1968: *Marx und Engels über Kunst und Literatur*.

Klingender, Francis D. 1947 (*1968*): *Art and the Industrial Revolution*.

Laing, David 1978: *The Marxist Theory of Art*.

Lifshitz, Mikhail 1933 (*1973*): *The Philosophy of Art of Karl Marx*.

Plekhanov, G. V. 1912 (*1953*): *Art and Social Life*.

Raphael, Max 1933 (*1980*): *Proudhon, Marx, Picasso: Three Studies in the Sociology of Art*.

Willett, John 1978: *The New Sobriety 1917–1933: Art and Politics in the Weimar Period*.

— 1980 (*1983*): 'Art and Revolution'. In Eric J. Hobsbawm *et al.* eds, *The History of Marxism*.

TOM BOTTOMORE

Asiatic society While the analysis of Asian societies was not central to the theoretical and empirical concerns of Marx and Engels in the nineteenth century, the nature of 'Asiatic society' or, more technically, the Asiatic mode of production (hereafter AMP) has subsequently assumed major conceptual and political significance in Marxism. The debate about the AMP has raised questions concerning not only the relevance of Marxist concepts outside the European context, but the character of materialist explanations of class society, revolutionary change and world history. The problematic status of the notion of 'Asiatic society' can be indicated in terms of a sharp dilemma. If the socio-economic specificity of Asiatic society is accepted the teleological assumptions of the conventional list of historical transitions (slave,

feudal, capitalist and socialist) may be avoided. However, in accepting the validity of the AMP, Marxists may also endorse the privileged position of Occidental over Oriental history. The dynamic and progressive character of the West is then uniquely contrasted with the stationary and regressive Orient; and it is then difficult to distinguish Marxist categories from traditional notions of 'Oriental Despotism'. The belief that Asiatic society is arbitrary, despotic and stagnant may thus become a justification for colonialism, in that external intervention is a necessary, however unfortunate, condition for internal change.

Marx and Engels first became interested in an analysis of Asiatic society in 1853 as a consequence of their journalistic criticisms of British foreign policy. In their *New York Daily Tribune* articles, they were influenced by James Mill (*History of British India*, 1821), by François Bernier (*Voyages contenant la description des états du Grand Mogol*, 1670) and by Richard Jones (*An Essay on the Distribution of Wealth and the Sources of Taxation*, 1831). On the basis of these sources, Marx and Engels claimed that the absence of private property, particularly private ownership of land, in Asiatic society was the basic cause of social stagnation. Periodic changes in the political organization of Asiatic society from dynastic struggles and military conquest had not brought about radical changes in economic organization, because ownership of the land and organization of agricultural activities remained with the state as the real landlord. The static nature of Asiatic society also depended on the coherence of the ancient village community which, combining agriculture and handicrafts, was economically self-sufficient. These communities were, for geographical and climatic reasons, dependent on irrigation which required a centralized administrative apparatus to co-ordinate and develop large-scale hydraulic works. Despotism and stagnation were thus explained by the dominant role of the state in public works and the self-sufficiency and isolation of the village community.

This preliminary sketch of Asiatic society was modified and extended by Marx and Engels to produce a more complex view of the AMP in their mature work. In the *Grundrisse*, Marx noted a crucial difference in the urban history of the Orient and Occident. Whereas in feudalism the existence of politically independent cities as locations for the growth of the production of exchange values was crucial for the development of a bourgeois class and industrial capitalism, the Oriental city was the artificial creation of the state and remained subordinate to agriculture and the countryside; it was merely 'a princely camp' imposed on the economic structure of society. Marx now placed special emphasis on the communal ownership of land by self-sufficient, autarchic villages which were the real basis of the social unity represented by the state.

The AMP was thus conceived as one form of communal appropriation which could, in principle, occur outside Asia. A similar approach to the AMP as representing a version of communal appropriation appeared in *Capital* where Marx returned to the self-sufficiency of the Asiatic village and the unity of handicrafts and agriculture as the ultimate foundation of Oriental despotism and social immutability. In *Capital* it is the simplicity of production at the village level which defines the essential feature of Asiatic stability: 'the secret of the unchangingness of Asiatic societies'. The surplus product of these communities was appropriated in the form of taxation by the state so that ground rent and taxation coincided.

Although there has been considerable debate as to the essential characteristic of Asiatic society – absence of private property, dominance of the state over irrigation works, self-sufficiency of villages, unity of handicrafts and agriculture, simplicity of production methods – in the analyses of Marx and Engels the point of these diverse features was to place the stationariness of Asiatic society in relation to Occidental development, and negatively to identify those factors in European feudalism which were conducive to capitalist development. Within the Orientalist perspective Asiatic society was typified by an overdeveloped state apparatus and an underdeveloped 'civil society', whereas in Europe the obverse obtained. In Asiatic society, those social arrangements which were closely associated with the rise of a bourgeois class – free markets, private property, guild structure and bourgeois law – were absent, because the centralized state dominated civil society. The absence of private property ruled out the development of social classes as agents of social change. At the village level, all the inhabitants may be regarded as an exploited class existing in a state of 'general slavery', but it is difficult to identify the dominant class within Asiatic society. The caste system which Marx and Engels regarded as a primitive form of class relationship was clearly not relevant to the analysis of China, Turkey and Persia. In the absence of internal mechanisms of social change, one implication of Marx's analysis of India was that British imperialism had become, however unintentionally, the principal exogenous force promoting the dissolution of the AMP. In their *New York Daily Tribune* articles, Marx and Engels argued that the British, by creating private property in land, had revolutionized Indian society by exploding the stationary AMP. The railway system, free press, modern army and modernized forms of communication would provide the institutional framework for social development in India. On the basis of these articles it has been claimed (Avineri 1969) that Marx's account of British imperialism leads to the proposition that the more extensive the forms of imperialism the more profound the consequences for modernization. Asiatic specificity ultimately provides a justification, albeit covert, for imperial expansion. It is because the AMP has strong ideological implications that Marxists have often argued for the demolition of this particular concept.

The concept of the AMP has experienced a long history of demolitions, resurrections and refurbishings. While Marx in the Preface to *A Contribution to the Critique of Political Economy* (1859) treated the AMP as one of the 'epochs marking progress in the economic development of society', Engels did not refer to it in *The Origin of the Family, Private Property and the State* (1884). The importance of the concept came back into Marxist debate in the context of the revolutionary struggles in Russia. Different political strategies were associated with different conceptions of the character of Russian society as feudal, capitalist or Asiatic. Marx and Engels had first referred to Tsarist Russia as 'semi-Asiatic' in 1853; Engels developed the notion of the isolation of the Russian commune as the basis of Oriental despotism in *Anti-Dühring* (1877). In the period 1877 to 1882, Marx wrote a number of letters to the editorial board of the *Otechestvenniye Zapiski*, Zasulich, and Engels, outlining his views on Russian social structure and the possibility of revolution. The issue was whether the Russian commune could provide the foundation of socialism or whether it represented a social brake on political development.

Marx and Engels argued that the Russian commune could provide a basis for socialism where capitalist relations of production had not penetrated too deeply into the countryside. In addition, a revolution in Russia had to coincide with working-class revolutions in Europe. The problem of Russia as a 'semi-Asiatic' society continued to play a major role in debates concerning revolutionary strategy. Plekhanov, rejecting the populists' utopian view of Russian history, saw the commune as the basis of Russian absolutism and attacked proposals for land nationalization as a restoration of the AMP and Oriental despotism. These debates over Asiatic society hinged on the question of a deterministic unilinear view of history versus multilinear perspectives. The validity of AMP was crucial to multilinear approaches because it implied that Marxism was not committed to a mechanistic evolutionary scheme in which historical stages followed each other according to necessary laws. The unilinear scheme – primitive communism, slave, feudal, capitalist and socialist – came to prevail after the Leningrad conference of 1931 rejected the relevance of the AMP to the analysis of Asian societies. The decision was confirmed by Stalin's adherence to a mechanistically unilinear perspective; rejection of the AMP meant that Asian societies were subsequently subsumed under the categories of slavery or feudalism.

In the post-war period, discussion of Asiatic society has been stimulated by Wittfogel's *Oriental Despotism*. Empirically, Wittfogel was concerned with the implications of centralized management of irrigation for the social structure of China. The theoretical inspiration for Wittfogel's study of hydraulic economy in his *Wirtschaft und Gesellschaft Chinas* came from Weber's application of the notion of 'patrimonial bureaucracy' to Chinese history. For Wittfogel, the concept of the AMP raised two fundamental issues. First, it pointed to the whole question of the relationship between man and nature; his study of the 'cultural geography' of social formations based on public ownership of irrigation works was aimed at the fundamental processes of productive labour connecting hu-

man groups to nature. Second, it posed the question of whether it was possible to have a society in which the dominant class did not own the means of production, but controlled the state apparatus and the economy as a bureaucratic class. Wittfogel later published *Oriental Despotism* in 1957 as a 'comparative study of total power'; the polemical thrust of this study was the argument that the communist leadership suppressed the concept of the AMP after 1931 because the idea of a ruling class controlling the means of administration without ownership of private property indicated a continuity of political power from Tsarist to Stalinist Russia. Since the party officialdom had replaced the traditional bureaucracy, Asiatic despotism had been preserved.

The process of de-Stalinization contributed to a revival of interest in the AMP in the 1960s. Under the impetus of the 'structuralist' Marxism of Althusser, the analysis of modes of production became part of a re-emphasis on the scientific status of historical materialism. Precise formulations of the laws of accumulation within various modes of production promised a rigorous Marxist alternative to theories of modernization and development in conventional social science. Interest in the AMP was one aspect of a more general trend in Marxism to produce concepts of dependency (see DEPENDENCY THEORY), uneven development and underdevelopment (see UNDERDEVELOPMENT AND DEVELOPMENT) in order to grasp the effects of capitalist expansion on peripheral economies. The AMP has often appeared useful as an alternative to unilinear theories of stages of development. Furthermore, as an alternative to slavery and feudalism, the idea that Asiatic society has particular features recognized the specificity of Oriental societies. Despite these alleged theoretical advantages, the concept of Asiatic society and the AMP remains problematic. The application of the feudal mode of production to Asia and Africa has often been criticized on the grounds that it is too vague to incorporate the empirical complexity and diversity of the societies within these regions. In practice, the notion of 'Asiatic society' has proved equally vague and uncertain. In Wittfogel, for example, a variety of societies exhibiting extreme variations in development and organization – Tsarist Russia, Sung China, Mamluk Egypt, Islamic Spain, Persia, Hawaii –

are embraced by the single concept of 'hydraulic society'. In a similar fashion, Marx used the term 'Asiatic society' to describe not only China and India, but also Spain, the Middle East, Java and pre-Columbian America. The concept of the AMP has been used promiscuously to describe almost any society based on communal ownership and self-sufficient villages where capitalist market relations are absent. While there are numerous empirical objections to the application of the AMP to particular societies, the AMP is also riddled with theoretical problems. It is difficult to see, for example, how self-sufficient, autonomous villages could be compatible with a centralized state which must intervene in the village economy. In addition, the social characteristics of Asiatic society appear to be caused by purely technological factors associated with large-scale irrigation rather than by the relations of production; the theory of Asiatic society involves assumptions about technological determinism which are incompatible with historical materialism in which relations determine forces of production. Finally, the explanation of the origins of the state in Asiatic society presents innumerable problems. In the absence of class struggles, the state has to be explained as the consequence of conquest or in terms of its functions in relation to public works.

The problem of 'Asiatic society' is in fact far more profound than these technical issues would suggest. The AMP had a negative importance in Marxism in that its theoretical function was not to analyse Asiatic society but to explain the rise of capitalism in Europe within a comparative framework. Hence, Asiatic society was defined as a series of gaps – the missing middle class, the absent city, the absence of private property, the lack of bourgeois institutions – which thereby accounted for the dynamism of Europe. 'Asiatic society' was thus a manifestation in Marxism of an Orientalist problematic which can be traced back through Hegel, Montesquieu and Hobbes to Greek political philosophy. Marxism often unwittingly inherited the language of traditional discourses on arbitrary rule which had been forged in the debate over European absolutism. 'Asiatic society' has to be seen, therefore, as a central element within an Orientalist tradition which has enjoyed a remarkable, but pernicious, resilience within Western philosophy. See also NON-

CAPITALIST MODES OF PRODUCTION; LANDED PROPERTY AND RENT; STAGES OF DEVELOPMENT.

Reading

Avineri, Shlomo, ed. 1969: *Karl Marx on Colonialism and Modernization*.

Bailey, Anne M. and Llobera, Josep R. 1981: *The Asiatic Mode of Production*.

Hindess, Barry and Hirst, Paul Q. 1975: *Pre-Capitalist Modes of Production*.

Krader, Lawrence 1975: *The Asiatic Mode of Production*.

Mandel, Ernest 1977: *The Formation of the Economic Thought of Karl Marx*.

Melotti, Umberto 1972 (1977): *Marx and the Third World*.

O'Leary, B. 1989: *The Asiatic Mode of Production*.

Said, Edward W. 1978: *Orientalism*.

Sofri, Gianni 1969: *Il modo di produzione asiatico: storia di una controversia marxista*.

Turner, Bryan S. 1978: *Marx and the End of Orientalism*.

Wittfogel, Karl A. 1957: *Oriental Despotism: A Comparative Study of Total Power*.

BRYAN S. TURNER

Austro-Marxism   The name given to a school of Marxist thought which flourished in Vienna from the end of the nineteenth century to 1934, but particularly in the period up to the first world war, its most eminent members being Max Adler, Otto Bauer, Rudolf Hilferding and Karl Renner. The main influences upon the school, leaving aside the more diffuse effects of the creative upsurge in Viennese intellectual and cultural life at the beginning of this century, were, as Bauer (1927) noted, the powerful current of neo-Kantianism and positivism in philosophy, the emergence of new theoretical orientations in the social sciences (notably marginalist economics), and the need to confront specific social problems in the multinational Habsburg Empire.

The initial public manifestation of a new school of thought was the foundation in 1904 of the *Marx-Studien*, edited by Adler and Hilferding and published irregularly until 1923, in which all the major early works of the Austro-Marxists appeared. This elaboration of a distinctive style of Marxist thought was confirmed by the establishment in 1907 of a new theoretical journal, *Der*

Kampf, which soon came to rival Kautsky's *Die Neue Zeit* as the leading European Marxist review. At the same time the Austro-Marxists were active in promoting workers' education and in the leadership of the rapidly growing Austrian Social Democratic party (SPÖ).

The conceptual and theoretical foundations of Austro-Marxism were elaborated chiefly by Adler, who conceived Marxism as 'a system of sociological knowledge . . . the science of the laws of social life and its causal development' (Adler 1925, p. 136). In his earliest major work (1904) Adler analysed carefully the relation between causality and teleology, and here, as well as in later writings, he emphasized the diversity of forms of causality, insisting that the causal relation in social life is not 'mechanical' but is mediated by consciousness. This idea is expressed strongly in a discussion of ideology (1930 p. 118) where Adler argues that even 'economic phenomena themselves are never "material" in the materialist sense, but have precisely a "mental" character'. The fundamental concept of Marx's theory of society was seen by Adler as 'socialized humanity' or 'social association' and treated by him in neo-Kantian fashion as being 'transcendentally given as a category of knowledge' (1925); i.e. as a concept furnished by reason, not derived from experience, which is a precondition of an empirical science. It was the formulation of this concept, Adler argued, which made Marx the founder of a genuine science of society.

Adler's conception of Marxism as a system of sociology provided the framework of ideas which largely inspired and directed the work of the whole school. This is very evident in Hilferding's economic analyses. In his critical study of marginalist economic theory (1904) Hilferding opposes to the individualist 'psychological school of political economy' the thesis that Marx's theory of value rests upon a conception of 'society' and 'social relations', and that Marxist theory as a whole 'aims to disclose the social determinism of economic phenomena', its starting point being 'society and not the individual'. In the preface to *Finance Capital* (1910) Hilferding refers specifically to Adler's work in asserting that 'the sole aim of any [Marxist] inquiry – even into matters of policy – is the discovery of causal relationships'. Hilferding's object in *Finance Capital* was indeed to disclose

the causal factors in the most recent stage of capitalist development, through an analysis of the growth of credit money and of joint-stock companies, the increasing influence of the banks, and the rise to a dominant position in the economy of monopolistic cartels and trusts. In the final part of the book he deduced from these changes the necessity of an imperialist stage of development and outlined a theory of imperialism (see COLONIALISM; IMPERIALISM AND WORLD MARKET) which provided the basis for the later studies by Bukharin and Lenin.

The importance of Marxism conceived as a sociological theory can also be seen in the studies of nationality by Bauer and Renner. Bauer's classic work, *Die Nationalitätenfrage und die Sozialdemokratie* (1907), set out to provide a theoretical and historical analysis of the nation and nationality, and led to the conclusion: 'For me, history no longer reflects the struggles of nations; instead the nation itself appears as the reflection of historical struggles. For the nation is only manifested in the national character, in the nationality of the individual; and the nationality of the individual is only one aspect of his determination by the history of society, by the development of the conditions and techniques of labour.' Renner devoted his attention more to the legal and constitutional problems of the nationalities in the Habsburg Empire (which gave rise to nationalist movements that competed with the socialist movement for popular support), and he developed the interesting idea, in the context of its time, of a transformation of the Empire, under socialist rule, into a 'state of nationalities' which might eventually provide a model for the socialist organization of a future world community (see Renner 1899, 1902).

But Renner is best known for his pioneering contribution to a Marxist sociology of law, *The Institutions of Private Law and their Social Functions* (1904). In this work he adopts as his starting point the existing system of legal norms and seeks to show how the same norms change their functions in response to changes in society, and more particularly, to changes in its economic structure. In the concluding section however he poses as major problems for a sociology of law some broader questions about how the legal norms themselves change and the fundamental causes of such changes. Here, as elsewhere in his writings, it is clear that Renner attributes to law an active role in maintaining or modifying social relations, and does not regard it as a mere reflection of economic conditions; and he cites as consonant with this view some of Marx's comments on law in the introduction to the *Grundrisse*. Adler also contributed to formulating the general principles of a Marxist sociology of law in his critique (1922) of Kelsen's 'pure theory of law' which treats law as a closed system of norms, the analysis of which is confined to showing the logical interdependence of the normative elements and excludes any inquiry into either the ethical basis of law or its social context. In the course of his study Adler examined in some detail the differences between a sociological and a formal theory of law.

Besides their major works described above the Austro-Marxists published many other sociological studies of considerable interest. They were, for example, among the first Marxists to examine systematically the increasing involvement in the economy of the 'interventionist state'. In a series of articles on 'problems of Marxism' (1916) Renner noted 'the penetration of the private economy down to its elementary cells by the state; not the nationalization of a few factories, but the control of the whole private sector of the economy by willed and conscious regulation'. He continued: 'State power and the economy begin to merge . . . the national economy is perceived as a means of state power, state power as a means to strengthen the national economy. . . . It is the epoch of imperialism.' Similarly, in essays published between 1915 and 1924, Hilferding developed, on the basis of his analysis in *Finance Capital*, a theory of ORGANIZED CAPITALISM, in which the state is seen as beginning to assume the character of a conscious, rational structuring of society in the interests of all. In organized capitalism the conditions exist for development in either of two directions: towards socialism and the fruition of a rational collective ordering of social life, if the working class is able to seize state power; towards a corporate state if the capitalist monopolies maintain their political dominance. In Italy and Germany the latter possibility was realized in the form of fascism, and Bauer (1936) provided one of the most systematic Marxist accounts of the social conditions in which the fascist movements were able to emerge and triumph (see FASCISM). Hilferding

himself, in his later writings, and especially in his unfinished work *Das historische Problem* (1941), outlined a radical revision of historical materialism which would assign to the state, and above all the modern nation state, an independent role in the formation of society. In the twentieth century, he argued specifically, there had been a profound 'change in the relation of the state to society, brought about by the subordination of the economy to the coercive power of the state. The state becomes a totalitarian state to the extent that this process of subordination takes place . . .' (see TOTALITARIANISM).

The Austro-Marxists also devoted much attention to the changing class structure in twentieth-century capitalist societies, and to its political implications (see CLASS). In a substantial essay on the 'metamorphosis of the working class' (1933), written in the context of the defeat and destruction of the working-class movement in Germany, Adler noted that 'already in Marx's work the concept of the proletariat displays a certain differentiation', with workers in the production process forming its main body, the industrial reserve army of the unemployed (see RESERVE ARMY OF LABOUR) its second layer, and beneath these two the lumpenproletariat. But he goes on to argue that the development of capitalism has produced such changes in the class structure of the proletariat that it represents a new phenomenon, and 'it is doubtful whether we can speak of a single class'. In this new proletariat, according to Adler, there are several distinct strata which have given rise to three basic, often conflicting, political orientations: that of the labour aristocracy, comprising both skilled workers and office employees; that of the organized workers in town and country; and that of the permanent or long term unemployed. Adler argues further that even among the main body of workers the development of organizations has produced a fatal division of labour between the growing stratum of salaried officials and representatives who are active in taking decisions, and the largely passive membership. The weakness of the working class in the face of fascist movements was due, he concluded, to this differentiation of socio-economic conditions and political attitudes.

Renner, writing after the second world war (see especially the posthumously published

Wandlungen der modernen Gesellschaft, 1953), concentrated his attention on the growth of new social strata – public officials and private employees – constituting what he called a 'service class' of salaried employees whose contract of employment 'does not create a relationship of wage labour'. This new class, which has emerged alongside the working class, tends to merge with the latter at its boundary, and Renner also notes that 'the trade union struggle has achieved for large sections of the working class a legal status which resembles that of officials' (p. 214). He concludes by deploring the superficial and careless approach of many Marxists to 'the real study of class formation in society, and above all the continuous restructuring of the classes', and asserts that 'the working class as it appears (and scientifically was bound to appear) in Marx's *Capital* no longer exists' (ibid.).

From a different aspect, and at an earlier date, Bauer also made an important contribution to the study of classes in his comparative account of the situation of workers and peasants and the relations between them in the Russian and German revolutions, and in his detailed analysis of the Austrian revolution (1923). He also examined in various writings (see especially Bauer 1936) the emergence of a new dominant class in the USSR as the dictatorship of the proletariat was transformed into the dictatorship of an all-powerful party apparatus.

After the first world war the Austro-Marxist school was eclipsed to some extent by the rise to a position of dominant international influence of Marxist-Leninist orthodoxy, especially in the period of Stalinism; and it was then largely destroyed in 1934 by the triumph of Austrian fascism. But the past decade has seen a considerable revival of interest in Austro-Marxism, and it is now widely discussed again, both as a general framework for a Marxist sociology – notwithstanding the fact that its '*positivist*' orientation brings it within the ambit of the renewed critique of positivism in the social sciences – and as a body of substantial research into major problems of structure and change in the advanced capitalist societies.

Reading

Bauer, Otto 1927 (*1978*): 'Was ist Austro-Marxismus?' Trans. in Bottomore and Goode eds *Austro-Marxism*.

Bottomore, Tom and Goode, Patrick eds 1978: *Austro-Marxism*.

Heintel, Peter 1967: *System und Ideologie*.

Kolakowski, Leszek 1978: *Main Currents of Marxism*. vol. 2, ch. XII.

Leser, Norbert, 1968: *Zwischen Reformismus und Bolschewismus. Der Austromarxismus als Theorie und Praxis*.

Mosetić, Gerald 1987: *Die Gesellschaftstheorie des Austromarxismus*.

TOM BOTTOMORE

automation   Marx's discussion of the development of the LABOUR PROCESS into one which uses MACHINERY AND MACHINOFACTURE is predicated on his discovery of the tendency of capital continually to try to escape from its dependence upon labour and LABOUR POWER. Machinery as objectified labour confronts living labour within the labour process as the power which controls it; living labour becomes a mere appendage of the machine. And since the purpose of the introduction of machinery is to increase relative SURPLUS VALUE by reducing necessary labour time as much as possible, the question arises as to what is possible. Can machinery be developed into a completely automatic system under the capitalist mode of production, emancipating workers from labour, and freeing capital from its dependence on an unpredictable and potentially troublesome human factor?

First, each individual capital is forced to pursue mechanization as a means of cheapening its products by the process of COMPETITION. Moreover because of the way in which each capital realizes surplus value (SEE PRICE OF PRODUCTION AND THE TRANSFORMATION PROBLEM), that capital will not appear to lose anything by reducing the proportion of capital it advances as variable capital. But what is true for each individual capital is not true for capital as a whole; since a given quantity of labour always produces, under given conditions, the same amount of VALUE in the same period of time, reducing the quantity of labour reduces the total value produced. Increases in productivity reduce necessary labour and as long as necessary labour is not reduced to zero, the rate of surplus value can increase indefinitely; but automation involves no workers at all, hence no valorization and thus zero surplus value.

This is the typical tension of the capitalist mode of production; tendencies arising from USE VALUE considerations coexist in contradiction with tendencies arising from value considerations, and are all produced by the same process of mechanization in pursuit of relative surplus value. The most general way of posing this is in terms of the FORCES AND RELATIONS OF PRODUCTION, and this is how Marx deals with automation in the *Grundrisse* ('The Chapter on Capital') where he talks of machinery as 'the most appropriate form of the use value of fixed capital', but 'it does not at all follow that therefore subsumption under the social relation of capital is the most appropriate and ultimate social relation of production for the application of machinery' (pp. 699–700). Only under communist relations would this be true, in a society which is based upon 'the free development of individualities, and hence not the reduction of necessary labour time so as to posit surplus labour, but rather the general reduction of the necessary labour of society to a minimum, which then corresponds to the artistic, scientific etc. development of the individuals in the time set free, and with the means created, for all of them' (p. 706).

But this is not possible under the social relations of capitalism, in which capital simultaneously tries to minimize necessary labour time, and posits labour time as the sole measure and source of wealth. With automation, however, the development of the collective worker, of the social individual, reaches its apogee; labour time can no longer be the measure of wealth, and exchange value no longer the measure of use value. Thus the tendency of increasing mechanization must ultimately founder on the capital relation, for automation requires the destruction of the latter. The tendency then is for capital to work 'towards its own dissolution as the form dominating production' (p. 700), but the realization of such an immanent law of capitalist production requires the active revolt of the working class. (See also *Capital* I, chs. 15 and 32, and ACCUMULATION; ECONOMIC CRISES; FALLING RATE OF PROFIT.)

SIMON MOHUN

B

Bakunin, Michael Born 30 May 1814, Pre-mukhino; died 16 January 1876, Berne. Baku-nin, the son of an aristocratic Russian land-owner, was the founder of ANARCHISM as an international revolutionary movement and Marx's principal adversary in the first of THE INTERNATIONALS. As a Young Hegelian Baku-nin stressed the importance of the negative in the dialectical process: 'The passion for destruction is a creative passion, too!' (Dolgoff 1971, p. 57). In becoming a social revolutionary, he was in-fluenced by Wilhelm Weitling and PROUDHON. In his early career, however, his libertarian ideas were expressed mainly in support of a concerted movement of the Slav peoples in their struggles against the autocratic rulers of Russia, Germany and Austria. By the part he played in several insurrections, 1848–49, he gained a reputation as a formidable revolutionary. Captured after the failure of the Dresden uprising, he was jailed for seven years and then exiled to Siberia, from where he escaped in 1861. After the failure of the Polish revolt of 1863 he ceased to believe in the revolutionary potential of national libera-tion movements, whose statist aspirations he oposed. He then sought to promote social re-volution on an international scale. His distinc-tively anarchist ideas were developed in a vari-ety of organizations, including the semi-secret International Alliance of Socialist Democracy which in 1868 aplied to join the First Interna-tio-nal. The application was rejected but, after the Alliance declared itself dissolved, its Geneva branch was admitted. Within the International's sections, Bakunin's ideas gained increasing sup-port, especially in Spain, southern Italy, and parts of France and Switzerland. A bitter factional struggle then ensued which reached a climax at The Hague Congress, 1872. On Marx's instiga-tion, Bakunin was expelled on the ground that the Alliance was being maintained as an inter-national secret society with policies opposed to

those of the International and aimed at disrupting it. The expulsion, accompanied by the decision to transfer the seat of the General Council from London to New York, split the International in two, both parts of which expired within the next five years.

In the course of the controversy, the differ-ences between Marxism and anarchism as rival revolutionary theories were crystallized. The differences included conflicting views about how the International should be organized, Marx arguing for centralizing of the movement, Bakunin insisting on a federal structure based on autonomous sections. Two further ideologi-cal differences may be noted. (i) While Marx believed that the bourgeois state had to be over-thrown, he insisted that in its place the proletar-iat should establish its own state which, as clas-ses were abolished as a result of the socialization measures taken, would then (in Engels's phrase) 'wither away'. Bakunin, in contrast, argued that the state, and the principle of authority it em-bodied, must be abolished in the course of the social revolution. Any DICTATORSHIP OF THE PROLETARIAT would become, he predicted, a dictatorship *over* the proletariat and result in a new, more powerful and vicious system of class rule. (ii) Marx believed that the proletariat could act as a class only by constituting itself a distinct political PARTY, opposed to all the old parties formed by the possessing classes; politi-cal action by the proletariat, including action within the parliamentary arena to win conces-sions favourable to the development of the class, was therefore necessary. In contrast, Bakunin shared Proudhon's belief that all political par-ties, without exception, were 'varieties of abso-lutism'; he therefore opposed political action in the Marxist sense. While he believed that re-volutionaries should be organized, sometimes even secretly, he saw their task as essentially one of arousing and encouraging the oppressed classes – peasants and other marginal groups as well as urban workers – to overthrow the existing order by their own direct action. On its ruins, the people would then construct 'the future social organization . . . made solely from the bottom upwards, by the free association or federation of workers, firstly in their unions, then in communes, regions, nations and finally in a great federation, international and universal' (Lehning 1973 p. 206).

In his 'Conspectus of Bakunin's *Statism and Anarchy*' (1874–5), Marx reiterated his view that, so long as other classes exist, the proletariat 'must employ *coercive* measures, that is, government measures'. Bakunin, he also observed, 'understands nothing about social revolution; all he knows about it is political phrases. Its economic prerequisites do not exist for him. . . . The basis of Bakunin's social revolution is the will, and not the economic conditions.'

Reading

Carr, E. H. 1937: *Michael Bakunin.*
Dolgoff, Sam ed. 1971: *Bakunin on Anarchy.*
Lehning, Arthur ed. 1973: *Michael Bakunin: Selected Writings.*
Marx, Engels, Lenin 1972: *Anarchism and Anarcho-Syndicalism.*

GEOFFREY OSTERGAARD

banks *See* FINANCIAL CAPITAL; FINANCIAL CAPITAL AND INTEREST.

base and superstructure The building-like metaphor of base and superstructure is used by Marx and Engels to propound the idea that the economic structure of society (the base) conditions the existence and forms of the STATE and social consciousness (the superstructure). One of the first formulations of this idea appears in *German Ideology* pt. I where a reference is made to 'the social organization evolving directly out of production and commerce, which in all ages forms the basis of the state and of the rest of the idealistic superstructure'. However, the notion of superstructure is not used only to indicate two dependent societal levels, namely, the state and social consciousness. At least once the term seems to refer to the consciousness or worldview of a class: 'upon the different forms of

property, upon the social conditions of existence, rises an entire superstructure of distinct and peculiarly formed sentiments, illusions, modes of thought and views of life. The entire class creates and forms them out of its material foundations and out of the corresponding social relations' (*18th Brumaire* III). Nevertheless, most of the time the metaphor is used to explain the relationship between three general levels of society, whereby the two levels of the superstructure are determined by the base. This means that the superstructure is not autonomous, that it does not emerge out of itself, but has a foundation in the social RELATIONS OF PRODUCTION. Consequently, any particular set of economic relations determines the existence of specific forms of state and social consciousness which are adequate to its functioning and any change in the economic foundation of a society leads to a transformation of the superstructure.

A more detailed description of what is understood by base is given by Marx in a passage which has become the classical formulation of the metaphor: 'In the social production of their life, men enter into definite relations that are indispensable and independent of their will, relations of production which correspond to a definite stage of development of their material productive forces. The sum total of these relations of production constitutes the economic structure of society, the real foundation, on which rises a legal and political superstructure and to which correspond definite forms of social consciousness. The mode of production of material life conditions the social, political and intellectual life process in general' (Preface to *A Contribution to the Critique of Political Economy*). The economic structure is not, therefore, conceived as a given set of institutions, productive units or material conditions; it is rather the sum total of production relations entered into by men, or, in other words, the class relations between them. As Marx puts it, 'it is always the direct relation of the owners of the conditions of production to the direct producers – a relation always naturally corresponding to a definite stage in the development of the methods of labour and thereby its social productivity – which reveals the innermost secret, the hidden basis of the entire social structure, and with it the political form of the relation of sovereignty and dependence, in short, the corresponding specific form of the state' (*Capital* III, ch. 47, sect. II).

Yet the character of the relationship between base and superstructure is more complicated than appears from these formulations. Marx is aware that the determination by the base can be misunderstood as a form of economic reductionism. That is why he further characterizes this relationship as historical, uneven, and compatible with the effectivity of the superstructure. As far as the first aspect is concerned Marx affirms that 'in order to examine the connection between spiritual production and material production, it is above all necessary to grasp the latter itself not as a general category but in *definite historical* form. Thus for example different kinds of spiritual production correspond to the capitalist mode of production and to the mode of production of the Middle Ages. If material production itself is not conceived in its *specific historical* form, it is impossible to understand what is specific in the spiritual production corresponding to it and the reciprocal influence of one on the other' (*Theories of Surplus Value*, vol. I, ch. IV). It is worth noting that although the specificity of the spiritual production is determined by the historical forms of material production, spiritual production is said to be capable of exercising 'reciprocal influence' on material production. In other words, the superstructure of ideas is not conceived as a mere passive reflection but it is capable of some effectivity.

Second, Marx is aware that material production develops unevenly with respect to artistic production and legal relations, as for instance in the relation between Roman private law and capitalist production, or in the relation between Greek art and undeveloped productive forces. As he puts it, 'in the case of the arts, it is well known that certain periods of their flowering are out of all proportion to the general development of society, hence also to the material foundation . . . the skeletal structure as it were, of its organization' (*Grundrisse*, Introduction). But the problem is not so much to understand that certain artistic or legal forms may correspond with undeveloped material conditions: Greek art is based on Greek mythology and this in turn is a primitive way of propitiating natural forces which are not well understood or mastered, so that, in Engels's terms, these false

conceptions have 'a negative economic factor as their basis' (letter to C. Schmidt, 27 October 1890). The real problem is that Greek art is still highly regarded and even counts as a norm or model in more advanced modes of production. Marx's attempt to explain this in terms of the inherent charm of the historic childhood of mankind is clearly insufficient, but at least shows an awareness that the social determination of art and legal forms does not necessarily restrict their validity for other epochs (see ART).

Third, Marx underlines the effectivity of the superstructure when he answers the objection that the economic determination of the superstructure applies only to capitalism, not to feudalism or classical antiquity where Catholicism or politics played the main role. Marx reaffirms the principle of determination by saying that 'the Middle Ages could not live on Catholicism, nor the ancient world on politics', but he adds that 'it is the mode in which they gained a livelihood that explains why here politics, and there Catholicism, played the chief part' (*Capital* I, ch. 1). Althusser and other structuralist authors have interpreted this quotation in the sense of a distinction between 'determination' and 'dominance', according to which the economy is always determinant in the last instance but does not always play the dominant role; it may determine that either of the two superstructural levels be dominant for a certain period of time. Whether or not this distinction can be drawn from Marx's quotation is debatable, but at least the text shows that determination by the base does not reduce politics and ideas to economic phenomena. This aspect has been rendered as the 'relative autonomy' of the superstructure.

Engels, in turn, combats a reductionist interpretation of the base–superstructure image by emphasizing the 'ultimate supremacy' of, or 'determination in the last instance' by, the economy which nevertheless 'operates within the terms laid down by the particular sphere itself' (letter to C. Schmidt 27 October 1890). He moves away from the idea of a mechanical causality whereby one level, the economy, is supposed to be the cause and the other levels, the superstructures, its effects. The notion of determination 'in the last instance' allows him to replace this conception by a 'dialectical' idea of causality whereby the ultimately determining factor does not exclude determination by the superstructures which, as secondary causes, can produce effects and 'react' upon the base (letter to F. Mehring, 14 July 1893). And to reinforce the point Engels adds that 'neither Marx nor I have ever asserted more than this. Hence if somebody twists this into saying that the economic factor is the *only* determining one, he transforms that proposition into a meaningless, abstract, absurd phrase' (letter to J. Bloch, 21–22 September 1890).

Engels further characterizes the relationship between the various effective determinations as an interaction among various superstructural elements, and between them and the base, which nevertheless 'takes place on the basis of economic necessity, which *ultimately* always asserts itself' (letter to W. Borgius, 25 January 1894). This account has been criticized for transposing into the base–superstructure relationship Hegel's conception of the Nature–Notion relationship; that is to say, for understanding the relationship between primary and secondary causes as the relationship between the necessary and the accidental. The effectivity of the superstructures is thus dissolved into an 'endless host of accidents'. At all events, Engels's account has enjoyed an immense prestige among Marxists.

Although Engels tries very hard to counter the mechanistic and deterministic interpretations of the base–superstructure metaphor which infiltrated the development of Marxism in the 1880s, he does not succeed in reversing a trend which in part his own writings contribute to establish. The absence of a notion of practice (see PRAXIS) from Engels's later writings, and the idea of a dialectics of nature separate from social activity which creeps into them, played an important role in the development of reductionist approaches to base and superstructure. The situation was made even worse by the lack of access which the first two generations of Marxists had to Marx's early philosophical works and to *The German Ideology*, where the idea of practice was most forcefully expressed. Indeed, in the absence of a mediating concept of practice the spatial image of base and superstructure lends itself to some problematic interpretations.

On one hand, the superstructure of ideas can be treated as a secondary phenomenon, a mere reflection whose reality is ultimately to be found in the production relations. Consciousness is thus emptied of its specific content and significance and is reduced to economic relations. Some of Lenin's formulations have occasionally given this impression. For example in an early work the evolution of society is seen as a process of 'natural history' which can be understood only by focusing on the relations of production. Lenin claims that Marx in *Capital* explains the economic structure only by the relations of production and that in so doing he accounts at the same time for the corresponding superstructures (1893, p. 141). It is as though the superstructures do not need to be analysed in themselves. Later, Lenin confirms this view by stating that 'materialism in general recognizes objectively real being [matter] as independent of consciousness, sensation, experience, etc., of humanity. Historical materialism recognizes social being as independent of the social consciousness of humanity. In both cases consciousness is only the reflection of being, at best an approximately true (adequate, perfectly exact) reflection of it' (1962, p. 326). These statements are in stark contrast with Lenin's better known, and certainly non-reductionist, elaborations of the importance of political organization and revolutionary theory.

On the other hand, some interpretations tend to separate 'levels' of the spatial image as if they were distinct 'totalities' or 'areas' which are somehow external to one another and which emerge in a sequential order. Plekhanov, for instance, lists five such levels: (1) the *state of the productive forces*; (2) the *economic relations* these forces condition; (3) the *socio-political system* that has developed on the given economic 'basis'; (4) the *mentality of men living in society*, which is determined in part directly by the economic conditions obtaining, and in part by the entire socio-political system that has arisen on that foundation; (5) the *various ideologies* that reflect the properties of that mentality. (1908, p. 70). What this spatial and sequential construction fails to convey is the crucial fact that all these 'levels' are produced by men's practical activity. The various 'levels' of society are taken as separate given entities and there is no explanation as to how the social totality emerges. If the problem is posed in these terms, the notion of determination becomes difficult: how can the economy as an objective instance produce art or theory as a different objective instance?

Ultimately, the base–superstructure metaphor does not succeed in conveying a precise meaning. This is partly because it has been asked to play two roles simultaneously: to describe the development of specialized levels of society brought about by capitalism and to explain how one of these levels determines the others. It seems adequate to perform the first function; that is to say, it helps describe the development of institutional differentiation and of specific 'fields' of practice – economic, political and intellectual – which are presided over by specialized apparatuses. But it seems less adequate to explain the determination of politics and social consciousness, or to account for the emergence of each level as part of the social totality, in so far as it is an inevitably static image which tends to reduce dynamic aspects such as class struggle or practice to one specific level separated from others. Hence the determination of the superstructure by the base becomes an external mode of causation.

Reading

Hall, Stuart 1977: 'Rethinking the "Base and Superstructure" Metaphor'. In J. Bloomfield ed. *Class, Hegemony and Party*.

Larrain, Jorge 1983: *Marxism and Ideology*.

Lenin, V. I. 1893 (*1960*): 'What the "Friends of the People" Are and How They Fight the Social Democrats'.

— 1908 (*1962*): *Materialism and Empirio-Criticism*.

Plekhanov, G. 1908 (*1969*): *Fundamental Problems of Marxism*.

Williams, Raymond 1977: *Marxism and Literature*.

JORGE LARRAIN

Bauer, Otto Born 5 September 1881, Vienna; died 4 July 1938, Paris. Studied philosophy, law and political economy at the University of Vienna. In 1904 Bauer sent Karl Kautsky an article on the Marxist theory of economic crises for publication in *Die Neue Zeit*, and was thereafter a regular contributor. He was asked by Viktor Adler, leader of the Austrian Social Democratic Party (SPÖ), to write a study of the problem of nationalities and nationalism, which was published in 1907 and became the classic Marxist work on the subject. In the same year he became parliamentary secretary of the SPÖ, and with Adolf Braun and Karl Renner he founded the party's theoretical journal *Der Kampf*, of

which he was the principal editor. After the collapse of the Austro-Hungarian Empire Bauer was briefly (1918–19) Secretary of State for Foreign Affairs. In 1919 he strongly opposed the idea of a Bolshevik-style revolution (on the Hungarian model) in Austria, and in the following years he elaborated his conceptions of the 'slow revolution' and 'defensive violence'. In this context he published a comprehensive study of the Austrian revolution, and several analyses of the Russian revolution (the most important collected, in a French translation, in Bourdet 1968). Among his later writings there is a notable study of fascism (1936) and an analysis of the rationalization of the capitalist economy after the first world war (1931). After the insurrection of 1934 Bauer had to leave Austria, and lived first in Brno (Czechoslovakia), then in Paris. (See AUSTRO-MARXISM.)

Reading

Bauer, Otto 1907: *Die Nationalitätenfrage und die Sozialdemokratie*.

— 1923 (*1970*): *Die Österreichische Revolution*.

— 1931: *Kapitalismus und Sozialismus nach dem Weltkrieg*, vol. i, *Rationalisierung oder Fehlrationalisierung?*

— 1936 (*1978*): 'Fascism'. In Bottomore and Goode eds. *Austro-Marxism*.

— 1968: *Otto Bauer et la révolution*, ed. Yvon Bourdet.

Braunthal, Julius 1961: *Otto Bauer: Eine Auswahl aus seinem Lebenswerk*.

TOM BOTTOMORE

Benjamin, Walter Born 15 July 1892, Berlin; died 27 September 1940, Port Bou, Spain. Benjamin is possibly the most important cultural theorist within the Marxist tradition. Little known during his lifetime, he has become widely influential since the second world war. However, the precise implications of his work remain a matter of debate between those who see him as an other-worldly and rather tragic figure blessed with almost mystical talents, and those who prize him for his hard-headed Marxism.

Benjamin's earliest work drew on a sophisticated interest in theology. His first major article, on Goethe's novel *The Elective Affinities*, was an attempt to confront the amoralistic symbolism of early twentieth-century cultural theory with his own rather puritanical ethics. This developed, in the doctoral dissertation 'Origin of German Tragic Drama', into a full-blown critique of the unpolitical 'stoicism' of intellectual life seen against seventeenth-century Lutheran drama. This work, completed when Benjamin was thirty-three, was the most comprehensive theoretical statement he produced. But it was also, as he said, 'the end of my German literature cycle'. From the mid-1920s onwards Benjamin devoted himself more or less exclusively to the problems raised by a Marxist understanding of CULTURE, and from that perspective the classical canon of academic literary history could only play a very subsidiary role. One external factor also influenced this change; the University of Frankfurt, to which Benjamin had submitted the work, rejected it and thereby shattered his hopes of a university career.

Between 1925 and 1933 Benjamin lived mainly by feuilleton journalism, and became close to Brecht and other left-wing intellectuals of the time. Although he decided against joining the Communist Party, his visit to Moscow in the winter of 1926/7 confirmed and deepened his interest in the cultural life of the new Soviet state. This was reflected in the lively and polemical articles (mainly reviews) he wrote during this time. The Nazi seizure of power obliged Benjamin to leave Berlin and deprived him of most of his journalistic livelihood. But he was able to obtain commissions from the Frankfurt Institute for Social Research and this, together with other small sources of income, enabled him to resume his writing in Paris. During these years he published a number of major theoretical pieces in the Institute's journal. The first, 'The Present Social Situation of the French Writer', analysed the progress of bourgeois intellectuals – like Benjamin himself – from a purely cultural avant-garde into organized political involvement. Most of the rest of his work for the Institute was associated with his projected history of nineteenth-century French ideologies, the so-called 'Arcades' complex. This included the famous 'The Work of Art in the Age of Mechanical Reproduction', which illuminated the sense in which 'art' was inseparable from its environment of technology and social class. The theory of *Technik* developed by Benjamin here and in the article on Eduard Fuchs is fundamental to his understanding of the Marxist position that ideas and culture have no independent history. The two articles on Baudelaire – only one, 'On Some Motifs in Baudelaire', was printed at the time – integrated Benjamin's understanding of class, technology and culture into a wider critique of fascism and reactionary ideology generally. Benjamin drew heavily on Freud and on the fascist anthropology of Ludwig Klages for these very remarkable late pieces.

Thus far only work produced for publication by Benjamin himself – work which gives a reasonably coherent picture of the development of his thought – has been mentioned. Since his death, however, there has been enormous pressure to dissociate him from the more straightforwardly Marxist, Brechtian position to which he would most easily be assimilated. Capitalizing on the obscurity of the 'Origin of German Tragic Drama', and making use of unpublished fragments mainly from earlier years, friends of Benjamin such as Adorno and Gershom Scholem have attempted to represent him as an arcane cabbalist whose politics were always subordinate to a utopian messianism. Certainly so far as the major contemporary publications go this interpretation is difficult to sustain. Nonetheless, Benjamin's final piece, the 'Theses on the Philosophy of History', does pose serious difficulties for a Marxist understanding. Written after the traumatic shock of the 1939 Nazi–Soviet pact, it is entirely pessimistic about organized political involvement, and envisages intellectual activity as a magical remembrance, and revolution as the utopian cessation of time. However, any inconsistencies in Benjamin's work need not detract from the fundamental principles of Marxist cultural analysis established in the major texts of the mature period.

Reading

Benjamin, Walter 1972–: *Gesammelte Schriften.*

— 1973: *Illuminations.*

— 1977: *Origin of German Tragic Drama.*

— 1977: *Understanding Brecht.*

— 1979: *One-Way Street and Other Writings.*

Roberts, Julian 1982: *Walter Benjamin.*

Scholem, Gershom 1982: *Walter Benjamin: History of a Friendship.*

Wolin, Richard 1982: *Walter Benjamin: An Aesthetic of Redemption.*

JULIAN ROBERTS

50 BERNAL

Bernal, John Desmond Born 10 May 1901, Nenagh, Co. Tipperary, Ireland; died 15 September 1971, London. Bernal was called 'Sage' by his friends and admirers because of the breadth of his learning and the depth and scope of his insight into natural and social phenomena. One friend called him 'a sink of ubiquity'. He was, arguably, the most eminent of the 'red scientists' of the 1930s, whose influence was important to the conception of science in orthodox Marxism, especially in Britain and the USSR. As a scientist he did important work in X-ray crystallography which helped to lay the foundations of molecular biology. His catalytic role was as important as his own discoveries. Two of his pupils, Dorothy Hodgkin and Max Perutz, became Nobel Laureates. Bernal became an FRS and Professor at Birkbeck College, London, and was awarded both the Stalin (later tactfully changed to Lenin) Prize and the US Medal of Freedom with Palm. His imagination was perhaps too restless for him to focus long and deeply enough on a particular problem to lead to the highest scientific achievements as conventionally conceived. His approach to the solution of complex problems found a fitting outlet in his contribution to the scientific aspect of the second world war effort, especially in Combined Operations in the planning of D-Day, the largest sea-borne invasion in history.

Bernal became a communist at Cambridge in the early 1920s and was very active in propagating Marxist ideas among scientists. He was greatly influenced by the appearance of the Soviet Delegation at the 1931 International Congress of the History of Science and Technology in London, where Bukharin and others argued eloquently that science should be seen in relation to the development of production, contrary to conventional beliefs in the self-sufficient character of science. Bernal was by far the most enthusiastic and spell-binding exponent of the view that science closely reflects economic development and, probably more significantly, that it should be seen as a guide to social policy. He wrote numerous essays and books, the most influential being *The Social Function of Science* (1939) and *Science in History* (1954) which became and remain standard orthodox Marxist works on their topics. 'Bernalism' has come to mean that if the distortions caused by capitalist and other non-socialist socio-economic forma-

tions could be removed, society could be run along lines dictated by scientific rationality. Science is a beacon lighting the way to communism as well as the motor of progress; in socialist countries, Bernal thought, there is 'a radical transformation of science, one which throws it open to the whole people . . . [and this] must bring enormous new strength to the countries where it occurs' (1954, pp. 900–1). His views were influential in both Britain and the USSR and continued to be so in the latter, but he fell foul of the Cold War and the Soviet scandal of LYSENKOISM. He found it difficult to reconcile his loyalty to the Soviet model of progress with Stalinism and with the terrible destruction of scientific research, especially in his own field of biology. Having advocated the Soviet state as something like the perfect funding agency, he was increasingly faced with it as the opposite. He never spoke publicly against orthodox communism but became less and less influential in Britain as other ways of conceiving the social relations of science began to emerge, which were critical of the role of scientific and technological rationality in both capitalist and nominally socialist societies. Bernal played a major part in establishing the topic of the social relations of science in the British Association and was also active in the Pugwash Conferences; yet in 1949 he was, for cold war reasons, removed from the Council of the British Association. He was also active in promoting scientific trade-unionism, and his influence was important in the founding of the British Society for Social Responsibility in Science.

Bernal played a leading role in the approach within twentieth-century Marxism that treated science as an unequivocally progressive force, but many Marxists have subsequently been much more ambivalent about the role of experts and the fruits of their research. Until recently, socialists generally continued to treat science as relatively unproblematic, but critics of Bernalism and Marxist orthodoxy have increasingly argued that applying science itself to problems of social organization only begs the questions if the political and evaluative issues are excluded or left only implicit. Problems of social values, priorities and accountability have to be posed in their own terms on the terrain of culture, and not handed over to a new mandarinate or body of experts.

Reading

Bernal, J. D. 1939 (1967): *The Social Function of Science*.

— 1954 (1969): *Science in History*.

Bukharin, Nikolai *et al*. 1931 (1971): *Science at the Crossroads*.

Goldsmith, Maurice 1980: *Sage: A Life of J. D. Bernal*.

Goldsmith, Maurice and Mackay, A. L. 1966: *The Science of Science*.

Hodgkin, Dorothy 1980: 'J. D. Bernal'.

Rosenhead, Jonathan *et al*. 1982: 'Science at the Crossroads: Looking Back on 50 years of Radical Science'.

Wersky, Gary 1978: *The Visible College*.

Young, Robert M. 1980: 'The Relevance of Bernal's Questions'.

ROBERT M. YOUNG

Bernstein, Eduard Born 6 January 1850, Berlin; died 18 December 1932, Berlin. The son of a Jewish engine-driver, Bernstein worked in a bank from 1866 to 1878. He joined the German Social Democratic Workers' Party (*Eisenacher*) in 1871 and became a Marxist under the influence of Marx, and more particularly Engels, both of whom he met in 1880. From 1881 to 1890 Bernstein edited the party organ, *Der Sozialdemokrat* (which was illegal under Bismarck's anti-socialist law), first in Zurich and then in London where he lived from 1888 until his return to Germany in 1901. In London he became a close friend of Engels who made him his literary executor. At the same time he also associated with the Fabians and came under their influence.

From 1896 to 1898 Bernstein published a series of articles in *Die Neue Zeit* which sought to revise what he considered as outdated, dogmatic, unscientific or ambiguous elements in Marxism, while denying that he was rejecting its essential core. In 1899 he set out his ideas in their most comprehensive form in *Die Voraussetzungen des Sozialismus*, the major work of classical revisionism, where he disputed Marxist predictions about increasing industrial concentration and class polarization, arguing that far from disappearing the middle class was growing in size and complexity. Historical development, he contended, had shown that economic crises were becoming less rather than more acute and had invalidated the theory of increasing

working-class misery (*Verelendung*). A 'social reaction . . . against the exploiting tendencies of capital' was 'always drawing more departments of economic life under its influence'. He argued for a perspective of 'steady advance' by the working class as against 'a catastrophic crash'. Agreements should be sought with the liberal middle class and the peasantry against the bureaucratic authoritarian state, the Junkers and big business. The conquest of political power by the working class entailed an extension of its political and economic rights, which would gradually 'transform the state in the direction of democracy'. Democracy was 'at the same time means and end'. He rejected the idea of forcible REVOLUTION and of the DICTATORSHIP OF THE PROLETARIAT, and appealed to SOCIAL DEMOCRACY 'to appear what it in fact now is, a democratic, socialistic party of reform'. His views were strongly challenged inside Germany by KAUTSKY and LUXEMBURG and from outside by PLEKHANOV, concerned to defend the classical Marxist heritage. Although successive party congresses condemned Bernstein's views, he was a representative of German Social Democracy in the Reichstag from 1902 to 1906, 1912 to 1918 and 1920 to 1928. In further writings and lectures he extended his criticisms of Marxist views, and adopted neo-Kantian positions (see KANTIANISM AND NEO-KANTIANISM) from which he argued the case for socialism on ethical grounds.

During the first world war, Bernstein called for a peace settlement and in December 1915 he voted against war credits. After leaving the Social Democratic Party he joined the more left-wing Independent Social Democratic Party (USPD) in 1917. After the war he rejoined the Social Democratic Party and, in 1920–21, took part in drafting its programme. Appreciation of Bernstein has not only revived in German Social Democratic circles since the late 1970s. It has also been openly expressed since 1989 by certain leading Soviet ideologists who claim to see the growth of socialist structures and relations within contemporary capitalist societies (Yuri Krasin and Oleg Bogomolov) and wish to 'rehabilitate the statement of Eduard Bernstein, against which in our time we proclaimed an anathema: "The final aim is nothing; the movement is everything"' (Oleg Bogomolov). (See also REVISIONISM; SOCIAL DEMOCRACY.)

Reading

Bernstein, Eduard 1895 (1980): *Cromwell and Communism. Socialism and Democracy in the Great English Revolution.*

— 1899 (1961) *Die Voraussetzungen des Sozialismus und die Aufgaben der Sozialdemokratie.*

Cole, G. D. H. 1956: *A History of Socialist Thought* vol. III.

Colletti, Lucio 1969 (1972): 'Bernstein and the Marxism of the Second International'. In *From Rousseau to Lenin.*

Gay, Peter 1952: *The Dilemma of Democratic Socialism: Eduard Bernstein's Challenge to Marx.*

Kautsky, Karl 1899: *Bernstein und das sozialdemokratische Programm. Eine Antikritik.*

Luxemburg, Rosa 1899 (1970): *Reform or Revolution.*

Sweezy, Paul M. 1946: *The Theory of Capitalist Development.*

Tudor, H. and Tudor, J. M. eds. 1988: *Marxism and Social Democracy. The Revisionist Debate 1896–1898.*
                                       MONTY JOHNSTONE

Blanquism designates the central political doctrine of the great French revolutionary, Louis-Auguste Blanqui (1805–81). In the conspiratorial tradition of Babeuf and Buonarroti, Blanqui's aim was to organize a relatively small, centralized, hierarchical elite, which would carry out an insurrection to replace capitalist state power by its own revolutionary dictatorship. Believing that prolonged subjection to class society and religion prevented the majority from recognizing its true interests, he opposed universal suffrage until the people had undergone a long period of re-education under this dictatorship, based on Paris. Ultimately, under communism, there would be an 'absence of government' (quoted by Bernstein, *1971*, p. 312).

Marx and Engels greatly admired Blanqui as a courageous revolutionary leader. They allied themselves briefly with his supporters in 1850 (Ryazanov 1928) and in 1871–2, following the Paris Commune, before which Marx had tried unsuccessfully to draw Blanqui into the First International. However, they rejected the conspiratorial approach of the 'alchemists of revolution' who strove artificially 'to forestall the process of revolutionary development' (*NRZ Revue*, no. 4, 1850). In contrast to Blanqui, Marx and Engels conceived the proletarian movement as 'the self-conscious, independent movement of the immense majority' (*Communist Manifesto* sect. 1) and 'entirely trusted to the intellectual development of the working class, which was sure to result from combined action and mutual discussion' (Engels). Bernstein and others have described Marx's and Engels's 'Address to the League of Communists' (March 1850) as strongly 'Blanquist'. The Address however argued that the next stage of the revolution in Germany involved helping the petty bourgeois democrats to power, while the German workers would need to go through 'a lengthy revolutionary development' before themselves taking power.

The widespread notion that Blanqui originated the term dictatorship of the proletariat and that Marx took it from him is without foundation. Not only is it recognized by both Dommanget (1957, p. 171) and Spitzer (1957, p. 176) that Blanqui never used the expression, but Engels was at pains to emphasize the fundamental difference between this Marxian concept and the revolutionary dictatorship conceived by Blanqui. 'From Blanqui's conception of every revolution as the *coup de main* of a small revolutionary minority', Engels wrote, 'follows of itself the necessity of a dictatorship after it succeeds: the dictatorship, of course, not of the whole revolutionary class, the proletariat, but of the small number of those who carried out the *coup* and who are themselves already in advance organized under the dictatorship of one or a few individuals' (Programme of the Blanquist Commune Refugees, 1874).

The charge of 'Blanquism' was levelled by the Mensheviks (especially Plekhanov) against Lenin and Bolshevism both before and after the revolution of October 1917. Some recent writers argue that 'Lenin's guide to action is fundamentally derived from the tradition of Jacobin Blanquism translated into Russian terms by [the nineteenth-century populist] Tkachev' (Fishman 1970, p. 170). Lenin however repudiated Blanquism in April 1917 as 'a striving to seize power with the backing of a minority. With us it is quite different. We are still a minority and realize the need for winning a majority' ('Report on the Present Situation and the Attitude towards the Provisional Government'). The Bolsheviks claimed to have won this majority support for revolution in October 1917. Although this has been contested by their opponents, the

mass involvement of workers, peasants and soldiers through the Soviets certainly profoundly
distinguished the Bolshevik revolution from the
Blanquist model.

Reading

Agulhon, M. *et al.* 1986: *Blanqui et les blanquistes.*

Bernstein, Samuel 1970 *(1971): Auguste Blanqui and the Art of Insurrection.*

Blanqui, Louis-Auguste 1977: *Oeuvres complètes.* Vol. 1: *Écrits sur la révolution.*

Cole, G. D. H. 1956: *A History of Socialist Thought.* Vol. 1: *The Forerunners.*

Dommanget, Maurice 1957: *Les Idées politiques et sociales d'Auguste Blanqui.*

Draper, Hal 1986: *Karl Marx's Theory of Revolution.*

Fishman, William J. 1970: *The Insurrectionists.*

Johnstone, M. 1983: 'Marx, Blanqui and Majority Rule'.

Ryazanov, David Borisovich 1928: 'Zur Frage des Verhältnisses von Marx zu Blanqui'.

Spitzer, Alan B. 1957: *Revolutionary Theories of Louis-Auguste Blanqui.*

MONTY JOHNSTONE

Bloch, Ernst Born 8 July 1885, Ludwigshafen; died 3 August 1977, Stuttgart. Like his friends Lukács and Benjamin, Bloch was impelled by the horrors of the first world war towards Marxism, seeing in it a defence against the Armageddon which might otherwise engulf humanity. During the Nazi period Bloch was a refugee in the USA; thereafter he tried to find a foothold in the new East German republic, but his unorthodox Marxism gained little sympathy there and in 1961 he left to spend the rest of his life in Tübingen. He has since become a major influence far beyond Marxism.

Bloch's essayistic, unsystematic Marxism is (in the best sense) homiletic rather than analytical. At the core of his teaching lies a secularized Messianism, the Judaic doctrine that redemption is always possible in our time, in this world. He believed that while a 'redeemed' world would inevitably be radically different from this one – and in that sense would be a 'utopia' – it was nonetheless possible without having to resign oneself to the Christian eschatology of death and rebirth. This theme, first taken up in the *Spirit of Utopia* (1918), reaches its full development in *The Principle of Hope* (1959). Here

Bloch re-reads the Aristotelian dichotomy of potency (matter) and act (intellect) in terms of the progressive realization of potency in a world fully illuminated by reason. The Scholastics' doctrine that primordial matter is first cause of the universe is thus interpreted horizontally, in our history, rather than vertically, in terms of an inaccessible heaven. Marxism itself is part of the historical 'figuration' of this process; in his book on Thomas Münzer (1921), for example, Bloch perceives the sixteenth-century Anabaptist revolution as a prefiguration of what is only now being fully realized in the Bolshevik revolution. History, says Bloch, in a term also echoed in Walter Benjamin's 1940 'Theses', is 'the persistently indicated' *(das stetig Gemeinte)* which fires the struggles of the present.

Reading

Benjamin, Walter 1940: 'Theses on the Philosophy of History'. In *Illuminations.*

Bloch, Ernst 1967– : *Gesamtausgabe.*

(which includes:)

1918: *Geist der Utopie.*

1921: *Thomas Münzer als Theologe der Revolution.*

1959: *Das Prinzip Hoffnung.*

1971: *On Karl Marx.*

Hudson, Wayne 1982: *The Marxist Philosophy of Ernst Bloch.*

JULIAN ROBERTS

Bolshevism the term Bolshevism, though often used synonymously with LENINISM, refers to the practice of, or the movement for, Marxist socialist revolution, whereas Leninism is the theoretical analysis (theory and practice) of socialist revolution. Lenin was the founder of this political tendency but it is an approach to revolutionary social change shared by many Marxists (Stalin, Trotsky, Mao Tse-tung). Bolshevism was born at the Second Congress of the Russian Social Democratic Labour Party (RSDLP) in 1903. From that date, Lenin recognized the existence of Bolshevism as 'a stream of political thought and as a political party'. In the discussion at the Congress of Clause 1 of the party's rules, Lenin and his supporters forced a split with MARTOV which centred on the conditions for membership of the RSDLP. Lenin advocated an active and politically committed party membership, unlike the trade-union based and not necessarily participatory membership of other social-democratic parties at that time. The nascent party split into two wings on this issue: the Bolsheviks (or 'majority' faction derived from the Russian word *bol'shinstvo*) and the MENSHEVIKS (the 'minority' or *men'shinstvo*). It was not until the Seventh (April) Conference of the party in 1917, that the term 'Bolshevik' officially appeared in the party title (Russian Social-Democratic Labour Party (Bolsheviks)); from March 1918 the party was called the Russian Communist Party (Bolsheviks) and in December 1925 the name was again changed to All-Union Communist Party (Bolsheviks). The term was no longer used as a description of the Soviet party from 1952, when the name was finally changed to Communist Party of the Soviet Union.

Underlying the Bolshevik position was a political strategy which emphasized active engagement in politics with the Marxist political party as the 'vanguard' or leader of the working class. The party was to be composed of militant, active Marxists committed to the 'socialist revolution', while those who merely sympathized with the socialist idea, and inactive members, were to be excluded from membership. The party has the task of providing leadership in the revolutionary struggle with the bourgeoisie (and other oppressive ruling groups, such as the autocracy); it also has an important role in bringing Marxist revolutionary theory and revolutionary experience to the masses, since in the Bolshevik view the masses do not spontaneously adopt a class-conscious political outlook. It is a party of a 'new type', in which decision-making is based on the principle of 'DEMOCRATIC CENTRALISM'. Members participate in the formation of policy and in the election of leaders, but when policy has been decided all members are responsible for carrying it out, and complete loyalty to the leadership is required. Only in this way, it is argued, can the party be an effective weapon of the proletariat in its revolutionary struggle with the bourgeoisie. Lenin had in mind a model of party organization apposite to the oppressive political conditions of Tsarist Russia, whereas Bolsheviks living in more liberal societies have emphasized more strongly the democratic element. There is thus an ambiguity or tension in Bolshevism between its centralist and democratic components, with different activists stressing the appropriateness of one or the other concept.

The successful seizure of power by the Bolshevik party in Russia in 1917 had repercussions for other socialist parties. At its Second Congress in 1920, the Communist International was organized on the model of the Russian party with twenty-one points defining the conditions of membership (see Carr 1953, pp. 193–6). Henceforth Bolshevism became a movement on an international scale.

With the ascendancy of Stalin in Soviet Russia, Bolshevism became associated with his policies: rapid industrialization, socialism in one country, a centralized state apparatus, the collectivization of agriculture, the subordination of the interests of other communist parties to those of the Soviet party. Under Stalin an important role was given to the superstructure (see BASE AND SUPERSTRUCTURE), in the form of the state, which he thought would establish the economic base of socialism through socialist industrialization. Once the attainment of this goal had been proclaimed in the USSR in 1936 Stalin took an economistic view of socialism, assuming that with the further development of the productive forces a socialist superstructure would develop. Stalinists also saw the Soviet state as the political expression of the (world) working class. Thus Bolshevism, in the form given to it by Stalin, combines an economistic view of the building of socialism with an instrumental view of politics.

While Bolshevism was seen by the Soviet leaders as a unitary political movement, there have been some significant differences within it. Major divergences may be seen in the policies of Trotsky and his followers in the Fourth International (see TROTSKYISM) and in the theory of Maoism. The Fourth International, while strictly defending the principle of party hegemony, called for greater participation by the membership and more effective control of the leadership. The Stalinist version of Bolshevism is seen as 'degenerate', with the leaders exercising an illegitimate dominating role over the working class. Furthermore, the Fourth International emphasized the global nature of capitalism and the impossibility of completing the building of 'socialism in one country'. The leadership of the Bolshevik movement had to create the conditions for the world revolution and the Russian revolution was interpreted as a means to this end. The principal contribution of the

Maoists has been to stress the role of changes in the superstructure, independently of those in the base, as necessary to the evolution of socialism. Rather than seeing changes in social relationships as following the changes in the development of productive forces, as the Soviet party emphasized, Maoists have stressed the importance of creating socialist relations between people even before the economy has reached a high level of maturation. Such relationships should be manifested in direct participation by the masses, and in minimizing differentials between different types of workers and between cadres and the masses. The ideological role of the state in rooting out capitalist tendencies in a socialist society, and in implanting socialist ideas in the masses, is also strongly emphasized.

Marxist opponents of Bolshevism have made fundamental criticisms of its doctrine and practice. Rosa LUXEMBURG opposed in principle the idea of a centralized party organization and party hegemony, arguing that this restricted the revolutionary activity of the working class. Trotsky, when in opposition to Lenin before the October Revolution, also claimed that the party would become a substitute for the working class. The MENSHEVIKS adopted a more evolutionary version of Marxism, regarded the revolutionary theory and tactics of the Bolsheviks as premature, and considered that revolutionary change could only occur in the most advanced capitalist countries through a trade-union based socialist party. The domination of the state in societies under Bolshevik rule is seen as resulting from the backwardness of the productive forces and the lack of sufficient consciousness among the mass of the people to carry out a socialist revolution. From this point of view, Bolshevism is voluntaristic and politically opportunist.

The orthodox view in communist states and in Bolshevik parties outside remained that it is the only correct strategy for the assumption and consolidation of power by the working class, though this conception was increasingly criticized from the 1970s by political tendencies such as EUROCOMMUNISM. These critical arguments were taken up by proponents of the opposition movements in Eastern Europe and the Soviet Union, and with the collapse of the communist regimes after 1989 the influence of Bolshevism as a political doctrine and practice has largely disappeared.

Reading

Carr, E. H. 1953: *The Bolshevik Revolution, 1917–1923*, vol. 1.

Corrigan, P., Ramsay, H. R. and Sayer, D. 1978: *Socialist Construction and Marxist Theory: Bolshevism and its Critique.*

Harding, N. 1977 and 1981: *Lenin's Political Thought*, vols. 1 and 2.

Knei-Paz, B. 1978: *The Social and Political Thought of Leon Trotsky.*

Lane, D. S. 1981: *Leninism: A Sociological Interpretation.*

Lenin, V. I. 1902 (*1961*): 'What is to be Done?'

Lukács, G. 1924 (*1970*): *Lenin.*

Luxemburg, R. 1961: 'Leninism or Marxism'. In *The Russian Revolution and Marxism or Leninism.*

Meyer, A. G. 1957: *Leninism.*

Stalin, J. 1924 (1972): 'Foundations of Leninism'. In B. Franklin ed. *The Essential Stalin.*

DAVID LANE

Bonapartism In the writings of Marx and Engels this refers to a form of regime in capitalist society in which the executive part of the state, under the rule of one individual, achieves dictatorial power over all other parts of the state, and over society. Bonapartism thus constitutes an extreme manifestation of what, in recent Marxist writing on the state, has been called its 'relative autonomy' (e.g. Poulantzas 1973). The main instance of this form of regime in Marx's lifetime was that of Louis Bonaparte, the nephew of Napoleon I, who became Napoleon III after his *coup d'état* of 2 December 1851. That episode inspired one of Marx's most important and glittering historical writings, *18th Brumaire*. For his part, Engels also paid considerable attention to the rule of Bismarck in Germany, and found in the Bismarckian regime many parallels with Bonapartism.

For Marx and Engels, Bonapartism is the product of a situation where the ruling class in capitalist society is no longer able to maintain its rule by constitutional and parliamentary means; but where the working class is not able to affirm its own hegemony either. In *The Civil War*, after Napoleon III's Second Empire had collapsed under the impact of defeat in the Franco-Prussian War, Marx said that Bonapartism 'was the only form of government possible at a time when the bourgeoisie had already lost, and the working class had not yet acquired, the faculty of ruling the nation' (ch. 3). Similarly, Engels said in *The Origin of the Family* that while the state was generally the state of the ruling class, 'by way of exception, however, periods occur in which the warring classes balance each other so nearly that the state power, as ostensible mediator, acquires, for the moment, a certain degree of independence of both' (ch. 9). These formulations stress the high degree of independence of the Bonapartist state; but its dictatorial character merits equal emphasis.

The independence of the Bonapartist state, and its role as 'ostensible mediator' between warring classes, do not leave it, in Marx's phrase, 'suspended in mid air'. Louis Bonaparte, he also said, 'represented' the small-holding peasantry, the most numerous class in France, by which he may be taken to have meant that Louis Bonaparte claimed to speak for that class, and was supported by it. But Louis Bonaparte, Marx also said, claimed to speak for all other classes in society as well. In fact, the real task of the Bonapartist state was to guarantee the safety and stability of bourgeois society, and to make possible the rapid development of capitalism.

In their writings on the state of the Bonapartist type, Marx and Engels also articulate an important concept about the state, namely the degree to which it represents the interest of those who actually run it. In *18th Brumaire*, Marx speaks of 'this executive power with its enormous bureaucratic and military organization, with its extensive and artificial state machinery, with a host of officials numbering half a million, besides an army of another half million, this appalling parasitic body, which envelops the body of French society like a caul and chokes all its pores . . .' (ch. 7). The Bonapartist state did not in fact choke *all* of France's pores, as Marx acknowledged in *The Civil War*; for it was under its sway, he wrote then, that 'bourgeois society, freed from political cares, attained a development unexpected even by itself' (ch. 3). But this does not detract from the point that the quasi-autonomous Bonapartist state seeks to serve its own interest as well as that of capital.

Reading

Draper, Hal 1977: *Karl Marx's Theory of Revolution.* Vol. I: *State and Bureaucracy.*

Poulantzas, Nicos 1973: *Political Power and Social Classes.*

Rubel, Maximilien 1960: *Karl Marx devant le Bonapartisme.*

RALPH MILIBAND

bourgeoisie   Engels described the bourgeoisie as 'the class of the great capitalists who, in all developed countries, are now almost exclusively in possession of all the means of consumption, and of the raw materials and instruments (machines, factories) necessary for their production' (*Principles of Communism*, 1847); and as 'the class of modern capitalists, owners of the means of social production and employers of wage labour' (note to the 1888 English edn of the *Communist Manifesto*). The bourgeoisie, as in this sense the economically dominant class which also controls the state apparatus and cultural production (see RULING CLASS), stands in opposition to, and in conflict with, the working class, but between these 'two great classes' of modern society there are 'intermediate and transitional strata' which Marx also referred to as the MIDDLE CLASS.

Marxist studies of the bourgeoisie over the past century have concentrated on two issues. One concerns the degree of separation between the bourgeoisie and the working class (the polarization), and the intensity of class conflict between them, particularly in conditions of a steady growth in numbers of the middle class. Here a division has emerged between those who attribute considerable social and political importance to the new middle class, and also to rising levels of living and political liberalization (e.g. Bernstein 1899, Renner 1953), and those who emphasize the 'proletarianization' of the middle class (Braverman 1974), and consider that there has been little change in the character of political struggles. The second important issue is that of the nature and role of the bourgeoisie in advanced capitalist societies, and in particular the extent to which, with the massive development of joint-stock companies on one side, and of state intervention on the other, managers and high state officials have either merged with or replaced the 'great capitalists' as the dominant group or groups in society, as proponents of the 'managerial revolution' have claimed. Marxist analyses of this situation have differed considerably, and two main positions have emerged.

Poulantzas (1975) begins by defining the bourgeoisie, not in terms of a legal category of property ownership but in terms of 'economic ownership' (i.e. real economic control of the means of production and of the products) and 'possession' (i.e. the capacity to put the means of production into operation). By these criteria the managers, because they carry out the functions of capital, belong to the bourgeoisie regardless of whether or not they are legal owners of capital. One problem with this type of analysis is that it is then easy to argue that the dominant group of managers and party officials in the existing socialist societies is also a bourgeoisie, since it is characterized by 'economic ownership' and 'possession', and the term is then denuded of any precise historical or sociological meaning. So far as high officials (and state officials more generally) are concerned, Poulantzas treats them as a category defined by their relation to the state apparatus, without paying much attention to the increasing role of the state in production, which transforms the functions of some officials into those of economic management.

Other Marxists – and notably Hilferding in his studies of ORGANIZED CAPITALISM – have analysed these phenomena in quite a different way, treating the growth of corporations and the great expansion of the state's economic activities as a major change in capitalism which moves it farther along the road to socialism. But in Hilferding's view this progressive socialization of the economy could only be completed by taking power from the bourgeoisie and transforming an economy organized and planned by the great corporations into one which was planned and controlled by the democratic state. Some recent studies have departed radically from this conception, and Offe (1972) has argued that the 'new forms of social inequality are no longer directly reducible to economically defined class relationships', and that the 'old frame of reference of structurally privileged interests of a ruling class' has to be replaced by new criteria for analysing the management of system problems, which 'has become an objective imperative, transcending particular interests'. A similar view has been taken by other 'critical theorists' of the later Frankfurt School, who concentrate on bureaucratic-technocratic domination rather than on the economic, social and political dominance of the bourgeoisie.

A very different analysis of the recent development of capitalism has been provided by those Marxists who stress the continuing crucial importance of the legal ownership of the means of production. Thus Mandel (1975) analyses the international centralization of capitalism through the multinational corporations and the banks (see FINANCE CAPITAL), which he suggests may be accompanied by the rise of a new, supranational bourgeois state power. He goes on to consider possible variants of the relationship between international capital and national states, including the creation of a supranational imperialist state in Western Europe, already taking shape in the EEC. On this view the most significant feature in the post-1945 development of capitalism is the formation of an international bourgeoisie. More generally, it has been argued that while there has been a partial dissociation between legal ownership and economic ownership in large corporations, nevertheless 'formal legal ownership is in general a *necessary* condition for economic ownership' (Wright 1978); or, in other terms, that the extent of 'separation of ownership from control' has been greatly exaggerated, and a 'propertied class' still dominates the economy (Scott 1979).

Reading

Bottomore, Tom and Brym, Robert J. eds. 1989: *The Capitalist Class: An International Study.*

Mandel, Ernest 1975: *Late Capitalism.*

Offe, Claus 1972: 'Political Authority and Class Structures: An Analysis of Late Capitalist Societies'.

Poulantzas, Nicos 1975: *Classes in Contemporary Capitalism.*

Scott, John 1979: *Corporations, Classes and Capitalism.*

Wright, Erik Olin 1978: *Class, Crisis and the State.*

TOM BOTTOMORE

Brecht, Bertolt   Born 10 February 1898, Augsburg; died 14 August 1956, Berlin.

Playwright, poet, and theorist of the theatre, Brecht began his writing career as a lively and original *poète maudit* with a love of things American ('Of Poor B.B.', *Baal*, *In the Jungle of the Cities*), and also sought to rescue the German stage from excesses both sentimental and expressionistic.

The economic crises of the Weimar Republic bore in upon Brecht, resulting by 1928 in a resolution to forge a 'theatre of the scientific age'. Cool, entertaining, yet didactic scripts, sets, acting and direction would present the dilemmas of modern society where the individual alone is helpless ('One is none', the theme of *A Man Is a Man*) and only new ways of thinking, organization, and productivity 'When man helps man' (theme of *The Baden Learning Play*) can rehumanize a life which the blind self-seeking of capitalism has rendered barbarous.

This moral vision the sceptical and erudite Brecht complemented with a lifelong study of the works of Marx, and to some extent of Lenin. While involved with preliminary studies for his play *St Joan of the Stockyards* Brecht discovered *Capital*. He mentioned to E. Hauptmann (one of many collaborators) that he 'had to know it all' (October 1926). Twenty years later he was putting the *Communist Manifesto* to 'the highly reputable verse form of Lucretius's *De rerum natura*, on something like the unnaturalness of bourgeois conditions' (Völker 1975, pp. 47, 134).

Brecht's Marxism was shaped in part by the scientistic claims of the German Communist Party, and in part by the intellectual mentors whom he accepted as friends and peers, foremost among them Fritz Sternberg, Korsch and Benjamin. Brecht rejected the dialectics of Adorno as not *plumpe* (materialistic), and he satirized the Frankfurt School group as court intellectuals for the bourgeois era (*Tui-Roman, Turandot*). Lukács's theory of literary realism Brecht rejected as undialectical and tending to suppress the imagination and productivity of readers (see 'Breadth and Variety of the Realist Way of Writing'), and he expressed his detestation of the literary-political power wielded by Lukács from Moscow.

Brecht himself lacked influence in the USSR. Kindred artist-thinkers, such as his friend Sergei Tretyakov or the director V. Meyerhold were exterminated, and only *The Threepenny Opera* was produced in Brecht's lifetime. Slipping into exile from Germany on the day Hitler came to power, Brecht hoped to be eventually successful on the commercial stages of Broadway; but he neither ingratiated himself with investors nor persuaded the American left that he had important wares to offer. His years in Santa Monica

and New York (1941–47) encouraged an opportunistic slippage in his method while only marginally increasing the accessibility of his work. He returned to Europe to implement the plays and methods with his own company, the Berlin Ensemble (led by his wife, the great actress Helene Weigel); its tours provided the definitive theatrical praxis of the 1950s in France, Great Britain, Italy, and Poland.

Brecht aimed to be the Marx of the post-capitalist, post-subjectivist theatre. The recipes which he offered to elucidate his practice – the notion of 'epic' (later, 'dialectical') theatre, and the 'distance'-creating techniques of acting, directing and writing – are indispensable readings in modern aesthetics. But the proof of the pudding must be in the eating, and such plays as *The Mother, St Joan of the Stockyards, The Measures Taken, Mother Courage, The Resistible Rise of Arturo Ui, Caucasian Chalk Circle,* and *Galileo Galilei* have an innate productivity which teaches dialectical objectivity as it draws the audience in and entertains.

Reading

Bentley, Eric 1981: *The Brecht Commentaries, 1943–80.*

Brecht, Bertolt 1961: *Plays* ed. Eric Bentley.

— 1964: *Brecht on Theater* ed. John Willett.

— 1971: *Collected Plays* ed. Ralph Manheim and John Willett.

— 1976: *Poems 1913–1956* ed. John Willett and Ralph Manheim.

Ewen, Frederic 1967: *Bertolt Brecht.*

Fuegi, John 1972: *The Essential Brecht.*

Munk, Erika 1972: *Brecht: A Collection of Critical Pieces.*

Schoeps, Karl H. 1977: *Bertolt Brecht.*

Völker, Klaus 1975: *Brecht Chronicle.*

Willett, John 1968: *Theatre of Bertolt Brecht*, 3rd rev. edn.

LEE BAXANDALL

British Marxist historians Arguably, British Marxist historiography began with Marx himself working in the British Museum on the making and dynamic of the capitalist mode of production. However, 'British Marxist historians' refers in particular to a generation of scholars who, since the late 1930s, have made critical and commanding contributions to their respective fields of historical enquiry and, comprehended as a historical and theoretical tradition, have significantly shaped not only the development of the historical discipline, especially the writing of *social* history, but also Marxist thought, and radical-democratic and socialist historical consciousness. This 'generation' includes the more senior figures of Cambridge economist Maurice Dobb (see DOBB, MAURICE) and journalists and writers Dona Torr and Leslie Morton, but its central figures have been the relatively younger historians, Rodney Hilton, Christopher Hill, Eric Hobsbawm, George Rudé, Edward Thompson, Dorothy Thompson, John Saville and Victor Kiernan.

The intellectual and political formation of this generation began in the 1930s in the shadows of the world depression, the triumph of Nazism and fascism in Central Europe and Spain, and the ever-increasing likelihood of a Second World War. Convinced that the Soviet Union represented a progressive alternative model of economic development and the foremost antagonist to the further expansion of fascism, and also that the British Labour Party was inadequate to the challenge of the contemporary crisis and the making of socialism, these older and younger historians (the latter were, in most cases, students at the universities of Cambridge or Oxford in this period) joined the Communist Party, believing they might contribute to the advance of working-class struggle through their scholarly labours. Thus, following the war and the return to civilian life, they organized themselves into the Communist Party Historians' Group in order to elaborate and propagate a – or, as they apparently believed at the time, *the* – Marxist interpretation of English and British history.

During the heyday of the Historians' Group, 1946–56, its membership was sufficiently large to permit the establishment of 'period sections' and, in addition to the work undertaken by its individual members, the group itself formulated and initiated a variety of cooperative and collective research and publishing efforts (e.g. Saville *et al.* 1954). However, in 1956–7, in the wake of Khruschev's speech on STALINISM to the Twentieth Congress of the Communist Party of the Soviet Union, the Soviet invasion of Hungary, and the failure of the British Communist Party to oppose the invasion and

democratize itself, the Historians' Group all but collapsed as many of its members resigned from the party in protest.

The several initiatives of the Historians' Group met with limited success beyond communist and Marxist circles; although it should be noted that one particular endeavour, the journal *Past and Present*, though not formally a Group project, and not intended to be merely a journal of Marxist historical studies, was founded in 1952 by several of its central figures (Hilton, Hill, Hobsbawm, Dobb and John Morris) and later became the premier English-language journal in the field of social history. Nevertheless, it is now recognized that the intellectual and political exchanges and comradeship which membership in the Historians' Group afforded were both crucial to the historians' later individual and collective accomplishments and fundamental to the emergence of a distinctly British Marxist historical tradition, that is, to the development of its particular problematics and perspectives.

The original influence of Dobb, Morton and Torr on the formation of the tradition must be noted here. It was Dobb's *Studies in the Development of Capitalism* (1946) addressing the question of the TRANSITION FROM FEUDALISM TO CAPITALISM, along with the debates to which it gave rise, both in the Historians' Group and (internationally) in the pages of the American journal, *Science and Society* (Hilton 1976, continuing to this day in, for example, 'the Brenner debate', Aston and Philpin 1985), which established the historical problematic and framework not only for the group's deliberations but also for the historians' continuing effort in favour of the development of a Marxist synthesis or 'grand narrative' of English and British history. Morton's and Torr's influence can be seen in the historians' commitment to the writing of that narrative as 'people's history', that is, a history not limited to the lives and actions of the elites or ruling classes, but encompassing as well those of 'the common people' or 'lower orders'. Indeed, Morton's *A People's History of England* (1938) was a pioneering text in the historians' campaign to 'democratize' the past both in the sense of extending the bounds of *who* was to be included in the essential historical record and in that of making it available and accessible to a popular and working-class audience. And Torr must also be recognized for having insisted that group members reject economistic, deterministic and fatalistic readings of history, thereby imbuing the work of the younger historians with a sense of the role of human consciousness and agency in the *making* of history.

Shaped by the experience and aspirations of the Historians' Group, the younger British Marxist historians produced their major scholarly writings in the decades following the mid-1950s, effectively recasting their respective fields of study in the process: Rodney Hilton, medieval and peasant studies (e.g. Hilton 1973, 1984); Christopher Hill, sixteenth and seventeenth-century studies and the English Revolution (e.g. Hill 1964, 1972); George Rudé, Eric Hobsbawm and E. P. Thompson, late eighteenth- and early nineteenth-century social history and the study of popular movements (e.g. Rudé 1964, 1980, Hobsbawm and Rudé 1969, Hobsbawm 1964, Thompson 1963); John Saville and Dorothy Thompson, nineteenth-century labour studies and Chartism (e.g. Saville 1987, Thompson 1984); and V. G. Kiernan and Eric Hobsbawm on European history and imperialism (e.g. Kiernan 1972, 1982, Hobsbawm 1962, 1977, 1987).

Yet beyond their outstanding individual accomplishments, there have been four paramount contributions which the British Marxist historians have made as a 'collective'. The first has been the development of 'class-struggle analysis'. Derived from the *Communist Manifesto*, the central working hypothesis of the historians has been that 'The history of all hitherto existing society is the history of class struggle.' Thus, the medieval world was not harmoniously organized into three estates but was an order of struggle between lords and peasants; the conflicts of the seventeenth century were not a mere civil war but a 'bourgeois revolution' driven by struggles of the lower orders as well; the eighteenth century was not conflict-free but shot through with antagonisms between 'patricians and plebeians' (i.e. 'class struggle without class', Thompson 1987b); and the Industrial Revolution entailed not only economic and social changes but, in the course of the conflicts between 'Capital and Labour', a dramatic process of class formation determined in great part by the agency of workers themselves. Revisions have been made to these stories but the centrality of class struggle

persists. Moreover, such struggle has not been limited to moments of outright rebellion or revolution. The historians enlarged the scope of what is to be understood as 'struggle'; thus, forcing a reconsideration of an array of popular collective actions, we now have 'resistance' along with rebellion and revolution as part of our historical vocabulary.

The second contribution, linked to people's history, has been the pursuit and development of 'history from below' or, more critically, 'history from the bottom up'. The British Marxist historians have sought to redeem, or *reappropriate*, both the experience and the agency of the lower orders – peasants, artisans and workers. The classic statement of this perspective and aspiration was offered by E. P. Thompson: 'I am seeking to rescue the poor stockinger, the Luddite cropper, the "obsolete" handloom weavers, the utopian artisan and even the deluded follower of Joanna Southcott, from the enormous condescension of posterity . . .' (1963). The *Annales* historians of France can be seen as having initiated 'history from below'; they did not, however, pursue it with an interest in class struggle and 'agency' as have the British historians (see ANNALES SCHOOL; HISTORIOGRAPHY). It must be noted that although history from below/the bottom up has most often been equated with people's history, it was originally conceived of as a 'critical perspective', that is, a commitment to comprehending history from the vantage point of the oppressed and exploited. Thus, history from the bottom up has not been limited to the study of the lower classes, but has also provided for the critical study of ruling classes and their modes of domination (especially in the work of Kiernan, e.g. 1980, 1988).

The third contribution has been the recovery and assemblage of a 'radical democratic tradition', asserting what might be called 'counter-hegemonic' conceptions of liberty, equality and community (see HEGEMONY). In Gramscian fashion, the historians have revealed not a history of political ideas originating inside the heads of intellectuals, but a history of popular ideology standing in dialectical relationship to the history of politics and ideas. Alongside Magna Carta we are offered the Peasant Rising of 1381; outside of Parliament in the seventeenth century we encounter Levellers, Diggers and Ranters; in the eighteenth century we hear not only Wilkes but also the crowds of London asserting the 'rights of the freeborn Englishman'; and, in the Age of Revolution, we are reminded that within the 'exceptionalism' of English political life there were Jacobins, Luddites and Chartists. At the same time, the British Marxists do have their 'intellectuals': John Ball and his fellow radical priests, Milton and Winstanley; Wilkes, Paine and Wollstonecraft; Wordsworth and Blake; and Cobbett, Owen, Jones, Marx and Morris (see MORRIS, WILLIAM).

Finally, another contribution of primary importance is that, by way of class-struggle analysis, history from the bottom up and the recovery of the radical democratic tradition, the historians have effectively helped to undermine the great 'grand narratives' of both Right and Left. Their writings directly challenged the Whig version of history in which the development of English life and freedoms is comprehended as a continuous evolutionary and progressive success. And they also helped to clear away the (supposedly) Marxist presentation of history in which historical development is conceived of in unilinear, mechanical and techno-economistic terms (see DETERMINISM; HISTORICAL MATERIALISM). The narrative they themselves have been developing may not have become the schoolbook version of past and present, but it has definitely shaped and informed radical-democratic and socialist historical consciousness in Britain.

The British Marxist historians have influenced work across the humanities and social sciences: literary and cultural studies; women's studies; labour, slavery and peasant studies; and even critical legal studies. In particular, however, the British Marxist historical tradition is being carried forward in both Britain and the United States: in Britain through the work of the Society for the Study of Labour History and the History Workshop movement of socialist and feminist historians; and in the United States, on the one hand by social historians who, affiliated with such groups as MARHO and *Radical History Review*, are exploring the experiences and struggles of peasants (internationally), farmers (in America) and artisans and workers generally, and on the other hand by economic historians and historical sociologists interested in economic development and social change, especially the question of the transition from feudalism to capitalism. Indeed, the influence of the British Marxist historical tradition has been so strong in North America that at least one response to the question of whether or not the tradition will continue beyond the original generation of historians might be that it is continuing as an Anglo-American tradition.

Reading

Hobsbawm, Eric 1978: 'The Historians' Group of the Communist Party'. In Maurice Cornforth, ed. *Rebels and Their Causes*.

Johnson, Richard 1979: 'Culture and the Historians'. In J. Clarke, C. Critcher and R. Johnson, eds. *Working-Class Culture: Studies in History and Theory*.

Kaye, Harvey J. 1984: *The British Marxist Historians*.

— 1988: 'George Rudé, Social Historian'. In George Rudé, *The Face of the Crowd: Selected Essays of George Rudé*, ed. Harvey Kaye.

— 1988: 'V. G. Kiernan, Seeing things historically'. In Victor Kiernan, *History, Classes and Nation-States: Selected Writings of V. G. Kiernan*, ed. Harvey Kaye.

— 1990: 'E. P. Thompson, the British Marxist Historical Tradition and the Contemporary Crisis'. In Harvey Kaye and Keith McClelland, eds. *E. P. Thompson: Critical Perspectives*.

Samuel, Raphael 1980: 'The British Marxist Historians I'.

Schwarz, Bill 1982: 'The People in History: The Communist Party Historians' Group, 1946–56'. In Richard Johnson et al., eds. *Making Histories: Studies in History-Writing and Politics*.

HARVEY J. KAYE

Bukharin, Nikolai Ivanovich Born 9 October 1888, Moscow; executed 15 March 1938, Moscow. The son of teachers, Bukharin joined the Bolsheviks in 1906. After his third arrest in Moscow, he escaped abroad in 1911, settling in Vienna, where he made a critical study (1919) of the Austrian marginal utility school of economics. Deported from Austria to Switzerland in 1914, he attended the Bolshevik anti-war conference in Berne in February 1915. In this period he clashed with LENIN over the latter's support for the right of national self-determination. However, in 1915 Lenin wrote an approving introduction to *Imperialism and World Economy*, in which Bukharin argued that internal capitalist competition was being replaced more and more by the struggle between 'state capitalist trusts'. In 1916 Bukharin wrote articles which, while accepting the need for a transitional proletarian state, urged 'hostility in principle to the state' and denounced the 'imperialist robber state' which had to be 'blown up' (*gesprengt*). After initial objections from Lenin, these ideas were reflected the next year in his own *State and Revolution*.

After periods in Scandinavia and the USA Bukharin returned to Moscow in May 1917, after the February Revolution. Elected to the party's Central Committee three months before the October Revolution, he remained a full member until 1934, and was a candidate member from 1934 to 1937. He edited the party daily, *Pravda*, from December 1917 to April 1929. In 1918 Bukharin was a leader of the 'Left Communists' opposing the signing of the Brest-Litovsk treaty with the Germans and calling for a revolutionary war. In the party debate on the role of the trade unions in 1920–21, he favoured incorporation of the trade unions into the state machine.

Bukharin's *ABC of Communism*, written jointly with PREOBRAZHENSKY in 1919, and *Economics of the Transformation Period*, written in 1920, bear the imprint of his 'Left Communist' outlook at that time, which he was later to abandon. His *Historical Materialism: A System of Sociology*, which appeared the next year, represents a substantial attempt to explain and popularize Marxism as a sociological theory. Along with an interesting critique of the ideas of Max Weber and Stammler, he discusses Robert Michels's arguments about 'oligarchy' and the 'incompetence of the masses'. He considered that this 'incompetence' could be overcome in a socialist society, and was himself to attach very great importance to raising the cultural level of the new proletarian ruling class as an antidote to the danger of degeneration. GRAMSCI (1977, pp. 419–72) and LUKÁCS (1972b, pp. 134–42) were critical of the sociological conception of Marxism in Bukharin's *Historical Materialism*, which they also criticized for deterministic and undialectical positions. In his 'Testament', in December 1922, Lenin described Bukharin as 'a most valuable and major theorist' who was 'also rightly considered as the favourite of the whole Party'. However, somewhat paradoxically, he added that 'his theoretical views can be classified as fully Marxist only with great reserve, for there is something scholastic about him (he has

never made a study of dialectics, and, I think, never fully understood it)' (*Collected Works* 36, p. 595).

After the introduction in 1921 of the New Economic Policy which permitted free trade inside Soviet Russia, Bukharin undertook a thorough reappraisal of his ideas. From the end of 1922 he advocated a gradualist strategy of Russia 'growing into socialism'. He foreshadowed the theory of 'socialism in one country', first enunciated by STALIN in December 1924, and became its foremost ideological protagonist. Deeply influenced by Lenin's last articles, written in 1923 (CW 33, pp. 462–502), he argued for the long-term continuation of NEP's mixed, market economy and the strengthening of socialist elements within it. To this end he advocated the step-by-step development of state-owned industry, with special attention to light industry producing consumer goods, alongside the promotion of peasant co-operatives on a voluntary basis. The alliance between the working class and the peasantry should be reinforced on the basis of an expanding and balanced trade between industry and agriculture. In 1925–7 Bukharin was closely allied with Stalin in seeking to implement this policy and in opposing Trotskyist proposals favouring accelerated industrialization to be made possible by 'pumping' resources out of the peasantry. He argued strongly against Preobrazhensky whose 'law of primitive socialist accumulation' sought to underpin this.

In 1928–9 Bukharin came into conflict with Stalin, who made an abrupt turn to all-out industrialization, financed by 'tribute' extracted from the peasantry, and a crash programme of COLLECTIVIZATION. He attacked this policy and the 'extraordinary measures' used to enforce it as constituting the 'military and feudal exploitation of the peasantry'. Publicly attacked as a right deviationist in 1929, he was removed from the editorship of *Pravda*, from work in the Communist International which he had led since 1926, and subsequently from the Politbureau.

From 1934 to 1937 Bukharin was editor of *Izvestia*. In 1935 he played an important role in the commission drafting the new Soviet constitution (adopted in 1936). In 1937 he was expelled from the party. A year later he was tried and sentenced to death for treason and espionage at the third great Moscow Trial. He was finally rehabilitated juridically, along with other defendants, by the Soviet Supreme Court in February 1988 and politically by the Soviet Communist Party, which restored him to membership five months later.

In the post-Stalin period much interest and sympathy has developed, particularly in socialist countries from Yugoslavia to China, for Bukharin as the representative of a humanist, non-coercive socialism and a consumer-oriented mixed economy. Since 1988 there has been a Bukharin renaissance in the Soviet Union with the republication of his writings in hundreds of thousands of copies and the appearance of biographies (including a Russian translation of Stephen Cohen's pioneering study), articles, conferences and exhibitions dealing with his life and work. He has been increasingly presented there as having offered the main socialist alternative to Stalin's brutally implemented policy of forced collectivization and to the Stalinist conception of socialism as a super-centralized, authoritarian command economy. However there is much argument and debate among Soviet historians, as in the West, on how realistic and consistent an alternative way forward Bukharin did offer to the USSR in the particular national and international context of the time. (See also LENIN; PREOBRAZHENSKY; SOVIET MARXISM; STALINISM.)

Reading

Bergmann, T. and Schäfer, G. eds. 1990: *'Liebling der Partei': Nikolai Bucharin.*

Bukharin, Nikolai Ivanovich 1917–18 (1972): *Imperialism and World Economy.*

— 1919 (1927): *Economic Theory of the Leisure Class.*

— (with Preobrazhensky, E. A.) 1919 (1968): *ABC of Communism.*

— 1920 (1971): *Economics of the Transformation Period.*

— 1921 (1925): *Historical Materialism: A System of Sociology.*

— 1982: *Selected Writings on the State and the Transition to Socialism.*

Cohen, Stephen F. 1974: *Bukharin and the Bolshevik Revolution: A Political Biography 1888–1938.*

Harding, Neil 1981: *Lenin's Political Thought*, vol. 2, chs 3, 5 and Conclusion.

Heitman, Sidney 1969: *Nikolai I. Bukharin. A Bibliography with Annotations.*

Lewin, Moshe 1975: *Political Undercurrents in Soviet Economic Debates. From Bukharin to the Modern Reformers.*

MONTY JOHNSTONE

bureaucracy From the beginning the problem of bureaucracy played a relatively important role in Marxist thought. Marx formed his theory of bureaucracy on the basis of his personal experience of the malfunctioning of the state administration at the time of the Moselle district famine (see his articles in the *Rheinische Zeitung*, 17, 18 and 19 January 1843). He deduces the notion of bureaucracy from the bureaucratic relationship existing between the powerholding institutions and the social groups subordinated to them. He calls this an essential social relation which dominates the decision-makers themselves. Thus, according to Marx, a bureaucratic state administration, even if it runs matters with the best intentions, the most profound humanity, and the greatest intelligence, is not able to fulfil its actual task but reproduces the phenomenon that in everyday life is called bureaucratism. These apparatuses act in accordance with their own particular interests which they represent as public or general interests, and so they impose themselves upon society: 'The bureaucracy has the essence of the state, the spiritual life of society, in its possession, as its *private property*. The universal spirit of bureaucracy is *secrecy*, the mystery, which it secures internally by hierarchy, and against external groups by its character as a closed corporation' (Marx, *Critique of Hegel's Philosophy of the State*, comments on paras 290–7).

In spite of their original radical criticism of bureaucracy Marx's and Engels's assessment of its real function is by no means free from presuppositions that have not been confirmed by the historical experiences of the last century and a half. Marx, both in his early essays and in later writings, limited the problem of bureaucracy to the state administration, and thought that life (i.e. production and consumption) begins where its power ends. Thus, in the *18th Brumaire* (pt. VII), he described the executive power in France as an 'enormous bureaucratic and military organization, with its elaborately stratified and ingenious state machinery, and a horde of officials numbering half a million alongside an army of another half million, this dreadful parasitic substance which envelops the body of French society like a caul and chokes all its pores', the effect of which was that 'every *common* interest was immediately separated from society and counterposed to it as a higher *general* interest, torn from the self-activity of the members of society and made the object of government activity'; and he concluded that all revolutions so far had 'perfected this machine instead of smashing it'. However, since the middle of the last century managements of a bureaucratic character have gained more and more influence in the economy, especially in the larger industrial plants. Marx and Engels never perceived that the white-collar staff of the factories are the bearers of the same essential social relations as the state management apparatus, and they wrote about the increasing role of clerical workers and managers in industry only as a simple empirical fact ('The conductor of an orchestra need not be the owner of the instruments of its members', *Capital* III, ch. 23).

Their other great error is connected with their image of the future socialist society. They failed to take into consideration that bureaucratic formations might survive, reproduce themselves and become dominant even after the abolition of private ownership of the means of production. Some of their ideas even cleared the ground for the apologetics of state management in the East European countries; for example, in their view, the national economy of the future socialist society would work as a 'single great enterprise', and the principle of authority should by all means be maintained in the field of production (Engels, 'On Authority'). Their conception of the society of free producers is connected only incoherently with their earlier views on bureaucracy.

The varied and pluralistic Marxist thought of the present day bears the marks of both these errors, in the West as well as in the East. In the highly industrialized Western societies the process of bureaucratization has continued in diverse forms and has reached a high level. The power of management in business enterprises has expanded while the influence of the state administration on economic decisions has grown considerably. At the same time the leadership of trade unions and political parties has become more and more bureaucratic. Marxism

failed to react to these processes in good time, or in an effective way, so that the analysis of the changes has been left mainly to social scientists of other schools (beginning with Max Weber and Michels; see CRITICS OF MARXISM).

All this has had a twofold negative effect on Marxism. On the one hand, in radical communist movements there has survived an anachronistic, romantic anti-capitalism which does not take into consideration the growing importance of the struggle against bureaucratism. This is a serious obstacle for the Eurocommunist trends (see EUROCOMMUNISM) because it hinders the development of a realistic and critical socialist analysis of the existing power relations in the West. On the other hand, in the revisionist-reformist orientations (i.e. in SOCIAL DEMOCRACY) this outlook has favoured the rise of a pro-bureaucratic trend instead of an anti-bureaucratic one. The main slogan of industrial bureaucracy became 'participation' (e.g. the West German *Mitbestimmungsrecht*) which in practice ensures an almost total control over the workers' movements.

In the East, at first in Russia, new types of socio-economic formation emerged on the ideological basis of LENINISM, as a consequence of the 'great Eastern schism' in Marxism. This has also had a primarily anti-capitalist and not an anti-bureaucratic character. After the second world war these formations were extended to the countries of Central and Eastern Europe. In these countries the abolition of private ownership of the means of production failed to bring about a diminution of bureaucracy, which in fact even increased considerably. Thus, parliamentary control over the state administration was eliminated, as well as capitalist control over enterprise management, but neither of them was replaced by new forms of non-bureaucratic social control.

This state management model was opposed by a self-management ideology and practice in Yugoslavia after 1949, but in the course of time the ideology has acquired an apologetic character, defending a practice in which the self-management organs for the most part work in a formal way while the bureaucratic apparatuses play a dominant role. It may be argued, therefore, that one of the principal conditions for a renaissance of Marxist thought both in the West and in the East is now a relevant and practically effective criticism of bureaucratism. (See also BONAPARTISM; STATE.)

Reading

Hegedüs, András 1976: *Socialism and Bureaucracy.*

Luxemburg, Rosa 1922 *(1961): The Russian Revolution.*

Michels, R. 1911 *(1949): Political Parties.*

Mills, C. Wright 1951: *White Collar.*

Webb, Sidney and Beatrice 1920: *Industrial Democracy.*

Weber, Max 1921 *(1947):* 'Bureaucracy'. In H. H. Gerth and C. Wright Mills, eds. *From Max Weber.*

ANDRÁS HEGEDÜS

C

Capital (*Das Kapital*) Marx's greatest work, containing the most developed fruits of his scientific enquiries. It is most famous as a three-volume work, *Capital*. The first volume was published in German in 1867; volume II was published by Engels in 1885, two years after Marx's death; and volume III, edited by Engels, appeared in 1894. But it is really a four-volume book, for Marx envisaged his work on the history of economic theory, first published by Kautsky in 1905–10 as *Theories of Surplus Value*, as the fourth part of the whole.

In *Capital* we find the reasoning behind Marx's most famous propositions: they include the idea that production (rather than trade and commerce) is at the root of capitalist progress and decline; that capitalism is the first system in history to be based on constant revolutionary changes in economic relations; that it requires a reserve army of the unemployed; that it has a tendency towards concentrating economic power in monopolies; and that economic crises are inseparable from capitalism. Throughout *Capital* Marx shows how the development of capitalism along these lines is based on the conflict between labour and capital. The creation and development (and differentiation) of the working class and capitalist class, at least in their economic roles, is its story.

Capital presents Marx's mature science of history ('historical materialism') applied to the analysis of capitalism, although it is largely confined to the economic dimension. Out of the many questions with which Marx implicitly confronts the reader, four provide a continuing theme linking the whole: How does the capitalist economy reproduce itself? How did it arise from pre-capitalist societies? What is the internal dynamic of its development, expansion and degeneration? And how do the surface appearances of capitalism differ from and hide the underlying relationships and forces?

These questions demand both abstract analysis and discussion of the dramatic historical experience of capitalism's birth, operation and growth, and the two are combined with extraordinary power in *Capital*. For many readers the powerful, meticulous historical passages describing the enclosures and the violent birth of capitalism in Britain, the later struggles of capitalist employers over the English Factory Acts, or the conditions of life in the workshop and outside it are the essence of *Capital*. Their empirical soundness is accepted, Marx's underlying passion does not undermine his careful attention to the data and the events almost seem to speak for themselves to unravel the nature of capitalism. But they cannot really speak for themselves, and the strength of Marx's description lies in the way he relates it to the laws of capitalism laid bare in his abstract analysis of economic categories.

Reading that analysis shows Marx's use of his dialectical method at work. He outlined a key aspect of his method in the *Grundrisse*, his rough draft, where he stated that to understand capitalism we have to analyse its most simple, abstract categories and, from their interrelations and contradictions, construct the increasingly complex categories that correspond to everyday phenomena. *Capital* is written on that principle. Of the many examples it contains of that method, the clearest is the fact that *Capital* begins with a highly abstract analysis of the simple concept 'commodity' and on that basis step by step builds analyses of such complex phenomena as money, capital, the reserve army of the unemployed, circulation and reproduction, the credit system, crises, and the rise of monopoly capital. At each step, the dialectical contradictions inherent in each category are the basis for the more complex categories; for example, the properties of money are derived from the contradictory relation of use value and exchange value in commodities.

The way Marx divides this subject matter between the first three volumes of *Capital* also gives a very clear indication of the structure of his analysis as it proceeds from one level of abstraction to another. The first, a critical analysis of 'capitalist production', is in terms of capital-in-general and in it Marx lays bare the secret of the essential characteristic all forms of capital have, self-expansion. He shows that capital's expansion is founded on the generation and appropriation of surplus value achieved through capital's control of the production process. That lays the foundation for the second volume's analysis of the 'process of circulation of capital', also in terms of capital-in-general. And in volume III, the essential but more complex reality of inter-capitalist competition is analysed as capital-in-general is transformed into many-capitals. There the transformation of surplus value into profit, interest and rent is explained as well as the dynamic operation of everyday market forces on production, and the operation of the credit system.

That procedure of analysing capital at successive levels of abstraction means that the economic categories are themselves continually transformed. Just as the concept of surplus value which is appropriate in the analysis of capital-in-general is changed into forms such as profit in the context of many-capitals, so the concept of value in volume I is related to price of production, market values and market prices in volume III. As the 'transformation problem', the transformation of value into prices of production (and surplus value into profit) has occupied a central place in discussions of Marx's economics since the publication of *Capital*. Critics of Marx have claimed that logical flaws in the transformation destroy the foundations of his economics, while defenders have argued in various ways that the transformation can only be understood in the context of Marx's dialectical method. (See also VALUE AND PRICE, SURPLUS VALUE AND PROFIT, CRITICS OF MARXISM.)

Those debates over the internal structure of *Capital* should not obscure the fact that it is a very open text. Not only is its logical argument linked to the real experience of capitalism through Marx's historical and contemporary social narrative but, in addition, its theoretical arguments themselves are incomplete and open to development. For example, the famous propositions regarding the tendency of the rate of profit to fall and the causes of economic crises are presented in a fragmentary and incomplete manner which invite rather than close off further work.

Another dimension of its openness is that the existing four volumes of *Capital* were never intended to be the whole of Marx's work on the economics of capitalism. Marx's 1857 outline for his major work conceived it as six books, the last three of which were to deal with the state, foreign trade and the world market. The material envisaged in 1857 for his first three books was incorporated, in a different form, in the first three volumes of *Capital* as we know them, but Marx never fulfilled his plan for works on the state, foreign trade and the world market, although it seems they were not abandoned. Subsequent work on these central features of capitalism has, therefore, been taken well beyond Marx's own comments.

Similarly, the links between economic relations and cultural, political and social relations were left open in *Capital*. Therefore its analysis of the economic location of classes and their changes was a starting point for class analyses which integrate class consciousness and class politics rather than an attempt to enclose classes in their economic grooves. (See BASE AND SUPERSTRUCTURE; CLASS.)

The place of *Capital* in Marx's work as a whole is contested. Many have emphasized its roots in his earlier work and the continuous development of essentially Hegelian concerns such as Hegel's dialectic and Marx's early concepts of alienation. But others see *Capital* as the zenith of a completely different body of mature work. The former are best represented by Rosdolsky whose analysis of *Capital*'s roots in the *Grundrisse* illuminated the role of concepts developed by Marx from his study of Hegel. The foremost exposition of the alternative 'mature Marx' thesis is that of Althusser and his collaborators, who argued that *Capital* was the ultimate product of an 'epistemological break' between his early and late work. In their view *Capital* presents the social relations of capitalism as relations within and between structures without either individuals or classes having any role as the subjects of history. (See also HEGEL AND MARX; STRUCTURALISM; GRUNDRISSE.)

For Marx himself, writing *Capital* was a

crucial part of his work to assist the proletariat in its task as capitalism's gravedigger, and for both him and Engels their labours over *Capital* were inseparable from their efforts to build the International Working Men's Association and the national workers' parties (see INTERNATIONALS). Although *Capital* is often seen now as an academic text to be picked over by intellectuals, or as a source of dogma for the propagandists of former communist regimes, its greatest strength is that for more than a century it has been read and reflected on by generations of working people in the vanguard of struggles for socialism. There is no doubt it will also wield such influence in the future.

Reading

Althusser, L. and Balibar, E. 1970: *Reading 'Capital'*.
Rosdolsky, R. 1968 (1977): *The Making of Marx's 'Capital'*.

LAURENCE HARRIS

capital In everyday speech, the word 'capital' is generally used to describe an asset owned by an individual as wealth. Capital might then denote a sum of money to be invested in order to secure a rate of return, or it might denote the investment itself: a financial instrument, or stocks and shares representing titles to means of production, or the physical means of production themselves. And depending on the nature of the capital, the rate of return to which the owner has a legal right is either an interest payment or a claim on profits. Bourgeois economics broadens the usage of the term still further, by letting it also denote any asset of whatever kind which can be used as a source of income, even if only potentially; thus a house could be part of an individual's capital, as could also specialized training enabling a higher income to be earned (human capital). In general, then, capital is an asset which can generate an income stream for its owner. (See VULGAR ECONOMICS.)

Two corollaries of this understanding are, first, that it applies to every sort of society, in the past, in the present and in the future, and is specific to none; and second, that it posits the possibility that inanimate objects are productive in the sense of generating an income stream. The Marxist concept of capital is based on a denial of these two corollaries. Capital is something

which in its generality is quite specific to capitalism; while capital predates capitalism, in capitalist society the production of capital predominates, and dominates every other sort of production. Capital cannot be understood apart from capitalist relations of production (see FORCES AND RELATIONS OF PRODUCTION); indeed, capital is not a thing at all, but a social relation which appears in the form of a thing. To be sure, capital is about money-making, but the assets which 'make' money embody a particular relation between those who have money and those who do not, such that not only is money 'made', but also the private property relations which engender such a process are themselves continually reproduced. Marx writes:

> capital is not a thing, but rather a definite social production relation, belonging to a definite historical formation of society, which is manifested in a thing and lends this thing a specific social character. . . . It is the means of production monopolized by a certain section of society, confronting living labour-power as products and working conditions rendered independent of this very labour-power, which are personified through this antithesis in capital. It is not merely the products of labourers turned into independent powers, products as rulers and buyers of their producers, but rather also the social forces and the . . . form of this labour, which confront the labourers as properties of their products. Here, then, we have a definite and, at first glance, very mystical, social form, of one of the factors in a historically produced social production process. (*Capital* III, ch. 48)

Capital is accordingly a complex category, not amenable to a simple definition, and the major part of Marx's writings was devoted to exploring its ramifications.

Not every sum of money is capital. There is a definite process which transforms money into capital, which Marx approaches by contrasting two antithetical series of transactions in the sphere of CIRCULATION: selling commodities in order to purchase different ones, and buying commodities in order subsequently to sell. (See COMMODITY.) Denoting commodities by C and money by M these two processes are C-M-C and M-C-M respectively. But the latter process only makes sense if the sum of money at the end is larger than the sum at the beginning, and, assuming away contingent fluctuations between the VALUE of a commodity and its money form, this does not seem to be possible. (See also VALUE AND PRICE.) For if exchange were not the exchange of value equivalents, value would not thereby be created, but just transferred from loser to gainer; yet if value equivalents are exchanged, the problem remains of how money can be made. Marx resolves this apparent contradiction by focusing on the one particular commodity whose USE VALUE has the property of creating more value than it itself has: this commodity is LABOUR POWER. Labour power is bought and sold for a wage, and the commodities subsequently produced by workers can be sold for a greater value than the total value of inputs: the value of labour power, together with the value of the means of production used up in the production process. But labour power can only be a commodity if workers are free to sell their capacity to work, and for this to occur the feudal restrictions on labour mobility must be broken down, and workers must be separated from the means of production so that they are forced into the labour market. (Marx analyses these historical preconditions as the primary or PRIMITIVE ACCUMULATION of capital.)

Consequently, the typical C-M-C series of transactions denotes the commodity labour power being sold for a wage, which is then used to purchase all those commodities necessary to reproduce the worker. Money is not here acting as capital at all. By contrast, the M-C-M series of transactions comprises the advance of money by the capitalist for inputs which are then transformed into outputs and sold for more money. Unlike the wage, which is spent on commodities which are consumed and hence disappears entirely, the capitalist's money is merely advanced to reappear in a greater quantity. Here money is transformed into capital on the basis of the historical process whereby labour power becomes a commodity, and the series of transactions should properly be written M-C-M', where $M' = M + \Delta M$, ΔM being SURPLUS VALUE. M-C-M' 'is . . . therefore the general formula for capital, in the form in which it appears directly in the sphere of circulation' (*Capital* I, ch. 4). Since capital is a process of the expansion of value, it is some times defined as 'self-expanding value', or equivalently the 'self-

valorization of value'. Capital is value in motion, and the specific forms of appearance assumed in turn by self-valorizing value are all accordingly forms of capital. This is easy to see if the general formula for capital is written more fully:

$$M - C \underset{\diagdown\ MP}{\overset{\diagup\ LP}{}} \ldots P \ldots C' - M'$$

where LP denotes labour-power, MP the means of production, P the process of production which transforms inputs C into outputs of greater value C', and M and M' are as before. M and M' are both money capital, or capital in money form; C is productive capital; and C' is commodity capital. The whole movement is called the 'circuit of capital', in which capital is a value which undergoes a series of transformations, each of which corresponds to a particular function in the process of valorization. Money capital and commodity capital pertain to the sphere of circulation, productive capital to production; and the capital that assumes these various forms at different stages in the circuit is called 'industrial capital', embracing every branch of production governed by capitalist relations.

Industrial capital is the only mode of existence of capital in which not only the appropriation of surplus-value or surplus product, but also its creation, is a function of capital. It thus requires production to be capitalist in character; its existence includes that of the class antagonism between capitalists and wage-labourers . . . The other varieties of capital which appeared previously, within past or declining social conditions of production, are not only subordinated to it and correspondingly altered in the mechanism of their functioning, but they now move only on its basis, thus live and die, stand and fall together with this basis. (*Capital* II, ch. 1)

(See also FINANCE CAPITAL; FINANCIAL CAPITAL AND INTEREST; MERCHANT CAPITAL; CREDIT AND FICTITIOUS CAPITAL; and generally FORMS OF CAPITAL AND REVENUES.)

The capitalist is the possessor of money which is valorized, but this self-valorization of value is an objective movement; only to the extent that this objective movement becomes the capitalist's subjective purpose does the possessor of money become a capitalist, the personification of capital. It is the objective movement of value expansion rather than the subjective motives for profit-making which is crucial here; whereas the latter are quite contingent, the former defines what it is that every single capital has in common. In terms of their ability to expand their value, all capitals are identical: what Marx calls 'capital in general'. Of course the profit accruing to each capital is an outcome of COMPETITION, but no more can be shared out than is actually produced in the production process since circulation creates no value. It follows that in order to understand the appearances of many capitals in competition, the content of these appearances must first be considered. Marx writes of

the way in which the immanent laws of capitalist production manifest themselves in the external movement of the individual capitals, assert themselves as the coercive laws of competition, and therefore enter into the consciousness of the individual capitalist as the motives which drive him forward . . . a scientific analysis of competition is possible only if we can grasp the inner nature of capital, just as the apparent motions of the heavenly bodies are intelligible only to someone who is acquainted with their real motions, which are not perceptible to the senses. (*Capital* I, ch. 12)

'Capital in general' appears as many competing capitals, but the latter presupposes a differentiation of capitals according to their composition, use values produced and so on; and such differentiation, organized by competition, determines the profit share of each capital in the total surplus value produced by them all. (See SURPLUS VALUE AND PROFIT; and PRICE OF PRODUCTION AND THE TRANSFORMATION PROBLEM.) In this profit form, capital seems to be productive of wealth, independent of labour; to understand this appearance requires examination of how surplus value is produced by capital, of how capital is a process continually taking the antithetical forms of money and commodities, of how capital is a social relation attached to things. It is only the analysis of 'capital in general' which allows analysis of the class character of bourgeois society; only after analysis of how the surplus labour of the working class is appropriated as value by capital can it be determined how and why the appearances of competition generate the illusions that this is not the case.

Thus the analysis of 'capital in general' must precede that of 'many capitals', capital's essence before that of its forms of appearance, valorization in production before that of the realization of value in circulation.

In the production process the purchased inputs play different roles. First, consider the means of production. Raw materials are completely consumed, hence lose the form in which they entered the LABOUR PROCESS; the same is true for the instruments of labour (although this may take several cycles of production). The outcome is a new use value, the product; use values of one sort are transformed by labour into use values of another sort. Now value can only exist in a use value – if something loses its use value, it loses its value. But since the production process is one of transformation of use values, then as the use values of the means of production are consumed, their value is transferred to the product. Thus the value of the means of production is preserved in the product, a transfer of value mediated by labour, considered in its particular useful or concrete character as labour of a specific type. But means of production are just one of the elements of productive capital; Marx defines 'constant capital' as that portion of capital advanced which is turned into means of production and does not undergo any quantitative alteration of value in the production process.

Secondly, consider labour; any act of commodity-producing labour is not only labour of a particular useful sort; it is also the expenditure of human labour power in the abstract, of labour in general, or of ABSTRACT LABOUR. It is this aspect which adds fresh value to the means of production. Just as concrete labour and abstract labour are not two different activities, but the same activity considered in its different aspects, so too the preservation of the value of the materials of labour and the addition to this value of new value are not the results of two different activities. The same act of adding new value also transfers the value of the means of production, but the distinction can only be understood in terms of the two-fold nature of labour. Thus Marx defines 'variable capital' as that part of capital advanced which is turned into labour power, and which, first, reproduces the equivalent of its own value, and secondly, produces value additional to its own equivalent, a surplus value, which varies according to circumstances.

The elements of capital are thereby distinguished, first with respect to the labour process according to whether they are objective factors (means of production) or subjective factors (labour power) and secondly with respect to the valorization process according to whether they are constant or variable capital. The distinction between constant and variable capital is unique to Marx's work; it is also central to his understanding of the capitalist mode of production. Once he had developed it, he could use it to criticize the analysis of capital by earlier economists, who tended to employ the different distinction between 'fixed' and 'circulating' capital. These categories are employed with respect to a chosen time period (for example, a year), and the elements of capital are considered according to whether they are totally consumed within the time period (circulating capital – typically labour power and raw materials), or whether they are only partially consumed within the period, depreciating only a portion of their value to the product (fixed capital – typically machines and buildings). Marx was severely critical of the way in which this distinction was centrally employed. In the first place the distinction applies only to one form of capital, productive capital; commodity and money capital are ignored. And in the second place:

The sole distinction here is whether the transfer of value, and therefore the replacement of value, proceeds bit by bit and gradually, or all at once. The all important distinction between variable and constant capital is thereby obliterated, and with it the whole secret of surplus value formation and of capitalist production, namely the circumstances that transform certain values and the things in which they are represented into capital. The components of capital are distinguished from one another simply by the mode of circulation (and the circulation of commodities has of course only to do with already existing, given values). . . . We can thus understand why bourgeois political economy held instinctively to Adam Smith's confusion of the categories 'fixed and circulating capital' with the categories 'constant and variable capital', and uncritically echoed it from one generation

down to the next. It no longer distinguished at all between the portion of capital laid out on wages and the portion of capital laid out on raw materials, and only formally distinguished the former from constant capital in terms of whether it was circulated bit by bit or all at once through the product. The basis for understanding the real movement of capitalist production, and thus of capitalist exploitation, was thus submerged at one blow. All that was involved, on this view, was the reappearance of values advanced. (*Capital* II, ch. 11)

This is one of the most important instances of FETISHISM, whereby the social character attached to things by the process of social production is transformed into a natural character possessed by the material nature of these things. Marx's concept of capital and its division into constant and variable components is crucial for unravelling this real inversion. It provides the analytical basis for his discussion of the production of surplus value, of the portion of surplus value which is reinvested or capitalized, and generally of the laws of motion of capitalist production (see ACCUMULATION).

In summary, capital is a coercive social relation; this relation is attached to things, whether commodities or money, and in money form comprises the accumulated unpaid surplus labour of the past appropriated by the capitalist class in the present. It is thus the dominant relation of capitalist society.

SIMON MOHUN

capitalism A term denoting a mode of production in which capital in its various forms is the principal means of production. Capital can take the form of money or credit for the purchase of labour power and materials of production; of physical machinery (capital in the narrow sense); or of stocks of finished goods or work in progress. Whatever the form, it is the private ownership of capital in the hands of a class – the class of capitalists to the exclusion of the mass of the population – which is a central feature of capitalism as a mode of production.

The word 'capitalism' is rarely used by non-Marxist schools of economics, as Tawney and Dobb were to point out. But even in Marxist writings it is a late arrival. Marx, while he uses the adjective 'capitalistic' or talks of 'capitalists', does not use capitalism as a noun either in the *Communist Manifesto* or in *Capital* I. Only in 1877 in his correspondence with Russian followers did he use it in a discussion of the problem of Russia's transition to capitalism. This reluctance to employ the word may have been due to its relative modernity in Marx's day. The OED cites its first use (by Thackeray) as late as 1854.

The suffix 'ism' can be used to denote a phase of history (Absolutism), a movement (Jacobinism), a system of ideas (millenarianism) or some combination of them. Thus, socialism is both a mode of production (a phase of history) and a system of ideas. The word capitalism however rarely denotes the system of ideas propagating a certain mode of production. It stands only for a phase of history. But this limited use does not lend clarity to the concept. As a phase of history, its lines of demarcation have always been a matter of controversy, its origins being pushed farther back or brought forward to suit particular theories of its origin; and especially in recent years its periodization has also been hotly disputed. There are also attempts to widen the concept by prefixing adjectives such as MONOPOLY CAPITALISM; STATE MONOPOLY CAPITALISM. (See also PERIODIZATION OF CAPITALISM.)

Controversies concerning the origins and periodization of capitalism arise from the tendency to emphasize one out of many features which can be said to characterize this mode, and it will be useful therefore to list these features. As a mode of production, capitalism can be said to be characterized by:

(a) Production for sale rather than own use by numerous producers: this contrasts with simple commodity production.

(b) A market where LABOUR POWER is bought and sold, the mode of exchange being money wages for a period of time (time rate) or for a specified task (piece rate): the existence of a market with the implied contractual relation contrasts with earlier phases of slavery or serfdom.

(c) Predominant if not universal mediation of exchange by the use of money. In taking the money form, capital permits the maximum flexibility to its owner for redeployment. This aspect also gives a systemic role to banks and financial intermediaries. Pure barter is an ideal-

ized contrast to use of money, but the actual incidence of pure barter is limited. The contrast should be made with earlier phases where, while limited use of coins was made, the possibility of debt/credit instruments for purchase/sale was non-existent except for examples of consumption loans to the feudal nobility advanced by nascent merchant capital (see MONEY; MERCHANT CAPITAL; FINANCE CAPITAL).

(d) The capitalist or his managerial agent controls the production (labour) process. This implies control not only over hiring and firing workers but also over the choice of techniques, the output mix, the work environment and the arrangements for selling the output: the contrast here is with the putting-out system or with alternative modern protosocialist forms such as the cooperative, the worker-managed firm, worker-owned and/or state-owned firms.

(e) Control of financial decisions: the universal use of money and credit facilitates the use of other people's resources to finance accumulation. Under capitalism, this implies the power of the capitalist entrepreneur to incur debts or float shares or mortgage the factory buildings to raise finance. Workers are excluded from this decision but will suffer from miscalculation by the capitalist, e.g. default leading to bankruptcy. The capitalist however has to contest control with lenders and/or shareholders. Some writers (e.g. Berle and Means 1932) saw widespread shareholding, with passivity of the share holders, as a sign of a new phase marked by a divorce between ownership and control (see JOINT-STOCK COMPANY), and another (Drucker 1976) has characterized share ownership by pension funds on behalf of workers participating in pension schemes as socialism. These intimations of the passing of capitalism are intended to suggest that the crucial element is control, whether accompanied by ownership or not. The contrast here would be with central financial control by a planning authority in socialism.

(f) Competition between capitals: the control of individual capitalists over the labour process and over the financial structure is modified by its constant operation in an environment of COMPETITION with other capitals either producing the same commodity or a near sub stitute, or just fighting for markets or loans. This increasing competition operates as an impersonal law of value forcing the capitalist to adopt new techniques and practices which will cut costs, and to accumulate to make possible the purchase of improved machinery. This constant revolution in value is an important feature of the dynamics of capitalism. Competition is to be interpreted broadly, and not narrowly as the perfect competition of neo-classical economics which is more likely in simple commodity production. It is competition which strengthens the tendency towards concentration of capital in large firms. It is to neutralize competition that monopolies and cartels emerge. The constant revolution in technology imposes new forms such as the multiproduct firm or even the multinational firm. But these various forms do not eliminate competition, they only modify the form in which the firm faces it. Some writers (e.g. Galbraith 1967) have argued that the modern large corporation can plan to insulate itself from the market, but recent experience of the US automobile and steel industries in the face of international competition points to the limitations of such a view.

The origins of capitalism are traced variously to the growth of merchant capital and external trade or to the spread of monetary transactions within feudalism via commuting of feudal rent and services. This debate concerns the TRANSITION FROM FEUDALISM TO CAPITALISM and pertains mainly to Western European experience where capitalism first emerged. Whatever the reasons for its origins, the period from about the fifteenth century to the eighteenth century is generally accepted as the merchant capital phase of capitalism. Overseas trade and colonization carried out by the state-chartered monopolies played a pivotal role in this phase of capitalism in Holland, Spain, Portugal, England and France. Maritime trade became cheaper than overland trade on account of the invention of fast ships, and hitherto (by Europe) undiscovered areas were linked in a trade involving slaves, precious metals and simple manufactures.

The industrial phase opened with the upsurge in power-using machinery known as the Industrial Revolution. Starting in England in the cotton spinning industry, the revolution spread across different industries, mainly universalizing the use of the steam engine, and across different countries of Western Europe and North America. This phase saw the parallel growth of the science of POLITICAL ECONOMY and the ideology of *laissez-faire*. It was marked by a struggle to curtail or eliminate the role of the state in the control of the labour market, of foreign trade and of domestic trade, and the theories of Adam Smith and Ricardo became powerful weapons in this battle (see VULGAR ECONOMICS). In England at least, the ideological battle for *laissez-faire* was won in the 1840s with the repeal of the Corn Laws, the passing of the Banking Act and the repeal of the Navigation Acts. The reform of the Poor Law rationalized state support of the poor and the indigent, in line with *laissez-faire* doctrines. The role of the state in capitalism, though minimized in the ideology of *laissez-faire* and modest in the English experience, remained substantial in the later development of the capitalist mode in France, Germany, Italy and Russia. The only other case paralleling the English experience is the United States of America.

There is a tendency, however, to characterize this middle phase of capitalism – industrial capitalism in a period of rapid growth and technical progress, consisting of individually owned small firms with minimal state participation and widespread competition – as somehow a natural phase. Subsequent phases have therefore been labelled MONOPOLY CAPITALISM, FINANCE CAPITAL, late capitalism etc. The monopoly (finance) capitalist phase is said to date from around the turn of this century when large-scale industrial processes became possible with the advent of the Second Industrial Revolution. In so far as each of the characteristics listed above is considered an essential feature of capitalism, various authors have heralded the demise of capitalism. *Laissez-faire* ideologists (Friedman, Hayek) have pointed to the growth of collective bargaining, and of legislation to regulate the adverse consequences of economic activity, as a sign of departure from classical capitalism. Marxist writers have seen the growing size of monopolies, or the dominant role of the state, as signs of the ill health or old age of capitalism. The role of the nation state in helping capital to seek markets overseas, often in politically controlled colonies, was seen by Lenin as marking the imperialist stage – the highest stage of capitalism. The role of the state internally, in alleviating the realization problem by public spending in the post-Keynesian era, was regarded by liberal economists (Shonfield 1965, Galbraith 1967) as heralding a new era in capitalism, and some social democrats also took this view (e.g. Crosland 1956).

In most modern capitalist countries, however, the features listed above are still recognizable: predominant private ownership of means of production, use of debt-credit to finance accumulation, buying and selling of labour power, and capitalist control, more or less hindered, over hiring and firing and choice of techniques. Internationally, capitalist economies have become more open rather than less so, and the advanced capitalist countries have faced competition from countries previously underdeveloped or outside the Western European orbit. For all these economies, private profit remains the major impetus to entrepreneurial activity and the major signal and source for initiating and fulfilling accumulation plans.

This is not to deny that capitalism has changed and evolved. The major influences on its evolution have been both technological and social in the broad sense. Successive waves of innovation starting from the steam engine and the harnessing of steam power in the railways, steel-making and electrical products, the chemical revolution which affected agriculture as well as industry, steamships as well as the recent inventions of radar and electronics, have changed capitalism in terms of the requirements of individual capital, the possibilities of control and its extent and reach. Simultaneously, political and social struggles for an extension of the franchise, for political rights of free speech and assembly, for freedom of conscience, have changed the legislative and administrative environment within which capitalism operates. There is of course a variety of political forms which the state in capitalist countries takes – fascist, authoritarian, republican, democratic, monarchical etc. – but the growth of communication and consciousness of international events has meant that everywhere there has been a democratic thrust which has forced states of whatever political colour to accommodate, or to counter with effective repression, popular demands for greater rights of control over the economic process. Marxist discussions of the capitalist STATE reflect these considerations (e.g. Miliband 1969, Poulantzas 1973).

Those who emphasize the worker's lack of control over the labour process as the crucial form of subordination of labour to external forces (see ALIENATION) characterize the economies of the Soviet Union, China and East European countries as forms of qualified capitalism. Given the lack of private ownership (in non–agricultural activities at least), they affix the adjective 'state' or 'state monopoly' to capitalism in order to characterize these economies. There is also a much looser use of this label to denote the growth of state involvement in private ownership capitalist economies (see STATE MONOPOLY CAPITALISM). Some writers thus call the US economy state monopoly capitalist. The term state capitalism was used by Lenin to denote an interim phase of the Soviet economy where some sectors were state owned but the capitalist mode prevailed in large parts of the economy. Lenin then cited the example of Germany during the first world war as a capitalist economy run by the state as a single trust. This was seen as the limit of the process of CENTRALIZATION AND CONCENTRATION OF CAPITAL, predicted by Marx. Lenin emphasized the different political context of Soviet Russia from that of Germany and therefore treated state capitalism as a progress beyond the capitalist phase. Subsequent writers, and especially Trotsky, have taken what others call state capitalism to be a degenerate phase of socialism or a sign of socialism not yet achieved.

The prevalence of scarcity and the persistent pressure to accumulate in these societies, as well as in the newly decolonized countries of Asia and Africa, have led some writers to propose that it is industrialization rather than capitalism that should be used to describe this phase of world history. The most prominent exponent of this view is W. W. Rostow (1960), who put forward a periodization scheme that consciously eschewed the Marxist categories of modes of production in favour of stages marked off by economic measures such as output per capita, savings ratio, etc. The common labelling of all societies as capitalist, with or without prefixes such as state or monopoly, encourages the notion of convergence of different societies towards a universal stage of high consumption and advanced technology. This is intended to contrast with Marx's view of capitalism as a specific and transitory historical phase on the way to socialism. While Rostow's schematization has been much criticized by Marxist as well as non-Marxist writers, it has endured as a catch-phrase. The questions it raises for Marxists are: will capitalism prove to be a transitory phase? Can socialist forms go in parallel with capitalism? What is the nature of post-capitalist societies and what are the paths whereby such societies can achieve socialism? (see TRANSITION TO SOCIALISM).

Reading

Berle A. and Means, G. C. 1932: *The Modern Corporation and Private Property*.

Crosland, C. A. R. 1956: *The Future of Socialism*.

Drucker P. 1976: *The Unseen Revolution: How Pension Fund Socialism Came to America*.

Galbraith, J. K. 1967: *The New Industrial State*.

Hilton R. ed. 1976: *The Transition from Feudalism to Capitalism*.

Miliband, R. 1969: *The State in Capitalist Society*.

Poulantzas, N. 1973: *Political Power and Social Classes*.

Rostow, W. W. 1960: *The Stages of Economic Growth*.

— ed. 1963: *The Economics of Take Off Into Self Sustained Growth*.

Shonfield A. 1965: *Modern Capitalism*.

MEGHNAD DESAI

cartels and trusts *See* monopoly capitalism.

caste In the 1850s Marx devoted much attention to India (see especially his articles in the *New York Daily Tribune* and various passages in the *Grundrisse*), but he was primarily interested in the existence of 'communal ownership' in the village community, the general character of ASIATIC SOCIETY, and the impact of British capitalism upon Indian society; and he had little to say about caste as such (see Thorner 1966). His main reference to it is in 'The Future Results of British Rule in India' where he asks whether 'a country not only divided between Mohammedan and Hindoo, but between tribe and tribe, between caste and caste; a society whose framework was based on a sort of equilibrium, resulting from a general repulsion and constitutional exclusiveness between all its members' was not 'the predestined prey of conquest'? On the effects of capitalism Marx concluded that 'modern industry, resulting from the railway system, will dissolve the hereditary divisions of labour, upon which rest the Indian castes, those decisive impediments to Indian progress and Indian power'.

Few later Marxists have attempted to analyse or explain the caste system. Those who have done so have generally tried to assimilate the broad fourfold division of the *varnas* to a class system; thus Rosas (1943) argues that in India the caste system obscures the nature of class society, while feudal forms often obscure the character of India as an Asiatic society (p. 159). However, he concedes that the caste system in all its complexity, involving the existence of innumerable small local caste groups (*jatis*), is unique to India, and that its development there cannot be definitively explained on the basis of present knowledge (p. 162). An Indian historian sympathetic to Marxism (Kosambi 1944) nevertheless criticizes Rosas's account as 'obliterating too many details to be useful' (p. 243). On the other hand, non-Marxist scholars have recognized that there are important class elements in the caste system; Srinivas (1959) observes that 'a caste which owned land exercised an effective dominance, regardless of its ritual status', while Béteille (1965) argues that 'in traditional society, and even fifty years ago . . . the class system was subsumed under the caste structure [and] ownership and nonownership of land, and relations within the system of production, were to a much greater extent associated with caste' (p. 191).

In the main, however, scholars have come to regard the local caste groups (*jatis*) as status groups in Max Weber's sense (Béteille 1965, p. 188; see also CLASS; CRITICS OF MARXISM), which are defined by 'styles of life' rather than by their place in a system of production. From this point of view castes fall into a category which Marx and Engels themselves distinguished when they wrote that 'in the earlier epochs of history, we find almost everywhere a complicated arrangement of society into various orders, a manifold gradation of social rank' (*Communist Manifesto*, sect. I). The question is whether such a 'manifold gradation', and as a particular instance of it, the caste system, can be fully explained within the scheme of historical materialism, or whether some *ad hoc* explanations are required in these cases (e.g. the influence of religion upon caste; see Dumont 1967, and HINDUISM), though still perhaps influenced by the Marxist conception of history as a 'guide to study' (as Engels expressed it in a letter to C. Schmidt, 5 August 1890). The latter possibility derives support from the fact that both Marxist and non-Marxist scholars recognize a close interconnection between caste and class. Moreover, economic development in India has begun to effect important changes in the caste system, one of the most significant being the emergence of 'caste associations' as important economic interest groups (Bailey 1963, pp. 122–135). It is clear, however, that the study of caste by Marxist historians, anthropologists and sociologists is still in its infancy (see MARXISM IN INDIA).

Reading

Bailey, F. G. 1963: *Politics and Social Change: Orissa in 1959*.

Béteille, André 1965: *Caste, Class and Power: Changing Patterns of Stratification in a Tanjore Village*.

Dumont, Louis 1967 (1970): *Homo Hierarchicus: The Caste System and its Implications*.

Kosambi, D. D. 1944: 'Caste and Class in India'.

— 1956: *An Introduction to the Study of Indian History*.

Rosas, Paul 1943: 'Caste and Class in India'.

Srinivas, M. N. *et al.* 1959: 'Caste: A Trend Report and Bibliography'.

Thorner, Daniel 1966: 'Marx on India and the Asiatic Mode of Production'.

TOM BOTTOMORE

centralization and concentration of capital
Capital has two distinct aspects. In relation to the labour process it exists as a concentrated mass of means of production commanding an army of workers; and in relation to an individual capitalist it represents that portion of social wealth which is concentrated in his hands as capital. These aspects of capital are in turn differentially operated on by two distinct processes: the process of increasing concentration through accumulation, which Marx calls the *concentration of capital*; and the process of increasing concentration through competition and credit, which he calls the *centralization of capital*.

Accumulation is the reinvestment of profit in newer, more powerful methods of production. Newer methods imply an increasing minimum scale of investment and a rising ratio of capital invested per worker – hence an increasing concentration of capital vis-à-vis the labour process. At the same time, even though accumulation tends to increase the amount of capital at the disposal of an individual capitalist, the division of property among members of a family, the splitting-off of new capitals from old ones, and the birth of new capitals, all tend to increase the number of capitalists themselves and therefore decrease the social capital concentrated in any one hand. Accumulation being comparatively slow in relation to these latter factors, the net effect on ownership tends to be a decentralization. On balance, therefore, accumulation concentrates capital in the labour process but tends to decentralize its ownership.

Competition and credit, on the other hand, increase concentration on both fronts. Competition favours large-scale investments because of their lower costs of production, while the credit system allows individual capitalists to gather together the large sums necessary for these investments. The concentration of capital in the labour process thereby proceeds much faster than that permitted by the mere accumulation of capital. At the same time, because competition destroys weaker capitalists and the credit system enables the strong to swallow up the weak, they lead to a gathering up of the ownership of capitals which more than compensates for the decentralizing tendencies associated with accumulation alone.

On the whole, therefore, capitalism is attended by the increasing capitalization of production, as well as an increasing centralization of the ownership of social capital (*Capital* I, ch. 23; *Capital* III, ch. 15; *Theories of Surplus Value*, III). In Marx's analysis both of these phenomena arise out of the battle of competition, and in turn serve to intensify it. In bourgeois economics, however, the very concept of 'perfect' or 'pure' competition implies that *any* concentration or centralization at all is the antithesis of competition. *Once one identifies the bourgeois conception with the reality of competition in early capitalism and/or with Marx's own analysis of it*, the historical fact of increasing concentration and centralization appears to be *prima facie* evidence of the breakdown of competition, of the rise of 'imperfect' competition, oligopoly and monopoly. Within Marxist economics, the dominant tradition originating with HILFERDING and developed by Kalecki, Steindl, Baran and Sweezy, makes exactly this double identification. This leads its proponents to argue that modern capitalism is ultimately regulated by the outcomes of the balance of *power* between monopolists, workers, and the state (see ECONOMIC CRISES). On the opposing side, Varga (1948) and some more recent writers have argued that concentration and centralization have actually intensified competition, as opposed to negating it, and that the empirical evidence on profitability actually provides support for Marx's theory of competition (Clifton 1977, Shaikh 1982). Lenin, it should be noted, is claimed by both sides. Needless to say, this debate has major implications for the analysis of modern capitalism and the current crisis.

Reading

Clifton, James 1977: 'Competition and the Evolution of the Capitalist Mode of Production'.

Shaikh, A. 1982: 'Neo-Ricardian Economics: A Wealth of Algebra, a Poverty of Theory'.

Varga, E. 1948: *Changes in the Economy of Capitalism Resulting from the Second World War*.

ANWAR SHAIKH

chance and necessity. *See* determinism; historical materialism.

Christianity   In modern society, Marx wrote in his early essay 'On the Jewish Question', men have freed themselves from the incubus of religion by relegating it to the personal sphere, cut off from the public hurly burly of competition. In this separation he saw an index of the alienation of man from man, making it impossible for the individual to be a full human being. Still, it was a necessary step forward, and the Reformation which inaugurated it was a revolutionary advance (Introduction: 'Critique of Hegel's Philosophy of Right'). He considered Christianity, with its fixation on individual man and soul, and especially its Protestant, bourgeois version, the creed most appropriate to an economy of anonymous commodity-exchange (*Capital* I, ch. 1, last section). Engels was pursuing the same idea when he contrasted Lutheranism

with the Calvinism of his own ancestors, and he viewed Calvinism as the more mature, more fully urban, and republican in temper (*Feuerbach*, sect. 4). It was a faith, he declared, fit for the most boldly aspiring bourgeois or early capitalist groups of its time; he interpreted its dogma of predestination as rooted in the unpredictability of success or failure in the business arena (Introduction to English edition of *Socialism: Utopian and Scientific*).

In 1847 Marx was inveighing against the notion that Christian doctrine could offer an alternative to communism; it meant nothing more than cowardly submission, when what the working class needed was courage and self-respect (Marx and Engels, *On Religion*, p. 83). In the *Communist Manifesto* (sect. 3) Christian socialism was dismissed as a feudal conservative trick, easily seen through by the workers. But Marx was soon recognizing that in a mainly peasant country such as France clerical influence could still be very weighty; hence the armed intervention by the French government to restore papal rule in Rome (*Class Struggles*, sect. 2). Several years later, on a tour of the Rhineland, he could not help feeling that social Catholicism, with Bishop Ketteler of Mainz as its exponent, was having an insidious effect on labour (letter to Engels, 25 September 1869).

Engels explained the Reformation as made possible by Germany's economic development and the country's growing share in international trade. In his work on the Peasant War of 1524–25 he treated it as a first attempt at a national revolution, bourgeois or anti-feudal, frustrated by lack of combination between burghers and peasants, while the lowest strata, the disinherited, standing outside society, could only indulge in unrealizable dreams of an ideal world of the future, in the spirit of the millenarian element in early Christianity; their Anabaptism was the first faint gleam of modern socialism (ch. 2).

In his later years Engels turned repeatedly to the problem of the origin and early growth of Christianity. A religion which had played so massive a part in world history, he wrote in his essay on Bruno Bauer, a pioneer in the field, could not be dismissed as mere deception; what was needed was to comprehend the conditions out of which it emerged. Mass misery in the Roman empire, with no hope of material relief, turned instead to thoughts of spiritual salvation; it learned to blame its own sinfulness, from which the Atonement offered deliverance. The tenet of original sin was the sole Christian principle of equality, he declared in *Anti-Dühring* (pt. 1, ch. 10), and was in harmony with a faith for slaves and the oppressed. But he was to go beyond this, and near the close of his life drew a parallel between the early Christians and the working-class movement of his own day, both starting among the downtrodden masses, yet Christianity becoming in time the religion of state, and socialism now, he had no doubt, assured of speedy victory (*On Religion*, p. 313). In a final pronouncement, at the end of his introduction to an edition of Marx's *Class Struggles* in 1895, he paid tribute to the early Christians as 'a dangerous party of revolt', ready to defy emperors and undermine authority by refusing to offer sacrifice at their altars.

Several Marxists of the next generation were drawn to the subject of Christian origins. Kautsky was the one who explored it most thoroughly, besides touching on later Christian history in various of his writings; he traced for instance the effect of the French Revolution on German theology in its adoption of the Kantian ethic as the base for a challenge to materialism (1906, pp. 66–7). It was he who took the most unflattering view of early Christianity. He stressed the utility of a creed of servile submission for slave-owners who otherwise could only maintain their power by force. He refused to admit any refining or softening influence by it, as its resources and status improved, on the harshness of Roman society, and preferred to ascribe any amelioration to objective causes, political or economic (*1925*, pp. 165–7). Later official Marxism has often returned a similar verdict. 'The Christian teaching of atonement', in the words of the Soviet scholar Prokofev, 'reflects the impotence, feeling of doom, and helplessness of the oppressed working masses' (*1967*, p. 464). But LUXEMBURG, besides being touched by the consolation their faith brought to the poor who had nothing to hope for in this world, was impressed by the element of property-sharing among the early Christians, even though this could have only limited meaning because it was a communism of consumption, not of production. She was writing amid the turmoil of the 1905 revolution, and complaining of the way

socialists were being vilified by the priests.

Since then there has been a great deal of Marxist thinking in western Europe about Christianity in various historical and political contexts. In Catholic countries, where the strength of the Church as a prop of conservatism has remained great, this thinking has necessarily often been on practical lines, as with Gramsci in an Italy under fascist rule partnered by the Church. In England, where Marxist historians have found one of their most fruitful themes in the seventeenth-century conflicts, they have seen religion playing a positive and dynamic, though not an independent part, with Calvinism the ideology of the newly risen propertied classes, offshoots of Anabaptism that of the propertyless. Another question very much in the foreground has been the connection between Methodism and the industrial revolution. Many have agreed with the conclusion that while Methodism gave the inchoate working class some useful lessons, its general effect was to 'retard the political development' of the workers (Thomson 1949, p. 23).

But every religious movement has both a progressive and a reactionary thrust, the same writer declared. 'There are two Christs', one of the rulers, one of the toilers (Thomson 1949, p. 4). In recent decades there have been breaks in the old hostility of the Churches to communism, at least as unremitting as its to them, and room has been found by both sides for the 'dialogues' which Marxists like Garaudy in France and Klugmann in Britain were active in promoting. Frequent support has been given by Christians and Churches to progressive causes, including colonial rebellions. Marxists may have to ask whether they have turned their backs too decidedly in the past on the fact that socialism itself is in many ways the offspring of Christianity.

Reading

Garaudy, Roger 1970: *Marxism and the Twentieth Century*.

Hill, Christopher 1964: *Society and Puritanism in Pre-Revolutionary England*.

Kautsky, Karl 1906 (*1918*): *Ethics and the Materialist Conception of History*.

— 1908 (*1925*): *Foundations of Christianity: A Study in Christian Origins*.

Luxemburg, Rosa 1905: *Socialism and the Churches*.

McLellan, David 1987: *Marxism and Religion*.

Prokofev, V. I. 1959 (*1967*): 'Religious and Communist Morality'.

Thompson, E. P. 1963: *The Making of the English Working Class*.

Thompson, George 1949: *An Essay on Religion*.

V. G. KIERNAN

cinema and television Marxists have been interested in cinema for three main contrasting reasons: its popularity, its intrinsic modernity and its potential for realism. When Lenin made his famous statement (later echoed by Mussolini) that 'for us the cinema is the most important of all the arts', he was little concerned with art but more with the cinema's ability to reach large audiences previously untouched by other means of expression. For Soviet film-makers of the 1920s such as Sergei EISENSTEIN, on the other hand, cinema was an art (the 'tenth muse') but one whose properties permitted the development of new expressive techniques not possible in literature and theatre: for Eisenstein, the montage of film images could be used as a means of representing the operations of the materialist dialectic. Meanwhile Dziga Vertov (the pseudonym of Denis Arkadevich Kaufman, 1896–1954) developed practices of documentary based on the idea of the camera as a mechanical eye, which 'saw' the world more accurately than the human eye and provided greater immediacy than verbal reportage.

These three forms of interest were soon, however, to prove mutually incompatible. The kind of cinema that has been popular the world over is neither modernist nor particularly realist. Popular cinema derives its narrative forms from the nineteenth-century novel and theatre, and its realism consists more often in making created things look real than in allowing the already real to display itself directly to the spectator. Even in the Soviet Union, the officially sanctioned socialist realism from the early 1930s onwards eschewed filmic realism as such in favour of narrative models which differed from Hollywood only in their value systems. As applied to the cinema, socialist realism was a compromise between an obligation to be 'correct' in the portrayal of historical development and the desire to attract audiences to stirring and reasonably truth-like stories. Meanwhile modernism and realism also

diverged, with documentary realism subordinated to increasingly practical purposes and modernist experiment confined to minority forms of film-making.

In the 1920 and 1930s, however, Marxist thinking on cinema could afford to be prescriptive about what the cinema ought to be: theorists were not yet resigned to the idea that it might have become irredeemably other than they would like it. Much of the debate centred on whether the cinema had an 'essence', and if so how this essence could related to surrounding realities. Against writers like Béla Balázs, who thought cinema's specificity lay in its unique way of making the world visible, Eisenstein maintained that the cinema produced its effects constructively, through the montage of contrasting elements: the cinema related to reality not by passively reflecting it but by dialectically reshaping it. The general tendency was to treat the cinema as an art, made by artists but under industrial conditions. The British documentarist Paul Rotha memorably described it as 'the great unsolved equation between art and industry'. Most Marxists took the general view, shared by other intellectuals, that capitalist control of the cinema was to be deplored, but the grounds for deploring it varied. For some it was axiomatic that films would reflect the ideology of their makers, here assumed to be capitalists. Others argued that the pursuit of profit was paramount and its effects could only be corrupting: films would be made, not to reflect the capitalist class's own world view, but to anaesthetize the masses with banality. Films produced within the capitalist industry were therefore prized when they appeared to stand out against these tendencies, either ideologically or aesthetically. Charlie Chaplin was praised on both counts, but the early Walt Disney was also admired (until his right-wing views put him beyond the pale), as were John Ford and the German émigré Fritz Lang.

Before 1945 there were very few Marxist makers of feature films outside the Soviet Union. Bertolt BRECHT attempted, with *Kuhle Wampe* (1932, directed by Slatan Dudow), a filmic equivalent of his radical dramaturgy. Jean Renoir was an enthusiastic supporter of the Front Populaire in the late 1930s. But for the most part the activity of Marxists was confined to documentary and agitational film-making, to which film-makers like the 'flying Dutchman' Joris Ivens brought an incisive quality of social analysis lacking in the work of their non-Marxist contemporaries.

After 1945, realism was dominant. In Italy the ideas of Antonio GRAMSCI and György LUKÁCS provided a successful counterweight to the socialist realist orthodoxy, still in force in the Soviet Union and other socialist countries. Among Italian film-makers associated with so-called neo-realism, Luchino Visconti was most clearly identified with this trend. But in France the non-Marxist phenomenological realism of André Bazin gained ground among critics and film-makers. The French New Wave was heavily influenced by Bazin, but in the run-up to the radical upheavals of 1968 Jean-Luc Godard broke loose from his former mentors and began to make films which set out simultaneously to challenge both bourgeois society and the conventional film language which (Godard argued) helped to naturalize bourgeois social relations at an ideological level. The influence of the philosopher Louis ALTHUSSER also made itself felt in theory and criticism, not only in France but also in Britain and (by the late 1970s) in North America.

The new theory was hostile to any idea of realism, including (and sometimes especially) Marxist variants of it, such as the critical realism of Lukács. Using arguments from psychoanalysis and semiotics, writers in Cahiers du Cinéma in France and Screen in Britain argued that it is an illusion to believe that films (or other art works, for that matter) produce rounded representations of 'reality' to be apprehended in their totality by the subject. The process by which a film is received has to be seen as contradictory in all its aspects. The viewing subject is not a reflective consciousness but engages psychically with the work at an imaginary level. The work itself is also necessarily contradictory, for reasons to do as much with its material conditions of production as with its inherent semiotic heterogeneity. This contradictoriness has to be recognized and exploited – by film-makers as well as by critics and theorists. There is nothing particularly progressive in making films with a socialist message if the film style is such as to cover over the contradictions of the film text and the spectator's engagement with it. Conversely, films that appear at first sight to be totally under the sway of bourgeois ideology may well contain unsuspected progressive elements. In a famous study of John Ford's 1939 bio-pic Young Mr Lincoln, the editors of Cahiers du Cinéma argued that the power of the film – both for audiences at the time and for analysts coming after – lies in its inability to resolve its contradictions at any level. Thus the attempt by 20th Century-Fox – itself internally contradictory – to situate Lincoln and the Republican Party in relation to Roosevelt's New Deal is in further contradiction with the distinct ideological slant imparted by Ford as director; this contradiction, however, does not exist merely within the work (or in facts external to the work) but needs to be activated in the spectator through various mechanisms of which the most remarkable, in Young Mr Lincoln, is what the authors call the 'castrating stare' of the hero which establishes Lincoln as phallic icon.

The particular application of Lacanian psychoanalysis practised by the Cahiers writers and their followers has been widely questioned – not least by feminists. But it had the merit of pointing to an absence in traditional Marxist analyses of the cinema and other art forms – their lack of a theory of subjectivity. The strength of Marxist writing on the cinema (and on the mass media in general) has lain in its attention to economic determinations and, to a lesser extent, the articulation of the economic and the ideological. It has proved less productive in relating these determinations to specifically aesthetic concerns and to questions of subjective apprehension. A Marxist theory of cinema, giving due weight to all these concerns, has yet to be written.

In the 1980s, the attention of Marxist writers on popular culture and the mass media has been increasingly directed towards television. At first, television and cinema might seem to present similar probems for Marxist analysis. Both are audio-visual moving-image media and both are technologically based industries with predominantly a mass audience. But there are major differences in their overall organization and, above all, in their mode of reception. Television is a much more journalistic medium than cinema. Also, until very recently it has tended to be state controlled to a far greater degree than cinema on the one hand or the press on the other. This has meant that Marxist analysis of television has hitherto been directed at least as much to ideology and politics as to economics. With deregulation, however, television worldwide is becoming more overtly commercial, bringing questions of economics and 'media imperialism' back to the forefront. An even more important difference is that the experience of television is less of discrete aesthetic objects than of a 'flow' of programmes (as Raymond WILLIAMS put it) whose reception takes place, not in a special locale people pay to enter, but in ordinary domestic space. This affects the nature of the economic relationship to the extent that the viewer does not pay directly to receive particular programmes, but the principal effect is ideological: the construction of the viewer as a particular type of individual and social being. Television in general becomes a process for attracting and holding viewers in their domestic space – where they are addressed less and less in their role as citizens to be informed, and more and more as consumers to be invited to stay tuned and to consume not only more television but also the products advertised thereon. This is a phenomenon of a scale and complexity entirely without historical precedent. It has also come about very rapidly. Whereas (say) the development of printing took several centuries to achieve its effects on a mass scale, television and its associated technologies have succeeded within fifty years in producing a revolution not only in everyday life but in such diverse fields as the conduct of diplomacy and warfare. This revolution has, however, taken place almost entirely within capitalist economic relations and the commodity form in particular. With the recent loosening of the state monopoly on television in both European· and Third World countries, Marxist analysis has therefore shifted its focus from the use of the medium as an instrument of state to the far more complex task of charting the imbrication of ideological functions with the operation of processes of exchange within a capitalist economy, a task which is only just beginning to be addressed.

Reading

Bazin, André 1967, 1971: *What is Cinema?* (2 vols).

Eisenstein, Sergei 1987: *Nonindifferent Nature*, trans. Herbert Marshall.

— 1988: *Writings, 1922–34*, ed. Richard Taylor.

— 1991: *Towards a Theory of Montage*, ed. Michael Glenny and Richard Taylor.

Ellis, John, ed. 1977: *Screen Reader I: Cinema/ Ideology/Politics.*

Guback, Thomas 1969: *The International Film Industry.*

Vertov, Dziga 1984: *Kino-Eye: The Writings of Dziga Vertov*, ed. Annette Michelson.

Williams, Christopher, ed. 1980: *Realism and the Cinema: A Reader.*

Williams, Raymond 1974: *Television: Technology and Cultural Form.*

GEOFFREY NOWELL-SMITH

circulation In Marxist theory a clear distinction is drawn between the sphere of PRODUCTION, from which SURPLUS VALUE originates, and the sphere of EXCHANGE in which commodities are bought and sold and finance is organized. During the ACCUMULATION of capital, there is a constant movement between these two spheres of activity and this constitutes the circulation of CAPITAL. If 'A Critical Analysis of Capitalist Production' is the subject of *Capital* I, 'The Process of Circulation of Capital' is the subject of *Capital* II (while *Capital* III also integrates relations of DISTRIBUTION and is subtitled 'The Process of Capitalist Production as a Whole').

The circulation of capital can be considered from the perspective of an individual capitalist and gives rise to the circuit of industrial capital: $M - C \dots P \dots C' - M'$. MONEY capital M is advanced to purchase C, MEANS OF PRODUCTION and LABOUR POWER. These are then joined to begin the process of production and constitute the elements of productive capital P. Commodity capital C' is the result of the LABOUR PROCESS and this embodies surplus value. The sale or realization of these commodities returns the circuit to the money form but it is quantitatively expanded to M' to include PROFIT. The circuit can now be renewed possibly expanding to accommodate accumulation. ... P ... constitutes the sphere of production and this interrupts the sphere of exchange in the circulation of capital just as the sphere of exchange interrupts the sphere of production since commodities must be both bought and sold as well as produced for the circulation to continue.

For capital as a whole, circulation integrates many such individual industrial circuits. In doing so different economic balances have to be established. In USE VALUE terms, appropriate proportions of means of production and means of CONSUMPTION have to be produced and exchanged so that production can be undertaken and labour employed in the various sectors of the economy. In terms of exchange value prices must be established and money or credit be available such that capitalists and workers can obtain the appropriate commodities in the appropriate proportions and with profit where required. Bourgeois economics, and some economists within the Marxist tradition who look at these relations of circulation in class terms, take one or other of these balances as a focus for analysis, with its breakdown constituting an explanation of crisis and recession. Marx can be considered to have done much the same in emphasizing the anarchy of capitalist production, but he adds a third balance to be established, and one that combines the use value and exchange value balances of the other two. This is circulation as a balance in value relations. It is only by doing this that the contradictions of capitalist production come to the fore in the analysis of the circulation process.

This follows from the results that Marx has established in *Capital* I in his analysis of capitalist production. Marx shows that as value relations are being formed so they are being transformed by the accumulation of capital that reduces values by promoting productivity increase through the introduction of MACHINERY. If circulation is analysed in abstraction from production, only the possibility of ECONOMIC CRISES is apparent on the basis of given use value, exchange value or value relations. The necessity of crisis in economic relations can only follow from the circulation of capital as it coordinates the accumulation process through exchange. It is this which preoccupies Marx in his discussion of the law of the tendency of the FALLING RATE OF PROFIT.

Different schools of political economy within Marxism have arisen according to how the circulation process has been perceived, although these perceptions are usually not made explicit. For underconsumption theories, circulation of capital is determined by the level of demand and is situated predominantly in the movement of exchange relations. For neo-Ricardians, circulation is determined by relations of distribution which are seen as embodying an inverse relation between wages and profit. Fundamentalists, or

the capital-logic school, determine circulation in production but confine contradictions to the sphere of production rather than seeing them as being a result of circulation as a whole with production as determinant.

Reading

Fine, Ben 1975: *Marx's 'Capital'*, ch. 7.

— 1980: *Economic Theory and Ideology*, ch. 2.

— and Harris, Laurence 1979: *Rereading 'Capital'*, ch. 1.

BEN FINE

city state.   *See* ancient society.

civil society   Although the term 'civil society' was used by writers such as Locke and Rousseau to describe civil government as differentiated from natural society or the state of nature, the Marxist concept derives from HEGEL. In Hegel, *die bürgerliche Gesellschaft*, or civil or bourgeois society, as the realm of individuals who have left the unity of the family to enter into economic competition, is contrasted with the state, or political society. It is an arena of particular needs, self-interest, and divisiveness, with a potential for self-destruction. For Hegel it is only through the state that the universal interest can prevail, since he disagrees with Locke, Rousseau or Adam Smith that there is any innate rationality in civil society which will lead to the general good.

Marx uses the concept of civil society in his critique of Hegel and German idealism, in such writings as 'On the Jewish Question', 'Contribution to the Critique of Hegel's Philosophy of Right: Introduction' and *Economic and Philosophical Manuscripts*. His discussion is in the Hegelian language of that period of his work. The term practically disappears in later works although it can be argued that some of the implications which his earlier discussion has for his view of politics remain. Civil society is also used in his early writings as a yardstick of the change from feudal to bourgeois society. Defined by Marx as the site of crass materialism, of modern property relations, of the struggle of each against all, of egotism, civil society arose, he insists, from the destruction of medieval society. Previously individuals were part of many different societies, such as guilds or estates each of which had a political role, so that there was no separate civil realm. As these partial societies broke down, civil society arose in which the individual became all important. The old bonds of privilege were replaced by the selfish needs of atomistic individuals separated from each other and from the community. The only links between them are provided by the law, which is not the product of their will and does not conform to their nature but dominates human relationships because of the threat of punishment. The fragmented, conflictual nature of civil society with its property relations necessitates a type of politics which does not reflect this conflict but is abstracted and removed from it. The modern state is made necessary (and at the same time limited) by the characteristics of civil society. The fragmentation and misery of civil society escape the control of the state which is limited to formal, negative activities and is rendered impotent by the conflict which is the essence of economic life. The political identity of individuals as citizens in modern society is severed from their civil identity and from their function in the productive sphere as tradesman, day-labourer, or landowner.

In Marx's analysis two divisions grow up simultaneously, between individuals enclosed in their privacy, and between the public and private domains, or between state and society. Marx contrasts the idealism of universal interests as represented by the modern state and the abstractness of the concept of a citizen who is moral because he goes beyond his narrow interest, with the materialism of real, sensuous man in civil society. The irony according to Marx is that in modern society the most universal, moral, social purposes as embodied in the ideal of the state are at the service of human beings in a partial, depraved state of individual egotistical desires, of economic necessity. It is in this sense that the essence of the modern state is to be found in the characteristics of civil society, in economic relations. For the conflict of civil society to be truly superseded and for the full potential of human beings to be realized, both civil society and its product, political society, must be abolished, necessitating a social as well as a political revolution to liberate mankind.

Although GRAMSCI continues to use the term to refer to the private or non-state sphere, including the economy, his picture of civil society is very different from that of Marx. It is not simply a sphere of individual needs but of organizations, and has the potential of rational self-regulation and freedom. Gramsci insists on its complex organization, as the 'ensemble of organisms commonly called "private"' where HEGEMONY and 'spontaneous consent' are organized (Gramsci 1971, pp. 12–13). He argues that any distinction between civil society and the state is only methodological, since even a policy of nonintervention like *laissez-faire* is established by the state itself (ibid. p. 160). In his notes, the metaphors he uses to describe the precise relationship between the state and civil society vary. A fully developed civil society is presented as a trench system able to resist the 'incursions' of economic crises and to protect the state (ibid. p. 235), while elsewhere in a note contrasting Russia in 1917, with its 'primordial' and undeveloped civil society, with countries in the West, the state is described as an outer ditch behind which stands a sturdy and powerful system of defence in civil society (ibid. p. 238). Whereas Marx insists on the separation between the state and civil society, Gramsci emphasizes the interrelationship between the two, arguing that whereas the everyday, narrow use of the word state may refer to government, the concept of state in fact includes elements of civil society. The state narrowly conceived as government is protected by hegemony organized in civil society while the hegemony of the dominant class is fortified by the coercive state apparatus. Yet the state also has an 'ethical function' as it tries to educate public opinion and to influence the economic sphere. In turn, the very concept of law must be extended, Gramsci suggests, since elements of custom and habit can exert a collective pressure to conform in civil society without coercion or sanctions.

In any actual society the lines of demarcation between civil society and the state may be blurred, but Gramsci argues against any attempt to equate or identify the two, be it in the works of various Italian fascist thinkers or by the French Jacobins. And while he accepts a role for the state in developing civil society, he warns against perpetuating statolatry or state worship (ibid. p. 268). In fact, the withering away of the state is redefined by Gramsci in terms of a full development of the self-regulating attributes of civil society.

Where in Marx's writings civil society is portrayed as the terrain of individual egotism, Gramsci refers to Hegel's discussion of the estates and corporations as organizing elements which represent corporate interests in a collective way in civil society, and the role of the bureaucracy and the legal system in regulating civil society and connecting it to the state (Razeto Migliaro and Misuraca 1978). He points out, however, that Hegel did not have the experience of modern mass organizations, which Marx also lacked despite his greater feeling for the masses (op. cit. p. 259). These differences may relate to Gramsci's emphasis on the need to analyse the actual organization of civil society and the interconnections between the state and society including the economy. It should be pointed out that in both Marx and Gramsci the term 'civil society' contains elements from both the economic base and the non-political aspects of the superstructure (see BASE AND SUPERSTRUCTURE), and therefore does not fit neatly into this metaphor.

A reading of the concept of civil society in both Marxist and non-Marxist thinkers leads to an examination of the concept of politics itself. It involves the relationship between individuals, and between individuals and the community, a view of society as organized or not, the delineation of public and private. Although the term disappears in Marx's later works, the theme of the withering away of politics as a separate sphere uncontrolled by society, and its substitution by a new type of democracy reappears in *The Civil War in France*, is found in Lenin's *State and Revolution*, and is further developed by Gramsci.

Most recently civil society has occupied a prominent place in debates in Eastern Europe as a result of the challenge to the socialist regimes there, and has entered discussions in the West about changes in the role of the state, the concept of citizenship, and the need to protect civil liberties.

Reading

Bobbio, N. 1979: 'Gramsci and the Conception of Civil Society'. In Mouffe ed. *Gramsci and Marxist Theory*.

Colletti, L. 1975: Introduction to Karl Marx, *Early Writings*.

Gramsci, A. 1929–35 (1971): *Selections from the Prison Notebooks*.

Keane, J. ed. 1988a: *Civil Society and the State*.

— 1988b: *Democracy and Civil Society*.

Razeto Migliaro, L. and Misuraca, P. 1978: 'Teoria della burocrazia moderna'. In *Sociologia e marxismo nella critica di Gramsci*.

Texier, J. 1979: 'Gramsci, Theoretician of the superstructures'. In Mouffe ed. *Gramsci and Marxist Theory*.

ANNE SHOWSTACK SASSOON

class   The concept of class has a central importance in Marxist theory, though neither Marx nor Engels ever expounded it in a systematic form. In one sense it was the starting point of Marx's whole theory; for his discovery of the proletariat as 'the idea in the real itself' (letter to his father, 10 November 1837), a new political force engaged in a struggle for emancipation, led him directly to an analysis of the economic structure of modern societies and its process of development. During this period (1843–44) Engels, from the perspective of political economy, was making the same discovery which he outlined in his essays in the *Deutsch-Französische Jahrbücher* (1844) and developed in *The Condition of the Working Class* (1845). Thus it was the class structure of early capitalism, and the class struggles in this form of society, which constituted the main reference point for the Marxist theory of history. Subsequently, the idea of CLASS CONFLICT as the driving force of history was extended, and the *Communist Manifesto* asserted, in a famous phrase, that 'the history of all hitherto existing society is the history of class struggles'; but at the same time Marx and Engels recognized that class was a uniquely prominent feature of capitalist societies – even suggesting in the *German Ideology* (vol. I, sect. I C) that 'class itself is a product of the bourgeoisie' – and they did not undertake any sustained analysis of the principal classes and class relations in other forms of society. Kautsky, in his discussion of class, occupation and status (1927), argued that many of the class conflicts mentioned in the *Communist Manifesto* were in fact conflicts between status groups, and that Marx and Engels were quite aware of this fact since in the same text they observed that 'in the earlier epochs of history, we find almost everywhere a complicated arrangement of society into various orders, a manifold gradation of social rank', and contrasted this situation with the 'distinctive feature' of the bourgeois epoch, when 'society as a whole is more and more splitting up into two great hostile camps, into two great classes directly facing each other – bourgeoisie and proletariat'. Yet there is clearly a sense in which Marx wanted to assert the existence of a major class division in all forms of society beyond the early tribal communities, as when he argues in general terms that 'it is always the direct relation between the owners of the conditions of production and the direct producers which reveals the innermost secret, the hidden foundation, of the entire social edifice' (*Capital* III, ch. 47).

Most later Marxists have followed Marx and Engels in concentrating their attention on the class structure of capitalist societies, and they have had to deal with two main questions. The first concerns precisely the 'complications' of social ranking or stratification in relation to the basic classes. In the fragment on 'the three great classes of modern society' which Engels published as the final chapter of *Capital* III, Marx observes that even in England, where the economic structure is 'most highly and classically developed . . . intermediate and transitional strata obscure the class boundaries'; and in discussing economic crises in the *Theories of Surplus Value* (ch. 17, sect. 6) he notes that he is disregarding for the purpose of his preliminary analysis, among other things, 'the real constitution of society, which by no means consists only of the class of workers and the class of industrial capitalists'. Elsewhere in the *Theories of Surplus Value* he refers explicitly to the growth of the MIDDLE CLASS as a phenomenon of the development of capitalism: 'What [Ricardo] forgets to emphasize is the continual increase in numbers of the middle classes . . . situated midway between the workers on one side and the capitalists and landowners on the other . . . [who] rest with all their weight upon the working basis and at the same time increase the social security and power of the upper ten thousand' (ch. 18, sect. B 1d). Further on he says again, with respect to Malthus, 'his greatest hope . . . is that the middle class will increase in size and the working proletariat will make up a constantly diminishing proportion of the total population (even if it grows in absolute numbers). That is, in fact, the

tendency of bourgeois society' (ch. 19, sect. 14). These observations do not fit easily with the idea of an increasing polarization of bourgeois society between 'two great classes'; and since the middle class has continued to grow, Marxist social scientists, from Bernstein to Poulantzas, have been obliged repeatedly to examine the political significance of this phenomenon, especially in relation to the socialist movement.

The second question concerns the situation and development of the two principal classes in capitalist society, BOURGEOISIE and proletariat (see WORKING CLASS). In the *18th Brumaire* (sect. VII) Marx gave this negative definition of a fully constituted class: 'In so far as millions of families live under economic conditions of existence that separate their mode of life, their interests, and their culture from those of the other classes, and put them in hostile opposition to the latter, they form a class. In so far as there is merely a local interconnection among these small-holding peasants, and the identity of their interests begets no community, no national bond, and no political organization among them, they do not form a class.' In the *Poverty of Philosophy* (ch. 2, sect. 5), describing the emergence of the working class, Marx expressed the same idea in positive terms: 'Economic conditions had in the first place transformed the mass of the people into workers. The domination of capital created the common situation and common interests of this class. Thus this mass is already a class in relation to capital, but not yet a class for itself. In the struggle, of which we have only indicated a few phases, this mass unites and forms itself into a class for itself. The interests which it defends become class interests.' Among later Marxists, Poulantzas (1975) has rejected (as a Hegelian residue) this distinction between 'class-in-itself' and 'class-for-itself', arguing as though classes sprang into existence fully equipped with CLASS CONSCIOUSNESS and a political organization, in specific opposition to the view expounded by Lukács (1923) which attributed crucial importance to the development of class consciousness, conceived as being brought to the proletariat from outside by a revolutionary party (see also LENINISM). Most Marxists, in fact, have recognized (increasingly in the past three decades) that in the case of the working class the development of a 'socialist' or 'revolutionary' consciousness poses problems which require more careful and thorough study. 'Class interest' itself is no longer conceived (as it was in general by Marx) as an objective and unambiguous 'social fact', but rather as having a sense which is constructed through interaction and discussion out of the experiences of everyday life and the interpretations of those experiences in political doctrines, hence as something which may assume diverse forms, as is indicated in one way by the historical divisions in the working-class movement. At one extreme some Marxists (e.g. Marcuse 1964) have suggested that a distinctive class interest and class consciousness of the working class is virtually extinct as a consequence of its more or less complete assimilation into advanced industrial society; while others have questioned fundamentally the view that political action is determined mainly by class relations (Wellmer 1971) or have rejected the conception of RULING CLASS interests in an era of comprehensive state regulation of social life (Offe 1972; see also FRANKFURT SCHOOL). In a less extreme way the socialist movement in advanced capitalist societies has been seen as depending only partly upon the working class, and increasingly upon an alliance of various groups (see EUROCOMMUNISM); a position which gains plausibility from the prominence in recent years of radical political movements which are not class-based, among them the women's movement, the green movement and diverse ethnic and national movements (see FEMINISM; NATIONALISM; RACE).

Such questions are, if anything, even more germane to the study of class structure in non-capitalist societies. In the ASIATIC SOCIETY, as Marx defined it, the development of classes as the principal agents of social change seems to be excluded by the absence of private property, and the dominant group in this type of society may be seen as comprising not the owners of the means of production but the controllers of the state apparatus. In ancient (slave) society (see SLAVERY) the lines of actual social conflict are far from clear – though the distinction between master and slave obviously is – and Marx himself referred sometimes to the class struggles between freeman and slave, sometimes to those between creditors and debtors. There are also difficulties in identifying the social conflicts which led to the decline of feudalism, and Marxists have been in substantial disagreement about

the part played by class struggles between lords and serfs, and on the other hand, the significance of the emergence of a new class – the town burgesses – and of the conflict, which Marx emphasized, between town and country (see FEUDAL SOCIETY; STAGES OF DEVELOPMENT; TRANSITION FROM FEUDALISM TO CAPITALISM). A more general issue is that of the place of the peasantry in the CLASS STRUCTURE and its political role in different types of society. Marx, as has been noted, did not regard the peasants of nineteenth-century France as a class in the full sense, still less a revolutionary class; but the socialist revolutions of the twentieth century have taken place mainly in peasant societies, and sections of the peasantry have played an important part in revolutionary movements, as they still do in many Third World countries, although they may often be led by urban based parties or by urban intellectuals (see AGRARIAN QUESTION; COLONIALISM; COLONIAL AND POST-COLONIAL SOCIETIES; PEASANTRY).

An issue of a different kind which has confronted Marxists of the present generation concerns the emergence of a new class structure in the state socialist societies. In broad terms, two alternative approaches can be distinguished. The first asserts that a new dominant class, stratum or elite has established itself in power. Thus Trotsky, while denying that a new class had appeared in the USSR, regarded the bureaucracy as the ruling group in a 'degenerated workers' state'. The most thorough recent study is that by Konrád and Szelényi (1979 p. 145) who argue that 'the social structure of early socialism' is a class structure, 'and indeed a dichotomous one. . . . At one pole is an evolving class of intellectuals who occupy the position of redistributors, at the other a working class which produces the social surplus but has no right of disposition over it'. But they continue: 'This dichotomous model of a class structure is not sufficient for purposes of classifying everyone in the society (just as the dichotomy of capitalist and proletarian is not in itself sufficient for purposes of assigning a status to every single person in capitalist society); an ever larger fraction of the population must be assigned to the intermediate strata'. The second approach is best exemplified by Weselowski's analysis (1979) of the transformation of the class structure in Poland in which he argues that there has been a gradual disappearance of class differences as a result of the declining importance of the relationship of individuals to the means of production, and that this is accompanied by a diminution in secondary differences related to the nature of work and to attributes of social position such as income, education and access to cultural goods. Hence Weselowski excludes the idea of a new dominant class and strongly emphasizes the decomposition of class domination, but at the same time he recognizes that status differences persist, as do conflicts of interest between different social groups and strata. In judging these alternative conceptualizations of the social structure of socialist societies two issues are crucially important. The first is whether there has been a real change in the relation of individuals to the means of production, in the sense of genuine public, collective control rather than a new form of 'economic ownership' and 'possession' (i.e. effective control, not legal ownership; see PROPERTY) by a specific social group which exercises power through the party and state apparatuses. The second is whether the conflicts in socialist societies are only between status groups or whether they have a broader class character, as various social upheavals in these countries in the 1950s and 1960s suggested.

The overthrow of the communist dictatorships in Eastern Europe in 1989 was accomplished, however, by broad popular movements rather than by a particular class, and these events indicate that the principal division in the state socialist societies was one between a ruling elite of a distinctive type, and the mass of the population which was subordinated to it. This was, therefore, a kind of stratification *sui generis*, not wholly comparable with other forms of stratification and class structure, though sharing some features with them. The eventual outcome of these revolutions is not yet clear, but in so far as capitalist economies are reintroduced, a class system similar to that in Western Europe will also re-emerge, and in some cases has already appeared, along with its political concomitants (see CRISIS IN SOCIALIST SOCIETY).

Marxist studies since the end of the nineteenth century have made it abundantly clear that class structure is a much more complex and ambiguous phenomenon than appears from most of the writings of Marx and Engels, who were greatly influenced in their views by the undoubted salience of class relations in early capitalism, and above all by the irruption into political life of the working-class movement. An array of problems briefly mentioned here – among them the transformations of class structure in capitalist and socialist societies and their political implications, the constitution and role of classes in the Third World, the relation of classes and class struggles to other social groups, including nations, and to other forms of social conflict – remain as a challenge to more profound and rigorous investigations. To use Marx's own words, they will not be resolved by 'the passe-partout of a historical-philosophical theory' (draft letter to Mikhailovsky 1877) but by an analysis in each separate case of the 'empirically given circumstances'.

Reading

Bottomore, Tom 1991: *Classes in Modern Society*, 2nd edn.

Carchedi, Guglielmo 1977: *On the Economic Identification of Social Classes*.

Giddens, Anthony 1973: *The Class Structure of the Advanced Societies*.

Konrád, George and Szelényi, Ivan 1979: *The Intellectuals on the Road to Class Power*.

Nicolaus, Martin 1967: 'Proletariat and Middle Class in Marx'.

Ossowski, Stanislaw 1957 (1963): *Class Structure in the Social Consciousness*.

Poulantzas, Nicos 1975: *Classes in Contemporary Capitalism*.

Weselowski, W. 1979: *Classes, Strata and Power*.

Wright, Erik Olin 1978: *Class, Crisis and the State*.

TOM BOTTOMORE

class conflict In the words of the *Communist Manifesto*: 'The history of all hitherto existing society is the history of class struggles.' But this thesis has been qualified in various ways since it was first formulated. Engels modified it to refer to *written* history (note to the English edn 1888) in order to take account of the early communal societies in which class divisions had not yet emerged. Subsequently Kautsky (1927) argued that some of the class struggles mentioned in the *Communist Manifesto* were in fact conflicts between status groups, and that this view conformed with Marx's and Engels's own observation in the same text that pre-capitalist societies were all characterized by 'a manifold gradation of social rank'. In the case of feudal society, for example, there has been disagreement among Marxist historians about the nature and significance of class conflict, some emphasizing the importance of peasant revolts, others drawing attention to the complexity of class affiliations and divisions (see STAGES OF DEVELOPMENT; TRANSITION FROM FEUDALISM TO CAPITALISM). Marx and Engels themselves indicated – and this came to be the general Marxist view – that the major classes are most clearly differentiated, class consciousness most fully developed, and class conflict most acute, in capitalist society, which constitutes in these respects a culminating point in the historical evolution of class-divided forms of society. From this perspective modern class struggles have a central importance in Marxist theory, because their outcome is conceived as a TRANSITION TO SOCIALISM; that is, to a classless society.

It is understandable, therefore, that subsequent Marxist research and debate should have concentrated to a very great extent upon the development of class conflict in modern times, from the emergence of working-class movements in the nineteenth century to the present day. The crucial issue is whether, over this period, there has in fact been an intensification of class conflict. Within Marxism the first to question this idea explicitly – though Marx and Engels had already suggested some doubts in their references to the labour aristocracy and to a more general *embourgeoisement* of the working class, at least in Britain – was Bernstein (1899) who contended that it was evident by the end of the nineteenth century that a polarization of classes and an intensification of class conflict were not occurring. Among the factors he adduced to explain this changing situation were the growth of the MIDDLE CLASS, the growing complexity of the class structure, and rising levels of living; these themes have figured prominently in all subsequent discussions. Recent historical studies have also drawn attention to other features: thus Foster (1974) in a study of the labour movement in three nineteenth-century English towns examines in detail 'the development and decline of a revolutionary class consciousness in the second quarter of the century', and explains the decline as a result of changes

associated with liberalization (extension of the suffrage, growth of mass parties, legal recognition of trade unions) which made possible a reimposition of capitalist authority. Clearly, this is a process which has been repeated in different forms in later historical periods. A particular problem has always been posed by the development of American society, where neither a mass socialist party nor political class struggles on an extensive scale have ever emerged; and 'American exceptionalism' has been the object of much sociological analysis, Marxist and other, since the early years of this century (see Sombart 1906). This situation has led some Marxists and other radical thinkers in the USA to make very sweeping revisions of Marxist theory: for example Mills's dismissal (1960) of the conception of a fundamental class conflict (and of the working class as the primary agent of social change) as a 'labour metaphysic', or Marcuse's broadly similar argument (1964) about the incorporation of the working class into advanced capitalist society.

Another kind of issue is posed by the conflicts in the socialist countries of Eastern Europe, where it is a matter of deciding whether movements of opposition and rebellions, such as those of 1956 (Hungary), 1968 (Czechoslovakia), or 1981 (Poland), and the upheavals of 1989 were class conflicts, or if not, what social forces they represented. Here the interpretation depends upon a prior judgement about whether a new class structure had been formed in these societies, and in particular whether there was a new ruling class (see CRISIS IN SOCIALIST SOCIETY.) It is also evident that in some of these societies national struggles have acquired considerable importance (see, for example, Carrère d'Encausse 1978), and this phenomenon has a much wider significance, for in the western capitalist countries too, in the past few decades, social conflicts have involved not only, or even mainly, classes, but national, ethnic or religous groups, as well as a number of broad social movements – feminist, ecological, anti-nuclear.

In the event, the overthrow of the Communist dictatorships in Eastern Europe at the end of 1989 was largely the outcome of a conflict between a ruling elite of a distinctive type and a broad democratic movement, rather than a conflict between classes. Since then, however, new divisions and conflicts have emerged in the post-communist societies, to some extent in the form of class conflict as a capitalist economy is re-established, and most dramatically in the growth of increasingly strident nationalist movements.

The task of present-day Marxist analysis is to comprehend these diverse struggles in the framework of a consistent theory, and to determine empirically the specific importance of class conflicts in diverse structural and historical conditions. This also involves – as a number of recent Marxist studies (e.g. Poulantzas 1975) demonstrate – re-examining class conflict in the late twentieth century, not simply in terms of a confrontation between bourgeoisie and proletariat, but more in terms of alliances between various social groups which on one side dominate and direct economic and social life and on the other side are subordinated and directed.

Reading

Foster, John 1974: *Class Struggle and the Industrial Revolution.*

Katusky, Karl 1890 *(1910): The Class Struggle.*

Lenin, V. I. 1917 (1964): 'The State and Revolution'.

Poulantzas, Nicos 1975: *Classes in Contemporary Capitalism.*

Tilly, Louise A. and Tilly, Charles eds 1981: *Class Conflict and Collective Action.*

TOM BOTTOMORE

class consciousness   From an early stage Marx made a distinction between the objective situation of a class and subjective awareness of this situation; that is, between class membership and class consciousness. In a strict sense social distinctions first take the form of 'classes' in capitalist society, because only in this case is membership of social groups determined solely by the ownership (or control) of the means of production or exclusion therefrom. In pre-bourgeois estates-society a legally sanctioned order of estates was superimposed upon differences in the ownership of means of production. An aristocrat always remained an aristocrat, and as such the possessor of definite and exactly circumscribed privileges. The system of property relations was hidden behind the structure of estates. The estates system harmonized fairly well with the system of property relations only so long as land remained the most important means

of production and for the most part the property of the aristocracy and the church. But with the rise of the urban bourgeoisie and the development of mercantile, manufacturing and finally industrial capital, and as the (partly ennobled) bourgeoisie intruded upon the domain of large-scale agricultural interests, this harmony was increasingly undermined. Estate consciousness is fundamentally distinct from class consciousness. Membership of an estate is as a rule hereditary, and it is clearly apparent from the ascribed rights and privileges or exclusion therefrom. Class membership, however, depends upon becoming aware of one's position within the production process; hence it often remains concealed behind a nostalgic orientation to the old estates system, particularly in the case of bourgeois, petty-bourgeois and peasant 'intermediary strata'.

Marx describes the emergence of class consciousness in the bourgeoisie and the proletariat as a consequence of the increasingly political struggle of the *tiers état* with the ruling classes of the *ancien régime*. He illustrates the difficulties in the development of class consciousness by the example of the French small-holding peasants who use their voting rights to subjugate themselves to a lord (Napoleon III) instead of establishing themselves in a revolutionary way as the dominant class:

> In so far as millions of families live under economic conditions of existence that separate their mode of life, their interests, and their culture from those of other classes, and put them in hostile opposition to the latter, they form a class. In so far as there is merely a local interconnection among these small-holding peasants, and the identity of their interests begets no community, no national bond, and no political organization among them, they do not form a class. They are consequently incapable of enforcing their class interests in their own name, whether through a Parliament or through a Convention. They cannot represent themselves, they must be represented. Their representative must at the same time appear as their master, as an authority over them … (*18th Brumaire*, sect. VII)

The formation of class consciousness in the proletariat can be seen as the counterpart of the necessary miscarriage of political class consciousness among the small peasants. In this case the initially limited conflit (e.g. a trade union struggle in a particular enterprise or branch of industry) is widened on the basis of an identity of interests until it becomes a common affair of the whole class, which also creates an appropriate instrument, in the form of a political party. Collective labour in large factories and industrial enterprises, and the improved means of communication required by industrial capitalism, facilitate this unity. The process of formation of class consciousness coincides with the rise of a comprehensive class organization. They mutually support each other.

Marx is quite aware that the understanding and active pursuit of the common interests of the whole class can often come into conflict with the particular interests of individual workers or groups of workers. At the least it can lead to conflicts between the short-term and short-sighted interests of individual skilled workers in their own social advancement, and those of the class as a whole. For this reason particularly great importance is attached to *solidarity*. The differentiation of the wage structure and the temptations of increasing affluence have usually brought about a weakening of class solidarity and hence of class consciousness in highly industrialized societies. In this process the 'isolating effect' of individual competition for prestige consumer goods, which has reached at least parts of the working class, may perhaps play a similar role to the 'natural isolation' of the French small-holding peasants in 1851.

According to Kautsky and Lenin an adequate, that is to say *political*, class consciousness can only be brought to the working class 'from outside'. Lenin maintained further that only a 'trade union consciousness' can arise spontaneously in the working class; i.e. a consciousness of the necessity and utility of the representation of trade union interests against those of capital. Political class consciousness can only be developed by INTELLECTUALS who, because they are well educated and informed and stand at a distance from the immediate production process, are in a position to comprehend bourgeois society and its class relations in their totality. But the class consciousness developed by intellectuals, which is laid down in Marxist theory, can only be adopted by the working class, not by the bourgeoisie or petty bourgeoisie. As the

organizational instrument for transmitting class consciousness to the empirical working class, Lenin conceives a 'new type of party', the cadre party of professional revolutionaries. In contrast to this Leninist conception Luxemburg gave prominence to the role of social experience, the experience of class struggle, in the formation of class consciousness. Even errors in the course of class struggles can contribute to the development of an appropriate class consciousness which guarantees success, while the patronizing of the proletariat by intellectual elites leads only to a weakening of the ability to act, and to passivity.

Lukács developed a kind of metaphysics of class consciousness which was immediately and decisively condemned by Leninist and Social-Democratic Marxists alike. However, Lukács's formulations actually correspond perfectly with Leninist theory, as does his conception of the role of the party. Lukács's definition of class consciousness proceeds, like Lenin's, from the thesis that 'adequate', or political, class consciousness must have as its content

> society as a concrete totality, the system of production at a given point in history and the resulting division of society into classes. . . . By relating consciousness to the whole of society it becomes possible to infer the thoughts and feelings which men would have in a particular situation if they were able to assess both it and the interests arising from it in their impact on immediate action and on the whole structure of society. That is to say, it would be possible to infer the thoughts and feelings appropriate to their objective situation. . . . Class consciousness consists in fact of the appropriate and rational reactions 'imputed' to a particular typical position in the process of production. This consciousness is, therefore, neither the sum nor the average of what is thought or felt by the single individuals who make up the class. And yet the historically significant actions of the class as a whole are determined in the last resort by this consciousness and not by the thought of the individual – and these actions can be understood only by reference to this consciousness. *(1971*, pp. 50–1)

A class whose consciousness is defined in this way is thus nothing other than a 'historical imputed subject'. The empirically existing class can only (successfully) act if it becomes conscious of itself in the way prescribed by this definition, or – in Hegelian language – transforms itself from a 'class in itself' to a 'class for itself'. If a particular class like the petty bourgeoisie is in fact incapable of this, or (like the German proletariat in 1918) fails to accomplish the transformation fully, then its political action will also necessarily miscarry. The problem with Lukács's definition is that it can be exploited by political elites which, invoking their 'possession' of a theory of imputation, patronize or indeed demoralize the real proletariat. (See also CLASS; CLASS CONFLICT; IDEOLOGY; WORKING CLASS.)

Reading

Lukács, György 1923 (1971): History and Class Consciousness.

Mann, Michael 1973: Consciousness and Action Among the Western Working Class.

Mészáros, Isván ed. 1971: Aspects of History and Class Consciousness.

IRING FETSCHER

collectivization   In Marxist theory the collective farm represents a type of ownership specific to the socialist mode of production. It is an intermediate stage of ownership between private and state farming, differing from the latter because ownership is exercised by a subset of the population (usually a village community) rather than by the state on behalf of the whole people. In practice, collective farms have differed little from this theoretical conception, and although the ownership of the principal means of production has usually been formally exercised by the state, control has been vested in local peasant communities. However, collectivization has rarely involved the complete elimination of the private sector; depending on the country and the time period, anything from one to 20 per cent of arable land has been privately controlled, and the breeding of pigs and the growing of vegetables by households has been commonplace.

The collective farm is a Marxist response to the exploitation and inadequate development of the forces of production created by the capitalist mode of production. According to Marx and Lenin the growth of capitalist relations of production gradually leads to the demise of the feudal mode of production in agriculture, and although small-scale peasant farming may persist over many decades during a transition period, the peasantry will eventually polarize into wage labourers and large-scale capitalist farmers employing wage labour. As Marx and Lenin acknowledged, this process did lead in Europe to some development of the forces of production, but this is necessarily inhibited by capitalist relations of production. Labour productivity is low because farm workers are alienated. The persistence of small-scale peasant farming over many years prevents the full exploitation of those on-farm economies of scale that can be reaped via investment in machinery. Private ownership constrains the development of the large-scale water conservancy projects essential for raising farm yields, especially in rice-based economies, and instead there is continual conflict over ownership of water and compensation for land occupied by irrigation projects. It also precludes the full mobilization of the farm workforce in directly productive activities because women are occupied by domestic tasks. Collective farming avoids all these problems by restoring ownership of the means of production to the peasantry. It thereby promotes mechanization, eliminates ownership disputes and liberates female labour power via communal provision of child care. Furthermore, the restoration of ownership puts an end to alienation and therefore offers autonomy and opportunities for self-realization to the farm labourer.

Nevertheless, early Marxist writings were careful to stress the necessity of a long period of transition from private to collective farming. Marx believed that the Tsarist commune could evolve into a genuine collective but only if the state provided the funds necessary for the purchase of agricultural machinery ('First Draft of the Letter to Vera Zasulich', 1881, in Marx and Engels CW 24). And Lenin, along with other Bolsheviks in the early days of the Soviet Union, insisted that collectivization had to be voluntary; the peasants were not to be forced into collectives, even though the state possessed the capacity to impose such a change:

We have millions of individual farms in our country, scattered and dispersed throughout remote rural districts. It would be absolutely absurd to reshape these farms in any rapid way, by issuing an order or bringing pressure to bear from without. . . . the peasants are far too practical and cling far too tenaciously to the old methods of farming to consent to any serious change merely on the basis of advice or book instructions. (Lenin 1919, p. 196)

it will take a whole historical epoch to get the entire population into the work of the cooperatives through the New Economic Policy. At best we can achieve this in one or two decades . . . Without this historical epoch, without universal literacy, without a proper degree of efficiency, without training the population sufficiently to acquire the habit of book-reading, and without the material basis for this, without a sufficient safeguard against, say, bad harvests, famine, etc. – without this we shall not achieve our object. (Lenin 1923, p. 470)

The same arguments are to be found in the writings and speeches of Trotsky and Bukharin in the early 1920s, and in those of Mao and other members of the Chinese Communist Party before 1955.

But in the event, these warnings were disregarded. Both in the Soviet Union (1928–32) and in China (1955–6), collectivization was coercive and preceded the mechanization of agriculture. For Stalin, the justification was the perceived military threat and the need to secure adequate grain for the cities. Bitter criticism from Trotsky (see, for example, Trotsky 1937), and others who remained faithful to the Leninist vision, was rendered futile in the end by their removal from power. Kamenev, Zinoviev and Bukharin met a similar response which, by the late 1920s, made possible the coercive solution. Mao, by contrast, argued (wrongly) that peasant enthusiasm was enormous and was being held back by no more than a conservative leadership. For many 'liberal' and even socialist writers, it was this 'premature transition' which ensured that collectivization was not only a failure but also a disaster (Selden 1982). In particular, in the absence of mechanization, the enforced reliance on a labour-intensive technique of production created insoluble difficulties. As collectivization was coercive, the collective work-force was not self-motivated, and therefore an

elaborate system of incentives and supervision was required to ensure satisfactory labour productivity. However, it is virtually impossible to design such a system because of the peculiar characteristics of farm work, notably the spatial dispersion of the workforce, the sequential nature of production (which prevents year-round specialization) and the mediation of climate (Nolan 1988). These types of problems, it has been argued, explain the greater reliance placed on tenancy rather than wage labour by landowners in poor capitalist economies. Moreover, collective farms and their members have enjoyed little operational independence. Output quotas have been imposed from above and strict controls on labour migration have been enforced. As a result, the opportunities for autonomy and self-realization emphasized by Lenin and Marx have been few indeed.

The long-run consequences of a 'premature transition' for farm sector performance have therefore been disastrous. Although yields have increased over time, these have been achieved by continual increases in labour inputs rather than as a result of improvements in labour productivity so that per capita rural incomes have remained stagnant. Furthermore, the process of collectivization led directly to famines on a scale never seen in capitalist economies. A recent estimate by a Soviet specialist put the death toll in the 1932–3 famine at three million (Danilov, cited in Davies 1989, p. 177). In China, as many as 30 million excess deaths occurred in the famine of the early 1960s (Ashton et al. 1984).

Although the scale of death in these two famines is historical fact, the causal link between famine and collectivization is tendentious. The Soviet famine was a consequence not of collectivization per se but of its very speed. As was shown in China, where the process was completed by 1957, it is possible to collectivize successfully if a gradual transition via mutual aid and cooperation precedes full-blown collective ownership. That country's own famine is better seen as a consequence of the de facto abandonment of material incentives within communes, combined with the diversion of farm labour into rural iron and steel production. Incentive systems did not 'fail' in China during 1958–62; they were not tried.

The suggestion that collectivization guarantees the stagnation of long-term labour productivity is more difficult to refute. However, the strong form of this argument – that labour productivity will be stagnant *even if* modern capital inputs are available – is not convincing. Of course, there are few direct economies of scale in rice production when farms are very large, not least because of the essentially aquatic environment. But even in China, rice production accounts for little more than 40 per cent of all grain production and average farm size in both the 1930s and the 1980s was so small – average farm size of 0.5 hectares divided into ten non-contiguous plots scattered throughout the village in 1988 – that economies were there to be exploited. In other words, it has to be recognized that the schedule relating farm size and land productivity is upward sloping over part of the range. Further, there is a wide range of off-farm operations, including crop processing and water conservancy, where economies of scale do exist and where modern capital goods will raise productivity dramatically. The classic 'liberal' response is that these sorts of benefits can be reaped via voluntary cooperation but it is rather naive to suppose that voluntary cooperative formation will take place, even if partially subsidized by the state. Poor peasants quite rightly fear 'cooperative capture' by rich peasants, who then proceed to manipulate cooperative policy to suit their own interest. Moreover, collective farms have performed well when investment resources have been made available. Output grew very quickly during the Khrushchev years despite the concentration of investment in the misconceived virgin lands scheme and the excessive emphasis on grain production. The surge in farm output that occurred in China between 1977 and 1981 – *before* decollectivization – was a direct consequence of the massive investment in water conservancy projects undertaken during the Maoist period combined with the injection of modern fixed and working capital that began in earnest in 1977.

The weak form of the anti-collective argument admits that collectivization does make possible some economies of scale. However, given the non-availability of modern investment goods in China and in the Soviet Union at the time of collectivization, it would have made more sense to have persevered with private farming, thereby at least ensuring a well-motivated farm workforce. In other words, if

one accepts the strategic threat posed to China, the Soviet Union and Vietnam at the time of their collectivization, and therefore their decision to divert investment away from agriculture and towards the production of weapons, collectivized agriculture was impracticable. But even this weak form of the argument ignores the genuine achievements of collective farming. The distribution of income in China by the 1970s was one of the most equal in the world, even though a majority of collective managers (cadres) granted themselves privileged access to the meagre supply of consumer durables. It is hard to see how such a degree of equality could have been achieved without collective farms and the abolition of private ownership of the means of production. There are those who argue that universal poverty is not socialism, but neither is socialism synonymous with the sort of inequalities that have emerged in China in the 1980s. Moreover, collectivization did a great deal to promote the development of the forces of production. It is probable that agriculture was a net recipient of resource transfers in both China and the Soviet Union (Ellman 1989), and therefore Stalin's defence of collectivization, that it would provide a surplus to finance accumulation and especially the development of heavy industry, may have been without foundation (though measurement of such flows is notoriously difficult). Nevertheless, collective farms made possible the mobilization of the rural labour force on an unprecedented scale and this in turn enabled vast water conservancy projects, and infrastructure construction, to be undertaken, both of which played a crucial role in raising farm yields.

Finally, the achievements of collectivized agriculture need to be contrasted with those of agriculture in comparable developing countries and not with some ideal type. The rural development of both India and Brazil since 1950 has been remarkably unimpressive (especially when allowance is made for hitherto uncultivated land exploited by Brazil) and it is with these two that China and the USSR ought to be compared. Moreover, although farm output has grown quite quickly in some capitalist developing countries, hardly any have combined growth with equity. Taiwan has arguably succeeded, but only by virtue of a unique constellation of peculiarly favourable factors – US aid and an influx of skilled labour from the mainland. For the majority of developing countries, it has proven easy enough to design a system of progressive taxation but much more difficult to avoid evasion or soaring collection costs.

The record of collectivized agriculture has been rather less good than many Marxists hoped. Nevertheless, it is unclear that overall performance – that is, development of the forces of production and the eradication of exploitation – has been any worse than in the majority of capitalist economies. Rather, when one recognizes that China, the USSR and Vietnam have all been confronted with a hostile international environment, the achievements of their agricultural sectors must rank as considerable.

Reading

Ashton, Basil, Hill, Kenneth, Piazza, Alan and Zeitz, Robin 1984: 'Famine in China'.

Davies, R. W. 1989: *Soviet History in the Gorbachev Revolution*.

Ellman, M. 1989: *Socialist Planning*.

Lenin, V. I. 1899 (*1960*): *The Development of Capitalism in Russia*.

— 1919 (*1965*): 'Speech delivered at the First Congress of Agricultural Communes and Agricultural Artels'.

— 1923 (*1966*): 'On Cooperation'.

Mao Zedong 1955 (*1971*): 'On the Question of Agricultural Cooperation'.

Nolan, Peter 1988: *The Political Economy of Collective Farms*.

Selden, M. 1982 (*1988*): 'Cooperation and Conflict'. In *The Political Economy of Chinese Socialism*.

Trotsky, L. 1937 (*1972*): *The Revolution Betrayed*.

CHRIS BRAMALL

colonial and post-colonial societies The age of modern COLONIALISM began with the global expansion of trade and conquest by European powers. A distinction must be drawn between pre-capitalist colonial rule, notably that of the Iberian powers in Central and Latin America, and the new colonialism that was associated with the birth, development and global expansion of West European capitalism, beginning with the commercial revolution of the sixteenth century and itself entering into successive phases of development. The object of pre-capitalist colonialism was direct extraction of tribute from subjugated peoples and its essential mechanisms were those of political control. By contrast, in the case of the new colonialism, associated with the rise of capitalism, the objectives and mechanisms were essentially economic – direct political control was not essential, though sometimes advantageous. The emphasis was on a search for raw materials and, especially after the industrial revolution in Britain, for markets. Realization of both these objectives entailed a restructuring of the economies of the colonized societies. Associated with that primary thrust was territorial conquest, with or without the elimination of indigenous populations of conquered territories, and the establishment of white settlers or slave plantations and mining enterprises. Except in the latter cases, given the economic pre-eminence and naval power of Britain, the principal imperialist power of the day, direct rule was not essential to secure the purposes of the new colonialism, or imperialism as it soon came to be called. Many countries that remained formally independent soon came under the economic domination of world imperialism. It was only in the late nineteenth century, faced with the German challenge above all, that there was a new scramble for colonial conquest, a fresh redivision of the world; the bid for direct colonial rule was now largely a pre-emptive strategy *vis-à-vis* rival imperialist powers rather than an indispensable condition of the colonial relationship itself. Too sharp a distinction between colonial and non-colonial societies of the Third World would therefore be misleading, though not without some significance.

To avoid confusion between pre-capitalist colonialism and capitalist world domination, with or without conquest and direct colonial rule, the term 'imperialism' is often used for the latter (see IMPERIALISM AND WORLD MARKET). But a distinction must then be made between the 'old imperialism' of early capitalism and the 'new imperialism' of mature capitalism in the late nineteenth century, the era of MONOPOLY CAPITALISM which was the subject of Lenin's famous tract *Imperialism – the Highest Stage of Capitalism*. This was associated with the pre-eminence of FINANCE CAPITAL, a drive for export of capital and also fierce inter-imperialist rivalry that culminated in two world wars. As for the world dominated by imperialism, both its phases entailed a forcible transformation of pre-capitalist societies and the establishment of a new international division of labour, whereby their economies were internally disarticulated and integrated externally with the metropolitian economies. They were no longer self-sufficient locally but were now to concentrate on production of raw materials and food demanded by the advanced capitalist countries, very often becoming precariously dependent on monoculture. On the other hand they provided markets for manufactured products supplied by the advanced capitalist countries. The Leninist theory of imperialism emphasizes above all the fact that they were profitable fields for investment of metropolitan capital. This was originally mainly in plantations and extractive industries, but later also in labour-intensive light manufacturing which takes advantage of cheap labour in the colonies. It has been argued in recent years that the emphasis on the quantum of capital exported is misplaced, for the most significant aspect of the new imperialism is the hierarchical relationship, in 'partnership', that is established between metropolitan capital and indigenous capital originating in the colony, on the basis of the former's control over sophisticated modern technology; so that the actual extent of metropolitan control over the colonized economy greatly exceeds the nominal value of metropolitan capital invested in it.

The nature of these economic relationships provides a key for understanding the problems of post-colonial societies. By the middle of the twentieth century much of the Third World was subject to direct colonial rule. With the rise of national liberation movements and, not least, a change in the balance of world forces, with the emergence of the Soviet bloc and also the emergence of American economic power which was no longer prepared to accept the monopoly of political control exercised by weak European powers over a large part of the globe, a process of decolonization began with the independence of South Asian countries in 1947. The fact that many of the newly independent countries opted for non-alignment in the context of the Cold War, reinforced by their rhetoric of socialism, encouraged many scholars to hail the Third World countries as exemplars of a new path to economic and social development, neither capitalist nor communist. But the dependent nature of their economies, organically linked and financially indebted to Western imperialist countries, which was manifest, dispelled such notions. The

concept of dependence on metropolitan capital soon came to be accepted as the alternative definition of their status – some extreme interpretations of dependence implying political subjugation as well as economic domination (see DEPENDENCY THEORY).

The notion of post-colonial societies recognizes a more complex alignment of class forces. In societies subjected to colonial domination pre-capitalist structures were undermined and new structures necessary for capitalist development were established. This not only allowed metropolitan capital to develop but also created conditions for the development of indigenous capital in industry as well as in commerce and agriculture. In colonial societies the colonial state is the instrument of the metropolitan bourgeoisie and is deployed against indigenous classes where their respective rights clash. But that is no longer the case in post-colonial societies, where the state is no longer controlled directly by the metropolitan bourgeoisie. The theory of the post-colonial state suggests that the classical Marxist conception of the STATE as the instrument of a single ruling class, or, in structuralist interpretations of the Marxist theory of the state, as the relatively autonomous reproducer of the social formation in the interests of the whole of that class, cannot be applied in an unproblematic way to the new conditions. The metropolitan bourgeoisie is no longer in unquestioned command of the state apparatus, although it continues to wield considerable influence. Its relationship with the post-colonial state is further complicated by the fact that it now stands in competition with the bourgeoisies of other advanced capitalist countries, as well as with the indigenous classes, for influence over the state. The latter now attempt to use the post-colonial state to advance their own particular class interests, but they too do not have unqualified command over it, for it is subject in some degree to the influence of powerful metropolitan capitalist classes. Indeed, it is argued that no single one of these classes qualifies as 'the ruling class', for that would exclude the powerful presence of the others in post-colonial societies.

The notion of post-colonial societies is also based on the conception of a single peripheral capitalist mode of production in which the various classes are all located, the metropolitan bourgeoisies having a structural presence in these societies. There is therefore no structural contradiction between these competing classes, and they have a common interest in the preservation of the capitalist social order that the post-colonial state upholds. Subject to this, the post-colonial state enjoys autonomy *vis-à-vis* each of these classes taken by itself, for only by virtue of such autonomy does it mediate their competing interests. Thus the post-colonial society, while being capitalist, possesses a class configuration and a state that is distinct from those found in advanced capitalist countries as well as in countries under colonial rule.

Reading
Alavi, Hamza 1972: 'The State in Post-Colonial Societies'.
— et al. 1982: *Capitalism and Colonial Production*.
— and Shanin, Teodor eds 1982: *Introduction to the Sociology of the 'Developing Societies'*.
Brewer, Anthony 1980: *Marxist Theories of Imperialism: A Critical Survey*.
Goulbourne, Harry 1979: *Politics and State in the Third World*.
Magdoff, Harry 1978: *Imperialism: From the Colonial Age to the Present*.

HAMZA ALAVI

colonialism Marxist analyses of colonialism have approached it by focusing on several general issues. First, they have tried to establish that direct political control of non-capitalist societies was in some way a result of the reproductive requirements or tendential developments of European and American industrial capitalist economies in the nineteenth century. Second, they have examined the political, economic and ideological effects of industrial capitalist entry into non-capitalist societies. In this, they have been concerned primarily with the results of these effects for the development of socialism in both the industrial capitalist and colonized societies; consequently, they have tended to focus on the forms of colonial capitalist development created and perpetuated by the colonizing powers, and on the implications of this. Finally, they have assessed the possible consequences of socialist developments in colonial societies for socialist transformation in colonizing countries. These problems have been approached

from within different theoretical and political perspectives in the Marxist tradition, and the varying answers given have laid down parameters for Marxist debates on the nature of post-colonial capitalist and socialist development (see COLONIAL AND POST-COLONIAL SOCIETIES).

Much of the writings of Marx and Engels on colonialism are commentaries on the results of British colonial rule in India and China, contained in articles and letters, the most detailed of which were written by Marx on India in 1853. At this time Marx was working on drafts of the *Grundrisse*, one of whose sections – 'Forms that preceded capitalist production' – deals in passing with the effects of colonial rule on non-capitalist modes of production, and particularly on the Asiatic mode of production (see ASIATIC SOCIETY). These brief writings indicate that Marx and Engels considered the relation between industrial capitalist development and colonial control and expansion a complex one – irreducible to the 'basic' economic tendencies offered as explanations by many later Marxist writers. They argued that colonial control was necessary not simply as a means for gaining access to markets and raw materials, but also as a means for excluding rival industrial nations, and in cases where the reproduction of non-capitalist economies was particularly resistant to capitalist penetration. They thus placed colonial control within a general economic context of a need for markets, raw materials, and investment outlets, to which, however, its presence and operation was not always reducible. The analysis of the resistance of non-capitalist modes of production to industrial capitalist entry was further developed in *Capital* III, where Marx stressed the importance of the colonial state for transforming those non-capitalist modes whose political level was crucial for their reproduction (as, for example, in the Asiatic mode of production).

To many critics there seem to be two contradictory strands in Marx's analysis. When, for example, he analyses the effects of colonialism on Indian society, he shows how the economy is undermined by the forcible destruction of the textile industry and the neglect of state-organized public works; yet, in an apparent paradox, he also states that colonial rule is beneficial, in that it introduces an economic system which can revolutionize production, introducing technological changes which will benefit the indigenous population in the long term. This seemingly contradictory notion of the colonial impact being detrimental yet beneficial became the focus for Marxist debates on the 'colonial question'.

The analysis of the impact of colonialism in breaking down non-capitalist modes of production and transforming them in a capitalist direction was further developed by Luxemburg. From an underconsumptionist perspective which viewed colonial control as a means for destroying self-sufficient natural economies in the interests of a capitalism whose reproduction was hindered by a continual lack of effective demand, Luxemburg posited four destructive industrial capitalist mechanisms. Natural economies could be undermined by the introduction of a commodity economy and an internal separation of trade from agriculture, or they could be coercively undercut by a forcible possession of their fertile land, raw materials and labour power. Only colonialism could achieve this undermining successfully; it came as a last resort, when the operation of economic mechanisms such as trade, investment and monetarization had failed to restrict the reproduction of the natural economy.

With the work of Hilferding, colonial control began to be viewed more specifically as the outcome of developments in a particular phase of industrial capitalist growth. Hilferding associated colonialism with the rise to dominance of FINANCE CAPITAL, and the resultant increase in the export of capital from industrial capitalist economies in the late nineteenth century. This laid the basis for an exacerbation of the conflicts between industrial nation states over the annexation and consolidation of colonial areas (see NATIONALISM; WAR). Lenin extended and popularized Hilferding's analysis, arguing that the export of capital to colonized areas would lead to an expansion and deepening of capitalist development. His polemic against Kautsky's theory of 'ultra-imperialism' focused on inter-imperialist rivalry between nation states limiting their possibilities for cooperative exploitation of colonized areas; this, together with his adherence to Marx's notions of capitalist penetration as ultimately progressive, laid the basis for one strand of the debate on colonialism in the Third International. The other strands

rested on Kautsky's premiss, or on Bukharin's (and Hilferding's) insistence that capitalist production, rather than spreading evenly through the colonial economy, would remain confined to sectors operating in the interests of the industrial capitalist economies. Lenin's perspective was most importantly extended by the Indian Marxist, M. N. Roy, and later by Eugene Varga; the arguments on the necessary sectoral confining of capitalist production were best represented by Pronin.

These debates on the forms of capitalist development promoted through colonial control, together with the differing analyses of their effects on the class structure and the state, laid the basis for the emergence of theories of underdevelopment (see UNDERDEVELOPMENT AND DEVELOPMENT) and dependency (see DEPENDENCY THEORY), together with criticisms of them in the post-independence 'neo-colonial' period; the central issue remained whether or not industrial capitalist reproduction necessarily required the imposition of a specific form of colonial capitalism which undermined the domestic sector and led to the impoverishment of the indigenous population.

The Marxist perspective on colonialism has been subjected to detailed criticism, the most important focusing on the following points:

(i) Colonialism was not particular to any specific phase in the development of the industrial capitalist economies. Although annexation and expansion did intensify in the late nineteenth century, the evidence is insufficient to establish the Marxist case in general, and Lenin's analysis in particular.

(ii) The economic arguments for the existence of a particular 'imperialist' stage of capitalist development are weak, if not unsustainable. Several authors, notably Barratt-Brown (1974), Warren (1980), and O'Connor (1970), have specified the major limitations: that 'finance capital' – defined as the dominance of banking over industrial capital – only prevailed in a minority of industrial capitalist states; that the export of capital did not increase dramatically in the latter part of the nineteenth century; that it was not simply a matter of profit rates being higher in the colonies, but rather the mass of profit realizable, and this was far greater in the industrialized economies; that the decay and technological retardation of capitalist progress which Lenin associated with the need to export capital is little evidenced in the nineteenth and early twentieth centuries.

(iii) Whatever the multitude of links in the chain between the actions of the colonial state and the reproductive requirements of the industrial capitalist economies, Marxist analyses of colonialism have always ultimately reduced the former to the latter. This economic determinism has severely restricted the analysis of such aspects as the colonial class structure, with its continual reproduction of economic groupings whose existence cannot be explained simply by the reproductive needs of industrial capitalism.

(iv) Analysis of the societies that existed before the colonial impact has been either ignored or placed within all-embracing residual categories whose generality has rendered them heuristically valueless. Such categories are Luxemburg's concept of a pre-capitalist self-sufficient natural economy, or the notion that pre-colonial societies were simply equivalent to European feudal formations before the advent of capitalism.

(v) The focus on the possibilities of a colonial capitalism creating the basis for a transition to a socialist economy has led to a political and theoretical obsession with the emergence of a national bourgeoisie. This has further restricted the possibilities of a rigorous Marxist analysis of classes and the state in colonial societies.

Reading

Barratt-Brown, M. 1974: *The Economics of Imperialism*.

Clarkson, S. 1979: *The Soviet Theory of Development*.

Hilferding, R. 1910 *(1981)*: *Finance Capital*.

Lenin, V. I. 1916 *(1964)*: *Imperialism: the Highest Stage of Capitalism*.

Luxemburg, R. 1913 *(1951)*: *The Accumulation of Capital*.

O'Connor, J. 1970: 'The Economic Meaning of Imperialism'. In R. Rhodes ed. *Imperialism and Underdevelopment*.

Pronin, A. 1940: *India*.

Roy, M. N. 1922: *India in Transition*.

Varga, Eugene 1948: *Changes in the Economy of Capitalism Resulting from the Second World War*.

Warren, B. 1980: *Imperialism: Pioneer of Capitalism*.

JOHN G. TAYLOR

colonial liberation movements   Colonial rule provoked, chiefly by its economic pressures, a multitude of grassroots discontents, sometimes erupting into fighting. Out of this incoherent unrest, organized movements struggled into existence, seeking concessions on one front or another, and advancing by stages to demands for independence. Among these the Indian National Congress, founded in 1885, was the most prominent. It benefited from the more legal or constitutional character of British rule compared with any of the other empires; and after years of gradually broadening its base it was given a strong impetus by the strains and tensions of the 1914–18 War. This had a radicalizing effect on the whole colonial world. A drifting apart of aspirations focused on national liberation, and others extending to internal social reform as well, was accelerated.

When Marxism began to travel outside Europe it faced many novel problems. A Marxist theory of colonialism had been sought for seriously only after about 1900, and it was concerned primarily with European causes and consequences. But after the failure of the Russian revolution of 1905, Lenin was looking to colonial revolt as a powerful reinforcement to the revolutionary movement in Europe, somewhat as Marx had come to think that freedom for Ireland would be the beginning of the end for British capitalism. Marxists had often been critical of nationalism in Europe, but its dangers for Asia were scarcely yet in sight, and liberation movements there were expected to develop in a progressive direction. Communism in Asia was always to have a strongly nationalist colouring.

Serious Marxist study of the colonial world, and participation in its struggles, had their starting point with the Bolshevik revolution of 1917, all the more because of its ramifications into Russian Asia. The Bolsheviks were soon eager to extend it still further, and the 'Congress of Peoples of the East' at Baku in September 1920 was organized with the aim of spreading the anti-imperialist flame across Asia. Russia's own revolution had indeed aroused widespread interest and applause in many lands. In the absence of an appropriate working-class basis, and because of police repression directed against all progressive movements, reformist socialism could find little of a foothold. Those who were drawn towards socialist ideals, at first mostly individuals of the educated classes who had some access, in spite of censorship, to Western ideas, had no alternative but to try to form communist parties, affiliated to the new world movement launched in 1919. These parties were closely modelled on the Bolshevik, a pattern that suited them well enough because they were oftener than not compelled to work underground, as Bolshevism had been in Tsarist Russia.

At the early congresses of the Third International (see INTERNATIONALS) the Indian pioneer M. N. ROY spoke for Asians impatient to make revolutions for themselves, instead of waiting for the working class in Europe to take power and open the door for them. He even argued, reversing Western calculations, that the European parties would be unable to carry out their revolutions until the Eastern countries did so first, thus crippling imperialism and with it capitalism. Roy was far too sanguine. But struggle for survival hardened the colonial communist parties, and their adherents displayed a devotion to their cause surpassed by no other political organization anywhere. Their activity was concentrated among the poverty-stricken masses, and they had considerable success in winning support: in India, for instance, among the workers; in China among the peasants. Conditions were less favourable to growth in the field of theory, despite the always high proportion of intellectuals and students among them. Practical problems absorbed their energy; these might, as in China or French Indochina, be of a largely military character, since planning for armed insurrection often seemed the only road. Membership of the Third International made possible some contacts among the scattered parties, although communications were usually difficult. Its periodical congresses were a forum for reviews of the world situation and discussion of the tactics best adapted to it. Inevitably dependence for guidance, and at times for material aid, was chiefly on Moscow, which could not always have a clear understanding of complications arising in countries like India or China, and might be inclined to steer policies in the light of Soviet interests. This might entail abrupt shifts, like the one made by the Seventh Congress in 1935 from sectarian self-isolation to united-front tactics in face of the menace of fascism.

From the outset, the International and its member parties in the bigger and economically more developed colonies had to debate relations with 'bourgeois nationalism', and whether communists should be willing to cooperate with movements like the Indian National Congress, linked with the more modern-minded of the propertied classes, or should build a basis of their own among the workers and peasants. The latter view was upheld in 1919 by M. N. Roy, while Lenin was more in favour of cooperation. To get bourgeois parties to fall in with this was seldom easy, and frictions were many, as they had been within nationalist movements in nineteenth-century Europe. Indian workers were increasingly being exploited by Indian rather than British mill-owners, and Indian peasants by Indian landlords more than by British tax collectors.

A related issue concerned the economic effects of imperialism on colonies. There was disagreement concerning the industrial growth that India, in particular, owed to the First World War and was then able to sustain, as to whether it amounted to economic 'decolonization', and might divert the bourgeoisie away from political militancy. Another question, faced earlier by Russian socialism, was whether a backward country must go through a period of full capitalism before socialism could be practicable. With the apparent success of the USSR in building a socialist economy, after the Five Year Plans began, it could be hoped that colonial countries would be able to follow its example.

Religion was a card that bourgeois spokesmen could play against communism, above all in India with its two powerful and mutually hostile creeds. Marxism was not ready with a sociology of religion, and colonial Marxists were not making much headway towards one. The Indian National Congress was born in 1885, and was well established as a liberal party of the educated before socialism came to challenge it. Gandhi broadened its popular basis after 1918, developing a non-violent ideology tinged with Hinduism which had more appeal to the middle classes than to the workers or peasants. Communists regarded it as timidly reformist, and stood aside from some of the Congress's spells of confrontation with the government, especially in 1942 when they were backing the Allied war effort because the USSR was now in the war; their party suffered for this in national esteem.

In China, religion was far less a factor, and modern-style capitalism was less expansive, confined to the coastal towns. During the turmoil of the early 1920s there was a short period of collaboration between communists and the middle-class Kuomintang, led by Sun Yat-sen. He held liberal, even socialist or 'welfarist' views, and his party needed the popular support that the communists could bring against the provincial 'warlords' who had usurped power. Once these were displaced, and with Sun Yat-sen now dead, the help and counsel of Moscow were discarded; from 1928 the Kuomintang and the country fell under the reactionary dictatorship of Chiang Kai-shek, who enjoyed Western backing.

Defeated in the towns, the Communist Party, with Mao Tse-tung as its new leader, turned to the peasantry, thus departing from the traditional Marxist tenet that only an industrial working class could be the proper vanguard of revolution. Japanese invasion gave the party a fresh chance; there has been controversy about whether it won its way to the front and finally triumphed in the civil war against Chiang Kai-shek on the strength of its championship of the peasantry against landlordism and a corrupt semi-feudal government, or on the strength of its energetic leadership in the conflict with Japan. It came to power in 1948–9 without a strong working class to give it ballast, but equally without a strong capitalist class to impede it.

In regions where communists were fewer than in Vietnam, such as Burma and Indonesia, many nationalists had welcomed the Japanese as liberators, and this left a legacy of division. In Indonesia the two wings (communist and nationalist) joined in 1945 to drive out the Dutch, but 1965 was to see a nationalist government with foreign backing crush the Communist Party after allegations that it was plotting to seize power, and then carry out a large-scale massacre of its supporters. In the Philippines, power was handed over by the USA to an elite consisting mainly of rich landowners, who had been content with mild constitutional opposition; communists then headed a smouldering peasant resistance. In Malaya, a guerrilla rising against the British was launched in 1948, but failed because of the country's ethnic, as well as social,

divisions; most of the insurgents were immigrant Chinese, who received little sympathy from the native Malay population. It was to conservative Malay leaders that power was eventually handed over.

In Africa, Marxism found its way much more slowly, but it played a prominent part in the rebellions in all the three Portuguese territories, and made itself felt in Rhodesia and in the anti-apartheid movement in South Africa. Class divisions have mattered far less than in Asia; on the other hand, ethnic differences have in some areas been an analogous weakness. Soviet material aid counted, and, in Angola, Cuban troops. Russian withdrawal from the Third World, noticeable for some time, can be expected to continue. If Marxism is to survive as a force there, it will clearly have to go through much overhauling and adaptation. One task to be undertaken everywhere will be a critical review of communist policies and methods, and their successes and failures, in the era of struggle against colonialism. Indian Marxists have made a useful start by beginning to reconsider their estimate of what Gandhi represented in Indian history.

Reading

Jean Chesneaux *et al.* 1972 (1977): *China from the 1911 Revolution to Liberation.*

Fanon, Frantz 1961 (1967): *The Wretched of the Earth.*

Gupta, S. Datta 1980: *Comintern, India and the Colonial Question, 1920–37.*

Hodgkin, Thomas 1981: *Vietnam: The Revolutionary Path.*

Melotti, Umberto 1972 (1977): *Marx and the Third World.*

Nagai, Yonosuke and Iriye, Akira eds 1977: *The Origins of the Cold War in Asia.*

Nehru, Jawaharlal 1936: *An Autobiography.*

Pomeroy, William J. 1970: *American Neocolonialism: Its Emergence in the Philippines and Asia.*

Spence, Jonathan D. 1982: *The Gate of Heavenly Peace: The Chinese and their Revolution, 1895–1980.*

Wolf, Eric R. 1971: *Peasant Wars of the Twentieth Century.*

V. G. KIERNAN

commodity All human societies must produce their own material conditions of existence. The commodity is the form products take when this production is organized through exchange. In such a system products once produced are the property of particular agents who have the power to dispose of them to other agents. Agents who own different products confront each other in a process of bargaining through which they exchange the products. In exchange a definite quantity of one product changes places with a definite quantity of another. The commodity, then, has two powers: first, it can satisfy some human want, that is, it has what Adam Smith calls USE VALUE; second, it has the power to command other commodities in exchange, a power of exchangeability that Marx calls VALUE. Because commodities exchange with each other in definite quantitative proportions each commodity can be thought of as containing a certain amount of value. The whole mass of commodities produced in a period can be seen as a homogeneous mass of value, though looked at in another way it is a heterogeneous collection of different and incomparable use values. As values commodities are qualitatively equal and differ only quantitatively in the amount of value they contain. As use values commodities are qualitatively different, since each product is specific and cannot be compared with another.

The labour theory of value analyses this mass of value as the form the total social labour expended takes in a commodity-producing system. The labour that produces commodities can thus be thought of either concretely, as labour of a particular kind which produces a particular use value (in the way that weaving is a particular kind of labour that produces cloth), or abstractly, as being the source of value in general, as ABSTRACT LABOUR.

Value becomes visible as exchange value when commodities confront each other in exchange, and exchange value comes to have an existence independent of any particular commodity as MONEY. The quantity of money for which a particular commodity can be bought or sold is its price. The prices of individual commodities may deviate from their values as measured by the amount of abstract labour they contain; on average or in the aggregate the total money price of commodities newly produced must equal their total value (see VALUE AND PRICE; PRICE OF PRODUCTION AND THE TRANS-

FORMATION PROBLEM). The commodity, analytically, is the dialectical union of use value and value. The analysis of the commodity form is the basis for the theory of abstract labour and the theory of money.

The theory of the commodity establishes the fundamental categories within which capital can be described and analysed. Capital is value which expands through the process of production and exchange. A capitalist starts production with a certain amount of money, which he uses to purchase labour power and means of production; the resulting product he sells for more money than the amount originally advanced, the excess being the surplus value. Thus capital is a form which rests on the existence of a commodity system of production and the emergence of the money form of value. The basic concepts used to describe and study capital, the commodity, money, purchase, sale, and value, are grounded in the analysis of the commodity form of production.

Labour expended in commodity production is social labour. The product is not consumed by its immediate producer, but by someone else who obtains it through exchange. Commodity producers depend on other producers to provide them, through exchange, with their required means of production and subsistence. But labour in commodity production appears to producers as their own private labour, expended independently of the society as a whole to meet their private wants and needs through exchange on the market. The real complex relations a commodity producer has with other human beings through the social division of labour promoted by commodity production are reduced to impersonal and uncontrollable market forces. The producers, whose world is in fact created by the people, see themselves as existing in a world of things, the commodities. The commodity form of production simultaneously makes private labour social as products are exchanged, and fragments social labour into private labour. This confusion of relations between people with relations to things is the fundamental contradiction of commodity production. Marx calls it the *fetishism of commodities* (see COMMODITY FETISHISM), the process by which the products of human labour come to appear as an independent and uncontrolled reality apart from the people who have created them. The historical mission of socialism, in Marx's view, is to transcend not just the contradictions of capitalist production, but the contradictions of the commodity form on which capitalist production rests.

The concept of the commodity is used by Marx to analyse forms which arise on the basis of a well-developed commodity production and exchange, but which are not themselves in the primitive sense commodities, that is, products produced for a system of exchange. For example labour power is sold for a price, the wage, and hence appears on the market as a commodity, though labour power is not produced as a commodity, nor does its value arise directly from the labour expended in producing it. In economies with highly developed financial markets, capital itself becomes a 'commodity', in the sense that it has a price (the rate of interest) and is exchanged on a market (see CREDIT AND FICTITIOUS CAPITAL; FINANCIAL CAPITAL AND INTEREST). In both these cases the concept of the commodity is used by analogy and extension rather than in its primitive sense.

Reading

Rubin, Isaak I. 1928 (1972): *Essays on Marx's Theory of Value*, chs. 1 to 5 and 7.

DUNCAN FOLEY

commodity fetishism   Marx's analysis of commodity fetishism is more or less confined to *Capital* I (ch. 1, sect. 4). Having established that COMMODITY production constitutes a social relationship between producers, a relationship that brings different types, skills and quantities of labour into equivalence with each other as values (see VALUE), Marx enquires how this relationship appears to the producers or more generally to society. For the producers, it 'is presented to them as a social relation, existing not between themselves, but between the products of their labour'. The social relationship between tailor and carpenter appears as a relationship between coat and table in terms of the ratio at which those things exchange with each other rather than in terms of the labours embodied in them. But Marx is quick to point out that this appearance of commodity relations as a relationship between things is not false. It exists, but conceals the relationship between the pro-

ducers: 'the relations connecting the labour of one individual with that of the rest appear, not as direct social relations between individuals at work, but as what they really are, material relations between persons and social relations between things'.

Marx's theory of commodity fetishism is never taken up again explicitly and at length, in *Capital* or elsewhere. Nevertheless its influence can clearly be discerned in his criticisms of classical political economy. Commodity fetishism is the simplest and most universal example of the way in which the economic forms of capitalism conceal underlying social relations; for example whenever CAPITAL, however understood, rather than SURPLUS VALUE is seen as the source of profit. The simplicity of commodity fetishism makes it a starting point and example for analysing non-economic relations. It establishes a dichotomy between appearance and concealed reality (without the former necessarily being false) which can be taken up in the analysis of IDEOLOGY. It discusses social relations conducted as and in the form of relations between commodities or things and this has application to the theory of REIFICATION and ALIENATION. (See also FETISHISM.)

Reading

Fine, Ben 1980: *Economic Theory and Ideology*, ch. 1.

Geras, Norman 1972: 'Essence and Appearance: Aspects of Fetishism in Marx's *Capital*'. In R. Blackburn ed. *Ideology in Social Science*.

Mohun, Simon 1979: 'Ideology, Knowledge and Neoclassical Economics'. In F. Green and P. Nore, eds., *Issue in Political Economy*.

BEN FINE

communism   Marx referred to communism – the word originated in the secret revolutionary societies of Paris in the mid-1830s – in two different but related senses: as an actual political movement of the working class in capitalist society, and as a form of society which the working class, through its struggle, would bring into existence. In the first sense – influenced not only, in all probability, by Lorenz von Stein's account (1842) of the proletariat and communism ('the response of a whole class') but also by his personal contacts with French communists in the *Ligue des Justes* – he wrote that 'the whole historical development, both the *real* genesis of communism (the birth of its empirical existence) and its thinking consciousness, is its comprehended and conscious process of becoming' (*EPM*, 3rd MS). A few years later in the *Communist Manifesto* he and Engels asserted that 'the Communists do not form a separate party opposed to other working-class parties . . . have no interests separate and apart from those of the proletariat as a whole', and are distinctive only in always emphasizing 'the common interests of the entire proletariat' and representing 'the interests of the movement as a whole'.

During the second half of the nineteenth century the terms SOCIALISM and communism came to be generally used as synonyms in designating the working-class movement, though the former was far more widely employed. Marx and Engels themselves followed this usage to some extent and they did not take strong exception even to the name 'Social Democratic' (see SOCIAL DEMOCRACY) which was adopted by some socialist parties, notably the two largest of them, in Germany and Austria, although Engels still expressed reservations, saying that while 'the word will pass muster' it remained unsuitable 'for a party whose economic programme is not merely socialist in general but specifically communist, and whose ultimate political aim is to overcome the entire state and consequently democracy as well' (foreword to the 1894 collection of his 1871–5 essays in the *Volksstaat*). Only after 1917, with the creation of the Third (Communist) International and of separate communist parties engaged in fierce conflict with other working-class parties, did the term communism again acquire a quite distinctive meaning, similar to that which it had around the middle of the nineteenth century, when it was contrasted, as a form of revolutionary action aiming at the violent overthrow of capitalism, with socialism as a more peaceful and constitutional movement of cumulative reform. Subsequently – and in particular during the period of Stalinism – communism came to have a further meaning: that of a movement led by authoritarian parties in which open discussion of Marxist theory or political strategy was suppressed, and characterized by a more or less total subordination of communist parties in other countries to the Soviet party. It is in this sense that communism can now be seen as a distinctive political movement of the twentieth

century, which has been extensively studied and criticized not only by opponents of Marxism (as is natural enough) but by many Marxists. Claudin (1975) has provided one of the most comprehensive accounts of the degeneration of the communist movement in a study of the failures of Comintern policy in the 1930s (in Germany, in the popular fronts of that period, and in China), and of the decline of Soviet political influence since the Yugoslav secession, the 1950s revolts in Eastern Europe, and the breach with communist China. 'With the death of Stalin', Claudin concludes, 'the communist movement entered its historical decline.' An analysis which is similar in many respects, written from inside Eastern Europe, and proposing ways to re-establish a viable socialist project in that region, is that of Bahro (1978). In Western Europe the crisis of the communist movement brought into existence, and was also expressed in, EUROCOMMUNISM which, through its emphasis on the value of the historically evolved Western democratic institutions and its tentative rapprochement with social democracy, seemed to mark the beginning of a new phase in which the sharp separation between communism and socialism as political tendencies might once again become attenuated.

The second sense of communism – as a form of society – was discussed by Marx on various occasions, in both early and late texts, though only in very general terms since he disclaimed any intention of writing '(Comtist) recipes for the cookshops of the future'. In the *Economic and Philosophical Manuscripts* (Third Manuscript) he wrote that 'Communism is the *positive* abolition of *private property*, of *human self-alienation*, and thus the real *appropriation* of *human* nature, through and for man. It is therefore the return of man himself as a *social*, that is, really human, being; a complete and conscious return which assimilates all the wealth of previous development.' Later he and Engels gave this conception a more precise sociological meaning by specifying the abolition of classes and of the division of labour as preconditions for a communist society: thus, in the *German Ideology* (vol. I, sect. I C), Marx argued that in order to achieve such a society it would be necessary for individuals to 're-establish their control over these material powers and abolish the division of labour. This is not possible without a community. . . . The illusory community in which, up to the present, individuals have combined, always acquired an independent existence apart from them, and since it was a union of one class against another it represented for the dominated class not only a completely illusory community but also a new shackle. In a genuine community individuals gain their freedom in and through their association.' It was in this sense too that Marx and Engels referred to early tribal societies – without private property, class divisions, or an extensive division of labour – as primitive communism. In subsequent works Marx emphasized the economic character of the future communist society, as a 'society of associated producers', arguing in *Capital* III (ch. 48) that freedom in the economic sphere could consist only in 'the fact that socialized humanity, the associated producers, regulate their interchange with nature rationally, bring it under their common control, instead of being ruled by it as by some blind power'.

Only in the *Critique of the Gotha Programme* did Marx distinguish between two stages of communist society: an early phase, when it has just emerged from capitalist society, in which the individual is paid for his labour and buys consumer goods (i.e. EXCHANGE persists); and a higher phase in which each person contributes to society according to his ability and draws from the common stock according to his needs. It was Lenin, in *State and Revolution*, who gave currency to a description of these two stages as 'socialism' and 'communism' (though Tugan-Baranovsky (1908) had suggested this usage earlier), and the terminology then became part of Leninist orthodoxy. But although official pronouncements in the USSR and other countries of Eastern Europe until recently still referred to these two stages, this is not the focal point of present-day discussions among Marxists, which have to do mainly with two issues that arise from the actual experiences of existing socialist countries. One concerns the role of the market in a socialist system, or rather, as market relations are increasingly introduced, the effective operation of a 'socialist market economy', which is seen as bringing both greater economic efficiency through a more rational allocation of resources in production and distribution, and a substantial decentralization of decision-making to 'self-managed' public enterprises of all kinds as well

as to small-scale privately owned businesses (see especially Brus 1972, 1973). This should, however, be viewed in the context of the continuing allocation of a large part of the gross national product by non-market mechanisms in the form of extensive social services, though this is now also a feature of the developed capitalist societies.

The second issue concerns Marx's view of human needs and the organization of human labour to satisfy those needs in communist society, which has formed a vague background to Marxist conceptions of the future social order but has been little studied in an explicit way until recent years, again in relation to the practical problems of socialism. One important study (Heller 1976) points to some inconsistencies in Marx's own conception. In the *Grundrisse* the alienation of labour (its externally imposed character) is overcome and it also becomes *travail attractif*, a vital need, since 'all labour becomes essentially intellectual labour, the field for the self-realization of the human personality'; but in *Capital* (III, ch. 48), while alienation ceases, labour does not become *travail attractif*, for 'the sphere of material production . . . remains a realm of necessity', and 'the true realm of freedom' begins only beyond it, in leisure time. Hence there remains an obligation to work (i.e. a constraint) in the society of associated producers. A solution of the problem within Marx's own work is to be found, Heller argues, in the idea that in this type of society a new 'structure of needs' will emerge, and everyday life will not be built around productive labour and material consumption, but around those activities and human relationships which are ends in themselves and become the primary needs. But she recognizes, on one side, the immense difficulties that remain in determining what are 'true social needs' in the realm of production and of ensuring that *everyone* has a voice in deciding how productive capacity should be allocated (a problem of even more staggering proportions if communist society is conceived, as it should be, as a global society); and on the other, that Marx's ideas on the new system of needs are utopian – but fruitful in as much as they establish a norm against which to measure the quality of present-day life. In a similar way Stojanović (1973), who sees the main prospects for essential innovations in Marxism in its critical confrontation with socialist society as it now exists, argues that the construction of a developed socialist society 'is possible only if approached from the standpoint of mature communism'; that is to say, from the standpoint of a moral (even utopian) norm.

In recent Marxist discussions of a future classless society the distinction between socialism and communism as 'lower' and 'higher' stages has lost much of its importance, and seems indeed simplistic. The movement towards such a society may pass through many stages, at present quite unforeseeable, and it may also experience interruptions and regressions. What now seems important to most participants in the debate is the need for a more profound empirical and critical study of existing social institutions, practices, and norms, in both capitalist and socialist countries, from the point of view of their inherent potentialities for development towards Marx's ideal, together with a more rigorous elaboration of the moral norms of a socialist society (see ETHICS; MORALS). Wellmer's argument (1971, pp. 121–2), which rejects the notion of 'an economically grounded "mechanism" of emancipation' and claims that it is 'necessary to include socialist democracy, socialist justice, socialist ethics and a "socialist consciousness" among the components of a socialist society to be "incubated" within the womb of a capitalist order', can just as well be applied to the existing socialist countries, with due regard to their specific characteristics and problems. (See also EQUALITY; SOCIALISM.)

Reading

Bahro, Rudolf 1978: *The Alternative in Eastern Europe.*

Brus, Wlodzimierz 1972: *The Market in a Socialist Economy.*

— 1973: *The Economics and Politics of Socialism.*

Claudin, Fernando 1975: *The Communist Movement: From Comintern to Cominform.*

Heller, Agnes 1976: *The Theory of Need in Marx.*

Lenin, V. I. 1917c (1969): 'State and Revolution'.

Moore, Stanley 1980: *Marx on the Choice between Socialism and Communism.*

Müller, Hans 1967: *Ursprung und Geschichte des Wortes 'Sozialismus' und seiner Verwandten.*

Stojanović, Svetozar 1973: *Between Ideals and Reality: A Critique of Socialism and its Future.*

TOM BOTTOMORE

Communist Manifesto Written in December 1847 and January 1848 at the behest of a small and mainly German revolutionary group, the Communist League, founded in the summer of 1847, it was published in London in February 1848 under the title *Manifest der Kommunistischen Partei*. Although it appeared under the names of both Marx and Engels, its main author was Marx, but a number of its ideas and formulations are to be found in Engels's *Principles of Communism*, written in October 1847.

The first English translation of the *Communist Manifesto*, by Helen Macfarlane, was published in the Chartist journal, *The Red Republican*, whose editor was Julian Harney, between June and November 1850. A new translation by Samuel Moore in 1888 was edited and supplied with notes by Engels. To mark the centenary of the *Manifesto*, the National Executive Committee of the Labour party decided in 1947 on the publication of a new edition. This appeared in 1948 with a lengthy introduction by Harold J. Laski.

The *Manifesto* is the product of a period of intense intellectual and political activity for Marx and Engels, during which they fashioned a new 'world-view'. Much was added by both men in subsequent years to that 'world-view'; but the *Manifesto* nevertheless forms the essential framework for what later came to be known as Marxism – a term which Marx himself never used.

One of the most remarkable features of the *Manifesto* is its perception, at a time when industrial capitalism was still in its early stages, of the revolutionary impact it was bound to have for the whole world, and of 'the most revolutionary part' which the bourgeoisie was called upon to play. 'The bourgeoisie', Marx and Engels wrote, 'cannot exist without constantly revolutionizing the instruments of production, and thereby the relations of production, and with them the whole relations of society . . . Constant revolutionizing of production, uninterrupted disturbance of all social conditions, everlasting uncertainty and agitation distinguish the bourgeois epoch from all earlier ones.' However, the *Manifesto* proclaimed, the bourgeoisie had also brought into being its 'gravediggers', the modern proletariat. In due course, and as a result of many struggles over objectives large and small, the working class would assume a revolutionary role and liberate itself and the whole of society from minority rule and class domination. For whereas 'all previous historical movements were movements of minorities, or in the interests of minorities', the proletarian movement 'is the self-conscious, independent movement of the immense majority, in the interests of the immense majority'. Nor was this emancipation conceived in national terms alone; on the contrary it would encompass the whole world, a notion encapsulated in the closing words of the *Manifesto*: 'Working Men of All Countries, Unite!'

One section of the *Manifesto* concerns the role of communists in this process; and it is noteworthy that, despite its title, the document affirms that 'the communists do not form a separate party opposed to other working-class parties.' Their role was rather to be 'the most advanced and resolute section of the working-class parties of every country'.

The final section of the *Manifesto* consists of a sharp critique of contemporary currents of thought which, though critical of the existing social order, proposed alternatives to it which Marx and Engels denounced as spurious or inadequate. They readily acknowledged that what they called 'Critical-Utopian Socialism and Communism' was 'full of the most valuable materials for the enlightenment of the working class'; but they also condemned it for its repudiation of class struggle and its rejection of revolutionary activity.

In prefaces which they wrote for later editions, Marx and Engels said that some aspects of the *Manifesto* needed amendment, notably the immediate programme of reforms which it proposed; but they also said that they stood by the 'general principles' laid down in the document. In the preface of 1872 to the third German edition of the *Manifesto*, they also emphasized that the experience of the revolution of 1848, and particularly of the Paris Commune of 1871, had shown that 'the working class cannot simply lay hold of the ready-made state machinery, and wield it for its own purposes'; and this was repeated by Engels in the 1888 preface to the English edition. The point was to be given central importance in Lenin's 'State and Revolution', published in 1917.

The *Communist Manifesto* is the most influential political pamphlet ever written. It has been translated into dozens of languages and it has been an inspiration to successive generations throughout the world. Its appearance in 1848 was a major landmark in the history of socialism; and for all the amendments and qualifications which it requires, the passage of time has scarcely dimmed the sweep and power of its message.

RALPH MILIBAND

competition For Marx competition is both an elusive and a complex category. On the one hand it belongs to the very inner nature of CAPITAL, which is inconceivable without it. On the other hand, as Rosdolsky (1968) has demonstrated, much of Marx's theory of capitalist PRODUCTION is to be derived by abstraction from competition. Rosdolsky even goes so far as to suggest that it is only at the level of *Capital* III that it is necessary for Marx to introduce competition. Up to that point the analysis, for Rosdolsky, concerns capital in general as opposed to many capitals in competition. Rosdolsky takes his observation too far but he does make clear the extent to which Marx's analysis of production by capital is a relation between capital and labour that exists independently of the competition it generates within classes. Accordingly, Marx is often seen to emphasize the role played by competition as the mechanism by which the laws of capitalism operate or exert coercion. As such, competition is to be understood at many different levels of complexity as the more concrete aspects of the capitalist economy come to be analysed. Here there is a contrast with bourgeois economics and with Marxism within the Sraffian (see SRAFFA) or neo-Ricardian tradition (see RICARDO AND MARX) where competition between capitalists is introduced at the outset.

It is because competition is so complex, involving the most immediate relations between individual capitals, that Marx ultimately resolved to deal with it systematically only in sequels to *Capital*, but his death prevented him from embarking upon this project. Nevertheless, scattered throughout *Capital* and elsewhere are many references to the significance of competition, and if these are gathered together we can construct a picture of Marx's approach to this subject. At the most general level he constantly refers to the misleading impressions which are given by the processes of competition, and emphasizes, for topic after topic, that the appearances of economic relations engendered by competition are the exact opposite of their true basis. This is usually the result of the divorce between the perspective taken by individual economic agents and their relationship to the economy as a whole. For example the transformation between VALUE AND PRICE, in the competition that equalizes the rate of PROFIT, gives the impression that profit is derived from the whole capital advanced, whereas the source of profit is to be derived exclusively from SURPLUS VALUE which depends immediately upon variable capital alone.

In discussing LANDED PROPERTY AND RENT in particular, Marx reveals the structure of value and price formation, and this is crucial for analysis of competition. Within a sector of the economy each individual capital will be characterized by a more or less unequal level of productivity. The associated individual levels of value will generate a normal or market value with respect to which some capitals will yield surplus profits and some deficient profits. The range of individual values within the sector is determined predominantly by the different sizes of capital that have been accumulated. Competition forces those with lower than normal productivity (and size of capital) into ACCUMULATION and, in this way, a SOCIALLY NECESSARY LABOUR time is established as a norm within the sector. Simultaneously, other capitals seek surplus profits by increasing capital advanced above the norm. Competition then leads to a market value and associated minimum size of capital, with the one decreasing as the other increases. At the level of production, competition concerns the extraction of surplus value, whether this is absolute or relative. The means of competition is through increase of size of capital whether to create greater COOPERATION or DIVISION OF LABOUR and whether or not there is a transformation of the LABOUR PROCESS through the further introduction of MACHINERY AND MACHINOFACTURE.

Between sectors of the economy, competition acts to form prices of production from market values (see PRICE OF PRODUCTION AND THE TRANSFORMATION PROBLEM). This relationship between value and price is based upon mobility of capital between the sectors and the tendency to establish an average or normal rate of profit. In this, a fully developed credit system is crucial for Marx, as it makes available the finance for mobility between sectors (as well as for accumulation within sectors).

At the most complex level there is a divergence of market price from price of production according to the most immediate factors affecting supply and demand, which are more or less temporary. These include, for example, divergences in the value of wages from the value of labour power as an effect of the price of consumption goods. More generally it can be seen that the relationship between value, price of production and market price holds a correspondence with the three forms of capital in the individual circuit, of productive, money and commodity capital respectively. The aggregate CIRCULATION of commodities includes expenditures as revenue (wages and profits for capitalist CONSUMPTION) and not simply expenditure as capital, and it is this which explains divergence of market prices from prices of production even though the structure and process of price of production formation determines market price formation.

The preceding analysis is formal since it is concerned primarily with the logical structure of competition in the accumulation of capital and process of price formation. But Marx also analyses the forms of competition on a historical basis, different mechanisms predominating at different stages of development of the MODE OF PRODUCTION. For the earliest stage of development of capitalism, accumulation is predominantly through concentration (see CENTRALIZATION AND CONCENTRATION OF CAPITAL) and the tendency for the rate of profit to be equalized does not operate. Commodities tend to exchange at their values and competition is based upon the greater or lesser restrictions in the markets for commodities and LABOUR POWER. At the higher level of development associated with accumulation through centralization, there is a historical transformation in price formation with the mobility of capital between sectors stimulated by the credit system. Marx here makes an implicit PERIODIZATION OF CAPITALISM, one which Lenin was to take up in his study of imperialism as the stage of MONOPOLY CAPITALISM.

In this work, and elsewhere, Lenin emphasizes that monopoly and competition are not mutually exclusive opposites but that the latter intensifies with the development of the former. This is despite the centralization of capital and the accompanying phenomena of cartel formation and interrelations between industrial and banking capital. Within modern Marxism, however, various writers have argued that monopoly and competition are mutually exclusive and that the former has increased at the expense of the latter. Writers such as Baran and Sweezy conclude that the imperative of capital accumulation is thereby eroded and capitalism suffers from a chronic tendency to stagnation. They see Marx's analysis as now inappropriate, and relevant only to the nineteenth-century period. In contrast it can be observed that Marx's theory of competition is at its most complex precisely for those conditions for which monopoly capitalism is established.

Reading

Baran, P. and Sweezy, P. 1964: *Monopoly Capitalism*.

Cowling, K. 1982: *Monopoly Capitalism*.

Fine, B. 1979: 'On Marx's Theory of Agricultural Rent'.

Rosdolsky, R. 1968 (1977): *The Making of Marx's 'Capital'*.

Weeks, J. 1982: *Capital and Exploitation*.

BEN FINE

Condition of the Working Class in England

Very few works as full of meaning and vitality as this have ever been written by so young an author. Engels was 24 when it was composed, late in 1844 and early in 1845 – he was always a very quick worker – from materials gathered during his first stay in England during 1842–4. He was attached to a Manchester mill in which his father held a partnership, but most of his energy must have been given to finding out all he could about the mill-workers and their lives, in the harsh grip of the Industrial Revolution. He studied all the statistical information available; his own explorations of Manchester and its environs make his impressions of scenes and human beings vivid for readers even after a century and a half. Engels was a keen student of literature, and had tried his hand at poetry and drama. In many ways he was a late-comer of the Romantic generation, and he expresses here his appreciation of 'Shelley, the genius, the prophet' and Byron's 'bitter satire upon our existing society'.

The book is an Inferno-like vision of the horrors of poverty, hunger, slum housing and chronic insecurity. It would be painfully depressing if it did not have a positive side as well. Engels looked on Steam, the giant of the new age, as a liberator as well as tyrant. The working class it was calling into existence, driven by the intolerable pressures of its life, would before long band together, as it was learning to do through strike actions, and overthrow its exploiters. With them the whole divisive class structure would collapse. This glowing confidence in the future had something akin to the old millenarian dreams, familiar to Engels from his religious upbringing, of a bad world ending in cataclysm, a new one dawning.

His early sojourn in Manchester and the book that came out of it can be seen as a prelude to all that followed in the great partnership between himself and Marx. This started in the summer of 1844 when Engels was in Paris on his way back to Germany. They joined forces next year in Brussels, and Engels took his friend on a visit to London and Manchester. Marx greatly admired his book, and echoes of it can be heard in their first two joint works, mainly written by Marx: *The Holy Family* (1845) and *German Ideology* (1845–6), the latter an attempt to work out an interpretation of history and see what future it was pointing to. In the following years the *Condition of the Working Class in England* may be said to have become an integral if buried part of the foundations of Marxist political philosophy.

It may have fixed there somewhat too firm a faith in the revolutionary destiny of the industrial working class. That class was indeed destined to play a great part in history, as Marx and Engels were among the first to see; but not the one they expected. Ironically its militant political movement in Britain, Chartism, was very close to its end, the failure of 1848, when Engels encountered it. And when he and Marx had to retreat to England after the failure of their German revolution in 1849, Engels had to return to the drudgery of business life in Manchester. He could scarcely now bring out an English edition of his book, with its fiery denunciation of the Manchester bourgeoisie. It lay unknown to Britain, not translated until 1886, and then in America.

V. G. KIERNAN

consumption Consumption of products of human labour (use-values) is the way in which human beings maintain and reproduce themselves both as individuals and as social individuals, i.e. both in the physical-mental sense (as human beings with a given personality) and in a concrete social-historical framework (as members of a given social formation, in a specific historical period). Under capitalism, i.e. generalized commodity production ('market economy'), consumption takes essentially the form of consumption of commodities, the two main exceptions being consumption of goods produced inside the household and consumption under subsistence farming. Consumption is subdivided into two large categories: *productive consumption*, which includes both consumption of consumer goods by producers, and consumption of means of production in the productive process; and *unproductive consumption*, which includes all consumption of goods which do not enter the reproduction process, do not contribute to the next cycle of production. Un-productive consumption comprises essentially consumption of consumer goods by non-productive classes (the ruling class, unproductive labour, etc.), and consumption of both consumer goods and investment goods by the non-productive sectors of the state (the military and the state administration sector).

Consumption has both a physiological and a historical dimension. These are tied to what Marx calls the 'system of human needs', which also fall into the same two categories. Basic physiological needs must be distinguished from historically determined needs, originating from new developments of the productive forces and a changed relationship of forces between social classes ('popularization' of consumer goods and services previously reserved to the ruling class; see VALUE OF LABOUR POWER). But with the growth of large-scale industry, generalized mechanization of labour, constant differentiation of commodities, and growing physiological and nervous wear and tear of labour power, consumer goods become more and more determined by technical innovations and changes in

the sphere of production. Capitalist consumption therefore depends more and more upon capitalist production. This involves both a broadening of the sphere of consumption and a potential deterioration of its quality. It implies in any case a growing manipulation of the consumer by capitalist firms, in the production, distribution and publicity spheres.

Under socialism, and even more so under communism, on the contrary, production would be increasingly determined by consumers. The consciously expressed needs of the consumers (and their democratically established priorities) would more and more determine the pattern of production. Production for need would substitute itself for production for profit, for maximizing income, or for production's sake, and the accumulation of more and more material goods (less and less useful at that) would cease to be a key goal of consumption once the basic needs were satisfied. Consumption would tend to become more humanly creative, i.e. creative of a universally developed human personality, and of richer mutual relations between human beings. (See also EQUALITY.)

Reading
Heller, Agnes 1976: *The Theory of Need in Marx.*
ERNEST MANDEL

contradiction Although the concept may be used as a metaphor for any kind of dissonance, strain or tension, it first assumes a distinctive meaning in the case of human (or more generally goal-oriented) action, where it specifies any situation which allows the satisfaction of one end only at the cost of another, i.e. a bind or constraint. An *internal contradiction* is then a double-bind or self-constraint, where a system, agent or structure S is blocked from performing with one system rule R because it is performing with another R'; or where a course of action pursued, T, generates a countervailing, inhibitory, undermining or otherwise opposed course of action, T'. Formal *logical contradiction* is a species of internal contradiction, whose consequence for the subject is axiological *indeterminacy*: 'A and −A' leaves the course of action (or belief) undetermined.

In the Marxist tradition *dialectical contradictions* have been characterized in contrast to both (α) exclusive or 'real' oppositions or conflicts (Kant's *Real-repugnanz*), in that their terms or poles presuppose each other, so that they constitute an *inclusive opposition*; and (β) formal logical oppositions, in that the relations involved are *meaning-* (or content-) *dependent*, not purely formal, so that the negation of A does not lead to its abstract cancelling, but to the generation of a new, higher, more inclusive content. Associated with the first contrast is the theme of the 'unity of opposites', the trademark of all Marxist *ontological* dialectics from Engels to Mao Tse-tung. Associated with the second are the themes of 'determinate negation', immanent critique and totalization, the trademark of Marxist *relational* dialectics from Lukács to Sartre. In both respects dialectical contradictions are held to be characteristically concrete.

In Marx's mature economic writings, the concept of contradiction is employed to designate *inter alia*: (a) logical inconsistencies or intra-discursive theoretical anomalies; (b) extra-discursive oppositions, e.g. supply and demand as involving forces or tendencies of (relatively) independent origins which interact in such a way that their effects tend to cancel each other out – in momentary or semi-permanent equilibria; (c) historical (or temporal) dialectical contradictions; and (d) structural (or systemic) dialectical contradictions.

Type (c) involves forces of non-independent origins operating so that a force F either tends to produce or is itself the product of conditions which simultaneously or subsequently produce a countervailing force F', tending to frustrate, annul, subvert or transform F. Examples of such contradictions are those between the relations and forces of production and between capital and the organized struggle of the working class. Such historical contradictions are grounded in the structural contradictions of CAPITALISM (d), which provide *ab initio* the formal conditions of their possibility. The most important of these are, for Marx, the contradictions between the concrete useful and abstract social aspects of labour and between the use-value and value of the COMMODITY – which is immediately manifest in the distinction between the relative and equivalent value forms, and externalized in the contradictions between the commodity and MONEY, and wage-labour and capital. All these contradictions are 'dialectical', both (α) in that

they constitute real inclusive oppositions, as their terms existentially presuppose each other, and (β) in that they are systematically or internally related to a mystifying form of appearance.

Dialectical contradictions of type (c) and (d) in Marx are both subject-specific and empirically grounded. Yet there is a long line of criticism in Marxist, as well as non-Marxist, thought (from Bernstein to Colletti) which holds that the notion of dialectical contradictions in reality is incompatible with (i) formal LOGIC, and hence coherent discourse and/or (ii) scientific practice, and hence MATERIALISM. This is not so. For inclusive oppositions, whether within being (cf. (α)') or between being and thought (cf (β)'), may be both consistently described and scientifically explained. It is only if contradictions are committed (as distinct from described) that there is any violation to the principle of non-contradiction; and provided thought is included within a stratified reality (not hypostatized) its fetishistic or otherwise categorically mystifying character involves no scientific absurdity. (See also KNOWLEDGE, THEORY OF.)

Reading

Bhaskar, Roy 1986: *Scientific Realism and Human Emancipation*.

Colletti, Lucio 1975b: 'Marxism and the Dialectic'.

Godelier, M. 1966 (1972): 'System, Structure and Contradiction in *Capital*'.

Lukács, G. 1923 (1971): *History and Class Consciousness*.

ROY BHASKAR

cooperation   Marx devotes a separate chapter of *Capital* I to the concept of cooperation. It follows the analysis of the production of absolute and relative SURPLUS VALUE. It is in turn followed by an examination of the mode of development of the capitalist LABOUR PROCESS through the stages of MANUFACTURE and MACHINERY AND MACHINOFACTURE. As such, it is, with the DIVISION OF LABOUR, an important link between the abstract concepts of absolute and relative surplus value and the more complex analysis of the specifically capitalist methods of production. Cooperation is simply defined in ch. 13: 'When numerous labourers work side by side, whether in one and the same process, or in different but connected processes, they are said to cooperate, or to work in cooperation.' This definition is notable for being independent of any one specific mode of production. Much the same is true of many of Marx's observations on the subject. For example: 'When the labourer cooperates sytematically with others, he strips off the fetters of his individuality, and develops the capabilities of his species.' More generally, those of Marx's observations which are independent of a specific mode of production are usually derived from a perspective focusing on the USE VALUE aspect of cooperation. He thereby argues that cooperation leads to the creation of the collective power of labour that exceeds the sum of the constituent parts. Nevertheless, as is clear from the quotations immediately above, even in its general aspect cooperation is seen in social and not reified terms. Moreover the general analysis is run together with the aspects specific to capitalism, co-operation as a (surplus) value relation between producers. Cooperation is well known under previous modes of production, but it is only under capitalism that it can be systematically exploited because of the availability of wage labourers who can be congregated in numbers. Moreover, COMPETITION makes that possibility a necessity since the collective power of labour must be utilized to produce at a SOCIALLY NECESSARY LABOUR time. Consequently, in the context of competition consideration of capitalist co-operation alone is sufficient to demonstrate the need for the individual and social ACCUMULATION of capital, even as the collective part of labour creates economy in the use of means of production.

Cooperation is also examined from the two aspects of use value and value for the characteristics of supervision. Cooperating labour requires an organizing influence in any circumstances, but for capitalist production this organizing role is inextricably entangled with the role of disciplining workers in the labour process for the extraction of surplus value. The greater productivity that results appears to derive from and therefore to be credited to the power of capital or the capitalist. This tends to conceal the role played by labour as the source of (surplus) value.

BEN FINE

cooperative association   There is no systematic treatment of cooperation in the sense of the cooperative movement or particular forms of cooperative production in Marx's and Engels's work, but there are more references to the subject, and more favourable ones, than is sometimes supposed. Lowit (1962) has collated them helpfully, and the principal references are mentioned below.

A few general points may be made. Cooperative associations, whether actually existing ones or as the cells of a future possible mode of production (the 'associated mode of production' of Capital III) are not considered, in Marx's work, in and for themselves but always in the general perspective of working-class emancipation. Secondly, 'utopian socialism' is not an epithet primarily directed at cooperatives or cooperation. The cooperative idea itself is not condemned, only deformations of it. Thus state-aided cooperatives in Prussia, and socialist advocacy of them by Lassalle, are attacked by Marx. Cooperative stores are regarded as surface scratches on the face of capitalism, unless they form part of productive associations within the forces and relations of production and 'the organized forces of society' (state power) get transferred through working-class activity, to the producers themselves. Cooperation, for Marx, is the negation of wage labour. In its positive form, 'associated labour plying its toil with a willing hand, a ready mind and a joyous heart', it could make 'hired labour' as archaic as capitalism had already made slave or serf labour (Marx, Inaugural Address, 1864). But within capitalism, forms of cooperative association were bound to bear the husks of the old system as well as the seeds of the new. Such contradiction was, however, a recommendation of cooperation rather than a reason for passing it by on the other side. The Inaugural Address sets out the main lines of argument on this topic clearly. The cooperative movement was already a 'Great Fact', representing a preliminary victory for the political economy of labour over that of property. It had already shown, and by deed rather than argument, that masters were not necessary for large-scale production. For this very reason it had acquired many false friends between 1848 and 1864, 'philanthropic middle-class spouters' anxious to use it for their own quack purposes. These had to be resisted, as did any tendency towards localism and self-sufficiency. Cooperation could never defeat monopoly unless it was developed to national dimensions. Only political power could enable it to escape from 'the narrow circles of the casual efforts of private workmen'.

Marx was impatient with those who could not see capitalism as riven with contradiction, not all of which was compatible with its continued existence. During the 1860s and 1870s he insisted upon the possibility and (partial) visibility of communism, in working-class practice and 'in the lap of capitalist production'. His views on cooperation, in the sense used here, were part of that insistence. Since they have not been emphasized much in the subsequent history of dominant forms of Marxism they are worth highlighting through quotation. 'The vulgus is unable to conceive the forms developed in the lap of capitalist production separate and free from their antithetical capitalist character' (*Capital* III, ch. 23). From a political point of view, Marx thought, this should have become evident through the associative forms of the Paris Communards. But:

It is a strange fact. In spite of all the tall talk and all the immense literature for the last 60 years, about the emancipation of labour, no sooner do the working men anywhere take the subject into their own hands with a will, than up rises at once all the apologetic phraseology of the mouthpieces of present society with its two poles of capital and wage slavery . . . as if capitalist society was still in its purest state of virgin innocence, with its antagonism still undeveloped, with its delusions still unexploded, with its prostitute realities not yet laid bare. (*Civil War in France*, sect. III)

From an industrial point of view the cooperative factories of the labourers themselves represented a similar working-class produced, future-present, internal-external, or *material* dialectic so characteristic of Marx's perception of capitalism. These factories

themselves represent within the old form the first sprouts of the new, although they naturally reproduce, and must reproduce, everywhere in their actual organization all the shortcomings of the prevailing system. But the antithesis between capital and labour is overcome with them, if at first only by way of making the associated labourers into their

own capitalist, i.e. by enabling them to use the means of production for the employment of their own labour. They show how a new mode of production naturally grows out of an old one, when the development of the material forces of production and of the corresponding forms of social production have reached a particular stage. Without the factory system arising out of the capitalist mode of production there could have been no cooperative factories. Nor could these have developed without the credit system arising out of the same mode of production. The credit system is not only the principal basis for the gradual transformation of capitalist private enterprise into capitalist stock companies, but equally offers the means for the gradual extension of cooperative enterprises on a more or less national scale. The capitalist stock companies, as much as the cooperative factories, should be considered as transitional forms from the capitalist mode of production to the associated one, with the only distinction that the antagonism is resolved negatively in the one and positively in the other. (*Capital* III, ch. 27)

(See also COUNCILS; SELF-MANAGEMENT).

Reading
Lowit, T. 1962: 'Marx et le mouvement coopératif'.
                                        STEPHEN YEO

corporation *See* joint-stock company.

councils During the lifetime of Marx and Engels only one movement foreshadowed the workers' Councils and Soviets of the twentieth century: the PARIS COMMUNE. Like the later movements, it arose quite spontaneously and represented an extremely democratic form of popular power, which Marx praised as marking a new stage in the revolutionary movement.

The first Soviet was formed in St Petersburg in October 1905. Although local in character and very short-lived it was ascribed an extremely important role in the 1905 Revolution by one of its leading participants, Trotsky: 'The Soviet organised the working masses, directed the political strikes and demonstrations, armed the workers, and protected the population against pogroms' (Trotsky, 1905). He argued that it was an 'authentic democracy' since it did not have an upper and lower chamber as most Western democracies do: it dispensed with a professional bureaucracy and the voters had the right to recall their deputies at any moment. It was based upon the working class in the factories, and the extent of its power was simply to be a workers' government 'in embryo'.

Although Soviets were to be much more prominent in the 1917 Revolution, neither Lenin nor Trotsky wrote a general theoretical treatise on them as a form of political organization. Lenin especially seems to have regarded the Soviets, much more broadly based than in 1905, as possible means to the end of seizing power and destroying the bourgeois state. But as they fell under the influence of the Mensheviks he withdrew the slogan 'All Power to the Soviets' and looked for other organizational means – such as the factory committees, more narrowly based on the employed working class – to achieve his end. During all these changes of tactics, he was concerned to emphasize the need for destroying the bourgeois state and replacing it with a new kind of state to govern the transition to socialism; and in this argument saw himself as merely restating the basic theories of Marxism. Thus *State and Revolution* (1917) largely consists in a reaffirmation of the writings of Marx and Engels. In September and October 1917, as the Soviets resumed their revolutionary character, Lenin defined them as being the new bearers of state power. In his most important article before the Revolution, 'Can the Bolsheviks Retain State Power?' (1917) he claimed that the Soviets were a new state apparatus which 'provides an armed force of workers and peasants; and this force is not divorced from the people, as was the old standing army, but is very closely bound up with the people . . .'. He emphasized that it was far more democratic than any previous state apparatus, in that it could prevent the growth of a bureaucracy of professional politicians, and could vest in the people's elected representatives both legislative and executive functions. As against anarchists and syndicalists, he argued strongly for the centralization of Soviet power.

Trotsky shared Lenin's ideas on the Soviets throughout the 1917 Revolution, but he conceptualized the situation which existed during this period as one of *dual power*. Either the

bourgeoisie would dominate the old state apparatus, making only minor alterations for its own purposes, in which case the Soviets would eventually be destroyed; or the Soviets would form the foundation of a new state, which would destroy both the old governmental apparatus, and the rule of those classes which it served. After the seizure of power, Lenin constantly stressed the irreconcilability of Soviet power with bourgeois democracy, regarding the former as the direct expression of the power of the working class. Accordingly, after winning a majority (with the Left Social-Revolutionaries) in the Soviets, he dissolved the Constituent Assembly, justifying this step on the ground that the Soviets represented a higher form of democracy than that of bourgeois parliaments. In 'The Immediate Tasks of the Soviet Government' (1918) he justified another measure distinguishing the two types of state: 'The socialist character of Soviet, i.e. *proletarian*, democracy, as concretely applied today, lies first in the fact that the electors are the working and exploited people; the bourgeoisie is excluded.'

Lenin and Trotsky represented the extreme left-wing position on workers' councils, but in the wave of revolutions which swept over Central and Western Europe after 1918, in which workers' councils played a prominent part, their views did not prevail. During this period, there were two other political positions. The right wing, represented by such figures as Ebert and Cohen in Germany, who in any case have a rather tenuous connection with Marxism, regarded the councils simply as caretaker organizations to be abolished as soon as the institutions of parliamentary democracy could be established. The most representative Marxist position was occupied by figures of the 'Centre', such as Kautsky and Adler (1919), who attempted to reconcile both extremes. In *The Dictatorship of the Proletariat* (1918), Kautsky conceded that the Soviet organization was one of the most important phenomena of our time, but he violently objected to the Bolsheviks' dissolution of the Constituent Assembly, and to their attempts to make an organ of government of the Soviets, which hitherto had been the fighting organization of a class. In particular, he severely criticized the exclusion of members of the bourgeoisie from the Soviets, on the grounds that in Germany it would mean the disenfranchisement of large numbers of people; the criteria for exclusion were very unclear; and excluding opponents would prevent the formation of a political class consciousness in the proletariat, since it would be deprived of any experience of political struggle. Ultimately, the Soviet government as established by the Bolsheviks was bound to become the dictatorship of a party within the proletariat.

While all the writers discussed so far examined the Soviet form in relation to immediate political questions, Gramsci (1977) undertook a more theoretical analysis, sometimes verging on utopianism, of the nature of the councils; and speculated on their relationships with other proletarian organizations. The Factory Council (which Gramsci equated with the Soviet) is not only an organization for fighting the class struggle, but 'the model of the proletarian State. All the problems inherent in the organization of the proletarian State are inherent in the organization of the Council'. To link these institutions, and order them into a highly centralized hierarchy of powers will be to create a genuine workers' democracy, prepared to replace the bourgeoisie in all its essential functions of administration and control. No other type of proletarian organization is suited to this task. The trade unions are a form of capitalist society, not a potential successor to that society; they are an integral part of capitalism, and have an essentially competitive, not communist, character, because they organize workers not as producers, but as wage-earners, selling the commodity labour power.

Workers' Councils (Soviets, *Arbeiterräte*), which were politically oriented, must be distinguished from Factory Councils (Works' Councils, *Betriebsräte*) which were concerned with the economic administration of individual factories. Factory Councils were primarily regarded as an instrument for achieving 'industrial democracy'. This was a concept advanced by a rather diverse group of thinkers, including non-Marxists such as Sydney Webb and G. D. H. Cole, and the Marxists Korsch and Bauer. The last expressed the idea as follows (1919):

By the establishment of factory committees, we arrive in the factory at a constitutional monarchy: legal sovereignty is shared between the boss, who governs the enterprise like a hereditary monarch, and the factory committee, which plays the role of Parliament. Beyond this stage, one goes on to the republican constitution of industry. The boss disappears; the economic and technical direction of industry is entrusted to an administrative council.

The difficulties inherent in this rather utopian view of the political potential of factory councils were exposed by Renner (1921). He pointed out that economic democracy based on factory councils could only represent limited and sectional identical interests, and that conflicts of interest *between* different classes or groups could only be settled by political means – by political democracy, rather than by the dictatorship of the councils, in his argument. Thus he saw economic democracy, of which factory councils represented only one form, and which had already been successful in England under other forms (cooperatives, trade unions, etc), as being the complement to the political democracy of parliaments.

After the failure of the revolutions in Central Europe, and the decline in the importance of the Soviets in the USSR, there was very little theoretical writing on the significance of the councils, with the exception of Pannekoek's International Communists of Holland and Mattick's Council Communist Group, with which Korsch was associated. Both groups attributed to the councils a much more crucial role in political revolutions than any previous theorists had done, and saw the power of the Soviets as an indicator of the success of a revolution. Thus they criticized the USSR for not maintaining the power of the councils. They tended to identify councils as the specific form of working-class power, and as such a spontaneous form of working-class organization which should not be subordinated to the dictates of the revolutionary party.

Reading

Adler, Max 1919: *Demokratie und Rätesystem.*

Anweiler, Oskar 1958 (1974): *The Soviets: The Russian Workers, Peasants and Soldiers Councils, 1905–1921.*

Bauer, Otto 1919: *Der Weg zum Sozialismus.*

Briciance, Serge 1978: *Pannekoek and the Workers' Councils.*

Gramsci, Antonio 1977: *Selections from Political Writings 1910–1920.*

Kautsky, Karl 1918 (1919): *The Dictatorship of the Proletariat*.

Korsch, Karl 1922: *Arbeitsrecht für Betriebsräte*.

— 1969: *Schriften zur Sozialisierung*.

Lenin, V. 1. 1917b (1964): 'Can the Bolsheviks Retain State Power?'

— 1918a (1965): 'The Immediate Tasks of the Soviet Government'.

Renner, Karl 1921 (1978): 'Democracy and the Council System'. In Bottomore and Goode, eds. *Austro-Marxism*.

PATRICK GOODE

credit and fictitious capital In its simplest form the sale of a commodity consists of the EX-CHANGE of the commodity for MONEY. The seller of the commodity may, however, accept in place of money itself the promise of the purchaser to pay in the future. In this case the seller extends *credit* to the purchaser, and they enter a new relation as *creditor* and *debtor* until the promise to pay is fulfilled. The debtor may settle the debt to the creditor by transferring money, in which case money functions as means of payment. But in well-developed credit systems debtors often pay by handing over other agents' promises to pay the creditor. In many cases these promises cancel each other out (for example, if A owes B $1,000, B owes C $1,000, and C owes A $1,000, the debts can simply be offset against each other) without the intervention of money. In major commercial centres where credit transactions are concentrated, money mediates only a small fraction of the values transferred through mutually offsetting credits.

Thus credit substitutes for money in the CIR-CULATION of commodities and the transfer of VALUE. Credit reduces the costs of holding valuable commodity money and accelerates the turnover of capital. Banks centralize credit for capitalist firms. Instead of individual capitalists extending credit to one another and incurring the costs of collection and the risks of loss inherent in credit transactions, they may all extend credit to a bank in the form of deposits, and draw credit as they require it from the bank in the form of loans. Alternatively the bank may achieve the same end by endorsing or 'accepting' individual capitalists' promises to pay, undertaking to make good with the bank's funds if the original issuer defaults. This process substitutes the bank's credit for the original debtor's. Finally, the bank may accept a private promise to pay and issue its own promises (bank notes) in exchange. The bank receives a profit on these transactions by leading at an interest rate higher than the interest rate it pays on its own borrowing, or, in the case of acceptances, by 'discounting' the private promises to pay, buying them at less than their face value and collecting them at their face value.

The growth of credit creates a potentially unstable chain of financial interdependencies, since every agent counts on being paid by its debtors in order to pay its creditors. A substantial failure to pay arising, for instance, from a decline in sales of commodities in a crisis of realization, can set off a credit crisis or panic, in which every agent seeks to turn credit into money and demands payment in money (see ECONOMIC CRISES). Since this is not possible, the pressure first raises interest rates sharply, and then results in bankruptcies and takeovers of the weakest capitals.

Marx distinguishes between credit, which is extended to facilitate purchase and sale of commodities, and loans of capital, in which no commodity purchase is involved. The lender of capital entrusts money to a capitalist borrower with the aim of participating, in the form of interest, in the SURPLUS VALUE which will arise from the use of the money to finance capitalist production (see FINANCIAL CAPITAL AND IN-TEREST). In fact, credit and loan transactions have a similar form and are closely intertwined in highly developed capitalist financial systems, the same institutions, such as banks, often acting as intermediaries in both kinds of transaction.

Loans of capital in specific forms may also generate fictitious capital. In the corporate or joint-stock form of organization of a capitalist firm, the ownership of the firm and its assets is vested in transferable shares, each of which has the right to a fraction of the residual profit of enterprise of the firm (see FORMS OF CAPITAL AND REVENUES). The original owners of these shares invest actual money capital in the firm. If the shares are sold by the original owners, the money paid for them does not enter the firm's circuit of capital, but is simply revenue for the seller. The firm continues to circulate the original capital, augmented by whatever part of the surplus value generated by it has been accumulated by the firm. In this situation the ownership shares of the firm represent a claim on a certain flow of income arising from the residual profit of enterprise. Holders of money can either lend their money and receive a flow of interest on it, or buy shares and receive a flow of dividends. The price of shares will be established to make them attractive as investments, in competition with loans, given the higher risk attached to the flow of residual profit relative to the flow of interest. But this price of shares may exceed the value of the capital actually invested in the firm's operations. Marx calls this excess *fictitious capital*, since it is part of the price of shares which does not correspond to the capital value actually participating in the firm's production. For example, suppose that a firm which has no debt and no taxes to pay, has $100 million in capital and realizes the average rate of profit of 20 per cent per year by making a profit of $20 million each year. Suppose there are 1 million shares outstanding, each of which has a claim to $20 per year in profit. If the rate of interest on loans is 5 per cent per year, and the riskiness of the dividend flow leads investors to require a 10 per cent per year return on shares, each share will be priced at $200, and the million shares as $200 million. The $100 million by which the share price exceeds the $100 million in actual capital Marx calls the fictitious capital.

In general, fictitious capital can arise whenever a stream of revenue is 'capitalized' in this way by financial markets. The state debt, for instance, corresponds to no capital investment, and is purely a claim to a certain fixed part of the tax revenues. Still, the financial markets treat state debt as though it were a productive investment and establish a capital value for it in relation to the interest rate on loans. (See also FINANCE CAPITAL.)

Reading

Hilferding, Rudolf 1910 (*1981*): *Finance Capital*, pt. II.

DUNCAN FOLEY

crime   Several themes appear in Marxist writings on crime. First, crime is analysed as the product of class society. In *The Condition of the Working Class*, Engels argued that the degrada-tion of English workers brought about by the extension of factory production deprived them of volition and led inexorably to crime. Poverty provided the motivation, and the deterioration of family life interfered with the proper moral education of children. Yet Engels noted that crime is an individual response to oppression, ineffective and easily crushed. For this reason, workers soon turned to collective forms of class struggle. Yet the class hatred nurtured by these collective responses continued to give rise to some forms of individualistic crime.

In other writings ('Outlines of a Critique of Political Economy', 'Speech at Elberfeld', *Anti-Dühring*), Engels attributed crime to the competitiveness of bourgeois society, which gave rise not only to the crimes committed by impoverished workers, but also to fraud and other deceptive business practices. Marx, citing criminal statistics from France and Philadelphia, argued that crime was a product less of a country's particular political institutions than of 'the fundamental conditions of bourgeois society in general' ('Capital Punishment').

It followed from this view of crime causation that repressive police measures could not eliminate crime, only contain it. The eradication of crime necessitated radically transformed social conditions. The advance of civilization had already reduced the level of violent crime (but was increasing property crime); a communist society, by supplying individuals' needs, eliminating inequality, and ending the contradiction between individual and society, would 'put the axe to the root of crime' (Engels, 'Speech at Elberfeld'). Marx later noted that the ascendance of the working class in the Paris Commune had virtually ended crime (*The Civil War in France*).

Willem A. Bonger, a Dutch social democrat (one of many late nineteenth- and early twentieth-century criminologists influenced simultaneously by Marxist thought and by non-Marxist positivism), elaborated on the connection between capitalism and crime by arguing that the competitiveness of capitalism give rise to egoism – the pursuit of individual self-interest to the detriment of others. Although socially harmful, egoistic behaviour is found among all classes; ruling-class political strength gives its particular types of exploitative behaviour at least partial immunity from being treated as criminal. For this reason, the working class is over-represented in crime statistics. Crime, he thought, would disappear only when socialism abolished the social sources of egoism. More recent Marxist analyses of crime have attempted to understand criminality among subordinate classes as an adaptation to, or resistance to, class domination; and the criminality of the ruling class as an instrument of class domination. As class relations in a given social formation change, so do patterns of crime (Taylor et al. 1973, 1975; Hay et al. 1975; Thompson 1975; Pearce 1976; Greenberg 1981, pt. II).

A second theme in this literature has been the critique of criminal justice. One dimension of this critique has concerned the failure of law enforcement in capitalist societies to fulfil its own stated ideals of fair and even-handed enforcement. In articles published in *Vorwärts* in 1844, Engels noted that English criminal procedure (e.g. property qualification for jury service) operated to the advantage of the wealthy classes. Invidious discrimination in law enforcement has been given continuing attention in American radical criminology. Another dimension has concerned the ideological aspects of criminal justice. Marx and Engels began this critique in *The Holy Family*, and Marx took it up again in 'Population, Crime and Pauperism' where he criticized philosophical justifications of punishment for their abstraction, their failure to situate criminals in the concrete social circumstances that gave rise to their crimes. Recent writings have advanced the critique of ideology through analyses of criminological explanations of crime causation, crime control policy, and the depiction of crime in the mass media (Taylor et al. 1973, 1975; Pearce 1976; Hall et al. 1978; Clarke 1978).

At another level the critique of criminal justice has taken the form of a political economy of crime control. Rusche and Kirchheimer (1939) explained historical changes in punishment practices from the Middle Ages to the twentieth century in terms of labour control. During times of labour scarcity, penal institutions (the prison, the workhouse, the galleys) could be used to provide employers or the state with a steady supply of coerced labour at low cost, while during periods of labour surplus, punishment could be used to control a potentially explosive surplus population. Though it has been criti-

cized as economistic (see ECONOMISM) this analysis has been extended and refined in contemporary accounts of the origins and subsequent transformation of the juvenile court, the prison and the police, and in the way short-run changes in punishment policy are related to the business cycle. Along somewhat different lines Quinney (1977) has suggested that crime contributes to the fiscal crisis of the state. To maintain its legitimacy the state must increase its expenditure on crime control in response to the increases of crime engendered by capitalism. As it does this, its ability to ensure the continued accumulation of capital is threatened. Thus crime is implicated in the contradictions of capitalism. A third theme in Marxist writings on crime has been the analysis and critique of criminal law, but these writings will not be reviewed here.

Some of Marx's own comments on crime concern matters unrelated to these three themes. In an ironic passage in *Theories of Surplus Value* (vol. I, Appendix 'Digression on unproductive labour') Marx deals with the social consequences of crime. Commenting on the proposition that all remunerative occupations are useful, he noted that by this criterion crime is also useful. It gives rise to the police, the court, the hangman, even the professor who lectures on criminal law. Crime, Marx went on, alleviates the monotony of bourgeois existence and provides the plots for great literature. It removes unemployed labourers from the job market and employs others in law enforcement, thereby preventing competition from reducing wages too far. In stimulating preventative efforts, crime advances technology. Here Marx anticipates functionalist analyses of the complex interconnections between the deviant and the normal in social life. Although Marx and Engels usually took official figures for arrests and trials as valid indicators of crime, in 'Population, Crime and Pauperism' Marx pointed out that these statistics reflect at least in part the somewhat arbitrary ways offences are labelled. An over-readiness to resort to the criminal law, he suggested, may create crimes as well as punish them. This passage foreshadows the work of contemporary sociological analyses of the labelling of deviant behaviour.

Reading

Bonger, Willem A. 1905 (1916): *Criminality and Economic Conditions*.

Cain, Maureen and Hunt, Alan, eds. 1979: *Marx and Engels on Law.*

Greenberg, David F., ed. 1981: *Crime and Capitalism: Readings in Marxist Criminology.*

Phillips, Paul 1981: *Marx and Engels on Law and Laws.*

Quinney, Richard 1977: *Class, State and Crime.*

Taylor, Ian, Walton, Paul, and Young, Jock 1973: *The New Criminology: For a Social Theory of Deviance.*

— 1975: *Critical Criminology.*

Thompson, E. P. 1975: *Whigs and Hunters: The Origin of the Black Act.*

DAVID GREENBERG

crisis in capitalist society   Traditionally Marxists have conceived a crisis as the breakdown of the operating principles of society. In capitalist society such a breakdown is held to be generated by the accumulation process determined by the tendency of the rate of profit to fall (see ECONOMIC CRISES). But a distinction must be drawn between, on the one hand, a partial crisis or collapse and, on the other, a crisis which leads to the transformation of a society or social formation. The former refers to such phenomena as the political-business cycle which involves seemingly endless booms followed by sharp downturns in economic activity and which is an endemic feature of capitalism. The latter refers to the undermining of the core or organizational principle of a society; that is, to the erosion or destruction of those societal relations which determine the scope of, and limits to, change for (among other things) economic and political activity.

Marx identified the organizational principle of capitalist society as the relationship of wage labour and capital; and he formulated the fundamental contradiction of this type of society as that between social production and private appropriation, that is social production for the enhancement of particular interests. Assuming that Marx was right about this, the following questions arise: have events in the last hundred years altered the way in which the fundamental contradiction of capitalism affects society's dynamics? Has the logic of crisis changed from the path of crisis-ridden growth and unstable accumulation to something fundamentally different? If so, what are the consequences for patterns of social struggle?

Marx accurately predicted a general tendency in all capitalist societies towards capital intensive industries and increased concentration of capital. Later Marxists have documented how firms and industries have become increasingly interdependent (Gurland 1941, Neumann 1944; Baran and Sweezy 1966). While it is useful to analyse present-day capitalism in terms of a number of sectors (the competitive and oligopolistic private sectors, the residual labour sector and the state sector) it is striking how the fortunes of many enterprises and industries are interrelated. The network of interdependencies ensures, at best, a delicate economic equilibrium. Any disturbance or disruption of economic life can potentially ramify throughout the system. A bankruptcy of a large firm or bank, for example, has implications for numerous apparently sound enterprises, whole communities, and hence for political stability. Accordingly, if the economic and political order of present-day societies is to be sustained, extensive state intervention is required. Viewed in this light the twentieth-century burgeoning of state activity, the expansion of 'interventionist machinery', can be seen as inevitable. The extensive effects of changes within the system (high rates of unemployment and inflation at the troughs and peaks of the political-business cycle) and/or the impact of external factors (shortages of raw materials as a result of international political events, for instance) have had to be carefully managed.

The attempt to regulate economic activity and sustain growth, an attempt which is associated closely with Keynes and the idea of fiscal and monetary management (and which was a marked feature of political life from the 1950s to the early 1970s), deepened the state's involvement in more and more areas (see STATE MONOPOLY CAPITALISM). This involvement itself generated difficulties which suggest that even if particular states were successful in minimizing economic fluctuations, this was only achieved by staving off problems and potential crises (Habermas 1973). In order to avoid economic crisis and political upheaval, governments and states had to shoulder an increasing share of the costs of production. In addition, in order to fulfil their increasingly diversified roles, they had to expand their bureaucratic structures, thus increasing their own internal complexity. This growing complexity in turn entailed an increased need for cooperation and, more importantly, required an expanding state budget. The state must finance itself through taxation and loans from capital markets, but it could not do this in a way which would interfere with the accumulation process and jeopardize economic growth. These constraints helped to create a situation of almost permanent inflation and crisis in public finances (O'Connor 1973). If the state cannot develop adequate policy strategies within the systematic constraints it encounters, the result is likely to be a pattern of continuous change and breakdown in policy and planning (Best and Connolly 1976). The problems are so deeply structured that it seems very unlikely indeed that any government can reverse these developments for anything other than the shortests of periods. Attempts to 'roll back the state' in the 1980s and early 1990s have only achieved limited success (see Held 1989).

The political consequences of this situation have been interpreted in different ways. If economic problems and the ensuing struggles between nation states do not lead to war, a deepening crisis of legitimacy, Habermas (1973) and Offe (1972) have argued, will face Western class democracies. The state is enmeshed in contradictions: intervention in the economy is unavoidable yet the exercise of political control over the economy risks challenging the traditional basis of the legitimacy of the whole social order – the belief that collective goals can properly be realized only by private individuals acting in competitive isolation and pursuing their aims with minimal state interference. The state's very intervention in the economy and other spheres draws attention to issues of choice, planning and control. The 'hand of the state' is more visible and intelligible than 'the invisible hand' of the market. More and more areas of life are seen by the general population as politicized, that is as falling within its (via the government's) potential control. This development, in turn, stimulates ever greater demands on the state; for example, for participation and consultation over decisions. If these demands cannot be met within available alternatives the state may face a 'legitimation crisis'. Struggles over, among other things, income, control over the work place, the nature and quality of state goods and services, might spill beyond the

boundaries of existing institutions of economic management and political control. Under these circumstances the fundamental transformation of the system cannot be ruled out; it is unlikely to result from one event, such as an insurrectional overthrow of state power, but more likely to be marked by a process of continuous erosion of the existing order's capacity to be reproduced and the progressive emergence of alternative institutions.

Those who have sketched this scenario have tended to underestimate and play down the social forces which fragment, atomize and hence privatize people's experiences of the social world. Factors such as differentiated wage structures, inflation, crisis in government finances and uneven economic development, which disperse the effects of economic crisis on to 'groups' such as consumers, the elderly, the sick, schoolchildren, are all part of a complex series of developments which combine to make the fronts of class opposition repeatedly fragmented and less comprehensible (Held 1982, 1989). A striking feature of these tendencies has been the emergence in many Western societies of what have been called 'corporatist arrangements'. The state, in its bid to sustain the continuity of the existing order, often favours selectively those groups whose acquiescence and support are crucial: oligopoly capital and organized labour. Representatives of these 'strategic groups' (trade union or business confederations) then step in alongside the state's representatives to resolve threats to political stability through a highly informal, extra-parliamentary negotiation process, in exchange for the enhancement of their corporate interests (Schmitter 1977; Panitch 1977; Offe 1980). Thus a 'class compromise' is effected among the powerful but at the expense of vulnerable groups, for example the elderly, the sick, non-unionized, non-white, and vulnerable regions, such as those areas with 'declining' industries no longer central to the economy (Held and Krieger 1982). Thus crucial fronts of social struggle can be repeatedly fragmented. Under these circumstances political outcomes remain uncertain.

But there are trends which enhance the possibility of a severe crisis. The favouritism towards dominant groups expressed by corporatist strategies and/or 'special' bargains erodes the electoral/parliamentary support of the more vulnerable groups, which may be required for the survival of a regime. More fundamentally, corporatist arrangements may erode the mass acceptability of institutions which have traditionally channelled conflict; for example party systems and conventions of collective bargaining. Thus new arrangements may backfire, encouraging the formation of movements opposing the status quo, based on those excluded from key decision-making processes, such as shop floor workers and shop stewards, those concerned with ecological issues, and the women's movement activists (Offe 1980).

While there is widespread scepticism about conventional politics, there is also, however, considerable uncertainty about alternatives to the status quo: Cold War attitudes and, of course, the rise and demise of Stalinism have discredited socialist ideas in the eyes of many. There is considerable uncertainty about what kind of institutions there might be and also about what general political *directions* should be taken. Thus there is reason to believe that the oft-expressed scepticism and remoteness many people feel in relation to dominant political institutions might be the basis of further political dissatisfaction in the future. But as possibilities for antagonistic stances against the state are realized, so too are the germs of a variety of other kinds of political movement, e.g., movements of the New Right. Anxiety about directionless change can fuel a call for the re-establishment of tradition and authority. This is the foundation for the appeal by the 'new' conservatives – or the New Right – to the people, to the nation, to many of those who feel so acutely unrepresented.

It is important to stress that trends such as these, in all their complexity and ambiguity, cannot be interpreted independently of international conditions and pressures. The capitalist world was created in dependence on an international market and is ever more dependent on international trade. The multiplicity of economic interconnections between nation states which are beyond the control of any one such state (Wallerstein 1974), disproportional economic development and uneven economic development generally within and between advanced industrial societies and Third World countries, enhance the likelihood of intensive struggles over who is at the centre and on the periphery of the economic order, and over who controls what resources. What cannot be ignored is the highly contingent, inherently dangerous nature of the international system of nation states, which has its origins before capitalist development but has been profoundly influenced by it (Poggi 1978).

In order to understand crisis tendencies today, therefore, a differentiated analysis of international conditions which form the constraints on, and the context of, the politics of modern societies is necessary. It is precisely the intersection of processes and events in national arenas – crisis of particular state forms, emergence of new social and political movements, conflicts in the relation between regimes, parties and economic institutions – with international developments, which have been the crucial determinants of transformative crises that affect the organizational principle of society (Skocpol 1979). But it is hard to see how such an account can take the form prescribed by classical Marxism with its emphasis on, for instance, history as the progressive augmentation of the forces of production or history as the progressive evolution of societies through class struggle (Giddens 1985). Developments within and between societies seem to have burst the boundaries of this conceptual scheme. The theoretical tools of Marxism are inadequate as a basis for a theory of crisis today.

Reading

Best, Michael and Connolly, William 1976: *The Politicized Economy.*

Giddens, Anthony 1985: *The Nation-State and Violence.*

Gurland, A. R. L. 1941: 'Technological Trends and Economic Structure under National Socialism'.

Habermas, Jürgen 1973 (1976): *Legitimation Crisis.*

Held, David 1982: 'Crisis Tendencies, Legitimation and the State'. In John Thompson and David Held eds., *Habermas: Critical Debates.*

— 1989: *Political Theory and the Modern State.*

— and Krieger, Joel 1982: 'Theories of the State: Some Competing Claims'. In Stephen Bernstein *et al.* eds. *The State in Capitalist Europe.*

O'Connor, James 1973: *The Fiscal Crisis of the State.*

Offe, Claus 1972: *Strukturprobleme des kapitalistischen Staates.*

— 1980: 'The Separation of Form and Content in Liberal Democratic Politics'.

Panitch, 1977: 'The Development of Corporatism in Liberal Democracies'.

Poggi, Gianfranco 1978: *The Development of the Modern State*.

Schmitter, P. C. 1977: 'Modes of Interest Intermediation and Models of Societal Change in Western Europe'.

Skocpol, Theda 1979: *States and Social Revolutions*.

Wallerstein, Immanuel 1974: *The Modern World System*.

DAVID HELD

crisis in socialist society   The idea of crisis in a socialist society has formed, until recently, no part of Marxist thought. On the contrary, socialism was conceived as a definitive resolution of the contradictions and crises of capitalism which Marxist theory was primarily concerned to analyse. Marx and Engels themselves refused to speculate about the economic and social arrangements of the future society, which they saw as developing on its own foundations, but they clearly assumed that this would be a harmonious development, no longer riven by class conflicts, in which the 'associated producers' would act collectively (and somehow spontaneously) to promote the common good. Some Marxists of the following generation, to be sure, recognized that the construction of a socialist economy and society, far from being a simple matter, would present a variety of problems. Kautsky (1902), in his text on 'the day after the revolution', examined some of these, while Otto Bauer (1919) argued that the process of socialist construction, after the working class had gained political power, would necessarily be slow and difficult, since 'it must not only achieve a more equitable distribution of goods, but also improve production; it should not destroy the capitalist system of production without establishing at the same time a socialist organization which can produce goods at least as effectively.' In general, however, Marxists were ill-prepared for the task of developing a new economy, as Neurath (1920) observed with reference to the Commission on the Socialization of Industry established in Germany in 1918: 'The technique of a socialist economy had been badly neglected. Instead, only criticism of the capitalist society was offered'; in consequence 'long-winded, sterile debates took place, showing disagreements of all sorts.'

But it was in Russia after 1917 that the problem became most acute, compounded by industrial backwardness and the havoc wrought by war, civil war and foreign intervention. In the 1920s, vigorous debates took place, involving particularly Lenin, Bukharin and Preobrazhensky; debates which became increasingly focused, however, on rapid industrialization (Erlich 1960) and on what was called 'building socialism in one country', until they were ended by Stalin's dictatorship, already foreshadowed in the total dominance of the Communist Party, and his policies of forced INDUSTRIALIZATION and COLLECTIVIZATION. After 1945 this totalitarian system (see TOTALITARIANISM) was imposed on the countries of Eastern Europe (although Yugoslavia began to escape from it in 1950), but after Stalin's death in 1953 its instability gradually increased, as was shown by a succession of revolts in the 1950s and 1960s. The signs of crisis became still more marked from the beginning of the 1970s and then multiplied rapidly in the following decade (in China as well as in Europe), culminating in the upheavals at the end of 1989 which initiated a radical restructuring of society.

The crisis can reasonably be described as 'general' in the sense that it profoundly affected the whole social framework – economic, political, social and cultural. In the economic sphere, the problems of highly centralized planning in more advanced, diversified and changing economies steadily increased (see ECONOMIC PLANNING), and the idea of an alternative 'socialist market economy' (see MARKET SOCIALISM) was widely debated and vigorously advocated in diverse forms. In the Soviet Union this combination of planning with markets now provides the context in which economic reforms are being undertaken, but in some East European countries there has been a more sweeping rejection of any kind of economic planning and social ownership by the new regimes, and powerful movements to re-establish a capitalist free-market economy have emerged.

The political crisis was just as severe, and more immediately important, in the movements of revolt, whose main demands were for the restoration of democracy, free elections, an end to the communist monopoly of power and, in particular, the elimination of the ubiquitous secret police forces. The political opposition also demanded a liberation of cultural life from censorship, an end to the imposition of dogmatic Marxism as an official doctrine and the establishment of freedom of the press and other media; and many of its most prominent leaders were writers, artists, teachers and students. The main impetus for the opposition movements came from these popular demands for democracy and basic rights of citizenship, including the right to form associations, independent of state control, throughout civil society. In Eastern Europe generally the movements were directed against the whole existing political system, and only in the Soviet Union from the mid-1980s (and in a different context in Yugoslavia) were the changes initiated within the communist regime itself. But in these two countries, by the end of the decade, the problems of the regimes had increased as freedom of political debate was extended, new parties were formed and free elections began to take place; and the difficulties were exacerbated by the rapid renaissance of long-suppressed national feeling and nationalist movements (which also affected Eastern Europe as a whole). Opposition movements also developed in China during the 1980s, and although they were violently suppressed in the summer of 1989 it is evident that widespread discontent with economic conditions and the absence of democracy persists, and the existing regime remains unstable.

The crisis in the countries of 'real socialism', which was analysed particularly in a series of monographs on 'Crises in Soviet-type Systems' (Mlynar 1982–9), and the dramatic changes initiated during the winter of 1989–90, pose major problems for Marxist thought. In the first place, the theory of history needs to be reconsidered. If some of the East European countries now restore capitalism, then that historical scheme which predicted a necessary, or at any rate probable, transition from capitalism to socialism has to grapple with the unexpected phenomenon of a transition from socialism to capitalism. It is true that the question can be resolved by arguing, as many Marxist critics of the Soviet-type societies – among them Kautsky, the Austro-Marxists, Trotsky, the thinkers of the Yugoslav *Praxis* group and of the Frankfurt School – have done, that these societies were not socialist but 'state capitalist' or 'degenerated workers' states' or 'totalitarian state econo-

mies', in which a new ruling class or elite had emerged or was on the way to establishing itself.

Yet in that case another, perhaps the most important, historical problem arises; namely, to explain how it was that revolutions inspired by Marxism produced as their consequence oppressive and eventually crisis-ridden societies. The development of this kind of analysis and explanation will involve, without any doubt, a radical reorientation of Marxist thought. Classical Marxism was concerned above all with the analysis of capitalism and its development, but in the future Marxists will be obliged to give at least equal attention to the historical experience of socialism and socialist movements. These new studies will entail a more fundamental reconsideration of such Marxist concepts as CLASS, HUMAN NATURE and REVOLUTION, as well as quite new conceptions of political power and economic structure.

At the centre of the crisis in socialist societies have been the contradictions between the idea that the 'associated producers' determine the economic and social conditions of their lives and 'make their own history', and the reality of political dictatorship, domination of the economy by a privileged social group, and mounting difficulties in planning and regulating the economy through a centralized apparatus. It is these 'contradictions of socialism' which now require the most thorough and serious analysis.

Reading

Bottomore, Tom 1990: *The Socialist Economy: Theory and Practice.*

Golubović, Z. and Stojanović, S. 1986: *The Crisis of the Yugoslav System (Crises in Soviet-type Systems*, no. 14).

Mlynar, Zdenek (director) 1982–9: *Crises in Soviet-type Systems*, nos 1–16.

Neurath, Otto 1920 (*1973*): 'Lecture to Sociological Society of Vienna'. In Marie Neurath and Robert S. Cohen, eds. *Empiricism and Sociology.*

Nuti, Domenico Mario 1988: 'Perestroika: Transition from Central Planning to Market Socialism'.

TOM BOTTOMORE

critical theory   *See* Frankfurt School.

critics of Marxism   A systematic critical examination of Marxist theory began in the last decade of the nineteenth century. In economics, the earliest critical comments, to which Marx himself replied (1879–80), seem to be those in the second edition of Adolph Wagner's *Allgemeine oder theoretische Volkswirthschaftslehre, Erster Teil, Grundlegung* (1879). More substantial critical discussions developed after the publication of the third volume of *Capital* in 1894; notably Werner Sombart's long review essay 'Zur Kritik des ökonomischen Systems von Karl Marx' (1894) and Böhm-Bawerk's *Karl Marx and the Close of his System* (1896). Critics of Marx's theory of the capitalist economy take its logical coherence as their criterion. Böhm-Bawerk typifies those who attempt to demolish the theory in favour of neo-classical economics, and for generations Marxists such as Hilferding had to confront his critique. Steedman (1977) typifies those whose critique, although trenchant, is offered in an attempt to strengthen Marxism; he applies the framework formulated by Sraffa (as a critique of neo-classical economics) to the assessment of Marx's logic, but the effect is to argue for the jettisoning of the whole structure of Marx's theory. The main areas of criticism have been Marx's theories of value, of the source of profit, and of the falling rate of profit; well chosen targets because of their centrality to the whole system.

Marx's concept of value, relating it to socially necessary ABSTRACT LABOUR, has often led to the criticism that the identification of labour as the element rendering commodities commensurate in exchange is arbitrary (Böhm-Bawerk 1896, Cutler *et al.* 1977). More attention has been given to attacks on the 'transformation problem', interpreted as Marx's claim to be able to show the relation between values and prices of production (and SURPLUS VALUE AND PROFIT). Critics take production prices to be an observable category and argue that the validity of value theory in explaining experiential phenomena depends on whether it is able (or necessary) to generate those prices. Bortkiewicz (1907) demonstrated that Marx's own quantitative solution is incomplete, and he and later writers (Dmitriev 1904, Seton 1957) provide alternative solutions. Steedman argues that Samuelson's verdict (1971) that values are 'an irrelevant detour' on the road to production prices is correct, since in Sraffa's system (or Bortkiewicz's or Dmitriev's) values and prices

are each directly derivable from physical input data. This view has acquired considerable support, and has stimulated strong opposition from Marxists (see Elson 1979, Steedman *et al.* 1981).

Value concepts in *Capital* enable Marx to analyse surplus value as the basis of profit. However, Steedman shows that in his own system positive surplus value is not a necessary condition for positive profit (if fixed capital or joint production exist); following Morishima (1974) a concept of surplus labour different from that of Marx is required. If surplus value is not the source of profit (or a necessary condition for it) the explanation of profit must lie outside Marx's theory. Böhm-Bawerk argued against Marx that profits are due to the productivity of means of production and the time preference of capitalists; they are a reward for waiting. That theory remains at the centre of neo-classical economics. And Schumpeter (1976), in dismissing value theory, identified the continuous existence of profits with innovation and entrepreneurship, while criticizing Marx for neglecting the proper role of entrepreneurship in capitalism.

Besides the theory of the source of profit, the law governing its movement (for Marx 'the most important law') has attracted arguments that the logic involved in deducing the law of the tendency of the rate of profit to fall is false. At a general level many writers have noted that Marx's assumptions are not sufficient to yield an empirical prediction concerning falls in the rate of profit (calculated in terms of values or production prices), and some have drawn the implication from this that Marx's law has no substance (Hodgson 1974). A more rigorous critique, which attempts to prove that capitalists' choice of new techniques can never lead to a fall in the profit rate unless real wages rise, apparently contradicting Marx's assumptions about the effect of technical progress, was proposed by Okishio (1961) and placed in a Sraffian framework by Himmelweit (1974) and Steedman (1977) (see FALLING RATE OF PROFIT).

Although those criticisms are concerned with logical faults in Marx's argument, in general the fault can only be demonstrated by using a theoretical structure (such as that of Sraffa) which does not employ Marx's method of abstraction (see Fine and Harris 1979). One critic,

Keynes, however, just washed his hands of Marx and Engels. Looking to them for 'a clue to the economic riddle', he wrote: 'I can discover nothing but out-of-date controversialising' (letter to Bernard Shaw, 1 January 1935). In fact Marx anticipated Keynes in his attack on Say's Law and the Quantity Theory of Money, but left-wing Keynesians with a sympathy for some aspects of Marxism have rejected the theoretical foundation of Marx's propositions. For example, Joan Robinson (1942) argues that 'none of the important ideas which he expresses in terms of the concept of *value* cannot be better expressed without it' and she rejects Marx's related concepts of exploitation and surplus value. Thus Keynesian, neo-classical and Sraffian critics all base their criticisms on an argument that Marx's value theory is either redundant or false.

In sociology, two of the founding fathers of the modern discipline – Max Weber and Émile Durkheim – elaborated their ideas to some extent in conscious opposition to the Marxist theory of society. This is most apparent in the work of Weber, who not only selected for analysis problems closely akin to those treated by Marx (the origins and development of Western capitalism, the significance of social classes and of the labour movement, the nature of the modern state and political power), but also criticized explicitly, though briefly, the 'materialist conception of history'. It may be argued, as it was by Karl Löwith (1932), that both Marx and Weber were primarily concerned with the fate of human beings in modern capitalist society, the one interpreting it in terms of 'alienation', the other in terms of 'rationalization'; and that their respective conceptions of social science correspond with the actual division of society between bourgeoisie and proletariat. Weber's general criticism of historical materialism was that it constituted only *one* possible perspective on history, resting upon a particular value orientation, and that other perspectives were equally possible; and he illustrated this by showing the part that religious ideas (the Protestant ethic) might have played in the development of capitalism, while insisting firmly that he did not propose to substitute for a one-sided 'economic interpretation' an equally one-sided 'spiritualist interpretation' (Weber 1904). In his detailed studies Weber (1921) qualified the Marxist view of the paramount importance of

class and class conflict by emphasizing the role of status groups, disputed the Marxist conception of the state, and came close to the elite theorists in his notion of political power, while emphasizing especially the independent role of the national state. He also attributed a particular importance to the growth of bureaucracy, and based part of his criticism of Marxist socialism on the contention that the socialist movement would be more likely to produce a 'dictatorship of the official' than a 'dictatorship of the proletariat' (1924).

Durkheim, although he did not take up to the same extent Marxist problems (perhaps because Marxist thought and the socialist movement were less developed in France than in Germany), did nevertheless confront Marx's theory of society on several occasions, in reviews of Marxist works in the *Année sociologique* and elsewhere, in his discussion of the 'abnormal forms of the division of labour' (1893), and in his lectures on socialism (1928), though these were abandoned before reaching a systematic examination of German (Marxist) socialism. He recognized (1897) as a particular merit of the Marxist theory that it set out to explain social life 'not by the notions of those who participate in it, but by more profound causes not perceived by consciousness' (p. 648), but considered that, in general, it attributed too much importance to economic factors and to class struggles. Thus he argued (1893, 1897) that class conflict was a secondary phenomenon arising from the lack of regulation of the new kind of industrial society and division of labour which had emerged in Europe; and he opposed to the Marxist concept of the state, the idea of the state as the 'intelligence' and moral agent of society as a whole (1950).

During this period there also appeared a criticism of Marx's theory within Marxism, by Eduard Bernstein (1899). One of his main contentions was that a polarization of classes was not taking place, due to rising levels of living and the growth of the middle class; and this theme has since been prominent both in reinterpretations of Marxist theory (e.g. Renner's conception (1953) of the 'service class', Poulantzas's analysis (1975) of the 'petty bourgeoisie' in present-day capitalism), and in criticisms of it (e.g. Parkin 1979). The debate about class in recent years has given rise both to conceptions of a 'new working class' (Mallet 1975) or a new class structure (Touraine 1971) (see WORKING CLASS), and to the study of non-class social movements such as ethnic movements (see RACE) or the women's movement (see FEMINISM) in relation to class conflict. It has also produced new studies of social stratification, and of the possible emergence of new class structures, in socialist societies (e.g. Konrád and Szelényi 1979).

An important later sociological criticism of Marxism is to be found in the work of Karl Mannheim (especially *Ideology and Utopia* 1929) who attempted to supersede Marx's theory of IDEOLOGY by a more general sociology of knowledge. His criticism and revision had three main features: (i) it rejected a direct association between consciousness and economic interests in favour of a correlation between a 'style of thought' and a set of attitudes related indirectly to interests; (ii) it treated Marxism itself as the ideology of a class, arguing that all social thought had a 'relational' character and could not claim to embody scientific 'truth'; (iii) it conceived other social groups besides classes (e.g. generational groups) as having a significant influence upon consciousness. More recently, sociological criticism of Marxist theory has come from two other major sociologists. Raymond Aron, from a standpoint much influenced by Weber, denies the claim of the 'economic interpretation' to be a science of history and emphasizes the independence of politics from the economy; and in a more general study he has examined critically the Marxism of Sartre (himself in many respects a major critic of Marxism) and Althusser (Aron 1970). C. Wright Mills, also influenced by Weber, though much less critical of Marxism as a whole, took a rather similar view of the separation between the economic and political spheres, and preferred the term 'power elite' to ruling class (which, he thought, presupposed a correspondence between economic and political power).

Much recent criticism of Marxist theory has indeed focused on the problem of the state and politics. Many critics, proceeding from a 'democratic pluralist' perspective (e.g. Lipset 1960), have sought to show that Marxist political theory presents a false picture of Western political systems: there is no 'ruling class' able to impose its will on the state and turn it into its 'instrument'. In any case, the nature of Western political systems, with the political and electoral competition which they make possible, prevents the state from pursuing for any length of time policies unduly favourable to any particular class or group. From a different perspective, critics have also argued that the notion of the 'relative autonomy of the state' did not go far enough (see STATE); and that Marxists failed to take adequate account of the fact that the state, situated in an international context, and competing with other states, had its own concerns, above and beyond the interests of all classes and groups in society (e.g. Skocpol 1979).

Another major theme in recent criticism and reassessment of Marxist theory is that concerning its status as a 'science of history', though this debate too goes back to Weber. Habermas (1979) in his 'reconstruction' of historical materialism argues, in conformity with his general criticism of Marxist 'positivism' (see FRANKFURT SCHOOL; POSITIVISM), that the early stages of social development have to be conceived not only in terms of social labour and material production, but also in terms of familial organization and norms of action, both crucially dependent upon language. More sweeping criticisms of the Marxist theory of history have been made, from opposite directions, by Popper and Althusser, on the grounds of its alleged HISTORICISM. On the other side, an 'old-fashioned historical materialism' (Cohen 1978) emphasizing the determining influence of the growth of productive forces has been strongly defended by some recent writers. But there are also more detailed problems in the Marxist theory, concerning especially transitions from one form of society to another, and the role of classes in them.

Great difficulty has been encountered in harmonizing complicated factual detail, such as modern research brings to light in an endless flood, with broadly conceived general formulae. This has exposed Marxists to the charge of biased selection of evidence that will fit into their scheme; of giving undue prominence, for example, in the study of European revolutions which has been one of their hunting-grounds, to any indications of class struggle. Whether class struggle has really run through history, or how widely in history 'classes' can be identified, has been very frequently queried. Insistence on them by Marxism has been felt to be part of what Heilbroner (1980) has called 'its tacit teleology, its unstated millennial assumptions' (p. 87).

Crucial to historical materialism has been the concept of the 'mode of production', yet in Marx's writings 'nowhere is it formulated with precision' (Shaw 1978, p. 31); and when Marxists have debated its obscurities, and still more the problem of how the economic base is related to the ideas, religion, laws, accompanying it, they have found themselves far from agreement. They can be taxed, as Marx himself has been, with tending to 'oscillate between loose and stringent versions' of the connection between 'base and superstructure' (Evans 1975, p. 67). A medievalist who has raised wide-ranging objections to Marxist theory argues that patterns of thought and behaviour can alter very markedly without any concomitant shift in the productive system: differences between the Europe of Charlemagne and the Europe of Barbarossa are much more significant than any underlying continuity of economic methods (Leff 1969, pp. 137–40).

Equally hard to work out convincingly has been the process or processes by which one 'mode', or socioeconomic structure, has given place to another, particularly in earlier epochs. Many critics have taken Marx's theory of historical change to be at bottom one of technological change. Marxists have usually repudiated this, though it may have to be admitted that, as Gandy says (1979), Marx sometimes 'carelessly slips towards technological determinism' (p. 131). But it cannot be said that they have provided an alternative answer combining sufficient precision with sufficient generality. In this context too the weight to be ascribed to ideas and ideals, and their degree of autonomy, are problematical. Rubel has spoken of an 'insoluble contradiction' in Marx's own thinking between economic determinism and creative humanism (1981, p. 51). Marx's successors have more often than not skirted round the issue of the ethical component in history (see ETHICS; MORALS). And all these perplexities are being compounded nowadays by the question of whether history has obeyed the same or similar 'laws' everywhere. It is increasingly having to be recognized that Marxist theory grew out of Western European experience. Its application so far by Western writers to other regions (e.g. to countries such as India) has drawn much criticism

from their own scholars, both Marxist and non-Marxist.

The most substantial critical examination of Marxist thought as a whole in recent years is undoubtedly Leszek Kolakowski's *Main Currents of Marxism*, which distinguishes between the value of Marxism as 'an interpretation of past history' and its 'fantasy' character as a political ideology, and argues that while the intellectual legacy of Marx has been largely assimilated into the modern social sciences – so that as an independent explanatory system or method Marxism is 'dead' – as an efficacious political doctrine it is simply 'a caricature and a bogus form of religion'. The events of the late 1980s, beginning with major changes in the Soviet Union, and reaching a climax in the revolutions in Eastern Europe at the end of 1989 which brought about the collapse of the communist regimes, make desirable a reappraisal of this argument. It is not so much that the intellectual legacy of Marx has been assimilated to some extent into the modern social sciences, although that has certainly occurred, in diverse ways. More important is that the continuing critical examination of Marxist conceptions such as those of human nature, the role of classes in social change, revolution, the structure of socialist society – which are major components of a very distinctive and powerful theory of society – now needs to take account also of the questions raised by these new historical developments as well as by alternative social theories (see CRISIS IN SOCIALIST SOCIETY).

As to Marxism as a political doctrine, it is evident that in its Soviet version it has been a failure throughout Eastern Europe, but there is little reason to doubt that in other forms, of which there are many, it does in fact possess the capacity to generate a body of rational norms for a socialist society. At all events we reject the proposition that Marxism is no more than a 'bogus form of religion' (what would be the 'authentic' form?), though it is true that in some versions, as an all-embracing world view, it did acquire a transcendental and dogmatic character. Other kinds of Marxist thought, however, have remained within the theoretical and empirical norms of scientific enquiry, in which respect they are closer to the spirit of Marx's own work; and the way for their future development has now been made much easier by the disappearance of the communist regimes in Europe and the consequent demise of 'official' Marxism.

Reading

Bernstein, Eduard 1899 (1961): *Evolutionary Socialism*.

Böhm-Bawerk, Eugen von 1896 (1949): *Karl Marx and the Close of his System*, ed. Paul M. Sweezy.

Bortkiewicz, L. von 1907 (1949): 'Zur Berechtigung der grundlegenden theoretischen Konstruktion von Marx im dritten Band des *Kapital*'. English trans. in Sweezy (ed.) 1949.

— 1952: 'Value and Price in the Marxian System'.

Cutler, A. *et al.* 1977: *Marx's Capital and Capitalism Today*, vol. 1.

Dmitriev, V. K. 1904 (1974): *Economic Essays on Value Competition and Utility*.

Elson, Diane ed. 1979: *Value: The Representation of Labour in Capitalism*.

Evans, M. 1975: *Karl Marx*.

Gandy, D. R. 1979: *Marx and History*.

Habermas, Jürgen 1979: 'Toward a Reconstruction of Historical Materialism'. In *Communication and the Evolution of Society*.

Heilbroner, R. L. 1980: *Marxism: For and Against*.

Himmelweit, S. 1974: 'The Continuing Saga of the Falling Rate of Profit – A Reply to Mario Cogoy'.

Hodgson, G. 1974: 'The Theory of the Falling Rate of Profit'.

Kolakowski, Leszek 1978: *Main Currents of Marxism*.

Lipset, S. M. 1960: *Political Man*.

Löwith, Karl 1932 (1982): *Max Weber and Karl Marx*.

Mannheim, Karl 1929 (1936): *Ideology and Utopia*.

Morishima, M. 1974: 'Marx in the Light of Modern Economic Theory'.

Okishio, N. 1961: 'Technical Change and the Rate of Profit'.

Parkin, Frank 1979: *Marxism and Class Theory: A Bourgeois Critique*.

Robinson, Joan 1942: *An Essay on Marxian Economics*.

Schumpeter, J. A. 1976: *Capitalism, Socialism and Democracy*.

Seton, F. 1957: 'The Transformation Problem'.

Skocpol, T. 1979: *States and Social Revolutions*.

Steedman, Ian 1977: *Marx after Sraffa*.

— *et al.* 1981: *The Value Controversy*.

Weber, Max 1904 (1976): *The Protestant Ethic and the Spirit of Capitalism*.

— 1918 (1978): 'Socialism'. In J. E. T. Eldridge (ed.), *Max Weber: The Interpretation of Social Reality*.

THE EDITORS

culture This is not an indigenously Marxist concept in the sense in which IDEOLOGY may be said to be. The concept has often been used in ways particularly repellent to most Marxists, whether to defend the notion of 'art for art's sake' or, in a very different use of the term, to reject a materialist approach in anthropology (Sahlins 1976). Yet many of the most important twentieth-century discussions of AESTHETICS, and more generally cultural questions, have been by Marxists. Moreover, there is a crucial cultural dimension to the whole Marxist and socialist project, and questions of culture and ideology have been so central to Western Marxism that some writers have identified a distinct trend of 'culturalist' Marxism.

We have already noted two uses of the term culture which can be taken as the extreme poles of its use. In one, it denotes the aesthetic domain of, in particular, ART and LITERATURE and the relations between them. At the other end of the spectrum are anthropological uses of the term to denote the 'whole way of life' of a society, often construed in an idealist way as founded upon meanings, values and so on. Somewhere between these two extremes we find the cluster of senses most fully developed within German idealist thought, in which culture is seen as the realm of objective mind or spirit and its embodiment in human institutions. Here 'culture' retains its original sense of cultivation and development, *Bildung*, sometimes identified with civilization and sometimes distinguished from it as something more profound, but almost always given a strongly positive evaluation.

Not surprisingly, few Marxist writers have identified themselves whole-heartedly with any of these uses, in so far as they suggest a separation between different aspects of human practice – a separate sphere of aesthetic production or a separate realm of ideas or values with its own intrinsic logic. But the concept of culture, in both Marxist and non-Marxist uses, can also express an attempt to break down these distinctions and, in Marxist thought, to develop a materialist account of the interrelations between ideas and other aspects and conditions of human praxis. It is culture, in its broadest sense, which is at issue in Marx's famous contrast between 'the worst of architects' (who at least plans his or her constructions) and 'the best of bees' (*Capital* I, ch. 5).

In other words the concept of culture is at the heart of the conception of consciousness as conscious existence, in which consciousness is seen both as bound up with an existing state of affairs and as a condition which makes it possible to change that state of affairs. In a crude form of Marxism, this gives rise to a dualistic conception of culture, seen paradoxically as both a reflection of an economic base and a propagandist weapon in the class struggle. This can be illustrated by the otherwise puzzling coexistence of a 'reflection' theory of knowledge (in which knowledge appears as a simple reflection of an independently existing reality) and a realist aesthetic on the one hand; and on the other, an instrumental conception of intellectual production which stresses the virtues of partisanship (on the right side).

In the circumstances of the Russian revolution it is not surprising that this instrumental attitude is the most prominent theme in Lenin's concept of cultural revolution, and in his and Trotsky's polemics against the Proletkult movement which aimed to create a new proletarian culture. The latter was certainly partisan, but in ways which Lenin and Trotsky considered irrelevant and counter-productive. For them, the emergence of a socialist culture was a long-term prospect, whose foundations had to be set by the extension of literacy and education and the creation of a new socialist intelligentsia, which would take up and incorporate what was valuable in bourgeois culture (just as it would incorporate the more advanced methods of work organization, such as Taylorism). The concept of cultural revolution was taken up in the GDR and other socialist countries in the 1950s. In China, however, the Cultural Revolution of the 1960s attacked bourgeois culture in a way which was more in the spirit of the radicals against whom Lenin's polemics were addressed.

Despite his conservatism on aesthetic questions, Lenin's concept of cultural revolution seems to have set the tone for the very broad concept of culture which is prominent in present-day discussion in the socialist countries. In the USSR it is often linked to the concept of 'way of life' (*byt*), in a way which comes close to the early sense of culture as *Bildung*. (The constitution of the German Democratic Republic, for example, included not just the arts but 'physical culture, sport and tourism' as 'elements of socialist culture'.)

WESTERN MARXISM is generally seen as beginning with Lukács and Gramsci, and this is certainly the starting point of a tradition which has been very much concerned with questions of culture; indeed it is hardly too much to see them as the twin progenitors of subsequent work in this area. Lukács was reared on German neo-Kantianism, and his essay of 1920 on 'Old and New Culture' is a Marxist reformulation of a concept of culture derived from this tradition in general and Simmel in particular. Lukács defined culture in opposition to civilization as 'the ensemble of valuable products and abilities which are dispensable in relation to the immediate maintenance of life. For example, the internal and external beauty of a house ... in contrast to its durability and protectiveness'. Culture in this sense is destroyed by capitalist production for the market, and since 'the sociological precondition of culture is man as an end in himself', a new culture, whose features are at present unpredictable, is only possible with the coming of socialism. Lukács's later work was largely devoted to aesthetics. In addition, *History and Class Consciousness* concerns the development of a proletarian world view in contrast to the reified thought-forms of bourgeois Europe.

Lukács's early works formed the basis of Goldmann's work in the sociology of literature and the history of ideas, and he was also one of the crucial influences on the critical theory of the FRANKFURT SCHOOL, whose central figures in this connection are Adorno, Horkheimer and Marcuse. Adorno also engaged in important exchanges with Benjamin, who was only marginally connected w th the Institute for Social Research, and witl Brecht. A Jorno's aesthetics is much the most developed, but he shared with Horkheimer and Marcuse a broader concept of culture which may owe a good deal to Freud's use of the term in 'i he Future of an Illusion (1927) and *Civilization and its Discontents* (1930). Marcuse's formulation in his essay 'On the Affirmative Concept of Culture' is fairly representative:

There is a general concept of culture that . . . expresses the implication of the mind in the historical process of society. It signifies the totality of social life in a given situation, in so far as both the areas of ideational reproduction (culture, in the narrower sense, the 'spiritual world') and of material reproduction ('civilisation') form a historically distinguishable and comprehensible unity. (1968, p. 94)

Culture in this sense was not to be seen as independent and understood 'in terms of itself', but nor was it a mere reflection of an independently existing base. In the aesthetic sphere,

> the task of criticism must be not so much to search for the particular interest-groups to which cultural phenomena have to be assigned, but rather to decipher the general social tendencies which are expressed in these phenomena and through which their powerful interests realise themselves. Cultural criticism must become social physiognomy. (Ibid. p. 30)

Culture, analysed in terms of COMMODITY FETISHISM and (especially by Adorno) REIFICATION, appeared in two main forms. The first is what Marcuse called 'affirmative culture'. Affirmative culture in the bourgeois world is, as religion was for Marx, 'the sigh of the oppressed creature, the heart of a heartless world: the soul of soulless conditions. It is the opium of the people' ('Critique of Hegel's Philosophy of Right: Introduction'). As Marcuse put it:

> By affirmative culture is meant that culture of the bourgeois epoch which led in the course of its own development to the segregation from civilisation of the mental and spiritual world as an independent realm of value that is also considered superior to civilisation. Its decisive characteristic is the assertion of a universally obligatory, eternally better and more valuable world that must be unconditionally affirmed: a world essentially different from the factual world of the daily struggle for existence, yet realisable by every individual for himself 'from within'; without any transformation of the state of fact. (Ibid. p. 95)

Culture, and art in particular, thus has an ambiguous role: it upholds the desires for freedom and happiness (the *promesse de bonheur*) which are thwarted in modern societies, but projects them into an illusory sphere and thus affirms the status quo by 'pacifying rebellious desire' (ibid. p. 121). The concept of culture, as Adorno later argued, is bound up with administration.

But if traditional bourgeois culture at least upheld a kind of transcendence, this is absent in the 'culture industry' which Adorno and Horkheimer analysed in their *Dialectic of Enlightenment* (1947). Here, the commodity principle is carried to its extreme, not just in 'aesthetic' production but even in the sphere of the personality, which 'scarcely signifies anything more than shining white teeth and freedom from body odours and emotions' (p. 167). Marcuse saw this process of the 'commodification of culture as the collapse of "higher culture" into "material culture" '; in which the former loses its critical potential. Culture, like sex, becomes more accessible, but in a degraded form (1964, ch. 3). Even the most radical criticism of this state of affairs is recuperated as just another commodity: Marcuse's *One-Dimensional Man* was a considerable commercial success. Any attempt to develop a genuinely alternative culture (Marcuse was more optimistic about such possibilities than Adorno and Horkheimer) seems to be a mere clutching at straws.

Habermas, the leading figure of the second generation of critical theory, has given much less attention to cultural questions, but he is increasingly turning to this theme in his analysis of legitimacy in modern civilization and is developing a concept of cultural modernity in which rationalized social processes are increasingly withdrawn from the common-sense understanding of those who are subject to them. This approach may provide a more general and powerful analysis of the processes identified by the earlier critical theorists.

If there is a reasonably clear line of influence from Lukács's Marxist reformulation of the German tradition of cultural criticism, then Gramsci's stress on the cultural dimension of socialist politics in societies where the bourgeoisie rules less by force than by HEGEMONY has been crucial, in a more diffuse way, for contemporary Marxists as diverse as Raymond WILLIAMS and ALTHUSSER. The focus on culture is clearest in Britain, in the work of Williams, the historian Edward Thompson, and members of the Birmingham Centre for Contemporary Cultural Studies founded by Richard Hoggart. However, even those who have criticized this approach on the basis of French STRUCTURALISM share an equal, though differently formulated concern with superstructural phenomena (Eagleton 1976 and Johnson, in Barrett *et al.* 1979). This is also true of the important work of Pierre Bourdieu and his associates in France, which uses the notions of symbolic and cultural capital to trace the reproduction of class relations in educational systems and politics as well as in 'cultural consumption' in a narrower sense (Bourdieu and Passeron 1970, Bourdieu 1979). Imperialism, too, has been seen to be a cultural as well as an economic and military phenomenon. Here the advanced countries' virtual monopoly of television, book, magazine and news agency output is merely one aspect of a process in which the Third World is exposed to a Western 'business culture' in the sphere of production and to a consumer culture which encourages the misallocation of resources (Schiller 1976).

It remains to be seen how far Western Marxism will retain its somewhat one-sided preoccupation with superstructures, whether conceived in terms of culture, ideology, or more diffuse notions of signification and representation. It is clear, however, that there is an increasing awareness (partly due to FEMINISM) of the interrelation of production and reproduction, and it seems likely that Marxists will come to think less in terms of 'culture with a capital K' and more in terms of the complicated mechanisms of cultural production and reproduction within existing modes of production.

The importance attached in Western Marxism to issues of culture and ideology is of course by no means just a matter of theory. What Trent Shroyer (1973) called 'cultural Marxism' was an important element, though more in Europe than in North America, in the 'counter-culture' of the 1960s (Roszak, 1970). This in turn has had a very considerable, if diffuse, influence on 'alternative' thinking, 'post-materialist' values and the emergence of new social movements, especially the Green movement (Ingleheart 1977, Weiner 1981). At the same time, of course, much of the opposition to the Marxist-Leninist dictatorships in the USSR and Eastern Europe was expressed in literary forms.

A further tightening of the connection between the concepts of culture and ideology has resulted from the growing recognition of the importance of the mass media as a focus of theories of ideology (Thompson 1990, Müller-Doohm 1990). Marxist thinkers and those close to Marxism have played a crucial part in the study of popular culture, especially in the United Kingdom, where 'cultural studies' has become a recognized academic discipline. As in earlier theorizing about culture, popular culture has been variously seen as a form of ideological hegemony imposed on the masses, and as a more or less autonomous expression of ordinary people's ways of life. (Hall 1980, Williams 1981; see also MORRIS, WILLIAM.)

Reading

Adorno, Theodor 1955 (1967): *Prisms*.

— and Horkheimer, Max 1947 (1972): *Dialectic of Enlightenment*.

Barrett, Michèle *et al*. eds. 1979: *Ideology and Cultural Production*.

Bourdieu, Pierre 1979: *La Distinction*.

— and Passeron, Jean-Claude 1970 (1977): *Reproduction in Education, Society and Culture*.

Eagleton, Terry 1976: *Criticism and Ideology*.

Freud, Sigmund 1927: 'The Future of an Illusion'.

— 1930: 'Civilisation and its Discontents'.

Goldmann, Lucien 1971 (1976): *Cultural Creation in Modern Society*.

Hall, Stuart 1990: 'Cultural Studies: Two Paradigms'.

Lukács, György 1920 (1970): 'The Old Culture and the New Culture'.

— 1923 (1971): *History and Class Consciousness*.

Marcuse, Herbert 1964 (1968): *One-Dimensional Man*.

— 1968: *Negations: Essays in Critical Theory*.

Sahlins, Marshall 1976: *Culture and Practical Reason*.

Schiller, Herbert 1976: *Communication and Cultural Domination*.

Thompson, John 1990: *Ideology and Modern Culture*.

Williams, Raymond 1981: *Culture*.

WILLIAM OUTHWAITE

D

Darwinism Charles Darwin published *Origin of Species* in 1859 and summarized his findings as the 'laws' of inheritance, variability, population increase, struggle for life, and natural selection entailing divergence of character and the extinction of less improved forms. On 18 June 1862, Marx wrote to Engels of his amusement that 'Darwin recognizes among beasts and plants his English society with its division of labour, competition, opening of new markets, inventions and the Malthusian "struggle for existence".'

But Marx genuinely admired the way that Darwin focused on 'the history of natural technology, i.e. the formation of the organs of plants and animals', and he argued that increased attention should be paid to 'the history of the productive organs of man in society' (*Capital* I, ch. 15). More specifically he drew an analogy between the two realms: Darwin observed that natural selection promotes a high degree of specialization in plant and animal organs when they perform very specific functions, and Marx found a similar pattern in the development of tools in modern industry. 'The manufacturing period simplifies, improves and multiplies the implements of labour', he wrote, 'by adapting them to the exclusive and special functions of each kind of worker' (*Capital* I, ch. 14). Thus Marx admired the way that Darwin's theory could establish, without teleology, a pattern arising from events that are in themselves indeterminate with respect to final outcome.

However, Marx's enthusiasm for the form of Darwinian explanation did not lead him to reproduce Darwin's natural history in his own study of human development. Marx did not employ Darwinian 'laws' in explaining transitions in human history that he identified as particularly important: the transition from an animal-like existence to a human one, from communitarian exchange to exchange among 'private' individuals, from commodity production to capital-ism, and from capitalism to communism (*Capital* I, chs 2, 16, 32). When social Darwinists 'explained' history in terms of human biology, population pressure, competition for survival and evolution of the species through selection, Marx reacted with derision. His theory assigned crucial importance to the changes which humans initiate, for whatever reasons, in their MODE OF PRODUCTION. While it is true that in 1873 Marx sent Darwin an inscribed copy of *Capital*, he did the same for others, and there is now no convincing reason to believe that he intended to dedicate any part, edition or translation of *Capital* to Darwin. That story arose from misattributed events in the life of Edward Aveling. Most probably Marx wanted to interest a sharp and influential mind in his own theory of society and was not seeking through Darwin the imprimatur of 'science' that so mesmerized Engels.

Engels drew his own ambiguous analogy between Marx's work and Darwin's when he announced in his 'Speech at the Graveside of Karl Marx' (1883) that 'just as Darwin discovered the law of development of organic nature, so Marx discovered the law of development of human history.' But it is highly questionable whether the positivist presumptions attributed by Engels to Marx and Darwin in common fit either scientist at all. Neither was concerned to limit science to 'proximate' or causal explanations – systematic correlations between attributes of an entity and its environment.

Engels also attempted, as Marx did not, to integrate the two theories in his own 'The Part Played by Labour in the Transition from Ape to Man' (written 1876, published 1895–6). In Engels's view the initial development of human history depended crucially on the evolution of human labour, as natural selection operated on variations in physiological organs and intellectual capacities. But this gave way in his account to a theory of inherited finesse in the transmission of learned behaviour from individuals to offspring that was somewhat un-Darwinian. Then in his widely read work, *Origin of the Family, Private Property and the State* (1884) Engels introduced an explicitly Darwinian theory into his account of the further development of human society. He argued that marriage forms had evolved from a supposed original condition of promiscuous intercourse to ever more restricted sexual relationships leading eventually to modern monogamy and the oppression of women. Natural selection was said to benefit those clans in which marriage among relatives was forbidden.

But Engels did not succeed in uniting Darwinian natural history with his overall theory that 'economic relations [are] the determining basis of the history of society' (Engels to Starkenburg, 25 January 1894). Despite occasional remarks about historical evolution, including the selection and extinction of races, nations and classes, Engels did not consistently embrace a social Darwinist theory of the survival of the fittest in human history. Rather he generally supported a Marxist theory that the 'whole history of mankind' has been a history of 'class struggles, contests between exploiting and exploited, ruling and oppressed classes' (1888 Preface to the *Communist Manifesto*).

In fact 'progress' in human productive activities and the struggles between exploiters and exploited do not fit readily into a scheme in which selection ensures that the 'fittest' merely survive and reproduce. Both Darwin and Marx attempted to separate qualitative judgements on human progress from bare facts of survival or extinction. However, some Marxists, such as KAUTSKY and PANNEKOEK, sought to reconcile the progressive struggle for existence espoused by social Darwinists with the class struggle for communism espoused by Marxists. But it was extremely difficult to argue for revolution in terms of a struggle for life when proletarians were defined as the underdogs of capitalist society. Moreover it was also extremely difficult to argue for revolution in terms of natural inevitability, when it was voluntary action in politics that was required. Soviet anthropologists have attempted a theoretical amalgamation of (1) an economic imperative in human development with (2) a role for individual volition and (3) a Darwinian pattern of selection among groups, but this work is necessarily speculative as there

is little available to us that could count as evidence.

Darwin presumed that plants and animals, his subject matter, were incapable of significant volition beyond an urge for survival and reproduction, so any analogy between his natural history of non-human populations and Marx's historical theory of human society must necessarily be limited. Marx presumed that contemporary humans could in principle learn enough about their environment, both natural and social, to enable them to form communistic intentions and to take appropriate political actions, thus decisively influencing their own development as social individuals.

Reading

Ball, T. 1979: 'Marx and Darwin: A Reconsideration'.

Carver, T. 1982: 'The "Guiding Threads" of Marx and Darwin'.

— 1985: 'Engels's Feminism'.

Farr, J. 1984: 'Marx and Positivism'.

Gellner, E. 1987: 'How did Mankind Acquire its Essence? or The Paleolithic October'.

Kelly, Alfred 1981: *The Descent of Darwin: The Popularization of Darwinism in Germany 1860–1914*.

Warren, M. 1987: 'The Marx–Darwin Question: Implications for the Critical Aspects of Marx's Social Theory'.

TERRELL CARVER

De Leon, Daniel Born 14 December 1852, on the island of Curaçao off the coast of Venezuela; died 11 May 1914, New York. The son of wealthy parents who belonged to a long-established Sephardic Jewish community, he was sent to Europe in 1866 to continue his education, first at the Gymnasium in Hildesheim, then for two years at the University of Leiden. In 1872 he moved to the USA, became a law student at Columbia University in 1876 and subsequently a teacher in the law faculty. De Leon first espoused radical causes in 1886 when he took the side of striking New York tramway workers against his conservative academic colleagues, and a few years later he abandoned his university career. In the meantime his radicalism had been reinforced by reading Henry George's *Progress and Poverty* (1879) and Edward Bellamy's *Looking Backward* (1887), but he soon became disillusioned with the policies of the protest movements they inspired, and he was finally converted to socialism by reading Marx. In 1890 he joined the Social Labour Party (SLP), quickly became its outstanding propagandist, and launched in 1891 its newspaper, *The People*, which he continued to edit for the rest of his life.

De Leon published no major work of social theory which would have established him as a leading Marxist thinker, but through his translations and his numerous speeches, articles and pamphlets he made an important contribution to the diffusion of Marxist ideas during the early phase of the American socialist movement. He translated (for the publishing house of the SLP) works by Marx, Engels, Kautsky, Bebel and others, making this Marxist literature available for the first time to a larger body of American workers. In his own writings, which for the most part expounded Marxist views in the context of current economic and political issues, he set out particularly to free Marxist socialist thought from the charge that it was an 'alien' European doctrine, and to emphasize its character as a necessary development out of an indigenous, radical democratic, American tradition.

Throughout his life, indeed, De Leon was committed to the idea of socialism as a largely 'spontaneous' movement from below (in which respect his ideas had some affinity with those of Rosa Luxemburg), yet at the same time he wanted to organize the SLP as a strictly disciplined party (resembling more closely the later Leninist model) which would diffuse Marxist ideas of socialism and class struggle in the trade union movement. Most later historians of American socialism have been highly critical of his sectarianism in relation to the labour movement as a whole and the trade unions in particular, although a recent study (Coleman 1990) gives a more sympathetic account of his ideas and activities. At all events, his intransigence over questions of doctrine and tactics led to numerous defections from the SLP, and while the party extended its national organization in the early 1890s its membership and influence never approached that of the Socialist Party of America (SPA) led by Eugene Debs. Nor was it more successful in converting the American trade unions to socialism. De Leon's enthusiasm at the founding of the Industrial Workers of the World (IWW) in 1905 led him to expound a theory of socialist industrial unionism and

peaceful revolution (De Leon 1952) which is perhaps his most original contribution to socialist thought, but the IWW itself began to decline from 1907 and the influence of the SLP again receded. In spite of his gifts as a thinker and propagandist, De Leon's influence on the socialist movement and on American Marxist thought was limited, and also short-lived; later Marxist studies in the USA, in the social sciences, history or philosophy, have made little or no reference to his work.

Reading

Buhle, Paul 1987: *Marxism in the USA*.
Coleman, Stephen 1990: *Daniel de Leon*.
De Leon, Daniel 1931: *Industrial Unionism: Selected Editorials by Daniel de Leon*.
— 1952: *Socialist Landmarks: Four Addresses*.
Peterson, Arnold 1941: *Daniel de Leon: Socialist Architect*.
Seretan, L. G. 1979: *Daniel de Leon: The Odyssey of an American Marxist*.

                                TOM BOTTOMORE

democracy   From his earliest writings Marx was committed to the ideal of direct democracy. His early conception of such democracy involved a Rousseauesque critique of the principle of representation, and the view that true democracy involves the disappearance of the state and thus the end of the separation of the state from civil society, which occurs because 'society is an organism of solidary and homogeneous interests, and the distinct "political" sphere of the "general interest" vanishes along with the division between governors and governed' (Colletti 1975, p. 44). This view reappears in Marx's writings about the Paris Commune, which he admired for its holding every delegate 'at any time revocable and bound by the formal instructions of his constituents': so 'instead of deciding once in three or six years which member of the ruling class was to misrepresent the people in parliament, universal suffrage was to serve the people, constituted in Communes' (*Civil War in France*, pt. III). Partly because this was his view, Marx never addressed the procedural issue of what forms collective choice or decision-making should take under communism, whether at the lower or higher stage.

Marx's view of bourgeois democracy

(characterized by universal suffrage, political liberties, the rule of law and political competition) was, however, complex and sensitive to its contradictory possibilities. Of the bourgeois democratic republic he wrote (*Class Struggles in France*, pt. II), that its constitution sanctions the social power of the bourgeoisie while withdrawing the political guarantees of this power, forcing it 'into democratic conditions, which at every moment help the hostile classes to victory and jeopardise the very foundations of bourgeois society'. Beginning with Engels's 1895 Introduction to that work, one strand in Marxism has focused on this latter possibility, envisaging the eventual victory of socialism through the ballot box and parliament. Notable exponents of this idea were Kautsky at that time and many so-called 'Eurocommunists' in our own (see EUROCOMMUNISM).

By contrast, Lenin sharply disagreed with Kautsky's view, holding that 'it is natural for a liberal to speak of "democracy" in general; but a Marxist will never forget to ask: "for what class?"' (Lenin 1918b (*1965*), p. 235). Bourgeois democracy like any other form of state was a form of class rule, to be 'smashed' and replaced by the DICTATORSHIP OF THE PROLETARIAT in the form of soviets. The implications of this view, which has been the dominant one in this century among all Leninists and Trotskyists, are clear: an insurrectionary politics of the transition, an insensitivity to the differences between bourgeois forms of state, and a tendency to regard the suspension of bourgeois democratic freedoms in socialist societies as not incompatible with the socialist project.

An alternative, if embryonic, Marxist tradition can be seen in the thought of Gramsci, for whom the development of popular forces within bourgeois democracies through political mobilization and organization and the development of a counter-hegemonic culture, might encourage the expansion of whatever possibilities for socialist transformation they may contain. Such a view begins to come to grips, as neither of the others does, with the problem of democratic consent and how to win it for socialism.

On the issue of democracy under socialism neither classical Marxism nor Marxism-Leninism has had much to say in detail (albeit for different reasons), though some schools of thought (e.g. AUSTRO-MARXISM) opposed to

Marxism-Leninism did discuss it critically. More recently, many thinkers in Eastern Europe sought to grapple with the question of how (if at all) 'actually existing socialism' might be democratized, but, ironically enough, such voices were scarcely heard in their own societies until the end of the 1980s.

Reading

Bahro, Rudolf 1978: *The Alternative in Eastern Europe.*

Brus, Wlodzimierz 1972: *The Market in a Socialist Economy.*

— 1975: *Socialist Ownership and Political Systems.*

Colletti, Lucio 1968 (*1972*): *From Rousseau to Lenin.*

— 1975: Introduction to Karl Marx, *Early Writings.*

Hunt, Alan ed. 1980: *Marxism and Democracy.*

Hunt, Richard N. 1974: *The Political Ideas of Marx and Engels.*

Maguire, John M. 1978: *Marx's Theory of Politics.*

Marković, Mihailo 1982: *Democratic Socialism: Theory and Practice.*

Miliband, Ralph 1977: *Marxism and Politics.*

                                    STEVEN LUKES

democratic centralism   This term has been applied by communist parties primarily to designate the often widely varying forms of inner-party organization which they operate. It also came to be proclaimed by the USSR and other communist regimes as the principle of state organization (as in the Soviet Constitution, Article 3).

Although the term is not to be found in Marx and Engels, the Rules of the League of Communists worked out with their participation in 1847 combine both the democratic and centralist elements of which democratic centralism claims to provide a dialectical synthesis (see appendices 1 and 10 to Marx and Engels, *Collected Works*, 1975, vol. 6, pp. 585–8, 633–8). In the leadership of the First International (see INTERNATIONALS) they sought in 1871–2 to increase the powers of the General Council and centralize its actions. However, they criticized 'the "strict" organization' enforced by J. B. von Schweitzer in the General Association of German Workers (see i.a. Engels to Marx, 24 September 1868), which Schweitzer's paper defended as 'democratic centralization' (*Der Social Demokrat*, Berlin, 7 October 1868. This seems to be the first place where this expression is to be found). In a number of letters at the end of his life, Engels insisted on the need for freedom of expression for the different trends in the rising workers' parties.

Democratic centralism was first specifically formulated as the organizing principle of a Marxist party by both Bolshevik and MENSHEVIK factions of the Russian Social Democratic Labour Party (RSDLP) at their separate conferences at the end of 1905 and unanimously approved at their party's unity congress the next year. The temporary spell of freedom won in the Russian revolution of 1905–7 meant that they could now apply democratic principles of organization where this had been impossible in the previous harsh conditions of illegality, as Lenin had indicated in 1902 in 'What is to be done?'. In 1906 Lenin specified that there was now agreement in the RSDLP on 'guarantees for the rights of all minorities and for all loyal opposition, on the autonomy of every party organization, on recognizing that all party functionaries must be elected, accountable and subject to recall'. He saw the observance of these principles as 'a guarantee that the ideological struggle in the party can and must prove fully consistent with strict organisational unity, with the submission to all the decisions of the unity congress' ('Appeal to the Party by Delegates to the Unity Congress', CW 10, p. 314), at which the Bolsheviks had been in a minority. Lenin pithily summed up democratic centralism as 'freedom of discussion, unity of action' ('Report on the Unity Congress of the RSDLP', CW 10, p. 380). In these years Lenin considered that democratic centralism was quite compatible with the existence of factions (the 1960–70 English edition of Lenin's *Collected Works* gives an intentionally weak translation of *fraktsia* as section, wing or group wherever Lenin refers to the legitimacy of factions in the RSDLP). The Bolsheviks abandoned this loose conception of democratic centralism in 1912 when they constituted themselves as a party separate from the Mensheviks, whom they attacked as 'liquidators' of the illegal party organization. 'The principle of federation, or of equality for all "trends", shall be unreservedly rejected', wrote Lenin in 1914 ('Report to the Brussels Conference', CW 20, p. 518).

In the period following the February revolution of 1917, the Bolsheviks, in the new conditions of legality, developed into a broader revolutionary mass party. It continued in the first years after the October revolution to decide its policy at congresses at which different platforms were openly argued for and voted on. However at the Tenth Congress in 1921, worried about the critical situation in which Soviet Russia then found itself, Lenin secured the adoption of a resolution outlawing factions in the party. This was not intended to end further democratic discussion in the party. However, in the framework of the one-party system (see PARTY) now being established, it provided a serviceable handle for Stalin to use to consolidate his own power. By the late 1920s, political debate was supplanted by 'monolithic unity' enforced from above.

At the Seventeenth Congress of the Communist Party of the Soviet Union (CPSU) in 1934, new party rules were adopted which defined democratic centralism in four points which many communist parties throughout the world were to incorporate into their own rules: election of all leading bodies of the party; their periodic accountability to their respective party organizations; strict party discipline and the subordination of the minority to the majority; decisions of higher bodies to be absolutely binding on lower bodies and on all party members. The democratic element in these rules proved nugatory in the face of Stalin's arbitrary mass purges, stage-managed congresses and uncontested elections. Gorbachev has recognized that not only in the Stalin period but right up into the 1980s democratic centralism in the CPSU was 'largely replaced by bureaucratic centralism', which entailed an 'excessive growth of the role played by the party apparatus at all levels' and led to 'power abuse and moral degeneration' (Gorbachev 1988, pp. 74–5).

In the debates leading up to the Twenty-eighth Congress of the CPSU in July 1990, opposing platforms were published in the party press for the first time since the 1920s. One of these, the Democratic Platform, attacked democratic centralism as an obstacle to the criticism of decisions and to minorities generating innovative ideas. It called for a restoration of freedom for factions and for a federal structure for the party in accordance with the federal state structure of the USSR. Demands for full autonomy, or in some cases secession from the CPSU as effected by the majority of the former Lithuanian Communist Party, have been increasingly voiced in Communist parties in Soviet union republics.

The Twenty-eighth Congress of the CPSU adopted revised party rules. On Gorbachev's proposal, it was decided to retain the term 'democratic centralism', along with the stipulation that 'a decision taken by a majority is binding on all.' However, the new rules then added: 'The minority has the right to defend its positions at party meetings, conferences, congresses, meetings of executive and control organs, in the party's mass media, [and] to make co-reports.' While laying down that the creation of factions is not allowed, the rules now grant 'the rights of Communists to unite around platforms in the course of discussions'. Although a federal party structure is not conceded, the Communist parties of union republics are characterized as 'independent' though operating on the basis of 'the fundamental programmatic and statutory principles of the CPSU'. The congress policy statement, 'Towards a Humane, Democratic Socialism', states that 'the CPSU resolutely rejects democratic centralism in the form that it took in the conditions of the administrative command system and rigid centralization.' Responding to pressure, the commitment to 'the renewal of the principle of democratic centralism' contained in its pre-congress draft was dropped.

The Third (Communist) International (1919–43), which saw itself as 'a single communist party of the entire world', included the implementation of democratic centralism in a particularly harsh form, entailing 'iron discipline' as one of the 21 conditions of admission laid down by its Second Congress in 1920 (Degras 1971, vol. 1, pp. 164, 171).

After the dissolution of the Communist International in 1943, communist parties were no longer committed to democratic centralism on an international level. However, its application within each party was influenced by the Soviet Union's Stalinist model, although naturally with essential differences between those parties holding state power and the others. Only from 1956, under the influence of Khrushchev's criticisms of Stalin at the Twentieth Congress of the CPSU, did a growing number of communist parties begin to revise this version of democratic centralism theoretically and practically in recognition of

'a serious error – too great an emphasis on centralism and an insufficient emphasis on democracy' (Communist Party (of Great Britain) 1957, p. 36).

Gramsci spoke of the 'elastic formula' offered by democratic centralism (Gramsci, *Selections from the Prison Notebooks*, 1971, p. 189). In practice some kind of combination of democracy and centralism is also envisaged by a wide range of bodies not connected with the Leninist tradition. The desirability or expediency of harsher or milder forms of party discipline arouses controversy in both communist and non-communist organizations. Robert Michels before the First World War wrote that 'the struggles within the modern democratic parties over this problem of centralization versus decentralization are of great scientific importance' (Michels 1959, p. 199). He perceived 'extremely strong centralizing and oligarchical tendencies' (p. 43) among the social democratic parties, which he especially studied. It is no accident that such tendencies were to reach their apogee in one-party states like Stalinist Russia, where nominal commitment to democratic election was in practice supplanted by the 'hierarchic investiture' explicitly rejected by Marx (*Civil War in France*, sect. III).

The East European upheavals of 1989 have led to an intensification of the debate on these questions in many of the world's communist parties. Most of the parties emerging out of the debris of former East European communist parties have rejected as compromised the term democratic centralism, as did the Italian Communist Party, now called the Democratic Party of the Left (PDS). Other communist parties retain the term, arguing that what is historically discredited is not democratic centralism as such but the suppression of its democratic constituent. The majority of the French Communist Party leadership defends the term against an unprecedented challenge from within its own ranks. The concept and practice of democratic centralism, along with the term itself, are today more than ever a source of sharp controversy. (See also BOLSHEVISM; LENIN; STALINISM.)

Reading

Communist Party (of Great Britain) 1957: *The Report of the Commission on Inner Party Democracy* (majority and minority reports).

Degras, J. ed. 1956–65 (1971): *The Communist Inter-national 1919–1943: Documents.*

Gorbachev, M. 1988: *Report to the Nineteenth All-Union Conference of the CPSU.*

Hunt, R. N. 1974: *The Political Ideas of Marx and Engels,* vol. 1, chapter 8.

Johnstone, M. 1980: 'Uno strumento politico di tipo nuovo; il partito leninista d'avanguardia'. In E. J. Hobsbawm *et al.*, eds. *Storia del Marxismo,* III/1.

Komintern und Revolutionäre Partei: Auswahl von Dokumenten und Materialien 1919–1943, 1986.

Liebman, M. 1973 (1975): *Leninism under Lenin.*

McNeal, Robert H. (general ed.) 1974: *Resolutions and Decisions of the Communist Party of the Soviet Union.*

Martov, Y. O. and Dan, F. I. 1926: *Die Geschichte der russischen Sozialdemokratie.*

Waller, Michael 1981: *Democratic Centralism: An Historical Commentary.*

MONTY JOHNSTONE

dependency theory   A school of thought which explains the underdevelopment of poor countries and regions as a product of capitalist development in wealthy countries. This approach originated in Latin American writing (see MARX-ISM IN LATIN AMERICA), especially in the two decades ending in 1980, and, although it is in decline as an academic school, similar ideas continue to inform radical popular movements.

Dependency theory is a broad approach with several variants sharing three main ideas. First, the process of capitalist growth in Europe, North America, and elsewhere, impoverished countries in Latin America, Africa and Asia, and their continued growth generates further poverty in the latter. In other words, underdevelopment (see UNDERDEVELOPMENT AND DEVELOPMENT) is created as a product of a continuing process; it is not an inherent condition of backwardness or failure to catch up. Second, that process of 'developing underdevelopment' operates through capitalism's global economic relations, 'the world market', which have historically been dominated by Europe and the United States. Third, global economic relations have a definite spatial structure, for the periphery (underdeveloped countries) is exploited by the metropolitan centre (advanced capitalist countries). The metropolis–periphery or centre–periphery concept is also used to describe the structure of economic relations within coun-

tries; the wealthy urban centres are metropolises exploiting the rural hinterland as the periphery.

The differences and nuances within these common positions partly relate to the diverse origins of the dependency school, since some writings grew out of a Marxist tradition while others emanated from a Latin American structuralism which reflected struggles to achieve national economic development. The writings of Marx and Engels on COLONIALISM and 'pre-capitalist modes of production' such as 'the Asiatic mode' (see ASIATIC SOCIETY) led some Marxists to believe that the countries of Latin America, Asia and Africa would follow paths of capitalist development partly mirroring North America and Europe's. Colonialism itself could be seen as facilitating this by its destruction of old social structures. Within classical Marxism, this view of development as evolutionary, linear progress was challenged by Luxemburg, who saw capitalism's reproduction and accumulation in terms of a global system of exploitation, and Lenin, who conceived of the system as imperialism (see IMPERIALISM AND WORLD MARKET) with super-exploitation.

Such Marxist ideas of a global system of imperialism were one impetus for dependency theory (especially in Cardoso's writings), but a particular feature of Latin American dependency theory is its definition of EXPLOITATION which owed much to the unorthodox concept of surplus promulgated by Baran and Sweezy in their theory of MONOPOLY CAPITALISM. Latin American structuralism, which was the other progenitor of dependency theory, was a theoretical rationalization of the development and trade strategies pursued by Latin American countries after the Second World War. The weakness of their export markets, dramatized first by the global depression of the 1930s and the disruption of world trade during the war, led to a policy of reducing dependency on the world market by developing 'import substitution' industries oriented to the home market instead. As a development strategy, these attempts to escape from dependency were linked to populist political movements and were given coherence by the Economic Commission for Latin America under Raul Prebisch. The writings of Sunkel, Paz, and Pinto are closest to this tradition. In the English-speaking world the best-known dependency theorist is André Gunder Frank who, like dos

Santos and Marini, attempted to build a more autonomous *dependencia* theoretical tradition. And Frank's work, in turn, has strong parallels with Wallerstein's WORLD SYSTEM theory of global capitalism.

At the heart of debates over dependency theory is the question of how exploitation occurs on an international scale. The seminal writings of Frank typify the central idea that exploitation occurs through trade between the centre and periphery. Some sought the theoretical underpinning for this idea in the concept of UNEQUAL EXCHANGE, and it was argued that empirically a long-run tendency for the terms of trade of Third World countries to worsen was a symptom of such exploitation through trade. These ideas seemed to justify the view that profits are transferred to the metropolis through systematically 'unfair' trade; that this loss caused a deterioration of the Third World's economies and prevented their own accumulation; and that strategies of import substitution could succeed by de-linking countries from the world market. But the notions of unequal exchange and declining terms of trade have been criticized on both theoretical and empirical grounds.

From a Marxist perspective, debates over those concepts have been part of a more fundamental critique of the concept of exploitation used by dependency theorists like Frank, and, beyond that, of the concepts of class relations implied by the theory. The idea of unequal exchange locates exploitation in the sphere of exchange, and in its simplest form can be expressed as the view that exploitation occurs because the Third World has to buy dear and sell cheap. The main Marxist critique of this exchange-based view is that Marx's theory of capitalism locates exploitation in the process of production. Exploitation by the capitalist class controlling production employing wage labourers is a long way from the notion of exploitation through trade, and the distinction is the basis of Brenner's cogent criticism of dependency theory. Another dimension of the same divide is that, whereas Marxist exploitation is in terms of SURPLUS VALUE, the profits appropriated in dependency theory are conceived as the somewhat different category of 'surplus'.

These distinctions between Marxist and dependency theorists relate to their wider conceptions of social structure, history and the state; the latter's emphasis on exploitation of one country (or region) by another contrasts with Marxist emphases on exploitation of one class by another. Although many dependency theorists do give class structure and conflict an important place in their analysis, especially in critical analysis of the role of the national bourgeoisie, the school has been criticized for giving primacy to centre–periphery relations instead of class relations. Marxist criticisms of the school's class analysis have been mounted from an alternative position based on analysis of modes of production. Laclau's classic critique views the clash between capitalism and other modes of production, with its contradictory results, as the motor of history in the Third World and a determinant of the state: a view counterposed to dependency theorists' analysis of centre–periphery relations within an all-embracing world capitalism.

Debates of this character stimulated changes in dependency theorists' writings at the same time as the case was weakened by historical changes. The rise of Newly Industrialized Countries made it clear that integration into the world capitalist market does not inevitably cause relative or absolute decline and may, as Warren's reading of Marxist classics suggested, generate strong industrial outposts of capitalism. Moreover, the hegemony in the 1980s of the market- and trade-oriented policies of the financial and aid institutions effectively liquidated the state agencies and strategies that had provided much of the rationale for dependency theory. Consequently, dependency theory no longer exists as a living, distinct theoretical school, but that should not cause us to underestimate its significance. In relation to Africa (Amin, Rodney) and the Caribbean (Beckford, Girvan), as well as Latin America, its ideas had a strong influence on anti-imperialist politics and development strategies. In the 1970s the strategies of Jamaica under Manley, and Tanzania under Nyerere, and UNCTAD's New International Economic Order were strong examples of its influence and there is no doubt that elements of *dependencia* ideas have passed into general political discourse and continue to thrive there.

Reading

Amin, Samir 1974: *Accumulation on a World Scale*.
Blomström, Magnus and Hettne, Björn 1984: *De-*

velopment Theory in Transition. The Dependency Debate and Beyond: Third World Responses.

Brenner, Robert 1977: 'The Origins of Capitalist Development: A Critique of Neo-Smithian Marxism'.

Cardoso, Fernando H. and Faletto, E. 1969: Dependency and Development in Latin America.

Frank, André Gunder 1966: 'The Development of Underdevelopment'.

— 1967: Capitalism and Underdevelopment in Latin America: Historical Studies of Chile and Brazil.

Laclau, Ernesto 1971: 'Feudalism and Capitalism in Latin America'.

Larrain, Jorge 1989: Theories of Development.

Rodney, Walter 1972: How Europe Underdeveloped Africa.

BJÖRN HETTNE

determinism Normally understood as the thesis that for everything that happens there are conditions such that, given them, nothing else could have happened. Thus, impressed by the spectacular astronomical success of Newtonian physics, de Laplace contended that given only knowledge of the total mechanical state of the universe at a given moment of time, nothing 'would be uncertain and the future, as the past, would be present to [our] eyes' (1814 (1951), p. 4). In the influential philosophical form articulated by Hume (1739–40 (1965)) and Mill it appears as *regularity determinism*, viz that for every event x there is a set of events $y_1 \ldots y_n$ such that they are regularly conjoined under some set of descriptions. However, reflection in recent philosophy of science on the conditions under which deterministic outcomes are actually possible (from which determinism as a metaphysical thesis derives its plausibility) suggests that apart from a few special – experimentally established or naturally occurring – closed contexts, laws set limits rather than prescribe uniquely fixed results; and that, in general, laws must be analysed as the tendencies of mechanisms rather than as the invariant conjunctions of events; so that the law-like bond or nomic connection is neither contingent nor actual but necessary and real (Bhaskar 1979). From this perspective the only sense in which science presupposes determinism is the (non-Humean, non-Laplacean) sense of *ubiquity determinism*, i.e. the ubiquity of real causes and hence the possibility of stratified explanations. 'Determinism', as normally understood, can then be seen to rest on both the error of supposing that because an event was historically caused to happen, it was bound to happen before it was caused (a confusion of 'determination' and 'predetermination'), and on a naive actualist ontology of laws.

In a Marxist context the debate about determinism has revolved around the questions of whether determinate or perhaps even dated future outcomes (conditions, states of affairs, events etc.) are (a) inevitable, (b) predictable and (c) fated (in the sense of being bound to transpire whatever people do). At (a) Marx and Marxism are pulled in two directions. Formally Marx identifies the laws of the capitalist economy, such as that of the falling rate of profit, as tendencies subject to counter-influences; and he clearly acknowledges the multiplicity of causes or determinations operating on historical outcomes. 'An economic base which in its principal characteristics is the same [may manifest] infinite variations and gradations, owing to the effect of innumerable external circumstances, climatic and geographical influences, historical influences from the outside etc.' (*Capital* III, ch. 47, sect. 2). At the same time he wishes to avoid eclecticism: 'In all forms of society it is a determinate production and its relations which assigns every other production and its relations their rank and influence. It is a general illumination in which all other colours are plunged and which modifies their specific tonalities. It is a special ether which defines the specific gravity of everything found within it' (*Grundrisse*, Introduction). The tension is clearly visible in Engels's well-known letter to Bloch (21 September 1890): 'The economic situation is the basis, but the various elements of the superstructure . . . also exercise their influence upon the course of events . . . and in many cases preponderate in determining their form. There is an interaction in which, amid the endless host of accidents, the economic movement finally asserts itself as necessary'. In his influential essay 'Contradiction and Overdetermination' (1965 (1969)), Althusser attempted to meet the desiderata of avoiding both monism, whether of an economic reductionist (e.g. Kautsky, Bukharin) or historical essentialist (e.g. Lukács, Gramsci) kind, and pluralism, in his concept (borrowed from Freud) of '*overdetermination*'; arguing that it is the economy which determines which relatively autonomous level of the superstructure is conjuncturally or epochally dominant. (See Marx: 'it is the manner in which the [ancient world and the Middle Ages] gained their livelihood which explains why in one case politics, in the other case Catholicism, played the chief part' (*Capital* I, ch. 1, sect. 4).)

At the most abstract level it seems that Marx is committed to an *integrative* (asymmetrically structured) *pluralism* both within historical materialism and as between historical materialism and various supplementary, or even alternative, explanatory schemes. But within the latter category it may be important to distinguish the case where some determination not described within historical materialism (e.g. the weather) acts as a genuinely independent cause, from the case where its efficacy is subject to the mediation of the historical process as described by historical materialism. In any event, given the complexity and heterogeneity of the multiple causes of events within human history, Marxism is only most implausibly interpreted as a deterministic theory in sense (a).

Superficially at least history seems characterized by a plurality, as well as a multiplicity, of causes. In this respect there is a clear tension between Marx's Preface to the *Critique of Political Economy* and his Preface to the first edition of *Capital* I, where he remarks that 'the country that is more developed industrially only shows, to the less developed, the image of its own future', which suggests a unilinear view of history; and the ringing denunciation in his letter to Mikhailovsky (November 1877) of those who would convert his 'historical sketch of the genesis of capitalism in Western Europe into a historico-philosophical theory of the general path every people is fated to tread, whatever the circumstances in which it finds itself', and the many passages in the *Grundrisse*, which suggest a multilinear view of history.

Turning to (b), it need only be noted here that – with the exception of one or two obviously rhetorical flourishes – all Marx's predictions are conditional, and subject to the operation of *ceteris paribus* clauses, so that he is not a historicist in Popper's sense (see HISTORICISM).

On (c) it would seem clear that Marx is not a fatalist. For him what happens in the future will happen because or at least in virtue of, not despite, whatever men and women do; any other view would constitute a gross reification of the historical process and be contrary to Marx's repeated assertions that it is 'men who make history'. On the other hand, if Marx is not a fatalist, Gramsci (1910–20 (*1977*)) still saw fit to characterize 1917 as 'the revolution against Karl Marx's *Capital*'; and a line of criticism most recently expressed by Habermas (1971)¯ and by Wellmer (1981) has seen Marx's approving quotation in the Afterword to the second edition of *Capital* I from a reviewer's description of his method as '[proving] the necessity of the present order of things, and the necessity of another order into which the first must inevitably pass . . . whether men believe or do not believe it, whether they are conscious of it or not', as indicative of an objectivistic misunderstanding of his own scientific practice.

Just as the general issue of determinism has become intertwined with that of 'free will', so that of necessity has become entangled with that of freedom. In an interesting passage in *Capital* III (ch. 48), Marx juxtaposed two concepts of freedom; the first consisting in the rational regulation and minimization of necessary labour, the second consisting in the 'development of human energy' as 'an end in itself'. It is unclear whether Marx conceived such free creative activity, in communism, as totally unconstrained/unconditioned by social forms (mediations) and historical circumstances. In any event Engels, in *Anti-Dühring* (pt. I, ch. 11), advanced a general metaphysical theory of freedom of a rather different hue, arguing that: 'Freedom does not consist in the dream of independence from natural laws, but in the knowledge of these laws, and in the possibility this gives of making them work towards definite ends.' While Engels attributed the provenance of this notion to Hegel, it seems likely that Engels's aphorism was understood by him and by orthodox Marxists generally more in the Baconian and positivist senses that nature obeys us only if we obey it, and that knowledge is power, than in any Spinozist or Hegelian sense. If this interpretation of Engels is correct, the clear difference remains between the natural and social cases, that in the social sciences knowledge or action is not external to the necessities described. On the other hand it was just such an apparent dislocation of agency from the social process, as naturalistically described, which became the hallmark of the positivistic evolutionism (see POSITIVISM) of the Second International and the historical justificationism (or ultra-voluntarism) of the Third International. In his influential essay 'On the Role of the Individual in History' (1908) Plekhanov attempted to show that a belief in determinism was compatible with a high level of political activity, allowing that individuals could 'change the individual features of events and some of their particular consequences', but not their 'general trend' (p. 169). While Adler and the Austro-Marxists attempted in a variety of ways to reconcile finalism and causality, a purposive account of human agency with a non-voluntarist conception of social forms, the general thrust of WESTERN MARXISM has been anti-naturalist and anti-causalist, as well as anti-determinist. This tendency reached its apogee perhaps in Sartre's attempt to ground the intelligibility of history in the freely chosen projects of individuals, while at the same time insisting upon the multiple orders and levels of mediation to which the forces ordinarily described in historical materialism are properly subject: in Sartre, as in Fichte, it is determination, not freedom (or the possibility of emancipation), which needs to be explained. (See also DIALECTICS; INDIVIDUAL; KNOWLEDGE, THEORY OF; MATERIALISM; REALISM; SCIENCE.)

Reading

Adler, Max 1904 (1978): 'Causality and Teleology'. In Bottomore and Goode, eds. Austro-Marxism.

Althusser, Louis 1965 (1969): 'Contradiction and Overdetermination'. In For Marx.

Bhaskar, Roy 1979: The Possibility of Naturalism.

Cohen, G. A. 1978: Karl Marx's Theory of History.

Giddens, A. 1981: A Contemporary Critique of Historical Materialism.

Plekhanov, G. 1908 (1969): 'On the Role of the Individual in History'. In Fundamental Problems of Marxism.

Sartre, Jean-Paul 1963: The Problem of Method.

Timpanaro, S. 1975 (1976): 'Engels and Free Will'. In On Materialism.

Wellmer, A. 1988: 'Critique of Marx's Positivism'. In Bottomore ed. Interpretations of Marx.

Williams, R. 1976: 'Determinism'.

ROY BHASKAR

Deutscher, Isaac Born 3 April 1907, Chrzanów near Cracow; died 19 August 1967, Rome. Was born into a religious Jewish family and destined to be a Talmudic scholar, but renounced his religious beliefs during his youth, and joined the outlawed Polish Communist party in Warsaw in 1927. He was expelled from the party in 1932 for his opposition to the line which then prevailed in regard to fascism, namely that it was no greater threat to the working class than was social democracy. Deutscher was associated with the Trotskyist opposition to Stalinism, but became a member of the Polish Socialist Party. He opposed the formation of the Fourth (Trotskyist) International in 1938 on the ground that the conditions for its effectiveness did not exist. He left Warsaw for London in 1939, and served in the Polish Army from 1940 to 1942. Thereafter he combined journalism for such papers as The Economist and The Observer with the writing of essays and books, and with occasional lecturing and broadcasting. He delivered the Trevelyan Lectures at Cambridge University in the session 1966–67; these were published as The Unfinished Revolution: Russia 1917–1967 (1967).

Deutscher's main writings were his 'political biography' of Stalin, and his three-volume work on Trotsky. These are outstanding examples of biography in the Marxist mode, and are also notable for their literary quality. In these and other writings, Deutscher set out to present a balanced appraisal of the Soviet experience. He was a consistent and severe critic of Stalin and Stalinism; but he allied his condemnation with a positive assessment of what had been achieved by the 'revolution from above' which Stalin had engineered. A major theme of Deutscher's writings was that a new working class was coming into being in the Soviet Union, which would in time fulfil the promise of the 'unfinished revolution' begun in October 1917.

Reading

Deutscher, Isaac 1949 (1967): Stalin: A Political Biography.

— 1954: The Prophet Armed: Trotsky 1879–1921.

— 1959: The Prophet Unarmed: Trotsky 1921–1929.

— 1963: The Prophet Outcast: Trotsky 1929–1940.

— 1967: The Unfinished Revolution.

— 1968: The Non-Jewish Jew.

— 1969: Heretics and Renegades and Other Essays.

Horowitz, David 1971: *Isaac Deutscher. The Man and his Work*.

Syré, L. 1984: *Isaac Deutscher – Marxist, Publizist, Historiker. Sein Leben und Werk 1907–1967*.

RALPH MILIBAND

dialectical materialism Dialectical materialism has been widely thought of as the PHILOSOPHY of Marxism, in contrast and relation to Marxist science, distinguished as historical materialism. The term was probably first used by Plekhanov in 1891. It was in that first generation after Marx's death that 'Diamat' (a shorthand term which became current especially in the USSR) emerged, as the work of Marx and Engels gave way to that of their followers. Marxism itself crystallized out of that transition, and dialectical materialism was constitutive of it (see MARXISM, DEVELOPMENT OF). The first generation of Marxists was dominated by the two most famous books of the founders, Marx's *Capital* and Engels's *Anti-Dühring*. The former represented the basic economic science of historical materialism. It was Engels in *Anti-Dühring* who was regarded as having presented in its 'final shape' (Plekhanov 1908, p. 23) the philosophy of Marxism. Dialectical materialism was a powerful force in the Second International, and following the Russian revolution it became essential to communist party orthodoxy.

On its own understanding dialectical materialism is cross-bred from the union of two bourgeois philosophies: the mechanistic MATERIALISM of the Scientific Revolution and Enlightenment, and Hegel's idealist DIALECTICS. The mechanicism of the former, which is incompatible with dialectics, and the IDEALISM of the latter, which is incompatible with materialism, are rejected and opposed as 'metaphysical' and 'ideological'. The result is a philosophy in the sense of a 'world outlook', 'the communist world outlook' as Engels calls it (*Anti-Dühring*, Preface to 2nd edn): a body of theory taken to be true of concrete reality as a whole, and conceived as in a sense scientific, as a kind of 'natural philosophy' generalizing and supported by the findings of the special sciences as they advance to maturity, including the social science of historical materialism. Thus, whereas Marx's theoretical work is a study of society, Engels founded dialectical materialism by developing a 'dialectics of nature' (*Dialectics of Nature*), based on the claim that 'in nature . . . the same dialectical laws . . . force their way through as those which in history govern . . . events' (*Anti-Dühring*, Preface to 2nd edn). The central theories of dialectical materialism, then, are presented as scientific laws of a completely general kind, governing 'nature, society, and thought' (*Anti-Dühring*, pt. I, ch. XIII). The political point of such a theory, as of Engels's distinctive contribution generally, is to argue the scientificity of Marxism, recruiting for historical materialism the support of the cognitive authority enjoyed by NATURAL SCIENCE, and at the same time depriving of that support other political and cultural movements currently claiming it, like Dühring's work, or 'social Darwinism' (Benton, in Mepham and Ruben 1979, vol. II, p. 101).

The combination of materialism with dialectics transforms both. Properly understood, the materialism of dialectical materialism is not, like its traditional ancestor, reductive. It does not reduce ideas to matter, asserting their ultimate identity. It holds, dialectically, that the material and the ideal are different, in fact are opposites, but within a unity in which the material is basic or primary. Matter can exist without mind, but not vice versa, and mind was historically emergent from matter and remains dependent on it. It follows that the mature special sciences form a unified hierarchy with physics at their base, though they are not reducible to physics. It follows also, in epistemology, that physics gives us knowledge of a mind-independent objective reality. What the component of dialectics asserts is that concrete reality is not a static substance in undifferentiated unity but a unity that is differentiated and specifically contradictory, the conflict of opposites driving reality onwards in a historical process of constant progressive change, both evolutionary and revolutionary, and in its revolutionary or discontinuous changes bringing forth genuine qualitative novelty. It is as such an emergent novelty that the mind is understood by this materialist version of dialectics. At the most basic intellectual level of logic, the contradictory nature of reality is taken to imply that contradictory statements are true of reality and consequently to require a special dialectical logic that supersedes formal logic, with its essential principle of non-contradiction (see CONTRADICTION; LOGIC).

Thus the fundamental laws of dialectical materialism are: (1) the law of the transformation of quantity into quality, according to which gradual quantitative changes give rise to revolutionary qualitative changes; (2) the law of the unity of opposites, which holds that the unity of concrete reality is a unity of opposites or contradictions; (3) the law of the NEGATION of the negation, which claims that in the clash of opposites one opposite negates another and is in its turn negated by a higher level of historical development that preserves something of both negated terms (a process sometimes represented in the triadic schema of thesis, antithesis, and synthesis).

There is no doubt that Marx's theory of society is both materialist and dialectical, and claims to be scientific. If it is justified in claiming the cognitive advantage of scientificity it must have important continuities with the established natural sciences. But it may be that there are other and more reliable continuities than the one argued for by Engels and by dialectical materialism, namely a shared content constituting a very general theory about reality as a whole, 'the communist world outlook'. In any case, there is a problematic tension in the union of dialectics and materialism, especially the materialism of the natural sciences with its strong tendencies towards mechanistic reductivism and detached objectivism. It is that emphasis on the natural sciences and on historical materialism as a natural science of society that is distinctive, within Marxism, of dialectical materialism. In consequence, dialectical materialism has pressed historical materialism towards ECONOMISM, the supposition that, as the material base of society, only the economy, and even perhaps only its 'most material' aspect, productive technology, has real causal efficacy, the political and theoretical superstructure being epiphenomenal. Lenin and Mao Tse-tung, both committed exponents of 'the communist world outlook', resisted economism, but its anti-revolutionary effects were present in the Marxism of the Second International and later Communist Party orthodoxy.

In the 1920s and 1930s, as the Russian revolution degenerated into Stalinist tyranny and party bureaucracy, the general domination of Marxist philosophy by dialectical materialism began to crumble outside the USSR and give way to a second Marxist philosophy, Marxist humanism. Its leading theorists were Lukács and Korsch, and their rejection of the materialism of the natural sciences and their Hegelian emphasis on dialectic seemed to be confirmed by the rediscovery of Marx's early philosophical writings. These Hegelianizing tendencies have themselves been heavily attacked by the schools of Althusser and Della Volpe in the last two decades. In contrast to this Western Marxism, SOVIET MARXISM has in general continued to adhere to 'Diamat', though there has been a recent tendency to reject the conception of a special dialectical logic superseding formal logic.

Reading

Colletti, L. 1969 (1973): Marxism and Hegel.

Jordan, Z. A. 1967: The Evolution of Dialectical Materialism.

Lenin, V. I. 1908 (1962): Materialism and Empirio-Criticism.

— 1895–1916 (1961): Philosophical Notebooks.

Mao Tse-tung 1937 (1967): 'On Contradiction'.

Mepham, J. and Ruben D.-H., eds. 1979: Issues in Marxist Philosophy.

Norman, R. and Sayers, S. 1980: Hegel, Marx and Dialectic.

Plekhanov, G. V. 1908 (1969): Fundamental Problems of Marxism.

Stalin, J. V. 1938 (1973): Dialectical and Historical Materialism. In B. Franklin ed. The Essential Stalin.

Wetter, G. A. 1958: Dialectical Materialism.

ROY EDGLEY

dialectics Possibly the most contentious topic in Marxist thought, raising the two main issues on which Marxist philosophical discussion has turned, viz the nature of Marx's debt to HEGEL and the sense in which Marxism is a science. The most common emphases of the concept in the Marxist tradition are as (a) a method, most usually scientific method, instancing *epistemological* dialectics; (b) a set of laws or principles, governing some sector or the whole of reality, *ontological* dialectics; and (c) the movement of history, *relational* dialectics. All three are to be found in Marx. But their paradigms are Marx's methodological comments in *Capital*, the philosophy of nature expounded by Engels in *Anti-*

Dühring, and the 'out-Hegeling Hegelianism' of the early LUKÁCS in *History and Class Consciousness* – texts which may be regarded as the founding documents of Marxist social science, dialectical materialism, and WESTERN MARXISM respectively.

There are two inflections of the dialectic in Hegel: (a) as a logical process; and (b) more narrowly, as the dynamo of this process.

(a) In Hegel the principle of idealism, the speculative understanding of reality as (absolute) spirit, unites two ancient strands of dialectic, the Eleatic idea of dialectic as *reason* and the Ionian idea of dialectic as *process*, in the notion of dialectic as a self-generating, self-differentiating and self-particularizing *process* of reason. The first idea begins with Zeno's paradoxes, moves through the differing Socratic, Platonic and Aristotelian dialectics, on via the practice of medieval disputation to Kantian critique. The second typically assumes a dual form: in an *ascending* dialectic, the existence of a higher reality (e.g. the Forms of God) is demonstrated; and in a *descending* dialectic, its manifestation in the phenomenal world is explained. Prototypes are the transcendent dialectic of matter of ancient scepticism and the immanent dialectic of divine self-realization of neo-Platonic and Christian eschatology from Plotinus and Eriugena onwards. Combination of the ascending and descending phases results in a quasi-temporal pattern of original unity, loss or division and return or reunification; or a quasi-logical pattern of hypostasis and actualization. Combination of the Eleatic and Ionian strands results in the Hegelian Absolute – a logical process or *dialectic* which actualizes itself by alienating itself, and restores its self-unity by recognizing this alienation as nothing other than its own free expression or manifestation; and which is recapitulated and completed in the Hegelian System itself.

(b) The motor of this process is dialectic more narrowly conceived, which Hegel calls the 'grasping of opposites in their unity or of the positive in the negative' (1812–16 (1969), p. 56). This is the method which enables the dialectical commentator to observe the process by which categories, notions or forms of consciousness arise out of each other to form even more inclusive totalities, until the system of categories, notions or forms as a whole is completed. For Hegel truth is the whole and error lies in one-sidedness, incompleteness and abstraction; it can be recognized by the contradictions it generates, and remedied through their incorporation in fuller, richer, more concrete conceptual forms. In the course of this process the famous principle of *sublation* is observed: as the dialectic unfolds no partial insight is ever lost. In fact the Hegelian dialectic progresses in two basic ways: by bringing out what is implicit, but not explicitly articulated, in some notion, or by repairing some want, lack or inadequacy in it. 'Dialectical', in contrast to 'reflective' (or analytical), thought grasps conceptual forms in their systematic interconnections, not just their determinate differences, and conceives each development as the product of a previous less developed phase, whose necessary truth or fulfilment it is; so that there is always a tension, latent irony or incipient surprise between any form and what it is in the process of becoming.

The most important phases in the development of Marx's thought on Hegelian dialectic are (i) the brilliant analysis of its 'mystified' logic in the *Critique of Hegel's Philosophy of the State*, resumed in the final manuscript of the *Economic and Philosophical Manuscripts*, where Hegel's idealist concept of labour moves centre-stage; (ii) in the immediately following works, *The Holy Family*, *The German Ideology*, and *The Poverty of Philosophy* the critique of Hegel is subsumed under a ferocious polemical assault on speculative philosophy as such; (iii) from the time of the *Grundrisse* on, a definite positive re-evaluation of Hegelian dialectic occurs. The extent of this re-evaluation remains a matter of lively controversy. Two things seem, however, beyond doubt: that Marx continued to be critical of the Hegelian dialectic as such and yet believed himself to be working with a dialectic related to the Hegelian one. Thus he says apropos of Dühring: 'He knows very well that my method of development is *not* Hegelian, since I am a materialist and Hegel is an idealist. Hegel's dialectics is the basic form of all dialectics, but only *after* it has been stripped of its mystified form, and it is precisely this which distinguishes *my* method' (letter to Kugelmann, 6 March 1868). And in the Afterword to the 2nd edn. of *Capital* I he writes: 'The mystification which the dialectic suffers in Hegel's hands by no means prevents him from being the first to present its general forms of motion in a comprehensive manner. With him it is standing on its head. It must be inverted to discover the rational kernel within the mystical shell.' These two metaphors – of the inversion and of the kernel – have been the subject of almost theological speculation. The kernel metaphor seems to indicate that Marx thought it possible to extract part of the Hegelian dialectic – against both (i) the Young Hegelian and Engelsian view that a complete extraction of the dialectical method from Hegel's system is possible and (ii) the view of positivistically-minded critics from Bernstein to Colletti that no extraction at all is possible, that the Hegelian dialectic is totally compromised by Hegel's idealism. Unfortunately Marx never realized his wish 'to make accessible to the ordinary human intelligence, in two or three printer's sheets, what is *rational* in the method which Hegel discovered and at the same time mystified' (Marx to Engels, 14 January 1858).

Whatever Marx's debt to Hegel, there is a remarkable consistency in his criticisms of Hegel from 1843 to 1873. (a) Formally, there are three principal targets of attack – Hegel's inversions, his principle of identity and his logical mysticism. (b) Substantively, Marx focuses on Hegel's failure to sustain the autonomy of nature and the historicity of social forms.

(a) (1) Hegel is guilty, according to Marx, of a three-fold inversion of subject and predicate. In each respect Marx describes Hegel's position as an inversion, and his own position as an inversion of Hegel's – the inversion of the inversion. Thus Marx counterposes to Hegel's absolute idealist ontology, speculative rationalist epistemology, and substantive idealist sociology, a conception of universals as properties of particular things, knowledge as irreducibly empirical, and civil society (later modes of production) as the

foundation of the state. But it is unclear whether Marx is merely affirming the contrary of Hegel's position or rather transforming its problematic. In fact, he is usually doing the latter: his critique is aimed as much at Hegel's terms and relations as his 'inversions'. Marx conceives infinite mind as an illusory projection of (alienated) finite beings and nature as transcendentally real; and the Hegelian immanent spiritual teleology of infinite, petrified and finite mind is replaced by a methodological commitment to the empirically-controlled investigation of the causal relations within and between historically emergent, developing humanity and irreducibly real, but modifiable nature. Nor does Marx clearly differentiate the three inversions which are identified in Hegel. Their distinctiveness is however implied by Marx's second and third lines of criticism, pinpointing Hegel's reductions of being to knowing (the 'epistemic fallacy') and of science to philosophy (the 'speculative illusion').

(2) Marx's critique of Hegel's principle of identity (the identity of being and thought *in* thought) is duplex. In his *exoteric* critique, which follows the line of Feuerbach's transformative method, Marx shows how the empirical world appears as a *consequence* of Hegel's hypostatization of thought; but in his *esoteric* critique, Marx contends that the empirical world is really its secret *condition*. Thus Marx notes how Hegel presents his own activity, or the process of thinking generally, transformed into an independent subject (the Idea), as the demiurge of the experienced world. He then argues that the content of the speculative philosopher's thought actually consists in uncritically received empirical data, absorbed from the existing state of affairs, which is in this way reified and eternalized. The following diagram illustrates the logic of Marx's objection.

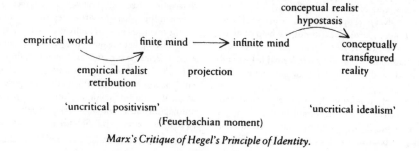

Marx's Critique of Hegel's Principle of Identity.

Marx's analysis implies (i) that conservatism or apologetics is intrinsic to the Hegelian method, not as the left Hegelians supposed, a result of some personal weakness or compromise, and (ii) that Hegel's logical theory is inconsistent with his actual practice, in that his dialectical steps turn out to be motivated by non-dialectical, unreflected, more or less crudely empirical considerations.

(3) Marx's critique of Hegelian 'logical mysticism', and the parthenogenesis of concepts and ideological conjuring tricks it allows, turns on a critique of the notion of the autonomy or final self-sufficiency of philosophy (and ideas generally). But here again it is unclear whether Marx is advocating (i) a literal inversion, i.e. the absorption of philosophy (or its positivisitic supersession) by science, as is suggested by the polemics of the *German Ideology* period; or rather (ii) a transformed practice of philosophy, viz as heteronomous, i.e. as dependent upon science and other social practices but with relatively autonomous functions of its own, as is indicated by his (and Engels's) own practice.

(b) Marx's critique of Hegel in the *Economic and Philosophical Manuscripts* locates two conceptual lacunae: (1) of the *objectivity* of nature and being generally, conceived as radically other to thought, i.e. as independently real and neither causally dependent upon nor teleologically necessitated by any kind of mind; and (2) of the distinction between *objectification* and ALIENATION – for in rationally transfiguring the present, historically determined, alienated forms of human objectification as the self-alienation of an absolute subject, Hegel conceptually pre-empts the possibility of a truly human, non-alienated mode of human objectification. More generally, in contrast to Hegel for whom 'the only labour ... is *abstract mental labour*' (*Economic and Philosophical Manuscripts*, end of Third Manuscript) labour for Marx always (1) presupposes 'a material substratum ... furnished without the help of man' (*Capital* I, ch. 1, sect. 2) and (2) involves real transformation, entailing irredeemable loss and finitude and the possibility of genuine novelty and emergence. So any Marxian dialectic will be objectively conditioned, absolutely finitist and prospectively open (i.e. unfinished).

One possibility raised by Marx's critique of Hegel's philosophy of identity is that the dialec-

tic in Marx (and Marxism) may not specify a *unitary* phenomenon, but a number of *different* figures and topics. Thus it may refer to patterns or processes in philosophy, science or the world; being, thought or their relation (ontological, epistemological and relational dialectics); nature or society, 'in' or 'out of' time (historical v. structural dialectics); which are universal or particular, trans-historical or transient etc. And within these categories further divisions may be significant. Thus any epistemic dialectic may be metaconceptual, methodological (critical or systematic), heuristic or substantive (descriptive or explanatory); a relational dialectic may be conceived primarily as an ontological process (e.g. Lukács) or as an epistemological critique (e.g. Marcuse). Such dialectical modes may be related by (a) a common ancestry and (b) their systematic connections within Marxism *without* being related by (c) their possession of a common essence, kernel or germ, still less (d) one that can be read back (unchanged) into Hegel. Marx may still have been positively indebted to Hegelian dialectic, even if in his work it is totally *transformed* (so that neither kernel nor inversion metaphor would apply) and/or *developed* in a variety of ways.

The most common positive theories of the Marxian dialectic are (i) as a conception of the world (e.g. Engels, DIALECTICAL MATERIALISM, Mao Tse-tung); (ii) as a theory of reason (e.g. Della Volpe, Adorno); and (iii) as essentially depending upon the relations between them (or thought and being, subject and object, theory and practice etc.) (e.g. Lukács, Marcuse). There is little doubt that in Marx's own self-understanding the primary emphasis of the concept is *epistemological*. Often Marx uses 'dialectical' as a synonym for 'scientific' method. In the Afterword to the 2nd edn of *Capital* I he quotes the St Petersburg reviewer's distinctively positivistic description (see POSITIVISM) of his method, commenting 'when the writer describes so aptly ... the method I have actually used, what else is he describing but the dialectical method?' However, it seems clear that Marx's method, though naturalistic and empirical is not positivist, but rather *realist* (see REALISM); and that his epistemological dialectics commits him to a *specific* ontological and a *conditional* relational dialectics as well. In a letter to J. B. Schweitzer (24 January 1865), Marx observes that 'the secret of scientific dialectics' depends upon comprehending 'economic categories as the theoretical expression of historical relations of production, corresponding to a particular stage of development of material production'. Marx's dialectic is scientific because it explains the contradictions in thought and the crises of socio-economic life in terms of the particular contradictory essential relations which generate them (ontological dialectic). And Marx's dialectic is historical because it is both rooted in, and (conditionally) an agent of, the changes in the relations and circumstances it describes (relational dialectic).

Corresponding to Marx's distinction between his empirically-controlled mode of inquiry and his quasi-deductive method of exposition, we can distinguish his critical from his systematic dialectics. The former, which is also a practical intervention in history, takes the form of a triple critique – of economic doctrines, agents' conceptions, and the generative structures and essential relations which underlie them; and it incorporates a (historicized) Kantian moment (first stressed by Max Adler), in which the historical conditions of validity and practical adequacy of the various categories, theories and forms under attack are meticulously situated. Marx's critical dialectics may perhaps best be regarded as an empirically open-ended, materially conditioned and historically circumscribed, dialectical phenomenology.

Marx's systematic dialectics begins in Capital I, ch. 1, with the dialectics of the commodity and culminates in Theories of Surplus Value with the critical history of political economy. Ultimately, for Marx, all the contradictions of capitalism derive from the structurally fundamental contradictions between the use value and the value of the commodity, and between the concrete useful and abstract social aspects of the labour it embodies. These contradictions, together with the other structural and historical contradictions they ground (such as those between the forces and relations of production, the production and valorization process, wage-labour and capital etc.) are (i) real inclusive oppositions, in that the terms or poles of the contradictions existentially presuppose each other and (ii) internally related to a mystifying form of appearance. Such dialectical contradictions violate neither the principle of non-contradiction – for they may be consistently described; nor the law of gravity, for the notion of a real inverted (mis)representation of a real object, generated by the object concerned is readily accommodated with a non-empiricist, stratified ontology, such as that to which Marx is committed (see CONTRADICTION). Marx conceives these fundamental structural contradictions as themselves a historical legacy of the separation of the immediate producers from (i) the means and materials of production, (ii) each other, and hence (iii) the nexus of social relations within which their action on (and reaction to) nature takes place. It is undeniable that there is more than a trace here of a modified Schillerian schema of history as a dialectic of original undifferentiated unity, fragmentation, and restored but differentiated unity. Thus Marx says: 'It is not the unity of living and active humanity with the natural, inorganic conditions of their metabolic exchange with nature, and hence their appropriation of nature, which demands explanation, or is the result of a historical process, but rather their separation from these inorganic conditions of human existence and this active existence, a separation which is completely posited only in the relation of wage-labour and capital' (Grundrisse, 'Chapter on Capital', Notebook V). He may have regarded this as empirically established. But in any event it would be unduly restrictive to proscribe such a conception from science: it may, for instance, function as a metaphysical heuristic, or as the hardcore of a developing research programme with empirical implications, without being directly testable itself.

It is not Marx's so called 'dialectical' definitions or deviations, but his dialectical explanations, in which opposing forces, tendencies or principles are explained in terms of a common causal condition of existence, and critiques, in which inadequate theories, phenomena etc. are explained in terms of their historical conditions, which are distinctive. Why does Marx's critique of political economy take the apparent form of an Aufhebung (sublation)? A new theory will always set out to save most of the phenomena successfully explained by the theories it is seeking to supersede. But in saving the phenomena theoretically Marx radically transforms their descriptions, and in locating the phenomena in a new critical-explanatory ambit, he contributes to the process of their practical transformation.

Is Marx indebted, in his critical or systematic dialectics, to Hegel's conception of reality? The three keys to Hegel's ontology are (1) realized idealism, (2) spiritual monism and (3) immanent teleology. In opposition to (1), Marx rejects both the Hegelian absolute and the figure of constellational identity, conceiving matter and being as irreducible to (alienations of) spirit and thought; against (2), Althusser has correctly argued that differentiation and complexity are essential for Marx, and Della Volpe has rightly stressed that his totalities are subject to empirical, not speculative, confirmation; as for (3), Marx's emphasis is on causal, not conceptual, necessity – teleology is limited to human praxis and its appearance elsewhere 'rationally explained' (see Marx to Lassalle, 16 January 1861). Most important of all, for Marx initiating a *science* of *history*, ontological *stratification* and *becoming* are irreducible, whereas in Hegel, where they are treated in the logical spheres of Essence and Being, they are dissolved into actuality and infinity respectively (and thence into the self-explanatory realm of the Notion). In all philosophically significant respects, Marx's ontology is as much at variance with Hegel's as it is with that of the atomistic

velopment of nature, human society and thought' (*Anti-Dühring*, pt. I, ch. 13); laws which can be 'reduced in the main to three' (*Dialectics of Nature*, 'Dialectics'): (1) the transformation of quantity into quality and vice-versa; (2) the interpenetration of opposites; and (3) the negation of the negation.

There are ambiguities in Engels's discussion: it is unclear whether the laws are supposed to be more or less a priori truths or super-empirical generalizations; or indispensable for scientific practice or merely convenient expository devices. Besides the notorious arbitrariness of Engels's examples, the relevance of his dialectics for Marxism, conceived as a putative social science, may be questioned, especially as Engels is opposed to any reductive materialism. While the evidence indicates that Marx agreed with the general thrust of Engels's intervention, his own critique of political economy neither presupposes nor entails any dialectics of nature, and his critique of apriorism implies the a posteriori and subject-specific character of claims about the existence of dialectical or other types of processes in reality. The relations between the Marxian, Engelsian and Hegelian positions can be represented as follows:

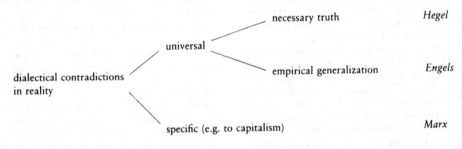

empiricism, which is the target of Engels's later philosophical works, which Marx in his youthful critique had shown that Hegelian idealism tacitly presupposes.

The three commonest positions on dialectics are that it is nonsense (e.g. Bernstein), that it is universally applicable, and that it is applicable to the conceptual and/or social, but not the natural, domain (e.g. Lukács). Engels stamped his immense authority on the second, universalist, position. According to him, dialectics is 'the science of the general laws of motion and de-

The very supposition of a dialectics of nature has appeared to many critics, from Lukács to Sartre, as categorically mistaken, in as much as it involves anthropomorphically (and hence idealistically) retrojecting onto nature categories, such as contradiction and negation, which only make sense in the human realm. These critics do not deny that natural science, as part of the socio-historical world, may be dialectical; what is at issue is whether there can be a dialectics of nature *per se*. Patently there are differences between the natural and social spheres.

But are their specific differences more or less important than their generic similarities? In effect the problem of the dialectics of nature reduces to a variant of the general problem of naturalism, with the way it is resolved depending upon whether dialectics is conceived sufficiently broadly and society sufficiently naturalistically to make its extension to nature plausible. Even then one should not expect a unitary answer – there may be dialectical polarities and inclusive oppositions in nature, but not dialectical intelligibility or reason. Some apologists for Engels (e.g. P. Ruben) have argued that (1) the epistemic interrogation of nature by man and (2) man's historical emergence from nature presupposes Schellingian 'points of indifference' (or dialectical identity) to sustain the intelligibility of the 'transcategorial' links. Yet both epistemic homogenization or equating (in measurement or experiment) and historical emergence (in evolution) presuppose the praxis-independence of the relevant natural poles. Any dialectical relation between humanity and nature takes the un-Hegelian aspect of an *asymmetrically* internal relation (social forms presuppose natural forms, but not the reverse); so that any epistemological or ontological identity occurs only within an overreaching materialist *non-identity*.

In the short run the paradoxical outcome of Engels's intervention was a tendency, in the evolutionist Marxism of the Second International, to a hypernaturalism and monism in many respects comparable to the positivism of Haeckel, Dühring *et al.* that Engels had been consciously opposing. But in the longer run certain formal consequences of Engels's appropriation of the Hegelian dialectic (in which reflectionism acted as an epistemic surrogate for the principle of identity, and a processual worldview underpinned a homology of form) asserted themselves: the absolutization or dogmatic closure of Marxist knowledge, the dissolution of science into philosophy, even the transfiguration of the status quo (in the reconciling *Ansicht* of Soviet Marxism).

If Engels had unwittingly established the naturalized *process* of history as a 'new absolute', Lukács attempted to show that the *goal* of history was the true realization of that very absolute which Hegel had vainly sought in contemplative philosophy, but which Marx had finally found in political economy: in his discovery of the destiny and role of the proletariat as the identical subject-object of history. In both Engels and Lukács 'history' was effectively emptied of substance – in Engels, by being 'objectivistically' interpreted in terms of the categories of a universal process; in Lukács, by being 'subjectivistically' conceived as so many mediations or moments of a finalizing unconditioned act of self-realization, which was its logical ground.

Despite these original flaws, both the dialectical materialist and Western Marxist traditions have produced some notable dialectical figures. Within Western Marxism, besides Lukács's own dialectic of historical self-consciousness or subject-object dialectics, there are Gramsci's theory/practice, Marcuse's essence/existence and Colletti's appearance/reality contradictions, all of more or less directly Hegelian provenance. In Benjamin dialectic represents the discontinuous and catastrophic aspect of history; in Bloch it is conceived as objective fantasy; in Sartre it is rooted in the intelligibility of the individual's own totalizing activity; in Lefebvre it signifies the goal of de-alienated man. Among the more anti-Hegelian Western Marxists (including Colletti), the Della Volpean dialectic consists essentially in non-rigid, non-hypostatized thinking, while the Althusserian dialectic stands for the complexity, preformation and overdetermination of wholes. Poised between the two camps, Adorno emphasizes, on the one hand, the immanence of all criticism and, on the other, non-identity thinking.

Meanwhile, within the dialectical materialist tradition, Engels's third law was unceremoniously dropped by Stalin and the first law relegated by Mao Tse-tung to a special case of the second, which from Lenin onwards increasingly discharged most of the burden of the dialectic. Certainly there were good materialist credentials (as well as political motives) for these moves. The negation of the negation is the means whereby Hegel dissolves determinate being into infinity. On the other hand, as Godelier has pointed out, dialectical materialists have rarely appreciated the differences between the Marxian *unity* and the Hegelian *identity* of opposites. Within this tradition Mao is noteworthy for a potentially fruitful series of distinctions – between antagonistic and nonantagonistic contradictions, principal and secondary contradictions, the principal and secondary aspects of a contradiction etc. – and for stressing, like Lenin and Trotsky, the 'combined and uneven' nature of their development.

In its long and complex history five basic threads of meaning of dialectic, each of which is more or less transformed within Marxism, stand out. (1) From Heraclitus, *dialectical contradictions*, involving inclusive oppositions or conflicts of forces of non-independent origins, are identified by Marx as constitutive of capitalism and its mode of production. (2) From Socrates, the elenchus or *dialectical argument* is on the one hand transformed under the sign of the class struggle, but on the other continues to function in some Marxist thought as, under 'ideal conditions' (in Gramsci, a communist society; in Habermas, an 'unconstrained consensus') a norm of truth. (3) From Plato, *dialectical reason* takes on a range of connotations from conceptual flexibility and novelty – of the sort which, subject to empirical, logical and contextual controls, plays a crucial role in scientific discovery and development – through enlightenment and demystification (Kantian critique) to the depth rationality of materially grounded and conditioned practices of collective self-emancipation. (4) From Plotinus to Schiller, *dialectical process* of original unity, historical fragmentation and differentiated unity, remains, on the one hand, as the counterfactual limits or poles implied by Marx's systematic dialectics of the commodity form, and acts, on the other, as a spur in the practical struggle for socialism. (5) From Hegel, *dialectical intelligibility* is transformed in Marx to include both the causally generated presentation of social objects and their explanatory critique – in terms of their conditions of being, both those which are historically specific and praxis-dependent and those which genuinely are not. (See also DETERMINISM; KNOWLEDGE, THEORY OF; LOGIC.)

Reading

Althusser, L. 1965 (1969): *For Marx*.

Bhaskar, R. 1986: *Scientific Realism and Human Emancipation*.

Colletti, L. 1969 (1973): *Marxism and Hegel*.

Della Volpe, G. 1950 (1980): *Logic as a Positive Science*.

Kolakowski, L. 1978: *Main Currents of Marxism* vol. 1, ch. 1.

Lukács, G. 1923 (1971): *History and Class Consciousness*.

Marcuse, H. 1941 (1955): *Reason and Revolution*.

Stedman-Jones, G. 1973: 'Engels and the End of Classical German Philosophy'.

Wood, A. W. 1981: *Karl Marx*.

ROY BHASKAR

dialectics of nature   One of the most striking legacies of the prestige of nineteenth-century science was its influence on the Marxism of the Second International and on SOVIET MARXISM. Engels, in a series of polemical and exploratory ruminations on science and nature from the point of view of Marxism, attacked Dühring's 'revolution in science' in *Anti-Dühring* and made numerous notes and speculations on the *Dialectics of Nature*. These involved an attempt to integrate certain conceptions of historical materialism into the philosophy of nature – to show, in effect, that Marxism could formulate laws of nature and that a single ontology could embrace nature and humanity. Analytic tools which can be used to gain insight into natural and social processes were thereby reduced to dialectical laws. Engels appeared to be exploring the fit between nineteenth-century scientific findings, theories and debates on the one hand, and dialectical conceptions on the other; e.g., in his reflections on 'The Part Played by Labour in the Transition from Ape to Man'. Subsequent codifiers of this approach transformed it into a sclerotic form of Marxist metaphysics which laid down the putative laws of being (see MARXISM, DEVELOPMENT OF). In particular, dialectics of nature offers three universal theorems: thesis – antithesis – synthesis, or 'negation of the negation' as the law of all development; the transformation of quantity into quality as an explanation of how evolutionary change becomes revolutionary change; the interpenetration of opposites as a fundamental dialectical relationship (see DIALECTICS). As a philosophy of science dialectics of nature has found little favour in the West. In the Soviet Union, China and Eastern Europe it has been taken very seriously indeed, but it has the air of a catechism rather than a growing and deepening tradition (see PHILOSOPHY).

Reading

Graham, Loren R. 1973: *Science and Philosophy in the Soviet Union.*

Kolakowski, Leszek 1978: *Main Currents of Marxism.* vol. 2, ch. 15.

Wetter, Gustav, A. 1952: *Dialectical Materialism.*

ROBERT M. YOUNG

dictatorship of the proletariat This is a crucial concept in Marx's political thought, and also in Leninism. In a letter to J. Wedemeyer (5 March 1852) Marx denied that he had discovered classes or class struggles, but insisted that 'what I did that was new was to prove (1) that the existence of classes is only bound up with particular phases in the development of production; (2) that the class struggle necessarily leads to the dictatorship of the proletariat; (3) that this dictatorship itself only constitutes the transition to the abolition of all classes and to a classless society . . .'.

Nowhere, however, does Marx define precisely what he meant by the concept. In *Class Struggles* he speaks of revolutionary socialism and communism as involving the 'declaration of the permanence of the revolution, the class dictatorship of the proletariat as a necessary intermediate point on the path towards the abolition of class differences in general . . .' (ch. 3); and in the *Critique of the Gotha Programme* he also said that 'between capitalist and communist society lies a period of revolutionary transformation from one to the other. There is a corresponding period of transition in the political sphere and in this period the state can only take the form of a revolutionary dictatorship of the proletariat' (sect. 4). But these and other references in Marx's writings to the dictatorship of the proletariat do not explain it any further.

There is, however, one major text of Marx which may be taken to constitute an elaboration of what he meant by the concept, namely the pamphlet he wrote on the Paris Commune in 1871, *The Civil War in France*. Marx said later that the Commune was 'merely the rising of a city under exceptional conditions', and that 'the majority of the Commune was in no wise socialist, nor could it be' (letter to F. Domela-Nieuwenhuis, 22 February 1881). Engels, on the other hand, in an Introduction to *The Civil War in France* for a new German edition, said in

1891: 'Look at the Paris Commune. That was the Dictatorship of the Proletariat'; and in the light of Marx's view of the Commune, this is a warranted claim.

For Marx, the significance of the Paris Commune ('the political form at last discovered under which to work out the economical emancipation of labour', *Civil War in France*, ch. 3) was that, unlike all previous revolutions, it had begun to dismantle the state apparatus and given power to the people: 'the whole initiative hitherto exercised by the state was laid into the hands of the Commune', whose municipal council was elected by universal suffrage and a majority of whose members 'were naturally working men, or acknowledged representatives of the working class'. 'The Commune was to be a working, not a parliamentary body, executive and legislative at the same time.' It got rid of the police, suppressed the standing army, and replaced it by the armed people. Like the rest of public servants, 'magistrates and judges were to be elected, responsible and revocable'; and all public service had to be done at workmen's wages. 'The Communal constitution', Marx also said, 'would have restored to the social body all the forces hitherto absorbed by the state parasite feeding upon, and clogging the free movement of, society' (ibid. ch. 3). In short, Marx saw the Commune as an attempt to give power to the working class and to bring into being a regime as close to direct democracy as was possible.

This points to the fact that the dictatorship of the proletariat, in Marx's view of it, was meant literally: in other words, that he meant by it not only a form of *regime*, in which the proletariat would exercise the sort of hegemony hitherto exercised by the bourgeoisie, with the actual task of government being left to others, but also as a form of *government*, with the working class actually governing, and fulfilling many of the tasks hitherto performed by the state.

This view of the dictatorship of the proletariat as being both a form of regime and a form of government found its strongest expression in Lenin's 'State and Revolution', written on the eve of the October Revolution of 1917 and closely based on Marx's interpretation of the Paris Commune. The work, however, does not deal with a major problem connected with the concept, namely the role of the party. For there is clearly a very great difference between the 'dictatorship of the proletariat' on the one hand, and the 'dictatorship of the proletariat under the guidance of the Party' on the other; and it is the latter formula which came to prevail, both in theory and practice.

The same problem is present in an additional and very important meaning of the concept: this is its interpretation as the ruthless suppression by the proletariat of its enemies in the course of revolution and in the transitional period between capitalism and socialism (see TRANSITION TO SOCIALISM). 'The revolutionary dictatorship of the proletariat', Lenin wrote at the end of 1918, 'is power won and maintained by the violence of the proletariat against the bourgeoisie, power that is unrestricted by any laws' ('The Proletarian Revolution and the Renegade Kautsky'). This came to mean the use of repression by the state and its coercive organs, under loose legal provisions, and in the name of the proletariat.

It is the repressive aspect of the concept which has tended to be emphasized by its critics; and it is because it has come to be widely associated with the dictatorship of the party and the state over the whole of society, including the proletariat, that it has proved an embarrassment to the leaders of communist parties in capitalist countries. Many such parties have now officially expunged the dictatorship of the proletariat from their party programmes.

Reading

Balibar, Étienne 1977: *On the Dictatorship of the Proletariat.*

Draper, Hal 1977: *Karl Marx's Theory of Revolution.* Vol. II: *The Politics of Social Classes.*

Kautsky, Karl 1918 (*1919*): *The Dictatorship of the Proletariat.*

Lenin, V. 1. 1917 (*1964*): 'The State and Revolution'.

– 1918 (*1965*): 'The Proletarian Revolution and the Renegade Kautsky'.

RALPH MILIBAND

Dietzgen, Josef Born 9 December 1828, Blankenburg, near Cologne; died 15 April 1888, Chicago. Dietzgen was a largely self-educated philosopher who received qualified praise from Marx and Engels; his followers credited him with no less than the articulation of a science of

understanding that complemented Marxism.

Dietzgen received limited education before he began work in his father's tannery, when his recreational reading included the *Communist Manifesto*. Repressive reaction to the events of 1848 drove him to the United States for several years, and in 1859 he returned there and settled in Alabama until the outbreak of the Civil War. In 1864 he undertook supervision of a tannery operated by the Russian government in St Petersburg, and there wrote his first work, 'The Nature of Human Brainwork, Described by a Working Man'. On his return to the Rhineland he wrote for the social democratic press, attended the Hague Congress of the International and stood as a candidate for the Reichstag. His last years were spent in the United States, where he completed his major work, *The Positive Outcome of Philosophy*.

Dietzgen was a strenuous opponent of speculative thought who insisted on the need for an inductive method based on sensory experience. He believed that humanity needed to be liberated from traditional religion and from those metaphysical systems that separated mind from matter, fact from value. His own monist philosophy claimed to furnish the proletariat with a unified dialectical system in which 'everything is the essence of everything, everything is contained in the all, everything related, everything interconnected, everything interdependent'. In his later writings he moved from questions of epistemology to propound a religion of social democracy that was scientific in its premises and yet offered the promise of redemption through heightened proletarian consciousness.

Dietzgen's early writings earned qualified public praise from Marx, who presented him to the Hague Congress of the First International as 'our philosopher'; and from Engels, who in *Ludwig Feuerbach and the Outcome of Classical German Philosophy* credited him with the independent discovery of the materialist dialectic. In private correspondence Marx and Engels were more patronising about his deficiencies of formal education.

Dietzgen later attracted a considerable international following. English translations of his principal writings were published by Charles Kerr in 1906; Russian translations appeared at the same time; a collected German-language edition followed in 1911. Lenin enlisted

Dietzgen in his assault on the empirio-criticists but distinguished between the cosmic excesses of the 'muddleheaded' Dietzgen and the strictly realist contribution of Dietzgen the atheist. Orthodox communists became more critical of Dietzgen in the 1920s when his more ardent disciples pressed his claim to have extended and completed the philosophical foundations of Marxism, and his ideas became confined to the fringes of working-class education.

Reading
Dietzgen, J. 1906: *Philosophical Essays.*
— 1906: *The Positive Outcome of Philosophy.*
Macintyre, S. 1974: 'Joseph Dietzgen and British Working-class Education'.
— 1980: *A Proletarian Science: Marxism in Britain 1917–1933.*
Ree, J. 1984: *Proletarian Philosophers: Problems in Socialist Culture in Britain, 1900–1940.*

STUART MACINTYRE

distribution For Marx relations of distribution differ between one form of society and another, as was understood by J. S. Mill; but unlike other writers Marx argued that they are derived from RELATIONS OF PRODUCTION.

> The so called distribution relations, then correspond to and arise from historically determined specific social forms of the process of production . . . The view which regards only distribution relations as historical, but not production relations, is . . . solely the view of the initial, but still handicapped, criticism of bourgeois economy. (*Capital* III ch. 51)

At the centre of Marx's theory of PRODUCTION is the EXPLOITATION of one class by another. The corresponding extraction of surplus labour yields a distributional relationship between the classes. But it is one that can only be understood in its quantitative and qualitative dimensions by reference to the relations of production. Let us illustrate this in the context of capitalism, although Marx has much to say about distributional relations under communism in the *Critique of the Gotha Programme.*
The basic distributional relationship is between CAPITAL and labour, each represented in the form of revenue by PROFIT and WAGES. Accordingly, a distributional analysis of capital-

ism views it as a conflict over exploitation as expressed in an inverse relationship between profit and wages. For Marx, however, profits are derived from the production of SURPLUS VALUE, through the coercion of labourers to work over and beyond the labour time required to produce the wage goods. The distribution between profits and wages is then derived from the relations of production. Wages are *advanced* as a *precondition* of production, and profits, as the form of surplus value in EXCHANGE, are the *result* of production, itself a conflict between capital and labour over the LABOUR PROCESS. Consequently, distributional relations under capitalism are not to be seen primarily, as in the Sraffian school of Marxism, as a conflict between the two classes over the shares of a net product but as the result of a conflict over production in which the classes are not situated symmetrically.
The production of surplus value reveals the nature of the distributional relations between capital and labour. But surplus value itself has to be distributed. Among industrial capitalists, and given the mobility of capital through CREDIT, there is a tendency for surplus value to be distributed as profit in proportion to capital advanced – the formation of PRICES OF PRODUCTION AND THE TRANSFORMATION PROBLEM. Surplus value is also appropriated in other forms such as RENT, for which the relations of landed property are crucial, and INTEREST, for which FINANCIAL CAPITAL must be analysed. In addition, COMPETITION is the most complex and concrete arbiter of distribution allowing, for example, wages to include a portion of surplus value from time to time, when the market for LABOUR POWER is advantageous to wages.

BEN FINE

division of labour Marx defines the social division of labour as 'the totality of heterogeneous forms of useful labour, which differ in order, genus, species and variety' (*Capital* I, ch. 1). He then points out that such a division of labour is a necessary condition for commodity production, for without mutually independent acts of labour, performed in isolation from one another, there could be no commodities to exchange with one another on the market. But the converse is not true: commodity production is not a necessary condition for a social division of labour to exist; primitive communities have a division of labour, but their products do not become commodities. Similarly, and more to the point, the division of labour within a factory is not the result of workers exchanging their individual products. This suggests that there are two quite different divisions of labour to be considered. First, there is the social division of labour, understood as a complex system of all the different useful forms of labour which are carried on independently of one another by private producers, a division of labour in exchange, between individual, independent, competing capitalists (in the case of capitalism). Secondly, there is the division of labour between workers, each of whom performs a partial operation, all operations being performed simultaneously; what is produced is the social product of the collective worker. This is a division of labour in production, between capital and labour within the production process, and while it is mutually related to the division of labour in exchange, the origins and development of the two divisions are quite different. (See CAPITAL; COMMODITY; EX-CHANGE; VALUE.)

Consider first the social division of labour. This exists in all types of society and originates in differences in human physiology, differences which are used to further particular ends depending upon the particular social relations which predominate. Further, different communities have access to different means of production and means of subsistence in their natural environments, and these differences prompt a mutual exchange of products as different communities come into contact with one another. Thus exchange within and between social units (the family, the tribe, the village, the community or whatever) provides an impetus for the specialization of production and hence a division of labour. However, with the development of capitalism, products are gradually converted into commodities, and a division of labour emerges within the production process, a specifically capitalist creation, which interacts with the social division of labour in the following way. The pursuit of valorization and hence surplus value (see ACCUMULATION) amalgamates previously independent handicraft producers into one production process in a single location under the control of capital; in this manner the division of labour in production develops at the expense of the social division of labour. At the same time, production in particular labour processes is broken down into its constituent elements, each becoming a separate production process; in this manner the social division of labour develops at the expense of the division of labour in production. But the forces of production developed by capital increase at such a pace that both divisions of labour expand, continually demarcating and revising the lines drawn between them. Thus it is the compulsion to accumulate which structures the capitalist division of labour, and not the limits imposed by the extent of the market. (See COOPERATION; LABOUR PROCESS; MANUFACTURE.)

Despite this continual interaction, the specialization that occurs in production under capital's control is quite different in kind from that which occurs in the exchange between different capitals. First, the division of labour in exchange only links all the different production processes which exist in so far as those processes produce commodities; different labours are only connected through the products of those labours as commodities, a connection which is only realized in the activities of purchase and sale. By contrast, in the division of labour in production no single worker produces a commodity; each worker is just a component of the collective worker, the sum total of all the specialized activities. And the only activities of purchase and sale which occur are the purchases by the capitalist of the labour-power of the required number of workers.

Secondly, the division of labour in society requires a wide distribution of the means of production among a large number of independent producers. But the division of labour within production presupposes a concentration of the means of production as the exclusive private property of the capitalist.

Thirdly, the way in which the two divisions of labour are organized is quite different. As regards the division of labour in society, what Marx calls 'the play of chance and caprice' (*Capital* I, ch. 14) have their sway, resulting in a seemingly arbitrary distribution of capitals between the various branches of social labour. While each capitalist is constrained by the necessity of producing a use value, and ultimately constrained by profitability considerations, these constraints only impinge upon the capitalist through price fluctuations. Thus the social division of labour is enforced *a posteriori*, by the process of COMPETITION. By contrast, 'chance and caprice' have no sway at all in the production process; each worker has a definite function, combining in determinate proportions with other workers and with means of production. The division of labour in production is planned, regulated and supervised by the capitalist, since it is a mechanism which belongs to capital as its private property; it is thus enforced *a priori* by the coercive powers of capital. Marx concludes that 'in the society where the capitalist mode of production prevails, anarchy in the social division of labour and despotism in the manufacturing division of labour mutually condition each other' (*Capital* I, ch. 14). And what is true for manufacturing is even more true in machinofacture, in which the process by which labour is subordinated to the means of production is realized to its fullest extent. (See MACHINERY AND MACHINOFACTURE.)

Finally, this contrast between 'anarchy' and 'despotism' is reinforced by bourgeois ideology. The organized division of labour within production is celebrated as the organization which increases the productive power of capital, the lifetime confinement of workers to partial operations which stunt and distort their human capacities being conveniently ignored. But every conscious attempt to regulate the disorganized social division of labour, to control it, to plan it according to socially agreed criteria, is promptly denounced as a dangerous encroachment upon individual freedom, the rights of private property, and the initiative or entrepreneurship of the individual capitalist. Bourgeois ideology thus tends to analyse the division of labour in terms of the allocation of individuals to jobs according to preferences and to skills (whether innate or acquired), to celebrate specialization as the source of increased growth and productivity, and in general to ignore the division of labour as the product of particular economic and social relations. Historically specific categories and institutions are thus treated as eternal, rather than as transitory; since individual preferences and technologies of production will always exist, it is easy to ridicule as hopelessly utopian the conception of Marx and Engels that

in communist society, where nobody has one exclusive sphere of activity but each can become accomplished in any branch he wishes, society regulates the general production and thus makes it possible for me to do one thing today and another tomorrow, to hunt in the morning, fish in the afternoon, rear cattle in the evening, criticize after dinner, just as I have a mind, without ever becoming hunter, fisherman, herdsman, or critic. (*German Ideology*, vol. I, sect. IA1)

Such a criticism is however quite misconceived. The major thrust of Marx's analysis of capitalism is to demonstrate how and why the products of human labour dominate the producers themselves, how objectified labour in its existence as capital exerts its dominance over living labour through the seemingly objective laws of supply and demand. And one of the corollaries of this is that a division of labour is forced upon individuals by the society which they themselves create. Now production is of course always an activity of objectifying labour in products, but the class relations under which such objectification occurs are critical for determining whether

as long as a cleavage exists between the particular and the common interest, as long, therefore, as activity is not voluntarily, but naturally, divided, man's own deed becomes an alien power opposed to him, which enslaves him instead of being controlled by him . . . this fixation of social activity, this consolidation of what we ourselves produce into a material power above us . . . is one of the chief factors in historical development up till now. (Ibid.)

This is a characteristic inversion of capitalism whereby what is subject is rendered object, and vice versa. Consequently, Marx and Engels treat the abolition of the division of labour as synonymous with the abolition of private property relations; people will only be free when they gain control over production and exchange, consciously planning them. With the abolition of the commodity-form, the social characteristics of labour will no longer appear as the objective characteristics of the products of labour; as a social relation between objects, movements of which control the producers themselves. Rather the reverse; these real inversions will disappear with the abolition of a division of labour based on private property.

Obviously some sort of social division of labour will still be necessary in order for the material conditions of human life to continue to be produced and reproduced. True freedom is only possible outside the sphere of actual production; within production, freedom

> can only consist in socialized man, the associated producers, rationally regulating their interchange with Nature, bringing it under their common control, instead of being ruled by it as by the blind forces of Nature; and achieving this with the least expenditure of energy and under conditions most favourable to, and worthy of, their human nature. (*Capital* III, ch. 48)

Thus instead of 'despotism' controlling the division of labour in production, that division will be controlled by democratic planning by the producers themselves. Instead of 'anarchy' controlling the social division of labour, 'society . . . has to distribute its time in a purposeful way, in order to achieve a production adequate to its overall needs; just as the individual has to distribute his time correctly in order to achieve knowledge in proper proportions or in order to satisfy the various demands on his activity' (*Grundrisse*, 'The Chapter on Money').

The developing potentialities of machinery, and in particular of AUTOMATION, under socialized relations of production, will permit such an economy of time in production that for the first time a 'true realm of freedom' will be created outside material production, comprising 'that development of human energy which is an end in itself' (*Capital* III, ch. 48). Then we will have

> the free development of individualities, and hence not the reduction of necessary labour time so as to posit surplus labour, but rather the general reduction of the necessary labour of society to a minimum, which then corresponds to the artistic, scientific etc. development of the individuals in the time set free, and with the means created, for all of them. (*Grundrisse*, 'The Chapter on Capital')

In this manner the division of labour will be abolished. (See also COMMUNISM.)

SIMON MOHUN

Dobb, Maurice H.   Born 24 July 1900, London; died 17 August 1976, Cambridge. The foremost Marxist economist of twentieth-century Britain. Having studied at Cambridge and London he obtained his first teaching post at Cambridge in 1924 and his work there until and after retirement profoundly influenced Marxist academic thought on the rise of capitalism, socialist planning, value theory, and the history of bourgeois economics. The strength of his academic work owes much to the fact that he was an active political militant and addressed his theoretical work, particularly that on socialist planning, to practical problems. In autobiographical notes in 1978 Dobb emphasized his political activism as a communist; he was a member of the Communist Party from 1922 until his death.

Studies in the Development of Capitalism (1946) examines the 'laws of motion' of feudal production which led to its crisis and dissolution, rejecting the thesis that the external force of growing exchange and trade was causative. This and related work determined the issues for others' subsequent work (see TRANSITION FROM FEUDALISM TO CAPITALISM). His many publications on socialist planning from 1928 to *Socialist Planning: Some Problems* (1970) were concerned with the relationship of market and plan, and with the appropriate balance between production of means of production and of consumption goods. His work on value theory and bourgeois economics stood almost as a lone representative of Marxist economics in Britain for some years. His interpretation of value theory was influenced especially in later works (1970, 1973) by Ricardo and by Sraffa, with whom he collaborated in publishing Ricardo's *Works*.

Reading

Cambridge Journal of Economics 2. 2 (Maurice Dobb Memorial Issue).

Dobb, M. H. 1925: *Capitalist Enterprise and Social Progress.*

— 1928: *Wages.*

— 1937: *Political Economy and Capitalism.*

— 1946: *Studies in the Development of Capitalism.*

— 1955: *On Economic Theory and Socialism.*

— 1965 (1978): 'Random Biographical Notes'.

— 1969: *Welfare Economics and the Economics of Socialism.*

— 1970: *Socialist Planning: Some Problems.*

— 1973: *Theories of Value and Distribution Since Adam Smith: Ideology and Economic Theory.*

Hilton, R. H. ed. 1976: *The Transition from Feudalism to Capitalism.*

LAURENCE HARRIS

domestic labour Mentioned by Engels (*Origin of the Family*, ch. II, IX), Bebel, Lenin, Trotsky and others as contributing to the economic oppression of women by removing them from social production, domestic labour became a recognized category of Marxist thought with the modern feminist movement (see FEMINISM), as Marxist feminists sought the material basis of women's oppression under capitalism. Previous Marxist writings on women had tended to locate the economic oppression of women purely in their disadvantaged position in the labour market, which followed from their main responsibilities within the home, while the FAMILY itself was seen as a superstructural institution whose effects were primarily ideological. The focus on domestic labour was supposed to rectify this somewhat contradictory position by recognizing that labour went on within the family too, that indeed the most significant form of the sexual division of labour was between domestic labour within the family (mostly performed by women) and wage labour for capital (performed by both sexes but predominantly by men). By extending the scope of labour to include most women's labour it was hoped to provide a materialist account of women's oppression.

The debate was fuelled by disputes over the demand for wages for housework, the protagonists of which claimed that domestic labour was productive labour producing SURPLUS VALUE for capital because it produced a particular commodity, LABOUR POWER. In these respects the home was just like a capitalist factory except that housewives were unwaged. They were therefore a section of the working class but one even more exploited than those who received wages. All the above descriptions were challenged by those opposed to wages for housework, who claimed that the demand would only enshrine women's place in the home and that domestic labour went on under relations of production which differed from those of wage labour for capital in many more respects than simply being unwaged.

The common ground was that domestic labour was the production of use values within the home, for direct consumption by members of the producer's family, which contributed to the reproduction of labour power. Unlike wage labour for capital it was subject to little DIVISION OF LABOUR, COOPERATION or specialization. The debates centred on which of Marx's categories applied to domestic labour, its products, its relations of production and its workers.

First, it was argued that domestic labour was not commodity production, therefore did not produce value, and *a fortiori* could not be a source of surplus value. This argument could be made on two grounds. The first rested on the special character of the commodity labour power, which far from being a commodity 'like any other' (see VALUE OF LABOUR POWER) differs from all others in that it is not produced by any labour process. Instead it is an attribute of living human beings who are themselves maintained (though not produced) by their own consumption of use values, some of which are produced by domestic labour. The other argument against seeing labour power as the product of domestic labour rested on the availability of substitutes for much domestic labour on the market. If the housewife who bakes bread at home is producing labour power, why not the baker who produces bread for sale? If we were to extend this logic, labour power would be the product of many industries, and its production certainly not the *differentia specifica* of domestic labour (see Harrison 1973).

Indeed, it was argued, domestic labour was to be distinguished not by its products but by its relations of production which are not those of value production. Because the products of domestic labour are not produced for sale its labour process is not subject to the operation of the law of value, the coercive force of competition which ensures that labour time is kept to a minimum in the production of commodities. It is only under such conditions that the notion of SOCIALLY NECESSARY LABOUR time has any social meaning. Without the operation of the law of value, there is no process whereby labour takes on the attribute of ABSTRACT LABOUR, which alone constitutes the substance of value (see Himmelweit and Mohun 1977). So if domestic labour did not produce value, it certainly could not produce surplus value, but that did not necessarily mean that no surplus could be produced by domestic labour and extracted in some form other than value. If it could be shown that there is a form of surplus extraction specific to domestic labour, then such labour would constitute a separate mode of production and housewives as domestic labourers would form a distinct class, undergoing a kind of exploitation different from that of the working class (see Delphy 1977, Gardiner 1973, Harrison 1973, Molyneux 1979).

Against this, it was argued that domestic labour cannot constitute a mode of production because its relations of production are not capable of self-reproduction. For domestic labour does not produce its own means of production, but is applied to commodity inputs produced under capitalist relations of production. The argument that it should be seen as a 'client' mode of production dependent on, though distinct from, the capitalist mode failed to recognize that the relation between the two was indeed a symbiotic one – capitalist production being dependent on domestic labour for its supply of labour power. Rather it was the traditional notion of the capitalist mode of production which needed redefinition if the criterion of being at least theoretically capable of independent self-reproduction, and thus appropriate to the characterization of an epoch of history, was to remain the *sine qua non* of a mode of production (see Himmelweit and Mohun 1977). If this was accepted there was no need to characterize housewives as a separate class. And the distinction between productive and unproductive labour, being relevant only to wage workers, did not apply to them. For productive labour is labour from which a profit is extracted by capital and this involves two exchanges: one when labour power is bought and another when the products of its use are sold. Domestic labour is involved in neither exchange: its products are not sold, nor is it wage labour (see Dalla Costa 1973, Fee 1976).

If the capitalist mode of production were to be redefined to include domestic labour it would comprise two forms of labour, the division between which would not define different classes. But this specification no longer differentiates the

workers involved in each form of labour; there is no necessity for this division of labour to coincide with a division between people at all. While this might match the reality of the double shift of employed women's lives, it provides no explanation of the sexual division of labour in which domestic labour is largely women's work.

Seccombe (1980) argued that the explanation of the sexual division of labour could not come from a specification of the capitalist mode of production alone. Even if the conception of a mode of production were to be reformulated to include the 'mode of subsistence', the relations by which the producing class consumes and reproduces its labour power, an explanation would still be needed of why in the capitalist mode this predominantly takes the specific form of the nuclear family. The capitalist mode of subsistence is characterized by individual consumption carried on within private households autonomous from control by capital, a mode of subsistence the working class has fought for and continues to defend in struggles over their living conditions and time away from work. However, the form these households take and the division of labour within them has been conditioned by 'patriarchy', another powerful historical force, dependent on the existence of private property but distinct from and not determined by the capitalist mode of production. The nuclear family is 'patriarchal' in that men have the effective possession of household property, the control of family labour and sexual and custodial rights over wives and children. Marx and Engels thought that the propertyless condition of the working class would erode the basis for the patriarchal family, but they were mistaken in this because they failed to distinguish between property in the means of subsistence and property in the means of production. While the proletariat has remained propertyless in the latter sense, it has managed to struggle for living conditions in which the accumulation of household property becomes possible and has thus, in what Seccombe calls 'breadwinner power', recreated the conditions for patriarchy.

The domestic labour debate was rarely concerned with domestic labour outside capitalism. Nevertheless, reference was frequently made to the differences between domestic labour under capitalism and domestic production in earlier NON-CAPITALIST MODES OF PRODUCTION. In particular, when domestic production was the main means by which a household earned its subsistence, either directly or through commodity production, all members would have worked under the same relations of production. Even though there was a sexual (and age-based) division of labour in which the male head of household controlled the labour of other members, all members visibly contributed to the maintenance of the household; indeed there would have been little separation between tasks necessary for the production of goods and those required for the reproduction of household members.

Further, it can be argued that the modern domestic unit has little historical connection with the unit that formed the basis of household production. For the latter was effectively destroyed by the Industrial Revolution and it was working-class struggle that won, at its most successful, the wages needed to maintain a working-class household within which not all members needed to take employment, personal life could take place and domestic labour was needed (Curtis 1980). For, as has been pointed out for parts of the Third World today, domestic labour requires there to be a household within which it can be performed (Molyneux 1979). Capitalist relations including the reproduction of labour power can be maintained, at a very basic level, without conceding the minimal living conditions in which domestic labour becomes possible.

The domestic labour debate was concerned to uncover the material basis of women's oppression. None of its participants managed to locate that basis within domestic labour itself. At most, the specific oppression of domestic workers was explained, with reference to other explanatory frameworks such as 'patriarchy' to say why it

was women who tended to be those workers. To move beyond this, the specific content of domestic and wage labour would have to be analysed using concepts which distinguish between men and women and do not reproduce the GENDER-blindness of existing Marxist categories. For domestic labour the recognition of gender must arise as soon as questions about human REPRODUCTION are raised. Interestingly, it is around these questions that the debate started, and it is to them that a return will have to be made if women's oppression is to be analysed as such, rather than that of a particular category of workers involved in domestic labour. For this elision to be avoided, the relation between domestic labour conceived of as private labour performed within the home and as labour involved in reproduction will have to be clarified.

Reading

Curtis, Bruce 1980: 'Capital, State and the Origins of the Working-Class Household'. In Bonnie Fox ed. *Hidden in the Household*.

Dalla Costa, M. 1973: 'Women and the subversion of the community'. In *The Power of Women and the Subversion of the Community*.

Delphy, C. 1977: *The Main Enemy*.

Fee, T. 1976: 'Domestic Labour: an analysis of housework and its relation to the production process'.

Gardiner, J. 1975: 'Women's Domestic Labour'.

Harrison, J. 1973: 'Political economy of housework'.

Himmelweit, S. and Mohun, S. 1977: 'Domestic Labour and Capital'.

Molyneux, M. 1979: 'Beyond the Domestic Labour Debate'.

Seccombe, W. 1980: 'Domestic Labour and the Working Class Household'. In Bonnie Fox ed. *Hidden in the Household*.

SUSAN HIMMELWEIT

E

ecology Although Marx and Engels regard the enormous expansionist tendency of the capitalist mode of production as a necessary condition for the transition to socialism, they nonetheless stress the destructive violence of this mode of production. As Marxist theory developed, however, the first point of view was increasingly emphasized in a one-sided manner, until finally Stalin saw the superiority of socialism over capitalism only in the ability of the former to provide the optimal conditions for the growth of the productive forces.

In *The Condition of the Working Class* Engels already mentions the devastating effects of the expansion of industry on the natural environment, while Marx observes that 'the capitalist transformation of the production process is at the same time the martyrdom of the producers' and 'every advance in capitalist agriculture is an advance in the art, not only of robbing the worker, but also of robbing the soil'; such progress therefore leads in the long run to the 'ruin of the permanent sources of this fertility [of the soil]' (*Capital* I, ch. 13). 'Capitalist production, therefore, only develops the techniques and organization of the social process of production by simultaneously undermining the sources of all wealth: land and the worker' (ibid.). In *Capital* III (ch. 46) Marx expressly refers to the obligation of human beings to preserve the ecological preconditions of human life for future generations: 'From the standpoint of a higher socio-economic formation [i.e. socialism] individual private ownership of the earth will appear just as much in bad taste as the ownership of one human being by another. Even a whole society, a nation, or all contemporary societies taken together, are not the absolute owners of the earth. They are only its occupants, its beneficiaries, and like a good paterfamilias have to leave it in improved condition to following generations.'

Reading
Bahro, Rudolf 1980: *Elemente einer neuen Politik, zum Verhältnis von Ökologie und Sozialismus.*
Fetscher, Iring 1982: 'Fortschrittsglaube und Ökologie im Denken von Marx und Engels'. In *Vom Wohlfahrtsstaat zur neuen Lebensqualität.*
Leiss, William 1972: *The Domination of Nature.*
Martinez-Alier, Juan 1987: *Ecological Economics.*

IRING FETSCHER

economic backwardness *See* agrarian question.

economic crises In discussing crisis theories, we must distinguish *general crises*, which involve a widespread collapse in the economic and political relations of reproduction, from the partial crises and business cycles which are a regular feature of capitalist history. In capitalist production the individual desire for profit periodically collides with the objective necessity of a social division of labour. Partial crises and business cycles are merely the system's intrinsic method of reintegrating the two. When the system is healthy, it recovers rapidly from its built-in convulsions. But the unhealthier it is, the longer become its convalescences, the more anaemic its recoveries, and the greater the likelihood of its entering a long phase of depression. In the United States, for example, though there have been thirty-five economic cycles and crises in the 150 years from 1834 to the present, only two – the Great Depressions of 1873–93 and 1929–41 qualify as general crises. The question which now confronts the capitalist world is whether or not the Great Depression of the 1980s will some day be added to this list (Mandel 1972; Burns 1969).

In analysing the capitalist system, Marx constantly refers to its 'laws of motion'. For instance, he speaks of the *tendency* of the rate of profit to fall as a general law, while at the same time presenting various *counteracting tendencies* 'which cross and annul the effects of the general law'. So the question naturally arises: How does a 'law' emerge from tendency and counter-tendency? There are two basic ways to answer this. One possibility is to conceptualize the various tendencies as operating on an equal footing. Capitalism gives rise to a set of *conflicting tendencies*, and the balance of forces existing at a particular historical 'conjuncture' then determines the system's final direction. In this perspective, structural reform and state intervention appear to have great potential, because under the right circumstances they can tip the balance and hence actually regulate the outcome. This general perspective, as will be seen, underlies most modern Marxist crisis theories and has important political implications.

Marx, on the other hand, had a rather different approach to the subject. For him, it was crucial to distinguish between the *dominant* tendency and various subordinate countervailing ones, because the latter operate within the limits provided by the former. Because the dominant tendencies arise out of the very nature of the system itself and endow it with a very powerful momentum, the subordinate tendencies effectively operate within moving limits and are *channelled*, so to speak, in a definite direction. (Within these limits the subordinate tendencies may well function as merely conflicting tendencies on an equal footing.) From this vantage point, those structural reforms, state intervention, and even class struggles which leave the basic nature of the system unchanged have limited potential, precisely because they end by being subordinated to the intrinsic dynamic of the system.

We can now identify two main types of crisis theories, corresponding to the two different methodological approaches to capitalist history: *possibility theories*, based on the notion of law as the resultant of conflicting tendencies, in which general crises occur if and when there is a certain conjunction of historically determined factors; and *necessity theories*, based on the notion of law as the expression of an intrinsic dominant tendency that subordinates countervailing ones, in which the periodic occurrence of general crises is inevitable (though, of course,

the specific form and timing is determined, *within limits*, by historical and institutional factors). We shall see how modern Marxist theories of crisis exemplify these two approaches.

Possibility Theories

Here we can identify two main groups: underconsumption/stagnation theories, and wage squeeze theories.

A. Underconsumption/Stagnation Theories

In capitalist society the money value of its net product is equal to the sum of the wages paid to workers *plus* the profits accruing to capitalists. Since workers get paid less than the total value of the net product, their consumption is never sufficient to buy it back: workers' consumption generates a 'demand gap', and the greater the share of profits to wages in value added, the greater this demand gap. Of course capitalists do consume a portion of their profits, and this helps to fill some of the gap. Nonetheless, the bulk of their income is saved, not consumed, and in Keynesian fashion these savings are viewed as a 'leakage' from demand whose ultimate basis remains the restricted income and consumption of the masses. If this portion of the demand gap corresponding to capitalists' savings were not filled, part of the product would not be sold, or at least not at normal prices, so that the whole system would contract until profits were so low that capitalists would be forced to consume all their income – in which case, there would be no (net) investment and hence no growth. The internal economic logic of a capitalist economy is thus said to predispose it towards stagnation.

Of course the demand gap can be filled not only by consumption but also by investment demand (the demand for plant and equipment). The greater this demand, the higher the level of production and employment in the system at any moment of time, the faster it grows. In the end, therefore, the final motion of the system depends on the interplay between the tendency towards stagnation created by the savings plans of the capitalists, and the countervailing tendency towards expansion created by their investment plans. Capitalists save because as individual capitalists, they must try to grow in order to survive. But they can invest only when the objective possibilities exist, and these in turn depend on two factors. Specifically, the *foundation* for large-scale commerce and trade is provided when the hegemony of a particular capitalist nation (Britain in the nineteenth century and the USA in the twentieth) allows it to orchestrate and enforce international political and economic stability. And the *fuel* for large-scale investment is provided when a critical mass of new products, new markets, and new technologies all happen to coincide. When foundation and fuel coexist expansionary factors will be ascendant. On the other hand as the fuel runs out and the inter-capitalist rivalries increasingly undermine the foundation, at some point the contractionary factors reassert themselves and stagnation becomes the order of the day – until, of course, a new hegemonic order (perhaps forged through a world war) and a new burst of discoveries initiate yet another epoch of growth.

None of this is fundamentally altered by the question of monopoly power. In modern capitalism, a few powerful firms are said to dominate each industry, and by restricting output and raising prices they are able to redistribute income in their favour at the expense of workers and of smaller capitalist firms. Since larger capitalists save a higher proportion of income, total savings rise; on the other hand, in order to keep up prices and profits the bigger firms restrict investment in their own industries, thus curtailing the available investment outlets. By increasing the demand gap and simultaneously weakening investment opportunities, monopolies theoretically make stagnation virtually unavoidable. Of course, *in practice*, post-war 'monopoly capitalism' has until recently 'enjoyed a secular boom . . . in many respects exceeding anything in its earlier history' (Sweezy). And so, once again, the absence of actual stagnation is explained by the presence of unusually strong countervailing factors: post-war US hegemony, new products and technologies, and military expenditures.

Within such a framework, it is obvious that any economic intervention which strengthens and directs the expansionary factors can in principle overcome the threat of stagnation. Keynesian economics, for instance, claims that the state, either through its own spending or through its stimulation of private spending, can achieve socially desired levels of output and employment and thus *determine, in the final instance, the laws of motion of the capitalist economy* (see KEYNES AND MARX). The under consumptionists do not deny this possibility. They merely claim that it is not currently practical, because modern capitalism is characterized by monopoly, not competition: monopoly increases capitalism's tendency towards stagnation; when this stagnation sets in the state counters it by stimulating aggregate demand; but then monopolists respond by raising prices rather than expanding output and employment (as would competitive firms). The resulting stalemate between state power and monopoly power thereby produces stagnation-with-inflation: 'stagflation' (Sweezy; Harman 1980; Shaikh 1978). If the state retreats from this struggle and retrenches, we then get a recession or possibly a depression. From this point of view the appearance of a crisis is an essentially political event, due to the unwillingness of the state to tackle the monopolies. Keynesian theory claims that the state has the economic capability to manage the capitalist system, *and once this premise is accepted*, both the existence of a crisis and the recovery from it are questions of the *political ends* toward which this capability is applied. Thus one is led to conclude that a political programme of curtailing monopolies through price controls, regulation, and forceful economic planning will break the back of inflation, while increased social welfare expenditures and even higher wages will benefit *not only the working class but also the capitalist system as a whole* (by reducing the demand gap). The economic contradictions of the system can be therefore displaced onto and resolved within the political sphere, provided sufficient pressure can be brought to bear on the state.

Sweezy himself studiously avoids drawing the political conclusions inherent in his argument, though he does warn that capitalists themselves may discover new ways to manage the system (1979, *Monthly Review* 31.3 pp. 12–13). But others are much less reticent. (See, for instance, Harrington 1972 ch. XII and 1979 p. 29; various issues of *Dollars and Senses*, particularly October 1979 and July–August 1981; and Gordon *et al.* 1982 pp. 589–91.)

B. Wage Squeeze Theories

Wage squeeze theories attempt to link general crises to a sustained fall in the rate of profit (see FALLING RATE OF PROFIT). The starting point is the recognition that when real wages rise and/or the length and intensity of the working day diminishes, the potential rate of profit falls – other things being equal. In Marxist terms a fall in the rate of surplus value produces a fall in the general rate of profit, *ceteris paribus*. However, this is simply to say that a rise in real wages (adjusted for the length and intensity of work) lowers the rate of profit *relative to its trend*. If the rate of profit tends to fall independently of this, then the rise in (adjusted) real wages merely exacerbates the pre-existing fall in the rate of profit. This, as we shall see in the next section, is what Marx argues. But if the rate of profit otherwise tends to rise, then only a sufficiently rapid rise in real wages can account for an actual fall in the rate of profit. This is typically the claim made by the wage squeeze theorists, who assume that in the absence of changes in the real wage, technical change tends to raise the rate of profit and the ratio of profits to wages.

In one version of the theory, this rising profit rate then directly fuels an investment boom; in the other version, which is really an extension of underconsumption/stagnation theory, the rising profit–wage ratio and increasing monopoly power exacerbate the demand gap and hence the system's tendency towards stagnation, but the state is able to offset this and thereby sustain the boom. In either case, *if* the boom lasts long enough for the market for labour to get so tight and workers to get so militant that their wage demands produce a sustained fall in the actual rate of profit, then a crisis eventually breaks out. Typically, the wage squeeze theory looks for real wages rising faster than productivity as evidence that it is labour which stands behind the crisis.

For instance, the conventional mathematical treatment of the so-called choice of technique implies a rising profit rate unless real wage increases reverse its course (Shaikh 1978a, pp. 242–7). This is cited by most modern proponents of the wage squeeze, such as Roemer (1979), Bowles (1981), and Armstrong and Glyn (1980). Others, such as Hodgson (1975, pp. 75–6), simply cite the empirical stability of the organic composition as a feature of modern capitalism. Finally Kalecki (*1971*) is usually cited as the source of the argument that state intervention turns an underconsumption tendency into a wage squeeze. It should be noted that even within the conventional choice of technique literature a real wage rising relative to *productivity* is neither necessary nor sufficient to generate a falling rate of profit. This is easily shown from the diagrams in Shaikh (1978a, p. 236) in which the maximum wage rate (the vertical intercept) is the net product per worker.

What is important to note here is that because the crisis occurs only when workers' wage increases become 'excessive', there is plenty of room in this theory for a vision of capitalism which can deliver both rising real wages to workers *and* a rising rate of profit to capitalists. From this point of view, the state can in principle engineer a recovery if both workers and capitalists make sufficient concessions, and it can prevent future crises if both sides display some moderation. It is characteristic of possibility theories in general that because they end by endowing the state with the power to determine the basic laws of motion of capitalism, both the expectations and the promises of their proponents come to depend heavily on the notion that even under capitalism, politics *can* command the system. *If this premise is false, then, at the very least, the tactics and strategy surrounding it are open to serious question.* This, as we shall see next, is exactly what necessity theories of crisis imply.

Necessity Theories

The principal modern necessity theory is Marx's theory of the falling rate of profit. In the past, even some versions of underconsumption theory (such as Luxemburg's) were necessity theories, but it is generally conceded that this was primarily due to a mistaken understanding of the logic of their own argument. The law of the falling rate of profit attempts to explain why capitalism goes through long periods of accelerated growth which are necessarily followed by corresponding periods of decelerated growth and eventual crises. What underconsumption theories explain through apparently external factors such as bursts of discoveries, Marx explains through internal factors based on the movements of the potential rate of profit.

The driving force of all capitalist activity is profit, and surplus value is its hidden basis. In order to extract as much surplus value as possible, capitalists must increase the length and/or intensity of the working day, and above all increase the productivity of labour. And in order to compete effectively against other capitalists, they must simultaneously achieve lower unit production costs. *The increase of fixed capital is the solution to both problems.* In brief, the growth of fixed capital relative to labour (the mechanization of production) is the principal means of raising the productivity of labour, and the growth of fixed capital relative to output (the capitalization of production) is the principal means of reducing unit production costs. It can be shown, however, that the growth of fixed capital also tends to lower the rate of profit on the more advanced methods of production (see references cited in FALLING RATE OF PROFIT). For the individual capitalists who first adopt these larger, more capital-intensive methods, their lower unit costs enable them to reduce prices and expand at the expense of their competitors, thus offsetting the smaller rate of profit by means of a larger share of the market. But for the system as a whole, this causes the average rate of profit to drift downwards. Though various factors can temporarily counteract this trend, they operate within strict limits, so that the secular fall in the rate of profit emerges as the *dominant tendency.*

Over a long period of time, the effects of this downward trend in the rate of profit on investment produce a 'long-wave' in the mass of total potential profit, which first accelerates, then decelerates and stagnates. In the latter phase investment demand falls off and excess capacity becomes widespread, while the lack of new investment slows down productivity growth so that real wages may for a time rise *relative* to productivity. In other words, both underconsumption and wage squeeze phenomena appear as *effects* of the crisis of profitability. But they do not *cause* general crises, because there are built-in mechanisms within capitalist accumulation which adjust capacity to effective demand, and which keep wage increases within the limits of productivity increases (*Capital* I, ch. 25, sect. 1; Garegnani 1978).

Each general crisis precipitates wholesale destruction of weaker capitals and intensified attacks on labour, which help restore accumulation by increasing centralization and concentration and by raising overall profitability. These are the system's 'natural' recovery mechanisms. But due to the secular fall in the rate of profit, each succeeding long upswing is characterized by generally lower long-term rates of profit and growth, *so that in the capitalist dominated world the problems of stagnation and worldwide unemployment worsen over time.* Because these problems arise from capitalist accumulation itself and not from either insufficient competition or excessive wages, they cannot be simply 'managed' away by state intervention *no matter how progressive its intent.* Politics cannot and will not command the system unless it is willing to recognize that the capitalist solution to a crisis *requires* an attack on the working class, and that the socialist solution in turn requires an attack on the system itself. As Yaffe (1976) notes, the characteristic reliance of possibility theories on the power of the state may be a dangerous illusion. (See also CRISIS IN CAPITALIST SOCIETIES.)

Reading

Armstrong, P. and Glyn A. 1980: 'The Law of the Falling Rate of Profit and Oligopoly; A Comment on Shaikh'.

Bowles, S. 1981: 'Technical Change and the Profit Rate: A Simple Proof of the Okishio Theorem'.

Burns, A. F. 1969: *The Business Cycle in a Changing World*, table 1.1, pp. 16–17.

Garegnani, P. 1978: 'Notes on Consumption, Investment and Effective Demand: A Reply to Joan Robinson'.

Harman, C. 1980: 'Theories of Crisis'.

Hilferding, Rudolf, 1910 (*1981*): *Finance Capital*, pt. IV.

Hodgson, G. 1975: *Trotsky and Fatalistic Marxism.*

Jacoby, Russell 1975: 'The Politics of Crisis Theory: Towards a Critique of Automatic Marxism II'.

Kalecki, M. 1943 (*1971*): 'The Political Aspects of Full Employment'. In *Selected Essays.*

Mandel, E. 1972 (*1975*): *Late Capitalism.*

Roemer, J. E. 1979: 'Continuing Controversy on the Falling Rate of Profit: Fixed Capital and Other Issues'.

Shaikh, A. 1978a: 'An Introduction to the History of Crisis Theories'. In *U.S. Capitalism in Crisis.*

— 1978b: 'Political Economy and Capitalism'.

Sweezy, Paul 1979–82: Leading articles in *Monthly Review* 31 (3, 6), 32 (5), 33 (5, 7), 34 (2).

Yaffe, D. 1976: 'Hodgson and Activist Reformism'.
ANWAR SHAIKH

Economic and Philosophical Manuscripts This title was chosen by the Soviet editors for the first publication (1932) of manuscripts written in Paris by Marx in 1844. The work is also known as *1844 Manuscripts* and as *Paris Manuscripts*. It is really the first version of Marx's lifelong project, which he called his 'critique of political economy'. The manuscripts are in rough draft only, with a good part missing. The early editors re-ordered the material in accordance with Marx's apparent intentions. The first publication of the manuscripts as near as possible to their original form (1982) is in the new *MEGA*. There are a number of English translations; the best is probably still the first, that is, Milligan's of 1959 which is the basis of that in *Collected Works* 3.

These manuscripts need (but repay) careful study because of their unfinished, fragmentary, multi-layered character, and the adoption in new senses of philosophical terminology borrowed from HEGEL and FEUERBACH. There are also difficulties in translating such terms: in particular, both *Entfremdung* and *Entäusserung* could be rendered as 'alienation', so translators' notes should always be consulted.

Crammed within Marx's surviving 50,000 words is a complex and visionary prospectus, situating his reading of political economy, his views on communism and his response to Hegel within a profound new theoretical framework. Evident in many places is Marx's enthusiastic reception of Feuerbach; but Feuerbach's contemplative naturalism is thoroughly surpassed in Marx's key idea of the self-creation of humanity through material labour.

When the *Economic and Philosophical Manuscripts* were first published, their importance was recognized by Marcuse (1932) in Germany and Lefebvre (1939) in France. In the USA they first became known to a wider public in a volume introduced by Erich Fromm (1961).

The diffusion of the work in the 1950s and 1960s created enormous interest because Marx's theory of ALIENATION therein was perceived as a startlingly new perspective on capitalist society which complemented (or, some felt, could replace) the familiar theory of exploitation. However, because the category of 'alienation' is not evident in the chapter titles of *Capital* (1867), a fierce debate broke out over the question of the relation of these works. Should one speak of a 'young' and 'old' Marx with a *break* between? And a break, perhaps, between 'philosophy' and 'science'? And if so – which should one value? (See Mészáros 1970, Petrović 1967, Althusser 1965, Mandel 1971.) The 'continuity thesis' gained some support with the availability of Marx's *Grundrisse* (1857–8) from 1953.

In sum, no intellectual event since his death altered the reception of Marx so much as the publication of these manuscripts. The manuscripts were the most important reference for self-styled 'Marxist humanism'. Today, Marx's reflections on Humanity and Nature are seen as a relevant (if ambiguous) legacy.

Reading
Arthur, C. J. 1986: *Dialectics of Labour: Marx and his Relation to Hegel*.
Fromm, Erich 1961: *Marx's Concept of Man*.
Marcuse, Herbert 1932 (*1983*): 'The Foundations of Historical Materialism'. In *From Luther to Popper*.
CHRISTOPHER J. ARTHUR

economic planning The nineteenth-century founders of socialist theory said very little about economic planning. Marx and Engels deliberately eschewed detailed discussion of future social organization on the grounds that it was utopian. They confined themselves instead to occasional general statements, as in Engels's reference to 'the replacement of the anarchy of social production by a socially planned regulation of production in accordance with the needs both of society as a whole and of each individual' (*Anti-Dühring*, pt. III, ch. 2).

Early in the twentieth century, however, theoretical criticism of socialism developed on the assumption that public ownership of the means of production would necessarily involve centralized economic planning. This gave rise to the so-called 'socialist calculation debate' that reached its high point in the 1930s, with Mises and Hayek arguing that in such a system rational economic calculation would be impossible and Oskar LANGE, above all, arguing the contrary.

The debate concerned whether a Pareto-efficient allocation of resources (an idealized benchmark used by neo-classical economists to evaluate welfare) could be achieved in the absence of markets and prices for means of production. The traditional account of the debate is that Mises had argued that this was theoretically impossible and, when his argument was refuted, Hayek argued that while it might be possible in theory it was impossible in practice. Hayek is usually interpreted as having based his argument on the impossibility of gathering and processing the information that would be needed to work out centrally an efficient allocation of resources. He is taken to have argued that in practice an efficient allocation of resources could result only from the operation of market forces, with market-determined prices having the central role of conveying information to decentralized decision-makers.

Lange took up this challenge and showed that it was possible to combine public ownership of the means of production with decentralized decision-making through the use of 'accounting prices'. These prices would be set by a central planning board, not by the market, and would be varied until planned supply and demand were equal. The outcome would be a Pareto-efficient general equilibrium identical to that existing in the perfectly competitive general equilibrium of neo-classical economics. On this interpretation, Lange got the better of the debate, but recent Austrian critics have argued that the interpretation is wrong, and claim that Hayek was not concerned with the conditions needed for a static Pareto-efficient allocation of resources. They insist that his concern was the process of resource *re*allocation resulting from the continuous responses of decentralized decision-makers to the ever changing information available to them, with market-determined prices having the role of co-ordinating their independent decisions.

Not all Marxists adopted Lange's solution of seeking to simulate the market mechanism and demonstrate that an economy based on public ownership of the means of production could arrive at an allocation of resources with the same efficiency properties as one based on private ownership. Maurice DOBB, in particular, argued that economic planning is desirable precisely because it enables outcomes that differ from those produced by the operation of market forces. From this perspective, the essence of economic planning is that it makes possible the co-ordination of interdependent decisions before they are implemented. It substitutes the conscious planned co-ordination of decisions *ex ante* for the market mechanism's unplanned *ex post* co-ordination as atomistic decision-makers respond to changing market prices and profit opportunities.

Interdependence in economic activity is most pronounced in relation to major investment. Dobb stressed the significance for planning of the distinction between unavoidable uncertainty and the uncertainty that arises from the necessary lack of knowledge on the part of atomized decision-makers of their rivals' intended actions. Investment decisions in capitalist economies are made on the basis of expectations of future profitability. Future profitability depends in part on the combined effect of all simultaneously undertaken projects. However, in fragmented, atomistic, market-based decision-making, individual investment decisions are made in ignorance of the actions of others. Hence, the expectations underlying them will in general not be realized.

Economic planning enables this interdependence to be taken into account. Investment decisions, to be rational, should be made on the basis of the expected future pattern of relative costs and prices not the existing pattern. Uncertainty about the actions of others prevents atomized decision-makers from making estimates of the future that are as good as is possible in a planned economy. In a planned economy, major investments bringing about non-marginal changes can be planned together and co-ordinated in advance before resources are committed.

These inescapable realities have led to the adoption of forms of economic planning from time to time in advanced capitalist and less developed countries. This was most pronounced in the case of Britain during the Second World War, when planning was introduced in order to mobilize the entire economy for the war effort. It was generally accepted then that planning is a superior allocating mechanism when a major mobilization or redeployment of resources is desired. Similar arguments informed widespread adoption of economic plans in developing countries, although for various reasons these proved to be mainly paper exercises with little practical effect. In the three decades following the Second War War, most advanced capitalist countries adopted measures of state intervention to promote restructuring and international competitiveness, ranging from indicative planning to industrial policy. Even after the neo-liberal challenge of the 1980s and 1990s, it is still the case that in no capitalist country is the allocation of resources left entirely to the operation of market forces.

However, economic planning has been primarily associated with the Soviet Union and, by extension, Eastern Europe. The Soviet system of central planning was developed during the 1930s after the adoption of the First Five Year Plan in 1929 and began to be dismantled 60 years later. Its distinctive form was shaped by the successive objectives of rapid industrialization, mobilization for the 'Great Patriotic War' against the Nazi invaders, post-war reconstruction and the prosecution of the Cold War. It was the vehicle for rapid economic growth and regional development, maintained full employment and low rates of inflation, and was associated with some increase in standards of living and cultural development. It coexisted with appalling repression and violation of individual freedom and was the vehicle for arbitrary decision-making, inefficiency and waste, widespread pollution and environmental degradation, endemic shortage, and lack of consumer satisfaction.

The Soviet model was a highly centralized administrative command system based on annual plans that consisted of binding targets for every enterprise, covering output quantities and destinations and input use and sources. The principal method used to draw up the plan was that of 'material balances'. This involved a statement of planned uses and sources of supply for each major product, with initial inconsistencies between interdependent balances being dealt with through one or more rounds of iterative revision. The information used to construct the plan was supplied by the enterprises and, since the incentive system consisted of bonuses related to target fulfilment, enterprises had an incentive to supply biased information in order to obtain easy targets.

The model had systemic weaknesses relating to information and motivation that were held in check as long as priority planning prevailed, with resources concentrated on a limited number of sectors, and non-priority areas, notably the consumer goods sector, treated as a residual. By the mid-1970s, however, the Soviet economy was stagnating and living standards and welfare provision were deteriorating. The advent of the Gorbachev era in 1985 initiated a prolonged process of attempted reform whose outcome is at present still very uncertain. In the meantime, most countries of Eastern Europe have overthrown their communist regimes and are well along the road to the introduction of economies based in some way on market forces, although the form may vary from country to country.

Parallel changes have occurred in the ideas of socialist theorists in the West. The historical antithesis between plan and market has been largely abandoned and some form of MARKET SOCIALISM has emerged as the principal economic model advocated by socialist economists. However, the experience of Eastern Europe, particularly of the New Economic Mechanism introduced in Hungary in 1968, has led to increasing scepticism about the possibility of anything resembling earlier Marxist concepts of economic planning. The basic argument is that for enterprises to have an incentive to make efficient use of the resources and local knowledge at their disposal, they must be fully autonomous. They can only be fully autonomous if they make their own decisions, including investment decisions, and benefit or suffer according to whether or not they are successful. This requires a capital and labour market, with investment decisions being co-ordinated and resources reallocated through the operation of market forces.

In some models of market socialism, enterprises are publicly owned, in others they are workers' cooperatives; in neither case are they owned by capitalists and in this sense they are not privately owned. However, if they are fully autonomous and rewarded or penalized according to their success, in another sense they are privately owned; the existence of fragmented decision-making by atomistic enterprises precludes anything that can be reasonably thought of as economic planning. An important role is envisaged in these models for fiscal and monetary policy, as well as for industrial policy and sometimes even indicative planning. However, the conscious *ex ante* co-ordination of major interdependent investment decisions that was considered by Dobb to be the essence of economic planning has been effectively abandoned. Today only a minority of Marxist economists reject market socialism. Those who do, argue for some form of participatory planning that envisages not a return from state to *de facto* private ownership but an advance to social ownership.

Reading

Brus, Wlodzimierz and Laski, Kazimierz 1989: *From Marx to the Market: Socialism in Search of an Economic System.*

Buchanan, Allen 1985: *Ethics, Efficiency, and the Market.*

Devine, Pat 1988: *Democracy and Economic Planning: The Political Economy of a Self-governing Society.*

Dobb, Maurice 1955: *On Economic Theory and Socialism.*

— 1960: *An Essay on Economic Growth and Planning.*

— 1974: 'Some Historical Reflections on Planning and the Market'. In C. Abramsky 1974: *Essays in Honor of E. H. Carr.*

Horvat, Branko 1982: *The Political Economy of Socialism.*

Lavoie, Don 1985: *Rivalry and Central Planning: The Socialist Calculation Debate Reconsidered.*

Nove, Alec 1983: *The Economics of Feasible Socialism.*

PAT DEVINE

economism A concept developed by Lenin in several articles of 1899 ('Retrograde Trend in Russian Social-Democracy', 'Apropos of the *Profession de foi*', etc. in *Collected Works*, vol. 4), which criticized some groups in the Russian social democratic movement for separating political from economic struggles and concentrating their efforts on the latter; an attitude which Lenin associated with 'Bernsteinian ideas' (see BERNSTEIN). 'If the economic struggle is taken as something complete in itself,' he wrote, 'there will be nothing socialist in it.' In a later article (1901) Lenin defined 'economism' as *a separate trend* in the social democratic movement, with the following characteristic features: a vulgarization of Marxism which

downgraded the conscious element in social life; a striving to restrict political agitation and struggle; a failure to understand the need 'to establish a strong and centralized organization of revolutionaries'. His pamphlet of 1902 'What is to be Done'? was directed primarily against economism, made a distinction between trade-unionist politics and social democratic politics, and denounced 'bowing to spontaneity' (i.e. the notion of a spontaneous movement towards socialism as an outcome of economic development).

Lenin used the term, therefore, mainly in the context of practical politics, and it took its place in the broader framework of his ideas about the need for a centralized and disciplined party which would bring a developed class consciousness to the working class from outside (see LENINISM). But economism also has a theoretical significance, as a form of Marxism which emphasizes (and in the view of its critics overemphasizes) the determination of social life as a whole by the economic base (see BASE AND SUPERSTRUCTURE), and in general insists upon the determinism of Marx's theory. Gramsci (1971, part II, sect. I) begins his discussion of economism by considering its political manifestations – identifying economism with syndicalism, *laissez-faire* liberalism, and various other forms of 'electoral abstentionism', which all express some degree of opposition to political action and the political party. He goes on, however, to relate it to a particular theoretical orientation in the social sciences, namely 'the iron conviction that there exist objective laws of historical development similar in kind to natural laws, together with a belief in a predetermined teleology like that of a religion'.

In recent debates, economism has been most strongly, though very inadequately, criticized by the structuralist Marxists (see STRUCTURALISM) in the course of their rejection of the base/superstructure model and of teleology. Poulantzas, in his study of the Communist International's policy towards fascism (1974), argues that the policy was based upon a particular kind of economism which reduced imperialism to a purely economic phenomenon (a process of linear economic evolution), explained fascism in Italy by the economic backwardness of the country, and did not expect fascism in Germany, which had a highly industrialized, advanced economy. Economism, in its various shades of meaning, and the criticisms of it, raise some fundamental questions (which have also been put in other terms) about the precise role of economic (and technological) development in Marx's theory of history (see HISTORICAL MATERIALISM), and in particular about how much weight should be assigned to this development as against the (relatively) independent influence of ideology, class consciousness, and political action seen as a manifestation of human agency.

Reading

Gramsci, Antonio, 1929–35 (*1971*): 'Some Theoretical and Practical Aspects of Economism'. In *Selections From the Prison Notebooks*, pt. II.

Lenin, V. I. 1902 (*1961*): 'What is to be Done?'

TOM BOTTOMORE

education The elements of a Marxist conception of education appear, from the 1840s, in many works of Marx and Engels (e.g. *Capital* I, ch. 13; *German Ideology*, vol. I, pt. 1; *Critique of the Gotha Programme*, sect. IV; *Principles of Communism* (Engels 1847)). A more coherent theory of education has been gradually built up on this basis. A major impetus was given to it by the October Revolution and its need for a Marxist educational praxis (Lenin, Krupskaya, Blonskij, Makarenko). In fact, Marxist educational theory is essentially *a theory of practice*. Some of the major figures contributing to it were Bebel, Jaurès, Zetkin, Liebknecht, Gramsci, Langevin, Wallon, Sève. A host of researchers are currently engaged in further developing it. The main components of the theory are the following:

(i) Free public education, compulsory and uniform for all children, assuring the abolition of cultural or knowledge monopolies and of privileged forms of schooling. In the original formulations, this had to be an education in institutions. The reason given then was to prevent the bad living conditions of the working class from hindering the overall development of children. Later, other objectives were made explicit, such as the necessity to weaken the role of the family in social reproduction; to bring up children under less unequal conditions; to utilize the socializing force of the community. Indeed, the most successful revolutionary educa-

tional experiments, from Makarenko to the Cuban schools, have taken place in institutional settings.

(ii) The combination of education with material production (or, in one of Marx's formulations, the combination of instruction, gymnastics and productive work). The objective implied here is neither a better vocational training, nor the inculcation of a work ethic, but rather the closing of the historical gap between manual and mental work, between conception and execution, by assuring to all a full understanding of the productive process. While the theoretical validity of this principle is widely recognized, its practical application (as shown by the many short-lived or only partly successful experiments) presents problems, especially under the conditions of rapid scientific and technological change.

(iii) Education has to assure the all-round development of the personality. With re-united science and production, the human being can become a producer in the full sense. On this basis, all his or her potentialities can unfold. A universe of needs then appears, activating the individual in all spheres of social life including consumption, pleasure, creation and enjoyment of culture, participation in social life, interaction with others, and self-fulfilment (auto-creation). The realization of this objective requires, among other things, the transformation of the social division of labour, a formidable task as yet only at its beginnings.

(iv) The community is assigned a new and vast role in the educational process. This changes the in-group relations of the school (a switch from competitiveness to cooperation and support), implies a more open relation between school and society, and presupposes a mutually enriching and active dual relation between the teacher and the taught.

The theory sketched above is not closed. There are dilemmas concerning the interpretation of, or the praxis corresponding to, the above principles. There are also current debates (both among Marxists, and between Marxists and non-Marxists) about the theory of personality; the 'nature–nurture' controversy; the role of school and education in social reproduction, and their innovative potential within prevailing social determinisms; and the relative importance of the contents, the methods and the structuring of education in promoting social change.

Reading

Apple, M. W. 1979: *Ideology and Curriculum.*

Bebel, August 1879 (*1886*): *Women and Socialism.*

Bourdieu, P. and Passeron, J. C. 1977: *Reproduction in Education, Society and Culture.*

Bowles, S. and Gintis, H. 1976: *Schooling in Capitalist America.*

Ferge, Zsuzsa 1979: *A Society in the Making*, ch. 4.

Freire, Paolo 1970: *Pedagogy of the Oppressed.*

Gramsci, Antonio 1973: *L'alternativa pedagogica.*

Jaurès, Jean 1899: *Le socialisme et l'enseignement.*

Langevin, Paul 1950: *La pensée et l'action.*

Lenin, V. I. 1913 (*1963*): 'The Question of Ministry of Education Policy'.

— 1920 (*1966*): 'The Tasks of the Youth Leagues'.

— 1920 (*1966*): 'On Polytechnic Education. Notes on Theses by Nadezhda Konstantinovna'.

Lindenberg, D. 1972: *L'Internationale communiste et l'école de classe.*

Manacorda, M. A. 1966: *Marx e la pedagogia moderna.*

ZSUZSA FERGE

Eisenstein, Sergei Born 22 January 1898, Riga; died 11 February 1948, Moscow. Eisenstein was trained as an engineer, but abandoned his education during the 1917 Russian Revolution and volunteered for the Red Army, first as a technician and then as a stage designer, producer and actor during the ensuing Civil War. After demobilization in 1920 he joined the First Proletkult Workers' Theatre as a designer and producer.

In a period of general artistic ferment, the Proletkult group was concerned to overthrow what it perceived as the hegemony of bourgeois 'high art' forms and replace them with elements drawn from more proletarian-orientated 'low' mass art forms, such as the circus or music-hall. Several years' experimentation and collaboration with other artistic revolutionaries, such as Vsevolod Meyerhold in theatre or Lev Kuleshov or the Petrograd Eccentrism group in cinema, led Eisenstein in 1924 to produce a play set in a gas works in an actual gas works, with an audience composed of the people who worked there. This audience did not appreciate the experiment and its failure persuaded him that theatre was too limited a medium for an effective revolutionary culture. As he put it, 'the horse bolted and the cart fell into cinema'.

Eisenstein's subsequent career was devoted to cinema and to the development of cinema as an effective political weapon. Using cinema as a focus, he also tried to develop an overarching theory of culture based on what he saw as the basic tenets of Marxism. Eisenstein's Marxism was *not* a mere façade. In one of his first theoretical articles, written in 1923, he argued that the essence of any artistic activity was the collision between individual attractions, each bringing to that collision their own set of associations which would trigger off a chain of reactions in the audience's mind. This notion, which he called a 'montage of attractions', was based on his understanding of the basic processes of the Marxian dialectic: thesis, antithesis, synthesis.

In the course of the 1920s Eisenstein was one of a number of Soviet film-makers who tried to distinguish cinema's legitimacy as an art form independent of theatre. While they all homed in on montage as the key specific element in cinema, it was Eisenstein who developed the notion of montage as collision. Since he also argued that 'all art is conflict', he regarded montage and hence also cinema as central to revolutionary art as a whole. The idea of conflict led him to the concept of 'intellectual montage' as the central element in 'intellectual cinema', as exemplified in his revolutionary anniversary film *October* in 1927. Eisenstein argued that intellectual montage, unlike the comforting, even soporific, linear narrative of 'bourgeois' cinema, would, through the collision of attractions and their concomitant associations, provoke the audience into an objective and logical assessment of the arguments presented to them. Emotional and moral outrage at an individual atrocity depicted on the screen would be intellectualized into a broader rejection of the political system behind the atrocity. The purpose of Eisenstein's intellectual cinema thus had much in common with BRECHT's theory of alienation.

The failure of the cinema avant-garde to mobilize audiences led Eisenstein to reconsider and redefine his methodology. After nearly three years in the West, he returned to the USSR in May 1932 to find his film-making career blocked by misunderstandings, both deliberate and accidental, with the authorities. He devoted his time increasingly to teaching at the Moscow Institute of Cinema and to writing. His attempts to devise an all-embracing aesthetic theory based on the fundamental principles of montage and the dialectic, encompassing in particular music, painting and sculpture, were encapsulated in the drafts for *Towards a Theory of Montage* and *Nonindifferent Nature* but the theory itself remained incomplete at the time of his death.

Nevertheless, Eisenstein's films and theoretical writings combine to suggest to subsequent generations at least the outlines of a theory of dialectical objectivity, of what he himself termed 'the building to be built'.

Reading

Aumont, Jacques 1987: *Montage Eisenstein*.

Christie, Ian and Elliott, David 1988: *Eisenstein at Ninety*.

Eisenstein, Sergei 1942: *The Film Sense*.

— 1949: *Film Form, Essays in Film Theory*.

— 1968: *Film Essays and a Lecture*.

— 1970: *Notes of a Film Director*.

— 1985: *Immoral Memories. An Autobiography*.

— 1987: *Nonindifferent Nature*.

— 1988: *Selected Works, 1: Writings, 1922–34*.

— 1991: *Selected Works, 2: Towards a Theory of Montage*.

Leyda, Jay and Voynow, Zina 1982: *Eisenstein at Work*.

RICHARD TAYLOR

elite   The elite theories were constructed, notably by Vilfredo Pareto and Gaetano Mosca, in conscious opposition to Marxism, and contradicted the Marxist view in two respects. First, they asserted that the division of society into dominant and subordinate groups is a universal and unalterable fact. In Mosca's words (1939, p. 50): 'Among the constant facts and tendencies that are to be found in all political organisms, one is so obvious that it is apparent to the most casual eye. In all societies – from societies that are very meagrely developed and have barely attained the dawnings of civilization, down to the most advanced and powerful societies – two classes of people appear – a class that rules and a class that is ruled.' Second, they defined the ruling group in quite a different way; Pareto mainly in terms of the superior qualities of some individuals which gave rise to elites in every sphere of life, Mosca in terms of the

inevitable dominion of an 'organized minority' or 'political class' over the unorganized majority, though he too referred to the 'highly esteemed and very influential' personal attributes of this minority. But Mosca also introduced many qualifications, and eventually outlined a more complex theory (closer to Marxism) in which the political class itself is influenced and restrained by a variety of 'social forces' (representing different interests) and is connected with a large sub-elite that is a vital element in ensuring political stability. This led Gramsci (1949) to say that Mosca's 'political class is a puzzle . . . so fluctuating and elastic is the notion', though elsewhere he concluded that it meant simply the intellectual section of the ruling group.

The impact of these views upon Marxism is well illustrated by the case of Michels, whose study of political parties (1911) has been described as 'the work of someone who has passed over from revolutionary Marxism to the camp of elite theory' (Beetham 1981, p. 81). Michels, disillusioned with the leadership of the German Social Democratic party, asked why socialist parties deviate into reformism and concluded that the leaders necessarily become divorced from the membership and assimilated into the existing social elites. His 'iron law of oligarchy' – drawing upon the ideas of Pareto and Mosca, and to some extent of Max Weber – formulates the conditions under which this divorce occurs and the leaders come to constitute a dominant elite in the party. It is partly because of the contrast between the ability and determination of the leaders, further nurtured by education and experience, and the 'incompetence of the masses'; partly because, as a minority, they are better organized and also control a bureaucratic apparatus.

Bukharin (1921) responded to part of Michels's argument by saying that the incompetence of the masses is a product of present-day economic and technical conditions and would disappear in a socialist society; hence there is no universal law of oligarchy. Among recent Marxists, Poulantzas (1973) briefly reviewed the elite theories and still more briefly dismissed them as not providing any explanation of the basis of political power (which is scarcely accurate). Other Marxists or *sympathisants* have been more inclined to incorporate some elements of elite theory into their own conceptions, and certainly to recognize that difficult (though not necessarily unanswerable) questions have been posed, especially by Michels. The thinker who went furthest in accepting elite theory (strongly influenced by Weber's concept of power) is Mills (1956) who used the term 'power elite' rather than 'ruling class', because in his view the latter is a 'badly loaded phrase' which presupposes that an economic class rules politically, and 'does not allow enough autonomy to the political order and its agents'. He went on to distinguish three major elites – economic, political and military – in American society, and then faced, but did not resolve, the difficulty of showing that these three groups actually form a single power elite, and how they are bound together. Others (e.g. Miliband 1977) have discussed elites mainly in terms of the state bureaucracy, and particularly in relation to the question of whether the USSR and other socialist countries can be described as being dominated by a bureaucratic 'power elite'. This raises difficult problems in the analysis of political power in such societies, and notably whether the ruling group should more properly be conceived, in Marxist terms, as an elite, or as a class which effectively 'possesses' the means of production (see CLASS).

More generally, Marxist political theory still needs to develop a more precise concept of elites, and to examine in a more comprehensive and rigorous way the relation between elites and classes, particularly in relation to socialist regimes and to the distinction between leaders and followers not only in social life as a whole, but in socialist parties themselves.

Reading

Beetham, David 1981: 'Michels and his critics'.

Bottomore, T. B. 1966: *Elites and Society*.

Michels, Roberto 1911 (1949): *Political Parties*.

Mills, C. Wright 1956: *The Power Elite*.

                                TOM BOTTOMORE

emancipation According to standard liberal views, freedom is the absence of interference or (even more narrowly) coercion. I am free to do what others do not prevent me from doing. Marxism is heir to a wider and richer view,

stemming from such philosophers as Spinoza, Rousseau, Kant and Hegel, of freedom as self-determination. If, in general, freedom is the absence of restrictions upon options open to agents, one can say that the liberal tradition has tended to offer a very narrow construal of what these restrictions can be (often confining them to deliberate interferences), of what the relevant options are (often confining them to whatever agents in fact conceive or choose), and of agents (seen as separate individuals, pursuing their independently conceived ends, above all in the market-place). Marxism invokes wider notions of the relevant restrictions and options, and of human agency.

More specifically Marx and later Marxists tend to see freedom in terms of the removal of obstacles to human emancipation, that is to the manifold development of human powers and the bringing into being of a form of association worthy of human nature. Notable among such obstacles are the conditions of wage labour. As Marx wrote, 'the conditions of their life and labour and therewith all the conditions of existence of modern society have become . . . something over which individual proletarians have no control and over which no social organisation can give them control' (*German Ideology*, vol. I, IV, 6). Overcoming such obstacles is a collective enterprise and freedom as self-determination is collective in the sense that it consists in the socially cooperative and organized imposition of human control over both nature and the social conditions of production: 'the full development of human mastery over the forces of nature as well as of humanity's own nature' (*Grundrisse*, Notebook V, Penguin edn., p. 488). It will only be fully realized with the supersession of the capitalist mode of production by a form of association in which 'it is the association of individuals (assuming the advanced stage of modern productive forces of course) which puts the conditions of the free development and movement of individuals under their control'. Only then 'within the community has each individual the means of cultivating his gifts in all directions' (*German Ideology*, vol. I, IV, 6).

What this form of association – embodying collective control, association or community, the development of manifold individuality and personal freedom – would look like, Marx and

Engels never say, nor do they ever consider possible conflicts among these values, or between them and others. Marxism tends to treat consideration of such matters as 'utopian'. But such a vision of emancipation is plainly integral to the entire Marxist project: a point clearly grasped by so-called 'Critical Theory', which postulates such a vision as a vantage-point from which to criticize actual (and perhaps unemancipateable) societies (see FRANKFURT SCHOOL).

Marxism's wider and richer view of freedom has often led Marxists to understate, even denigrate both the economic and the civic freedoms of liberal capitalist societies. Though Marx plainly valued personal freedom, he did, in *On the Jewish Question*, see the right to liberty as linked to egoism and private property, and elsewhere wrote of free competition as limited freedom because based on the rule of capital and 'therefore [sic] at the same time the most complete suspension of all individual freedom' (*Grundrisse*, Notebook VI, Penguin edn, p. 652). More generally, he tended to see exchange relations as incompatible with genuine freedom. Later Marxists have followed him in this, and, especially since Lenin, they have often shown a pronounced tendency to deny the 'formal' freedoms of bourgeois democracy the status of genuine freedoms.

Such formulations are theoretically in error and have been practically disastrous. There is no essential link between liberal freedom and either private property or egoism; neither economic competition nor exchange relationships are inherently incompatible with the freedom of the parties concerned (nor indeed is the pursuit of self-interest implicit in both necessarily incompatible with emancipation, unless this is defined as based on universal altruism); and the limited character of bourgeois political and legal freedoms does not make them any the less genuine. It is a mistake to think that unmasking bourgeois ideology entails exposing bourgeois freedoms as illusory, rather than showing them to be in some cases (such as the freedom to accumulate property) precluding other more valuable freedoms and in others (such as the freedom to dissent) as applied in far too limited a fashion. In practice the failure to call liberal freedoms freedom has legitimized their wholesale suppression and denial, all too often in the name of freedom itself.

Reading

Berlin, Isaiah 1969: *Four Essays on Liberty*.

Caudwell, Christopher 1965: *The Concept of Freedom*.

Cohen, G. A. (1983): 'The Structure of Proletarian Unfreedom'.

Dunayevskaya, Raya 1964: *Marxism and Freedom from 1776 until Today*.

Horkheimer, Max and Adorno, Theodor W. 1947 (1973): *Dialectic of Enlightenment*.

Ollman, Bertell 1971 (1976): *Alienation: Marx's Conception of Man in Capitalist Society*.

Selucký, Radoslav 1979: *Marxism, Socialism, Freedom*.

Wood, Allen W. 1981: *Karl Marx*.

STEVEN LUKES

empires of Marx's day   Marx and Engels gave much thought to empires, of very heterogeneous kinds; in old Europe the Roman, further away the not long since decayed Mughal empire in India, and the now tottering Manchu power in China. European expansionism of their own time they viewed in much the same light as they did capitalism inside Europe. Both were brutish and detestable in themselves, but necessary goads to progress for those who suffered from them. Africa and Asia being stuck in a rut, an immense gap had opened, they were convinced, between those regions and even the most backward states of Europe. Marx had high praise for Count Gurowski, a Russian spokesman of the Panslavism repugnant to him as a tool of tsarist influence, for advocating not 'a league against Europe and European civilization', but a turning away towards the 'stagnant desolation' of Asia as the proper outlet of Slav energies. There 'Russia is a civilizing power' (*Eastern Question*, no. 98). No Asian empire could be credited with any such virtue, even the Turkish with its one foot in Europe. It was clear to Marx that the semi-barbarous condition of the Balkan region was largely due to the Turkish presence; if its peoples won freedom they would soon develop a healthy dislike of tsarist Russia, to which as it was they were forced to look for protection (*Eastern Question*, no. 1).

Fourier's disciples worked out blueprints for a sort of utopian imperialism along with their utopian socialism, and took a special interest in north Africa as a field for French expansion, which they hoped might take place through a largely pacific process of fraternizing with the inhabitants. Marx and Engels had no such rosy illusions, but like nearly all Europeans they regarded the French conquest of Algeria as an advance of the frontiers of civilization. Much later, at the time of the British occupation of Egypt, Engels was ready to bet ten to one that the nationalist leader Arabi Pasha had no higher wish than to be able to fleece the peasants himself, instead of leaving it to foreign financiers to fleece them; 'in a peasant country the peasant exists solely to be exploited'. One could sympathize with the oppressed masses, he added, and condemn 'the English brutalities while by no means siding with their military adversaries of the moment' (letter to Bernstein, 9 August 1882).

But this general viewpoint did not prevent him and Marx from being alert to the diversity of local situations, motives, and methods. No single theory of IMPERIALISM such as later Marxists have tried to construct can incorporate all their responses. Marx did not welcome all colonial conquests, if only because they might hamper what he considered more important business inside Europe, as in the case of the second Burma war. Deploring its approach in 1853 he declared that Britain's wars in that quarter were its most inexcusable: no strategic danger could be alleged there, as on the North-West Frontier, and there was no evidence of the supposed American designs. There was in fact no reason for it except 'the want of employment for a needy aristocracy' – a factor that later Marxist study of British imperialism may have greatly underestimated. He observed too that with the cost of conflicts in Asia 'thrown on the shoulders of the Hindus', a collapse of India's finances might not be far away ('War in Burma', 30 July 1853). In the same year, attributing rebellion and chaos in China to the pressure of British intervention and trade, he raised, prophetically, the question of 'how that revolution will in time react on England, and through England on Europe' ('Revolution in China and in Europe', 14 June 1853).

In 1883 during a French campaign in Indochina Engels singled out as the latest inspiration of imperialism in tropical areas 'the interests of stock exchange swindles', at work now 'openly and frankly' in both Indochina and Tunisia

(letter to Kautsky, 18 September 1883). Again, later Marxist theory committed to the Hobson-Hilferding-Lenin doctrine of capital export as the soul of imperialism has given too little attention to more elementary readings like this of capitalism and its operations. The following year he described Dutch rule in Java as 'an example of state socialism', the government organizing production of cash crops for export, and pocketing the profits, 'on the basis of the old communistic village communities' (letter to Bebel, 18 January 1884). Java showed once more, he thought, like India and Russia, 'how today primitive communism furnishes . . . the finest and broadest basis of exploitation and despotism 'and how much its disappearance was to be hoped for (letter to Kautsky, 16 February 1884).

A highly specific feature of the British empire, with Russia's position in Siberia as a sole and distant parallel, was its inclusion of very large colonies of settlement with scarcely any native inhabitants. Marx, like most later Marxists took far less interest in these than in territories like India, but he devoted the final chapter of *Capital* I to Gibbon Wakefield's plan of organized emigration. This was designed to extend the English social order to the colonies, by controlling sales of land and keeping its price high, in order to prevent settlers from having their own farms, which in Wakefield's view would mean fragmentation of property and prevent economic development. Marx cited his lament over an entrepreneur who brought a mass of workers to western Australia, only to find that they all decamped as soon as they arrived. Here was an excellent illustration of the true nature of capitalism: money could only become capital when there was labour for it to exploit.

Engels was expecting the 'colonies proper', like those in Australia, to become independent before very long (letter to Kautsky, 12 September 1882). Visiting Canada briefly in 1888 he was unfavourably impressed by its torpor (he saw chiefly French Canada), and thought that within ten years it would be glad to be annexed to the USA, already gaining economic control, and that Britain would raise no objection (letter to Sorge, 10 September 1888). In Marx's eyes the old plantations, now transformed by the abolition of slavery, came into the category of 'colonies'. In 1865 he and Engels shared the widespread public indignation at the 'Jamaica infamies', as Engels called them in a letter to his friend (1 December 1865), the bloodthirsty repression following a small disturbance among blacks suffering from economic hardships. In the Pacific British settlers were not long in developing ambitions of their own; and in 1883 Engels commented on a scheme to grab New Guinea, as part of the search for what was virtually slave labour for the Queensland sugar plantations (letter to Kautsky, 18 September 1883).

Ireland, partly the first victim of English imperialism, partly the first field of Anglo-Scottish colonizing, deeply interested Marx and Engels all through their lives in England. Engels, who planned to write its history, was struck when visiting the island in 1856 by its poverty and backwardness (letter to Marx, 23 May). Marx took careful note of the economic shift, after the Famine and the breakdown of the old rackrenting system, from agricultural to pastoral, with evictions to enable farms to be consolidated, and a further stream of emigration (letter to Engels, 30 November 1867). Baffled by the failure of the British working class after Chartism to show any militant political spirit, he found one cause in the ability of industrialists to utilize cheap labour from Ireland, and so divide the workers: the English workman hated the Irish blackleg, and looked down on him as a member of an inferior race. If British forces were withdrawn, he wrote, agrarian revolution in Ireland would not be long delayed, and the consequent overthrow of the landed aristocracy would lead to the same happening in England, and open the way to the overthrow of capitalism (letter to Meyer and Vogt, 9 April 1870). The reasoning may seem less convincing than Marx's often was, as if in this case he was clutching at a straw.

Reading

Mashkin, M. N. 1981: *Frantsuzkie sotsialisti i demokrati i kolonial'nii vopros 1830–1871* (French socialists and democrats and the colonial question).

V. G. KIERNAN

empiricism   The Marxist tradition has generally been hostile to empiricism, at least in name, but neither the precise object nor the grounds for this hostility have always been clear. To an extent this stems from the fact that, in contrast to (and indeed partly as a result of) his earlier critique of idealism, Marx's critique of empiricism was never systematically articulated as a critique of a philosophical doctrine or system, but rather took the substantive form of a critique of vulgar economy. Both Marx and Engels then attempted to repair this omission at the philosophical level by appealing, albeit in different ways, to 'DIALECTICS' for the missing antiempiricist ingredient in their epistemology.

While never subscribing to empiricism, the young Marx and Engels, especially in the works of 1844–47, espouse some characteristically empiricist themes: they expressly reject apriorism and any doctrine of innate ideas, conceive of knowledge as irreducibly (even exclusively) empirical, tend to deprecate abstraction as such and veer in the direction of a Baconian inductivism. By the time of *Capital* I, however, Marx's methodological commitment to what is known as 'scientific realism' is fully formed. 'Vulgar economy', he declares, 'everywhere sticks to appearances in opposition to the law which regulates and explains them' (pt. III, ch. II); contrariwise, 'scientific truth is always paradox, if judged by everyday experience, which catches only the delusive appearance of things' (*Value, Price and Profit*, pt. VI). Empiricism sees the world as a collection of unconnected appearances, ignores the role of theory in actively organizing and critically reorganizing the data provided by such appearances, and fails to identify its function as the attempt to re-present in thought the essential relations generating them. Laws are the tendencies of structures ontologically irreducible to, and normally out of phase with, the events they generate; and knowledge of them is actively produced as a social, historical product. Thus in opposition to the empiricist reification of facts and the personification of things Marx is committed to a distinction between the (transitive) process of knowledge and the (intransitive) reality of objects.

Both the dialectical materialist and Western Marxist traditions have polemicized against empiricism. But it can be argued that the former, in virtue of its 'reflectionist' theory of knowledge, ignores the transitive dimension and reverts to a contemplative form of 'objective empiricism', effectively reducing the subject to the object of knowledge. In Western Marxism the anti-empiricist polemic has normally functioned as part of an attempt to sustain, against both DIALECTICAL MATERIALISM and bourgeois thought, concepts held to be essential to authentic Marxism – e.g. totality (Lukács), structure (Althusser) or determinate change (Marcuse). However, the tradition has often veered in the direction of apriorism, overlooking both Marx's early critique of rationalism and the massive empirical infrastructure of Marx's mature scientific work. And in this way it can also be argued, following the line of the early Marx's critique of Hegel (especially in the *Critique of Hegel's Philosophy of the State*) that, in effectively ignoring the intransitive dimension, the tradition tends to a form of 'subjective idealism', tacitly identifying the object with the subject of knowledge.

Marx's work was anti-empiricist, but not anti-empirical. In as much as this distinction is respected, Marxism can once more take up the option of becoming an empirically open-ended, historically developed, practically oriented research tradition rather than a closed system of thought. (See also KNOWLEDGE, THEORY OF; MATERIALISM; REALISM.)

Reading

Adorno, T. 1966 (1973): *Negative Dialectics*.

Della Volpe, G. 1950 (1980): *Logic as a Positive Science*.

ROY BHASKAR

Engels, Friedrich Born 28 November 1820, Barmen; died 5 August 1895, London. The eldest son of a textile manufacturer in the Wuppertal in Westphalia, Engels was brought up a strict Calvinist and on leaving Gymnasium was trained for a merchant's profession in Bremen. From school onwards, however, he developed radical literary ambitions. He was first attracted to the democratic nationalist writers of the Young Germany movement in the 1830s and then fell increasingly under the sway of HEGEL. Taking the opportunity of military service to delay his mercantile career, he went to Berlin in 1841 and became closely involved with the Young Hegelian circle around Bruno Bauer. There, he achieved brief fame for his pseudonymous attacks upon Schelling's critique of Hegel.

In the autumn of 1842, Engels left for England to work in his father's firm in Manchester. Under the influence of Moses Hess he was already a communist, and, following the latter's *European Triarchy*, believed England destined for social revolution. A stay of almost two years in the textile district and contact with Owenites and Chartists distanced him from the Bauer circle. The experience, registered in *The Condition of the Working Class*, convinced him that the working class, a distinctively new force created by the 'industrial revolution', would be the instrument of revolutionary transformation. Between leaving England and writing his book, Engels had his first serious meeting with Marx. Because they found they shared a common position against the Bauer group and had been similarly impressed by the importance of the working-class movement outside Germany, they agreed to produce a joint work stating their position, *The Holy Family*. This marked the beginning of their lifelong collaboration. At that time the communism they espoused remained strongly influenced by FEUERBACH, though distinctive in the far greater importance they attached to the working class and politics.

From the beginning of 1845 however, partly under the impact of Stirner's critique of Feuerbach in *The Ego and His Own*, Marx clarified his theoretical position, in relation both to Feuerbach and to the Young Hegelians. This marked the beginning of a distinctively 'Marxist' conception of history. According to his own account, Engels's role in this process was secondary. Nevertheless, his work on political economy and on the relationship between the industrial revolution and the development of class consciousness in England contributed vital elements to Marx's overall synthesis. Moreover, Engels contributed substantially to their unfinished joint work setting out the new conception, the *German Ideology*.

The period between 1845 and 1850 was one of extremely close collaboration. Engels broke off relations with his father and devoted himself full time to political work with Marx in Brussels and Paris. Their joint ambition was to win German communists to their own position and to forge international links with foreign working-class movements on the basis of a common revolutionary proletarian platform. To this end, they joined the German League of the Just (renamed the Communist League) and produced for it the *Communist Manifesto* on the eve of the 1848 revolution. During the revolution, Engels worked with Marx in Cologne on the *Neue Rheinische Zeitung*. Threatened with arrest in September 1848, he went to France, but returned early in 1849 and from May to July participated in the final stages of armed resistane to the victory of counter-revolution. His interest in military affairs dated from this period and his general interpretation of the revolution was recorded in *Revolution and Counter-Revolution in Germany* (1851–2).

After some time in Switzerland and London where the Communist League finally broke up, Engels settled in Manchester in 1850 and rejoined the family firm. There he stayed until 1870. In addition to his successful business activity, he helped the impoverished Marx family, remained Marx's principal political and intellectual companion, and applied their common position in a wide array of journalistic contributions. It was also from the late 1850s that he became increasingly interested in establishing dialectical connections between the materialist conception of history and developments in the natural sciences (see NATURAL SCIENCE). His unfinished work around these themes was eventually collected together and published in Moscow in the 1920s as the *Dialectics of Nature*.

In 1870 Engels was able to retire comfortably and move to London. As Marx's health became more fragile, Engels undertook an increasing share of their political work, in particular the running of the First International in its last years. It was in this political role that Engels intervened against the positivist currents in the German Social Democratic Party, to produce *Anti-Dühring* – the first attempt at a general exposition of the Marxist position. This work and abridgements from it like *Socialism: Utopian and Scientific* formed the basis of his immense reputation among the new socialist movements between 1880 and 1914. Further works, notably *Origin of the Family* and *Ludwig Feuerbach*, consolidated his position as a philosopher of even greater importance than Marx during the epoch of the Second International. After Marx's death in 1883, Engels spent most of his time editing and publishing the second and third volumes of *Capital* in 1885 and 1894. But he also took an active part in the

formation of the Second International (see INTERNATIONALS), which he saw both as the best vehicle for the further development of socialism and as a barrier against the danger of a destructive war between France and Germany. He was just beginning work on the fourth volume of *Capital* (subsequently published as *Theories of Surplus Value*), when he died of cancer.

Before 1914, Engels enjoyed an unparalleled reputation. He, far more than Marx, was responsible for the diffusion of Marxism as a world view within the socialist movement (see MARXISM, DEVELOPMENT OF). After 1914 and the Russian revolution, however, his standing was more contested. While Soviet Marxists accentuated the apparent scientism of his writings as part of an official philosophy of 'dialectical materialism', Western socialists accused him of positivism and revisionism. Both lines of interpretation are guilty of serious defects, for Engels belonged to a pre-positivist generation. Next to Marx himself, his mentors were Hegel and Fourier and his interpretation of socialism should be understood in that light.

Reading

Carver, Terrell 1981: *Engels*.
— 1983: *Marx and Engels: The Intellectual Relationship*.
Henderson, W. O. 1976: *The Life of Friedrich Engels*.
McLellan, David 1977: *Engels*.
Marcus, S. 1974: *Engels, Manchester and the Working Class*.
Stedman Jones, Gareth 1978 (1982): 'Engels'. In Eric Hobsbawm *et al.* eds, *History of Marxism*, vol. I.

GARETH STEDMAN JONES

equality Marxist theory recognizes two kinds of equality, corresponding with the two phases of post-revolutionary society. In the first phase the principle 'From each according to his abilities, to each according to the amount of work performed' prevails. This principle of distribution – contrary to the claims of defenders of present-day capitalist society – will first be realized only in post-revolutionary society, where all other criteria according to which distribution has taken place will have been abolished as illegitimate and unjust. However, because differences in individual achievement are at least partly due to differences in talent and ability which are either innate or the product of environmental conditions, and because family situations and conditions of life of different individuals differ so greatly (from differences in physique and the corresponding needs for clothing and nourishment, to the differing burdens imposed by differences in family size, etc.), this principle of distribution does not yet amount to a *just* equality (equal treatment). In as much as an *'abstractly equitable'* yardstick is formally applied *to all individuals*, they receive in fact *materially unequal treatment.*

The principle 'From each according to his abilities, to each according to his needs' corresponds with the higher communist phase of post-revolutionary society. Only under communism will there be really equal treatment of unequal human beings with all their necessarily unequal needs. A musician, for example, will receive the musical instrument which he needs even though he does not perform publicly, and so on. It is of course presupposed here that the universal striving for ever more possessions will have disappeared of itself in a society which guarantees a materially adequate livelihood for everyone and in which there are no longer hierarchies of power and prestige. In reply to the widespread criticism that this perspective is 'utopian', one can point to the spontaneous emergence of 'post-material values' in many highly industrialized societies. When everyone is assured of satisfying activities (and the possibility of varying them), and social relations sustain and express these activities, the drive for possessions, it may be argued, will decline of its own accord and a 'rational moderation' will become established.

Reading

Heller, Agnes 1976: *The Theory of Need in Marx.*

IRING FETSCHER

ethics The socialism propounded by Marx is not based on a subjective moral demand but on a theory of history. Marx, like Hegel before him, regards history as progressive. However, the progress made in the course of history is dialectically achieved; that is to say, it is realized in and through contradiction. For Marx, the process of historical development is by no means over; present-day capitalist society is not the end and goal of history. According to his theory of history, the function of the capitalist mode of production consists in the creation of the material presuppositions of a future socialist society and of communism. History itself is moving towards the realization of a better, more humane social order, and conscious insight into this objective tendency of history enables the industrial proletariat to hasten the historical process, to 'shorten the birth pangs of the new society'. Compared with such efficacious insight into history, the merely subjective moral demand always shows itself to be powerless. In asserting this, Marx takes over the Hegelian critique of moralism; yet a moral judgement is nevertheless immanent in the Marxist theory of history. The promotion of historical development can only be declared a worthwhile task if history is moving towards what is 'better', towards the 'emancipation of humanity' which will be achieved in the form of the emancipation of the proletariat. (See PROGRESS.)

Marx's critique of political economy is certainly not intended as a moral judgement on the capitalist mode of production, but seeks to demonstrate its immanent contradictions which point beyond this mode of production. Nonetheless his critique embodies unambiguous moral valuations. The 'exploitation of man by man', the REIFICATION of social relations between human beings as relations between 'things' (MONEY, the COMMODITY), the destruction of the living presuppositions of all production, nature and humanity: all these indications of the negative consequences of the capitalist mode of production contain moral valuations. Since Marx, however, regards all phases of this mode of production, including the phase of colonialist expansion, as historically necessary presuppositions of the future socialist society, he is obliged to accept these negative aspects. In an article on British rule in India he wrote:

England, it is true, in causing a social revolution in Hindostan, was actuated only by the vilest interests, and was stupid in her manner of enforcing them. But that is not the question. The question is, can mankind fulfil its destiny without a fundamental revolution in the social state of Asia? If not, whatever may have been the crimes of England she was the unconscious tool of history in bringing about the revolution. (*New York Daily Tribune*, 25 June 1853)

Only with the advent of socialism will this contradictory way of bringing about progress be overcome:

When a great social revolution shall have mastered the results of the bourgeois epoch, the market of the world and the modern powers of production, and subjected them to the common control of the most advanced peoples, then only will human progress cease to resemble that hideous pagan idol, who would not drink nectar but from the skulls of the slain. (Ibid. 8 August 1853)

Marx and Engels themselves express divergent opinions as to whether there will be morality in future socialist society, and if it proves necessary, what form it should take. In his early writings Marx seems to believe that there will be no longer be a morality which prescribes norms of behaviour for the individual. Thus he writes, in agreement with Helvétius and the French materialists:

If enlightened self-interest is the principle of all morality it is necessary for the private interest of each person to coincide with the general interest of humanity. . . . If man is formed by circumstances, these circumstances must be humanly formed. (*The Holy Family*, ch. VI)

Engels, however, assumes that history displays a progression towards higher and higher types of morality, which would seem to imply that the morality of the victorious proletariat will eventually become the universal morality of humanity. The claims of previous moralities to universal validity were indeed illusory. Thus Feuerbach's ethical theory 'is designed to suit all ages, all peoples and all conditions; and for that very reason it is never and nowhere applicable. In relation to the real world it remains just as impotent as Kant's categorical imperative. In reality every class, and even each profession, has its own morality, which it also violates whenever it can do so with impunity' (*Ludwig Feuerbach*, ch. III).

The changes in Marxist ethical theory are connected with those in the theory of history and in historical circumstances. To the extent that the unity of fact and value within the historical process was dissolved, and replaced by a positivistic theory of progress, the need for an ethical supplementation of Marxism arose. While most revisionists (Bernstein, Staudinger, etc.) sought this supplementation in neo-Kantianism (see KANTIANISM AND NEO-KANTIANISM), Kautsky (1906) resorted to a crude naturalism, in which morality was attributed to the 'social' drives to be found among the 'higher mammals'. Lenin, however, faced with the practical necessity of intervening actively and extensively in the historical process, and with the backward condition of Russia, reduced socialist ethics to the task of advancing and accelerating the class struggle and the victory of the proletariat:

morality is what serves to destroy the old exploiting society and to unite all the working people around the proletariat, which is building up a new, a communist society. (Lenin 1920)

Clearly, the thesis implicitly underlying this definition is that 'communist society' is morally superior to the existing capitalist society. This total instrumentalization of ethics, however, poses the question of the relation between means and end. Kolakowski (1960, pp. 225–37) has argued that there are means which are in principle inappropriate for attaining a moral goal (such as a really humane society). The retrospective justification of 'evil' as an inevitable means of accomplishing progress (as in Marx's article on India) is different in principle from the conscious planning and utilization of 'evil' means by a revolutionary party. (See also IDEOLOGY; JUSTICE; MORALS.)

Reading

Bauer, Otto 1905–6: 'Marxismus und Ethik', *Die Neue Zeit*, XXIV. Partly translated in Bottomore and Goode, eds. *Austro-Marxism.*

Kautsky, Karl 1906 (1918): *Ethics and the Materialist Conception of History.*

Kolakowski, Leszek 1960: *Der Mensch ohne Alternative.*

Lenin, V. I. 1920 (1966): Speech at 3rd Komsomol Congress, 2 October 1920.

Stojanović Svetozar 1973: *Between Ideals and Reality,* ch. 7.

IRING FETSCHER

Eurocommunism A movement of strategic and theoretical change begun in the 1970s by many communist parties in capitalist democracies – the mass parties of Italy, Spain and France, as well as numerous smaller parties – in response to the 1956 XXth Congress of the Soviet party (CPSU) and events surrounding it (the Hungarian and other revolts in socialist societies, the Sino-Soviet split, the rise of *détente* in international politics), together with dramatic changes in the social structure of advanced capitalism following from the long post-war economic boom. By the 1970s major European communist parties were aware that political success would henceforth depend on their capacity to appeal to new constituencies beyond the working class – in particular to 'new middle strata' – and to construct workable alliances with other political forces.

De-Bolshevization was the core of Eurocommunism, as commitments to policies and methods derived from earlier Third International experience were greatly attenuated. For Eurocommunist parties the 'road to socialism' was to be peaceful, democratic and constructed primarily out of the raw materials present within the national society. Socialism itself was to be democratic, again in accordance with the logic of domestic social development. Resort to Soviet institutional patterns – one-party 'proletarian dictatorships' in particular – and replication of the Soviet model more generally were ruled out. In most cases 'de-Stalinization' and democratization in the party's internal life were also proposed. These processes also implied renunciation of Soviet hegemony over the international communist movement.

The Italian Communist Party (PCI) was the first practitioner of Eurocommunism (the term itself was first coined by an Italian journalist) after the enunciation of its 'historic compromise' strategy in 1973. The PCI envisaged the beginning of its trajectory towards socialism through alliance with the ruling Christian Democrats around a vigorous programme of democratic reforms (Hobsbawm 1977). The Spanish party (PCE), emerging from decades of clandestinity under Franco, then opted for a similar approach involving loyal communist participation in the construction of a new, and advanced, Spanish democracy (Carrillo 1977). The French party (PCF), engaged in an effort to

come to power in alliance with the Socialists around a Common Programme of democratic reforms, moved in a similar direction at its XXIInd Congress in 1976, when its allegiance to the Soviet model and the DICTATORSHIP OF THE PROLETARIAT was abandoned (Marchais 1973 and PCF 1976). The distinctive Eurocommunist approaches of these three parties led them to frustrate Soviet goals of recentralizing the international communist movement around a pro-Soviet line at the East Berlin Conference of communist parties in 1976.

The early hopes of Eurocommunism had been dashed by the 1980s. In Italy the PCI, after major electoral gains in 1976 and entrance into the majority bloc (although not the government), gained little from the Christian Democrats in return for its parliamentary support. By 1980, faced with a political impasse and the effects of economic crisis, its electoral and mass – especially union – power had begun to decline. The PCI nonetheless persisted on its Eurocommunist course, even if 'historic compromise' gave way to a revived 'Union of the Left', with the Italian Socialist Party (PSI), as a strategy. Thus in 1981 the PCI broke dramatically with the CPSU over the declaration of martial law in Poland to destroy *Solidarnösc*, announcing that the progressive energies of the Soviet Revolution had been spent. Henceforth a *terza via* – a third, Eurocommunist, way to socialism – was imperative.

The Spanish party failed to make its mark either electorally or in terms of trade-union strength (through the Workers' Commissions) in the first years of the new Spanish democracy. Instead a new Social Democratic party rapidly accumulated most of the resources which the PCE coveted and which its Eurocommunist strategy was designed to capture. Partly in consequence, by the early 1980s the PCE had fallen victim to schismatic regionalist and factional disputes, in which the unwillingness of its Secretary-General, Santiago Carrillo, to allow the democratization of the party's internal life was a central issue. Decline and marginalization seemed inevitable.

The French party followed yet another road. Like the PCE, the PCF had Eurocommunized 'from above', changing its strategic outlook without changing its internal life. Thus when the *Union de la Gauche* proved electorally too profitable for the Socialists, the PCF leadership abruptly decreed a complete change of course after 1977. Eurocommunism was abandoned in favour of a re-assertion of older forms of identity – *ouvrièrisme*, anti-Social Democrat sectarianism, pro-Sovietism – with the goal of thwarting the further growth of Socialist strength. In the process pro-Eurocommunist forces inside the party were obliterated. The 1981 presidential elections in France showed that this retreat from Eurocommunism had probably hastened, rather than halting, PCF decline. In the wake of the Mitterrand/Socialist victory, however, the PCF was forced by circumstances and its desire to accede to ministerial posts to change its strategy again, back towards Left unity. It was reluctant, however, to return to any full-fledged Eurocommunist posture, in particular maintaining a markedly pro-Soviet international stance.

Thus Eurocommunism, greeted in the 1970s as a plausible new trajectory for Left success situated between the equally unpromising paths of traditional communism and social democracy, had demonstrated serious weaknesses by the 1980s. In some cases – the PCE and PCF – change had come too late and was too incomplete to prevent a rejuvenated Social Democratic movement from successfully occupying contested political terrain. In the Italian case Eurocommunism was more fully embraced, but success was still elusive.

Reading

Carrillo, Santiago 1977: *Eurocommunism and the State*.

Claudin, Fernando 1979: *Eurocommunism and Socialism*.

Hobsbawm, Eric ed. 1977: *The Italian Road to Socialism*, interview with Giorgio Napolitano.

Lange, Peter and Maurizio, Vannicelli 1981: *Eurocommunism: A Casebook*.

Mandel, Ernest 1978: *From Stalinism to Eurocommunism*.

Marchais, Georges 1973: *Le Défi démocratique*.

Parti Communiste Français (PCF) 1976: *Le Socialisme pour la France*.

Poulantzas, Nicos 1978: *State, Power, Socialism*.

Ross, George 1982: *Workers and Communists in France*.

GEORGE ROSS

exchange 'The wealth of societies in which the capitalist mode of production prevails appears as an "immense collection of commodities".' Thus Marx opens *Capital* and it follows that exchange is the most immediate economic relation under capitalism. All individuals of all classes necessarily participate in exchange, unlike PRODUCTION for example. But exchange is only a moment in the CIRCULATION of CAPITAL as a whole. In order to understand its significance it is necessary to penetrate analytically beyond its most obvious effects and reveal the class relations upon which it is based.

At the most immediate level, exchange presents itself as simple commodity circulation, $C_1 - M - C_2$ (see *Capital* I, ch. 3, sect. 2a). Commodities C_1 are exchanged for money M which is in turn exchanged for different commodities C_2. The motive involved is to substitute one set of use values C_2 for another C_1. In principle, the values involved in the sequence of exchanges could vary: what one trader gains, the other loses. But in aggregate the total VALUE exchanged must remain unchanged. For bourgeois society it is a principle that there should be equality in exchange, summarized in the maxim: fair exchange is no robbery. Accordingly Marx sets himself the task of showing how EXPLOITATION can exist even in circumstances of fair exchange.

Consider the exchanges involved in the general formula of capital $M - C - M'$ (*Capital* I, ch. 4). Here MONEY is exchanged against commodities which in turn generate more money, and hence SURPLUS VALUE. This is only possible if one of the commodities purchased is a source of greater value than it costs itself. The COMMODITY concerned is LABOUR POWER and its existence in a form in which it can be exchanged against money capital goes to the roots of capitalism's class RELATIONS OF PRODUCTION. The ideology of the bourgeoisie is to emphasize the freedom of exchange, the sanctity of property and the pursuit of self-interest. It is these very characteristics of exchange that conceal underlying class relations. Marx summarizes the situation sarcastically as follows:

The sphere of circulation or commodity exchange within whose boundaries the sale and purchase of labour-power goes on, is in fact a very Eden of the innate rights of man. It is the exclusive realm of Freedom, Equality, Property and Bentham. Freedom, because both buyer and seller of a commodity, let us say of labour-power, are determined only by their own free will. They contract as free persons, who are equal before the law. Their contract is the final result in which their joint will finds a common legal expression. Equality, because each enters into relation with the other, as with a simple owner of commodities, and they exchange equivalent for equivalent. Property, because each disposes only of what is his own. And Bentham, because each looks only to his own advantage. The only force bringing them together, and putting them into relation with each other, is the selfishness, the gain and the private interest of each. Each pays heed to himself only, and no one worries about the others. And precisely for that reason, either in accordance with the pre-established harmony of things, or under the auspices of an omniscient providence, they all work together to their mutual advantage, for the common weal, and in the common interest. (*Capital* I, ch. 6)

It is clear that exchange involves a relation between producers (and non-producers). It thereby creates an equivalence between different types of labour, forming ABSTRACT LABOUR as the substance of value. This formation of value is, and is expressed as, a relationship between the USE VALUES of commodities and is consequently characterized as COMMODITY FETISHISM. It is taken to an extreme by the role of money in exchange which dictates that everything should have its price. Social relations between producers are, and are expressed as, material relations between things. This is a necessary accompaniment of capitalist economic relations. But matters go even further. So powerful is the ideology and influence of the market in correspondence to the 'immense wealth of commodities' that it tends to fashion social relations in general in its own image. This is true, for example, of other forms of exchange which are not the exchange of commodities. To the superficial mind and to the economic agents involved, the buying and selling of INTEREST bearing capital in the form, say, of bonds or the renting of LANDED PROPERTY seem to be specific cases of exchange in practice. By contrast, for Marx, they are specific forms in which surplus value can be appropriated. They do not involve commodities directly even if they result in rent and interest which appear to be prices.

More generally the influence of exchange extends beyond economic relations, even to those where the market is itself not directly involved. For example, marriage becomes a more or less implicit form of contract between the partners. More generally, the atomization of individuals under bourgeois society causes relations between them to be governed by relations of private property even where exchange is itself absent. So fetishized economic relations are carried over into social relations in general. This is most notable at the level of ideology where it is inconceivable for the bourgeois mind to see non-capitalist relations in terms other than wages, profits and commodity exchange.

Because exchange is the most immediate of economic relations, it is easily taken to be the cause of economic developments. Just as the virtues of *laissez-faire* are associated with the freedom and harmony of exchange, so ECONOMIC CRISES are seen as a failure of the market mechanism. Such is the thrust of Keynesianism and also of the idea that trade unions force WAGES above the level at which harmony can be achieved between demand and supply of labour. For UNDERDEVELOPMENT AND DEVELOPMENT, UNEQUAL EXCHANGE is seen as a causal factor by some, although for Marx it was essential to explain general phenomena of capitalism on the basis of *equality* in exchange. In part, such an equality is a tendency within capitalism, while COMPETITION as the necessary accompaniment of exchange tends to present appearances as the opposite of the underlying reality.

Reading
For relevant reading *see* CIRCULATION.

                                          BEN FINE

exploitation Used by Marx in two senses, the first being the more general one of making use of an object for its potential benefits; thus, the exploitation of natural resources, of a political situation, or of moral hypocrisy: 'in relation to the traffic in children, working-class parents have assumed characteristics that are truly revolting and thoroughly like slave-dealing. But the pharisaical capitalist . . . denounces this bestiality which he himself creates, perpetuates and exploits. . . .' (*Capital* I, ch. 15, sect. 3). In one sense, therefore, exploitation is a useful, catch-all derogatory term of unique polemical force, and so very much part of Marx's critical assault on capitalism.

It has another more precise meaning which makes it a central concept of HISTORICAL MATE-RIALISM. In any society in which the forces of production have developed beyond the minimum needed for the survival of the population, and which therefore has the potential to grow, to change and to survive the vicissitudes of nature, the production of a surplus makes possible exploitation, the foundation of class society. Exploitation occurs when one section of the population produces a surplus whose use is controlled by another section. Classes in Marxist theory exist only in relation to each other and that relation turns upon the form of exploitation occurring in a given MODE OF PRODUCTION. It is exploitation which gives rise to CLASS CONFLICT. Thus different types of society, the classes within them, and the class conflict which provides the dynamic of any society can all be characterized by the specific way in which exploitation occurs. Under capitalism, exploitation takes the form of the extraction of SURPLUS VALUE by the class of industrial capitalists from the working class, but other exploiting classes or class fractions share in the distribution of surplus value (see FORMS OF CAPITAL AND REVENUES). Under capitalism, access to the surplus depends upon the ownership of property, and thus the exploited class of capitalism, the proletariat, sell their labour power to live; though they too are divided into fractions by the specific character of the labour power which they own and sell (see also LABOUR PROCESS; DIVISION OF LABOUR; MIDDLE CLASS; CLASS CONSCIOUSNESS).

Capitalism differs from NON-CAPITALIST MODES OF PRODUCTION in that exploitation normally takes place without the direct intervention of force or non-economic processes. The surplus in the capitalist mode arises from the specific character of its production process and, especially, the manner in which it is linked to the process of EXCHANGE. Capitalist production generates a surplus because capitalists buy workers' labour-power at a wage equal to its value but, being in control of production, extract labour greater than the equivalent of that wage. Marx differed from the classical political economists, who saw exploitation as arising from the unequal exchange of labour for the wage. For Marx, the distinction between labour and labour power allowed the latter to be sold at its value while the former created the surplus. Thus exploitation occurs in the capitalist mode of production behind the backs of the participants, hidden by the facade of free and equal exchange (see COMMODITY FETISHISM).

> The sphere of circulation or commodity exchange, within whose boundaries the sale and purchase of labour-power goes on, is in fact a very Eden of the innate rights of man. [But if we] . . . in company with the owner of money and the owner of labour-power, leave this noisy sphere, where everything takes place on the surface and in full view of everyone, and follow them into the hidden abode of production, on whose threshold there hangs the notice 'No admittance except on business', here we shall see, not only how capital produces, but how capital is itself produced. The secret of profit making must at last be laid bare! (*Capital* I, ch. 6)

But 'profit-making' is just capitalist exploitation. Its secret gave rise to the study of political economy; and since Marx disclosed it orthodox economics has been devoted to covering it up again. No previous mode of production required such intellectual labour to unearth, display, and re-bury its method of exploitation, for in previous societies the forms of exploitation were transparent: so many days of labour given, or so much corn claimed by representatives of the ruling class. Capitalism is unique in hiding its method of exploitation behind the process of exchange, thus making the study of the economic process of society a requirement for its transcendence.

Exploitation is obscured too by the way the surplus is measured in the capitalist mode of production. The rate of profit ($s/(c+v)$) calculates surplus value as a proportion of the total capital advanced, constant and variable, the ratio of interest to individual capitals, for it is according to the quantity of total capital advanced that shares of surplus value are appropriated. But as capital expands the rate of profit may fall, concealing a simultaneous rise in the rate of exploitation defined as the ratio of surplus to necessary labour, the rate of surplus value, s/v (see FALLING RATE OF PROFIT).

Recently members of the school of ANALYTICAL MARXISM have questioned whether Marx was correct to accord the concept of exploitation such a fundamental place in his condemnation of capitalism. Roemer (1988) defines individuals to be exploited if the labour they expend in production is greater than the labour embodied in the goods they can purchase from the revenues they gain from production. Roemer's definition purposely talks of individuals rather than classes and makes no mention of the social relations of production. This is so that he can then use it to demonstrate that neither wage-labour nor any specific class structure is a prerequisite of exploitation defined in this way. Indeed, workers may hire means of production rather than the other way round and still be exploited. The purpose of this exercise is to show that the unfairness of capitalism is based not on the wage-labour relation between classes but on the differential ownership of alienable means of production between individuals. It is this unequal distribution of assets that makes an exploitative exchange of labour power beneficial for both sides. The causes of this inequality of distribution, rather than the exploitation which results from it, constitute for Roemer the basis of his 'ethical' critique of capitalism.

Against this, it has been argued that Roemer's use of the formal methods of modern microeconomics leads him to lose sight of Marx's objective: to uncover the laws of motion of a specific mode of production, capitalism. Thus the fact that in Roemer's model it does not matter whether capital hires workers or the other way round shows that his model of capitalism is incompletely specified. It is capital *control* of the workers' labour process which allows the exploitation of the working class to take place in the process of production, through 'the formal subsumption of labour to capital', and any formal model which does not recognize that social characteristic of capitalism will of necessity fail to capture its essential relation of exploitation (Lebowitz 1988).

Reading

Lebowitz, Michael 1988: 'Analytical Marxism'.
Luxemburg, Rosa 1925 (1954): *What is Economics?*
Roemer, John 1988: *Free to Lose.*

SUSAN HIMMELWEIT

F

---

falling rate of profit The law of the falling rate of profit expresses the results of Marx's analysis of the basic forces which give rise to the long-term rhythms of capitalist accumulation: long periods of accelerated growth which are necessarily followed by corresponding periods of decelerating growth and eventual widespread economic convulsions. The Great Depression of the 1930s was one such period, and according to some Marxists the capitalist world once again hovers on the brink. It should be noted that this sort of generalized economic crisis (see ECONOMIC CRISES) is quite different from shorter-term cyclical fluctuations such as business cycles, or partial crises caused by specific events such as crop failures, monetary disturbances, etc. Business cycles and partial crises are explained by more concrete factors, and their rhythms are superimposed, so to speak, on the long-term one (Mandel 1975). The fact that they may trigger a general crisis when the underlying conditions are ripe only emphasizes the importance of first analysing the underlying movements themselves.

The driving force of capitalist activity is the desire for profits, and this compels each individual capitalist to battle on two fronts: in the labour process, against labour over the production of surplus value; and in the circulation process, against other capitalists over the realization of surplus value in the form of profits. In the confrontation with labour, *mechanization* emerges as the dominant form of increasing the production of surplus value, whereas in the confrontation with other capitalists it is the *reduction of unit* production costs (unit cost-prices) which emerges as the principal weapon of competition.

In brief, Marx argues that more advanced methods of production will involve larger, more capital-intensive plants in which at normal capacity utilization the unit production costs will be lower. Greater quantities of fixed capital per unit output are the *primary means* through which economies of scale are achieved. Because larger-scale plants enable a given number of workers to process a greater amount of raw materials into a correspondingly greater amount of product, both raw materials and output per unit of labour tend to rise together. At the same time, the greater amount of fixed capital per unit output implies higher depreciation charges and higher auxiliary materials costs (electricity, fuel, etc.) per unit output. Thus for more advanced methods, the higher capitalization (capital advanced per unit output) implies higher unit non-labour costs (unit constant capital c) while the higher productivity implies lower unit labour costs (unit variable capital v). On balance, the unit production cost $c + v$ must decline, so that the latter effect must more than offset the former. Under given technical conditions, as the limits of existing knowledge and technology are reached, subsequent increases in investment per unit output will call forth ever smaller reductions in unit production costs. This, it can be shown, implies lower transitional rates of profit for the lowest cost methods, and hence (from the Okishio Theorem), a falling general rate of profit.

It can be shown that the above pattern implies that the more advanced methods tend to achieve a lower unit production cost at the expense of a lower rate of profit. Competition, nonetheless, forces capitalists to adopt these methods, because the capitalist with the lower unit costs can lower his prices and expand at the expense of his competitors – thus offsetting his lower *rate* of profit by means of a larger *share* of the market. As Marx notes, 'each individual capital strives to capture the largest possible share of the market and supplant its competitors . . .' (*Theories of Surplus Value*, pt. II, ch. XVII). In terms of Marxist categories the above process can be shown to imply that the organic composition of capital will rise faster than the rate of surplus value, even when real wages as well as the length and intensity of the working day are constant, so that the general rate of profit falls independently of any impetus on the part of labour (Shaikh 1978, 1980).

Marx notes that various counteracting influences act to slow down and even temporarily reverse the falling rate of profit. Higher intensity of exploitation, lower wages, cheaper constant capital, the growth of relatively low organic composition industries, the importation of cheap wage goods or means of production, and the migration of capital to areas of cheap labour and natural resources can all act to raise the rate of profit by raising the rate of exploitation and/or lowering the organic composition of capital. But precisely because these counter-tendencies operate within strict limits, the secular fall in the rate of profit emerges as the *dominant tendency*.

A falling rate of profit leads to a generalized crisis through its effect on the mass of profit. On already invested capital, any fall in the rate of profit reduces the mass of profit; on the other hand, accumulation adds to the stock of capital advanced and thus adds to the mass of profit so long as the new capital's rate of profit is positive. The movement of the total mass of profit therefore depends on the relative strengths of the two effects. But a falling rate of profit progressively weakens the incentive to accumulate, and as accumulation slows down the negative effect begins to overtake the positive one, until at some point the total mass of profit begins to stagnate. It is in this phase that the crisis begins, though of course its specific form is conditioned by concrete institutional and historical factors. It should be noted, incidentally, that the above process implies a 'long-wave' in the mass of profit, which first accelerates, then decelerates, stagnates, and eventually collapses in the crisis. The phenomena of long-waves in capitalist accumulation can therefore be explained by a *secular* fall in the rate of profit, as opposed to (say) a rising-and-falling rate of profit as in Mandel (1975).

Opponents of this theory generally argue that, in the bourgeois economic notion of 'perfect competition', such a process is logically excluded, and that in any case the empirical evidence does not support it. In either case it is easy to show that neither conclusion holds up once the neo-classical economic theory and/or data upon which they base themselves are critically examined. (Shaikh 1978, 1980; Perlo 1966; Gordon 1971. Perlo is a Marxist and Gordon an orthodox economist; both find that the conventional method of estimating the capital stock seriously underestimates it, and this in turn implies a serious overestimation of the rate of profit.)

Ceteris paribus, higher wages and improved working conditions directly lower profits and also spur further mechanization, thereby doubly intensifying the built-in tendency for the rate of profit to fall. However, as Marx emphasizes, these and other struggles focused on reform of the system necessarily operate within strict limits arising from profitability, mobility of capital, and (world-wide) competition, and therefore remain constrained by the basic dynamics of capitalist accumulation. A similar argument can be made for the limits of state intervention.

Each crisis precipitates wholesale destruction of weaker capitals and intensified attacks on labour. These are the system's 'natural' mechanisms for a recovery. Each succeeding recovery in turn results in more concentration and centralization, and generally lower long-term rates of profit and growth. Thus, though the contradictions worsen over time, *there is no final crisis until workers are sufficiently class conscious and organized to overthrow the system itself* (Cohen 1978, pp. 201–4). (See also CRITICS OF MARXISM; ECONOMIC CRISES.)

Reading

Gordon, R. 1971: 'A Rare Event'.

Mandel, E. 1972 (1975): *Late Capitalism*.

Perlo, V. 1966: 'Capital Output Ratios in Manufacturing'.

Shaikh, A. 1978: 'Political Economy and Capitalism. Notes on Dobb's Theory of Crisis'.

— 1980: 'Marxian Competition versus Perfect Competition'.

— 1982: 'Neo-Ricardian Economics: A Wealth of Algebra, A Poverty of Theory'.

ANWAR SHAIKH

false consciousness.   *See* ideology.

family Marxist analysis of the family is still dominated by Engels's *The Origin of the Family*. Engels argued that the bourgeois family rested on a material foundation of inequality between husband and wife, the latter producing legitimate heirs for the transmission of property in return for mere board and lodging. He described this relation as a form of prostitution, contrasting mercenary bourgeois marriage with the 'true sex love' allowed to flourish in a proletariat where husband and wife attained an equality of exploitation through wage labour.

This analysis has been subjected to criticism on every possible count, but it remains a uniquely materialist account of the family and has the considerable merit of attempting to explain the different family forms characteristic of different classes. Engels's account, however, is based on the dubious evolutionary anthropology of L. H. Morgan, underplays the palpable domination of men in the proletarian family as 'residual', and fails to consider the domestic division of labour and the burdens imposed on women undertaking a 'double shift' of wage labour along with childcare and housework at home.

Notwithstanding such criticisms, the main points of Engels's observations form the basis of official family policy, as Molyneux (1981) has argued, in the Marxist-Leninist tradition. The USSR may stand as a model for these policies. An emphasis on drawing women into productive labour is combined with social provision of childcare facilities and an official ideology that exalts the 'working mother'. Lenin himself argued for the socialization of housework but, as feminist critics (see FEMINISM) point out, such socialization was never understood as involving men undertaking domestic chores. In this respect the Cuban Family Code, enjoining husbands to share housework and childcare equally with their wives, represents a unique development in socialist reformulation of the family.

Marx himself did not develop an analysis of the family independently of that produced by Engels, and indeed the evidence suggests that his own conception of the family was naturalistic and uncritical. Without defending his assumptions Marx tends to imply, in his discussion of wages and the reproduction of labour power, for instance, that workers are male and that women and children are simply a threatening source of substitution and cheap competition.

In Marxist thought as a whole the family occupies a vexed position. The *Communist Manifesto* calls for 'the abolition of the family', but such calls have tended to be transmuted into the far weaker project of abolishing the bourgeois family in favour of a proletarian, socialist, family. Such a 'socialist family' has tended to rest on an assumed heterosexual serial monogamy, and falls far short of critiques of the family in more general radical thought. Marxist thought on the family has therefore tended to be less uncompromisingly critical than utopian socialist, libertarian, anarchist and feminist positions.

Marxist analysis of the family in the twentieth century finds its high point in the recognition by the FRANKFURT SCHOOL that the family is a *social* institution and ideology, despite all the appearances of its character being private. Debates in the 1950s and 1960s tended to descend to popular conundrums as to whether the family had been 'taken over' by the state or was in 'decline'.

Recent analysis has focused on two areas, the first being historical interpretation of different family forms. Many Marxist historians accept that the form of family dominant in the West today is characteristic of the nineteenth-century bourgeoisie as a class, and this recognition has led to more detailed specification of family forms as they vary historically, by class, by ethnic group and so on. A second major interest lies in the relevance of psychoanalysis in an interpretation of the family – though this approach remains controversial within Marxism.

Not least of the problems encountered in analysis of the family is that of definition. Historically two distinct meanings of the term – (1) kinship arrangements and (2) the organization of the household – have tended to become conflated into a notion of co-residing kin. It must be conceded, however, that the *ideological* resonance of the family extends far beyond this formal definition. (See also DOMESTIC LABOUR; GENDER; KINSHIP.)

Reading

Barrett, Michèle and McIntosh, Mary 1991: *The Antisocial Family*.

Davidoff, Leonore and Hall, Catherine 1986: *Family*

Fortunes: Men and Women of the English Middle Class, 1780–1850.

Molyneux, Maxine 1981: 'Socialist Societies Old and New: Progress towards Women's Emancipation'.

MICHÈLE BARRETT

fascism   The rise of fascist movements, and the establishment of fascist regimes in several European countries during the 1920s and 1930s confronted Marxist thinkers with a new and urgent problem for analysis. There were two main issues: (i) what economic and social conditions gave rise to fascism, and (ii) what made possible the victory of fascism and the destruction of the working-class movement in some countries? In a series of pamphlets and articles written between 1930 and 1933 Trotsky sketched the main features of fascism, though he was primarily concerned to formulate an effective political strategy which would enable the working-class movement to halt the fascist advance in Germany. Fascism, he argued, is the expression of a profound structural crisis of late capitalism, and results from the tendency of monopoly capitalism (as noted by Hilferding) to 'organize' the whole of social life in a totalitarian fashion (see TOTALITARIANISM), while the social basis of the fascist mass movements is the petty bourgeoisie or middle class. A more systematic general analysis of fascism was undertaken by Bauer (1936), who regarded it as 'the product of three closely interconnected processes'. First, the first world war expelled large numbers of people from bourgeois life, turning them into *déclassés*, who after the war formed the fascist 'militias' and 'defence leagues' with their militaristic, anti-democratic and nationalist ideologies. Second, the post-war economic crisis impoverished a large part of the lower middle class and peasantry, who then forsook the bourgeois-democratic parties and rallied to the militias. Third, the economic crises reduced the profits of the capitalist class, and in order to restore them by raising the level of exploitation it needed to break the resistance of the working class, and this seemed difficult or impossible to achieve under a democratic regime.

Several members of the FRANKFURT SCHOOL also made detailed studies of the rise of fascism. Neumann, in a classic study of National Socialist Germany (1942), argued that 'in a monopolistic system profits cannot be made and retained without totalitarian political power . . . that is the distinctive feature of National Socialism' (p. 354), and he went on to describe the regime as a 'command economy', or more broadly as 'totalitarian monopoly capitalism'. In Germany, Neumann claimed, the process of CENTRALIZATION AND CONCENTRATION OF CAPITAL, leading to monopoly, had proceeded farther than elsewhere and this, together with the exceptional severity of the economic crisis in Germany, accounted for the strength of fascism. A somewhat different analysis was made by Pollock in essays written between 1932 and 1941; while agreeing about the importance of monopoly capitalism Pollock emphasized more strongly the role of the interventionist state and described the system as 'state capitalism' (a term which Neumann regarded as a *contradictio in adjecto* which 'cannot bear analysis from an economic point of view'). Finally, from 1945 onwards, Adorno and Horkheimer in association with several American social scientists undertook a series of studies on prejudice – dealing in particular with the 'authoritarian personality' and anti-Semitism – with the aim of exploring the psychological basis of fascist movements (see especially Adorno *et al.* 1950; see also PSYCHOANALYSIS).

Some more recent studies of fascism, while largely accepting the main elements of the foregoing analyses which relate fascism to monopoly capitalism, acute economic crisis, and the threatened position of large sections of the middle class, have also raised additional points. Poulantzas (1974), in a study which is mainly devoted to a critical examination of the doctrine and policy of the Third International and the communist parties of Italy and Germany in their confrontation with fascism (and notably their characterization of Social Democracy as 'social fascism'), nevertheless also discusses some more general questions, in particular the specific nature of fascism in relation to other forms of the 'exceptional capitalist state', which include Bonapartism and various types of military dictatorship. Mason, in a short essay (1981) on unresolved problems in Marxist accounts of fascism, refers particularly to the significance of Hitler as a leader and of anti-Semitism; and he suggests that the Third Reich may have been a 'unique regime', thus drawing attention to an important general issue – for although the conditions for the rise of fascism can emerge in all advanced capitalist societies, its victory may well depend upon specific national circumstances and historical traditions. Finally, it seems necessary to take more account of phenomena such as unemployment which other writers (though also some Marxists, among them Adler and Bauer) have emphasized; thus Carsten (1967) notes that 'it was in particular from the ranks of the unemployed that the S.A. [the National Socialist storm troops] during these years [1930–32] recruited a private army of 300,000 men'. From both Marxist and other studies it may be concluded, therefore, that an acute economic crisis can promote not only greater working-class radicalism but also the rapid growth of right-wing political movements.

Reading

Adorno, Theodor W. *et al.* 1950: *The Authoritarian Personality.*

Bauer, Otto 1936 (*1978*): 'Fascism'. In Bottomore and Goode, eds. *Austro-Marxism.*

Beetham, David ed. 1984: *Marxists in face of Fascism.*

Carsten, F. L. 1967: *The Rise of Fascism.*

Mason, Tim 1981: 'Open Questions on Nazism'. In R. Samuel ed. *People's History and Socialist Theory.*

Neumann, Franz 1942 (*1944*): *Behemoth: The Structure and Practice of National Socialism.*

Pollock, Friedrich 1975: *Stadien des Kapitalismus.*

Poulantzas, Nicos 1974: *Fascism and Dictatorship.*

Trotsky, Leon 1930–33 (*1971*): *The Struggle Against Fascism in Germany.*

TOM BOTTOMORE

feminism The place of feminism in Marxist thought is the subject of controversy. On the one hand it can be argued that feminism – seen as women's equality with men – is essentially a doctrine of liberalism and the enlightenment, owing little to revolutionary Marxism. On the other hand it has been claimed that the liberation of women from oppression and exploitation could only be achieved as part of the human liberation that socialist revolution alone could bring about.

Certainly it would be correct to identify historically quite distinct tendencies in feminism. In Great Britain and the USA the longest tradition is that of democratic, liberal, feminism directed towards obtaining equal rights and opportunities for women. In the nineteenth century much of this work was focused on removing educational and professional barriers, but the impetus behind these reforming campaigns was often quite militant. The culmination of this 'equal rights' militancy came with the violent struggles of the early twentieth-century suffragettes in their fight for the vote. Recent victories for 'equal rights' feminism have been the British Equal Pay and Sex Discrimination legislation and the US equivalents, and many reforms in social policy, employment and so on are now being campaigned for.

A second dominant tradition in feminism can be identified as more 'separatist' in character. Feminist utopias have often depicted communities of women where the supposedly violent, militaristic, hierarchical and authoritarian characteristics of men are mercifully absent. This strand of feminist thought inclines to pessimism on the question of ameliorating male brutality and advises the establishment of female communities and the strengthening of women's relationships to each other. Historically this tradition has tended to involve a sentimentalization of, rather than an erotic approach to, relationships between women, but in this respect as in others the contemporary inheritors of separatist feminism take a less conciliatory and respectable stance. The present-day women's liberation movement, formed in Great Britain and the USA in the late 1960s (and represented in such early classic texts as Firestone and Millett), draws its political impact from an uncompromising critique of male brutality (physical and mental) and male power (economic, political and military). Many feminists argue that male domination (patriarchy) is the primary social division and of more significance than divisions of class or race.

A third strand of feminism aligns the struggle for women's liberation with more general socialist perspectives and politics. It is important to note that the present-day feminist movement in Great Britain has been less influenced politically by the Marxist-Leninist tradition than it has been inspired by utopian socialism, libertarianism, Maoism, anti-colonialism and anarchism. 'Consciousness-raising', for example, is a central strategy of feminism, owing a great deal to Fanon and Mao Tse-tung. It is no coincidence that these particular socialist traditions take very seriously questions of ideology, consciousness and cultural revolution.

What, then, is the place of feminism in Marxist thought proper? There are as many answers to this question as there are interpretations of Marx. Feminism is clearly compatible with the spirit of justice, egalitarianism and personal fulfilment that is to be found in the alienation theory of the young Marx. It is more difficult to see how the mature Marx of *Capital* left room for any consideration of gender in his detailed analysis of the dynamic on which capitalism rests. In general, humanist interpretations of Marx tend to be more compatible with feminism than anti-humanist stances. In recent years, however, followers of Althusser have tried to argue (from an anti-humanist position) that the oppression of women can be understood in terms of the requirements of capitalist reproduction (through the FAMILY) of the labour force and social relations of production. These arguments have not proved altogether convincing, not least because they attempt to explain with reference to the needs of capitalism as a system a phenomenon (the oppression of women) that appears to exist in all known modes of production.

Considerable tension has existed between Marxist and feminist thought and political practice, and Marx himself offers in his own writings little encouragement of feminism. Engels, on the other hand, as well as producing his immensely influential analysis of the FAMILY, adopted throughout his life a more auspicious attitude to feminism. Although Marxists have often regarded feminism as one of a number of 'bourgeois deviations' from the revolutionary path, while feminists have often regarded Marxism as unwilling to give priority to gender equality, there can be no doubt that a basis for mutual sympathy and alliance has existed for some time. Outside feminist thought itself there is no tradition of critical analysis of women's oppression that could match the incisive attention given to this question by one Marxist thinker after another. Lenin, Trotsky, and Bebel, in particular, built on the work of Engels in this area. The policies of societies attempting to implement a Marxist transition to socialism have invariably attached considerable weight to the emancipation of women. Even in the USSR, which many critics see as less radical than newer

socialist societies such as Cuba, the position of women compares very favourably with the situation in neighbouring countries. (This is particularly clear if Soviet Central Asia, say, is compared with adjoining states like Iran.)

The history of feminism in the communist movement can be traced through the biographies of women such as Klara Zetkin and Alexandra KOLLONTAI. Marxist-inspired regimes have, by and large, failed to rise to the feminist critique of oppressive personal and family relations, but they have nevertheless pushed on with material improvements in women's situation and a substantial measure of legislative and policy reforms. Certainly it can be demonstrated that feminism is treated with more respect in Marxist-inspired programmes than it is by those regimes that have recently come to power on the basis of religious fundamentalism of one kind or another. (See also DOMESTIC LABOUR.)

Reading

Banks, Olive 1981: *Faces of Feminism.*

Firestone, Shulamith 1970: *The Dialectic of Sex.*

Millett, Kate 1971: *Sexual Politics.*

Mitchell, Juliet 1976: 'Women and Equality'. In J. Mitchell and A. Oakley eds. *The Rights and Wrongs of Women.*

Rowbotham, Sheila 1974: *Women, Resistance and Revolution.*

MICHÈLE BARRETT

fetishism   In capitalist society, Marx argues, material objects have certain characteristics conferred on them in virtue of the prevailing social relations, and are regarded as if such characteristics belonged to them by nature. This syndrome, pervasive of capitalist production, he calls fetishism, its elementary form being the fetishism of the COMMODITY, as repository, or bearer, of VALUE. His analogy is religion, in which people bestow upon some entity an imaginary power. However, the analogy is inexact, for the properties bestowed on material objects in the capitalist economy are, Marx holds, real and not the product of imagination. But they are not natural properties. They are social. They constitute real powers, uncontrolled by, indeed holding sway over, human beings; objective 'forms of appearance' of the economic relationships definitive of capitalism. If these forms are taken for natural, it is because their social content or essence is not immediately visible but only disclosed by theoretical analysis.

Although it is not always appreciated, Marx's doctrine of fetishism and his theory of value are indissolubly linked. They highlight the peculiar form that is assumed by expended labour in bourgeois society. Labour itself is universal to human societies. But it is only with the production and exchange of commodities, generalized under capitalism, that it gains expression as an objective property of its own products: as their value. In other types of economy, both communal and exploitative, labour can be recognized directly for what it is, a social process. It is overtly regulated and coordinated as such, whether by authority or by agreement. Under capitalism, by contrast, individual producers of commodities work independently of one another and what coordination there is comes about impersonally – behind their backs so to speak – via the market. They all function within an elaborate DIVISION OF LABOUR. Yet this social relation between them is only effected in the form of a relation between their products, the commodities they buy and sell; the social character of labour appears only indirectly, in the values of those commodities, whereby, being all equally embodiments of labour, they are commensurable. Things become the bearers of a historically specific social characteristic.

The illusion of fetishism stems from conflation of the social characteristic and its material shapes: value seems inherent in commodities, natural to them as things. By extension of this elementary fetishism, in the role of MONEY, one particular thing, for example gold, becomes the very incarnation of value, pure concentrate apparently of a power that, in fact, is social. Similarly, in capital fetishism, the specific economic relations that endow means of production with the status of CAPITAL are obscured. The powers this commands, all the productive potentialities of social labour, appear to belong to it naturally, a mystifying appearance whose supreme expression is capital's capacity, even without assistance from productive labour, to generate INTEREST.

In the properties conferred upon the objects of the economic process, therefore, veritable powers which render people subject to the latter's dominance, the peculiar relationships of capitalism wear a kind of mask. This gives rise to illusions concerning the natural provenance of these powers. Yet the mask itself is no illusion. The appearances that mystify and distort spontaneous perception of the capitalist order are real; they are objective social forms, simultaneously determined by and obscuring the underlying relations. This is how capitalism *presents itself*: in disguise. Thus the reality of social labour is concealed behind the values of commodities; thus, too, WAGES conceal EXPLOITATION since, equivalent only to the value of LABOUR POWER, they appear to be an equivalent for the greater value that labour power in operation creates. What is actually social appears natural; an exploitative relationship seems to be a just one. It is the work of theory to discover the essential hidden content in each manifest form. However, such forms or appearances are not thereby dissolved. They last as long as bourgeois society itself. With communism, according to Marx, the economic process will be transparent to, and under the control of, the producers. (See also COMMODITY FETISHISM.)

Reading
Cohen, G. A. 1978: *Karl Marx's Theory of History*, ch. V and appendix I.
Geras, Norman 1971: 'Essence and Appearance: Aspects of Fetishism in Marx's *Capital*'.

NORMAN GERAS

feudal society Although their historical interests were wide, Marx and Engels were primarily interested in the definition of the capitalist MODE OF PRODUCTION. Their writing about feudalism tended to mirror that interest, as well as focusing on the transition between the feudal and the capitalist modes of production. They were concerned with the 'existence form' of labour and the manner in which the products of labour were appropriated by ruling classes. The analogy between the two modes of production, therefore, was between the appropriation of surplus value by capitalists, in industrializing or industrial societies, who employed proletarians as individuals to produce commodities, and the appropriation of feudal rent, in a primarily agrarian society, by feudal lords, from their peasant tenants, who were small-scale producers of their own subsistence needs with a labour force based on the family.

Even its final money form, feudal rent was distinguished by Marx from capitalist ground rent, whose level was ultimately determined by the general rate of profit on capital. The level of feudal rent was determined – apart from such basic factors as the fertility of the soil and the efficiency of peasant cultivation – by the ability of the feudal ruling class to exercise non-economic forms of compulsion in the extraction of rent. Non-economic compulsion implies that there is no market bargaining between landowners and tenants to produce a level of rent determined by the supply of, and the demand for, land, but that the tenants are compelled to pay rent because of the superior force exercised by the landowner. In the settled society which feudalism became this force was legitimated by the institution of SERFDOM. Peasants, being legally unfree, were deprived of property rights, though they had rights of use. They were obliged to surrender their labour, or the product of their labour, over and above what was needed for family subsistence and the simple reproduction of the peasant household economy.

Feudal society was seen by Marx and Engels as intermediate, chronologically and logically, between the slave society (see SLAVERY) of the ancient world and the world of capitalists and proletarians in the modern era. This model is, however, inadequate to explain the peculiar characteristics of western feudalism from which the capitalist mode of production, as we know it, developed. The ancient world cannot simply be characterized in terms of a relationship between slaves working on plantations or in mines, and their owners. There was probably always a minority of slaves and a majority of free and semi-free peasants and artisans. Surplus labour was realized more in the form of rent and tax than as the unpaid toil of the captive slave. On the other hand some slaves are found well into the feudal era, working on the estates of landlords up to the tenth century (even until the eleventh century in England). And although juridical serfs constituted an important, though fluctuating, element among the medieval European PEASANTRY there was always a high proportion of peasants of free status. Does this mean, therefore, that from the Marxist standpoint there is no way of differentiating feudal society from other pre-capitalist societies? The short definition given above of the basic

features of the feudal mode of production does less than justice to Marx and Engels, who, without exploring the overall evolution of medieval feudalism, nevertheless saw it as a historical process. They were not only interested in the transition from feudalism to capitalism but also in the impact of the Germanic tribes on the decaying Roman Empire, and speculated on the specific forms of medieval society as a synthesis arising from this impact. This was not taken far, but it suggests that a Marxist understanding of feudal society should depend on seeing it as a historical development, not as a static set of relationships between two principal and contending classes, the landowners and the peasants. That does not mean, of course, that it would be possible to understand the feudal economy and society without an understanding of that relationship and the special (and changing) character of the coercion which was embedded in it. But there was a good deal more to feudal society than the exploitation of peasants by landowners, and their resistance to it.

In the first place we must understand not only the 'existence form' of labour, but the 'existence form' of landed property. This brings us to the institution which gave its name to feudalism, namely the 'fief' (Latin *feodum, feudum*), one of the main topics (rather neglected by Marxists) of bourgeois historiography. The classical fief was a piece of landed property held by a vassal from a lord in return for military service, or the giving of aid and counsel. It was a specific expression of a more general relationship within the feudal ruling class. This potent relationship was lordship and vassalage, expressed by the oath of fealty and long pervading the ethos of the ruling class. It can be traced back to the relationship between Roman magnates and their clients, and especially to that between Germanic warrior leaders and their followers. The latter gave their loyalty, service and counsel in the expectation of gifts from the profits of war – that is, plunder. The landed fief was, in part, the later equivalent of redistributed plunder, first developed in the period of relative stabilization under the hegemony of the Carolingians.

It is the lord–vassal relationship and its expression in property-holding through the fief which has determined medieval and modern perceptions of feudal society, rather as the factory system determined perceptions of capitalism. It used to be thought that the fief was mainly developed in the Loire–Rhine area and in Norman England. It has, however, been demonstrated recently that by the end of the eleventh century, the fief and other features of feudalism, such as vassalage and decentralized jurisdictional power, were also to be found in Catalonia, Aragon, southern France and northern Italy. The concept was sufficiently strong, as Engels noted, to reach its 'classic expression of the feudal order' in, of all places, the *Assizes* of the ephemeral crusader Kingdom of Jerusalem.

The lord–vassal relationship was a significant bonding element even in the strongest early medieval states – the Carolingian and Ottoman empires, the English and Anglo-Norman kingdoms. It was all the more important when some state powers fragmented. Because of the bad communications and localized character of the economy, effective rule could only be exercised over a relatively small area. Within the duchy, the county or the area controlled by a castellan, the network of lord–vassal relationships was the basis of cohesion. It was ideologically reinforced by religious institutions (bishops and abbeys, themselves feudal landowners). It was exercised primarily through jurisdiction. The right to hold a court for their vassals, who attended it as suitors, advisors and declarers of custom, was the main way in which lords exercised power in feudal society, settling disputes and punishing breaches of law and custom. The court was also an administrative organ for levying taxes and raising military forces. In so far as the size of states was increased (as in the case of the feudal monarchies) it was, in the first place, by extending the hierarchy of control through jurisdiction. The creation of taxation systems, bureaucracies and permanent armies was secondary.

The jurisdictional system described above was concerned with the relationship – by no means always peaceful – between the lords and vassals who were all part of an essentially military aristocracy. Jurisdictional power was even more essential for the maintenance of landowner control over the peasantry. It must be stressed that the relationship between great lords and their free vassals was not analogous to that between the landowning class as a whole and peasant tenants. Military vassals were free men, their family rights in their estates, though

not entirely inviolable, could not be challenged without serious cause. And although changes in allegiance might provoke accusations of treason, such changes were by no means impossible. But even peasants who were of free personal status had little opportunity for freedom of movement and freedom to dispose of their property, much less so those of unfree status. Over the latter, their lord's jurisdiction was exercised in order to force them to do unpaid labour services on the demesne (home farm) and to pay various dues in kind, or even money, which were levied on the family holding. By the twelfth century (though the tempo of development varies considerably in different parts of Europe) the scope of jurisdictional exaction had considerably increased. The decentralization of feudal power meant that the petty lords of villages were able to tax all inhabitants (whether tenants or not), to force them to grind their corn at the lord's mill, press their grapes in his wine press, bake their bread in his oven – for a consideration. They paid money fines to him when they were judged for delinquency in his court, fines for leave to marry off a daughter and a more or less heavy death duty.

This complex variety of exactions from the peasantry raises the question of the definition of feudal rent in its essence. For some Marxists the essential feudal rent was labour service on the demesne, an obvious way by which the ruling class appropriated surplus labour. For them, the development of rent in kind and in money was peripheral, simply a sign of the breakdown of the feudal mode of production in the west – in contrast to its maintenance, with large demesnes and servile labour rent, in Eastern Europe from the sixteenth to the eighteenth centuries. This view is difficult to sustain in view of the fluctuations over time of demesne cultivation by means of labour rent. If it was characteristic of Carolingian Francia in the ninth century, of England in the thirteenth century and of Poland in the seventeenth century, it was also of diminished importance in eleventh-century France, twelfth- and fourteenth-century England and thirteenth- to fourteenth-century Eastern Europe. One cannot but conclude that it is not correct to identify only one form of feudal rent as characteristic of feudal society at its full development.

The addition of the profits of private jurisdiction to 'ordinary' feudal rent in western Francia from the eleventh century directs our attention to the nature of those profits. They, and much of the rent from holdings, were often received in money form. To pay rents and fines in money, to use money in order to buy exemptions and even charters (this happened as early as the late twelfth century), peasants must have been producing surpluses over subsistence and reproduction needs. These surpluses must have been sold for cash on the market, as commodities. What then was the role of commodity production in feudal society?

It is clear that, side by side with a subsistence economy, there was a market economy. Probably the greatest part of the social product (mainly food stuffs) never went onto the market. Most of the non-marketed produce was consumed within the peasant household or was transferred in kind from peasant to lord. There was also a lord's subsistence economy, for although part of the demesne product went to the market, a considerable proportion was directly consumed in aristocratic households, in the lavish establishments of high ecclesiastics and in the frequent feasting of retainers.

Pressure to market farm produce came from two directions. After all, the social division of labour between cultivation, manufacture, praying, ruling and waging war, was already ancient before the arrival of feudalism. Such a division implied the production of food surpluses by the cultivators in order to allow the full- or part-time activities of the others to be undertaken. According to the circumstances of the time – land/labour ratio, level of technology, disturbance of production by warfare (invariably a form of plunder) – the disposable surplus could vary considerably in amount or availability. When feudal society began to stabilize in the eleventh century, in the manner described above, peasants were able to produce surpluses, for conditions became relatively peaceful, population began to grow and there are indications of technological progress. Local and regional markets for the exchange of agricultural and manufactured products began to emerge from the mass of villages and hamlets.

Another essential component in the growth of commodity production in medieval feudal society was the special needs of the ruling class. To an important extent these were inherited from the consumption habits of the ruling classes of the Roman Empire, carried over by high-ranking churchmen (archbishops, bishops, abbots) of aristocratic origin. What was consumed was only partly a matter of enjoyment: it was also a matter of display and reward – in other words it had a political function. The consumption goods included silks, spices, Mediterranean fruits and wines. What especially characterized them was that to begin with they were relatively small in bulk and high in price, and that they were produced a long way from the place of consumption – the Middle and Far East in particular. These goods were the commodities of international trade which in a stable feudal society could not be obtained, or at any rate only sporadically, by means of warfare and plunder. The feudal ruling class needed money to buy them, money which was obtained through rent and jurisdictional profits, and which peasants obtained by selling their surplus product on the local markets.

Feudal aristocratic demand stimulated the growth of key cities on international trade routes which became great mercantile centres (e.g. Venice, Cologne, Bruges, London). Demand was also focused at points of political and administrative importance, where permanent establishments of rulers, clerics, armed retainers and officials were set up. Thus high-price luxury goods would be redistributed to the seats of great abbeys and bishoprics, and to fortified centres of feudal power, including monarchical and regional capitals. Furthermore, to the goods of international trade, again sustained by upper-class demand, was added a new range of commodities of European manufacture, especially high quality woollen textiles. This led to a further wave of urbanization in central Italy, the Low Countries and elsewhere, encouraging the addition of grain, oil, wine and timber to the goods of international trade.

Marketing, manufacture and urbanization increased the numbers of such classes as city merchants, retail traders and artisans. The problem has been raised whether these constituted antagonistic or even revolutionary elements within feudalism. Sometimes the problem is put another way. If, in feudal society, production was for use, did not the development of production for the market contradict, and ultimately erode, the feudal social order?

Capitalism, in Marxist terms, is not possible

until the shape of society and economy is largely determined by the exploitation by owners of capital of a class of propertyless wage workers. The problem of the TRANSITION FROM FEUDALISM TO CAPITALISM is concerned predominantly with this issue; but not exclusively, because the problem of the formation of capital is also involved, not to mention the social and political processes by which capitalists replace feudal aristocracies as the ruling class.

To what extent did the development of commodity production, of long-distance trade, of specialized manufacturing centres and of urbanization undermine the feudal mode of production, based as it was on the relationship of two main classes, landowners and peasants? The degree of urbanization in feudal society varied. England's medieval urban population possibly fluctuated between 10 per cent and 15 per cent. Specialized areas (like the Low Countries) could have more than 30 per cent. Advanced urbanization was typified by big cities: Venice, Florence, Milan and Genoa may have had about 100,000 inhabitants at the end of the thirteenth century; Paris may have had 200,000; London 50,000. More to the point, however, is the social structure of the cities. In important respects this mirrored rather than contrasted with the countryside. The basic unit of production was the artisan workshop with a labour force no bigger than that of the middling peasant holding. The basic unit of retail marketing was the shop or market stall of the huckster, run by one or two individuals. Even the warehouses of rich wholesale merchants would have a labour force of tens rather than hundreds. The only big concentrations of dependents would be in the households of the clan-like families of the mercantile elites – and these were, if anything, replicas of aristocratic feudal households rather than anticipations of the modern factory system. In every big city there were also large numbers of uprooted and marginalized persons, mostly rural immigrants. But these in no way constituted a proletariat.

One must conclude that the medieval city presented no fundamental contrast or threat to the feudal order. The interests of the bourgeois élites of the medieval cities were not basically antagonistic to those of the feudal aristocracy. It is true that those élites obtained varying levels of political autonomy and jurisdictional privilege,

mainly in the twelfth and thirteenth centuries. Having done so, they fitted snugly into the hierarchy of feudal lordship. Even in Italy, where the power of the mercantile bourgeoisie was such that it achieved some local hegemony over the petty aristocracy of the countryside, one should not imagine a partial victory of capitalism. There was rather a fusion than a conflict between merchant capitalists and the feudal interest. The bourgeois rulers of the great Italian cities were doing for Europe's feudal rulers and aristocracies as a whole what the lesser merchants of the northern cities were doing on a lesser scale – provisioning and moneylending. As feudalism in crisis was sucked more and more into war, so its rulers more and more needed cash which merchant-banker usurers provided. And, as always, usurers and aristocratic borrowers fed on each other, needed each other.

The fundamental antagonism in feudal society was between landlords and peasants. The conflict was mostly concealed, sometimes overt as in the great peasant risings of the late Middle Ages. It was fundamental in another sense. Peasants, in their communities and as controllers of the self-contained family enterprise, were not *economically* dependent on lords. For this reason their potentialities for resistance were not negligible. Hence, if the level of rent was determined not so much by market forces as by the relative strength of the antagonists, a strengthening of peasant resistance reduced the level of rent transferred to the ruling class – and of tax to the state. This was one of the roots of the crisis of the feudal order.

If we are to define 'feudal society' in broader terms than simply 'the feudal mode of production', the political and ideological dimensions must not be neglected. As we have seen power, by and large, was exercised through jurisdiction. Jurisdiction was politics, so that one could say that the means by which landowners extracted surplus from peasants was political rather than economic. As feudal society became more complex, as the favourite occupation of the ruling class – warfare – became centralized and coordinated, jurisdiction had to be reinforced by another form of surplus extraction – taxation, which was mainly war taxation. But this taxation had to be extracted with the least possible offence to the landed interest and the bourgeois élite, that is by consent through periodically summoned assemblies (e.g. Parliament, Estates General), an extension of the conciliar element in feudal relations.

These assemblies tended to reflect the current official view of the social order, rather than how society really was. In the French and Spanish kingdoms and the German principalities, the assemblies were based on a tripartite division of society, between the church, the nobility and the 'third estate' (the towns). This reflected the ideological vision of the divinely created society of orders, divided between those who prayed (the clergy), those who fought (the nobility) and those who worked (peasants). In this organic view of society the orders of the body politic were mutually supportive and had defined roles outside which no one born or appointed to a particular order (or estate) must step. To do so would not only be a crime against the social order but a sin against God. The doctrine dates back to at least the ninth century and was promulgated especially by the clergy. It became the received social wisdom until deposed by various doctrines of bourgeois individualism in the seventeenth century. As urbanization developed the doctrine had to accommodate social classes other than the three original orders, but the message of social harmony and immobility remained the same. It was never effectively challenged by the medieval bourgeoisie. The nearest approach to a challenge came from a spokesman for the peasantry, in the second half of the fourteenth century, the Englishman John Ball, preaching: 'When Adam delved and Eve span, who was then the gentleman?'

Reading
Anderson, P. 1974b: *Passages from Antiquity to Feudalism.*
Bloch, Marc 1961: *Feudal Society.*
Bois, G. 1976: *Crise du Féodalisme.*
Bonnassie, Pierre (forthcoming): *From Slavery to Feudalism.*
Centre d'études et de recherches marxistes 1974: *Sur le Féodalisme.*
Dobb, M. 1946 (1963): *Studies in the Development of Capitalism.*
Duby, Georges 1973 (1974): *The Early Growth of the European Economy: Warriors and Peasants.*
— 1986: *The Three Orders: Feudal Society Imagined.*
Geremek, B. 1968: *Le Salariat dans l'artisanat parisien aux XIIIe–XIVe siècles.*
Hilton, R. 1973: *Bond Men made Free.*
Kuchenbuch, L. and Michael, B. eds. 1977: *Feudalismus – Materialien zur Theorie und Geschichte.*
Kula, W. 1976: *Economic Theory of the Feudal System.*

R. H. HILTON

Feuerbach, Ludwig   Born 28 July 1804, Landshut, Bavaria; died 13 September 1872, Nuremberg. Noted materialist philosopher whose *Essence of Christianity* (1841), with its doctrine that religion is the projection of human wishes and a form of alienation, attracted world attention, and whose critique of HEGEL and of religion had an important influence on the young Marx and Engels.

The son of a noted, and for his time progressive, jurist and criminologist (Paul Johann Anselm von Feuerbach), Feuerbach came to philosophy by way of theology, beginning his studies at Heidelberg in 1823. In 1824 he moved to Berlin and attended Hegel's lectures; in 1825 he lost his religious faith, became a philosophical Hegelian and transferred to the Faculty of Philosophy, completing his degree at Erlangen in 1828. His *Thoughts on Death and Immortality* (1830) caused a scandal by denying the immortality of the soul. In 1829 he had become a *Dozent* in philosophy at Erlangen and he continued lecturing until 1832, when he stopped in protest against the university's failure to appoint him professor because of his antireligious views. He lived the rest of his life as a private scholar, publishing in the 1830s a number of pioneering studies in the history of modern philosophy, followed by articles increasingly critical, from a 'materialist' standpoint, of Hegel's idealism. *The Essence of Christianity* (1841) and *Basic Propositions of the Philosophy of the Future* and *Preliminary Theses for the Reform of Philosophy* (both 1843) created a generation of Feuerbachians, following him in rejecting monarchism, the claims of Absolute Reason and of religion as illegitimate attempts to abstract human powers from man, to substitute thought for man thinking, and to set these up to dominate man. Further studies of religion followed and on the outbreak of the revolution of 1848 Feuerbach was hailed, at least by his students at Heidelberg, as its intellectual father and hero – though he himself took a passive and sceptical attitude to it, believing that Germany was not yet sufficiently emancipated from theological illusions to become a republic. In 1850 Feuerbach was converted to the medical materialism of Moleschott, and summed up his view that man is determined by the nature and quality of his food rather than by homilies against sin, in the German pun 'Man is what he eats'. He wrote little of consequence after that except some fragments on ethics, and no longer attracted public attention. In 1868 he read Marx's *Capital* and praised it for its exposure of horrible, inhuman conditions; in 1870 he joined the Social Democratic Party.

Feuerbach was neither a systematic nor a carefully consistent philosopher; he threw off aphorisms and ideas and has not left behind him a coherently worked out and carefully analysed position on any of the major problems of philosophy that are central to his work. Both his 'materialism' (perhaps better described as a naturalistic, non-atomistic empiricism) and his theory of knowledge are matters for interpretation and possible dispute. Marx's treatment of him in the *Theses on Feuerbach* as a contemplative materialist who neglected the active side of mind is simply wrong; so is the charge that he saw *praxis* only in its 'dirty Jewish' (Marx's term for vulgarly practical) aspects. Greatly influential in Germany in the 1840s, and in Russia and France still in the 1850s and 1860s, Feuerbach has had later receptions and revivals, and from becoming the leading anti-theological figure of the nineteenth century, he has become a central figure in twentieth-century theology with its elevation of man as the content of religion. Feuerbach's elevation of love as the principle of union between human beings, his doctrine of the I-Thou as the minimum content of all truly human activities (thinking, speech and love) have appealed to modern theologians and to some other philosophers standing on the margins of technical developments, but they have not much interested Marxists. Feuerbach's critique of religion, his conception of alienation, his 'materialism' and his critique of Hegel have in recent years attracted renewed study and become part of the new philosophical treatment of Marxist thought. Marx himself saw Feuerbach's critique of religion as ending in the proposition that man is the highest being for man,

and thus providing the starting-point for a truly revolutionary philosophy. Feuerbach's claim that Hegel reverses the role of subject and predicate, treating man as an attribute of thought instead of thought as an attribute of man, is certainly one source of Marx's decision to 'turn Hegel on his head', and Feuerbach's genetic critical method of inquiry, seeking the origin and function of such social institutions as religion, is applied by Marx to the state in 1843 and may be said to be one of the ingredients of his materialist conception of history. It is only with the discovery and rediscovery of Marx's early philosophical writings, however, that the relationship between Marx and Feuerbach has come to be thoroughly studied and well understood. Marx himself saw Feuerbach as an important but passing phase in his own intellectual development and maintained no lasting interest in him, though he did order from London, in the 1860s, the seven volumes of Feuerbach's collected works. Engels's *Ludwig Feuerbach*, though an important text in the development of official Soviet dialectical materialism, is neither a valuable study of Feuerbach's own philosophy nor a major contribution to a sophisticated Marxist philosophical position. Among classical Marxists, and philosophers working in the Soviet Union until recently, there has been much lip-service to Feuerbach as an important but inadequate forerunner of Marxism, but only one serious study, by A. M. Deborin (1923). Deborin's claim that Feuerbach was an important philosopher and that Marxism is a variety of Feuerbachianism, on which the first edition of the book ended, was removed from subsequent editions, and his incorrect estimation of the relationship between Feuerbach and Marx was one of the charges made against him when he was denounced and removed from his philosophical post at Stalin's behest. Kamenka's study (1970) treats Feuerbach as important historically and as basically sound in his non-atomistic empiricism, his active theory of mind and his critique of religion, but does not regard him as a systematic or great philosopher. Wartofsky (1977) treats Feuerbach as raising much more profound issues and attempts to show that Feuerbach's philosophical development is of the deepest significance for a dialectical understanding of the progress of thought.

Reading

Feuerbach, Ludwig 1841 (1957): *The Essence of Christianity.*

— 1843 (1966): *Principles of the Philosophy of the Future.*

— 1851a (1873): *The Essence of Religion.*

— 1851b (1967): *Lectures on the Essence of Religion.*

— 1967: *The Essence of Faith according to Luther.*

Kamenka, Eugene 1970: *The Philosophy of Ludwig Feuerbach.*

Wartofsky, Marx W. 1977: *Feuerbach.*

The Collected Works of Feuerbach, published in ten volumes in his own lifetime, were edited by Bolin and Jodl in 1903–11 and were reprinted as thirteen volumes in twelve, with supplementary material, by the Fromann Verlag/Günter Holzboog in Stuttgart-Bad Canstatt under the editorship of Hans-Martin Sass in 1960–4. The fullest German-language edition of Feuerbach will be the projected sixteen-volume critical edition being issued by the East German Akademie-Verlag, Berlin, under the editorship of Werner Schuffenhauer.

EUGENE KAMENKA

Finance Capital   When HILFERDING'S study of 'the latest phase of capitalist development' was published in 1910 it was greeted as a major original contribution to Marxist economic theory. Otto Bauer (1909–10) wrote that the book could almost be regarded as a further volume of *Capital*, while Kautsky (1911) described it as a brilliant demonstration of the fruitfulness of the Marxist method applied to phenomena which Marx himself, in the unfinished volumes of *Capital*, had not been able to analyse fully. Subsequently, Lenin's (1916) study of imperialism drew heavily upon Hilferding's 'very valuable theoretical analysis', and Bukharin referred to it as the 'starting point and essential inspiration' of his book *Imperialism and World Economy* (1918) which Lenin had read in manuscript before completing his own study. The book also had a wider influence, outside Marxist circles, for example on Schumpeter's writings and in particular his monograph on imperialism (1919).

But Hilferding's theory of imperialism was derived from a much broader analysis of the major changes in the capitalist economy – the great expansion of credit money through the flotation of joint stock companies and bank lending, the increasing concentration and centralization of capital in large corporations, the formation of cartels and trusts controlling whole industries, and the growing power of the banks in the economic system – a process characterized above all by the development of 'an ever more intimate relationship' between bank and industrial capital in which the banks were the dominant partners. Hilferding summarized his main thesis by saying that 'taking possession of six large Berlin banks would mean taking possession of the most important spheres of large scale industry.'

This thesis was later criticized by other economists, including some Marxists, who argued that Hilferding's analysis was based too exclusively upon the dominance of the banks. More recent writers, however, have defended the thesis while introducing qualifications and pointing to some unresolved problems (see FINANCE CAPITAL). März (1968) argued that the banks did play an important part in the development of industry from the mid-nineteenth century and that close organizational and personal links between bank and industrial capital did grow up; and he suggested that this situation only began to change in Western Europe after 1945, with the nationalization of many banks and the greatly expanded role of the state in promoting and financing industrial development. Hilferding himself later qualified his main thesis to some extent in essays on ORGANIZED CAPITALISM published between 1915 and the mid-1920s, where he argued that in conjunction with the dominance of large corporations and banks the increasing involvement of the state in the regulation of the economy had brought an important element of planning into economic life and prepared the way for socialist planning.

Finance Capital gave a major impetus to Marxist studies of the development of capitalism, and although the original thesis has been modified and refined in various ways, it did undoubtedly focus attention upon two essential features – the growth of giant corporations and the immensely important role of financial institutions – which are even more evident in the last decade of the twentieth century.

TOM BOTTOMORE

finance capital   The only form of capital that was not theorized by Marx but has become established as a valid category for twentieth-century Marxist theory. It is a form quite distinct from others such as financial, interest-bearing, or money capital. In the concept first promulgated by Hilferding (1910) it has two central characteristics: first, it is formed by the close integration of financial capital in the hands of banks, with industrial capital; and second, it arises only at a definite stage of capitalism. The existence of finance capital, thought Hilferding, has major implications for capitalism, being seen as integral to the development of monopolies (see CENTRALIZATION AND CONCENTRATION OF CAPITAL), to IMPERIALISM, and to the prospects for the overthrow of capitalism. It was these dynamic aspects which gave finance capital a significant place in the writings of Lenin and Bukharin, and have ensured that the debate over it has persisted to the present. Its significance for the application of Marxist theory to twentieth-century conditions was, indeed, implied by Kautsky and Bauer in their reception of Hilferding's book, FINANCE CAPITAL, as the completion of Marx's preliminary ideas on the stage of capitalism that was only just emerging before his death. (See Bottomore 1981 and Coakley 1982 for the connections between Hilferding's work and that of his contemporaries.)

The integration of financial and industrial capital, in a general sense, is not specific to finance capital. Throughout capitalism the existence of specialized financial capitalists holding, exchanging, borrowing, and lending money is possible only because of their articulation with the productive sectors; it is only by lending money to industrial capitalists that they can appropriate surplus value through interest, and only by operating the payments and foreign exchange systems for the transactions of the whole economy that they can appropriate surplus value through profit (see FINANCIAL CAPITAL AND INTEREST). However, it is the specific manner in which the two types of capital are integrated that distinguishes finance capital, and the essence of it is that the relationship ceases to be at arm's length; as Hilferding wrote, finance capital arose from the forces that 'bring bank and industrial capital into an ever more *intimate* relationship' (emphasis added). Moreover, it is an intimacy in which the banks are the dominant partners, controlling industry and forcing change upon it.

Hilferding and Lenin, with different emphasis, identified three channels through which the banks' control of industry is exerted. First, the rise of the JOINT-STOCK COMPANY enabled banks to take controlling shareholdings in industrial firms, and this facilitated not only control but a merging of identities so that 'banks . . . become to a greater and greater extent industrial capitalists' (Hilferding 1910, p. 225). Second, the 'personal link-up' (Lenin 1916, p. 221) achieved through the appointment of bank directors to the boards of industrial firms and vice versa, and the fact that the same persons who hold major shareholdings in banks hold them in industry too. Finally, the banks obtain detailed knowledge of 'their' industrial firms' affairs by the fact that they handle their financial transactions; they know the state of their bank balance day by day and they handle the credit (bills of exchange) generated in the course of the firms' everyday business. It is significant that the concept of finance capital was not developed with respect to financial capital in general dominating industrial capital; the channels of control were those by which a particular institutional form of the former, banks, interlocked with and dominated an institutional embodiment of the latter, joint-stock companies. Indeed, the framework was even more specific, for although they referred to other countries, Hilferding and Lenin did base their ideas primarily upon their observation of the system that dominated industrial Central Europe where the 'universal bank' was typical. Whereas commercial banks in the United Kingdom have historically concentrated on handling payments and giving short-term credits to industry, taking the view that industrialists know more about industry than bankers, the German universal bank has combined such functions with holding shares, floating share issues and holding directorships in industry.

The idea of an articulation between banks and industrial firms with the former dominating is, as such, static, but the essence of the idea of finance capital is that it is typical of a stage in the history of capitalism, and therefore both the product of historical forces and the generator of forces which would themselves transform the world. For Lenin (1916) finance capital was not itself a stage of capitalism but was, instead, an intrinsically prominent feature of the stage called monopoly capitalism or imperialism (see

PERIODIZATION OF CAPITALISM). Monopoly capitalism was the stage in which competition between many capitals came to take the form of domination of whole industries by a handful of giant enterprises, trusts or cartels, but finance capital was an essential characteristic of it. Finance capital was not the interlocking of any bank with any firm but 'the bank capital of a few very big monopolist banks, merged with the capital of the monopolist associations of industrialists' (Lenin 1916, p. 266). The picture was one of giant trusts dominated by bankers and wielding enormous power. In the hands of non-Marxists a similar picture informed populist and even fascist attacks on 'the power of finance' in the first half of this century, but Hilferding, Lenin and Bukharin saw their task as uncovering the laws that governed finance capital's rise and its future. Finance capital was generated by the operation of two phenomena that Marx had identified. Concentration and centralization had created monopolistic firms in industry, while the rise of a modern credit system had concentrated into the hands of banks the savings of the whole community; the merging of the two was the outcome of monopolistic firms having nowhere else to go for the large blocks of finance needed to facilitate their accumulation, while the banks had no profitable alternative to investing their large inflows of funds in industry. Moreover, the merger in the form of finance capital was itself an impetus to the development of further monopolies as blocks of financial-industrial capital attempted to gain further control over the anarchy of their markets. In this process the promotion of new industrial enterprises by banks was an important strategy which generated a special form of profits, promoter's profits, through the promotion itself.

The creation of monopolies, which both underlay and was given added impetus by finance capital, was seen by Lenin as inseparable from the *internationalization* of capital in imperialism. In his introduction to Bukharin's *Imperialism and the World Economy* (1917) he explained the growth of finance capital by arguing that at

> a certain stage in the development of exchange, at a certain stage in the growth of large-scale production, namely, at the stage that was

reached approximately at the end of the nineteenth and the beginning of the twentieth centuries, commodity exchange had created such an internationalisation of economic relations, and such an internationalisation of capital, accompanied by such a vast increase in large scale production, that free competition began to be replaced by monopoly. (p. 11)

Again, though, this was seen as a two-way relationship. Imperialism was a condition of the monopolies which were the condition for finance capital, but finance capital was itself the motive force for, and a defining characteristic of imperialism. Lenin's *Imperialism, the Highest Stage of Capitalism* (1916), expresses it in this way:

> The characteristic feature of imperialism is *not* industrial *but* finance capital. It is not an accident that in France it was precisely the extraordinarily rapid development of *finance* capital and the weakening of industrial capital, that from the eighties onwards, gave rise to the extreme intensification of annexationist (colonial) policy. (p. 268)

The emphasis on finance capital, distinct from industrial or other forms of capital, as the characteristic of imperialism was the fulcrum for Lenin's and Bukharin's theoretical criticisms of other Marxist views. Lenin (1916) attacked Kautsky's view that imperialism was characterized by industrial capital seeking the subjugation of agrarian areas, while Bukharin, in 'Imperialism and the Accumulation of Capital' (in Luxemburg and Bukharin 1972), bases his general critique of Luxemburg's theory of imperialism partly on the ground that she fails to distinguish the specific form of capital which underlies imperialism, finance capital, from capital in general.

Lenin and Bukharin argued that reality contradicted a view of imperialism as appropriation of agrarian areas or as, according to Luxemburg, the expansion of capital into non-capitalist areas in its search for markets; for imperialism at the turn of the century was characterized by expansion into areas where capitalist industry was already established. (Bukharin took the French occupation of the Ruhr in 1923 as his example, while Lenin mentioned German designs on Belgium, and French designs on Lorraine.) This imperialist struggle for industrial, as well as non-industrial, economies, could only be explained by the dominance of finance capital. It was symptomatic of a struggle to re-divide the world rather than simply expand into virgin territory, and re-division was imperative because of finance capital's domination and maturity. For in the years before the first world war finance capital had reached maturity by establishing a world system in which financial capital and productive capital were exported until the whole world was linked with one or another block of finance capital. In Lenin's view: 'finance capital, literally, one might say, spreads its net over all countries of the world.... The capital-exporting countries have divided the world among themselves in the figurative sense of the term. But finance capital has led to the actual division of the world' (1916, p. 245). Since the world was thus divided, further competitive development of the trusts necessarily involved a struggle for re-division.

That struggle was seen as a principal element in the genesis of imperialist war so that for Lenin and Bukharin war was seen as a necessary concomitant of finance capital's domination. In this they diverged from Hilferding, for although his theory of imperialism, with finance capital at its centre, was the foundation for that of the better known writers, he did not regard war as the inevitable outcome of imperialist rivalry. And whereas Bukharin and Lenin thought that the imperialism of finance capital only changed the conditions under which socialist revolution would overthrow capitalism and smash its state, Hilferding saw the state's subordination to finance capital and the interventionism to which the trusts pushed it as laying the foundation for a system (which he later called 'organized capitalism') that could be readily taken over and, without transformation, used by the proletariat. It was this above all that marked the political divisions between Hilferding and Lenin.

Debates over the manner in which imperialist war and the regulation of capitalism by trusts and the state would affect the balance of power between classes and the prognosis for capitalism are, however, at one remove from the question of power that is at the core of finance capital: the enormous economic, social and political power that it appeared to concentrate in the hands of banks and of the handful of capitalists that control them. The validity of the concept of finance capital for later capitalist societies has hinged on the question whether this power, predicated on the dominance of banks over industrial corporations to which they are tied, does exist. The debate on this question, which Sweezy initiated in a 1941 article and subsequent book (1942), has concerned principally the empirical question of whether data on shareholdings and interlocking directorships confirm that the channels of control identified by Hilferding do exist, and it has concentrated on the United States. The theoretical problems in the concept of finance capital – the meaning of dominance, power and integration in the relationship between banks and firms – have hardly been discussed.

Sweezy argued that Hilferding and Lenin had witnessed the emergence of capitalism into a new stage, MONOPOLY CAPITALISM, and that the dominance of bankers had been only a transitional phenomenon in its gestation: 'Bank capital, having had its day of glory, falls back again to a position subsidiary to industrial capital' (1942, p. 268). A significant challenge to this thesis came from Fitch and Oppenheimer (1970) and Kotz (1978) who argued that major banks do control large firms in the United States (although whereas the theory of finance capital emphasized the strength this brings to the trusts, Fitch and Oppenheimer pointed to the debility induced in railways and power companies by banks' policies). An important mechanism of control (in addition to boardroom representation) was seen to be the management of corporate stock by US banks' trust departments on behalf of pension funds and individuals, giving some banks effective control over strategic blocks of shares. In Kotz's work the holdings of other financial institutions within banking groups were also examined, and in the case of Britain, the work of Minns (1980) has demonstrated that banks' management of pension funds' portfolios has given them control over substantial blocks of shares and at least the prima facie possibility of using that to control industry's development. Whether such power is, in fact, exercised in modern America and Britain remains an unanswered question. Their involvement in the merger waves through which capital was centralized in the two decades from the early 1960s, and in the restructuring of industry in the economic crises of the 1970s and 1980s, is beyond question, although difficult to document and quantify; but whether they dominated and gave impetus to these changes in a significant way, as implied by the concept of finance capital, is less clear.

The theoretical coherence of the concept of finance capital, as opposed to the empirical validity of the thesis of bank domination, has remained unquestioned, but in fact it is not unproblematic. The main difficulty is that two distinct entities, financial capital in the hands of banks and industrial capital organized in corporations, are conceived as merging but yet remaining distinct to the extent that one remains dominant over the other. That notion is sustainable as long as 'merging' is interpreted in a loose sense to mean that the elements while remaining distinct are articulated with each other through definite channels and are mutually transformed through their connection. But although some of the transformations have been enumerated in the concept (such as the increased degree of monopoly in industrial capital), Hilferding, Lenin and Bukharin reflected the problem by collapsing the characteristics of finance capital into those of one or other of its elements. Although Hilferding noted the 'relative independence' of finance capital, in places he slipped into arguing that bank capital simply became industrial capital: 'the banks ... become to a greater and greater extent industrial capitalists' (1910, p. 225) while Lenin, in his Introduction to Bukharin (1917), slipped into endowing finance capital with the same characteristic of universality as Marx attributed to financial capital (in the form of interest-bearing capital): 'finance capital, a power that is peculiarly mobile and flexible, peculiarly intertwined at home and internationally, peculiarly devoid of individuality and divorced from the immediate processes of production. . . .'

A different problem which is, nevertheless, related to that of the nature of the merger and transformation of the elements of finance capital is the identification of financial capital with banks and of industrial capital with firms whose activities are only industrial. It has meant that forms of articulation between financial and industrial capital which are not comprised in links between banks and firms are excluded from

theoretical consideration (and from much empirical investigation), although the concept of finance capital purports to be more general. As an example of the empirical weakness that results from this theoretical restriction, modern multinational corporations encompass industrial production, commercial activities, *and* the banking activities of money dealing and control of investment funds (in the form of retained earnings and reserves and in the form of borrowing on the same wholesale money markets as banks draw upon); they integrate financial and industrial (and merchant) capital, but since this occurs within themselves the concept of finance capital defined in terms of banks and firms cannot be strictly applied.

For Marxist political strategies the question of the modern validity of the concept ultimately turns on whether finance capital generates a political or economic power which has to be broken if capitalism is to be overthrown. Hilferding and Lenin pointed to the concentration of power that it generated; the latter argued that 'literally several hundred billionaires and millionaires hold in their hands the fate of the whole world', while the former thought that 'taking possession of six large Berlin banks would mean taking possession of the most important spheres of large-scale industry and would greatly facilitate the initial phases of socialist policy during the transition period'. In the 1980s it remains true that the construction of socialism would require the overthrow of the independent power of the banks, but the reasons for this have more to do with their character as financial capital than with their dominant position within finance capital. With some exceptions (the Japanese economy being the most prominent) the power of banks within the capitalist system is not primarily the consequence of their direct involvement in and control of industry even though that involvement does exist. It arises from the structural power that their (and other) financial capital exerts in the foreign exchange and money markets, determining interest and exchange rates that influence the whole economy. It also arises from the discretionary power private banks have acquired to move credit on an international scale, but this credit is financial capital not bank capital tied to industry; it was exemplified in the 1970s by the international banking system becoming the principal source of credit for some third world and socialist governments, a position that gives them great power but does not constitute finance capital.

Reading

Bottomore, Tom 1981: 'Introduction to the Translation'. In Hilferding, *Finance Capital*.

Bukharin, Nikolai 1917 (1972): *Imperialism and the World Economy*.

Coakley, Jerry 1982: 'Finance Capital'.

Fitch, Robert and Oppenheimer, Mary 1970: 'Who Rules the Corporation?'

Hilferding, Rudolf 1910 (1981): *Finance Capital*.

Kotz, David 1978: *Bank Control of Large Corporations in the United States*.

Lenin, V. I. 1916 (1964): 'Imperialism, The Highest Stage of Capitalism'.

Luxemburg, Rosa and Bukharin, Nikolai 1972: *Imperialism and the Accumulation of Capital*.

Minns, Richard 1980: *Pension Funds and British Capitalism*.

Sweezy, Paul 1942: *The Theory of Capitalist Development*.

LAURENCE HARRIS

financial capital and interest In developed capitalist society financial capital plays a significant role as a mass of capital existing outside the production process, giving the appearance of being independent of it, and yet affected by and affecting it in several ways. Financial capital passes through several forms including equities, bonds and loans. Although HILFERDING developed a Marxist theory of their complex interrelations, Marx himself focused attention on interest-bearing capital and the forms of fictitious capital (titles to revenue) associated with it (see Harvey 1982, ch. 9).

Interest-bearing capital is a commodity which is alienated from its owner for a specific period of time. In Marx's theory it does not include loans, such as consumer credit, to workers (categorized as usury), but concerns only loans to capitalists engaged in production. Using those loans to finance production surplus value is produced and a portion of it is paid to the financial capitalist lenders in the form of interest; the exchange value of interest-bearing capital is the interest that has to be paid, while its ability to finance the production of surplus value is its use value.

The factors which govern the movement of the interest rate and of the mass of interest are unclear in Marx's own writings. In *Capital* III pt. V he emphasizes that the interest rate is determined by 'accidental' forces of demand and supply, reflecting the balance of strength between financial and industrial capitalists. Since they are essentially fractions of the same class there is no law which yields a definite determination, whereas there is for forms of revenue, such as wages, which reflect the fundamental division between the two great classes of capitalism. Nevertheless interest, either its rate or its mass, is seen as being limited by the total rate of profit generated by production, and the law of a falling rate of profit together with the development of banking and a rentier stratum was expected to lead to a long run decline in the level of interest. In the short term, fluctuations of the interest rate were seen as the product of the underlying trade cycle; the interest rate being generally low in the phase of prosperity but rising to a peak as economic crises break. Hilferding (1910) bases these movements on the disproportionalities between sectors that arise in the course of the cycle and extends the analysis to show how these cyclical movements of the interest rate in turn affect financial activity over the cycle, and can precipitate financial crises even before the onset of a generalized economic crisis (although the former remains 'only a symptom, an omen, of the latter crisis').

In Marx's theory, interest-bearing capital, although ultimately dependent on industrial capital, stands outside and is a more universal, unfettered category. In that it parallels the character of externality, universality, and freedom which Marx attributes to money *vis à vis* commodities (in *Capital* I). Similarly, the rate of interest appears as a purer category than the rate of profit; it is calculated transparently and yields a single figure (although here Marx was exaggerating) compared with the multitude of different profit rates on different capitals. (See also FORMS OF CAPITAL AND REVENUES; CREDIT AND FICTITIOUS CAPITAL.)

Reading

Harris, Laurence 1976: 'On Interest, Credit and Capital'.

Harvey, David 1982: *The Limits to Capital.*

Hilferding, Rudolf 1910 (*1981*): *Finance Capital.*
LAURENCE HARRIS

force. *See* violence.

forces and relations of production Throughout the mature Marx's economic works the idea that a contradiction between forces and relations of production underlies the dynamic of the capitalist mode of production is present. More generally, such a contradiction accounts for history existing as a succession of modes of production, since it leads to the necessary collapse of one mode and its supersession by another. And the couple, forces/relations of production, in any mode of production underlies the whole of society's processes, not just the economic ones. The connection between them and the social structure was stated in some of Marx's most succinct sentences:

> In the social production of their life men enter into definite relations that are indispensable and independent of their will, relations of production which correspond to a definite stage of development of their material productive forces. The sum total of these relations of production constitutes the economic structure, the real basis on which rises a legal and political superstructure. . . . (*Contribution to the Critique of Political Economy,* Preface)

The power of the contradiction between relations and forces to act as the motor of history is also stated in the same place: 'at a certain stage of their development, the material productive forces of society come in conflict with the existing relations of production . . . within which they have been at work hitherto'; and 'from forms of development of the productive forces these relations turn into their fetters', thereby initiating social revolution.

The productive forces were conceived by Marx as including means of production and labour power. Their development, therefore, encompasses such historical phenomena as the development of machinery, changes in the LABOUR PROCESS, the opening up of new sources of energy, and the education of the proletariat. There remain, however, several elements whose definition is disputed. Some writers have included science itself as a productive force (not just the changes in means of production that result), and Cohen (1978, ch. II) includes geographical space as a force.

Relations of production are constituted by the economic ownership of productive forces; under capitalism the most fundamental of these relations is the bourgeoisie's ownership of means of production while the proletariat owns only its labour power. Economic ownership is different from legal ownership for it relates to the control of the productive forces. In a legal sense the workers with rights in a pension fund may be said to own the shares of the companies in which the pension fund invests and thus to be, indirectly, legal owners of their means of production (although even this interpretation of the legal position is open to criticism on the grounds that share ownership is a legal title to revenue rather than to means of production); but if so, they are certainly not in control of those means of production and hence have no economic ownership (see PROPERTY).

The manner in which the development of the forces and relations of production occurs, and the effects of this development, have been the subject of one of the main controversies in Marxist thought. The most straightforward interpretation of the celebrated passage from the *Preface* is this: within a mode of production there is a correspondence both between forces and relations, and as a result of this, between the relations of production and legal, ideological and other social relations (the second correspondence being one between BASE AND SUPERSTRUCTURE). The correspondence appears to be one where the forces of production are primary, the relations of production are determined by the forces, and they themselves determine the superstructure. These respective positions of the three elements in the chain of causation acquire significance from their implications for historical development. Thus, the development of the forces of production *leads to* a contradiction between them and the relations of production (which 'turn into their fetters'), and the intensification of this contradiction *leads* to the breakdown of the existing mode of production and its superstructure. One problem with this interpretation of the central historical role of forces and relations of production turns on the central question. Is it valid to conceive of the forces of production as the prime movers?

In the revival of Marxist theory in the third quarter of this century this particular interpretation of Marx's thesis has been subjected to considerable criticism. An important consideration for some was that the thesis appeared to carry a political implication which was rejected: it was argued that Stalin's policy of rapid industrialization with its forced collectivization and political repression stemmed from his conception of the primacy of the forces of production (and that Trotsky shared this conception), so that if the productive forces in the Soviet Union could become those of modern industry, socialist relations of production would have their proper basis. Moreover, Marx's own writings appeared to be ambiguous on the primacy of the productive forces, and in places he writes as though the relations of production dominate and generate changes in the forces. In *Capital* I, for example, especially in the discussion of the development of the real subsumption of labour to capital (in a manuscript chapter 'Results of the Immediate Process of Production' which was first published in 1933), Marx writes as though the capitalist relations of production revolutionize the instruments of production and the labour process. Such formulations need not be a problem for the idea that the forces of production are primary if Marxism were to offer a conception of the articulation between forces and relations such that they interact, but with the forces being determinant, in some sense, both of the relations and of the way the two elements interact. But Marx's own texts are silent on this, and some writers have argued that they preclude the possibility of such interaction between two distinct elements because they collapse or 'fuse' forces and relations together, with the forces becoming a form of the relations (Cutler *et al.* 1977, ch. 5; Balibar 1970, p. 235).

The idea that the productive forces are primary, despite the problems it presents, has been vigorously reasserted by Cohen (1978; see also Shaw 1978). Cohen demonstrates the coherence of the thesis in its own terms and argues that it does have a valid, logical centrality in Marx's own writing. The basic difficulty in understanding the connection between forces and relations of production is that whereas the two are seen as necessarily compatible with each other within a mode of production, one of them has to develop in such a way that a contradiction or incompatibility matures; their progress, therefore, has an element of asymmetry, and it has to be a systematic rather than accidental asymmetry. Thus 'compatibility' cannot mean mutual and even determination. It could mean that the relations develop, causing development of the forces, which then react back on the relations but in such a way that the effect of relations on forces is multiplied while that of forces on relations is muted; if that occurred the relations of production would be primary but the maturation of the forces would run up against the 'fetters' which characterize the contradiction. Cohen, however, does not adopt this interpretation. Instead, he argues that the development of the forces is primary because it results from a factor which is, in a sense, exogenous; there is a motive force which lies outside the forces and relations of production and acts first upon the former. For Cohen, this motive force is human rationality, a rational and ever-present impulse of human beings to try to better their situation and overcome scarcity by developing the productive forces.

Cohen's emphasis upon human beings' rational pursuit of their interest in overcoming material want is the weak link, and a crucial one, in his defence of Marx's view on the primacy of the forces of production. As Levine and Wright (1980) argue, even if the action of human interests is seen in the context of class interests, thereby avoiding a non-Marxist individualism, it neglects the question of class *capacities*. The interests of a class do not guarantee its effectivity in shaping history. Levine and Wright define class capacities 'as those organizational, ideological and material resources available to classes in class struggle' and argue that the 'transformation of interests into practices is the central problem for any adequate theory of history'. This, of course, becomes a particularly acute issue when the theory of the forces and relations of production confronts the problem of the type of contradiction that will lead to the collapse of the capitalist mode of production and the installation of socialism. Writers who argue for the importance of class capacity as well as class interests in carrying through such a transformation see themselves as postulating the significance of class struggle in contrast to the economic determinism of an inexorable working out of the contradictory development of forces and relations in response to some basic human interest. (See also HISTORICAL MATERIALISM.)

Reading
Balibar, E. 1970: 'The Basic Concepts of Historical Materialism'. In Althusser and Balibar, *Reading Capital*.

Cohen, G. A. 1978: *Karl Marx's Theory of History: A Defence*.

Cutler, A. *et al.* 1977: *Marx's Capital and Capitalism Today*, vol. 1.

Levine, A. and Wright, E. O. 1980: 'Rationality and Class Struggle'.

Shaw, William H. 1978: *Marx's Theory of History*.

LAURENCE HARRIS

forms of capital and revenues Capital as a social relation is a dynamic phenomenon following a circuit of capital in which it takes on different forms at different points of the circuit. If we start with capital in the form of money (M), it is transformed into commodities (means of production and labour power) to become then productive capital (P). The outcome of the process of production is commodity capital (C') which has to be realized through sale and thus retransformed into money capital. In that sense capital assumes different forms but M and C' by themselves are lifeless; it makes more sense to talk of capital having specialized functions within each stage of the circuit.

Productive capital, P, is a process. It is the factory or farm at work. In the case of a hypothetical, unsophisticated capitalist system the enterprise that runs the factory may also have full control over dealing in commodities and money, but in reality these processes have been specialized functions and are distinct forms of capital. *Merchant capital* has the specialized function of dealing in commodities. It is typified by the great trading houses that make profits by buying and selling the raw materials for industry or by the High Street multiple stores that trade in finished commodities (the C in the circuit), but there is a multitude of intermediate forms. To the extent that banks simply deal in money (the M in the circuit) by exchanging it they, too, are operating a type of merchant capital. However, the development of the monetary sys-

tem in relation to these operations gives rise to CREDIT and the development of a different, specialized form of *interest-bearing capital* (see FINANCIAL CAPITAL AND INTEREST). Interest-bearing capital is engaged in the process of lending money capital to industrial capital so that the initial M in the circuit of industrial capital is advanced from that source.

Parts IV and V of *Capital* III are concerned with these specialized forms of capital. They are an important element in validating Marx's claim to be able to explain the complexities of the world from principles uncovered by examining highly abstract, general categories, for Marx reaches these chapters after having examined the nature of capital in its undifferentiated form. In *Capital* I and II, and the early parts of *Capital* III, Marx presents the laws of capital in general, and of many industrial capitals in competition, and he believed that the specialized forms of capital could only be understood on the basis of these laws. In particular, the earlier analysis uncovers the way in which SURPLUS VALUE is produced and distributed between industrial capitals, whereas in Parts IV, V and then VII of *Capital* III the question is how this surplus value is distributed in various types of revenue between different specialized forms of capital. The actors change from being industrial capital alone, to industrial capital plus merchant capital plus interest-bearing capital. And whereas in the earlier analysis surplus value takes the form of PROFIT, now industrial capital receives only profit-of-enterprise while interest-bearing capital receives a portion of surplus value as interest and merchant capital also receives profit, commercial profit, which is a deduction from the total surplus value. The revenues received by merchant capital and interest-bearing capital, and their separation from the other forms of surplus value, merit further analysis.

Merchant capital, operating in the sphere of circulation does not directly generate surplus value, but it does appropriate as profit some of the surplus value that is generated in the only place possible, the sphere of production in capitalist industry and agriculture. Merchants do more than simply buy commodities for resale; in order to accomplish their role they also expend capital upon the labour power of shop-workers, clerks and so on. However, this labour is unproductive according to Marx's definition (see PRO-

DUCTIVE AND UNPRODUCTIVE LABOUR); it does not directly produce surplus value, although by reducing the costs of circulation below what they would have been if non-specialist industrial capitalists had undertaken it, it may indirectly contribute to it. Given that merchant capital does not generate surplus value in a process of production controlled by it, its profit is obtained from its dealings with industrial (and agricultural) capital. Merchants buy commodities from industry below their value and sell them at their value. The difference, which they appropriate, has a tendency to equal the general rate of profit; competition ensures that the rate of profit accruing to merchants on the capital they advance equals that accruing to industrialists on their capital, and each equals the total surplus value divided by the total of the (merchant and industrial) capital.

That consideration of commercial profit ignores the deduction of interest; and the nature of interest-bearing capital, too, is considered by concentrating on its relation to industrial capital alone. Interest is paid by industrial capitalists out of their profits, and what remains is profit-of-enterprise, a proportion of the total. Marx considered that the proportions which result from this division are a matter of 'accidental' forces of demand and supply, so that no general principles determining the rate of interest (or rate of profit-of-enterprise) could be postulated except as general limits to the range of values it could take.

The final type of revenue which derives from surplus value is RENT, but this return to land-ownership is not the same as a return on a specialized form of capital.

The specialized forms of capital are more than simply the basis for the division of surplus value into different types of revenue, for the development of each has an important historical impact. Although merchant capital depends on industrial capital for the source of its profits, it arose in an early form before industrial capital. Indeed, the role of trade and plunder in the rise of capitalism, the process of PRIMITIVE ACCUMULATION, means that merchant capital was crucial for amassing the resources and stimulating the growth of social relations that were necessary for capitalism. The early monopolistic trading companies were its typical representatives in this respect. However, although merchant capi-

tal lay at the origins of capitalism in Europe, it has been argued that its predominance in Europe's relations with the Third World has blocked the ability of the countries of Africa, Asia and Latin America to undertake capitalist development. Kay (1975) argues that merchant capital within Europe lost its independence as industrial capitalism developed, and therefore did not hinder the development of the latter, the rise of a class making profits through organizing production. In many countries of the Third World, however, merchant capital has continued to predominate, at least until recently, and to exercise a great deal of independence in pursuing profits through trading rather than developing capitalist production. Kay argues that this independence has had a paradoxical character at least since the mid-nineteenth century when it 'both retained and lost its independence'. Independence was retained in the sense that it was the only form of capital in the underdeveloped countries, but since, in the world as a whole, it coexisted with industrial capital it had to modify its actions to act partially as agent for the latter in the Third World. As an agent it had to trade in the manner required by industrial capital (shipping raw materials and food to the capitalist countries and selling their manufactures in the poor countries), and only had to influence local production in the minimal manner necessary to serve Europe's need for raw materials and food (see UNDERDEVELOPMENT AND DEVELOPMENT).

Interest-bearing capital's role in history is identified by Marx partially in terms of the impact of the credit system on the centralization of capital (see CENTRALIZATION AND CONCENTRATION OF CAPITAL) and, particularly, on the formation of JOINT-STOCK COMPANIES. These developments were seen as marking a new stage (see PERIODIZATION OF CAPITALISM) and as having a significant effect. They give rise to one of Marx's counteracting tendencies to the FALLING RATE OF PROFIT, since those who advance capital to the joint-stock companies are thought to accept a lower yield as a result of the dominance of interest as the form of surplus value. And they give rise to a change in class composition as the actually functioning capitalist is differentiated from the owners of the capital which the industry uses. Interest-bearing capital, however, does not rest unchanged once it arises; it develops more complex characteristics and Hilferding (1910) and others in particular have identified its transformation into FINANCE CAPITAL as especially important.

Reading
Hilferding, Rudolf 1910 (1981): *Finance Capital.*
Kay, G. 1975: *Development and Underdevelopment: A Marxist Analysis.*

LAURENCE HARRIS

Frankfurt school The genesis of the Frankfurt school, which emerged in Germany during the 1920s and 1930s, is inseparable from the debate over what constitutes Marxism, or the scope of a theory designed with a practical intent, to criticize and subvert domination in all its forms. In order to grasp the axes around which its thought developed it is essential to appreciate the turbulent events which provided its context: the defeat of left-wing working-class movements in Western Europe after the first world war, the collapse of mass left-wing parties in Germany into reformist or Moscow-dominated movements, the degeneration of the Russian revolution into Stalinism and the rise of fascism and Nazism. These events posed fundamental questions for those inspired by Marxism but prepared to recognize how misleading and dangerous were the views of those who maintained either that socialism was an inevitable part of 'history's plan', or that 'correct' social action would follow merely from the promulgation of the 'correct' party line.

The Frankfurt school can be associated directly with an anti-Bolshevik radicalism and an open-ended or critical Marxism. Hostile to both capitalism and Soviet socialism, its writings sought to keep alive the possibility of an alternative path for social development; and many of those committed to the New Left in the 1960s and 1970s found in its work both an intriguing interpretation of Marxist theory and an emphasis on issues and problems (bureaucracy and authoritarianism, for instance) which had rarely been explored by the more orthodox approaches to Marxism.

The ideas of the Frankfurt school are generally referred to under the heading 'critical theory' (Jay 1973; Jacoby 1974). But critical theory, it should be emphasized, does not form a

unity; it does not mean the same thing to all its adherents (Dubiel 1978; Held 1980). The tradition of thinking which can be loosely referred to by this label is divided into two branches. The first was centred around the Institute of Social Research, established in Frankfurt in 1923, exiled from Germany in 1933, relocated in the United States shortly thereafter and reestablished in Frankfurt in the early 1950s. The Institute's key figures were Max Horkheimer (philosopher, sociologist and social psychologist), Friedrich Pollock (economist and specialist on the problems of national planning), Theodor Adorno (philosopher, sociologist, musicologist), Erich Fromm (psychoanalyst, social psychologist), Herbert Marcuse (philosopher), Franz Neumann (political scientist, with particular expertise in law), Otto Kirchheimer (political scientist, with expertise in law), Leo Lowenthal (student of popular culture and literature), Henryk Grossman (political economist), Arkadij Gurland (economist, sociologist), and, as a member of the 'outer circle' of the Institute, Walter Benjamin (essayist and literary critic). The Institute's membership is often referred to as the 'Frankfurt' school. But the label is a misleading one, for the work of the Institute's members did not always form a series of tightly woven, complementary projects. To the extent that one can legitimately talk of a 'school', it is only with reference to Horkheimer, Adorno, Marcuse, Lowenthal, Pollock and (in the early days of the Institute) Fromm; and even among these individuals there were major differences of opinion. The second branch of critical theory stems from Jürgen Habermas's recent work in philosophy and sociology, which recasts the notion of critical theory. Others who have contributed to this enterprise include Albrecht Wellmer (philosopher), Claus Offe (political scientist and sociologist) and Klaus Eder (anthropologist) (Wellmer 1974).

The following account refers to the pre-eminent members of the Frankfurt school – Horkheimer, Adorno, Marcuse and Habermas; the key contributors to date in elaborating a critical theory of society. The idea of such a theory can be specified by a number of common strands in their work. The extension and development of the notion of critique, from a concern with the conditions of possibility of reason and knowledge (Kant), to a reflection on the emergence of spirit (Hegel),

and then to a focus on specific historical forms –
capitalism, the exchange process (Marx) – was
furthered by them. They tried to develop a critical
perspective in the discussion of all social practices,
that is, a perspective which is preoccupied by the
critique of ideology – of systematically distorted
accounts of reality which attempt to conceal and
legitimate asymmetrical power relations. They
were concerned with the way in which social
interests, conflicts and contradictions are expressed in thought, and how they are produced
and reproduced in systems of domination. Through
an examination of these systems they hoped to
enhance awareness of the roots of domination,
undermine ideologies and help to compel changes
in consciousness and action.

Trained primarily as philosophers, all the critical theorists wrote major appraisals of the
German philosophical heritage. These works
were conceived as both analyses and interventions, for their goal was to break the grip of all
closed systems of thought and to undermine traditions which had blocked the development of the
critical project. All four thinkers retained many
of the concerns of German idealism – for example,
the nature of reason, truth and beauty – but
reformulated the way these had been understood
by Kant and Hegel. Following Marx they placed
history at the centre of their approach to philosophy and society (e.g. Marcuse 1941). But
while each of them maintained that all knowledge is historically conditioned, they contended
that truth claims can be rationally adjudicated
independently of particular social (e.g. class)
interests. They defended the possibility of an
autonomous moment of criticism (Horkheimer
1968; Adorno 1966).

Much of the work of the critical theorists
revolved around a series of critical dialogues
with important past and contemporary philosophers and social thinkers. The main figures of
the Frankfurt school sought to engage with and
synthesize aspects of the work of, among others,
Kant, Hegel, Marx, Weber, Lukács and Freud.
For Habermas certain traditions of Anglo-
American thought are also important, especially
linguistic philosophy and the recent philosophies of science. The motivation for this enterprise appears similar for each of the theorists –
the aim being to lay the foundation for an
exploration, in an interdisciplinary research
context, of questions concerning the conditions

which make possible the reproduction and
transformation of society, the meaning of culture, and the relation between the individual,
society and nature.

The acknowledgement that Marxism became
a repressive ideology in its Stalinist manifestation – thereby confirming that its doctrines do
not necessarily offer the key to truth – constitutes one of the crucial premises of critical
theory. It allows recognition not only of the fact
that 'classical' Marxist concepts are inadequate
to account for a range of phenomena (Stalinism,
fascism, among other things), but also that the
ideas and theories of, for example, Weber and
Freud provide vital clues to problems that face
Marxists – why revolution in the West was
expected and why it has not occurred. The
critical theorists' concern to assess and, where
applicable, develop non-Marxist thought does
not represent an attempt to undermine
Marxism; rather, it is an attempt to reinvigorate
and develop it. Accordingly, while they acknowledge the central importance of Marx's
contribution to political economy, this is regarded as an insufficient basis for the comprehension of contemporary society. The expansion of the state into more and more areas, the
growing interlocking of 'base' and 'superstructure', the spread of what they called the 'culture
industry', the development of authoritarianism,
all implied that political economy had to be
integrated with other concerns. Hence, political
sociology, cultural criticism, psychoanalysis
and other disciplines found a place in the framework of critical theory. By raising issues concerning the division of labour, bureaucracy, patterns of culture, family structure as well as the
central question of ownership and control, the
Frankfurt school decisively broadened the terms
of reference of critique and helped to transform
the notion of the political.

Their work set out to expose the complex
relations and mediations which prevent modes
of production – perhaps the most central refer-
ent of the Marxian corpus – from being characterized simply as objective structures, as things
developing 'over the heads' of human agents.
They took issue, specifically, with the 'determinist' and 'positivist' interpretation of historical
materialism, which emphasized unalterable stages
of historical development (driven by a seemingly autonomous economic 'base') and the

suitability of the methodological mode of the natural sciences for understanding these stages. The latter interpretation of Marx corresponds, they argued, to a form of thought which Marx himself had rejected – 'contemplative materialism', a materialism which neglected the central importance of human subjectivity. The traditional standpoint of orthodox Marxism (e.g. the doctrines of the German Communist Party) failed to grasp the significance of examining both the objective conditions of action and the ways in which these conditions are understood and interpreted. An analysis of the components of, for example, culture or identity formation is necessary because 'history is made' by the 'situated conduct of partially knowing subjects'. The contradiction between the forces and relations of production does not give rise to a fixed crisis path. The course of the crisis, the nature of its resolution, depends on the practices of social agents, and on how they understand the situation of which they are a part. Critical theory is addressed to the examination of the interplay between structure and social practices, the mediation of the objective and subjective in and through particular social phenomena.

While there are significant differences in the way they formulated questions, the critical theorists believed that through an examination of contemporary social and political issues they could elucidate future possibilities which, if realized, would enhance the rationality of society. However, they were not merely concerned with explicating what is latent nor, as Horkheimer and Adorno often put it, with 'remembering' or 'recollecting' a past in danger of being forgotten – the struggle for emancipation, the reasons for this struggle, the nature of critical thinking itself; they also contributed new emphases and ideas in their conception of theory and practice. Marcuse's defence, for instance, of personal gratification (against those revolutionaries who maintained an ascetic and puritanical outlook); of individual self-emancipation (against those who would simply argue that liberation follows from changes in the relations and forces of production); and of fundamental alternatives to the existing relationship between humanity and nature (against those who would accelerate the development of existing forms of technology): all constitute a significant departure from traditional Marxist doctrines (Marcuse 1955). Hork-

heimer, Adorno and Marcuse never advanced, however, a rigid set of political demands. For it is a central tenet of their thought, as of Habermas's also, that the process of liberation entails a process of *self-emancipation* and *self-creation*. Accordingly, Leninist vanguard organizations were appraised critically because it was thought that they reproduced a chronic division of labour, bureaucracy and authoritarian leadership. Although the critical theorists did not produce a sustained political theory, they stood in the tradition of those who maintain the unity of socialism and liberty and who argue that the aims of a rational society must be prefigured in and consistent with the means used to attain that society.

Throughout the 1930s and 1940s, the Institute of Social Research, under Horkheimer's directorship, pursued research and analysis in a number of different areas, including individual identity formation, family relations, bureaucracy, state, economy and culture. Although what has become known as 'Frankfurt' social theory often began from familiar Marxian axioms, many of the conclusions reached ran counter to traditional Marxist theory as their findings highlighted many obstacles to social transformation in the foreseeable future. The following constellation of elements was central to their account of contemporary developments in capitalist society.

First, they identified a trend towards increasing integration of the economic and political. Monopolies emerge and intervene in the state, while the state intervenes to safeguard and maintain economic processes.

Second, the increasing interlocking of economy and polity ensures the subordination of local initiative to bureaucratic deliberation, and of the market allocation of resources to centralized planning. Society is coordinated by powerful (private and public) administrations increasingly self-sufficient but oriented single-mindedly towards production.

Third, with the spread of bureaucracy and organization, there is an extension of the rationalization of social life, through the spread of instrumental reason – a concern with the efficiency of means to pre-given goals.

Fourth, a continual extension of the division of labour fragments tasks. As tasks become increasingly mechanized there are fewer chances for the worker to reflect upon and organize his or her own labour. Knowledge of the total work process becomes less accessible. The majority of occupations become atomized, isolated units.

Fifth, with the fragmentation of tasks and knowledge the experience of class diminishes. Domination becomes ever more impersonal. People become means to the fulfilment of purposes which appear to have an existence of their own. The particular pattern of social relations which condition these processes – the capitalist relations of production – are reified. As more and more areas of social life take on the characteristics of mere commodities, reification is reinforced, and social relations become ever less comprehensible (see COMMODITY FETISHISM; EXCHANGE). Conflict centres increasingly on marginal issues which do not test the foundation of society.

The Frankfurt school's analysis of these processes set out to expose the particular social basis of seemingly anonymous domination and to reveal, thereby, what hinders people 'coming to consciousness of themselves as subjects' capable of spontaneity and positive action. In pursuing this theme attention was focused on an assessment of the way in which ideas and beliefs are transmitted by 'popular culture' – the way in which the personal, private realm is undermined by the external (extra-familial) socialization of the ego.

Horkheimer and Adorno believed that the products of the great artists of the bourgeois era, as well as those of the Christian Middle Ages and the Renaissance, preserved a certain autonomy from the world of purely pragmatic interests (Horkheimer and Adorno 1947). Through their form or style, these artists' works represented individual experiences in such a way as to illuminate their meaning. 'Autonomous' art, as Adorno most often called it, produces images of beauty and order or contradiction and dissonance – an aesthetic realm, which at once leaves and highlights reality (see AESTHETICS; ART). Its object world is derived from the established order, but it portrays this order in a non-conventional manner. As such, art has a cognitive and subversive character. Its 'truth content' resides in its ability to restructure conventional patterns of meaning.

By their day, the Frankfurt theorists maintained, most cultural entities had become commodities, while culture itself had become an 'industry'. The term 'industry' here refers to the 'standardization', and the 'pseudo-individualization' or marginal differentiation, of cultural artefacts (for example, television Westerns or film music) and to the rationalization of promotion and distribution techniques. Without regard for the integrity of artistic form, the culture industry concerns itself with the 'predominance of the effect'. It aims primarily at the creation of diversions and distractions, providing a temporary escape from the responsibilities and drudgery of everyday life. However, the culture industry offers no genuine escape. For the relaxation it provides – free of demands and efforts – only serves to distract people from the basic pressures on their lives and to reproduce their will to work. In analyses of television, art, popular music and astrology, Adorno particularly tried to show how the products of the 'industry' simply duplicate and reinforce the structure of the world people attempt to avoid. They strengthen the belief that negative factors in life are due to natural causes or chance, thus promoting a sense of fatalism, dependence and obligation. The culture industry produces a 'social cement' for the existing order. (Adorno did not hold that this was the fate of all art and music. He never tired of emphasizing, for example, that Schönberg's atonal music preserves a critical, negative function.) Through an examination of modern art and music, the Frankfurt school sought to assess the nature of various cultural phenomena. In this inquiry they tried to show how most leisure activities are managed and controlled. The spheres of both production and consumption have crucial influences on the socialization of the individual. Impersonal forces hold sway not only over individuals' beliefs but over their impulses as well (see CULTURE).

Using many psychoanalytic concepts, the school examined the way society constitutes the individual, producing social character types. They found that in the socialization process, the importance of parents is dwindling. As families provide ever less protection against the overpowering pressures of the outside world the legitimacy of the father's authority is undermined. The result is, for example, that the male child does not aspire to become like his father, but more and more like images projected by the culture industry in general (or by fascism in Nazi Germany). The father retains a certain power, but his demands and prohibitions are, at best, poorly internalized. The father's power, therefore, appears arbitrary. In this situation the child retains an abstract idea of force and strength, and searches for a more powerful 'father' adequate to this image. A general state of susceptibility to outside forces is created – to fascist demagogues, for instance.

The classic study, *The Authoritarian Personality* (Adorno et al. 1950), aimed at analysing this susceptibility in terms of a personality syndrome which crystallizes under pressures such as these. The study endeavoured to establish interconnections between certain character traits and political opinions which might be regarded as potentially fascist, such as aggressive nationalism and racial prejudice (see RACE). It revealed a 'standardized' individual whose thinking is rigid, prone to the use of stereotypes, blindly submissive to conventional values and authority, and superstitious. The study showed how deeply ideology was ingrained, and why it was that people might accept belief systems 'contrary to their rational interests'. The authoritarian character type was juxtaposed with an autonomous individual capable of critical judgement.

The Frankfurt school's accounts of contemporary culture, patterns of authoritarianism etc., were intended to help foster the struggle for emancipation, although, it must be added, the precise meaning of this project was subject to dispute among the school's members. None the less, it is clear that their work exhibits a paradox, particularly embarrassing since they maintain that the potentialities for human and social change must be historically based; they offer a theory of the importance of fundamental social transformation which has little basis in social struggle. Their expansion of the terms of reference of critique and the notion of the political constitute an important step in holding together the tensions of their position. It is precisely because they saw no inevitable transformation of capitalism that they were so concerned with the criticism of ideology and thus helping to create awareness of the possibility of a break with the existing structure of domination. But the tensions in the main arise from a questionable thesis – a thesis which led them to underestimate both the significance of certain types of political struggle and the importance of their own work for these struggles.

One of their main concerns was to explain why revolution, as envisaged by Marx, has not occurred in the West. In trying to account for the absence of revolution they tended to underrate the complexity of political events. Their assumption that change should have occurred through a decisive break with the existing order led them to give undue weight to the power of the forces operating to stabilize society. In attempting to explain why what they expected was absent, they exaggerated the capacity of 'the system' to absorb opposition. As a consequence, critical theory lost sight of a range of important social and political struggles both within the West and beyond it – struggles which have changed and are continuing to change the face of politics (see CRISIS IN CAPITALIST SOCIETY). Yet although they were not always able to appreciate the changing constellation of political events, their interest in theory and critique, in analysis of the many forms of domination which inhibit radical political movements, had considerable practical impact. Their work in these domains stands as an integral and important part of the Marxist tradition.

There are other criticisms that can be made of the Frankfurt school's positions, although they will not be pursued here (Anderson 1976; Held 1980; Thompson 1981; Geuss 1982). Significantly, some of the most important defects have been addressed in the writings of the second generation of critical theorists, most notably by Habermas, who has developed his ideas in a framework which substantially differs from that of Horkheimer, Adorno or Marcuse. In particular he has probed further into the philosophical foundations of critical theory, attempting to explicate its presuppositions about rationality and the 'good society' and has recast its account of the developmental possibilities of capitalist society (Habermas 1968, 1973). His work is still in the process of development (see HABERMAS), testifying to the fact that the elaboration of a critical theory of society is a project still very much alive, even if we cannot at this time uncritically appropriate many of its doctrines (see also KNOWLEDGE, THEORY OF; WESTERN MARXISM).

Reading

Adorno, Theodor 1966 (1973): *Negative Dialectics*.

Adorno, Theodor and Horkheimer, Max 1947 (1973): *Dialectic of Enlightenment*.

Adorno, Theodor *et al.* 1950: *The Authoritarian Personality.*

Anderson, Perry 1976: *Considerations on Western Marxism.*

Dubiel, Helmut 1978: *Wissenschaftsorganisation und politische Erfahrung.*

Geuss, Raymond 1982: *The Idea of a Critical Theory.*

Habermas, Jürgen 1968 (*1971*): *Knowledge and Human Interests.*

— 1973 (*1976*): *Legitimation Crisis.*

Held, David 1980: *Introduction to Critical Theory: Horkheimer to Habermas.*

Horkheimer, Max 1968 (*1972*): *Critical Theory.* (This volume consists of essays written in the 1930s and early 1940s.)

Jay, Martin 1973: *The Dialectical Imagination. A History of the Frankfurt School and the Institute of Social Research, 1923–1950.*

Marcuse, Herbert 1941: *Reason and Revolution.*

— 1955 (*1966*): *Eros and Civilization.*

Thompson, John 1981: *Critical Hermeneutics.*

Wellmer, Albrecht 1974: *Critical Theory of Society.*

DAVID HELD

freedom. *See* emancipation; determinism.

Fromm, Erich Born 23 March 1900, Frankfurt am Main; died 18 March 1980, Locarno. The only child of an orthodox Jewish wine merchant, Fromm studied law in Frankfurt, then sociology, psychology and philosophy in Heidelberg, and until 1926 also received instruction in the Talmud. In 1924 he began a course of psychoanalysis, continued until 1929, when he became one of the founders of the South German Institute of Psychoanalysis in Frankfurt. The following year he began his collaboration with the FRANKFURT SCHOOL as a member of the Institute of Social Research and contributed to its journal a notable essay (1932) in which, partly influenced at first by the ideas of Wilhelm Reich (Funk 1983, p. 55; Springborg 1981, ch. 8), he set out to establish a relation between PSYCHOANALYSIS and Marxism by extending Freud's explanations in terms of the history of the individual to include the class location of the family and the historical situation of social classes. These ideas were subsequently developed in his model of the 'social character' (1942) and in his analysis of Marx's conception of HUMAN NATURE (1961).

In 1933 Fromm emigrated to the United States and the following year settled in New York as a practising psychoanalyst while continuing his work with the Frankfurt Institute, now in exile at Columbia University. Here he pursued a study of the 'authoritarian character' and contributed a long theoretical essay to a collective volume (which also included essays by Horkheimer and Marcuse) published in 1936. By this time, however, there were profound disagreements between Fromm and other leading members of the Institute, and his commitment to an increasingly sociological (and also more empirical and Marxist) reinterpretation of psychoanalysis provoked in due course critical rejoinders by Adorno (1946) and Marcuse (1955). Fromm left the Institute in 1938, and thereafter, but particularly from 1949 when he moved to Mexico City and began teaching in the National University, his writing became more directly concerned with political issues, analysed in both sociological and psychological terms.

One principal field of activity was the peace movement, and associated with this a renewed analysis of aggression which resulted in a major work of psychoanalytic theory (1973), drawing also on studies in animal psychology and anthropology. The other main field of work was represented by his studies of contemporary societies, in his critical analysis of the pathological features of capitalism and of the authoritarian socialist alternative (1956), as well as by his support for the dissident democratic socialists of Eastern Europe, his exposition of a socialist humanism (1965), and his particularly close contacts with the Yugoslav philosophers and sociologists of the 'Praxis' group.

Reader

Fromm, Erich 1932 (*1971*): 'The Method and Function of an Analytical Social Psychology: Notes on Psychoanalysis and Historical Materialism'. In *The Crisis of Psychoanalysis.*

— 1942: *The Fear of Freedom.*

— 1956: *The Sane Society.*

— 1961: *Marx's Concept of Man.*

— ed. 1965: *Socialist Humanism.*

— 1973: *The Anatomy of Human Destructiveness.*

Funk, Rainer 1983: *Erich Fromm.*

Springborg, Patricia 1981: *The Problem of Human Needs and the Critique of Civilisation.*

TOM BOTTOMORE

G

gender Neither Marx nor Engels explicitly addressed the question of gender in the form it has been posed by modern social science, namely the explanation of those differences between men and women which are social constructs as opposed to naturally given sexual differences. Nevertheless, some of their work can be seen as a contribution to the explanation of the social construction of gender.

Marx and Engels, and much of the subsequent Marxist tradition, talk about the issue as the 'Woman Question'. Thus, in common with bourgeois social science where the representative individual is implicitly masculine, for Marx the representative proletarian is a male wage-labourer. This is sometimes implicit as, for example, in his assumption that all those without other access to the means of production have to sell their labour power for a wage. This ignores the fact that households usually share resources, albeit unequally, and so may contain other members, supported by the earnings of a wage-labourer, who also have no access to the means of production but do not have to sell their own labour power. Since these last two attributes are used interchangeably by Marx to define the working class, it leaves the class position of financially dependent women unclear.

In other places, the assumed maleness of the typical worker is made explicit. Thus, for example, the value of labour power is 'determined, not only by the labour-time necessary to maintain the individual adult labourer, but also by that necessary to maintain his family' and when his wife and children are employed, too, that 'spreads the value of the man's labour-power over his whole family. It thus depreciates his labour-power' (*Capital* I, ch. 15, sect. 3(a)). Women and children are therefore seen as supernumerary members of the proletariat whose sex and age differentiate them from the typical male. Marx notes that it was the introduction of ma-

chinery in the mills that enabled women (and children), despite their lesser strength, to be employed; indeed women's natural docility and dexterity can make them preferable workers for capital, as does the fact that they are cheaper and so can be used to undercut men's wages. So from this formulation it appears that the problem Marx set himself was to explain how it is that some workers are female, rather than the converse question of explaining why most of those who sell their labour power are male, and women's position in the labour force (and in society more generally) is discussed in relation to that of men.

Further, embedded in the explanations he gives are some naturalistic assumptions about the capacities and desirable roles of men and women, which stand closer to the Victorian ideal of a breadwinning husband supporting a financially dependent wife and children at home than Victorian reality ever did. Similarly, his castigation of the immorality of the way women were employed to work together with men in certain occupations owes as much to contemporary bourgeois morality as to his obviously genuine horror at their working conditions. Nevertheless, he makes it clear that he sees the cooperative working together of individuals of both sexes and all ages as a source of human emancipation; though not under the brutal conditions of capitalist exploitation. And even under capitalism the employment of women is potentially liberatory, since it creates the economic conditions for a higher form of family and better relations between the sexes (ibid. sect. 9).

Perhaps reflecting the difference in their personal lifestyles, Engels appears to have been more prepared than Marx to see through the morality of his day to recognize how much of men's and women's roles were socially constructed. However, the whole thrust of Engels's *Origin of the Family, Private Property and the*

State is based on an unquestioned sexual division of labour which is used to explain why it was men who developed private property in the means of production that they then wished to pass on to identifiable biological heirs; it was the overthrow of mother right and consequent enforced monogamy and domestication of women which constituted for Engels the 'world historical defeat of the female sex' (*Origin of the Family*, ch. II, sect. 3). He shared Marx's view of the potentially liberatory effects of capitalist wage-labour for women, not only in enabling them to play an equal role with men in social production, but also freeing them from domestic labour. However, 'to bring the whole female sex back into public industry' depended on the abolition of private property, and for this 'the characteristic of the monogamous family as the economic unit of society [would have to] be abolished' (ibid, sect. 4).

Thus both Marx and Engels can be seen as engaged, even if not centrally, in the explanation of gender roles, but in doing so they both made naturalistic assumptions. Further, their view gave little centrality to the struggle of women. The members of their revolutionary class, the proletariat, were typically envisaged as male, and women's emancipation was seen as a relatively unproblematic result of capitalist and subsequent socialist development. Bebel, Lenin, Zetkin and Trotsky developed the political content of some of these ideas, notably adding demands for married women's property rights, freedom from violence and divorce on demand, but stayed within the same basic framework of the Woman Question, within which questions of gender remained subsidiary of those of class.

The revival of FEMINISM in the late 1960s brought a renewed interest in gender. Initially 'Marxist feminism' distinguished itself from other types of feminism by its insistence that gender divisions had to be explained within a materialist framework, which was interpreted to mean by the class relations of capitalism. Within this framework, questions of gender tended to be treated as superstructural, with the roles of men and women in the family and segregation within paid employment both being seen as ideological side-effects of capitalist production relations. On the family, the DOMESTIC LABOUR debate was an attempt to move beyond this and to locate the explanation of gender divisions within the material base. This was done by including within it in the production relations of housework, thus explaining women's position by the specific production relations into which they entered, not just those of the working class as a whole. However, while the debate was useful in showing that the family was a site of material production, it failed to develop any new analysis and only made use of existing Marxist concepts.

Within paid employment, (married) women were seen as a RESERVE ARMY OF LABOUR for capital who could be called on in periods when insufficient men were available, and used at all times to keep down wage levels. Married women could function as such a reserve because their role within the family ensured that they were not wholly dependent on their own wages. However, the evidence that since the Second World War, despite higher individual turnover rates, married women as a whole were in the labour force to stay and were no more disposable than men threw into doubt the usefulness of this particular Marxist concept for the analysis of gender differences in employment (Bruegel 1979).

Other approaches attempted to broaden the meaning of the material to include also relations of sexuality and/or human REPRODUCTION, noting that women's oppression pre-dated and therefore could hardly be explained entirely in terms of the capitalist mode of production. Mitchell (1974) tried a synthesis of psychoanalytic and Marxist approaches to produce a structuralist account of women's oppression. She used the concept of patriarchy within her work, a radical feminist term which had previously been shunned by Marxists as introducing an ahistorical reductionist element into what had to be explained historically. Rubin (1975) had suggested that patriarchy be seen as a *form* of sex/gender system, by analogy with the way capitalism is seen as a form of mode of production. Eisenstein (1979) called contemporary society 'capitalist patriarchy', Hartmann (1979) talked of 'a partnership of patriarchy and capital' and a long debate surfaced about how the relation between two such structures should be theorized (Eisenstein 1979, Sargent 1981). By this time, Marxist feminism was beginning to see itself less as an application of Marxism to a particular question and more as a critique and extension of traditional Marxism: in particular of a materialism that insisted that everything, including gender relations, could be explained by reference to the mode of production and class relations.

More recent accounts have thrown doubt on the value of such overarching accounts. Barrett (1988) has argued that the process by which women's oppression became embedded in capitalism should be seen as historically contingent and not in any essentialist sense a logical necessity for capitalist production relations. Since then many Marxist feminists, particularly those previously working within an Althusserian framework and subsequently influenced by post-structuralism, have drifted away from Marxism – dismissing previous attempts to explain gender divisions and women's oppression within Marxism as feminists doing Marxism's 'theoretical housework', that is, seeing how to tidy up Marxism so as to incorporate gender and make it more respectable in feminist terms, rather than a serious attempt to look at women's oppression in its own right. However, while this critique might have some validity, it does not mean that the question of gender has no continued relevance for Marxism; rather it must be taken as a sign of the failure of Marxism to tackle the question adequately up to now.

Reading

Barrett, Michèle 1988: *Women's Oppression Today: Problems in Marxist Feminism.*

Breugel, Irene 1979: 'Women as a Reserve Army of Labour'.

Eisenstein, Zillah ed. 1979: *Capitalist Patriarchy and the Case for Socialist Feminism.*

Hartmann, Heidi 1979: 'The Unhappy Marriage of Marxism and Feminism: Towards a More Progressive Union'.

Mitchell, Juliet 1974: *Psychoanalysis and Feminism.*

Rubin, Gayle 1975: 'The Traffic in Women: Notes on the "Political Economy" of Sex'. In Rayna Reiter, ed. *Toward an Anthropology of Women.*

SUSAN HIMMELWEIT

geography Geographical knowledge deals with the description and analysis of the spatial distribution of those conditions (either naturally occurring or humanly created) that form the material basis for the reproduction of social life. It also tries to understand the relations between such conditions and the qualities of social life achieved under a given MODE OF PRODUCTION.

The form and content of geographical knowledge depends upon the social context. All societies, classes, and social groups possess a distinctive 'geographical lore', a working knowledge of their territory and of the spatial distribution of use values relevant to them. This 'lore', acquired through experience, is codified and socially transmitted as part of a conceptual apparatus with which individuals and groups cope with the world. It may be transmitted as a loosely defined spatial-environmental imagery or as a formal body of knowledge – geography – in which all members of society or a privileged elite receive instruction. This knowledge can be used in the quest to dominate nature as well as other classes and peoples. It can also be used in the struggle to liberate peoples from so-called 'natural' disasters and from internal and external oppression.

Bourgeois geography, as a formal body of knowledge, underwent successive transformations under the pressure of changing practical imperatives. Concern for accuracy of navigation in earlier centuries gave way later on to cartographic practices designed to establish private property and state territorial rights. At the same time the creation of the world market meant 'the exploration of the earth in all directions' in order to discover 'new, useful qualities of things' and so promote the 'universal exchange of products of all alien climates and lands' (Marx, *Grundrisse*, p. 409). Working in the tradition of natural philosophy, geographers such as Alexander von Humboldt (1769–1859) and Carl Ritter (1779–1859) set out to construct a systematic description of the earth's surface as the repository of exploitable use values (both natural and human) and as the locus of geographically differentiated forms of economy and social reproduction. By the late nineteenth century, geographical practices and thought were deeply affected by direct engagement in the exploration of commercial opportunities, the prospects for PRIMITIVE ACCUMULATION and the mobilization of labour reserves, the management of Empire and colonial administration. The division of the world into spheres of influence by the main imperialist powers also gave rise to geopolitical perspectives in which geographers such as Friedrich Ratzel (1844–1904) and Sir Halford Mackinder (1861–1947) dealt with the struggle for control over space, i.e. over access to raw materials, labour supplies and markets, in direct terms of geographical control. In recent years, geographers have concerned themselves with the 'rational management' ('rational' usually from the standpoint of accumulation) of natural and human resources and spatial distributions.

Two strongly opposed currents of thought stand out in the history of bourgeois geography. The first, deeply materialist in its approach, nevertheless holds to some version of environmental or spatial determinism (the doctrine that forms of economy, social reproduction, political power, are determined by environmental conditions or location). The second, deeply idealist in spirit, sees society engaged in the active transformation of the face of the earth, either in response to God's will or according to the dictates of human consciousness and will. The tension between these two currents of thought has never been resolved in bourgeois geography. The latter has, in addition, always preserved a strong ideological content. Although it aspires to universal understanding of the diversity of social life, it often cultivates parochial, ethnocentric perspectives on that diversity. It has often been the vehicle for transmission of doctrines of racial, cultural, or national superiority. Ideas of 'geographical' or 'manifest' destiny, of 'the white man's burden' and of the 'civilizing mission' of the bourgeoisie, are liberally scattered in geographical thought. Geographical information (maps, for example) can be all too easily used to prey upon fears and promote hostility between peoples, and so justify imperialism, neo-colonial domination, and internal repression (particularly in urban areas).

Marx and Engels paid little attention to geography as a formal discipline, but they frequently drew upon the works of geographers (such as Humboldt) and their historical materialist texts are suffused with commentary on matters geographical. They implied that the fundamental opposition in bourgeois thought could be bridged. They argued that by acting upon the external world and changing it we thereby also changed our own natures, and that although human beings made their own histories they did not do so under social and geographical circumstances of their own choosing. But Marx, evidently concerned to distance himself from the determinist current in bourgeois thought, usually downplayed the significance of environmental and spatial differentiations. The result is a somewhat ambivalent treatment of geographical questions.

For example, Marx often made it sound as though there was a simple unilinear historical progression from one mode of production to another. But he also accepted that ASIATIC SOCIETY possessed a distinctive mode of production, in part shaped by the need to build and maintain large scale irrigation projects in semi-arid environments. He also later attacked those who transformed his 'historical sketch of the genesis of capitalism into an historico-philosophical theory of the general path of development prescribed by fate to all nations', and argued that he had merely sought to 'trace the path by which, in Western Europe, the capitalist economic system emerged from the womb of the feudal economic system' (letter to *Otechestvenniye Zapiski*, November 1877). Even in Western Europe, considerable variation existed because of the uneven penetration of capitalist social relations under local circumstances showing 'infinite variations and gradations in appearance' (*Capital* III, ch. 47).

Marx also sought an analysis of capitalism's historical dynamic without reference to geographical perspectives on the grounds that the latter would merely complicate matters without adding anything new. But in practice he is forced to recognize that the physical productivity of labour is affected by environmental conditions which in turn form the physical basis for the social division of labour (*Capital* I, ch. 16). The value of labour power (and wage rates) consequently vary from place to place, depending upon reproduction costs, natural and historical circumstances. Differential rent can also in part be appropriated because of differentials in fertility and location. To the degree that such differentials create geographical variation in wage and profit rates, Marx looks to the mobilities of capital (as money, commodities, production activity, etc.) and labour as means to reduce them. In so doing he is forced to consider the role of geographical expansion – colonization, foreign trade, the export of capital, bullion drains, etc. – on capitalism's historical dynamic. He accepts that geographical expansion can help counteract any tendency towards falling profit rates but denies that the crisis tendencies of capitalism can be permanently assuaged thereby. The contradictions of capitalism are merely projected onto the global stage. But Marx does not attempt any systematic analysis of such processes. A planned work on crises and the world market never materialized.

Marx's commentaries possess a unifying theme. Though nature may be the subject of labour, much of the geographical nature with which we work is a social product. The productive capacities of the soil, for example, are neither original nor indestructible (as Ricardo held) because fertility can be created or destroyed through the circulation of capital. Spatial relations are also actively shaped by a transport and communications industry dedicated, in the bourgeois era, to the reduction of turnover time in the circulation of capital (what Marx called 'the annihilation of space by time'). Distinctive spatial configurations of the productive forces and social relations of capitalism (investment in physical and social infrastructures, URBANIZA-TION, the territorial division of labour, etc.) are produced through specific processes of historical development. Capitalism produces a geographical landscape in its own image, only to find that that image is seriously flawed, riddled with contradictions. Environments are created that simultaneously facilitate but imprison the future paths of capitalist development.

Subsequent Marxist work often failed to appreciate the subtly nuanced 'geographical lore' omnipresent in Marx's and Engels's texts. Lenin's *Development of Capitalism in Russia* is an early exception. The dominant tendency was to view nature and hence geographical circumstance as unproblematically social. Karl Wittfogel (1896–) attempted to reintroduce geographical determinism into Marxist thought; though seriously flawed, his work reopened the question of the relations between mode of production and environmental conditions. The practical requirements of reconstruction, planning, industrial and regional development in the Soviet Union also led to the emergence of geography as a formal discipline within a Marxist framework. A deep and almost exclusive concern with the development of the

productive forces on the land was associated with an analysis in which the concrete development of such productive forces was seen as the moving force in a geographically differentiated social history. This style of thinking flowed westward, mainly through the work of French geographers such as Pierre Georges (1909–).

The study of imperialism and the world market (a topic which Marx had left untouched) introduced a more explicitly spatial imagery into Marxist thought in the early years of the twentieth century. Hilferding, Lenin, Bukharin, and Luxemburg dramatically unified themes of exploitation, geographical expansion, territorial conflict and domination, with the theory of accumulation of capital. Later writers pursued the spatial imagery strongly. Centres exploit peripheries, metropolises exploit hinterlands, the first world subjugates and mercilessly exploits the third, underdevelopment is imposed from without, etc. (see DEVELOPMENT AND UNDERDEVELOPMENT). Class struggle is resolved into the struggle of the periphery against the centre, the countryside against the city, the third world against the first. So powerful is this spatial imagery that it freely flows back into the interpretation of structures even in the heart of capitalism. Regions are exploited by a dominant metropolis in which ghettos are characterized as 'internal neo-colonies'. The language of *Capital* (the exploitation of one class by another) tends to give way in some Marxist work to a compelling imagery in which people in one place exploit those in another. There was, however, very little in this Marxist tradition which grappled with the concrete processes whereby class antagonisms are translated into spatial configurations, or with the way in which spatial relations and organization are produced under the imperatives of capitalism.

New life was breathed into these questions during the 1960s, as the radical critique of bourgeois geography gathered strength. The attempt to reconstitute formal geographical understandings from a socialist perspective had some peculiar advantages. Traditional bourgeois geography, dominated by conservative thinkers attached to the ideology of empire, was nevertheless global, synthetic and materialist in its approach to ways of life and social reproduction in different natural and social environments. It was a relatively easy target for criticism and lent itself easily to historical materialist approaches. Yet there was little to appeal to in Marxist geographical thought and only a brief flurry of an indigenous radical tradition in the anarchism of Elisée Reclus (1830–1905) and Kropotkin (1842–1921).

The radical thrust initially concentrated on a critique of ideology and geographical practice. It called into question the racism, classism, ethnocentrism and sexism in geographical texts and teaching. It attacked the dominantly positivist stance of geographers as a manifestation of bourgeois managerial consciousness. It exposed the role of geographers in imperialist endeavours, in urban and regional planning procedures directed towards social control in the interests of capital accumulation. It sought to uncover the hidden assumptions and class biases within geography through a thorough critique of its philosophical basis.

But it also sought to identify and preserve those facets of geography relevant to socialist reconstruction and to merge the positive aspects of bourgeois geography with a reconstituted understanding of the geography buried in Marx's and Engels's texts. The more mundane techniques – from mapping to resource inventory analysis – appeared usable (as the Soviet experience had shown), but were too close to bourgeois practice for comfort, and the assumption of their social neutrality was troubling. Something more was needed. Bourgeois geographers had long sought to understand how different peoples fashion their physical and social landscapes as a reflection of their needs and aspirations and they had also shown that different social groups – children, the aged, social classes, whole cultures – possess different and often non-comparable forms of geographical knowledge. It was a short step to create a more dialectical view, based on Marx's thesis that by acting upon and changing the external world we change our own natures. From this a new agenda for geography could be constructed – the study of the active construction and transformation of material environments (both physical and social) through particular social processes, together with critical reflection on the geographical knowledge (itself contributory to those social processes) which resulted. It follows that contradictions within a social process (such as those founded on the antagonism between capital and labour) are necessarily manifest in both the actual geographical landscape (the social organization of space) and our interpretations of that landscape.

Marxist geographical inquiry is in its infancy in the West. It seeks the reformulation of bourgeois questions, and new perspectives on Marxist theory and practice. It seeks deeper insights into how different social formations create material and social landscapes in their own image. It explores how capitalism transforms and creates nature as new productive forces embedded in the land and sets in train irreversible and often damaging processes of ecological change. It examines how spatial configurations of productive forces and social relations are created and with what effects – uneven geographical development, the spatial integration of world capitalism through the geographical mobility of capital and labour. It seeks to explain how the exploitation of people in one place by those in another (peripheries by centres, rural areas by cities) can arise in a social formation dominated by the antagonism between capital and labour. It investigates how spatial organization (e.g. segregation) relates to the reproduction of class relations. Above all, geographers seek understanding of how crises are manifest geographically, through processes of regional growth and decay, inter-regional competition and restructuring, the export of unemployment, inflation, surplus productive capacity, degenerating into inter-imperialist rivalries and war.

Reading

Anuchin, V. 1977: *Theoretical Problems of Geography.*

Gregory, D. 1978: *Ideology, Science and Human Geography.*

Harvey, D. 1982: *The Limits to Capital.*

Johnston, R. J. ed. 1986: *The Dictionary of Human Geography.*

Kidron, M. and Segal, R. 1981: *The State of the World Atlas.*

Peet, R. 1977: *Radical Geography.*

Quaini, Massimo 1974 (1982): *Geography and Marxism.*

DAVID HARVEY

German Ideology Marx and Engels wrote together the bulky manuscript of *Die deutsche*

Ideologie in Brussels in 1845 and 1846. The proposed subtitle was 'Critique of Modern German Philosophy according to its representatives Feuerbach, B. Bauer, and Stirner, and of German Socialism according to its various prophets.' As this indicates, the object of the work was mainly polemical. But the intention was to introduce the basic ideas of HISTORICAL MATERIALISM to the public at the same time. Unable to find a publisher, they 'abandoned the manuscript to the gnawing criticism of the mice', as Marx (1859) later put it: it was indeed, as he said then, primarily intended as a work of self-clarification, wherein they marked themselves off from their past associations with the movement of YOUNG HEGELIANS.

They were able to do this because for the first time they had jointly arrived at their 'big idea' – the materialist conception of history – and thus they were able to criticize all ideology from this perspective. They held that all the post-Hegelian tendencies – whether ethical socialism (Grün) or individualist anarchism (Stirner), whether idealist (Bauer) or materialist (FEUERBACH) – all shared the same fault of over-estimating the battle of ideas, failing to recognize the source of their ideas, as well as of ideology in general, in the material conditions of life. Ideas spring from the soil of specific social systems. If 'the ideas of the ruling class are in every epoch the ruling ideas', then historians who take them at face value thereby share 'the illusion of the epoch'.

It is argued that the production and reproduction of the material basis of social life underpins everything else. This means that 'a sum of productive forces, a historically created relation of individuals to nature and to one another . . . is handed down to each generation from its predecessors . . . and prescribes for it its conditions of life.' Therefore 'circumstances make men just as much as men make circumstances.' This leads to a new view of communism itself. It is not an eternal truth, 'an *ideal* to which reality will have to adjust itself', but a result of premises created in the movement of history, which give rise to 'a *real* movement which abolishes the present state of things'. Among 'the forms of intercourse' (as Marx called relations of production at this time) most attention is paid to the DIVISION OF LABOUR; the discussion is marked by the influence of both Smith and Fourier; it issues in a notorious prediction about the abolition of the

division of labour under communism.

In spite of Engels's (1886/8) later verdict that it showed only 'how incomplete our knowledge of economic history was at that time', the first chapter ('Feuerbach') especially is an indispensable source for expressions of 'the materialist outlook'. (Unfortunately it is the least 'finished', leading earlier editions to reorder the materials: *Collected Works* 5 has it as close as possible to the MS.) Since the first publication of chapter 1 in the 1920s, and of the whole in 1932, it has been an important reference for Marxist debates on IDEOLOGY.

Reading

Arthur, C. J. 1986: 'Marx and Engels: *The German Ideology*'. In G. Vesey, ed., *Philosophers Ancient and Modern*.

                    CHRISTOPHER J. ARTHUR

Goldmann, Lucien Born 20 June 1913, Bucharest; died 3 October 1970, Paris. During his studies in Vienna in the 1930s Goldmann became acquainted with Lukács's early work – especially 'The Metaphysics of the Tragedy' (from *Soul and Form*), *The Theory of the Novel*, and *History and Class Consciousness* – which exercised a profound and lasting influence on his thought. Other major influences came from Jean Piaget's 'genetic epistemology' and, in the 1960s, from Marcuse's thesis about ORGANIZED CAPITALISM as master of its inner contradictions: an idea to which Goldmann's *Sociology of the Novel* and his new edition of *The Human Sciences and Philosophy* bear witness.

Taking his inspiration from Lukács's discussion of CLASS CONSCIOUSNESS, Goldmann formulated his own conceptual framework of critical understanding. It centred on the notions of 'the partial identity of subject and object' which makes possible the production of the 'coherent world view' of a 'transindividual subject'. In Goldmann's view only the latter is objectively capable of attaining the philosophically and artistically/literarily significant level of a 'maximum possible consciousness', in contrast to the contingencies and limitations of individual consciousness. Hence the real subject of cultural creation is the 'collective subject' which articulates the 'significant structures' of historical consciousness, in response to the needs and determinations of a social group or class as situated within the dynamic social totality.

After publication of his two doctoral dissertations (one on Kant, in Zurich and the other on Racine and Pascal, in Paris) which involved detailed historical investigation, Goldmann's interest shifted to primarily methodological and meta-theoretical issues, discussed in essays collected in numerous volumes, after their original publication in polemical contexts. Writing in France at the height of the popularity of STRUCTURALISM, he tried to define his own position as a critical voice within the orbit of, but in opposition to, what he called the dogmatic one-sidedness of the latter, naming his own approach 'genetic structuralism' so as to insist on its historical dimension. His most popular work was, to his great surprise, a volume of essays *Towards a Sociology of the Novel*, reprinted several times in large editions. Reviving some central tenets of Lukács's *Theory of the Novel*, it stressed the power of REIFICATION in a much more extreme form than the Hungarian philosopher, wedding the original themes of Lukács's early work to the vision of Marcuse's *One Dimensional Man*, and finding the key to understanding the 'new novel' in the claimed disappearance of active mediation from the massively reified world of contemporary capitalism. The concept of negativity occupied an increasingly great role in his thought at this time, equating 'structuration' with 'destructuration' and insisting that 'the evolution of industrial societies has created some irreversible situations' (Goldmann 1966, p. 19). Against such a background, seen as a devastating social paralysis, he greeted May 1968 enthusiastically, as an act of liberation. However, he did not live long enough to translate his more optimistic political perspectives into a new theoretical vision as he hoped.

Reading

Goldmann, Lucien 1948 (1971): *Immanuel Kant*.
— 1952 and 1966 (1969): *The Human Sciences and Philosophy*.
— 1956 (1967): *The Hidden God*.
— 1958: *Recherches dialectiques*.
— 1964 (1975): *Towards a Sociology of the Novel*.
— 1970: *Structures mentales et création culturelle*.
— 1977: *Lukács and Heidegger*.
— 1981: *Method in the Sociology of Literature*.
Naïr, Sami 1981: 'Goldmann's Legacy'.
Williams, Raymond 1971: 'Literature and Sociology: in Memory of Lucien Goldmann'.

ISTVÁN MÉSZÁROS

Gramsci, Antonio. Born 22 January 1891, Ales, Sardinia; died 27 April 1937, Rome. Born in the impoverished island of Sardinia of lower middle-class parents, Gramsci won a scholarship in 1911 to the University of Turin. There he was influenced by the work of the Italian idealist philosopher, Benedetto Croce. Impressed by the Turin working-class movement, he joined the Italian Socialist Party (PSI) in 1913, and began writing for socialist newspapers. His experience of a backward peasant culture and an industrial city influenced his view that any socialist revolution in Italy required a national-popular perspective and an alliance between the working class and the peasantry. The need for the working class to go beyond its corporate interest, and the political role of culture and ideology would remain a constant theme in his work. Gramsci hailed the October Revolution as invalidating any reading of Marx's *Capital* which might suggest that revolution had to await the full development of capitalist forces of production (see FORCES AND RELATIONS OF PRODUCTION), and as an example of a social change made by the mass of society rather than an elite. A socialist transformation of society was defined throughout his work as the expansion of democratic control.

In 1919 Gramsci helped to found a new Turin socialist weekly, *L'Ordine Nuovo*, to translate the lessons of the Russian Revolution into the Italian context by providing a voice for the rapidly developing factory council movement (see COUNCILS). Influenced by Sorel's idea that the productive sphere could provide the basis for a new civilization, Gramsci wrote that the factory councils helped to unite the working class, and allowed workers to understand their place in the productive and social system and to develop the skills required to create a new society and a new type of state in a period when the bourgeoisie could no longer guarantee the development of the forces of production. The only way to destroy the old society and maintain working-class power was to begin to build a new order. Thus the roots of Gramsci's concept of HEGEMONY can be found in this period (Buci-Glucksmann 1979). The context of new working-class institutions was the decline in the role of the individual entrepreneur, increased investment by the banks and the state, and the crisis of liberal democracy as a result of this change in the relationship between the political, social and economic spheres. The fascist offensive in 1920–21 led Gramsci to analyse its mass base in disaffected sections of the petty bourgeoisie which were used as instruments by the large landowners, parts of the industrial bourgeoisie, and elements in the state machinery. Fascism, he wrote, could provide a new basis of unity for the Italian state, and he predicted a coup d'état although he tended to overestimate the fragility of the new regime.

In January 1921 Gramsci helped to found the Communist Party (PCI). From 1922 to 1924, he worked for the Comintern in Moscow and Vienna amidst debates about what policy should be followed to build socialism in the Soviet Union, and about the relationship between socialists and the new communist parties in the West. Elected to the Italian Parliament in 1924, he returned to Italy where he took over the party leadership and engaged in a struggle to transform the PCI from the sectarianism of its early years into a party rooted in the mass movement. Gramsci was arrested in November 1926 and sentenced to more than twenty years imprisonment. The starting point for his studies in prison, he wrote, would be an examination of the political function of the intellectuals. Working on several notebooks and different themes at the same time, subjected to the prison censor and the haphazard availability of sources, Gramsci eventually filled thirty-four notebooks. A single note often combines several concepts and is embedded in a particular debate or historical reference, and there are several versions of many of them, so that no chronological or unilinear description of his ideas in the *Prison Notebooks* is possible.

Gramsci analysed the unification of Italy, in particular the role of Italian intellectuals and the way in which the new nation-state was the result of a 'passive revolution', in which the mass of the peasantry gave at most passive consent to the new political order. He divides the INTELLECTUALS into organic intellectuals, which any new progressive class needs to organize a new social order, and traditional intellectuals, who have a tradition going back to an earlier historical period. He defines intellectuals very widely to include all those who have 'an organisational function in the wide sense' (Gramsci 1971, p. 97). All human beings, he argues, have rational or intellectual capabilities, although only some at present have an intellectual function in society.

Intellectuals organize the web of beliefs and institutional and social relations which Gramsci calls hegemony. Thus he redefines the state as force plus consent, or hegemony armoured by coercion (Gramsci 1971, p. 263), in which political society organizes force, and CIVIL SOCIETY provides consent. Gramsci uses the word 'state' in different ways: in a narrow legal-constitutional sense, as a balance between political and civil society; or as encompassing both. Some writers criticize his 'weak' view of the state which overemphasizes the element of consent (Anderson 1976–7), while others stress that Gramsci is trying to analyse the modern interventionist state where the lines dividing civil and political society are increasingly blurred (Sassoon 1980). He argues that the nature of political power in advanced capitalist countries, where civil society includes complex institutions and mass organizations, determines the only strategy capable of undermining the present order and leading to a definitive victory for a socialist transformation: a war of position, or trench warfare; while the war of movement, or frontal attack, which was successful in the very different circumstances of tsarist Russia, is only a particular tactic. Influenced by Machiavelli, Gramsci argues that the Modern Prince – the revolutionary party – is the organism which will allow the working class to create a new society by helping it to develop its organic intellectuals and an alternative hegemony. The political, social and economic crisis of capitalism can, however, result in a reorganization of hegemony through various kinds of passive revolution, in order to pre-empt the threat by the working-class movement to political and economic control by the ruling few, while providing for the continued development of the forces of production. He includes in this category fascism, different kinds of reformism, and the introduction in Europe of scientific management and assembly-line production.

In relation to his ideas on the intellectuals,

Gramsci suggests that whereas professional philosophers develop the skill of abstract thought, all human beings engage in a philosophical practice as they interpret the world, albeit often in an unsystematic and uncritical form. Philosophy becomes in Marx's phrase 'a material force' with effects on the 'common sense' of an age. A philosophical system must be placed in historical perspective, in the sense that it cannot be criticized simply at an abstract level but must be related to the ideologies which it helps various social forces to generate. As a 'philosophy of praxis', Marxism can help the masses become protagonists in history as more and more people acquire specialized, critical intellectual skills, and a coherent world view. Gramsci attacks two positions influential in his own day which reinforced the passivity and resignation reflected in the phrase, 'we must be philosophical about it': the idealism of Croce and what he considered Bukharin's simplistic and mechanical interpretation of Marxism. This approach is echoed in Gramsci's critical look at literature, folklore and the relationship between popular and 'high' or 'official' culture which had to be analysed from the point of view of how intellectuals as groups related to the mass of the population and the development of a national-popular culture.

After years of ill health Gramsci died in 1937 from a cerebral haemorrhage. A variety of debates developed as his works began to be published after the second world war (Jocteau 1975; Mouffe and Sassoon 1977). Among the questions raised are whether the crucial dimensions of his thought are Italian or international, the relationship of his ideas to those of Lenin, the connection between different periods in his work, and his relationship while in prison to the PCI and to developments in the Soviet Union. Recent interpretations point to an embryonic theory of socialism and a contribution to a critical examination of the experience of existing socialist societies. His influence on the post-second world war PCI, and the relation of his ideas to EUROCOMMUNISM, is also a matter of debate.

Reading

Anderson, P. 1976–77: 'The Antinomies of Antonio Gramsci'.
Buci-Glucksmann, C. 1979: *Gramsci and the State*.
Davidson, A. 1977: *Antonio Gramsci: Towards an Intellectual Biography*.
Fiori, G. 1965 (1970): *Antonio Gramsci: Life of a Revolutionary*.
Francioni, G. 1984: *L'officina gramsciana. Ipotesi sulla struttura dei 'Quaderni del carcere'*.
Gramsci, A. 1929–35 (1971): *Selections from the Prison Notebooks*.
— 1975: *Quaderni del Carcere I-IV*.
— 1977: *Selections from Political Writings, 1910–1920*.
— 1978: *Selections from Political Writings, 1921–1926*.
— 1985: *Selections from Cultural Writings*.
— 1990: *Bibliografia gramsciana*.
Jocteau, G. C. 1975: *Leggere Gramsci: una guida alle interpretazioni*.
Mouffe, C. ed. 1979: *Gramsci and Marxist Theory*.
Mouffe, C. and Sassoon, Anne S. 1977: 'Gramsci in France and Italy'.
Sassoon, Anne S. 1980 (1987): *Gramsci's Politics*.
— ed. 1982: *Approaches to Gramsci*.
ANNE SHOWSTACK SASSOON

Grünberg, Carl Born 10 February 1861, Focşani, Rumania; died 2 February 1940, Frankfurt am Main. After studying law at the University of Vienna Grünberg became a judge and then practised for a time as a lawyer, but at the same time continued his research in agrarian history and the history of socialism. In 1893 he founded (with others) the *Zeitschrift für Wirtschafts- und Sozialgeschichte*. From 1894 to 1899 he was a lecturer in the University of Vienna; he became professor of political economy in 1909, and thus the first 'professorial Marxist' in a German-speaking university. In 1924 he was appointed as the first Director of the Frankfurt Institute of Social Research (see FRANKFURT SCHOOL) but was obliged to retire in 1928 after a stroke. Grünberg's contribution to Marxist thought was threefold. First, he was the teacher of all the leading Austro-Marxist thinkers, and has been called 'the father of Austro-Marxism'. Second, in 1910 he founded the famous *Archiv für die Geschichte des Sozialismus und der Arbeiterbewegung* (*Grünberg-Archiv*) to which all the principal Marxists of the period contributed, and the aim of which he described as being to provide a general view of socialism and the labour movement based upon the specialized investigations of individual scholars and research groups. Third, in his brief period as Director he launched the Frankfurt Institute on its course of fruitful historical research and theoretical debate; although this was given a very different direction under his successor, Max Horkheimer.

Reading

Grünberg, Carl, ed. 1910–30: *Archiv für die Geschichte des Sozialismus und der Arbeiterbewegung*, vols I–XV.
Festschrift für Carl Grünberg zum 70. Geburtstag. 1932.
Indexband zu Archiv für die Geschichte des Sozialismus und der Arbeiterbewegung. 1973. Includes a biography of Grünberg by Günther Nenning.

TOM BOTTOMORE

Grundrisse *Grundrisse* ('outlines') is the title ordinarily given to a large manuscript written by Marx in 1857–8. He had already been working away at his *magnum opus* on economics for several years but the impression that a fresh wave of revolutionary upheaval was about to burst on Europe impelled him to sketch out the main lines of his work in a frantic spurt of activity lasting six months. This outline extends to about 800 closely printed pages. But perhaps the length is not so surprising given that the whole work was to have comprised six parts, of which the volumes of *Capital* are but a fragment, albeit a substantial one.

The *Grundrisse* was never meant for publication. It was only made available in the original in 1941 in Moscow and in English translation in 1973. Yet by many it soon came to be seen as Marx's central work. There are two main reasons for this. The first is that the *Grundrisse* is central in a literal sense. The early writings of Marx were imbued with a Hegelian philosophical humanism which seemed a far cry from much of the rather dry economics of the later

Marx. The *Grundrisse* provided the missing link in that it contains, together with the outlines of Marx's economics, discussion of such concepts as alienation which are reminiscent of much of Marx's early works and generally shows the continuing influence of Hegel on Marx's economic concepts. Secondly, the *Grundrisse* has a wider perspective than that of *Capital*. It is clear that Marx was eventually able to complete only a part of his projected work and thus that the *Grundrisse* contains discussions of matters that he was not able to include in his later published work. In fact, the three volumes of *Capital* form the first part of the six-part 'Economics' that Marx in 1857 intended to write. Such important topics as the state, international division of labour and the world market were to be analysed in the other parts; the *Grundrisse* gives us clues as to how Marx would have dealt with these questions. Moreover, these discussions are linked with digressions of a much wider nature such as the relation of the individual to society, the influence of automation and the problems of increasing leisure, the nature of pre-capitalist economic formations, the revolutionary nature of capitalism and its inherent universality, and so on.

More generally, the *Grundrisse* gives the reader the sense of Marx in his workshop, fashioning his own economic concepts by refining and reshaping those of the classical tradition and matching Ricardo with Hegel. At the same time, it is a work that is difficult to read in that its note form makes it disorganized and allusive. But it shows Marx's extraordinary ability to combine subtle analysis with broad historical vision and the richness of this text will provide exciting material for reflection for many years to come.

Reading

McLellan, David 1973: *Marx's Grundrisse*.

DAVID MCLELLAN

H

Habermas, Jürgen Born 18 June 1929, in Düsseldorf, Habermas studied philosophy, history, psychology and German literature at the University of Göttingen, and then in Zurich and Bonn, where he obtained his doctorate in 1954. After working as a journalist, he became, in 1956, Adorno's assistant at the reconstituted Institute for Social Research in Frankfurt, where he participated in an empirical study on the political awareness of students, published in 1961. From 1959 to 1961 he worked on his *Structural Transformation of the Public Sphere* (1962). After a period as Professor of Philosophy at Heidelberg, Habermas returned to Frankfurt in 1964 as Professor of Philosophy and Sociology, where he delivered the inaugural lecture on 'Knowledge and Interest' reprinted in 1968 in the book of the same name. His other works of this period are the essays entitled *Theory and Practice* (1963), a survey work on *The Logic of The Social Sciences* (1967) and some further essays grouped under the title *Technology and Science as Ideology* (1968).

The year 1968 was also of course the year of major student-led protest, in West Germany as elsewhere. Habermas participated very fully in the movement, welcoming its intellectual and political challenge to the complacency of West German democracy (and incidentally its supersession of the gloomy diagnosis in his own *Student und Politik* of the unpolitical orientation of West German students). Although he came to criticize its extremism, he has continued to take a very positive view of the long-term effect of the movement in terms of values in the Federal Republic, while deploring the short-term legacy of its failure: a decline into apathy or desperate terrorism.

In 1971 Habermas left Frankfurt for Starnberg, Bavaria, to take up, along with the natural scientist C. F. von Weizsäcker, the directorship of the newly created Max Planck Institute for the Study of the Conditions of Life in the Scientific-Technical World. In an environment which attracted some of the most brilliant younger sociologists in the country, he published an enormous amount of material, including the well known *Legitimation Crisis* (1973) and culminating with the *Theory of Communicative Action* (1981). In 1982, he returned to Frankfurt to the chair in Sociology and Philosophy which he still occupies. His most recent major work, *The Philosophical Discourse of Modernity*, was published in 1985.

If Max Weber has been described as a bourgeois Marx, Habermas might be summarily characterized as a Marxist Max Weber. Like Weber, he is basically a thinker rather than a man of action but one who intervenes in political issues when something, as he often puts it, 'irritates' him. His collected 'political writings' – a broad category which includes occasional lectures and interviews – run to several volumes. Although he rejects Weber's doctrine of the value-freedom of science, he insists, like Weber, on the distinction between scholarly and political discourse (Dews 1986, p. 127). Like Weber, and Karl Jaspers in the post-war period, he has operated in some way as the intellectual conscience of Germany, with a public profile higher than one would expect of someone who has not sought out a political role.

Habermas combines a deep grounding in the philosophical tradition with a remarkable openness to a wide variety of contemporary philosophical and social theories. Entire books could be written about the respective influences on him of Kant and Hegel, Marx and Weber, Parsons and Piaget, and so on. The most important source is, however, without question the broad Marxist tradition which also inspired the original Frankfurt Institute for Social Research. His relationship to Frankfurt critical theory was rather less immediate than is often assumed. In intellectual terms, Habermas is closer to the Institute's earlier programme, grounding its critique in an inter-disciplinary synthesis drawn from various social sciences. But if he was dissatisfied with the form of Adorno and Horkheimer's thought from *Dialectic of Enlightenment* (1947) onwards, he shared their substantive preoccupation with the way in which enlightenment, in the form of instrumental rationality (rationality of means rather than ends), turns from a means of liberation into a new source of enslavement. As early as the late 1950s, as he claimed in a recent interview, 'My problem was a theory of modernity, a theory of the pathology of modernity, from the viewpoint of the realization – the deformed realization – of reason in history' (Dews 1986, p. 96).

In Habermas's early work, this preoccupation took three forms. First, a working through of the classical philosophical texts: Marx and Weber, but also Kant, Fichte and Hegel – not to mention the Greeks. Second, a preoccupation with technology and the attempt to construct a 'left' alternative to the technological determinism arising in part from Heidegger and in post-war Germany from Arnold Gehlen and Helmut Schelsky. Third, and relatedly, a concern with the conditions of rational political discussion, or practical reason, in the conditions of modern technocratic democracy. The first of these themes predominates in *Theory and Practice*; the second can be found in Habermas's early journalism and in *Technology and Science as Ideology*; the third theme occurs in both these works, but is first addressed in *Student und Politik* and *Structural Transformation of the Public Sphere*.

Taken as a whole, *Theory and Practice* has three main themes which recur in Habermas's later work: (1) a critical evaluation of the Marxist tradition; (2) some reflections on the possibility of what he later called the 'reconstruction' of historical materialism; and (3) a methodological comparison between the unity of empirical and normative, or technical and 'practical' issues, to be found in Aristotle, in natural law theory and in Marxism, on the one hand, and the scientistic, ostensibly value-free approach of the modern social sciences, on the other. In *Knowledge and Human Interests* (1968), Habermas undertook a historically based critique of positivism in both the natural and the social sciences. Then in the 1970s, he

gradually developed his own 'theory of communicative action', now conceived not as a philosophical foundation for the social sciences, but as itself a *self-reflexive* social theory 'concerned to demonstrate its own critical standards' (1984, p. xxxix). A communicative action, distinguished from instrumental or strategic action, occurs wherever people make assertions to other people about what is or should be the case. From this core notion, Habermas develops theories of truth/morality, human evolution and political legitimacy, as well as a philosophy of history. This sees modernity as an 'uncompleted project of, *inter alia*, realising certain universally justifiable Enlightenment values' and is correspondingly hostile towards the prophets of 'post-modernity'.

Should Habermas be considered a Marxist thinker? He has always accepted the label, though his Marxism, like that of the FRANKFURT SCHOOL, is anything but orthodox, and his abiding and growing concern with the discursive foundations of ETHICS, in particular, marks him off from most Marxists and even neo-Marxists. But if at times it seemed that his description of himself as a Marxist was little more than an expression of solidarity with the victims of West German McCarthyism, he has shown an abiding concern with what at one stage he called the reconstruction of HISTORICAL MATERIALISM: its restatement in what he considers to be more adequate terms. In any case, there can be little doubt that he will be remembered as one of the crucial thinkers of the second half of this century.

Reading

Bernstein, R. J. 1985: *Habermas and Modernity*.

Dews, P. ed. 1986: *Autonomy and Solidarity: Interviews with Jürgen Habermas*.

Ingram, D. 1987: *Habermas and the Dialectic of Reason*.

McCarthy, T. 1978: *The Critical Theory of Jürgen Habermas*.

Roderick, R. 1986: *Habermas and the Foundations of Critical Theory*.

Thompson, J. and Held, D. eds. 1982: *Habermas: Critical Debates*.

White, S. K. 1988: *The Recent Work of Jürgen Habermas: Reason, Justice and Modernity*.

WILLIAM OUTHWAITE

Hegel, Georg Wilhelm Friedrich Born 27 August 1770, Stuttgart; died 14 November 1831, Berlin. The son of a revenue officer, Hegel studied philosophy, classics and theology at the University of Tübingen, then became a private tutor, first in Berne and subsequently in Frankfurt. In 1801 he became a university lecturer (*Privatdozent*), and in 1805 professor, at the University of Jena, and his first major work, *The Phenomenology of Mind* (1807), was written there. From 1808 to 1816 he was rector of the Aegidiengymnasium in Nürnberg, then professor at Heidelberg (1816–18), and at Berlin where he remained from 1818 until his death and where a Hegelian school began to form.

Hegel's philosophy was important for Marx in two respects. First, he was profoundly influenced by Hegel's critiques of Kant, and by his philosophy of history. Secondly, he took over Hegel's dialectical method in its most comprehensive form, that of the *Logic*, and used it to lay bare the dynamic structure of the capitalist mode of production. In his critique of knowledge Kant restricted human claims to genuine scientific knowledge to the realm of 'appearance', stating that knowledge can only result from the combined action of forms of intuition and categories inherent in the knowing subject on one side, and of externally produced sense data on the other. Beyond this relationship, established by critical reflection, there remains the 'thing-in-itself' which is in principle unknowable. What human beings can know is only 'appearance'. Hegel, however, maintained against Kant that appearance and essence necessarily belong together, and that the innermost structure of reality corresponds with that of the self-knowing human spirit. In theological terms this means that God (the Absolute) comes to self-knowledge through human knowledge. The categories of human thought are thus at the same time objective forms of Being, and logic is at the same time ontology.

Hegel interprets history as 'progress in the consciousness of freedom'. The forms of social organization correspond with the consciousness of freedom, and hence consciousness determines being. The consciousness of a historical epoch and a people is expressed above all in religion, 'which is where a people defines for itself what it holds to be the true. . . . Religion is a people's consciousness of what it is, of its highest being'

(*The Philosophy of History*). Peoples who worship a stone or animal as their 'god' thus cannot be free. Free social and political relations first become possible with the worship of a god in human form or a 'spirit' (the 'holy spirit'). Historical progress passes through want and privation, suffering, war and death and even the decline of whole cultures and peoples. Hegel remains convinced however that through these historical struggles a higher principle of freedom, a closer approximation to the truth, a higher degree of insight into the nature of freedom gradually emerges. The direction of human history is towards Christianity, the Reformation, the French Revolution and constitutional monarchy. Progress in religious conceptions and philosophical ideas corresponds with social and political progress.

The YOUNG HEGELIANS, through whom Marx became acquainted with Hegel's philosophy, used their master's doctrine as a weapon of criticism against the Prussian monarchy, which had become conservative. In so doing, they went beyond Hegel's conception of the state as a constitutional monarchy administered by enlightened state officials. While Hegel regarded only philosophically educated officials as possessing a developed insight into the unity of subjective spirit (the individual human being) and objective spirit (the state), the Young Hegelians held that all citizens could acquire it. For this reason they also demanded that the merely allegorical religiosity of traditional Christianity should be overcome by generalizing the philosophical insight of Hegelian logic. The idea of humanity was to take the place of the allegorically represented God of Christianity:

> Humanity is the union of two natures: god become man, infinity objectified in finitude, a finite spirit which remembers its infinity. It is the miracle worker, in so far as, in the course of human history, it masters nature, both within human beings and outside them, ever more completely, and subordinates nature as the impotent material of its own activity. It is without sin in so far as the process of its development is blameless; defilement is a characteristic only of individuals, while in the species and in history it is transcended. (D. F. Strauss 1839)

(See also HEGEL AND MARX.)

Reading

Avineri, Shlomo 1972: *Hegel's Theory of the Modern State*.

Hegel, G. W. F. 1807 *(1931)*: *The Phenomenology of Mind*.

— 1812 *(1929)*: *The Science of Logic*.

— 1821 *(1942)*: *The Philosophy of Right*.

— 1830–1 *(1956)*: *The Philosophy of History*.

Hyppolite, Jean 1955 *(1969)*: *Studies on Marx and Hegel*.

Kojève, A. 1947: *Introduction à la lecture de Hegel*.

Löwith, Karl 1941 *(1964)*: *From Hegel to Nietzsche. The Revolution in Nineteenth-Century Thought*.

IRING FETSCHER

Hegel and Marx   Marx's thought shows the influence of Hegel's dialectical philosophy in many ways. He first became acquainted with it during his student days in Berlin, adopting in the first place a republican interpretation of Hegel's philosophy of history such as was represented by, for example, Eduard Gans. Like Hegel, Marx interprets world history as a dialectical progression, but following Feuerbach's materialist reinterpretation of Hegel, Marx comprehends 'material labour as the essence, as the self-validating essence, of humanity' (*Economic and Philosophical Manuscripts*). Marx's critical reformulation of Hegel's philosophy of history consists in the elimination of the fictitious subject of world history, the so-called 'world spirit', and in the prolongation of the dialectical process of historical development into the future. That realm of freedom which Hegel asserted to be fully realized here and now, lies for Marx in the future as a real possibility of the present. The dialectic of productive forces and productive relations which effects historical progress offers in contrast to Hegel's dialectic of world spirit no guarantee that the realm of freedom (see EMANCIPATION) will be realized; it presents only the objective possibility of such a development. Should the historically possible revolutionizing of society not come about, then a relapse into barbarism (Luxemburg) or the 'common ruin of the contending classes' (Marx) is also possible.

In place of the constitutional bourgeois state, which for Hegel constituted the end point of historical development, Marx puts forward the concept of 'the free association of producers'. This is a social order which dispenses with any kind of coercive force standing over and above it, and whose members manage their own affairs through consensus. For Hegel, the process through which an individual liberates himself from his natural existence, from external coercion, is a process of 'spiritualization'; through philosophical insight into his objective situation, the individual comes to see that what *appeared* to be external constraints upon his will are in fact necessary conditions of his existence as a thinking being with a will of its own, and with this insight comes reconciliation with the objective reality. Hegel and conservative Hegelians held that such insight, reconciliation and liberation could only be perfectly attained by philosophically educated state officials, while the YOUNG HEGELIANS, generalizing this idea, identified the process of 'spiritualization' with that of the individual's maturation to citizenship. Nonetheless, in both interpretations the individual is left with a certain 'double identity': on the one hand, he is a natural individual feeling himself to be subject to external and coercive forces; on the other hand, he is a 'spiritual being' possessed of the knowledge that that which apparently denies him his freedom is in fact his freedom and reality itself. Liberation is reconciliation. For Marx, however, liberation is only possible when this duplication of human identity into human being and citizen, into natural individual and spiritualized being, is no longer necessary, has been overcome; when human beings no longer have to objectify their own social constraints in an 'alien essence standing over and above them' – the state (later also capital). Despite all his criticisms of Hegel Marx nevertheless retains the Hegelian conviction that humanity makes PROGRESS in the course of history. He also adopts – indeed as a matter of course – Hegel's Eurocentrism; and his own Eurocentrism is at its most obvious in his writings on India and China.

In Marx's work on the 'critique of political economy' a second influence of Hegel makes itself felt. The comprehension of this influence is particularly essential for an adequate understanding of Marx's main work, *Capital*, for it concerns the method which underlies his analysis of the capitalist mode of production. Here Marx makes use of Hegel's dialectical method, which he claims to have put (back) on its feet, in order to present the internal dynamic and systematic structure of capitalist production. The capitalist system of production relations constitutes a totality, that is to say, an all-inclusive unity which for this very reason must be examined and presented as an interconnected whole. However, empirical research and the processing of specific empirical data must precede the presentation of the totality. The dialectical self-movement of the at once subjective and objective categories, value, money and capital, must be a feature of the object under investigation, not the result of an externally imposed methodological scheme. Marx stresses the difference between his way of handling empirical relationships and facts and that of Hegel who, as Marx maintained in his early *Critique of Hegel's Philosophy of the State*, develops a scheme of categories first – in his *Logic* – and then presents social institutions such as the family, civil society, the state and their internal structures in abstract conformity with his scheme. According to Marx the only adequate dialectical exposition of an object of investigation is one which is sensitive to the dynamic and structural individuality of the object. The self-moving 'subject' of the capitalist mode of production, that for the sake of which capitalist production takes place at all, is capital itself, which is, however, not something independently real, but rather something which arises out of the unconscious interaction and collaboration of individuals and classes, and which will therefore disappear once capitalist society has been transcended. It is not a real subject of production but a 'pseudo-subject'. For this reason it is at best misleading to assert that Marx's category of 'capital' plays the same role in his thought as does the category of 'spirit' in Hegel's thought and system. Whereas the (World) spirit according to Hegel's idealist philosophy actually produces history, capital is only the seemingly real subject of the capitalist mode of production. The *actual* 'subjectlessness' of this mode of production (Althusser) is by no means only a methodological achievement of Marx; the idea that capital on the one hand objectively appears as the independently real subject of production yet on the other is not 'really real', is not really an independent subject at all, contains an implicit criticism of the mode of production which constitutes it. The free association of producers, according to Marx, is destined to take the place of capitalism, a social order which ruthlessly

and short-sightedly exploits nature, in which individuals and classes are determined by the structural laws of the mode of production to serve the 'pseudo-subject', capital. The free association of producers, so Marx maintains, will regulate the metabolic interchange between society and nature rationally and, in contrast to capitalist society – where production is subservient and responsive only to the interests of capital – its production will be directed towards satisfying the producers' material requirements and their needs for (social) activity, social life and individual development. It will, as the real subject of production, take the place of the 'pseudo-subject', capital, the mere objectively existing 'appearance' of a subject of production. Only in this not yet realized subject will the Hegelian World Spirit find its empirical embodiment.

Marx only used Hegel's dialectic methodologically and tacitly to ground his belief in historical progress. Engels, however, in *Anti-Dühring*, attempted to go beyond this, to draft a kind of materialist dialectical ontology and theory of development (see MATERIALISM). Out of this attempt, which owed indeed more to Darwin and nineteenth-century natural science and scientific world-views than to Hegel, so-called 'dialectical materialism' arose, to whose further development and elaboration Plekhanov, Lenin, Stalin and a series of Soviet thinkers contributed.

Reading

Colletti, Lucio 1969 (1973): *Marxism and Hegel*.

Fetscher, Iring 1967 (1970): 'The Relation of Marxism to Hegel'. In *Karl Marx and Marxism*.

Hyppolite, Jean 1955 (1969): *Studies on Marx and Hegel*.

Korsch, Karl 1923 (1970): *Marxism and Philosophy*.

Lichtheim, George 1971: *From Marx to Hegel and Other Essays*.

Marcuse, Herbert 1941: *Reason and Revolution: Hegel and the Rise of Social Theory*.

Negt, Oskar, ed. 1970: *Aktualität und Folge der Philosophie Hegels*.

Riedel, Manfred 1974: 'Hegel und Marx'. In *System und Geschichte*.

Wolf, Dieter 1979: *Hegel und Marx*.

IRING FETSCHER

hegemony Any definition of hegemony is complicated by the use of the word in two diametrically opposed senses: first, to mean domination, as in 'hegemonism'; and secondly, to mean leadership, implying some notion of consent. Thus Mao Tse-tung used 'hegemonism' to indicate a kind of domination by one country over another which was not imperialism. The second meaning is more usual in Marxist writing. Anderson (1976–7) has pointed out that both the Mensheviks and Lenin used the word to indicate political leadership in the democratic revolution, based on an alliance with sections of the peasantry. Buci-Glucksmann (1979) discusses how it was used by Bukharin and Stalin in the 1920s. Its full development as a Marxist concept can be attributed to Gramsci. Most commentators agree that hegemony is the key concept in Gramsci's *Prison Notebooks* and his most important contribution to Marxist theory. In his pre-prison writings, on the few occasions when the term is used, it refers to a working-class strategy. In an essay written just before he was imprisoned in 1926, Gramsci used the word to refer to the system of alliances which the working class must create to overthrow the bourgeois state and to serve as the social basis of the workers' state (Gramsci 1978, p. 443). About the same time he used the term to argue that the Soviet proletariat would have to sacrifice its corporate, economic interests in order to maintain an alliance with the peasantry and to serve its own general interest (ibid. p. 431).

In his *Prison Notebooks* Gramsci goes beyond this use of the term, which was similar to its use in debates in the Communist International in the period, to apply it to the way in which the bourgeoisie establishes and maintains its rule. Two historical examples which he discusses in this context are the French Revolution and the Italian Risorgimento, in which he contrasts the extended basis of consent for the new French state with the limited consent enjoyed by the state in unified Italy. In discussing the different manifestations of bourgeois domination he draws on such thinkers as Machiavelli and Pareto when he describes the state as force plus consent. In modern conditions, Gramsci argues, a class maintains its dominance not simply through a special organization of force, but because it is able to go beyond its narrow, corporative interests, exert a moral and intellectual leadership, and make compromises (within certain limits) with a variety of allies who are unified in a social bloc of forces which Gramsci calls the historical bloc. This bloc represents a basis of consent for a certain social order, in which the hegemony of a dominant class (see RULING CLASS) is created and re-created in a web of institutions, social relations, and ideas. This 'fabric of hegemony' is woven by the intellectuals who, according to Gramsci, are all those who have an organizational role in society. Thus, he goes beyond the definition of the state as the instrument of a class used by Marx, Engels and Lenin.

Although Gramsci writes that the institutions of hegemony are located in CIVIL SOCIETY, whereas political society is the arena of political institutions in the legal constitutional sense, he also says that the division is a purely methodological one and stresses the overlap that exists in actual societies (Gramsci 1971, p. 160). Indeed, in the political conditions of expanding state intervention in civil society, and of reformism as a response to demands made upon the political arena as trade unions and mass political parties are organized, and as the economy becomes transformed into so-called 'organized capitalism', the form of hegemony changes and the bourgeoisie engages in what Gramsci calls passive revolution. Thus the material basis of hegemony is constituted through reforms or compromises in which the leadership of a class is maintained but in which other classes have certain demands met. The leading or hegemonic class is thus in Gramsci's definition truly political because it goes beyond its immediate economic interests (which it may have fought for in the political arena) to represent the universal advancement of society. Thus, Gramsci employs the concept of hegemony to argue that any economistic notion of politics or ideology which looks for an immediate economic class interest in politics and culture is incapable of an accurate analysis of the political situation and of the balance of political forces and cannot produce an adequate understanding of the nature of state power (see ECONOMISM). Consequently it is inadequate as a basis for a political strategy for the working-class movement.

Gramsci's approach to what he defined as an attempt to develop a Marxist science of politics has various implications. A fully extended hegemony must rest on active consent, on a collective will in which various groups in society unite. Gramsci thus goes beyond a theory of political obligation resting on abstract civil rights to argue that full democratic control develops in the highest form of hegemony. Yet his analysis of various forms of hegemony, such as that which came to dominate the Italian Risorgimento, shows that the limited nature of consent can lead to a weak basis for a political order, which may come to rely increasingly on force. Hegemony, it may be argued, cannot be reduced to legitimation, false consciousness, or manipulation of the mass of the population, whose 'common sense' or world view, according to Gramsci, is made up of a variety of elements, some of which contradict the dominant ideology, as does much of everyday experience. What a dominant, hegemonic ideology can do is to provide a more coherent and systematic world view which not only influences the mass of the population but serves as a principle of organization of social institutions. Ideology in his view does not simply reflect or mirror economic class interest, and in this sense it is not a 'given' determined by the economic structure or organization of society but rather an area of struggle. It organizes action through the way it is embodied in social relations, institutions and practices, and informs all individual and collective activities (Mouffe 1979).

Gramsci defines the special historical project of the proletariat as the creation of a 'regulated society' in which hegemony and civil society, or the area of consent, is fully expanded and political society, or the area of constraint, is diminished. This implies that the proletariat must create a continuous expansion of consent in which the interests of various groups come together to form a new historical bloc. In developing a strategy towards this end, a new hegemony must harness and systematize elements of popular ideas and practice. The concept of hegemony is thus the basis of Gramsci's critical analysis of folklore and popular culture and his discussion of religion and of the relationship between the systematic philosophy of the philosophers and the unsystematic philosophy or world view of the mass of the population.

Various questions have been raised about Gramsci's concept of hegemony. Some have to do with the adequacy of his analysis of bourgeois state power and the strategic conclusions he draws from this (Anderson 1976–77).

One aspect of this debate concerns the extent to which working-class hegemony can or must be developed before state power is transformed and the extent to which it remains the task of a socialist state to develop hegemony. Other questions concern the role of the revolutionary party in creating proletarian hegemony. Some writers emphasize the homogeneous, or unitary and possibly totalizing, character of hegemony; while others stress its diverse elements which are not necessarily rooted in economically defined classes, and the way in which it represents the coming together of quite different groups, with the compromises this implies. Some recent interpretations claim that hegemony not only provides a conceptual tool for an analysis of bourgeois society, and for the development of a strategy of transition to socialism, but can also be used to analyse the achievements and the limits of socialist societies themselves. In addition it has been used as the basis of a 'post-Marxist' critique of the class basis of Marxist analysis.

Reading

Anderson, P. 1976–77: 'The Antinomies of Antonio Gramsci'.

Buci-Glucksmann, C. 1979: *Gramsci and the State*.

— 1982: 'Hegemony and Consent'. In A. S. Sassoon ed. *Approaches to Gramsci*.

De Giovanni, B. *et al.* 1977: *Egemonia, stato, partito in Gramsci*.

Femia, J. 1981: *Gramsci's Political Thought. Hegemony, Consciousness and the Revolutionary Process*.

Gramsci, A. 1929–35 (1971): *Selections from the Prison Notebooks*.

— 1978: *Selections from Political Writings 1921–1926*.

Laclau, E. and Mouffe, C. 1985: *Hegemony and Socialist Strategy*.

Mouffe, C. 1979: 'Hegemony and Ideology in Gramsci'. In C. Mouffe ed. *Gramsci and Marxist Theory*.

Sassoon, A. S. 1980: *Gramsci's Politics*.

                    ANNE SHOWSTACK SASSOON

Hilferding, Rudolf Born 10 August 1877, Vienna; died 10 February 1941, Paris. After studying medicine at the University of Vienna Hilferding practised as a doctor until 1906 (as he did again during his military service from

1915 to 1918), but he was profoundly interested in economic problems from his high school days. From 1902 he was a frequent contributor on economic subjects to *Die Neue Zeit*, and in 1904 he published his rejoinder to Böhm-Bawerk's criticism (from the standpoint of Austrian marginal utility theory) of Marx's economic theory, in a book which Paul Sweezy (1942) called 'the best criticism of subjective value theory from a Marxist standpoint'. Also in 1904, with Max Adler, Hilferding founded the *Marx-Studien*. In 1906 he was invited to Berlin to teach in the German Social Democratic Party (SPD) school, and later became the foreign editor of *Vorwärts*. In 1914 he joined the left wing of the SPD in opposing war credits, and after the war he edited the journal of the Independent Social Democratic Party (USPD), *Freiheit*. Having acquired Prussian citizenship in 1920 he was appointed to the Reich Economic Council, was a member of the Reichstag from 1924 to 1933, and Minister of Finance in two governments (1923 and 1928/29). After the Nazi seizure of power he had to go into exile, and in 1938 he moved to Paris; after the fall of France he moved to the unoccupied zone, but was eventually handed over to the German authorities by the Vichy government and died in the hands of the Gestapo. He is best known for his major analysis of 'the latest stage of capitalist development', *Finance Capital*, and for his subsequent writings on ORGANIZED CAPITALISM. (See AUSTRO-MARXISM; FINANCE CAPITAL.)

Reading

Gottschalch, Wilfried 1962: *Strukturveränderungen der Gesellschaft und politisches Handeln in der Lehre von Rudolf Hilferding*.

Hilferding, Rudolf 1904 (1949): *Böhm-Bawerk's Marx-Critique*, ed. Paul Sweezy.

— 1910 (1981): *Finance Capital*.

Kurotaki, M. 1984: *Zur Todesursache Rudolf Hilferdings*.

TOM BOTTOMORE

Hinduism   Marxist interest in Hinduism goes back to Marx himself, though he made no regular study of it. To him it was the ideology of an oppressive and outworn society, and he shared the distaste of most Europeans for its more lurid features. 'A more monstrous combination than any of the divine monsters startling us in the Temple of Salsette', was his summing up of British despotism in India grafted on to Asiatic despotism; and he was as sceptical as his Indian followers were to be of any notion of a Hindu 'golden age' of the past (*The First Indian War of Independence*, p. 156). In this century Marxism outside India has concerned itself with Hinduism chiefly as part of the subject of RELIGION in general; inside the country it has been to a great extent preoccupied with practical issues concerning Hinduism in recent times, its place in the national movement, and the communal passions which resulted in independence being accompanied by partition and massacre.

As Romila Thapar notes, the name 'Hinduism' is something of an anachronism when used of ancient India, but is a convenient label for the religion growing, some two millennia ago, out of the Vedic cult of the Aryan invaders. It was a highly composite one, scarcely definable with any accuracy in terms of beliefs, a mixture of Aryan and Dravidian thinking, not without some influences from Buddhism and Jainism. Thapar points to the concept of an Absolute, emerging in the Upanishads or later Vedic compositions, and then assuming the guise of a trinity, of creator, sustainer, and destroyer, in which can be recognized a reflection of the order of nature, birth and life and death. Subsequently the first deity of the three, Brahma, fell into the background, while the other two, Vishnu and Shiva – the latter an Aryan-Dravidian hybrid associated with fertility rites – survived as two paramount deities, dividing the allegiance of Hindus. Later times saw a shift from ceremonial practices towards *bhakti*, or the quest for an individual communion with God and often ecstatic devotion to him, as 'the dynamic form of later Hinduism' (Thapar 1966, pp. 131–3). Towards the end of the Middle Ages teachers like Kabir and Nanak gave a new turn to *bhakti* by incorporating Islamic ideas into it; they may be taken to have given expression to the feelings in that troubled age of humbler townsmen, and rural artisans in contact with urban life (p. 308).

Personal devotion, like any version of mysticism, was in a way an escape from priestly hegemony; but all this time Brahmin ascendancy had been upheld and even intensified. One aspect of its organization was the temple, as an institution with rich financial resources. A study of medieval south India shows large benefactions to temples from merchants or trading guilds, probably intended to secure higher social status and prestige for the donors, as well as spiritual blessings (Jha 1976).

An essay by R. S. Sharma (1966, ch. 1) charts currents of opinion about old India and Hinduism in modern writings, some of them inspired by historical materialism. In another essay he observes that in the Rig Veda 'the main concern of the prayers is the material prosperity of the Aryans' (1976, p. 39); he might well have added that one main concern at least of the *dharma*, or religious code of Hinduism, was the prosperity of men of the higher castes, as against both lower strata and women. As he points out elsewhere, frequently in the texts women and *sudras*, the drudges of the CASTE system, were 'lumped together in the same category', these two evidently representing 'the most condemned sections of society' (1966, pp. 29, 32). Those like the law-giver Manu who formulated the principles of the *dharma*, D. Chattopadhyaya remarks, reveal 'an intense hostility to free thinking or rationalism'; not surprisingly, because mystification as well as coercion was needed to uphold a social order where 'the vast millions of toiling masses are to be kept reconciled to servitude' (1976, p. 83). Chattopadhyaya gave prominence to an opposite, agnostic tradition in Indian thought, and agreed with the view of several scholars that Buddhism must have owed much to the early Samkhya school of philosophers: each was 'deliberate and categorical' in rejecting the notion of deity (1969, p. 95).

Some related matters were raised by Namboodripad, a communist party leader as well as a historian of his own southern province of Kerala. This region adopted Brahminism, but preserved various features of its own old social practices, and unlike northern India was moving during the Middle Ages towards a feudal species of private ownership of land. In the course of this transition an extensive polemical literature was thrown up in support of the dominant class and its religious ideology; one objective was the elimination of Buddhism (1952, ch. 3).

A well-known Indian Buddhist communist, Rahul Sankrityayana, among many other works wrote a critical narrative in fictional form of the evolution of Hinduism through the centuries. Of late years the Marxist approach has been utilized in part by other religious writers seeking clues to the history of their own or other religions; a good example is provided by two Catholics, Houtart and Lemercinier, working in India and Sri Lanka. They look on the myths of the Vedic Aryans as reflecting at first the needs of a migratory life, and then, as they developed a distinct pantheon, the change to settled agriculture. From the priest's role as intercessor it came to be held that 'only a god was capable of speaking to the gods', so that the Brahmin, whose function 'expressed the inability of the group to resolve its contradictions', became himself a divine being. A lower-class individual could rise in the scale, but only on condition of fully accepting the social order. Thus 'any social movement based on religion was impossible' (1980, pp. 36–8, 45). Here is a striking contrast between Hinduism and Christianity.

During the nineteenth century many progressive Indians, with Ram Mohun Roy as their pioneer, made it their first aim to liberate the minds of their countrymen from the more morbid strands of the complex fabric of faith, custom, and ritual. But the rise of a national liberation movement brought with it an energetic revival of Hinduism in all its aspects, better and worse. Another Christian spokesman in India, Wielenga, in the course of an open-minded scrutiny of Indian Marxism, goes into the conflict of ideas between it and the revivalist mentality (1976, pp. 113 ff.). A succinct statement on this can be found in a work by Palme Dutt, the Indian theoretician of the British Communist Party. Leaders with no up-to-date understanding of politics, he wrote, had tried to build nationalism on 'the still massive forces of social conservatism in India', and 'the supposed spiritual superiority' of old India over modern Europe. He referred to propagandists like Tilak and Aurobhindo Ghosh, the setting up of a Cow Protection Society and the holding of national festivals in honour of the elephant-headed godling Ganesh and the goddess of destruction Kali. Devoted patriots though they were, these men made themselves in effect 'champions of social reaction and superstition, of caste division and privilege' (1940, pp. 291–2, 294).

Gandhi was inevitably regarded as the new oracle of resurgent Hinduism. He was turning political issues into religious phrases, and talking of *Ram Rajya*, God's reign, as the Utopia to be hoped for, the golden age to be restored, instead of socialism. He was preaching abandonment of machinery and the rest of modernity, and return to the simple village existence of the past. All this his admirers imagined, wrote Dutt, to be the aspiration of the true India, the peasantry, whereas in reality it was no more than the nostalgia of a section of 'the bewildered petty bourgeoisie, harassed and endangered by processes of remorseless economic change', and hankering for 'the comfort of some rock of ancient certainty' (pp. 510–1). Jawaharlal Nehru himself, disciple of Gandhi though he was, often as a socialist deeply tinged with Marxism, felt bewildered by what seemed 'a glorification of poverty', a relic of bygone epochs when humanity 'could only think in terms of scarcity' (Norman 1965, vol. 1, pp. 85–6).

Nehru consoled himself with the thought that Gandhi, with his crusade on behalf of the Untouchables in particular, was 'gently but irresistibly' undermining orthodoxy, and that he was doing far more to shake India up than any armchair theorists of the left (vol. 1, pp. 299–300). Uncompromising opposition to Gandhi and his cherished Hindu convictions meant that communists were cut off in a considerable measure from the mainstream of the patriotic struggle, and incurred the risk of an isolation similar to that of socialists in Ireland. Since the coming of independence a number of them, like Mukerjee, have felt obliged to revise their estimate of the Mahatma and his services to India, but his identification with retrograde Hinduism has continued to be a stumbling-block. Some at least of their misgivings have proved well warranted. Bettelheim's survey of free India has much to say about the contagion of caste in local and national elections. Friction with the still large Muslim minority smoulders on, and occasionally erupts. The 'soul of India' so much talked of by conservatives, Namboodripad wrote, is no more than the spirit of Hinduism, and 'those who champion this theory slip into the chauvinistic Hindu idea that non-Hindus are aliens' (1966, p. 295).

Reading

Barun De, *et al.* eds. 1976: *Essays in Honour of Professor S. C. Sarkar.*

Bettelheim, Charles 1968: *India Independent.*

Chattopadhyaya, Γebinprasad 1969 (*1980*): *Indian Atheism: A Marxist Approach.*

— 1976: 'Social Function of Indian Idealism'. In Barun De, *op. cit.*

Dutt, R. Palme 1940: *India Today.*

Houtart, François and Lemercinier, Geneviève 1980: *The Great Asiatic Religions and their Social Functions.*

Jha, D. N. 1976: 'Temple and Merchants in South India c. AD 900–AD 1300'. In Barun De, *op. cit.*

Namboodripad, E. M. S. 1952: *The National Question in Kerala.*

— 1966: *Economics and Politics of India's Socialist Pattern.*

Norman, Dorothy ed. 1965: *Nehru, the First Sixty Years.*

Sankrityayana, Rahul 1942 (*1947*): *From Volga to Ganga (Ganges).*

Sharma, R. S. 1959: *Aspects of Political Ideas in Ancient India.*

— 1966: *Light on Early Indian Society and Economy.*

— 1976: 'Forms of Property in the Early Portions of the Rg Veda'. In Barun De, *op. cit.*

Thapar, Romila 1966: *A History of India*, vol. 1.

Wielenga, Bastiaan 1976: *Marxist Views on India in Historical Perspective.*
                                            V. G. KIERNAN

historical materialism The term refers to that central body of doctrine, frequently known as the materialist conception of history, which constitutes the social-scientific core of Marxist theory. According to Engels's 1892 introduction to *Socialism: Utopian and Scientific*, historical materialism

> designate[s] that view of the course of history which seeks the ultimate cause and the great moving power of all important historic events in the economic development of society, in the changes in the modes of production and exchange, in the consequent division of society into distinct classes, and in the struggle of these classes against one another.

Engels credited Marx with being the originator of historical materialism, which he saw as one of Marx's two great scientific discoveries (the other being the theory of surplus value), while Marx wrote that Engels had arrived at the materialist conception of history independently. In accord with the theory itself they stressed the historical and material preconditions of its formulation.

Although scholars disagree about the degree of continuity of various themes between Marx's early and later writings, few would deny that the materialist view of history which Marx and Engels began to hammer out at the time of *German Ideology* (1845/46) – though not without its intellectual antecedents – constitutes that which is, and was believed by them to be, distinctive of their world view. Earlier adumbrations of this conception in their writings may or may not demonstrate that one or the other of them had already reached a recognizably Marxist perspective prior to 1844–5. At this time, however, they began quite self-consciously to utilize historical materialism as, in Marx's words, the 'guiding thread' of all their subsequent studies.

Historical materialism is not, strictly speaking, a philosophy; rather, it is best interpreted as an empirical theory (or, perhaps more accurately, a collection of empirical theses). Thus Marx and Engels frequently underscore the scientific character of their enterprise, and *German Ideology* claims that its approach rests not on philosophically derived abstractions or dogmas, but rather on observation and an accurate depiction of real conditions; in short, on premises that 'can thus be verified in a purely empirical way'. Occasionally, Marx and Engels offer simple a priori arguments in favour of historical materialism, but these are not very compelling. A theory which makes such bold claims about the nature of history and society can be vindicated, if at all, only by its ability to provide a viable research programme for social and historical investigations.

These claims receive their most memorable statement in a very compact passage from Marx's 'Preface' to *A Contribution to the Critique of Political Economy*. Although the reliability of the 'Preface' has not gone unchallenged, its authority is bolstered by the fact that Marx refers to it at least twice in *Capital* as a guide to his materialist perspective. The themes of the 'Preface' reverberate throughout the Marxian corpus and must, of course, be interpreted in the light of the elaboration they receive elsewhere. In the 'Preface' Marx contends that the economic structure of society, constituted by its relations of production, is the real foundation of society. It is the basis 'on which rises a legal and political superstructure and to which correspond definite forms of social consciousness'. On the other hand society's relations of production themselves 'correspond to a definite stage of development of [society's] material productive forces'. In this manner, 'the mode of production of material life conditions the social, political and intellectual life process in general'.

As the society's productive forces develop, they clash with existing production relations, which now fetter their growth (see FORCES AND RELATIONS OF PRODUCTION). 'Then begins an epoch of social revolution' as this contradiction divides society and as people become, in a more or less ideological form, 'conscious of this conflict and fight it out.' The conflict is resolved in favour of the productive forces, and new, higher relations of production, whose material preconditions have 'matured in the womb of the old society', emerge which better accommodate the continued growth of society's productive capacity. The bourgeois mode of production represents the most recent of several progressive epochs in the economic formation of society, but it is the last antagonistic form of production. With its demise the prehistory of humanity will come to a close.

As the above illustrates, a core thesis of historical materialism – though one which some Marxists have eschewed – is that the different socio-economic organizations of production which have characterized human history arise or fall as they enable or impede the expansion of society's productive capacity. The growth of the productive forces thus explains the general course of human history. The productive forces, however, include not just the means of production (tools, machines, factories and so on), but labour power – the skills, knowledge, experience, and other human faculties used in work. The productive forces represent the powers society has at its command in material production.

The relations of production, which are said to correspond to society's productive level, link productive forces and human beings in the process of production. These relations are of two broad types: on the one hand those technical relations that are necessary for the actual production process to proceed; on the other the relations of economic control (which are legally manifested as property ownership) that govern access to the forces and products of production.

The contrast is between the material work relations and their socio-economic integument, and Marx pointedly criticizes those who confound the two. Types of economic structure are differentiated by their dominant social production relations. 'Whatever the social form of production, labourers and means of production always remain factors of it. . . . The specific manner in which [their] union is accomplished distinguishes the different economic epochs of the structure of society from one another' (*Capital* II, ch. 1).

The related concept MODE OF PRODUCTION is similarly equivocal. Sometimes Marx uses it in the restricted sense of the technical nature or manner of producing, as when capitalism is said to introduce 'constant daily revolutions in the mode of production'. More frequently, Marx employs the concept in a second sense, namely that of the *social* system (or manner or mode) of producing, which is carried on within, and as a result of, a certain set of ownership relations. Thus, capitalist relations of production define a specific connection between people and productive forces, while the capitalist mode of production involves the production of commodities (see COMMODITY), a certain manner of obtaining surplus, labour time determination of value, and so on. (In addition, Marx sometimes uses 'mode of production' to encompass both the technical and social properties of the way production proceeds.) More than one mode of production may subsist within any actual social formation, but the Introduction to the *Grundrisse* maintains that 'in all forms of society there is one determinate kind of production which assigns ranks and influence to all the others'.

The expansion of the productive forces determines the relations and mode of production which obtain because, as Marx wrote to Annenkov, 'men never relinquish what they have won'. In order to retain 'the fruits of civilization' they will change their way of producing – either their material or social relations of production or both – to accommodate the acquired productive forces and facilitate their continued advance. The resulting economic structure in turn shapes the legal and political superstructure. Thus the productive forces do not fashion the social world directly. Only the broad contours of history, the main forms of society's socio-economic evolution, are set by the development of society's productive capacity.

The relations of production can influence the momentum and qualitative direction of the development of the productive forces. Capitalism in particular is distinguished by its tendency to raise society to a productive level undreamt of before. This is in line with historical materialism, however, since Marx's thesis is that the relations of production which emerge do so precisely because they have the ability to promote the development of society's productive capacity. Relatedly, it is often noted that the productive forces which marked the birth of capitalism are not those forces – for example, the factories and machinery typical of large-scale mechanized production – that are distinctive of capitalism. Historical materialism, though, envisages the emergence of capitalism as a response to the then existing level of productive forces.

Some present-day Marxists deny the dominant role of the productive forces in favour of the idea that relations and forces are mutually determining. But while Marx certainly allows for their interaction and indeed describes specific instances of the relations of production influencing the productive forces, in all his general theoretical pronouncements the basic determination runs the other way. Because historical materialism sees the productive forces as enjoying explanatory primacy, it is able to give an answer to the question of why in general different socio-economic formations arise when they do.

The legal and political institutions of society are clearly superstructural for Marx: their fundamental character is determined by the nature of the existing economic structure. Which other social institutions are properly part of the superstructure is a matter of debate (see BASE AND SUPERSTRUCTURE). Certainly Marx thought that the various spheres and realms of society reflect the dominant mode of production and that the general consciousness of an epoch is shaped by the nature of its production. The Marxist theory of IDEOLOGY contends, in part, that certain ideas originate or are widespread because they sanction existing social relations or promote particular class interests. The economy's determination of legal and political structures, though, will tend to be relatively direct, while its influence over other social realms, culture, and consciousness generally is more attenuated and nuanced. Historical materialism perceives a general hierarchy among the realms of social life, but these relations must be elaborated, not just for society in general, but also for each specific type of socio-economic organization. It is a law for Marx that the superstructure is derived from the base, but this is a law about laws; in each social formation, more specific laws govern the precise nature of this general derivation. In line with this, an important footnote in *Capital* I (ch. 1, sect. 4) suggests that the mode of production of an era determines the relative importance of the various spheres of the social world of that period. The nature and strength of the mechanisms hypothesized by the base-superstructure metaphor, however, are among the most vexed and controversial questions of historical materialism. Marx's theory does not view the superstructure as an epi-phenomenon of the economic base, nor overlook the necessity of legal and political institutions. It is precisely because a superstructure is needed to organize and stabilize society that the economic structure brings about those institutions that are best suited to it. Nor are superstructure and base related like a statue and plinth; that superstructures affect or 'react back on' the base is one of the fundamental tenets of historical materialism.

Law, in particular, is necessary to 'sanction the existing order' and grant it 'independence from mere chance and arbitrariness' (*Capital* III, ch. 47). This function itself gives the legal realm some autonomy since the existing relations of production are represented and legitimated in an abstract, codified form, which in turn fosters the ideological illusion that the law is entirely autonomous with respect to the economic structure. In addition, under capitalism the 'fictio juris of a contract' between free agents obscures the real nature of production, in particular, the 'invisible threads' which bind the wage-labourer to capital (*Capital* I, ch. 23). In precapitalist societies, for example in feudalism, tradition and custom perform a similar stabilizing function and may also win a degree of autonomy. There, the true nature of the social relations of production is obscured by entanglement with the relations of personal domination which characterize the other spheres of feudal life.

Marx's stress on class analysis, surprisingly

absent from the 'Preface', connects with the above themes of historical materialism in several significant ways. In the social organization of production, people stand in different relations to the forces and products of production and in any given mode of production these relations will be of certain characteristic sorts. The individual's economic position as that is understood in terms of the existing social production relations establishes certain material interests in common with others and determines class membership. Hence follow the familiar definitions of the bourgeoisie and proletariat by reference to the purchase and sale, respectively, of labour power (and the underlying ownership or non-ownership of the means of production).

A central thesis of historical materialism is that class position, so defined, determines the characteristic consciousness or world view of its members. For example Marx's discussion of the Legitimists and Orleanists in *18th Brumaire* emphasizes that on the basis of its socio-economic position each class creates 'an entire superstructure of distinct and peculiarly formed sentiments, illusions, modes of thought and views of life'. The differing material interests of classes divide them and lead to their struggle. Classes differ in the extent to which their members perceive themselves as a class, so that antagonisms between classes may not be discerned by the participants, or may be understood only in a mystified or ideological form (see CLASS CONSCIOUSNESS).

The ultimate success or failure of a class is determined by its relation to the advance of the productive forces. In the words of *German Ideology*, 'the conditions under which definite productive forces can be applied are the conditions of the rule of a definite class of society'. That class which has the capacity and the incentive to introduce or preserve the relations of production required to accommodate the advance of the productive forces has its hegemony ensured. Thus Marx thought that the eventual success of the proletarian cause, like the earlier rise of the bourgeoisie, was guaranteed by the fundamental currents of history while, for example, the heroic slave revolts of the ancient world were doomed to failure. Historical materialism views class rule, hitherto, as both inevitable and necessary to force the productivity of the direct producers beyond the subsistence level. 'No antagonism, no progress', states *The Poverty of Philosophy* (ch. I). 'This is the law that civilization has followed. . . . Till now the productive forces have been developed by virtue of this system of class antagonism.' The productive progress brought by capitalism, however, eliminates both the feasibility of, and the historical rationale for, class rule. Since the state is primarily the vehicle by which a class secures its rule, it will wither away in post-class society.

Historical materialism contends that class conflict and the basic trajectory of human history is accounted for by the advance of the productive forces. Their advance, however, must be understood in terms of a theoretical model that reveals the character of the specific modes of production involved. Such a theory will be very abstract with regard to any particular society. Thus, for example, Marx presents the evolution of capitalism in abstraction from the specific physiognomy of any particular capitalist nation state. *Capital* underwrites the claim that socialism is 'inevitable', but by the same token it does not empower one to predict the arrival of socialism at any particular time or place – only to affirm that the tendency of capitalist development is such as to bring it about. Nor does the specific course of each society simply repeat some universal dialectic of forces and relations of production. Societies are rarely isolated, untouched and uninfluenced by productive advances outside them. Accordingly, every social group of the globe is not fated to pass through the same stages of economic development, nor is the evolution of any particular social formation solely a matter of internal productive events. Although historical materialism permits countries to lag behind or even skip steps, their course must still be accounted for within the over-arching pattern of socioeconomic evolution, and that development is due to the productive forces.

The 'Preface' designates the Asiatic, ancient, feudal, and modern bourgeois modes of production as the major epochs in humanity's advance, but these mark the general stages of socioeconomic evolution as a whole – not the steps which history obliges every nation, without exception, to climb (see STAGES OF DEVELOPMENT). In a famous letter of November 1877, Marx characteristically denied propounding 'any historico-philosophical theory of the *marche*

générale imposed by fate upon every people'; but this oft-quoted remark does not amount to a rejection of historical determinism. Marx could consistently believe in a necessary, productive-force-determined evolution of history without holding that every social group is preordained to follow the same course. It seems likely, in fact, that Marx would have been willing to revise his particular tabulation of historical periods (or at least the pre-feudal ones), since he did not analyse in detail humanity's early modes of production. Modification of Marx's historical schema as well as of his analysis of capitalism (and the projected transition to socialism) is in principle compatible with the basic tenets of historical materialism. It should be borne in mind that historical materialism does not pretend to explain every last detail of history. From its broad purview, many historical events, and certainly the specific forms they take, are accidental. Nor does the theory seek to explain scientifically individual behaviour, though it attempts to situate that behaviour within its historical confines. In so far as there are ineluctable tendencies in history, these result from, not despite, the choices of individuals. The explanatory ambitions of historical materialism as a social-scientific theory do not commit it to philosophical determinism.

Because historical materialism is so central to Marxism, diverse political and intellectual currents in Marxism have frequently distinguished themselves by their differing interpretations of that theory. One fairly standard interpretation has been presented above, but controversy rages over the basic concepts and theorems of the theory, and the relative importance of its various components. The task of rendering historical materialism as an empirically plausible theory without reducing it to a collection of truisms has proved very formidable. Given the far-ranging claims of the theory and the lack of an interpretative consensus, an accurate assessment of its viability is exceedingly difficult.

Reading

Balibar, Étienne 1970: 'The Basic Concepts of Historical Materialism'. In Louis Althusser and Étienne Balibar, *Reading 'Capital'*.

Bukharin, Nikolai 1925: *Historical Materialism*.

Cohen, G. A. 1978: *Karl Marx's Theory of History: A Defence*.

Evans, Michael 1975: *Karl Marx*.

McMurtry, John 1978: *The Structure of Marx's World-View*.

Plekhanov, Georgii V. 1972: *The Development of the Monist View of History*.

Shaw, William H. 1978: *Marx's Theory of History*.

Witt-Hansen, J. 1960: *Historical Materialism: The Method, the Theories*.

Wood, Allen W. 1981: *Karl Marx*.

WILLIAM H. SHAW

historicism The uses of the term 'historicism' are, in Marxist thought, almost as protean as its original meanings in pre-Hegelian German social thought. There are two main senses:

First, there is the historicism associated with the work of Karl Popper. For Popper, Hegel and Marx are guilty of the misguided and noxious view that history has a pattern and a meaning that, if grasped, can be used in the present to predict and fashion the future. The conflation of metaphysics and history involved in Popper's version of historicism may have been present in Hegel but it is not characteristic of the main thrust of Marx's work. It was Marx's view that history itself had no meaning beyond that which men in their varying stages of development assigned to it. It is also obvious that there have been subsequent versions of Marxism where allegedly superior insight into the 'laws of history' helped to justify and sustain the totalitarian politics Popper associated with historicism. Equally, the question of whether Marx's own thought is to be judged historicist is bound up with the question of its scientific character, with his critique of utopianism, and with the status of his predictions.

The second current sense of the term – in many ways the opposite of the above – is found in the historical relativism of the 'return to Hegel' in the works of the young Lukács, Korsch, and to some extent, Gramsci. Korsch, referring explicitly to Hegel, claimed that 'we must try to understand every change, development and version of Marxist theory, since its original emergence from the philosophy of German idealism, as a necessary product of its epoch'. In the same sense, Gramsci, in his critique of Bukharin could refer to Marxism as an 'absolute historicism'. The main critic of this version of Marxism is Althusser who in the fifth chapter of *Reading 'Capital'* makes historicism,

together with humanism, the main object of his attack. Principally involved in this debate are, once again, the nature of Marx's science and also the complex question of the relationship of Marx to Hegel. (See also HEGEL AND MARX; HISTORICAL MATERIALISM; MARXISM, DEVELOPMENT OF; PROGRESS.)

Reading

Althusser, Louis and Balibar, É. 1970: *Reading 'Capital'*.

Gramsci, Antonio 1929–35 (*1971*): 'Critical Notes on an Attempt at Popular Sociology'. In *Selections from the Prison Notebooks*.

Korsch, Karl 1923 (*1970*): *Marxism and Philosophy*.

Lukács, Georg 1923 (*1971*): *History and Class Consciousness*.

Popper, Karl R. 1957: *The Poverty of Historicism*.

DAVID MCLELLAN

historiography Germans with their lack of a national state and history, the *German Ideology* (pt. I, sect. 1A) declared, could not think realistically about the past as Frenchmen or Englishmen could, but imagined that the motive force of history was religion. Marx continued to take a poor view even of the most eminent German historians, like Ranke, 'the bouncing little root-grubber', who reduced history to 'facile anecdote-mongering and the attribution of all great events to petty and mean causes' (letter to Engels, 7 September 1864). Of non-Germans, Guizot was one who had early impressed Marx, with a study of the English revolution and recognition of its affinities with 1789; though he was not slow to find faults in Guizot's handling of it, especially as being too narrowly political.

Engels was more of a born historian than his friend, drawn both to the writing of history and to the theory of how it ought to be written. Incomprehension of the historical process was one of very many failings with which he taxed Eugen Dühring. He accused him of seeing only a repulsive record of ignorance, barbarity, violence, to the neglect of the hidden evolution going on 'behind these noisy scenes on the stage' (*Anti-Dühring*, pt. 1, ch. 11; pt. 2, ch. 2). In the same work he insisted that political economy must be treated as a '*historical* science', since it dealt with material constantly changing (pt. 2, ch. 1). Some historians, in England for instance, were just beginning to be conscious of their bad habit, which Engels complained of in a letter to Mehring (14 July 1893), of breaking history up into religious, legal, political, and so on, as if these were all separate compartments.

It has been a criticism of Engels himself that in setting out to compose a work such as his book on the peasant war of 1524–5 in Germany he was not seeking truth through original research so much as taking from previous publications whatever would support a preconceived thesis. In later days at any rate he was fully aware of the danger of over-simple procedures, and at the very end of his life he was planning a thorough revision of his *Peasant War*. He had as a pupil the young Kautsky, whom at first he felt in duty bound to criticize unsparingly for his slapdash style of work, worsened by an Austrian schooling which neglected careful preparation. He had 'absolutely no idea of what really scientific work means', Engels wrote to Bebel in 1885 (24 July). Kautsky profited by instruction, and went on to make important contributions. He emphasized the great practical influence of historical knowledge on events, military above all. He made shrewd comments on the way history was written by non-Marxists. Mommsen's admiring portrait of Caesar first appeared in 1854, he pointed out, a few years after 1848 and the Paris workers' insurrection, at a time when Napoleon III was being exalted by many liberals, especially in Germany, as saviour of society, and was himself helping to promote a cult of Julius Caesar (1908, p. 168).

In Russia leading socialists like Lenin took history no less seriously. Bukharin had much to say about the idealism which he found running through historiography and other social sciences, from Bossuet with his notion of the record of the past as manifestation of God's guidance of man, down to Lessing, Fichte, Schelling, Hegel, and obscuring everything with 'downright mysticism, or other tomfoolery' (1921, p. 59). After the 1917 revolution use had to be made of any historians available, as of experts in all other departments, but with an endeavour to shepherd them towards the Marxist point of view. In 1925 a Society of Marxist Historians was set up in which the old Bolshevik and historian Pokrovsky had a leading part as intermediary between scholars and officialdom.

He began, Enteen (1978) shows, by trying to temper the wind to the shorn sheep of the old school, and to foster peaceful coexistence between Marxist and non-Marxist; but by 1928 this was becoming difficult, and from 1931 Stalin's heavy-handed intervention was casting a blight, as Deutscher was to write, on the ambitious and enthusiastic plans with which Soviet historiography had set out, and the history of the Bolshevik party sponsored by Stalin, 'that bizarre and crude compendium of Stalinist myths', was held up as a model. 'Western historiography', Deutscher added, 'has rarely been guilty of wholesale falsification, but it has not been innocent of suppression of facts.' Deutscher was paying tribute to E. H. Carr, as 'the first genuine historian of the Soviet régime', though 'primarily of institutions and policies', with less interest than a Marxist would have in social underpinnings (1955, pp. 91–5).

It was not in the Soviet Union alone that history was suffering propagandist distortions. Among the chief problems Gramsci set himself in prison was that of weighing up the tendencies represented by his countryman Croce's two main historical works, on nineteenth-century Europe and Italy. Gramsci thought it wrong of Croce to begin them at 1815 and 1871, thus omitting the struggles of the French Revolutionary and Napoleonic era, and the Risorgimento: such a choice suggested a desire to steer readers towards unrevolutionary ideas about the present, which, as things were, meant steering them towards fascism (1971, pp. 118–19).

It was not hard for Soviet spokesmen to retort to Western criticism when, in the Cold War years, the objectivity on which Western scholarship prided itself was so heavily compromised in America, and in a much lesser degree in Europe, with recovery slow and as yet not complete. One counter-attack was directed against the proliferating literature in America on Soviet nationalities policy. It was accused of identifying itself with the propaganda of Ukrainian and Central Asian nationalist émigrés, and misrepresenting such things as the opening up of Kazakhstan to grain production as 'colonization', on a par with that of the American West at the expense of its native inhabitants (Zenushkina 1975, pp. 9, 284). A writer who pressed these charges admitted on the other hand that Soviet writings during the turmoil of the 1920s were often uncritical:

'Soviet history as a science was still in its infancy' (ibid. pp. 14–15).

More generally the Soviet writer I. S. Kon in 1960 blamed Western historians for succumbing to reactionary religious thinking, like that of Jacques Maritain who was reviving the Christian philosophy of history as governed by the transcendental, or of Berdyaev with his pessimistic depreciation of this world and its affairs by comparison with eternity. In the West any evolutionary vision was being abandoned, Kon asserted, in favour of the concept of 'multiple, independent, self-contained cycles, "cultures" (Spengler), "civilizations" (Toynbee), or, to use Rothacker's expression, "styles of life"'; or in favour of relativism like that of C. Beard, according to which every historian, every generation, has a valid right to a private image of the past (Kon 1960). Another Soviet critic, Glezerman, joining in the continuing controversy between Marxists and Weberians, found fault with the latter for seeing no more in feudalism or capitalism than abstract conceptions, mental constructs. Toynbee's scheme of world history he regarded as designed to combat Marx's division of it into modes of production, substituting detached 'civilizations' for socio-economic formations. He noted how current bourgeois scholarship, as represented for instance at the Third World Congress of Sociology in 1956, was renouncing any thought of historical progress or development, and putting in its place the neutral label of 'change' (Glezerman 1960, pp. 179, 183–4).

Against any tendencies towards obscurantism or inertia a powerful countercurrent was represented by the journal *Annales* (see ANNALES SCHOOL), which has done much to put France in the lead among history-writing nations. Founded in the inter-war years, under the inspiration of Marc Bloch and Lucien Febvre, with Fernand Braudel as an outstanding successor, in the 1950s and 1960s it achieved a unique position. It set itself militantly against all blinkered or hidebound ways of thinking, confronting them with a large vision of history as the leading social science, a guide to all others. Lending a strong impetus to research it encouraged all kinds of novel speculation and experimental method, amid which Marxism was able to exert a distinct influence, and at the same time acquire fresh vitality by freeing itself from Soviet stereotypes.

In Britain a similar new departure came independently with the launching in 1952 of another journal of history and historical ideas, *Past and Present*. This was initiated by a communist group, not however as a definitively Marxist organ but as openmindedly rational and progressive, a break with the cramping prejudices of the Cold War. It evolved after its early years into something still more broadly liberal, and acquired a special place and reputation in the English-speaking world while remaining a journal where Marxist interpretations were at home. Thanks to widening debate and exchange of ideas the gulf between Marxist and other thinking in Western historiography has greatly narrowed, and the importance of the former is nowadays acknowledged; though the latter has been attracted of late to some new approaches, such as 'bio-history' or 'psycho-history', scarcely to be reconciled with Marxist methodology. It must be added that in the past decade there have been symptoms in some Western quarters of a desire to reverse the growing intellectual influence of Marxism by disparaging its methods and achievements.

Reading

Bukharin, N. I. 1921 (1925): *Historical Materialism. A System of Sociology*.

Deutscher, Isaac 1955 (1969): *Heretics and Renegades*.

Enteen, George M. 1978: *The Soviet Scholar-Bureaucrat. M. N. Pokrovskii and the Society of Marxist Historians*.

Glezerman, G. 1960: *The Laws of Social Development*.

Gramsci, Antonio 1929–35 (1971): *Selections from the Prison Notebooks*.

Kon, I. S. 1960 (1967): 'The Idea of Historical Change and Progress'. In M. Jaworsky ed. *Soviet Political Thought*.

Lukács, Georg 1937 (1962): *The Historical Novel*.

Zenushkina, L. 1975: *Soviet Nationalities Policy and Bourgeois Historians*.

V. G. KIERNAN

History and Class Consciousness First published in Berlin in 1923, this collection of closely interconnected essays by György LUKÁCS is one of the most influential theoretical works of the twentieth century. Written between March 1919 – when Lukács was People's Commissar for

Education and Culture in the short-lived Hungarian Council Republic – and Christmas 1922, *History and Class Consciousness* has deeply affected debates in sociology, politics and philosophy ever since.

The essays of this volume range from the discussion of 'Class Consciousness', 'The Marxism of Rosa Luxemburg' and 'The Changing Function of Historical Materialism' to assessing the nature of 'Orthodoxy in Marxism' and the relationship between 'Legality and Illegality', sketching at the same time the outlines of a 'Methodology of the Problem of Organization'. However, by far the most important essay of *History and Class Consciousness*, making up nearly one half of the entire volume, is 'Reification and the Consciousness of the Proletariat'. One of the principal achievements of this study is that it reconstructed with great insight Marx's theory of alienation ten years prior to the publication of the *Economic and Philosophical Manuscripts of 1844*, even if it did so in a Hegelian key. Moreover, it offers, in another section of the same essay, a powerful critique of the 'antinomies of bourgeois thought', together with the elaboration of their positive counterpart, summed up by Lukács as 'the standpoint of totality'.

History and Class Consciousness argued that the individual can never become the orienting measure of philosophy, or indeed of emancipatory action. For he is of necessity confronted by 'a complex of ready-made and unalterable objects which allow him only the subjective responses of recognition or rejection. Only the class can relate to the whole of reality in a practical revolutionary way' (*1971*, p. 193), on condition that its members free themselves from the paralysing force of 'reified objectivity'. This could be accomplished in Lukács's view only by successfully articulating the proletarian standpoint of totality in a morally fitting institutional form. The collective agency of revolutionary transformation was therefore characterized by the author of *History and Class Consciousness* in terms of '*imputed*' or '*ascribed consciousness*', opposing the latter to the '*psychological consciousness*' of the empirically existing proletariat, dominated by the reified objectivity of the capitalist system. At the same time, he insisted that class consciousness was also the ETHICS of the proletariat, and its party could not

be considered the 'organized incarnation of proletarian class consciousness' unless it fully lived up to its historical role of being 'the incarnation of the ethics of the fighting proletariat' (p. 42). In this way, Lukács counterposed an idealized conception of the party to the ongoing bureaucratization of the communist movement, criticizing such developments under the code-name of 'the parties of the old type'. As a result he was severely attacked by high-ranking Comintern figures, including Zinoviev. Only in 1967 could he openly defend the achievements of *History and Class Consciousness* in a long preface to the new edition, distancing himself from it on philosophical grounds – mainly on account of its Hegelian ingredients – from the vantage point of his systematic *Ontology of Social Being*.

The activist stance of *History and Class Consciousness*, stressing the seminal importance of ideology, was always the secret of its success. It not only influenced Gramsci, Korsch and some major figures of the FRANKFURT SCHOOL (e.g. Benjamin and Marcuse) in the 1920s and 1930s, but made a considerable impact even in the 1950s in France (from Merleau-Ponty's praise of it as the originator of WESTERN MARXISM to the intellectuals grouped around the journal *Arguments*), and in the late 1960s on the student movement, particularly in Germany.

Yet this ideology-centred activism was also one of the most problematical characteristics of this work. For the author greatly underestimated the material power of global capital, describing its adaptive features as 'the capitulation of the class consciousness of the bourgeoisie before that of the proletariat' (p. 67). In this spirit, he postulated that the reason why capitalism was not yet collapsing was because 'the *objectively* extremely precarious position of bourgeois society is endowed *in the minds of the workers* with its erstwhile stability' (p. 31). Thus he anticipated 'the certainty that capitalism is doomed' (p. 43) on methodological grounds, insisting that the victory 'can be *guaranteed methodologically* – by the dialectical method' (ibid.). He thought that the real issue was the proletariat's '*ideological crisis*' (p. 67) both in theoretical and in organizational terms, concluding that the outcome of the 'final battle depends on closing the gap between the psychological consciousness and the imputed one' (p. 74). The adoption of Hegel's 'identical

Subject/Object' in characterization of the new historical agency – rightly described in the 1967 Preface to *History and Class Consciousness* as an attempt to 'out-Hegel Hegel' – and the role ascribed to methodology (restated uncritically in the same preface) were well in tune with this noble voluntarist vision of ideology and the 'struggle for consciousness' that it advocated (p. 68).

Reading

Cerutti, Furio *et al.* 1971: *Geschichte und Klassenbewusstsein Heute.*

Lukács, György 1923 (1971): *History and Class Consciousness.*

Merleau-Ponty, Maurice 1955 (1973): *Adventures of the Dialectic.*

Mészáros, István, ed. 1971: *Aspects of History and Class Consciousness.*

ISTVÁN MÉSZÁROS

Horkheimer, Max Born 14 February 1895, Stuttgart; died 7 July 1973, Nuremberg. Studied at the universities of Munich, Freiburg and Frankfurt, initially in psychology but later primarily in philosophy. Completed his doctorate on Kant in 1923. He became enormously influential as director of the Institute of Social Research in Frankfurt from 1930, bringing together those who became known as the FRANKFURT SCHOOL. Although trained as a philosopher, his broad knowledge of the social sciences proved decisive in the School's development (Dubiel 1978; Held 1980). He was critical of the type of Marxism promulgated by the Second and Third Internationals, taking issue, specifically, with all 'determinist' and 'positivist' interpretations of historical materialism. The philosophical and political regeneration of Marxism was the centre of his work.

Under Horkheimer's directorship the Institute of Social Research was oriented to the development of a critical theory of society. Although his position changed considerably over time, he emphasized at least three elements in this project. First, there was the idea of a critique of ideology which he took to be similar in structure to Marx's critique of capitalist commodity production and exchange. Second, there was a stress on the necessity of reintegrating disciplines through interdisciplinary research.

Third, there was an emphasis on the central role of PRAXIS in the ultimate verification of theories: the claim of critique to be the 'potential critical self-awareness of society' had to be upheld in practice.

Among Horkheimer's most important achievements are an elaboration of the philosophical basis of critical theory and a critique of empiricism and positivism (1947), a major analysis (with Adorno) of the origin and nature of instrumental reason (1947), an account of the commodification of modern culture (1968), an exploration of the way authoritarianism crystallizes at the intersection of the economic structure of capitalist society and its ideological superstructure, that is at the point of the patriarchal family (1939), and a vast array of commentaries on contemporary culture and politics (1974).

Reading

Adorno, Theodor and Horkheimer, Max 1947 (1972): *Dialectic of Enlightenment.*

Dubiel, Helmut 1978: *Wissenschaftsorganisation und politische Erfahrung.*

Held, David 1980: *Introduction to Critical Theory: Horkheimer to Habermas.*

Horkheimer, Max 1939: 'Die Juden und Europa'.

— 1947: *Eclipse of Reason.*

— 1968 (1972): *Critical Theory.* (This volume includes 'Art and Mass Culture', 'Authority and the Family' and 'Traditional and Critical Theory', essays written in the 1930s and early 1940s.)

— 1974: *Notizen 1950 bis 1969 und Dämmerung.*

Schmidt, Alfred 1974: *Zur Idee der Kritischen Theorie: Elemente der Philosophie Max Horkheimers.*

DAVID HELD

human nature The notion of human nature involves the belief that all human individuals share some common features. If these are construed as actually manifested characteristics, the notion of human nature is descriptive. The notion is normative when it embraces potential dispositions which tend and ought to be manifested under appropriate conditions.

The descriptive concept embraces an increasingly rich amount of reliable objective information about human beings in history. These data constitute the empirical scientific ground for any sound theory of human nature. Yet a purely descriptive approach suffers from the customary weakness of positive science and historiography. (1) As a consequence of the academic division of labour and narrow specialization there is a tendency to reduce human nature to only one of its dimensions; biological (aggressivity, jealous concern about territory, subordination to the dominant male), sociological (prohibition of incest in the view of Lévi-Strauss), or psychological (*libido* and other instincts in Freud). (2) The descriptive concept is supposed to be value free, but this claim is usually false; empirical scientific research is invariably guided by certain (more or less unconscious) interests and at least implicitly it involves some value-laden conceptions. If the claim were true, however, the descriptive concept would lack important practical insights into basic constraints and optimal possibilities for human self-development. (3) The dichotomy between structuralism and historicism cannot be overcome within the descriptive concept. Analytical, structure-oriented empirical research programmes construe human nature as a set of permanent ahistorical models of behaviour. A historical approach emphasizes differences in behavioural patterns, in customs and norms, in different places and times; it ends in relativism.

The normative point of view escapes relativism and provides a theoretical foundation for critical analysis and evaluation. However it often has a metaphysical character, i.e. it postulates a structure of human beings the validity of which cannot be tested even in principle. Hobbes, for example, considered that an egoistic desire for power was the basic feature. This desire is manifested only in a state of nature, which is a hypothetical construct; consequently, no possible evidence either confirms or refutes Hobbes's theory. Preference for one such theory over another does not depend so much on good reasons showing that one fits reality better than another, but is a matter of a particular interest. In this sense normative conceptions tend to have an ideological function. By construing certain historically limited forms of human life as natural, lasting, necessary ones, they rationalize and legitimate particular interests of dominant social groups. There is hardly any great ideologue who does not try to 'derive' his theories from an appropriate 'image' of man. Machiavelli's advice to his imaginary prince not to rule by law alone

but also to resort to force, follows from his view of man as 'ungrateful, fickle, false, coward, covetous'. Cruelty is advisable because 'it is much safer to be feared than loved'. All conservative advocates of law and order derive the legitimacy of a coercive state machinery from the view of human beings as naturally egoistic, aggressive, acquisitive, primarily interested in the satisfaction of their own appetites. All ideologues of *laissez-faire* capitalism agree with Malthus (1798) that men are 'really inert, sluggish, averse from labour, unless compelled by necessity'. As liberalism gradually gives way to state-bureaucratism, domination and hierarchy are more and more stressed as central genetic characteristics of the human species. According to Desmond Morris (1967): 'As primates we are already loaded with the hierarchy system. This is the basic way of primate life.'

Correlations between ideologies (see IDEOLOGY) and conceptions of human nature can be expressed in three simple rules: *Status quo* ideologies tend to develop sceptical views. One variant of this scepticism is reluctance to endorse any structural change because there are animal instincts in human beings which must not be unleashed. Another variant is the rejection of the very idea of human nature as a metaphysical concept. In the absence of any anthropological ground for a long-range project of radical social change the only reasonable alternative is held to be cautious growth governed by the method of trial and error. Future-oriented theorists, radically opposed to the injustices of existing society, tend to be very optimistic in their conceptions of human nature. Sometimes the faith in essential human goodness compensates for the hopelessness of the situation and the difficulty of the revolutionary task. The more an ideology is past-oriented, and expresses the interests of those who hope to restore historically obsolete structures of domination, the gloomier and more cynical its view of human beings, who are considered basically evil (lazy, aggressive, egoistic, greedy, acquisitive, even brutish). The worse their image, the less hope for any project of social improvement, the more justification for restrictions of freedom.

Marx described his position as a unity of naturalism and humanism. Naturalism is the view that man is part of nature. He has not been created by some transcendental spiritual agency, but is the product of a long biological evolution, which at a certain point enters a new specific form of development, human history, characterized by an autonomous, self-reflective, creative way of acting – PRAXIS. Thus man is essentially a *being of praxis*. Humanism is the view that as a being of praxis man both changes nature and creates himself. He acquires more and more control over blind natural forces and produces a new humanized natural environment. On the other hand he produces a wealth of his own capacities and needs, which then becomes a starting point for a new self-development.

Marx did not develop a systematic theory of human nature but he made several contributions of lasting value (not only in his early philosophical writings but also in his mature scientific works). First, he showed how human nature can be constructed as a dynamic, historical concept without lapsing into relativism. It must include both universal invariants and constituents that vary from epoch to epoch: 'If one wants to judge all human acts, movements, relations etc. in accordance with the principle of utility one must first deal with human nature in general and then with human nature as modified in each historical epoch' (*Capital* I, ch. 22). Second, Marx transcended the dichotomy between egoistic individualism and abstract, primitive collectivism. A human individual is at the same time a *unique person*, concerned with self-affirmation and objectification of his subjective powers, and a social being, since all his powers are socially moulded and his creative activity satisfies the needs of others. 'It is above all necessary to avoid postulating "society" once again as an abstraction over against the individual. The individual *is* a social being' (*Economic and Philosophical Manuscripts*, Third manuscript). Third, Marx gave new life to Aristotle's distinction between *actuality* and *potentiality*. No matter how degraded and alienated actual human existence might be, man always preserves a potential for emancipation and creativity. Fourth, Marx specified the conditions under which human potentiality is crippled and wasted: the division of labour, private property, capital, state oppression, false ideological consciousness. Their abolition is a necessary condition of universal emancipation.

When Marx's views (expounded in various fragments, against different opponents at different stages of his development) are put together, considerable difficulties become apparent. There is a normative concept of human nature in the *Economic and Philosophical Manuscripts*, in terms of human freedom, productivity, creativity, sociality, wealth of needs, increasing power of the human senses. One year later in the *Theses on Feuerbach* Marx defines human essence as an '*ensemble* of social relations'. The latter is a descriptive concept which cannot be used for a critique of the existing society. The normative concept is completely optimistic. Negative human characteristics are interpreted as mere facticity, as transient features likely to disappear when the unfavourable conditions which produced them are removed. However, many experiences during the turbulent and dramatic century since Marx's death suggest that the evil may be more deep-rooted. Moreover, the concept of human nature lacks an inner dialectic. Since it is a historical concept, and its development cannot be determined by external causes, the source of man's self-creation must be in the inner contradictions of human nature. Rather than qualifying the positive as the 'essence', and the negative as the 'facticity', one has to recognize the conflict of general human dispositions in the 'essence' itself.

There is a basic division among Marxists on the issue of human nature and the humanist tradition in Marx. Official ideology in the countries of 'real socialism' dismisses the very idea of a general human nature because of its alleged incompatibility with the BASE AND SUPERSTRUCTURE model and with the theory of class struggle. The only general characteristics which human beings have, according to the requirements of historical materialism, are those which are determined by a definite mode of production and must have a class character. Marxist STRUCTURALISM (e.g. Althusser) follows the same line in a more sophisticated way, introducing the idea of an unbridgeable gap between various types of social structure. Consequently, there is no transepochal human nature which undergoes a process of totalization (see TOTALITY).

For those Marxists who identify themselves as humanists and critical theorists the concept of human nature is of crucial importance for at least two reasons. First, radical social critique is ultimately a critique of the human condition and without knowing what human beings are it would not be possible to establish what is negative in the human condition in various epochs. Second, the concept of human history would lose any sense, and would have to disintegrate into histories of various epochs, had there not been something invariant through all changes; namely, the human being in history. Some Marxist humanists offer rather uncritical orthodox interpretations of basic issues, leaving the problems open, while others try to solve them by reconstructing historical materialism and Marx's philosophical anthropology. Rigid determinism in history is rejected and the view is adopted that the emancipation and self-realization of man as a being of free and creative activity (praxis) is not necessary but only possible. Analysis of human potential for praxis leads to the establishment of a set of universal human capacities (e.g. unlimited cultivation of the senses, symbolic communication, conceptual thinking and problem-solving, autonomous innovative activity, ability to harmonize relations with other individuals in a community). These are not essences but latent dispositions which are constantly in conflict with opposite dispositions (to act heteronomously and repetitively, even destructively, to substitute dominating power for creative power, to use communicative means in order to set up barriers rather than bridges towards other communities, to act aggressively). The conflict of these opposite dispositions (which enters into the descriptive concept of human nature) constitutes the source of historical dialectics.

The normative concept of human nature, which provides the ground of the entire humanist critique, presupposes a basic criterion of evaluation of various conflicting dispositions. Those dispositions would be judged positive, and worth attempting to realize, which are (1) specifically human and (2) responsible for historical periods of truly impressive development. Thus only humans, of all living organisms, communicate in symbols and think conceptually. Life in peace, freedom and creativity has made accelerated evolution and the flowering of culture possible. Aggressiveness and destructiveness brought about periods of stagnation and decay. While these are all recognized as constituents of actually existing human nature, the potential for *praxis* is the ideal end which gives a sense of direction to human self-creation in history.

Reading

Althusser, Louis 1965 (1969): For Marx.

Fromm, Erich 1961: Marx's Concept of Man.

— 1973: The Anatomy of Human Destructiveness.

Hobbes, Thomas 1651: Leviathan, pt. I, ch. 13.

Lukács, György 1923 (1971): History and Class Consciousness.

Marković, Mihailo 1974: The Contemporary Marx, ch. IV.

Petrović, Gajo 1967: Marx in the Mid-Twentieth Century.

Schaff, Adam 1963: A Philosophy of Man.

Venable, Vernon 1945 (1966): Human Nature: The Marxian View.

MIHAILO MARKOVIĆ

I

idealism Marx was opposed to idealism in its metaphysical, historical and ethical forms. Metaphysical idealism sees reality as consisting in, or depending upon (finite or infinite) minds or (particular or transcendent) ideas; historical idealism locates the primary or sole motor of historical change in agency, ideas or consciousness; ethical idealism projects an empirically ungrounded ('higher' or 'better') state as a way of judging or rationalizing action. Marx's anti-idealism, or 'materialism', was not intended to deny the existence and/or causal efficacy of ideas (on the contrary, in contradistinction to reductionist materialism, it insisted upon it), but the autonomy and/or explanatory primacy attributed to them.

Marx's works between 1843 and 1847 may be regarded as an extended critique of idealism, in the course of which he and Engels at once settled accounts with their 'erstwhile philosophical conscience' and began to chart the terrain of their proto-scientific investigations. This critique was composed in a double movement: in the first, characteristically Feuerbachian, moment ideas are situated as the properties of finite embodied minds; in the second, distinctively Marxian, moment, these minds are in turn situated as products of historically developing social relations.

As Marx worked through the first moment it was initially focused on the Hegelian DIALECTIC and consisted in a critique of Hegel's triple subject-predicate inversions, directed against Hegel's absolute idealist ontology, speculative rationalist epistemology, and substantive idealist sociology, and of the Hegelian identification of the topics of the inversions – first of the reduction of being to knowing, whose esoteric condition Marx isolates as an uncritical positivism, then of the reduction of science to philosophy, whose consequence Marx shows to be the total pliability of ideology. Having completed the Feuerbachian critique of idealism, Marx now replaces the Feuerbachian problematic of a fixed HUMAN NATURE with the historico-materialist problematic of a developing human sociality: 'The human essence is no abstraction inherent in each single individual. In its reality it is the ensemble of social relations' (*Theses on Feuerbach*, 6th thesis). At the same time Marx insists that history is '*nothing* but the activity of men in pursuit of their ends (*The Holy Family*); he is as anxious to avoid ontological hypostases as essentialist individualism, REIFICATION as much as voluntarism, as he formulates his conception of the reproduction and transformation of social forms, and the historical process generally, in human PRAXIS or labour.

While Engels and Lenin both conducted vigorous polemics against scepticism and subjective idealism, the dialectical materialist tradition they inaugurated has often lapsed into a dogmatic and contemplative materialism. On the other hand WESTERN MARXISM, launched by Lukács and Korsch, in re-emphasizing the subjective and critical aspects of Marx's materialism, has often tended to some form or other of epistemological idealism. Marx's 'ethical naturalism' was rejected both by the Kantians of the Second International and by many of the humanist and existentialist philosophies that sprang up in the post-second world war post-Stalin period. At the same time the exact meaning and status of HISTORICAL MATERIALISM is a matter of dispute at the present time. So, in one way or another, the issue of idealism remains, as it was in the beginning, near the centre of Marxist thought. (See also KNOWLEDGE, THEORY OF.)

ROY BHASKAR

ideology Two strands of previous critical philosophical thought directly influence Marx's and Engels's concept of ideology: on the one hand the critique of religion developed by French materialism and by Feuerbach, and on the other, the critique of traditional epistemology and the revaluation of the subject's activity carried out by the German philosophy of consciousness (see IDEALISM) and especially by Hegel. Yet whereas these critiques did not succeed in connecting religious or metaphysical distortions with specific social conditions, the critique by Marx and Engels seeks to show the existence of a necessary link between 'inverted' forms of consciousness and men's material existence. It is this relationship that the concept of ideology expresses by referring to a distortion of thought which stems from, and conceals, social contradictions (see CONTRADICTION). Consequently, from its inception ideology has a clear-cut negative and critical connotation.

In contrast with a purely synchronic reading of Marx's writings, it is necessary to consider the concept of ideology within the context of various stages of Marx's intellectual development while denying any dramatic 'epistemological break' between them. A basic nucleus of meaning finds new dimensions as Marx develops his position and tackles new issues. The first stage comprises Marx's early writings and extends to 1844. The hallmark of this period is a philosophical debate in which the main points of reference are Hegel and Feuerbach. The term ideology still does not appear in Marx's writings, but the material elements of the future concept are already present in his critique of religion and of the Hegelian conception of the state which are described as 'inversions' concealing the real character of things. The Hegelian 'inversion' consists in converting the subjective into the objective and vice-versa, so that starting from the assumption that the Idea necessarily manifests itself in the empirical world, the Prussian state appears as the self-realization of the Idea, as the 'absolute universal' which determines civil society instead of being determined by it.

However, the Hegelian inversion is not the product of an illusory perception. If Hegel's point of view is abstract it is because 'the "abstraction" is that of the political state'. (*Critique of Hegel's Philosophy of the State*, The Legislature). In this sense it is maintained that the source of the ideological inversion is an inversion in reality itself. The same idea informs

Marx's critique of religion. Although he accepts Feuerbach's basic tenet that man makes religion and that the idea that God makes man is an inversion, he goes further than Feuerbach in arguing that this inversion is more than a philosophical alienation or mere illusion; it expresses the contradictions and sufferings of the real world. The state and society produce religion, 'which is an inverted consciousness of the world, because they are an inverted world' ('Critique of Hegel's Philosophy of Right, Introduction'). The religious inversion compensates in the mind for a deficient reality; it reconstitutes in the imagination a coherent solution which is beyond the real world in order to make up for the contradictions of the real world.

The second stage begins with the break with Feuerbach in 1845 and lasts until 1857. This is a period dominated by Marx's and Engels's construction of HISTORICAL MATERIALISM, when the general premises of their approach to society and history are elaborated and the Feuerbachian orientation of the first stage is definitely abandoned. In this context the concept of ideology is introduced for the first time. The idea of an inversion is retained, but now Marx extends it to cover the critique which the YOUNG HEGELIANS had carried out of religion and of Hegel's philosophy. Marx realizes that their critique is dependent on very Hegelian premises because they believe that the task is to liberate men from mistaken ideas. 'They forget, however,' Marx says, 'that to these phrases they themselves are only opposing other phrases, and that they are in no way combating the real existing world' (*German Ideology*, vol. I, pt. I). So the inversion Marx now calls ideology subsumes both old and young Hegelians and consists in starting from consciousness instead of material reality. Marx affirms on the contrary that the real problems of humanity are not mistaken ideas but real social contradictions and that the former are a consequence of the latter.

In effect, as long as men, because of their limited material mode of activity, are unable to solve these contradictions in practice, they tend to project them in ideological forms of consciousness, that is to say, in purely mental or discursive solutions which effectively conceal or misrepresent the existence and character of these contradictions. By concealing contradictions the ideological distortion contributes to their reproduction and therefore serves the interests of the ruling class. Hence ideology appears as a negative and restricted concept. It is negative because it involves a distortion, a misrepresentation of contradictions. It is restricted because it does not cover all kinds of errors and distortions. The relationship between ideological and non-ideological ideas cannot be interpreted as the general relationship between error and truth. Ideological distortions cannot be overcome by criticism, they can disappear only when the contradictions which give rise to them are practically resolved.

The third stage starts with the writing of the *Grundrisse* in 1858 and is characterized by the concrete analysis of advanced capitalist social relations which culminates in *Capital*. The term ideology all but disappears from these texts, yet the pertinence of Marx's economic analyses for the concept is shown by the sustained use and reworking of the notion of inversion. Marx had already arrived at the conclusion that if some ideas distorted or 'inverted' reality it was because reality itself was upside down. But this relationship appeared unmediated and direct. The specific analysis of capitalist social relations leads him to the further conclusion that the relationship between 'inverted consciousness' and 'inverted reality' is mediated by a level of appearances which are constitutive of reality itself. This sphere of 'phenomenal forms' is constituted by the operation of the market and competition in capitalist societies and is an inverted manifestation of the sphere of production, the underlying level of 'real relations'. As Marx puts it:

everything appears reversed in competition. The final pattern of economic relations as seen on the surface, in their real existence and consequently in the conceptions by which the bearers and agents of these relations seek to understand them, is very much different from, and indeed quite the reverse of, their inner but concealed essential pattern and the conception corresponding to it. (*Capital* III, ch. 12)

Hence, ideology conceals the contradictory character of the hidden essential pattern by focusing upon the way in which the economic relations appear on the surface. This world of appearances constituted by the sphere of circulation does not only generate economic forms of ideology but is also 'a very Eden of the innate rights of man. There alone rule Freedom, Equality, Property and Bentham' (*Capital* I, ch. 6). To this extent the market is also the source of bourgeois political ideology: 'equality and freedom are thus not only perfected in exchange based on exchange values but, also, the exchange of exchange values is the productive real basis of all *equality* and *freedom*' (*Grundrisse*, 'The Chapter on Capital'). But of course the bourgeois ideology of freedom and equality conceals what goes on beneath the surface process of exchange where 'this apparent individual equality and liberty disappear and prove to be inequality and unfreedom' (ibid.).

From the very early critique of religion to the unmasking of mystified economic appearances and of seemingly libertarian and equalitarian principles, there is a remarkable consistency in Marx's understanding of ideology. The idea of a double inversion, in consciousness and reality, is retained throughout, although in the end it is made more complex by distinguishing a double aspect of reality in the capitalist mode of production. Ideology, therefore, maintains throughout its critical and negative connotation, but is used only for those distortions which are connected with the concealment of a contradictory and inverted reality. In this sense the often-quoted definition of ideology as false consciousness is not adequate in so far as it does not specify the kind of distortion which is criticized, thus opening the way for a confusion of ideology with all sorts of errors.

Soon after Marx's death the concept of ideology began to acquire new meanings. At the beginning it did not necessarily lose its critical connotation, but a tendency arose to give that aspect a secondary place. These new meanings took two main forms; namely, a conception of ideology as the totality of forms of social consciousness – which came to be expressed by the concept of 'ideological superstructure' – and the conception of ideology as the political ideas connected with the interests of a class. Although these new meanings were not the result of a systematic reworking of the concept within Marxism, they finally displaced the original negative connotation. The causes of this process of displacement are complex. In the first place, elements of a neutral concept of ideology can be found in some formulations of Marx and Engels themselves. Despite a basic thrust in the direction of a negative concept, their writings are not exempt from ambiguities and unclear statements which occasionally seem to indicate a different direction. Gramsci, for instance, often quotes the passage in which Marx refers to legal, political, philosophical – 'in short, ideological forms in which men become conscious of this conflict and fight it out' (Preface to *A Contribution to the Critique of Political Economy*) in order to sustain his interpretation of ideology as the all-encompassing superstructural sphere in which men acquire consciousness of their contradictory social relations (Gramsci *(1971)*, pp. 138, 164, 377). Engels, in turn, mentions on a few occasions the 'ideological superstructure', the 'ideological spheres' and the 'ideological domain' with sufficient generality to make it possible for someone to believe that ideology covers the totality of forms of consciousness (*Anti-Dühring*, ch. 9).

Another important contributory factor in the evolution towards a positive concept of ideology is the fact that the first two generations of Marxist thinkers after Marx did not have access to *German Ideology* which remained unpublished until the mid-1920s. Hence Plekhanov, Labriola and, most significantly, Lenin, Gramsci and Lukács in his early writings were not acquainted with Marx's and Engels's most forceful argumentation in favour of a negative concept of ideology. In the absence of this work, the two most influential texts for the discussion of the concept were Marx's 1859 'Preface' and Engels's *Anti-Dühring*, which were frequently quoted by the new generations of Marxists. Yet these two texts contain important ambiguities and certainly make no adequate distinction between the base–superstructure relationship and the ideological phenomenon. So progressively the idea of an ideological superstructure became established through the writings of authors like Kautsky, Mehring and Plekhanov. But until 1898 none of the authors of the first generation openly called Marxism itself an ideology.

The first thinker who posed the problem as to whether Marxism is an ideology was Bernstein. His answer is that although proletarian ideas are realistic in their direction, because they refer to material factors, which explain the evolution of societies, they are still thought reflexes and therefore ideological. In identifying ideology with ideas and ideals, Bernstein does no more than repeat what Mehring and Kautsky had already said. But he draws the obvious conclusion they had not drawn; namely, that Marxism must be an ideology. It is symptomatic of the absence of any clear idea about a negative concept of ideology that although Bernstein was already under attack for his 'revision' (see REVISIONISM) of Marx, none of his Marxist critics took him up on this issue. This shows that the first generation of Marxists did not consider it of the essence of Marxism to defend a negative concept of ideology.

However, the most important cause of the evolution in the concept of ideology is positive and lies in the political struggles of the last decades of the nineteenth century, especially in Eastern Europe. Marxism focuses its attention on the need to create a theory of political practice and therefore its development became more and more related to class struggles and party organizations. In this context the political ideas of the classes in conflict acquired a new importance and needed to be theoretically accounted for. Lenin provided the solution by extending the meaning of the concept of ideology. In a situation of class confrontation, ideology appears connected with the interests of the ruling class and its critique connected with the interests of the dominated class; in other words, the critique of the ruling class ideology is carried out from a different class position, or – by extension – from a different ideological point of view. Hence, for Lenin, ideology becomes the political consciousness linked to the interests of various classes and, in particular, he focuses on the opposition between bourgeois and socialist ideology. With Lenin, therefore, the process of change in the meaning of ideology reaches its culmination. Ideology is no longer a necessary distortion which conceals contradictions but becomes a neutral concept referring to the political consciousness of classes, including the proletarian class.

Lenin's conception became most influential and has played a crucial role in shaping new contributions to the subject ever since. This is apparent in Lukács, for instance, who, from his early essays, uses the terms ideology or ideological to refer both to bourgeois and proletarian consciousness, without implying a necessary negative connotation. Marxism, for Lukács, is 'the ideological expression of the proletariat' or 'the ideology of the embattled proletariat', indeed its 'most potent weapon' which has led to bourgeois 'ideological capitulation' (Lukács 1923, pp. 258–9, 227 and 228). If bourgeois ideology is false it is not because it is ideology in general, but because the bourgeois class situation is structurally limited. However, bourgeois ideology dominates and contaminates the psychological consciousness of the proletariat. Lukács's explanation of this phenomenon goes beyond Lenin's account. Whereas for Lenin the ideological subordination of the proletariat was the result of the bourgeoisie possessing an older ideology and having more powerful means of disseminating ideas, for Lukács it is the very situation and practice of the proletariat within the reified appearances of the capitalist economy that induces the proletariat's ideological subordination. On the other hand, as Lukács himself recognized later in life, he consistently overrates the role of ideology and ideological struggle in his early writings, to the point that they seem to become a substitute for real political practice and real class struggle.

Lenin's approach to ideology also influenced Gramsci, who explicitly rejected a negative conception. However, Gramsci's idea of the negative conception does not correspond with that of Marx, but rather refers to 'the arbitrary elucubrations of particular individuals' (Gramsci 1971, p. 376). Hence he propounds a distinction between 'arbitrary ideologies' and 'organic ideologies', and concentrates upon the latter. Ideology in this sense is 'a conception of the world that is implicitly manifest in art, in law, in economic activity and in all manifestations of individual and collective life' (ibid. p. 328). But ideology is more than a system of ideas; it has to do also with a capacity to inspire concrete attitudes and provide orientations for action. Ideology is socially pervasive in that men cannot act without rules of conduct, without orientations. Hence, ideology becomes 'the terrain on which men move, acquire consciousness of their position, struggle, etc.' (ibid. p. 377). It is in and by ideology, therefore, that a class can exercise HEGEMONY over other classes, that is, can secure the adhesion and consent of the broad masses. Whereas Lenin and Lukács treated ideology at the level of theory, Gramsci distinguishes four degrees or levels of ideology; namely, philo-sophy, religion, common sense and folklore in a decreasing order of rigour and intellectual articulation.

Gramsci broke fresh ground by analysing in a highly suggestive manner the role of INTELLEC-TUALS and ideological apparatuses (education, media etc.) in the production of ideology. Whereas Lenin and Lukács had not been able to bridge the distance between socialist ideology and spontaneous consciousness, between the 'ascribed' consciousness and the psychological consciousness of the class, Gramsci finds a double current of determinations between them. True, socialist ideology is developed by intellectuals, but there cannot be an absolute distinction between intellectuals and non-intellectuals and, moreover, the class itself creates its organic intellectuals. So there is no question of a science being introduced from without into the working-class; rather the task is to renovate and make critical an already existing intellectual activity. Marxist ideology does not substitute for a deficient consciousness but expresses a collective will, a historical orientation present in the class.

The existence of two major conceptions of ideology within the Marxist tradition is the source of many debates. Some authors of the present day believe that only one of these versions is the truly Marxist one, whereas others, unable to accept a difference between Marx and Lenin, try to reconcile both versions. This is so with Althusser who has presented the most influential exposition of ideology in the last two decades. He distinguishes a theory of ideology in general, for which the function of ideology is to secure cohesion in society, from the theory of particular ideologies, for which the former general function is overdetermined by the new function of securing the domination of one class. These functions can be performed by ideology in so far as it is 'a representation of the imaginary relationship of individuals to their real conditions of existence' (Althusser 1971, p. 153) and in so far as it interpellates individuals and constitutes them as subjects who accept their role within the system of production relations. On the other hand Althusser also affirms the existence of dominated ideologies which express the protest of exploited classes. Althusser insists that science is the absolute opposite to ideology, but at the same time he describes ideology as an objective level of society which is relatively autonomous.

The difficulty of this approach lies in the fact that it is impossible to reconcile the existence of a revolutionary ideology with the assertion that all ideology subjects individuals to the dominant system. Moreover, it is very difficult to reconcile ideology as a misrepresentation opposed to science with ideology as the objective superstructure of society, unless the superstructure contains nothing but ideological distortions and science is located elsewhere, but this is also problematic.

Reading
Althusser, Louis 1971: *Lenin and Philosophy.*
Gramsci, Antonio 1929–35 (*1971*): *Selections from the Prison Notebooks.*
Larrain, Jorge 1979: *The Concept of Ideology.*
— 1983: *Marxism and Ideology.*
Lenin, V. I. 1902 (*1961*): 'What is to be done?'
Lukács, G. 1923 (*1971*): *History and Class Consciousness.*

JORGE LARRAIN

imperialism and world market   Of all the concepts in Marxist theory imperialism is perhaps the one used most eclectically and with greatest disregard for the theoretical basis upon which it rests. The most common use of the term is in narrow reference to the economic and political relationship between advanced capitalist countries and backward countries. Indeed, since the second world war the word imperialism has become synonymous with the oppression and 'exploitation' of weak, impoverished countries by powerful ones. Many of the writers who present such an interpretation of imperialism cite Lenin as a theoretical authority, though Lenin sharply criticized Kautsky for defining imperialism in this way.

Imperialism refers to the process of capitalist ACCUMULATION on a world scale in the era of MONOPOLY CAPITALISM, and the theory of imperialism is the investigation of accumulation in the context of a world market created by that accumulation. The theory has three elements: (1) the analysis of capitalist accumulation, (2) the PERIODIZATION OF CAPITALISM into eras, and (3) the location of the phenomenon in the context of the political division of the world into 'countries'. Since the first element implies the second, there remain only two discrete elements.

These combine to produce closely related but distinct lines of inquiry: (1) the relations among advanced capitalist countries ('imperialist rivalry'); (2) the impact of capitalism on non-capitalist social formations (articulation of MODES OF PRODUCTION); and (3) the oppression of people subjugated by the rule of capital ('the National Question', see NATION). Within orthodox Marxist theory, the work of Lenin forms the basis of the theory of imperialism. His most famous work on the subject is a pamphlet by the same name, but it is a mistake to take this as Lenin's theoretical contribution to the analysis of the development of capitalism on a world scale. The theoretical basis of what Lenin called 'a popular outline' is to be found in two long essays which he wrote almost two decades earlier, 'On the So called "Market Question"', and 'A Characterization of Economic Romanticism'. The purpose of these two essays is both to defend Marx's theory of accumulation against underconsumptionist arguments and thereby develop a theory of the capitalist world market, and to demonstrate the progressive nature of capitalism, in order to criticize utopian socialism (see also PROUDHON).

In his pamphlet on imperialism, Lenin gave a now famous list of the characteristics of the phenomenon: (1) the 'export of capital' becomes of prime importance, along with the export of commodities; (2) production and distribution become centralized in great trusts or cartels; (3) banking and industrial capital become merged; (4) the capitalist powers divide the world into spheres of influence; and (5) this division is completed, implying a future inter-capitalist struggle to re-divide the world. The first of these characteristics, the 'export of capital', is frequently taken as the single identifying factor of the imperialist era. The term is ambiguous, however, as Lenin pointed out in his two theoretical essays. The ambiguity arises because commodities are capital, one of the forms which capital assumes in its circuit, $M–C \ldots P \ldots C'-M'$ (money capital – productive capital – commodity capital, then money capital again).

Before considering why imperialism is characterized by the export of money and productive capital the use of the word export must be considered. Imperialism is not characterized in the literature by the term movement of capital, but by the specific word export which introduces explicitly a division between capital movements which are national and those which are international. Since no transformation occurs in capital merely by passing a border or customs post, this analytical division must be justified by an explanation of what political boundaries imply for the movement of capital. In other words, one must explain why additional concepts are required (such as imperialism itself) in order to move from an abstract capitalist society to a more concrete formulation which considers the division of the world in terms of countries. Clearly involved here is the meaning attached to the concept of a country. The explicit treatment of political divisions is what distinguishes Lenin's concept of imperialism from Kautsky's. In the Leninist formulation, the export of capital occurs in the context of a world divided by different ruling classes, whose power is represented by the STATE of each country. Thus, the export of capital implies the mediating role of states and the potential conflict of ruling-class interests. This potential conflict can be between capitalist states (inter-capitalist rivalry), or between a capitalist state and a pre-capitalist state or ruling class (articulation of modes of production and the national question). Lenin placed particular stress on inter-capitalist rivalry, developing his central political conclusion that accumulation in the imperialist era generates a tendency towards inter-capitalist wars. It is in this framework that he identified the first world war as an imperialist war and that the Comintern similarly identified the second world war until the Nazi invasion of the Soviet Union.

Kautsky, on the other hand, defined imperialism as the relationship between advanced capitalist countries and under-developed countries ('agrarian areas'), and explicitly argued that the conflicts among the ruling classes in the advantaged capitalist countries tended to disappear during the imperialist era. These two keystones of Kautsky's theory have tended to characterize the literature on imperialism since the end of the second world war, most clearly in DEPENDENCY THEORY. This literature has placed all the emphasis upon imperialist domination of backward countries, with the implicit or explicit view that the United States' capitalist class has been strong enough since the second world war to reduce all other capitalist classes to client status.

Which of these interpretations of imperialism is correct is both an empirical and a theoretical issue. The theory of imperialism as developed by Lenin follows from Marx's theory of accumulation. Capitalism represents a particular form of class society and its particular laws of development reflect the manner in which a surplus product is extracted from direct producers. This extraction of a surplus product occurs in production, and in capitalist society is predicated upon the buying and selling of LABOUR POWER. It is the buying and selling of labour power which both reflects the essential nature of capitalism and determines that essential nature. It reflects the separation of workers from means of production (see PRIMITIVE ACCUMULATION), and once this separation is achieved, the COMMODITY status of labour power dictates the manner in which capitalist society reproduces itself. This reproduction must be achieved through the circulation of commodities: dispossessed workers must be paid wages in order to purchase the commodities which they can no longer produce themselves; capitalists must sell commodities in order to obtain the money capital to purchase labour power and the means of production and re-initiate the production process.

Thus capitalist society is reproduced by a constantly repeated cycle of exchange, production, and realization (the circuit of capital) and it is for this reason that Marx described capital as self-expanding VALUE. Capital initiates the reproduction process by exchanging a given amount of value in the form of money for labour power and the means of production, and from production emerges a mass of commodities of expanded value which must be realized as money capital. This process of self-expansion, in the context of COMPETITION, proceeds on a growing scale and is the theory of the expansion of capital. This theory of the expansion of capital is completely general, abstracting from any spatial context. Once we come to consider the political division of the world no special theory of capital expansion is required. This theory, developed by Marx in *Capital*, is in contrast to the analysis of underconsumptionists, notably Luxemburg, who reject the conclusion that capitalism is self-reproducing and therefore find it necessary to specify a special theory of the movement of capital between geographic areas.

The approach of Marx leads to an explicit

periodization of capitalism in order to account for the international movement of capital in its different forms (money capital, productive capital and commodity capital). As noted, capital is by its nature expansionary. In the early stage of capitalist development the scope for the movement of money and productive capital is limited because of the underdevelopment of the social relations of production. During what Marx called the 'stage of manufacture', capitalist credit institutions are relatively underdeveloped, making movement of money capital difficult, both within capitalist social formations and between these and pre-capitalist formations. Further, in this early stage of capitalist development, a great part of the world was pre-capitalist and the role of money extremely limited, so the movement of money and productive capital was limited by the social relations outside the capitalist social formations. As a consequence the international movement of capital in this period was primarily of commodity capital (trade), and this trade progressively developed a world market for capitalist production. In this trade manufactured commodities of capitalist origin tend to be exchanged for raw materials and food products produced within pre-capitalist social relations (such as New World slavery).

The consequence of this trade for the pre-capitalist social formations is a matter of considerable controversy and central to the theory of imperialism, specifically with regard to the analysis of the articulation of modes of production. Some authors argue that trade alone is sufficient to make pre-capitalist social formations predominantly capitalist in nature (Sweezy *et al.* 1967), and that during the nineteenth century the underdeveloped areas of the world were in fact so transformed (see NON-CAPITALIST MODES OF PRODUCTION). Marx, however, argued that trade alone, dominated by MERCHANT CAPITAL, tends to rigidify pre-capitalist relations. Following this line of argument, one concludes that the initial development of the world market tended to block the development of capitalism in what Lenin called 'backward' countries or colonial and semi-colonial areas. Thus, in this period of manufacture, the expansion of capitalism transformed the social relations and developed the productive forces in the capitalist countries, but blocked the same transformation and development elsewhere.

However by the second half of the nineteenth century capitalism had entered into the stage of what Marx called Modern Industry (*Capital* I, esp. chs. 13–14), characterized by the production of relative surplus value, accompanied by the centralization of capital and the development of credit institutions to facilitate that centralization. This began the epoch referred to as MONOPOLY CAPITALISM, as production on an increasingly larger scale (concentration) generated a tendency towards monopolization on a national and international scale. In the theoretical formulation of Marx and later Lenin this process of monopolization was accompanied by intensified competition. This also is a controversial point. As pointed out, Kautsky interpreted monopolization literally, as the opposite of competition, signalling the end of inter-capitalist rivalry. Bukharin and Preobrazhensky took a middle position, arguing that in the stage of monopoly capitalism, competition is eliminated within capitalist countries, but continues between capitalist countries. The term STATE MONOPOLY CAPITALISM has been used to describe such a situation.

Following the argument of Marx and Lenin, the combination of monopolization and intensified competition ushers in the epoch of imperialism. Among the capitalist countries this generates a tendency towards inter-capitalist war, and in the economic sphere the conflict assumes the form of the export of capital. The development of the credit system facilitates the integration of financial and industrial capital (see FINANCE CAPITAL), so the export of money capital becomes possible on a large scale. Throughout the imperialist epoch the export of money capital (and productive capital, considered below) was and is largely among advanced capitalist countries, and the same is true for the movement of commodity capital. This reflects the underdevelopment of both the social relations and the productive forces in the backward countries. The two central debates in the literature over imperialism are whether intercapitalist rivalry characterizes the epoch, and the impact of the export of money capital and particularly productive capital upon underdeveloped areas. The second issue, from a Marxist perspective, is whether capital export in these forms tends to transform underdeveloped countries and develop capitalism there. If this is the case, capitalism in the epoch of imperialism would be considered progressive, in so far as the tendency for capitalism to reproduce itself in underdeveloped countries would imply the progressive development of the productive forces and the emergence of the proletariat as an important force in the class struggle.

It is at this point in the theory of imperialism that the explicit consideration of the political division of the world becomes necessary. If, as Marx argued, exchange alone does not bring about the development of capitalism, then force is necessary in order to break down the pre-capitalist social relations which block the development of a free wage labour force, and use of force requires control of the state. Going back to Lenin, a school of Marxist thought has argued that the ruling classes in the advanced capitalist countries tend to ally with the pre-capitalist ruling classes in backward countries and that this alliance prevents the local bourgeoisie in backward countries from successfully bringing about a bourgeois revolution which would gain them state power (see NATIONAL BOURGEOISIE). And without state power the local bourgeoisie remains weak and capitalism underdeveloped.

In this analysis capitalism itself is considered progressive, but the imperialist domination of the world by capitalist ruling classes blocks its development in the underdeveloped world. The local bourgeoisie is seen as a potentially anti-imperialist force because of its contradictions with the imperial bourgeoisie. A number of writers, most notably Mao Tse-tung, conclude from this that the revolutionary struggle in underdeveloped countries has two stages, an initial anti-imperialist stage to overthrow the combined rule of pre-capitalist classes and imperial capital, followed by a stage of socialist revolution. The first stage, called the New Democracy by Mao Tse-tung, involves an alliance of the proletariat, the peasantry, and the local bourgeoisie, or at least the elements of the latter that have strong contradictions with imperial capital.

The general proposition that a primarily anti-imperialist struggle is a precondition for socialist revolution in a country dominated by a pre-capitalist ruling class is relatively uncontroversial. Controversy rages, however, over how to analyse imperialism when an underdeveloped country is predominantly capitalist. Some argue

that once countries become predominantly capitalist, they can be expected to develop to a level and structure similar to that of currently advanced capitalist countries, and that this is in fact occurring in countries such as Brazil and Mexico (Warren 1973). Dependency theorists, on the other hand, reject this even as a possibility, and use the term 'dependent capitalist development' (or 'distorted' capitalist development) to describe predominantly capitalist social formations in the underdeveloped world. While the term has its attractiveness it is commonly used in a quite subjective way, and the characteristics which dependency theory attributes to 'dependent capitalism' were in general characteristics of the currently developed capitalist countries in their early stages of capitalist transformation. One characteristic which is different is that the currently underdeveloped countries must undergo capitalist transformation in an epoch in which the world is already dominated by capitalist powers. Dependency theorists base their entire analysis upon this fact, so that the whole dynamic of underdeveloped countries becomes a mere response to external domination, and the term imperialism is used in the extremely limited sense of the relations between advanced capitalist and backward countries. Further, the dependent capitalist development postulated by the dependency theorists is logically dependent upon the proposition that competition has been eliminated in and among advanced capitalist countries. It is the alleged absence of competition which makes imperial capital interested in limiting capitalist development in underdeveloped countries as an aspect of protecting their monopolistic positions. This literal view of monopoly capitalism has come under considerable attack in recent years (Clifton 1977; Weeks 1981).

It is not too much to say that after the time of Lenin the theory of imperialism largely stagnated, with the contributions after the second world war being of an empirical nature. However, in the 1970s theoretical debate re-emerged, prompted by objective conditions, namely the development of capitalism in the underdeveloped world. This development renders partial at best an analysis of underdevelopment based upon an imperial pre-capitalist alliance blocking the development of capitalism. At the other extreme, the dependency view that capitalism is general in the underdeveloped world but 'dependent' or 'distorted' requires an unacceptably large number of *ad hoc* arguments in order to incorporate the obviously successful capitalist accumulation in a number of underdeveloped countries. The result is a healthy theoretical unrest among Marxist writers and a renewed interest in intercapitalist rivalry as a possible explanation of the dynamics of accumulation in the epoch of monopoly capitalism. (See also DEPENDENCY THEORY; MARXISM IN LATIN AMERICA.)

Reading

Brewer, A. 1980: *Marxist Theories of Imperialism: A Critical Survey.*

Bukharin, Nikolai 1917–18 (1972): *Imperialism and World Economy.*

Clifton, J. A. 1977: 'Competition and the Evolution of the Capitalist Mode of Production'.

Hilferding, Rudolf 1910 (1981): *Finance Capital.*

Hilton, Rodney ed. 1976: *The Transition from Feudalism to Capitalism.*

Kemp, T. 1967: *Theories of Imperialism.*

Lenin, V. I. 1916 (1964): *Imperialism.*

Warren, B. 1973: 'Imperialism and Capitalist Industrialization'.

Weeks, John 1981: *Capital and Exploitation.*
                                          JOHN WEEKS

individual In *Theories of Surplus Value* Marx wrote that 'although at first the development of the human species takes place at the cost of the majority of human individuals and even classes, in the end it breaks through this contradiction and coincides with the development of the individual; the higher development of the individual is thus only achieved by a historical process during which individuals are sacrificed' (pt. II, ch. ix). As this passage shows, Marx saw world history as the story of the unfolding of human powers, operating, until the end of class society, behind men's backs through social relations that are 'indispensable and independent of men's wills' (*Critique of Political Economy*, Preface) but, with the abolition of capitalism, making possible a world under the control of associated producers, cooperating in community, developing many-sided individuality and experiencing personal freedom.

As a philosophy of history, then, Marxism proposes a theory of the development of the individual (like many other nineteenth-century theories). As social science it discounts explanations in terms of individuals' purposes, attitudes and beliefs, preferring to treat these as themselves matters to be explained. On the other hand, like every macro-theory, it requires a micro-theory to work; but it does not focus attention on the details of such a theory. As a theory of ideology, it postulates that individualistic theories and modes of thought, especially those couched in terms of abstract individuals, taken out of historical context, are 'Robinsonades', after Robinson Crusoe (*Critique of Political Economy*, Introduction), concealing the underlying social relations (above all relations of production) that in turn explain individual thought and action. 'Man', Marx wrote, 'is not an abstract being squatting outside the world' ('Critique of Hegel's Philosophy of Right: Introduction'). And as a vision of the good society and human fulfilment, it postulates a notion of fully-developed, many-sided individuality that is measurable according to no predetermined yardstick (albeit realizable only under conditions of social unity and the collective control of nature) that has clear links with German Romanticism.

Marxism has therefore relatively little to say about the micro-level of human interaction, about the nature of the individual human psyche, about personal relations or about the relations between the state and the individual or between the public and private spheres. Marxism sees the individual as a social product (as Althusserian 'structuralist' Marxism has stressed) and yet it requires a theory of individual human behaviour and social interaction to underpin historical materialism; and its goal (as Marxist humanists have seen) is both to explain and engage in the process of bringing about the end of reified social relations of production and intercourse, subjugating them 'to the power of the united individuals', for 'the reality which communism creates is precisely the basis for rendering it impossible that anything should exist independently of individuals, in so far as reality is nevertheless only a product of the preceding intercourse of individuals' (*German Ideology*, vol. I, IV, 6).

Reading

Lukács, Georg 1923 (1971): *History and Class Consciousness.*

Lukes, Steven 1973: *Individualism*.

Macpherson, C. B. 1962: *The Political Theory of Possessive Individualism*.

Plamenatz, John 1975: *Karl Marx's Philosophy of Man*.

Tucker, D. F. B. 1980: *Marxism and Individualism*.

STEVEN LUKES

industrialization Though the *term* 'industrialization' is absent from the work of Marx and Engels, the *concept* is clearly present. Marx distinguishes 'Modern Industry' or 'The Factory System' or 'The Machinery System' from earlier forms of capitalist production, cooperation and MANUFACTURE. Modern Industry is distinguished from manufacture by the central role of *machinery*. 'As soon as tools had been converted from being manual implements of man into implements of a mechanical apparatus, of a machine, the motive mechanism also acquired an independent form, entirely emancipated from the restraints of human strength. Thereupon the individual machine sinks into a mere factor in production by machinery' (*Capital* I, ch. 13, sect. 1). In parallel with manufacture, Marx distinguishes two stages in the development of the machinery system. In the first stage, 'simple cooperation', there is only a 'conglomeration in the factory of similar and simultaneously acting machines' using a single power source. In the second stage, a 'complex system of machinery', the product goes through a connected series of detailed processes carried out by an interlinked chain of machines. When this complex system is perfected and can carry out the entire process of production with workers only as attendants, it becomes an 'automatic system of machinery' (ibid. ch. 13, sect. 1).

The conversion of hand-operated tools into instruments of a machine reduces the worker to a 'mere' source of motive power, and as production expands, the limits of human strength necessitate the substitution of a mechanical motive power for human muscles. In the factory system, all the machines are driven by a single 'motive force', the steam engine, but Marx stresses that the steam engine existed long before Modern Industry and that it 'did not give rise to any industrial revolution ... on the contrary, the invention of machines ... made a revolution in the form of steam-engine necessary' (ibid. ch.

13, sect. 1). An important stimulus to the improvement of the steam engine was the new means of communication and transport required by modern industry. Ocean and river steamers, railways, locomotives and telegraphs all required 'cyclopean machines' for their construction, and such machines (steam hammers, boring machines, mechanical lathes) required a large motive force under perfect control. Maudsley's slide-rest facilitated the refinements in construction of steam engines required for such control (ibid. ch. 13, sect. 1). In the factory with an automatic machinery system, workers are reduced to attendants of machines, and there is a growing 'separation of the intellectual powers of production from manual labour' since an even lower level of skill is required than in manufacture (ibid. ch. 13, sect. 4: for subsequent development of this theme see Braverman 1974).

'Modern Industry' also transforms agriculture. Machines are introduced, along with industrially produced chemicals, and other new techniques. The greater amounts of capital required to compete in agriculture completes the removal of peasants from the land, and the new machinery displaces many agricultural labourers and impoverishes others. The transfer of population to the towns is thus accelerated, and the division between town and country becomes complete. The industrialization of agriculture impoverishes the soil, as well as the agricultural labourer (ibid. ch. 13, sect. 10). In both industry and agriculture, the introduction of machinery and its domination of ever more sectors of production creates a 'surplus population' or a RESERVE ARMY OF LABOUR (see also POPULATION) as living labour is displaced by machinery (ibid. ch. 23, sect. 3 and Engels, *Socialism: Utopian and Scientific*, sect. 3).

Although capitalist forms of production existed before industrialization, 'modern industry' is none the less the highest form of such production, and the form which finally sweeps aside all others and establishes the domination of the capitalist mode of production in economics and of the bourgeoisie in politics. Modern industry achieves economic domination by subordinating and then destroying domestic industry and manufacture in town and countryside, and capturing the entire home market for itself (*Capital* I, ch. 13, see also Lenin 1899). At the same time competition between capitalists produces a continual improvement and expansion of machinery and of the factory system, thus causing continuous revolutions in both the FORCES AND RELATIONS OF PRODUCTION in society. 'Modern Industry never looks upon . . . the existing form of a process as final. The technical basis of that industry is therefore revolutionary, while all earlier modes of production were essentially conservative' (Capital I, ch. 13, sect. 9).

Although Marx dates the beginnings of modern industry in England to the last third of the eighteenth century, he locates its most rapid period of development between 1846 and 1866 (ibid. ch. 23, sect. 5). Its repercussions however were not restricted to England. Having revolutionized international means of communication and transport, modern industry destroys the handicraft industry of foreign countries by its cheap commodities, and thus creates a new international division of labour in which one part of the world produces raw materials for the industries of another part (ibid. ch. 13, sect. 7).

Marx and Engels were concerned solely with capitalist industrialization, but later Marxists used their analysis as the basis of a theory and practice of industrialization under socialism. Although 'crash' industrialization in the USSR is usually identified with Stalin (see STALINISM; SOVIET MARXISM), PREOBRAZHENSKY was the first Marxist to attempt to adapt Marx's analysis of capitalist industrialization to Soviet conditions. In this adaptation particular emphasis was given to the importance of the constant capital sector in accumulation and industrial expansion (see Capital II, ch. XXI, and REPRODUCTION SCHEMA). Under Stalin, this led to the stress on capital goods industries (or 'heavy industries') which has since been a marked feature of industrialization in the Soviet Union and Eastern Europe.

Reading

Braverman, H. 1974: Labour and Monopoly Capital: The Degradation of Work in the Twentieth Century.

Lenin, V. I. 1899 (1960): The Development of Capitalism in Russia: The Process of the Formation of a Home Market for Larger-Scale Industry.

Preobrazhensky, E. 1926 (1965): The New Economics.

GAVIN KITCHING

intellectuals Marxism has been concerned both with the part played by intellectuals in history, and with the relationship between socialist intellectuals and movements. On the first issue Marx and Engels saw intellectuals as sharply divided into conservatives and progressives. The former and more numerous they linked with their conception of IDEOLOGY, as a protective cocoon of beliefs spun round itself by any society, mainly to the advantage of its dominant classes. These illusions have been the concern of men habituated by widening division of labour, and separation of mental from physical activity, to abstract, unreal thinking (German Ideology, pt. 1 sects. 1a, 1b; Engels to Mehring, 14 July 1893). Narrow specialization they deemed as cramping to academic as to manual workers (Venable 1946, pp. 54, 129).

By contrast, Engels paid tribute to thinkers of times like the Renaissance, whose minds moved freshly and vigorously amid the stir and bustle of active life (Dialectics of Nature, Introduction). Such individuals, he and Marx assumed, expressed and clarified the impulses of new, advancing classes or social currents. Men such as Bayle, whom in an early laudatory essay on French materialism (Holy Family, ch. VI, sect. 3d) Marx singled out as the overthrower of all metaphysics, could readily be identified as spokesmen or allies of the French bourgeoisie, preparing for its long-delayed challenge to monarchy and aristocracy.

Marx and Engels were aligning themselves in analogous fashion with the new industrial working class. But relations with this nearly illiterate mass could not be the same as those of intellectuals with any previous movement; on what they could or should be, neither of the two left any conclusive statement. One complication was that they had from the first an exceptionally poor opinion of middle-class dabblers or meddlers in socialism in the Germany of their day, as pretentious, half-baked scholars. In the Communist Manifesto (sect. 3), deriding 'German' or 'True' Socialism, they accused these word-spinners of converting French ideas into meaningless abstractions, figments of fancy. Engels's massive polemic against Dühring reveals all the dislike he and Marx felt for such pseudo-intellectualism, and their anxiety about the risk of the labour movement being fuddled and misled by it (cf. Marx and Engels to

Bebel and others, September 1879).

They hoped, intermittently, that the working class would find its own way to socialism. But there were few signs of this happening, and very few proletarian thinkers like Joseph DIETZGEN were coming forward. To Lenin it seemed apparent that beyond the simple point of trade unionism ideas could only come to the working class from outside. As Plekhanov put it Marxists should be proud to serve as intellectuals to the revolutionary workers (1908, p. 28). Lenin had very mixed feelings about the intelligentsia, however, especially in Russia, where his diatribes on its shortcomings are reminiscent of Marx's on educated Germans. It was flabby, slipshod, irresolute; these strictures deepened after the failure of the 1905 revolution, when Lenin felt that even Bolshevik intellectuals were succumbing to defeatism, and some of them were taking refuge in empty fantasy. He was capable of telling Gorky that he welcomed their desertion, and their replacement in the ranks by workers. Still, not many days later he assured his friend that he had no desire to keep intellectuals out, 'as the silly syndicalists do', and that he was fully aware of how indispensable they were to the labour movement (letters of 7 and 13 February 1908). In fact 79 out of 169 leading Bolsheviks before 1917 had higher education, and 15 per cent of the rank and file had been to universities (Liebman 1973, p. 100).

Lecturing on socialism to an attentive professional audience Kautsky felt hopeful of a sufficient number of such people changing allegiance. He assured them that socialism would bring to intellectual and artistic work not only more public patronage but greater freedom as well: any attempt at government control in this sphere would be foolish, and the watchword should be 'Communism in material production, anarchism in the intellectual' (1902, pp. 178–9, 183). With the Bolshevik revolution came a practical test, under unfavourable conditions because of Russia's backwardness. Lenin pointed out that in every field it was necessary to employ the old intelligentsia, who must – but the same was true of the working class – be re-moulded, re-educated (1920a, p. 113). The technical intelligentsia had a particular importance. Rapid industrialization by Stalinist methods brought the regime into collision with it, while other sections were subjected to strict control. Educated

men had in any case been far too few, and a new corps was being raised, at first recruited as far as possible from the working class, and trained to loyalty and efficiency more than to independent thinking. Similar difficulties were encountered later in China, where they were worsened by the country's being still more retarded, and not made any easier by the Cultural Revolution which at times seemed prepared to dispense with intellectuals altogether and return to primitive communism.

In Western Europe much thought was given to the question by Gramsci, who distinguished between the 'traditional' intelligentsia of any country, regarding itself as a separate class or community – an unreal detachment reflected in all idealist philosophy – and the thinking groups that each class (except the peasantry) produced 'organically' from its own ranks (1957, pp. 118–20). He hoped to see more intellectuals from the working class, though his definition was broad enough to include all strata of directing and organizing personnel: the intellectuals required nowadays, he wrote, were practical builders of society, not simply talkers. He noted as a regular feature of modern life a heavy rate of unemployment among 'middle intellectual strata' (1957, pp. 122–3).

In the West, diminishing faith in the working class as the bringer of socialism has led to greater weight being attached to the intelligentsia. No professed Marxist could go nearly so far as Wright Mills, in America, in elevating the intelligentsia to the place of fulfiller of the progressive mission left vacant by working-class default. But Western Marxism has paid increasing attention to the influence of ideas on history, and therefore to the men and women most concerned with them. With this has come a heightened recognition that if socialism is to have a future it must enlist knowledge and art on its side, as well as bread-and-butter interests.

Reading

Davidson, Alastair 1977: *Antonio Gramsci: Towards an Intellectual Biography.*

Gandy, G. Ross 1979: *Marx and History. From Primitive Society to the Communist Future.*

Gramsci, Antonio 1957: *'The Modern Prince' and other writings.*

Kautsky, Karl 1902 (1916): *The Social Revolution.*

— 1906 (*1918*): *Ethics and the Materialist Conception of History.*

Lenin, V. I. and Gorky, M. 1973: *Letters, Reminiscences, Articles.*

Liebman, Marcel 1973 (*1975*): *Leninism under Lenin.*

Plekhanov, G. V. 1908–10 (*1973*): *Materialismus Militans.*

Seliger, Martin 1977: *The Marxist Conception of Ideology.*

Venable, Vernon 1946: *Human Nature: the Marxian View.*

Mills, C. Wright 1962: *The Marxists.*

V. G. KIERNAN

interest. *See* financial capital and interest.

internationalism This was central to the thought and activity of Marx and Engels, who gave a class basis (proletarian internationalism) to the idea of human brotherhood proclaimed by the French Revolution. Engels, in 1845, contrasted 'the fraternisation of nations, as it is now being carried out everywhere by the extreme proletarian party' with 'the old instinctive national egoism and the hypocritical private-egotistical cosmopolitanism of free trade'. Whereas the bourgeoisie in each country had its own special interests, 'the proletarians in all countries have one and the same interest, one and the same enemy, and one and the same struggle' ('The Festival of Nations in London'). Marx and Engels saw this common interest as lying not only in cooperation across frontiers to defend immediate class interests but also in bringing about 'a great social revolution (which) shall have mastered the results of the bourgeois epoch, the market of the world and the modern powers of production, and subjected them to the common control of the most advanced peoples' (Marx, 'The Future Results of British Rule in India').

When Marx and Engels joined the League of Communists in 1847, its old motto 'All Men are Brothers' was changed to 'Proletarians of all Countries, Unite!' In specifying what distinguished the communists they placed first the fact that 'in the national struggles of the proletarians of the different countries, they point out and bring to the front the common interests of the entire proletariat, independently of all nationality' (*Communist Manifesto*, pt. 2). At the same time they recognized that 'though not in substance, yet in form, the struggle of the proletariat with the bourgeoisie is at first a national struggle. The proletariat of each country must, of course, first of all settle matters with its own bourgeoisie' (ibid., pt. 1) . Marx emphasized that 'there is absolutely no contradiction in the *international* workers' party striving for the establishment of the Polish nation' ('For Poland': emphasis in original). And Engels insisted that 'a sincere international collaboration of the European nations is only possible if each of these nations is entirely autonomous in its own house' (Preface to 1892 Polish edition of *Communist Manifesto*). Marx, working for the independence of Ireland, saw it as a stimulus to social revolution in England (letter to S. Meyer and A. Vogt, 9 April 1870).

If the First International was formed 'to afford a central medium of communication and cooperation between Working Men's Societies existing in different countries' (General Rules of IWMA, drafted by Marx), Marx and Engels did not see such an organization as always essential to internationalism. Engels wrote in 1885 that the First International had become 'a fetter' on the international movement, which 'the simple feeling of solidarity based on the understanding of the identity of class position suffices to create and to hold together' ('On the History of the Communist League', conclusion). Engels's expectations were over-optimistic, but the problem was not solved by the formation of the Second International, which with the outbreak of war in 1914 broke down in an upsurge of nationalism.

Lenin, from 1914, urged that internationalists should work for 'the conversion of the present imperialist war into a civil war' ('The War and Russian Social-Democracy', *CW* 21, p. 34). He also argued for self-determination for the oppressed nations of Tsarist Russia (and elsewhere) 'not because we have dreamt of splitting up the country economically, or of the ideal of small states, but, on the contrary, because we want large states and closer unity and even fusion of nations only on a truly democratic, truly internationalist basis, which is *inconceivable* without the freedom to secede' ('The Revolutionary Proletariat and the Right of Nations to Self-Determination, ibid. pp. 413–14: emphasis in original). He placed increasing emphasis during and after the war on the need for 'a union between revolutionary proletarians of the capitalist, advanced countries, and the revolutionary masses of those countries where there is no or hardly any proletariat, i.e. the oppressed masses of colonial, Eastern countries' against imperialism (Report on the International Situation and the Fundamental Tasks of the Communist International, at Second Comintern Congress, *CW* 31, p. 232). In this context he approved a modification of the famous slogan of the *Communist Manifesto* to read: 'Workers of all countries and oppressed peoples, unite!' (Speech at a Meeting of Moscow Activists, ibid., p. 453). He insisted that 'proletarian internationalism demands, first, that the interests of the proletarian struggle in any one country should be subordinated to the interests of that struggle on a world-wide scale, and, second, that a nation which is achieving victory over the bourgeoisie should be able and willing to make the greatest national sacrifices for the overthrow of international capital' (Preliminary Draft Theses on the National and the Colonial Questions for the Second Comintern Congress, ibid., p. 148).

Lenin and the Bolsheviks expected that the Russian Revolution of October 1917 would herald an international socialist revolution. Its isolation led to the atrophy, under Stalin, of much of the internationalism of the Lenin period and the growth of national egoism and big power hegemony. These evils did not disappear after the second world war when this isolation was ended but, as the Soviet government statement of 30 October 1956 acknowledged, there occurred 'violations and mistakes which belittled the principle of equal rights in the relations between socialist states' (*Soviet News*, 31 October 1956). Subsequently mutual assistance (particularly important for countries like Cuba, Vietnam and Angola) and attempts to integrate 'the world socialist system' were accompanied by a revival of nationalism and conflicts between some of these states. These included wars, notably between Vietnam, Kampuchea and China, and military intervention (presented as 'internationalist assistance against counter-revolution') notably against Czechoslovakia in 1968. The latter action has now been recognized by the Soviet government and the four other invading states to have been 'unlawful' and to have 'interrupted the process of demo-

cratic renewal in Czechoslovakia, and [to have] had lasting negative effects' (Statement of 4 December 1989). National tensions have increasingly sharpened and flared up also within the USSR and other multinational states of the former 'socialist bloc' (as well as in Yugoslavia), sometimes assuming violent forms. Such developments constitute a most serious challenge to Marxists, who had traditionally assumed that 'in proportion as the antagonism between classes within the nation vanishes, the hostility of one nation to another will come to an end' (*Communist Manifesto*, pt. 2).

From the late 1960s the term 'proletarian internationalism' came to be used by the Soviet (CPSU) and closely associated communist parties to denote the uncritical acceptance which they sought for Soviet policies and actions. It was therefore increasingly rejected by 'Eurocommunist' parties, which had become openly critical of Soviet hegemony. The Italian Communist Party (PCI) counterposed to it the concept of 'a new internationalism' encompassing wide links with other progressive organizations but 'without particular or privileged links with anybody' (Resolution of PCI Leadership, 29 December 1981, Berlinguer 1982, p. 28). Such a broader notion of internationalism embracing communists, socialists, social democrats, Third World liberation movements and wider sections of world opinion around a defence of 'universal human values' has in recent years been strongly advocated by Gorbachev and the CPSU. However the Japanese Communist Party reproaches the Soviet position with a 'one world-ism' which falsely counterposes the struggle against nuclear war to the class struggle in the interests of its state diplomacy, and from Cuba Castro criticizes it for playing down the anti-imperialist struggle. The debate continues. (See also INTERNATIONALS; NATION; NATIONALISM.)

Reading

Berlinguer, Enrico 1982: *After Poland. Towards a New Internationalism*.

Deutscher, Isaac 1964 (1972): *Marxism in Our Time*.

Fuwa, Tetsuzo 1982: *Stalin and Great Power Chauvinism*.

Gorbachev, Mikhail 1987: *Perestroika. New Thinking for Our Country and the World*.

Johnstone, Monty et al. 1979: 'Conflicts between Socialist Countries'.

Klugmann, James 1970: 'Lenin's Approach to the Question of Nationalism and Internationalism'.

Lenin, V. I. 1970: *On the National Question and Proletarian Internationalism*.

Miliband, Ralph 1980: 'Military Intervention and Socialist Internationalism'.

MONTY JOHNSTONE

Internationals, the

The First International (*The International Working Men's Association*, 1864–76) was an international federation of working-class organizations based on Western and Central Europe, where the labour movement was reviving after the defeats of 1848–49. Although founded by the spontaneous efforts of London and Paris workers, expressing solidarity with the 1863 Polish national rising, Marx (from 1864 to 1872) and Engels (from 1870 to 1872) were to play the key role in its leadership. Marx immediately recognized that 'real "powers" were involved', but that it would 'take time before the reawakened movement allows the old boldness of speech' (letter to Engels, 4 November 1864), which had characterized the much smaller international cadres' organization, the League of Communists, led by Marx and Engels from 1847 to 1852. He therefore drew up and secured the acceptance of an Inaugural Address and Rules framed so as to provide a basis for cooperation with the Liberal leaders of the British trade unions, as well as the continental followers of Proudhon, Mazzini and Lassalle. The International admitted both individual members and affiliated local and national organizations. Its General Council, elected at its (normally) annual congresses, had its seat in London until 1872.

In the early years of the International, Marx, who drafted almost all the documents issued by the General Council, restricted himself to 'those points which allow of immediate agreement and concerted action by the workers' (letter to Kugelmann, 9 October 1866). These included actions against export of strikebreakers, protests against the maltreatment of Irish Fenian prisoners and the struggle against war. As the International developed, Marx succeeded in securing the adoption of demands of an increasingly socialist character. Thus, in 1868, despite a dwindling

Proudhonist opposition, the IWMA, which began without any specific commitment to public ownership, had declared for collective ownership of the mines, railways, arable land, forests and communications.

The PARIS COMMUNE of 1871 represented a turning point in the history of the IWMA. Engels was to describe Paris's spring revolution as 'without any doubt the child of the International intellectually, although the International did not lift a finger to produce it' (letter to Sorge, 12–17 September 1874). The International's French supporters, mainly Proudhonists, played an important part in it and the General Council organized a campaign of international solidarity. Marx secured the endorsement of his passionate historical vindication of the Commune, *The Civil War in France*, by a majority of the General Council, in whose name it was issued as an Address. The experience of the Commune, as well as the growth of working-class suffrage, led Marx and Engels to place great emphasis on the need for effective forms of political action. In September 1871, on their initiative, the IWMA at its London Conference came out officially for the first time in favour of the 'constitution of the working class into a political party' (see PARTY). This objective was incorporated into the new Rule 7a, drawn up by Marx and adopted at the Hague Congress of the International in 1872, which also specified that 'the conquest of political power becomes the great duty of the proletariat'.

These positions were opposed by Bakunin and his supporters in the International who, from anarchist premises (see ANARCHISM), argued for abstention from politics. Bakunin's International Alliance of Socialist Democracy had applied to enter the IWMA in 1868. Notwithstanding his distaste for its programme, Marx the next year supported the admission of its sections into the International on the principle that the IWMA should 'let every section freely shape its own theoretical programme' (*Documents of the First International*, vol. 3, pp. 273–7, 310–11). The conflict between the supporters of Marx and of Bakunin, which escalated in the International from 1869 to 1872, centred above all on how the IWMA should be organized. Bakunin attacked the 'authoritarianism' of the General Council, while at the same time seeking to place the International under the tutelage of a hierarchically organized secret society or societies controlled by himself. Faced with state repression from without and Bakuninist disruption from within, Marx and Engels argued for the powers of the General Council to be increased. Bakunin won support for his opposition to this in Switzerland, Italy, Spain and Belgium, as well as securing the backing of a substantial portion of the British.

The Hague Congress of 1872 brought together sixty-five delegates from thirteen European countries, Australia and the USA, a larger number than at any previous congress. It granted increased powers to the General Council and expelled Bakunin and his comrade, Guillaume, from the IWMA for trying to organize a secret society within the International, accompanied by a more contentious finding of fraud against Bakunin. The congress also approved by a narrow majority a proposal in the name of Marx and Engels and their supporters to move the seat of the General Council to New York. A significant motive for this was probably a fear that in London it might come under the control of the French Blanquist émigrés (see BLANQUISM), with whom they had had to ally themselves to secure the defeat of Bakunin. This was effectively to mark the end of the IWMA, which was finally dissolved at a conference in Philadelphia in 1876. An 'anti-authoritarian' International, which sought to take over the mantle of the IWMA, enjoyed some initial success, but found itself hopelessly split by 1877 and held its last, purely anarchist, rump congress in 1881.

The following years saw an important growth of national workers' parties, mostly of a more of less Marxist character, which the IWMA had, expecially in 1871-2, worked so hard to promote. Marx, until his death in 1883, and Engels, even on the eve of the founding congress of the Second International, had opposed attempts 'to play at international organizations which are at present as impossible as they are useless' (letter to Laura Lafargue, 28 June 1889). He was however subsequently to give the new International important support and advice.

The Second International (1889-1914) was effectively founded at a Marxist-organized International Workers' Congress held in Paris in July 1889. Like the First International it was based essentially on the European labour movement, but was very much larger than its prede-

cessor. Largely dominated by German Social Democracy, many of its affiliated parties had secured – or were in the process of securing – a mass basis. By 1904 they were participating in elections in twenty-one countries and had won more than 6.6 million votes and 261 parliamentary seats. By 1914 they had a membership of four million and a parliamentary vote of twelve million. The Second International was essentially a loose federation of parties and trade unions. In 1900 an International Socialist Bureau, with a technical and coordinating rather than a directive function, was established in Brussels with Camille Huysmans as its full-time secretary. In most affiliated parties, with the principal exception of the British Labour Party (admitted in 1908), Marxism was the dominant ideology, though other trends and influences were also present. These included initially the anarchists who, following defeats on the question of political struggle at the congresses of 1893 and 1896, were excluded from the International. The two theorists who, after Engels's death in 1895, contributed most to the character of the official Marxism of the Second International were KAUTSKY and PLEKHANOV.

The International held its congresses every two to four years to decide on common actions and to debate questions of policy. Among the former was the organization, from 1890, of demonstrations in every country every May Day in support of an eight-hour day. Struggles between right, left and centre trends, originating first in national parties, were carried into the international arena. The Paris Congress of 1900 sharply debated the question of 'Millerandism': whether it was permissible to join a bourgeois government as the French socialist Millerand had done the previous year. Finally a compromise resolution, drafted by Kautsky, was adopted which allowed that such a step might be acceptable as 'a temporary expedient... in exceptional cases' if sanctioned by the party (quoted by Braunthal 1966, vol. 1, pp. 272-3).

The next congress, meeting in Amsterdam in 1904, was asked to give international approval and validity to the resolution condemning the revisionist ideas of Bernstein passed by the German Social Democratic congress at Dresden the previous year. This led to a major and impressive debate on strategy in which the German Social Democratic leader, Bebel, defended his party against charges from the French socialist leader, Jaurès, that its doctrinal rigidity was responsible for a frightening contrast between the growth in its electoral support and its inability to change the Kaiser's autocratic régime. Congress gave its support to the Dresden resolution by 25 votes to 5, with 12 abstentions, but the revisionists remained in the International as in the German party, both of which they permeated with their ideas (see REVISIONISM).

Another important issue of controversy was COLONIALISM, which had already been unanimously condemned by the International's congress of 1900, at the time of the Boer War. However a majority of the colonial commission of the Stuttgart Congress seven years later argued that they should 'not reject all colonial policies in all circumstances, such as those which, under a socialist regime, could serve a civilising purpose' (Braunthal, ibid. p. 318). After a hard-hitting debate this view was rejected by 127 votes to 108 and a resolution passed condemning 'capitalist colonial policies [which] must, by their nature, give rise to servitude, forced labour and the extermination of the native peoples' (Braunthal, ibid. p. 319).

The struggle against war was pivotal to the International and had, since its foundation, been reflected in congress resolutions. It dominated the Stuttgart Congress of 1907, meeting as the clouds of war were gathering over Europe. The final resolution adopted there unanimously – despite serious differences in the debate – incorporated an amendment submitted by LENIN, LUXEMBURG and MARTOV which, after urging the exertion of 'every effort in order to prevent the outbreak of war', went on: 'In case war should break out anyway, it is [the labour movements'] duty to intervene in favour of its speedy termination, and with all their powers to utilize the economic and political crisis created by the war to rouse the masses and thereby to hasten the downfall of capitalist class rule' (Braunthal, ibid. p. 363). This was reaffirmed at the next two congresses. That of Basle in 1912, the last before the war, became a moving demonstration for peace and called – again unanimously – for revolutionary action if war came. The outbreak of the first world war two years later showed approval of such words 'to be only a thin veneer, covering deeply ingrained nationalism' (Deutscher 1972, p. 102). The leading parties of the Second International gave their support to the war waged by their own governments and thereby brought about the ignominious collapse of the International. This was the culmination of a whole period of capitalist expansion and the national integration of the labour movement.

Only the Russian, Serbian, Italian, Bulgarian (Tesnyak), Romanian and US parties – together with small groups inside other parties – remained true to the principles repeatedly extolled by the International. Some unsuccessful wartime attempts were made, particularly by parties in neutral countries, to revive the Second International, whose International Bureau had been moved to Holland. In 1919, however, at a conference at Berne, a shadowy version of the old Second International was reconstituted ('Berne International') and held its first congress at Geneva the next year with seventeen countries represented. In 1921 left socialists from ten parties, including the German Independent Social Democratic Party (USPD), the Austrian Social Democrats (SPÖ) and the British ILP, met in Vienna to constitute the International Working Union of Socialist Parties ('Vienna Union'), nicknamed the 'Two-and-a-Half International'. It saw itself as the first step towards an all-embracing International. In 1923, at a congress in Hamburg, it united with the revived Second International to form the *Labour and Socialist International*, which ceased to function in 1940.

It was succeeded in 1951 by the present *Socialist International*, which is a loose association of the main Socialist and Social Democratic Parties throughout the world with its headquarters in London. Its Eighteenth Congress, held in Stockholm in 1989, re-elected Willy Brandt as its president and adopted a Declaration of Principles placing great emphasis on the securing of peace and disarmament, environmental protection and improved North–South relations. Of its 51 affiliated parties with full membership (1989), 23 are in Third World countries, where its growth in recent years has been most rapid. The Italian Communist Party, which has now become the Democratic Party of the Left (PDS), and some former communist parties in Eastern Europe have expressed a desire to seek affiliation.

The Third International (1919–43) Following the disintegration of the Second International at the outbreak of the first world war, Lenin wrote in November 1914: 'The Second International is dead, overcome by opportunism. . . . Long Live the Third International . . .' ('The Position and Tasks of the Socialist International', CW 21 p. 40). This Third International – called the Communist International, or Comintern – was founded in Moscow in March 1919 on the initiative of the Bolsheviks after the victory of the 1917 October Revolution in Russia and at a time of revolutionary upsurge in Central Europe. Speaking at its first congress, Lenin expressed the prevailing mood and expectations when he declared that 'the founding of an international Soviet republic is on the way' (CW 28, p. 477). He later defined 'recognition of the dictatorship of the proletariat and Soviet power in place of bourgeois democracy' as 'the fundamental principles of the Third International' (CW 31, pp. 197–8). A 'World Union of Socialist Soviet Republics' (Degras 1971, vol. 2, p. 465) was to remain its official objective throughout its whole existence, though it was to recede into the background after 1935. At its second congress in Moscow in July–August 1920 there were delegates from parties and organizations in forty-one countries, and consultative delegates, among others, from the French Socialist Party and the German USPD, a majority at whose congresses would vote before the end of the year to affiliate to the Comintern. Concerned that the new International was threatened with dilution by unstable Social Democratic elements, the congress laid down its draconic Twenty-One Conditions of affiliation. All parties desiring affiliation had to 'remove reformists and centrists from all responsible positions in the workers' movement', and combine legal with illegal work, including systematic propaganda in the army. Defining the epoch as one of 'acute civil war', it demanded 'iron discipline' and the greatest possible degree of centralization both under the party centres, nationally, and, internationally, under the Comintern executive whose decisions were binding between congresses (ibid., vol. 1, pp. 166–72).

In its Statutes the Comintern declared that 'it breaks once and for all with the traditions of the Second International, for whom only white-skinned people existed'. Its task was to embrace and liberate working people of all colours. The Second Congress adopted Theses on the National and Colonial Question, largely drafted by Lenin, which emphasized the need for an anti-imperialist alliance of national and colonial liberation movements with Soviet Russia and working-class movements fighting capitalism (ibid., vol. 1, pp. 138–44). Lenin's pamphlet, 'Left-Wing' Communism – an Infantile Disorder, written in 1920, sought to combat 'leftist' tendencies in the Comintern and argued the case for a principled communist participation in parliamentary elections and work inside reactionary trade unions. It was such trends that he confronted at the third Comintern congress in 1921, when he saw that the revolutionary wave had receded, the communist parties outside Russia represented a minority of the working class, and the previous offensive revolutionary tactics, modelled essentially on Russian experience, were no longer appropriate for the West. The congress called for a united front of working-class parties, nationally and internationally, to fight for the immediate needs of the working class. Arising from this, a conference of the executives of the Comintern, the Second International and the Vienna Union was held in Berlin in 1922, but disagreements prevented its follow-up with subsequent collaboration.

After the failure of the hoped for German revolution in October 1923, the Comintern recognized that a period of relative capitalist stabilization had set in. During the next few years the internal struggles of the Soviet Party were carried into the Comintern. After many bitter battles the Trotskyist opposition to Stalin's policies on Socialism in One Country, the Anglo-Russian Trade Union Unity Committee, and the strategy and tactics to be followed in the Chinese revolution of 1925–27 was defeated, and Trotsky was expelled from the Comintern Executive in September 1927. The Sixth Congress of the Comintern in 1928 adopted a comprehensive programme, largely drafted by Bukharin. It also ushered in the Comintern's 'third period', in which social democracy was denounced as 'social fascism', and proposals for a united front with its leaders were rejected. In 1931 the Comintern executive stated that it was necessary to stop drawing a line 'between fascism and bourgeois democracy, and between the parliamentary form of the dictatorship of the bourgeoisie and its open fascist form' (quoted in Sobolev 1971, p. 313). The disastrous effects of this policy, above all in Germany, led from 1933 to a revision of Comintern strategy. In March 1933, following the establishment of the Nazi dictatorship, the Comintern executive publicly recommended its affiliated parties to approach the central committees of Social Democratic Parties with proposals for joint action against fascism. This led subsequently to united action between communists and socialists in France. The seventh, and last, Comintern congress in 1935, representing over three million communists (785,000 in capitalist countries) in sixty-five parties, made a powerful case for a united front of working-class parties and its extension to a broader Popular Front to stem the tide of fascism. In his main report Dimitrov emphasized that the choice was now not between proletarian dictatorship and bourgeois democracy, but between bourgeois democracy and an open terrorist bourgeois dictatorship represented by fascism. The Comintern's new strategy helped to inspire the Popular Fronts in France and Spain. It mobilized international support for the struggle of the Spanish republic against fascism, as well as for the Soviet government's proposals for a peace front of the USSR and the Western bourgeois democracies to check fascist aggression.

The Comintern, which was always effectively dominated by the Soviet Communist Party, gave its full support to Stalin's purges of the 1930s, in which some of its leading members perished and which led to the dissolution of the Polish Communist Party in 1938 on trumped up charges. Following the German–Soviet non-aggression pact of August 1939 and on Stalin's direct instructions, the Comintern revised its strategy based hitherto on its crucial differentiation between the Western bourgeois democracies and the fascist states. From 1939 to 1941 it condemned the war as unjust, reactionary and imperialist on both sides. After the German attack on the Soviet Union in June 1941 it gave its unstinting support to the Soviet Union and its Western allies in their struggle against the Axis powers. The Comintern was dissolved in June 1943 on the proposal of its presidium, which argued that the different conditions under which the greatly expanded international communist movement now had to work made its direction from an international centre impossible. The dissolution was also intended to placate Stalin's Western allies (see Claudin 1972).

In addition to the Young Communist International (1919–43), which was officially a section of the Communist International, a number of 'sympathizing mass organizations for definite special purposes' were set up on the initiative of the Comintern and worked under its effective leadership. They comprised in particular: the Red International of Labour Unions, or Profintern (1921–37); International Red Aid, or International Class War Prisoners' Aid (1922 till World War Two); Workers' International Relief (1921–35); the Peasant International, or Krestintern (1923–c.1933).

In 1988 the Soviet Communist Party, which holds the extensive Comintern archives in Moscow, decided to make them more accessible to researchers from all over the world. Along with this a more critical debate on and treatment of Comintern history has opened up among Soviet historians.

The Fourth International was founded in 1938 on the initiative of Trotsky from small groups of his supporters in opposition to the Second and Third Internationals, which it condemned as 'counter-revolutionary'. Describing itself as the 'World Party of the Socialist Revolution', it has remained extremely small and has been subject to serious splits (see TROTSKYISM). (See also INTERNATIONALISM.)

Reading

Braunthal, Julius 1961–71 (1966–80): *History of the International*, vols 1–3.

Claudin, Fernando 1972 (1975): *The Communist Movement. From Comintern to Cominform.* Pt. 1.

Cole, G. D. H. 1954–60: *A History of Socialist Thought.* vols 2–5.

Collins, Henry and Abramsky, Chimen 1965: *Karl Marx and the British Labour Movement. Years of the First International.*

Degras, Jane ed. 1956–65 (1971): *The Communist International 1919–1943: Documents.* vols. 1–3.

Deutscher, Isaac 1964 (1972): 'On Internationals and Internationalism'. In *Marxism in Our Time.*

Documents of the First International.

Documents of the Fourth International. The Formative Years. (1933–40) 1973.

Joll, James 1955 (1975): *The Second International 1889–1914.*

Sobolev, A. I. *et al.* 1971: *Outline History of the Communist International.*

MONTY JOHNSTONE

Islam Classical Marxism had relatively little to say about the structure and history of Islam as a world religion. The comments of Marx and Engels on Islam are tantalizingly suggestive, but equally incomplete. In a letter to Engels discussing the nature of Asiatic society, Marx posed the central question to which no adequate answer has yet been provided: Why does the history of the East *appear* as a history of religions? More concretely, Engels in an article on the history of early Christianity for *Die Neue Zeit* grasped one of the fundamental processes of Islamic social structure, namely the political oscillation between nomadic and sedentarized cultures. In a commentary on Islam which reproduced Ibn Khaldun's theory of the circulation of tribal elites, Engels observed that Islam is a religion perfectly adapted to Arab townsmen and nomadic Bedouin: 'Therein lies, however, the embryo of a periodically occurring collision. The townspeople grow rich, luxurious and lax in the observation of the "law". The Bedouins, poor and hence of strict morals, contemplate with envy and covetousness these riches and pleasures' ('On the History of Early Christianity', in Marx and Engels, *On Religion* (1957)). The poor nomads periodically unite together behind a prophet to oust the decadent town-dwellers, reform moral conduct and restore the pristine faith. Within a few generations, the puritanical Bedouin have themselves become individualistic in morals and lax in religious observance; once more, a Mahdi arises from the desert to sweep the towns clean and the cycle of political domination is repeated. The constant transformations of political leadership did not, however, correspond with any fundamental reorganization of the economic base of society which remained remarkably stationary (see ASIATIC SOCIETY).

While Engels interpreted a number of messianic and sectarian movements in Islam as manifestations of this perennial conflict between nomads and townsmen, it is possible to approach Islam itself as an effect of this contradictory fusion of nomadic pastoralism and sedentarized society. Islam, originating from the *hijra* (the migration of the Prophet from Mecca to Medina) of 622 AD, has to be understood as part of the mercantile culture of the trade centres of the Arabian peninsula. Whereas social scientists like Max Weber have treated Islam as 'a warrior religion', Islam was primarily the religion of urban elites who were enjoying the economic rewards of the expanding trade passing though Mecca, which in the seventh century had come to dominate the Arabian economy. Islam, as the blending of urban piety and tribal virtue, provided a new principle of political integration based on faith rather than blood, organized around loyalty to a prophet and universalistic values. By uniting the fissiparous tribes within a single religious community under urban, commercial leadership, Islam protected trade and proved a peculiarly dynamic social and political force. After the death of the Prophet Muhammad in 632, the new religion rapidly established its dominance in the Middle East and North Africa by 713, despite the division between the followers of 'Ali (Shi'ites) and the supporters of 'the rightly guided caliphs' (Sunni Muslims) over the question of political succession.

The early success of the expanding Islamic community, which was the fusion of an urban merchant elite and Bedouin nomadic warriors, is partly explained by the military weakness of surrounding empires (Sassanian and Byzantine), partly by the integrative force and simplicity of Islamic ideology, and partly by the system of patronage which Islam created in relation to protected and dependent populations of Christian and Jewish tribes in the so-called 'millet system'. These Islamic conquests did not therefore pulverize the social structures of the social formations within which the Islamic faith became dominant. Islam spread as a series of patrimonial empires with the following constitutive features: (1) the ownership of land was controlled by the state and distributed to landlords in the form of non-inheritable prebends; however, in addition to prebendal ownership, there was tribal land and religious property (*waqf* property); (2) the state bureaucracy was staffed by slaves and a slave army developed as a social buffer between the royal household, the prebendal cavalry and the urban population; (3) urban culture and religious piety were shaped, especially in the more advanced societies of North Africa and the Middle East, by the interests and lifestyle of a merchant class, whose wealth depended on inter-continental trade in luxuries, and of the religious leaders (the *ulama*) whose control of the law (the *Shari'a*) contributed to their social pre-eminence.

In the period of expansion and consolidation (700–1500) before the fragmentation of Islamicate society into three empires (Safavi, Timuri and Ottoman), in addition to mercantile wealth based on luxury goods (spices, silk, scent and jewellery), papermaking, textiles, carpets, leatherwork and pottery were rapidly expanded, despite the economic drag resulting from the Mongol irruptions in the thirteenth and fourteenth centuries. Islamic Spain, in particular, became a great centre of agrarian development, shipbuilding, mining and textiles. The economic surplus which resulted from conquest, expansion and growth of handicrafts became the basis of a civilized, rational, court culture through royal patronage of science, medicine and the arts. A sophisticated, genteel (*adab*) culture emerged among the polite classes around the royal courts which became the vehicle of worldly values in literature, music and the fine arts. This *adab* culture became somewhat separate and remote from the more rigid religious values. In this way, Islam became the creative vehicle of Greek philosophy and science which, via Islamic Spain, provided the intellectual basis of the Renaissance.

The absence of indigenous capitalist development in Islamic society represents a major issue for Marxist historiography. The idea that the beliefs of Muslims, the fatalism of Islamic theology or the legal norms against usury prohibited the development of capitalist society has been rejected by Marxists. For example, Rodinson (1974) showed that the prescriptions relating to economic behaviour in the Qur'an (God's recitation) and *Sunnah* (orthodox practices of the Prophet) did not inhibit economic development; on the contrary, a capitalist sector did develop in Islam which was similar to developments in Europe. There were, however, three limitations on the expansion of this sector: (1) the self-sufficiency of the local village economy; (2) the dominance of the state in the guild system, trade relations and land tenure; and (3) periodic checks on socio-economic development following nomadic invasions. One problem with Rodinson's argument is the equation of trade and mercantile capital with capitalist relations of production. In Islam, inter-continental trade, which was the main source of capital accumulation, was controlled by a small group of merchants who played almost no role in local production and distribution. Although the rural surplus was appropriated by towndwellers through the mechanism of taxation, there was little economic exchange between town and country because peasant needs were satisfied locally. The role of trade in Islamic societies provides an illustration of Marx's argument that, while trade disintegrated traditional economic relations in Europe, its corrosive consequences depended on the nature of the productive communities between which trade occurred. Thus the social structures of ancient communities of Asia were hardly disturbed by such inter-continental trade.

While Marx and Engels expected the development of capitalist relations to liquidate religious belief and identity, Islam has so far proved highly resistant to the secularizing impact of capitalist transformation. This resilience, a consequence of Islamic responses to imperialism and colonialism, can be divided into two stages. In the first, there was a broad movement of religious reform, aimed at suppressing rural and magical practices associated with Sufism and veneration of saints. There was thus a renewed emphasis on literacy, Qur'anic orthodoxy and ritual simplicity; urban literate piety was superimposed on the mass religiosity of the countryside. Reformed Islam was simultaneously a return to Qur'anic tradition and an attempt to render Islam compatible with modern industrial, secular society. In the second stage, Islam assumed a militant, anti-colonial, populist stance in which the *ulama* emerged as representative of the urbanized poor, unemployed youth and alienated students. Because the mosques, *madrasah* (religious schools) and *ulama* enjoyed popular support from the masses, puritanical, militant Islam could emerge as a principal source of opposition to client regimes in Africa and Asia.

In the late twentieth century, various fundamentalist movements in Islam have challenged the secularization of religious values and the Westernization of traditional culture. Militant Islam is able to function on a world scale precisely because of the creation of a global capitalist system of production, trade and communication. Although there are important differences between these radical religious movements, the Muslim Brotherhood (in Egypt), the Islamic party in Pakistan and Islamic resurgence in Malaysia share a number of common features: rejection of Westernization and consumerism, combined with the view that Marxism has failed to appeal to the masses. However, in the case of Iran, the revolutionary quality of Shi'ism is a combination of traditional themes of martyrdom with a new theory of clerical sovereignty in a context of severe economic and social disruption. With a global population of approximately 600 million Muslims, militant Islam is now not only a source of political disruption in the client states of the West, but equally in the Soviet Union and to a lesser extent in China, where Islam has survived Stalinization and the Cultural Revolution.

Reading

Ashtor, E. 1976: *A Social and Economic History of the Near East in the Middle Ages*.

Gellner, Ernest 1981: *Muslim Society*.

Hodgson, Marshall G. S. 1974: *The Venture of Islam*.

Rodinson, Maxime 1971: *Mohammad*.

— 1974: *Islam and Capitalism*.

— 1979: *Marxism and the Muslim World*.

Roff, W. R. ed. 1987: *Islam and the Political Economy of Meaning*.

Turner, Bryan S. 1974: *Weber and Islam: A Critical Study*.

BRYAN S. TURNER

J

Jaurès, Jean   Born 3 September 1859, Castres (Languedoc); assassinated 31 July 1914, Paris. A brilliant student, from a modest middle-class family, Jaurès became a university teacher, with a very wide range of interests, and a fluent writer and speaker. Early drawn to politics, he was elected to the Assembly from his native region, the Tarn, in 1885, and in 1893, by now definitely a socialist, as candidate of the Tarn miners after a long strike. A firm republican and democrat, he was active in the defence of Dreyfus and the campaign for separation of church and state. He did not join the more intransigent or Marxist wing of the socialist movement, but he had much respect for Marx, whom he frequently cited. Engels, it must be said, was one of a number of Marxists who thought poorly of him, especially as an economist (letter to Lafargue, 6 March 1894). As a historian Jaurès was a pioneer in the study of the social bases of the French Revolution, and tried to combine Marx's historical materialism with recognition of ideals and their influence (Lévy 1947, p. xiv); his aim was to hold up socialism as the legitimate heir and fulfilment of the Revolution. He was quite prepared to speak in terms of class struggle, and he looked to the working class to lead France forward, with the support of the peasantry. He insisted on the significance of the worker as emancipated individual, not merely as a unit in a mass. Very much a patriotic Frenchman, he worked out a plan of army reform, published in 1910, based on universal, short-term service, which was designed to make the army more effective as well as democratic. But he was an eloquent advocate of peace, with great faith in the International as its bulwark. As war approached in 1914 he was pleading for restraint when he was murdered by a nationalist fanatic.

Reading
Jackson, J. Hampden 1943: *Jean Jaurès, his Life and Work.*

Jaurès, Jean 1898–1902 (1922–24): *Histoire socialiste.*

— 1901: *Études socialistes.*

— 1910: *L'Armée nouvelle.*

Lévy, Louis ed. 1947: *Anthologie de Jean Jaurès.*

Pease, Margaret 1916: *Jean Jaurès, Socialist and Humanitarian.*

Rappoport, Charles 1915: *Jean Jaurès, l'homme, le penseur, le socialiste.*

V. G. KIERNAN

joint-stock company   The joint-stock company broadly developed from the middle of the nineteenth century onwards, replacing the family-owned firms to an increasing extent. Today, practically all large-scale firms, outside the public sector, have that juridical form. Its generalization corresponds with two basic trends of the capitalist mode of production. On the one hand, every large sum of money reserve ('savings') has the tendency to transform itself into money capital, i.e. to aspire to partake in the general distribution of total socially produced surplus value. Before the appearance of the joint-stock company, this could only be done by depositing these savings in financial institutions (above all banks). But such deposits generally receive only a rather low rate of interest, much below average profit. Through the joint-stock company, whoever acquires stocks from a capitalist firm can expect a somewhat higher rate of return on his capital than depositing it with a bank, especially taking into account the long-term value appreciation of that capital. On the other hand, the tendency towards growing CENTRALIZATION AND CONCENTRATION OF CAPITAL implies that larger and larger firms emerge, disposing of greater and greater amounts of capital.

They therefore need to acquire capital over and above that of their founders. With the appearance of the joint-stock company, capitalists who lose their independent businesses and are owners of a certain amount of money savings can still remain involved in current capitalist business, be it in a 'passive' way. If they acquire stocks in larger firms, their income (and in a certain sense, their economic fate) still remains tied to the success or failure of those firms.

However, by buying stocks in a given company, an owner of money capital becomes a victim of the process of centralization of capital. He loses the right to dispose freely of his money capital, by abandoning it to those who actually run the company (the directors, the managing board etc., according to the rules and customs of various capitalist countries, which allow many variations of titles and functions). In fact, jurisprudence or even straightforward commercial law or bankruptcy law in several countries has established that the stockholder is not entitled to a part of a company's assets proportional to his share of the total stocks issued by that company. Ownership of stocks only entitles the owner to a pro-rata part of current income in the form of *distributed profits* (dividends). Those who actually run the company can generally manage to get a larger share of the total profit, which can be seen as the sum total of *entrepreneurial profit* and of interest (on stocks, bonds and other debts such as bank credit). They may receive special allowances for attending board meetings (called *tantièmes* in French and German). They can vote themselves large directors' or managers' salaries, pensions, expense account allowances, free services (cars, mansions, yachts, vacations, hospital bills etc.) They can receive preferential stocks or easy speculative profits through new stock options. This larger share will be important especially during the initial floating of the stock; Hilferding (1910) called that differential entrepreneurial gain *promoter's profit* (see FINANCE CAPITAL).

With the generalization of the joint-stock company, *a growing duplication of capital* occurs. On the one hand, there is a 'real' physical capital: buildings, machinery and other equipment, raw material stocks, commodity stocks, money deposited in the banks and used for the current payment of wages, etc. On the other hand, there are stocks and bonds deposited in safe-deposit boxes or kept in safes, appearing occasionally in the stock market. Marx calls this second form of capital *fictitious capital*: for evidently, this 'duplication' of capital does not correspond to any increase in total value of real assets, or total value currently produced, or total surplus value currently produced and (re)distributed. The value of this fictitious capital oscillates on a long-term basis around the value of the 'real assets', but can occasionally differ markedly from it, thereby making e.g. *take-over bids* profitable for speculators when it falls signicantly below the value of the real assets. More generally, the expansion of the joint-stock company and the emergence of the *stock market* creates a powerful stimulus for speculation, which initially was only centred around the public debt and the stocks of a few special adventuristic firms like the various East India companies which sprang up in Western Europe in the seventeenth century, or Law's speculative ventures in France in the eighteenth century.

Stock market speculation does not determine the *ups and downs of the industrial cycle*. It tries to anticipate them. The prices of a given stock, at a given moment, on the stock exchange will depend upon the expected earnings of the firm (more precisely: distributed earnings, i.e. dividends) and the current rate of interest. But as these expectations are never precise, and can often be proved wrong through later developments, all kinds of factors (rumours about the state of the business of the firm, information about the general state of the business in a given industrial branch, a given country or even a wider geographical area in which the main part of the firm's business is being conducted, rumours about the personal finances or even the health of the firm's main director(s) etc.) can immediately influence a given stock's rating in the stock market. 'Insiders' who possess real information as against unfounded rumours, large-scale speculators who have a lot of money (or bank credit) at their disposal, can try to influence these rates in order to make handsome profits through buying and selling, or selling and buying. Obviously, all these speculations in no way directly increase the total amount of the surplus value available for distribution among the bourgeois class as a whole. But they can significantly alter the way it is distributed among various groups of capitalists. And they can even influence, at least in the short run, the rate of effective (productive) capital accumulation. For example if a firm wants to expand its 'real assets', needs additional cash for buying them and tries to float an issue of new stocks in order to finance this expansion, but this issue hits a depressed stock market, the issue might fail, the expansion of 'real assets' will not take place, and thereby a process of expanded material production and expanded value production might be arrested or reversed.

Some of the ruses used by founders of joint-stock companies or speculators basing themselves upon 'inside information' come close to outright robbery. As this is robbery of many capitalists by a small group of them, it is regarded more severely by bourgeois society than are those various processes, basic to the system, through which capitalists large and small rob the workers or the petty bourgeoisie. Therefore, after serious cases of such misappropriation, capitalist countries generally enact legislation to control more strictly the operations both of joint-stock companies and of the stock exchange, in order to make the gravest outrages more difficult. Nevertheless, the fleecing of 'the public' by stock market speculators continues to be widespread in many capitalist countries.

Over the last fifty years the generalization of the joint-stock company, the running of the big capitalist firms through directors, boards of directors etc. has created a reinterpretation of contemporary capitalism as being run by managers in contrast with the 'old capitalism' run by the owners. The works of Berle and Means (1933), James Burnham (1943) and Galbraith (1967) are the main landmarks of that interpretation. There is obviously a kernel of truth in these reinterpretations. In *Capital* III Marx himself, many decades before these authors, drew attention to a growing divorce between formal ('naked') ownership of capital, and the capacity of *operatively disposing of capital*, a difference between 'passive' capitalists and 'functioning' capitalists (*fungierende Kapitalisten*), i.e. those entrepreneurs who actually manage and operate firms. There is no doubt that this distinction, which is inherent in capital as such, has been greatly enhanced by the generalization of the joint-stock company. The real controversy therefore, concerns something else, namely

whether 'managers' constitute a new social class, with interests apart and different from those of the juridical owners of capital, or whether whatever difference of interest and behaviour exists between them is a *functional difference within the same social class*, the bourgeoisie.

These questions can be answered at two levels. At the level of general social interest, it seems obvious that managers and stock holders, whether large or small, have the same common interest to extract the maximum of surplus value from the workers, to maximize the profits and the accumulation of capital of 'their' firm(s). This flows automatically from the iron law of competition, i.e. from the existence of private property in the *economic* and not the purely juridical sense of the word (of what Marx calls 'many capitals'). Only if there were no more than a single firm in the whole world would this rule lose its relevance. As long as this is not the case, one cannot discern any fundamental difference in economic behaviour between the so-called top managers and big capitalists in general. After all, maximization of profit and of capital growth (capital accumulation) is a basic characteristic of capitalism and the capitalist class since its inception, and not an idiosyncrasy of managers. At the level of personal social interests, top managers are by no means propertyless. Their huge income and access to special privileges (inside information, stock options etc.) also enable them to *accumulate private capital on a large scale*. This is certainly a very small fraction of the total capital which they manage, but in absolute figures it is substantial and can even be enormous; and it puts them squarely into the same social class as other private owners of capital, with the same basic interest of defending surplus value extraction and private property in general, for the whole capitalist class.

Finally, the assumption that through the growing power of top managers the key financial groups ('monopolists') who actually control the majority of large corporations have lost control is dubious, to say the least. Techniques of control may have been differentiated or changed. Some finance groups may have seen their power decline while others have seen it grow (e.g. the Morgans versus the Rockefellers in the USA). Some 'new' barons may have emerged at the top level in periods of rapid capitalist expansion (e.g. the Texas oil interests in the USA after world war II). But there is hardly any evidence that propertyless managers are managing billion dollar corporations *against* the interests of billionaire stockholders.

So what remains of the change insisted upon by the participants in this controversy is the fact that there is a real division of interest *inside* the capitalist class between those who have the primary interest of seeing current profits distributed in the form of dividends and those who want most profit retained inside the corporation for growth. But this is a difference of interest between *rentiers* and *operative capitalists* (entrepreneurs), not between two different social classes. After all, if your current personal income is already very high there is no great incentive to increase it as much as possible since this would only increase tax liability and the income would be spent anyway. The rentiers spend, the managers direct current operations, and the big monopolists take the key financial decisions with regard to accumulation (expansion of the firm, differentiation of output, mergers etc.) The fact that they often own 'only' 5 or 10 per cent of capital (5 or 10 per cent of 10, 20, 30 billion that is to say) does not disprove this functional division of labour inside the capitalist class in any way. It only shows that joint-stock companies – the general meetings of stockholders notwithstanding – are just a device through which many capitalists are deprived of the capacity to dispose freely of their capital, in favour of a few capitalists who are very large and very rich indeed. (See also BOURGEOISIE; FINANCE CAPITAL.)

Reading

Berle, A. A. and Means, G. C. 1933: *The Modern Corporation and Private Property.*

Burnham, James 1943: *The Managerial Revolution.*

Galbraith, J. K. 1967: *The New Industrial State.*

Hilferding, Rudolf 1910 (*1981*): *Finance Capital.*

Mandel, E. 1975: *Late Capitalism.*

Scott, John 1979: *Corporations, Classes and Capitalism.*

ERNEST MANDEL

Judaism There are a number of reasons why Judaism is important in relation to Marx and

Marxism, though its substantive content has not featured in debate. First, it offered Marx an opportunity to consider the role of a religion in society – other than Christianity which was then an adjunct of the state – at a time when he was moving from democratic radicalism to historical materialism. Secondly, Marx was of Jewish origin and wanted to distance himself from that association. Thirdly, Marx has often been accused of being anti-Semitic. Most of the extant and continuing literature on the subject tends to concentrate on the latter two factors.

Marx was drawn into the debate on Jews and Judaism after the Jews of Germany, with strong support from an increasingly powerful liberal lobby, had been campaigning for half a century for civil emancipation and the abolition of their special tolerated status. For Marx, the critique of religion in Germany had been completed and he supported the demand for civil rights for Jews, partly because any structural change in the organization of the Christian state would be desirable in that it would undermine the foundations of an irrelevant social order, and partly because civil rights would only confer political emancipation, an insufficient but necessary precursor of the achievement of human emancipation. Marx did not join the debate on Jews spontaneously. He had followed with interest the demystification of Christianity which began with D. F. Strauss's seminal work, *The Life of Jesus* (1837). It was followed soon after by Feuerbach's *Essence of Christianity* (1841) and Bruno Bauer's systematic critique of theology. Feuerbach added an original dimension to the debate by leaving Christian theology intact and presenting it in anthropological terms, with the Christian god as man's projection of his spiritual self onto an imaginary divinity (Löwith 1941). Moses Hess completed this line of religious critique by the Young Hegelians, rejecting their 'theological consciousness' and calling for a *social* analysis of the human condition (Hess 1843).

When Bruno Bauer joined the debate on Jewish emancipation he followed the reasoning established in the German philosophical tradition. Fichte, the first to respond to the original demand for emancipation in the late eighteenth century, rejected it on the grounds that the isolation of the Jews was largely of their own making. As human beings they could claim human rights, but as dissenters in a Christian state they could not claim formal acceptance of their dissent, where Christians themselves were denied the right to dissent. Hegel, in a famous footnote in the *Philosophy of Right* (1821), also emphasized the human status of the Jews, but linked the question of civil rights to the acceptance of civil obligations. If, for example, Jews were willing to accept military service and Quakers were not, then Jews had a prior right to be emancipated. Bauer, however, preferred to follow Fichte. In two well-known essays (Bauer 1843) he rejected Jewish emancipation partly because the Jews were unwilling to free themselves of their Jewishness and also because Christians could not bestow freedom on Jews while they themselves were not free. It was at this point that Marx joined the debate with a critical analysis of Bauer's arguments. Like Hess, he called for a social analysis of religion and dismissed Bauer's contention that Jews would have to give up their Judaism to be eligible for civil equality. Religion was a private matter and the state had no right to intervene other than on issues concerning the individual as a citizen. Bauer's objections were theological and therefore invalid. There was, however, a social question and Marx agreed with Bauer that, if the Jews, who were numerically an insignicant section of the population (± 1%) could nevertheless exert an influence out of all proportion to their number, then this was due to their traditional concentration in trade and commerce, a position which gave them real political power. Marx elaborated on this and emphasized the importance of financial power, which had enabled the Jews not only to demand civil rights, but also to infiltrate their social and commercial values into the organization of civil society. The state needs the commercial function of the Jews and becomes 'Judaized' in its pursuit of money. Jewish exclusiveness, which serves their ethnocentric preoccupations is not determined, as Bauer had argued, by their refusal to accept a position in history, but, on the contrary, is a product of history which preserves the Jew as an essential element in the structure of civil society. It follows that, when Jews relinquish their social role as traders and hucksters, or the state frees itself of its need for commercialism, the Jews and their dedication to the mystical egoism of their religious tradition, will vanish.

Marx's main argument was set out in two review essays on Bauer in the solitary issue of the *Deutsch-Französische Jahrbücher* (1844). The first essay is an incisive presentation of the relationship between church and state in which Bauer's theological position is demolished. The second essay, which deals with the social roles of Jews and Judaism, is a short, vehement polemic, written in an aggressive, virulent style, full of assertions and assumptions, which owe little to the empirical realities of Jewish life in the first half of the nineteenth century, or to the intellectual traditions of Judaism. When they were first published, the essays made no impact and the only known review of them in a Jewish newspaper of the time, welcomed Marx's support of the Jewish claim for emancipation (see Carlebach 1978). The polemical character of the second essay raised no comment, probably because the intemperate language in which it was couched was quite commonplace in the 1840s. With the advent of formal anti-Semitic movements in the wake of the successful outcome of the Jewish struggle for emancipation in the last quarter of the nineteenth century, renewed attention was focused on Marx's essays, by both protagonists and opponents of Marxism. Jews also had to take a position on Marx's essays, particularly those who were attracted by socialism in one form or another. It was in this context that a large literature was generated, which strove to resolve two questions. Was Marx Jewish in a more meaningful sense than mere biological descent and was he anti-Semitic or, more accurately, did he share the conviction of the anti-Jewish lobby that Jews and Judaism were inimical to the interests and well-being of nations, groups or social classes?

Regarding the first question, there have been many attempts to depict Marx as a 'prophet' in Old Testament tradition (Künzli 1966), as a secular Jew steeped in a Jewish ethical tradition, as a self-hating Jew or as a Jewish apostate (Carlebach 1978). Marx has also frequently been described as a Jew by 'race', with all the character implications this carries in racialist theories. Marx himself did not comment on this subject except to acknowledge his origins. Apart from a literary appreciation of the Hebrew prophets, there is no evidence that Marx was, or felt himself to be, Jewish or influenced by the Judaic tradition. With the advent of the Nazi era and the mass extermination of the Jews of Europe, the question of Marx's anti-Semitism has become a more sensitive issue. As one Jewish socialist put it, the call for the emancipation of mankind from Judaism in 1843 has come too close to being a prescription for the events of 1943 (Jona Fink in Carlebach 1978, pp. 298 ff). Although we know that Marx was not averse to using offensive vulgarisms about some Jews (Silberner 1962), there is no basis for regarding him as having been anti-semitic. At the same time, there can be no doubt that his second essay on the Jews has been and continues to be used by those who propagate anti-Jewish views, in support of their various accusations against the Jews. It is also true that the misuse of Marx's essay began in his lifetime, without eliciting protest or comment from him.

The argument over Marx's relationship to Jews and Judaism goes on and is likely to continue (Pachter 1979, Hirsch 1980, Clark 1981) but rarely touches on the most interesting problem which Marx has raised about Judaism. That is, whether Judaism has survived through history or in spite of it. This question was elaborated by Moses Hess when he revived the idea of a national solution to the Jewish problem in 1862 (*Rom und Jerusalem*), but did not receive a great deal of attention until the emergence of political Zionism at the end of the nineteenth century. It then gave rise to a vigorous, though largely hostile debate, which nevertheless contributed substantially to the development of Marxist analyses of nationalism generally (Carlebach 1978, esp. chs. IX and X).

Reading

Bauer, Bruno 1843: *Die Judenfrage.*

— 1843: 'Die Fähigkeit der heutigen Juden und Christen frei zu werden'. In Herwegh, G. ed., *Einundzwanzig Bogen aus der Schweitz.*

Carlebach, Julius 1978: *Karl Marx and the Radical Critique of Judaism.*

Clark, Joseph 1981: 'Marx and the Jews: Another View'.

Hess, Moses 1843: 'Philosophie der Tat'.

Hirsch, Helmut 1980: *Marx und Moses, Karl Marx zur 'Judenfrage' und zu Juden.*

Künzli, Arnold 1966: *Karl Marx — Eine Psychographie.*

Löwith, Karl 1941 (1964): *From Hegel to Nietzsche.*

Pachter, Henry 1979: 'Marx and the Jews'.

Silberner, Edmund 1962: *Sozialisten zur Judenfrage.*

JULIUS CARLEBACH

justice Until quite recently there was little overt or extended theoretical reflection about the place that principles of justice occupy within Marxist thought. Two conflicting attitudes – as often as not in tension under the same pen – have been common in the tradition: on the one hand, explicit, sometimes fervent, disavowals of any reliance on considerations of justice, as being irrelevant to the case for socialism and against capitalism; on the other hand, a widespread use in practice of arguments precisely from justice, unreflectively or unknowingly yet time and again resorted to in Marxist social criticism.

From the early 1970s, however, an intensive interest among philosophers in the concept of distributive justice began to leave its imprint on the discussion of Marx's ideas, generating a considerable exegetical literature, itself polarized in accordance with the two traditionally conflicting attitudes. Principles of distributive justice concern the proper division of benefits and burdens within a society or other collectivity. Did Marx condemn capitalism in the light of any such principles?

Many say that he did not. They cite: (1) his insistence in *Capital* that the wage relation, as an exchange of equivalent values (labour power for the wage), involves no injustice to the worker; (2) Marx's polemic in *Critique of the Gotha Programme*, against socialist appeals to notions of 'fair distribution' or 'right'; (3) his view that standards of right and justice are internal to specific modes of production and, as such, historically relative; and (4) his characterization of morality in general as ideological, part of a dependent, changing superstructure.

Proponents of this viewpoint argue further: (5) that to impute to Marx a care for justice bends his meaning towards a narrow concern with reforming the sphere of distribution – income differentials, wage levels and the like – where in fact his aim was more fundamental and revolutionary, the transformation of production and property relations; (6) that the imputation denatures, also, his effort to identify the real historical forces leading to the overthrow of capitalism, substituting a project of ethical enlightenment he would himself have dubbed idealist; (7) that, as a juridical principle, justice could not anyway be implemented in a communist society, which Marx conceived as having no juridical apparatuses of state and law; and (8) that his vision of communism excluded those circumstances (of scarcity and conflict) which render norms of justice necessary, anticipating instead a distributive standard ('To each according to their needs') which lay *beyond* justice. (9) If Marx did condemn capitalism, finally, he did so, on this interpretation, in the light of values other than justice: primarily, freedom and self-realization.

Other commentators believe Marx did criticize capitalism as unjust. They argue: (1) that his description of the wage relation as an exchange of equivalents was merely provisional, applying to the sphere of circulation – and followed by a characterization of the production process in which he displayed that relationship as in truth exploitative: not a genuine exchange at all but appropriation by the capitalist of unpaid surplus labour; (2) that notwithstanding his own polemics against moralistic criticism, he presented exploitation as wrongful or unfair, calling it 'robbery' and 'theft'; (3) that by ranking, in *Critique of the Gotha Programme*, the principle of distribution according to need above the principle of distribution according to work and this in turn above the distributional norms of capitalism, Marx proffered, implicitly, transhistorical, non-relative criteria of moral ordering, a sort of hierarchy of standards of distributive justice; and (4) that his apparent statements of moral relativism expressed, in fact, a moral realism, specifying the material conditions necessary for achieving 'higher' standards of fairness, rather than denying that such historically transcendent ethical judgements could be made.

In addition, these commentators contend, (5) a concern with distribution is not intrinsically reformist, since, broadly conceived, distribution covers the most general division of social goods and bads, including the ownership of productive resources – a revolutionary preoccupation indeed. (6) Equally, while Marx did not think that moral criticism by itself was sufficient, still, as a complement to materialist historical analysis of the potential agencies of change, it had a place in his thought. (7) Categorizing principles of justice as juridical is too narrow; they can be envisaged also, independently of any instruments of coercion, as simply ethical principles for evaluating and determining the allocation of social benefits and burdens. (8) 'To each according to their needs' is such a principle, a norm of distributive justice, its aim an equal right to self-realization; even though viewed by Marx as to be achieved with the disappearance of coercive state apparatuses. (9) The distinction made in the opposing interpretation, finally, between his views of justice and of freedom, is exegetically arbitrary: so far as Marx did sometimes belittle ethical criticism or characterize moral norms as being historically limited or relative, freedom and other values figured alongside justice amongst his targets.

Partly because he was no moral philosopher, and indeed impatient with ethical advocacy and analysis, partly because of his play with 'dialectical' contradictions in expounding the nature of the wage relation, it is not possible to render all of Marx's ideas in this area consistent with one another. A resolution of the controversy requires some effort of intellectual reconstruction, an attempt to make the best sense that can be made of his various viewpoints. The most cogent such reconstruction broadly vindicates those who say Marx did think capitalism unjust.

Some sense can be made of the apparent evidence to the contrary; whereas no satisfactory answer has been given to the questions which trouble the opposing interpretation. For, first, there is no persuasive account of why Marx should have described exploitation as 'robbery' if he did not see it as a wrong. Second, the argument that he condemned the unfreedoms rather than the injustices of capitalism poses a spurious alternative: concerned, as he was, with the *distribution* of freedom, his criticism in this matter was itself a critique of injustice. Third, though obscured by some of what Marx himself says, the principle 'To each according to their needs' is both a principle of moral equality and – if we construe the notion of communist 'abundance' in any realistic fashion – a norm of distributive justice.

On the other hand, Marx's express refusal to offer criticism in terms of justice is explicable as being due to the narrow conception of this value which he (overtly) entertained: a conception associating justice with the prevailing norms internal to a.given social order; and with those norms, moreover, covering distribution in its most limited sense: distribution of consumption goods. But these two conceptual associations are not obligatory. There are broader notions of distributive justice than they define. Inasmuch as he did clearly regard the most general distribution of benefits and burdens under capitalism as, by some historically transcendent standards, morally objectionable, we must conclude that Marx thought capitalism unjust, on a broader conception of justice than the one he himself professed. Implicitly, his critique was a critique of social injustice. (See also ETHICS; MORALS.)

Reading

Arneson, Richard J. 1981: 'What's Wrong with Exploitation?'

Brenkert, George G. 1983: *Marx's Ethics of Freedom.*

Buchanan, Allen E. 1982: *Marx and Justice: The Radical Critique of Liberalism.*

Cohen, G. A. 1983: Review of *Karl Marx* by Allen W. Wood.

Cohen, Marshall, Nagel, Thomas and Scanlon, Thomas, eds. 1980: *Marx, Justice, and History.*

Geras, Norman 1985: 'The Controversy About Marx and Justice'.

Lukes, Steven 1985: *Marxism and Morality.*

Nielsen, K. and Patten, S. C., eds. 1981: 'Marx and Morality'.

Ryan, Cheyney C. 1980: 'Socialist Justice and the Right to the Labour Product'.

Wood, Allen W. 1981: *Karl Marx.*

Young, Gary 1978: 'Justice and Capitalist Production: Marx and Bourgeois Ideology'.

NORMAN GERAS

K

Kalecki, Michał Born 22 June 1899; died 17 April 1970, Warsaw. A Polish economist, Kalecki's early reading of Marx, Luxemburg and Tugan-Baranovsky and his studies of industrial behaviour were the basis of models of business cycles which he published from the early 1930s. Although he saw fluctuations in profits and investment as the key factors in the business cycle, his use of the concept of effective demand caused him to be widely regarded as a forerunner of Keynes and a theorist of left-wing Keynesianism. This view found a strange echo in 1968, when Kalecki was accused by Polish government-inspired economists of being an 'incomplete Marxist' and of having fallen under the influence of Keynes.

Throughout his life, Kalecki continued to refine his theory of business cycles in capitalist economies, and he also made fundamental contributions to the economic analysis of developing countries and socialist economies. His profound economic insights were usually advanced as an aid to practical policy-making. Thus, in his business cycles theory, he sought to explain the instability of capitalist economies, a feature which he regarded as the chief economic defect of capitalism, supplanting in an era of monopoly capitalism the absolute working-class immiseration of nineteenth-century capitalism. This instability, which was due to fluctuations in profits and investment, could be alleviated by government expenditures and the stimulation of investment, but only temporarily because of capitalists' hostility to any permanent regime of full employment.

In developing economies, Kalecki saw the key problem as being that of the financing of development where private capital accumulation is weak and immature, and the tax base for state-financed accumulation is narrow. This, in his view, accounts for the widespread tendency of those economies to economic stagnation, even under progressive, modernizing governments.

In socialist economies, he was mainly concerned with analysing how labour supply, investment and the supply of wage goods can be combined to obtain balanced growth in living standards. He regarded economic planning as essential for the coordination of a socialist economy, but such planning had to be balanced by workers' control in order to prevent the bureaucratization of the economy.

There are certain superficial similarities between Kalecki's business cycle theory and Keynes's macroeconomic analysis, such as their common use of concepts of effective demand. Kalecki also made virtually no use of the labour theory of value in his work. However, his analysis of capitalist and developing economies is firmly based on Marxist class categories. In its chief particulars, such as his theory of profits (which are determined by capitalists' expenditures on consumption and investment, the government deficit and the foreign trade surplus), investment (which is determined by profits and the existing capital stock), consumption (which is determined by total output and the distribution of income between wages and profits) and wages (which are determined by the degree of monopoly and the relative prices of raw materials), it is wholly different from that of Keynes and his followers. Kalecki's business cycle theory is derived from Marxian schemes of reproduction, from which he also deduced a Keynesian Investment Multiplier.

Kalecki also wrote a critique of econometrics based on historical materialism. His sympathies were always with the working class, and he regarded socialism as the only permanent solution to the problems and injustices of capitalism.

Reading
Kalecki, Michał 1971: *Selected Essays on the Dynamics of the Capitalist Economy 1933–1970.*

— 1972: *Selected Essays on the Economic Growth of the Socialist and the Mixed Economy.*

— 1976: *Essays on Developing Economies.*

— 1986: *Selected Essays on Economic Planning.*

— forthcoming: *Collected Works.*

Osiatyński, Jerzy 1988: *Michał Kalecki on a Socialist Economy.*

Sawyer, Malcolm 1985: *The Economics of Michał Kalecki.*

JAN TOPOROWSKI

Kantianism and Neo-Kantianism The work of the German philosopher Immanuel Kant (1724–1804) is seminal for any understanding of both modern theory of knowledge and modern social theory. In the theory of knowledge Kant's work effected a synthesis of elements of rationalism and empiricism through which the objectivity of scientific and commonsense judgements could be defended, and metaphysical speculation rejected. The formation of objective judgements requires the application of fundamental concepts, or 'categories', and 'forms of intuition' (space and time) to the contents of possible sensory experience. The mind makes an active contribution in organizing cognition, but falls into irresolvable contradiction when it moves beyond the bounds of possible sense-experience. It follows from this, however, that the world of which we have knowledge is the world of objects of possible experience: the world of 'phenomena', as distinct from things as they are 'in themselves', and independently of human cognitive faculties. But for purposes of practical and moral life – and even for the conduct of science itself – we cannot do without ideas whose objects are beyond the reach of sensory experience: such ideas as God, the freedom of the will, and immortality of the soul. As things-in-themselves ('noumena') such objects cannot be objects of knowledge, and fall within the domain of faith.

In the theory of knowledge, and allied disciplines such as history, philosophy and sociology of science, Kant's work has been an important source for critics of the almost universally dominant positivist and empiricist accounts of science and cognition (see EMPIRICISM; POSITIVISM; SCIENCE). The Kantian recognition of the active contribution of the knowing subject in the constitution of knowledge is a necessary presup-

position for any attempt to understand the history of science as anything other than the gradual accumulation of empirical facts, and is a necessary assumption for any sociology of science at all. But Kant's distinction between the realms of 'phenomena' and 'things-in-themselves' is both the site of serious difficulties in Kant's own position, and the source of important ambiguities in subsequent uses of Kantian ideas. Since cognition of things-in-themselves is ruled out in Kant's theory of knowledge, the way is open to a relativization of our knowledge of 'phenomena' or 'appearances' so that later critics of the idea of objectivity in science (from Hegel through to contemporary sociologists and philosophers of science such as Bloor and Feyerabend) have been able to make use of certain Kantian ideas to subvert Kant's own intellectual purposes.

For Marx, Engels and Lenin, Kant's theory of knowledge was defective in three related ways. First, it was held to be ahistorical in its account of the *a priori* contributions made by the mind in the constitution of knowledge: for Kant these fundamental concepts were universal properties of the mind whereas Marxists have tended to understand human cognitive powers as subject to historical transformation and development. Connectedly, whereas Kantianism locates the *a priori* conditions of objective knowledge in faculties of the mind, Marxism characteristically locates them in indispensable human social practices which have bodily as well as mental aspects. Finally, Engels and Lenin argued that the boundary between the world of knowable 'phenomena' and the unknowable 'things-in-themselves' was not, as Kantianism required, fixed and absolute, but was historically relative. The potential knowability of the world as it is, independent of and prior to the human subject, was seen as essential to the materialist world-view of Marxism.

The Kantian distinction between the world of appearances, the possible object of natural scientific knowledge, and the world of spirit, will and morality as objects of faith was also seminal for modern social theory. For HEGEL it became the foundation for an idealist social ontology and historical dialectic in which the absolute knowledge of self-realized spirit is the standpoint for a critique of scientific objectivity and materialism. For one modern Marxist thinker

(Colletti 1973) Marx's materialist inversion of Hegel should be understood as a return to materialist elements in Kant's philosophy. After the decline in the influence of Hegel in Germany, and the subsequent spread of positivist and materialist philosophical culture, a 'revolt' against positivism took the form of a return to Kant as a source for a new methodology and philosophical foundation for the cultural and historical sciences. This Neo-Kantian movement was diffuse both geographically and in the uses made of Kant's work, but characteristically a fundamental division was adhered to between the sciences of nature and those forms of knowledge which take human cultural and historical phenomena as their object. The fundamental concepts of meaning, value, and purpose, through which we organize our historical and cultural knowledge, in one sense function analogously to the forms of intuition and *a priori* categories in Kant's account of natural scientific knowledge. They differ, though, in that these concepts which found the human sciences are simultaneously the concepts through which human actors create the social world: the ultimate identity of subject and object of social scientific knowledge makes for a qualitatively different relationship between knowledge and its object in this domain of enquiry.

The philosophical Marxism associated with LUKÁCS, and Weberian sociology, both have their roots, intellectually and biographically in the Neo-Kantianism of Dilthey and Rickert. The philosophical basis of AUSTRO-MARXISM, and most notably the work of Max ADLER, was also Neo-Kantian. Philosophically, subsequent Marxism has been broadly divided between those tendencies for which the later work of Engels, and Lenin's 'Materialism and Empirio-Criticism' are paradigmatic, and various forms of Neo-Kantianism. The former offers a naturalistic/materialist perspective on the history of the human species as part of the order of Nature, and intelligible through essentially natural scientific forms of knowledge, while the latter perceives the natural and the human historical as divided by a deep gulf by virtue of the purposive, transformative character of human social practice, which requires forms of understanding qualitatively different from those of the natural sciences. (See also KNOWLEDGE, THEORY OF; PHILOSOPHY.)

Reading

Althusser, L. 1971: 'Lenin and Philosophy'. In *'Lenin and Philosophy' and other Essays*.

Bleicher, J. 1980: *Contemporary Hermeneutics*.

Colletti, L. 1973: *Marxism and Hegel*.

Hughes, H. S. 1959: *Consciousness and Society*.

Korner, S. 1955: *Kant*.

Lenin, V. I. 1908 (1962): 'Materialism and Empirio-Criticism'.

Lukács, G. 1923: *History and Class Consciousness*.

Outhwaite, W. 1975: *Understanding Social Life*.

TED BENTON

Kautsky, Karl Born 16 October 1854, Prague; died 17 October 1938, Amsterdam. Kautsky studied history, economics and philosophy at the University of Vienna, and while still a student contributed articles to the socialist press. In 1875 he joined the Austrian Social Democratic party, and when he moved to Zurich in 1880 became a friend of BERNSTEIN. From 1885 to 1890 he lived in London, working closely with Engels. On his return to Germany after the repeal of the Anti-Socialist Law, he quickly consolidated his position as the leading theorist of the Social Democratic Party (SPD), writing the theoretical section of the Erfurt programme (1891). He remained in the SPD until 1917, when he joined the breakaway Independent Social Democratic Party (USPD). Returning to the SPD in 1922, he failed to regain his former prominence. He emigrated to Prague in 1934, and died in exile in Amsterdam.

Kautsky was the leading Marxist thinker of the Second International in the period 1889–1914, and played a major role in establishing Marxism as a serious intellectual discipline. He edited *Die Neue Zeit* (from 1883 onwards), the first Marxist journal since 1848, and defended Marxist 'orthodoxy' against the 'revisionists' (see REVISIONISM), initially on a specific issue, the agrarian question (in *Die Agrarfrage* 1899), and then, in more general terms, against Bernstein. After working with Engels in the 1880s he translated Marx's *Poverty of Philosophy*, and later edited *Theories of Surplus Value*. He wrote a number of works popularizing Marx's economic and philosophical theories, and applied Marxism to the investigation of the origins of Christianity (1908) and the nature of utopian religious thought. His earliest intellectual orientation was towards natural-scientific materialism, in particular that of Buckle, Haeckel, and Darwin, and his conception of Marxism remained cast in this mould for the rest of his life. The summation of his view that Marxism is a natural-scientific materialism applied to society is *Die materialistische Geschichtsauffassung* (1927). This attachment to the more determinist aspects of Marxist theory brought him into increasing conflict with those who regarded Marxism as a guide to revolutionary action and not simply a method of analysis.

The Road to Power (1909) was the last of Kautsky's works which was accepted by all tendencies of Marxism, except the open 'revisionists'. Here he restated the need for the working class to undertake direct revolutionary action against the state power. Interestingly enough he considered that there was the possibility of an alliance between the working class of the metropolitan countries and the national liberation movements in the colonies. Thereafter he found himself increasingly under fire from the left wing of Marxism – beginning with his controversy with LUXEMBURG over the mass strike issue (Kautsky 1914). His equivocal stance towards the first world war, based on his theoretical conviction that imperialism was not a necessary result of the development of capitalism, was sharply condemned by Lenin. Kautsky's criticism of the Bolsheviks, his opposition to the DICTATORSHIP OF THE PROLETARIAT (1918), and his support for parliamentary democracy led to his being branded a 'renegade' by Lenin. He continued to voice these criticisms until the end of his life but increasingly withdrew from political involvement. Though he continued to write prolifically until his death, after the early 1920s he did not produce anything of the same quality as his earlier work.

Reading

Blumenberg, Werner 1960: *Karl Kautskys literarisches Werk. Eine bibliographische Übersicht.*

Kautsky, Karl 1899 (1988): *Die Agrarfrage.*

— 1908 (1925): *Foundations of Christianity: A Study of Christian Origins.*

— 1909: *The Road to Power.*

— 1914: *Der politische Massenstreik.*

— 1918 (1919): *The Dictatorship of the Proletariat.*

— 1927 (1988): *The Materialist Conception of History.*

— 1983: *Selected Political Writings.*

Steenson, Gary P. 1979: *Karl Kautsky 1854–1938.*

PATRICK GOODE

Keynes and Marx The most important common feature in the approaches of Marx and J. M. Keynes to economic problems and theory is their *macroeconomic character*, continuing a tradition which the Physiocrats had started and the classical economists (especially Ricardo) had perfected. The most important difference between them is that with Marx, the macroeconomic approach and evaluations are rooted in his specific theory of value and SURPLUS VALUE (the labour theory of value perfected by him), while with Keynes and his school, macroeconomic calculations are of a purely empirical and 'immediate' character (GNP calculations based upon government statistics), and not related to the neo-classical theory of value, on which he still bases himself. The latter is essentially microeconomic, without any possibility of statistical verification. This introduces, among other things, an explosive contradiction in Keynesian and post-Keynesian evaluations of capital (in the non-Marxist sense of the word), of which the British Cambridge school (Sraffa, Joan Robinson *et al.*) have shown all the devastating implications for neo-classical theory. The return to macroeconomic calculations (aided by Leontiev's input-output tables) is not however, with Keynes, an endeavour born from scientific research, but a pragmatic device for pursuing a given purpose; namely to *influence decisively the shaping of economic policies by the government*. Like Marx, Keynes rejected the neo-classical theorem that the capitalist system tended spontaneously, through the operation of the laws of the market, towards equilibrium and more or less guaranteed growth. But unlike Marx he rejected the idea that the business cycle (or industrial cycle) was an inevitable result of the operation of the laws of motion of the capitalist mode of production. He thought that a correct anticyclical government policy, especially (but not only) in the fields of taxation, money supply, credit expansion and contraction, interest rates ('cheap money'), public works, and especially budget deficits ('deficit financing') and budget surpluses, could guarantee full or nearly full employment and a significant rate of economic growth for long periods, if not for ever.

This assumption was based upon a specific theory of crisis (theory of the business cycle; see ECONOMIC CRISES) essentially in the 'underconsumptionist' tradition of Malthus, Sismondi, the Russian populists, Luxemburg and her school, Major Douglas and others. Like Marx, Keynes rejected 'Say's Law', according to which a given level of supply automatically creates its own demand. He saw the 'propensity to consume' (i.e. the relation between current production and current demand for that production) limited by the savings ratio, which was obviously higher for higher incomes than for lower ones. The level of national income was largely a function of the level of employment, and a policy of full employment was instrumental for a policy of sustained economic growth. These ideas were experimented with during Roosevelt's 'New Deal' in the USA, and after the second world war were put into practice in the USA, Britain, Holland, France, and Japan, and subsequently in almost all capitalist (OECD) countries.

While the contradiction between the tendency of capitalism to develop the productive forces without limit, and restricted mass consumption, is also fundamental for Marx's explanation of economic crises, his theory of crisis is based much less than that of Keynes upon a monocausal explanation of the cycle. Marx always combines the tendency towards overproduction of commodities with the tendency towards overaccumulation of capital (impossibility of valorizing additional capital at the given average rate of profit). For him, therefore, national income under capitalism is not only a function of the level of consumption and employment, but also a function of the rate of profit (in other words, the level of employment is also a function of the rate of profit). Therefore all the forces which promote full employment can only remain operative if they do not themselves undermine the rate of profit, or if they are not accompanied by other trends which do so. Likewise, all the forces which increase profits cannot achieve accelerated long-term growth if they do not at the same time lead to an expansion of the market for the 'final consumers', i.e. if they do not lead towards full employment. That is the basic problem of cyclical development which no government economic policy can solve in the long run.

As Keynes and his disciples were confronted, not with that general theoretical challenge, but with the challenge of large-scale unemployment in the 1930s, and the threat of a repetition of that unemployment after the second world war (when the armaments boom was supposed to be over), they tended to disregard the warnings by Marxists, and to concentrate their polemics on refuting the arguments of the 'orthodox' neoclassical liberals that their policies would lead to rapid inflation in the long run. Keynes even posited, as a shrewd bourgeois politician, that the working class and the trade unions would show less resistance to a slow erosion of real wages with a rising level of nominal wages and of inflation, than to a lowering of nominal wages under stable paper money. His disciples today, however, have adopted the position that it will be necessary to control wages in order to beat 'stagflation'. What the monetarists and Keynes himself wanted to achieve through existing government policies (for the monetarists, in the field of money supply), the neo-Keynesians want to achieve through an 'incomes policy' (i.e. through government control of wages), with or without the collaboration of the trade union bureaucracy, according to the possibilities.

Here the differences between Marxist and Keynesian proposals for achieving full employment are most striking. Keynes accepts the logic of the capitalist system, and places his proposals squarely within that framework. The big weakness of that system (which led, among other things, to the failure of the 'New Deal' to achieve *full employment*) is that while 'deficit spending' and general measures favourable to popular consumption can indeed temporarily increase sales and output of consumer goods, they can only lead the capitalists to increase productive investment if, simultaneously, they increase the rate of profit and the expectations of profit. This needs a sum of coinciding circumstances which are not generally given, and certainly not produced by Keynesian policies. For Marxists, on the other hand, there is no compulsion to accept the inner logic of the capitalist system. Priority is given to achieving a social goal, and to political strategies tending to create the preconditions for achieving it. This implies the need to create another economic system, with a different economic logic and relations of production; a transition towards socialism, the expropriation of the bourgeoisie, and the elimination of bourgeois state power.

Attempts to bridge the gap between Keynesian and Marxist projects have been made in the theoretical field (e.g. by KALECKI) and in the field of economic policies by the proponents of a 'mixed economy' with a strong public sector of the economy, capable of generating enough productive investment to neutralize the 'investment strike' by the private sector triggered off by the declining rate of profit. There is no evidence that such a model has ever worked or ever can work, that it is possible to combine in a single economy both the logic of production for profit and the logic of planned production for need. (See also CRITICS OF MARXISM.)

Reading

Kühne, Karl 1979: *Economics and Marxism.* vol. II, pt. IV.

Mattick, P. 1969: *Marx and Keynes: The Limits of the Mixed Economy.*

Robinson, Joan 1948 (*1968*): 'Marx and Keynes'. In Horowitz ed, *Marx and Modern Economics.*

Tsuru, Shigeto 1954 (*1968*): 'Keynes versus Marx: The Methodology of Aggregates'. In Horowitz ed. *Marx and Modern Economics.*

ERNEST MANDEL

kinship When anthropologists study 'kinship systems', they consider matters as diverse as systems of classification of social persons, recruitment to social groups, sex roles, control and transfer of resources, dynamics of residence and domestic relations, rules of marriage or inheritance, and sexual symbolism. For Marxists, however, these many issues can be understood only in the context of the modes of production within which kinship systems operate and of which they are a part, and only in a dynamic historical framework. From this viewpoint, kinship is an important object of study because it focuses on the central institutions and dynamics of some pre-capitalist societies, and on the articulation in all societies of broad processes of social development with everyday life. It is worth emphasizing that from both viewpoints, the object of study is a *social system* – the cultural recruitment of people to groups – which, while organizing the facts of biology (reproduction), remains distinct from them.

Kinship functions in all modes of production at some level. The principal problem for a Marxist analysis of kinship is to sort out the relationships between the structural constitution of groups and the various modes of production, emphasizing both the structural role of kinship and its role as a crucial element of ideological reproduction. In this context, relations of dominance, both within the kin group and in the society as a whole, are central.

Pre-state societies are composed of structurally-equivalent kin groups whose interrelations ('politics') are also constituted as 'kin' relations. There is a core distinction to be made between band societies (gatherer-hunters), which are essentially egalitarian, and lineage societies which, while egalitarian by modern standards, organize people into potentially competing sub-units which are typically the basis of production and consumption. Present-day band systems tend to occur in areas of marginal, limited resources, and the kinship systems of these societies are the idiom which articulates the flexibility of sub-group membership, inter-group cooperation, and shared territorial access to resources necessary to survival in such environments. The egalitarian nature of these societies extends to relations between the sexes: both women's productive role and their personal autonomy are recognized and highly valued (see PRIMITIVE COMMUNISM).

By contrast, kinship in lineage societies demarcates the boundaries between often competing, corporate social groups. These forms of kinship tend to occur in horticultural or pastoral societies, in which descent (matrilineal, patrilineal, or bilineal) is the idiom which defines restricted access to resources, a relation which has been erroneously glossed as a form of property, but is in fact a predecessor of property *proprement dit.* Competition in these societies occurs explicitly among lineages, the inter-marrying sub-groups of the larger whole, and is further expressed in intra-lineage status and rank (Rey 1975). These systems are thus significant because it is within them – and particularly at the intersection of inter- and intra-lineage ranking – that we find the origins of social hierarchy and class distinctions. It is also within these systems, in conjunction with both the transition from matrilocal to avunculocal and patrilocal residence, and the emergence of connections between marriage and property transfers, that we may best locate the origins of social-structural male dominance. Recent discussion in the Marxist-feminist literature has placed this status differentiation of women and men appropriately in its larger socio-economic context. (See, on intra- and inter-lineage ranking, Gough 1971, and Reich 1945; and on the emergence of structural male dominance, Engels, *Origin of the Family*, ed. Leacock 1972, and Reiter, ed. 1975, especially the selections by Gough and Sacks.)

In state societies other juridical and organizational principles displace kinship from the central place it occupies in band or lineage societies, although the lineage mode of production may be preserved as an encapsulated element of mixed-mode states. In such contexts, the subordinated kinship system retains most of its practical functions in the production and organization of subsistence and everyday life, but loses its control over surplus as well as its political autonomy. In these societies, nationalism is in conflict with kin-based identities, and the imperatives of surplus-extraction conflict with the functioning of popular corporate groups. Furthermore, it is in state society that male domination takes on a more comprehensive and rigid *institutional* form, and the national arena becomes a male domain. These tensions and contradictions may be absorbed ideologically in a limited sense, as the ruling elite transforms kinship ideology into the basis of the legitimation of the state and an idiom of surplus appropriation, but the general drift is towards undermining the integrity of the lineage and lineage mode. The West African kingdom of Dahomey exemplified this dynamic (Katz and Kemnitzer 1979), which is seen even more clearly in the development of feudal Europe where a longer historical record documents in more detail the absorption of kin-based organizations into the dominant, mercantile individualist state, with the state and market gradually assuming the functions of the kinship system, breaking it down into smaller and smaller units. This is not merely a matter of declining household size, but rather of the size and composition of the jural unit which confronts the state, and of the units of production, consumption, and mutual aid.

In the post-agrarian state, both capitalist and socialist, the process of proletarianization completes the elimination of the corporate aspects of kin-group functioning. Increasingly, people face the state as individuals; the socialization of labour is accompanied by the privatization of personal (i.e. family) life; thus productive labour is separated from kin relationships; and the family unit, while remaining in theory the unit of consumption and social reproduction, is further reduced in effect and size – most recently to two or even one person.

In capitalism specifically the family becomes located in the system's contradiction between the social production of wealth and its private accumulation. A considerable literature addresses the problematics of the nuclear family (see FAMILY; FEMINISM). Three further issues remain to be discussed here. The first involves the impact of colonialism on traditional, kin-based or proto-state societies. Although there is considerable variation, the colonial system seeks everywhere to keep the burden of social reproduction, the subsistence of its lower classes, outside its surplus-producing sphere of interest. In order to cope with the disorganizing effects on their subsistence base of the consequent partial proletarianization, and depending on the specifics of precolonial modes of production, the people re-order their social organization in various ways: e.g. communalized villages (see Marx's letter to V. Zasulich, 8 March 1881, and drafts of the letter, on the Russian communal village, in *Marx-Engels Archiv*, vol. I); closed corporate communities (Wolf 1957); strategically-adaptive women's networks involving 'fictive kin' (see Brown and Rubbo in Reiter, ed. 1975). In these processes, kin ideology is the enabling metaphor which infuses these new social arrangements with the legitimacy of traditional communal forms.

Analogous kin-based networks exist among the urban poor in the capitalist-imperialist centre. One of the clearest examples of this phenomenon is the elaboration of 'kin' networks (frequently including 'fictive kin'), such as that described by Stack (1974) in a community of American Black women. The adaptive strategies of these women mean not the circumscription of kin ties, but the extension of kin reciprocity along much broader lines which, as Stack points out, are crucial to and successful for survival, despite the fact that they run counter to the self-propelled achievement ethic of bourgeois culture.

These strategies of survival hinge on forms of economic cooperation, but rest also on resistance on the part of peoples to further integration as an underclass into the capitalist social order. The middle class, conversely, participating fully in bourgeois society, historically developed a form of the nuclear family incorporating the requirements of civil society into the structure of the kin group. In the face of the recent structural undermining of the nuclear family organization, the middle class has further elaborated its pattern of individualist, market-based contractual relations in the privatized 'personal' life. Thus, rather than extending a kin-based metaphor to 'non-kin', and with it the range of holistic demands of mutual aid and reciprocity, the middle class has used a market ethic in an effort to salvage the family group. Manifested by language and strategies such as 'negotiation', 'mediation', 'role-playing', and 'contract', the outcome of this trend is to limit sharply – to the parent-child pair and more rarely to the sibling group – the range of relationships in which the broad obligations and demands associated with kinship are operable. Other customary kin relations are subsumed within the category of 'friendship' which, as Rapp (1978) has suggested, may entail emotional support but carry no obligations of sharing of resources. These relations are thus individualized and attenuated by the separation of abstract and practical 'support'; they are, furthermore, terminable and, like the new nuclear family, subject to individual 'cost/benefit' analysis. Finally, the elaboration of a whole corps of professionals to administer and maintain these relationships completes this developmental process.

What is glossed as 'kinship' is the set of practices which constitutes the *immediate reproduction* of the social order. In the most basic pre-state social formations, kinship lies at the institutional and ideological core of society. With the advent of the agricultural state, there is introduced a rift in its functioning, between the role of kinship as ideology, and its role in both pragmatic 'everyday life' and *de facto* resistance to domination. With the integration of capitalism, kinship becomes, finally, articulated in the language of dominance itself.

Reading

Gough, Kathleen 1971: 'Nuer Kinship: A Re-examina-

tion'. In Beidelman ed. *The Translation of Culture: Essays in Honor of E. E. Evans-Pritchard.*

— 1975: 'The Origin of the Family'. In Reiter ed. *Toward an Anthropology of Women.*

Katz, N. and Kemnitzer, D. S. 1979: 'Mode of Production and Process of Domination: The Classical Kingdom of Dahomey'. In Leons and Rothstein, eds. *New Direction in Political Economy: An Approach from Anthropology.*

Leacock, E. B. 1972: 'Introduction' to Engels, *The Origin of the Family.*

Rapp, R. 1978: 'Family and Class in Contemporary America: Notes toward an Understanding of Ideology'.

Reich, W. 1945: *The Sexual Revolution.*

Reiter, R. ed. 1975: *Toward an Anthropology of Women.*

Rey, P.-P. 1975: 'The Lineage Mode of Production'.

Stack, C. 1974: *All Our Kin.*

Terray E. 1975: 'Classes and Class-consciousness in the Abron Kingdom of Gyaman'. In M. Bloch ed. *Marxist Analyses and Social Anthropology.*

Wolf, E. R. 1957: 'Closed Corporate Communities in Mesoamerica and Central Java'.

NAOMI KATZ and DAVID KEMNITZER

knowledge, theory of It is a truism that the tensions in Marxist thought between positivism and Hegelianism, social science and philosophy of history, scientific and critical (or humanist or historicist) Marxism, materialism and the dialectic etc. are rooted in the ambivalence and contradictory tendencies of Marx's own writings. Despite this, it is possible to reconstruct from his work perspectives (a) *in* and (b) *on* the theory of knowledge which transcend and partially explain the dichotomies within Marxism.

(a) Two epistemological themes predominate in Marx: (α) an emphasis on *objectivity*, the independent reality of natural, and the relatively independent reality of social, forms with respect to their cognition (i.e. realism, in the ontological or 'intransitive' dimension); (β) an emphasis on the role of work or *labour* in the cognitive process, and hence on the social, irreducibly historical character of its product, viz knowledge (i.e. 'practicism', in the narrowly epistemological or 'transitive' dimension). (α) is consistent with the practical modification of nature and constitution of social life; and Marx understands (β) as dependent on the mediation of intentional human agency or PRAXIS. Objectification in the senses of the *production* of a subject and of the *reproduction* or transformation of a social process must be distinguished both from objectivity qua externality, as in (α), and from the historically specific, e.g. alienated, forms of labour in particular societies – so 'objective' and its cognates have a four-fold meaning in Marx. These two inter-related themes – objectivity and labour – entail the epistemological supersession of empiricism and idealism, scepticism and dogmatism, hypernaturalism and anti-naturalism alike.

In his early writings Marx essayed a forceful and sporadically brilliant critique of idealism, which was the medium of his biographical *Ausgang* from philosophy into substantive socio-historical science, and provides the key to the subject matter of his new science. But he never engaged a comparable critique of empiricism. His anti-empiricism is available only in the practical, untheorized state of the methodological commitment to scientific realism implicit in *Capital*, together with a few scattered philosophical *aperçus*. One consequence of this critical imbalance has been the relative intellectual underdevelopment of the realist in comparison with the practicist pole within Marxist epistemology, and a tendency for it to fluctuate between a sophisticated idealism (roughly (β) without (α)) and a crude materialism (roughly (α) without (β)).

Marx's critique of idealism, which incorporates a vigorous critique of apriorism, consists in a double movement: in the first, *Feuerbachian* moment, ideas are treated as the products of finite embodied minds and in the second, distinctively *Marxian* moment, such embodied minds are in turn conceived as the products of historically developing ensembles of social relations. The first moment includes critiques of Hegel's subject-predicate inversions, the reduction of being to knowing (the 'epistemic fallacy') and the separation of philosophy from social life (the 'speculative illusion'). In the second anti-individualist moment, the Feuerbachian humanist or essentialist problematic of a fixed human nature is replaced by a problematic of a historically developing sociality: 'The human essence is no abstraction inherent in each single individual. In its reality it is the ensemble of social relations' (*Theses on Feuerbach*, 6th Thesis). 'The sum of the forces of production, capital and forms of social intercourse, which

each individual confronts as something given, is the real foundation of . . . the "essence of man"' (*German Ideology*, vol. I, pt. I, sect. 7). At the same time Marx wished to insist that 'history is nothing but the activity of men in pursuit of their ends' (*The Holy Family*, ch. VI, pt. 2). Thus Marx works his way towards a conception of the reproduction and transformation of the social process in and through human praxis; and of praxis as in turn conditioned and made possible by that process: 'Men make their own history but they do not make it just as they please; they do not make it under circumstances chosen by themselves, but under circumstances directly encountered, given and transmitted by the past' (*18th Brumaire*, sect. I). Did Marx suppose that under communism men and women would make history as they pleased, that process would be dissolved into praxis? The evidence is ambiguous (see DETERMINISM). In any event, the subject matter of *Capital* is not human praxis, but the structures, relations, contradictions and tendencies of the capitalist mode of production: 'individuals are dealt with here only in so far as they are the personifications of economic categories, the bearers (*Träger*) of particular class relations and interests' (*Capital* I, Preface).

Marx is never seriously disposed to doubt (1) simple *material object realism*, the idea that material objects exist independently of their cognition; but his commitment to (2) *scientific realism*, the idea that the objects of scientific thought are real structures, mechanisms or relations ontologically irreducible to, normally out of phase with and perhaps in opposition to the phenomenal forms, appearances or events they generate, is arrived at only gradually, unevenly and relatively late (see REALISM). However, by the mid-1860s scientific realist motifs provide a constant refrain: 'all science would be superfluous if the outward appearances and essences of things directly coincided' (*Capital* III, ch. 48). 'Scientific truth is always paradox, if judged by everyday experience, which catches only the delusive appearance of things' (*Value, Price and Profit*, pt. VI). In opposition to vulgar economy Marx claims to give a scientific, and in opposition to classical political economy a categorically adequate (non-fetishized, historicized), account of the real underlying relations, causal structures and generative mechanisms of capitalist economic life. Marx's method in fact incorporates three aspects: (a) a *generic scientific realism*; (b) a domain–*specific qualified* (or critical) *naturalism*; and (c) a subject–*particular dialectical materialism*. At (a) Marx's concern is, like that of any scientist, with a consistent, coherent, plausible and empirically-grounded explanation of his phenomena. At (b), his naturalism is qualified by a series of differentiae of social, as distinct from natural, scientific inquiry – the most important of which are the praxis-, concept- and space-time-dependence of social forms, the historical reflexibility necessitated by the consideration that the critique of political economy is part of the process it describes and the fact that neither experimentally established nor naturally occurring closed systems are available for the empirical control of theory (entailing reliance on explanatory, non-predictive criteria of confirmation and falsification). (In this respect the 'power of abstraction' which Marx invokes in *Capital* I, Preface, neither provides a surrogate for 'microscopes' and 'chemical reagents' nor does justice to Marx's actual empirical practice.) At (c), the particular character of Marx's explanations is such that they take the form of an *explanatory critique* of an object of inquiry which is revealed, on those explanations, to be *dialectically contradictory*. Marx's scientific critique is both of (i) conceptual and conceptualized entities (economic theories and categories; phenomenal forms) and (ii) the objects (systems of structured relations) which necessitate or otherwise explain them. At the first level, the entities are shown to be false *simpliciter* (e.g. the wage form), fetishized (e.g. the value form) or otherwise defective; at the second level, Marx's explanations logically entail *ceteris paribus* a negative evaluation of the objects generating such entities and a commitment to their practical transformation. The particular systemic dialectical contradictions, such as between USE-VALUE and VALUE, which Marx identifies as structurally constitutive of capitalism and its mystified forms of appearance give rise, on Marx's theory, to various historical contradictions which, on that theory, both tendentially subvert its principle of organization and provide the means and motive for its supersession by a society in which 'socialized mankind, the associated producers, regulate their interchange with nature rationally (bringing) it under their conscious control, instead of being ruled by it as by some blind power' (*Capital* III, ch. 48).

If for Marx idealism is the typical fault of philosophy, empiricism is the endemic failing of *common sense*. Marx sets himself against both the idealist ontology of forms, ideas or notions with its conceptual (or religious) totalities and the empiricist ontology of given atomistic facts and their constant conjunctions, in favour of the real world, conceived as structured, differentiated and developing and, given that we exist, a possible object of knowledge for us. Thus the essence of Marx's critique, in the *Theses on Feuerbach*, of the old 'contemplative materialism' is that it desocializes and dehistoricizes reality; so that, at best, it can merely prompt, but not sustain '*scientificity*'. And the essence of Marx's critique, in the final manuscript of the *Economic and Philosophical Manuscripts* and elsewhere, of the culmination of classical German Idealism in the philosophy of HEGEL is that it destratifies science and then dehistoricizes reality; so that it prompts, but cannot sustain '*historicity*'. So we arrive at the twin epistemic motifs of Marx's new science of history: materialism signifying its generic form (as a science), dialectic its particular content (as a science of history). But it is an index of the epistemological lag of philosophical Marxism behind Marx that, whether fused in dialectical materialism or separated in WESTERN MARXISM, its dialectic has remained cast in an essentially idealist mould and its materialism expressed in a fundamentally empiricist form.

Marx (and Engels) usually associate dogmatism with idealism and rationalism, and scepticism with empiricism; and in the *German Ideology* they firmly reject both. Their premises, they announce, are not 'arbitrary dogmas' but can be verified 'in a purely empirical way' (*German Ideology*, vol. I, pt, I, A). At the same time, they lampoon the kind of 'new revolutionary philosopher' who has 'the idea that men were drowned in water only because they were possessed with the *idea* of gravity' (ibid. Preface). Thus, on the one hand (in the transitive dimension), they initiate the idea of Marxism as an empirically open-ended research programme; and, on the other (in the intransitive dimension), they register their commitment to an objective ontology of transfactually active structures.

288 KNOWLEDGE, THEORY OF

(b) Marx's position *on* epistemology also revolves around two interrelated themes: an
emphasis (α) on the *scientificity* and (β) on the
historicity of the cognitive process (the themes,
of course, of the new science of history brought
to bear on the theory of knowledge). On the one
hand Marx represents himself as engaged in the
construction of a science, so that he is seemingly
committed to certain epistemological propositions (e.g. criteria demarcating science from
ideology or say art); and, on the other, he conceives all sciences, including his own, as the
product of (and a potential causal agent in)
historical circumstances, and must therefore be
committed to the possibility of historically explaining them. (α) and (β) constitute two aspects
(the 'intrinsic' and 'extrinsic' aspects) of the
cognitive process: (α) without (β) leads to *scientism*, the dislocation of science from the socio-
historical realm and a consequent lack of historical reflexity; (β) without (α) results in *historicism*, the reduction of science to an expression of
the historical process and a consequent judgemental relativism. These two aspects are united
in the project of an explanatory critique of
historically specific epistemologies.

However, the peculiar character of Marx's
route from philosophy into science was such
that, as in the case of his scientific realism, the
nature of his commitment to the intrinsic dimension remained untheorized. Indeed, following
an early phase in which Marx visualizes the
realization of philosophy in and through the
proletariat, his expressly articulated views
abruptly halt at a second positivistic phase in
which philosophy seems to be more or less
completely superseded by science: 'When reality
is depicted, philosophy as an *independent*
[emphasis added] branch of knowledge loses its
medium of existence. At the best, its place can
only be taken by the summing up of the most
general results, abstractions which arise from
the observation of the historical development of
men' (*German Ideology*, vol. I, pt. I, A). This
abstract-summative conception of PHILOSOPHY
was given the imprimatur of the later Engels and
became the orthodoxy of the Second International. However there is a patent contradiction
between Engels's theory and practice: his practice is that of an engaged underlabourer for
HISTORICAL MATERIALISM – a Lockean function
which Marx clearly approved. Moreover it is

difficult to see how Marxism can dispense with
epistemological interventions, and hence positions, so long as social conditions give rise not
just to the (philosophical) 'problem of knowledge', but to knowledge as a (practical, historical) problem. In any event, if there is a third
position implicit in Marx's practice, it is one in
which philosophy (and a fortiori epistemology)
is conceived as dependent upon science and
other social practices: i.e. heteronomously, as a
moment of a practical cognitive ensemble. As
such it would have nothing in common with
either the old Hegelian 'German professorial
concept-linking method' or the Lukácsian-
Gramscian view of Marxism as a philosophy,
rather than a (naturalistic) science, characterized by a totalizing vantage point of its own.

The main characteristics of the later Engels's
immensely influential philosophical intervention were: (1) a conjunction of a positivistic
conception of philosophy and a pre-critical
metaphysics of the sciences; (2) an uneasy synthesis of a non-reductionist (emergentist) cosmology and a monistic (processual) dialectics of
being; (3) espousal of such a universal dialectical ontology in harness with a reflectionist epistemology, in which thought is conceived as mirroring or copying reality; (4) a vigorous critique
of subjectivism and an emphasis on natural
necessity combined with a stress on the practical
refutation of scepticism. *Anti-Dühring* was the
decisive influence in the Marxism of the Second
International, while the combination of a dialectics of nature and reflection theory became the
hallmark of orthodox philosophical Marxism –
styled 'dialectical materialism' by Plekhanov
(following Dietzgen). Unfortunately Engels's
critique of the contingency of the causal connection was not complemented by a critique of its
actuality (a notion shared by Hume with Hegel)
or with co-equal attention to the mediation of
natural necessities in social life by human
praxis. Moreover despite his great insight into
particular episodes in the history of science –
e.g. his remarkable (post-Kuhnian!) Preface to
Capital II – the effect of his reflectionism was the
truncation of the transitive dimension and a
regression to contemplative materialism. Thus
the mainstream of the Second International, at
its best in the works of Kautsky, Mehring,
Plekhanov and Labriola, came to embrace a
positivistic and rather deterministic evolution-

ism (in Kautsky's case, arguably more Darwinian than Marxian); and concerned itself for the most part with systematizing, rather than developing or extending, Marx's work. Paradoxically – because if the main theme of Engels's intervention was materialism, its express intention had been to register and defend the specific autonomy of Marxism as a science – its outcome was a *Weltanschauung* not so very different from the hypernaturalist monisms – the 'mechanical' and 'reductive' materialisms – of Haeckel, Dühring *et al.*, which Engels had set out to attack.

Lenin's distinctive contributions were his insistence on the practical and interested character of philosophical interventions, and a clearer conception of the relative autonomy of such interventions from day-to-day science, both of which partially ameliorated the objectivist and positivist cast of Engels's thought. Lenin's philosophical thought moved through two phases: 'Materialism and Empirio-Criticism' was a reflectionist polemic designed to counter the spread of Machian ideas in Bolshevik circles (e.g. by Bogdanov); while in the *Philosophical Notebooks* Engels's polar contrast between materialism and idealism gradually took second place to that between dialectical and non-dialectical thinking. There was a robust, if short-lived, debate in the Soviet Union in the 1920s between those who, like Deborin, emphasized the dialectical side and those who, like Bukharin, emphasized the materialist components of dialectical materialism. Thus the two terms of Engels's epistemological legacy – 'dialectics' and 'materialism' – were both rejected by Bernstein, were accentuated at different times by Lenin, externalized as an internal opposition within Soviet philosophy between Deborin and the mechanists before being codified under Stalin as '*Diamat*', and became antithetical currents within Western Marxism.

In the thought of ADLER and the Austro-Marxists, Marxist epistemology became self-consciously critical, in Kantian terms, in two senses: analogously, in that Marx, like Newton, had enabled the formulation of a Kantian question, viz. how is socialization possible?; and directly, in that sociality was a condition of the possibility of experience in exactly the way that space, time and the categories are in Kant. For Adler, Marx's theory is to be understood as an empirically controlled critique, whose object – socialized humanity – is subject to quasi-natural laws, which depend for their operation upon intentional and value-oriented human activity.

None of the thinkers considered so far doubted that Marxism was primarily a science (cf. e.g. Bukharin's *Historical Materialism*). At the same time there was little, if any, emphasis on the authentically dialectical or Hegelian elements within Marx; for which, no doubt, the difficulties of Marx's exposition of the theory of value in *Capital* and the late publication of key early works were largely responsible. This situation now changed. Indeed, in the Hegelian Marxism expounded by Lukács (1923) which stimulated the work of the FRANKFURT SCHOOL and the genetic structuralism of Goldmann and provided an interpretative canon for Marx almost as influential as that of Engels, in Korsch (1923) and Gramsci (1971) the main emphases of the Engelsian tradition are dramatically reversed.

The chief generic features of their theory of knowledge are (1) historicism, the identification of Marxism as the theoretical expression of the working class, and of natural science as a bourgeois ideology, entailing the collapse of the intrinsic dimension of the cognitive labour process together with a rejection of Marxism as a social science in favour of Marxism as a self-sufficient or autonomous philosophy or social theory, with a comprehensive totalizing standpoint of its own; (2) anti-objectivism and anti-reflectionism, based on the idea of the practical constitution of the world, leading to the collapse or effective neutralization of the intransitive dimension of science and a corresponding epistemological idealism and judgemental relativism; (3) recovery of the subjective and critical aspects of Marxism (including in Lukács's case, the rediscovery of an essential ingredient of Marx's theory: the doctrine of FETISHISM), submerged in the positivistic scientism of the Second International.

Marxism is now fundamentally the expression of a subject, rather than the knowledge of an object; it is 'the theoretical expression of the revolutionary movement of the proletariat' (Korsch 1923, p. 42). Moreover it is not just self-sufficient – containing as Gramsci puts it, 'all the fundamental elements needed to constitute a total and integral conception of the world'

(1971, p. 462) – but distinguished precisely and only by this self-sufficiency. Thus for Lukács 'it is not the primacy of economic motives that constitutes the decisive difference between Marxism and bourgeois thought, but the point of view of the totality [a position reiterated in his later *Ontology of Social Being*] . . . the all-pervasive supremacy of the whole over its parts is the essence of the method which Marx took over from Hegel' (1923, p. 27). From this standpoint natural science itself expresses the fragmentary, reified vision of the bourgeoisie, creating a world of pure facts, segregated into various partial spheres and unrelated to any meaningful TOTALITY. Thus Lukács inaugurates a long tradition within Marxism which confounds science with its positivistic misrepresentation and starkly counterposes dialectical to analytical thought.

For Lukács the proletariat is the identical subject-object of history, and history (in the Lukácsian circle) is its realization of this fact. Historical materialism is nothing other than the self-knowledge of capitalist society, i.e. (on the circle) the ascribed consciousness of the proletariat which, in becoming self-conscious, i.e. aware of its situation as the commodity on which capitalist society depends, already begins to transform it. *Capital* I, ch. 1, sect. 4, on commodity fetishism 'contains within itself the whole of historical materialism, and the whole self-knowledge of the proletariat, seen as the knowledge of capitalist society' (ibid. p. 170). Lukács's epistemology is rationalist and his ontology idealist. More particularly, his totality is (as Althusser has pointed out) 'expressive', in that each moment or part implicitly contains the whole; and teleological, in that the present is only intelligible in relation to the future – of achieved identity – it anticipates. What Marx's ontology has, and both the Engelsian ontology (highlighting process) and the Lukácsian ontology (highlighting totality) lack, is structure.

For Gramsci the very idea of a reality-in-itself is a religious residue, and the objectivity of things is redefined in terms of a universal intersubjectivity of persons; i.e. as a cognitive consensus, asymptotically approached in history but only finally realized under communism, after a practical one has been achieved. Gramsci remarks that 'according to the theory of praxis it is clear that human history is not explained by

the atomistic theory, but that the reverse is the case: the atomistic theory, like all other scientific hypotheses and opinions, is part of the superstructure' (1971, p. 465). This encapsulates a double collapse: of the intransitive to the transitive, and the intrinsic to the extrinsic dimensions. In the first respect Gramsci's remark reminds one of Marx's jibe against Proudhon that like 'the true idealist' he is, he no doubt believes that 'the circulation of the blood must be a consequence of Harvey's theory' (*Poverty of Philosophy*, ch. 2, sect. 3). The historicity of our knowledge (as well as the distinct historicity of its objects) on which Gramsci quite properly wishes to insist does not refute, but actually depends upon, the idea of the otherness of its objects (and their historicity).

Lukács, Gramsci and Korsch all reject any dialectics of nature of an Engelsian type, but whereas Lukács does so in favour of a dualistic, romantic anti-naturalism, Gramsci and Korsch do so in favour of a historicized anthropomorphic monism. Whereas Lukács argues that the dialectic, conceived as the process of the reunification of original subject and estranged object, only applies to the social world, Gramsci and Korsch maintain that nature, as we know it, is part of human history and therefore dialectical. While in Gramsci's achieved (being-knowing) identity theory, intransitivity is altogether lost, on Lukács's theory, on which identity is the still-to-be-achieved outcome of history, intransitivity remains in two guises: (i) as an epistemically inert nature, not conceived in any integral relation to the dialectic of human emancipation; (ii) as the realm of alienation in human history, prior to the achievement of proletarian self-consciousness.

The principal epistemological themes of the 'critical theory' of Horkheimer, Adorno, Marcuse and (in a second generation) Habermas and their associates are (1) a modification of the absolute historicism of Lukácsian Marxism and a renewed emphasis on the relative autonomy of theory; (2) a critique of the concept of labour in Marx and Marxism; and (3) an accentuation of the critique of objectivism and scientism.

(1) is accompanied by a gradual decentering of the role of the proletariat and eventually results in the loss of any historically grounded agency of emancipation, so that – in a manner reminiscent of the YOUNG HEGELIANS – revolu-

tionary theory is seen as an attribute of individuals (rather than as the expression of a class) and displaced onto the normative plane as a Fichtean 'Sollen' or 'ought'. The consequent split between theory and practice, poignantly expressed by Marcuse – 'the critical theory of society possesses no concepts which could bridge the gap between present and future, holding no future and showing no success, it remains negative' (1964, p. 257) – underscored a pessimism and judgementalism which, together with its totally negative – romantic and undialectical – conceptions of capitalism, science, technology and analytical thought, place its social theory – conceived (as in historicist Marxism) as the true repository of epistemology – at some remove from Marx's. By the same token, this allowed it to illuminate problems which Marx's own optimistic rationalism and Prometheanism had obscured.

(2) The pivotal contrast of critical theory between an emancipatory and a purely technical or instrumental reason came increasingly, from Horkheimer's 'Traditional and Critical Theory' of 1937 (1968) to Habermas's *Knowledge and Human Interests* (1971), to be turned against Marx himself, in virtue of his emphasis on labour and his concept of nature purely as an object of human exploitation. Thus Marcuse (1955) conceives an emancipated society as one characterized neither by the rational regulation of necessary labour nor by creative work but rather by the sublimation of work itself in sensuous libidinous play. According to Habermas, Marx recognizes a distinction between labour and interaction in his distinction between the forces and relations of production but misinterprets his own practice in a positivistic way, thereby reducing the self-formation of the human species to work. However, it may be argued that Marx understands labour not just as technical action, but as always occurring within and through a historically specific society and that it is Habermas, not Marx, who mistakenly and uncritically adopts a positivistic account of labour, viz. as technical action, and more generally of natural science, viz. as adequately represented by the deductive-nomological model.

(3) Habermas's attempt to combine a conception of the human species as a result of a purely natural process with a conception of reality, including nature, as constituted in and by

human activity illustrates the antinomy of any transcendental pragmatism. For it leads to the dilemma that if nature has the transcendental status of a constituted objectivity it cannot be the historical ground of the constituting subject; and, conversely, if nature is the historical ground of subjectivity then it cannot simply be a constituted objectivity – it must be *in-itself* (and, contingently, a possible object for us). This is a point which Adorno, in his insistence on the irreducibility of objectivity to subjectivity, seems to have appreciated well. Indeed Adorno (1966) isolates the endemic failing of First Philosophy, including Marxian epistemology, as the constant tendency to reduce one of a pair of mutually irreducible opposites to the other (e.g. in Engelsian Marxism consciousness to being, in Lukácsian Marxism being to consciousness) and argues against any attempt to base thought on a non-presuppositionless foundation and for the immanence of all critique.

It will be convenient to treat together the work of (i) humanist Marxists, such as E. Fromm, H. Lefebvre, R. Garaudy, A. Heller and E. P. Thompson; (ii) existentialist Marxists, such as Sartre and Merleau-Ponty; (iii) East European revisionists, such as L. Kolakowski, A. Schaff and K. Kosik; and (iv) the Yugoslav *Praxis* group of G. Petrović, M. Marković, S. Stojanović and their colleagues. Despite their diverse formations and preoccupations, all share a renewed emphasis on man and human praxis as 'the centre of authentic Marxist thought' (*Praxis*, I, p. 64) an emphasis lost in the Stalinist era, whose recovery evidently owed much to the *Economic and Philosophical Manuscripts* (and, to a lesser extent, the new humanistic readings of Hegel's *Phenomenology* proposed by e.g. A. Kojève and J. Hyppolite). Two points are worth stressing: first, it is assumed that human nature and needs, although historically mediated, are not infinitely malleable; second, the focus is on human beings not just as empirically given but as a normative ideal – as de-alienated, totalizing, self-developing, freely creative and harmoniously engaged. The first signals an undoubted partial return from Marx to Feuerbach. Among these writers, Sartre's *oeuvre* is the most far-reaching and sustained attempt to ground the intelligibility of history in that of individual human praxis. But, as has been noted before, Sartre's starting point logically precludes his goal: if real transformation is to be possible then a particular context, some specific ensemble of social relations, must be built into the structure of the individual's situation from the beginning – otherwise one has inexplicable uniqueness, a circular dialectic and the abstract ahistorical generality of conditions (from 'scarcity' to the 'practico-inert').

By and large anti-naturalist Western Marxism from Lukács to Sartre has shown little concern with either ontological structure or empirical confirmation. These biases are separately corrected in the scientific rationalism of Althusser and other structuralist Marxists (such as Godelier) and the scientific empiricism and neo-Kantianism of Della Volpe and Colletti. In Althusser one finds most sharply formulated, in *For Marx* and (with E. Balibar) *Reading Capital*: (1) a novel anti-empiricist and anti-historicist conception of the social totality; (2) rudiments of a critique of epistemology coupled with a collapse of the extrinsic dimension ('theoreticism'); and (3) a form of scientific rationalism influenced by the philosopher of science G. Bachelard and the metapsychologist J. Lacan, in which the intransitive dimension is effectively neutralized, resulting in a latent idealism.

(1) Althusser reasserts the ideas of structure and complexity, on the one hand, and of irreducible sociality, on the other in his view of the social totality as an overdetermined, decentred complex, pre-given whole, structured in dominance. Against empiricism, it is a whole and structured, and its form of causality is not Newtonian (mechanistic); against historicism and holism it is complex and overdetermined, not an 'expressive totality', susceptible to an 'essential section' or characterized by a homogeneous temporality, and its form of causality is not Leibnizian (expressive). Against idealism, the social totality is pre-given; and against humanism, its elements are structures and relations, not individuals, who are merely their bearers or occupants. However, while Althusser wishes to insist against sociological eclecticism that the totality is structured in dominance, his own positive concept of structural causality is never clearly articulated.

(2) Although opposed to any reduction of philosophy to science or vice-versa, in maintaining that criteria of scientificity are completely intrinsic to the science in question, Althusser leaves philosophy (including his own) without any clear role; in particular, the possibilities of any demarcation criterion between science and ideology, or critique of the practice of an alleged science, seem ruled out. Epistemological autonomy for the sciences is accompanied by and underpins their historical autonomy, and the dislocation of science from the historical process presupposes and implies the inevitability of ideology (conceived as mystification or false consciousness) within it – a view at variance with Marx's.

(3) Although Althusser insists upon a distinction between the real and thought, the former functions merely as a quasi-Kantian limiting concept within his system, so that it easily degenerates into an idealism, shedding the intransitive dimension completely, as e.g. in 'discourse theory'. It is significant that just as Althusser sees Spinoza, not Hegel, as the true precursor of Marx, his paradigm of science is mathematics, an apparently *a priori* discipline, where the distinction between the sense and reference of concepts, and the theory-dependence and theory-determination of data, can be obscured. In short Althusser tends to buy theory at the expense of experience, as he buys structure at the price of praxis and the possibility of human emancipation.

If Lukács expresses the Hegelian current within Marxism in its purest form, Della Volpe draws out the positivist themes most exactly. The aim of his important work, *Logic as a Positive Science*, is the recovery of historical materialism as a tool of concrete empirically-oriented research and the revindication of Marxism as a materialist sociology or a 'moral Galileanism'. Della Volpe situates Marx's critique of Hegel as the historical climax of a line of materialist critiques of *a priori* reason extending from Plato's critique of Parmenides to Kant's critique of Leibniz. In it, Marx replaces the Abstract-Concrete-Abstract (A-C-A) Circle of the Hegelian dialectic with its 'indeterminate abstractions' by the Concrete-Abstract-Concrete (C-A-C or better C-A-C') Circle of materialist epistemology with its 'determinate rational abstractions', thus effecting a transition from 'hypostasis to hypothesis, from *a priori* assertions to experimental forecasts' (1980, p. 198). 'Any knowledge worthy of the name is science' (1978, p. 200), and science always conforms to this schema, which Marx is said to have elaborated in the Introduction to the *Grundrisse* and which, as Della Volpe interprets it, boils down to the familiar hypothetico-deductive method of Mill, Jevons and Popper.

Only four kinds of problems with the Della Volpean reconstruction can be indicated here. (1) It is supposed to apply indifferently to social science and philosophy as well as natural science. The upshot is a hypernaturalist account of social science and a positivist proleptic conception of philosophy shackled on to a view of science which is monistic and continuist within and across disciplines and buttressing a conception of Marx's own development as linear and continuous. (2) C-A-C is a purely formal procedure which works equally well for many theoretical ideologies. (3) Della Volpe never clearly differentiates theoretical precedents from historical causes: a latent historicism underpins the overt positivism of his work. (4) Most importantly, there are crucial ambiguities in the definition of the C-A-C' model. Does 'C' refer to a conceptualized problem or a concrete object, i.e. does the circle describe a passage from ignorance or from being to knowledge? If it is designed to do both, then the consequent empirical realism, in tying together transitive and intransitive dimensions, destratifies reality and dehistoricizes knowledge. Does 'A' refer to something real, as in transcendental realism and Marx, or merely ideal, as in transcendental idealism and pragmatism? Finally, does 'C'' refer to (i) presentation, (ii) test or (iii) application? The distinction between (i) and (ii) is that between Marx's order of presentation and inquiry; (ii) and (iii) that between the logics of theoretical and applied activity; (i) and (iii) that between the hierarchy of presuppositions of capitalist production elaborated in *Capital* and the kind of analysis of determinate historical conjunctures (the 'synthesis of many determinations' of the *Grundrisse* Introduction) which Marx essayed in the *18th Brumaire* or *The Civil War in France*.

The best known member of the Della Volpean school, Colletti, rejected even Della Volpe's restricted, purely epistemological, dialectics, contending that any dialectic excluded materialism, and criticized Della Volpe's hypernaturalist reconstruction of Marx for omitting the critical themes of reification and alienation. Colletti has, however, had great difficulty in reconciling these themes with his own unstratified empirical realist ontology and neo-Kantian conception of thought as other than being; and seems eventually to have settled on a split between the positive and critical dimensions of Marxism, thereby abandoning the notion of a scientific critique. There is in the work of Colletti, as in that of Habermas and Althusser (probably the three most influential recent writers on Marxist epistemology), a pervasive dualism: between thought as truth and as situated, objectivity as something in itself and as the objectification of a subject, man as a natural being and as the genus of all genera (the point at which the universe comes to consciousness of itself). While Colletti's work has been criticized in Italy (e.g. by Timpanaro) for neglecting the ontological aspects of materialism, both the Althusserian and Della Volpean tendencies in general seem vulnerable to scientific realist reconstructions of knowledge and Marxism. Between the theory of knowledge and Marxism, there will always, however, remain a certain tension. For, on the one hand, there are sciences other than Marxism, so that any adequate epistemology will extend far beyond Marxism in its *intrinsic* bounds; but, on the other, science is by no means the only kind of social practice, so that Marxism has greater *extensive* scope. There will thus always be a tendency for one or the other to be subsumed – as, within the concept of Marxist epistemology, epistemology becomes critically engaged and Marxism submits itself to a reason it displaces.

Reading

Adler, M. 1904–27 (1978): Selections on 'The Theory and Method of Marxism'.

Adorno, T. 1966 (1973): *Negative Dialectics.*

Althusser, L. 1965 (1969): *For Marx.*

Anderson, P. 1976: *Considerations on Western Marxism.*

Bhaskar, Roy 1986: *Scientific Realism and Human Emancipation.*

Della Volpe, G. 1950 (1980): *Logic as a Positive Science.*

Gramsci, Antonio 1929–35 (1971): *Selections from the Prison Notebooks.*

Habermas, Jürgen 1971: *Knowledge and Human Interests.*

Lukács, G. 1923 (1971): History and Class Consciousness.

Sartre, Jean-Paul 1963: The Problem of Method.

Stedman Jones, G. et al. 1977: Western Marxism: A Critical Reader.

                                    ROY BHASKAR

Kollontai, Alexandra Born 19 March 1872, St. Petersburg; died 9 March 1952, Moscow. Alexandra Kollontai was a figure of major controversy in the aftermath of the Russian revolution, and her name now stands for the spirit of revolutionary idealism defeated in the 1920s. Her life and work, little regarded by the Soviet authorities since her death, have now been appropriated by Western socialist feminists as an inspiration and a warning.

Kollontai joined the Bolsheviks in 1914 and by 1917 was on the Party's Central Committee. After the October revolution she became the only woman in Lenin's government when she was elected Commissar of Social Welfare. In 1920 she became Director of the Zhenotdel (women's department) of the party. She had already published many works criticizing the family and bourgeois sexual morality, and her uncompromising stance on these issues – often misrepresented as a 'free love' position – articulated an idealism and libertarianism on personal relations soon to be crushed by party policy on the family.

In 1920 she joined the Workers' Opposition within the Bolsheviks, increasingly disturbed by the bureaucratization, elitism and exclusive emphasis on production in Lenin's New Economic Policy. For this she inevitably fell from favour, being bitterly condemned by Lenin and banished by Stalin in 1922 to a minor diplomatic post in Oslo. From this date she escaped the Stalinist purges in which many of her left opposition comrades died, and rose to become the Soviet ambassador to Sweden.

Kollontai was a powerful writer and speaker and her popularity caused her and her ideas to be a thorn in the flesh of Soviet officialdom. Although decorated towards the end of her life she is largely ignored in the Soviet Union. In the West, however, she remains a source of inspiration to socialist feminists, her ideas passionately defended, her life and convictions admired and her fate seen as martyrdom to a male-dominated and bureaucratized party orthodoxy. Controversy about Kollontai is likely to continue, not least because she remained loyal to the party that had rejected her ideas, choosing peaceful exile rather than continued opposition.

Reading
Kollontai, Alexandra 1977: Selected Writings.
Porter, Cathy 1980: Alexandra Kollontai: A Biography.

                                MICHÈLE BARRETT

Korsch, Karl Born 15 August 1886, Todstedt, near Hamburg; died 21 October 1961, Belmont, Massachusetts. The son of a bank official, Korsch studied law, economics and philosophy at various universities, and obtained his doctorate at Jena. He became a member of the 'Free Student Movement' and subsequently, during his stay in England (1912–14), he joined the Fabian Society. After the first world war he moved rapidly leftwards, first joining the Independent Social Democratic Party (USPD), and then the Communist Party of Germany (KPD). During this time he participated actively in the COUNCILS movement. He was a leading member of the KPD from 1920 to 1926, writing prolifically for its newspapers and editing its theoretical journal Die Internationale (until 1924). Condemned as a 'revisionist' (see REVISIONISM) by Zinoviev at the Fifth Congress of the Communist International (1924), he was expelled from the KPD in 1926. He remained politically active in various splinter groups until he left Germany in 1934. In exile in the USA from 1938 until his death, he gradually moved away from the dominant forms of Marxism.

Korsch's most original contribution was undoubtedly Marxism and Philosophy (1923). Its aim was 'to understand every change, development and revision of Marxist theory, since its original emergence from the philosophy of German Idealism, as a necessary product of its epoch. . .'. He argued that Marxism itself had passed through three major stages: from 1843 to 1848 it was still thoroughly permeated with philosophical thought; from 1848 to 1900 the components of the theory of Marxism became separated into economics, politics, and ideology; finally, from 1900 to an indefinite future, Marxists came to regard scientific socialism as a

L

labour aristocracy   The phrase 'aristocracy of labour', as Hobsbawm (1964) notes, 'seems to have been used from the middle of the nineteenth century at least to describe certain distinctive upper strata of the working class' (p. 272). Marx and Engels, in one of their political reviews in the *Neue Rheinische Zeitung. Politisch-ökonomische Revue* (October 1850), noted that the Chartist movement had split into two factions, one revolutionary, to which 'the mass of workers living in real proletarian conditions belong', the other reformist, comprising 'the petty-bourgeois members and the labour aristocracy'. Subsequently, Lenin also associated reformism in the labour movement with the labour aristocracy; in particular, in his writings during the first world war he argued that 'certain strata of the working class (the bureaucracy in the labour movement and the labour aristocracy . . .), as well as petty bourgeois fellow-travellers . . . served as the main social support of these tendencies' to opportunism and reformism (*Collected Works*, vol. 21, p. 161). Max Adler, in a study of the working class in relation to fascism (1933), attributed to the labour aristocracy, as 'a numerically large privileged stratum', which 'has separated itself profoundly from the rest of the proletariat', responsibility for the diffusion of a conservative ideology. His analysis ultimately merges the notion of a labour aristocracy with that of *embourgeoisement* (which Engels had already introduced in letters of the 1880s and 1890s), and thus points to more recent debates. Hobsbawm (1964) concluded that the labour aristocracy in Britain at the end of the nineteenth century comprised about 15 per cent of the working class, and went on to consider changes in the twentieth century, noting particularly the 'new labour aristocracy' of white collar and technical workers. This suggests that the labour aristocracy is now a less significant phenomenon in present-day capital-

ist societies than the more general changes in the position of the working class and the growth of the new middle class.

Reading

Adler, Max 1933 (1978): 'Metamorphosis of the Working Class'. In Bottomore and Goode eds, *Austro-Marxism*.

Hobsbawm, Eric 1964: 'The Labour Aristocracy in Nineteenth-century Britain'. In *Labouring Men*.

Moorhouse, H. F. 1978: 'The Marxist Theory of the Labour Aristocracy'.

TOM BOTTOMORE

labour power   The capacity to do useful work which adds VALUE to commodities (see COMMODITY). It is labour power that workers sell to capitalists for a money wage. Labour power is to be distinguished from *labour*, the actual exercise of human productive powers to alter the use value of, and add value to, commodities. The products of labour can be bought and sold as commodities. But it is impossible to give an exact sense to the idea of buying and selling labour itself, productive activity. The producer who cannot sell the product of labour must sell the power to labour, promising to expend labour in the interest of and under the direction of the purchaser, in exchange for a sum of money, the wage.

The category of labour power arises in the labour theory of value in the explanation of the source of SURPLUS VALUE. The capitalist lays out money to buy commodities and later sells commodities for more money than he laid out. This is possible systematically only if there exists some commodity whose use adds value to other commodities. Labour power is precisely such a commodity and the only such commodity, since in buying and using labour power the capitalist extracts labour, and labour is the source of set of purely scientific observations without any immediate connection with the political struggle. It was a pioneering work, for as Korsch himself pointed out, the prominent Marxist thinkers of the Second International had paid little attention to philosophical questions. His achievement is all the more impressive in that neither Marx's *Economic and Philosophical Manuscripts* nor the *Grundrisse* were published until a decade or more later. In general, Korsch stressed the subjective, activist element of Marxist politics in contrast to the deterministic formulae of the 'orthodox Marxists' of the Second International.

Korsch's other important work, *Karl Marx* (1938), was written under quite different conditions, for he was no longer part of a broad political movement, and no longer thought that Marxism was the sole ideology appropriate to the workers' movement. The purpose of the book was 'to restate the most important principles and contents of Marx's social science in the light of recent historical events and of the new theoretical needs which have arisen under the impact of those events . . .'. He now concentrated on Marxism as a materialistic science, which has three basic principles: historical specification; its critical character; and its practical orientation. Marxism has a twofold content, based on these principles: the materialist conception of history; and political economy. To some extent, in relation to both the principles and content of Marxism as he now expounded it, he moved away from the philosophical positions of *Marxism and Philosophy* to a more positivist conception of Marxism. Perhaps the most valuable sections of *Karl Marx* are those

which set forth the basic propositions
ist political economy – at that time, a
neglected aspect of Marxism. It does
the pioneering spirit of *Marxism an*
ophy, yet it can stand comparison wi
basic expositions of the fundamental th
Marxism from any period, and is of cor
relevance today.

The greater part of Korsch's other w
consisted of ephemeral political jour
Two minor exceptions, however, are his *A
recht für Betriebsräte* (1922), which no
analysed a specific law (the 1920 Factory (
cils Law) from a Marxist standpoint, bu
considered the relationship between law
society in more general terms; and
materialistische Geschichtsauffassung (1
which provided an interesting critique of
philosophical bases of Kautsky's work of
same name. From the mid 1930s, as no
above, Korsch changed his view of the role
Marxism, and expressed his later position mo
clearly in his lecture notes 'Zehn Thesen übe
Marxismus heute' (1950) where he asserted tha
'all attempts to re-establish the Marxist theory
as a whole, and in its original function as a
theory of the working-class social revolution,
are now reactionary utopias'.

Reading

Goode, Patrick 1979: *Karl Korsch*.

Korsch, Karl 1922: *Arbeitsrecht für Betriebsräte*.

— 1923 (*1970*): *Marxism and Philosophy*.

— 1929: *Die materialistische Geschichtsauffassung*.

— 1938 (*1967*): *Karl Marx*.

— 1950 (*1965*): 'Zehn Thesen über Marxismus heute'.

PATRICK GOODE

value. The source of surplus value in the system of capitalist production as a whole lies in the fact that the value capitalists pay for labour power is smaller than the value which the labour they extract adds to commodities. The only other possible explanation of surplus value, that the capitalist buys commodities below their values or sells them above their value, can explain individual surplus values, but cannot explain surplus value in a whole system of production, since the value gained in this way must be lost by some other commodity producer.

The historical precondition for the appearance of labour power on the market for capitalists to buy is the emergence of a class of 'free' labourers: 'free' first in that they have the legal right to dispose of their labour power for limited periods in exchange negotiations with potential buyers; and 'free' as well from ownership of, or access to, their own means of production. Thus the appearance of labour power requires the dissolution of slavery and serfdom and all limitations on the right of people to dispose of their own labour power in exchange. It also requires the separation of the direct labourers from means of production so that they cannot produce and sell the product of their labour, and are forced to live by selling their labour power (see PRIMITIVE ACCUMULATION).

Though labour power appears in fully developed capitalist production as a commodity on the market, it has several peculiarities which distinguish it from other commodities, and give rise to important contradictions in the capitalist production system. First, though labour power appears as a commodity for sale on the market, it is not produced like other commodities. The production of labour power is an aspect of the biological and social REPRODUCTION of workers as human beings. This complex process of reproduction involves social relations which are in general different from capitalist or commodity relations. In well developed capitalist societies, for example, labour power is reproduced by household labour which does not receive a wage; in less developed capitalist countries labour power is often reproduced through surviving non-capitalist modes of production. These processes have their own logic and ideology; the pure logic of capitalist relations cannot assure in and of itself the reproduction of labour power (see DOMESTIC LABOUR).

Second, the use value of labour power is its capacity to produce value. Labour power is unlike other commodities in that in order to utilize it the purchaser, the capitalist, must enter into a whole new set of relations with the seller, the worker. The extraction of labour from labour power raises additional points of conflict between buyer and seller beyond the usual negotiation over the price of the commodity, in this case the wage; conflicts over the intensity and conditions of work. These antagonistic class conflicts fundamentally structure the technical and social aspects of capitalist production.

Finally, the sale of labour power alienates the worker from his or her own creative powers of production which it delivers into the hands of the capitalist, and from any control over the product of labour. In the emergence of labour power as a commodity the contradictions of the commodity form between use value and exchange value reappear as the ALIENATION of the worker from his or her labour and product.

Despite the substantial advances that had been made up to Ricardo's work in formulating a coherent theory of value, classical political economy was unable to resolve the confusion inherent in the concept of the 'value of labour', which in some contexts meant the wage, and in others the value produced by labour. Marx dissipates this confusion by splitting the concept of labour into the pair labour/labour power (*Capital* I, chs. 6 and 19). This allows us to see that the sale of labour power to the capitalist for a wage precedes production and the emergence of a value in the product; and to see the exact mechanism of the appropriation of a surplus value in capitalist production. Marx viewed the discovery of the distinction between labour power and labour as his most important positive contribution to economic science. (See also EXPLOITATION; SOCIALLY NECESSARY LABOUR; ABSTRACT LABOUR.)

DUNCAN FOLEY

labour process   At its simplest the labour process is the process whereby labour is materialized or objectified in USE VALUES. Labour is here an interaction between the person who works and the natural world such that elements of the latter are consciously altered in a purposive manner. Hence the elements of the labour process are three-fold: first, the work itself, a purposive productive activity; second, the object(s) on which that work is performed; and third, the instruments which facilitate the process of work. The objects on which work is performed, commonly provided by a previous labour process, are called 'raw materials'. The instruments of work comprise both those elements which are intrastructural or indirectly related to the labour process itself (canals, roads etc.), and those directly involved elements such as tools through which labour works on its object. These are always the result of previous labour processes, and their character is related both to the degree of development of labour and to the social relations under which the work is performed. The objects of work and the instruments of work together are called the 'means of production'. The alteration in the object of work effected by labour is the creation of a use value; identically, we say that labour has been objectified. Since the means of production are use values consumed in the labour process, the process is one of 'productive consumption'. And since use values are thereby produced, from the perspective of the labour process, the labour performed is 'productive labour'.

The labour process is a condition of human existence, common to all forms of human society: people with their labour, the active elements, on the one side, and the natural, inanimate world, the passive element, on the other. But to see how different human participants relate to one another in the labour process requires consideration of the social relations within which that process occurs. In the capitalist labour process, the means of production are purchased in the market by the capitalist. So too is LABOUR POWER. The capitalist then 'consumes' labour power by causing the bearers of labour power (workers) to consume means of production by their labour. Work is thereby performed under the supervision, direction and control of the capitalist, and the products produced are the property of the capitalist, and not the property of the immediate producers. The labour process is simply a process between things the capitalist has purchased – hence the products of that process belong to the capitalist (see CAPITAL; CAPITALISM).

These products are use values for the capitalist only in so far as they are bearers of exchange value. The purpose of the capitalist labour process is to produce commodities whose VALUE exceeds the sum of the values of labour power and means of production consumed in the process of production. Thus this production process is both a labour process creating use values, and a valorization process creating values, the latter only being possible because of the difference between the exchange value and the use value of labour power. It is crucial to the understanding of Marxian economics to distinguish the value of labour power from the value which expenditure of that labour power valorizes in the labour process. Unless the latter exceeds the former, no SURPLUS VALUE can be created. Further, capital has command over labour power, since people are forced to sell their labour power for a wage by virtue of their historical separation from access to the means of production other than through the wage transaction. And capital has command over labour, since the exercise of labour power is performed under the dictates of capital, whereby the working class is compelled to do more than is required for its own subsistence. Accordingly, capital is a coercive social relation.

Thus the labour process is concerned with the qualitative movement of production, a process with a definite purpose and content, producing a particular kind of product. The value-creating process considers the same process from a quantitative point of view, all elements of the process being conceived as definite quantities of objectified labour, measured according to socially necessary duration in units of the universal equivalent of value (see MONEY). Any process of commodity production is a unity of labour process and value-creating process. Once that value-creating process is carried on beyond a certain point we have the capitalist form of commodity production, or the capitalist production process, the unity of labour process and valorization process.

There is some terminological inexactitude in much modern Marxist writing on the capitalist production process, since this latter is often identified as the capitalist labour process rather than as a unity of labour and valorization process. It is important to maintain the distinction between the two processes in order to maintain the familiar Marxist duality of use value and value processes. The means of production under capitalism have a similar dual aspect. From the point of view of the labour process the means of production are the means for purposive productive activity, and the worker is ontologically related to the means of production as essential elements for the objectification of labouring activity in products. From the point of view of the valorization process, however, the means of production are the means for the absorption of labour. As the worker consumes means of production as the material elements of productive activity (labour process), so simultaneously do the means of production consume the worker in order that value is valorized (valorization process). Under capitalism, it is not that the worker employs means of production, but rather that the means of production employ the worker. Once the capitalist's money is transformed into means of production, the means of production at once are transformed into the capitalist's title to the labour and surplus labour of others, a title justified by the rights of private property, and maintained ultimately by the coercive forces of the capitalist state. Such an inversion of the relation between already objectified labour, or dead labour, and labour power in motion, or living labour, is characteristic of the capitalist mode of production, and is mirrored in bourgeois ideology as a confusion between the value of means of production on the one hand, and the property they possess, as capital, of valorizing themselves on the other. The means of production are then seen to be productive, when in fact only labour is capable of producing things. (See FETISHISM and COMMODITY FETISHISM for further details of this type of inverted consciousness).

The formulation that the means of production employ the worker under capitalism, rather than the converse, emphasizes the subordination of labour to capital. But Marx ('Results of the Immediate Process of Production') distinguishes two forms of what he calls 'the subsumption of labour under capital', forms which correspond to distinct historical periods in the prehistory and history of capitalism. The first form is found in the way in which capitalism emerges from earlier modes of production, and is concerned purely with an alteration in the way in which surplus labour is extracted. Marx calls this the 'formal subsumption of labour under capital' in order to describe a process whereby

capital subordinates labour on the basis of the same technical conditions of production (same level of development of the forces of production) within which labour has hitherto been performed. All personal relations of domination and dependency, characteristic of guild production in the feudal towns and peasant production in the feudal countryside, are dissolved in the cash nexus, whereby different commodity owners (of the conditions of labour, and of labour power) relate to each other solely on the basis of sale and purchase, to confront each other within the production process as capital and labour. Since this 'formal subordination of labour to capital' does not alter the labour process itself the only way in which surplus value can be extracted is by extending the length of the working day beyond necessary labour time. Formal subordination is thus associated with the production of absolute surplus value, seen by Marx as existing in Britain from the mid-sixteenth century to the last third of the eighteenth century, in which the labour process is characterized first by simple COOPERATION and later by MANUFACTURE. But with the advent of MACHINERY AND MACHINOFACTURE, the labour process is itself continuously transformed, or revolutionized in pursuit of productivity gains. Machinery becomes the active factor in the labour process, imposing continuous, uniform and repetitive tasks upon labour, which necessitates the imposition of a strict factory discipline. Moreover, the scientific knowledge which is the necessary concomitant to the introduction of machinery creates new hierarchies of mental and manual labour, as previous divisions of labour based on craft skills are eliminated (see DIVISION OF LABOUR). Marx calls large-scale industry with its production based on machinery the 'real subsumption of labour under capital' and associates it with the production of relative surplus value. Introduced into Britain by the 'industrial revolution', the real subsumption of labour under capital continually transforms the labour process in pursuit of the accumulation of value, and is generally taken to indicate the maturity of capitalism as a mode of production.

After Marx's writings on the subject there was little subsequent analysis of the capitalist production process by Marxists for about a hundred years. In part this was perhaps because of the very success of Marx's analysis: the development of factory production after Marx's death seemed emphatically to confirm his writings. But the harnessing of science in pursuit of productivity gains led to such an extraordinary growth of capitalism that, notwithstanding depression, fascism, world wars, and so on, there was a tendency among Marxists to regard advanced capitalist technology as the necessary form of organization of the labour process no matter what the social relations of production were. That is to say that the technology came to be seen as class-neutral and its authoritarian and hierarchical nature as a function of the prevailing relations of production. This was closely associated with a different view: an interpretation of history as dominated by the advance of the forces of production, the development of technology being seen as a smooth, linear process of advance, which determined what relations of production were appropriate at particular points of time. Technology, rather than class struggle, became the motor of history. Both views were given great impetus by the enthusiasm with which Lenin embraced Frederick W. Taylor's principles of 'scientific management' as one of the means by which the USSR was to catch up and overtake capitalism. Thus in 1918 Lenin remarked that Taylorism,

> like all capitalist progress, is a combination of the refined brutality of bourgeois exploitation and a number of the greatest scientific achievements in the field of analysing mechanical motions during work, the elimination of superfluous and awkward motions, the elaboration of correct methods of work, the introduction of the best system of accounting and control, etc. The Soviet Republic must at all costs adopt all that is valuable in the achievements of science and technology in this field. The possibility of building socialism depends exactly upon our success in combining the Soviet power and the Soviet organization of administration with the up-to-date achievements of capitalism. ('The Immediate Tasks of the Soviet Government', CW, 27, p. 259)

Such a strategy turned out to have crippling effects on the socialist development of Soviet society, as Soviet labour processes differed little from their capitalist counterparts. In retrospect this was, perhaps, not surprising, for Soviet industrialization depended upon the large-scale import of capitalist technology in the years 1929 to 1932, technology which was then copied; and the Soviet Union has always had problems in replicating anything approaching the dynamic of technological innovation in advanced capitalist countries. This is a clear if controversial example of how technology is determined by class relations, rather than the converse.

The major consequence in the West of the 'technologist' conception of history was that the Marxist analysis of the changing class structure of advanced capitalist countries stagnated, leaving the way clear for a variety of post-capitalist or post-industrial sociologies, which provided much of the ideological underpinning of social democratic revisionism, particularly in the 1950s. But from the late 1960s onwards, attention among Marxists gradually turned to the rediscovery of the capitalist labour process, as part of the revival of the Marxist analysis of capitalism. Within this development, the publication of Braverman's work (1974) proved enormously influential and stimulating to the development of Marxist analyses of processes of production and of the evolving class structure of advanced capitalist countries. (See Nichols 1980 for some examples.) Braverman's analysis was structured around capital accumulation as the fundamental dynamic of capitalism, restoring Marx's emphasis on the simultaneous expansion of production and degradation of labour. As regards the former, Braverman's analysis is concerned with MONOPOLY CAPITALISM, in which he emphasizes how the developments of management and of mechanization have been particularly important. The rise of the oligopolistic large firm, the changing structure of the market and the development of the economic activities of the state are integrated into the analysis in such a way that the changing structure of capital is shown to produce changes in the structure of the working class. In particular, Braverman emphasizes the changes in the character and composition of the RESERVE ARMY OF LABOUR, the importance of the sexual division of labour, and the changes in the labour process in the clerical and service industries and occupations. The other side of the coin is the degradation of labour, in particular of craft work, as capitalist organization of the labour process is continually concerned to cheapen labour, and to secure effective control over the labour process by abolishing all repositories of skill and knowledge which undermine capital's attempts to reorganize production. This latter constitutes for Braverman a general tendency towards the real subordination of labour to capital via the degradation of craft skills.

Criticisms of Braverman's work (Elger 1979 gives a good bibliography) tend in general to focus on his attempt to analyse the modern working class as a class 'in itself' rather than 'for itself', and his consequent eschewing of all analysis of working-class consciousness, organization and activities. This approach renders the working class a mere object of capital, passively accommodating to the changing dynamic of valorization, and this loses sight of the ways in which class struggle at the point of production is central to an understanding of the development of the capitalist labour process. (See also Rubery 1978.) Moreover, Braverman's analysis can be taken to imply that capitalist control and domination is completely and totally exercised within the production process, which fails to account for the significance of political relations and capitalist state institutions; if class relations within production are seen as frequently problematical for capital, political institutions and processes can be seen as rendering those problematic relations safe for capital.

Despite the passivity of Braverman's working class, both within the production process and beyond it (perhaps partially engendered by specifically American conditions, but see also Aglietta 1979, ch. 2), his work has been of fundamental importance in redirecting the attention of Marxists back to the capitalist labour process, and in providing a focus and reference point for the discussion of issues which are central to Marxist theory. (See also ACCUMULATION; CLASS CONSCIOUSNESS; EXPLOITATION; INDUSTRIALIZATION.)

Reading

Aglietta, Michel 1979: *A Theory of Capitalist Regulation. The US Experience*.

Berg, M. ed. 1979: *Technology and Toil in Nineteenth Century Britain*.

Braverman, Harry 1974: *Labour and Monopoly Capital*.

Elger, Tony 1979: 'Valorization and "Deskilling": A Critique of Braverman'.

Marglin, Stephen 1974–5: 'What Do Bosses Do? The Origins and Functions of Hierarchy in Capitalist Production. Pt. I'.

Nichols, Theo 1980: *Capital and Labour: Studies in the Capitalist Labour Process*.

Rubery, Jill 1978: 'Structured Labour Markets. Workers' Organization and Low Pay'.

Samuel, Raphael ed. 1977: 'The Workshop of the World: Steam Power and Hand Technology in mid-Victorian Britain'.

SIMON MOHUN

Labriola, Antonio Born 2 July 1843, Cassino; died 12 February 1904, Rome. After studying philosophy at the University of Naples he became a schoolteacher and lived in Naples until 1874 when he was appointed to a chair of philosophy in Rome. Influenced initially by Hegelianism and then by Herbart's associationist psychology he became a Marxist at the end of the 1880s, and thus the first 'professorial Marxist' in Europe. His best-known work in English is *Essays on the Materialist Conception of History* (1895–6), the first two volumes of a four-volume study of historical materialism (the last volume published posthumously in 1925). Labriola's Marxism was open and pragmatic, and even in his later work he refused to bring all his ideas within one all-embracing scheme of thought. The great value of the Marxist theory of history, in his view, was that it overcame the abstractions of a theory of historical 'factors': 'The various analytic disciplines which illustrate historical facts have ended by bringing forth the need for a general social science, which will unify the different historical processes. The materialist theory is the culminating point of this unification.' But this unifying principle had to be interpreted in a flexible way: 'The underlying economic structure, which determines all the rest, is not a simple mechanism, from which institutions, laws, customs, thought, sentiments, ideologies emerge as automatic and mechanical effects. Between this underlying structure and all the rest, there is a complicated, often subtle and tortuous process of derivation and mediation, which may not always be discoverable' (op. cit. pp. 149, 152). Labriola introduced Marxism into the originally syndicalist (see SYNDICALISM) Italian socialist movement, and he had a strong influence upon his pupil Benedetto Croce, who himself published several important essays on Marxism between 1895 and 1899 (see Croce 1913).

Reading

Labriola, Antonio 1895–6 (1904): *Essays on the Materialist Conception of History.*

— 1898 (1907): *Socialism and Philosophy.*

Dal Pane, Luigi 1935: *Antonio Labriola. La vita e il pensiero.*

TOM BOTTOMORE

Lafargue, Paul Born 15 January 1842, Santiago de Cuba; died 26 November 1911, Paris. Of very mixed ancestry, Lafargue came to France to study medicine, but was soon involved in left-wing politics, at first under the inspiration of Proudhon's ideas. Moving to London in 1866 he became an intimate of Marx's family, adopted his views, and married his daughter Laura. Settling permanently in Paris after 1880, he was soon a leading propagandist of the *Parti ouvrier français*, indefatigable in popularizing Marxist thinking in the labour movement, and always in close touch with Engels. One of the most versatile and attractive, if not the most orthodox, of all Marxist publicists, he was a militant anti-clerical; women's rights were among his interests; he investigated economic issues. In jail in 1883 he wrote one of his best-liked works, *The Right to be Lazy*, in which with some whimsical exaggeration he argued the case for more leisure for workers, a subject he was one of the first to take up. His colonial background helped to make him a critic of imperialism, and to interest him in the new fields of anthropology and ethnology. His most ambitious work, *Evolution of Property*, is a sparkling presentation of Marxist historical theory. (See also NATIONALISM; STAGES OF DEVELOPMENT.)

Reading

Girault, Jacques 1970: *Paul Lafargue: textes choisis.*

Lafargue, Paul 1883 (1907): *The Right to be Lazy.*

— 1910: *Evolution of Property from Savagery to Civilization.*

— (1959–60): *Frederick Engels, Paul and Laura Lafargue. Correspondence.*

Stolz, Georges 1938: *Paul Lafargue, théoricien militant du socialisme.*

V. G. KIERNAN

landed property and rent Marx's theory of capitalist agricultural rent is to be found in *Capital* III and in *Theories of Surplus Value* (predominantly pt II). Marx's starting point, and it is one that distinguishes his theory from nearly all others, is that rent is the economic form of class relations to the land. As a result rent is a property not of the land, although it may be affected by its varying qualities and availability, but of social relations.

Marx distinguishes as types of rent, differential rent and absolute rent. Differential rent itself consists of two types. Differences of land in fertility and location lead to equal capitals earning different returns within the agricultural sector. These differences are the basis for differential rent of the first type, DRI. When capitals of different size are applied to land they again earn different returns. Unlike industry in general, however, the associated surplus profits do not accrue to the individual capitalist with larger than normal capital. They may in part be appropriated as rent, this time of the second type, DRII. Marx's conclusion is that to the extent that access of capital to land within the sector is impeded by landed property, the intensive development of agriculture is obstructed. Capitalists' ability and incentive to pursue surplus profits within the sector are inhibited to the extent that rent can be appropriated.

While differential rent is concerned with COMPETITION between capitals within the agricultural sector, absolute rent is derived from competition between sectors of the economy in the formation of VALUE AND PRICE OF PRODUCTION. When capital flows into agriculture it is either invested intensively as for DRII or it is invested on new land. In this last case an absolute rent must be paid in the presence of landed property that does not allow free use of land. But this rent is not without limit in size. Marx argues that it is at most the difference between the value and price of production of agricultural commodities, this being a positive quantum of SURPLUS VALUE due to the lower ORGANIC COMPOSITION OF CAPITAL in agriculture.

There has recently been a revival within Marxism of an interest in rent theory following analyses of the role of landed property in urban crises (see URBANIZATION). Much of the resulting literature has rejected Marx's theory of absolute rent by replacing it with a monopoly rent, in which case there is no limit on the level of rent above price of production. Moreover there is no reason for the organic composition to be lower in agriculture. Fine (1979) argues that this is a misinterpretation of Marx's theory and demonstrates that the limits on absolute rent are to be derived from the intensive development of agriculture as an alternative to its extension onto new lands. Ball (1977) argues that there can be no general theory of rent, but that the specific historically developed relation between capital and land must be the basis for theory. Moreover, the organic composition must not be confused with the value composition of capital. Marx derives absolute rent from impediments to intensive ACCUMULATION within agriculture and this is associated with a lower organic not value composition of capital. A different approach is adopted by Murray (1977) who, while supporting Marx's propositions, assumes that they have general applicability to landed property. Accordingly the existence and role of differential and absolute rent can be presumed independently of the form of landed property.

It must be recognized that these differing interpretations of, and breaks with, Marx's analysis are in part the result of the poor state of preparation of Marx's analysis whether in *Capital* III or in *Theories of Surplus Value*. The material presented often constitutes pages of tables of hypothetical prices and differential rents. Fine argues that these are present precisely because prices and rents cannot be derived from the presumed technical relations of production between capital, labour and land. It depends upon what constitutes normal capital and normal land in value determination and here the historical and social relation between the two must enter into the analysis.

In *Capital* III Marx also considers the development of pre-capitalist ground rent. He periodizes feudal rent into three types forming a logical sequence. These are labour rent, rent in kind and money rent. These three forms of rent are associated with different stages of development of feudal society, the last for example, presupposing a certain growth of COMMODITY production by which money can be obtained to pay the rent in cash. Nevertheless despite commodity production the mode of production remains feudal. As for private accumulation, Marx's analysis here is of relevance for modern

analyses of UNDERDEVELOPMENT since money forms of feudal rent persist where pre-capitalist societies are confronted by capital.

In *Theories of Surplus Value*, Marx elaborates his own position on the question of rent and criticizes other writers. Ricardo, for example, has a concept of differential rent alone, apart from a monopoly rent which could obtain in any sector of the economy. For Ricardo, rent is precisely a property of the land, of nature, and all landed property does is to determine who should receive it. Smith does admit the possibility of absolute rent in so far as he subscribes to a components theory of price in which price is made up of independently determined portions of wages, profits and rents. But this theory is itself incoherent since these three forms of revenue cannot be independently determined since they are confined to sum to net output. By criticizing these and other writers Marx attempts to demonstrate that rent can only be adequately understood by examining the social relationship between capital and land. This is a value relationship which is distorted, as compared to industry in general, by the condition of access to the land. As a result surplus value is appropriated in various forms of rent (which can only be distinguished analytically) and whatever the levels of rent, landed property has an effect on the development of those industries which are particularly sensitive to land as a means of production.

Reading

Ball, M. 1977: 'Differential Rent and the Role of Landed Property'.

— 1980: 'On Marx's Theory of Agricultural Rent: a Reply to Ben Fine'.

Clarke, S. and Ginsberg, N. 1976: 'The Political Economy of Housing'.

Edel, M. 1976: 'Marx's Theory of Rent: Urban Applications'.

Fine, Ben 1979: 'On Marx's Theory of Agricultural Rent'.

— 1980: 'On Marx's Theory of Agricultural Rent: A Rejoinder'.

— 1982: *Theories of the Capitalist Economy*, chs 4 and 7.

Fine, Ben and Harris, Laurence 1979: *Rereading 'Capital'*, ch. 7.

Murray, R. 1977: 'Value and Theory of Rent'.

BEN FINE

Lange, Oskar Ryszard Born 27 July 1904 in Tomaszow Mazowiecki; died 5 October 1965 in a London hospital. The son of a German textile manufacturer, he became an economist, econometrician, statistician, socialist thinker and statesman. Lange studied law and economics at Poznan and Krakow (Jagiellonian) universities, obtained a Ph.D. in economics and became a docent at the latter university. In 1934 he was awarded a Rockefeller Foundation fellowship for studies in the USA and England, spending most of his time (extended to two years) at Harvard University, studying under Schumpeter, and at the London School of Economics. For the next ten years he taught at several American universities, mainly at Chicago, and in 1945 became ambassador of the Polish People's Republic in Washington DC and subsequently the representative of Poland at the UN Security Council. In 1948 he returned to Poland where he combined teaching with political activity.

A convinced socialist, Lange regarded Marxist economics as the most promising theory of social development. Simultaneously he was fascinated by neo-classical economics, particularly by the theory of general equilibrium. After the 'Keynesian revolution' he attempted in several studies to reconcile and integrate these two theories, showing Keynes's theory as a special case of general equilibrium theory. He regarded this theory, however, as very far from reality, since in contemporary economies monopolies and state intervention are destroying the mechanism of free competition. Thus, in his view, neo-classical economics, particularly welfare economics, is better able to analyse the management of a socialist economy than to describe a capitalist economy.

In the Western literature (far beyond economics), the best known part of Lange's writings is his theory of MARKET SOCIALISM. He took part in a great debate on economic calculation in a socialist economy, initiated by Mises and Hayek. Rejecting their contention that without a market to determine real prices of production factors, and without private ownership, a rational economy is impossible, Lange argued that public ownership permits better (fuller) use of the competitive mechanism than contemporary capitalist economies, which suffer from frictions caused by monopolistic corporation practices.

In his model there is a real market for consumption goods and labour and an artificial market for capital goods. A Central Planning Board was to fix prices of capital goods and correct them according to the changes in stocks. Thus, the CPB would imitate a market and by this method of management (by 'the trial and error method') would respect consumers' preferences. Managers of socialist firms would have to obey two rules imposed on them by the CPB: to produce goods to the point at which prices are equal to marginal costs, and to minimize average costs. Lange did not deny that a bureaucratization of economic life is a real danger even within such a form of socialism. He only hoped that managers subject to democratic control would be better than the private corporate executives responsible to nobody. This classical model (known also as the Lange-Lerner model, since Lange corrected his original text following Lerner's criticism) provoked many polemics and a variety of interpretations. The liberal economists usually criticized it for giving too much discretion to the CPB, which would be unable to react to market signals quickly enough, leaving the national economy rather rigid, whereas socialists attacked it for giving up planning. One can say that at different periods Lange accepted the arguments of both sides. During world war two his views evolved in the direction of a mixed market economy, in which only key industries (monopolies) would be socialized. He also seemed to drop his idea of fixing prices for capital goods by the CPB. For these reasons he refused to prepare a second edition of his work. After returning to Poland, Lange became one of the theoreticians of a command economy and central planning with a limited (subordinated) market and workers' participation.

In the second half of the 1950s Lange became an idol of the supporters of revisionism and of reform economics, the essence of which was plan *cum* market or central planning *cum* decentralized management. Like Otto Bauer in the 1930s, he believed that Stalinist industrialization creates preconditions for a socialist welfare state and thus for a political emancipation of the working class and 'socialist' intelligentsia. When hopes for crucial reforms in Poland expired, he devoted his efforts to popularizing new, specialized branches of economics, such as econometrics, economic cybernetics, linear programming, etc. In the late 1950s, Lange undertook the very ambitious task, in a treatise entitled *Political Economy*, of synthesizing the contemporary stage of knowledge in this branch of science (Western and Marxist). Contrary to his earlier attempts, this time he tried to base his treatise on Marxist economics (very much influenced by a 'Leninist' interpretation). On the other hand, using the principle of economic rationality as a methodological justification, he wanted to absorb all essential achievements of modern Western economics. But of the planned three volumes of this *magnum opus* Lange managed to complete only the first.

Reading

Kowalik, Tadeusz 1987: 'Oskar Lange'. In *The New Palgrave: A Dictionary of Economics*, vol. 3.

Lange, Oskar 1963: *Political Economy*, vol. 1.

— 1970: *Papers on Economics and Sociology.*

— 1973–86: *Dziela* (Works), vols. 1–8. In Polish.

Lange, Oskar and Taylor, Fred M. 1938 *(1964): On the Economic Theory of Socialism*, edited and with an introduction by Benjamin E. Lippincott.

TADEUSZ KOWALIK

Lassalle, Ferdinand Born 13 April 1825, Breslau; died 31 August 1864, Geneva. One of the strangest figures in the history of socialism, Lassalle was the son of a prosperous Jewish businessman. As a philosophy student at Berlin he became a YOUNG HEGELIAN and progressive, and during the 1848 revolution was associated with Marx and the *Neue Rheinische Zeitung*. Arrested, he was acquitted in May 1849 by a jury. In 1858 he published a bulky study on Hegelian lines of the Greek philosopher Heraclitus the Obscure, and in 1861 another of law and the evolution of legal ideas. He returned to public affairs in 1859 with a pamphlet on the Italian war, and more actively when the constitutional crisis between monarchy and parliament broke out in Prussia in the early 1860s. In 1863 he organized Germany's first socialist party, the General Union of German Workers, with all authority concentrated in his own hands.

Seven years younger than Marx, Lassalle always showed considerable respect for him, helped him with money and publishing arrangements, urged him to complete the writing of

Capital, and on a visit to London in 1862 proposed a newspaper to be directed by them jointly. Marx, and still more Engels, were far from reciprocating this friendliness; they disliked Lassalle's inordinate vanity, his lavish and dissolute style of living, and his flamboyant demagogy, and they distrusted his ideas. His miscellaneous writings won very little approval from them; as an economist, he seemed to them to show much ignorance of the subject, as well as to be plagiarizing from Marx. All the same, they were shocked by his early death, the result of an absurd duel arising from a disappointment in love.

They disapproved most strongly of Lassalle's political tactics in his last years. Realizing that the German bourgeoisie was incapable of a serious revolutionary struggle, and with a good deal of the German nationalist in him, he withdrew from support of the Liberals, and negotiated with Bismarck, in the vain hope of achieving through him and the monarchy the two grand aims he set before the workers' movement in his 'Open Letter' or manifesto of February 1863. One of these was universal, equal suffrage, to democratize the state; the other was to make the state no longer a mere 'nightwatchman' or policeman, as he blamed *laissez-faire* liberals for considering it, but an active participant in social change, granting credits to workers' cooperatives through which the economy would be gradually socialized.

His party grew with a slowness that greatly chagrined him, and could make no headway in Berlin, but his barnstorming methods made him an effective popularizer, and his organization as well as his name outlived him. In 1875 when the party agreed to merge with a rival body led by William Liebknecht and August Bebel, who stood closer to Marx, the latter was indignant to find that the programme adopted, at a meeting at Gotha, contained far more Lassallean than Marxist ideas. Marx wrote an elaborate criticism of it, objecting for instance to the perpetuation of the so-called 'iron law of wages' which Lassalle had endorsed, and pointing out that he had attacked only capitalists, not landlords. Not until 1890 however was the programme altered. A final summing up of Lassalle by Engels, in a letter to Kautsky of 23 February 1891, is very severe. Among later Marxists he continued to be given praise as the originator of the socialist movement in Germany, and he was one of the heroes of socialism who were honoured with memorials in Russia soon after the Bolshevik revolution.

Reading

Bernstein, Eduard 1891 (*1893*): *Ferdinand Lassalle as a Social Reformer.*

Footman, David 1946: *The Primrose Path. A Life of Ferdinand Lassalle.*

Morgan, R. 1965: *The German Social Democrats and the First International 1864–1872.*

Oncken, Hermann 1920: *Lassalle. Eine politische Biographie.*

V. G. KIERNAN

law   Marxism is often seen as sharing with radical revolutionary socialism and anarchism a profound hostility to law, a belief that law protects property, social inequality and class domination and that the need for law will disappear in a truly human, cooperative society. Marx himself, though he began his university career as a law student, quickly lost interest in the subject and wrote nothing systematic or sustained on questions of legal theory, legal history or the place of law in society. In his youthful period as a Left Hegelian and radical democrat (1842–3), he took the radical Hegelian view that 'true' law was the systematization of freedom, of the internal rules of 'universal' coherent human activities and could therefore never confront human beings from outside as a form of coercion, seeking to determine them as though they were animals. In 1844–7, in the process of developing a still mainly philosophical critique of society based on private property, Marx took the view that actual, existing law was a form of alienation, abstracting the legal subject and legal duties and legal rights from concrete human beings and social realities, proclaiming formal legal and political equality while tolerating, and indeed encouraging economic, religious and social servitude, divorcing man as a legal subject and man as a political citizen from the economic man of civil society. With his proclamation and working out of the materialist conception of history from 1845 onward, Marx developed the view that law was essentially epiphenomenal, part of the superstructure (see BASE AND SUPERSTRUCTURE), a reflection of the viewpoints, the needs and interests of a ruling class produced by development in the productive FORCES AND RELATIONS OF PRODUCTION that constitute the economic base of social development.

Marx's mature view that law is a form of class domination can be reconciled with his two earlier views and, in fact, subsumes them. But while the critique of law as a form of alienation sees law as a system of abstract concepts, the critique of law as a form of class domination, especially in the hands of Engels, treats law as a set of state-sanctioned commands. All three views lead to the conclusion that in the truly human, unalienated society of communism there will be no law as an external coercive force confronting individuals. In his *Critique of the Gotha Programme* (1875) Marx distinguished the stage after the revolution when bourgeois habits have not yet disappeared, when the 'narrow horizons of bourgeois right (law)' cannot yet be transcended and each works according to his capacity and receives according to his contribution, from the ultimate stage when each contributes according to his capacity and receives according to his need. Engels proclaimed that at this stage, when private property and class division had disappeared, the state and law will wither away since both, as organs of class rule, would have lost their *raison d'être*.

Much of the Marxist and non-Marxist discussion of Marx's and Engels's view of law has concentrated on the more general problems of the materialist conception of history – whether the relationship between law and the superstructure generally and the economic base is to be understood causally or functionally, whether a causal relationship can allow, as Engels believed, for limited reaction back from the superstructure onto the base (two-way determinism), whether there are in society relatively independent structures, and whether law is such a structure. Critics have argued that law can determine the character of economic production and that legal conceptions and realities, such as ownership, are part of the very definition of Marx's relations of production and therefore cannot be determined by them. Defenders have tried to show that Marx's use of terms like 'appropriation' and 'ownership' refers to infra-legal facts, though on the determinist view this still leaves the problem why law should be necessary to secure power achieved and defined without it. Some Marxist writers, especially in the Soviet Union and Soviet bloc countries, have treated law as a material force and, in recent years, as in some form necessary for any society whatever, having elements that are class-based and elements that reflect general conditions and needs of human societies.

Only two Marxist legal theorists, Karl Renner and E. B. Pashukanis (1891–?1937) have attracted interest and respect among non-Marxist legal theorists. Renner, rejecting the view that law is epiphenomenal and insisting that legal concepts are part of the description of the mode of production, focused on the continuity and comparatively unchanging definitions of legal concepts across greatly different modes of production. He argued that legal norms were neutral and relatively stable, based on human relationships and activities found in a wide range of societies. But such norms were brought together into legal institutions and clusters of legal institutions in different ways to perform different social functions according to the mode of production in which they were serving a function. The property norm, in some sense necessary in any society whatever to indicate who would be responsible for what, was undergoing a fundamental transformation in social function as a result of the fact that the development of bourgeois society was destroying the private, initially household, character of property and giving it a public and social character. E. B. Pashukanis, on the contrary, saw law as fundamentally a commercial phenomenon, reaching its apogee in bourgeois society. It was based, for him, on the abstract individuality, equality and equivalence of the legal parties. It treated all legal institutions, including the family, criminal law and the state, on the model of the contract between individuals and its *quid pro quo*. Law was thus fundamentally different from administration, which emphasizes duties rather than rights, and in socialism subordination to the common good rather than formal equality, sociotechnical norms rather than individuals, unity of purpose rather than conflict of interests. Under fully developed socialism, policy and plan would replace law.

The development of legal thought in countries ruled by Marxist-Leninist parties now stands in fundamental contradiction with growing West-ern radical emphasis on the class nature of law, and belief in replacing it with voluntary, informal and participatory procedures. Official Soviet theory has long defined law as the totality of state-sanctioned norms securing the basis and nature of the relevant mode of production and thus advantageous to the ruling class. But Khrushchev's proclamation that the dictatorship of the proletariat had ended in the USSR and that the Soviet state was now the State of All the People has been followed by an ever-increasing elevation of the importance of law in socialist society – administratively, educationally, ideologically. It is said to ensure stable and predictable social life, to organize production and to protect the individual and his rights. Law is now seen as the regular, necessary, fair and efficient means of steering society in conditions of social ownership. Like the state, it is allegedly a fundamental element in human affairs, which has been captured and distorted in the class interest in class societies, but which will not wither away when class disappears and which has elements of a non-class nature within it.

Reading

Cain, Maureen and Hunt, Alan eds. 1979: *Engels on Law.*

Hazard, John N. 1969: *Communists and their Law: A Search for the Common Core of the Legal Systems of the Marxian Socialist States.*

Kamenka, Eugene and Tay, Alice Erh-Soon 1978: 'Socialism, Anarchism and Law'. In Eugene Kamenka, Robert Brown and Alice Erh-Soon Tay eds. *Law and Society: The Crisis in Legal Ideals.*

Pashukanis, E. B. 1979: *Selected Writings on Marxism and Law.*

Renner, Karl 1904 (1949): *The Institutions of Private Law and their Social Function.*

EUGENE KAMENKA

legal Marxism A critical and scholarly interpretation of Marxism developed by P. B. Struve, M. I. Tugan-Baranovsky, N. A. Berdyaev, S. N. Bulgakov and S. L. Frank, which exerted its greatest influence in Russia in the period 1894 to 1901. Its main preoccupations were the merits (and deficiencies) of Marxism as a heuristic device and a plausible account of historical development. It stressed, in particular, the progressive role of capitalism and its modernizing,

Westernizing and civilizing significance for contemporary Russia. Its aim, as expressed by Struve, was to provide 'a justification of capitalism' even to the extent of appearing pro-capitalist both to its friends and to its populist opponents.

The Legal Marxists devoted little attention to Marxism as a mobilizing ideology of the working class, and generally avoided active involvement in the political organizations of Russian social democracy. Their political abstentionism stemmed partly from the scholarly disposition of the group, but was reinforced by the constraints governing the legal publication of Marxist ideas in Russia. After the arrest and exile in 1895–6 of most of the political leaders and theorists of the revolutionary wing of Russian social democracy the Legal Marxists became the most important publicists of Marxism in its application to Russia. Through their books and through their influential journals (*Novoe Slovo*, 1897 and *Nachalo*, 1898) they largely succeeded in displacing POPULISM as the dominant current of thought amongst the intelligentsia. Their journals also provided outlets for the publication of the theoretical writings of the 'illegals' in prison, exile or underground.

They were, from the outset, critical not only of many of Marx's conclusions but also of important aspects of his method. Struve anticipated many of the revisionist ideas of Bernstein and was, arguably, more thoroughgoing than the latter in exposing the methodological and empirical inadequacies of the theory of the catastrophic collapse of capitalism and the capacity of the proletariat to effect a social revolution. The Legal Marxists came to believe that historical materialism bore no necessary relation to philosophical materialism and they became increasingly concerned with the need for an ethical basis for socialism (see ETHICS). They were led towards neo-idealism and Kantian moral philosophy (see KANTIANISM AND NEO-KANTIANISM). Frank, Berdyaev and Bulgakov were eventually to become prominent philosophers of religion. The Legal Marxists were among the first to explore and develop Marx's accounts of the development of the market under capitalism and his REPRODUCTION SCHEMA. Tugan-Baranovsky was the first to develop a Marxist theory of ECONOMIC CRISES, emphasizing the disproportionality of

development of producer-goods and consumer-goods industries in explaining the periodicity of capitalist crises.

By 1902 Struve had become the editor of the first liberal journal in Russia and led the other members of his group into the proto-liberal Union of Liberation in 1903. From 1901 onward the group had suffered the fierce invective of Lenin and Plekhanov who diagnosed in the group's evolution the classic example of a typical regression from critical theoretical and economic analysis to philosophical eclecticism and thence to REVISIONISM and liberalism.

Reading

Berdyaev, N. A. 1937: *The Origin of Russian Communism*.

Kindersley, R. 1962: *The First Russian Revisionists: A Study of Legal Marxism in Russia*.

Luxemburg, R. 1913 (1951): *The Accumulation of Capital*.

Mendel, A. P. 1961: *Dilemmas of Progress in Tsarist Russia: Legal Marxism and Legal Populism*.

Pipes, R. 1970: *Struve*, 2 vols. Vol. 1: *Liberal on the Left*.

Struve, P. B. 1933–5: 'My Contacts and Conflicts with Lenin'.

NEIL HARDING

Lenin V. I. Pseudonym of Vladimir Ilich Ulyanov. Born Simbirsk (now Ulyanovsk) 22 April 1870; died 21 January 1924, Gorki. Unquestionably the most influential political leader and theorist of Marxism in the twentieth century, Lenin revitalized its theory of revolution by stressing the centrality of class struggle led by a tightly organized PARTY. He elaborated a theory of IMPERIALISM as the final stage of capitalism preparatory to an international proletarian revolution establishing and maintaining itself through force in a transitional DICTATORSHIP OF THE PROLETARIAT. He led the Bolshevik Party in the October Revolution of 1917 and established the world's first socialist state. Through the Communist International (see INTERNATIONALS) which he inspired, his views spread throughout the world, serving to define modern COMMUNISM in its opposition to SOCIAL DEMOCRACY.

Lenin was born into a moderately well-to-do and scholarly family. His father was an inspector of schools of liberal if moderate views with a high sense of public duty who died when Lenin was sixteen years of age. In the following year, when Lenin was sitting his final school examinations, his elder brother, Alexander, was executed for his part in a plot to assassinate the tsar. It can hardly be doubted that these events had a traumatic effect upon the youthful Lenin but such was his extraordinary resilience that he passed his examinations with the highest possible marks and was admitted to Kazan University. He had not been there long before he was expelled for participating in a student protest meeting and thereafter he devoted himself wholly to revolutionary activity, as did his surviving brother and two sisters.

Lenin's first substantial work, *What the 'Friends of the People' Are . . .*, was published in 1893. Its objective was to undermine the economic, social and political ideas of Russian POPULISM – a persistent theme of Lenin's writings up to 1900. He had already established himself as the leader of the St Petersburg Marxists and was influential in directing them away from in-depth propaganda to mass economic agitation. Arrested in December 1895 he continued to write from prison in support of the great strikes of 1896. Exiled to Siberia he completed work on his massive *Development of Capitalism in Russia* (1899), arguably the fullest account in Marxism of the earlier phases of the evolution of capitalism.

In 1900 Lenin joined forces with Plekhanov's group in Geneva. He conceived the plan of a national newspaper (*Iskra*) to articulate the grievances against tsarism and to act as the scaffolding for a disciplined party of professional revolutionaries which would lead the democratic revolution. He summarized his views on party objectives and the organizational forms necessary, in conditions of illegality, to fulfil them in his programme 'What Is To Be Done?' (1902).

In the revolution of 1905 Lenin believed economic measures against feudal landholding to be more important than constitutional projects. Accordingly he stressed the importance of land nationalization as the measure to split the bourgeoisie from the landowners, promote the rapid development of capitalism in the countryside, and draw the poor peasants alongside the proletariat. (For his position in 1905, his opposition to Trotsky's permanent revolution, and to the Menshevik line of conceding leadership to the liberals, see his *Two Tactics of Social Democracy in the Democratic Revolution.*)

In order to explain the outbreak of war in 1914 and the patriotic stance of many socialist leaders Lenin turned to the theory of monopoly or finance capitalism developed by Hilferding and Bukharin. In 1916 he produced what is arguably his most influential and characteristic book *Imperialism, the Highest Stage of Capitalism*. He maintained that a new and final epoch of capitalism had arisen in which monopoly replaced competition and the concentration of capital and class divisions of society had reached their extremes. Export of capital had replaced export of goods, and the economic territory of the whole world had been subjected to the parasitic exploitation of the most powerful capitalist states. Economic monopoly found its complement in political uniformity and the erosion of civil liberties; society and state were subordinated to the interests of finance capital. Capitalism in the epoch of imperialism, Lenin concluded, had become militaristic, parasitic, oppressive and decadent. It had, however, concentrated production in trusts and cartels, and capital in the banks, and had thereby greatly simplified the task of bringing the whole economy under social control and ownership. It had itself created 'a complete material basis for socialism'.

By the spring of 1917 all the elements of Lenin's theory of revolution had come together. International war and economic collapse made an international socialist revolution imperative, there was no other way out of barbarism. The bureaucratic-militarist state-capitalist trust was to be replaced by organs of popular democracy, administrative organs of the PARIS COMMUNE type whose modern forms were the Soviets (see COUNCILS). The simplified administrative structures of the banks and the trusts would enable all to participate in the economic administration of society. These libertarian views on the proper nature of the socialist state Lenin elaborated in his *State and Revolution* (1917). In October 1917, having captured a majority in the principal urban and military soviets, Lenin spurred the Bolshevik Party to assume power in a relatively bloodless coup.

From the spring of 1918 onwards Lenin's writings altered considerably in tone. As chairman of the Council of People's Commissars he was confronted by a mounting series of crises: urban famine, collapse of transport and of the army, foreign intervention and civil war. His preoccupations now were to ensure the most efficient mobilization of the régime's scarce resources, to instil firm discipline and accountability and to insist upon the authority of the centre. The emphasis now was upon the accountability of lower party (and state) organs to higher ones and this was crucial to Lenin's account of democratic centralism. The self-administration and decentralization of the Commune model was replaced by a more austere version of the dictatorship of the proletariat which, Lenin acknowledged, had to be exercised by its party. It was this model of the party/state absorbing the energy of the class that was projected through the Communist International in which Lenin reposed such faith. He remained convinced that without the swift extension of the revolution to Europe the prospects for socialism in Russia would be slight.

With the end of intervention and the civil war, resentment built up against the centralized dictatorial regime which the Bolsheviks had established. In March 1921 Lenin led his party into the strategic retreat of the New Economic Policy with its considerable relaxation in the terms of peasant freedom of trade. Simultaneously however, he insisted upon greater discipline within the party, a ban on factions and a severe line against non-party critics. Lenin envisaged a prolonged period of a mixed economy before the socialist sector could significantly expand and this situation, he insisted, required renewed vigilance and discipline.

Not until his last writings of late 1922 and 1923, after a second stroke had forced his effective retirement, did Lenin have leisure to reflect on what had been built in Russia. He was disturbed that the state apparatus had replicated many of the worst abuses of the tsarist state, that communists were high-handed, incompetent administrators, and increasingly divorced from the people. Some, including Stalin, had become so rude that they ought to be deprived of their powers (December 1922, 'Letter to the Congress'). The apparatus was, moreover, swollen out of all proportion to the useful work it did, and Lenin proposed drastic reductions in its size. He was unsure whether even the party was

capable of preserving socialist values in a land where industry (and the proletariat) had suffered so severely and where it was surrounded by a peasant mass. His final proposals were that the party and the state should fuse their best personnel in one exemplary institution which might keep alight a glimmer of socialism in isolated, backward Russia ('Better Fewer but Better', and 'How We Should Reorganise the Workers' and Peasants' Inspection' (1923)).

Lenin was, by any standards, an extraordinary man. Totally dedicated to the revolutionary cause he subordinated every aspect of his life to its service. As a leader his decisiveness and determination, the thoroughness of his theoretical analyses and of his practical preparations gave him unequalled authority and prestige within the Bolshevik Party and the Soviet Government. He was exacting of himself and had equally exacting expectations of his colleagues. He was by nature personally modest and lived a frugal, almost austere life. He was genuinely discomforted by extravagant praise and attempts to make of him a hero. After his death in January 1924, he was, against his express wishes to the contrary, interred with great ceremony in a mausoleum in Red Square, was canonized by Party and State and memorialized in innumerable ways in his own country and throughout the communist movement.

Lenin was the founding father of modern communism, and communist regimes and communist parties continue to venerate his writings and personal example and still feel obliged to justify their present policies by reference to his thought. (See also BOLSHEVISM; LENINISM.)

Reading

Carr, E. H. 1966: *The Bolshevik Revolution*.

Cliff, T. 1975–79: *Lenin*.

Harding, N. 1982: *Lenin's Political Thought*.

Lenin, V. I. (1960–70): *Collected Works*.

Lewin, M. 1967 (1969): *Lenin's Last Struggle*.

Liebman, M. 1975: *Leninism under Lenin*.

Rigby, H. 1979: *Lenin's Government Sovnarkom 1917–1922*.

Shub, D. 1948: *Lenin*.

Ulam A. B. 1965: *Lenin and the Bolsheviks*.

Wolfe, B. D. 1956 (1966): *Three Who Made a Revolution*.

NEIL HARDING

Leninism Marxist-Leninists conceive 'Leninism' to be the development of the scientific understanding of society propounded by Marx and Engels. As such it is a science of the laws of development of nature and society, which elucidates the causal relationships between man and society and the advance to the classless society of communism. The major components of Marxism-Leninism are dialectical and historical materialism as a method of analysis, political economy as the study of the class relationships to the means of production and the level of productive forces, and the theory of scientific communism (the structure and process of communist societies). More narrowly defined, Leninism is that tendency within Marxist thought which accepts the major theoretical contributions of Lenin to revolutionary Marxism. Specifically, it is an approach to the seizure of power for and by the proletariat and the building of socialist society, which legitimates revolutionary action by the party on behalf of the working class. It may be distinguished from BOLSHEVISM which is the political practice or political movement based on Leninism.

Leninists see Marxism as a revolutionary class PRAXIS which is concerned above all with the conquest of power, and they stress the role of the communist party as a weapon of struggle. The party is composed of class-conscious Marxists and is organized on the principle of democratic centralism. The danger of trade unionism as a basis for a socialist party is that its focus is too narrow and is predicated on the improvement of economic conditions, not on revolutionary activity. Rather than relying on the spontaneous development of consciousness in the working class, Leninists see the party as a catalyst bringing revolutionary theory and political organization to the exploited masses. 'Without a revolutionary theory . . . there can be no revolutionary movement.' For Marxist-Leninists, the seizure of power is the result of revolutionary struggle and initially the DICTATORSHIP OF THE PROLETARIAT is established under the hegemony of the party. Leninists reject the notion that the capitalist state can be taken over and made to serve the interests of the proletariat, or that socialism can be achieved through evolutionary means.

Leninists regard capitalism as an international and imperialist phenomenon. The laws of accumulation in the advanced capitalist countries lead to crises of overproduction of commodities and capital, and to a tendency for the rate of profit to fall; the search for profits leads to the export of capital and to a temporary stabilization of the capitalist world. Imperialism entails the division of the world between the dominant advanced industrial nations and the colonial societies which are forced into the world system, and it led to military conflict between these nations in world war I. This in turn produced a destabilization of the world capitalist system, and created favourable conditions for revolution. Lenin opposed the policies of the Second International which justified the social democratic movement's participation in national wars. Imperialism also led to uneven development and a shift in the focus of revolutionary socialist upheaval to the East; and for Lenin Russia was the paradigmatic case. The 'weakest link' of capitalism is located in the 'underdeveloped' or semi-colonial areas where the indigenous bourgeoisie is weak but there is enough industrialization to create a class-conscious proletariat. On the other hand, the metropolitan bourgeoisie is able, by virtue of the excess profit obtained from colonial tribute, to placate temporarily part of its own working class. The idea of socialist revolution in 'underdeveloped' countries leads to the inclusion of the PEASANTRY as an agent of revolutionary change. According to Lenin and Mao Tse-tung the peasantry first becomes an important social force in the bourgeois revolution, and then the poor and middle peasantry become a major support of the working class in the creation of a socialist order. After the socialist revolution in the East, however, the contradictions of capitalism in the metropolitan countries become greater and lead to world revolution. Only on a world scale can socialist revolution be consummated.

Compared with classical Marxism, Leninism gives a greater role to revolutionary 'toilers' (workers and peasants) rather than to the revolutionary proletariat as such, to the 'underdeveloped' or semi-colonial countries rather than the advanced capitalist countries; and it emphasizes the leading role of the party rather than the spontaneous activity of the working class (see PARTY). Rosa Luxemburg was a principled opponent of Leninism on this issue, stressing the importance of spontaneous class consciousness.

The success of the Bolsheviks in the Russian Revolution has led many Leninists to identify Leninism with the practice of the Soviet state, as 'representing' the dictatorship of the proletariat on a world scale. This view is particularly associated with Stalin and his supporters, who argued that the interest of the world proletariat was identical with that of the Soviet Union. After Lenin's death, and during the ascendancy of Stalin, Leninism became an ideology of legitimation used by the rulers of the Soviet Union and their supporters in the world communist movement. Stalin described Leninism as 'Marxism in the era of imperialism and of the proletarian revolution. . . . Leninism is the theory and tactics of the dictatorship of the proletariat in particular' (1934). Leninism in this sense became a doctrine which involved the subordination of the world communist parties to the interests of the USSR. Opposition to Stalin and to the hegemony of the Soviet Party over the world communist movement (see COMMUNISM) led to claims by other Marxists to be the true inheritors of Lenin's revolutionary praxis, the most important groups being the followers of Trotsky and Mao Tse-tung. Both groups are Leninist in the sense that they advocate the leading role of the party, the primacy of revolutionary political action, support for the October Revolution and for Lenin's methodological approach. A third, more revisionist group is to be found among the adherents of EURO-COMMUNISM who argue that Lenin's policies were specific to the Russia of his time. For them the essential feature of Leninism is its approach to such issues as political leadership and the concrete analysis of capitalism. On this view, a more open and democratic, less centralized communist party is relevant to Western conditions, and different class and political alliances are required if the communist party is to achieve power in the context of parliamentary democracy.

While holding to the belief in class struggle these thinkers see greater political advantage from participation in, and utilization of, the capitalist state apparatus, which is regarded as a necessary element in defending and extending workers' rights under capitalism. In particular, they see the idea of the dictatorship of the proletariat as a specific application of Leninism rather than its substance, and consider such an aim no longer apposite to the struggle of the European proletariat. Such views were extended by the adoption by the leadership of ruling communist parties in Europe and the Soviet Union of the reform policies associated with the doctrine of *perestroika*. The 'leading role' of the Communist Party is sometimes abandoned or conceived in open competition with other parties and groups in the context of political and economic pluralism. Other components in Leninism (the primacy of revolutionary struggle, the dictatorship of the proletariat, Lenin's political approach) have been abandoned.

Reading

Carrillo, S. 1977: 'Eurocommunism' and the State.

Corrigan, P., Ramsay, H. R. and Sayer, D. 1978: Socialist Construction and Marxist Theory: Bolshevism and its Critique.

Harding, N. 1977 and 1981: Lenin's Political Thought.

Knei-Paz, B. 1978: The Social and Political Thought of Leon Trotsky.

Lane, D. 1981: Leninism: A Sociological Interpretation.

Lenin, V. I. 1902 (1961): 'What is to be done'?

— 1916 (1964): 'Imperialism, the Highest Stage of Capitalism'.

— 1917c (1969): 'The State and Revolution'.

Luxemburg, R. 1922 (1961): 'Leninism or Marxism'. In The Russian Revolution.

Meyer, A. G. 1957: Leninism.

Stalin, J. V. 1934 (1973): 'Foundations of Leninism'; 'Problems of Leninism'. In B. Franklin ed. The Essential Stalin.

DAVID LANE

liberation theology   The first theoretical construction of Christian faith elaborated in the Third World with the aim of presenting freedom from oppression as a matter of universal religious significance. Of Latin American origin and dating from the 1960s, liberation theology fuses concepts from the social sciences with biblical and theological ideas. In particular, in its use of Marxist and neo-Marxist social theory it may be superficially read both by undiscerning theologians and sympathetic sociologists as a form of radical social theory incorporating a secular ethic of justice. Indeed, a recent official response of the Catholic church to liberation theology questions the epistemological status of a theology which attempts to unite the materialist foundations of Marxism and the transcendent elements of Christianity (Congregation for the Doctrine of the Faith 1984).

The hybrid form of liberation theology creates an initial impediment to definition. One might go further and say that the use of the noun in the singular, 'theology', to describe the corpus of liberation literature, as if it were in any way comparable to classical systematic theology, is misleading. There are a number of liberation theologies: Black Liberation Theology (Cone 1969); Jewish Theology of Liberation (Ellis 1987); Asian Liberation Theology (Suh Kwang-sun 1983); and Latin American Liberation Theology (Haight 1985). In addition to these, there is so-called political theology, influenced by the FRANKFURT SCHOOL, which may be described as a liberation theology for Western capitalist society (Metz 1969). In other words, there are 'liberation theologies' rather than one 'liberation theology'.

Even if a univocal description is not available, these theologies may be linked together under one title because they share assumptions about the need for contemporary theology to be oriented by three values: first, the analysis of oppression and its corresponding form of liberation; second, the employment of social analysis and theory as a corrective to the 'privatized' mode of traditional theology; and, third, the use of the paradigm of liberation from the Book of Exodus.

Oppression and liberation

The distinctive mode of theologizing developed in liberation studies came from the combination of detailed empirical analysis of forms of oppression and the sociological and political analysis of these forms. In Latin America, the education theories of Paulo Freire (1970) promoted descriptions of poverty and powerlessness among the masses. In the course of establishing new forms of adult education, it came to be realized that the socio-economic analysis of Marx was effective in identifying these forms of oppression as inevitable consequences of the alliance of wealth and power specific to capitalism. Those theologians who were reflecting along with the people on the experience of poverty began to speak of 'structures of oppression', and, interpreting the situation theologically, they adopted the term 'structures of sin'.

It is not clear whether liberation theologians have made textual connections between their own mode of theologizing and Marx's particular analysis of oppression in his *Critique of Hegel's Philosophy of the State* (1843). But the similarities are striking. Marx identifies the oppressing class by its 'embodiment of a limitation' . . . 'which gives general offence' (in terms of liberation theology this might be the sinful structures which create widespread poverty); or by the deficiency of a particular sphere which becomes 'the notorious crime of a whole society' (which might describe the place of the Nazi holocaust in Jewish Liberation Theology) (Marx 1844, in *Early Writings*, 1975).

The progression from a personal and psychological understanding of the foundations of theology to a sociological interpretation of reality is typical of liberation theology. For instance, the Catholic church's recommendation of a subjective lifestyle of poverty has been replaced in liberation theology by an objective 'option for the poor'. Since the church compromised itself with the oppressing wealth-owning class, it must now identify with the poor in the struggle for liberation. This recommendation to 'a fundamental option for the poor' reflects Marx's view that 'if one class is to be the class of liberation *par excellence*, then another class must be the class of oppression' (1975, p. 254).

Marx's conclusion (with its own strange theological echoes) that social oppression of this kind means 'the total loss of humanity, which can therefore redeem itself only through the total redemption of humanity' (p. 256) presents in secular form the eschatological theme of the struggle to establish the universal Kingdom of God (with its social and political consequences) which is at the heart of liberation theology.

The echoes of a principle of universal brotherhood in this kind of statement might bring down on the liberation theologian who quoted them Marx's own imprecation on that 'gibberish about universal love of man'. Nevertheless, there are passages in the *Economic and Philosophical Manuscripts* which recall the theme of solidarity in liberation theology; and the conclusion of Marx's review of Bauer's *The Jewish Question* is a reminder of the same theme.

Radical social theory

In deprivatizing the Christian message, the development and nature of liberation theology cannot be understood without seeing it in part as a reaction, first, against the individualism of classical Western theology, and secondly, against the consensus theoretical approach of traditional Catholic social thinking. Two influences were brought to bear in correcting the first weakness: German political theology, which was defined by Metz (1968, p. 3) as 'a critical corrective to the tendency of contemporary theology to concentrate on the private individual'; and the recovery of the social meaning of the Gospel by Latin American Christians engaged in the struggle for justice. Liberation theology attempted to correct the second weakness by drawing on Marxist contributions to demonstrate that the analysis of social oppression entails a theory of conflict and action. It has tried to be selective in its use of Marxist insights, to avoid accepting, that is, the Marxist system; but many Christian commentators are doubtful if the analysis can be used without also accepting the materialist interpretation of history.

What distinguishes the approach of liberation theology from preceding forms, and, more importantly, what constitutes its distinctive epistemology is summed up in its use of the term PRAXIS. Western theologians were trained in a tradition that gave primacy to theoretical knowledge. First came truth, and then its application. Liberation theologians question this order. They give primacy to action; praxis comes before theory; orthopraxis comes before orthodoxy. Without denying the usefulness of this approach to theology, it may be asked if this use of praxis is anything more than Aristotle's use of the term to describe those matters which have to do with life in the *polis*; whereas in Marx 'praxis' has specific reference to that action connected with the relationships of production. Once again, the intimate connections between the notion of praxis in Marxism and the materialist interpretation of reality must create difficulties for theological interpretation of history.

The Exodus paradigm

It would be misleading, however, to discuss liberation theology as if its coherence depended exclusively on exact correspondence with a definitive Marxism, especially at a time when Marxism finds itself more and more incapable of keeping intact the universalistic nature of its economic propositions. At this point Marxism may have something to learn from liberation theology.

In 1921, Ernst Bloch, in his original and independent interpretation of Marxism, argued against Engels and others that the language used by Thomas Münzer in the Peasant War of 1524 was not a disguised form of secular political aims, but an expression of deeply felt religious experiences which also fostered political commitment. In liberation theology, the Book of Exodus occupies a central and paradigmatic place in promoting Christian endeavour to break the bonds of oppression. In the story of Exodus, faith and politics are set together; the action of the people and the action of God are one; political fact and theological event run together. Looked at from the point of view of the liberation process itself, the Book of Exodus identifies two moments: liberation from (the oppression of the Pharaoh); and liberation to (the Promised Land). It is this paradigm that directs much of liberation theologizing. Already in 1968, the Conference of Latin American Bishops in their famous Medellin document (which officially inaugurated liberation thematics) referred to the revolutionary force of reflecting on liberation in Exodus; and Gutierrez (1973, p. 159) remarks that 'it remains vital and contemporary due to similar historical experiences which the people of God undergo.'

Reading

Boff, L. 1985: *Church, Charism and Power.*

Boff, L. and Boff, C. 1987: *Introducing Liberation Theology.*

Bonino, J. 1983: *Towards a Christian Political Ethics.*

Concilium, 189 Special Column, 1987, pp. 1–133.

Cone, J. 1969: *Black Theology and Black Power.*

Congregation for the Doctrine of the Faith 1984: *Instruction on Certain Aspects of the Theology of Liberation.*

Ellis, M. H. 1987: *Towards a Jewish Theology of Liberation.*

Freire, P. 1970: *Pedagogy of the Oppressed.*

Gutierrez, G. 1973: *A Theology of Liberation.*

Haight, R. 1985: *An Alternative Vision: An Interpretation of Liberation Theology.*

Lane, D. 1984: *Foundations for a Social Theology.*

Marx, K. 1975: *Early Writings,* introduced by Lucio Colletti.

Metz, J.-B. 1968: 'The Church's Social Function in the Light of Political Theology'.

— 1969: *Theology of the World.*

A Monograph of Christian Jewish Relations, vol. 21, no. 1, Spring 1988.

Sobrino, J. 1978: *Spirituality of Liberation.*

Suh Kwang-sun, D. 1983: 'A Biographical Sketch of an Asian Theology'. In *Minjung Theology: People as the Subjects of History,* ed. Commission on Theological Concerns of the Christian Conference of Asia.

                                    FRANCIS P. MCHUGH

linguistics A branch of science which deals with the systematic description of the phenomena of particular languages and elaborates conceptual systems and theories suitable for that purpose. It compares languages and their varieties, explains the similarities and differences found among them, and creates theories explaining formal and functional characteristics of language. It also deals with philosophical questions, such as the origin of human language, its place within society, its relation to thought and reality, etc.

Marx and Engels dealt with the questions of linguistic theory sporadically, though in a fairly systematic way. The first set of Marx's observations relevant to linguistics and linguistic philosophy concerns the problem of the *essence* or *nature* of language. His social theory as expounded in *German Ideology* includes the thesis of the unity of material-social activity and language. Accordingly, communication is not just one of the functions of language. On the contrary, language presupposes, both logically and factually, the interaction among people: 'language, like consciousness, only arises from the need, the necessity, of intercourse with other men' (*German Ideology,* vol. I, pt. I A, 1). Hence a characteristic thesis of Marxist linguistic theory is that language is essentially, not just contingently or secondarily, a social phenomenon. This assumption, connected with the premise concerning the mutual presupposition of consciousness and language, primarily supports the thesis of the social nature of consciousness: 'Consciousness is, therefore, from the very beginning a social product . . .' (ibid.). The idea of

social determination seems to demarcate the Marxist conception of language from strong statements of innatism – the theory stressing the innate, biological determination of the faculty of language – and this is the ground for some of the Marxist criticisms of Chomsky's theory of language (see Ponzio 1973). It is also naturally opposed to speculations concerning the logical possibility of a private language, and this provides the possibility for a 'Marxist use' of Wittgenstein (see Rossi-Landi 1968). The thesis concerning the *social nature* of language was supplemented by Engels with the empirical hypothesis that language (like consciousness) originates from work. Since Engels it has been a common element in various Marxist approaches to trace the genesis of language back to work. The most radical elaboration of Engels's genetic hypothesis has been put forward by Lukács, who holds that work explains not only the origin but also the structural properties of language; work, in Lukács's view, is the basic model of all human activities including linguistic activity.

Another set of Marx's thoughts refers to the problem of the interrelation of language, thought and reality. According to these speculations, language and thought form an inseparable unity with regard to their functioning, as well as to their origin: language is the mode of being of thoughts. This conception, even in its actual phrasing, directly continues the traditions of post-Kantian 'Sprachphilosophie' and German philology (Herder, Schlegel, Bopp, the Grimm brothers, W. v. Humboldt). The thesis of the unity of thought and language, in the form proposed by Marx and Engels, is in some sense suggestive of a weak version of linguistic relativism, i.e. the thesis that linguistic structures determine different ways of thinking, world outlooks, etc. (Sapir-Whorf hypothesis, Neo-Humboldtianism, etc.). Most Marxists, however, reject linguistic relativism, since they generally take one or another version of reflection theory as their point of departure and lay stress on the universality of the forms of human thought. The contradiction thus arising may be resolved in several ways. The universality of human thinking may be related to the universal linguistic structures described by language typology. This view approaches universality from the point of view of language form.

Another solution would be the subsumption of speech under the category of activity (as it appears in speech act theory), or tracing language back to work as a universal condition of human life.

The third set of Marx's speculations with relevance to linguistic theory tackles the relation of social classes and ideologies. Considerations that can be interpreted on the semantic level seem to support the assumption of a 'bourgeois language' in the *German Ideology*. In addition, Marx points out that 'Ideas do not exist separately from language' (*Grundrisse*, p. 163), and that 'the ideas of the ruling class are in every epoch the ruling ideas . . .' (*German Ideology*, vol. I, pt. IA, 2). These considerations lead to the conclusion that linguistic usage bears the imprint of class relations and ideologies, and that the power of the ruling class extends to the use of language. A rather difficult question arises here: does language have the character of superstructure, as the ideologies embedded in it do? (see BASE AND SUPERSTRUCTURE; IDEOLOGY). The most likely answer seems to be that language, according to Marx, does not presuppose more than society itself taken in general (i.e. the necessarily collective nature of human activity), while its interrelation with concrete social-ideological structures is expressed on the level of the special subcodes of linguistic usage. The empirical aspects of that interrelation now belong to the domain of sociolinguistics.

The results of historical comparative linguistics or 'modern historical grammar' appearing in the works of Bopp, Grimm and Diez were often referred to by Marx and Engels as scientific standards to be followed. Engels himself dealt with comparative linguistic history. He summarized his findings in his manuscripts on ancient Germanic history, more specifically on the Age of the Franks and the Frankish language ('Zur Urgeschichte der Deutschen', and 'Fränkische Zeit', in Ruschinski and Retzlaff-Kresse 1974). For example, having studied the inflectional forms and phonetic characteristics of tribal dialects, he criticized the classification of German dialects which was based on the so-called second German vowel shift and considered every dialect as either High or Low German ('Fränkische Zeit'). Thus he contributed to a more precise reconstruction, both geographical and linguistic, of the Frankish dialect. These

manuscripts constitute the foundation of Marxist linguistics in so far as they consider linguistic development in accordance with the history of the community speaking the language, and connect the logical and the historical approach.

In linguistic theory, Marxism displayed two tendencies in the first half of the twentieth century. The first went back to Marx's theory of the relation between language and ideology. As interpreted by Lukács, some of Marx's analyses revealed the effects of reification upon language. In *History and Class Consciousness* Lukács hinted at the possibility of 'a philological study from the standpoint of historical materialism' to be carried out on that basis (Lukács 1923, p. 209, fn. 16). Essentially this is the path followed by Marxist semiotics since its beginnings in the 1960s, and this approach deals with 'linguistic alienation' among other subjects. As a result, linguistic theory has been enriched by categories such as 'linguistic work', 'linguistic tool', 'linguistic capital' etc. (Rossi-Landi 1975).

The thesis that language is a social and ideological phenomenon was interpreted by Soviet linguistics, influenced mainly by Marr's views, in the 1930s as implying that language has a class character and, as such, is part of the superstructure. According to Marr language came into being as a means of class rule, and was causally determined by class struggle at every phase of its development. Owing to the unity of the process of language creation (glottogony), all known languages could be reduced to the same elements, while the differences among languages were to be explained by the fact that they had emerged in different stages of the process of development. The class determination of languages meant, for Marr, that different languages represented the product of different classes, and not that of tribal, ethnic or national communities. Marr's view triumphed over the rival conceptions which had been formulated by Bakhtin (under the pseudonym Vološinov, in the *chef-d'oeuvre* of the age in linguistic philosophy, Vološinov 1973), who also considered language a socio-ideological phenomenon but did not regard language communities as coinciding with class distinctions. Various classes used the same language; hence, instead of supposing class struggle to determine language we should say that class struggle was going on within language itself. In his words: 'the sign becomes an arena of the class struggle' (1973, p. 23).

The second tendency, exerting a prolonged influence on Marxist studies of language, is in curious contrast to both Vološinov's and Marr's conception of the social nature of language. It is related to the Pavlovian theory of reflexes, which identifies language with the secondary signalling system. This view was less influential in linguistics in general than in the exposition – within the framework of dialectical materialism – of the doctrine concerning the interrelation of language and cognition. It was a paradox of the history of science and ideology that Pavlovian naturalism and Marrism should have been officially sanctioned teachings at one and the same time.

Stalin's article on linguistics put an end to the dominance of Marrism (Stalin 1950). Briefly, his main argument was that language cannot be assigned a place within the dichotomy of base and superstructure. According to Stalin, language should be interpreted on the pattern of working tools, since it is able to serve different social systems.

A remarkable attempt at applying and elaborating Pavlov's theory of reflexes was made by Lukács, who proposed a hypothesis concerning the so-called 'signalling system 1' within his theory of everyday life including everyday language (Lukács 1963, vol. 2, pp. 11–193). He also criticized Pavlov for his naturalism, and in later works he discussed language primarily as an element of social reproduction, as a means of the continuity of social life.

A fundamental question concerning the relation of Marxism to present-day linguistics is whether we can now speak of a 'Marxist linguistics' and, if so, in what sense. The history of Marxism indicates that there is a specific Marxist approach (of course, in several versions) to interpreting human language. Thus there exists a Marxist theory of the philosophy of language, which gives primacy to its social character and to social communication. This approach extends even to the explanation of structural aspects of language. However, at least in the present state of linguistics, this focus on the social character may be suspended in the course of devising a formal representation of grammatical structures, which after all is one of the

primary goals of modern theoretical linguistics. The question whether a theory has a Marxist character is to be decided not at the level of grammatical description, but on that level where our knowledge of human language is integrated with the totality of our knowledge.

Reading

Lukács, György 1923 (1971): *History and Class Consciousness.*

— 1963: *Die Eigenart des Ästhetischen.*

Ponzio, Augusto 1973: *Produzione linguistica e ideologia sociale. Per una teoria marxista del linguaggio e della communicazione.*

Rossi-Landi, Ferruccio 1968: 'Per un uso marxiano di Wittgenstein'.

— 1975: *Linguistics and Economics.*

Ruschinski, H. and Retzlaff-Kresse, B. eds. 1974: *Marx-Engels über Sprache, Stil und Übersetzung.*

Stalin, J. V. 1950: 'Marxism in Linguistics'.

Vološinov, V. N. 1973: *Marxism and the Philosophy of Language.*

KATALIN RADICS and JÁNOS KELEMEN

literature The aesthetic views of Marx and Engels were shaped and dominated by their ideas about literature (including the texts of dramas), while the other arts scarcely drew their attention. The thoughts, opinions, and incidental comments, offered for the most part in their correspondence, cumulate in several pungent, distinctly original contributions to literary theory (and thus criticism). But these Marxian themes do not form a comprehensive system of literary theory and they are not self-sufficient, being oriented primarily by what tradition terms the 'content' rather than the 'form' of writing. Moreover, subsequent Marxists have provided a treacherous if often stimulating 'tradition' in literary criticism, because their interpretations were tempered both by the ideological currents of the times and by their frequent ignorance of the substantial basis for the study of literature which Marx and Engels themselves had laid (the first brief anthology of their scattered writings on the subject was not published until 1933 edited by M. Lifshitz and F. P. Schiller, and little use was made of it until after 1945). Half a century elapsed after Engels's death before the pattern of the various themes began to be systematically elaborated and to provide a framework for Marxist studies of literature, although there were two notable early attempts to develop a Marxist literary theory, by Mehring (1893) and Plekhanov (1912).

The values which properly underlie the works of later Marxist writers in this field may be defined briefly in terms of the *presentation of reality*. The basis of analysis is Marx's theory of history, involving a dialectical and materialist method of study. Accordingly, Marxist literary theory and criticism can on no account be reduced to merely moralistic judgements, let alone to political encomia or denunciations. Literary studies, from this perspective, are bound to result in both ethical and behavioural reappraisals and decisions, but that is subsequent to the appropriation of the (literary) reality for purposes of understanding and analysis. The principal themes of concern to Marxists are class equivalents, the method and reception of realist writing, and alienation/disalienation in literary experience.

Class Equivalents

The isolation of important elements of the representation of reality in writing, in terms of social class, began before Marx, being introduced apparently by Mme de Staël. With the rise of industrial capitalism and an impoverished urban proletariat which replaced the peasantry as the principal mass social group, literary producers and critics alike became keenly aware of the relative instability of social formations and of the role of 'class' ethics and politics in shaping future society. Marx was but one of a generation of YOUNG HEGELIANS who, in Germany, grasped events in social life and in its literary representation as being historical and mutable. His first intention was to be a poet of incandescent fantasy and withering social criticism, like his friends E. T. A. Hoffman, Heinrich Heine and F. Freiligrath, but he abandoned this aim as he became more immersed in philosophical and social thought, in political journalism, and in political activity as a leading figure in the emergent international working-class movement.

Class was a crucial element in Marx's thought from the time of his discovery (in the early 1840s) of the proletariat as the 'idea in the real itself', and Marxist literary thought is necessarily oriented to the value-clusters in literary production and reception that social class affects. At the same time this theme has to be seen as emerging cumulatively from the insights as well as the errors of numerous critics of specific literary works. Indeed, the key concept for a class analysis of literature – that of class *equivalents* – was provided not by Marx or Engels but by Plekhanov, who may be regarded together with Mehring as one of the first Marxist literary theorists.

The notion of class equivalents can be applied to a range of correlatives in the literary work, from explicit statements of political views (more or less relatable to class affiliations), most often found in what the Young Hegelians called *Tendenz* writers, to what Marx more approvingly, in a letter to Freiligrath of 29 February 1860, described as enlistment in 'the party in the great historical sense', i.e. in the progressive movement of humanity. Marx remained sceptical, however, of the ability of most writers to make the leap from self-interest (class interest) to a truly universal literary empathy, but when this occurred, as in Balzac's novels (despite that author's professed dedication to monarchical principles) Marx saluted the achievement. On the other hand, he mocked even (or especially) socialist or radical authors who, while raising the banner of equality and fraternity, were still dominated by the influence of their class origins and position, Eugene Sue being an early target of his derision (in *The Holy Family*, ch. V; see also Prawer 1976, ch. 4).

Later Marxist analysis of the correlatives of class in literature has ranged widely, from the radical humanism of Bakhtin (1929, 1965) which emphasized class struggle (see Solomon 1979, pp. 292–300), to the 'genetic structuralism' of Goldmann whose works (1955, 1964, 1980) examine literature from the perspective of the 'world view' of a class which is expressed in it. Lenin's few texts on literature, based upon story analysis, are entirely superseded by such work, as are those 'vulgar' analyses which largely prevailed in Bolshevik literary criticism in the 1930s, in which the writer's class origins were treated as totally and permanently determining his attitudes and interests. This kind of analysis, which distorts the notion of 'class equivalents' into a simple process of labelling, was exemplified by Soviet critic V. Friche: more recently, however, it has been redeemed in a quite different context of thought by Sartre in his massive study of the class education of Flaubert. Needless to say, at the hands of sensitive critics, 'content' values are of interest chiefly in writing which will, in any case, command a readership because of its achievements as literature.

Realist Method

Quite substantial formulations by Marx and Engels provide a solid basis for relating the depiction of social classes to the narrative possibilities of writing. Here the neo-Hegelian notion of 'typicality' is central. Marx and Engels commented at length on the literary method of Lassalle in structuring his historical drama *Franz von Sickingen* (Marx to Lassalle 19 April 1859, Engels to Lassalle 18 May 1859), and these texts, together with some later letters of Engels deliberately refine their thesis concerning the representation of historical phenomena in fiction; thus Engels wrote to Margaret Harkness (early April 1888) about her novel, *A City Girl*: 'If I have any criticism to make, it is perhaps that your novel is not quite realistic enough. Realism, to my mind, implies, besides truth of detail, the truthful rendering of typical characters under typical circumstances'. Lukács's studies of realism in literature are the principal, if narrow, exegesis of this statement.

The exploration of the Marxian notion of literary realism only began with this statement, which can be just as true (even more true) of the writing of history as of fiction. Marx had praised fantasy-filled tales by Hoffmann and Balzac; there is no hint of the problems this poses when one reads Marxists who follow an untroubled 'reflection' theory of narrative depiction. Early Marxist writers, such as the American, L. Fraina (on dance, futurism), raised issues which Brecht and others would elaborate in the controversies of the 1930s and later about realism and modernism (see Bloch *et al.* 1977). Finally, the writings of Kafka seemed to pose the issues decisively. In the greater freedom of the post-Stalin era orthodox Marxist literary critics were confronted with the praise of Kafka by such 'renegades' from realism as Fischer, Garaudy and Fuentes. Since many Marxist or *marxisant* artists experimented freely with symbolism, fantasy, surrealism, allegory, and subjectivity through the years of orthodoxy in the USSR and in the intellectual circles which the Soviet ruling party dominated abroad, the way the issues were posed by communist editors and arbiters were highly misleading. An adequate history of the Marxist theory of realism will only be written when the accomplishments and assumptions of its film makers, poets, novelists, painters, industrial designers and other creative contributors have been properly assessed. It will be an immense and revealing task.

Alienation and Disalienation

Marx's notion of alienation is the underlying dimension of the class-struggle theme of his theory of history, and this is also true for the literary theory. What begins as a perception of (among other significant elements) the class equivalents in fiction, leads the perceptive and trained critic and theorist towards mythic, genre-based, and/or formal equivalents in the literary work of the consequences of conflict, confusion, and loss of species-potential in social life. Thus Marx said of the intended humanity-in-general of the heroine of Sue's novel *The Mysteries of Paris* that she in fact betrayed the narrowness of her author's mind and experience. And he remarked much more broadly that the industrial age had produced impoverishment of the creative imagination – the myths and aesthetic harmony of the ancient Greeks will be seen no more – while the characters of the dominant social class of capitalism are driven by concupiscence to the loss of those traits which the Renaissance had most prized in its ruling circles (*Grundrisse*, Introduction).

It would be possible to elaborate this philosophical dimension of Marx's and Engels's commentaries on individual literary works, and the results would dwarf much of the often far more detailed literary excurses of some of their Marxist followers. For the sense of rage against the degradation of the quality of life, and the warping of the potential for self-realization of our human species, is paramount in Marx's writings (particularly in the *Economic and Philosophical Manuscripts*). It is the motivating and magisterial element, and his awareness of disalienation (as Morawski 1974 terms it) as a moral possibility and a practical guideline contributes the fine edge of proportion and context to the rage that sets Marxism apart from other philosophies and historical theories of our era.

Application of what may be thought a quasi-utopian dimension to an empirical case of critical analysis is fraught with risk. The awareness of loss, of diminution, of ignorance, of confusion, and absence, may overwhelm the detailing of what is. Yet it is impermissible, in terms of method, to employ an approach which pragmatically assumes that the existent may be explained only up to a point before recourse is had to the available but absent, without setting out a conception of the alienated and the space in which it exists. Literature, and the arts generally, are the ideal sphere in which to do so. Bahro (1978) like other recent critical Marxists has emphasized the 'emancipating and humanizing power of all art'. For the artist, the writer, is a co-explorer of the problematic of alienation and disalienation, and aesthetic (literary) value is among the most tangible of the disalienating value-clusters conferred upon the public sphere. (See also AESTHETICS; ART.)

Reading

Baxandall, Lee 1968: *Marxism and Aesthetics: A Selective Annotated Bibliography*.

Bisztray, George 1978: *Marxist Models of Literary Realism*.

Bullock, Chris and Peck, David 1980: *Guide to Marxist Literary Criticism*.

Demetz, Peter 1967: *Marx, Engels and the Poets: Origins of Marxist Literary Criticism*.

Eagleton, Terry 1976: *Criticism and Ideology: A Study in Marxist Literary Theory*.

Goldmann, Lucien 1964 (1975): *Towards a Sociology of the Novel*.

Jameson, Fredric 1971: *Marxism and Form: Twentieth Century Dialectical Theories of Literature*.

Lukács, Georg 1964: *Realism In Our Time: Literature and the Class Struggle*.

Morawski, Stefan 1974: *Inquiries into the Fundamentals of Aesthetics*.

Prawer, S. S. 1976: *Karl Marx and World Literature*.

Weimann, Robert 1976: *Structure and Society in Literary History*.

Williams, Raymond 1977: *Marxism and Literature*.

                                        LEE BAXANDALL

logic   The work of Marx and Marxists is characterized by a self-conscious use of categories taken from the traditional table of logical categories. Important roles are given to negation, quantity,

relation, and necessity. The explanatory method of Marx and the Marxists evolves within the framework of these categories. The interpretation of the categories is a realist one; the categories are treated as forms of reality, which includes thought (see REALISM).

Categories

DIALECTIC is the most prominent feature of Marxist logic, but an understanding of dialectic rests on the Marxist view of the traditional categories.

Negation

It is a NEGATION as internal rather than external that is basic in Marxist logic. In looking for analogues in formal logic, which deals with propositional forms, one would find internal negation closer to the negation of the predication in 'All are *not* red' than to the negation of the proposition in '*Not* all are red'. A more direct account, though, must go beyond formal logic.

As a system develops every new determination negates that system in one of several ways. Either it adds itself to the system and thus posits a multiplicity where there was previously unity; there is now the system and in addition the determination that evolves from within the system. Or it destroys the system and thus posits itself as a unity where there was previously a different unity. Negation then, in its internal sense, is a process of the development of multiplicity from unity. Marx's critique of political economy was itself an internal negation. It was not a negation based on principles transcending society, but a negation based on the point of view of the working class within capitalism (see FRANKFURT SCHOOL).

Quantity

Exchange values (see VALUE) and ABSTRACT LABOUR are quantities that are fundamental in Marxist economic theory. The abstraction from the qualitative differences between use values (to get exchange values) and between concrete expenditures of labour (to get abstract labour) is crucial for Marxist theory building. This and other such abstractions are developed for the sake of the reverse process of explaining qualitative changes on the basis of quantitative ones. The variational law that qualitative changes arise from changes in quantity gives Marxism its materialist character (Engels, *Dialectics of Nature*, ch. 2). Quantity here has the meaning of extensive magnitude – parts outside parts. Whereas Hegel saw quantity as externality that was to be overcome in unity, Marxist materialism posits quantitative concepts as part of its basic theoretical structure (see IDEALISM).

Relation

Though relations among the parts of a quantity may be irreducibly external, Marxists make important use of internal relations. There will then be encompassing wholes within which such relations have their terms. The social relations of production are relations between actors in the encompassing social system. Social wholes still retain the role of logical subjects that cannot themselves be dissolved into cluster points for multiple relations (Zelený 1980, ch. 3). Social wholes have multiple aspects that are internally related (Marx, *Grundrisse*, Introduction). Thus an atomist world view is ruled out by the importance given to internal relations. A consequence of this is that a cause will have its effects not in isolation but as a cause empowered by being an aspect of a whole. In addition, when cause and effect are both aspects of one system, there is reciprocity or interaction since the change represented by the effect is a change in the system to which the cause belongs.

Necessity

Tendencies determine necessities. But there may be obstacles to realizing tendencies. Thus in contrast with the traditional modal relations, necessity does not imply actuality, but at best possibility. If something is necessary then, if and when it does happen, its occurrence is grounded in a tendency. The obstacles to tendencies are not always adventitious; the negativity of wholes is a basis for conflicting or contradictory tendencies within those wholes. Because of such conflict, necessity and also scientific law point to ideal developments rather than actual ones (Hegel, *Science of Logic* 1929 edn vol. 2, sect. 2, ch. 1 (C) (b); and Marx, *Capital* III, ch. 13).

The tendency for the workplace to become socialized leads necessarily to the social ownership of the means of production. This tendency, though, is matched by the tendency to discipline the workforce, which leads necessarily to less

and less control by workers of the work process. Neither of these ideal developments – each of which unfolds with necessity – corresponds to the actual workplace.

Dialectical logic

Reality is dialectical because changes in it arise from contradictions (see CONTRADICTION). Non-Marxists have difficulty in countenancing contradictions, and Marxists debate their nature among themselves.

Contradictions

To understand contradictions it suffices to bring together several of the above categories. First, the poles of a contradiction are contained within a whole and are thus internally related. Second, contradictions themselves reflect the negativity of reality whereby multiplicity arises from unity. Not all such contradictions are formal contradictions like 'a is red and a is not red'. Formal contradictions are a special case of 'a is H and a is G', which represents a multiplicity – H and G – within unity – a – and is hence the basic kind of contradiction. If H and G were external determinations, as in the Platonic theory of predication, there would be no tension between the unity of a and its determinations. But here the determinations are internal.

Third, the tension between unity and multiplicity resolves itself through change. The specific kind of change is set by the tendencies associated with each pole of the contradiction. The interaction of these tendencies is a negation of a negation; the original negation is the positing of multiplicity within a unitary whole and the subsequent negation is the change brought about by the tension between unity and multiplicity (Engels, *Anti-Dühring*, ch. 13; also Fisk 1979, ch. 4).

Alternative logics

One basis for the non-Marxist rejection of contradictions is the conviction that a contradiction implies anything. Thus in a dialectical system anything could be proved. However, in formal systems within which implication is interpreted as an 'entailment' or a 'relevance' relation, contradictions can be isolated without everything being provable. Even more interesting is the fact that a complete formal system with entailment can be constructed within which certain propositions and their negations are both theorems and yet the classical law of non-contradiction – not (A and not A) – is a theorem (Routley and Meyer 1976). The significance of this is that there is no conclusive reason in formal logic for rejecting the view that the world supports some formal contradictions. *A fortiori* there is no conclusive reason in formal logic for rejecting the view that the world supports contradictions of the more basic but looser kind expressing a tension between unity and multiplicity. This attempt to show that an inconsistent world is possible runs counter to the Kantian view that contradictions belong to thought alone. On the Kantian view dialectic must be relegated to thought and thus cannot be made part of the material world.

Explanatory method

The dialectical view does not give a full plan for explanation, but it suffices to distinguish Marxist explanatory method in the social sciences from its competitors.

Abstraction

Theory and practice are both parts of social existence. Their tendencies towards isolation are never fully realized. As conflicting moments of social existence they interact. Owing to the fact that quantitative changes underlie qualitative ones, this interaction must be compatible with the view that the framework for explaining concepts and hypotheses is practice. This contrasts with the view that they originate as creations of mind, a view that runs into sceptical questions about whether there is a reality they represent. Theoretical concepts are abstract, but not because they are creations of mind. Their abstractness has its beginnings in practice (Sohn-Rethel 1978, ch. 5). In practice certain aspects of a reality are dealt with to the neglect of the totality. A concept represents aspects of reality emphasized in actual or possible practice.

A theory as a whole, such as Marxist economics, is abstract in that it represents tendencies of only one rather limited aspect of social existence. To be useful in obtaining concrete claims, an abstract theory must be combined with claims about other aspects of social existence. The economic, the political, gender relations, and ideology are all aspects of our society (Althusser 1969, ch. 6). The view that there is one theory of all these aspects seems incompatible with the abstractness of theories and the selective nature of practice. Still, on the historical materialist postulate, the theory of any one of these aspects will set out economic theory as its framework of operation.

Determination

Marxists explain things by finding what determines them (see DETERMINISM). Yet within Marxism there is a shifting back and forth between two views of determination. One view is that determination is a matter of antecedents stimulating, generating, or providing the occasion for consequents. Suspicion as to whether this can be the end of the matter comes from considering how this view of determination fits with dialectic. If relations are internal to wholes and depend for what they are on those wholes, then determination – as a relation of stimulation or generation – must itself be determined by underlying features of wholes. So the second view is that determination is a matter of the natures of wholes making possible relations within them. Since these views are not incompatible but complementary, it is important to recognize that both kinds of determination have their place in Marxism (Balibar 1968, ch. 1, sect. 3; Fisk 1981).

The materialist interpretation of history posits a primary role for economic theory in explanation (see HISTORICAL MATERIALISM). This primacy admits of explication not in terms of determination as antecedent stimulation but only in terms of the natures of wholes making such antecedent stimulation possible within them. The economic is primary in social science in much the way a paradigm in physical science is primary (Kuhn 1970, ch. 5).

Teleology

The teleological character of much Marxist explanation cannot be disputed. Sometimes a development of the means of production *calls for* a change in the relations of production; sometimes the preservation of the relations of production *calls for* a change in the means of production. Claims of this sort cannot be represented simply in terms of antecedent stimulation, yet antecedent stimulation is involved in them. The idea is that we explain an event on the ground that if it were to occur it would be the stimulus for some desirable state of affairs (Cohen 1978, ch. 9). The assembly line is explained by the fact that if there were an assembly line the production worker could be more easily disciplined. Teleological explanation does not eliminate the need for determination by the underlying features of wholes. It is only within a certain kind of social whole – one in which exploitation serves the privileged – that the existence of the assembly line will arise simply because it makes disciplining workers easier.

Levels of reality

The status of the superstructure and of appearances is debated among Marxists (see BASE AND SUPERSTRUCTURE). The economic base determines the superstructure of consciousness (Marx, *Contribution to the Critique of Political Economy*, Preface). This can be interpreted in view of the two kinds of determination. To claim that the superstructure is caused by the economic base as an antecedent stimulus leaves insuperable problems about how there could even be an economic base without a developed system of consciousness. This leads one to attempt to interpret the base–superstructure metaphor by way of the second type of determination. The base is then an economic framework within which a mixture of cultural, political, and also economic circumstances can stimulate changes of consciousness.

Appearances are not the sensations of the empiricist foundations of knowledge (see EMPIRICISM). Appearances, such as the appearances of exchange values as objective characters of products, are ideological in nature. The appearance-reality distinction is then a social distinction in the way the sensation-theory distinction of empiricism was never intended to be. Appearances need to be criticized with the tools of theory and not used as a basis for theory (*Capital* I, ch. 1, sect. 4).

Relativity

The overall explanatory logic of Marxism is a logic of relativity. Theories and concepts are formed within practice in order to advance it. Thus they are relative to given objective circumstances. Only if the interconnectedness of things within wholes were abandoned could concepts and theories be held to transcend practice. In addition, causal and teleological connections are relative to the wholes that make them possible and thus they have no universal scope.

Marxist views of concepts differ from those that emphasize the relativity of reference to language. Such views start with language and inevitably are trapped within language. But for Marxists the relativity of concepts is to social, and ultimately class, circumstances that themselves embody physical systems. This is then a materialist rather than an idealist relativity.

Many Marxists accept the relativity implied by the unity of theory and practice up to a point, but they look for an escape beyond practice. Some look for the escape through the view that in the deliverances of the senses we get reality as it is (Lenin 1927, ch. 2, sect. 5). Others look for the escape through giving privileged status to the perspective of the proletariat – a perspective that unlike others allows for an undistorted view of reality (Lukács 1923, sect. 3). These views clash with the dialectical view that gives concepts and theories a relative character.

Reading

Althusser, Louis 1970: *For Marx*.

Balibar, Étienne 1970: 'The Basic Concepts of Historical Materialism'. In L. Althusser and É. Balibar, *Reading 'Capital'*.

Cohen, G. A. 1978: *Karl Marx's Theory of History*.

Fisk, Milton 1979: 'Dialectic and Ontology'. In J. Mepham and D.-H. Ruben eds, *Issues in Marxist Philosophy*, vol. 1.

— 1981: 'Determination and Dialectic'.

Hegel, G. W. F. 1812–16 (1929): *Science of Logic*, vol. 2.

Kuhn, Thomas S. 1970: *The Structure of Scientific Revolutions*.

Lenin, V. I. 1908 (1962): *Materialism and Empirio-Criticism*.

Lukács, Georg 1923 (1971): 'Reification and the Consciousness of the Proletariat'. In *History and Class Consciousness*.

Routley, Richard and Meyer, Robert K. 1976: 'Dialectical Logic, Classical Logic, and the Consistency of the World'.

Sohn-Rethel, Alfred 1978: *Intellectual and Manual Labor*.

Zelený, Jindrich 1980: *The Logic of Marx*.

MILTON FISK

long waves   The theory of long waves of economic development, encompassing several business cycles, was initiated by Marxist economists like Parvus (Helphand) and van Gelderen at the beginning of the twentieth century. But it became traditionally associated with the contribution of two outstanding academic economic historians, the Russian Kondratiev and the Austrian Schumpeter. Generally it is referred to as the theory of the 'Kondratiev cycle'.

Kondratiev, a former vice-minister in the Kerensky government during the Russian revolution of 1917, founded under the Soviet government an Institute of Studies of the World Economic Conjuncture (*Weltkonjunktur*) which was one of the first, if not the first, of this kind in the world. His empirical studies led him rapidly to the conclusion that economic waves of around fifty years duration could be discerned in the history of capitalism since the beginning of the nineteenth century: twenty-five years of upsurge followed by twenty-five years of decline. The essential tool for determining these long cycles was the movement of prices, but with consequences in the fields of output and income. Roughly speaking he saw three such Kondratiev waves: one between the Napoleonic wars and 1848; a second between 1848 and the end of the nineteenth century, and a third starting from that time. Stalinist repression brought Kondratiev's activity to a sudden and tragic end in 1928. He disappeared in the Gulag, and was finally rehabilitated in 1988.

The Austrian economist Joseph Schumpeter, for a short time Minister of Finance during the first Austrian Republic, integrated the concept of the Kondratiev cycle into his general theory of business cycles, worked out in a seminal book which appeared under that title in 1939. But where for Kondratiev the correlation between agricultural prices and industrial prices is the basic motor of the long cycle, Schumpeter's theory, much more sophisticated and balanced, puts the emphasis on innovative investment in general, with a particular emphasis on industrial investment. This explanation is at least partially an extension of Marx's explanation of the normal 7–10 year business cycles, in which the upsurge depends on the renewal of fixed capital (machinery and buildings) which generally is neither piecemeal nor, at least not in several successive cycles, realized with an identical technology. It implies technological innovation.

The weak aspect of Schumpeter's long cycle theory, which is in any case an impressive intellectual achievement, lies in its excessive reliance on the appearance of innovative personalities (entrepreneurs) as the triggering force for an upswing 'Kondratiev'. This makes the economic movement dependent on biological, or biological-educational (environmental) accidents. The question of whether technological innovations are bunched, and whether they are cyclical or anti-cyclical within the Kondratiev cycles – whether it is innovation or the 'popularization', the massive application, of previous innovations which really triggers off the upswing 'Kondratiev' – has been an object of great controversy and much empirical research during the last decade.

During the long boom after world war two, the long waves/long cycle theory of economic conjuncture went out of fashion. While some empirical work continued to be carried on, especially by Forrester at MIT, and while several economists concentrated on the problem of the determinants of long-term growth, they did not study determinants of long-term decline, which was generally considered as excluded once and for all.

Again it was in Marxist circles that the study of long-term conjunctural movements was revived in the mid-1960s, and the present author made an early contribution. His ideas, first formulated in an article in 1965, then developed at length in his book *Late Capitalism* (1972), were finally treated more extensively in *Long Waves of Capitalist Development* (1979). Starting from remarks made by Leon Trotsky in a polemic with Kondratiev in the mid-1920s, 'long waves' are distinguished from 'long cycles'. The concept of 'long cycles' implies a more or less automatic movement similar to that of the normal business cycle. The slump generates forces leading to the boom, in the same way as the boom liberates forces leading to the slump. Likewise, an 'expansive' Kondratiev would liberate forces leading to a 'depressive' Kondratiev, which in turn would liberate forces for a new twenty-five years' expansion.

It is argued that there is an asymmetry between the movement from an expansive long wave into a depressive long wave on the one hand, and the movement from a long depression into a long expansion on the other hand. The first one is endogenous. The second one is not automatic. It needs outside system-shocks: a radical change in the average rate of profit (and of surplus value) as a result of wars and counter-revolutions; a radical broadening of the market, e.g. as a result of the discovery of new gold fields and the emergence of a hegemonic power on the world market capable of making its paper money 'as good as gold' etc. This means that one cannot take a regular time-scale for granted. There is no average duration of the 'Kondratiev' of twenty-five years. They vary between twenty and thirty-five years. This is an additional reason for calling them 'long waves' rather than 'long cycles'.

The prime movers of the long waves are the average rate of profit and the dimension of the world market. Only when both expand more or less simultaneously can the effects of a 'popularized' technological revolution come into their own. This theory has the additional characteristic of integrating long-term cumulative effects of the class-struggle (of a relatively autonomous class-struggle cycle) into the long waves of capitalist development.

Other Marxist economists have made significant contributions to the 'long waves' theory, especially the French economist Boccara, the East German economic historian Kuczynski and the Soviet economist Menshikov. With the partial exception of Boccara, they tend to accept the 'long cycle' theory, i.e. the automatic upswing after a long depression. Menshikov gives this a more sophisticated mathematical expression. The American economist Gordon has insisted particularly on the general conditions of capital accumulation as co-determining long wave movements. Immanuel Wallerstein and André Gunder Frank have attempted to extend the 'long cycles' backward to the sixteenth century, if not earlier, and emphasized the central importance of 'world accumulation of capital' at the expense of the Third World, trying to return primarily to price movements rather than movements of material output as key indicators of 'long waves'.

Reading

Dupriez, Léon 1947: *Des mouvements economiques généraux.*

Kondratiev, N. D. 1926: *Die Langen Wellen der Konjunktur.*

Mandel, Ernest 1980: *Long Waves of Capitalist Development.*

Menschikow, Stanislaw 1989: *Lange Wellen in der Wirtschaft.*

Schumpeter, Joseph 1939: *Business Cycles.*

ERNEST MANDEL

Lukács, György (Georg) Born 13 April 1885, Budapest; died 4 June 1971, Budapest. Lukács had a long and intense life as a philosopher, literary critic, and (between 1919 and 1929) one of the leaders of the Hungarian Communist movement. Author of many books, his first publications appeared in 1902 and he completed his *Prolegomena to a Social Ontology* nearly seventy years later, shortly before his death, leaving in sketchy outline his last intended work: his memoirs, appropriately entitled *Gelebtes Denken (Lived Thought)*.

Before 1918 Lukács was committed to an objective idealist system, influenced by Plato, Kant, Hegel and Kierkegaard. (Lukács was the first to revive the work of the latter, back in 1908.) A friend of Georg Simmel, Max Weber and Ernst Bloch, he spent much time in Germany, later writing many of his works in German. In Hungary during the first world war he was the intellectual leader of a 'Sunday Circle', in association with Frigyes Antal, Béla Balázs, Béla Fogarasi, Arnold Hauser, Karl Mannheim, Karl Polányi, Wilhelm Szilasi, Charles de Tolnay, Eugene Varga and others. In 1917 Lukács and his friends organized the 'Free School of the Sciences of the Spirit' in which Bartók and Kodály also participated. His main works in this period were *Soul and Form*, 1910; *History of the Development of Modern Drama*, 1911; *Aesthetic Culture*, 1913; *The Theory of the Novel*, 1916; and the *Heidelberg Philosophy of Art* as well as the *Heidelberg Aesthetics* – started in 1912 and abandoned in 1918 – published posthumously.

During the last year of the war Lukács wholeheartedly embraced the Marxist outlook and in December 1918 he joined the Communist Party. During the months of the Hungarian Commune in 1919 he was Minister ('People's Commissar') for Education and Culture, appointing several of his friends and associates (Antal, Bartók,

Kodály, Mannheim, Varga and others) to important political/cultural positions. After the collapse he escaped from the country and, until 1945, returned only for clandestine party work, defying the death sentence passed on him by Horthy's judges. He spent the years of his emigration in Austria, Germany and Russia, returning to the Chair of Aesthetics at Budapest University in August 1945.

Lukács's Marxist period shows five distinctive phases of activity:

(1) 1919–1929. As one of the leaders of the Hungarian Communist Party, Lukács was heavily involved in day-to-day political struggle, vitiated by internal factional confrontations, constantly under fire from Béla Kun and his friends in the Third International. Many of his writings were concerned with political/agitational issues and with the elaboration of a viable political strategy, culminating in the *Blum Theses*. Written in 1928 and advocating perspectives very similar to the 'Popular Front' (adopted as official Comintern policy seven years later, after Dimitrov's speech), they arrived rather prematurely and were condemned by the Comintern as 'a half-social-democratic liquidationist theory'. His main theoretical writings of this period were collected in three volumes: *History and Class Consciousness*, 1923; *Lenin: A Study on the Unity of his Thought*, 1924; and *Political Writings 1919–1929*. Of these, *History and Class Consciousness* – condemned by the Comintern through Bukharin, Zinoviev and others – exercised an enormous influence, from Korsch to Benjamin and Merleau-Ponty and from Goldmann to Marcuse and to the student movement of the late 1960s.

(2) 1930–1945. Condemned to abandon active politics through the defeat of his 'Blum Theses', Lukács wrote mainly essays in literary criticism and two major theoretical works: *The Historical Novel*, 1937 and *The Young Hegel*, 1938. His literary studies were later collected into volumes entitled *Studies in European Realism*, *Goethe and his Age* and *Essays on Thomas Mann*. Theoretically this period was marked by a modification of his earlier views on 'reflection' and by his rejection of the 'identical subject-object' (as expressed in *History and Class Consciousness*), following the publication of Marx's *Economic and Philosophical Manuscripts* and

Grundrisse, and Lenin's *Philosophical Notebooks*. For a brief period he was imprisoned, in 1941, and was released on the intervention of Dimitrov who shared his perspectives.

(3) 1945–1949. After his return to Hungary Lukács was heavily involved in cultural/political activity, publishing many literary essays and popular philosophical articles, and he founded and presided intellectually over the cultural monthly *Forum*. In 1949 he was violently attacked by the party ideologues Rudas, Horvath and Révai for the views expressed in his volumes *Literature and Democracy* and *For a New Hungarian Culture* which recalled the perspectives of the *Blum Theses*. These attacks (joined by Fadeev and other Russian figures) signalled the complete Stalinization of culture and politics in Hungary, and compelled Lukács to withdraw to his philosophical studies.

(4) 1950–1956. He embarked on some major works of synthesis of which two were completed in this period: *The Destruction of Reason* and *Particularity as an Aesthetic Category*. In 1956 he wrote *The Meaning of Contemporary Realism*, and in October he became Minister of Culture in Imre Nagy's short-lived government. After the suppression of the uprising, he was deported with the other members of the government to Romania, returning to Budapest in the summer of 1957.

(5) 1957–1971. In this period he completed two massive syntheses: a work on AESTHETICS (*The Specific Nature of the Aesthetic*, 1962) and a social ontology (*Towards an Ontology of Social Being*, 1971) of which three chapters appeared in English: *Hegel* (1978); *Marx* (1978); and *Labour* (1980).

Lukács's major achievements range over a wide area, from aesthetics and literary criticism to philosophy, sociology and politics. In aesthetics, in addition to many works in which he developed a Marxist theory of realism, from a strongly anti-modernist stance, he produced one of the most fundamental and comprehensive syntheses of the theory of art and literature. In philosophy, as a principal figure of WESTERN MARXISM, he constantly championed the cause of dialectics against various forms of irrationalism and mechanical materialism and dogmatism, elaborating in *History and Class Consciousness* a theory of alienation and REIFICATION well before the belated publication of

Marx's seminal works on the subject, as well as producing a monumental and still little understood social ontology in his last ten years of activity. In sociology it was his theory of CLASS CONSCIOUSNESS which made the greatest impact, strongly influencing the 'sociology of knowledge' and the FRANKFURT SCHOOL as well as more recent theories. And in politics he is primarily remembered for his ideas on organizational matters and as one of the first advocates of the 'Popular Front' and of a mass-based political participation in the 'Peoples' Democracies'.

Reading

Benseler, Frank ed. 1965: *Festschrift zum achtzigsten Geburtstag von Georg Lukács.*

Goldmann, Lucien 1977: *Lukács and Heidegger.*

Löwy, Michel 1976: *Pour une sociologie des intellectuels révolutionnaires: l'évolution politique de Lukács 1909–1929.*

Merleau-Ponty, Maurice 1955 (1973): *Adventures of the Dialectic.*

Mészáros, István 1972: *Lukács's Concept of Dialectic.*

Oldrini, Guido ed. 1979: *Lukács.*

Parkinson, G. H. R. ed. 1970: *Georg Lukács: The Man, his Work and his Ideas.*

Pinkus, Theo ed. 1974: *Conversations with Lukács.*

ISTVÁN MÉSZÁROS

lumpenproletariat Marx (*18th Brumaire*, pt. V) described the lumpenproletariat as the 'refuse of all classes', 'a disintegrated mass', comprising 'ruined and adventurous off-shoots of the bourgeoisie, vagabonds, discharged soldiers, discharged jailbirds . . . pickpockets, brothel keepers, rag-pickers, beggars' etc., upon whom Louis Bonaparte relied in his struggle for power. It is in a similar context, in analysing the rise of fascism, that later Marxists have also made occasional references to the lumpenproletariat, though this notion does not have a very prominent place in their analysis. Bauer (1936) distinguished as important elements in the fascist movements the *déclassés* who were unable to find their way back into bourgeois life after the first world war, and the impoverished masses of the lower middle class and peasantry; but when he observed that 'the whole lumpenproletariat' was driven to the fascists it is not clear what he included in this category, and he emphasized

more strongly the extent to which unemployed workers could be recruited to the fascist ranks. Trotsky, in his writings on fascism (1971), referred briefly to 'the transformation of even larger groups of workers into the lumpenproletariat', but gave much greater attention to the petty bourgeoisie as the social basis of fascist mass movements.

The main significance of the term lumpenproletariat is not so much its reference to any clearly defined social group which has a major sociopolitical role, as in drawing attention to the fact that in extreme conditions of crisis and social disintegration in a capitalist society large numbers of people may become separated from their class and come to form a 'free floating' mass which is particularly vulnerable to reactionary ideologies and movements.

TOM BOTTOMORE

Luxemburg, Rosa Born 5 March 1871, Zamość, Poland; died 15 January 1919, Berlin. The youngest of five children in a fairly well-to-do and cultured middle-class Jewish family, Rosa Luxemburg grew up in Warsaw. She was an intelligent and academically successful girl of independent spirit and, rebelling against the restrictive regime then prevalent in the schools of Russian Poland, she became involved in socialist political activity from early youth. In 1889 she had in consequence to leave Poland to avoid arrest and went to Zurich. Here she enrolled in the university, studying first mathematics and natural sciences, then political economy; and at length completed a doctoral dissertation on Poland's industrial development. Active at the same time in the political life of the revolutionary *émigrés* from the Russian Empire and opposing the nationalism of the Polish Socialist Party, in 1894 she took the lead with Leo Jogiches, a comrade similarly engaged, in creating the Social Democracy of the Kingdom of Poland: he was its main organizer, she its ablest intellect and voice. The two of them had formed what was to be a long and intense relationship, the close political tie between them surviving a later personal estrangement. In 1898, wanting a wider political stage for her energies, Rosa Luxemburg moved to Germany.

Henceforth she was prominent in the important debates within European socialism. She made her mark at once during the revisionist controversy (see REVISIONISM) with her *Social Reform or Revolution*, still perhaps the best general Marxist riposte to reformism. While capitalism endured, she contended, its crises and contradictions could not be subdued and to suggest otherwise, as Bernstein had, was to cut the very heart out of Marxism, denying the objective foundations of the socialist project and turning it into an abstract ethical utopia. The workers' movement had indeed to struggle for reforms through trade-union and parliamentary activity. But as these would never suffice to abolish capitalist relations of production, it must not lose sight of its ultimate goal: the conquest of power for revolution. In 1904, in *Organizational Questions of Russian Social Democracy*, Luxemburg intervened in the dispute between Lenin and the Mensheviks, criticizing the former for his conception of a tightly centralized vanguard party; an attempt, as she saw it, to hold the working class in tutelage. Her themes here – characteristic of all her work – were the independent initiative, the self-activity, of the workers, their capacity to learn through their own experience and their own mistakes, the need accordingly for a broadly based democratic organization. She had other disagreements with Lenin in these years. Although she deplored national as every other kind of oppression, she did not support, as he did, either the independence of Poland or, more generally, the slogan of a *right* of nations to self-determination.

However, their common response to the 1905 revolution drew them closer; they both envisaged for Russia a bourgeois revolution, to be carried through under the leadership, and by the methods of struggle, of the proletariat. In the mass actions of the Russian workers Luxemburg thought to have discovered, in addition, a strategic idea of international relevance and began to urge it upon German Social Democracy, speaking in this as in other things for the left of the organization. In her *Mass Strike, Party and Trade Unions*, she proposed the mass strike as the form *par excellence* of proletarian revolution. Spontaneous expression of the creative power of the broadest masses and antidote to bureaucratic inertia, it linked political with economic struggles, and immediate with more far-reaching demands, in what was potentially a global challenge to the capitalist order. In 1910 this view led to her break with Kautsky, when he rallied to the cautious, purely electoralist, policy of the party leadership. Another of her preoccupations was imperialism, with its threat of war, and in 1913 in her major theoretical work, *The Accumulation of Capital*, she set out to explain its underlying cause. A closed capitalist economy, she argued, without access to noncapitalist social formations, must break down through inability to absorb all the surplus value produced by it. Imperialism was a competitive struggle between capitalist nations for what remained of the non-capitalist environment but, by eroding the latter, it led towards the universal sway of capitalist relations and inevitable collapse of the system.

Luxemburg led the opposition to the first world war in Germany. Intellectual standard-bearer of the revolutionary internationalists gathered in the Spartacus League, in her *Junius Pamphlet* and other writings she denounced Social Democracy's patriotic stance as a betrayal. She had to spend most of the war in prison and there she wrote *The Russian Revolution*, in solidarity and sympathy with Lenin, Trotsky and the Bolsheviks, endorsing their attempt at socialist revolution; yet critical of their land and nationalities policy, above all of their curtailment of socialist democracy, and of their tendency in this connection to make a virtue out of unfortunate necessities. Freed in late 1918 to participate in the German revolution, she was brutally murdered by right-wing officers after the crushing of an abortive rising in Berlin.

Rosa Luxemburg's work has sometimes been interpreted as a species of political fatalism, on account of her theory of inevitable capitalist breakdown; and as displaying a boundless faith in the spontaneity of the masses. However this is to misunderstand or caricature her. The collapse of capitalism presented the proletariat with alternatives: on the one side, crisis, reaction, war, finally catastrophe and barbarism; on the other side, socialism. Active struggle for socialism was therefore necessary and urgent. For her, true to a central Marxist theme, the substance of this struggle was indeed provided by the spontaneous, self-emancipatory efforts of the working class. But she did not deny the need for organization, nor the importance of Marxist theory and able leadership. The division between her and Lenin has often been exaggerated. They were united by as much. Luxemburg's lifelong concern for democracy and liberty was unambiguously that of a revolutionary Marxist and should not be confused with the criticisms of this tradition by other traditions – liberal, reformist or anarchist – completely alien to her.

Reading

Basso, Lelio 1975: *Rosa Luxemburg.*

Davis, Horace B. ed. 1976: *The National Question. Selected Writings by Rosa Luxemburg.*

Ettinger, Elzbieta 1987: *Rosa Luxemburg: A Life.*

Frölich, Paul 1972: *Rosa Luxemburg.*

Geras, Norman 1976: *The Legacy of Rosa Luxemburg.*

Howard, Dick ed. 1971: *Selected Political Writings of Rosa Luxemburg.*

Looker, Robert ed. 1972: *Rosa Luxemburg. Selected Political Writings.*

Luxemburg, Rosa 1913 (*1963*): *The Accumulation of Capital.*

Luxemburg, Rosa and Bukharin, Nikolai 1972: *Imperialism and the Accumulation of Capital.*

Nettl, J. P. 1966: *Rosa Luxemburg.*

Waters, Mary-Alice, ed. 1970: *Rosa Luxemburg Speaks.*

NORMAN GERAS

Lysenkoism   The term originated with the career, influence and scandal of Trofim Denisovich Lysenko (born 1898, Karlovka in Poltava Province, Ukraine; died 20 November 1976, USSR). Lysenko was an obscure plant breeder who made extravagant claims that by treating seeds with temperature and moisture and other simple techniques he could dramatically alter the seasonal patterns of crops and their yields. He also claimed that the beneficial effects of these changes could be passed on to subsequent generations – the inheritance of acquired characteristics. His method, claims and theories flew in the face of the developing science of plant genetics. The result was that biological and agricultural theory and practice in the Soviet Union and countries influenced by it were in total opposition to the international community of scientists and agriculturalists. From 1927, when he first became known, until 1948 when the backing of Stalin ended all opposition to his power, Lysenko rose until he controlled all disciplines touched by conceptions of heredity. Western genetics was denounced and its Soviet practitioners persecuted, imprisoned and in some cases killed. His power was unchallenged until Stalin's death in 1953, after which it waned but waxed again under Khrushchev's patronage until both were deposed in 1965. In the West, Lysenkoism was treated as an object lesson: don't interfere with the relative autonomy and value neutrality of science. Political interference in science produces untoward scientific, technological and social results. Lysenkoism was successfully used as a stick with which to beat socialist and communist ideas about science and society, especially during the Cold War. It alienated many progressive scientists and had serious effects in the history, philosophy and social studies of science.

There is no doubt that Lysenkoism decimated research in Soviet genetics and related fields, though it has been argued that it had surprisingly little measurable effect on the already troubled crop production in the Soviet Union. It was disastrous both as a patronage system and as a basis for scientific methodology. The main problem, however, is that the crudity of the Lysenkoist scandal effectively precluded the pursuit of more complex questions about the relations between social, political and economic forces on the one hand, and the role of experts on the other. Lysenko rose as a peasant or proletarian scientist partly because bourgeois scientists in the Soviet Union were so unwilling to cooperate. When Lenin's compromise with the bourgeois experts ended, the attempt to achieve 'a cultural revolution' and promote 'red scientists' caught many unqualified opportunists in its net. Similarly, the need for a grain surplus to feed the urban proletariat and to export in order to buy capital goods for industrialization led to extreme measures (see Stalin, 'On the Grain Front', 1928). The ease with which criticisms can be made of Soviet science, technology and agricultural policy has helped to divert attention from the subtler but not less important ways in which Western political, economic and ideological priorities have shaped research and development. 'Lysenkoism' has served as a smokescreen behind which complacency can grow about capitalist control over research and development in the more subtly mediated patronage system of Western research. Before Sputnik (1957) the Western system was also thought to be vastly more successful; since then the emphasis on military expenditure has led to heavy military patronage in Western research and development, as well as a growing reliance on direct customer-contract relations in setting research tasks. As a theoretical basis for genetics and agriculture, Lysenkoism is wholly discredited. As an object lesson and an invitation to look more deeply into the process of setting priorities in research and development it can be said to have many lessons still to teach.

Reading

Graham, Loren 1973: *Science and Philosophy in the Soviet Union.*

Huxley, Julian 1949: *Soviet Genetics and World Science: Lysenko and the Meaning of Heredity.*

Joravsky, David 1970: *The Lysenko Affair.*

Lecourt, Dominique 1977: *Proletarian Science? The Case of Lysenko.*

Lewontin, Richard and Levins, Richard 1976: 'The Problem of Lysenkoism'. In H. and S. Rose eds. *The Radicalisation of Science.*

Medvedev, Zhores A. 1969: *The Rise and Fall of T. D. Lysenko.*

Safonov, V. 1951: *Land in Bloom.*

Stalin, Joseph 1928 (*1953*): 'On the Grain Front'. In *Problems in Leninism.*

Young, Robert M. 1978: 'Getting Started on Lysenkoism'.

Zirkle, Conway 1949: *Death of a Science in Russia.*

ROBERT M. YOUNG

M

machinery and machinofacture Whereas under MANUFACTURE instruments of production are the manual implements of workers and their use is constrained by the strength and agility of human beings, with the development of large-scale, or modern, industry characterized by the use of machinery all such constraints are swept away. A machine is a combination of motor mechanism, transmitting mechanism, and tool which may perform an operation carried out by workers, but is quite independent of the organic limitations constraining the operation of the tools of the handicraft worker. However, machines do not simply substitute for labour in those operations which the DIVISION OF LABOUR in manufacture has already simplified: the dependence of the manufacturing division of labour on human specialization and skill (what Marx calls a subjective principle) is replaced by an entirely objective process, characterized by objective relations between the number, size and speed of machines, hence by continuity of production and by implementation of the automatic principle (see AUTOMATION). Modern capitalist industry uses machines to produce machines, and only in so doing creates for itself an adequate technical foundation, an entirely objective organization of production, in which the cooperative character of the LABOUR PROCESS has become a technical necessity, and which confronts the worker as a pre-existing material condition of production. Production by machinery is sometimes called 'machinofacture' to distinguish it from the manufacture of handicraft production.

The increases in productivity resulting from COOPERATION and the division of labour are forces of social labour which the capitalist can appropriate gratis. The same is not true with respect to the instruments of labour. The value of the machine is transferred to the product over the economic lifetime of the machine (which must be distinguished from the 'moral depreciation' arising out of the difference between the economic and the physical lifetimes of the machine). Compared with the tool under the manufacturing form of production, under machinofacture the part of the product's value which is transferred to it from the machine is a greater proportion of the total value of the product although the latter is smaller absolutely. The productivity of the machine can accordingly be measured in terms of the human LABOUR POWER it replaces: in general, to introduce machinery in order to cheapen the product requires that less labour be expended in producing the machine than is displaced by employment of that machine. But since capitalists pay for labour power rather than for labour, the limits to capitalist use of machinery are fixed by the difference between the value of the machine and the value of labour power replaced by it. This suggests that the scope of application for machinery in communist society is very much greater than in bourgeois society. And whereas in the former society the introduction of machinery serves to reduce the burden of work upon the people, in capitalist society, machinery is designed purely to increase the productivity of labour and hence is the driving-force for the production of relative surplus value (see VALUE; SURPLUS VALUE; ACCUMULATION).

But machines cannot themselves produce surplus value. Surplus value can only be produced by the variable part of CAPITAL, and the amount produced depends upon the rate of surplus value and upon the number of workers employed. For any given length of the working day the use of machinery can only increase the rate of surplus value via cheapening commodities, thereby reducing the value of labour power by reducing the number of workers employed by a given amount of capital. Variable capital, that is, must be transformed into constant capital.

This compulsion is at the heart of the Marxian dynamics of capitalism, and Marx argued that it has several consequences.

First, machinery – the most powerful means for reducing labour time – becomes under capitalist relations means whereby the whole working-class family is transferred into simple labour time at capital's disposal for its own valorization. Labour power is exploited more intensively; workers are de-skilled and compelled to work at the dictates of the machine; the factory is the scene of strict discipline, an autocratic capitalist state in miniature which caricatures the social regulation of the labour process; and science, nature and social labour, embodied in the system of machinery, and constituting the power of the capitalist, confront the worker in the labour process as the domination of dead labour over living labour. In every labour process which is also a valorization process, the objective reality is that 'it is not the worker who employs the condition of his work, but rather the reverse, the conditions of work employ the worker' (*Capital* I, ch. 15). Secondly, as machinery is substituted for workers, it produces a surplus working population, a RESERVE ARMY OF LABOUR, fluctuations in which in turn regulate WAGES and assure, under normal conditions, the appropriation of surplus value by capitalists. Thirdly, the tendency to increase constant capital at the expense of variable capital creates what Marx calls 'an immanent contradiction' within the sphere of production, since only living labour produces any value at all, yet that quantity of living labour must be reduced in order to increase the rate of surplus value. This has definite implications for the analysis of tendential movements in the composition of capital (see ORGANIC COMPOSITION OF CAPITAL; VALUE COMPOSITION OF CAPITAL) and for the analysis of the rate of profit (see FALLING RATE OF PROFIT; ECONOMIC CRISES).

SIMON MOHUN

manufacture Marx defines manufacture as that form of COOPERATION which is based on the DIVISION OF LABOUR, and whose basis is handicraft production (*Capital* I, ch. 14). In Britain manufacturing was the dominant form of capitalist production from the middle of the sixteenth century to the last third of the eighteenth century. Manufacture originates in two different ways. First, there are those products which are the outcome of various independent handicraft processes (Marx uses the examples of the manufacture of a carriage or of watches, and calls this 'heterogeneous manufacture', *Capital* I, ch. 12). These independent handicraft workers are assembled together in a single workshop, under the control of a capitalist, and then in the course of time the independent processes are broken down into various detailed operations which become the exclusive functions of particular workers. Each worker becomes only a partial worker, and the whole manufacturing process is the combination of all the partial operations. Second, there are those articles which are wholly produced by an individual handicraft worker in a succession of operations (Marx uses the examples of the manufacture of paper, or needles, and calls this 'organic manufacture', ibid.). Again, these workers are simultaneously employed in one workshop, initially all doing the same work. The work is gradually divided up, until the COMMODITY is no longer the individual product of an independent handicraft worker, but is the social product of a workshop of handicraft workers, each of whom performs only one of the constituent, partial operations. Either way a division of labour is introduced, or further developed in the production process. Machinery is little used, except for simple processes which must be conducted on a large scale, with the application of great force (though the sporadic use of machinery in the seventeenth century was important in providing a practical basis for mathematics, stimulating the creation of mechanics). This means that the manufacturing period never attains a technical unity, and the only item of machinery specifically characteristic of the period is what Marx calls the 'collective worker' – the one-sidedness of each worker's specialization compels him or her to work as part of the collective worker with the regularity of a machine.

But as a consequence of the specialization arising out of the division of labour in manufacturing, workers are the more separated from the means of production, for what is lost by specialization is concentrated in the capital which employs them: the social productive power of capital is vested in the collective worker, and this increases only through the impoverishment of the individual productive power of labour. The division of labour in manufacturing not only specializes workers and combines them into a single mechanism; it thereby creates an organization of social labour which develops new productive powers of labour for the benefit of capital, and at the same time it creates historically new conditions for the domination of capital over labour. The division of labour in manufacturing, then, is a particular method of creating relative SURPLUS VALUE. However, it is a limited method. Handicraft skill remains the technical basis of production, and the skill hierarchies which manufacture develops create an important autonomy for labour from capital. There is no objective framework of manufacture which is independent of the workers themselves; manufacture is essentially an artificial economic construction based on handicraft production in the towns and domestic industries in the countryside. Without machinery there is no way in which capital can break through the lifelong attachment of workers to their partial functions, and this narrow technical basis means that capital is constantly concerned with problems of maintaining labour discipline, which it can only do by force. It requires the development of machinery to abolish the roles of craft and skill as the regulating principle of social production.

Finally, the period of manufacturing sees the rise and development of political economy as an independent science. Whereas writers in the ancient world were concerned with quality and USE VALUE, by the time of the early manufacturing period, writers (from W. Petty onwards) were beginning to develop the principle of reducing the labour time necessary for the production of commodities, a developing emphasis on quantity and exchange value (see VALUE). Indeed, Marx calls Adam Smith 'the quintessential political economist of the period of manufacture' (*Capital* I, ch. 12) because of the emphasis he places on the division of labour, and because of the way he sees the social division of labour through the prism of the division of labour in manufacturing. (See also ACCUMULATION; LABOUR PROCESS.)

SIMON MOHUN

Mao Tse-tung (Mao Zedong) Born 26 December 1893, Shaoshan, Hunan Province, China; died 9 September 1976, Peking. Mao's importance as a practitioner of Marxism, or in any case as a leader who carried out a revolution inspired by what he believed to be Marxist principles, is generally recognized. There is, on the other hand, lively and as yet unresolved controversy as to whether he in fact made any original theoretical contributions, and if so, whether these constituted a development or a perversion of Marxism. It is hard to deny that Mao not only did, but said, distinctive and significant things. Whether or not these innovations were authentically Marxist in character is a moot point, but a case can be made for the view that they were, at least in part. Mao has often been praised, or attacked, as a 'peasant revolutionary'. While he did indeed attribute to the peasants a role, and above all a degree of initiative, greater than is commonly regarded as orthodox, the problem of what he did with, or to, Marxism can perhaps best be approached by considering first the structure of Chinese society as a whole, and the conclusions he drew from it.

China in the 1920s, when Mao began his apprenticeship in revolution, was of course economically a very backward country. This meant that, whatever might be said about the hegemony of the proletariat (or of its vanguard), the Communist Party had to rely on the peasantry as the greatest single social force supporting the revolutionary cause. But Chinese society was not (as Trotsky imagined) primarily capitalist in character, nor was it simply 'feudal' or 'semi-feudal'. It included, in addition to a limited but rapidly growing number of urban workers, and Chinese entrepreneurs or 'national bourgeois', a small but extremely powerful landlord class, the peasants (rich and poor, landed and landless), and a rich variety of other categories, from artisans and hawkers to 'compradors' in the service of foreign capitalists, and from bureaucrats and militarists to monks, bandits, and rural vagabonds. This complex social structure derived from the coexistence of elements and strata dating from different historical epochs, and shaped both by indigenous and by foreign influences.

The consequences of this situation are reflected in the concepts of the 'principal contradiction', and the 'principal aspect of the principal contradiction', which play so large a part in Mao's interpretation of dialectics. Marx, it is hardly necessary to point out, would never have posed the question, with reference to France or England in the nineteenth century, 'Which contradiction is primary today?' He took it as axiomatic that the key contradiction was that between the proletariat and the bourgeoisie, and that this would remain the case until the conflict was resolved by socialist revolution. Mao, on the other hand, saw it as his more urgent practical task to determine, in the light of what he regarded as a Marxist analysis, where the decisive cleavages should be drawn, both in China and in the world. In a sense, of course, he was simply following a line of analysis sketched out by Marx, and further developed by Lenin (and Stalin) according to which not only the peasants, but other classes and groups in a pre-capitalist society could participate in the democratic stage of the revolution, and the behaviour of various classes in a given country could be affected by the fact of foreign domination. But Mao systematized and elaborated these ideas, and drew from them philosophical conclusions to which he attributed general validity.

It is, arguably, this dimension of his approach to revolution, in conjunction with his view that practice was primary, and theory secondary or derivative, which has led to such a wide range of often categorically opposed interpretations of Mao and his ideas. On the one hand, those who stress the flexibility of his tactics and his skill in adapting himself to changing circumstances can argue (as have Soviet Marxists since the 1960s) that Mao was either a capitulationist, because of the concessions he made, in 1938, in 1945, and in the early 1950s, to the 'national bourgeoisie', or a wholly unprincipled opportunist, or both. But conversely, those who are struck rather with his emphasis on class struggle, proletarian values, and the implacable carrying of the revolution through to the end, have characterized him (especially since the late 1950s) as the most radical of all the major leaders and theorists in the international communist movement.

There are elements of truth in both these perspectives, it may be argued, first with reference to his tactics, and then with reference to more general principles of his thought. Perhaps the most crucial single issue is that of what Mao meant by 'proletariat'. He was aware, of course, at least from the late 1920s onwards, of the leading role assigned by Marxism to the urban working class, and in principle he accepted this axiom. Undoubtedly his understanding of the term 'proletariat' was in some way coloured by the literal meaning of the Chinese expression *wu-ch'an chieh-chi* (propertyless class), but he consistently recognized the hegemony in the revolution of the urban proletariat. A more important and significant ambiguity, which has frequently been underscored, is that surrounding the relation between objective proletarian class nature, and proletarian ideology or proletarian virtue.

As early as 1928, Mao suggested that rural vagabonds and other such elements could be transformed into proletarian vanguard fighters by a combination of study, and participation in revolutionary practice, and this strain runs through the ensuing half century of his thinking. It manifested itself particularly, as everyone knows, in the 'Cultural Revolution' of 1966–67, but even at that time, Mao did not adopt (as is sometimes argued) a wholly subjective definition of class in general, and the proletariat in particular. He combined objective and subjective criteria in a complex and shifting pattern dictated partly by expediency, but partly by his belief in the importance of subjective forces in history. With reference to this broader topic, it has been argued by Arthur Cohen (1964) that Mao could not possibly have put forward the view that in certain circumstances, the superstructure played the 'leading and decisive role' in historical change, until the way had been opened by Stalin's writings of 1938 and 1950. The recently discovered original 1937 text of 'On Contradiction' proves that Mao did in fact adopt such a position before Stalin. This may be seen as the root of the tendencies, now stigmatized as 'voluntarist' by the Chinese themselves, which emerged in Mao's thought, and in the party's policies, during the Great Leap and the Cultural Revolution. It should be added, however, that while Chinese Marxists today thus criticize an *excessive* emphasis on subjective forces, the predominant view is that 'man's conscious action' should not be underestimated as an historical force.

Apart from the point mentioned at the beginning of this entry about the significance of Mao's stress on the need to distinguish the 'principal contradiction' in each case, the most important aspect of his dialectics is the reduction of the three laws of Hegel and Marx to one: the unity and struggle of opposites. This was prefigured in 'On Contradiction' in 1937, when he said that the law of the unity of opposites was 'the fundamental law of thought', thus apparently giving it higher status than the negation of the negation, and the transformation of quantity into quality. In 1964, he explicitly repudiated the last two laws, saying that he 'did not believe' in the negation of the negation, and that the transformation of quantity into quality was merely a special case of the unity of opposites. This development in Mao's thinking has been seen by some as a manifestation of traditional Taoist dialectics of the *yin* and the *yang*, and by others as reflecting Stalin's influence. There is no doubt, in any case, that logically it went hand in hand with Mao's increasing tendency to view historical development as an ambiguous and problematic process, and the continued forward progress of the revolution as something of a miracle, against the grain of the revisionist tendencies inherent in all of us.

What, then, were Mao's positive contributions to Marxism? First, the concept of the 'mass line', which did not mean, even in theory, let alone in practice, handing the revolutionary struggle (before 1949) or the running of the country (after 1949) over to the people themselves, but which nevertheless introduced an element of democratic participation from below (within strict limits, and under party guidance) almost wholly absent from the Leninist and Soviet tradition. Secondly, while he sometimes outrageously exaggerated the capacity of the masses, when mobilized under correct leadership, to transform nature and society virtually at will, he did introduce into (or perhaps superpose on) the Marxist philosophy of history, as commonly understood by most WESTERN MARXISTS, the idea that human change must accompany and support economic and technical progress, and not simply arise from it as a kind of by-product. His ideas regarding the participation of the bourgeoisie in the revolution, before and after 1949, while largely derived from those of Lenin (the revolutionary-democratic dictatorship of the workers and peasants) and Stalin (the four-class bloc), integrated non-proletarian elements into the revolutionary process in China to a degree which carried a step farther the synthesis between national and social revolution in

Asia. (Some of course will regard this as a good thing, and others will not.) He launched a great war on bureaucracy, carried out in ways so violent, unjust, and chaotic as to be largely counter-productive, but none the less placing the problem on the agenda for the future. Finally, to return to the aspect of Mao's thought evoked at the beginning, he by no means stood on its head the Marxist and Leninist axiom of working-class leadership over the peasants; the workers, as he put it in 1959, were the 'elder brothers' in this relationship. But he tried to combine this principle (of which he did not, perhaps, perceive all the implications, at least as they appeared to Marx) with the conviction that the centre of gravity of Chinese society was to be found in the countryside, and that the peasantry must play an active part in building a new socialist China. This problem, too, he raised but did not solve, and the contradictions between rural and urban China remain after his death; but for better or for worse it is unlikely that the conventional Marxist schema of salvation through industrialization and workers educating peasants will ever be adopted in future without significant modifications in the directions Mao sketched out.

Reading

Cohen, Arthur A. 1964: *The Communism of Mao Tse-Tung.*

Hsiung, James Chieh 1970: *Ideology and Practice. The Evolution of Chinese Communism.*

Mao Tse-tung 1961–77: *Selected Works.*

— 1974: *Miscellany of Mao Tse-tung Thought.*

Schram, Stuart R. 1969: *The Political Thought of Mao Tse-tung.*

— 1977: 'The Marxist'. In Dick Wilson ed. *Mao Tse-tung in the Scales of History.*

— ed. 1974: *Mao Tse-tung Unrehearsed.*

Starr, John Bryan 1979: *Continuing the Revolution. The Political Thought of Mao.*

Womack, Brantly 1982: *The Foundations of Mao Zedong's Political Thought.*

STUART R. SCHRAM

Marcuse, Herbert Born 19 July 1898, Berlin; died 30 July 1979, Munich. Completed his military service during the first world war, and shortly afterwards became involved in politics in a soldiers' council in Berlin. He left the Social

Democratic Party after brief membership in 1919, protesting against its betrayal of the council movement (see COUNCILS). He studied philosophy at Berlin and Freiburg and was for a brief time a student of both Heidegger and Husserl. Concerned from the outset with the interrelation between philosophy and politics, Marcuse joined the Institute of Social Research in 1933 (the year it was forced to leave Nazi Germany) and subsequently became a key figure in the FRANKFURT SCHOOL. He settled in the United States after the second world war. Although many of his ideas were similar to those elaborated by the two other leading members of the school – Horkheimer and Adorno – he engaged more fully than they did with the interests of classical Marxism. His unambiguous commitment to politics and social struggle led him to become a prominent spokesman and theorist of the New Left in the 1960s and early 1970s. It was through Marcuse's work, especially in North America, that the Frankfurt School's criticisms of contemporary culture, authoritarianism and bureaucratism became well known.

Marcuse's career represents a constant attempt to examine and reconstruct the Marxist enterprise. A preoccupation with the fate of revolution, the potentiality for socialism and the defence of 'utopian' (seemingly unobtainable) objectives, is apparent throughout his work. The goals of his critical approach to society are self-emancipation, the nurturing of a decentralized political movement and the reconciliation of humanity and nature. While the importance of the writings of the 'early Marx' is acknowledged by Horkheimer and Adorno, Marcuse places a greater emphasis on them and, in particular, on Marx's *Economic and Philosophical Manuscripts*. A general theory of labour and alienation provides a backdrop to all his writings. An elaborate integration of this theory with Freud's work marks, perhaps above all, the distinctiveness of Marcuse's project.

Marcuse's most important contributions to social and political theory include an early attempt to synthesize Heideggerian phenomenology and Marxism (1928), a re-examination of the theoretical and political significance of Hegel's *oeuvre* (1941), a reinvestigation of the relation between the individual and society through a synthesis of Marx and Freud (1955), a critical analysis of state socialism and industrial

capitalism (1958, 1964), a provocative assessment of modern science as a form of domination (1964) and an outline of a new aesthetics (1978).

Reading

Breines, Paul ed. 1970: *Critical Interruptions*.

Habermas, Jürgen ed. 1968: *Antworten auf Herbert Marcuse*.

Leiss, William 1974: *The Domination of Nature*.

Marcuse, Herbert 1928 (1969): 'Contribution to a Phenomenology of Historical Materialism'.

— 1941: *Reason and Revolution*.

— 1955: *Eros and Civilization*.

— 1958: *Soviet Marxism*.

— 1964: *One Dimensional Man*.

— 1978: *The Aesthetic Dimension*.

Robinson, Paul 1969: *The Sexual Radicals*.

DAVID HELD

market socialism A theoretical concept (model) of an economic system in which the means of production (capital) are publicly or collectively owned, and the allocation of resources follows the rules of the market (product markets, labour markets, capital markets). The term is often applied more loosely to cover the concepts of reforming the economic system of the countries of 'real socialism' (communist countries) away from command planning in the direction of market regulation (Yugoslavia from the early 1950s, Hungary after 1968, China, Poland, the USSR, as well as Bulgaria, in the 1980s). For ideological reasons the designation 'market socialism' was, however, largely avoided in some of the countries in question, with preference for the formula of 'socialist market' which was thought to be more acceptable for Marxists.

Marx's political economy had for a long time been interpreted to hold that socialism was incompatible with the market. Socialism makes the market redundant and overcomes its shortcomings as an allocation mechanism by bringing into the open the social nature of work, assigning it directly *ex ante* to a particular role in the economic process through the 'visible hand' of planning, which secures full utilization of resources, especially human, free of cyclical fluctuations.

After the Russian revolution of 1917, any application of the market mechanism was presented in the programmatic communist documents as only a temporary concession to underdevelopment (Programme of the Communist International, 1929, ch. 4). At the same time, however, the social-democratic wing of Marxism began to recognize the relevance of the market in a socialist economy (Kautsky 1922).

Theoretical debates on market socialism acquired a new dimension in the inter-war period, particularly after the republication by Hayek (1935) of an article by Mises, originally published in 1920, which categorically denied the possibility of rational economic calculation under socialism, because exchange relations between production goods and hence their prices could be established only on the basis of private ownership. Among the many attempts at refutation of this view (Taylor 1929; Dickinson 1933; Landauer 1931; Heimann 1932), probably the best known is that by Oskar LANGE (1936-7). Similar ideas have been developed in the same period by Abba Lerner (1934, 1936, 1937), hence the often used designation of 'Lange-Lerner solution'.

Lange not only denied the purely theoretical validity of Mises's stand (by pointing to Barone's (1908) demonstration of the possibility of dealing with the question through a system of simultaneous equations) but tried to present a positive solution. This was to consist of a 'trial and error' procedure, in which the Central Planning Board (CPB) performs the functions of the market where there is no market in the institutional sense of the word. In this capacity the CPB fixes prices, as well as wages and interest rates, so as to balance supply and demand (by appropriate changes in case of disequilibrium), and instructs managers to follow two rules: (1) to minimize average cost of production by using a combination of factors which would equalize marginal productivity of their money unit-worth; (2) to determine the scale of output at a point of equalization of marginal cost and the price set by the Board.

Most of the subsequent accounts of the inter-war debate acknowledged the validity of the theoretical argument presented by Lange, and accepted that Hayek retreated to a position of asserting the practical impossibility of reconciling socialism with rational economic calcula-

tion. This may be true when one follows – as Lange seems to have done – the type of model of static general equilibrium as developed by Walras (1954). However, the point made increasingly forcefully by new students of the inter-war debate (e.g. Lavoie 1985) is that the Mises/Hayek challenge has come from the positions of the Austrian school, with the emphasis on the dynamic properties of the competition process, the central figure of which is the entrepreneur. This leaves unanswered the question whether economic actors who are not principals operating on their own risk and responsibility but agents employed by a public body are actually capable of entrepreneurial behaviour.

Thus, Lange's 'competitive solution' had the merit of advancing the idea of an alternative to command planning as well as showing the indispensability of scarcity prices for rational allocation of resources under socialism. At the same time, however, it could not provide an adequate theoretical base for change when market-orientated reforms were put on the practical agenda in countries of 'real socialism'.

The first attempt to apply the ideas of market socialism in practice came in the early 1950s in Yugoslavia, after the Stalin–Tito break. The Yugoslav Communist Party searched both for greater economic efficiency and for ideological legitimacy *vis-à-vis* Stalinism. The latter was found in self-management, and as self-managed economic units must be autonomous, this engendered the process of replacement of the command system by market coordination, albeit not conducted in a consistent way.

In the Soviet-bloc countries the main motive for the reform drive was the dissatisfaction with the command economy's performance when it came into the open after Stalin's death. In Poland a relatively comprehensive blueprint of systemic changes was worked out in 1956–7; similar ideas in Hungary were quelled as a result of the suppression of the popular uprising of 1956.

Subsequently, a long string of attempts at economic reforms – of various degrees of consistency, but heading in the same direction of increasing the role of the market, occurred in Eastern Europe: Czechoslovakia in 1958 and in 1967–8; the New Economic System in the German Democratic Republic in 1963; the 1965 so-called 'Kosygin reform' in the USSR and its

Bulgarian imitation; the Hungarian New Economic Mechanism introduced in 1968; repeated attempts at reform in Poland. However, at the beginning of the 1980s, out of all these attempts, only the Hungarian NEM remained basically operative; otherwise, what emerged were rather secondary modifications within the framework of the command system. On the other hand, the tendency to market-directed change persisted, clearly under the pressure of a progressive deterioration of economic performance, which reached crisis proportions in most communist countries in the 1980s. In 1978–9, China joined the reformist ranks, and from 1985 onwards 'radical economic reform' became one of the fundamental elements of Gorbachev's 'perestroika' in the USSR.

The reasons for the difficulties in carrying out the market-oriented economic reforms are seen (Brus 1979) in: (1) political resistance of the ruling elite; (2) vested interests of the administrative apparatus as well as of some sections of the workers who may feel threatened in their job security; (3) substantive obstacles to grafting a market mechanism onto the existing structures of planning and management, property rights and the monopoly of power of the Communist Party. As a result, countries which made some headway in the reform process (Yugoslavia, Poland, Hungary) not only found themselves in economic troubles worse than those of countries (Czechoslovakia, East Germany) which stuck to the old system (although non-systemic factors must be taken into account in any comparisons), but also actually failed to cross the threshold between administrative coordination and market coordination of the economy. The examination of the Hungarian NEM in this respect led to the conclusion that despite the abolition of obligatory output targets and physical allocation of producer goods, the overall effect of the reform by mid-1980s was merely a change from direct to indirect 'bureaucratic coordination' (Kornai 1986).

Experience seems to have shown that the earlier reform models based on the idea of a combination of central planning with a 'regulated market' by limiting market regulation mainly to the product market (Brus 1961), as well as on the acceptance of the dominant position of state ownership of means of production, have proved inadequate. In the course of the 1980s, the concepts of market-oriented change in communist countries have undergone sharp radicalization: the need for a capital market, both in the form of commercial banking and of dealing in securities, has been widely recognized (Tardos 1986, Lipowski 1988), and so has the need for a labour market, although sometimes not openly by name. Moreover, a successful market-oriented economic reform has become closely linked with fundamental transformation of the ownership structure (Abalkin 1988). One of the factors which evidently contributed to the reconsideration of the ownership issue was the experience of much more favourable results of systemic reforms outside the state sector (cooperatives, private enterprise) in Hungary, and particularly the initial spectacular success of the 'family production responsibility' in Chinese agriculture. The acknowledgement of the necessity for a wide-ranging change in the ownership structure was reflected towards the end of the 1980s in a number of legal measures in various communist countries: in the USSR in the legislation about 'arenda'/leasehold of land, buildings and equipment with the intention of maintaining the position of the state as a freeholder, but of introducing entrepreneurship to workers' collectives, partnerships or even individuals; in some other countries (Poland, Hungary) the principle of a mixed economy was adopted, with state enterprises, cooperative enterprises and private enterprises (the latter without limits on size and employment) intended to compete on equal terms.

This conceptual, and to some extent also practical, development poses the question of correspondence between economic and political transformations with renewed force. On the one hand, marketization involving increased enterprise freedom, particularly when accompanied by ownership changes, raises the political aspirations of the people, who feel less subjugated by the all-pervasive state. On the other hand, in view of the resistance of the ruling elites and their supporting strata, political pluralism becomes an indispensable instrument for effecting the transition from the old to the new economic system, as well as for guarding the latter's continuing existence. The objection based on examples of successful market economies with authoritarian political regimes (e.g. some of the 'newly industrialized countries' in Asia) was refuted by the reformers in communist countries as failing to recognize the true nature of the problems they were facing.

Consistent pursuit of market socialism – capital and labour markets, ownership restructuring, political pluralism – must be regarded as blurring the habitual distinctions between capitalism and socialism, and therefore denying to socialism the character of a bounded successor system to capitalism (Brus and Laski 1989). This is not necessarily tantamout to the abandonment of basic socialist policy objectives – full employment, equality of opportunity, social welfare – or of government intervention as the method to achieve them. What it does imply, however, is the abandonment of the concept of socialism as a grand design requiring total replacement of the past institutional framework; in other words abandonment of the philosophy of the revolutionary break in favour of continuity in change. From this point of view, market socialism as an aim of a consistent transformation of the countries of 'real socialism' may be said to share certain common features with market socialism as perceived by some Western social-democratic parties, including the British Labour Party (Fabian Society 1986), but any analogy must be very tentative both because of the starting position and because of the profoundly different conditions of struggle for achieving the desired aim, as well as of ideological implications.

The collapse of communist power in Eastern Europe in 1989 brought about renunciation of market socialism as an objective of systemic transformation; the aim became – more or less explicitly – a return to capitalist economy. However, the necessity to maintain, at least temporarily, a sizeable public sector and the programmatic adherence of some communist countries (including the two major ones, China and the USSR) to the principles of socialism may mean that issues associated with market socialism will retain some significance.

Reading

Abalkin, L. 1988: 'Obnovlenye sotsialisticheskoy sobstvennosti' (Renewal of Socialist Ownership).

Barone 1908 (1935): 'Ministry of Production in a Collectivist State'. In F. A. von Hayek, ed. *Collectivist Economic Planning*.

Brus, W. 1961 (1972): *The Market in a Socialist Economy*.

— 1979: 'East European Economic Reforms: What Happened to Them?'.

Brus, W. and Laski, K. 1989: *From Marx to the Market: Socialism in Search of an Economic System*.

Dickinson, H. D. 1933: 'Price Formation in a Socialist Community'.

Fabian Society 1986: *Market Socialism: Whose Choice? A Debate*.

Hayek, F. A. von 1935: *Collectivist Economic Planning*.

Heimann, E. 1932: *Sozialistische Wirtschafts- und Arbeitsordnung*.

Kautsky, K. 1922: *Die proletarische Revolution und ihr Programm*.

Kornai, J. 1986: 'The Hungarian Reform Process: Vision, Hopes and Reality'.

Landauer, C. 1931: *Planwirtschaft und Verkehrswirtschaft*.

Lange, O. 1936–7 (1948): 'On the Economic Theory of a Socialist Economy'. In O. Lange and F. Taylor, *On the Economic Theory of Socialism*, ed. B. Lippincott.

Lavoie, D. 1985: *Rivalry and Central Planning: The Socialist Calculation Debate Reconsidered*.

Lerner, A. 1934: 'Economic Theory and Socialist Economy'.

— 1936: 'A Note on Socialist Economics'.

— 1937: 'Statics and Dynamics in Socialist Economics'.

Lipowski, A. 1988: *Mechanizm rynkowy w gospodarce polskiej* (The Market Mechanism in the Polish Economy).

Mises, L. von 1920 (1935): 'Die Wirtschaftsrechnung im sozialistischen Gemeinwesen'. In English (Economic Calculation in a Socialist Community) in F. A. von Hayek, ed., *Collectivist Economic Planning*.

Tardos, M. 1986: 'The Conditions of Developing a Regulated Market'.

Taylor, F. 1929 (1948): 'The Guidance of Production in a Socialist State'. In O. Lange and F. Taylor, *On the Economic Theory of Socialism*, ed. B. Lippincott.

Walras, L. 1954: *Elements of Pure Economics*.

W. BRUS

Martov, Y. O. (Tsederbaum, Yulii Osipovich)
Born 24 November 1873, Constantinople (Istanbul); died 4 April 1923, Schömberg, Germany. Co-founder, with Lenin, of the St Petersburg Union of Struggle for the Emancipation of the Working Class (1895) and of the revolutionary

Marxist *Iskra* group (1900), Martov became the founder of Menshevism (see MENSHEVIKS) at the Second Congress of Russian Social Democracy (1903). Then, and thereafter, he challenged Lenin's organizational scheme of a narrow, highly centralized and elitist party of professional revolutionaries, advocating instead a broad, social democratic workers' party, adapted to Russia's illegal and (after the 1905 revolution) semi-legal conditions.

In the 1905 debate on power with Lenin and Trotsky, Martov upheld Plekhanov's doctrine of bourgeois revolution, inveighing against a premature socialist assumption of power, since objective economic and social prerequisites for socialism were missing in backward Russia and, pre-eminently, its ignorant petty-bourgeois masses still lacked the will to socialism. Social democrats had no right, Martov and fellow-Menshevik Alexander Martynov urged, to seize and use state power to 'neutralize the resistance of the petty bourgeoisie to the socialist aspirations of the proletariat'. But following Marx's advice to the German Communist League (1850), Martov assigned to Russian social democrats the role of a militant revolutionary opposition which, entrenched 'in organs of revolutionary self-government' such as Soviets, trade unions, workers' clubs, cooperatives and town dumas, would, in a situation of 'dual power', make the official bourgeois-democratic government implement 'democratic' policies.

A pillar of the Zimmerwald socialist peace movement during the war, and leader of the Menshevik-Internationalists in 1917, Martov opposed official Menshevism's 'revolutionary defencism' and 'coalitionism' and advocated a popular front government and, after the October revolution, a socialist coalition government, ranging from the Popular Socialists to the Bolsheviks.

Leader of the semi-loyal, semi-implacable Menshevik opposition party, Martov rejected Lenin's minority dictatorship as a flagrant departure from both Marx's majority concept of the DICTATORSHIP OF THE PROLETARIAT and the democratic practice of the PARIS COMMUNE. Martov urged that Marx had not envisaged the dictatorship of the proletariat as the state power of a 'conscious revolutionary minority' which, à la Lenin, imposed its will on an 'unconscious majority', making it the 'passive object of social experimentation'. He claimed that Marx's dictatorship of the proletariat represented the 'conscious will' of the proletarian majority, directing its 'revolutionary force' solely against the resistance of the 'ruling capitalist minority' to the 'legal transfer of political power to the working masses'.

In Martov's view, it was commitment to the 'state power of the toiling majority' which sharply divided 'revolutionary Marxists who call themselves social democrats' from the communists. The latter had not merely espoused 'the dictatorship of a revolutionary minority', but were bent on creating 'such institutions as would make it a permanent feature'. Martov has been seen as the authentic voice of Russian social democratic Marxism contesting Lenin's Bolshevik interpretation and practice of Marxism (see BOLSHEVISM).

Reading

Bourguina 1968: *Russian Social Democracy: The Menshevik Movement, a Bibliography*.

Getzler, Israel 1967: *Martov*.

— 1980: 'Martov e i menscevichi prima e dopo la rivoluzione'. In *Storia del Marxismo*, III.

Haimson, Leopold ed. 1974: *The Mensheviks*.

Martov, Julius 1938: *The State and the Socialist Revolution*.

ISRAEL GETZLER

Marx, Karl Heinrich Born 5 May 1818, Trier; died 14 March 1883, London. Social scientist, historian and revolutionary, Marx is undoubtedly the most influential socialist thinker. Although largely unheeded by scholars in his lifetime, the body of social and political ideas that he elaborated gained increasingly rapid acceptance in the socialist movement after his death in 1883. Until recently almost half the population of the world lived under regimes that claimed to be Marxist. This very success, however, has meant that the original ideas of Marx have often been obscured by attempts to adapt their meaning to a great variety of political circumstances. In addition, the delayed publication of many of his writings meant that only relatively recently has the opportunity arisen for a just appreciation of Marx's intellectual stature.

Marx was born into a comfortable middle-class home in Trier on the river Moselle in Germany. He came from a long line of rabbis on both sides of his family and his father, although intellectually a typical Enlightenment rationalist who knew Voltaire and Lessing by heart, had only agreed to baptism as a Protestant on pain of losing his job as one of the most respected lawyers in Trier. At the age of seventeen, Marx enrolled in the Faculty of Law at the University of Bonn and was receptive to the romanticism there dominant, particularly as he had just become engaged to Jenny von Westphalen, the daughter of Baron von Westphalen, a prominent member of Trier society who had already interested Marx in romantic literature and Saint-Simonian politics (see UTOPIAN SOCIALISM). The following year Marx's father sent him to the larger and more serious-minded University of Berlin where he remained for the next four years, during the course of which he abandoned romanticism for the Hegelianism which ruled in Berlin at that time (see HEGEL AND MARX; YOUNG HEGELIANS).

Marx became deeply involved in the Young Hegelian movement. This group, which contained such figures as Bauer and Strauss, were producing a radical critique of Christianity and, by implication, a liberal opposition to the Prussian autocracy. Finding a university career closed to him by the Prussian government, Marx moved into journalism and, in October 1842, became editor, in Cologne, of the influential *Rheinische Zeitung*, a liberal newspaper backed by Rhenish industrialists. Marx's incisive articles, particularly on economic questions, induced the government to close the paper and he decided to emigrate to France.

On his arrival in Paris at the end of 1843 Marx rapidly made contact with organized groups of *émigré* German workers and with the various sects of French socialists. He also edited the short-lived *Deutsch-französische Jahrbücher* which was intended to form a bridge between nascent French socialism and the ideas of the German radical Hegelians. During the first few months of his stay in Paris, Marx rapidly became a convinced communist and set down his views in a series of writings known as the *Economic and Philosophical Manucripts* which remained unpublished until around 1930. Here he outlined a humanist conception of COMMUNISM, influenced by the philosophy of Feuerbach and based on a contrast between the alienated nature of labour under capitalism and a communist society in which human beings freely developed their nature in cooperative production. It was also in Paris that Marx first formed his lifelong partnership with Engels.

Marx was expelled from Paris at the end of 1844 and moved (with Engels) to Brussels where he stayed for the next three years, visiting England, then the most advanced industrial country, where Engels's family had cotton-spinning interests in Manchester. While in Brussels Marx devoted himself to an intensive study of history and elaborated what came to be known as the materialist conception of history (see HISTORICAL MATERIALISM). This he set out in a manuscript (also published only posthumously as *German Ideology*) of which the basic thesis was that 'the nature of individuals depends on the material conditions determining their production'. Marx traced the history of the various modes of production and predicted the collapse of the present one – capitalism – and its replacement by communism. At the same time as this theoretical work Marx became involved in political activity, polemicizing (in *The Poverty of Philosophy*) against what he considered to be the unduly idealistic socialism of Proudhon and joining the Communist League. This was an organization of German *émigré* workers with its centre in London of which Marx and Engels became the major theoreticians. At a conference of the League in London at the end of 1847 Marx and Engels were commissioned to write a *Communist Manifesto* which was to be the most succinct expression of their views. Scarcely was the *Manifesto* published than the 1848 wave of revolutions broke in Europe.

Early in 1848 Marx moved back to Paris where the revolution first broke out and then on to Germany where he founded, again in Cologne, the *Neue Rheinische Zeitung*. The paper, which had a wide influence, supported a radical democratic line against the Prussian autocracy and Marx devoted his main energies to its editorship since the Communist League had been virtually disbanded. With the ebbing of the revolutionary tide, however, Marx's paper was suppressed and he sought refuge in London in May 1849 to begin the 'long, sleepless night of exile' that was to last for the rest of his life.

On settling in London Marx, optimistic about the imminence of a fresh revolutionary outbreak in Europe, rejoined the rejuvenated Communist League and wrote two lengthy pamphlets on the 1848 revolution in France and its aftermath entitled *The Class Struggles in France* and *The 18th Brumaire of Louis Bonaparte*. But he soon became convinced that 'a new revolution is possible only in consequence of a new crisis' and devoted himself to the study of political economy in order to determine the causes and conditions of this crisis.

During the first half of the 1850s the Marx family lived in a three-room flat in the Soho quarter of London and experienced considerable poverty. On arrival in London there were already four children and two more were soon born. Of these only three survived the Soho period. Marx's major source of income at this time (and later) was Engels who was drawing a steadily increasing income from his father's cotton business in Manchester. This was supplemented by weekly articles written as foreign correspondent for the *New York Daily Tribune*. Legacies during the late 1850s and early 1860s eased Marx's financial position somewhat, but it was not until 1869 that he had a sufficient and assured income settled on him by Engels.

Not surprisingly Marx's major work on political economy made slow progress. By 1857/8 he had produced a mammoth 800-page manuscript which was a rough draft of a work which he intended should deal with capital, landed property, wage-labour, the State, foreign trade and the world market. This manuscript known as *Grundrisse* or *Outlines* was not published until 1941. In the early 1860s he broke off his work to compose three large volumes, entitled *Theories of Surplus Value*, which discussed his predecessors in political economy, particularly Smith and Ricardo. It was not until 1867 that Marx was able to publish the first results of his work in volume I of *Capital*, devoted to a study of the capitalist process of production. Here he elaborated his version of the labour theory of VALUE and his conception of SURPLUS VALUE and EXPLOITATION which would ultimately lead to a FALLING RATE OF PROFIT and the collapse of capitalism. Volumes II and III were largely finished during the 1860s but Marx worked on the manuscripts for the rest of his life and they were published posthumously by Engels.

One of the reasons why Marx was so delayed in his work on *Capital* was that he devoted much time and energy to the First International (see INTERNATIONALS), to whose General Council he was elected on its foundation in 1864. Marx was particularly active in preparing for the annual Congresses of the International and in leading the struggle against the anarchist wing led by Bakunin. Although Marx won this contest, the transfer of the seat of the General Council from London to New York in 1872, which Marx supported, led to the swift decline of the International. The most important political event during the existence of the International was the PARIS COMMUNE of 1871 when the citizens of Paris, in the aftermath of the Franco-Prussian War, rebelled against their government and held the city for two months. On the bloody suppression of this rebellion, Marx wrote one of his most famous pamphlets – *The Civil War in France* – which was an enthusiastic defence of the activities and aims of the Commune.

During the last decade of his life Marx's health declined considerably and he was incapable of the sustained efforts of creative synthesis that had so obviously characterized his previous work. Nevertheless he did manage to comment substantially on contemporary politics, particularly in Germany and Russia. In Germany, he opposed, in his *Critique of the Gotha Programme*, the tendency of his followers Liebknecht and Bebel to compromise with the state socialism of Lassalle in the interests of a united socialist party. In Russia, in correspondence with Vera Zasulich he contemplated the possibility of Russia's bypassing the capitalist stage of development and building communism on the basis of the common ownership of land characteristic of the village *mir*. Marx was, however, increasingly dogged by ill-health and he regularly travelled to European spas and even to Algeria in search of recuperation. The deaths of his eldest daughter and his wife clouded the last years of his life.

Marx's contribution to our understanding of society has been immense. His thought is not the comprehensive system evolved by some of his followers under the name of DIALECTICAL MATERIALISM. The very dialectical nature of his approach meant that it was usually tentative and open-ended. Moreover, there was often a tension between Marx the political activist and

Marx the student of political economy. Many of his expectations about the future course of the revolutionary movement have, so far at least, failed to materialize. But his stress on the economic factor in society and his analysis of classes have both had enormous influence on history and sociology.

Reading

Avineri, S. 1968: *The Social and Political Thought of Karl Marx.*

Bottomore, T. ed. 1988: *Interpretations of Marx.*

Cohen, G. 1978: *Karl Marx's Theory of History: A Defence.*

Hunt, R. 1974: *The Political Ideas of Marx and Engels.*

McLellan, D. 1974: *Karl Marx: His Life and Thought.*

Ollman, B. 1971: *Alienation: Marx's Conception of Man in Capitalist Society.*

Plamenatz, J. 1975: *Karl Marx's Philosophy of Man.*

Rubel, Maximilien 1980: *Marx: Life and Works.*

DAVID MCLELLAN

Marx, Engels and contemporary politics At the heart of Marx's and Engels's approach to politics in their time lay their expectation of a proletarian revolution and their efforts to promote it. Once they had settled accounts with their erstwhile philosophical consciences Marx and Engels directed their attention to other revolutionary and socialist movements. Such rival theories as Utopian, Christian and true Socialism were dismissed in the *Communist Manifesto* (ch. 3) and elsewhere as being far from revolutionary, while certain contemporary revolutionary movements, on the other hand, were criticized as being too narrowly concerned with purely political revolution rather than with the wider social transformation which Marx and Engels believed should accompany it. Thus Engels, always willing to assist Marx in his disputes with Bakunin and the anarchists, later reproached the Russian Jacobin, P. N. Tkachev, who considered the socialist revolution more likely to occur in pre-capitalist Russia than in the more advanced West, with having 'still to learn the ABC of socialism' ('On Social Relations in Russia').

In rejecting Tkachev's notion Engels was adhering to the general conception of historical development expressed earlier in such works as the *Communist Manifesto* (and Marx's Preface

to *A Contribution to the Critique of Political Economy*). Nevertheless, their actual approach to politics, particularly later in Marx's career, at times seemed to demonstrate a willingness to depart from the strict canons of HISTORICAL MATERIALISM. This was, perhaps, notably the case in their (more particularly Marx's) assessments of developments in Russia as the essentially non-Marxist revolutionary movement gathered momentum there in the 1870s and early 1880s. Despite Engels's polemic with Tkachev and his own previous distrust of many Russian revolutionaries, Marx was, in the last few years of his life, somewhat more prepared to countenance the Populist notion of a specifically Russian road to socialism via the peasant commune (see RUSSIAN COMMUNE) although, in his public utterances at least, such a concession was not unconditional. Indeed, Marx's and Engels's hope, expressed in their preface to the Russian edition (1882) of the *Communist Manifesto*, that the Russian revolution would become the signal for the proletarian revolution in the West, so that each would complement the other, demonstrates their fundamental concern to see the proletarian revolution succeed in the economically more advanced countries of the West, which they considered to possess the material and cultural prerequisites of socialism.

Credited with an apparently ubiquitous and malign influence, the tsar's government was seen by Marx and Engels as the mainstay of much of the European order whose overthrow they sought. Their sympathy for Hungary and Poland, whose revolutions had been suppressed by Austria and Russia in 1849 and 1863 respectively, nevertheless stemmed perhaps less from the social character and outlook of the national movements in those countries than from their orientation on the international plane. The aspirations of other, chiefly Slavic, Eastern European peoples which conflicted with those of the Hungarians, Poles or 'civilization-bearing' Germans, on the other hand, were damned as 'counter-revolutionary', principally by Engels in his capacity as foreign editor of the *Neue Rheinische Zeitung*, the daily newspaper which Marx edited in 1848 and 1849 (see NATION; NATIONALISM).

It was in the pages of that journal as well as in subsequent articles that Engels advanced his notion, originally derived from Hegel, of 'historyless peoples'. Included in this category were the Basques, Bretons, Scottish Gaels, Czechs, Slovaks, Croats and other southern Slavs, 'remnants of a former population that was suppressed and held in bondage by the nations which later became the main vehicle of historical development' ('The Magyar Struggle', NRZ, 13 January 1849). On similar grounds, Engels supported Germany in its war against Denmark over control of Schleswig-Holstein in 1848 as 'the right of civilisation as against barbarism, of progress as against stability' ('The Danish–Prussian Armistice', NRZ, 9 September 1848).

Among the reasons Engels advanced for dismissing certain peoples as 'historyless' was his observation that, given their linguistic, cultural and geographical fragmentation, none of them could concentrate a sufficiently large number of their population into a suitably compact area of territory to develop a modern economy in it. Since the creation of such economies entailed the development of a market and a class structure on a nationwide basis, Marx and Engels, unlike some of their Austro-Marxist successors (see AUSTRO-MARXISM), tended to oppose notions of federalism, opting instead for large-scale unitary states. Thus the first of their *Demands of the Communist Party in Germany* (1848) was the creation of 'a single and indivisible republic'. With this aspiration, along with others expressed in 1848, unfulfilled, they were to view Prussia's lightning victory over Austria in 1866 as ultimately benefiting their cause since 'everything that centralises the bourgeoisie is of course advantageous to the workers' (Marx to Engels, 27 July 1866).

Although the Austro-Prussian War had not been their preferred means of advancing the process of German unification, Marx and Engels believed that, in certain instances, war itself could incidentally assist the cause of the proletarian revolution. In 1848 they called for a revolutionary war against Russia, not only to enable the Poles to free themselves from their tsarist oppressor but also as a means of consolidating the revolution at home. Even before this, Engels had viewed military conquest as a potential agency of social progress when he described the French conquest of Algeria as, despite its brutality, 'an important and fortunate fact for the progress of civilisation', just as he was to welcome 'the energetic Yankees' conquest of

California from 'the lazy Mexicans' ('Democratic Pan-Slavism, 1', NRZ, 15 February 1849). Later, as he and Marx expected a major economic crisis in the West, the outbreak of the Crimean War aroused their hopes that the allegedly half-hearted prosecution of the war by the 'Russian agent' Palmerston and others would provoke the intervention of 'the sixth great European power, Revolution' ('The European War', NYDT, 2 February 1854; *The Eastern Question*, p. 220). Despite his association at this period with the Russophobe Tory MP, David Urquhart, Marx's interest in the war stemmed less from any particular fondness for the Porte than from a concern with the interests of the revolution. Similar considerations influenced his attitude to the Franco-Austrian War of 1859 in which, despite his hostility to Habsburg control of northern Italy, he saw an Austrian defeat as likely to benefit the two European powers which were the most dangerous opponents of revolution, namely Russia and the France of Napoleon III. While Marx welcomed the latter's defeat in the Franco-Prussian War in 1870 he held that, once Bonaparte had capitulated, Germany was no longer waging a war of defence, but risked falling under increased Russian influence. In the Second Address he wrote for the International Working Men's Association (IWMA) in September 1870 he forecast, with remarkable prescience, the course German foreign policy was to follow until 1914: Germany would at first forge closer links with Russia, to be superseded, after a short respite, by preparations for a further, more widespread war, this time against 'the combined Slavonian and Roman races'.

If Marx tended to reserve his infrequent use of the term 'imperialism' for empires (notably the French Second Empire) in Europe, the problem of European COLONIALISM came to engage his attention somewhat more once he had settled in England. His and Engels's views of the non-European world were closely related to their conception of capitalism as a universalizing system, driven by its quest for markets and sources of raw materials towards constant expansion which would, in turn, pave the way for the coming of socialism. While such expansion might serve to postpone crises of capitalism in those more advanced areas where a proletarian revolution might otherwise occur, Marx and

Engels saw such upheavals as the Taiping rebellion as a possible means of precipitating 'the long-prepared general crisis, which, spreading abroad, will be closely followed by political revolution on the Continent' ('Revolution in China and Europe', NYDT, 14 June 1853).

While expressing strong moral condemnation of much Western policy in the East, from the 'wicked' opium trade to the reprisals following the Indian Mutiny, Marx and Engels nevertheless remained highly critical of traditional oriental society. In their eyes, 'old China' had been preserved only by her 'complete isolation', while life in India, about which Marx wrote much more extensively, had, at least until Western penetration, been consistently 'undignified, stagnatory and vegetative'. Resting on a foundation of isolated, self-sufficient village economies, Oriental despotism in India 'restrained the human mind within the smallest possible compass'. In destroying the economic foundations of such an order, English interference had 'thus produced the greatest, and . . . only *social*, revolution ever heard of in Asia' ('The British Rule in India', NYDT, 25 June 1853) (see ASIATIC SOCIETY). In subsequent decades Marx's writings on capitalism's impact on oriental societies tended less to stress its revolutionary character than to point to the destruction and suffering it caused. Yet in their analysis of the phenomenon of colonialism, Marx and Engels had pointed, as Lenin was later to do, to the possibility of workers in the metropolitan powers being 'bribed' with the spoils of empire. Thus Engels wrote to Marx on 7 October 1858 that 'the English proletariat is actually becoming more bourgeois, so that this most bourgeois of all nations is apparently aiming ultimately at the possession of a bourgeois aristocracy and a bourgeois proletariat alongside the bourgeoisie' (see LABOUR ARISTOCRACY). Prominent among the forces which Engels considered responsible for this embourgeoisement of the English workers was Ireland's position as 'England's first colony' (Engels to Marx, 23 May 1856). Antagonism between English and immigrant Irish workers, artificially fostered by the possessing classes, was seen by Marx as 'the secret of the impotence of the English working class' and of the capitalists' continued maintenance of power. He therefore declared that, where he had previously believed that Ireland's liberation would follow the triumph of the English working class, he had now reached the opposite conclusion that 'the decisive blow against the English ruling classes (and it will be decisive for the workers' movement all over the world) cannot be delivered *in England* but *only in Ireland*' (letter to Meyer and Vogt, 9 April 1870, emphasis in original).

Despite its shortcomings the English labour movement represented a useful ally, within the First International, in Marx's struggles against the influence of Proudhon and Bakunin. Yet in rejecting these doctrines it did not thereby espouse Marx's revolutionary politics. As Marx and Engels themselves recognized, the English workers had made some gains since the mid-1840s, notably with the passing of the Ten Hour Act and the growth of the cooperative movements. Similarly, many of the aims of the People's Charter had already been, or were likely to be, attained despite the fact that Chartism itself had gone into decline after 1848. During the International's first few years of existence, the Reform Act of 1867 and the improved conditions for trade-union organization served to reinforce the English labour leaders' beliefs that adoption of a reformist, rather than revolutionary, strategy might be enough to attain their goals. Indeed they could have been reassured by Marx's declaration at the Hague Congress of the International in 1872 that in such countries as England, the United States and perhaps Holland it might be possible for labour to do this by peaceful means.

Marx recognized that, although the English trade-unionists within the International's leadership did not always share his long-term political aspirations, their interest in such international questions as Poland's struggle, the movement for Italian unification and the American Civil War indicated a reawakening of the British labour movement from its long period of relative quiescence during the 1850s. Of these three issues, the cause of the Risorgimento enjoyed the widest support in England, not only among the workers but in other classes as well. Yet it was the one which Marx and his followers least expected to further their aims, given the strong influence of Marx's rival Mazzini in Italy and, to a lesser extent, in the International itself. In Marx's eyes Mazzini's policies were ill-considered, stronger on sentiment and moralizing rhetoric than on practical value to the needs of the Italian population, particularly of its peasantry. Besides being concerned about the influence of Mazzini and, later, Bakunin, Marx believed that, at the level of power politics, Italy's attainment of independence would be, in part, at the expense of Austria, which, whatever the character of her domestic politics, represented a potential buffer against Russian expansion.

In the case of the American Civil War, a development which divided English society much more than had the Risorgimento, Marx's *Inaugural Address of the IWMA* (1864) noted the support for the Confederacy shown by sections of the British upper classes. For Marx's cause, on the other hand, preservation of the Union was seen as a necessary precondition of future social, political and economic development. His and Engels's interest in the Civil War stemmed, at the moral level, from their abhorrence of slavery as well as from their hopes, on the strategic plane, that the shortage of cotton which the conflict was causing in England might contribute to the long awaited economic crisis in the metropolis of capitalism itself.

The third major international upheaval preceding and, in this case, to some extent occasioning the International's formation was the Polish uprising of 1863. In the early 1860s a common sympathy for Poland had indeed been one of the forces prompting the British and French labour movements towards closer cooperation, as the speeches of Odger and other founders of the International indicate. This sentiment was not shared, however, by such groups as the Proudhonians and, later, the Belgian César de Paepe, who contended that the restoration of Poland would simply benefit the nobility and clergy. Against such arguments Marx and Engels maintained, as they had done in 1848, that the partition of Poland constituted the link which held the Russian-Prussian-Austrian Holy Alliance together. The restoration of Poland, they therefore concluded, would not only undermine Prussia's pre-eminence in Germany, but also place 'twenty million heroes' between Europe and 'Asiatic despotism under Muscovite direction' (Speech to a Meeting on Poland, held in London on 22 January 1867). To those Polish revolutionaries such as Ludwik Waryński (1856–89) who maintained that the struggle for national independence was of lesser importance than the cause of the exploited and underprivileged classes Engels retorted that 'an international movement of the proletariat is possible only among independent nations'. (Engels to Kautsky, 7 February 1882).

Despite Engels's expression, in the early 1850s, of some misgivings, he and Marx remained committed to the cause of Polish independence, which they saw as likely to benefit that of socialism in Europe as a whole. Similar strategic considerations came to influence their approach to the revolutionary movement emerging in Russia in the 1870s and 1880s, especially as, with the Polish uprising and the Paris Commune both cruelly suppressed, the revolutionary tide seemed to be ebbing elsewhere. Strict adherence to their theories was not demanded of those revolutionaries actively combating the tsarist regime. Indeed, given his estimate of the tsar's influence in Europe, Marx had less admiration for his theoretically more 'orthodox' *émigré* Russian followers such as Plekhanov than for the more active Populists and Narodovol'tsy working for revolution within Russia itself. His approbation of the assassins of Alexander II in 1881, on the grounds that no alternative course was open, contrasted strikingly with his condemnation of such actions elsewhere in Europe, such as the attempts by Hödel and Nobiling to assassinate Kaiser Wilhelm I in 1878 and the Phoenix Park murders in Dublin in 1882.

Two years after Marx's death, Engels, usually more orthodox in matters of theory, declared that Russia in 1885 constituted 'one of the exceptional cases where it is possible for a handful of people to make a revolution', but he added that that very revolution might unleash forces beyond the control of the revolutionaries themselves (letter to Vera Zasulich, 23 April 1885). No such revolution occurred in Engels's remaining years, of course, and as the pace of Russia's industrialization accelerated towards the end of the century, he reckoned that Russia would, in all probability, have to follow the path of Western capitalist development rather than rely on the decaying peasant commune as the basis of a future socialist society. In drawing this conclusion, Engels vindicated the position of the Russian Marxists, as later expressed, for example, in Lenin's *Development of Capitalism in Russia*

(1899). (See also BLANQUISM; BONAPARTISM; EMPIRES OF MARX'S DAY; LASSALLE.)

Reading

Avineri, S. ed. 1968: *Karl Marx on Colonialism and Modernization: his despatches and other writings on China, India, Mexico, the Middle East and North Africa.*

Bloom, S. F. 1941: *The World of Nations: a study of the national implications of the World of Karl Marx.*

Collins, H. and Abramsky, C. 1965: *Karl Marx and the British Labour Movement: Years of the First International.*

Cummins, I. T. 1980: *Marx, Engels and National Movements.*

Davis, H. B. 1967: *Nationalism and Socialism – Marxist and Labour Theories of Nationalism to 1917.*

Haupt, G., Lowy, M. and Weill, C. eds. 1974: *Les Marxistes et la question nationale, 1848–1914.*

Kiernan, V. G. 1974: *Marxism and Imperialism.*

Molnár, E. 1967: *La Politique d'alliances du marxisme (18481889).*

Walicki, A. 1980: 'Marx, Engels and the Polish Question'.

IAN CUMMINS

Marxism, development of The term 'Marxism' was unknown in Marx's lifetime. His comment, reported by Engels, that 'all I know is that I am not a Marxist', was made with reference to phrases used by his son-in-law Paul Lafargue. It is of course impossible to infer from this that Marx rejected in principle the idea of a theoretical system emerging from his work, but it is evident that he did not claim to offer a comprehensive world view. Marx's and Engels's thought was first developed in the latter direction during the period of the Second International. Thus Plekhanov (1894) wrote that 'Marxism is a whole world view' and introduced the term DIALECTICAL MATERIALISM to describe it; while for Kautsky their work amounted to a comprehensive theory of evolution, embracing both nature and human society, of which a naturalistic ethic and a materialistic (biologistic) world view form part. Engels himself had taken the first step in this direction, at the request of the leaders of the German Social Democratic Party (SPD), in *Anti-Dühring* (1878), a work (in which Marx had collaborated to a small extent) that had a much greater influence on the consciousness of members of socialist parties than did Marx's own major work, *Capital*, of which only the first volume appeared in his lifetime (1867), the other two volumes being edited and published by Engels (1885, 1894) from Marx's manuscripts and notes.

Marx himself seems to have conceived his theoretical work primarily, if not exclusively, as a critique of political economy from the standpoint of the revolutionary proletariat, and as a materialist conception of history; materialist in the sense that the way in which material production is carried on (the technique of production in a broad sense) and is organized (in Marx's terminology, the 'relations of production', and in earlier texts also 'relations of intercourse'), is the determining factor in political organization and in the intellectual representations of an epoch. This conception was developed in conscious opposition to the subjective-idealist standpoint of the YOUNG HEGELIANS, who aimed to transform social and political conditions through a mere change in consciousness. Their view attained its extreme expression in the work of the anarchist thinker, Max Stirner, who urged his fellow citizens to 'expel the state and property from their minds' and to join together in a 'Union of the Free'. Against this, Marx shows that the state and property (money, etc.) are by no means only subjective fancies, which vanish from the world if they are ignored, but the reflection of real conditions, which nevertheless do not have to be accepted as eternal and inalterable.

The 'critique of political economy' – in conformity with this materialist conception of history – comprises not simply a critique of 'false representations', but also a critique of the objective (material, social) conditions which necessarily produce these representations (of classical bourgeois political economy). To this extent classical economic theory is not simply 'false' either, but an appropriate (if not perfect) reflection of the phenomena of the capitalist mode of production and its inner relations. Value, money, profit, surplus value, etc. are necessary phenomenal forms (objective categories) of this mode of production, which can therefore only disappear along with it. In principle this critical theory (like any scientific theory) can be adopted by any individual. But a *whole class* can only adopt it if its own existence is not bound up with the need to remain *unconscious* of the complex system of relations. The only class which can assimilate the critique of political economy without damage to itself is the proletariat; and indeed the assimilation of this critique is the necessary precondition for its emancipation. While individual members of the bourgeoisie (like Engels, for example) can transcend the limits of their class position, it is inconceivable for Marx that a whole class should commit suicide in this way. There is, one might say, an existential barrier that prevents the capitalist class from accepting Marx's theory, which it has an existential interest, on the contrary, in ignoring or refuting.

In opposition to the theories of revolution of Bakunin or Blanqui (see BLANQUISM), which emphasized the 'subjective factor', the sheer commitment to revolution, and held it to be possible (in principle) at any time, Marx argued that the objective conditions of revolution must already have matured before the proletarian revolution could be victorious. It is true that he was not able to say exactly what these objective conditions are. Sometimes he says that a revolution will not occur before the productive forces have developed to the fullest extent possible in an existing form of society. In this case, stagnation would be the precondition for revolution; and the 'tendency of the rate of profit to fall', formulated in *Capital* III (chs. 13, 14), suggests that the capitalist system will ultimately reach such a point of stagnation. Engels ('Soziales aus Russland', *Der Volksstaat*, no. 43, 1875) asserts that the social revolution pursued by modern socialism requires 'not only a proletariat to carry out this transformation, but also a bourgeoisie in whose hands the social productive forces have developed to such an extent that they make possible the definitive abolition of class distinctions'.

In the German labour movement, which developed rapidly after 1875 in spite of government repression, the actual impossibility of revolutionary changes and the necessity of a cultural consolidation of working-class organizations produced the need for a distinctive 'world view'; a need which was reinforced by the requirements of working-class education and by the exclusion of the working class from the dominant bourgeois (and vestigially feudal) culture. This led to the development of Marxism as an all-embracing doctrine about the world which often directly replaced religious conceptions. As a result, the leading Marxist thinkers, such as Kautsky and Plekhanov, introduced into it elements of the prevailing popular materialist ideology. Marx's conception of history was applied, by Engels and others, to pre-capitalist societies, and was seen as a scientific achievement analogous to Darwin's theory of evolution. What Darwin did for nature, Marx had done for human society. The Marxist world view, thus elaborated, created in the labour movement – not only in Germany – a consciousness of being borne along by an invincible objective process of development, and in this way reinforced its self-awareness. Haeckel (1843-1919), the popularizer of Darwinism, was much more significant for this world view than was Hegel and his dialectic. The discrepancy between the growing numerical strength of the SPD – the first almost completely Marxist party – and its political impotence, was concealed and compensated by the formation of a sub-culture of its own, the ideological basis of which was Marxism.

Still greater than in Imperial Germany, with its semi-constitutionalism, was the discrepancy between Marxist revolutionary hopes and socio-political realities in pre-revolutionary Russia. There, Marxism was conveyed to the small minority of the population already employed in large-scale industry by an intellectual elite. Lenin's theory of the PARTY expressed this relationship very clearly. Marxism was an all-embracing world view and political theory which had to be brought into the proletariat from outside by an organization created specifically for the purpose – the 'party of a new type'. The ideology – as this doctrine of Marxism as a world view was later called, quite uncritically, in the Stalin era – was intended to ensure the discipline and exclusiveness of the cadre party, and its incontestable claim to leadership. Thus the relation between the working class and working-class consciousness was reversed: first the cadre party, with the help of the intellectuals who belonged to it, developed this class consciousness, of which the 'Marxist world view' formed the core; and subsequently this consciousness was transmitted to the working class, which grew rapidly after the revolution. While

Lenin was still prepared to accept revisions of his theory, on the basis of empirical circumstances, the world view doctrine congealed into dogma in the period of construction of a bureaucratic state socialism under Stalin. Marxism became the official state and party doctrine, which was an obligatory outlook for all Soviet citizens. It was in this period, roughly from the end of the 1920s, that the Marxist world view became a straitjacket in which not only all citizens, but science and art, were confined. There was a 'Marxist linguistics', a Marxist conception of cosmology, genetics, chemistry, etc. When it became apparent – after Stalin's death and under the new leadership – that the petty tutelage of the natural sciences by party ideologists had enormously disadvantaged Soviet science and technology in comparison with the West, the tutelage was withdrawn in that sphere; but it remained in the social and cultural sciences, in art and literature, though with some degree of liberalization.

Marx's contributions to a critical theory were not improved, but rather devalued, by their incorporation into a Marxist world view. It is obvious that Marx was a convinced atheist, but he regarded religion as a necessary product of unfree social conditions and was sure that with the establishment of a free association of producers (under communism) it would completely disappear. In no sense did he advocate that a 'materialist ideology' should take the place of religion; his favourite motto – de omnibus dubitandum – would have made him sceptical about that. On the contrary, the emergence and persistence of such an ideology, and still more a state-imposed, authoritatively determined world view, can be interpreted, following Marx himself, as the expression of unfree social and political conditions; and the dogmatic world view of SOVIET MARXISM would vanish of its own accord if the social and political structures of bureaucratic domination, which this ideology merely serves, were transcended.

In opposition to the all-embracing world view of Soviet Marxism there has developed – beginning with the early works of Lukács and Korsch – a so-called WESTERN MARXISM, which above all rejects the incorporation of a dialectic of nature into Marxism, as was attempted from Engels onwards, and emphasizes the importance of the 'subjective factor' and of openness to criticism.

For this 'Western' or 'critical' Marxism, moreover, the application of Marxist criticism to Marxism itself, first advocated by Korsch (1923), has also become important. The inability to undertake such critical self-correction has led to the sterility of Soviet Marxism, in spite of the substantial financial resources which are available to it for research.

Since the 1920s a non-dogmatic Marxism has profoundly influenced Western thought in many fields. At Cambridge, Piero Sraffa, Joan Robinson and Maurice Dobb continued over several decades a Marxist critique of political economy in which, it is true, elements of neo-Ricardian theory were incorporated (see DOBB; RICARDO AND MARX; SRAFFA). In the USA, Paul Baran (1957) initiated a critical Marxist approach to problems of UNDERDEVELOPMENT AND DEVELOPMENT in the Third World. The influence of Marxism has grown considerably in the fields of sociology and history, often combined with that of Max Weber, and French historians of the Annales school, in particular, have drawn extensively and fruitfully upon a Marxist approach (see ANNALES SCHOOL; HISTORIOGRAPHY). Some of these Western contributions have been sharply criticized by 'orthodox' Marxists, but their own work since the death of Lenin, with a few exceptions (e.g. Preobrazhensky, Varga), has not been marked by any notable achievements. In so far as Soviet philosophy and social theory have made any progress it is in spite of, rather than on the basis of Marxism, and above all in highly specialized fields such as mathematical logic and cybernetics, which also have very important technological (including military) applications. One of the principal reasons for the much greater liveliness and originality of Marxist thought in the West is, no doubt, that it has remained open to the influence of other, non-Marxist, advances in the social sciences, philosophy and other disciplines.

Reading
Bukharin, Nikolai 1921 (1925): Historical Materialism: A System of Sociology.
Fetscher, Iring 1970: Karl Marx and Marxism.
Hobsbawm, Eric J. et al. eds. (1980–): The History of Marxism.
Kolakowski, Leszek 1978: Main Currents of Marxism.
Korsch, Karl 1923 (1970): Marxism and Philosophy.

— 1929: *Die materialistische Geschichtsauffassung: eine Auseinandersetzung mit Karl Kautsky.*

Lichtheim, George 1961: *Marxism: An Historical and Critical Study.*

Lukács, Georg 1923 (1971): *History and Class Consciousness.*

Marcuse, Herbert 1958 (1964): *Soviet Marxism: A Critical Analysis.*

Stalin, J. V. 1938: *Dialectical and Historical Materialism.*

Vranicki, Predrag 1972, 1974: *Geschichte des Marxismus.* (2 vols.).

IRING FETSCHER

Marxism and the Third World   Awareness of Marxism in most countries of the Third World has come largely through the colonial connection and has been closely bound up with anti-imperialist struggle. Imperialism has defined the principal issues in that context and has put its distinctive stamp on Marxist thought and practice in, and about, the Third World. The central questions have concerned the impact of metropolitan capital on pre-capitalist social structures, the emergence of new classes, and the resulting patterns of class alignments and class contradictions that underlie the development of those societies and the conditions of revolutionary struggle.

Classical Marxism, that of Marx and Lenin in particular, had a vision of the effects of the introduction of (metropolitan) capital in 'backward societies' that was belied by actual developments. While they exposed and deplored its destructive and exploitative character, they took the view, nevertheless, that once the structure of the capitalist mode of production was introduced in a society, it would impose its own logic of development, breaking down pre-capitalist structures and generating the dynamic of capital accumulation and growth, in the same way as it had done in metropolitan Europe. Lenin offered a specific model, in his study *The Development of Capitalism in Russia*, which has provided a framework in terms of which such development has been analysed. He put forward the concept of a social formation (the Russian one) in which there was more than one mode of production, the rising capitalist mode challenging the dominant feudal mode of production and the feudal state. The principal contradiction in Russian society was the opposition between these two modes of production, which would be resolved by the dissolution of the pre-capitalist mode. This alignment of class forces represented the stage of the bourgeois-democratic revolution, though in Russia that would be accomplished under a resolute proletariat rather than the weak bourgeoisie. This was a two-stage theory of revolution, for the bourgeois-democratic stage had to be completed before the socialist revolution could materialize. Lenin was emphatic about this, repudiating populist notions of by-passing capitalism in a one-stage socialist revolution (see POPULISM). Furthermore, the bourgeois-democratic revolution entailed a *dissolution* of pre-capitalist structures in the social formation. This is the framework in terms of which analyses of development in Third World societies have proceeded and to which recent debates refer.

Lenin extrapolated his analysis of the development of capitalism in Russia to colonial societies, as if capitalism in non-colonized societies was homologous with that in metropolitan societies; this is an issue that has come up in recent debates. According to Lenin, with the introduction of capitalism a mighty democratic movement was growing 'everywhere in Asia', as it was in Russia. But, unlike Russia, in the colonies it was the bourgeoisie that was in the van of the struggle for the bourgeois-democratic revolution, for there the bourgeoisie was *still* siding with the people. This was linked up with national movements, for the bourgeoisie needed the nation state to fulfil the needs of capitalist development. It was not until the Second Congress of the Comintern in 1920 that this analysis was related to the tasks of the world communist movement and its class alliances. Now a specific reference to imperialism was substituted for earlier references to capitalism in general. But no questions were raised as to whether there was a structural difference between the two beyond the idea that imperialism represented capital that was not indigenous. Lenin's draft theses on the National and Colonial Questions asked what communist parties should do about anti-colonial (and anti-feudal) bourgeois-democratic movements in the colonized world. He proposed that the communist movement should look for the 'closest alliance' with the national bourgeoisie of these countries and that the parties of the proletariat should 'support' (Lenin did not say: 'lead') the national liberation movements. In that historic debate Lenin's position was challenged by an Indian communist, M. N. ROY, who opposed the call for collaboration with the bourgeois movements, arguing that the Comintern should devote its energies exclusively to the creation and development of the organization of the colonial proletariat and the peasantry, promoting their class struggle, leading them to revolution and the establishment of soviet republics. Roy's schema evaded the difficulty that at the time the proletariat and the proletarian parties hardly existed in the colonies.

There were unresolved theoretical problems underlying the formulation that Lenin put forward in 1920, which nevertheless remains the basic point of departure of rival positions in Marxist movements with regard to revolutionary struggles in the Third World, to this day. Historical materialism, and Lenin's analytical framework, posits a necessary contradiction between the development of capitalism in a social formation and the previously dominant pre-capitalist (feudal) social structure, which is resolved by the dissolution of the latter. This entails the existence of antagonistic contradictions between the classes located in the respective modes and an irreconcilable class struggle between them. How can we then reconcile such a conception with the idea of an *alliance* between metropolitan capital and native feudalism in the colony, the two classes being located in a capitalist and a pre-capitalist mode of production respectively? Likewise there is no structural explanation of the conflict between the indigenous (national) bourgeoisie of the colony and the ruling metropolitan bourgeoisie, although both are located in the same, capitalist, mode of production. Nevertheless it is postulated that contradictions between the colonial national bourgeoisie on the one hand, and on the other the metropolitan bourgeoisie and the feudal classes, determine the structural contradictions underlying the national bourgeois democratic revolution in the colonies, defining alignments in the class struggle.

In the light of the 1920 debate Lenin did reformulate his position in one respect and accepted the substitution of the words 'revolutionary liberation movements' (which were to be supported by the communists) for his original

formulation, namely 'bourgeois democratic movements', acknowledging thereby that the colonial bourgeoisie was as capable of compromise with imperialism as of opposition to it, thus becoming reformist and not to be supported by the communists. This acknowledged a reality but left the theoretical issues referred to above even more tangled, for it was not clear what conditions would determine its character either way. This reformulation did not alter Lenin's basic position, for he maintained that: 'There is not the slightest doubt that every nationalist movement can only be a bourgeois democratic movement' and that it would be utopian to think otherwise. The distinction between the 'progressive national bourgeoisie' and the reformist bourgeoisie in later years became convenient designations used by the Soviet state to legitimate its dealings with post-colonial states, in accordance with the exigencies of Soviet interests.

In 1928 the policy formulated by the Comintern for colonial societies was slightly modified against the background of the débâcle in China where a policy of unqualified collaboration with the Kuomintang, the party led by the national bourgeoisie, was imposed upon the Chinese communists by the Comintern, but nevertheless ended in the counter-revolution of 1926–27 when the CCP was decimated by Chiang Kai-shek. At the Sixth Congress of the Comintern in 1928, the national bourgeoisie was no longer represented as the leader of the national democratic revolution, being given to vacillation and compromise. The possibility was envisaged of proletarian leadership, but the overall formulation was left ambiguous. The emphasis was on revolution from below and the thesis also emphasized that 'along with the national liberation struggle the agrarian revolution constitutes the axis of the bourgeois-democratic revolution in the chief colonial countries.' This was the point of departure of Maoism (SEE MAO TSE-TUNG). But the Comintern line veered again in 1935 at its Seventh Congress, when the Popular Front policy was adopted, and for the colonized world faith in the 'national bourgeoisie' was restored.

In the 1970s a wholly new conception was espoused by the CPSU and communist parties oriented towards it, who resurrected the populist notion of by-passing capitalism, in the name of Lenin, and applied it to the Third World. The long-established two-stage theory of revolution was replaced by the slogan of the 'Non-capitalist Path to Development' which, it was argued, is made possible by the existence of a powerful socialist bloc in the world today. It is a statist conception of revolution from the top; it may be more accurate to say that it is an evolutionary conception rather than a revolutionary one. In the Third World generally, it was argued, the bourgeoisie is weak and the working class has not yet become a leading force. Instead there exist possibilities for the creation of a 'State of National Democracy', with Soviet aid, ruled by a 'United National-Democratic Front' under the leadership of *any* democratic class, be it the workers or peasants, the urban petty bourgeoisie, progressive intellectuals, revolutionary military officers, or the (national) bourgeoisie. The main criterion of the 'State of National Democracy' is its opposition to imperialism and cooperation with the socialist bloc. It was suggested that 'the general framework of this revolution in the course of its fulfilment *goes beyond the framework of capitalism*', though it was not made clear why or how. This conception raised large questions about the Marxist class theory of the state and questions of class alignments and class contradictions.

Against this, as well as against other conceptions of a peaceful parliamentary road to the national democratic revolution under the leadership of the national bourgeoisie, the 'Maoist line' represents a commitment to revolutionary struggle from below. The Maoist label is a self-designation of such movements which are not necessarily supported or encouraged by the Chinese State. This identication derives from the rhetoric adopted by the Chinese in the context of Sino-Soviet polemics, and only in particular countries such as India and Indonesia have the Chinese themselves urged communists to embark on the strategy of armed struggle; not in other cases such as Pakistan with whose rulers they happened to have a friendly relationship. The Maoist line emphasizes the importance of armed struggle against imperialism and feudalism, great emphasis being placed on the agrarian revolution, the main force of the national democratic revolution that must precede the socialist revolution.

The alternative positions summarized above were formulated within the theoretical framework laid down by Lenin which predicated the necessary *dissolution* of pre-capitalist structures with the development of capitalism. Present-day Marxists concerned with predominantly small peasant societies (which they consider pre-capitalist), as in parts of Africa, find on the contrary that the development of capitalism, instead of dissolving such pre-capitalist peasant societies, appears to conserve them and to subordinate them to its needs. The peasant societies are markets for industrial production, and become producers of certain commodities for the market; above all, they are reproducers of cheap migrant labour power for employment in large capitalist enterprises. Instead of the dissolution of pre-capitalist modes, it is argued, in Third World societies where capitalism does not develop from within the societies but is imposed from the outside, it has the effect of 'conservation-dissolution' of pre-capitalist peasant societies. This theory of (symbiotic) 'articulation of modes of production' now enjoys a wide measure of acceptance.

An alternative conception (Alavi 1982) which challenges the articulation concept as functionalist and voluntaristic, abandoning a central conception in historical materialism (namely, the idea of contradiction between modes of production which is the hinge of history), is the view that pre-capitalist structures have in fact been dissolved in the Third World and what exists there is capitalism. It rejects the view that social relations of production on the land are any longer feudal. Likewise it is argued that present-day peasant societies are no longer able to reproduce themselves in the manner of pre-capitalist societies, as they did before the colonial transformation. Having been drawn into the circuit of generalized commodity production of the capitalist economy they can no longer subsist on the basis of localized self-sufficiency as before. Export of migrant labour power is also a result of their structural transformation. They are subsumed under capital. But this formulation poses a problem. The Marxist conception of capitalism is premised on the separation of the producer from the means of production. In the case of these peasant societies, however, it is clear that their subsumption under capital (if that is accepted to be the case) takes place without such a separation, for the peasant continues to own his means of production.

A variant of this view is the conception of the control of production which proposes that capitalism in the Third World has specific structural features, so that it is not homologous with metropolitan capitalism. Whereas in the metropoles there is an 'integrated' form of division of labour, with regard to the production of capital goods and consumer goods, it is disarticulated in the Third World, without a balanced development of the two branches of the economy, and with a dependence upon exports and imports. There are numerous variations in the representation of the relationships between the Third World and the metropolis, ranging from the extreme positions of 'dependency' theories which see Third World countries totally in the grip of imperialism to other formulations, such as that of 'dependent development' and the 'post-colonial state', which acknowledge a degree of autonomy of Third World economies and Third World states from advanced capitalist countries. (See also COLONIALISM; DEPENDENCY THEORY; MARXISM IN AFRICA; MARXISM IN INDIA; MARXISM IN LATIN AMERICA; PEASANTRY.)

Reading

Aguilar, L. E. 1968: *Marxism in Latin America.*

Alavi, H. A. 1982: 'The Structure of Peripheral Capitalism'. In H. Alavi and T. Shanin, eds. *Introduction to the Sociology of Developing Societies.*

Alavi, H. A. *et al.* 1982: *Capitalism and Colonial Production.*

Amin, S. (1976): *Unequal Development.*

Cardoso, F. H. and Faletto, E. 1979: *Dependency and Development in Latin America.*

Carrère d'Encausse, H. and Schram, S. R. 1965 (1969): *Marxism and Asia.*

Kahn, J. and Llobera, J. R. 1981: *The Anthropology of Pre-capitalist Societies.*

HAMZA ALAVI

Marxism in Africa While Marxism in Africa has had various meanings and applications, none of these has seriously affected the course of African history since one or other first appeared there, during the 1920s, as a distant trumpet note; but three of them, if with differing impact, have made their mark. These refer to Marxism as historical analysis or sociology; Marxism as a Moscow-inspired conspiracy; and Marxism as a guide to nation-state development. The first of these, introducing the concept and methodology of class structure and corresponding analysis, has achieved profound and far-reaching influence since the 1950s, even in schools of socio-political thought where no such parentage may be admitted; and this influence seems likely to continue.

Marxism as a Moscow-inspired conspiracy knew a fruitless life between c.1925 and 1939. It followed the rise of the Comintern which, through West European communist parties, set up or tried to set up organizations and targets for anti-colonial agitation and action, largely by way of the French Communist Party, the only one in Western Europe with the weight and potential capable of making its voice heard in colonies. No more than a handful of Africans appear to have worked professionally for the Comintern; and not much in detail is as yet (1990) known of the Comintern's African endeavours, while the little that is known derives chiefly from colonial police archives (e.g. Services de Liaison avec les Originaux des Territoires d'Outre-Mer – the 'Slotfom' series – in Section Outre-Mer des Archives Nationales, Paris; and Public Record Office, London) which reflect official suspicion as often as they offer usable data.

Generally, the Marxist project always suffered, whether in the period of the Comintern or later, from the doctrine that revolution must begin with the action of the 'proletariat', necessarily in those years in Europe and not in Africa, so that radical change in Africa must await radical change in Europe. Only in the 1950s did relevant European communist parties begin to accept the primacy of anti-colonial nationalism in preparing the conditions, as it was argued, for the emergence of genuinely revolutionary projects in Africa. South of the Sahara, communist parties were formed in South Africa (in 1921) and Sudan (in 1944), with one or two projected parties elsewhere (for instance, Angola in 1954); but their effectiveness even in South Africa, where an urban working class had begun to take shape, was reduced or nullified by the vagaries of Comintern policy, internal splits and official repression. North of the Sahara, such communist parties as appeared (for instance, Algeria) were little more than provincial branches of the French party, and with correspondingly little influence.

Marxism as a guide to nation-state development achieved a wider currency and attempted application after the 1940s, and was duly woven into a number of territorial programmes aimed at socialist reconstruction. Seen as a usable alternative to the general Western project of post-colonial development by capitalism, this application gained credit and prestige by virtue of the increasingly clear inability of the Western project to produce expansive structural change even in those newly independent countries, such as Ghana and Tanzania, where that project had been consistently attempted.

But these socialist policies, both from their many inherent faults and from adverse conditions imposed by the existing world economic order, notably in respect of inter-continental terms of trade, proved either disappointing in their results or an outright failure. Or else, in several countries where Marxist-type programmes were attempted with rigour and determination the project came to grief because it was modelled on the authoritarian and rigidly centralizing practice of the USSR or other communist countries. This was flagrantly the case, after 1975, in Mozambique and Angola where the accepted Soviet model asked for rapid urban and industrial expansion at the cost of rural communities, thus playing into the hands of Pretoria-organized banditries, or at a pace, as in the launching of cooperatives in rural areas, that conditions would not allow. A partial value of the Soviet model was briefly achieved in Ethiopia after 1976, at least in implementing land reform where latifondist or quasi-feudal relations of production had persisted until 1974; but progress after that was stifled by the stiffly dictatorial nature of the post-1976 Ethiopian regime, and by its refusal to address the issue of ethnic autonomies for non-Amhara communities. By the early 1980s all these Soviet-style programmes were completely discredited.

Compared with these failures or futilities, sometimes reaching verbalist absurdity as with the 'socialism' of the People's Republic of Congo (formerly French Moyen-Congo) or with the 'African Socialism' of Kenya and Senegal, Marxism as a sociology has continued to exercise a major intellectual influence in many parts of Africa. This has remained a factor of penetrating strength, however often misread by 'Cold War' distortions of the 'West' or doctrinal orthodoxies of the 'East', whether Soviet or Chinese. Invariably achieved in spite of such distortions and orthodoxies, this success has derived from the theory and practice of several African political thinkers who have sought to develop Marx's analysis (rather than models said to be based on that analysis) in terms of post-colonial needs. Of these rare but sometimes remarkable persons the most perceptive have been those who took themselves through the processes of acute anti-colonial struggle, most notably the Guinea-Cape Verdean revolutionary Amílcar Cabral (1924–73) and some of his fellow activists.

In the deepening ideological void of the 1980s, with the 'capitalist solution' confronted by increasing impoverishment or confusion and the 'socialist solution' by outright collapse, African thinkers in the heritage of Marx have tended to argue that the structural disasters of the colonial period can be overcome, and space cleared for democratic development, only by far-reaching devolutions of operative power to local communities, whether rural or urban, capable of understanding their condition and working to change it by methods of self-development and autonomous initiative. In their perception the dominant class will continue to remain in the industrialized world: to the extent that this external domination can be successfully challenged on behalf of large and indigenous majorities, the solution has to be a process of class alliance in Africa whereby rapidly increasing populations can be led to grasp the realities of the world as it is now, and, reacting to these realities, can find united means of autonomous self-assertion. In this context, the Marxist debate in Africa vigorously continues.

Reading

Allen, Chris 1989: *Benin.*

Cabral, Amílcar 1980: *Unity and Struggle: Selected Writings.*

Rudebeck, Lars 1983: 'On the Class Basis of the National-Liberation Movement of Guinea-Bissau'.

Simons, H. J. and Simons, R. E. 1969: *Class and Colour in South Africa 1850–1950.*

Szentes, Tamás 1973: *The Political Economy of Underdevelopment.*

BASIL DAVIDSON

Marxism in Eastern Europe The history of East European Marxism as a properly differentiated topic begins with the integration of this region into the Soviet bloc. Previously, the works of some major figures who originated from or ended up in the countries of today's Eastern Europe belonged to the history of SOVIET MARXISM (e.g. Dimitrov, Varga, Lukács between *c*. 1930 and 1945) or to what Merleau-Ponty called WESTERN MARXISM (e.g. Lukács 1918–29, Bloch). Similarly, if more controversially, only the non-orthodox approaches belong to the topic: the orthodoxy of the post-1945 period (its content, stages of development and social function) belongs to the career of *Soviet* Marxism in Eastern Europe. Finally, Yugoslav Marxism, though located geographically in this region, belongs intellectually, for the most part, to the Western Marxist body of thought.

Marxism in Eastern Europe should be analysed in terms of four distinct stages that involve, to be sure, different time sequences in the relevant countries: East Germany (GDR), Poland, Czechoslovakia and Hungary. In this context the term *revisionism* which has now come to mean the project of reforming the theory and practice of the existing regime, on the bases of its own (supposedly) Marxist-Leninist principles, needs to be supplemented by three others. First, the critical confrontation of the regime with the results of the recovery of the original Marxian philosophy and social theory, clearly different from the official versions, was aptly named (by Lukács) the *renaissance* of Marxism. The attempt to apply some version of the classical social theory of Marx directly to societies of the Soviet type, far rarer in Eastern Europe than in the West, is a logical consequence of this stage. Second, the project of developing critical theories of their own societies on the normative foundations of some major elements of Marx's social philosophy, and on the general model of his critique of political economy, but using entirely new analytical means, is best characterized as the *reconstruction* (Habermas) of Marxism. Third, the construction of post-Marxian critical perspectives based on the explicit intention to break with the tradition should nevertheless be called the *transcendence* of Marxism in the sense of cancellation/preservation (*Aufhebung*) to the extent that such an effort involves

important if only implicit continuities with 're-born' and 'reconstructed' varieties of the theory.

Evidently, *revisionism* is the most universal of all the stages of East European Marxism. (It is also the only one having a distinct parallel in the Soviet Union.) Revisionism is however also the most paradoxical stage. On the one hand it was indeed a confrontation of totalitarian ruling parties with their own original Marxist-Leninist principles, among which some relatively non-authoritarian ones were diligently selected. On the other hand revisionism also represented a clear opening for a democratic and pluralist challenge going far beyond any conceivable understanding of Leninism. The fact that these elements were sometimes actually mixed together by a single figure such as W. Harich does not make the mixture any less contradictory. Revisionism in theory was naturally enough best represented in the two officially permitted social scientific fields: philosophy and economics. In philosophy thinkers such as Lukács, Bloch and their students, Harich and his *Deutsche Zeitschrift für Philosophie*, the groups around the Polish student journal *Pro Prostu*, and the Hungarian 'Petöfi Circle', sought to eliminate from Marxism determinism and objectivism (neglect of human subjectivity and agency) in epistemology and anthropology, scientism and historicism in ethics. In many instances it was believed that a theory so revised would finally become the originally wished for vehicle not only of general reform (end of police repression, legal reform, elimination of censorship, reduction of administrative centralism) but also, for some revisionists at least, of democratization (workers' councils, free unions, free discussion and even pluralism in the ruling party, at times even the revival of a multi-party system). While in some cases (especially in Poland) such a programme was eventually seen as incompatible with any form of Leninism, elsewhere there were attempts to compare favourably the Lenin of the *Philosophical Notebooks* and *State and Revolution* (and even the trade-union debates) with the Lenin of *Materialism and Empirio-criticism* and *What is to be Done?* For most revisionists the consistent and uncompromising anti-Leninism already typified by Kolakowski lay still in the future.

In economics, revisionism represented at the very least the first intellectual context in which ideas of 'market socialism' (which had in part independent origins) could be fully represented. On a purely economic level to be sure there is a good deal of continuity among the approaches that characterize all stages of East European Marxism, including post-Marxian discussions of possible reform models. The desire to work out an optimal mix of central planning and decentralized market mechanisms goes back to O. Lange in Poland, and F. Behrens and A. Benary in East Germany, in the early 1950s, and the relevant theoretical models were greatly enriched in the period after 1956 by economists such as W. Brus, M. Kalecki, O. Sik, J. Kosta, and J. Kornai. What characterized these efforts in the context of revisionism as here defined was an almost exclusive focus on purely economic issues and an avoidance of the political and social prerequisites for the structural reform of the system. Such was more or less the position of the Czech economic reformers of the 'Prague Spring'. Elsewhere too, the economics profession would find little in common with the renaissance of Marxism, since the desire to stand by the original sources of the tradition was always the definition of dogmatism in this field. The programme of the reconstruction of Marxism on the other hand was bound to seem redundant to economists who were already utilizing non-Marxian concepts for the purpose of constructing models of a socialist economy, a problem area deliberately bypassed in the classical critique of political economy. Only the transcendence of Marxism was to have an echo in economics, but this influence is restricted to Poland (Lipinski, Kowalik and in exile Brus) and to a much lesser extent Hungary.

The renaissance of Marxism (also called 'philosophy of praxis') involved a general abandonment of Leninism and a return to the original sources and historical values of Marxism. The trend as a whole responded to the cynical ideological ritualism of the ruling parties in periods of the quiescence of social movements. Intellectually this stage of East European Marxism had a good deal in common with the Western New Left and the *Praxis* group in Yugoslavia. In Eastern Europe, however, the best results of the renaissance of Marxism were confined to philosophy. This involved above all a return to the young Marx, but also a rediscovery of the same philosophical concerns in the critique of political economy (A. Schaff, Kolakowski, Lukács, A. Heller, G. Márkus). Almost universal was the study and interpretation, in this context, of the writings of the young Lukács, Korsch and Gramsci. At times the original perspectives were enriched by relevant non-Marxist philosophical traditions, e.g. those of Heidegger (Kosik), Husserl (Vajda) and Neo-Kantianism (Heller). But in only one significant case, Modzelewski and Kuron's *Open Letter*, was a sophisticated version of the classical Marxian social theory applied to the Soviet-type systems. The theorists of the renaissance of Marxism were in fact well acquainted with the best versions of this classical theory (Márkus, Kis, Bence), but on the whole they were sceptical about the applicability of the class theory, the force relations model of social change, the value theory, the concept of commodity fetishism, and the notion of the state as superstructure, in East European contexts. Marx was thus preserved, but precisely as he did not want to be, as a philosopher. While it is unfair to argue (Szelenyi and Konrad 1979) that the philosophical utopianism of the renaissance of Marxism implied a neo-Bolshevik critique of Bolshevism, i.e. a critique hoping to replace the existing system under the aegis of ideas that can only degenerate into a defence of an equally authoritarian social order, the silence of the philosophers of praxis concerning social theory indicated a secret belief that they would not be able to utilize even the best version of the classical theory without a reversion to either mythology or vanguardism or both. And indeed while Kuron and Modzelewski guarded themselves against Leninism only by reviving the classical myths of the working class and council democracy (see COUNCILS), the last important theorist of the renaissance of Marxism, R. Bahro, writing in a very different context ten years later, openly re-established the links between the classical theory and Leninist politics.

The reconstruction and the transcendence of neo- and post-Marxism represent two responses to the new situation in Poland and Hungary. While on the level of the most recent discussions of political programmes in the alternative public spheres of the two countries post-Marxism is overwhelmingly dominant, on the level of theoretical output the achievement of neo-Marxism is certainly more impressive. This difference can in part be explained in terms of partially different origins. The year 1968 of course represents the final end of all illusions among critical intellectuals everywhere in Eastern Europe (except perhaps the GDR) concerning the structural reform of the systems from above. Not only the defeat of the Prague Spring, but especially the lesson that the ruling parties drew from it was significant. In the whole subsequent period these parties were staunchly determined not to risk any economic or administrative reforms that could spill over into politics or culture. Given this new attitude, those who came out of the tradition of East European Marxism were forced to realize that structural changes which would decisively alter the relationship of the party-state to society had to be introduced in one way or another from below. However, the ways in which such a possibility could be explored were decisively affected by the social contexts of the respective countries. In countries where the high level of repression blocked the possibility of establishing a more or less functioning alternative public sphere, no new language of political discourse could be developed, leading either to the continued use of the old concepts, if without enthusiasm (the pattern in the GDR), or to a retreat to the absolutely minimal position all those in opposition can agree upon, the language of human rights (Czechoslovakia). In the context of the timid Hungarian modernization from above, which was mainly confined to the economy but has resulted in the preservation of a relatively improved legal framework, the possibility of the development of an alternative public sphere (though without any relation to other social forces) has led to a discussion that is primarily theoretical in nature. In Poland finally, where the existence of a developed alternative public sphere has from the beginning been determined by the power and the requirements of a growing social movement, the discussion has been primarily political, practical. Whereas in Hungary the possibilities of structural change were, at least initially, explored on the level of an analysis of the dynamics of societies increasingly affected by a crisis of administrative and economic rationality and by the modernizing attempts from above ('crisis management') designed to deal with this situation, in Poland theorists tended to take the point of view of social movements exploring in practice the limits and plasticity of their social formation, a perspective hardly foreign to the philosophy of praxis.

The theoretical character of the discussion in Hungary and its neo-Marxist language has also been a function of the continued presence, until 1977 at least, of an influential intellectual circle, the Budapest Lukács School. The ties of this circle to parts of the Western New Left entailed a wider international audience which continued to speak a Marxist language. The programme of the reconstruction of Marxism grew out of this exchange, which involved a rather unique East European reception of Frankfurt and Starnberg varieties of 'Critical Theory'. Elsewhere only the Polish sociologist Staniszkis has participated in an analogous enterprise, which can be most generally described as an attempt to build a dynamic social theory around concepts derived variously from Weber, Polanyi, post-Keynesian economics, systems theory and Marx himself, preserving nonetheless the model character of the Marxian critical theory. On these bases important first steps were taken to analyse the new structure of economic reproduction in Soviet-type societies (Kis, Bence – 'Marc Rakovski' – Markus), the new forms of stratification (Hegedüs, Konrád, Szelényi), the political and ideological institutions (Feher, Heller), and the place of social movements in the social system (Staniszkis). Nevertheless while it has been occasionally possible from neo-Marxist perspectives to anticipate elements of the new politics of the opposition in Poland (Szelényi and Konrád, Hegedüs), more generally Marxist perspectives tended to occlude what in fact was *new* in the new social movement (Staniszkis, and on a different intellectual basis, Bahro). Writing at the very time when a social movement in Poland was already introducing from below innovations into the existing system on a hitherto unprecedented scale, neo-Marxist theorists tended to construct either a closed, almost unchangeable social structure apparently capable of withstanding or integrating reform elements from above or below (Rakovski, Markus, Feher, Heller, Staniszkis), or to work out models of social change on ultimately rigid historical materialist premises which led to illusory consequences concerning the probable triumph of a reformist, technocratic stage of state socialism (Szelényi and Konrád).

It was these theoretical problems, in the historical context of the full unfolding of the Polish social movement, that led to an almost universal replacement of neo-Marxism by post-Marxism also in Hungary, despite the fact that there was no chance of a Polish type of movement developing. Today neo-Marxist approaches are pursued on the whole by Hungarian (as against Polish) theorists in exile, who of course write for Western radical audiences, whereas the post-Marxist position has been dominant among most of the important theorists of the Polish (Modzelewski, Michnik, Kuron et al.) and Hungarian (Kis, Bence, Vajda et al.) internal oppositions. (Hegedüs and Staniszkis seem to be the only exceptions to the trend at home.)

Philosophically speaking post-Marxism is based on a reconsideration of the state and civil society problem first articulated by Hegel and the young Marx. It is in this context of course that post-Marxism is directly continuous with the work of the renaissance of Marxism. Following Kolakowski's lead, post-Marxist theorists tend to reject as inevitably authoritarian the Marxian solution to the problem of the alienation inherent in the state/civil society duality, namely, a democratic unification of state and society. They seek instead to defend or re-establish the institutional mediations (Vajda) between society and the state: legality, plurality, publicity. Accordingly, the new social movement could be interpreted (Kuron) as the active constitution or self-constitution of a civil society hitherto suppressed or subjugated or even obliterated by totalitarian states. Some of the most significant writings of the post-Marxists (Kolakowski, Kuron, Michnik) dealt with the strategic questions of establishing civil society, and as such they both anticipated and contributed to the Solidarity movement of 1980–81. Particularly noteworthy were the achievements of KOR in establishing new post-Leninist relations between intellectuals and workers. Nevertheless post-Marxist theoretical approaches have hardly even begun to confront two serious problems that arise in this context. First, on the philosophical level the rejection of Marx's solution to the civil society problem, however justified, has rarely led to a clarification by post-Marxist theorists of their relationship to the Hegelian and Marxian critique of the capitalist version of civil society. If this critique is simply dismissed

(Kolakowski), the theorist comes perilously close to an apology of capitalist society. If the critique is accepted at least in part (Vajda) the theorist has still to conceptualize the project of a possible version of civil society liberated not only from the authoritarian state, but also from its historical ties to capitalist societies. Many aspects of this problem were in fact creatively confronted by the Polish movement of 1980–81, but theoretical reflection even here lagged behind actual practice. Such a lag was pointed out by Michnik in a text smuggled out of Bialoleka prison.

On a second level too there existed a set of unsolved problems for post-Marxist approaches. Taking primarily the point of view of the social movement it was almost impossible to account adequately for either the objective constraints of the existing system or its self-induced difficulties, both of which decisively affect the field of action of those seeking to reconstitute civil society, given the impossibility of overthrowing the East European regimes altogether. So far, within the framework of post-Marxism, this problem has been addressed only by historical exploration of the differential traditions of societal independence in the various East European countries and the Soviet Union, which supposedly account for the stability of the system at the centre and instability at some of the peripheries. But while such a historicist turn helps to overcome the structuralist bias of neo-Marxist theories (Vajda 1981) its own relationship to social change is primarily retrospective. At best, when taken alone the approach is an important defensive response to the destruction of memory and traditions in the Soviet-type societies (Kundera). But its relevance to a dynamic social theory could be established only if historical and structural methods were brought together. The recently renewed interest of some post-Marxist theorists like Vajda in structural analysis, as well as the raising of the problem of a socialist civil society by some neo-Marxists like Szelényi indicates that all polemics aside there are important links between the two tendencies, whose very plurality indicates the health of some sectors of East European intellectual life.

Reading

Bahro, R. 1978: *The Alternative in Eastern Europe.*

Brus, W. 1975: *Socialist Ownership and Political Systems.*

Erard, Z. and Zygier, G. M. 1978: *La Pologne: une société en dissidence.*

Hegedüs, A. *et al.* 1974 (1976): *Die Neue Linke in Ungarn.*

Kolakowski, L. 1968: *Toward a Marxist Humanism.*

— 1978: *Main Currents of Marxism*, vol. III.

Konrád, G. and Szelényi, I. 1979: *The Intellectuals on the Road to Class Power.*

Labedz, L. ed. 1962: *Revisionism. Essays on the History of Marxist Ideas.*

Rakovski, M. 1978: *Toward an East European Marxism.*

Silnitsky, F. *et al.* eds. 1979: *Communism and Eastern Europe.*

Vajda, M. 1981: *The State and Socialism.*

ANDREW ARATO

Postscript

The collapse of the communist regimes has changed profoundly the conditions in which East European Marxism developed. The various phases of revisionist thought discussed in this entry were directed against political dictatorship and against the 'official' Marxism which provided its ideological support, but since these objects of criticism have now disappeared, so too has much of the *raison d'être* of a distinctive style of Marxist thought. In particular, the emphasis, in what is here termed 'post-Marxism', on the re-establishment of a civil society independent of the state is no longer necessary, and Marxist thinkers are now likely to become involved in the more general discussion, such as has been taking place among Marxists everywhere, about the specific nature of civil society in a democratic socialist system. Beyond this, however, some other preoccupations of the revisionists (shared with Western Marxists), in particular with MARKET SOCIALISM, now seem less relevant, at least for the time being, as some of the East European societies move towards the restoration of a capitalist market economy. More generally, it seems probable that post-Marxist schools of thought will predominate in the immediate future, but the eventual outcome of the intellectual confrontation between neo-Marxism, post-Marxism and other Marxist schools remains unclear while the new economic and social structures in Eastern Europe are still taking shape (see CRISIS IN SOCIALIST SOCIETY).

TOM BOTTOMORE

Marxism in India Contributions within the Marxist tradition in India have derived their major stimulus from the specificity and complexity of Indian society. Their concern has been more with the analysis of this complexity for the purpose of political praxis, applying wherever possible traditional Marxist categories, than with the development of a self-conscious Marxist theoretical tradition. Consequently, theoretical innovations have been a by-product of concrete analyses; and discussion has paid closer attention to the classics, not only of Marx and Engels, but of Lenin and also Mao, even when diverging from them, than in the contemporary West. Marxism in India may well resent being labelled 'Indian Marxism'.

An important area of discussion has been the nature of the pre-colonial social formation, the role of caste within it and the potentialities for capitalist development that existed. While the term 'feudalism' has been used to characterize the earlier social formation by Kosambi (1956) and Sharma (1965), both aware of its difference from the European model, and the former in particular emphasizing two contributory processes, 'feudalism from above' (alienation of tax rights by rulers) and 'feudalism from below' (the emergence of landowners from within the village), others (e.g. Mukhia) have objected to this usage, both on account of the concept becoming too inclusive, and also because of the connotation of an inevitable transition, but for colonial intervention, to capitalism. The term 'Asiatic mode of production' (see ASIATIC SOCIETY) is still occasionally used (e.g. by Namboodiripad 1966), but less and less frequently, mainly because it is thought not to do justice to the considerable stratification within the peasantry, the social divide between the peasants and labourers (the latter belonging generally to the 'untouchable' castes), the significant discontinuities that emerge over time, notwithstanding the continuity provided by caste ideology and the village as the unit of social organization, the growth of commercial production and the contradictions leading to peasant revolts. The main change relates to the growth of urban centres, craft production and central power, following the Muslim conquest, for which Habib suggests the neutral (but not altogether satisfactory) term 'medieval social formation'. The potentialities for capitalist development are variously estimated. Some think they were great; but others (for instance, Habib) are less sanguine, since it is only the surplus that was commoditized, peasant revolts were fragmented because of caste factors and often led by local lords ('zamindars') and artisan production was shackled by the nobility's control. The decline of science, following the victory of Shankara's philosophical idealism and the šuppression of materialist tendencies (Chattopadhyaya 1959), was an interlinked process of great importance.

There has not been much explicit controversy among Marxists on the overall economic impact of COLONIALISM; the attempt has rather been to fill in the picture (e.g. by Bagchi 1982). A nagging theoretical question, however, has remained: what is the relationship of colonial exploitation to the domestic exploitation of the working class in the metropolis? The easy part of the answer is: colonial labour is also exploited (even more ruthlessly) to provide cheap primary products, and in addition there is the direct 'drain' of surplus value. The difficult part is: the sale of British cloth in India is based on the exploitation of British labour; where do the displaced Indian artisans theoretically fit in? Since their dispossession does not add to the quantum of surplus value produced, does it play any *necessary* role in the process of capitalist development?

On the anti-colonial struggle, the question has been raised: since this struggle was multiclass, should the communists have striven for influence by playing down internal class struggle? One view would say that they should have, and that their not doing so in the 1930s and 1940s is what kept their influenced restricted (Bipan Chandra); others would argue that this would have made them tail behind the bourgeois leadership (note the collapse of the social democrats), that though 1947 was a crucial stage in the democratic revolution it is not the end of it, and that the struggle for proletarian leadership over the unfinished democratic revolution continues.

Some authors (R. Guha and others in *Subaltern Studies*) have questioned of late the tradi-

tional Marxist interpretations of popular struggles in the colonial period. Using non-'elite' data sources on some struggles of the 'subaltern classes' (Gramsci), they have emphasized the role of the 'autonomous' ideologies informing these struggles. While the attempt has unleashed a quest for new source material, provided a counterpoint to economic determinist interpretations and stimulated (indirectly perhaps) fresh Marxist research in the cultural and literary terrains, its departure from traditional class analysis has brought forth the charge that the protagonists of many of the 'subaltern' struggles thus highlighted were often a ragbag of different classes, their ideology not really 'autonomous' but a refracted form of the dominant caste ideology, so that 'subaltern studies' restrict rather than expand Marxist understanding for the purpose of praxis.

The political question of whether a proletariat-led democratic revolution, involving among other things radical land redistribution, still remains on the agenda in the post-independence period, and, if so, how and when conditions would 'ripen' for it, has implicitly permeated much of Marxist discussion on developments in recent years. A prime example is the debate on 'the mode of production in agriculture' (a misnomer since agriculture is not a separate entity), where the participants included Thorner, Rudra, Patnaik, Chattopadhyaya, Bhaduri, Alavi, Banaji, Sau and many others, and which raised a whole gamut of basic questions. Is the extent of use of wage labour *per se* an adequate index of the size of capitalist agriculture or is capitalism characterized by something more, namely that the accumulation process must be inherent to it (without which even Mughal India would have sizeable capitalism)? Is there a tendency towards capitalist development in agriculture (see AGRARIAN QUESTION), and on what empirical criteria can we identify it? Does the existence of such a tendency warrant the treatment of agriculture as *de facto* capitalist (or is Lenin's distinction between 'trend' and 'moment' important), in which case the programme of the agrarian revolution would have to be altered away from the issue of land redistribution? What are the characteristics of the capitalism emerging, i.e. landlord or peasant capitalism, and what are the limits to it? What is meant by semi-feudalism, what is its relationship with emerging capitalism and how does it constrain the productive forces? How can classes be identified empirically in an agrarian structure of this sort? Is the concept of the 'colonial mode of production' a useful analytical category, or is it merely descriptive? Though the debate subsided (rather than ended), echoes of it are still found in discussions of particular issues, e.g. the inter-sectoral terms of trade (Mitra 1977).

Another example is the discussion on the role of imperialism and the nature of the bourgeoisie (Bagchi 1982, Chandra 1988). The comprador bourgeoisie/national bourgeoisie distinction, infrequently used even in the colonial period (reflecting perhaps the discrimination against the local bourgeoisie in every sphere), and generally substituted by the concept of the 'dual nature' or 'contradictory character' of the bourgeoisie as a whole, was revived by some in the wake of the Chinese Cultural Revolution, when subscription to the theory of 'social imperialism' allowed a branding of the entire ruling class as comprador. The more prevalent view, however, sees the bourgeoisie as making compromises with imperialism and working out a *modus vivendi* even while struggling for some space of its own, the extent of its concessions depending on the acuteness of its domestic contradictions. The public sector is seen as a promoter of capitalism and a potential bulwark against imperialism (until metropolitan capital and agencies like the World Bank start directly penetrating it, as in recent years), rather than any harbinger of a non-capitalist path.

The role of CASTE in modern India, though discussed by some (e.g. Ranadive, Omvedt 1976), has not perhaps received the attention it deserves from Indian Marxists. The 'nationality' question, however, has occupied them for a long time. On the basis of the commonly held view that India was a country with many nationalities, the Communist Party had for years upheld (following Lenin) the right to self-determination of individual nationalities, and even supported partition in 1947 on the grounds that Muslims constituted a separate nationality. While the identification of religion with nationality may not find much support among Marxists today, the term 'nationality' being defined in a more orthodox manner, recent secessionist movements have revived the old question: if

India is a conglomeration of nationalities, is there any basis for the concept of an 'Indian nation', and should its integrity be defended against secessionist movements? (see NATIONALISM).

Many today would answer this question differently. For example, A. Guha (1982) has proposed the concept of a dual national consciousness, a pan-Indian nationalism, crystallized during the anti-colonial struggle, coexisting with the local, e.g. Bengali or Maharashtrian, nationality consciousness which dates back earlier; the corollary is that tendencies overemphasizing one to the exclusion of the other have a mutually reinforcing effect, and are potentially pernicious because of their disruptive consequences for common mass struggles. A parallel development spanning large sections of the political left has been to oppose secessionist movements (a departure from Lenin) as strengthening imperialism, while demanding much greater regional autonomy and genuine federalism (an approach that pre-dates and anticipates Gorbachev). (See COLONIAL AND POSTCOLONIAL SOCIETIES; HINDUISM.)

Reading

Bagchi, A. K. 1982: *The Political Economy of Underdevelopment.*

Byres, T. J. and Mukhia, H. eds. 1985: *Feudalism and Non-European Societies.*

Chandra, N. K. 1988: *The Retarded Economies.*

Chattopadhyaya D. P. 1959: *Lokayata: A Study in Ancient Indian Materialism.*

Guha, Amelendu 1982: *The Indian National Question: A Conceptual Frame.*

Habib, Irfan 1963: *Agrarian System of Mughal India.*

Kosambi, D. D. 1956 (1975): *An Introduction to the Study of Indian History.*

Mitra, Ashok 1977: *Terms of Trade and Class Relations.*

Namboodiripad, E. M. S. 1966: *Economics and Politics of India's Socialist Pattern.*

Omvedt, Gail 1976: *Cultural Revolt in a Colonial Society: The Non-Brahmin Movement in Western India, 1873–1930.*

Patnaik, U. ed. 1989: *Agrarian Relations and Accumulation: The Mode of Production Debate.*

Sharma, R. S. 1965: *Indian Feudalism c.300–1200.*

Subaltern Studies 1982– : ed. Ranajit Guha. Vols 1–6.

PRABHAT PATNAIK

Marxism in Latin America   The diffusion of Marxism in Latin America received an initial impulse with the formation of socialist and communist political parties during the first decades of this century. The official Marxism which was espoused in Latin America was Eurocentric and Marx's few, ill-informed, and superficial writings on Latin America did not help. The recognition of Marx's break with his Eurocentrism as revealed in his writings on Ireland, China, Turkey and the RUSSIAN COMMUNE, among others, has come late. José Aricó has done much through his writings (1980) and editorial work in propagating Marx's changed position on the peripheries of capitalism. Various generations of students throughout the Spanish-speaking world have learnt their Marxism from the Chilean Marta Harnecker who has written by far the most popular Marxist textbook (1969). Her brand of Marxism is of a structuralist-Althusserian kind (see STRUCTURALISM and ALTHUSSER).

The first and foremost Latin American Marxist who began to 'think Marx' from Latin America was José Carlos Mariátegui (1928). His writings were the first major challenge to the official Eurocentric Marxism in Latin America and opened the way to a Latin American Marxism. Mariátegui's analysis differed from official Marxism in a variety of ways. He rejected the deterministic as well as the social democratic revisionist strands in Marxism. He argued that the development of capitalism in Latin America differed from the classical European model because it did not eliminate pre-capitalist social relations of production and only intensified the domination of imperialist monopoly capital. Imperialist capital was linked to, and profited from, pre-capitalist relations. Furthermore, Mariátegui saw no scope for the development of an autochthonous or independent national capitalism since the NATIONAL BOURGEOISIE in Latin America was unable and unwilling to perform the progressive role it played in Europe. In his view the socialist revolution could not wait until capitalism had fully developed.

Mariátegui was also one of the first Marxists to highlight the revolutionary potential of the PEASANTRY. Additionally, he held that the indigenous peasant communities could constitute the germ of the socialist transformation in the Peruvian countryside. His pioneering analysis of the Indian issue challenged the prevailing view that the 'indigenous question' was a racial and cultural issue, arguing instead that it was rooted in the land tenure problem. In short, Mariátegui foreshadows some of the central issues of, and debates within, Latin American Marxism, articulating a position which from today's perspective is sometimes labelled as neo-Marxist or national Marxist.

Despite the pioneering writings of Mariátegui it was not until the 1960s that official Marxism (whose principal guardians were the communist parties) began to lose its dominance, being challenged by the Cuban revolution and the rise of neo-Marxism. This new Marxism in Latin America made a major contribution to the theory of REVOLUTION and TRANSITION TO SOCIALISM, to the analysis of internal relations of exploitation and domination through the conceptualization of internal colonialism, to Marx's theory of POPULATION through the concept of marginality, to the debate on MODE OF PRODUCTION, and above all to the theory of imperialism with DEPENDENCY THEORY.

A key contributor to the theory of revolution and transition to socialism is Ernesto 'Ché' Guevara, the most legendary Latin American Marxist. He was a revolutionary fighter in Cuba and elsewhere ('the heroic guerrilla'), a Marxist thinker, as well as a policy-maker in the Cuban revolutionary government. In his theory of revolution for the Third World he stressed the need for armed struggle and the importance of the peasantry. He argued that the guerrilla group (the insurrectionary *foco* or nucleus) is the catalyst which would bring about all the necessary objective and subjective conditions for the revolution. Similarly, with regard to the transition to socialism, he argued that it was necessary to forge a new consciousness (create the 'new man') which in turn would accelerate the development of the productive forces, and not the other way round as held by orthodox Marxists. For Guevara, material incentives were secondary to moral incentives in the building of the new society. It is of interest to note that Mandel sided with Guevara in Guevara's debate with Charles Bettelheim on the transition to socialism.

With regard to internal colonialism, González Casanova finds that many of the factors which defined a situation of COLONIALISM *between* countries also exist *within* some independent Third World countries (see Kay 1989). It is this similarity which prompts him to coin the term internal colonialism when referring to the latter. The analysis of internal colonialism challenges the dualism of modernization theory and criticizes orthodox Marxist theory for neglecting to explore the links between class, ethnicity and region. At first colonial and class relations appear intermixed, with the former being dominant. With the subsequent development of CAPITALISM, class relations increasingly enter into conflict with colonial relations. Internal colonialism – according to Rodolfo Stavenhagen – by maintaining ethnic divisions, impedes the development of class relations as ethnic consciousness overrides CLASS CONSCIOUSNESS.

The Marxist view on marginality originated as a critique of the modernization view on marginality and as a debate within Marxist theory (see Kay 1989). José Nun (1969) created a new category – 'marginal mass' – which he differentiated from the Marxist concepts of 'relative surplus population' and 'industrial reserve army of labour'. Likewise, Quijano (1974) proposed the concepts of 'marginal labour' and 'marginal pole of the economy' and wrestled with their relationship to existing Marxist categories. Quijano and Nun pinpoint the problem of marginalization as originating from the increasing control of foreign capital over the industrialization process in Latin America, accentuating its monopolization. Nun argues that the penetration of MULTINATIONAL CORPORATIONS into Latin America has created such a large relative surplus population that part of it is not only afunctional but even dysfunctional for capitalism. This part of the relative surplus population does not perform the function of an industrial reserve army of labour as it will never be absorbed into this hegemonic capitalist sector, even during the expansionary phase of the cycle, and therefore it has no influence whatsoever on the level of wages of the labour force employed by the hegemonic sector. Thus, in Nun's view, a new phenomenon, not foreseen by Marx, has emerged in the dependent countries. For this reason he feels justified in coining a new concept, i.e. 'marginal mass'.

Quijano's and Nun's theory of marginality has generated a lively debate, largely from a Marxist perspective. The discussion has centred on three major issues: (1) the extent to which the marginality concepts differ from Marx's industrial reserve army of labour; (2) the contribution of marginals to the process of capital accumulation and their articulation to the dominant mode of production; and (3) the relationship between marginality and dependency. With regard to (1) the critics query the need for new concepts and hold that existing Marxist categories are adequate. With regard to (2) they argue that the marginals' contribution to capital accumulation is far greater than suggested by the *marginalistas*, who are criticized for underestimating their significance for the reproduction of capitalism. The critics also put greater emphasis on analysing the social relations of production of the marginal sector, which they characterize as being largely non-capitalist but functional for capitalist accumulation. Finally, with regard to (3) they stress that marginality depends as much on internal as external factors.

Turning to dependency theory, at least two key positions can be differentiated: reformist and Marxist. The reformist dependency approach is best seen as a further development of the Latin American structuralist school originating in CEPAL (the Economic Commission for Latin America). Within the Marxist dependency camp are the writings of Ruy Mauro Marini, Theotonio Dos Santos, André Gunder Frank, Oscar Braun, Vania Bambirra, Aníbal Quijano, Edelberto Torres-Rivas and Alonso Aguilar, among others. The emergence of a Marxist theory of dependency arose out of a realization that Marx never fully tackled the question of COLONIAL AND POST-COLONIAL SOCIETIES. While the classical Marxist theory of IMPERIALISM addressed the new stages and aspects of capitalism, it was mainly concerned with the imperialist countries and had little to say on the underdeveloped countries, a gap which the Marxist *dependentistas* sought to fill. Furthermore, they are critical of the classical theories' progressive view of capitalism in Third World countries. For these reasons the Marxist *dependentistas* are sometimes referred to as neo-Marxists.

Among the Marxist dependency writers, Marini (*1973*) has made the most systematic theoretical effort to determine the specific laws which govern the dependent economies. Marini's central thesis is that dependence involves the over-exploitation – or super-exploitation – of labour in the subordinate nations (see EXPLOITATION). This over-exploitation of labour in the periphery arises out of the need of capitalists to recover part of the fall in the profit rate as a consequence of UNEQUAL EXCHANGE. In turn this over-exploitation of labour hinders the transition from absolute to relative SURPLUS VALUE as the dominant form in capital–labour relations and the accumulation process in the periphery, thereby underpinning their dependence. According to Marini the circuit of CAPITAL in dependent countries differs from that of central countries. In dependent countries the two key elements of the capital cycle – the production and circulation of commodities – are separated as a result of the periphery being linked to the centre through the over-exploitation of labour. Production in the Third World countries does not rely on internal capacity for consumption but depends on exports to the developed countries. Wages are kept low in the dependent countries because the workers' consumption is not required for the realization of commodities. Thus, the conditions are set for the over-exploitation of labour.

Turning now to the work of Frank, his main contribution to dependency analysis occurred before he actually used the term 'dependence' (1967), and is found in his central and well-known idea of 'the development of under-development' (see UNDERDEVELOPMENT AND DEVELOPMENT). Although dependency theory is best known to an English-speaking audience through the work of Frank, in retrospect his writings can best be considered as belonging to the WORLD-SYSTEM perspective. Thus it would be a mistake to consider him as the dependency writer *par excellence*.

The book by Cardoso and Faletto (1979) is considered by many as the key dependency text, but it is a matter of debate to what extent it can be situated within Marxism. The authors explore diversity within unity of the various historical processes, contrary to Frank's search for unity within diversity. Dependence is not regarded by them simply as an external variable, since they do not derive the internal national socio-political situation mechanically from external domination. Thus, they do not see dependency and imperialism as external and internal sides of a single coin, with the internal reduced to a reflection of the external. They conceive the relationship between internal and external forces as forming a complex whole and explore the ways in which they are interwoven. In contrast to some other dependency writers, such as Frank and Marini, Cardoso does not regard dependency as being contradictory to development; to indicate this he coins the term 'associated dependent development'.

Cueva's analysis (1976) provides an entry point into the discussion concerning the Marxist nature of the neo-Marxist dependency perspective. He regards their writings as non-Marxist. Furthermore, he does not accept the existence of a dependent mode of production and regards orthodox Marxist theory as adequate for analysing Latin American society. In denying that any specific laws of development are operative in the Third World, Cueva challenges the very core of dependency analysis.

The debate over the feudal or capitalist nature of Latin America's mode of production acquired a new life with the publication of Frank's book on Latin America (1967) in which he boldly and assertively argues that Latin America has been capitalist since the European conquest in the sixteenth century. The ensuing debate has similarities with the Marxist polemic on the TRANSITION FROM FEUDALISM TO CAPITALISM whose main protagonists were DOBB and Sweezy. The most influential critique of Frank is made by the Argentinian, Ernesto Laclau (1971), who castigates Frank for over-emphasizing the importance of exchange relations while ignoring production relations. In Laclau's view 'the pre-capitalist character of the dominant relations of production in Latin America was not only not incompatible with production for the world market, but was actually intensified by the expansion of the latter' (1971, p. 30). The significance of Frank's intervention was mainly political. By arguing that capitalism was the cause of Latin America's underdevelopment and responsible for its continuation, he challenged the orthodox Latin America communist parties, who argued that Latin America was still feudal and therefore the popular forces should support the bourgeoisie in its revolutionary task, which in turn would advance the socialist revolution. For Frank, and the Marxist *dependentistas*, the Latin American bourgeoisie is only perpetuating the development of underdevelopment and therefore, following the example of the Cuban revolution, capitalism itself has to be overthrown as only SOCIALISM can eliminate underdevelopment.

Reading

Aricó, José 1980 (1983): Marx y América Latina.

Cardoso, Fernando H. and Faletto, Enzo 1969: (1979): Dependency and Development in Latin America.

Cueva, Agustín 1976: 'Problems and Perspectives of Dependency Theory'.

Frank, André Gunder 1967 (1969): Capitalism and Underdevelopment in Latin America. 2nd edn., revised and enlarged.

Kay, Cristóbal 1989: Latin American Theories of Development and Underdevelopment.

Laclau, Ernesto 1971: 'Feudalism and Capitalism in Latin America'.

Liss, Sheldon B. 1984: Marxist Thought in Latin America.

Löwy, Michaël 1980: Le Marxisme en Amérique Latine de 1909 à nos jours.

Mariátegui, José Carlos 1928 (1971): Seven Interpretive Essays on Peruvian Reality.

Marini, Ruy Mauro 1972 (1973): Dialéctica de la dependencia.

Quijano, Aníbal 1974: 'The Marginal Pole of the Economy and the Marginalised Labour Force'.

CRISTÓBAL KAY

Marxist economics in Japan

Historical Background

Marxist economics first arrived in Japan in the early years of this century. The Japanese Social Democratic Party was banned on the day it was formed in 1901, but nevertheless provided the basis on which Marxist ideas spread and were influential primarily among non-academic active socialists. The first Japanese translation of the Communist Manifesto appeared in the weekly journal of the party in 1904 and an abridged introduction to Capital was published in 1907, while other books of Japanese origin sought to introduce Marxist ideas as a basis for socialism.

At this time Marxism was just one of a series of European (mainly German) ideas and institutions that had been rapidly imported wholesale into Japan since the Meiji restoration of 1868. The specific character of the transformation

this wrought in the structure of the Japanese economy has been the subject of some dispute among Japanese Marxists (see below), but it initiated an unprecedented rate of capitalist expansion and growth of foreign trade compared with the relatively slow growth of early European capitalism or even the later contemporary growth rates of the United States and Germany. Unlike these older capitalist economies, Japanese industrial capitalism was largely built on an infrastructure provided directly by the Meiji government which undertook the construction for sale of modern factories, docks and mines, enabling Japanese capital to compete with the industry of the advanced capitalist countries, though this relied heavily on the import of industrial techniques and technical knowledge. Imported institutional structures soon followed, with Prussia being particularly influential in providing a model for a Constitution in which the power of an elected assembly was tightly controlled and restricted by an executive responsible directly to the emperor and not to the assembly. The Meiji Constitution aimed for 'modernization' without any substantial transfer of power and Bismarckian Germany provided an appropriate model. The German 'historical school' which stressed the specificity of national and historical development was the dominant influence in social and economic thought at the time. This was clearly more appropriate to the heavily interventionist Japanese state than the laissez-faire policies of classical political economy which soon lost favour in the universities. Meanwhile Japan's own imperialist expansion through war with China in 1894–5 and with Russia in 1904–5, brought rapid expansion of capitalist industry and the growth of an impoverished proletariat, whose wages were held back by the still proportionately massive peasantry and rural unemployed.

The Russian revolution unleashed renewed interest and support for socialist movements in Japan as in Europe. The Japanese Communist Party was formed in 1922, and other socialist, popular front, worker and peasant parties were also formed in that period. Japanese capital responded to the world crisis by an intensification of the process of monopolization. The conglomerate 'Daibatsu' so characteristic of Japanese capitalism today had its roots in the cartels formed after the Russo-Japanese war, but it was in the interwar period that FINANCE CAPITAL became particularly integrated. Although the growth of these large firms led to the development and rapid growth of trade unions, urban wages and working conditions remained very backward with a massive reserve army remaining in the countryside, consisting of nearly half the working population which was still employed in agriculture and fisheries, compared with less than 20 per cent in manufactures (Itoh 1980, p. 16). While the socialist parties took up struggles between peasants and landowners, the demand for universal suffrage and trade-union issues, Marxist ideas began for the first time to enter the universities. Teaching posts in the newly created departments of economics and also in those universities which had no formal economics department, often went to teachers who had themselves been educated in Germany and were influenced by the flourishing Marxist culture of pre- and post-war Germany. The translation of Marxist works took off at a rate almost matching the growth of Japanese capital. While the first Japanese translation of the three volumes of *Capital* was not published until the early 1920s, by 1933 the world's first complete collected works of Marx and Engels, plus an index of a detail unequalled in other versions, was published in Japanese. Severe political repression in the 1930s had its effects on the development of Japanese Marxism. Nearly all Marxists lost their posts in the universities, and mass arrests and censorship effectively crushed any developments outside the universities as the Sino-Japanese conflict escalated into the second world war.

After the war academic Marxism became largely divorced from all political movements, socialist developments within the latter foundering as Japanese capitalism rapidly expanded. At the same time Marxism gained predominance in economics departments, becoming, for a time, in effect the orthodoxy. But with the expansion of academic interchange with the United States neo-classical and to some extent Keynesian economics gained a hold too, with numbers in the two main schools of Marxist and 'modern' (i.e. non-Marxist) economics now being roughly equal. The two schools have developed largely in isolation from each other, but the basic training in most Japanese universities

still consists of elements of both Marxist and non-Marxist economics, so that, unlike in the West, most Japanese neo-classical economists are aware of the elements of Marxism. This has led to some interesting eclectic developments, particularly in mathematical areas. Mathematical models have been used by Koshimura (1975) to extend Marx's reproduction schema to consider crises of disproportion, and by Okishio (1963, 1977) to model the tendency of the rate of profit to fall and the growth of the industrial reserve army. In a more encompassing way, Morishima (1973) has attempted to incorporate Marxism into Von Neumann growth theory. Modern econometric techniques have also been used by some Marxist economists in their empirical work.

The Debates
The controversies about the nature of the Japanese economy which took place during the 1920s and 1930s were not dissimilar in political implications from those which had occurred in Russia earlier in the century. The Comintern vacillated as to whether the next major transformation in store for Japan was to be towards a socialist revolution or whether Japan had still to undergo its bourgeois revolution before a socialist one could be initiated. The Japanese Communist Party eventually settled on the latter position in 1932, arguing that the Meiji Restoration had not brought capitalism to Japan, which still remained a basically feudal society. The supporters of this line became known as the Koza-Ha (feudalist) school and were opposed by the Rona-Ha (workers and peasants) school whose theoretical positions were adopted by the left wing of various socialist parties outside the official Communist Party.

In support of their position the Koza-Ha school pointed to the absolutist nature of the Japanese state, which had not been reformed in line with those of Western capitalist countries. The Meiji Restoration, it was argued, had been simply a set of reforms of the feudal land system, by which a rising capitalist class was accommodated into an alliance with the feudal landowners, in which the latter retained their dominance. The continued existence of high rents, paid largely in kind, in the numerically predominant impoverished agricultural sector lent support to their insistence that feudal exploitation of agricultural peasants was the dominant form of surplus extraction in Japan. On the other hand, the Rona-Ha school saw the Meiji Restoration as the Japanese bourgeois revolution, after which capitalist rather than feudal exploitation had been predominant within the Japanese economy, and argued that the class structure had changed with a rapid proletarianization of the peasantry.

Since the second world war a similar debate has taken place within the Koza-Ha school as to whether capitalism had eventually been brought to Japan with the postwar land reform imposed by the American occupation. Kurihara argued that as a result of the land reform the land-owning class had effectively been wiped out, but that this did not mean that capitalist development was taking place in agriculture. Rather, direct control by the state of the relations of production in agriculture meant that a form of STATE MONOPOLY CAPITALISM had been imposed from above. Orthodox Koza-Ha theorists continued to reject this view, for as Rona-Ha critics had pointed out, if the postwar land reform had introduced capitalist development of whatever form from above, the argument that the Meiji government could not have done so earlier was inconsistent. On the other side, if the Meiji Restoration had not been the bourgeois revolution because it had lacked a revolutionary subject and had been a reorganization imposed from above, that applied to postwar changes brought in by an occupying power too. Indeed, they argued, the occupation lent support to their insistence that Japan was still pre-capitalist; that it retained an internal semi-feudal structure, which was dominated by American imperialism ruling through the collaboration of the absolutist state. Again, this view lent support to the political priority of a bourgeois revolution. This theoretical position lost support in face of the growth of Japanese capitalism and indeed of Japan itself as a modern imperialist power from the 1950s. Nevertheless, the development of tendencies towards reformism within the Japanese Communist Party have their roots in this original position, while the development of positions close to those of EUROCOMMUNISM among the leadership of the party can be traced to the earlier characterization of parts of the economy as state monopoly capitalist. On the other hand, not surprisingly, the postwar land

reforms were analysed by Rona-Ha theorists as a capitalist reform of private landownership which was holding back capitalist development, against the power of large landowners. This position was held by the left wing of the Socialist Party who consistently argued for socialist revolution as the next stage in the democratization of Japan.

Two aspects of this debate about the character of the Japanese economy and the nature of the Meiji and postwar reforms were significant in methodological debates of the time, and they led eventually to the development of a third group, the Uno school of Japanese Marxism. First, the elements which had led the Koza-Ha school to characterize the Japanese economy as feudal were seen by their critics as the basis on which a specific type of capitalist development could be characterized. This raised questions about the relations between the abstract specification of a mode of production and its laws of motion, and the specific form these took in particular economies. Second, the vacillation of the orthodox (Koza-Ha) theoretical views, reflecting those of a political party, brought into question the relation between economic theory and political struggle. Kozo Uno, in *Principles of Political Economy* (1964) insisted that Marxism must recognize and clearly distinguish three levels of analysis:

(1) *Principles* derived, and developed where necessary, from Marx's analysis in *Capital*. At this level the purely economic laws of motion of capitalist production could be formulated. Uno argued that in *Capital* Marx used the early to mid-nineteenth-century British economy as his main example, because this economy was undergoing a development which made it move towards the paradigm case of a pure capitalist economy, and in consequence the abstraction of such basic principles could be made from it. Nevertheless the principles were abstractions to which some aspects of any real economy would not conform.

(2) The next level of analysis would develop a *stages theory* of the historical forms in which the laws of motion of capitalist development have operated throughout the world, and the policies to which they have given rise. Uno suggested three such stages: mercantilism, in which British merchant capital based on the woollen industry was dominant, then liberalism, dominated by

British industrial capital, centred on the cotton industry, and finally imperialism when finance capital, based on the development of heavy industry in Germany and the United States as well as Britain, was predominant.

(3) A third level, of *empirical analysis*, would consider the development of the economies of particular countries and would be appropriate for the analysis of transitional periods in which political considerations as well as those of a purely economic character would need to be analysed. Uno saw the whole era since the first world war as such a period, transitional between capitalism and socialism, and therefore, because political confrontations between socialist forces within and outside capitalist economies informed policy, this was no longer a pure stage of capitalist development. He maintained that a clear differentiation of these three levels of analysis would avoid the dilemma in which orthodox theory found itself when the development of Japanese capitalism did not conform to the model of capitalist development outlined in *Capital*. While the latter is at the level of principles, Japanese capitalist development must be analysed at the empirical level where the specific character of Japanese agriculture and class formation could be appreciated.

The Uno school has also had interesting contributions to make to the theory of VALUE and of crisis (see ECONOMIC CRISES), in keeping with the methodological prescriptions outlined above, and has shown a healthy lack of dogmatism uncharacteristic of much Japanese Marxism. It is this lack of dogmatism, shown in the way some members of the Uno school tend to claim some difference of approach from that of their founder, which may explain why this school has become better known to Western Marxists than other Japanese schools of Marxism. Two members have been particularly active in reaching out to Western audiences: Makoto Itoh, from Japan, has published widely in the West on both theoretical and empirical issues using Uno's three levels of analysis (Itoh 1980, 1988), and Thomas Sekine, now resident in Canada, has translated Uno's *Principles* for an English-speaking audience (Uno *1980*) and provided in his own work an interpretation of Uno's theory using Western developments in Marxist and bourgeois economics (Sekine 1984). Recently, a study group set up by Sekine

has led to the first non-Japanese writings on Uno and the relation of his work to Western Marxism: Albritton (1986) sees Uno's theory as providing an alternative to Althusserian structuralism, while Duncan (1983) compares Uno's approach to theory with that of E. P. Thompson to concrete history (see also Maclean 1981).

One of the most controversial aspects of Uno's Marxism is its insistence that economics can be independent of political and ideological movements. This has been exemplified by the development of the school in Japan which, although it has some adherents among the left wing of the Socialist Party, remains mainly an academic school, whose followers see their main contribution to socialist transformation as being the development of a scientific understanding of capitalism. This separation, and the limitations it has imposed on their work, may be inherent in the methodological separation of levels of analysis itself. For perhaps an over narrow focus on the laws of motion of capitalism leads to a neglect of the role of class struggle. Uno relegates this to the empirical, political level, but others would argue that class struggle can be seen as inherent in the process by which modes of production reproduce themselves and thus integral to their definition (and not just in transitional periods). The contradictions of capitalism such as those within the commodity form of LABOUR POWER, which Uno analyses at the level of principles as the basis of capitalist crises, are the result, and not only the cause, of class struggle. Those trends which have emphasized the need to see class struggle as endogenous to the laws of motion of capitalism may in this respect be more fruitful in generating analysis of the present state of the world economy.

Reading

Albritton, R. 1986: *A Japanese Reconstruction of Marxist Theory*.

Burkett, Paul 1983: 'Value and Crisis: Essays on Marxian Economics in Japan, A Review'.

Duncan, C. 1983: 'Under the Cloud of Capital: History Versus Theory'.

Itoh, Makoto 1980: *Value and Crisis, Essays on Marxian Economics in Japan*.

— 1988: *The Basic Theory of Capitalism*.

Kim, Soo Haeng 1982: 'The Theory of Crisis. A Critical Appraisal of some Japanese and European Reformulations'.

Koshimura, Shinzaburo 1975: *Theory of Capital Reproduction and Accumulation*.

Maclean, B. 1981: 'Kozo Uno's *Principles of Political Economy*'.

Morishima, Michio 1973: *Marx's Economics*.

Okishio, Nubuo 1963: 'A Mathematical Note on Marxian Theorems'.

— 1977: 'Notes on Technical Progress and Capitalist Society'.

Sekine, T. 1975: 'Uno-Riron: a Japanese Contribution to Marxian Political Economy'.

— 1984: *The Dialectic of Capital*, vol. I.

Uno, Kozo 1964 (1980): *Principles of Political Economy: Theory of a Purely Capitalist Society*.

SUSAN HIMMELWEIT

materialism In its broadest sense, materialism contends that whatever exists just is, or at least depends upon, matter. (In its more general form it claims that all reality is essentially material; in its more specific form, that human reality is.) In the Marxist tradition, materialism has normally been of the weaker, *non-reductive* kind, but the concept has been deployed in various ways. The following definitions attempt some terminological clarity at the outset. Philosophical materialism is distinguished, following Plekhanov, from historical materialism, and, following Lenin, from scientific materialism generally. *Philosophical materialism* comprises:

(1) *ontological materialism*, asserting the unilateral dependence of social upon biological (and more generally physical) being and the emergence of the former from the latter;

(2) *epistemological materialism*, asserting the independent existence and transfactual activity of at least some of the objects of scientific thought;

(3) *practical materialism*, asserting the constitutive role of human transformative agency in the reproduction and transformation of social forms.

Historical materialism asserts the causal primacy of men's and women's mode of production and reproduction of their natural (physical) being, or of the labour process more generally, in the development of human history. *Scientific materialism* is defined by the (changing) content of scientific beliefs about reality (including social reality). The so called '*materialist world-outlook*' consists of a looser set of (historically changing) practical beliefs and attitudes, a *Weltanschauung* (which may include e.g. a pro-scientific stance, atheism, etc.). This entry is mainly concerned with philosophical materialism, but its relation to historical materialism is briefly taken up.

The principal philosophically-significant connotations of Marx's '*materialist* conception of history' are: (a) a denial of the autonomy, and then of the primacy, of ideas in social life; (b) a methodological commitment to concrete historiographical research, as opposed to abstract philosophical reflection; (c) a conception of the centrality of human praxis in the production and reproduction of social life and, flowing from this, (d) a stress on the significance of labour, as involving the transformation of nature and the mediation of social relations, in human history; (e) an emphasis on the significance of nature for man which changes from the expressivism of the early works (especially the *Economic and Philosophical Manuscripts*) where, espousing a naturalism understood as a species-humanism, Marx conceives man as essentially at one with nature, to the technological Prometheanism of his middle and later works where he conceives man as essentially opposed to and dominating nature; (f) a continuing commitment to simple everyday REALISM and a gradually developing commitment to scientific realism, throughout which Marx views the man–nature relationship as asymmetrically internal – with man as essentially dependent on nature, but nature as essentially independent of man.

Only (c), Marx's new practical or transformative materialism, can be considered in any detail here. It depends upon the view that human is distinguished from merely animal being or activity by a double freedom: a freedom from instinctual determination and a freedom to produce in a planned, premeditated way. The general character of this conception is expressed most succinctly in the *Theses on Feuerbach* (8th thesis): 'All social life is essentially *practical*. All mysteries which lead theory to mysticism find their rational solution in human practice and in the comprehension of this practice.' The twin themes of the *Theses* are the passive, ahistorical and individualist character of traditional, contemplative materialism, and the fundamental role of transformative activity or practice in social life, which classical German Idealism had glimpsed, only to represent in an idealized and alienated form. It was Lukács who first pointed out, in *The Young Hegel*, that the nub of Marx's critique of Hegel's *Phenomenology of Mind* was that Hegel had identified, and so confused, objectification and alienation; by conceiving the present, historically specific, alienated forms of objectification as moments of the self-alienation of an Absolute Subject, he at once rationally transfigured them and foreclosed the possibility of a fully human, non-alienated, mode of human objectification. But once this distinction has been made a three-fold ambiguity in Marx's own use of 'objectivity' and its cognates remains; and its clarification becomes essential for Marx's materialism from at least the time of the *Theses on Feuerbach*. Thus the 1st Thesis implies, but does not clearly articulate, a distinction between (α) *objectivity* or externality as such and (β) objectification as the *production* of a subject; and the 6th Thesis entails a distinction between (β) and (γ) objectification as the *process* of the reproduction or transformation of social forms.

The 1st Thesis commits Marx to sustaining both the materialist insight of the independence of things from thought and the idealist insight of thought as an activity and hence to a distinction between (α) and (β), or in the terminology of the *Grundrisse* Introduction between real and thought objects, or in the terminology of modern scientific realism between the intransitive objects of knowledge and the transitive process or activity of knowledge-production. This distinction allows us to clarify the sense in which for Marx social practice is a *condition*, but not the *object*, of natural science; whereas it is *ontologically*, as well as *epistemologically* constitutive in the social sphere. Seen in this light, Marx's complaint against idealism is that it illicitly abstracts from the intransitive dimension the idea of an independent reality; while traditional materialism abstracts from the transitive dimension, the role of human activity in the production of knowledge.

The 6th Thesis proclaims a critique of all individualist and essentialist social theory, focused upon Feuerbach's humanism, and isolates man's historically developing sociality as the true key to the ills Feuerbach anthropologi-

cally explained. And it entails the distinction between (β) and (γ), intentional human activity and the reproduction or transformation of the antecedently existing, historically social forms, given as the conditions and media of that activity, but reproduced or transformed only in it.

Failure to distinguish adequately (α) and (β), as two aspects of the unity of known objects, has led to tendencies to both epistemological idealism (reduction of (α) to (β) from Lukács and Gramsci to Kolakowski and Schmidt) and traditional materialism (reduction of (β) to (α) from Engels and Lenin to Della Volpe and the contemporary exponents of 'reflection theory'). And failure to distinguish adequately (β) and (γ), as two aspects of the unity of transformative activity (or as the duality of praxis and structure) has resulted in both sociological individualism, voluntarism, spontaneism, etc. (reduction of (γ) to (β) as e.g. in Sartre); and determinism, reification, hypostatization etc. (reduction of (β) to (γ) as e.g. in Althusser). The 9th and 10th Theses expressly articulate Marx's conception of the differences between his new and the old materialism: 'The highest point reached by that materialism which does not comprehend sensuousness as practical activity, is the contemplation of single individuals and of civil society.' 'The standpoint of the old materialism is civil society; the standpoint of the new is human society, or social humanity.' The problem-field of traditional materialism is based on an abstract ahistorical individualism and universality: isolated Crusoes, externally and eternally related to one another and to their common naturalized fate. For Marx, this conception underlies the traditional problems of epistemology (see KNOWLEDGE, THEORY OF), and indeed PHILOSOPHY generally. For the contemplative consciousness, disengaged from material practice, its relation to its body, other minds, external objects, and even its own past states, becomes problematic. But neither these philosophical problems nor the practices from which they arise can be remedied by a purely theoretical therapy. Contra e.g. the Young Hegelian Stirner who believes 'one has only to get a few ideas out of one's head to abolish the conditions which have given rise to those ideas' (*German Ideology*, vol. 1, pt. III), 'the resolution of *theoretical* oppositions is possible only in a *practical* way, and hence is by no means a task of knowledge but a task of *actual* life; which philosophy could not resolve because it grasped the task *only* as a theoretical one' (*Economic and Philosophical Manuscripts*, 3rd MS). Hence 'the philosophers have only *interpreted* the world in various ways; the point is to *change* it' (11th Thesis).

It would be difficult to exaggerate the importance of Engels's more cosmological cast of materialism, elaborated in his later philosophical writings, especially *Anti-Dühring*, *Ludwig Feuerbach*, and *Dialectics of Nature*. It was not only the decisive moment in the formation of the leading theorists of the Second International (Bernstein, Kautsky, Plekhanov) but, as the doctrinal core of what subsequently became known as DIALECTICAL MATERIALISM, it provided the axis around which most subsequent debates have revolved. Writing in a context imbued with positivist and evolutionist (especially social Darwinist) themes (see DARWINISM; POSITIVISM), Engels argued: (a) against mechanical or 'metaphysical' materialism, that the world was a complex of processes, not fixed and static things; and (b) against reductive materialism, that mental and social forms were irreducible to, but emergent from, matter (as indeed its highest product). The immediate target of Lenin's later influential *Materialism and Empirio-Criticism* was the spread of Mach's positivist conceptions among his Bolshevik comrades such as Bogdanov.

Both Engels and Lenin utilize a number of different notions of materialism and idealism, which are treated as mutually exclusive and completely exhaustive categories, and generally speak of ontological and epistemological definitions of materialism as though they were immediately equivalent. But the mere independence of matter from human thought does not entail its causal primacy in being; it is consistent with the objective idealisms of Plato, Aquinas and Hegel. Certainly it is possible to argue that (1) and (2) above are intrinsically connected – in that if mind emerged from matter then a Darwinian explanation of the possibility of knowledge is feasible and, conversely, that a full and consistent realism entails a conception of man as a natural causal agent nested within an overreaching nature. But neither Engels nor Lenin specified the links satisfactorily. Engels's main emphasis is undoubtedly ontological and Lenin's epistemological; and may be represented thus:

the natural world is prior to and causally independent of any form of mind or consciousness, but not the reverse (Engels)

the knowable world exists independently of any (finite or infinite) mind, but not the reverse (Lenin).

A noteworthy feature of Engels's materialism is his stress on the practical refutation of scepticism. Pursuing a line of thought favoured by among others Dr Johnson, Hume and Hegel, Engels argued that scepticism – in the sense of suspension of commitment to some idea of an independent reality, known under some description or other – is not a tenable or serious position. Although theoretically impregnable, it was continually belied or contradicted by practice (including, he could have added, as Gramsci was later to intimate in his notion of theoretically implicit consciousness, the sceptic's own speech practice), particularly 'experiment and industry'. 'If we are able to prove the correctness of our conceptions of a natural process by making it ourselves . . . then there is an end to the Kantian ungraspable "thing-in-itself" ' (*Ludwig Feuerbach*, sect. 2). Whereas in Engels there is a pervasive tension between a positivistic concept of philosophy and a metaphysics of science, in Lenin there is clear recognition of a relatively autonomous Lockean or underlabourer role for philosophy in relation to historical materialism and the sciences generally. This is accompanied by (i) a clear distinction between matter as a *philosophical category* and as a *scientific concept*; (ii) emphasis on the practical and interested character of philosophical interventions in his doctrine of *partinost* (partisanship); (iii) the attempt to reconcile scientific change with the idea of PROGRESS (and, normatively, to counter dogmatism and scepticism respectively) in a distinction between 'relative' and 'absolute' TRUTH.

The hallmark of the dialectical materialist tradition was the combination of a DIALECTICS of nature and a reflectionist theory of knowledge. Both were rejected by Lukács in the seminal text of WESTERN MARXISM, *History and Class Consciousness*, which also argued that they were mutually inconsistent. Gramsci, redefining objectivity as such in terms of a universal inter-subjectivity, asymptotically approached in history but only finally realized under communism, went even further, claiming: 'It has been forgotten that in the case of [historical materialism] one should put the accent on the first term – "historical" – and not on the second – which is of metaphysical origin. The philosophy of praxis is absolute "historicism", the absolute secularization and earthliness of thought, an absolute humanism of history'. (Gramsci 1971, p. 465). In general, where Western Marxism has been sympathetic to dialectical motifs it has been hostile to materialism. For Sartre, for instance, 'no materialism of any kind can ever explain [freedom]' (Sartre 1967, p. 237), which is precisely what is distinctive of the human-historical situation. On the other hand, where Western Marxism has advertised its materialism, this has usually been of an exclusively epistemological kind, as in Althusser, Della Volpe and Colletti; and, where ontological topics have been broached, as in Timpanaro's (1976) important re-emphasis on the role of nature, and of the biological 'substructure' in particular, in social life, their discussion has often been vitiated by an unreflected empiricism in ontology.

In any discussion of materialism there lurks the problem of the definition of matter. For Marx's practical materialism, which is restricted to the social sphere (including of course natural science) and where 'matter' is to be understood in the sense of 'social practice', no particular difficulty arises. But from Engels on, Marxist materialism has more global pretensions, and the difficulty now appears that if a material thing is regarded as a perduring occupant of space capable of being perceptually identified and re-identified, then many objects of scientific knowledge, although dependent for their *identification* upon material things, are patently immaterial. Clearly if one distinguishes scientific and philosophical ontologies, such considerations need not, as Lenin recognized, refute philosophical materialism, But what then is its content? Some materialists have subscribed to the idea of the exhaustive knowability of the world by science. But what grounds could there be for this? Such cognitive triumphalism seems an anthropocentric, and hence idealist, conceit. On the other hand, the weaker supposition that whatever is knowable must be knowable by science, if not tautologous, merely displaces the truth of materialism onto the feasibility of naturalism in particular domains.

For such reasons one might be tempted to treat materialism more as a *prise de position*, a practical orientation, than as a set of quasi-descriptive theses, and more specifically as: (a) a series of denials, largely of claims of traditional philosophy – e.g. concerning the existence of God, souls, forms, ideals, duties, the absolute etc., or the impossibility (or inferior status) of science, earthly happiness etc.; and (b) as an indispensable ground for such denials, a commitment to their scientific explanation as modes of false or inadequate consciousness or IDEOLOGY. However, such an orientation both presupposes some *positive* account of science etc. and is in principle vulnerable to a request for normative grounding itself, so that a pragmatist reconstruction of materialism is hardly an advance on a descriptivist one. In both cases the problem of justification remains. In fact it may be easier to justify materialism as an account of science and scientificity than it is to justify materialism *per se*; and perhaps only such a *specific* explication and defence of materialism is consistent with Marx's critique of hypostatized and abstract thought (in the 2nd Thesis on Feuerbach).

Post-Lukácsian Marxism has typically counterposed Marx's premises to Engels's conclusions. But on contemporary realist reconstructions of science there is no inconsistency between refined forms of them. Thus a conception of science as the practical investigation of nature entails a *non-anthropocentric ontology* of independently existing and transfactually efficacious real structures, mechanisms, processes, relations and fields. Moreover such a *transcendental realism* even partially vindicates the spirit, if not the letter, of Engels's 'Two Great Camps Thesis'. For (a) it stands opposed to the *empirical realism* of subjective idealism and the *conceptual realism* of objective idealism alike, (b) pinpointing their common error in the reduction of being to a human attribute – experience or reason – in two variants of the 'epistemic fallacy' and (c) revealing their systematic interdependence – in that epistemologically, objective idealism presupposes the reified facts of subjective idealism and ontologically, subjective idealism presupposes the hypostatized ideas of objective idealism; so that upon inspection of their respective fine structures they may be seen to bear the same Janus-faced legend: empirical certainty/conceptual truth. Historical investigation also gives some grounds for Engels's view that materialism and idealism are related as dialectical antagonists in the context of struggles around changes in scientific knowledge and, more generally, social life. Finally it should be mentioned that a transcendental realist explication of materialism is congruent with an emergent powers naturalist orientation.

The importance of this last consideration is that, since Marx and Engels, Marxism has conducted a double polemic: against idealism and against vulgar, reductionist or 'undialectical', e.g. contemplative (Marx) or mechanical (Engels) materialism. And the project of elaborating a satisfactory 'materialist' account or critique of some subject matter, characteristically celebrated by idealism, has often amounted in practice to the endeavour to avoid *reductionism* (e.g. of philosophy to science, society or mind to nature, universals to particulars, theory to experience, human agency or consciousness to social structure) – the characteristic 'materialist' response – without reverting to a *dualism*, as would more than satisfy idealism. This in turn has usually necessitated a war of position on two fronts – against various types of '*objectivism*', e.g. metaphysics, scientism, dogmatism, determinism, reification, and against various formally counterposed, but actually complementary, types of '*subjectivism*', e.g. positivism, agnosticism, scepticism, individualism, voluntarism. It would be misleading to think of Marxist materialism as seeking a via media or simple Hegelian synthesis of these historic duals – it is rather that, in transforming their common problematic, both the errors and the partial insights of the old antagonistic symbiotes are thrown, from the new vantage point, into critical relief.

As defined at the outset, none of (1)–(3) entails historical materialism, which is what one would expect of the relations between a philosophical position and an empirical science. On the other hand, historical materialism is rooted in ontological materialism, i.e. presupposes a scientific realist ontology and epistemology, and consists in a substantive elaboration of practical materialism. Only the first proposition can be further commented upon here. Both Marx and Engels were wont to defend historical materialism by invoking quasi-biological considerations. In *The German Ideology* vol. I pt. I, they state: 'The first premiss of all human history is, of course, the existence of living human individuals. Thus the first fact to be established is the physical organisation of these individuals and their consequent relation to the rest of nature. . . . [Men] begin to distinguish themselves from animals as soon as they begin to *produce* their means of subsistence, a step which is conditioned by their physical organisation'. Marxists have, however, for the most part considered only one side of the natural-social relations, viz technology, describing the way in which human beings appropriate nature, effectively ignoring the ways (putatively studied in ecology, social biology, etc.) in which, so to speak, nature re-appropriates human beings.

Reading

Bhaskar, Roy 1986: *Scientific Realism and Human Emancipation*.

Gramsci, A. 1929–35 (1971): *Selections from the Prison Notebooks*.

Lenin, V. I. 1908 (1962): 'Materialism and Empirio-Criticism'.

Sartre, J.-P. 1962: 'Materialism and Revolution'. In *Literary and Philosophical Essays*.

Schmidt, A. 1962 (1971): *The Concept of Nature in Marx*.

Timpanaro, S. 1976: *On Materialism*.

Wetter, G. 1952 (1958): *Dialectical Materialism*.

Williams, R. 1980: *Problems in Materialism and Culture*.

ROY BHASKAR

matter.   *See* materialism.

means of production.   *See* forces and relations of production.

mechanical materialism   *See* materialism.

mediation   A central category of DIALECTICS. In a literal sense it refers to establishing connections by means of some intermediary. As such it figures prominently in epistemology (see KNOWLEDGE, THEORY OF) and LOGIC in general, and addresses itself to the problems of immediate/ mediated knowledge on the one hand, and to those of the syllogism – or 'mediated inference' – on the other. Thereby the diverse forms and varieties of knowledge may be assessed in terms of determinate rules and formal procedures which, however, must find their explanation and justification in the study of being, and not in some circular reference to their own framework of classification and stipulated validation. This is why the category of mediation acquires a qualitatively different significance in Marxist dialectic, which refuses to grant the autonomy of any traditional branch of philosophy and treats their problems – hence also those of 'mediation', inherited from past epistemology and logic, and in a special sense (as the 'intermediate' or the 'mean') from Aristotelian ethics – as integral parts of an adequate study of social being, with the TOTALITY of its objective determinations, interconnections and complex mediations.

Among the precursors of such a conception Aristotle occupies a very important place. For in defining virtue as 'a kind of mean, since . . . it aims at what is intermediate' he also insisted on the social/human specificity of his key term: 'By the *intermediate in the object* I mean that which is equidistant from each of the extremes, which is *one and the same for all men*; by the *intermediate relatively to us* that which is neither too much nor too little – and this is *not one, nor the same for all*' (Aristotle 1954 edn, pp. 37–8). In epistemology the problem presented itself as the necessity of mediating between the knowing subject and the world to which his knowledge referred, i.e., to 'proving the truth, that is, the reality and power, the this-sidedness [*Diesseitigkeit*] of his thinking' (*Theses on Feuerbach*, 2nd Thesis). Consequently, in demonstrating what was accessible to knowledge as well as the ways and forms of securing its successful accomplishment, the concept of human 'practice' as the true intermediary between consciousness and its object acquired an ever-increasing significance. Thus, well before Goethe could speak of 'Experiment as the Mediator between Subject and Object' (in an article bearing this title), Vico expressed his 'marvel that the philosophers should have bent all their energies to the study of the world of *nature*, which, since God made it, he alone knows; and that they should have neglected the study of the world of nations, or

civil world, which, *since men had made it, men could come to know*' (Vico 1744, p. 53).

Linked to this philosophical tradition – which culminated in the Hegelian dialectic – Marx rejected the one-sided immediacy of 'all hitherto existing materialism' and its narrow conception of practice as 'fixed only in its dirty-judaical form of appearance' (*Theses on Feuerbach*, 1st Thesis). While criticizing the use to which Hegel put his concept of mediation in his *Philosophy of Right* – in that he presented 'a kind of mutual reconciliation society' by means of some fictitious 'extremes which interchangeably play now the part of the extreme and now the part of the mean', so that 'each extreme is sometimes the lion of opposition and sometimes the Snug of mediation', notwithstanding the fact that 'Actual extremes cannot be mediated with one another precisely because they are actual extremes' (*Critique of Hegel's Philosophy of the State*, sect. B) – he also acknowledged Hegel's pathbreaking achievement in grasping 'the essence of *labour* and comprehending objective man – true, because real man – as the outcome of man's *own labour*' (Marx, *Economic and Philosophical Manuscripts*, Third Manuscript). In the same spirit Marx indicated labour (or 'industry') as the mediator between man and nature, thus identifying in the productive activity of the 'self-mediating natural being' the vital condition of human self-constitution. But whereas for Hegel the externalizing mediation of activity was synonymous with 'alienation', Marx pinpointed the historically specific and transcendable second order mediations of money, exchange and private property (which superimpose themselves upon productive activity as such) as responsible for the alienating perversion of productive self-mediation (see ALIENATION). Similarly the 'secret of the fetishism of the commodity' (*Capital* I, ch. I, sect. 4) was explained by the fact that the production of use value had to be mediated by and subordinated to the production of exchange value, in accordance with the requirements of a determinate set of social relations (see COMMODITY FETISHISM).

Lenin particularly stressed the dynamic transitional function of mediation; 'Everything is *vermittelt* = mediated, bound into one, connected by transitions. . . . Not only the unity of opposites, but the transition of every determination, quality, feature, side, property into every other' (Lenin, 1914–16, pp. 103, 222). He was also anxious to stress the practical foundation of the figures of logic as articulated in the Hegelian syllogism:

For Hegel action, practice is a *logical 'syllogism'*, a figure of logic. And that is true! Not, of course, in the sense that the figure of logic has its other being in the practice of man (= absolute idealism), but, vice versa: man's practice, repeating itself a thousand million times, becomes consolidated in man's consciousness by figures of logic. Precisely (and only) on account of this thousand-million-fold repetition, these figures have the stability of a prejudice, an axiomatic character. First premise: the good end (*subjective* end) versus *actuality* ('external actuality'). Second premise: the external *means* (instrument), (*objective*). Third premise or conclusion: the coincidence of *subjective* and *objective*, the test of subjective ideas, the criterion of objective truth. (Ibid. p. 217)

Here, as elsewhere in Marxist literature, the unity of theory and practice is articulated through the mediating focus of practical activity and its necessary instrumentality (see PRAXIS). Other important aspects of mediation involve NEGATION and the complex relations of 'concrete mediations' with 'concrete totality'.

Reading

Aristotle 1954: *The Nicomachean Ethics*.
Lenin 1914–16 (*1961*): 'Conspectus of Hegel's *Science of Logic*'.
Lukács, Georg 1972a: 'Moses Hess and the Problems of Idealist Dialectics'. In *Political Writings 1919–1929*.
Vico, Giambattista 1744 (*1961*): *The New Science*.

ISTVÁN MÉSZÁROS

Mehring, Franz Born 27 February 1846, Schlawe, Pomerania; died 28 January 1919, Berlin. In his early years Mehring was a well-known liberal journalist and critic of Bismarck's imperial policy, but from 1890 he became a socialist, and as editor of the *Leipziger Volkszeitung* associated himself with the left wing of the Social Democratic party (SPD). During the first world war he vigorously attacked the SPD policy of cooperation with the government, joined with Rosa Luxemburg in creating the

Spartakusbund and became a leading member of the Independent Social Democratic party (USPD) on its foundation in 1917. His death was hastened by the news of the murder in January 1919 of Liebknecht and Luxemburg. Mehring's principal contributions to Marxism were in history and literature. His *History of German Social Democracy* (1897–98) provided a broad survey of the political, social and intellectual development of Germany in the nineteenth century, and his life of Marx (1918) – the first full-scale biography – was notable among other things for its objective defence of Lassalle and Bakunin against some of Marx's criticisms. The most outstanding of his works, *Die Lessing-Legende* (1893), helped to establish a Marxist sociology of literature and of intellectual history, and he pursued this kind of study in his essays on modern literature. In his general expositions of historical materialism (e.g. in the appendix to *Lessing*) he was inclined to adopt a rather crude 'reductionist' approach, which elicited an implied criticism from Engels (letter of 14 July 1893), who observed that 'one point is lacking', namely a recognition that Marx and he (Engels) had put the main emphasis on the derivation of ideological notions from basic economic facts, and had 'neglected the formal side – the ways and means by which these notions, etc., come about [which] has given our adversaries a welcome opportunity for misunderstandings and distortions'.

Reading

Mehring, Franz 1893 (*1938*): *Die Lessing-Legende*.
— 1897–98: *Geschichte der deutschen Sozialdemokratie*.
— 1918 (*1936*): *Karl Marx*.

TOM BOTTOMORE

Mensheviks Between 1903 and 1912 a trend and a faction in the Russian Social Democratic Labour Party, and from 1912 an independent party taking that name (RSDLP). The second congress of the RSDLP in 1903 divided between the supporters of Lenin, who favoured 'personal participation in one of the Party organizations' as a condition of membership, and those of MARTOV and Axelrod, who proposed a looser formula. The former, who were to stand for a more disciplined and centralized party, gained a majority (*bol'shinstvo*) in the elections to the party's leading bodies, and came to be known as Bolsheviks. The latter were called Mensheviks (minoritarians) and favoured a broader party. Further differences between Mensheviks and Bolsheviks (see BOLSHEVISM) developed under the impetus of the 1905 Russian Revolution and concerned the nature of class leadership, alliances and objectives in such a bourgeois democratic revolution. Whereas the Bolsheviks argued that the working class should lead it, in alliance principally with the peasantry, the majority of Mensheviks envisaged its being led by the bourgeoisie and favoured alliances with the Liberals. The Mensheviks rejected the Bolshevik conception of working-class participation in a provisional government established by a bourgeois-democratic revolution, arguing the classical Marxist position that the workers' party should act as the 'extreme revolutionary opposition'. For the subsequent historical period they foresaw a scenario based on a West European model, where the organization and consciousness of a larger working class would gradually be developed with the growth of the productive forces and democratic institutions, and the objective and subjective bases would be created for an eventual advance to socialism.

After the defeat of the 1905 Revolution, in which they played an important role in the Soviets, many Mensheviks left the underground Party organizations in Russia to concentrate on work in legal front organizations. This led from 1908 to Lenin's charge of Menshevik 'liquidationism' in respect of the illegal party and the Bolsheviks' decision to constitute themselves as an independent party in 1912. However efforts were made by Martov and by his friends in Russia to develop a network of Menshevik illegal organizations, called 'Initiative Groups'. In 1914 most Mensheviks tended to take an internationalist position and to condemn the war as imperialist, but the right wing of the party, now joined by PLEKHANOV, supported the allies' war against Germany. However, after the Russian February Revolution (1917), the majority of the Mensheviks, who occupied a leading position in the Soviets, came to support the war under the slogan of 'revolutionary defensism'. They were opposed in this by the party's left wing, the Menshevik-Internationalists, led by Martov, who also strongly attacked

their party's decision of May 1917 to become junior partners in a bourgeois-socialist coalition cabinet. Between June and November 1917 the Mensheviks' cripplingly divided party drastically lost ground to the Bolsheviks in the Soviets and the country. In the elections to the Constituent Assembly in November they received less than 3 per cent of the votes as against 24 per cent cast for the Bolsheviks.

The Mensheviks were united in condemning the revolution of October 1917 as a Bolshevik *coup d'état*. At a conference in October 1918, however, the majority of the party, now led by Martov, modified its attitude to the Soviet government and gave it critical support in the civil war. It recognized the October Revolution as 'historically necessary' and as 'a gigantic ferment setting the whole world in motion'. This stand was condemned by a minority of right-wing Mensheviks, some of whom even participated in imperialist-backed anti-Soviet governments. From 1918 until its armed overthrow by Soviet and Georgian Bolshevik forces in 1921, a Menshevik government ruled in Georgia.

Although frequently subject to repression, the Mensheviks continued as a legal opposition until the Kronstadt Revolt of 1921 (which they welcomed but took no part in organizing) led effectively to the suppression of all non-Bolshevik parties. Lenin was also concerned not to allow the Mensheviks to make political capital out of the fact that important elements in their economic programme appeared to have been conceded by the Bolsheviks with the introduction at that time of the New Economic Policy permitting free trade. Widespread arrests of Mensheviks took place, while a number of their prominent leaders were allowed to leave for the West, where they were active first in the Two-and-a-half International and then in the Labour and Socialist International (see INTERNATIONALS). From 1921 till 1965 they published the Menshevik journal *Sotsialisticheskiy Vestnik* (Socialist Courier) from Berlin, Paris and then New York.

Inside the USSR former Mensheviks in the 1920s occupied a number of influential positions in Soviet planning and other institutions. From among them were drawn most of the defendants in the 1931 trial in Moscow of a mythical Menshevik 'Union Bureau'. They were forced to confess to economic sabotage and disruption and to working, in collaboration with West European imperialists and the Labour and Socialist International, to re-establish capitalism in the Soviet Union. Their guilt on these fictitious charges continued to be alleged in Soviet literature as late as 1986. It has more recently been called into question pending the imminent revision of their trial now that similar and related trials of the 1930s have already been quashed.

With the Soviet Union's rapid move since 1989–90 towards a multi-party system (see PARTY), Social Democratic parties and clubs have been formed in different parts of the USSR. At a congress in Tallinn in January 1990 their representatives founded a Social Democratic Association, which now has a parliamentary group in the Supreme Soviet. Its affiliated organizations in different Soviet republics, including a Russian Social Democratic Party formed in May 1990, draw in varying degrees on the Menshevik legacy alongside other traditions including Russian POPULISM. (See also BOLSHEVISM; LENINISM.)

Reading

Ascher, Abraham ed. 1976: *The Mensheviks in the Russian Revolution*.

Brovkin, V. N. 1987: *The Mensheviks after October: Socialist Opposition and the Rise of the Bolshevik Dictatorship*.

Carr, Edward H. 1950–3 (1966): *The Bolshevik Revolution, 1917–1923*.

Deutscher, Isaac 1964a (1966): 'The Mensheviks'. In *Ironies of History*.

Getzler, Israel 1967a: *Martov. A Political Biography of a Russian Social Democrat*.

Haimson, Leopold H. ed. 1974 (1976): *The Mensheviks. From the Revolution of 1917 to the Outbreak of the Second World War*.

Lane, David 1969 (1975): *The Roots of Russian Communism*.

Martov, Y. O. and Dan, F. I. 1926: *Geschichte der russischen Sozialdemokratie*.

1904 (1978): *Second Ordinary Congress of the RSDLP, 1903*.

Strada, Vittorio 1979: 'La polemica tra bolshevichi e menshevichi sulla rivoluzione del 1905'. In Hobsbawm, E. J. *et al.* eds. *Storia del Marxismo, II*.

MONTY JOHNSTONE

merchant capital The capitalist mode of production is characterized by specific social relations of production, namely free wage labour (buying and selling of LABOUR POWER) and the existence of the means of production in COMMODITY form. That is, capitalism involves not merely monetary exchange, but also the domination of the production process by capital. The life-cycle of capital has three moments in its continuous circuit, $M - C \ldots P \ldots C' - M'$. The first moment is the conversion of money capital into productive capital (M-C, exchange of money for labour power and the means of production), and is mediated by financial capital. In the second moment (sphere of production), there is a physical transformation of the means of production in production, and a new set of commodities emerges ($C \ldots P \ldots C'$). This moment is controlled by industrial capital. Finally, the commodities, or commodity capital, must be transformed into money capital, or realized. This third moment is the role of merchant capital.

The development of capitalism was not possible before the process of PRIMITIVE ACCUMULATION (creation of a free wage labour force), but products did enter into monetary exchange. There is some confusion about this point, particularly in the DEPENDENCY THEORY literature (Frank 1969; Wallerstein 1979), but Marxist writers are generally agreed that the epoch of capitalism coincides with the control of capital over the production process (Brenner 1977). Before the epoch of capitalism, in societies where commerce had developed there existed the *form* of capital without the essential social relations upon which capitalism is based. Merchant capital was characterized by the circuit M-C-M, in which the production process lies outside of the circuit of merchant capital, and capital is purely in the sphere of circulation, or mercantile.

There is some debate over the historical role of merchant capital in the transformation of social formations. Some (particularly Engels) have argued that merchant capital was the vehicle by which capitalism replaced feudal society. Marx, however, was quite clear in arguing that merchant capital 'is incapable by itself of promoting and explaining the transition from one mode of production to another', and 'this system presents everywhere an obstacle to the real capitalist mode of production . . .' (*Capital* III, ch. 20). He argued that merchant capital not only does not control the production process, 'but tends rather to preserve it as its precondition' (ibid.). Following this line of argument some writers have argued that the underdevelopment of currently backward countries reflects the debilitating effect of merchant capital on these countries during the period of European colonialism (1500–1850). Specifically, it is argued that merchant capital allied with the most reactionary elements of the local precapitalist ruling class, magnifying their power and blocking the emergence of capitalist relations of production (Kay 1975; Dore and Weeks 1979). This argument is closely related to the debate over the nature of IMPERIALISM.

While the term merchant capitalism is commonly encountered, it is somewhat of a misnomer. As noted above merchant capital is by definition divorced from the sphere of production, and each mode of production is defined by the social relations in which production is organized. Therefore, merchant capital cannot determine the basic nature of society, but rather superimposes itself upon societies whose essential character is determined independently of it. Merchant capitalism is not a definitive social and economic system, but rather a mechanism of control over the exchange of products for money.

Reading

Brenner, R. 1977: 'The Origins of Capitalist Development: A Critique of Neo-Smithian Marxism'.

Dore, Elizabeth and Weeks, John 1979: 'International Exchange and the Causes of Backwardness'.

Frank, A. G. 1969: *Capitalism and Underdevelopment in Latin America*.

Kay, G. 1975: *Development and Underdevelopment*.

Wallerstein, I. 1979: *The Capitalist World System*.

JOHN WEEKS

middle class   Marx and Engels used the term 'middle class' in various, not always consistent, ways. Engels, in the preface to *The Condition of the Working Class*, wrote that he had used the word *Mittelklasse* 'in the sense of the English middle-class or middle-classes corresponding with the French *bourgeoisie*, to mean that part of the possessing class differentiated from the aristocracy', and he repeated this usage in describing the development of the bourgeoisie in the feudal system (*Socialism: Utopian and Scientific*). Marx, however, used the term more in the sense of 'petty bourgeoisie', to designate the class or strata between the bourgeoisie and the working class; and on two occasions (in *Theories of Surplus Value*) he explicitly mentioned the increasing size of the middle classes as an important feature of the development of capitalism (see CLASS). Neither Marx nor Engels made a systematic distinction between different sections of the middle class, in particular between the 'old middle class' of small producers, artisans, independent professional people, farmers and peasants, and the 'new middle class' of clerical, supervisory, and technical workers, teachers, government officials, etc.

Later Marxists have been concerned with two main aspects of the middle class. First, they have analysed its political orientation in different contexts, but particularly in relation to fascism. Marx and Engels generally treated the petty bourgeoisie as being a conservative element in society, or as forming, with the labour aristocracy, a reformist element in workers' movements (*Neue Rheinische Zeitung Revue*, 1850); and in the 1920s and 1930s Marxists saw it as the main social basis of the fascist movements. But there is also, in the developed capitalist societies, the well-known phenomenon of 'middle-class radicalism', and it is impossible to advance very far in an analysis of the politics of the middle class without distinguishing the very diverse groups which compose it: shopkeepers, small producers, highly paid professional and managerial personnel (who merge into the bourgeoisie), lower paid professional, technical or supervisory workers, clerical workers, and so on. Even when these numerous sectional groups have been differentiated it is still difficult to arrive at a satisfactory classification – for example, 'upper' and 'lower' middle class – which would fully explain different political allegiances; indeed the latter seem to be strongly influenced by a variety of cultural factors and by specific political conditions.

The second aspect of the middle class which has attracted even more attention, is its growth in numbers. Bernstein (1899) advanced as one of the principal grounds for a revision of Marxist theory the fact that the 'middle class does not disappear' (assuming, not unreasonably, that the orthodox view of the polarization of classes required such a disappearance), and Renner (1953) later argued that the substantial growth of the 'service class' had fundamentally changed the class structure of capitalist societies. The major recent attempt to define the middle class, and to determine the boundary between it and the working class, was made by Poulantzas (1975), who used two criteria for this purpose; the distinction between productive and unproductive labour (productive workers being defined by him as those who produce surplus value and are directly engaged in material production), and that between mental and manual labour. The result of using these criteria is, as Wright (1978) has claimed, to make the working class very small, and the middle class very large in advanced capitalist societies, and this poses a problem about the future of the working-class movement which Poulantzas did not directly confront.

Other Marxists have taken an exactly opposite course in their analysis, arguing either that the middle class is being proletarianized as a result of the mechanization of office work and '*deskilling*' (Braverman 1974), or that technicians, engineers, professional workers in the public services and private industry, form part of a 'new working class' which showed its radical potential in the social movements of the late 1960s, especially in France (Mallet 1975). The proletarianization thesis is a direct counterpart of the thesis of the *embourgeoisement* of the working class, advanced mainly by non-Marxist sociologists but also to be found in a somewhat different form in the work of some Marxists (e.g. Marcuse 1964). A judgement on these opposed views can only be made ultimately in terms of the development of political attitudes and organizations; whether working-class parties do in fact attract the support of sections of the middle class which are proletarianized either in the sense of being 'deskilled' or of forming a new working class in their relation to the large corporations and the state, or whether 'centre' parties are able to grow as the representative bodies of distinct middle-class interests. Marxist analysis has now to deal with these two real tendencies in present-day capitalist societies, paying attention on one side to the lack of homogeneity and the strongly marked

historical fluctuations of political outlook which characterize the middle class, and on the other, to some of the defining features of its social position – its market situation and the influence of status considerations – which were particularly emphasized by Max Weber in opposition to the Marxist theory of class (see CRITICS OF MARXISM).

Reading

Abercrombie, Nicholas and Urry, John 1983: *Capital, Labour and the Middle Classes*.

Braverman, Harry 1974: *Labor and Monopoly Capital*.

Nicolaus, Martin 1967: 'Proletariat and Middle Class in Marx'.

Poulantzas, Nicos 1975: *Classes in Contemporary Capitalism*.

Renner, Karl 1953 (1978): 'The Service Class'.

Walker, P. ed. 1980: *Between Capital and Labour*.

Wright, Erik Olin 1978: *Class, Crisis and the State*.

TOM BOTTOMORE

mode of production Not used in any single, consistent sense by Marx, the term has since been elaborated as the core element of a systematic account of history as the succession of different modes of production (see HISTORICAL MATERIALISM; STAGES OF DEVELOPMENT). This account, which sees epochs of history (or their theoretical characterization) as defined by a dominant mode of production, and revolution as the replacement of one mode by another, was common in the 'economistic' Marxism of the Second International (see ECONOMISM; INTERNATIONALS), and was restated as the correct understanding of Marx's materialist conception of history by Stalin in *Dialectical and Historical Materialism*; thus becoming the foundation of 'Diamat' (see DIALECTICAL MATERIALISM), the official Comintern interpretation of Marxism. The authority for regarding this as Marx's own conception is the famous Preface to *A Contribution to the Critique of Political Economy*:

> In the social production which men carry on they enter into definite relations that are indispensable and independent of their will; these relations of production correspond to a definite stage of development of their material powers of production. The sum total of these

relations of production constitutes the economic structure of society – the real foundation on which rise legal and political superstructures and to which correspond definite forms of social consciousness. The mode of production in material life determines the general character of the social, political and spiritual processes of life. At a certain stage of their development, the material forces of production in society come into conflict with the existing relations of production, or – what is but a legal expression for the same thing – with the property relations within which they had been at work before. From forms of development of the forces of production, these relations turn into their fetters. Then comes the period of social revolution.

On this view the DIALECTIC consists of the parallel development of the two elements; the forces developing on the basis of given relations of production and their immanent contradiction becoming manifest only at a 'certain stage of their development' when 'these relations turn into their fetters'. (For a more extended discussion see FORCES AND RELATIONS OF PRODUCTION.) This has given rise to a determinist reading of the process of revolution; when the forces of production have outstripped the relations of production, revolution is not only possible but inevitable. The success of revolution in backward Russia and its failure in advanced Germany pointed, among other things, to the role of consciousness in the revolutionary process, and suggested that something in this determinist account was wrong. The economic base did not determine the superstructure in the direct, automatic way that Marx seemed to imply, and the collapse of a mode of production was not therefore such a clear cut matter as it had seemed to be. There appeared to be circumstances in which ideological and political factors overrode the economic, that is, the superstructure determined what was happening in the base, to the extent of bringing about or preventing a transformation in the mode of production (see BASE AND SUPERSTRUCTURE; DETERMINISM).

An attempt to deal with this problem, while retaining the mode of production as a central concept, has been made by Althusser particularly in Reading 'Capital' (with Étienne Balibar). Althusser rejects the notion of a base determining the superstructure; instead he sees the economic, political and ideological as levels, consisting of specific practices, which together form a structured totality, a social formation. The notion of determination is replaced by that of structural causality (see STRUCTURALISM). The mode of production remains a key concept in so far as it is the economic level, the mode of production, which 'determines' which of the different levels is 'dominant' in the interdependent structured totality. The economic sets limits, within which the other levels can be only 'relatively autonomous', by assigning functions necessary to the reproduction of the mode of production to those non-economic levels.

The mode of production, as defined by Althusser and Balibar, consists of two sets of relations or 'connections': 'the connection of real appropriation of nature' and 'the relations of expropriation of the product' (Althusser and Balibar 1970, glossary). These two sets of relations, it is claimed, correspond to Marx's characterization of all production by 'two indissociable elements: the labour process . . . and the social relations of production beneath whose determination this labour process is executed' (ibid.). The trouble with this formulation, as has been pointed out by critics (see Clarke 1980), is that it has immediately dissociated the indissociable; the labour process itself is seen as something ahistorical, while social relations are concentrated within the mode of appropriation of the product, i.e. within relations of property and distribution alone. By specifying a priori the boundaries and categories within which we must look for the socially specific, Althusser hypostasizes them and thus manages to hypostasize production itself. But Marx's fundamental criticism of bourgeois thought was that it eternalized the social relations of capitalism, and most crucially those of capitalist production.

Hence, although Althusser broke with earlier forms of crude economic determinism, by rejecting their reductionism, he did not differ fundamentally in his understanding of the economic base, the mode of production. The new relation he posited, in which the relative autonomy of non-economic levels depended on their necessity for the reproduction of the mode of production, created a separation between the characterization of the conditions of production, and of the conditions under which they can be reproduced; and this has been criticized as missing the essential idea of process and dialectic in Marx's work (Glucksmann 1972). An alternative approach, which also rejects the economic determinism of the Second and Third Internationals, by reformulating and broadening their conception of the mode of production, has arisen largely through the interest in Marx's own writings on the labour-process, stimulated by the publication in English in 1976 of a hitherto little-known manuscript originally intended as ch. 6 of *Capital* I; 'Results of the immediate process of production' (*Capital* I, Penguin edn. 1976). For Marx's own use of the term outside that chapter is definitely ambiguous with respect to the Althusserian dichotomy. On the one hand it is used to define the type of economic process, and basically the relations between people in the production and appropriation of the surplus (for example, in the passage from the 'Preface' cited above). At other times it seems to have a much less grand meaning, as in the chapter on 'Machinery and Modern Industry' in *Capital* I, where mechanization in single spheres of industry, such as the introduction of the hydraulic press, of the power loom and the carding engine, are all referred to as 'transformation(s) of the mode of production' in their appropriate sphere. In the 'Results' chapter, the consistency of the range of meanings becomes clear. By distinguishing between the formal and the real subsumption of labour under capital, Marx distinguishes between the formal conditions under which capitalist forms of exploitation take place (the 'Diamat' and Althusserian definition), and the actual production conditions to which those forms of exploitation lead and under which they are reproduced. So although the former may define the mode of production formally, they can only be reproduced as the latter; and the consequences, that is, the ways in which the mode of production does act as a base affecting the rest of society, depend on the real conditions, the conditions under which the mode of production can be reproduced. By consigning the non-economic levels to the role of reproduction, his critics would argue, Althusser is both recreating the reductionism he wished to avoid and impoverishing the concept of the mode of production to a formal, ahistorical shell (see

Banaji 1977; Glucksmann 1972; Clarke *et al.* 1980).

All sides in the debate would be happy to accept as a working definition of 'mode of production' the much used quotation from Marx (which incidentally does not use the term itself):

The specific economic form, in which unpaid surplus labour is pumped out of direct producers [and also that this] determines the relationship of rulers and ruled, as it grows directly out of production itself and in turn, reacts upon it as a determining element. Upon this, however, is founded the entire formation of the economic community which grows up out of the production relations themselves, thereby simultaneously its specific political form. It is always the direct relationship of the owners of the conditions of production to the direct producers – a relation always naturally corresponding to a definite stage in the development of the methods of labour and thereby its social productivity – which reveals the innermost secret, the hidden basis of the entire social structure. (*Capital* III, ch. 47, sect. II)

The dispute concerns the precise interpretation of this passage. All sides accept that what is crucial is the way in which the surplus is produced and its use controlled, for it is the production of a surplus which allows societies to grow and change. The disagreement concerns the extent to which the economic can be defined *a priori*, and formally distinguished from other 'levels'; whether determination means the operation of separate entities on each other, even if connected in a structured totality, or rather the immanent development of internal relations within an indivisible whole.

Reading

Althusser, L. and Balibar, É. 1970: *Reading 'Capital'*.

Banaji, J. 1977: 'Modes of Production in a Materialist Conception of History'.

Clarke, S. 1980: 'Althusserian Marxism'. In Clarke *et al. One-Dimensional Marxism*.

Clarke, S. *et al.* 1980: *One-Dimensional Marxism*.

Colletti, 1969 (1972): 'Bernstein and the Marxism of the Second International'. In *From Rousseau to Lenin*.

Glucksmann, A. 1972: 'A Ventriloquist Structuralism'.

Stalin, J. 1938: *Dialectical and Historical Materialism*.

SUSAN HIMMELWEIT

modernism and postmodernism As a general term in cultural history, modernism embraces an immense variety of aesthetic breaks with the European realist tradition. For the modernist text (poem, novel, painting, building, musical composition), aesthetic form no longer unproblematically 'reflects' a pre-given external social world, but becomes an object of attention, anxiety or fascination in its own right – to the point, indeed, where it may even seem to *constitute* the 'reality' it once supposedly mirrored. Favoured dates for the origins of the movement are 1848, when after the brutal suppression of the revolutions of that year classical or realist writing lurched into crisis in the works of Charles Baudelaire and Gustave Flaubert; or the 1880s, when a long series of accelerating aesthetic experimentalisms got underway: from Naturalism through Symbolism to Cubism, Expressionism, Futurism, Constructivism, Vorticism, Surrealism and others. The high point of modernism, by general consent, is the years from 1910 to 1930, after which modernist artists in Nazi Germany and Stalinist Russia were silenced or persecuted, and elsewhere in Europe a reaction towards realist aesthetics – social responsibility rather than individualist experiment in art – set in as a response to the increasing political polarization of the Continent.

Whether any single common defining feature could be distilled from the amazing range of aesthetic innovations of these years is doubtful: some modernisms celebrated a future of technology, speed and urban dynamism, others harked back to a primitivist past of settled *Gemeinschaft* and intuitive harmony with Nature; some sought to make their own aesthetic forms as sprawlingly encyclopaedic as the contemporary life that was their matrix, while others tried to distil from this vast, rushing process some minimalist formal perfection – a fleeting epiphany, a two-line Imagist *haiku*, a play by Samuel Beckett lasting all of twenty seconds, a nearly blank canvas. Moreover, modernists within the same camp moved to the most diverse political destinations: from Futurism, Vladimir Mayakovsky embraced Bolshevism, while Filippo Marinetti supported Mussolini; from Expressionism, Gottfried Benn supported Hitler, while Ernst Toller moved to the revolutionary left. Perhaps only the heightened attention to aesthetic form (itself justified from diverse and often incompatible ideological positions) is common to all the artists of this period. To offer any more specific defining features of modernism would be to risk making a movement out of a crisis – a cultural and social crisis whose key features would include the rise of mass culture, working-class and feminist militancy, the new technologies of the second industrial revolution, and the overwhelming experience of the new imperialist metropolises.

Throughout these same years a lively polemic took place within Marxism on the significance of modernism, coming to a head in the so-called 'Expressionism debate' of the 1930s. Mainstream Marxists, including Georg LUKÁCS, denounced modernism for its idealist abandonment of reflectionist epistemology, for its self-regarding, involuted 'formalism', its cult of the private psyche and intense inner experience as against the rounded portrait of man-in-society that realism was argued to paint, its preference for myth over history. Other Marxists, including Walter BENJAMIN, Bertolt BRECHT and Theodor ADORNO, welcomed the new movements in varying degrees and for varying reasons; and we might be inclined to see their work not just as 'Marxism *on* modernism' but rather as a distinctive 'modernist Marxism'. More recently, it has been argued that the intense emphasis on form in modernist culture was itself crucial in the development of a 'Western' or dialectical as opposed to an 'Eastern' or mechanical materialism – the former ironically including Lukács's own *History and Class Consciousness* (Lunn 1985).

In the last twenty or so years, our sense of modernism has again shifted with the emergence of postmodernism – initially in architecture but later across a range of cultural fields. The 'modernism' against which postmodernism first defined itself, though a narrow selection of the whole gamut of experiment during the earlier period, has accordingly come to dominate our recent definitions of early twentieth-century avant-garde aesthetics. It is now the austerely functionalist architecture of Le Corbusier and the International Style, or of Walter Gropius and the Bauhaus – stripped of ornament and all concessions to human individuality, rigidly rectilinear in construction and determinedly 'state of the art' in building techniques and materials (steel and reinforced concrete being particular favourites) – which has become the exemplary modernism. Modernist aesthetics could thus be seen as premised on a sharp, elitist binary division between 'high art' and 'mass culture', the gleaming white facades and flat roof of Le Corbusier's architectural sculpture versus the degraded, 'massified' urban fabric around it; and this definition of modernism (or what some theorists have come to call 'high modernism') is flexible enough to catch up certain contemporary experiments – the notoriously 'difficult' and allusive poetry of T. S. Eliot, for instance – which in most other respects have very little in common indeed with International Style architecture. Postmodernism, from the late 1960s, thus initially presented itself as a *populism*, a return to the demotic, vernacular, even mass commercial traditions after the long detour into uncompromising avant-garde elitism; its manifestos bear such titles as *Learning from Las Vegas* and *From Bauhaus to Our House*. Another, related, key motif was *historicism*, a relaxed return to the manifold styles of the past as a source of inspiration in the present, rather than a knee-jerk condemnation of them in the name of advanced technology and functionalist rationality. The equivalent of such architectural developments in the field of fiction is what Linda Hutcheon has termed 'historiographic metafiction', exemplified by such authors as Gabriel García Márquez, Günter Grass, John Fowles, E. L. Doctorow and Salman Rushdie. Novels of this kind return to questions of plot, history and reference which had once seemed to be exploded by modernist fiction's concern for textual autonomy and self-consciousness, but without simply abandoning these 'metafictional' preoccupations; the result is a paradoxical genre in which history is powerfully asserted and problematized in the same moment.

Postmodernism has, in general, been attractively open to cultural 'otherness', the repressed styles of the past but also marginalized voices in the present: women, gays, blacks, the Third World. This positive assessment of other voices, experiences and narratives has taken the form, in philosophy, of a suspicion of the 'grand metanarratives' whereby knowledge has been grounded in the past. The grand narratives of Enlightenment, with universal reason progressively triumphant over barbarous supersitition, and of Marxism, with its view of the proletariat

as universal revolutionary class, are seen as analogous to Gropius's or Le Corbusier's austere, geometrical white boxes, as incarnating a totalitarian rationality which brooks no difference, dissent or pluralism. Postmodernist philosophy, above all in the work of Jean-François Lyotard, instead stresses the relativity of knowledge, its context-dependency, preferring to speak of local, Wittgensteinian 'language games' rather than of 'reason', 'truth' or 'totality'. For postmodernism, Marxism is irredeemably in thrall to the repressive project of modernity, brutally reducing actual histories to the procrustean 'History' of class struggle or modes of production. Marxists have hit back by accusing postmodernism of a cult of 'pastiche' and 'schizophrenia', of erasing history into a mere play of depthless surfaces or of decentring the subject so radically as to render it incapable of political (or any other) action. As these charges and countercharges suggest, the debates between Marxism and postmodernism share many features with the earlier confrontation of modernism and Marxist politics; and they are being pursued today with as much urgency and confusion as was the latter in the 1920s and 1930s. If the most interesting development of those decades was not the rigid embittered polemics but the emergence of a flexible 'modernist Marxism' in the no man's land between the warring camps, so, too, today are we beginning to sense the shape of a possible synthesis, a 'postmodernist Marxism', which may already be signalled by the sudden centrality of geography in Marxist cultural studies; for the insertion of categories of space and place into Marxist theory takes on board the postmodern emphasis on locality or context without sacrificing Marxism's traditional political concerns.

Reading

Harvey, David 1989: *The Condition of Postmodernity*.

Hutcheon, Linda 1988: *A Poetics of Postmodernism*.

Jameson, Fredric 1984: 'Postmodernism, or the Cultural Logic of Late Capitalism'.

Lunn, Eugene 1985: *Marxism and Modernism*.

Lyotard, Jean-François 1979 (*1984*): *The Postmodern Condition*.

Williams, Raymond 1989: *The Politics of Modernism*.

TONY PINKNEY

money A general equivalent form of VALUE, a form in which the value of commodities appears as pure exchange value. The money form of value is inherent in the commodity form of production organized by exchange. In EXCHANGE a definite quantity of one commodity, say 20 yards of linen, is equated to a definite quantity of a second, say, one coat. In this equation the coat measures the value of the linen; the linen is a value relative to the coat, and the coat is the equivalent of the linen. This elementary value relation can be expanded to equate the 20 yards of linen to a definite quantity of every other commodity as its equivalent: the linen is equated to one coat, to 10 pounds of tea, to 40 pounds of coffee, or to 2 ounces of gold. In this expanded form of value every commodity in turn plays the role of equivalent. The expanded form of value can be inverted to the general equivalent form of value, in which one commodity is seen as measuring simultaneously the value of every other commodity. In the example given, if the linen is viewed as general equivalent, it measures the value of one coat, 10 pounds of tea, 2 ounces of gold, and so on. Any commodity can in principle serve as the general equivalent. The *numéraire* of neo-classical economic theory is a particular case of a general equivalent commodity.

Money is a *socially accepted* general equivalent, a particular commodity which emerges in social reality to play the role of general equivalent, and excludes all other commodities from that role. Any produced commodity could in principle serve as money; Marx usually refers to the money-commodity as gold, and argues that the natural properties of gold, its durability, uniformity and divisibility, make it particularly suited to function as the measure of pure exchange value. The money form of value is thus latent in and arises directly from the commodity form of production. The concept of a 'pure barter economy' in which well developed exchange relations exist without money has no place in Marx's theory of money; wherever the commodity form of production appears, money as a form of value will tend to develop as well, even if many transactions occur without the mediation of money as means of purchase. The most fundamental property of money in Marx's theory is its function as the measure of value of commodities. In this role the general equivalent

need not be physically present, since it is possible to express the price of a commodity in gold without actually exchanging the commodity for gold. Once a commodity emerges as a socially accepted general equivalent, definite quantities of the money-commodity come to be used as a *standard of price*, and bear special names, such as pound, dollar, franc, mark, peso, and so on. The state may play a role in regulating and manipulating the standard of price, just as it comes to regulate customary standards of weight, length, and other measures.

Since the money commodity is a produced commodity its value is determined by the same laws that determine the value of other commodities. If we abstract from all those factors that may make commodities exchange at ratios different from the ratios of ABSTRACT LABOUR contained in them, an amount of the money commodity containing one hour of abstract labour will buy a quantity of any other commodity that also embodies one hour of abstract labour. The value of the money commodity, like the value of other commodities, changes continually as the conditions of production change. Thus although the state can regulate the standard of price, that is, the amount of gold in the pound or dollar or whatever, it cannot regulate the value of the money commodity (gold) itself.

Once a money commodity emerges it begins to play other roles besides that of measure of value: as medium of circulation, as an immobilized hoard of value, as means of payment, and as universal money. As medium of circulation, money mediates the exchange of commodities. An exchange takes the form of the sale of a commodity for money, followed by the purchase of another commodity with the money (a process Marx describes by the diagram C-M-C, that is, Commodity-Money-Commodity). If we examine this process from a social point of view we see that a certain quantity of money is required to circulate a certain volume of commodities over a given time. This quantity depends on the value of the commodities and the value of the money-commodity, which together determine the money price of the mass of commodities circulated, and on the velocity of circulation of money, the number of transactions each piece of money can participate in during the period. In Marx's theory these factors determine the amount of money required to circulate commodities; the mechanisms by which this money is provided are a separate topic of inquiry. It is at this fundamental point that Marx's theory of money deviates from that of the 'quantity theory of money' which holds that the prices of commodities must rise or fall to equilibrate the money required in circulation to a predetermined existing quantity of money.

Since money makes only a fleeting appearance in commodity circulation, it is possible for tokens or symbols of the money commodity to replace it there as long as these tokens or symbols can in fact be converted into the money commodity at their face value. Thus small coins whose metallic content is less than their face value, or banknotes with negligible intrinsic value, can circulate in place of gold. A different case is the issuing of fiat money by the state without a guarantee of its convertibility into gold at its face value. Marx analyses this phenomenon on the assumption that gold continues to function as money alongside the fiat currency. This fiat money will circulate in place of gold, but if the state issues it in excess of the requirements of circulation, the fiat issue will depreciate against gold in market transactions until the gold value of the fiat issue is just sufficient to meet the requirements of circulation. In these circumstances the fiat money price of commodities will rise in proportion to the issue of the fiat money, but the mechanism of this change is the fall in the gold value of fiat money on the market. The gold prices of commodities continue to be determined by the conditions of production of gold and the other commodities, but a larger amount of the fiat money is needed to equal that gold price. Once again this result has a different basis and mechanism from the 'quantity theory of money', which predicts a general rise of money prices of commodities due to an increase in the quantity of money rather than a depreciation of the fiat money against a continuing commodity money general equivalent.

Because money mediates the exchange of commodities, purchase and sale are not identical, and Say's Law, the proposition that the offering of commodities for sale is equivalent to a demand to purchase other commodities, so that supply creates in the aggregate its own demand, does not hold. Since purchase is sep-arated from sale, exchange crises, in which commodities cannot be sold for money, are possible, though the positive determinants of crises lie in the particular relations of capitalist production (see ECONOMIC CRISES).

The circulation of money permits and requires the formation of hoards, stocks of money held either to facilitate circulation of commodities, or to accumulate the crystallized abstract labour of the society as an end in itself. The existence of hoards can provide the flexibility necessary to allow money in circulation to adapt to the requirements of circulation, though Marx in his general theory of money offers no account of the mechanisms through which money flows in and out of hoards. In capitalist crises hoarding expresses the unwillingness of capitalists to advance money capital in the face of collapsed markets. The accumulation of money by the hoarder is to be distinguished from the ACCUMULATION of value by the capitalist. The hoarder accumulates by throwing a greater value of commodities onto the market than he buys back. Though the hoarder withdraws money from circulation he withdraws no extra or surplus value, since the value of the commodities he has sold is just equal to the value of the money he holds. The hoard is a passive aggregation of money value. Capital, on the other hand, expands by a constant process of circulation, the use of money to buy commodities to undertake production, and the appropriation of a surplus value in selling the produced commodities.

The payment for commodities may be deferred if the seller extends CREDIT to the buyer. In this case money functions also as means of payment to repay debts. Credit can to a considerable extent substitute for money in the circulation of commodities, and can be seen as accelerating the velocity of money. In periods of crisis, however, money as means of payment reasserts its primacy when producers scramble to raise the real money necessary to cover their debts in the face of a widespread inability to turn commodities into money by selling them on the market.

When the same commodity emerges as money in several different countries, the money commodity also serves as universal money, settling international trade accounts and permitting the transfer of wealth between countries.

Money capital in Marx's theory is a stock of money held by a capitalist after selling commodities but before recommitting the value to production by spending it to buy labour power and means of production. Not all stocks of money are money capital, since money may be held by capitalist households to finance their consumption, or by workers' households or the state to finance their circuits of revenue and spending. Such reserves are potentially money capital, since they may be mobilized by capitalist firms which borrow them to employ as capital in the circuit of capital.

In modern capitalist economies the links between the monetary system and a general equivalent commodity have become highly attenuated, and the credit system normally functions without recourse to a commodity money. In these circumstances the value of the monetary unit does not depend on the costs of production of a money commodity, but is free to vary in response to the pressures on prices generated in the circuit of capital and the accumulation process. The basic structure of Marx's theory, which derives the money form of value from the commodity form of production, and tries to understand how the monetary system accommodates the circulation of commodities and money, still holds in this case, but the determination of the value of the money commodity by its cost of production must be replaced by the determination of changes in the value of the monetary unit in response to the contradictions of capital accumulation. Marx's theory of money shows that money in each of its moments mediates a social relation. When money functions as measure of value it expresses the equivalence of socially necessary abstract labour in exchange, the relation between commodity producers. Money in circulation permits the social validation of the products of private labour. The use of money as means of payment mediates the relation between debtors and creditors. Money capital expresses the capitalists' command over labour power. The role of the state in managing money must thus be seen as a managing of these social relations as well.

Reading

de Brunoff, Suzanne 1973 (1976): *Marx on Money.*

Hilferding, Rudolf 1910 (1981): *Finance Capital*, chs. 1 to 5.

DUNCAN FOLEY

monopoly capitalism   The idea that monopolies were characteristic of a new stage of capitalism emerging at the end of the nineteenth century was introduced into Marxism by Lenin and the theorists of FINANCE CAPITAL. However, the term monopoly capitalism acquired a different meaning and a new prominence from the book by Baran and Sweezy (1966) which had a major impact in reviving interest in Marxist economic theory in the mid-1960s. This book developed some of the ideas put forward by the two authors in their earlier work (Sweezy 1942, Baran 1957) and its theses have subsequently been sustained by a rich body of writing in *Monthly Review* and by major books such as that by Braverman (1974) written within the framework of the concept. Although Baran and Sweezy's work on monopoly capital revived interest in Marxist economics, especially in North and South America, it was revisionist in character. Faced with what appeared to be a stable and growing post-war capitalism they argued that the contradictions uncovered by Marx had been replaced by others and capitalism had developed new methods for containing them. The key change in capitalism's character, they argued, had been the replacement of competition between industrial capitals by monopolies; in other words the weight of each firm in the *markets* on which their commodities were sold increased and underwent a qualitative change. For Baran and Sweezy that was the defining characteristic of the stage of monopoly capitalism. Although they relied on Marx's law of CENTRALIZATION AND CONCENTRATION of capital to explain the *cause* of this development and root their concept in Marxist tradition, Baran and Sweezy took over a standard theorem of neo-classical economics to argue that its *effect* was an increase in monopolistic firms' profits.

In the concept of monopoly capitalism employed by Baran and Sweezy's school the burgeoning profits of monopolistic firms are given the status of a law which supersedes Marx's law of the FALLING RATE OF PROFIT. Arguing that total profits approximate 'society's economic surplus' Baran and Sweezy 'formulate as a law of monopoly capitalism that the surplus tends to rise both absolutely and relatively as the system develops' (1966, p. 72). They see this substitution of the tendency of the surplus to rise for the law of the falling rate of profit as the theoretical expression of the things that are 'most essential about the structural change from competitive to monopoly capitalism'. From this tendency stem some of the most prominent aspects of the new system, but it is important to note that their concept of 'economic surplus' is quite distinct from Marx's notion of SURPLUS VALUE.

Economic surplus is calculated at market prices instead of values, and more significantly, it rests on a normative judgment concerning the nature of socially necessary costs. For society, they argue, surplus is total output minus costs of production as long as the latter are socially necessary. Some business costs are excluded from this category on the grounds that they relate only to the sales effort; these include not only costs such as the wages of the sales force but also the cost of features of each commodity which are not strictly necessary to its basic function. Thus, as one example, an automobile's embellishments of chromework and eye-catching upholstery are costs not necessary to its basic function; they should not be included in socially necessary costs but should be conceived as an element of the surplus. Such arbitrary definition of commodities as (partially) not being use values is irrelevant for Marx's concepts of surplus value or PRODUCTIVE AND UNPRODUCTIVE LABOUR. Finally, the genesis of increases in the economic surplus is located in the process of EXCHANGE, market domination, whereas Marx's surplus value is founded upon the LABOUR PROCESS and its articulation with the process of valorization.

Braverman (1974), however, turns attention to the labour process under monopoly capitalism. In a remarkable historical and theoretical study he examines the rise of 'scientific management' which he connects with the beginnings of the monopoly capitalist stage, and he traces the transformations in the labour process, the deskilling of labour, and the shifts in occupational structure and position of the WORKING CLASS that have unfolded over subsequent years. In fact, however, the concept of monopoly capitalism developed by Baran and Sweezy (and its

elements such as the economic surplus) is not centrally employed in this study. Thus, despite his connection with Baran and Sweezy's work and his use of the title *Labor and Monopoly Capital* his study does not remedy the dominance of exchange considerations in those writers' concept of monopoly capital.

Baran and Sweezy, developing their argument in a tradition inspired by KALECKI (1954) and Steindl (1952), consider that the rising economic surplus leads to economic stagnation unless counteracted, for they postulate an inherent inability to employ the surplus or in other words, UNDERCONSUMPTION. Monopoly capitalism is characterized by the development of mechanisms to absorb the surplus and thereby maintain growth. These include the rise of military expenditure, expenditure on the huge and 'wasteful' sales efforts associated with mass consumption, and high state expenditure. To the extent that these do maintain monopoly capitalism's momentum, the potential for its overthrow by the exploited classes at its centre is weakened. Baran and Sweezy argue that the seeds of its downfall are to be found in Third World revolutions, and they anticipate these resulting from the contradictions generated by monopoly capitalism's imperialist expansion and its extraction of 'economic surplus' from the Third World.

Reading

Baran, Paul 1957: *The Political Economy of Growth.*

Baran, Paul and Sweezy, Paul 1966: *Monopoly Capitalism.*

Braverman, Harry 1974: *Labor and Monopoly Capital.*

Cowling, Keith 1982: *Monopoly Capitalism.*

Kalecki, Michal 1954: *Theory of Economic Dynamics.*

Steindl, Josef 1952: *Maturity and Stagnation in American Capitalism.*

Sweezy, Paul 1942: *The Theory of Capitalist Development.*

LAURENCE HARRIS

morals   The Marxist view of morals is paradoxical. On the one hand, it is claimed that morality is a form of ideology, that any given morality arises out of a particular stage of the development of productive forces and relations and is relative to a particular mode of production and particular class interests, that there are no eternal moral truths, that the very form of morality and general ideas such as freedom and justice cannot 'completely vanish except with the total disappearance of class antagonisms' (*Communist Manifesto*), that Marxism is opposed to all moralizing and that the Marxist critique of both capitalism and political economy is not moral but scientific. On the other hand, Marxist writings are full of moral judgments, implicit and explicit. From his earliest writings, expressing his hatred of servility through the discussions of alienation in the *Economic and Philosophical Manuscripts* and *German Ideology* to the excoriating attacks on factory conditions and inequalities in *Capital*, it is plain that Marx was fired by outrage, indignation and the burning desire for a better world. The same goes for Engels and most Marxist thinkers since. Indeed, at least in capitalist societies, it is arguable that most people who become Marxists do so for mainly moral reasons.

This paradox may be amply illustrated from Marxist texts. Consider Marx's scorn for Proudhon's and others' appeals to justice, and his rejection of moral vocabulary in the *Critique of the Gotha Programme*, alongside his bitter descriptions of capitalism's stunting, alienating effects on workers and his often-surfacing vision of communism, where the associated producers would work and live 'under conditions most favourable to, and worthy of, their human nature' (*Capital* III, ch. 48). Consider Engels's rejection of moral dogmas and his view that 'morality has always been class morality' alongside his belief in moral progress and in 'the proletarian morality of the future' (*Anti-Dühring*, pt. I, ch. IX). Consider Kautsky's, Luxemburg's and Lenin's attacks on 'ethical socialism' alongside their denunciations of capitalism's ills and their visions of socialism and communism. Compare Trotsky's view that all morality is class ideology and part of the 'mechanics of class deception' with his acceptance of 'the liberating morality of the proletariat' (1969, pp. 16, 37).

The paradox has been avoided by various deviant traditions within Marxist history: the Kantian-influenced Marxists and 'ethical socialists' of Germany and Austria, existentialist-influenced Marxists, above all in France, and dissident Marxists in Eastern Europe, especially Poland and Yugoslavia. Such deviations have tended to embrace the moral component of Marxism (whether in the form of categorical imperatives, existential commitments or humanist interpretations and principles), while rejecting or underplaying the anti-moral.

The paradox may perhaps begin to be resolved in two ways. First, by the suggestion that Marx and later Marxists have been confused or even self-deceived in their attitude to morality, falsely believing themselves to have dispensed with or gone beyond a moral point of view. Certainly, the positivist, scientist component in Marxism has encouraged this possibility. But the second proposed resolution cuts deeper. This involves drawing a distinction between the area of morality which concerns rights, obligations, justice, etc., which is identified by the German term '*Recht*'; and the area concerned with the realization of human powers, and freedom from the obstacles to that realization, which is best captured by what Marx called 'human emancipation' (see EMANCIPATION). Morality in the former sense is, arguably, from a Marxist point of view inherently ideological, since it is called forth by conditions – above all scarcity and conflicting interests – that arise out of class society, whose antagonisms and dilemmas it both misdescribes and purports to resolve. To morality *in this sense* Marxism holds a view exactly analogous to its view of religion: that the call to abandon such illusions is the call to abandon conditions which require such illusions. Remove scarcity and class conflict and the morality of *Recht* will wither away. The morality of emancipation demands the abolition of the conditions that require a morality of *Recht*.

This suggestion would make sense of two points various recent writers have noticed: that Marx appears to reject the view that capitalism is unjust, and that Marxism lacks a developed theory of rights. More generally, one may say that Marxism has an inspiring moral vision, but no developed theory of moral constraints, of what means are permissible in the pursuit of its ends. It does of course have a theory of ends, and since Lenin a plethora of tactical and strategic discussions of means, but with few exceptions, it has always resisted any discussion of this question from a moral point of view (see ETHICS; JUSTICE).

Reading

Buchanan, Allen E. 1982: *Marx and Justice: The Political Critique of Liberalism.*

Cohen, Marshall, Nagel, Thomas and Scanlon, Thomas eds. 1980: *Marx, Justice and History.*

Kamenka, Eugene 1969: *Marxism and Ethics.*

Kautsky, Karl 1906 (*1918*): *Ethics and the Materialist Conception of History.*

Lukes, Steven 1985: *Marxism and Morality.*

'Marx and Morality' 1981: Supplementary volume of the *Canadian Journal of Philosophy* 7.

Merleau-Ponty, Maurice 1947 (*1969*): *Humanism and Terror.*

Plamenatz, John 1975: *Karl Marx's Philosophy of Man.*

Rubel, Maximilien 1948: *Pages choisies pour une éthique socialiste.*

Stojanović, Svetozar 1973: *Between Ideals and Reality.*

Trotsky, Leon, Dewey, John and Novack, George 1969: *Their Morals and Ours: Marxist versus Liberal Views on Morality.*

Wood, Allen W. 1981: *Karl Marx.*

STEVEN LUKES

Morris, William Born 24 March 1834, Walthamstow, London; died 3 October 1896, Hammersmith, London. One of the foremost designers of his own, or any generation, William Morris founded a firm in 1861 that produced high quality textiles, wallpapers, carpets, furniture and stained glass for churches. In revolt against the shoddy, pretentious decoration produced by Victorian commerce, he saw the firm as an attempt to reform the decorative arts. Some of his designs became very popular and are still sold. He was also a talented craftsman, mastering twelve different crafts. His work inspired the arts and crafts movement. His Kelmscott Press, founded in 1890, set new standards in the design of type and in book production.

His passionate love of art and architecture, deepened by his early reading of Ruskin, moved him into the socialist movement of the 1880s. He became a socialist as an artist in revolt against the 'eyeless vulgarity', the 'sordid, aimless, ugly confusion' of 'modern civilisation'. In 1877 he founded the Society for the Protection of Ancient Buildings (SPAB – still active) and gave his first two public addresses: a speech as treasurer of the Eastern Question Association against Disraeli's war policies in the Balkans; and a lecture entitled *The Decorative Arts.* This was the first of his many public lectures on art and society. After a period of activity in the radical wing of the Liberal Party, he grew disillusioned with it and by 1882 had become a socialist or, as he always preferred to call himself, a communist, reading *Capital* in French. For the remainder of his life he undertook all the activities of a 'practical socialist', in the Social Democratic Federation, then in the Socialist League, editing its journal *The Commonweal,* and finally in the Hammersmith Socialist Society. He opposed the strategy of parliamentary reformism and what he called the 'state socialism' advocated by the Fabians. Change should be brought about by the workers themselves: 'By us, and not for us' should be their motto. He saw his main political activity as the endeavour to 'make socialists'. He stood for 'education towards revolution'.

William Morris's views on art, architecture, work and society were developed in many lectures such as *Art and Socialism, Useful Work versus Useless Toil, The Beauty of Life* and *The Aims of Art.* He held, following Ruskin, that art is the expression of human beings' pleasure in their work. Everyone could produce works of art given the right conditions, which could be obtained only under socialism, with its equality and its 'fellowship'. The nature of work should be transformed under socialism so that workers are able to express in it their creative imagination.

These ideas were confirmed by his knowledge of the Middle Ages when the labour of the craftsmen was often creative and enjoyable, and when they had control over their own work. Early in his life, deeply influenced by the Romantic Movement and the Pre-Raphaelites, he had developed a powerful historical imagination, enabling him to build up a vivid picture of medieval England as a community possessing values and art in sharp contrast with those of the Victorians.

These values were expressed in his poetry. His first book of verse, *The Defence of Guenevere* (1858) employs medieval themes. In 1868–70 his long narrative poem *The Earthly Paradise,* reworking classical, Nordic and Arabic legends, made him well known as a poet. In his search for alternative values he discovered the Icelandic sagas, admiring the qualities of courage, self-reliance and community spirit displayed in them. He translated many of them into English, and made the legend of Sigurd the Volsung into one of the finest narrative poems in English (1876). Later, in the cause of socialism, he used his poetic skill to compose *The Pilgrims of Hope*, commemorating the Paris Commune, and his famous *Chants for Socialists*.

Morris's views on the nature of the future socialist society were elaborated in his lectures on art and architecture and in many others such as *True and False Society*, *The Society of the Future*, *How We Live and Might Live*, *A Factory as it Might Be*. A factory would be a beautiful building, ornamented by its workers and set in spacious gardens. Furnished with a library and workshop, it would be a centre for the self-education of children and adults. Unrewarding work such as minding machines would be of short duration, taken turn and turn about. People should learn at least three crafts or occupations for 'variety of life is as much an aim of communism as equality of condition.' There would be no 'hierarchy of compulsion'; people would have control over their own work, working together in cooperatives. In the sphere of politics, society would be managed as a federation of communes.

These lectures laid the groundwork for his two socialist romances. In *A Dream of John Ball* (1886) he used his historical imagination to depict the contradictory way in which human society develops through the alternation of success and defeat, 'the change beyond the change'.

Morris's reflections about future society found their finest expression in *News from Nowhere* (1890), describing in fictional form a communist society where free and independent men and women are joyfully living together, where work has become a necessity and a pleasure, and where poverty, squalid cities, exploitation, competition and money have vanished. In writing his English utopia, his aim was to inspire people with hope for the future and to stimulate their imaginations about the nature of socialism. The place of utopianism in Marxism is much debated; Morris showed that it can be a significant element of Marxism, complementing theory with imagination.

Morris's love of nature, expressed in his de-

signs, his poems and his writings, and his distress at the destruction of the English countryside by the 'brutal squalor' of the industrial towns, made him a pioneer of the movement for the conservation of the environment. His work for the SPAB reflected his view that a beautiful old building is as much a part of nature as the fields and the trees. His writings on the relation between town and country – he wanted towns 'to be impregnated with the beauty of the countryside' – made him a precursor of the garden cities movement. His insistence on simplicity of lifestyle is also important. In his writings and in *News from Nowhere* Morris made a unique contribution to radical environmentalism.

Reading

Coleman, S. and O'Sullivan, P. 1990: *William Morris and News from Nowhere*.

Faulkner, Peter 1980: *Against the Age: An Introduction to William Morris*.

Mackail, J. W. 1899: *The Life of William Morris*.

Meier, Paul 1972 (1978): *William Morris: The Marxist Dreamer*. 2 vols.

Morris, William 1910–15: *Collected Works*.

— 1936: *William Morris: Artist, Writer, Socialist*. 2 vols.

— 1962 (1984): *William Morris, Selected Writings and Designs*, ed. Asa Briggs.

— 1968 (1974): *Three Works by William Morris: News from Nowhere, The Pilgrims of Hope, A Dream of John Ball*, ed. A. L. Morton.

— 1970: *News from Nowhere*, ed. James Redmond.

— 1973 (1984): *Political Writings of William Morris*, ed. A. L. Morton.

— 1984–7: *The Collected Letters of William Morris*, ed. Norman Kelvin. Vol. 1: *1848–80* (1984); vol. 2: part A, *1881–4*, part B, *1885–8* (1987); vol. 3 in preparation.

Thompson, E. P. 1955 (1976): *William Morris: Romantic to Revolutionary*. 2nd edn, shortened with postscript.

Watkinson, Ray 1966 (1990): *William Morris as Designer*.

ROGER SIMON

multinational corporations The term refers to capitalist enterprises which operate in more than one country. While such a broad definition could apply to the mercantilist trading houses which operated during the early phase of European colonialism (beginning in the seventeenth century), the term did not come into use until after the second world war, and refers specifically to a phenomenon of the monopoly stage of capitalism, in which there is an internationalization of industrial capital (see MONOPOLY CAPITALISM; PERIODIZATION OF CAPITALISM; FINANCE CAPITAL).

From a Marxist theoretical perspective the internationalization of industrial capital is explained by the development of capitalism itself. Expansion, or accumulation of VALUE, is inherent in the capitalist mode of production, and during the early phase of capitalist development this expansion was at the expense of pre-capitalist production largely within the national boundaries of the incipiently capitalist countries (see PRIMITIVE ACCUMULATION). In this early phase of development, which Marx called 'the stage of manufacture', the conditions did not exist for the export of money or productive capital. This was the period during which MERCHANT CAPITAL was powerful, controlling trade between capitalist and pre-capitalist areas. With the development of capitalism, the credit system also developed (see CREDIT AND FICTITIOUS CAPITAL; CENTRALIZATION AND CONCENTRATION OF CAPITAL), facilitating the export of money capital, which Lenin documented in his well-known pamphlet 'Imperialism: the Highest Stage of Capitalism' (1916) (see IMPERIALISM AND WORLD MARKET). The export of productive capital (fixed means of production), awaited the breakdown of pre-capitalist social formations in backward areas, since productive or industrial capital is based upon the exploitation of labour power in commodity form. This dissolution of pre-capitalist social formations began to occur on a world scale after the second world war (see NON-CAPITALIST MODES OF PRODUCTION; PEASANTRY).

As is to be expected, the export of productive capital from the advanced capitalist countries first took the form of investments in extractive activities and plantations, since these activities were for export and not dependent upon an internal market which only develops with the expansion of capitalist social relations of production (Lenin). Only when capitalism had expanded in the backward countries did the general export of productive capital (i.e. general

across manufacturing sectors) become possible. This general export of productive capital created the multinational corporation, with headquarters in one country and manufacturing facilities throughout the world.

The literature on multinational corporations is largely descriptive and of an eclectic theoretical orientation, particularly prone to use arguments based on DEPENDENCY THEORY. Within this literature, however, there is quite valuable work documenting the complex process of the internationalization of money and productive capital. Particularly important is the analysis of the transfer of technology from developed to underdeveloped countries. Empirical work on this issue relates to the major debate among Marxists as to whether the tendency of capitalism in its advanced stage is to develop or retard the productive forces on a world scale (see IMPERIALISM AND WORLD MARKET for elaboration of this point). Similarly, case studies of transfer-pricing (international exchanges among subsidiaries of the same corporation) and market sharing agreements among corporations are relevant to the debate over whether capitalism in the age of imperialism is still governed by the competitive contradiction among capitals.

Perhaps the most fundamental theoretical issue raised by the empirical literature is the relation between the capitalist class and the national state. Basic to most Marxist theories of capitalist rivalry is the link between a capitalist class and a state which pursues its interests in the international arena. For some writers the internationalization of capital results in the nationality of capitals becoming ambiguous, and the interests of multinational capital becoming so complex that they cannot be contained within the structure of a national state. This issue, along with others, indicates that a considerable synthesis of theory and empirical work remains to be accomplished in order to understand the internationalization of capital.

Reading

Lenin, V. I. 1893a (*1960*): On the So-called 'Market Question'.

Radice, H. ed. 1975: *International Firms and Modern Imperialism*.

JOHN WEEKS

N

nation It is noticeable in many of their writings that Marx and Engels were very conscious of national make-up or character. But nationality in itself was not a theme that greatly interested them; they looked forward to its speedy demise, and in the meantime were far more concerned with its component elements, social classes. Many nationalities were fading out already, in their view, such as the Welsh and the smaller Slav peoples, and for this they had no regret. Industrialism was hastening this process, they came to think very early, merging all civilized countries into a single economic whole; a bourgeoisie might still have its separate interests, but in the working class the national sense was extinct (*German Ideology*, vol. I, sect. IIb). In the *Communist Manifesto* (sect. 2) they declared that 'the working men have no country'.

Practical politics obliged them to take national issues more seriously, but it was left to their successors to systematize a Marxist view. This took shape first in the classical work of Bauer (1907; see AUSTRO-MARXISM) and then in Stalin's pamphlet of 1913. Nationality, Stalin wrote (in much the same terms as Bauer, though with some divergences), is not a racial or tribal phenomenon. It has five essential features: there must be a stable, continuing community, a common language, a distinct territory, economic cohesion, and a collective character. It assumes positive political form as a nation under definite historical conditions, belonging to a specific epoch, that of the rise of capitalism and the struggles of the rising bourgeoisie against feudalism. Reversing the original opinion of Marx and Engels, Stalin ascribed the advent of the nation to industry's need of a national market, with a homogeneous population and common market. It came about first in Western Europe, whereas further east a different, multinational state evolved, but now industry was spreading everywhere and kindling the same aspirations. All peoples of the Habsburg and tsarist empires which could qualify as nations were therefore entitled to claim independence. Among those excluded were the Russian Jews, as lacking a territory of their own. Their left-wing organization, the Bund, founded in 1897, had claimed national status for the Jews, and autonomy for itself from the Social-Democratic party. This led to a rupture, after heated disputes at the party's second congress in 1903 when there was much discussion of national issues and the Jewish in particular.

Stalin's formulation leaves various questions about earlier times; whether for example the Scots who resisted English conquest in the middle ages were not a nation, rather than a simple nationality, or whether the title can be denied to the Romans. It leaves some doubts about peoples in Western Europe which, even if not true nations formerly, now have movements claiming national status. Engels was convinced that Bretons, Corsicans and others were quite content with their incorporation into France (*The Role of Force in History*, sect. 6); if such was the case, it is evidently far less so today, and the same may be said of the Basques in Spain, the Scots, and others, among them peoples believed by Marx and Engels to be fated to extinction (see especially Engels, 'Democratic Pan-Slavism', *Neue Rheinische Zeitung*, 15 and 16 February 1849). In Asia further problems arise. It seems increasingly hard not to think of old Iran, China, Japan, as nations, or Vietnam with its thousand years of resistance to Chinese invasion. In Africa very few of today's political entities fulfil Stalin's five requirements, and nations as well as states are having to be forged by deliberate effort, as was Portuguese Guinea under the Marxist leadership of Cabral. (See also: NATIONALISM; BAUER; RENNER.)

Reading

Abdel-Malek, Anouar 1969: *Idéologie et renaissance nationale. L'Égypte moderne.*

Bauer, Otto 1907 (1924): *Die Nationalitätenfrage und die Sozialdemokratie.*

Cabral, Amilcar 1969: *Revolution in Guinea. An African People's Struggle.*

Chlebowczyk, Józef 1980: *On Small and Young Nations in Europe.*

Haupt, Georges *et al.* eds. 1974: *Les Marxistes et la question nationale, 1848-1914.*

Kann, R. A. 1950: *The Multinational Empire.*

Stalin, J. V. 1913 (1936): 'Marxism and the National Question'.

V. G. KIERNAN

national bourgeoisie The term is used exclusively in the context of backward or underdeveloped countries. One of the primary characteristics of backwardness is that pre-capitalist social relations coexist with and in some cases may be dominant over capitalist relations of production. While in an advanced capitalist country the class struggle can be analysed in terms of the conflict between the proletariat and the bourgeoisie, in backward countries it is necessary to consider the interaction among at least four classes: the emerging proletariat, the capitalist class, the pre-capitalist exploiting class, and the direct producers in the pre-capitalist mode of production. In backward countries the class struggle is rendered particularly complex for two reasons. First, from a classical Marxist viewpoint, there may be an antagonistic interaction between the two exploiting classes caused by the tendency for capitalism to undermine pre-capitalist society as it expands, and this antagonism proceeds concurrently with the emerging conflict between labour and capital. Second, imperialist domination of backward countries may involve oppression of the entire population to some degree, though support from pre-capitalist ruling elements may sometimes be needed (see COLONIAL AND POST-COLONIAL SOCIETIES; IMPERIALISM; NATIONALISM). These characteristics of backward countries have generated a sharp debate over the correct strategy for revolutionary transformation, and a central issue in this debate is whether the bourgeoisie in backward countries can play any role in the revolutionary struggle.

In this context it has been common to use the term national bourgeoisie to refer to a fraction of the capitalist class in underdeveloped countries which is anti-imperialist. This implies that it is a potential ally of the working class in the anti-imperialist struggle, a struggle characteristically supported by the petty bourgeoisie and the peasantry. Thus the term is normally defined with respect to the role of a part of the bourgeoisie in the political sphere. This manner of defining the national bourgeoisie is rather unsatisfactory, however, since it presupposes contradictions between fractions of the local bourgeoisie and imperialism. The term 'comprador bourgeoisie' is applied to the portion of the local bourgeoisie which tends to ally itself with imperialism. Some authors attempt to distinguish these two fractions of the bourgeoisie in backward countries by their relation to the means of production (Dore and Weeks 1977), and to deduce their political role from this relation.

According to this method the comprador bourgeoisie is defined as the portion of the local capitalist class whose capital is in circulation (commerce, banking, etc.). Involved exclusively in the circulation of commodities, this fraction of the local bourgeoisie is characteristically allied with capital from the imperialist countries, particularly MERCHANT CAPITAL. The national bourgeoisie, on the other hand, can be defined as the local bourgeoisie which has its capital in the sphere of production, within the national boundaries of the backward country. COMPETITION is inherent in capitalism, and competition between national and imperial capital provides the possibility that the national bourgeoisie can play an anti-imperialist role. Because of the higher development of the productive forces in the imperialist countries, national capital in underdeveloped countries is frequently at a disadvantage in the competitive struggle with imperial capital. In principle this can make the national bourgeoisie an ally in the national struggle for liberation from imperialist domination. It can, however, also have the opposite effect. Competitive disadvantage may compel fractions of the local capitalist class to ally themselves with imperial capital as suppliers or subsidiaries of MULTINATIONAL CORPORATIONS. Whether the national bourgeoisie will in practice be 'nationalist' at any moment depends upon the concrete circumstances prevailing in any particular social formation.

The possibility that the national bourgeoisie will participate in an anti-imperialist alliance arises not only from narrow economic interests. Imperialism tends to oppress all classes within backward countries, not only in the economic sphere, but also politically, socially and culturally. It is this oppression which contributes to the possibility that the national bourgeoisie may play a progressive role at certain historical moments and may enter into momentary alliances with the proletariat, or try to mobilize working-class support, against imperialism.

But any alliance between the proletariat and the national bourgeoisie is by its very nature an unstable one. The bourgeoisie exists through exploitation of the working class and personifies capital. In addition, it is nowadays usually the class which controls the state in underdeveloped countries, and so the class the proletariat must overthrow. Despite this essential antagonism most revolutionary theorists and leaders have argued that the proletariat should ally with the national bourgeoisie at particular historical moments in its revolutionary struggle to seize state power and to transform society. Lenin (1920) wrote that it was obligatory for the vanguard of the proletariat 'to [make] use of any, even the smallest rift between the enemies . . .' or among the bourgeoisie, and to '[take] advantage of any, even the smallest opportunity of winning a mass ally, even though this ally be temporary, vacillating, unstable, unreliable and conditional.' Most major revolutionary leaders have taken a similar position. In his writings on the Chinese revolution (1925–1927) Stalin recommended an alliance with the bourgeoisie, though he was careful to warn against the proletarian and peasant forces taking a subordinate position in such an alliance. Mao Tse-tung, who forged the alliance Stalin recommended, is popularly cited as a general supporter of alliances with the bourgeoisie. A careful reading of Mao's work, however, makes it obvious that he did not argue that an alliance with the bourgeoisie was a general strategy for revolution that had to be applied in all underdeveloped countries. On the contrary, he stressed that any alliance is the result of a specific historical conjuncture, and he warned against the adoption of unalterable formulas which are arbitrarily applied everywhere (1937). Mao Tse-tung was cautious in his advocacy of alliance with the national bourgeoisie, and concluded that 'when imperialism launches a war of aggression against a (semi-colonial) country, all of its various classes, except for some traitors, can temporarily unite in a national war against imperialism. . . . But . . . when imperialism carries on its oppression not by war, but by milder means . . . the ruling classes in semi-colonial countries capitulate to imperialism, and the two form an alliance for the joint oppression of the masses of the people' (ibid.). The same question was also the subject of long-continued debate in India (see ROY).

Reading

Dore, Elizabeth and Weeks, John 1977: 'Class Alliances and Class Struggle in Peru'.

Lenin, V. I. 1920a (1966): ' "Left Wing" Communism – An Infantile Disorder'.

Mao Tse-tung 1937a (1967): On Contradiction.

Stalin, Joseph 1925–1927 (1975): On Chinese Revolution.

ELIZABETH DORE

nationalism Nationalism is a subject on which Marx and Engels are commonly felt to have gone astray, most markedly in their earlier years, by greatly underestimating a force which was about to grow explosively. Emigrants in a foreign land, rationalistic in outlook, it was natural enough for them to have little comprehension of patriotic fervour. Their hopes fixed on class struggle, they could have little liking for a sentiment which professed to transcend social divisions, and blunted class consciousness. But events compelled recognition of the importance of national issues, and as practical organizers they could scarcely fail to understand that national environment and tradition were things a working-class movement could not ignore.

No part of their pronouncements on national questions has invited more criticism than the vehemence with which they condemned the minor Slav peoples of the Habsburg empire, during the revolutions of 1848–49, for turning against the stronger German-speaking Austrians and the Magyars, and thus helping conservatism to regain control. They were trying to fit all the heterogeneous forces astir in those years into black and white, reactionary and progressive; and through their spectacles the Austrians and Magyars were simply liberals, though in fact they were, as their attitude to national minorities showed, at least as strongly nationalistic or chauvinist. There was a moment when Engels wrote generously of the 'gallant Czechs', embittered by centuries of German oppression, but he could see no future for them, whether their side won or lost (*Neue Rheinische Zeitung*, 18 June 1848), and he repeated some far more intemperate language after the fighting was over. Much of this heat can be put down to suspicion that the Pan-Slavism which influenced some leaders meant support of Russia, the powerful ally of counter-revolution. Lenin (1916) rationalized this hostility in later days by arguing that Slav claims in 1848, however justifiable in themselves, were inopportune at that time, and it was right to want to subordinate them to the larger requirements of progress ('The Socialist Revolution and the Right of Nations to Self-Determination', CW 22, pp. 149–50).

Poland was too big a country to be thought of in the same way, and its efforts to regain its freedom had an appeal not only romantic but also political. Its independence would weaken tsarism, and establish a barrier between Russia and Germany, enabling the latter to develop without interference. Marx had, indeed, some misgivings as to whether Poland by itself would be viable (*On the Eastern Question*, article 59). A serious objection was that its liberty had been lost through the irresponsibility of the serf-owning nobility, and it was the same class that was in the van of the national movement, in alliance with the Catholic church, until the later nineteenth century. In the final section of the *Communist Manifesto* support was proclaimed for the more progressive wing which held that agrarian revolution was a necessary condition of national emancipation. Later Engels put the matter differently: Polish national liberation must come first, to make any social advance possible; no nation could fix its mind on any other goals before it was free from alien rule, and an international workers' movement could only flourish on the basis of a harmony of free peoples (letter to Kautsky, 7 February 1882). Still more than in the case of Poland, he and Marx came to regard independence for Ireland as vital, not from any particular esteem for its nationalism or leadership, but in the interests of progress in the British Isles as a whole.

Wars of national liberation were entitled to the support of socialists; but this was apt to be slippery ground, for each war inevitably had very mixed motives, some more questionable than others. Along with memories of older conflicts, or oppression, they left behind bitterness which made it harder for fraternal links among the workers of different nations to develop. All classes were affected, and governments were eager to keep anti-foreign feeling alive as a distraction from discontents at home. The split between the Marxist and Bakuninist wings of the socialist movement was not unconnected with Slavophil self-assertion against what could appear as German or Western ascendancy. Bakunin cherished hopes of a federation of Slav peoples, to ensure equal standing for them (Davis 1967, p. 42). Those who were trying to infuse Marxist ideas into the French labour movement, like Marx's son-in-law Lafargue, were often uncomfortably conscious of the bad feeling left by the defeat of 1870, and of mistrust of Marxism as a 'German' doctrine. In 1893 Lafargue, Guesde and others felt obliged to publish a manifesto rebutting accusations of anti-patriotism, which were the more easily brought against all the Left because of loose talk by anarchists (Lafargue to Engels, 23 June 1893). Jaurès, a socialist less fully committed to Marxism, and with a strong sense of the natural attachment of all people to their native land, interpreted the words of the *Communist Manifesto* about working men having no country as meaning that they had been wrongfully deprived of their place in the national life, and must recover it.

Italy and Germany had been divided countries striving for union; it was with peoples trying to break away from unwanted unions that Lenin's generation had usually to reckon. He himself was keenly aware of the complexities of the tsarist empire with its multitude of nationalities, all in varying degrees disgruntled with tsarist and Great Russian domination. His strategy called for a fine balance, not easily achieved in practice, between the duty of socialists in dominant countries to work for the liberation of oppressed nationalities, and that of socialists belonging to these others to oppose narrow, self-absorbed nationalism. What came to be the standard formulation of Bolshevik views was the pamphlet 'Marxism and the National Question' written in 1913 by Stalin very probably under Lenin's direction, and in any case corresponding faithfully enough with his mentor's views.

Like so many statements of Marxist principles it is a good deal entangled with the contemporary circumstances which gave rise to it. Stalin began by observing that since the defeat of the 1905 revolution, and with further spread of industry in the Russian empire to cause ferment, there had been a widespread turning away towards local nationalism; there was danger of this infecting the workers, and it was the business of socialists to resist it, a duty in which some in the minority regions had been found wanting. But minority nationalism could only be counteracted by a socialist pledge of full rights of self-determination. Stalin went on to a detailed critique of the programme adopted by the Austrian socialist leaders (see AUSTRO-MARXISM) for coping with the problem in the Habsburg empire, now transformed into the Dual Monarchy of Austria-Hungary with all the other nationalities straining at the leash. It was an attempt to satisfy their aspirations by a grant of full cultural autonomy, but this Stalin argued was quite inadequate; it had not averted a break-up of both socialist and trade-union movements into jarring national sections.

For Russians the grand problem was Poland. There the earlier rebelliousness of the land-owning gentry had ebbed away, and a newer one had not yet replaced it. Some Polish socialists, Luxemburg the most eloquent, took the view that support of nationalism now would be retrograde, and that unity of Polish and Russian workers had far higher claims. Against this position Lenin maintained that there could not be a healthy combination without recognition of Poland's right to freedom. In 1916 during the Great War, when all socialists were coming round to the principle of self-determination, he repeated afresh that the goal of socialism was to unite the nations and merge all peoples in one family, but this could not come about before each was given the opportunity to choose its own path ('The Socialist Revolution and the Right of Nations to Self-Determination', CW 22, p. 146).

An important factor in Marxist thinking after 1917 was that it was the established doctrine of a very large multi-national State, with an inheritance of many feuds from the past, even though Finland and the Baltic provinces as well as Poland had broken away. Complex measures were worked out to provide every ethnic community with a degree of self-government answering to its size and history, as well as full freedom of cultural self-development. But with levels of development so diverse, and memories often so painful, frictions were unavoidable. In his report to the sixteenth party congress Stalin dwelt on the menace of 'creeping deviations' of two opposite sorts: regional separatism, and Great Russian arrogance masquerading as internationalism and encouraging premature moves towards fusion of nationalities. Yet the strains of building the economy, under constant threat of renewed foreign invasion, meant that appeals had to be made to the patriotism of the masses, now, it could be thought, legitimate because purified from the perversions of class society. This reached its climax in the 'Great Patriotic War' of 1941–45, when an army mostly of peasants could not effectively be appealed to in the name of defence of socialism. An Order of Suvorov was instituted, and a film made to glorify that hero of tsarist imperialism. All this was far removed from Marx's sceptical rationalism.

To fuse socialism with nationalist revolt was the endeavour of James Connolly, who gave his life in the Dublin rising of 1916. In Ireland the experiment met with very little success. But separatist movements have been proliferating in Western, as formerly in Eastern Europe; and in some of them, such as the Scottish Nationalist, a socialist and Marxist element has been making itself felt. Communist parties have been inclined to see them as unwelcome distractions, or throwbacks, breaches of working-class solidarity. This has been so at times outside Europe too. Many Asian and practically all African countries include ethnic minorities whose aspirations may raise awkward questions. In both Iran and Pakistan the communist view, unpalatable to the Baluch minorities, has been that they should cooperate with progressives of other provinces instead of trying to set up as an independent nation.

But where a straightforward struggle against imperialism was being waged, fusion or linkage of socialism with nationalism won many successes. Lenin before 1914 was hailing the revolt of Asia as highly favourable for the success of socialism everywhere, and the Third International, very unlike its rival the Second, threw its weight fully behind COLONIAL LIBERATION MOVEMENTS. (It may be of interest to recall that Marx, writing his commentaries on the Indian Mutiny in 1857, could not conceal a lively sympathy with the rebels, premature and only very imperfectly national though he realized their movement to be.) In Asia, by contrast with Europe, modern nationalism and Marxist socialism were coming to the front more or less simultaneously, and the latter with its better organization and clearer theory might take the lead, as in China against the Japanese invasion, or in Vietnam against French rule. India was an exception; there, with the Western connection so old, and political activity tolerated, a national movement on liberal lines had a long start. There were chronic debates among Indian Marxists as to whether they should collaborate with it, and on what terms; their failure to gain more ground owed much to their seeming to stand aloof from the national struggle.

Whether in some other countries, China notably, the force which will eventually come to the top will be socialism or nationalism, it may be too early to say. In Europe the disbanding of the Comintern in 1943 was a milestone marking the end of what has been called the fully 'international' era of Marxism (Narkiewicz 1981, p. 84); since then the quarrel between the USSR and China has strengthened the tendency for each national party to look for its own way forward. Within the USSR itself, following relaxation of central controls in the later 1980s, there has been a striking recrudescence of national feeling, with separatist agitation in the Baltic republics and conflict in Transcaucasia between those old enemies, Armenians and Azerbaijanis. (See also NATION; REVOLUTION.)

Reading

Cummins, Ian 1980: *Marx, Engels and National Movements*.

Davidson, Basil 1967 (revised edn): *Which Way Africa? The Search for a New Society*.

Davis, Horace Bancroft 1967: *Nationalism and Socialism*.

Dunn, John 1970 (1989): *Modern Revolutions: an Introduction to the Analysis of a Political Phenomenon*.

Hodgkin, Thomas 1981: *Vietnam: The Revolutionary Path*.

Lenin, V. I. 1916b (1964): 'The Socialist Revolution and the Right of Nations to Self-Determination'.

Nairn, Tom 1977: *The Break-Up of Britain. Crisis and Neo-Nationalism*.

Narkiewicz, Olga A. 1981: *Marxism and the Reality of Power 1919–1980*.

Nimni, Ephraim 1991: *Marxism and Nationalism*.

Stalin, J. V. 1913 (1936): 'Marxism and the National Question'.

Torr, Dona ed. 1940: *Marxism, Nationality and War*.

Tuzmuhamedov, R. 1973: *How the National Question was Solved in Soviet Central Asia*.

V. G. KIERNAN

natural science The problem about natural science in the history of Marxism is that it has always provided a tempting alternative to idealism and utopianism. For many decades excerpts from Engels's *Anti-Dühring* published in pamphlet form as *Socialism: Utopian and Scientific* were the most popular Marxist text. Marx and Engels were both deeply imbued with the concept of science as progress which characterized nineteenth-century thought, and some of their most influential interpreters – Bernstein, Kautsky, Plekhanov – relied heavily on natural science models and analogies to uphold the scientific character of Marxism, especially ones drawn from the Darwinian theory of evolution. Where Marx and Engels had expressed nuanced judgements on DARWINISM, their theoretical interpreters relied on it as the theory linking conceptions of humanity and society to the methods and assumptions of science. Marx referred to Darwinism as the basis in natural history for their view of history (letter to Engels, 19 December 1860) and Engels, in his speech at Marx's graveside, referred to Marx's discovery of the basic law of human history as analogous to Darwin's discovery of the law of organic evolution. But both were equally struck by the image of living nature from which Darwinism was derived – the Malthusian law of struggle, Hobbes's law of all against all (Marx to Engels, 18 June 1862). Even in the writings which were most deferential to natural science, Engels interposed the concept of labour between apes and humans (*Dialectics of Nature*, ch. IX).

Both Marx and, especially, Engels were close students of scientific developments in mathematics, biology, physics and chemistry. Engels went much further than Marx in integrating dialectics with the laws of nature (see DIALECTICS OF NATURE). Marx was more concerned with science as a productive force and as a means of control of the workforce. He pointed out that 'natural science has penetrated all the more *practically* into human life through industry; it has transformed human life and prepared the emancipation of humanity, even though its immediate effect was to accentuate the dehumanisation of man'; and continued: 'natural science will abandon its abstract materialist, or rather idealist, orientation, and will become the basis of a *human* science, just as it has already become – though in an alienated form – the basis of actual human life. One basis for life and another for *science* is *a priori* a falsehood' (*Economic and Philosophical Manuscripts*. Third manuscript). In the *Grundrisse* Marx stressed the close links between industry and science and predicted that these would continue to grow ('Chapter on Capital', pp. 704–5) and in *Capital* I, in a chilling passage on technological innovations designed to control the workers, he quoted Ure: 'This invention confirms the great doctrine already propounded, that when capital enlists science in her service, the refractory hand of labour will always be taught docility' (ch. 13, sect. 5).

Many strands in Marxism stress its character as science, but when the term 'science' is unpacked, it is seen to be frequently invoked as part of a search for legitimacy, and often it is not natural science which is being referred to (see SCIENTIFIC AND TECHNOLOGICAL REVOLUTION). When natural science is intended, the reference is usually to the sources of scientific research in the needs of production. This was most eloquently shown in Boris Hessen's essay (in Bukharin 1931) on 'The Social and Economic Roots of Newton's "Principia"', which linked that most famous document in the scientific revolution to economic issues of the seventeenth century. Other essays in the same work stressed that scientific theory is the continuation of practice by other means. The idea of the self-sufficient character of science, Bukharin argued,

was false consciousness – a confusion of the subjective passions of the professional scientist with the objective social role of science. The social function of science in the production process remains (1931, pp. 19–21).

Gramsci argued that all scientific hypotheses are superstructures and that all knowledge is historically relative (*Prison Notebooks*, pp. 446, 468).

Matter as such, therefore, is not our subject but how it is socially and historically organised for production, and natural science should be seen correspondingly as essentially an historical category, a human relation . . . Might it not be said in a sense, and up to a certain point, that what nature provided the opportunity for, are not discoveries and inventions of pre-existing forces – and pre-existing qualities of matter – but 'creations' which are closely linked to the interests of society and to the development and the further necessities of the development of the forces of production? (Ibid. pp. 465–6)

The role of natural science and the development of science as a productive force have led to a weakening of the distinction between science and technology, so that the restructuring of capitalism around, e.g., microelectronics, biotechnology, and increasingly subtle means of pacing, surveillance and control, has led to a greater awareness of the need to carry on politics inside science, technology and medicine. On the whole, orthodox Marxists in the 'Diamat' tradition (see DIALECTICAL MATERIALISM) have treated scientific practices as value-neutral and above the class struggle (see BERNAL), while 'critical theorists' (see FRANKFURT SCHOOL), have seen the categories, assumptions and legitimating role of natural science as being at the heart of the problem of revolutionary transformation. As Marx and Engels said in the *German Ideology* (vol. I, sect. IA): 'We know only a single science – the science of history.'

Reading

Arato, Andrew 1973–74: 'Re-examining the Second International'.

Bukharin, Nikolai *et al.* 1931 (1971): *Science at the Crossroads*.

Gramsci, Antonio 1929–35 (1971): *Selections from the Prison Notebooks*.

Jacoby, Russell 1971: 'Towards a Critique of Automatic Marxism: The Politics of Philosophy. From Lukács to the Frankfurt School'.

Lichtheim, George 1961: *Marxism: An Historical and Critical Study.*

Radical Science Journal Collective 1981: 'Science, Technology, Medicine and the Socialist Movement'.

ROBERT M. YOUNG

nature It might be thought that since Marxism is a materialism, the category of 'nature' would be unproblematic, but this is far from the case. Marx's early notebooks included a critique of abstract materialism in the name of a materialism which focused on human industry. Nature exists independently, but for humanity it attains its qualities and meaning by means of a transformative relationship of human labour. Labour is neither nature nor culture but their matrix. Thus, although no Marxist would be happy to be labelled 'idealist' (a frequently used epithet in criticisms of those who stress the Hegelian strands in the Marxist tradition), few would want the naturalism of Marxism to be other than a critical one.

Nature is, for humankind, a matter of utility, not a power for itself. The purpose in trying to discover nature's autonomous laws is to subjugate nature to human needs, as an object of consumption or means of production (*Grundrisse*, 'Chapter on Capital', pp. 409–10). 'Industry is the actual historical relation of nature, and therefore of natural science, to man' (*Economic and Philosphical Manuscripts*. Third manuscript. The approach which historicizes nature is characteristic of the writings of Bukharin, (the early) Lukács, Gramsci, and the FRANKFURT SCHOOL. Its approach can be summarized in Lukács's words: 'Nature is a societal category. That is to say, whatever is held to be natural at any given stage of social development, however this nature is related to man and whatever form his involvement with it takes, i.e. nature's form, its content, its range and its objectivity are all socially conditioned' (1923, p. 234).

There are, however, at least two other strands in the Marxist tradition which tend to minimize the mediation of human history and human purposes in the idea of nature. The first – DIALECTICAL MATERIALISM – has its source in Engels, was developed in the Marxism of the Second International, and became official orthodoxy in Soviet philosophy. According to this approach, nature is not seen primarily in terms of human social mediations; rather, Marxist conceptions and categories are ontologized so that nature is not a human transformation of unknowable noumena but something which can be directly expressed in Marxist theory. If we follow nature and do not distort its true categories, socialism is assured. The second strand is closely related to dialectical materialism but has a more positivist cast and is better described as REALISM. Its adherents would deny that they have ontologized dialectical categories, and would argue rather that there is some version of a one-to-one correspondence between the categories of nature and those of knowledge. The philosophical writings of Lenin, Bhaskar and Timpanaro belong to this tendency, and are characterized by deference to the natural sciences and to social sciences based on natural science models.

One way of characterizing the three tendencies discussed here would be to say that the first group base their philosophy on a humanist critique of concepts of nature, and from this standpoint make searching analyses of the concepts and assumptions of the natural, biological and human sciences. The dialectical materialist group conflate concepts of nature and the sciences into a single set of dialectical laws. The realists tend to view concepts of nature through the methods and assumptions of the physical sciences and root the human sciences in the findings of biology.

Reading

Bhaskar, Roy 1978: *A Realist Theory of Science.*

Bukharin, N. I. *et al.* 1931 (1971): *Science at the Crossroads.*

Jay, Martin 1973: *The Dialectical Imagination.*

Joravsky, David 1961: *Soviet Marxism and Natural Science 1917–1932.*

Lukács, Georg 1923 (1971): *History and Class Consciousness.*

Marcuse, Herbert 1964: *One-Dimensional Man.*

Schmidt, Alfred 1962 (1971): *The Concept of Nature in Marx.*

Timpanaro, S. 1976: *On Materialism.*

ROBERT M. YOUNG

needs. *See* human nature.

negation In the Marxist sense this is not merely the mental act of 'saying no', as formalist/analytical philosophy treats it in its circularity, but primarily refers to the objective ground of such negating thought-processes without which 'saying no' would be a gratuitous and arbitrary manifestation of caprice, rather than a vital element of the process of cognition. Thus the fundamental sense of negation is defined by its character as an immanent dialectical moment of objective development, 'becoming', MEDIATION and transition.

As an integral moment of objective processes, with their inner laws of unfolding and transformation, negation is inseparable from positivity – hence the validity of Spinoza's dictum: 'omnis determinatio est negatio', all determination is negation – and all 'supersession' from 'preservation'. As Hegel puts it: 'From this negative side the immediate has become submerged in the Other, but the Other is essentially not the empty negative or Nothing which is commonly taken as the result of the dialectic: it is the Other of the first, the negative of the immediate; it is thus determined as *mediated*, – and altogether contains the determination of the first. The first is thus essentially contained and preserved in the Other' (Hegel 1812, vol. 2, p. 476.) In fully adhering to such a view in his comments on this passage, Lenin writes:

> This is very important for understanding dialectics. Not empty negation, not futile negation, not sceptical negation, vacillation and doubt is characteristic and essential in dialectics, – which undoubtedly contains the element of negation and indeed as its most important element – no, but negation as a moment of connection, as a moment of development, retaining the positive. (1914–16, p. 226)

In contrast to Feuerbach – who tends to overemphasize in a one-sided manner positivity, mythically inflating immediacy in his rigid rejection of Hegelian mediation and 'negation of the negation' – Marx and Engels assign a very important role to negation. Engels considers the 'negation of the negation' a general law of development of 'nature, history and thought; a law which holds good in the animal and plant kingdoms, in geology, in mathematics, in history and in philosophy' (*Anti-Dühring*, pt. I, ch. 13) and he also explores various aspects of this problematic in great detail in his *Dialectics of Nature*. Marx, too, insists on the vital importance of this law in the social-economic processes of capitalist development: 'The capitalist mode of appropriation, the result of the capitalist mode of production, produces capitalist private property. This is the first negation of individual property, as founded on the labour of the proprietor. But capitalist production begets, with the inexorability of a law of Nature, its own negation. It is the negation of negation. This does not re-establish private property for the producer, but gives him individual property based on the acquisitions of the capitalist era: i.e., on co-operation and the possession in common of the land and of the means of production' (*Capital* I, ch. 24 sect. 7). Thus through the negation of negation the 'positivity' of earlier moments does not simply reappear. It is preserved/superseded, together with some negative moments, at a qualitatively different, sociohistorically higher level. Positivity, according to Marx, can never be a straightforward, unproblematical, unmediated complex. Nor can the simple negation of a given negativity produce a self-sustaining positivity. For the ensuing formation remains dependent on the previous formation in that any particular negation is necessarily dependent on the object of its negation (*Economic and Philosophical Manuscripts*). Accordingly, the positive outcome of the socialist enterprise must be constituted through successive stages of development and transition (*Critique of the Gotha Programme*).

A radically different emphasis is given to negation by Sartre; not only in the 'nihilating *néantisation*' of his freedom-constituting 'For-itself' (1943), but even in his later reflections according to which 'the whirlpool of partial totalization constitutes itself as a negation of the total movement' (1960, p. 88), thereby foreshadowing the ultimate disintegration of the positively self-sustaining structures. Similarly in critical theory (see FRANKFURT SCHOOL) negation and negativity predominate, from Benjamin to Horkheimer and from Marcuse's *One-Dimensional Man* and *Negations* to Adorno's programmatic attempt 'to free dialectics from affirmative traits' (1966, p. xix). (See also DIALECTICS.)

Reading

Adorno, Theodor W. 1966 (1973): Negative Dialectics.

Hegel, G. W. F. 1812–16 (1929): The Science of Logic.

Lenin, V. I. 1914–16 (1961): Conspectus of Hegel's Science of Logic.

Sartre, Jean-Paul 1943 (1969): Being and Nothingness.

— 1960 (1976): Critique of Dialectical Reason.

ISTVÁN MÉSZÁROS

non-capitalist modes of production Marx argued that capitalism is merely one historically specific form in which the means of production and labour power are combined to reproduce the material conditions of life. Before the capitalist epoch the material conditions of life are reproduced through non-capitalist relations, as in much of the underdeveloped world today. The term non-capitalist modes of production, strictly speaking, includes post-capitalist societies, but here we shall be concerned with those social systems which are pre-capitalist, by which is meant that they historically precede the development of capitalism in a social formation, though they may be contemporaneous with capitalism on a world scale.

A MODE OF PRODUCTION in Marx's framework is defined by the manner in which production is organized, specifically in terms of the relationship between the direct producers and the exploiting class. This relationship, which Marx sometimes called the 'mode of exploitation' (or appropriation), refers to the manner in which the surplus product is extracted from the class of producers by the class of exploiters. In orthodox Marxist theory this relationship is the fundamental basis of society, determining, with allowance for historically concrete variations, the system of political control, ideology, and culture. Until recent years it was common for Marxists to summarize social development as passing through five modes of production, in the following chronological order: primitive communism, slavery, feudalism, capitalism and communism. Socialism would be included by those considering it to be a mode of production and excluded by those considering it merely as a transitional stage between the last two, without its own unique and definitive relations of production. In recent years, however, this proposed stage theory has come into question (see STAGES

OF DEVELOPMENT), and in particular the concept of a slave mode of production has been criticized, since history is rife with qualitatively different forms of SLAVERY (e.g. in both the ancient world and the New World).

The central element in defining a mode of production is the social relations of production which link producer to exploiter (with the obvious exception of modes without exploitation, primitive communism and communism). Marx's work was primarily concerned with identifying capitalist relations of production and feudal relations of production, with most emphasis on the former. A relative consensus can be found on the definition of European feudalism (see FEUDAL SOCIETY), which is characterized by self-contained production units ('manors') in which a class of peasants or serfs control subsistence plots to which they are tied by extra-economic coercion, and are compelled to render a surplus product to a landlord class. The term landlord is used advisedly, because ownership of land in the modern, legal sense by the exploiting class is neither necessary nor common in societies defined as feudal.

There exists considerably less agreement about the defining characteristics of other modes of production, of the past or currently extant. Most Marxists would accept the concept of an ancient mode of production, characterizing the Mediterranean basin from Classical Greece to the fall of Rome (Anderson 1974b; see also ANCIENT SOCIETY), but further consensus is difficult to achieve. Particularly with respect to backward countries, a number of hypothesized modes of production have failed to obtain general acceptance among Marxists; the lineage mode of production (Rey 1975), the colonial mode of production (Rey 1973 and Alavi 1975 – though the two writers use the term differently), and the Andean mode of production, to give the best known. More fundamental than these attempts to specify concrete social relations of production is the debate over whether non-capitalist modes of production are characterized by internal contradictions. The issue is whether the process of internal reproduction of these modes has inherent in it destabilizing forces which tend to undermine that same process of reproduction.

This is of course the argument that Marx made for capitalism. Put schematically, Marx argued that the process of the centralization of capital and the growth of the proletariat progressively undermine capitalism, thereby creating the conditions whereby it is overthrown by the working class. Whether all modes of production are analogously contradictory is a matter of considerable debate. Marx's ideas underwent change over time, as one would expect in any process of revolutionary and intellectual development, and on this issue as on others one can find different positions in his writings. In a much quoted passage (*Contribution to the Critique of Political Economy*, Preface) he states clearly that he considered all modes of production (with the exception of communism) to be inevitably undermined by the contradiction between the forces and relations of production. Engels (*Capital* III, Engels's supplementary note on 'The Law of Value and Rate of Profit') generally accepted this view, arguing that it is the development of the productive forces, an essentially autonomous development, that makes all societies transitory.

In his writings on India and China Marx coined the term 'Asiatic' mode of production, whose characteristic, among others, was its resistance to change of any kind and the absence of internal contradictions to undermine it. This argument has been extensively criticized by Anderson (1974b), and few hold it today (see ASIATIC SOCIETY). The position that Marx's analysis of contradictions is specific to capitalism has greater currency, argued eloquently by Colletti (1974) who interprets Marx as maintaining that the contradictions of capitalism derive from the opposition of USE VALUE and VALUE, which manifests itself in COMMODITY FETISHISM, in which social relations of exploitation are projected in the superstructure as relations of formal equality. This has the consequence of rendering the class struggle under capitalism not only antagonistic, but also contradictory in the sense of inherently unstable. If Colletti's argument is correct, a general theory of the conflict between the forces and relations of production cannot be deduced from the analysis of capitalism.

Colletti's argument notwithstanding, it remains the case that all class societies are characterized, at least potentially, by class antagonisms. On the basis of this truism it has been argued that all modes of production have as their basic dynamism the conflict between the direct producers and the exploiting class (Bettelheim 1974; Brenner 1977). Brenner maintains that it is this conflict, not the development of the productive forces, which undermines the process of reproduction in pre-capitalist modes of production and brings about their dissolution and transition to a new mode.

At the present stage of theory and practice there is general agreement on what is meant by capitalism, feudalism, and perhaps the 'ancient' mode of production. Considerably less agreement, if any, exists over other possible modes of production, and particularly over how to characterize the social formations of the underdeveloped world. This last is manifested in the extensive debate over the nature and possibility of capitalist transformation in underdeveloped countries (see IMPERIALISM; DEPENDENCY THEORY; UNDERDEVELOPMENT AND DEVELOPMENT).

Reading

Alavi, H. 1975: 'India and the Colonial Mode of Production'. In Miliband and Saville eds. *The Socialist Register*.

Anderson, P. 1974a: *Lineages of the Absolutist State*.

— 1974b: *Passages from Antiquity to Feudalism*.

Bettelheim, Charles 1974: *Les luttes de classes en URSS*, vol. 1.

Brenner, R. 1977: 'The Origins of Capitalist Development: A Critique of Neo-Smithian Marxism'.

Colletti, L. 1968 (1972): *From Rousseau to Lenin*.

Rey, P. P. 1973: *Les alliances de classes*.

— 1975: 'The Lineage Mode of Production'.

JOHN WEEKS

O

organic composition of capital   With the development of MACHINERY AND MACHINOFACTURE, the LABOUR PROCESS is continually transformed in capital's pursuit of increases in relative surplus value (see CAPITAL; SURPLUS VALUE). Mechanization enables the production of more use values in a given period of time by a worker, implying that the value of each produced use value falls (see USE VALUE; VALUE). But production of more use values can only occur if there is an increase in the relative quantity of means of production that one worker in a given time turns into products, and this in turn implies a decrease in the number of workers required per unit of means of production to produce a given output. Under capitalism, a productivity increase is always a reduction in the number of workers relative to the means of production with which they work. The ratio of the mass of the means of production to the labour which is required to employ them is called the 'technical composition of capital' (TCC), and is the composition of capital understood in use value terms. Since there is no way in which heterogeneous means of production and concrete labour can be measured, the TCC is a purely theoretical ratio, whose increase is, synonymous with a productivity increase.

The composition of capital can of course be measured in value-terms, but the result is by no means a simple concept, and is frequently misunderstood. If use values were unproblematically reflected by values, then as the ratio of means of production to labour rose, so *pari passu* would that ratio in value terms, the ratio of constant to variable capital. But since productivity increases reduce values, it is not at all clear what happens to the composition of capital in value terms; with the quantity of means of production rising, for example, and the value of a unit means of production falling, the product of the two together – constant capital – can increase, decrease or stay the same, depending upon the particular numbers involved. Within this framework, those who argue that the composition of capital in value terms necessarily rises are reduced to an assertion which cannot be substantiated except in terms of a dubious metaphysics concerning the essence of capital.

The issue however is important, since the dynamics of the composition of capital in value terms are central to Marx's analysis of the industrial cycle, of wage movements, of unemployment, and of the rate of profit (see ACCUMULATION; FALLING RATE OF PROFIT; RESERVE ARMY OF LABOUR; WAGES). The interpretation followed here is based on that proposed by Fine and Harris (1976, 1979), which is unambiguous and consistent with Marx's analysis (*Capital* I, ch. 23; III, ch. 8). Marx defines the 'organic composition of capital' (OCC) as the TCC in value terms. Inputs (means of production and labour power) are evaluated at their 'old' values, and abstraction is made from changes in values which occur as a result of the productivity increase. A change in the OCC is simply the value of a change in the TCC, and so changes in the OCC are directly proportional to changes in the TCC. By contrast, the 'value composition of capital' (VCC) is the TCC in value terms, where inputs are evaluated at their current or 'new' values, and differences between the VCC and OCC reflect changes in values which occur as a result of the productivity increase. (This suggests an index number interpretation which Steedman (1977, pp. 132–6) pursues.) Thus a rise in the TCC always produces a rise in the OCC, but the total effect is only captured in the VCC, which may or may not rise.

How then are these categories used? By approaching the analysis of accumulation from the perspective of what all capitals have in common – their ability to valorize themselves – Marx shows how relative surplus value is pursued by the introduction of machinery (a rising TCC) which continually develops the forces of production (see FORCES AND RELATIONS OF PRODUCTION). Input values accumulate as the scale of production expands, with workers working up more raw materials and using more machinery. At the same time, the unit values of outputs are falling, because of the productivity increases. Precisely how these values fall depends upon how values formed in production are realized in exchange (see COMPETITION). But because adjustment takes time, divergencies appear between the values of inputs as they result from previous production processes (the OCC), and those same inputs as they are evaluated in terms of the values emerging from current production processes (the VCC). Such discrepancies can be particularly marked for large blocs of fixed capital. 'Old' values must at some point be adjusted (devalued) to current values, and, if the discrepancies are particularly marked, this can involve a sharp break in the accumulation process (see ECONOMIC CRISES). Marx's various concepts of the composition of capital, then, are appropriate, not to some timeless, equilibrium growth process, but to a dialectical process whereby the essence of value relations (valorization through development of the forces of production) is continually confronted by the barrier of the forms of existence of those relations (as many capitals in competition), and adjustment can be quite discontinuously abrupt.

This account also suggests why so many Marxists have difficulty with the various compositions of capital: the valorization process comprises the complete circuit of capital, involving both PRODUCTION and CIRCULATION. Circulation is not an epiphenomenon of production, but neither is capital in general reducible to many competing capitals. Consequently the formation of values in production, and the realization of those values in competition can involve contradictory determinations; the various compositions of capital are categories intended to capture these real contradictions. (For recent debates see Fine and Harris 1976; Steedman et al. 1981. See also CONTRADICTION; DIALECTICS.)

Reading

Fine, Ben and Harris, Laurence 1976: 'Controversial Issues in Marxist Economic Theory'. In Miliband and Saville eds, Socialist Register.
— 1979: Rereading 'Capital'.
Steedman, Ian 1977: Marx After Sraffa.
— et al. 1981: The Value Controversy.

SIMON MOHUN

organized capitalism A term introduced by Rudolf Hilferding, in essays published between 1915 and the mid-1920s which attempted to define the changes in capitalist society during and after the first world war; largely a development of ideas already adumbrated in *Finance Capital* (1910) (see AUSTRO-MARXISM). The distinctive features of organized capitalism were seen as: (i) the introduction of a considerable degree of economic planning as a result of the dominance of large corporations and the banks, and of the increasing involvement of the state in the regulation of economic life; (ii) the extension of such planning into the international economy, leading to a 'realistic pacifism' in the relations between capitalist states; (iii) a necessary change in the relation of the working class to the state, in the sense that its aim now should be to transform an economy planned and organized by the great corporations into one planned and controlled by the democratic state. Hilferding's conception was criticized at the time by Bolshevik theorists (among them Bukharin) who regarded it as exaggerating the postwar stabilization of capitalism and encouraging reformist politics; but in the past decade it has attracted renewed attention and can be seen to have some affinities with recent versions of the theory of STATE MONOPOLY CAPITALISM.

Reading

Hardach, Gerd and Karras, Dieter 1975 (1978): A Short History of Socialist Economic Thought.
Hilferding, Rudolf 1915: 'Arbeitsgemeinschaft der Klassen?'
— 1924: 'Probleme der Zeit'.
Winkler, H. A. ed. 1974: Organisierter Kapitalismus: Voraussetzungen und Anfänge.

TOM BOTTOMORE

oriental despotism. *See* Asiatic society.

Origin of the Family, Private Property and the State The *Origin*, which was later to become a classic of the Marxist canon and a blueprint for socialist policies of women's emancipation, had a strange beginning. Marx had read, and extensively annotated, Lewis Henry Morgan's *Ancient Society* (1877), where Morgan had argued for a connection between the emergence of private property and the monogamous family form. On Marx's death, Engels decided to 'work up' these notes for publication, despite the fact that for some while he could not locate a copy of Morgan's book itself. The text of the *Origin* was written in less than three months in March to May 1884. A look back at Morgan shows that Engels drew not merely the raw anthropological data, but also the main lines of his historical thesis from *Ancient Society*, but he added perceptive insights into the implications of Morgan's argument for marriage and family practices in contemporary capitalism.

At the heart of the argument lies the proposition that early human societies were matrilineal, for the simple reason that prior to monogamous marriage descent has to be reckoned through the maternal line. It is only with the development of private property (initially the domestication of animals), and the consequent question of inheritance, that a motive for the more vexed patrilineal system of kinship begins to emerge. The modern monogamous family, so different from the clans and group marriages of earlier societies, is the result of this process. Engels saw property as the key to the difference between bourgeois marriage, where the wife's economic dependence on her husband was a form of prostitution, and the egalitarian marriage of the working class which reflected the fact that both wife and husband were wage labourers.

Social changes in the century or more since its publication have rendered much of the thesis irrelevant. Male domination in the proletarian family is now more widely recognized; feminism has largely freed middle-class women from their economic dependence on men; divorce is available for couples of any social class, and the state's role is more complex than protecting property interest through marriage law. Thus Engels's account of the state, class-based marriage patterns and the subordination of women is now sociologically dubious. In addition, a variety of factual and methodological challenges to the anthropological base of the theory have been made by critics.

The *Origin of the Family* has had, however, enormous influence within Marxist thought. Hyperbolically endorsed by Lenin as 'one of the fundamental works of modern socialism, every sentence of which can be accepted with confidence', it became the central text used by socialist regimes to emancipate women from confinement in the family and get them out into the public sphere of productive work. Flawed and disputed as the text undoubtedly is, it nonetheless also commands considerable interest from modern feminists as one of the few points where classical Marxism engaged with the 'woman question'.

Reading

Engels, Friedrich 1884 (*1985*): *The Origin of the Family, Private Property and the State*, introduced by Michèle Barrett (contains references to various modern discussions and critiques).

Krader, L. ed. 1972: *The Ethnological Notebooks of Karl Marx* (contains Marx's original notes).

Morgan, Lewis Henry 1877 (1974): *Ancient Society: Researches in the Lines of Human Progress from Savagery through Barbarism to Civilization*.

MICHÈLE BARRETT

overproduction   A situation in which various individual capitals, industries, sectors, experience difficulty in selling their entire output, leading to a general condition in which total output exceeds total demand. Given the unplanned character of capitalist competition, it is only by accident, or by theoretical idealization, that a situation of equilibrium can prevail in all branches, with output matching demand and capitalists' plans being realized. Overproduction is a concomitant of crises, but is disputed as a *cause* of them. Say's Law, on which classical and neo-classical political economy rest, denies the possibility of persistent overproduction and argues that the economy is capable of self-adjustment via movement of capital between activities, guided by the inequalities in the rate of profit. Overproduction theorists argue that the crisis is initiated by overproduction relative to demand in one activity and then spreads to other sectors, causing a cumulative disequilibrium rather than a restoration of equilibrium. Marx's schemes of expanded reproduction (see REPRODUCTION SCHEMA) were manipulated by

Tugan-Baranowsky to generate examples of a disproportionality in the output of the two departments leading to a general overproduction. Such manipulations of the scheme, which continue to be used, fail to explain the initial cause of the crisis in terms of capitalist behaviour, individual or collective, and hence remain controversial. (See also ECONOMIC CRISES; UNDERCONSUMPTION.)

Reading

Sweezy, Paul 1942: *The Theory of Capitalist Development*, ch. X.

MEGHNAD DESAI

P

Pannekoek, Antonie (German form: Anton) Born 2 January 1873, Vassen, Netherlands; died 28 April 1960, Wageningen, Netherlands. Studied mathematics at the University of Leyden and received a doctorate in astronomy 1902. Worked at the Leyden Observatory until 1906, later taught at the University of Amsterdam where he became Professor of Astronomy 1932. From 1906–14 Pannekoek lived in Germany, where he became a leading member of the left wing of the German Social Democratic Party (SPD), taught in the party school in Berlin until threatened with deportation, and contributed to *Die Neue Zeit*. His Marxism was distinctive in two respects. First, it developed directly out of natural science, via a study of the writings of the self-taught worker Joseph DIETZGEN (1828–88) to whom Engels (*Ludwig Feuerbach*, part iv) gave credit for the independent discovery of 'materialist dialectics'; and it was directed particularly to clarifying the relation between science and Marxism, notably in *Marxism and Darwinism* (1909). Second, in the sphere of political action, it issued in a theory of the revolutionary self-organization of the working class through workers' councils (see the articles in Bricianer 1978). From this position Pannekoek broke with the policies of the Third International in 1920, and later became a leading figure in the 'Council Communist' movement (see COUNCILS) along with Korsch and Gorter (see Smart 1978).

Reading

Bricianer, Serge 1978: *Pannekoek and the Workers' Councils*.

Pannekoek, Antonie 1909 (1912): *Marxism and Darwinism*.

— 1951 (1961): *A History of Astronomy*.

Smart, D. A. 1978: *Pannekoek and Gorter's Marxism*.

TOM BOTTOMORE

Paris Commune Analysis of the 1871 Paris Commune occupies a place of fundamental importance for Marx – in various writings, e.g. the addresses which compose *The Civil War in France* (1871) (together with the 1891 introduction by Engels) – and for Lenin, especially in *State and Revolution* (1917). Partially conflicting interpretations were also expressed by Kautsky, in *Terrorism and Communism* (1919), and by Trotsky in his preface to Talès, *La Commune de Paris* (1921).

The two-month Paris Commune did not result from any planned action and at no time benefited from the leadership of any individual or organization with a coherent programme. Significantly, however, a third of the elected members were manual workers and most of these were among the third who were activists in the French branch of the First International. The members of this government were chosen by the Parisian voters in a special election arranged by the Central Committee of the Paris National Guard, a week after the latter had unexpectedly found itself holding state power. This had occurred when the provisional French government had hastily withdrawn from the capital after some of its troops had fraternized with the populace on 18 March.

Marx felt that the 'measures of the Commune, remarkable for their sagacity and moderation, could only be such as were compatible with the state of a besieged town. . . . Its special measures could but betoken the tendency of a government of the people by the people'. As he reiterated in a letter to Domela Nieuwenhuis (22 February 1881) the Commune was merely 'the rising of a city under exceptional conditions and its majority was in no wise socialist nor could it be'. Yet if the Commune was not a socialist revolution, Marx nevertheless emphasized that its 'great social measure . . . was its own existence'. Far from being seen as a dogmatic model or formula for revolutionary governments of the future, the Commune, for Marx, was a 'thoroughly expansive political form, while all previous forms of government had been emphatically repressive'. Insisting upon this view of Marx, Lenin stressed that in this way the Commune had improvised a 'DICTATORSHIP OF THE PROLETARIAT'; i.e. a state which would give unprecedented control of all institutions, including the coercive ones, as the Commune was seen to have done, to the majority of voters (i.e. the workers); a state which would be most suitable for achieving the emancipation of labour through the establishment of a socialist society.

Since the Russian Revolution, Marx's whole emphasis on the democratic essence of the Commune has been disregarded, and in socialistically oriented regimes stress has been placed upon his brief criticism of the Commune's liberalism in time of war as justification for authoritarian monolithic one-party states (see Monty Johnstone, 'The Commune and Marx's Conception of the Dictatorship of the Proletariat and the Role of the Party', in Leith 1978). A discussion of recent historiographical issues is also included in Leith.

Reading

Leith, J. A. ed. 1978: *Images of the Commune*.

Marx, K. and Engels, F. (1986): *Collected Works* 22.

Schulkind, E. ed. 1972: *The Paris Commune: The View from the Left*.

Tersen, Bruhat Dautry 1970: *La Commune de 1871*.

EUGENE SCHULKIND

party Marx and Engels never developed a finished theory of political parties, which only at the end of their lives were beginning to assume the forms that we know today. Engels described parties as 'the more or less adequate expression of . . . classes and fractions of classes' (1895 Introduction to Marx, *Class Struggles*). Marx, in *18th Brumaire* (secs. 2 and 3) attributed the division between French Orleanist and Legitimist royalist parties to 'the two great interests into which the bourgeoisie is split – landed property and capital'. However he did not consider that every party struggle must necessarily reflect conflicting economic interests, seeing largely 'ideological' factors as the *raison d'être* of the bourgeois republicans as against the bourgeois

royalists. He described the French social democratic party as 'a coalition between petty bourgeois and workers'.

Advocacy of an independent proletarian party occupied a central position in the political thought and activity of Marx and Engels. 'In its struggle against the collective power of the propertied classes,' they argued, 'the working class cannot act as a class except by constituting itself into a political party, distinct from, and opposed to, all old parties formed by the propertied classes.' (Resolution, drafted by Marx and Engels, adopted at Hague Congress of First International, 1872.) They spoke of such a party in relation to widely varying types of organization. However, theoretical consciousness and the *Selbsttätigkeit* (spontaneous self-activity) of the working class complemented each other as constant elements in their conception of the party, combining in different proportions in different conditions. This idea finds its classical expression in the *Communist Manifesto* (1848), written by Marx and Engels on behalf of the League of Communists, of which they were leaders from 1847 to 1852. In the *Manifesto* they spoke of the communists' clearer theoretical understanding of 'the line of march, the conditions and the ultimate general results of the proletarian movement' (sect. 2), which they conceived as 'the self-conscious, independent movement of the immense majority, in the interest of the immense majority' (sect. 1).

The Second International, at its Amsterdam Congress of 1904, declared that, as there was only one proletariat, there should only be one socialist party in each country. Much Marxist thinking in this period reflected an economistic, quasi-fatalistic conception of an inexorable growth of these parties as a function of the growth and social position of the working class.

By contrast, there was always a strong activist element in Lenin's conception of the party, to which he accorded major theoretical and practical importance. As in Marx and Engels, there is more than one 'model' of the party to be found in Lenin, though all of them envisaged a centralized vanguard working to fuse socialist theory and consciousness with the spontaneous labour movement. His best known work on this theme, 'What is to be Done?' (1902), favoured a narrow, hierarchically organized cadres' party as most appropriate to the movement's stage of development and the conditions of illegality imposed by Tsarism at that time. However later, taking advantage of the greater freedom provided by the 1905 revolution, as subsequently by that of February 1917, he went all out for a broad mass party based on DEMOCRATIC CENTRALISM, with an elected, accountable and removable leadership. It was around the nature of the party that differences between Bolsheviks and Mensheviks first arose in 1903. The latter's criticism of Lenin and the Bolsheviks for excessive centralism was shared and amplified the following year by Trotsky (1904) and Rosa Luxemburg (1904).

In 'What is to be Done?' Lenin followed Kautsky in arguing that 'class political consciousness can be brought to the workers *only from without*, that is, only from outside the economic struggle' (1902, *CW 5*, p. 422, emphasis in original). He distinguished between 'trade union consciousness', which the workers could acquire spontaneously, and 'Social Democratic consciousness', which it was the party's function to develop among them (ibid. pp. 375, 421–2; see ECONOMISM). Lukács (1923) pushed this distinction further and counterposed the workers' 'psychological consciousness', empirically acquired, to 'imputed (*zugerechnetes*) consciousness', seen as 'the correct class consciousness of the proletariat and its organisational form, the communist party'.

In contrast to this conception, which Lukács later repudiated as 'essentially contemplative' and reflecting a 'messianic utopianism' (1967 Preface to Lukács 1923), Gramsci and Togliatti insisted: 'It is not necessary to believe that the party can lead the working class through an external imposition of authority . . . either with respect to the period which precedes the winning of power, or with respect to the period which follows it.' It could only lead if it really succeeded, 'as part of the working class, in linking itself with all sections of that class' (Lyons Theses, drafted in 1925 by Gramsci and Togliatti, in Gramsci 1978, pp. 367–8). Later, in prison, Gramsci wrote of the role of initiator of political change ('the modern prince') lying with 'the political party – the first cell in which there come together the germs of a collective will tending to become universal and total' (Gramsci 1971, p. 129).

A one-party system was nowhere envisaged by Marx and Engels. The PARIS COMMUNE of 1871, which Engels described as the DICTATORSHIP OF THE PROLETARIAT, was divided into a Blanquist majority and a mainly Proudhonist minority, with various political groups like the middle-class Alliance Républicaine des Départements functioning freely. Nor did the Bolsheviks in the October Revolution of 1917 see Soviet power as entailing the suppression of all other parties. In December 1917 Lenin drafted a decree providing for proportional representation in the Soviets (see COUNCILS) 'based on acceptance of the party system and the conduct of elections by organised parties' (Draft Decree on Right of Recall, *CW 26*, p. 336). After repressive measures were taken against the leaders of the capitalist Constitutional Democratic (Cadet) Party, and the Constituent Assembly was dissolved in January 1918 for refusing to recognize Soviet power, a multi-party system continued to operate within the Soviets. In January 1918 Lenin argued the superiority of the Soviet system on the grounds that, under it, 'if the working people are dissatisfied with their party they can elect other delegates, hand power to another party and change the government without any revolution at all' (Replies to notes at Extraordinary All-Russia Railwaymen's Congress, *CW 26*, p. 498). In July 1918 the revolt of the Left Socialist Revolutionary Party, with whom the Bolsheviks had collaborated in a coalition government from November 1917 to March 1918, led to their repression and elimination as the principal recognized opposition party. Although other left-wing parties like the MENSHEVIKS survived alternating spells of repression and toleration through the civil war (1918–20), with some of their leaders speaking at the Congresses of Soviets, they were completely suppressed following the Kronstadt Mutiny of 1921, with which they had associated themselves. Whilst not officially proclaimed, and doubtless regarded by Lenin as a temporary response to an emergency situation, a one-party system was then established, precluding the possibility of the Bolsheviks being constitutionally replaced by another party. At the Tenth Congress of the Communist Party in 1921 Lenin insisted that 'the dictatorship of the proletariat would not work except through the Communist Party' (Summing-up Speech at Tenth RCP(B) Congress, *CW 32*, p. 199). And Trotsky maintained that the party was 'entitled to assert its dictatorship even if that dictatorship temporarily clashed with the passing moods of the workers' democracy' (quoted by Deutscher 1954, pp. 508–9). The economic and social pluralism of the New Economic Policy (NEP) allowing free trade, introduced in 1921, was accompanied by a restriction of political pluralism. However, the abolition of NEP at the end of the 1920s was followed by its total suppression.

Under Stalin, power passed from the hands of the one licensed party into those of its leading group and then of Stalin personally (see DEMOCRATIC CENTRALISM and STALINISM). Stalin was responsible for the acceptance for many years by the international communist movement of the idea that a one-party system was a necessary feature of socialism. 'A party is part of a class, its most advanced part', he said in 1936. 'Several parties, and, consequently, freedom of parties, can exist only in a society in which there are antagonistic classes whose interests are mutually hostile and irreconcilable' (Stalin 1940, p. 579). Trotsky, opposing this conception, wrote: 'In reality classes are heterogeneous; they are torn by inner antagonisms, and arrive at the solution of common problems not otherwise than through an inner struggle of tendencies, groups and parties . . . Since a class has many "parts" – some look forward and some back – one and the same class may create several parties' (Trotsky 1937 (1957), p. 267).

The Stalinist model of the ruling communist party, to which all public bodies were subordinate, was followed in almost all the other socialist states which had come into being since the Second World War. This included the *nomenklatura* system whereby appointments not only in the party but also in the state and in voluntary organizations like trade unions (seen as 'transmission belts' for party directives) have to be approved by an appropriate party committee. In some of these states other political parties were allowed to exist, but only within a *bloc* or front, and on condition that they accepted the leading role of the Communist Party. Article 6 of the 1977 Soviet constitution laid down that the Communist Party was 'the leading and guiding force of Soviet society and the nucleus of its political system' and that it 'determines the general perspectives of the development of society and the course of the home and foreign policy of the USSR'. Similar formulations were inserted in the constitutions of most East European socialist states.

Gorbachev, initiating the process of democratization in the Soviet Union, saw it as entailing a 'pluralism of opinions' but not a pluralism of parties. However, by 1989–90, widespread and persistent demands were being put forward in the Soviet Union and in other socialist states from Hungary to Mongolia for a genuine multiparty system seen as an essential feature of democracy. Guarantees for the leading role of the Communist Party like Article 6 of the Soviet constitution were removed. The dramatic popular upsurge against the old autocratic systems in Eastern Europe in the last months of 1989 led to contested elections in which former communist parties, under changed names, were often defeated by other parties to whom they ceded the reins of government. In the Soviet Union there has been a mushrooming of political parties and proto-parties challenging the rule of the Communist Party, which is itself deeply divided. Gorbachev has stressed the need for the CPSU to end the practice of 'commanding and substituting for state and economic bodies'. It 'intends to struggle for the status of the ruling party. But it will do so strictly within the framework of the democratic process by giving up any legal and political advantages' (Gorbachev's report to the CPSU Central Committee, 5 February 1990). In a number of elected bodies (Supreme Soviets of Baltic republics, city Soviets in Moscow, Leningrad etc.) CPSU representatives in 1990 found themselves in a minority.

The Yugoslav Communist Party in 1952 changed its name to the League of Communists of Yugoslavia to emphasize its desire to cease directly managing society and become a political and ideological guiding force within a self-managing socialist system. However, in the absence of any legal opposition, it often swung back to its old dominating role. Philosophers of the Yugoslav *Praxis* group such as Mihailo Marković have argued that 'a democratic political life will require a plurality of political organisations: of various clubs, leagues, societies and unions', but not political parties seen as 'a specifically bourgeois form of political organisation characterised by struggle for power, authoritarian decision-making, hierarchy and ideological manipulation of the masses' (Marković 1982, pp. 144, 42). However, Yugoslavia enters the 1990s with the rise of a vigorous multi-party system, especially in Slovenia and Croatia where the League of Communists' successor parties have been defeated in elections by their political opponents.

The case for party pluralism under socialism, including rights for opposition parties which function within the law, has for very many years been argued *inter alios* by 'Eurocommunist' parties (see EUROCOMMUNISM) and a number of other communist parties. They see this as a necessary condition for democratic choice between alternative governmental programmes and for checking concentrations of power towards which one-party systems tend more strongly to gravitate. (See also: BOLSHEVISM; CLASS CONSCIOUSNESS; INTERNATIONALS; LENIN; MARX, ENGELS AND CONTEMPORARY POLITICS; MENSHEVISM; WORKING CLASS MOVEMENTS.)

Reading

Gramsci, Antonio 1929–35 *(1971)*: *Selections from the Prison Notebooks*, pt. 2/1.

Johnstone, Monty 1967: 'Marx and Engels and the Concept of the Party'.

— 1970: 'Socialism, Democracy and the One-Party System'. In *Marxism Today*, August, September and November.

Lenin, V. I. 1902 *(1961)*: 'What is to be Done?'

— 1907 *(1962)*: Preface. In *CW* vol. 13, pp. 100–8.

Lukács, Georg 1923 *(1971)*: *History and Class Consciousness*.

Luxemburg, Rosa 1904 *(1970)*: 'Organisational Questions of Russian Social Democracy'. In *Rosa Luxemburg Speaks*.

Miliband, Ralph 1977: *Marxism and Politics*.

Molyneux, John 1978: *Marxism and the Party*.

Trotsky, Leon D. 1904 *(1980)*: *Our Political Tasks*.
                                    MONTY JOHNSTONE

pauperization   Marx's analysis of capitalism leads him to identify two kinds of tendencies inherent in the system: inescapable or dominant tendencies, such as the creation of a RESERVE ARMY OF LABOUR or the tendency of the rate of profit to fall (see FALLING RATE OF PROFIT), which channel the counteracting factors in a certain direction and thus end by subordinating them; and escapable or coordinate tendencies, whose relentless pressure may nonetheless be offset by an opposite tendency of sufficient countervailing pressure.

In analysing the condition of the working class, Marx argues that capitalism inevitably creates and maintains a pool of unemployed and partially employed labour (the reserve army of labour) which, in conjunction with the limits given by considerations of the profitability, competition and mobility of capitals, necessarily prevents workers from raising real wages faster than productivity; in fact, real wages decline *relative* to the productivity of labour, or in Marxist terms, the rate of exploitation rises. The resultant widening gap between productivity and real wages enlarges the power of capital, and, therefore widens 'the abyss between the labourer's position and that of the capitalist ...'. The *relative impoverishment* of workers is an inherent feature of the capitalist system as a whole. Marx notes that real wages can rise provided they do 'not interfere with the progress of accumulation' (*Capital* I, ch. 23), and concludes that 'the tendency of the rate of labour exploitation to rise' is but a 'specific (form)' through which the growing productivity of labour is expressed under capitalism' (*Capital* III, ch. 14). In *Wage-Labour and Capital* (ch. 5) he notes that wages may rise if productive capital grows, but 'although the pleasures of the labourer have increased, the social gratification which they afford has fallen in comparison with the increased pleasures of the capitalist which are inaccessible to the worker, in comparison with the stage of development of society in general.'

The fact that real wages cannot generally increase beyond an upper limit in no way prevents capitalists from incessantly striving to *reduce* real wages as much as possible, and the objective lower limit to this tendency towards the *absolute impoverishment* of workers is provided by the conditions which regulate the availability of wage labour. Where the reserve army is large, for instance, real wages can be driven down even below subsistence because fresh workers become available as existing ones are 'used up' by capital. On the other hand, during boom periods when the reserve army has dried up in certain regions, then within the limits of the costs of the import of labour or the mobility of capital, real wages may rise simply due to the scarcity of *immediately available* labour. Even more importantly, workers' struggles as reflected in unionization and in social legislation can themselves regulate the terms on which labour is made available to capital, and except in periods of crisis, successfully overpower the capitalist attempts to lower real wages. The inherent pressure towards the absolute impoverishment of labour can therefore be offset under the right conditions.

Some modern Marxists such as Meek (1967) have argued, however, that whereas 'there is little doubt that Marx did anticipate that as capitalism developed *relative* wages [i.e. relative to property incomes] would decline, whatever happened to *absolute* wages' (p. 121), there has not in fact been an appreciable fall in relative wages in the advanced capitalist countries. Meek therefore concludes that there is a need to work out new 'laws of motion' of present-day capitalism (pp. 127–8). One such version of the new laws of motion argues that in the advanced capitalist countries there is neither 'absolute' nor 'relative' pauperization, so that pauperization in any form becomes confined to the peripheral underdeveloped countries (usually as a consequence of the development of metropolitan capital). This view is often allied with wage squeeze theories of crises in the centre (see ECONOMIC CRISES), because the absence of pauperization is equivalent to a constant or (more probably) a falling rate of surplus value. At the heart of this perspective, however, is the *empirical* claim that the rate of exploitation does not rise substantially. And it is precisely this claim which falls apart once even minimal attention is paid to the difference between Marxist categories and the orthodox economic categories in which modern national income accounts are expressed (Shaikh 1978, pp. 237–9).

Reading

Elliott, J.E. 1981: *Marx and Engels on Economics, Politics and Society.*

Meek, Ronald L. 1967: 'Marx's "Doctrine of Increasing Misery".' In *Economics and Ideology and Other Essays.*

Rosdolsky, R. 1968 (1977): *The Making of Marx's 'Capital'.*

Shaikh, A. 1978a: 'An Introduction to the History of Crisis Theories'. In *U.S. Capitalism in Crisis.*

Sowell, T. 1960: 'Marx's "Increasing Misery" Doctrine'.

ANWAR SHAIKH

peasantry   Marx and Engels were acutely aware of the historical significance of peasantries and of the importance of peasantries in the Europe of their own time (and elsewhere). Both, moreover, stressed the need to consider peasantries which were socially differentiated. Marx did so, for example, when considering the 'genesis of capitalist ground rent', and casting light on the transition from feudalism to capitalism (*Capital* III, ch. 47). By the late nineteenth century, European Marxists, including Engels, saw the continued existence in Europe of peasantries as constituting the AGRARIAN QUESTION: the reflection of an incomplete transition to capitalism. Central to the agrarian question was the fact of differentiated peasantries.

In the Soviet Union of the 1920s, a critical part of the debate on socialist transition centred on the implications of a large differentiated peasantry. Much fruitful work on this was done by the Agrarian Marxists, whose leader was L. N. Kritsman (Cox and Littlejohn 1984). In national liberation movements and in twentieth-century revolutions, particular strata of the peasantry have played an important, if controversial, role: some writers have stressed the role of poor peasants, others that of middle peasants (Byres in Rahman 1986). In present-day poor countries, peasantries which are socially differentiated loom large.

The term 'peasantry' is commonly used in Marxist discourse to identify a variety of forms of non-capitalist or non-socialist agricultural production. But it is, in such usage, a descriptive rather than an analytical category. Thus, attempts to identify a distinct peasant MODE OF PRODUCTION, to be added to those commonly employed (feudalism, capitalism, socialism, etc.), have not found an accepted place in Marxist analysis (Ennew, Hirst and Tribe 1977). The first such attempt, that of the important Russian neo-populist theorist of the peasantry, A. V. Chayanov, was not couched in Marxist terms, and cannot be so accommodated.

Kritsman provided the following definition of peasant agriculture, which translates peasantry into Marxist terms:

> Peasant farming is the farming of petty producers. A characteristic of them is the presence in their enterprise of their own means of production and its use by their own labour. In

other words . . . the relation between its own labour power and its own means of production alone can characterise a peasant farm. (Cited by Cox, in Cox and Littlejohn 1984, p. 25)

Peasantries with such characteristics, not themselves constitutive of a distinct mode of production, have existed within a variety of modes of production since the dawn of recorded history. In a materialist treatment, they are to be analysed in terms of the mode of production in which they are located, and via consideration of the distinguishing FORCES AND RELATIONS OF PRODUCTION of that mode. They are not autonomous entities, but are part of the existing RURAL CLASS STRUCTURE.

Kritsman's definition may be seen to identify peasant agriculture, in Marxist analytical terms, as an example of PETTY COMMODITY PRODUCTION. This is an illuminating way of treating peasantries in present-day poor countries, and in a range of historical situations, where peasants produce commodities for exchange. Bernstein (1979), for example, provides such a framework for the analysis of African peasantries.

Particularly influential in the treatment of differentiation of the peasantry are the formulations of Lenin (1899) and Mao (1933). Among present-day Marxists, Utsa Patnaik (1987) has contributed powerfully and originally to the analysis of differentiation. Here we should note the fundamental difference between Marxist and neo-populist conceptions. Neo-populists, such as Chayanov, stress *demographic* rather than social differentiation. This has been tested and rebutted for Russia, by Harrison (1977), and, for example, by Rahman (1986) for Bangladesh.

In this dynamic view, peasantries are seen to have sections which may show signs of movement towards proletarian status (a poor peasantry); sections which may contain the possibility of transformation into a capitalist class (a rich peasantry); and, indeed, sections which tend towards an 'archetypal' peasant condition (a middle peasantry), as identified by Kritsman. Such tendencies may be weakly developed, or they may be very strongly developed. Differentiated peasantries may well reproduce themselves at a particular level over long periods of time:

differentiation may remain, in a sense, quantitative. There is no necessary guarantee that any such peasantry will be transformed into a fully developed capitalist agriculture: that the processes underpinning differentiation generate qualitative change.

One distinguishes a *peasantry* from, on the one hand, a class of *wage labourers* and, on the other, from a class of *capitalist farmers*. A peasantry may ultimately, where a capitalist road is traversed, disintegrate irrevocably and be transformed into these latter two classes. But in conditions of economic backwardness, it will exist quite distinctly from them. It is to be distinguished, also, from a *landlord class*. We may pursue these distinctions in order to identify a Marxist view of the likely nature of peasantries in a variety of historical situations, and to establish some preliminary notion of what a socially differentiated peasantry entails.

A *pure wage labourer* has been separated from the means of production. He is 'free in the double sense that as a free man he can dispose of his labour power as his own commodity, and that on the other hand he has no other commodity for sale, is short of everything necessary for the realisation of his labour power' (*Capital* I, ch. 6). He has no possession of the means of production, and no access to the means of subsistence. He must, therefore, sell his labour power.

It is the mark of the *peasant*, by contrast, that he is not separated from the means of production in this complete sense. He may have lost land, and he may face the prospect of losing yet more. He may, in other words, have become, or be in process of becoming, a *poor peasant*. But for so long as he possesses land and possesses the instruments of production, he is a peasant. He may own land, or he may rent it, or he may do both. Whatever his means of access to land, a crucial distinguishing characteristic of a peasant is possession of that land. He may have been forced into selling his labour power to others to ensure his survival: again, a characteristic feature of a poor peasantry. But for so long as this is not his sole means of survival, he is a peasant.

Among the characteristics of a *capitalist farmer*, is that he is 'the owner of money, means of production, means of subsistence, who is eager to increase the sum of values [he] possesses, by buying other people's labour power' (*Capital* I, ch. 26). It is one of the prerequisites of a fully formed capitalist agriculture that 'the actual tillers of the soil are wage-labourers employed by a capitalist, the capitalist farmer who is engaged in agriculture merely as a particular field of exploitation for capital' (*Capital* III, ch. 37). The capitalist farmer appropriates surplus value exclusively via the wage relation: via his purchase, setting to work and exploitation of the labour power of others. That is a necessary, though not a sufficient, condition for the existence of capitalist agriculture.

A *peasant*, however, will use family labour. One may, ideally, conceive of an 'archetypal' peasant using only family labour. Where, further, the peasantry is socially differentiated, a *poor peasant* or *middle peasant* may have this as one of his characteristics. But a peasant – even a poor or middle peasant – may well use nonfamily labour. He may hire labour, as well as selling his own labour; in peak seasons (for example, at harvest time or, say, in rice cultivation at the time of transplanting) to release tight labour constraints, or even in a more prolonged way. Part of the peasantry – a rich peasantry – may constitute 'an exploiting, surplus appropriating class' (Patnaik 1976, p. A85). The major proportion of labour input on a rich peasant's land may, indeed, be wage labour. What marks the peasant off from the capitalist farmer is, however, his continuing recourse to family, manual labour.

A *landlord class* is one which owns land and rents it out to tenants: appropriating surplus via rent. A landlord may have some of his land cultivated, whether by peasants supplying labour in the form of labour rent, or by bonded labour, or via wage labour. Where, however, the predominant form of exploitation is rent we confront a landlord class. A *peasant* may well own his land, cultivate some of it and let some of it out at rent. He is not, however, thereby to be considered a landlord, or part of the landlord class. To the extent that he still cultivates it, that this constitutes a major part of his activity, and that he has the other distinguishing characteristic of a peasant, he must be designated a peasant – a rich peasant, or *kulak* – and not a member of the landlord class. The same logic applies to those peasants who lend money at usurious interest.

The perhaps significant differences among countries following the same road (be it capitalism or socialism) will hinge on variations in the extent and nature of differentiation of the peasantry (see Byres 1991 for the capitalist case). The distinction between countries embarking on separate roads derives, in part, from the very different role ascribed to differentiation in each road. For a successful *capitalist* road, unchecked processes of social differentiation, at least in some cases, may be essential. Under *socialism*, attempts to eradicate it in favour of collective structures may be made. Where *populist* strategies are followed, efforts to minimize it, or replace it with small, individual holdings, may be suggested.

Reading

Bernstein, Henry 1979: 'African Peasantries: A Theoretical Framework'.

Byres, T. J. 1986: 'The Agrarian Question and Differentiation of the Peasantry'. In Rahman 1986.

— 1991: 'The Agrarian Question and Differing Forms of Capitalist Agrarian Transition: An Essay with Reference to Asia'. In J. C. Breman and S. Mundle, eds. *Rural Transformation in Asia*.

Cox, Terry and Littlejohn, Gary eds. 1984: *Kritsman and the Agrarian Marxists*.

Ennew, Judith, Hirst, Paul and Tribe, Keith 1977: ' "Peasantry" as an Economic Category'.

Harrison, Mark 1977: 'Resource Allocation and Agrarian Class Formation: The Problem of Social Mobility among Russian Peasant Households, 1880–1930'.

Journal of Peasant Studies, from 1973 onwards (vol. 1, no. 1).

Lenin, V. I. 1899b (1960): *The Development of Capitalism in Russia*.

Mao Tse-tung 1933 (1967): 'How to Differentiate the Classes in the Rural Areas'. In *Selected Works*, vol. 1.

Patnaik, Utsa 1976: 'Class Differentiation within the Peasantry: An Approach to Analysis of Indian Agriculture'.

— 1987: *Peasant Class Differentiation: A Study in Method with Reference to Haryana*.

Rahman, Atiur 1986: *Peasants and Classes: A Study in Differentiation in Bangladesh*.

T. J. BYRES

periodization of capitalism As a theory of history Marxism is more than an application of dialectics to the transition from one mode of production to another; it encompasses, too, the historical changes that occur *within* the life of each mode. Capitalism, like other modes, is conceived as progressing through distinct stages; instead of moving along a smooth curve as its internal contradictions mature, it follows a broken path with distinct segments. Thus the stage that capitalism had reached by the third quarter of this century is recognized as being quite distinct from the competitive capitalism of *Capital's* paradigm and it is named, variously, as MONOPOLY CAPITALISM (Baran and Sweezy 1966) STATE MONOPOLY CAPITALISM (Boccara 1976), or late capitalism (Mandel 1975).

The idea that each MODE OF PRODUCTION has a history of its own is inherent in historical materialism, for the systematic progress of society from one mode of production to another can only be theorized in terms of the contradictions in one mode maturing to undermine it and lay the basis for the new. But why should that history be conceived in the form of distinct stages? The logic of such a periodization for capitalism is that there are significant transformations in the form taken by the relations of production (defined either narrowly or as the whole ensemble of social relations) as capitalism progresses. The contradictions inherent in capitalism, such as that between the FORCES AND RELATIONS OF PRODUCTION, intensify as the system matures but they are transformed in the process. These changes, affecting the whole spectrum of relations and the institutional framework of society in which they exist, give rise to distinct types of capitalism in the history of any society. However, while constructing the internal history of modes of production has in principle been a theoretical necessity, in practice the analysis of capitalism's stages has been driven by the pressure of reality, the *empirical* observation and description of historical changes that have already occurred. Lenin developed his theory of imperialism, and Baran and Sweezy promoted their concept of monopoly capitalism, as a result of the political need to come to terms with the changes in the system that the socialist movement was actually confronting, and to review the prognoses for the end of capitalism.

Some writers periodize capitalism into three successive stages, competitive capitalism, monopoly capitalism and state monopoly capitalism, but there are disagreements over the validity of these categories both individually and as a sequence. The debate has stemmed in part from different political perspectives: Mandel (1975) for example sees the concept of state monopoly capitalism as being tied to the political strategy of Communist parties. In part, though, it stems from theoretical ambiguities: the question of the appropriate principles for delineating the differences between stages has been neither resolved nor even fully considered (see the critical comments in Uno 1964, discussed in MARXIST ECONOMICS IN JAPAN).

The differences between the stages of capitalism lie in the degree to which production in its broad sense is socialized. Marx's view of the contradictory nature of the forces and relations of production focused on the increasingly socialized nature of production compared with private ownership of capital and appropriation of surplus value, but private ownership and appropriation themselves were seen as taking increasingly socialized forms as capitalism developed. Thus, in *Capital* III (ch. 27) Marx's succinct comments on joint-stock companies (which typify monopoly capitalism) noted that

> capital, which in itself rests on a social mode of production and presupposes a social concentration of means of production and labour-power, is here directly endowed with the form of social capital (capital of directly associated individuals) as distinct from private capital, and its undertakings assume the form of social undertakings as distinct from private undertakings. . . .

The successive stages of capitalism are marked by increasing socialization of every aspect of the economy. Production itself becomes increasingly socialized as the division of labour changes qualitatively. Thus, with the move from competitive capitalism to monopoly capitalism, the predominant method of production changes from one where absolute surplus value is produced to one in which relative surplus value is the mainspring of accumulation as machinery (see MACHINERY AND MACHINOFACTURE) dominated the labour process (what Marx calls the real subsumption of labour to capital). And with the machinofacture of monopoly capitalism, production is more highly socialized than in the previous stage: productive labour (see PRODUCTIVE AND UNPRODUCTIVE LABOUR) comes to take the form of the collective labourer, an integrated workforce instead of individualized craft workers, and the production of relative surplus value means that the production of surplus value in any one industry depends upon the productivity of all other industries directly or indirectly reducing the value of wage goods and hence the VALUE OF LABOUR POWER.

To separate the history of capitalism's increased socialization into distinct stages such changes in methods of production can be marked out (as in Friedman 1977), but changes in the forms of appropriation and in the structures and relations that guide and direct economic reproduction and the social division of labour show equally clear-cut divisions between the three stages of competitive, monopoly, and state monopoly capitalism. Under competitive capitalism surplus value is appropriated predominantly in the form of profit, and the division of labour is coordinated or guided by the markets on which commodities are sold. At the international level capital expands through exporting and importing commodities. Under monopoly capitalism, the credit system comes to dominate and work with the commodity markets to guide the social division of labour as it allocates credit away from unprofitable and towards profitable sectors. Interest becomes a predominant form in which surplus value is appropriated, forcing a division of profit into interest and profit-of-enterprise, and as Marx observes, the whole profit takes on the appearance of interest:

> Even if the dividends which they receive include the interest and the profit-of-enterprise ... this total profit is henceforth received only in the form of interest, i.e. as mere compensation for owning capital that is now entirely divorced from the function in the actual process of production, just as this function in the person of the manager is divorced from the ownership of capital. (*Capital* III, ch. 27)

When financial capital in this stage takes on the special dominance involved in FINANCE CAPITAL an additional form of appropriation, promoter's profit, becomes significant. And at the international level the social division of labour is, at this stage, effected by the export of capital as financial capital, identified by Hilferding, Bukharin and Lenin as the characteristic of imperialism; in fact imperialism was identified as a stage of capitalism coterminous with monopoly capital.

The most recent stage, state monopoly capitalism, is marked by the role of the state (articulated with the credit system and commodity markets) in coordinating the social division of labour. Through Keynesian macroeconomic policies, through public-sector production of goods and services (either as commodities or isolated from the market as in the case of free education), and through setting the framework for corporatist planning, indicative planning or incomes policies, the state in this stage plays an active role affecting the structure of the economy. And taxation as a form for the appropriation of surplus value becomes significant at this stage. At the world level, capital is internationalized in the form of productive capital within the MULTINATIONAL CORPORATIONS; production processes are divided between factories in different countries instead of capital being exported only in the form of traded commodities or foreign loans. In theories of this stage a close connection between the state and big, monopoly capital is usually assumed (see STATE MONOPOLY CAPITALISM).

The principles of periodization adopted here for capitalism have parallels with those used by Marx in periodizing feudalism. In *Capital* III ch. 47 Marx analysed the 'Genesis of Capitalist Ground Rent' in terms of three distinct stages of feudalism. The index of these stages (although not their whole character) was seen as given by the form in which surplus labour was appropriated; labour rent, rent in kind, and money rent, respectively. And with the different forms of appropriation distinct mechanisms governed the reproduction of the economy; coercion, contracts, and contracts plus markets (contracts denominated in money) respectively.

Poulantzas (1975), however, has argued that only capitalism can be periodized. He also differs in other respects from the approach taken here, arguing that capitalism cannot be periodized at the level of abstraction at which the mode of production is theorized but only at the level of the more complex SOCIAL FORMATION (the concept that, being at a lower level of abstraction, more fully captures the complexity and the appearance of actual societies). Baran and Sweezy (1966) propose quite a different scheme of periodization, postulating a simple division between the competitive capitalism on which Marx concentrated and the 'monopoly capitalism' that characterizes the most recent period. Their concept of the latter stage is quite different from the one employed here (see MONOPOLY CAPITALISM) and in addition does not separate monopoly and state monopoly capitalism. Their dividing line for discriminating the stages is not the changes in the form of all the relations and forces of production, reflecting increased socialization, but changes in the laws of accumulation that reflect one key change alone, the change in the market structure faced by firms as competition is transformed into monopoly. In the approach taken above, it is assumed that the basic contradictions of capitalism which produce its law of accumulation remain, but the form of the relations within which they occur changes; capitalism in each stage is affected by the law of the FALLING RATE OF PROFIT and ECONOMIC CRISES, and indeed, major economic crises usher in new stages (as the 1870s marked the start of monopoly capitalism and the 1930s of state monopoly capitalism in the major capitalist societies). For Baran and Sweezy, however, writing in the long post-war boom (albeit near its end) monopoly capital appeared to have transformed these laws.

Mandel's great study (1975) of the latest stage of capitalism does not follow the three-fold scheme outlined above, but his stage of late capitalism is little different from the state monopoly capitalism described here. More important, he examines at length the dynamic of the system, the laws of accumulation that give rise to the transformation of capitalism from one stage to another. His approach to this question is also similar in seeing the contradictions of accumulation that Marx identified as leading to the new stage, and in turn being promoted by the new structural relations of the new stage. In Mandel's work the transformations that occur at all levels of the economy from the new social division of labour in production to financing and the economic activity of the state, are theorized as an integrated whole.

Reading

Baran, Paul and Sweezy, Paul 1966: *Monopoly Capitalism*.

Boccara, Paul ed. 1969 (1976): *Traité d'économie politique: Le Capitalisme monopoliste d'état*.

Fine, Ben and Harris, Laurence 1979: *Rereading 'Capital'*.

Friedman, Andrew 1977: *Industry and Labour*.

Mandel, Ernest 1975: *Late Capitalism*.

Poulantzas, Nicos 1975: *Classes in Contemporary Capitalism*.

LAURENCE HARRIS

petty bourgeoisie. *See* middle class.

petty commodity production Often descriptively termed 'household production', 'PCP' has a major and contentious place in Marxism, if one often implicit in conflicting interpretations of the nature and dynamics of capitalism. It is a unity of individual or family labour and privately owned means of production producing commodities for exchange. This definition is encompassed in different views that it is (1) common to capitalism and other modes of production (what Marx called a 'simple' category); (2) a pre-capitalist or transitional category sooner or later destroyed by the development of capitalism; (3) a distinctive category of capitalism subject to continuous if uneven processes of destruction *and* re-creation.

All these positions (and variants of them) can claim support in different passages of Marx. Explaining the 'persistence' of PCP, especially in agriculture, by protracted or 'blocked' transitions to capitalism exemplifies the second position (see PEASANTRY, AGRARIAN QUESTION). Others explain PCP by its 'functions' for capitalism, that unpaid family labour cheapens or 'subsidizes' the value of commodities it produces; one variant of this is the concept of 'articulation of modes of production' (see MARXISM AND THE THIRD WORLD), which has affinities with Rosa Luxemburg's theory of imperialism.

In an important assessment and restatement, Gibbon and Neocosmos (1985) argue for the third position, quoting Marx in *Theories of Surplus Value*, vol. 3:

The independent peasant or handicraftsman is cut up into two persons. As owner of the means of production he is a capitalist, as labourer he is his own wage-labourer. As capitalist he therefore pays himself his wages and draws his profit on his capital; that is he exploits himself as wage-labourer, and pays himself in the surplus-value, the tribute that labour owes to capital. (p. 408)

Here PCP is a contradictory unity premised on a *prior* separation of capital and labour, the essential condition of capitalism, thereby distinguishing it from the unity of labour and means of production in pre-capitalist modes of production, and also suggesting its intrinsic instability, its tendency to decompose into one or other of its constituent 'persons':

The handicraftsman or peasant who produces with his own means of production will either gradually be transformed into a small capitalist who exploits the labour of others, or he will suffer the loss of his means of production . . . and be transformed into a wage-labourer. This is the tendency in the form of society in which the capitalist mode of production predominates. (p. 409).

How, to what extent and with what effects this tendency to class differentiation is realized always depends on specific historical conditions, analysed in concrete studies by Lenin (1899b) among others.

There are two distinct mechanisms of the destruction of PCP: in particular *branches of production* by competition from capitalist production; and the destruction of *individual* enterprises by competition between petty producers. Both manifest the proletarianization of petty producers unable to reproduce their means of production, while the second also embodies the possibility of some becoming capitalists.

Regarding the creation and re-creation of PCP, Lenin observed that 'A number of "new middle strata" are inevitably brought into existence again and again by capitalism . . .' ('Marxism and Revisionism', *CW* 15, p. 39). This does not require a functionalist or teleological explanation but is an *effect* of changes in the productive forces and social division of labour and in patterns of capital accumulation. The extent or mere existence of PCP, then, is not an index of 'backwardness'; rather it is the *types* of PCP in a particular branch of production or economy that reflect the level of development of the productive forces. These include highly capitalized family farms and home-based computer businesses in Western capitalism, as well as peasant and artisanal production in the Third World.

The essential difference between the productive forces of PCP and capitalist production is one of labour process, hence *social* rather than technical: the restriction of PCP to individual or family labour precludes any extensive specialization and complex cooperation in production (expressed by Marx as the 'collective worker').

An important reason for persisting views of PCP as pre- or non-capitalist has been its association with unitary and ahistorical notions of 'the' household or 'the' family. These are now untenable in the light of feminist investigation of sexual divisions of labour, property and income in household production and reproduction, and of how forms of gender inequality change in specific processes of commoditization. It has also problematized the idea of 'self-exploitation' (as in the first quotation from Marx above); the exploitation by men of the labour of women and children or other subordinate kin illustrates how the class positions of capital and labour combined in PCP can be distributed differentially between members of petty commodity enterprises.

In addition to the conflicting interpretations of capitalist development already noted, PCP has also been contentious because it generates petty bourgeois politics with its tendency to fluctuate erratically between alliances with the working class and with the bourgeoisie. If 'classes in the Marxist sense . . . are not simply given by capitalist relations, but need to be constituted through a specific political practice' (Gibbon and Neocosmos 1985, p. 183), the ideologies, demands and actions of petty producers have to be confronted and assessed in relation to proletarian and bourgeois practices in particular conjunctures of struggle. The politics no less than the economics of PCP should not be assigned then to 'the dustbin of history' in an *a priori* or mechanistic fashion.

An interesting footnote to current Marxist analysis is that investigation of PCP in the Third World has stimulated new thinking about its place in Western economies, e.g. in work on family farming, and on forms of PCP generated by recession and by post-Fordism.

Reading

Friedmann, Harriet 1980: 'Household Production and the National Economy: Concepts for the Analysis of Agrarian Formations'.

Gibbon, Peter and Neocosmos, Michael 1985: 'Some Problems in the Political Economy of "African Socialism"'. In Henry Bernstein and Bonnie K. Campbell, eds. *Contradictions of Accumulation in Africa: Studies in Economy and State.*

Redclift, Nanneke and Mingione, Enzo, eds. 1985: *Beyond Employment. Household, Gender and Subsistence.*

Scott, Alison MacEwen ed. 1986: *Rethinking Petty Commodity Production.*

Smith, John, Evers, Hans-Dieter and Wallerstein, Immanuel, eds. 1984: *Households and the World Economy.*

HENRY BERNSTEIN

philosophy As a form of socialism, Marxism is centrally a practical political movement. What distinguishes it within socialism is its combination of revolutionary practice with a radical and comprehensive social theory. But that theory aims and claims to be not (social or political) philosophy but rather social science. What then is the relation between that combined science and political practice on the one hand and philosophy on the other? And how does Marxism understand that relation?

Marx himself began his intellectual career as a philosopher, before making the transition to the science of historical materialism that culminated in *Capital.* What is the nature of that transition? And how is it related to that larger transition in European culture as a whole, by which philosophy in general ceded its position of intellectual dominance to science, first to natural science in the seventeenth century and then to social science in Marx's own century?

As Marxism is practically opposed to bourgeois politics, so it opposes also bourgeois theory and ideas. Nevertheless, bourgeois theories are not simply rejected: rather, they are, dialectically, absorbed and transformed. Predominantly, Marxist theory being centrally social science, it attacks the bourgeois social sciences while seeking to inherit the tradition of scientificity established by bourgeois culture in natural science: though it also sees natural science as historically changing, in particular as beginning to recognize and theorize the historicity of nature. In establishing these relations with bourgeois science, Marx and Marxism respond positively to three streams of bourgeois philosophy: Aristotelianism, the materialism of the Scientific Revolution and Enlightenment, and Hegel's DIALECTICS. But though key elements within these philosophies are appropriated, they are also transformed into a body of theory that stands in overall opposition to bourgeois philosophy. For Marxism, bourgeois philosophy is bourgeois ideology.

The main question to be asked is: does Marxism appropriate and oppose bourgeois philosophy by incorporating it into its own Marxist philosophy? Is there a distinctive Marxist philosophy, either in addition to or implicit in Marxist science? Or does historical materialism contradict and supersede philosophy as such? In the century since Marx's death the overwhelming answer that Marxism itself has given to these questions is that there is indeed a Marxist philosophy, so that it is in terms of that philosophy that Marxism's opposition to bourgeois philosophy is to be understood. In fact, the development of Marxism so far is generally theorized in accordance with the two Marxist philosophies that have successively held sway in the movement, the former most closely associated with the later work of Engels, the latter with the earlier work of Marx.

Dialectical Materialism

Marxism's first philosophy was DIALECTICAL MATERIALISM. A combination of scientific MATERIALISM and Hegel's dialectics, it holds that concrete reality is a contradictory unity whose contradictions drive it forward in a process of ceaseless historical change, evolutionary and revolutionary. Being contradictory, this reality can be truly described only by contradictory propositions and consequently requires a special dialectical LOGIC that supersedes formal logic with its principle of non-contradiction. The materialism of this view conceives matter and mind as themselves opposites within a unity in which the material is primary. Thus dialectical materialism is a 'world outlook' (Engels, *Anti-Dühring*, Preface to 2nd edn), a theory about the nature of reality as a whole. In particular, it claims to be instantiated in the special sciences, both natural and social, as they progress to maturity, constituting a Marxist version of 'the unity of science' and in the process arguing for the scientificity of historical materialism. As such, it sees itself as generalizing, and validated by, the findings of the sciences. Is dialectical materialism then philosophy or science?

Engels's argument on that question occurs in the Preface to the 2nd edn of *Anti-Dühring* and in the so-called 'Old Preface', originally written for the first edition but then rejected and assigned later to the materials for his *Dialectics of Nature*. His argument hardly justifies the tradition's tendency to regard dialectical materialism as philosophy. He claims that the developments in natural science that tend to confirm dialectical materialism are developments of *theoretical* natural science. By 'theoretical' here Engels is referring to the conceptual development of the sciences, and specifically to the relatively speculative development of concepts that though confirmed by, nevertheless go beyond, the strictly empirical evidence. Such concepts, he thinks, will tend to unify the separate special sciences. This process of non-empirical conceptual unification requires skills and ideas that have hitherto been the province of philosophy. But though Engels himself approaches the subject from philosophy, from the philosophies of materialism and dialectics, he thinks that probably developments within the natural sciences themselves will eventually 'make my work . . . superfluous' (*Anti-Dühring*, Preface to 2nd edn). His 'natural philosophy' will become 'theoretical natural science'. Philosophy as such will itself become superfluous, what is of value in it appropriated by and transformed into science.

Marxist humanism and Western Marxism
In the 1920s and 1930s, as the Russian Revolution regressed and 'Diamat' (a shorthand term for dialectical materialism current especially in the USSR) became essential to Communist Party orthodoxy, the hegemony of this first Marxist philosophy began to give way to a second. A loosely united tendency rather than a single well-defined set of doctrines, its earliest theorists were Lukács and Korsch, but at about the same time Marx's early philosophical writings were rediscovered and seemed to give support to this new philosophy rather than to dialectical materialism. Whereas 'Diamat' was a theory about reality as a whole, and saw people and society as instantiating universal natural processes, with social science as a natural science of society, the new tendency was humanist: it

reaffirmed the old humanist doctrine of 'man the measure of all things', asserting the centrality and distinctiveness of people and society and attacking not only the natural science model of social understanding but even science and technology themselves as bourgeois, and thus alienated and manipulative modes of enquiry and practice. Indeed, the characteristically Hegelian concept of ALIENATION, which is entirely absent from *Anti-Dühring* but essential to Marx's *Economic and Philosophical Manuscripts* (1844) was now, like that work itself, moved into a commanding position. With it came such related concepts as REIFICATION and FETISHISM, all apparently evaluative and ethical. But the focus was the conception of people as subjects, not objects; that is as centres of consciousness and values and thus essentially different from the rest of the natural order as depicted by science.

For dialectical materialism Marxist theory is predominantly scientific, and dialectical materialism itself is philosophy of science in the sense of 'natural philosophy', destined to lose its philosophical character and become fully scientific as 'theoretical natural science' develops. For Marxist humanism, on the contrary, Marxist theory is not primarily scientific but philosophical, any science occurring as an embedded part within the totalizing perspective of humanist philosophy. Its themes echo the general culture of the Romantic reaction against Enlightenment rationalism, the philosophical tradition they inherit chiefly the philosophy closest to Romanticism, German idealism: Kant (see KANTIANISM), Hegel, and the hermeneutic philosophy of the *Geisteswissenschaften*. All these agreed that reality as we know it does not exist independently of that knowledge but is (partly) constituted by it. Hermeneutics in particular rejected the empiricist doctrine of the unity of science and argued that understanding human and social affairs cannot have the same logic and methodology as empirical natural science: it is less like causally explaining events than understanding the meaning of ideas and language. In fact, understanding the language of a society is a large part of understanding that society itself. For in understanding their own language, participants have an understanding of their society that no science can undermine. The theoretical articulation of that understanding requires not the detached objectivity of empirical observation but 'empathy' with or even participation in the social activities under investigation, and is more conceptual and philosophical than empirical and scientific.

These tendencies have been more or less strongly present in the work of the FRANKURT SCHOOL, of SARTRE, and of the Marxism of contemporary Yugoslav dissident philosophers (expressed in the journal *Praxis*). But for the last two decades this Marxist humanism, and with it the high estimate of Marx's early philosophy, has come under attack from within Marxist philosophy, specifically from ALTHUSSER and his followers. Like the Italian school of Della Volpe, Althusser has opposed the Hegelian and idealist tendencies in Marxist humanism. He has argued that Marxist theory is centrally science but that implicit in historical materialism there is a Marxist philosophy, to be made explicit by analysis. As with dialectical materialism, then, this Marxist philosophy is philosophy of science. But in contrast to that, Althusser's Marxist philosophy is not 'natural philosophy', a world outlook that Marxism shares with the advanced natural sciences. Rather it is something closer to the orthodox conception of philosophy of science, namely epistemology: science is 'theoretical practice' and philosophy is 'theory of theoretical practice'. However, in his later self-criticism Althusser qualifies this conception, arguing that though still philosophy of science Marxist philosophy differs from science in being normative and ideological, and in particular political. By contrast with Marxist science, Marxist philosophy is 'politics in the field of theory', 'class struggle in theory' (Althusser 1976, p. 68 and p. 142).

Philosophy, idealism, and materialism

Marx began his intellectual career as a philosopher, acknowledging philosophy's traditional and definitive claim to intellectual supremacy in the field of ideas. But even in his early phase he became critical of that claim and with it of philosophy itself. He accepted the idea of 'the end of philosophy', not in its empiricist form as the replacement of *a priori* metaphysics by empirical science but instead conceiving the end or aim of philosophy as its realization and thus its end or supersession as superfluous. However, he came to see philosophy as being 'realized' not

in reality itself but rather in another form of theory, namely science. Of all types of theory it is science that is closest to reality and most capable of depicting it, whereas philosophy is a form of theory that subjects even its most penetrating insights to systematic distortion. For philosophy is constituted precisely by its search for the authorization of all (other) ideas within ideas themselves, and thus for ideas that form the eternally valid and *a priori* basis of thought in general. It is this search that compels philosophy to oscillate between *a priori* dogmatism and complete scepticism. Authorization by philosophy is something that science cannot have and does not need. Science has no foundations within theory itself. Indeed, all theory has its basis in material reality, but science is the only form of theory that recognizes this and thus the only form capable of adequately representing reality. Because of their material basis other forms of theory such as philosophy succeed in presenting something of that material reality, but in a mystified way. In superseding philosophy, science appropriates the contents of its insights but converts them into its own more adequate form.

It is this range of considerations and argument that Marx both condenses into his advocacy of materialism as against idealism and exemplifies in the construction of his own social science of historical materialism. The view that Marx advocates materialism *as a philosophy* is partly what is responsible for the conviction that there is a Marxist philosophy. Traditional materialism may be a philosophy, but it seems more consistent with the views of both Marx and Engels to hold that for them philosophy retains from religion a more or less residual idealism, so that philosophical materialism, though as such an advance on philosophical idealism, is still itself, as philosophy, idealist, its conceived basis for thought not material reality but (transcendentally) the necessary idea of material reality. The philosophical alternative to total scepticism is always some ontology, metaphysics, or epistemology. The non-philosophical alternative with its acknowledged basis in material reality itself is science. For science, knowledge of reality is possible, but no idea, however deeply embedded within the conceptual framework, is totally beyond question, all ideas ultimately requiring validation, however indirect, scientifically, in terms of their adequacy to reality.

Traditional epistemology conceives knowledge as the possession of some subject in relation to a known object. That knowledge is an idea of the object in the mind of the subject, and for materialism the object is paradigmatically 'material substance' or 'matter'. Given philosophy's classical starting point within the subject's ideas and its general commitment to 'the way of ideas', the sceptical problem arises of how such ideas can constitute knowledge of a material object that is external to and independent of ideas as such. Philosophical idealism holds that there is no such object. For Hegel's idealism, the object of knowledge is not material but ideal, the product of mind or spirit in an activity in which spirit objectifies or alienates itself. Alienation involves loss and illusion, loss of self and the illusion that what is lost is not spirit's own product but something other; and this sets the scene for Hegel's historical saga of recovery or reconciliation, a cognitive saga within consciousness and leading to the goal of Absolute Knowledge.

Marx transforms this philosophical idealism not into its philosophical counterpart, philosophical materialism, but into the elements of a science of society. In the process he develops a specifically social materialism, shifting the conception of the material from matter to (material) practice. The knowledge of nature acquired by the physical sciences is of an object which that knowledge itself asserts to be external to and independent of consciousness. But in accepting that much of the content of philosophical materialism, Marx rejects the individualist subject–object relation as its basis. Following Hegel, he stresses the acquisition of knowledge as an active socio-historical process of production, but gives this a materialist interpretation by arguing that as the content of knowledge is an abstraction from mental activity, so mental activity is an abstraction from (material) practice, and ultimately from the economic production of material goods. The traditional duality of thought and matter is thus mediated by material practice, a constant condition of our knowledge of nature. For social science, however, socio-historical practice is not only the unavoidable condition but also the object of knowledge (see KNOWLEDGE, THEORY OF).

Society, as an object of scientific knowledge, is a structure of practices, with material practice at its base. Though we do not produce nature, and certainly not by pure mental activity, as idealism holds, we do produce goods and artefacts, and in doing so we produce or reproduce, if not deliberately, our social relations and thus society itself. Here indeed, not with natural but with social objects and activities, there is alienation, a relation involving loss, illusion, and subjection: labour produces commodities, for instance, which are appropriated by capital and thus appear as capital's not labour's products, the product controlling the producer rather than the other way round. Society itself is such an alienated product, appearing to its members as a natural object beyond their power to change. But this alienation is not to be understood philosophically, as an eternal aspect of the human condition, but scientifically, as something subject to change, to a change, moreover, in which science can and must play an effectively practical role. The unity of the social structure is contradictory, a contradictory class structure with the contradictory mode of production of capitalism at its base. Under the pressure of these contradictions, society is changing towards a revolutionary situation in which the working class, armed with Marx's science as its theoretical IDEOLOGY, will eliminate these contradictions, bringing the social order under human control and in the process liberating themselves and mankind generally.

Scientific realism and dialectic

In rejecting the subject–object relation of traditional epistemology Marx rejects its specific form in EMPIRICISM. He does so in a single conception that, while finding support in modern philosophy of science, undermines not only empiricism but at the same time also the hermeneutic alternative and with it, further, the foundation of Wittgenstein's philosophical method in his theory of language. Appropriating and transforming an ancient philosophical doctrine, most famously presented in Plato, Marx holds that the empirical appearance of society, as with nature, is superficial and is contradicted by the character of its underlying reality. It is these real but superficial appearances that, being registered in the spontaneous ideas of participants in society, are conceptualized in ordinary language and as such more or less decisively enter and influence the theoretical work of a society. For Marx the real function of scientific theory is to penetrate the empirical surface of reality and discover the 'real relations', the underlying structures and forces, that generate both those 'phenomenal forms' and the fundamental historical tendencies of reality. Theoretical concepts in science are thus neither reducible to observation concepts, as for empiricism, nor are they subjective constructions imposed upon reality by theorists, as for idealism. They describe, more or less accurately, unobservable features of (material) reality. Marx's conception of science is realist (see REALISM), as has been argued by members of the recently developed English group of Marxist philosophers (see, e.g., Bhaskar 1979, Mepham and Ruben 1979).

It follows that for Marx a developed science includes concepts that are neither wholly empirical nor a priori: they go beyond the strictly empirical evidence yet stand or fall not 'philosophically' but scientifically, as part of a conceptual framework more or less adequate to reality. It follows also that a crucial element of scientific method is conceptual critique and innovation. As a social practice with a determinate historical and cultural location, Marx's science subjects the concepts of both ordinary language and existing theories to critical scrutiny, transforming this raw material by intellectual labour into a more adequate theoretical product. But since these current ideas are part of society itself, for social though not natural science the object to be understood and explained, Marx's science, in its critical opposition to those ideas, also seeks to explain them by tracing them back to their material conditions. Marx does not here succumb to the temptation so powerful in the 'sociology of knowledge', of supposing that a materialist explanation of thought is incompatible with its cognitive evaluation and thus embracing an incoherent sceptical relativism. On the contrary, tracing cognitively defective ideas to the material conditions that necessitate them, he reveals society, and in particular its dominant mode of production, as a mystifying object, as an object that generates an appearance that conceals its underlying reality and so confuses and mystifies its participants (Marx, Capital I, ch. 1, sect. 4, 'The Fetishism of Com-

modities'). This objective mystification is part of a process whereby society reproduces itself. It thus has a political function, supporting the ruling class in the class struggle. Marx's scientific criticism of other ideas and theories is therefore itself political. He reveals those ideas and theories as bourgeois ideology, and in criticizing them criticizes also the material conditions that necessitate them: for 'To call on them to give up their illusions about their condition is to call on them to give up a condition that requires illusions' ('Critique of Hegel's Philosophy of Right: Introduction'). In this way Marx's science repudiates that cardinal principle of bourgeois philosophy of science, the value-neutrality of science in relation to its object. That too is revealed as bourgeois ideology. But Marx's materialism is incompatible with the supposition that either these defective ideas or their mystifying material conditions can be changed by theoretical criticism alone. His science is part of that 'practical-critical' activity that he identifies as 'revolutionary' (Theses on Feuerbach, 1st thesis): not detached from, but an integral part of, the socialist movement that is effecting the practical overthrow of capitalism and bourgeois society. Marx's science is a science from the working-class point of view, and as such it enjoys the cognitive advantage both common to any rising class and peculiar to a class that no other class will supersede. Its scientificity is not merely compatible with but positively requires its status as proletarian ideology. Contrary to Althusser, it is science, not philosophy, that constitutes the Marxist side of 'class struggle in theory'.

These relations are theorized by the dialectic in its materialist form. From the point of view of bourgeois philosophy, the crucial and outrageous step that Marx takes is to extend the application of the logical category of CONTRADICTION from thought to material reality. This step becomes intelligible both as part of the foregoing argument and as a generalization of the concepts of alienation and fetishism. Whatever their resemblances, social science differs from the natural sciences studying inorganic reality in this respect, that thought as such is part of the reality that is the object of social science, namely society, and such thought therefore requires not only to be cognitively (scientifically) evaluated and criticized but also to be explanatorily comprehended in relation to its material conditions. The basic structures and forces that shape material life and labour also shape mental life and intellectual labour. Thus in seeking to reflect reality in its explicit content, thought will reflect the reality of material practice in implicit and structural ways that it may not itself recognize. This explanatory link between thought and action offers some scope for the possibility of analysing ideas in a way that will decipher reality's secrets. More importantly, it provides a channel through which the criticism of ideas can unite with the criticism of the (material) practices that necessitate such ideas. It is this unity that is categorized by the dialectical conception of contradiction, of which alienation is a special case. For science, contradiction is a critical category, a category of logic that implies the illogicality or irrationality of what it applies to. But practice as well as thought can be more or less irrational. For a dialectical science, systems of thought that are contradictory, embodying illusion and mystification, reflect the structural irrationalities of a system of (material) practice that is contradictory, in conflict with itself. Basically, it is those practical irrationalities that confuse and mystify the ideas of their participants. Marx's critique, then, involves a type of evaluation that falls under the category not of morality but of rationality.

These real social contradictions, however, are not 'philosophical', an eternal part of the human condition, but historically specific. The same holds for the other relevant philosophical doctrines. As the revolution eliminates society's structural contradictions, that structure will become more rationally organized, more accessible to the control of participants, and more intelligible to their spontaneous thought (*Capital* I, ch. 1, sect. 4, 'The Fetishism of Commodities'). The truth of hermeneutics, but not in its philosophical form, will be realized. So also for the truth of empiricism, as that of scientific realism is superseded. The contradiction between social appearance and reality will disappear, and with it the mystifying character of society. There will no longer be any need for, or even possibility of, theory, i.e. social science (Cohen 1978, p. 326).

This schema puts into place, and brings out the ultimate meaning of, the views of both Marx

and Engels about philosophy and its relation to materialism and idealism. For Marx's materialism not only religion and philosophy but all theory as such, including even social science, is in the last analysis idealist: it requires that most central of all forms of the division of labour, the division between manual and mental work, and with it a mystifying and alienating society. It is a mark of our present epoch that science is absorbing and superseding philosophy, transforming its content into a type of theory with a more materialist content, form, and mode of existence. But full social materialism is something to be historically realized in and as a practice, a social practice whose intelligibility and transparency will render it comprehensible to the spontaneous thought of its agents, without theory; and thus without the idealism, however residual, that is inseparable from a mode of activity requiring some detachment from the life of practice (*Theses on Feuerbach*, esp. the 8th thesis).

Reading

Althusser, L. 1976: *Essays in Self-Criticism.*

Althusser, L. and Balibar, É. 1970: *Reading 'Capital'.*

Bhaskar, R. 1979: The *Possibility of Naturalism.*

Cohen, G. 1978: *Karl Marx's Theory of History.*

Colletti, L. 1969 (1973): *Marxism and Hegel.*

Habermas, J. 1968 (1978): *Knowledge and Human Interests.*

Korsch, K. 1923 (1970): *Marxism and Philosophy.*

Lenin, V. I. 1895–1916 (1961): *Philosophical Notebooks.*

Lukács, G. 1923 (1971): *History and Class Consciousness.*

Mepham, J. and Ruben, D.-H. eds. 1979: *Issues in Marxist Philosophy.*

ROY EDGLEY

Plekhanov, Georgii Valentinovich Born 29 November 1856, Gudalovka, Tambov Province; died 30 May 1918, Terioki, Finland. He began his revolutionary career as an adherent of revolutionary POPULISM. Rejecting the then dominant line of political terrorism he was one of the first Populist agitators to concentrate upon the urban workers. By 1878 he was freely using Marxism in defence of his contention that communal landholding in the RUSSIAN COMMUNE was, and would remain, the dominant mode of production in Russia. In 1882 his translation of the *Communist Manifesto* was published with a foreword by Marx, and in the following year he published his first lengthy essay against Populism and formed the Emancipation of Labour Group in Geneva. The Group, dominated intellectually by Plekhanov, was the leading centre of Russian Marxism in the late nineteenth century. Its authoritative publications served to define the orthodoxy of Russian Marxism and deeply influenced Lenin's thought up to 1914.

Rightly considered the 'Father of Russian Marxism' Plekhanov, in the books, pamphlets and journals he wrote and edited, established not only a comprehensive critique of populism but gave Marxism an intellectual ascendancy in Russia and outlined the long-term strategy which dominated the movement down to 1914. Recognizing the unique and ill-developed character of the hybrid social and economic structure of Russia, Plekhanov insisted that the revolution would necessarily come in two stages. First there would be the democratic revolution against tsarism and the remnants of feudalism. The democratic revolution would accelerate the development of capitalism and therefore of class differentiation and provide those conditions of freedom of association and publication in which the second, or socialist revolution, would flourish. These two revolutions, though quite distinct in their objectives, would not necessarily be widely distant in time. Plekhanov also asserted that, owing to the peculiar weakness of the Russian bourgeoisie, the proletariat and its party would be obliged to lead the democratic revolution. The duties of the proletarian party in Russia were, therefore, exceptionally onerous and complicated, particularly given the relative smallness of its numbers and the backwardness of its consciousness. Plekhanov accordingly assigned to the Social Democratic intelligentsia a decisive role in bringing organization, consciousness, and cohesion to the working class. He maintained consistently that without the determined activism of 'the revolutionary bacilli of the intelligentsia' the movement could not succeed.

On a more general and international level Plekhanov established a reputation second only to Kautsky's as an innovative and authoritative theorist of Marxism. His *Development of the Monist View of History* traced the whole evolution of modern philosophical and social thought emphasizing particularly the contribution of Hegel and Feuerbach to Marx's mature thought, which Plekhanov was the first to characterize as DIALECTICAL MATERIALISM. He asserted that this dialectical and materialist method illuminated and unified all knowledge and he was a pioneer in applying it not only to politics, economics and philosophy, but also to linguistics, aesthetics and literary criticism. Because of his belief that economic determinism, applied in a dialectical way, was a sufficient world view and was necessary to the integrity of the mission of the proletariat, he reacted vehemently to any attempts to 'improve' upon Marxism by importing elements of other philosophies. He was therefore the principal defender of Marxist 'monism' against the eclecticism of Bernstein and his supporters.

From 1905 onwards Plekhanov's standing as a political leader of Russian Social Democracy declined rapidly, partly because of his hesitant attitude to the 1905 revolution, and he devoted himself increasingly to historical and philosophical studies. He became an outspoken 'defencist' (i.e. supporter of the war) in 1914 and returned to Russia in March 1917 after thirty-five years in exile. In the remaining months of his life he took a determined stand against what he felt to be the unprincipled activities of the Bolsheviks and deplored their seizure of power as premature and likely to produce disastrous consequences. In spite of this Lenin continued to hold his writings as a militant materialist in the highest esteem and they became essential reading for generations of activists in the Communist International and the Soviet Union.

Reading

Ascher, A. 1972: *Pavel Axelrod and the Development of Menshevism*.

Baron, S. H. 1962: 'Between Marx and Lenin: George Plekhanov'.

— 1963: *Plekhanov: The Father of Russian Marxism*.

Haimson, L. H. 1955: *The Russian Marxists and the Origins of Bolshevism*.

Plekhanov, G. V. 1885 (1961): *Our Differences*. 'Programme of the Social-Democratic Emancipation of Labour Group' In *Selected Philosophical Works*, vol. 1.

— 1894 (1961): *The Development of the Monist View of History.* In *Selected Philosophical Works*, vol. 1.

— 1898 (1940): *The Role of the Individual in History.*

— 1908 (1969): *Fundamental Problems of Marxism.* In *Selected Philosophical Works*, vol. 3.

NEIL HARDING

political economy A term often used synonymously with economics to indicate the area which studies resource allocation and the determination of aggregate economic activity. Its more specific meaning in a Marxist context relates to the corpus of work of certain writers who dealt with the distribution and accumulation of economic surplus, and the attendant problems of determination of prices, wages, employment, and the efficacy or otherwise of political arrangements to promote accumulation. This is mainly associated with the works of Adam Smith and Ricardo, and of such authors as Malthus, James Mill, J. S. Mill, McCulloch, Senior. Marx himself drew a sharp distinction between scientific political economy (Adam Smith and Ricardo, but mainly the latter; see RICARDO AND MARX), and vulgar political economy which developed after 1830 (see VULGAR ECONOMICS). Marx regarded his major work *Capital* as a critique of political economy, but in more recent times academic economists sympathetic to Marxism have used political economy as a label for radical economics to distinguish it from bourgeois or neo-classical economics. Yet another strand in academic economics, which also calls itself political economy, studies the interaction of democratic political processes and market determined economic relations. This body of work sees the political process, in so far as it is not based on market (commodity) relationships, as a distortion of the market economy.

All these strands, though seemingly disparate, have a common root in the work of Adam Smith, and the key to this work is the concept of an autonomous, self-regulating economy described as CIVIL SOCIETY. It was Adam Smith's genius to have seen the *probability* of the isolation of civil society from the political sphere (the state), its *capacity* for self-regulation if left unhindered, its *potential* for achieving a state of maximum benefit for all participants left free to pursue their own interests, and hence the *philosophical desirability* of bringing about such a state of affairs, in which civil society could become independent of the state.

While Adam Smith defined the ground from which subsequent developments and divergences stemmed, his work should be seen in its appropriate context. Apart from isolated earlier economists (most notably John Locke and Richard Cantillon) the origins of political economy are to be found in the eighteenth-century Enlightenment. The erosion of religious authority had posed the need for a new explanation of social events, and the growth of the natural sciences, especially in the work of Isaac Newton during the seventeenth century, indicated the possibility of arriving at such an explanation using the methods of science. One strand in the efforts to construct a science of social events was Montesquieu's *Esprit des lois*. His work was taxonomic and while producing a 'model' to explain the diversity of human social arrangements did not provide a dynamic explanation. A group of Scottish philosophers, carrying on a teacher-student succession through the century, created a body of work constituting the origins of social science, which they called political economy. Francis Hutcheson, Adam Ferguson, David Hume, Adam Smith, John Millar, Lord Kames were the principal members of this group. They produced collectively and cumulatively the idea of human history going through stages of growth, with the key to each stage, as well as the transition from one stage to another, the mode of obtaining subsistence in any society. Hunting, pastoralism, agriculture and commerce were identified as the four principal modes, and a variety of social circumstances – the nature of political authority, the growth of morals, the position of women, the 'class structure' – were all explained in terms of the mode of subsistence. This was not a monocausal explanation, nor a unilineal, unidirectional, or deterministic model of historical progress. It was a bold speculation, supported by extensive reading on the conditions in different societies as recorded by travellers, and by historical accounts of diverse nations from the Greek and Roman onwards (see STAGES OF DEVELOPMENT).

Adam Smith was not the most 'materialist' of the Scottish philosophers (John Millar was) but he was certainly the most influential and most famous. In the *Wealth of Nations* the four stages theory does not figure prominently, but the logic of that theory leads Smith to associate commerce with liberty. The growth of commerce and the growth of liberty mutually determine each other. Commerce could be seen as a key to prosperity, but only its unhindered pursuit would secure the maximum prosperity. Liberty is thus a key to the growth of commerce. Commerce, by spreading world-wide and making accumulation of wealth possible in liquid (i.e. transportable) form, renders merchants independent of political tyranny and hence increases the chances of the growth of liberty.

Writing at a very early stage of the Industrial Revolution Adam Smith saw the crucial importance of industrial production. Division of labour in industrial production made possible an unprecedented growth in output and productivity. If it was possible to sell this enhanced output over a wide market, then such division would prove profitable, and the profits could be ploughed back into further profitable activity. In locating the growth of wealth in the interaction between division of labour and growth of markets, Smith liberated economics from an agrarian bias such as the Physiocrats had imparted to it, or the narrow commercial bias that the Mercantilists had given it. Surplus did not originate in land alone, nor was the acquisition of treasure (precious metals) any longer the sole or desirable measure of economic prosperity. Thus wealth could take the form of (reproducible) vendible commodities. If the wealth holders then spent it productively in further investment wealth would grow.

The other aspect of Adam Smith's message was the need to let individuals pursue their self-interest unhindered by outside (political) interference. In arguing that individuals, in pursuing their self-interest, indirectly and inadvertently promoted the collective interest, Smith crystallized the concept of civil society as a self-regulating and beneficent arrangement. Individual rationality led to collective good; the seeming anarchy of the individual pursuit of selfish interest led to an ordered universe, an order brought about not by deliberate political action but unconsciously by the action of many individuals. The sphere of private interests thus became autonomous with respect to the sphere of public interest, the private individual was divorced from the citizen. But in contrast with

the previously held fears of a collapse of order, and a civil war among private interests in the absence of the state overseeing the economic domain, Smith provided a picture of harmony, beneficence and prosperity, due precisely to the *absence* of the state from the private sphere.

Thus civil society was shown to be autonomous, beneficent and capable of progress. Since wealth consisted of vendible, reproducible commodities, labour as the primary agent of production (and via division of labour the key to growth in productivity) was the obvious choice as a measure of value of these commodities. But labour was not only a *measure* of value; it was also conceived as a cause or source of value. If however labour was the source of all value, how could one justify the two major categories of non-labour income – rent and profits?

Subsequent work in political economy – defined broadly enough to include much of social science – grew out of these strands in Smith's writings. These are (i) the economic theory of historical progress; (ii) the theory of accumulation and economic growth through the division of labour and spread of exchange; (iii) the redefinition of wealth as comprising commodities, and not solely treasure, which sparked the criticism of mercantilist policies and the advocacy of Free Trade; (iv) the theory of individual behaviour which reconciled pursuit of self-interest with the collective good, providing a programme for *laissez-faire* and the minimal state; and (v) the labour theory of value which argued for labour as a measure and sometimes as a source of value.

Ricardo refined and reworked the more narrowly economic strands of Smith's work under (ii), (iii), and (v) above but ignored the theory of progress. Hegel derived from Smith the theory of progress and the notion of civil society which he used in his theory of the state. Marx came to the economics of Smith via his *Critique of Hegel's Philosophy of the State*. It was here that the notion of civil society and its separation from political society was central. Hegel tried to rationalize the Prussian hereditary monarchy as the ideal state by arguing that the separation of civil society from political society was the cause of a basic social division and as such a hindrance to historical progress. This contradiction between civil society as the sphere of selfish interests and political society as the sphere of public interest could only be reconciled, in Hegel's view, by political arrangements which stood above and outside civil society – 'supra-class' agencies. These were the system of estates, the bureaucracy, and the hereditary monarchy. In criticizing Hegel's theory, Marx counter-posed universal franchise, the proletariat and democracy as the triad which, unlike Hegel's, could supersede the contradictions of civil society by ushering in communism and so further-ing human self-realization. But Marx took the autonomy of civil society as a datum. His subse-quent researches led him away from the theory of the state to an examination of the theory of the functioning of civil society, i.e. to a critique of political economy.

Indeed, the theory of progress became histori-cal materialism in Marx's hands. His theory of value sharpened the contradiction implicit in the dual nature of labour as a measure as well as a source of value. While accepting the theory of accumulation, Marx sought to bring into ques-tion, by the method of an immanent critique, the beneficent aspects of the functioning of capital-ism. He used historical materialism to demons-trate the historicity of capitalism – capitalism as but a stage of history – and used the contradic-tion in value theory to fashion a theory of class struggle which in capitalism takes the form of the antagonism between labour and capital. He sought to demonstrate how individual pursuit of self-interest, far from leading to collective rationality or the public good, leads to recurring crises, and how the attempts of the capitalists to overcome these crises leads to an eventual breakdown of capitalism, and/or its superses-sion by socialism achieved through political struggle.

Thus Marx called his work a critique of politi-cal economy because he showed that its basic categories were historical and not universal. The purely economic became relative to its particu-lar epoch, and transitory. But subsequent de-velopments in economics have deliberately or unconsciously ignored Marx's critique. Neo-classical economics from the 1870s onwards ignored strands (i) and (v) in Adam Smith's work (and especially the latter), but took the theory of individual behaviour and the advo-cacy of free trade from him and fashioned it into a pure economic science. The theory of ACCU-MULATION was ignored by all except Marxists

until Schumpeter and the post-Keynesian wri-ters revived it. English economics under the influence of Marshall and Pigou pointed out the many exceptions to the simple equation of indi-vidual good and public good and fashioned an argument for state intervention to promote eco-nomic welfare. The autonomy of civil society, dressed up as the ability of the economy to achieve full utilization of resources, once again became an area of controversy after Keynes's critique of Say's Law (see UNDERCONSUMPTION). There has recently been a revival of *laissez-faire* ideology. In the hands of the Chicago School it is a double-pronged attack on the Marshall–Pigou argument for intervention in particular economic activities to correct the failure of the 'invisible hand', and on Keynes's arguments against the self-regulating nature of the eco-nomy. This new classical school claims the label of political economy by reverting to Smith's arguments, while ignoring the historical dimen-sions of classical political economy. One ten-dency in this revivalist school sees democracy as a hindrance to the efficient functioning of the free market and seeks to subordinate the politi-cal to the economic, i.e. to fashion the state in the image of civil society. Hence a definition of political economy as the theory of civil society is still broadly valid.

Reading

Desai, M. 1979: *Marxian Economics*, pp. 199–213.

Meek, R. L. 1967: 'The Scottish Contribution to Marxist Sociology'. In *Economics and Ideology*.

O'Malley, J. 1970: Editorial Introduction to Karl Marx, *Critique of Hegel's Philosophy of Right*.

Skinner, A. 1982: 'A Scottish Contribution to Marxist Sociology?' In Bradley and Howard, eds. *Classical and Marxian Political Economy*.

MEGHNAD DESAI

population   In his discussion of method in the Introduction to the *Grundrisse* Marx treats population as an example of a category which should be conceived as the concrete result of many determinations, a full understanding of which depends on the prior elucidation of 'more simple concepts' or abstractions. If population is considered in undifferentiated form, without prior consideration of the classes of which it is composed, which in turn depend upon the social relations of exploitation constituting a particular mode of production, it becomes an unwarranted and sterile abstraction. Hence Marx insists that 'every particular historical mode of production has its own special laws of population', the law of population under industrial capitalism being that of a 'relative surplus population' (*Capital* I, ch. 23). He rejects the naturalistic determinism of 'Parson' Malthus (for Marx's and Engels's judgements on Malthus see Meek 1953), pointing out that there is no necessary relation between the level of wages and the size of families, and insisting that the 'surplus population' which keeps wages down is not the result of the vicious habits of the working class, but of their labour for capital which 'produces both the accumulation of capital and the means by which [the working population] itself is made relatively superfluous' (ibid.). For working-class labour produces surplus value which, as accumulated capital, is used to buy those means of production (also produced by the working class) which, in replacing living by dead labour, replenish the RESERVE ARMY OF LABOUR, and ensure that a section of the population, in normal circumstances, remains surplus to the requirements of capital and therefore unable to find employment.

The central importance of the creation and retention of a surplus population for the capitalist mode of production is demonstrated by the attempts made in the early period of capitalism to prevent workers from emigrating during times of recession. In Britain until 1815 mechanics employed in machine working were not allowed to emigrate and those who attempted to do so were severely punished, while in the 'cotton famine' during the American Civil War, when vast numbers of cotton workers lost their jobs, working-class demands for state aid or voluntary national subscription to finance the emigration of some of the surplus population of Lancashire were refused. Instead, 'they were locked up in that "moral workhouse" of the cotton districts, to form in the future, as they had in the past, the strength of the cotton manufacturers of Lancashire' (*Capital* I, ch. 21).

It is a basic contradiction in the wage form that wages provide an income only for the employed, but the unemployed must be kept alive to form the surplus population available for future exploitation. Modern states have attempted to bridge that contradiction through the provision of unemployment benefits designed to provide a level of living far below that of the employed. But as controversy about state welfare benefit demonstrates (de Brunhoff 1978), they do not remove the contradiction itself, which remains as the expression of the special laws of population in the capitalist mode of production.

Few later Marxists have attempted to develop more fully a theory of population, a notable exception being the work of Coontz (1957) who argues that population growth, as well as the distribution of population, in the capitalist era, is determined by the demand for labour. In presenting this argument he draws to some extent on the work of Soviet demographers, especially Urlanis (1941) who analyses the growth of population in Europe in terms of economic development, and then emphasizes particularly the correlation between the decline in fertility during the last quarter of the nineteenth century and the transition from competitive capitalism to monopoly capitalism or imperialism. But Coontz has some criticisms of this account as not going beyond correlation 'to an analysis of the causal nexus or the *modus operandi* by which demand for labour governs its supply' (1957, p. 133), and he goes on to examine in greater detail both the demand for labour and the changing economic functions of the family.

Humphries (1987) attempts to rectify Engels's failure to deliver on his promise to accord 'the production of human beings themselves, the propagation of the species' a significant role in his materialist account of the family (see REPRODUCTION). She argues that the heterosexual family developed in pre-industrial times as a form of population control, mediating the contradiction between socialization into heterosexuality and economic scarcity. Within this framework, marriage and legitimate births reflect the economic space that was available for procreation, whereas illegitimacy indicates a failure of social control of fertility. The obsession of eighteenth- and nineteenth-century social commentators with the sexual behaviour of the working class and the rigid occupational segregation that developed should, Humphries argues, also be seen in this light as a concern with population control.

Marxists have also paid relatively little

attention to population questions in pre-capitalist forms of society. But Meillassoux (1975) argues that the domestic community, in existence since the neolithic period, remains the only economic and social system which manages the physical reproduction of human beings as an integrated form of social organization, through the control of women as 'living means of reproduction'. Capitalist production remains tied to this vestigial form through the patriarchal family, but that connection is being severed by the emancipation of women and minors, depriving the domestic unit of their labour power to deliver it direct to capital for exploitation. The patriarchal family, once indispensable for the reproduction of the 'free labourer', is becoming superseded and in this way the free labourer is being reduced to a condition of total alienation. Meillassoux can envisage labour power becoming a 'true commodity' produced under capitalist relations of production. This for him, provides a vision of totalitarianism far more barbaric than that invoked by the prospect of intervention in the family by even the most bureaucratic of socialist states.

From another aspect historians have been concerned with the influence of demographic changes. Marx himself, in the *Grundrisse* (section on 'Forms which precede capitalist production', pp. 471–514), referred to the significance of population growth and migrations (as well as warfare) in the development of early societies (e.g. Rome). More recently, Marxist and non-Marxist historians have engaged in a major debate about the importance of demographic changes in the 'crisis of feudalism' and the transition to capitalism in Western Europe (see Brenner 1976 and the ensuing symposium in *Past and Present*, nos. 78–80, 85, 97; also TRANSITION FROM FEUDALISM TO CAPITALISM), and one Marxist participant (Hilton 1978) recognizes that demographic and other aspects were important, though arguing that they should be seen in the context of a crisis of 'a whole socio-economic system', but concludes that research has not yet provided clear answers 'given the insufficiency of quantitative evidence about population, production and commerce'.

Like Meillassoux, Engels assumed that increasing control over nature and the development of the forces of production would require greater inputs of labour and thus greater control

over the production of people. But in a reply to Kautsky (1 February 1881) who had raised the problem of excessive population growth, often brought forward by critics of socialism, he observed: 'Of course the abstract possibility exists that the number of human beings will become so great that limits will have to be set to its increase. But if at some point communist society should find itself obliged to regulate the production of human beings, as it has already regulated the production of things, it will be precisely and only this society which carries it out without difficulty.' Lenin (1913) took a very hostile attitude to what he called 'reactionary and impoverished neo-Malthusianism', and Marxist-Leninist demographers in general have been strongly anti-Malthusian. But actual population policies in the USSR and Eastern Europe seem to have been influenced mainly by practical considerations, including the demand for labour and concern about declining fertility (see Besemeres 1980). In China, on the other hand, rapid population growth has led to very active measures to reduce fertility, again mainly for economic reasons. (See also REPRODUCTION.)

Reading

Besemeres, John F. 1980: *Socialist Population Policies: The Political Implications of Demographic Trends in the USSR and Eastern Europe.*

Brenner, Robert 1976: 'Agrarian Class Structure and Economic Development in Preindustrial Europe'.

Coontz, Sydney H. 1957: *Population Theories and the Economic Interpretation.*

de Brunoff, S. 1976 (1978): *The State, Capital and Economic Policy.*

Edholm, F., Harris, O. and Young, K. 1977: 'Conceptualising Women'.

Hilton, R. H. 1978: 'A Crisis of Feudalism'.

Humphries, Jane 1987: 'The Origin of the Family: Born out of Scarcity not Wealth'. In Sayers, Evans and Redclift eds. *Engels Revisited.*

Lenin, V. I. 1913b (1963): 'The Working Class and Neo-Malthusianism'.

Meek, Ronald L. ed. 1953: *Marx and Engels on Malthus.*

Meillassoux, C. 1975 (1981): *Maidens, Meal and Money: Capitalism and the domestic community.*

Past and Present 1978, 1979, 1982: Symposium on 'Agrarian Class Structure and Economic Development in Western Europe'.

Urlanis, B. T. 1941: *The Growth of Population in Europe*. (In Russian.)

TOM BOTTOMORE and
SUSAN HIMMELWEIT

populism   A protean concept which has been used to label rather diverse social and political movements, state policies and ideologies. Attempts to distil a general concept of populism are, by and large, unrewarding. But we can usefully distinguish four principal contexts in which the term has been used.

Populism refers, first, to radical North American movements in the rural south and west that arose during the last two decades of the nineteenth century, articulating principally demands of the independent farmers predominant in the American countryside (who were not peasants), giving voice to their suspicion of concentrations of economic power, especially of banks and financial institutions, big land speculators and railroad companies. They were concerned also with issues of fiscal policy and, especially, monetary reform and a demand for the free coinage of silver as an antidote for depression of agricultural prices.

Then there is Russian populism (*narodnichestvo*) which is the most significant example of populism in the present context, for it was closely involved in a debate with Marx, Marxism and Marxist movements. Venturi, in an authoritative work (1960), includes a wider range of movements under that rubric than later authorities (Pipes 1964, and Walicki 1969) seem willing to do. Russian populist movements drew their inspiration from the thought of Herzen and Chernyshevskii and their strategies from the ideas of Lavrov, Bakunin and Tkachev. They had their first full-fledged manifestation in the 'Going to the People' movement and the second *Zemlya i Volya* (Land and Liberty) movement of the 1870s, and according to Venturi reached their peak in the (elitist) terrorism of the *Narodnaya Volya* (Peoples' Will) movement of the 1880s. But Plekhanov and following him recent authorities such as Walicki regard *Narodnaya Volya* as a negation of what is essential to populism. It is as a broad current of thought that Russian populism continues to be of interest – one that was differentiated within itself and influenced both revolutionary and non-revolutionary individuals and movements. Its central conceptions were a theory of non-capitalist development, and the idea that Russia could and should by-pass the capitalist stage and build a socialist, egalitarian and democratic society on the strength of the peasant commune and petty commodity production; it was hostile to large-scale organization of production.

Russian populist thought was formed under a strong influence of Marx's analysis of capitalist development. *Capital* I was translated into Russian by a populist, Nicolai Danielson, and the works of Marx and Marxists were closely studied by populist intellectuals. But unlike Marx himself, populists read into his work only a devastating critique of capitalist development and its alienating effects, looking upon it as a retrogressive rather than a progressive social process. Russia could avoid going through that because of the existence of the peasant commune (see RUSSIAN COMMUNE) as a potential basis for building socialism. Marx himself did not reject this idea out of hand, as evidenced by his letter to Vera Zasulich on the subject (8 March 1881) and his Preface to the Russian edition of the *Communist Manifesto* where he acknowledged the possibility that the commune might serve as a starting point for a communist development provided it was 'the signal for a proletarian revolution in the West'.

Lenin located the ideology of populism, historically and sociologically, as a protest against capitalism from the point of view of small producers, especially the peasantry whose position was being undermined by capitalist development but who, nevertheless, wanted a dissolution of the feudal social order. While characterizing populist ideology as economic romanticism, a backward-looking petty bourgeois utopia, Lenin opposed one-sided condemnation of populism, as is shown in his polemic against the Legal Marxist Struve on the subject. He also distinguished between the more radical, antifeudal and democratic ideology of the earlier populist movements and writers, and the rightwing tendencies of later populist intellectuals such as Mikhailovsky who represented primarily a reaction against capitalist development. But even about contemporary populism he wrote: 'It is clear that it would be absolutely wrong to reject the whole of the Narodnik programme indiscriminately in its entirety. One must clearly distinguish its reactionary and progressive sides' ('The Economic Content of Narodism').

The third context in which the term populism has been deployed is that of state ideologies in countries of Latin America, where it is a political strategy employed by weak indigenous bourgeoisies to forge an alliance with subordinate classes against agrarian oligarchies, on terms that do not give an independent weight to the subordinate classes that are brought into play, in order to promote industrialization. This is an antithesis of populism as an ideology of rural based movements in conflict with dominant powers in the state. The paradigmatic cases of populism in Latin America, in this sense, are those of Brazil under Vargas and his heirs and Peronism in the Argentine. But, it must be added, the term has been used sufficiently loosely to make it applicable to a variety of configurations of state power and its bases amongst the people in practically every country of Latin America and elsewhere. An essential feature of populism in this sense is its rhetoric aimed at mobilization of support from underprivileged groups and its manipulative character for controlling 'marginal' groups. There is a strong emphasis on the role of the state. But, again, it essentially revolves around a style of politics based on the personal appeal of a leader and personal loyalty to him underpinned by an elaborate system of patronage. The populist ideology is moralistic, emotional, and anti-intellectual, and non-specific in its programme. It portrays society as divided between powerless masses and coteries of the powerful who stand against them. But the notion of class conflict is not a part of that populist rhetoric. Rather it glorifies the role of the leader as the protector of the masses. Such a political strategy might be better described as personalism rather than populism, and in this form it has some affinities and connections with fascism.

Finally we might consider a case where populism refers to a state ideology, but one which espouses a vision of society and national development which resembles that of the Russian populists. The most outstanding and consistent example (so far) of this approach to national development is that of Tanzania, which aims at a rural-based small-scale strategy of development, eschewing large-scale industry and engag-

ing in the rhetoric at least of a non-capitalist path of development, even though, being enmeshed in the network of world capitalism, it finds it difficult to evade altogether the imperatives of capital and the penalties for disregarding them.

Reading
Ionescu, G. and Gellner, E. eds. 1969: *Populism.*
Kitching, G. 1982: *Development and Underdevelopment in Historical Perspective.*
Lenin, V. I. 1893b (*1960*): 'What the "Friends of the People" are'.
— 1894 (*1960*): 'The Economic Content of Narodism'.
di Tella, Torcuato 1965: 'Populism and Reform in Latin America'. In Claudio Veliz ed. *Obstacles to Change in Latin America.*
Venturi, F. 1960: *Roots of Revolution.*
Walicki, A. 1969: *The Controversy over Capitalism.*
Weffort, F. C. 1970: 'State and Mass in Brazil'. In I. L. Horowitz ed. *Masses in Latin America.*
HAMZA ALAVI

positivism Auguste Comte (1798–1857) is generally recognized as the founder of positivism, or 'the positive philosophy'. Comte's primary intellectual-cum-political project was the extension of natural scientific methods to the study of society: the establishment of a scientific 'sociology'. His conception of scientific method was evolutionary and empiricist: each branch of knowledge passes through three necessary historical stages: theological, metaphysical, and, finally, 'positive', or 'scientific'. In this final stage reference to ultimate, or unobservable causes of phenomena is abandoned in favour of a search for law-like regularities among observable phenomena. In common with modern empiricist philosophers of science, Comte was committed to a 'covering-law' model of explanation according to which explanation is symmetrical with prediction. Predictability of phenomena is, in turn, a condition of establishing control over them, and this is what makes possible the employment of science in technology and engineering.

For psychological and systematic reasons, according to Comte, the passage of the human sciences into the 'positive' or scientific stage has been delayed, but is now on the historical agenda. The essentially critical and therefore 'negative' philosophy of the Enlightenment knew well how to bring down the old order of society, but the consolidation of a new order will require the extension of the positive philosophy to the study of humanity itself. Once the domain of the human sciences is brought under the disciplines of empirical science, intellectual anarchy will cease, and a new institutional order will acquire stability from the very fact of consensus. Knowledge of the laws of society will enable citizens to see the limits of possible reform, while governments will be able to use social scientific knowledge as a basis for piecemeal and effective reform which will further underwrite the consensus. The new order of society – scientific-industrial society – would have science as its secular religion, functionally analogous to the Catholicism of the old order of society.

Positivism became a more-or-less organized international political and intellectual movement, but its central themes have achieved a diffusion in present-day society immensely wider than the reach of any particular movement. The more vigorous and systematic 'logical positivism' or 'logical empiricism' of the Vienna Circle became the most influential tendency in the philosophy of science in the twentieth century, while the project of extending the methods of the natural sciences (as interpreted by empiricist philosophy) to the social sciences has until recent decades been the dominant tendency of thought in these disciplines. Evolutionary, or 'stages' theories of the development of society, in which differences in the forms of property and social relations are subordinated to the supposedly determining effects of technology have a clear positivist ancestry, and have likewise been enormously influential.

Within Marxism itself, the philosophical conception of historical materialism as a science, and the advocacy of a union between this science and revolutionary political practice, have made possible positivist and neo-positivist Marxisms. Otto Neurath, one of the leading members of the Vienna Circle in the 1920s and 1930s, advocated the development of empirical sociology on a 'materialist foundation'. This empirical sociology would develop the theory of Marx and Engels as a basis for the planned reorganization of social life. Socialist planning

could be seen as analogous to experimentation in the physical sciences, and the greater the scale of the reorganization of society, the greater the stimulus it would give to sociological theory. The anti-metaphysical and anti-theological tendency of empirical science and its associated world-view had always offended the ruling classes of the day. The extension of empirical science to society is likewise resisted by today's ruling class, which depends on religion and metaphysics to create illusions in the minds of the masses. Neurath's conception of science, like that of the other members of the Vienna Circle, linked it closely with empirical predictions, and therefore with technology. The connection between Marxism and practice can, in this way, be understood as a form of large-scale project of 'social engineering'. The REVISIONISM of the Second International rests upon such a conception of Marxism as an empirical science linked to a practice of social engineering, but a similar conception also played a part in the constitution of what has become known as STALINISM. In its Stalinist forms, the scientific status of historical materialism is underwritten by a 'scientific world-outlook' which effectively dogmatizes its basic propositions, and legitimates an autocratic technocracy in terms of 'iron laws' of history.

Theorists of the FRANKFURT SCHOOL of 'critical theory' have been among the foremost critics of the 'social engineering' conception of the relation between theory and practice. A genuinely emancipatory social theory will be reflexive and interpretative, alive to the potentialities which lie beyond the current situation, rather than tied obediently to the depiction of its empirical reality. For thinkers such as Habermas and Wellmer, the most potent forms of human domination in present-day societies rely upon the technocratic ideology which is the legacy of positivism, and they discover a 'latent positivism' in Marx's own thought (Wellmer 1971). Accordingly, theorizing in the Marxist tradition can be emancipatory only to the extent that it eradicates its conception of itself as scientific, and abandons the technocratic ideology to which that conception belongs. Against the critical theorists, it can be argued that they are insufficiently thorough in their critique of positivism. First, their rejection of a naturalistic programme for the social sciences relies on a failure to criticize adequately positivist and empiricist philosophies of the natural sciences. Secondly, they follow the positivists in supposing there to be an essential connection between science and 'technical rationality'. It is arguable here that a distinctive contribution of Marxism has been its attempt to develop a conception of science as both objective and emancipatory, and indeed both Wellmer and Habermas concede that critical self-reflection needs to be complemented by generalizing, causal analyses of the sort traditionally provided by science. (See also KNOWLEDGE, THEORY OF; SCIENCE.)

Reading

Andreski, S. ed. 1974: *The Essential Comte.*

Ayer, A. J. 1936 (1946): *Language, Truth and Logic.*

Benton, T. 1977: *Philosophical Foundations of the Three Sociologies.*

Giddens, A. ed. 1974: *Positivism and Sociology.*

Habermas, J. 1986b (1971): *Knowledge and Human Interests.*

Marcuse, H. 1964: *One-Dimensional Man.*

Neurath, O. 1973: *Empiricism and Sociology.*

Wellmer, A. 1974: *Critical Theory of Society.*
                                        TED BENTON

Poulantzas, Nicos Born 21 September 1936; died 3 October 1979, Paris. A Greek Communist and Marxist theorist who spent his most productive years in Paris, Poulantzas both belonged to the Greek Communist Party of the Interior and was influential in theoretical debates on the French left. Outside France he is best known for his analysis of the relative autonomy of the capitalist state. He held various academic posts in Paris – his last being that of Professor of Sociology at the University of Vincennes. Poulantzas committed suicide on 3 October 1979.

Following a law degree in Greece, Poulantzas moved to France in 1960. He continued working on law for his doctorate (of 1965) but also began a turn towards state theory inspired by neo-Gramscian political theory and Althusserian Marxism. In his pioneering book *Political Power and Social Classes* (1968), Poulantzas grounded the relative autonomy of the capitalist type of state in its institutional separation from capitalist production. Since capitalist exploitation did not require extra-economic coercion,

the capitalist state could be organized as a national-popular state. The struggle among political forces to win hegemony in this context was the means through which a capitalist power bloc could be organized and the dominated classes disorganized. In maintaining the social cohesion of a class-divided society, the capitalist state helped to promote continued accumulation.

This important book first appeared in English after Poulantzas had become known through a controversy in *New Left Review*. He had criticized Ralph Miliband for explaining the state's capitalist nature in terms of its control by procapitalist forces; his own view was that the state's objective place in capitalist society ensured its capitalist character whoever controlled it (1969). Miliband replied that Poulantzas allowed no space for the class struggle or state autonomy and attributed too much influence to structural constraints (1970). Neither critique was fully justified but the Miliband–Poulantzas debate has marred anglophone appreciation of Poulantzas's work ever since.

Poulantzas himself turned to consider the nature of German and Italian fascism (1970), changing domestic and international class relations in contemporary capitalism (1974), the collapse of the military dictatorships in Greece, Portugal and Spain (1975) and the drift towards authoritarianism in the current stage of capitalism (1978). In each case his interest was awakened as much by current problems of political strategy as by abstract theoretical considerations. Thus his first book was intended as a critique of the orthodox communist theory of state monopoly capitalism, economic reductionism and humanism; his work on fascism criticized the view that Greece and France were becoming fascist; his work on classes discussed US imperialism, the new middle classes and class alliance; his work on the military dictatorships was a reflection on problems of democratization; and his last book dealt with authoritarian statism, new social movements and problems of a democratic transition to democratic socialism. Before his untimely death, Poulantzas had completed the political transition from support for Marxism-Leninism to a democratic socialism which denied a vanguard role for communist parties and stressed the contribution of new social movements.

Reading

Jessop, B. 1985: *Nicos Poulantzas: Marxist Theory and Political Strategy*.

Miliband, R. 1970: 'The Capitalist State – Reply to Poulantzas'.

Poulantzas, N. 1968 (1973): *Political Power and Social Classes*.

— 1969: 'The Problem of the Capitalist State'.

— 1970 (1974): *Fascism and Dictatorship*.

— 1974 (1975): *Classes in Contemporary Capitalism*.

— 1975 (1976): *Crisis of the Dictatorships*.

— 1978: *State, Power, Socialism*.

BOB JESSOP

praxis Refers in general to action, activity; and in Marx's sense to the free, universal, creative and self-creative activity through which man creates (makes, produces) and changes (shapes) his historical, human world and himself; an activity specific to man, through which he is basically differentiated from all other beings. In this sense man can be regarded as a being of praxis, 'praxis' as the central concept of Marxism, and Marxism as the 'philosophy' (or better: 'thinking') of 'praxis'. The word is of Greek origin, and according to Lobkowicz 'refers to almost any kind of activity which a free man is likely to perform; in particular, all kinds of business and political activity' (1967, p. 9). From Greek the term passed into Latin and thence into the modern European languages. Before it entered philosophy the term was used in Greek mythology both as the name of a rather obscure goddess, and also in a number of other meanings. Another modern writer, Fay Weldon, who used Praxis as the name for the heroine of a novel (1978), gives the following explanation: 'Praxis, meaning turning point, culmination, action; orgasm; some said the goddess herself.' The term was used in early Greek philosophy, especially in Plato, but its true philosophical history begins with Aristotle, who attempts to give it a more precise meaning. Thus although he sometimes uses the plural form (*praxeis*) in describing the life activities of animals and even the movements of the stars, he insists that in a strict sense the term should be applied only to human beings. And although he sometimes uses the term as a name for every human activity, he suggests that praxis should be regarded as only one of the three basic activities of man (the two

others being *theoria* and *poiesis*). The suggestion is made in the context of a division of the sciences or knowledge, according to which there are three basic kinds of knowledge – theoretical, practical and poietical – which are distinguished by their end or goal: for theoretical knowledge this is truth, for poietical knowledge the production of something, and for practical knowledge action itself. Practical knowledge in turn is subdivided into economic, ethical and political. Both by its opposition to theory and poiesis, and by its division into economics, ethics and politics, the concept of praxis in Aristotle seems rather stably located, but he does not adhere firmly to such a concept. On several occasions he discusses the relation between theoria and praxis as a kind of basic opposition in man, whereby he seems to include poiesis in praxis or to brush it aside as something marginal. On the other hand he sometimes seems to restrict praxis to the sphere of ethics and politics (leaving aside economics), or simply to politics (in which case ethics is included in politics). Moreover, on some occasions he seems to identify praxis with eupraxia (good praxis) as opposed to dyspraxia (bad praxis, misfortune). However it would be misplaced to regard all those complications as a sign of confusion; they express rather a profound understanding of the complexity of the problems.

In Aristotle's own school the question of whether to divide all human activity into two or three fields was decided in favour of a division into the theoretical and the practical, and this dichotomy was also accepted in medieval scholastic philosophy. Difficulties with classifying applied sciences and arts such as medicine or navigation (which seemed to fit into neither the theoretical nor the practical sciences) led Hugh of St Victor to propose *mecanica* as a third element (in addition to *theorica* and *practica*), but the suggestion found no echo. On the other hand, in a small treatise entitled *Practica geometriae*, he introduced the distinction between a 'theoretical' and a 'practical' geometry, thus suggesting the use of 'practical' in the sense of 'applied'; this suggestion was immediately widely accepted, and the use of 'praxis' for the 'application of a theory' has survived until our own day. Francis Bacon gave a prominent place to the concept of praxis in this sense, and at the same time insisted that true knowledge is that which brings fruits in praxis. Regardless of whether they agreed with Bacon's view, many philosophers in the period between Bacon and Kant had a similar conception of practical knowledge, as applied knowledge useful for life. Thus D'Alembert in his Preliminary Discourse for the *Encyclopédie* divided all cognitions into three groups: 'purely practical', 'purely theoretical', and those which attempted 'to achieve possible usefulness for praxis from the theoretical study of their object'. However, the Aristotelian view that practical knowledge is an independent knowledge of the principles of human activity (especially political and ethical) can be found in many other authors. Thus Locke, who made a trichotomous division of all knowledge and science into *fysikè*, *praktikè*, and *semeiotikè* defined *praktikè* as 'the skill of rightly applying our own powers and actions, for the attainment of things good and useful. The most considerable under this head is ethics' (1690, vol. II, p. 461).

In Kant we find modifications of the two traditional concepts: (1) praxis as the application of a theory, 'the application to the cases encountered in experience', and (2) praxis as the ethically relevant behaviour of man. The first sense is especially prominent in his essay 'On the saying: "This may be right in theory, but does not hold good for praxis".' The second concept, much more important for Kant, is the basis of his distinction between pure and practical reason, and the corresponding division of philosophy into the theoretical and the practical. Thus, in the *Critique of Pure Reason*, Kant distinguishes between 'theoretical cognition' as one through which I come to know *what there is* and 'practical cognition' through which I imagine *what there should be*'. This concept of the practical receives a further refinement when Kant insists that a knowledge can be regarded as practical as opposed either to theoretical or to speculative knowledge: 'Practical cognitions are namely either (1) *Imperatives* and so far opposed to *theoretical* cognitions; or they contain (2) *reasons for possible imperatives* and are so far opposed to *speculative cognitions*' (1800, p. 96). On the other hand Kant insists that despite the distinction between the theoretical (or speculative) and the practical, reason is 'in the last analysis only one and the same'. The unity of reason is secured through the primacy of practical reason (or rather practical use of reason) over the theoretical (or speculative). 'Everything comes to the *practical*' and '*morality*' is the '*absolutely practical*'. The Kantian division of philosophy into theoretical and practical reappears with modifications and supplements in Fichte, who insisted even more strongly than Kant upon the primacy of practical philosophy; and in Schelling, who tried to find a higher third member, which would be 'neither theoretical nor practical, but both at the same time'.

Hegel, like Schelling, accepted the distinction between the theoretical and the practical, placed the practical above the theoretical and also thought that their unity must be found in a third, higher moment. However, he saw as one of the basic defects of Kantian philosophy that the 'moments of the absolute form' were externalized as separate parts of the system. Hence he refused to divide philosophy into theoretical and practical, and in his system, which on a different principle is divided into logic, philosophy of nature, and philosophy of spirit, the distinction between the theoretical and the practical reappears (and is repeatedly transcended in a higher synthesis) in each of the three parts. Thus the distinction between the theoretical and the practical has a place equally in the sphere of pure thought (in logic), of nature (more specifically in organic life), and of human reality (in the 'finite spirit'). The distinction as elaborated in logic finds its imperfect realization in nature and an adequate one in man. As applied to man, theory and praxis are two moments of the finite spirit in so far as he is a subjective spirit, man as individual. Individual praxis is higher than theory, but neither of them is 'true'. The truth of theory and praxis is freedom, which cannot be achieved at the individual level, but only at the level of social life and social institutions, in the sphere of 'objective spirit'. And it can be adequately known and thus completed only in the sphere of the 'absolute spirit', through art, religion and philosophy.

In Hegel's system praxis became one of the moments of absolute truth, but at the same time lost its independence. The first Hegelian to propose that this 'moment' of absolute truth should be taken out of the system and turned against it was Cieskowski (1838) who defended the Hegelian system as the system of absolute truth, but argued that this truth had to be realized through 'praxis' or 'action'. It is not clear whether Marx ever read the book, but his friend Moses Hess was strongly influenced by it. Thus in *The European Triarchy* (1842) and in 'Philosophy of Action' (1842) Hess also advocates a philosophy of praxis and insists: 'The task of the philosophy of spirit now consists in becoming a philosophy of action.' In Marx the concept of praxis became the central concept of a new philosophy which does not want to remain philosophy, but to transcend itself both in a new meta-philosophical thinking and in the revolutionary transformation of the world. Marx elaborated his concept most fully in the *Economic and Philosophical Manuscripts* and expressed it most pregnantly in the *Theses on Feuerbach*, but it was already anticipated in his earlier writings. Thus in his doctoral dissertation (*The Difference Between the Democritean and Epicurean Philosophy of Nature*, pt. I, ch. IV) he insisted on the necessity for philosophy to become practical. 'It is a psychological law that the theoretical mind, having become free in itself, turns into practical energy, and emerging as *will* from the shadow world of Amenthes turns against the worldly reality which exists without it'; and in 'Critique of Hegel's Philosophy of Right: Introduction' (*Deutsch-Französische Jahrbücher* 1844) he proclaims praxis as the goal of true philosophy (i.e. of the criticism of speculative philosophy) and revolution as the true praxis (praxis à la hauteur des principes).

In the *Economic and Philosophical Manuscripts* Marx elaborated his view of man as a free creative being of praxis, in both a 'positive' and a 'negative' form, the latter through a critique of human self-alienation. As for the former he writes that 'free, conscious activity is the species-character of the human being', and that 'the practical construction of an *objective world*, the *work upon* inorganic nature, is the confirmation of man as a conscious species-being' (1st MS, 'Alienated Labour'). What is meant by human practical production in this context is explained by contrasting the production of man with the production of animals: 'They [animals] produce only in a single direction, while man produces universally. They produce only under the compulsion of direct physical need, while man produces when he is free

from physical need and only truly produces in freedom from such need. Animals produce only themselves, while man reproduces the whole of nature. The products of animal production belong directly to their physical bodies, while man is free in face of his product. Animals construct only in accordance with the standards and needs of the species to which they belong, while man knows how to produce in accordance with the standard of every species and knows how to apply the appropriate standard to the object. Thus man constructs also in accordance with the laws of beauty' (ibid.). In the *Economic and Philosophical Manuscripts* Marx sometimes seems to suggest that theory should be regarded as one of the forms of praxis. But then he reaffirms the opposition between theory and praxis and insists on the primacy of praxis in this relationship: 'The resolution of *theoretical* contradictions is possible *only* in a *practical* way, only through the practical energy of man' (ibid. 3rd MS, 'Private property and Communism'). In the *Theses on Feuerbach* the concept of praxis, or rather 'revolutionary praxis', is central: 'The coincidence of the changing of circumstances and of human activity or self-changing can be conceived and rationally understood only as revolutionary praxis' (3rd thesis); and again: 'All social life is essentially *practical*. All the mysteries which lead theory towards mysticism find their rational solution in human praxis and in the comprehension of this praxis' (8th thesis). In the *Economic and Philosophical Manuscripts* Marx as a rule opposes 'labour' to 'praxis' and explicitly describes 'labour' as 'the act of alienation of practical human activity', but he is sometimes inconsistent, using 'labour' synonymously with 'praxis'. In the *German Ideology* he insists strongly on the opposition between 'labour' and what he previously called praxis, and upholds the view that all labour is a self-alienated form of human productive activity, and should be 'abolished'. The non-alienated form of human activity, previously called praxis, is now called 'self-activity', but despite this change in terminology Marx's fundamental ideal remains the same: 'the transformation of labour into self-activity'. It remained the same in the *Grundrisse* and in *Capital* too.

For various reasons Marx's concept of praxis was for a long time forgotten or misinterpreted. The misinterpretation began with Engels, who in his speech at Marx's graveside claimed that Marx had made two chief discoveries: the theory of historical materialism and the theory of surplus value. This initiated the widespread view that Marx was not a philosopher but a scientific theorist of history and a political economist. Only one thesis on praxis became widespread and popular (again owing to Engels), namely that praxis is a guarantee of reliable knowledge and the ultimate criterion of truth. Engels expressed this thesis as follows: 'But before there was argumentation, there was action. *Im Anfang war die Tat* [In the beginning was the deed]. . . . The proof of the pudding is in the eating' (Introduction to English edn *Socialism: Utopian and Scientific*), and similarly: 'The most telling refutation of this [scepticism and agnosticism] as of all other philosophical crotchets, is praxis, namely experiment and industry' (*Ludwig Feuerbach*, sect. II). The text is extremely important because it gave an interpretation of praxis which became widespread: praxis as experiment and industry.

The view of praxis as the decisive argument against agnosticism, and as the ultimate criterion of truth, was defended and elaborated by Plekhanov and Lenin. As Lenin wrote: 'The viewpoint of life, of praxis, should be the first and the basic viewpoint of the theory of knowledge' (1909), but he tried to interpret it in a more flexible way by arguing that 'the criterion of praxis can never in fact *fully* prove or disprove any human view' (ibid.). Plekhanov and Lenin also followed Engels in holding that Marx's historical and economic theories needed as a foundation a new version of the old philosophical materialism. Hence they elaborated the doctrine of DIALECTICAL MATERIALISM, finally canonized by Stalin (1938). In this famous short text Stalin quoted the no less famous pronouncement of Engels on praxis and pudding, and insisted on the role of praxis as a criterion and basis of epistemology, while at the same time he tried to show the importance of theory for praxis, and more specifically the relevance of the basic tenets of dialectical and historical materialism for the 'practical activity of the party of the proletariat'. Mao Tse-tung also referred to praxis on several occasions, and in his essay 'On praxis' (1937), with the aid of quotations from Lenin (and one from Stalin) tried likewise to elaborate a view of the 'unity of knowing and doing' and of praxis as the criterion of truth (*Selected Works of Mao Tse-tung*, vol. I, pp. 295–309).

Labriola seems to have been the first who, inspired by Marx's *Theses on Feuerbach*, tried to interpret Marxism as a 'philosophy of praxis', and used that name for Marxism. Following Labriola's example (and challenged by Gentile's and especially Croce's criticism of Marx) Gramsci also called Marxism the 'philosophy of praxis' and tried to elaborate it in the spirit of Marx , sometimes even against Marx himself (as, for example, when he praised the October Revolution as a revolution against Marx's *Capital*; i.e. against the deterministic elements in Marx). But his elaboration of the philosophy of praxis, written under most difficult conditions, is uneven and sometimes inconsistent (returning to Engels's view of praxis as experiment and industry). At an earlier time the philosophy of praxis received a stronger impetus from the work of Lukács, who heavily attacked Engels's concept of praxis: 'Engels's deepest misunderstanding consists in his belief that the behaviour of industry and scientific experiment constitutes praxis in the dialectical, philosophical sense. In fact, scientific experiment is contemplation at its purest' (1923, p. 132). According to Lukács himself the concept of praxis was the 'central concern' of his book, but his dispersed comments on it are less clear than his critical remarks on Engels's interpretation. At all events, Lukács's account of praxis was a great stimulus for further discussion, though in a later self-criticism he said that his own conception of revolutionary praxis was 'more in keeping with the current messianic utopianism of the Communist left than with the authentic Marxist doctrine' (ibid. Preface to new edn 1971).

In his writings of the 1920s Korsch also argued that Marxism was a 'theory of social revolution' and a 'revolutionary philosophy', based on the principle of the unity of theory and praxis, more precisely on the unity of 'theoretical criticism' and 'practical revolutionary change', the two conceived as 'inseparably connected actions' (1923). But unlike Lukács he was largely satisfied with the current interpretation of 'praxis' and quoted with approval Engels's consideration of praxis as pudding-eating. The concept of praxis was also elaborated independently by Marcuse in the late 1920s (greatly influenced by Heidegger's *Sein und Zeit*) and in the early 1930s (stimulated by the publication of Marx's *Economic and Philosophical Manuscripts*). Thus Marcuse argued (1928) that Marxism was not a self-sufficient scientific theory but a 'theory of social activity, of historical action', more specifically 'the theory of proletarian revolution and the revolutionary critique of bourgeois society'. Identifying the concepts 'radical action' and 'revolutionary praxis' he discussed the relation between praxis, revolutionary praxis and historical necessity. A more elaborate discussion of the concept of 'praxis' itself, and its relation to 'labour', is to be found in a later paper (1933) which still remains one of the most important Marxist analyses of praxis. Here Marcuse identifies 'praxis' with 'doing' (*Tun*), and treats 'labour' as a specific form of praxis. It is not the only praxis (play is a praxis too), but as the activity through which man secures his bare existence, it is a privileged form which the 'very praxis of human existence' of necessity 'demands'. In elaborating the view that 'not every human activity is work' Marcuse recalls Marx's distinction between the 'realm of necessity' (material production and reproduction) and the 'realm of freedom'. Beyond the 'realm of necessity', Marcuse maintains, human existence remains praxis, but praxis in the realm of freedom is basically different from that in the sphere of necessity; it is the realization of the form and fullness of existence and has its goal or end in itself.

In the 1950s and 1960s a number of Yugoslav Marxist philosophers, in their attempts to free Marx from Stalinist misinterpretations and to revive and develop the original thought of Marx, came to regard the concept of praxis as the central concept of Marx's thought. According to their interpretation, Marx regarded man as a being of praxis, and praxis as free, creative and self-creative activity. More specifically some of them suggested that Marx used 'praxis' for the Aristotelian 'praxis', 'poiesis' and 'theoria'; not however for every 'praxis', 'poiesis' and 'theoria', but only for 'good' praxis in any of these three fields. 'Praxis' was thus opposed not to poiesis or theoria, but to 'bad', self-alienated praxis. The distinction between good and bad praxis was not meant in an ethical sense, but as a fundamental ontological and anthropological distinction, or rather a distinction in metaphilosophical revolutionary thinking. Therefore instead of talking about good and bad praxis, they preferred to talk about authentic and self-alienated praxis, or simply about praxis and self-alienation. The first issue of the journal *Praxis* which they established in 1964 was devoted to a discussion of the concept.

The concept of praxis has played an important role in the work of several recent Marxist thinkers (e.g. Lefebvre 1965, Kosik 1963), and notably among the thinkers of the FRANKFURT SCHOOL, for whom the relation between theory and praxis was always a primary interest, though they have paid more attention to 'theory' (and more specifically 'critical theory') than to the other term of the relation 'praxis'. One later representative of the school in particular, Habermas, has attempted to formulate the concept of praxis in a new way, by making a distinction between 'work' or 'purposive rational action' and 'interaction' or 'communicative action': the former being 'either instrumental action or rational choice or their conjunction . . . governed by *technical rules* based on empirical knowledge', or by strategies based on analytic knowledge; the latter 'symbolic interaction . . . governed by binding consensual norms' (1970, pp. 91–2). According to Habermas social praxis as understood by Marx included both 'work' and 'interaction', but Marx had a tendency to reduce 'social praxis to one of its moments, namely to work' (ibid.).

Finally, some current controversies may be briefly mentioned. While there is general agreement that the concept of praxis should be reserved for human beings, disagreement persists on how it should be applied. Some thinkers regard praxis as one aspect of human nature or action, which should therefore be studied by some particular philosophical discipline (e.g. ethics, social and political philosophy, theory of knowledge, etc.), but others argue that it characterizes human activity in all its forms. The latter viewpoint has sometimes been called (with an undertone of criticism) 'anthropological Marxism', but some who accept it regard the concept of praxis as more ontological than anthropological, going beyond philosophy as a separate activity towards some more general 'thinking of revolution'.

A second question concerns the extent to

which the concept of praxis can be defined or clarified. Thus some have maintained that as the most general concept, used in defining all other concepts, it cannot itself be defined; whereas others have insisted that although it is very complex it can to some extent be analysed and defined. The definitions range from that which treats it simply as the human activity through which man changes the world and himself, to more elaborate ones which introduce the notions of freedom, creativity, universality, history, the future, revolution, etc. Those who define praxis as free creative human activity have sometimes been criticized for proposing a concept which is purely 'normative', and 'unrealistic'. If by 'man' we mean a being which really exists, and by 'praxis' what human beings really do, then it is evident that there has always been more unfreedom and uncreativity in human history than the converse. In response to such criticisms, however, it has been claimed that the notion of free creative activity is neither 'descriptive' nor 'normative', but expresses essential human potentialities; something different both from what simply *is* and from what merely *ought* to be.

Lastly, some of those who regard praxis as free creative activity have gone on to define praxis as revolution. Against this it has been objected that it involves a return to the idea of praxis as a form of political action; but those who hold the view maintain that revolution should not be understood as a kind of political activity, nor even merely as radical social change. In the spirit of Marx, revolution is conceived as a radical change of both man and society. Its aim is to abolish self-alienation by creating a truly human person and a human society (Petrović 1971).

Reading
Bernstein, Richard 1971: *Praxis and Action: Contemporary Philosophies of Human Activity.*

Bloch, Ernst 1971: *On Karl Marx.*

Kosik, Karl 1963 (1976): *Dialectics of the Concrete.*

Lefebvre, Henri 1965: *Métaphilosophie: Prolégomènes.*

Lobkowicz, Nicholas 1967: *Theory and Practice: History of a Concept from Aristotle to Marx.*

Lukács, Georg 1923 (1971): *History and Class Consciousness.*

Marković, Mihailo 1974: *From Affluence to Praxis. Philosophy and Social Criticism.*

Petrović, Gajo 1971: *Philosophie und Revolution.*

Schmied-Kowarzik, Wolfdietrich 1981: *Die Dialektik der gesellschaftlichen Praxis.*

Sher, Gerson S. 1977: *Praxis: Marxist Criticism and Dissent in Socialist Yugoslavia.*

GAJO PETROVIĆ

Preobrazhensky, Evgeny Alexeyevich. Born 1886, Oryol Province, Russia; died 1937. Joined the Russian Social Democratic Party when he was seventeen, and worked for the Bolsheviks, primarily in the Urals, until the end of the Civil War. In 1920 he was elected a full member of the Central Committee, and became one of the party's three secretaries for a short time. From 1923 to 1927, he was the leading economic theorist of the successive left oppositions within the party, calling for a greater emphasis on industrialization and linking the economic difficulties of the country to the bureaucratization of party life under Stalin's leadership. With the increasing emphasis on industrialization Preobrazhensky was one of the first of the former Left Opposition to break with Trotsky and attempt a reconciliation with Stalin. He was readmitted to the Party, expelled again in 1931, readmitted in 1932, recanted his 1920s positions in 1934, but was arrested and imprisoned in 1935 and summarily shot in prison in 1937 (Haupt and Marie 1974).

Preobrazhensky is best known for his writings on inflation and the finance of industrialization in an isolated and backward agricultural economy. Once the Soviet economy had recovered from war and civil war, it was clear that in order to increase industrial capacity considerable investment was necessary, investment whose income-generating effects would be felt long before the desired output-generating effects would be realized. The consequent inflationary imbalance would threaten the worker-peasant alliance, jeopardizing both the economic and the political bases of the New Economic Policy established by Lenin in 1921. Preobrazhensky argued that inflationary imbalance existed anyway. The revolution on the land had created a structure of peasant household farms, peasants were accustomed to consuming more of their own produce, and only interested in delivering their surplus to the towns in exchange for industrial commodities. Hence with the economy restored to its 1913 level of output, there was a substantial increase in demand for industrial goods which was not matched by any increase in industrial capacity. Preobrazhensky emphasized that 'maintaining the equilibrium between the marketed share of industrial and agricultural output at prewar proportions . . . means sharply upsetting the equilibrium between the effective demand of the countryside and the commodity output of the town' (1921–27, pp. 36–7). But the industrial investment, which would in the long run generate the required increase in industrial capacity, would in the short run only exacerbate the shortfall between industrial capacity and effective demand. A large increase in investment was required, directed towards capacity-expanding heavy industry, but this could not be financed from within the industrial sector itself, which was too small, nor from foreign sources, because of political boycotts and the limited availability of agricultural exports to finance imports. Hence the agricultural sector had to bear the burden of the increase in investment. This was to be done by diverting a portion of the excess demand from the peasantry out of consumption into investment, and this would simultaneously solve the inflationary imbalance of the Soviet economy. State trading monopolies would replace the market mechanism, purchasing agricultural goods at low prices and selling industrial goods at higher prices, thereby turning the rate of exchange between state industry and private agriculture to the advantage of the former. Preobrazhensky called this mechanism of unequal exchange, via a monopoly pricing policy by the state, 'primitive socialist accumulation', by analogy with Marx's primary or PRIMITIVE ACCUMULATION in the last part of *Capital* I (esp. ch. 24). There was no suggestion of analogy in the methods of accumulation, however. This policy would also strike hardest at the richer stratum of peasants thereby curbing the danger of the growth of rural capitalism.

Preobrazhensky was opposed by Bukharin who argued that the peasantry would refuse to market its surplus, unless on the basis of equal exchange, and that planning should be seen as 'an anticipation of what would establish itself (post factum) if regulation was spontaneous'

(Brus 1972, p. 54). But Preobrazhensky's 'law of primitive socialist accumulation' was an economic regulator which coexisted with, and contradicted, the 'law of value' as a regulator deriving from the maintenance of COMMODITY production and private property relations. His thesis of the two regulators was thus designed to capture the antagonism between socialized and privatized relations of production in the transition period (see TRANSITION TO SOCIALISM).

Preobrazhensky's economics must be seen in terms of his commitment to democracy, to socialism, and to internationalism. He consistently advocated greater democratization; conceived Soviet industrialization as a means rather than an end, in which the essential was to construct socialized relations of production; and was always hostile to the doctrine of 'socialism in one country', arguing that the revolution could not succeed in constructing socialized relations of production in isolation from socialist revolutions in the more advanced capitalist countries. (For a dissenting view, see Day 1973, 1975, and for a rebuttal Filtzer 1978.)

Preobrazhensky was one of the most creative and important Marxist economists of this century. His use of the REPRODUCTION SCHEMA in his concrete analysis of the Soviet economy, his theorization of the transition, his thesis of the two regulators, his insistence upon economic forms as social processes, and his analysis of the possibilities of industrialization, make him one of the very few economists to date who have developed Marxian economics rather than repeated Marx's economics. (See also BOLSHEVISM; COMMUNISM; DICTATORSHIP OF THE PROLETARIAT; PEASANTRY; STALINISM; UNDERDEVELOPMENT AND DEVELOPMENT.)

Reading

Brus, W. 1972: *The Market in a Socialist Economy.*

Day, R. B. 1973: *Leon Trotsky and the Politics of Economic Isolation.*

— 1975: 'Preobrazhensky and the Theory of the Transition Period'.

Erlich, A. 1960: *The Soviet Industrialization Debate, 1924–1928.*

Filtzer, Donald A. 1978: 'Preobrazhensky and the Problem of the Soviet Transition'.

Gregory, P. R. and Stuart, R. C. 1981: *Soviet Economic Structure and Performance.*

Haupt, G. and Marie, J. J. 1974: *Makers of the Russian Revolution*, pp. 191–201.

Preobrazhensky, Evgeny 1921–7 (1980): *The Crisis of Soviet Industrialization.*

— 1922 (1973): *From NEP to Socialism.*

— 1926 (1965): *The New Economics.*

SIMON MOHUN

price of production and the transformation problem The concept of price of production is intended to explain the tendency for the rate of PROFIT on stocks of invested capital to be equalized across different sectors in capitalist production (abstracting from differences i risk, market power, technical innovativeness, a⌐d so on), within the framework of the labour theory of VALUE, which holds that value produced is proportional to labour time expended in COMMODITY production. If value produced were proportional to labour time expended, and wages were uniform over sectors, the SURPLUS VALUE, the difference between value newly produced in a stage of production and wages, would also be proportional to labour expended. Abstracting from rent, surplus value appears to the capitalist as profit, and the ratio of surplus value to capital invested as the rate of profit. But if capital invested per unit of labour expended is not uniform across sectors (and there is no reason in general to suppose that it will be) then the ratio of surplus value to capital invested, that is, the rate of profit, will be different across sectors. This raises the theoretical problem of how to reconcile the equalization of the rate of profit with the labour theory of value.

Marx (*Capital* III, chs. 8–10) proposed as a general solution to this problem that the prices of commodities might systematically deviate from their values as determined by the labour embodied in them so as to equalize the rate of profit. But in this process, he argued, the law that only labour produces value would be respected, because the total value produced and the total surplus value would remain unchanged; Marx saw the deviation of prices from value as a redistribution of a given aggregate surplus value among different sectors of production. What does it mean for prices to correspond to, or deviate from, values? Price is the amount of MONEY which buys a commodity. Value, according to the labour theory of value, reflects

the amount of social, necessary, abstract labour time embodied in the commodity (see SOCIALLY NECESSARY LABOUR; ABSTRACT LABOUR). In order to speak coherently of the relation between money price and labour value we must specify the relation between abstract labour time and money, the amount of abstract labour time the monetary unit represents, which we might call the value of money. Prices correspond to values if the prices of commodities multiplied by the value of money equal the labour time embodied in the commodity. Prices deviate from values if the price of a commodity, multiplied by the value of money, is larger or smaller than the labour time embodied in the commodity.

Marx's solution to the problem of reconciling the labour theory of value with the tendency for profit rates to be equalized begins by assuming that all commodities have prices which accurately express the labour time expended on them. As we have seen, if capital invested per unit of labour time expended differs across sectors, at these initial prices profit rates will vary from sector to sector. Marx then proposes that the capitalization of profit rates raises the prices of those commodities with lower than average profit rates and lowers the prices of those with higher than average profit rates, in such a way as to distribute the constant amount of total surplus value. Since he makes no adjustment of variable capital or constant capital in this process, the aggregate value newly produced, $s + v$, and hence the labour time equivalent of the unit of money are unchanged. Marx continues this adjustment of prices until the rates of profit are all equal to the original average rate of profit. The resulting prices he calls *prices of production*; they are prices at which profit rates are equalized and at which the total surplus value is proportional to surplus labour time. In the process all that has happened is a redistribution of the predetermined surplus value. All the results of the labour theory of value analysis of capitalist production continue to hold in the aggregate, and are modified in particular sectors only by this redistribution. The rate of profit in the end is exactly equal to the average rate of profit at the initial prices.

Although Marx's analysis is abstract, it represents the real process of unfettered competition among capitals. If profit rates in one sector exceed the average, capital will flow into the high profit sector, and COMPETITION will force prices in that sector down until the profit rate equals the average. This analysis abstracts, of course, from barriers to competition, which might in reality prevent the equalization of profit rates. Marx acknowledges that these barriers exist in reality, but argues that they can be analysed only after the case of unfettered competition has been studied.

Marx's solution has been criticized on the ground that as the prices of produced commodities change, the cost of those same commodities as inputs to production or as elements of workers' subsistence will also change. Marx, in holding the value of constant and variable capital unchanged in each sector through the transformation, neglects this link between sales prices of commodities and costs. Later attempts to correct this solution have shown that it is impossible in general to maintain all of the following important results Marx claims: (1) equalization of profit rates; (2) conservation of surplus value and variable capital; (3) conservation of constant capital; (4) conservation of the original average rate of profit. The solutions proposed all achieve (1), the equalization of profit rates, but have to abandon some other of the four results.

These solutions can be grouped into two broad classes, depending on what additional restrictions the solution respects. The first group holds constant in the transformation the physical bundle of commodities consumed by workers, and *a fortiori* the labour time embodied in those commodities. In a very general model of production it is possible to find prices and a wage which equalize rates of profit across sectors and permit workers to buy an arbitrary predetermined bundle of subsistence goods as long as that bundle is not so large as to make production of a surplus product impossible. In these solutions it is impossible in general to hold the value of both surplus value and variable capital invariant (or to put it another way, impossible to make the value of money and surplus value both invariant). Critics of the labour theory of value have used this result to argue that the labour theory of value is redundant in the analysis of capitalist production, since there is no coherent sense in which actual surplus value can be rigorously seen as the result of surplus labour time (see Seton 1957; Medio 1972).

The second group of solutions equalize profit rates holding constant the ratio of aggregate surplus value to aggregate variable capital (or, what amounts to the same thing, holding constant the value of money and the total surplus value). These solutions, since they conserve surplus value in a rigorous sense, do retain an active theoretical role for the labour theory of value, and respect the argument that surplus labour time is the source of surplus value. In these solutions the purchasing power of the wage may change in the transformation process, so that in general the consumption of workers may change, as will the labour actually embodied in workers' consumption. What does remain constant is the abstract labour equivalent workers receive in the wage (see Lipietz 1982; Dumenil 1980, Foley 1982). Neither of these groups of solutions exhibits in general Marx's results (3) and (4): the conservation of the value of constant capital or the constancy of the average rate of profit.

The price of production expresses a more concrete theory of capitalist relations than do pure labour values, since it takes into account the specifically capitalist form of commodity production in allowing for equalization of the rate of profit through the competition of capitals. Prices of production are only a step towards a fully concrete theory of price, since innovations, shortages and gluts, and restrictions on competition, may force market prices to deviate even from the prices of production for a longer or shorter time. Some writers on the transformation problem have emphasized this qualitative aspect; that Marx's method of abstraction makes it necessary to move from values to prices of production to market prices. For values are revealed by abstracting from competition between capitals in different sectors, and permit the explication of the source of surplus value in the contradiction between capital as a whole and labour; prices of production relate to a level of abstraction where such competition exists and total surplus value is distributed between different capitals; while market prices no longer abstract from the full complexity of competitive forces. Those who emphasize the significance of the transformation for Marx's method of abstraction, and its ability to reveal hidden layers oppose writers who, examining only quantitative solutions, argue that value theory is redundant since prices of production cannot be derived from it on the assumptions Marx thought important, but can be derived directly from technological and wage data.

Reading

Dumenil, G. 1980: *De la valeur aux prix de production.*

Foley, D. 1982: 'The Value of Money, the Value of Labour-power and the Marxian Transformation Problem'.

Lipietz, A. 1982: 'The So-called Transformation Problem Revisited'.

Medio, Alfredo 1972: 'Profits and Surplus Value'. In E. Hunt and J. Schwartz, eds. *A Critique of Economic Theory.*

Seton, Francis 1957: 'The Transformation Problem'.

DUNCAN FOLEY

primitive accumulation Marx defines and analyses primitive accumulation in *Capital* I, pt. VII. Having examined the laws of development of production by capital, he is concerned with the process by which capitalism is itself historically established. His understanding of capitalism is a precondition for this, as is his more general analysis of MODE OF PRODUCTION. This follows from the necessary focus upon how one set of class relations of production becomes transformed into another. In particular, how is it that a propertyless class of wage labourers, the proletariat, becomes confronted by a class of capitalists who monopolize the means of production?

Marx's answer is disarmingly simple. Since pre-capitalist relations of production are predominantly agricultural, the peasantry having possession of the principal means of production, namely land, capitalism can only be created by dispossessing the peasantry of the land. Accordingly the origins of capitalism are to be found in the transformation of relations of production on the land. The freeing of the peasantry from land is the source of wage labourers both for agricultural capital and for industry. This is Marx's central observation and he emphasizes it by ironic reference to the 'so-called secret of primitive accumulation'. Many of his contemporaries saw capital as the result of abstinence, as an original source for accumulation. Marx's point is that primitive accumulation is not an accumu-

lation in this sense at all. Abstinence can only lead to accumulation of capital if capitalist relations of production are already in existence. For Marx, the 'secret' is to be found in the revolutionary and broader reorganization of existing relations of production rather than in some quantitative expansion of the provision of means of production and subsistence, and he illustrates his argument by reference to the Enclosure Movement in Britain. But he also examines the sources of capitalist wealth and the legislation forcing the peasantry into wage labour and disciplining the proletariat into the new mode of life.

Marx's concept is relatively clear but there is dispute about whether it is a valid framework for analysing the transition to capitalism. Even if Marx's illustration for the case of Britain is considered to be correct, it cannot be taken as typical of the establishment of capitalism elsewhere; in Europe for example. This has led writers such as Sweezy to argue that exchange is the active force in the disintegration of pre-capitalist relations and consequently that the origins of capitalism are to be found in cities, the centres of commerce. Sweezy was responding to Dobb (1946) who had taken a position similar to that of Marx, as developed further in *Capital* III when considering the historical genesis of capitalist ground rent and merchant capital. For Dobb, capitalism arises out of the internal contradictions of pre-capitalist societies for which commerce is at most a catalyst and for which agricultural relations of production are the most significant.

The debate between Dobb and Sweezy, with other contributions, is collected in Hilton (1976) (see also TRANSITION FROM FEUDALISM TO CAPITALISM). It is not simply an exercise in history since it has profound implications for the way in which underdevelopment is understood today (see UNDERDEVELOPMENT AND DEVELOPMENT). The question is whether capitalism is to be analysed in terms of the extension and penetration of exchange relations from outside, or of developing internal class relations with particular reference to landed property. Brenner (1977) argues that the first view, associated with Sweezy, Frank and Wallerstein among others, has its intellectual origins in the work of Adam Smith and is a departure from Marxism.

In *The New Economics*, PREOBRAZHENSKY

proposed the notion of primitive socialist accumulation. This term embraced a series of policies, designed for the Soviet economy in the 1920s, to appropriate resources from the wealthier classes to aid socialist construction through state planning. Lenin's *Development of Capitalism in Russia* is a classic application of Marx's theory of primitive accumulation to prerevolutionary economic development in Russia.

Reading

Aston, T. and Philpin, C. (eds) 1985: *The Brenner Debate*.

Brenner, R. 1976: 'Agrarian Class Structure and Economic Development in Pre-Industrial Europe'.

— 1977: 'The Origins of Capitalist Development'.

Dobb, M. 1946 (1963): *Studies in the Development of Capitalism*.

Hilton, Rodney ed. 1976: *The Transition from Feudalism to Capitalism*.

Laclau, E. 1971: 'Feudalism and Capitalism in Latin America'.

Marglin, S. 1974: 'What Do Bosses Do?'

Preobrazhensky, E. 1926 (1965): *The New Economics*.

BEN FINE

primitive communism This refers to the collective right to basic resources, the absence of hereditary status or authoritarian rule, and the egalitarian relationships that preceded exploitation and economic stratification in human history. Long a subject for comment by travellers from stratified state societies to their hinterlands, an influence on humanist writings (such as More's *Utopia*), and a source of inspiration to political rebels and experimental socialist communities, the concept was first given detailed ethnographic embodiment in 1877 by Lewis Henry Morgan. Building on his first-hand knowledge of the Iroquois, Morgan in *Ancient Society* described the 'liberty, equality and fraternity of the ancient gentes' (1877, p. 562), and in *Houses and House-Life of the American Aborigines* (1881) he detailed how 'communism in living' was reflected in the village architecture of native Americans.

In *Origin of the Family* Engels worked from Marx's copious notes on *Ancient Society* (see Krader 1972), as well as from the text itself, to analyse primitive communism and the processes of its transformation. He applied to the data of Morgan and others the concept that was central to Marx's analysis of capitalism, the transition from production for use to production of commodities for exchange; and he added his own thinking on the concomitant transformation of communal family relations and gender equality to individual families as economic units and female subordination.

The establishment of anthropology as a discipline at the close of the nineteenth century coincided with a general challenge to the reality of social evolution and primitive communism as outlined by Engels (Leacock 1982). The predominating anthropological stance was that private property and class differences were human universals that simply grew from lesser to greater importance in politically organized stratified society (e.g. Lowie 1929). This stance was in turn countered by arguments supporting the Morgan/Engels thesis, most notably by the British archaeologist Gordon Childe (1954) and the American social anthropologist Leslie White (1959). Theirs and other work led after mid-century to the virtual acceptance of primitive communism as a reality, although it was usually referred to by some politically less loaded term such as egalitarianism (Fried 1967). Present-day texts in anthropology commonly point out that in egalitarian societies rights to resources were held in common; such property as was owned was purely personal; such status as existed was not inherited but in direct response to proven wisdom, ability and generosity; and chiefly people were no more than 'firsts among equals' in an essentially collective decision-making process.

The application of Marxist concepts to the analysis of non-stratified societies, especially by French anthropologists, has recently produced a considerable literature, often sharply polemical, on the primitive communist mode or modes of production (Seddon 1978). A problem with some of this literature is the failure to distinguish between fully communistic peoples and those in the process of class transformation (Hindess and Hirst 1975). The erroneous assumption that all so-called primitive peoples were communistic at the time of European expansion follows in part from Morgan's overestimation of democracy among the highly stratified Aztecs of Mexico, and from Engels's acceptance of this and others of Morgan's mistaken classifications. A further problem with many analyses of primitive communal societies is the failure to define changes brought about in them by European colonialism. As a consequence, some Marxist anthropologists, like many non-Marxists, erroneously contend that women were subordinate to men even in otherwise egalitarian societies (Leacock 1982).

Reading

Childe, V. Gordon 1954: *What Happened in History.*

Fried, Morton H. 1967: *The Evolution of Political Society.*

Hindess, Barry and Hirst, Paul Q. 1975: *Pre-Capitalist Modes of Production.*

Krader, Lawrence, ed. 1972: *The Ethnological Notebooks of Karl Marx.*

Leacock, Eleanor 1981: 'Marxism and Anthropology'. In Bertell Ollman and Edward Vernoff eds. *The Left Academy.*

— 1982: *Myths of Male Dominance.*

Lowie, Robert H. 1929: *The Origin of the State.*

Morgan, Lewis Henry 1877 (1974): *Ancient Society.*

— 1881 (1965): *Houses and House-life of the American Aborigines.*

Seddon, David ed. 1978: *Relations of Production: Marxist Approaches to Economic Anthropology.*

White, Leslie, A. 1959: *The Evolution of Culture.*

ELEANOR BURKE LEACOCK

Prison Notebooks When Antonio Gramsci was sent to prison by a fascist court in 1928, the intention was clear. 'For twenty years we must stop this brain functioning', declared the Public Prosecutor. The results were the contrary. Between 1929 and 1935, when he became too ill to work, Gramsci produced thirty-three notebooks, which were rescued when he died in April 1937 and eventually published in the postwar period. Many would consider them one of the most original contributions to twentieth-century thought. At the same time, their note form, the wide range of Gramsci's concerns, difficulties in tracing the sequence in which he worked and his open-ended approach mean that, while they are a rich source of new concepts and highly original insights which have had a wide influence both in intellectual work and political practice, any attempt at a definitive

systematization confronts enormous hurdles and is most probably impossible. Amending his original outline more than once, redrafting a large proportion of the notes, Gramsci worked on several notebooks and focused on several subjects at the same time, with themes often cutting across notebooks, and individual notes containing more than one concept. The result, as Francioni has shown, is that even the critical Italian edition has some serious defects, while the first Italian edition, and those in other languages which derive from it, often constrain the notes within categories that are inaccurate reflections of Gramsci's thinking.

It could be argued that Gramsci's aim is nothing less than to refound Marxist theory in the light of both the latest developments of capitalism and the first concrete attempt to build socialism, viewed as challenges not only to Marxism but to modern thought in general. Rooted in the debates about revisionism and in the communist movement, he re-reads Marx to disentangle him from Marxism in order to intervene in the crisis of both the theory and the practice of the working-class movement in the 1920s and 1930s. This crisis is viewed as part and parcel of a long process of transformation which requires a confrontation with unprecedented developments such as Fordism, fascism, modern mass culture, increasingly complex civil society or the interventionist state. Convinced that any effective theory had to struggle to avoid being trapped by outmoded concepts and language, Gramsci read widely, seeking insights from thinkers like Croce but also from what might appear surprising sources, Sorel or even certain fascist thinkers, since they appeared to him to capture significant aspects of contemporary reality, even though he was highly critical of the conclusions they drew.

Thus he provides both a re-reading of Marx in the light of new questions, and novel tools which are still useful today. The enormous complexity of both the form and the content of the notebooks reflects Gramsci's approach to a reality which could not be captured by any schema. The fragments come to be joined in the mind of the reader, who necessarily creates a text according to contemporary questions and categories. This is probably one reason why the insights they contain maintain such fascination and why they provoke such widespread debate.

Reading

Francioni, G. 1984: *L'Officina gramsciana. Ipotesi sulla struttura dei 'Quaderni del Carcere'*.

Gramsci, A. 1929–35 (1971): *Selections from the Prison Notebooks*, ed. Quintin Hoare and Geoffrey Nowell Smith.

— 1975: *Quaderni del carcere I–IV*.

Mangoni, L. 1987: 'La genesi delle categorie storico-politiche nei Quaderni del carcere.'

Sassoon, Anne S. ed. 1982: *Approaches to Gramsci*.

— 1980 (1987): *Gramsci's Politics*.

ANNE SHOWSTACK SASSOON

production If in the world of politics Marxism is associated with the struggle for communism, in its theory it is identified with the fundamentally determining role played by production. Each society is characterized by a definite configuration of socially and historically constituted FORCES AND RELATIONS OF PRODUCTION which constitute the basis upon which other economic and social relations rest.

In the social production of their life, men enter into definite relations that are indispensable and independent of their will, relations of production which correspond to a definite stage of development of their material productive forces. The sum total of these relations of production constitutes the economic structure of society, the real foundation, on which rises a legal and political superstructure and to which correspond definite forms of social consciousness. The mode of production of material life conditions the social, political and intellectual life process in general. (Marx, *Contribution to the Critique of Political Economy*, Preface)

Continuing this famous passage Marx goes on to suggest that the passage from one MODE OF PRODUCTION to another is to be understood on the basis of the determining role played by production. Yet, equally important, Marx qualified these observations as 'the general result at which I arrived and which, once won, served as a guiding thread for my studies'. This is not to suggest that Marx considered any revision of his conclusions to be likely, but that his analysis depended upon further logical and historical investigation. The materialist conception of history (see HISTORICAL MATERIALISM) is not to be

considered as some ready made formula for revealing the secrets of social organization and development.

This is apparent from the controversy within Marxism that surrounds, for example, the question of DETERMINISM and the relation between BASE AND SUPERSTRUCTURE. But it is an issue that bears upon the understanding of production itself. In his Introduction to the *Grundrisse* (sect. 2c), Marx concludes in a general discourse 'not that production, distribution, exchange and consumption are identical, but that they all form the members of a totality, distinctions within a unity', having observed earlier (sect. 2a) that 'not only is production immediately consumption and consumption immediately production . . . but also, each of them, apart from being immediately the other and apart from mediating the other, in addition to this creates the other in completing itself, and creates itself as the other'. This all follows, for example, from society as a system of REPRODUCTION and from consumption within the labour process of means of production. Marx then proceeds to a similar discourse on the relation between DISTRIBUTION and production. It all serves to illustrate that these economic categories are not identical but that there are definite relations between them. Moreover, while 'a definite production thus determines a definite consumption, distribution and exchange as well as *definite* relations between these differing moments . . . production is itself determined by the other moments' (sect. 2c).

Accordingly there is no simple relation between production and the rest of the economy, mode of production, or social formation. Indeed, even what constitutes an object of production is ambiguous. For a slave society the reproduction of the species can be an act of production in so far as slaves can be bought and sold. By contrast, for capitalism it is essential for the defining characteristic of LABOUR POWER as a COMMODITY, that the process of reproduction lies outside the realm of production by capital. This example illustrates the difficulty and dangers of identifying general and ahistorical categories such as production. It leads, however, to the understanding that production and its related moments are always social in a specifically historical form and that these must be studied to extract the specific forms of determination and definition that they involve: 'In all forms of society there is one specific kind of production which predominates over the rest, whose relations thus assign rank and influence to the others. It is a general illumination which bathes all the other colours and modifies their particularity' (*Grundrisse*, Introduction sect. 3).

In *Capital*, Marx does from time to time treat production as a general category in order to illuminate its specific forms for capitalism. For example, the LABOUR PROCESS involves the working up of a set of raw materials into final products in which the original materials are often visible within the product, as in weaving. In the case of capitalist production such raw materials represent constant capital and it is this which is preserved in the commodity product as the form of preservation of the initial values and use values. By the same token, the fact that it is VALUE that is preserved and necessarily added during production is concealed, and this is even more so for SURPLUS VALUE.

If production is at once both a general category and one with definite social and historical characteristics, a crucial element in specifying the latter for Marxism is the mode of production and the associated class relations and forces of production. These in turn can be specified further by reference to general categories such as EXPLOITATION, ownership of means of production, the level of technology etc. But it would be a mistake to see Marx's or Marxism's understanding of production as being exclusively preoccupied with material production. At a general level it is concerned with the reproduction of the social formation as well as of the economy. Marx is clear that society *produces* its political, ideological as well as its economic relations, whereas there is a tendency under capitalism, for example, to identify production with capital alone or more generally with wage labour. Marxism has emphasized that a RULING CLASS must produce the means of legitimation, that the proletariat must be reproduced by DOMESTIC LABOUR etc. In each case, productive activity is involved, most of which is not directly engaged by capital and much of which is non-material in content. While these activities may be 'illuminated' by, rather than identified with, capitalist production they are nonetheless production and must be understood as such. The same is true in the realm of ideas that are pro-

duced by the activities and relations in which we are involved as much as, if not more than, by the act of thinking itself (see COMMODITY FETISHISM, for example).

The production of ideas, of conceptions, of consciousness, is at first directly interwoven with the material activity and the material intercourse of men, the language of real life. Conceiving, thinking, the mental intercourse of men, appear at this stage as the direct efflux of their material behaviour. The same applies to mental production as expressed in the language of politics, laws, morality, religion, metaphysics, of a people. Men are the producers of their conceptions, ideas – real active men, as they are conditioned by a definite development of their productive forces and of the intercourse corresponding to these, up to its furthest forms. (*German Ideology*, vol . I, sect. IA)

BEN FINE

productive and unproductive labour The distinction between productive and unproductive labour has recently become an important one in Marxist political economy. The increasing number of state employees not engaged in COMMODITY production has presented the analytical problem of explaining their role and significance. At the same time attention has focused upon the CLASS position of such workers; to what extent do they form a part of the working class or at least a trustworthy ally of it?

Marx's own analysis is to be found at the beginning of *Capital* II and in the *Theories of Surplus Value*. His definition of productive labour seems quite clear and the concept of unproductive labour follows as wage labour that is not productive. Productive labour is engaged by CAPITAL in the process of production for the purpose of producing SURPLUS VALUE. As such productive labour concerns only the relations under which the worker is organized and neither the nature of the production process nor the nature of the product. Opera singers, teachers and house-painters just as much as car mechanics or miners may be employed by capitalists with profit in mind. This is what determines whether they are productive or unproductive.

In Marx's time the vast majority of unproductive labourers were commercial workers, domestic or personal servants and state administrative employees. Commercial workers are unproductive for Marx because they are not involved in production, which is the sole source of surplus value for capital as a whole, even if their activities result in commercial profits for their employers. Nevertheless Marx and Engels do refer to the commercial proletariat, suggesting that being unproductive does not bar a worker from membership of the working class, as has been suggested by some Marxists (e.g. Poulantzas 1975).

The importance of Marx's distinction is that most of his analysis is concerned with productive labour (for example, the ways in which capitalist production develops). This is the basis on which unproductive labour can be examined in its dependence upon surplus value as a source of wages, but it is not an analysis of unproductive labour as such. This would require an examination of the relations under which that unproductive labour is organized and why it has not been dissolved by capitalist production. This may be for structural reasons, such as the separation between production and exchange in the case of commercial workers, or for historical reasons as in the struggle to provide welfare services (health, education) or to privilege a profession (doctors).

One school of thought, however (see Gough 1972), has essentially rejected the distinction between productive and unproductive labour, arguing that all wage labour is identically subject to exploitation irrespective of whether it is employed directly by capital or not. Others (see Fine and Harris 1979) have denied this on the grounds that it reduces exploitation to a generalized concept of performing surplus labour. This would not only result in abolishing the distinction between categories of productive and unproductive labour as wage-earners, but would also fail to distinguish between exploitation under capitalism as opposed to feudalism, for example. Nevertheless, it is generally agreed that there is no simple relation between the economic criterion of productive and unproductive labour and the potential for membership and formation of the working class, which also depends upon political and ideological conditions. But how this is so is itself a controversial matter.

Reading

Fine, Ben and Harris, Laurence 1979: *Rereading 'Capital'*, ch. 3.

Gough, I. 1972: 'Marx's Theory of Productive and Unproductive Labour'.

— 1973: 'On Productive and Unproductive Labour: A Reply'.

Poulantzas, Nicos 1975: *Classes in Contemporary Capitalism*.

Wright, Erik O. 1978: *Class, Crisis and the State*.

BEN FINE

profit. *See* surplus value and profit.

progress A conception of progress clearly underlies Marx's theory of history (see HISTORICAL MATERIALISM) though it is nowhere fully expressed. In a brief note at the end of his introduction to the *Grundrisse*, referring to the relation between the development of material production and of artistic production, Marx comments that 'the concept of progress is not to be understood in its familiar abstraction'; in the *Preface* of 1859 he arranges the principal modes of production in a series as 'progressive epochs in the economic formation of society'; and in the same text he defines the conditions in which 'new, higher relations of production' can appear. The fundamental elements of this largely implicit conception are two-fold. First, that cultural progress – 'the complete elaboration of human potentialities', human emancipation in the broadest sense – depends upon 'the full development of human mastery over the forces of nature' (*Grundrisse*, pp. 387–8), that is, upon the growth of productive powers, and in modern times especially, upon the advance of science. Second, that progress is not regarded, as in the evolutionist theories of Comte and Spencer for example, as a gradual, continuous and integrated process, but as characterized by discontinuity, disharmony, and more or less abrupt leaps from one type of society to another, accomplished primarily through class conflict.

Many later Marxists have accepted, or set out more explicitly, this view of progress, not only in everyday political discourse where such expressions as 'progressive forces' and 'progressive movements' are commonplace, but also in academic writing. Thus, the Marxist archaeologist Gordon Childe (1936) claimed to be vindicating the idea of progress in showing how economic revolutions had promoted civilization. From another aspect, Friedmann (1936) argued that Marxism has incorporated and extended the idea of progress formulated in the eighteenth century by the thinkers of the bourgeois revolutions, and continues to express a belief in progress which the bourgeoisie has now abandoned. More recently Hobsbawm, in his introduction (1964) to a section of the *Grundrisse* dealing with pre-capitalist economic formations, argues that Marx's aim is 'to formulate the *content* of history in its most general form', and 'this content is progress'; for Marx 'progress is something objectively definable' (p. 12). In a different way progress is an important, though largely unexamined, concept in the more Hegelian versions of Marxism (see LUKÁCS; FRANKFURT SCHOOL) which regard the historical process as, in some sense, a progressive movement of emancipation.

On the other hand there have always been Marxists who sought to limit the significance of the idea of progress, which opens the way for the introduction of value judgments into what they consider a purely scientific theory. This was the position of some thinkers of the Second International (e.g. Kautsky and most of the Austro-Marxists) who held strictly to the notion of 'economic determinism', though they were obliged on various occasions to confront the question of the ethical aims of socialism (Kautsky 1906). It is also that of many recent structuralist Marxists, notably Althusser, who are concerned above all to establish the rigorously scientific character of Marxism in opposition to ideological thought, which includes all forms of HISTORICISM.

Reading

Childe, V. Gordon 1936: *Man Makes Himself.*

Cohen, G. A. 1978: *Karl Marx's Theory of History: A Defence.* ch. 1.

Friedmann, Georges 1936: *La crise du progrès.*

Hobsbawm, Eric 1964b: 'Introduction' to Karl Marx, *Pre-Capitalist Economic Formations.*

Kautsky, Karl 1906 (*1918*): *Ethics and the Materialist Conception of History.*

TOM BOTTOMORE

proletariat. *See* working class.

property In Marxist social theory the notion of property and some related categories (property relations, forms of property) have a central significance. Marx did not regard property only as the possibility for the owner to exercise property rights, or as an object of such activity, but as an essential relationship which has a central role in the complex system of classes and social strata. Within this system of categories the ownership of means of production has outstanding importance. Lange (1963) says that according to Marxist theory such ownership is 'the "organizing principle" which determines both the relations of production and the relations of distribution'.

Marx and Engels held that it is the changes in forms of property which mainly characterize the succession of socioeconomic formations. This idea led to a strict periodization of the history of humanity (primitive communism, slavery, Asiatic society, feudal society, capitalism, socialism, communism) which became even more simplified in the orthodox versions of Marxism (see Ojzerman 1962, pt. II, ch. 1; STAGES OF DEVELOPMENT). One valuable feature of Marx's and Engels's original classification, however, was that it challenged the assumption commonly made in the West at that time that bourgeois forms of property must everywhere be the norm, and thus stimulated much historical research into land rights in medieval Europe or in pre-British India, for example, as well as anthropological research which has shown the absence of private property, at least in land, among many tribal peoples (see PRIMITIVE COMMUNISM; TRIBAL SOCIETY).

In modern Marxist thought this rigid historical scheme is, in many respects, beginning to dissolve. Thus, the debates of the 1960s on ASIATIC SOCIETY (see Tökei 1979) encouraged this process, and efforts to analyse property relations in the Roman and Germanic societies in a more realistic way have a similar effect. Marx had already discussed, on several occasions, these diverse forms of property; e.g. 'Property, then, originally means – in its Asiatic, Slavonic, ancient classical, Germanic form – the relation of the working (producing or self-reproducing) subject to the conditions of his production or reproduction as his own. It will therefore have different forms depending on the conditions of this production' (*Grundrisse,*

p. 495). Those who favour modernizing Marxist thinking lay particular stress on the need to analyse adequately the property relations and forms in countries where the private ownership of means of production has been eliminated. According to Stalinism, by taking the means of production into state ownership in the most important branches of the economy, and by collectivization of agriculture, small industry and small trade, the property problem has actually been solved; and it remains only to transform cooperative property into public (state) property. In order to answer the question whether the problem of property in these countries will remain or not, it is necessary to introduce the concept of *possession*, which means the exercise of ownership and property rights as distinct from juridical ownership (see Hegedüs 1976). If the real situation is analysed with the help of this notion, two fundamental controversies unfold:

(a) The exercise of possession possibilities by the state administration versus the exercise of property rights by the whole society. This involves mainly the problem of state management, but a similar dilemma arises at the local level too, concerning exercise of possessional possibilities by the local professional administration versus exercise of property rights by the local community.

(b) The exercise of possession possibilities by the professional apparatus of economic enterprises versus the exercise of property rights by the enterprise collectives. This problem emerges first in large and medium-scale firms, both in the state and cooperative sectors. Within the same framework, in small-scale industry and trade, there is a possibility for the development of relatively independent associations of producers which might introduce a new form of socialist ownership.

This quasi-socialist property form has become bankrupt in East and East-Central Europe with the collapse of the monolithic Stalinist power structures. The main trends of change in property relations in this area are now privatization and re-privatization. The former chiefly increases the private property of the rich and influential strata, while the latter gives back to the former owners their collectivized or nationalized wealth. Besides these trends, one can also observe some tendencies which suggest the emergence of authentic socialist ownership. Such are, first of all, the following:

– cooperatives which are being formed voluntarily by small owners, mainly in agriculture;

– transfer of a part of the shares in larger enterprises to the workers;

– property associations through which the workers themselves run their enterprises;

– workers' organizations emerge which regard it as their function to exercise workers control over the economic bureaucracy.

All these historical experiences confirm the necessity of revising the Marxist theory of property.

Reading

Bernstein, Eduard 1891b: *Gesellschaftlichen und Privateigentum.*

Hegedüs, András 1976: *Socialism and Bureaucracy,* ch. VII.

Kautsky, Karl 1887 (1912): *Karl Marx: Ökonomische Lehren.*

— 1927: *Die materialistische Geschichtsauffassung in der Staat und die Entwicklung der Menschheit.*

Lange, Oskar 1963: *Politische Ökonomie.*

Ojzerman, T. I. 1962: *Formirovanije Filoszofii Marxism.*

Stalin, J. V. 1924b (1945): *Problems of Leninism.*

Tökei, F. 1979: *Essays on the Asiatic Mode of Production.*

ANDRÁS HEGEDÜS

Proudhon, Pierre-Joseph Born 15 January 1809, Besançon; died 16 January 1865, Passy. Proudhon, a self-educated French artisan of peasant stock, was the first person to use 'anarchy' in a non-pejorative sense to refer to his ideal of an ordered society without government. In his prolific writings are to be found many of the basic ideas of ANARCHISM and also of French SYNDICALISM. Believing that 'the abolition of exploitation of man by man and the abolition of government are one and the same thing' (see Thomas 1980, pp. 212–13), he argued that working men should emancipate themselves, not by political but by economic means, through the voluntary organization of their own labour – a concept to which he attached redemptive value. His proposed system of equitable exchange between self-governing producers, organized individually or in association and financed by free credit, was called 'mutualism'. The units of the radically decentralized and pluralistic social order that he envisaged were to be linked at all levels by applying 'the federal principle'. In *The Holy Family* (ch. 4, sect. 4) Marx praised Proudhon's *What is Property?* (1840) as a 'great scientific advance', making possible for the first time 'a real science of political economy'. But in *The Poverty of Philosophy* (ch. 2), the first major presentation of Marx's own 'critique of political economy', Proudhon was severely and vituperatively condemned for his attempt to use Hegelian dialectics and for his failure to rise above 'the bourgeois horizon'. Instead of recognizing that 'economic categories are only the theoretical expressions, the abstractions of the social relations of production', Proudhon, 'holding things upside down like a true philosopher', saw in actual relations 'nothing but the incarnation of these . . . categories'.

Reading

Edwards, Stewart ed. 1969: *Selected Writings of Pierre-Joseph Proudhon.*

Thomas, Paul 1980: *Karl Marx and the Anarchists.*

Woodcock, George 1956: *Pierre-Joseph Proudhon.*

GEOFFREY OSTERGAARD

psychoanalysis The branch of psychology which is associated with the work of Sigmund Freud (1856–1939) and stresses the importance of unconscious impulses. Freud believed that the root of much human thinking and behaviour could be traced to the forces of the 'id': i.e. to those sexual and aggressive urges which are frequently repressed from the conscious parts of the mind. Much of the emphasis of psychoanalysis is in the treatment and explanation of neuroses and other psychological disturbances. However, Freud also formulated a psychoanalytic theory of society, which, he believed, conflicted with Marxist theory: he stressed the unconscious psychological motivations underlying organized social behaviour, whereas Marxists pointed to the importance of economic factors. According to Freud, changes in the economic structure of society would not lead to basic changes in HUMAN NATURE. Thus he argued that

the 'new order' being created in the Soviet Union would not produce fundamental psychological changes, but that the Soviet rulers would 'still have to struggle for an incalculable time with the difficulties which the untameable character of human nature presents to every kind of social community' (1932, p. 181).

Psychoanalytic theory and treatment has been officially rejected in the Soviet Union, and Lenin is reputed to have criticized psychoanalysts for their bourgeois practice of 'poking about in sexual matters' (Rahmani 1973, p. 9). On the other hand, Trotsky, who had encountered Freud's ideas in Vienna before the first world war, was more sympathetic to psychoanalysis. In 1926 he declared that Freud's approach was as materialist as Pavlov's (see PSYCHOLOGY) and he argued that 'the attempt to declare psychoanalysis incompatible with Marxism and simply turn one's back on Freudianism is too simple' (Trotsky 1973a, p. 234). As with other matters, Trotsky's view did not prevail in the USSR.

In the West a number of Marxist theorists, particularly in Germany, attempted to reinterpret Freudian concepts in order to develop new ways of understanding the topics of ALIENATION and IDEOLOGY. Such theorists included Adorno, Horkheimer, Marcuse and Erich Fromm of the FRANKFURT SCHOOL, and Wilhelm Reich (1897–1957), who was a pupil of Freud and was also, until his expulsion, a member of the German Communist Party.

It was argued that instinctual repression, as described by psychoanalytic theory, could be seen as alienating humans from their natural state. Whereas Freud had argued that sexual repression was necessary to all organized social life, this was now challenged. Reich linked sexual repression to male-dominated society in general, and to capitalism in particular. Marcuse attempted to resolve the conflict between Freudian and Marxist approaches by suggesting that Freud's theory of instinct contained a hidden theory of society which paralleled that of Marx. In *Eros and Civilization* Marcuse outlined a 'dialectic of civilization' which described history in terms of the antagonism between Eros and Thanatos (the Freudian sexual and aggressive instincts). As in Reich's earlier writings, this argument raised the possibility of a future revolutionary liberation, achieved by the triumph of Eros over Thanatos, which would end political and economic domination, together with sexual alienation.

Psychoanalytic concepts were also used to understand ideology in modern capitalist society and to explain why large sections of the population adhered to political beliefs which, from a Marxist perspective, do not represent their economic interests. The most startling example of this sort of 'false consciousness' was the support for National Socialism in Germany (see FASCISM). Reich, in *The Mass Psychology of Fascism*, argued that Marxists should understand the irrationality of fascist support in terms of a reaction to sexual repression. Fromm, who was like Reich a practising psychoanalyst, agreed that ideology should be examined in terms of its unconscious roots, but he laid less stress on sexuality. He discussed (1942) the prejudices of the fascist supporter in terms of authoritarian and sado-masochistic tendencies, which, he argued, were widespread in advanced capitalism, particularly among the petty bourgeoisie. Fromm's description of the underlying psychology of the fascist personality resembles Sartre's portrayal of anti-Semitism. Like Fromm, Sartre was critical of orthodox psychoanalytic explanations, which concentrated upon repressed sexuality, but he accepted the basic idea that the prejudiced person projects inner psychic conflicts onto innocent victims. Fromm's account also resembles the analysis of *The Authoritarian Personality*, in which Adorno, under the general guidance of Horkheimer, collaborated with American psychologists in order to investigate the psychological roots of prejudice and anti-Semitism. In such studies of prejudice, the psychological themes are often more obviously apparent than the specifically Marxist ones.

The use of psychoanalytically based concepts has been continued in more recent analyses of ideology. For example, Balibar has suggested that there are parallels between Marxist and Freudian approaches, pointing out the 'epistemological analogies between Marx's theoretical work and Freud's' (Althusser and Balibar 1970, p. 243). In common with other Marxist theorists, Althusser and Balibar draw upon 'unconventional' interpretations of psychoanalytic theory – in this case, they have been influenced by the work of Jacques Lacan, who stresses the linguistic, rather than primarily sexual, structure of the unconscious.

Reading

Adorno, T. W. 1951 (*1978*): 'Freudian theory and the pattern of Fascist propaganda'. In *The Essential Frankfurt School Reader*, ed. A. Arato and E. Gebhardt.

Adorno, T. W., et al. 1950: *The Authoritarian Personality*.

Freud, S. 1932: *New Introductory Lectures on Psycho-Analysis*. In *Complete Psychological Works*, vol. 22.

Fromm, E. 1942: *Fear of Freedom*.

— 1971: *The Crisis of Psychoanalysis: Essays on Freud, Marx and Social Psychology*.

Marcuse, H. 1955 (*1966*): *Eros and Civilization*.

Reich, W. 1942 (*1975*): *The Mass Psychology of Fascism*.

Sartre, J. P. 1948: *Portrait of the Anti-Semite*.

Trotsky, L. 1973a: *Problems of Everyday Life and Other Writings on Culture and Science*.

MICHAEL BILLIG

psychology   Marx's and Engels's comments on psychology and the study of human consciousness form part of their general criticism of idealism and their defence of materialism. In the German Ideology they argued that the way people think and feel must be examined from a materialist view of society, for 'life is not determined by consciousness, but consciousness by life' (vol. I, pt. I, A). This position assumes that man has a changing psychological nature and that, as society develops, new forms of consciousness emerge. Thus, Marx in the *Economic and Philosophical Manuscripts* suggested that 'the history of industry' was 'the open book of man's essential powers, the perceptibly existing human psychology', and went on to state that any psychology which ignored the historical development of industry 'cannot become a genuine, comprehensive and real science' (Third Manuscript).

The criticism of idealist psychology also involved attacking metaphysical notions of consciousness as unscientific. Engels emphasized that mental states had a material basis in physiology. For example, he asserted that 'we simply cannot get away from the fact that everything that sets men acting must find its way through their brains' and in this way 'the influences of the external world upon man express themselves in his brain, [and] are reflected therein as feelings, thoughts, impulses, volitions' (*Ludwig Feuerbach*, ch. II).

This physiological theme was taken up by Lenin in his criticisms of idealist philosophy; according to Lenin, 'the scientific psychologist has discarded philosophical theories of the soul and set about making a direct study of the material substratum of psychical phenomena – the nervous processes' (1894, p. 144). In *Materialism and Empirio-Criticism* (which was written in 1908 and was to have an immense effect on the development of Soviet psychology) Lenin specifically attacked Wilhelm Wundt, who was one of the principal founders of experimental psychology in Germany, and accused him of adhering 'to the confused idealist position' (p. 58). In his discussion of perception, Lenin claimed that sensations were a reflection of the external world and suggested that psychologists should describe this process in purely physical terms: 'you must . . . simply say that colour is the result of the action of a physical object on the retina' (p. 52).

The need to develop an empirical psychology based upon Marxist principles was recognized by leading Russian theorists in the years following the Revolution. At that time there were a number of different schools of psychology in Russia, but a pattern for future developments was set in 1921, when Lenin signed an edict giving I. P. Pavlov special privileges. Throughout the Stalinist period, Pavlovian psychology was encouraged at the expense of other theories, the culminating point being reached in 1950 when Pavlovianism was declared to be the sole acceptable psychological approach for Marxism-Leninism.

Pavlov (1850–1936) studied behaviour in terms of reflexes and physiological processes. His most famous work, conducted before the Revolution, had shown that the natural response (unconditioned reflex) of dogs to salivate when presented with food could be generalized (become a conditioned reflex), so that dogs would salivate to the sound of a bell, if bell and food had been previously presented together sufficiently often. Pavlov banned the use of mentalistic concepts (such as *thinking, feeling, anticipating*, etc.) from his laboratory and sought to explain human consciousness in terms of conditioned and unconditioned reflexes. He argued

in favour of 'basing the phenomena of psychical activity on physiological facts, i.e. of uniting the physiological with the psychological, the subjective with the objective' (1932, p. 409).

In addition to being attracted to the physiological materialism of Pavlov's approach, the Soviet authorities also praised Pavlov for his belief in the 'extraordinary plasticity' and 'immense potentialities' of human beings; they saw an affinity between their own efforts to create a new type of society and Pavlov's belief that 'nothing is immobile, unyielding; everything can always be attained, changed for the better, if only the proper conditions are created' (p. 447). A similar belief in human plasticity was shared by American behaviourist psychology, which, nevertheless, has been consistently criticized in the Soviet Union.

While there was official encouragement in the USSR for Pavlov, who neither joined the Communist Party nor related his psychology to Marxist philosophy, the works of other psychologists, who deliberately sought to create a Marxist psychology, were suppressed. For example, the theories of L. S. Vygotsky (1896–1934) were officially branded as 'idealist' in 1936. Vygotsky had criticized the physiological emphasis of 'reflexology', and had argued that Marxists should not consider humans as merely reacting to the external environment, but should also take into account how humans actively create their environment, which in turn gives rise to new forms of consciousness. Particularly in his pioneering studies of children's thought, Vygotsky sought to create a psychology which would be 'subject to all the premises of historical materialism' (1934, p. 51), and he stressed that social and historical factors combine to produce in language a tool which guides thought.

Since the death of Stalin, the influence of Pavlov has declined in the USSR (and more latterly within Chinese psychology as well), whereas Vygotsky's theories, as developed by his pupils A. R. Luria and A. N. Leontiev, have increased in importance. The concept of 'activity' has replaced the concept of 'reflex' and is now a dominant feature of Soviet psychology, affecting all levels of analysis from physiological to social psychology. Although Western psychologists might tend to use different theoretical concepts, much of the empirical work of psychologists such as Vygotsky and Luria has been internationally accepted.

In the West the work of Soviet psychologists has not led to the development of a specifically Marxist psychology. Those Western Marxists with an interest in psychology have tended either to turn towards PSYCHOANALYSIS or to concentrate upon demonstrating the limitations of Western psychology. For example, much criticism has been directed against the hereditarian tradition of Western psychology which views the achievements of individuals and ethnic groups as reflecting innate, biological capacities, rather than social conditions. However, within Western psychology, it is not only Marxist theorists who argue that such psychological theories are racist and elitist in their presuppositions and faulty from a scientific viewpoint; in consequence the criticisms of particular Western schools of thought are frequently not undertaken from a psychological perspective which is specifically Marxist. (See also DARWINISM; HUMAN NATURE; SCIENCE.)

Reading

Billig, M. 1982: *Ideology and Social Psychology.*

Brown, L. B. ed. 1981: *Psychology in Contemporary China.*

Joravsky, D. 1977: 'The Mechanical Spirit: the Stalinist Marriage of Pavlov to Marx'.

Kozulin, A. 1984: *Psychology in Utopia: Toward a Social History of Soviet Psychology.*

Lenin, V. I. 1908 (1962): *Materialism and Empirio-Criticism.*

McLeish, J. 1975: *Soviet Psychology: History, Theory and Content.*

Pavlov, I. P. 1932 (1958): *Experimental Psychology and Other Essays.*

Rahmani, L. 1973: *Soviet Psychology: Philosophical, Theoretical and Experimental Issues.*

Sève, L. 1974 (1978): *Man in Marxist Theory and the Psychology of Personality.*

Vygotsky, L. S. 1934 (1986): *Thought and Language.*

Wertsch, J. V. ed. 1981: *The Concept of Activity in Soviet Psychology.*

MICHAEL BILLIG

Q

quality and quantity. *See* dialectics.

R

race   The concepts of race and race relations are necessarily ones which raise doubts among Marxist sociologists. On the one hand they seem to suggest biologistic, or at least culturalist, explanations of social and institutional phenomena. On the other hand they seem to refer to forms of social bonding in political contexts which compete with those which arise from class formations. A Marxist explanation of race as a factor in politics has therefore to address itself to the relations between what may be thought of as normal institutional relationships and class formation, and the types of situation thought of as being concerned with 'race relations'.

In fact the notion that political behaviour and political relations can be seen as having a genetic origin receives very little support among either biologists or social scientists An overall classification of the human species into races is thought to have little usefulness or relevance for explaining political differences, and even the more limited notion of biological 'populations' with a common gene-pool cannot by itself explain the actual empirical groupings which come to act politically and compete for resources. Such groupings clearly have origins of a different sort, including especially those arising from the differential relation which groups have to the means of production. It is sometimes argued more convincingly that ethnic ties, usually thought of as deriving from culture or religion, have an independent role in the development of social and political formations. Marxist sociology, however, may still argue that different ethnic groups are placed in relations of cooperation, symbiosis or conflict by the fact that as groups they have different economic and political functions.

Since Marxism was first developed in a European context and was applied to the analysis of relations to the means of production and class formation in capitalist industrial societies, it was always likely that its concepts of class and class struggle would require extension when they were applied to other societies and particularly at the colonial periphery. This is now beginning to occur and it is this type of extension of Marxist class analysis which has some leverage in relation to problems commonly thought of as problems of race and ethnicity. It is all too limited and insular a Marxism which sees class struggle as arising within limited national and ethnically homogeneous units. Capitalism always moves towards being a world-wide phenomenon and the capitalist system always has to be understood as a world economic system. Within that framework a useful unit of analysis is the world-wide empires which arose with the overseas expansion of some European powers, politically and economically, from the sixteenth to the nineteenth centuries. In such units there was no simple division of the population into a single bourgeoisie and a single proletariat, but rather the development of multifarious and different relationships to the economic and political order by all manner of ethnic and racial groups seeing themselves as having distinct and divided interests.

The notion that those social systems which did not have the characteristics of the advanced capitalist societies were 'feudal' or 'oriental' has given way among many Marxist scholars in recent times to the notion that along with the classical development of capitalism and class struggle in the North-West European metropolises from the sixteenth century onwards, there also developed two peripheries, on the one hand a 'second serfdom' within which ancient institutions took on a new subordinate role within world capitalism, and on the other hand the new forms of colonial settlement in the Americas, Asia and Africa. It was in these latter situations that the characteristic form of political interaction came to be thought of – though mainly by non-Marxists – as being a matter of race relations.

The class analysis of colonial societies is infinitely complex (see COLONIAL AND POST-COLONIAL SOCIETIES). It always has a central core that derives from the basic form of economic exploitation, which may take such forms as plantation agriculture using imported slaves or indentured workers, the enforced dependency of peasantries, and various forms of tax-farming. A further accretion of groups, however, takes place in newly constituted or reconstituted colonial societies, including freedmen, coloured people and poor whites who belong fully to neither the exploiting nor the exploited groups, secondary traders from third countries, white settlers from the metropolis who arrive as free farmers, capitalist entrepreneurs or free artisans, and the distinct cadres of missionary clergy and administrators. In the interaction between these groups there is both class struggle of one form or another within the basic structures of exploitation and a struggle between colonial estates in defence of their special interests. Since the different groups involved are usually recruited and sometimes imported from different racial, ethnic and national backgrounds the struggle between them is often seen as a race or ethnic struggle.

Superimposed on such colonial social formations, however, are other tendencies which arise from their later development. The pure colonial form, often characterized by what Max Weber called 'booty capitalism', tends to be superseded by more classical *laissez-faire* forms involving *inter alia* slave emancipation and land reform; different groups acquire political ascendancy in the move towards colonial independence; the colonial economic system becomes more or less, though always imperfectly, incorporated in a developing world capitalist system; and the forces of change and revolution are torn between national and class models of revolution. Within this changing class order the language of racial difference frequently becomes the means whereby men allocate each other to different social and economic positions. Sometimes this process of allocation takes a simple form of the classification of all individuals in one or other grouping, so that being either White or Black in the United States of America or East Indian or

Afro-Caribbean in Guyana provides a basic structuring principle, or a form in which a more fluid racial order reflects differentiation of status as in many parts of Latin America or the Caribbean.

Within one Marxist problematic of 'class-in-itself' becoming 'class-for-itself' the persistence of groupings based on race and ethnicity may sometimes be viewed as a transient form of false consciousness which will be superseded in due time by true CLASS CONSCIOUSNESS. Racial and ethnic consciousness, however, appears recalcitrant to this transformation. Such recalcitrance may not be based upon false consciousness at all, but upon a realistic understanding that the relationship of a group to the political as well as the economic order is a distinct one and that it has its own particular interests to defend. Some of the classical race relations situations in the modern world are to be found in the United States, the Republic of South Africa, and in a variety of post-colonial plural societies. In the United States the descendants of slaves have had to compete with free immigrant workers in a newly created capitalist metropolis and have had to struggle for a place within a political order based upon those free immigrant workers. In South Africa a White economy with its own internal processes of class struggle also exploits native labour through the institutions of the labour compound, the urban location and the rural reserve. In post-colonial societies like Malaysia and Guyana the descendants of workers of differing ethnic origins compete for resources and political power and influence.

The metropolitan class struggle itself, however, does not remain immune from these processes. Emigration of both entrepreneurs and workers to the opportunities on offer elsewhere leaves gaps in metropolitan society which are filled by workers from poorer countries, and particularly from the colonial periphery. The latter are often excluded from acceptance as normal workers, because of the past experiences of, and linkages with, the colonial social order. In circumstances in which a metropolitan working class has won a degree of incorporation into the prevailing order in the form of citizenship or welfare rights, the colonial worker may find himself in the position of belonging to an underclass. This may not mean, as has been suggested in the United States, a group which is a despairing mass caught up in a culture of poverty and a tangle of pathologies, but rather the emergence of independent class struggle mobilized around national, ethnic and race ideologies. On the other hand the collapse of a welfare state consensus might lead either to a perceived need by metropolitan workers to ally themselves with the ultra-exploited colonial workers, or to racist scapegoating in which the colonial workers are blamed for the loss of rights which they suffer in conditions of economic crisis.

The use of the concept of race and race relations should not, therefore, be confined to a secondary hypothesis, in which an independent element is seen as disturbing normal processes of capitalist development and class struggle, even though such a secondary hypothesis may have its uses. What the type of analysis used here suggests is that the exploitation of clearly marked groups in a variety of different ways is integral to capitalism and that ethnic groups unite and act together because they have been subjected to distinct and differentiated types of exploitation. Race relations and racial conflict are necessarily structured by political and economic factors of a more generalized sort.

Reading

Brenner, Robert 1977: 'The Origins of Capitalist Development: A Critique of Neo-Smithian Marxism'.

Cox, Oliver Cromwell 1948 (1970): Caste, Class and Race.

Mason, Philip 1970: Patterns of Domination.

Rex, John 1982: Race Relations in Sociological Theory.

Van Den Berghe, Pierre 1978: Race and Racism; A Comparative Perspective.

Wallerstein, Immanuel 1974: The Modern World System: Capitalist Agriculture and the Origins of the World Economy.

Zubaida, Sami ed. 1970: Race and Racialism.

                                        JOHN REX

realism Marx is committed to realism at two levels: (1) *simple*, commonsense *realism*, asserting the reality, independence, externality of objects; (2) *scientific realism*, asserting that the objects of scientific thought are *real structures* irreducible to the events they generate. (1) includes for Marx both the essential independence of nature and the generally extra-logical character

of existence (whether social or natural), i.e. that 'the real subject remains outside the mind, leading an independent existence' (*Grundrisse*, Introduction). (2), which both justifies and refines (1), incorporates the ideas that explanatory structures, generative mechanisms or (in Marx's favoured terminology) essential relations are (a) ontologically distinctive from, (b) normally out of phase with and (c) perhaps in opposition to the phenomena (or phenomenal forms) they generate. Thus Marx remarks that 'all science would be superfluous if the outward appearances and essences of things directly coincided' (*Capital* III, ch. 48); criticizes Ricardo's procedure of so called violent or forced abstraction, which consists in treating phenomena as the direct expression of laws, without taking account of the complex ways in which the laws and/or their effects are mediated (*Theories of Surplus Value*, chs 10–11, 13, 15–18, passim); and comments 'that in their appearances things often represent themselves in inverted form is pretty well-known in every science except political economy' (*Capital* I, ch. 19). (a)–(c) correspond to three moments of the disjuncture between the domains of the real and the actual situated in modern realist philosophy of science. Marx's criticism of the classical economists as well as his concrete historical studies show that he recognized besides: (i) the *stratification*, (ii) the *internal complexity* and (iii) *differentiation* of reality. Thus an abstraction can be faulted if it fails to grasp either the stratification or the internal complexity of a domain of reality (e.g. if it isolates a necessary connection or relation from others essential to its existence or efficacy); and the differentiation of reality allows for the possibility of the multiple determination of concrete historical events by agencies or mechanisms of (relatively or absolutely) *independent* origins, as well as for the coherence of the determining agencies or mechanisms in a common causal condition of existence or a totality.

While Marx is never seriously disposed to doubt (1), his commitment to (2) develops only gradually with his deepening investigation of the capitalist mode of production. In the *Economic and Philosophical Manuscripts* Marx, under the influence of Feuerbachian sensationalism, is critical of abstraction *per se*, and *en route* to the scientific realism of *Capital* toys with quasi-

Kantian and quasi-Leibnizian as well as Hegelian and positivist views of abstraction. Despite the abundant textual evidence for Marx's simple and scientific realism, both are controversial; the latter has only recently been recognized, and an entire tradition has interpreted Marx as rejecting the former. This begins with Lukács's rejection of any distinction between thought and being as a 'false and rigid duality' (1971, p. 204), Korsch's characterization of it as 'vulgar socialist' and Gramsci's dismissal of realism as a 'religious residue', and proceeds down to the extraordinary claims made on behalf of Marx by e.g. Kolakowski that the very existence of things 'comes into being simultaneously with their appearance as a picture in the human mind' (1958, p. 69) and Schmidt that 'material reality is from the beginning socially mediated' (1971, p. 35) and 'natural history is human history's extension backwards' (ibid. p. 46).

One reason for this is no doubt that Marx never clearly set out the theoretical distinction (towards which he is groping in the *Grundrisse* Introduction) between two kinds of object of knowledge, the *transitive* object of knowledge-production, which is a social product and actively transformed in the cognitive process, and the *intransitive* object of the knowledge produced, which is a (relatively or absolutely) independent, transfactually efficacious structure or mechanism. That is, Marx never brought into systematic relation the two dimensions in terms of which he thought of human knowledge, viz the transitive dimension of *praxis* and the intransitive dimension of *objectivity*. Because Marx's originality lay in his concepts of practice and of the labour process, it was easy for his realism to get lost or vulgarized or assimilated to that of some pre-existing philosophical tradition (e.g. Kantianism). Secondly, Marx never explicitly undertook a critique of empiricism comparable to the critique of idealism which formed his pathway from philosophy into social-historical science. The result is that Marx's scientific realism is available only in, so to speak, 'the practical state' and in a few scattered methodological asides. Moreover given Marx's own positivistic tendency (see POSITIVISM), especially in the *German Ideology*, to identify philosophy with realism or ideology as such, orthodox Marxists in the Engels mould have prematurely concluded that any realism

must be obvious or ideological, i.e. in some way pre-empt science. Thus the possibility of a transcendental realism, Lockean or Leninist in function, but critical and dialectical in form – a philosophy *for* science – has seemed, until very recently, foreclosed. Together these considerations help to account for the fact that Marxist epistemology (see KNOWLEDGE, THEORY OF) after Marx has tended to fluctuate between a vulgarized, hypernaturalist and dogmatic realism, as expressed e.g. in the dialectical materialist tradition, and some variety of epistemological idealism, normally anti-naturalist and judgementally relativist, as has been dominant in WESTERN MARXISM.

Clearly scientific realism, at the level of generality at which it is formulated, can isolate only some of the epistemically significant features of Marx's scientific practice. Thus Marx conceived the deeper reality of essential production relations, in terms of which he sought to explain the manifest phenomena of economic life and to criticize political economy, as internally contradictory, historically-developing and dependent upon the phenomenal forms and everyday activities it governed. And he understood his own practice as part of the process it studied, critically and self-reflexively engaged with it. But Marx never satisfactorily theorized the epistemological limits on any natural science-based realism; nor did he perhaps ever finally rid himself of a residual rationalism in dealing with the problems posed by the differentiation of reality.

While realism can readily ground Marx's concept of laws on tendencies, there is an epistemologically significant ambiguity in Marx's way of characterizing the laws he is investigating: sometimes, e.g. in the Preface to *Capital* I, they are seen under the aspect of tendencies working with iron necessity towards inevitable results; at other times, e.g. in the *Grundrisse*, they are seen as nothing but the alienated powers of human beings destined to be returned to them. These two notions can certainly be formally reconciled. But this raises the question of whether according to Marx one of the results towards which the logic of capitalism was leading was not precisely the dissolution of society's 'transcendentally realist' character. Such a surmise, which is given added interpretive plausibility by the peculiarly concrete nature of Marx's route to scientific realism, would not, if it turned out to be fulfilled, refute scientific realism (for in such a society the concept 'science' would lack any application to itself), but rather the thesis of an inevitable role for social science. (See also DETERMINISM; DIALECTICS; MATERIALISM; TRUTH.)

Reading

Bhaskar, Roy 1978: A Realist Theory of Science.

Gramsci, A. 1929–35 (1971): Selections from the Prison Notebooks.

Kolakowski, Leszek 1958 (1969): 'Karl Marx and the Classical Definition of Truth'. In Marxism and Beyond.

Lukács, G. 1923 (1971): History and Class Consciousness.

Mepham, J. and Ruben, D. H. eds. 1979: Issues in Marxist Philosophy, vols. I–III.

Ruben, D. H. 1977: Marxism and Materialism.

Sayer, D. 1979: Marx's Method.

Schmidt, A. 1962 (1971): The Concept of Nature in Marx.

Zelený, Jindřich 1980: The Logic of Marx.

ROY BHASKAR

reformism Reformism is best understood as one major position in a long-standing debate on the nature of the transition to socialism and on the political strategy most appropriate to its attainment. Since the 1890s at least, debate has raged within the socialist sections of the labour movements of advanced capitalism on a related set of questions to which the writings of Marx and Engels gave only the most ambiguous of answers: whether the transition to socialism could be achieved without violence; whether that transition would be a gradual and smooth process of incremental social change or one best characterized by struggle and crisis culminating in a decisive moment of social transformation; and whether its attainment was possible through the exploitation by the working class of existing political institutions (most notably the parliaments and elected executives of the bourgeois democratic state) or only by the supplementation or even replacement of those state structures by new avenues of socialist struggle and new forms of popular administration. Different packages of answers to those questions have been provided by different socialist parties

and theorists at various times since 1890, but for forty years after 1917 the choice of answers tended to be a relatively straightforward one: between a revolutionary (more properly, insurrectionary) path to socialism that derived its inspiration from Lenin; and a reformism that could be traced back to the writings of Kautsky and to the political practice of pre-1914 German Social Democracy.

It is important to distinguish reformism from the less ambitious politics of social reform. As Miliband (1977, p. 155) has observed,

there has always existed a trend in working class movements . . . towards social reform; and this is a trend which, in so far as it has no thought of achieving the wholesale transformation of capitalist society into an entirely different social order, must be sharply distinguished from the 'reformist' strategy, which has insisted that this was precisely its purpose.

It is important to recognize that insurrectionary socialists and reformists have not disagreed on the need for socialism. Their disagreement has focused instead on the manner of its attainment, and on what goes with that, 'the scale and extent of the immediate economic and social transformation' (ibid. p. 178) that the transition to it necessarily entails. For at least two generations after 1917, the revolutionary current in Western Marxism tended to see that transition as necessarily violent in character and insurrectionary in form, involving struggle outside (as well as occasionally within) existing political institutions, and culminating in the replacement of the bourgeois state by the DICTATORSHIP OF THE PROLETARIAT. The advocates of reformism, on the other hand, believed in the possibility of achieving socialism by constitutional means. They looked first to win the battle for majority control of the democratic state, then to use their position as the democratically elected government to superintend a peaceful and legal transition to socialism. It is this belief 'in the possibility of attaining socialism by gradual and peaceful reform within the framework of a neutral parliamentary State' (Anderson 1980, pp. 176–7) that constitutes the defining belief of the reformist route to socialism.

The reformist current in the socialist movements in advanced capitalist societies has been and remains a powerful one. Social democratic parties (see SOCIAL DEMOCRACY) have long made it the defining element of their strategy; and the political practice (and latterly the theorizing) of many West European communist parties has gravitated towards it in the wake of those parties' growing disenchantment with the Soviet Union and the insurrectionary route to power. Both sets of parties have been pulled to reformism by the obvious problems of that insurrectionary alternative – not least its unpopularity, its violence and its vanguardism – and by 'the extremely strong attraction which legality, constitutionalism, electoralism, and representative institutions of the parliamentary type have had for the overwhelming majority of people in the working-class movements of capitalist societies' (Miliband 1977, p. 172). But though popular, reformism too has its problems – especially the seemingly inexorable propensity of reformist parties to slide from a commitment to socialism towards the less arduous pursuit of social reforms and electoral advantage within capitalism, and the associated difficulties which even resolute reformists experience of dismantling capitalism incrementally and without precipitating reactionary violence. Far from proving an effective route to socialism, reformist parties have more normally been the crucial political mechanism through which the working class has been incorporated into a subordinate position within a strengthened bourgeois order (as in Britain, Norway, Sweden, West Germany and Austria); alternatively, on those rare occasions when they have been more resolute, they have been the harbingers, not of socialism, but of the violent suppression of workers by repressive capitalist states (as in Germany in 1933, and Chile forty years later). (On this, see Anderson 1980, p. 196.)

The contemporary dilemma of socialists in Western Europe can be said to turn still on the paradox of reformism: on the apparent unpopularity of any strategy that is not reformist, and the impossibility of effectively implementing any strategy that is. This paradox lies behind the propensity of both Left Eurocommunists and left-wing social democrats to seek a 'third way' to socialism that is neither reformist nor insurrectionary. For them, the simple search for a parliamentary majority, or for a brief period of dual power before the dismantling of the bourgeois state, has to be replaced by a strategy which seeks both a parliamentary victory and 'the unfurling of forms of direct democracy and the mushrooming of self-management bodies' (Poulantzas 1978, p. 256). For them, reformism is not 'a vice inherent in any strategy other than that of dual power', but rather 'an ever latent danger', to be avoided by struggle within and outside the State in a 'long process of transformation' (ibid. pp. 258, 263). More orthodox revolutionaries remain unconvinced, seeing in a new rhetoric the old reformist propensity to underestimate the problems of class violence and the centrality of class struggle in the transition to socialism (see Mandel 1978, pp. 167–87). The question of which of these positions, if any, is correct must remain the central issue to be resolved by socialists in Western Europe in the last years of the century.

Reading

Anderson, P. 1980: *Arguments within English Marxism*.

Claudin, F. 1979: *Eurocommunism and Socialism*.

Hodgson, G. 1977: *Socialism and Parliamentary Democracy*.

Mandel, E. 1978: *From Stalinism to Eurocommunism*.

Miliband, R. 1977: *Marxism and Politics*.

Poulantzas, N. 1978: *State, Power, Socialism*.

Salvadori, M. 1979: *Karl Kautsky and the Socialist Revolution*.

Wright, E. O. 1978: *Class, Crisis and the State*.

DAVID COATES

regulation   The 'regulation approach' was first developed in the middle of the 1970s by some French economists with Marxist origins: Michel Aglietta, Robert Boyer, Alain Lipietz. At the time, it was a reaction against the structuralist orientation of Althusser's school (see ALTHUSSER, STRUCTURALISM). Whereas this insisted on the automatic, impersonal REPRODUCTION of capitalism, the new approach emphasized the contradictory character of capitalism, the difficulty of solving contradictions between expectations and the projects of agents, and the necessity for society to construct a compromise solving its contradictions for a period of time.

'Regulation' thus denotes the way a social system reproduces itself despite and through its own contradictions. The concrete modes of regulation are subject to variations over time (through crises and social struggles). So capitalism experiences a succession of *patterns of development*, which should be analysed from three different angles:

(1) As *model (or paradigm) of industrialization*: the general principles governing the evolution of the organization of labour during the period of the model's supremacy.

(2) As *regime of accumulation*: the macroeconomic principles describing the compatibility over a prolonged period of the transformations in production conditions and in the types of use of social output.

(3) As *mode of regulation*: the way expectations and the contradictory behaviours of individual agents are adjusted to the collective principles of the regime of accumulation. These forms of adjustment may include cultural habits as well as institutional features such as laws, agreements, etc.

The regime of accumulation therefore appears as the macroeconomic *result* of the workings of the mode of regulation, *based* on a model of industrialization.

Using a term first proposed by Gramsci, regulationists labelled the hegemonic pattern of development after World War Two 'Fordism'. Its *industrial paradigm* included the Taylorist principles of rationalization through the separation between the planning and the execution of labour, plus continual mechanization. Taylorism thus achieved the 'real subordination' of labour to capital to an unprecedented degree. Yet regulationists believe that in a 'post-Fordist' model, the contradictions of the labour process could be solved through more negotiated workers' involvement. At all events, Taylorism led to dramatic gains in productivity, entailing the over-production crisis of the 1930s. The solution (increased wages) finally triumphed through World War Two, leading to a new *regime of accumulation*, characterized as follows:

(a) Mass production with polarization of skills, high productivity ' growth, growing capital–output ratio (in volume, but not in value).

(b) Constant sharing-out of value-added, hence the real income of wage-earners growing in parallel with productivity.

(c) Hence the rate of profit remained rather stable, with full employment of productive capacity and the labour force.

In other words, the 'Fordist compromise' consisted in a match between mass production and mass consumption. But what forces could finally induce individual bosses to accept that compromise, which was in conformity with their middle-term interests? This was the task of the new *mode of regulation*, which included to a greater or lesser extent:

(a) Social legislation on increasing minimum wages, and a strong collective bargaining mechanism, inducing *all* the bosses to grant annual improvements in real wages parallel to gains in national productivity.

(b) A developed welfare state granting to nearly all the population the status of consumer, even in the case of temporary or indefinitely prolonged incapacity to earn money from one's work: illness, unemployment, retirement and so on.

(c) A credit money supply regulated by central banks, issued by private banks according to the needs of the economy (and not according to a stock of gold).

As may be seen, 'Fordism' is a national-based pattern of development. After they had studied (econometrically and historically) its 'golden age', regulationists studied the reasons for its breakdown. First, the Taylorist paradigm developed its own contradictions. Second, internationalization put the mode of regulation at bay.

Later, regulationists extended their work to international regulation, current attempts to establish new patterns, and so on. Their methodology was adopted by a growing stream of scholars worldwide, including geographers, sociologists, historians, extending it to new fields. That, however, led to some misunderstandings. The *result* of the first generation of research (the 'Fordist case') is often confused with the methodology of the regulation approach. The insistence that *some* mode of regulation should exist (for a pattern of development to be stabilized) led to the idea that the mode of regulation is a *functional* requirement of capitalism. In fact, social processes 'invent' new modes of regulation and new patterns in the same movement. The insistence of regulationists on the necessity of *some* social compromise led to the idea that they are reformists. In fact, the regulationists' political positions extend from moderate social democracy to Green movements.

However, as a methodology, the regulation approach appeared to have an application wider than simply within Marxist theory. In fact, 'regulation' matters the moment 'contradiction' and 'dialectics' matter, and that is the main improvement brought to Marxism by this approach. But in a situation where Marxism is in disarray, this has led many regulationists to give up Marxism . . . and keep 'regulation'.

Reading

Aglietta, Michel 1976 (1979): *A Theory of Capitalist Regulation: The US Experience.*

Boyer, Robert 1986: *La théorie de la régulation: une analyse critique.*

Lipietz, Alain 1983: *Le monde enchanté. De la valeur à la crise inflationniste.*

— 1985: *Mirages et miracles: Problèmes de l'industrialisation dans le Tiers Monde.*

ALAIN LIPIETZ

reification   The act (or result of the act) of transforming human properties, relations and actions into properties, relations and actions of man-produced things which have become independent (and which are imagined as originally independent) of man and govern his life. Also transformation of human beings into thing-like beings which do not behave in a human way but according to the laws of the thing-world. Reification is a 'special' case of ALIENATION, its most radical and widespread form characteristic of modern capitalist society.

There is no term and no explicit concept of reification in Hegel, but some of his analyses seem to come close to it e.g. his analysis of the *beobachtende Vernunft* (observing reason), in the *Phenomenology of Mind*, or his analysis of property in his *Philosophy of Right*. The real history of the concept of reification begins with Marx and with Lukács's interpretation of Marx. Although the idea of reification is implicit already in the early works of Marx (e.g. in the *Economic and Philosophical Manuscripts*), an explicit analysis and use of 'reification' begins in his later writings and reaches its peak in the *Grundrisse*, and *Capital*. The two most concentrated discussions of reification are to be found in *Capital* I, ch. I sect. 4, and in *Capital* III, ch. 48. In the first of these, on COMMODITY FETISHISM, there is no definition of reification but basic

elements for a theory of reification are nevertheless given in a number of pregnant statements:

The mystery of the commodity form, therefore, consists in the fact that in it the social character of men's labour appears to them as an objective characteristic, a social natural quality of the labour product itself . . . The commodity form, and the value relation between the products of labour which stamps them as commodities, have absolutely no connexion with their physical properties and with the material relations arising therefrom. It is simply a definite social relation between men, that assumes, in their eyes, the fantastic form of a relation between things . . . This I call the fetishism which attaches itself to the products of labour, so soon as they are produced as commodities, and which is therefore inseparable from the production of commodities . . . To the producers the social relations connecting the labours of one individual with that of the rest appear, not as direct social relations between individuals at work, but as what they really are, thinglike relations between persons and social relations between things. . . . To them their own social action takes the form of the action of things, which rule the producers instead of being ruled by them.

In the second discussion, Marx summarizes briefly the whole previous analysis which has shown that reification is characteristic not only of the commodity, but of all basic categories of capitalist production (money, capital, profit, etc.). He insists that reification exists to a certain extent in 'all social forms insofar as they reach the level of commodity production and money circulation', but that 'in the capitalist mode of production and in capital which is its dominating category . . . this enchanted and perverted world develops still further'. Thus in the developed form of capitalism reification reaches its peak:

In capital-profit, or still better capital-interest, land-ground rent, labour-wages, in this economic trinity represented as the connection between the component parts of value and wealth in general and its sources, we have the complete mystification of the capitalist mode of production, the reification [*Verdinglichung*] of social relations and immediate coalescence of the material production relations with their historical and social determination. It is an enchanted, perverted, topsy-turvy world, in which Monsieur le Capital and Madame la Terre do their ghost-walking as social characters and at the same time directly as things. (*Capital* III, ch. 48)

As equivalent in meaning with *Verdinglichung* Marx uses the term *Versachlichung*, and the reverse of *Versachlichung* he calls *Personifizierung*. Thus he speaks about 'this personification of things and reification of the relations of production'. He regards as the ideological counterparts of 'reification' and 'personification', 'crude materialism' and 'crude idealism' or 'fetishism': 'The crude materialism of the economists who regard as the *natural properties* of things what are social relations of production among people, and qualities which things obtain because they are subsumed under these relations, is at the same time just as crude an idealism, even fetishism, since it imputes social relations to things as inherent characteristics, and thus mystifies them' (*Grundrisse*, p. 687).

Despite the fact that the problem of reification was discussed by Marx in *Capital*, published partly during his lifetime, and partly soon after his death, which was generally recognized as his master work, his analysis was very much neglected for a long time. A greater interest in the problem developed only after Lukács drew attention to it and discussed it in a creative way, combining influences coming from Marx with those from Max Weber (who elucidated important aspects of the problem in his analyses of bureaucracy and rationalization; see Löwith 1932) and from Simmel (who discussed the problem in *The Philosophy of Money*). In the central and longest chapter of *History and Class Consciousness* on 'Reification and the Consciousness of the Proletariat', Lukács starts from the viewpoint that 'commodity fetishism is a *specific* problem of our age, the age of modern capitalism' (p. 84), and also that it is not a marginal problem but 'the central structural problem of capitalist society' (p. 83). The 'essence of commodity-structure', according to Lukács, has already been clarified, in the following way: 'Its basis is that a relation between people takes on the character of a thing and thus

acquires a "phantom objectivity", an autonomy that seems so strictly rational and all-embracing as to conceal every trace of its fundamental nature: the relation between people' (p. 83). Leaving aside 'the importance of this problem for economics itself' Lukács undertook to discuss the broader question: 'how far is commodity exchange together with its structural consequences able to influence the *total* outer and inner life of society?' (p. 84). He points out that two sides of the phenomenon of reification or commodity fetishism have been distinguished (which he calls the 'objective' and the 'subjective'): '*Objectively* a world of objects and relations between things springs into being (the world of commodities and their movements on the market). . . . *Subjectively* – where the market economy has been fully developed – a man's activity becomes estranged from himself, it turns into a commodity which, subject to the non-human objectivity of the natural laws of society, must go its own way independently of man just like any consumer article.' (p. 87). Both sides undergo the same basic process and are subordinated to the same laws. Thus the basic principle of capitalist commodity production, 'the principle of rationalization based on what is and *can be calculated*' (p. 88) extends to all fields, including the worker's 'soul', and more broadly, human consciousness. 'Just as the capitalist system continuously produces and reproduces itself economically on higher levels, the structure of reification progressively sinks more deeply, more fatefully and more definitively into the consciousness of man' (p. 93).

It seems that the problem of reification was somehow in the air in the early 1920s. In the same year as Lukács's book appeared, the Soviet economist I. I. Rubin published his *Essays on Marx's Theory of Value* (in Russian; see Rubin 1972), the first part of which is devoted to 'Marx's Theory of Commodity Fetishism'. The book was less ambitious than Lukács's (concentrating on reification in economics) and also less radical; while Lukács found some place for 'alienation' in his theory of reification, Rubin was inclined to regard the theory of reification as the scientific reconstruction of the utopian theory of alienation. Nevertheless, both Lukács and Rubin were heavily attacked as 'Hegelians' and 'idealists' by the official representatives of the Third International.

The publication of Marx's *Economic and Philosophical Manuscripts* was a great support for the kind of interpretation of Marx begun by Lukács, but this was fully recognized only after the second world war. Although the discussion of reification never became as extensive and intense as that about alienation, a number of outstanding Marxists such as L. Goldmann, J. Gabel and K. Kosik have made valuable contributions to it. Not only have the works of Marx and Lukács been discussed afresh, but also Heidegger's *Being and Time*, which concludes with the following remarks and questions: 'That the ancient ontology works with "thing-concepts" and that there is a danger "of reifying consciousness" has been well known for a long time. But what does reification mean? Where does it originate from?... Why does this reification come again and again to domination? How is the Being of consciousness positively structured so that reification remains inadequate to it?' Goldmann maintained that these questions are directed against Lukács (whose name is not mentioned) and that the influence of Lukács can be seen in some of Heidegger's positive ideas.

A number of more substantial questions about reification have also been discussed. Thus there has been much controversy about the relation between reification, alienation, and commodity fetishism. While some have been inclined to identify reification either with alienation or with commodity fetishism (or with both), others want to keep the three concepts distinct. While some have regarded alienation as an 'idealist' concept to be replaced by the 'materialist' concept of 'reification', others have regarded 'alienation' as a philosophical concept whose sociological counterpart is 'reification'. According to the prevailing view alienation is a broader phenomenon, and reification one of its forms or aspects. According to M. Kangrga 'reification is a higher, that is the highest form of alienation' (1968, p. 18), and reification is not merely a concept but a methodological requirement for a critical study and practical 'change, or better the destruction of the whole reified structure' (ibid. p. 82).

Reading
Arato, Andrew 1972: 'Lukács's Theory of Reification'.
Gabel, Joseph 1962: *La réification*.
Goldmann, Lucien 1959: 'Réification'. In *Recherches dialectiques*.
Kangrga, Milan 1968: 'Was ist Verdinglichung?'
Löwith, Karl 1932 (*1982*): *Max Weber and Karl Marx*.
Lukács, Georg 1923 (*1971*): *History and Class Consciousness*.
Rubin, I. I. 1928 (*1972*): *Essays on Marx's Theory of Value*.
Schaff, Adam 1980: *Alienation as a Social Phenomenon*.
Tadić, Ljubomir 1969: 'Bureaucracy – Reified Organization'. In M. Marković and G. Petrović eds. *Praxis*.

GAJO PETROVIĆ

relations of production.   See forces and relations of production.

religion   Marx and Engels began their thinking about society in a Germany where, as Engels said later, straightforward political activity was scarcely possible, and progressive aspirations found vent largely in criticism of orthodox religion, that buttress of the social and political order (*Feuerbach*, sect. 1). Hegel's evolutionary approach to history showed that the simple materialism of the eighteenth-century philosophers was inadequate: it was not enough to suppose that CHRISTIANITY and all the other religions had been hatched by impostors (Engels, 'Bruno Bauer and Early Christianity'). What was needed, Marx wrote in his 'Critique of Hegel's Philosophy of Right: Introduction', was an analysis of the human conditions and relations that made them indispensable to mankind. Religion was an expression of man's imperfect self-awareness: not man as abstract individual, but social man, or the human collective. It was a distortion of man's being, because society was distorted. In some of Marx's most celebrated words it was the heart of a heartless world, the opium – or painkiller – of the suffering masses. The way to real happiness was for men to free themselves from the kind of life that made them crave this substitute. Self-emancipation, Marx added, was not merely desirable: it was man's *duty* to realize his highest potential by throwing off everything that kept him imperfect and degraded.

In one of the *Theses on Feuerbach* (4th thesis) Marx complained that while that liberal critic of religion recognized its earthly roots, he failed to see that it could only be uprooted by a reorganization of society. Feuerbach was not in fact desirous of getting rid of it, Engels wrote in his later study (*Feuerbach*, sect. 3), but only of reconstructing it; he viewed history as a succession of religious transformations, instead of material, social changes with religious accompaniments. In their youth at least Marx and Engels were over-optimistic about the speed or completeness with which such changes could bring enlightenment. Even industrialism in capitalist guise, they were ready to believe, could deliver those whose lives were shaped by it from religious illusions, well in advance of socialism. By commercializing all relationships, they wrote in the *German Ideology* (pt. 1, sect. 1), industry was doing its best to wipe out both religion and morality, or reduce them to a transparent lie. (Possibly a century and a half later it may be said to have made good progress in that direction.) They were too confident that religious belief could take no hold on the working class, which they were inclined to think of as more of a *tabula rasa* than it really was. All such unrealities, they held, would be dispersed by experience, rather than by argument, but the new proletariat had never suffered from them, or had by now long since shed them.

A still more striking token of trust in history's wastepaper-basket was the assertion in Marx's early essay 'On the Jewish Question' that if Jews could be relieved of the burden of their present life of huckstering, JUDAISM would quickly fade away. More deliberately in *Capital* I (ch. 1, last sect.) Marx repeated his conviction that religious delusions have no function but to throw a veil over the irrationalities of the system of production, and will come to an end when men enter into rational relations with one another and cure the social whole of its distempers.

Marx thought about religion most systematically in his youth; Engels came back to the subject repeatedly, perhaps an after-effect of a religious upbringing from which he had extricated himself not without some pangs. As a historian he found plenty of scope in his book on the Peasant War of 1524–25 in Germany to discuss the interplay of politics and religion during a revolutionary crisis. In the so-called 'religious wars' of sixteenth- and seventeenth-century Europe, he argued, as in medieval collisions between Church and heresy, the reality to

be explored was class struggle, waged over competing material interests; whereas the academic German mind could discern nothing but theological disputes, thus taking the illusions of past epochs about themselves at their face value (ch. 2). This may seem a purely negative approach to religion, but it allows for the possibility that deviant trends arising in protest against official cults are inspired by new, progressive social currents. This was so above all in the case of the Reformation.

In the last chapter of *Anti-Dühring* Engels returned to the theme of religion as a freakish projection of the forces overshadowing human existence. These were at first the powers of nature, generating a varied mythology, and later, no less alien and until lately as mysterious, the social order. He thought of the single deity of monotheism, in whom the attributes of all earlier divinities came to be gathered together, as a personification of the abstract idea of humanity. This emergence of monotheism was traced afresh in *Feuerbach* (sect. 2). Here Engels was facing the fact that religious concepts appear to stand further apart than any others from material life, and to be the most completely detached from it; also that they have not sprung directly from contemporary life, but are borrowed from a distant past. His answer was that every 'ideology', to fulfil its purpose – to satisfy us with ideas to the exclusion of reality – must necessarily develop out of inherited, long-cherished materials. But the changes that religious ideas go through respond to shifts in social conditions and class relations.

Early socialists in Eastern Europe were surrounded by a vast peasant population, steeped most deeply in Russia in religiosity of a peculiarly superstitious sort which had always been very much at the service of the tsars. A diversity of other Christian cults and non-Christian religions in the tsarist empire helped to complicate the situation. A determined struggle against all religion seemed essential for progress. Hence Plekhanov's uncompromising stand on the strictest materialism, and his admiration for what he called the finest flowering of materialistic thought, in the writings of the eighteenth-century *philosophes*; he fully agreed with an early dictum of Engels that religion had exhausted all its possibilities (*Materialismus Militans*, pp. 13, 20). But his environment made it easier for him to see that it could still have a strong retrogressive influence on working-class strata, not yet fully class-conscious. He was indignant at the drift of some prominent progressives, after the failure of the revolution of 1905, into a sort of mysticism brought on by lassitude and disillusion, which took the form of the 'God-building' associated especially with Lunacharsky.

This was a matter of still more serious concern to Lenin. Engels had warned against the folly of trying to abolish religion by compulsion, as some Blanquist members of the Paris Commune had wanted to do ('Programme of the Blanquist Commune Refugees'). Lenin agreed, but he was aware that religious infection was not limited to recreant intellectuals, but could be found among some workers, unnerved by the blind energies of capitalism which chronically menaced them with unforeseeable calamities. Religion should be a private matter, he wrote (26 May 1909), so far as the state was concerned; it could not be so for a socialist party, but this did not mean that believers were banned from membership if they were also *bona fide* socialists. Atheism had no place in the party programme. Since the hold of religion rested on the play of economic forces, the working class could not be protected against it by declarations, but only by the struggle against capitalism, and unity in this was of far more moment than unanimity over the affairs of heaven ('The Attitude of the Workers' Party to Religion', CW 15). There may be a certain difference of emphasis in Stalin's statement in 1913 that the party should defend the free exercise of their faiths by all communities, but must denounce all religion as an obstacle to progress (*Marxism and the National Question*, sect. 6).

When the party came to power in Russia this obstacle was felt more concretely. In his *Historical Materialism* Bukharin took a forceful line on it, theoretical and practical. He dismissed, as Marxism may always have been too ready to do, the alternative or supplementary derivation of religion from man's condition as individual, his fear of death as well as of life, and, in early times, of departed spirits (p. 172). It was only logical, Bukharin argued, for a young and revolutionary working class to be materialist in outlook, just as it was for a senile ruling class to sink into religious torpor (p. 58). He ridiculed the celes-

tial hierarchy of the Orthodox Church as a close parallel to the tsarist bureaucracy, with St Michael as commander-in-chief of the angelic hosts (p. 176). But religion must be opposed actively; there was no sense in waiting for anything to die out of its own accord (p. 180). Inevitably a tendency grew for believers to be considered of dubious loyalty to the new order, and unfit for responsible positions.

Tentative explorations of the religious past by Marx and Engels were soon being followed up by their successors, notably by Kautsky in the field of early Christian history. Pannekoek (1938, pp. 26–7) among others made much of the brevity of the bourgeoisie's attachment to materialism, its philosophy during its period of coming to the front; it was scared off by the eruption of mass discontent during the French Revolution, and fell back on religion as a means of keeping the masses in their place. Such a volte-face, Marxists held, was something that their dialectical view of history could explain, as the old simple materialist outlook could not. They were looking further back too, into the beginnings of religion as well as of a particular religion like Christianity. In the early part of his work (1906) on the evolution of ethics Kautsky was intrigued as Engels had been by the coming of monotheist and moralizing creeds out of the cults of the old amoral deities. In this field of prehistory or anthropology Marxism has since made a decided mark. It has been observed that the Durkheim school has had much in common with it, but that instead of taking the social structure as a given fact Marxism thinks in terms of developing processes of interaction between men and their environment. The same commentator adds that in practice both schools have allowed for more autonomy of religious evolution than their stricter formulae might seem to admit (Robertson 1972, pp. 19, 21).

Marx and Engels were led by their growing interest in the world outside Europe to speculate about other faiths than the Christian. Oriental history, Marx noted, often seemed to wear the appearance of a history of religions (letter to Engels, 2 June 1853). In one of his articles on India (June 1853) he made a suggestive point by saying that proximity in India of luxurious wealth and abject poverty was reflected in HINDUISM with its medley of 'sensualist exuberance' and 'self-torturing asceticism'. He remarked too that helpless dependence on Nature could find expression in worship of nature-gods or animals. Later Marxists have followed up this interest in the character of other religions, particularly ISLAM.

Some regions outside Europe have now for a good many years had Marxists of their own to examine their record. In India these have often been drawn to the study of ancient times, and of both Brahminism and Buddhism. A thoroughgoing iconoclasm made Kosambi (1962, p. 17) tax the country's best-loved and immensely influential scripture, the Gita, with 'dexterity in seeming to reconcile the irreconcilable', and 'slippery opportunism'. Chattopadhyaya (1969) emphasizes the strong materialist tradition that was part of India's thinking in its best times, and writes of Jainism and Buddhism as in origin atheist philosophies, overlaid in course of time by the superstitions with which India was always rife. More Marxist investigation of later times might have been expected, but communal tensions have made this delicate ground. It must be confessed that Indian communists before the partition in 1947 failed, like the equally secularist Nehru, to comprehend the enormous destructive force of religious animosities. In China the path-finding Marxist historian Kuo Mo-jo associated ancestor-worship in antiquity with the advent of private property, and the worship of a supreme deity with that of a central political authority which required heavenly warrant (Dirlik 1978, pp. 150, 156). It may indeed be said that, like Marx at the outset of his intellectual life, Marxism has found in the historical scrutiny of religion one of its most stimulating tasks.

Reading

Bukharin, Nikolai 1921 (1925): *Historical Materialism: A System of Sociology.*

Chattopadhyaya, Debiprasad 1969: *Indian Atheism: A Marxist Approach.*

Dirlik, Arif 1978: *Revolution and History. The Origins of Marxist Historiography in China, 1919–1937.*

Kosambi, D. D. 1962: *Myth and Reality; Studies in the Formation of Indian Culture.*

Lenin, V. I. 1909 (1963): 'The Attitude of the Workers' Party towards Religion' (26 May 1909).

Pannekoek, Antonie 1938 (1948): *Lenin as Philosopher.*

Robertson, Roland 1972: *The Sociological Interpretation of Religion.*

Seliger, Martin 1977: *The Marxist Conception of Ideology.*

Thomson, George 1941: *Aeschylus and Athens. A Study in the Social Origins of the Drama.*
                                          V. G. KIERNAN

Renner, Karl   Born 14 December 1870, Unter-Tannowitz, Moravia; died 31 December 1950, Vienna. After completing his secondary school education Renner joined the army in order to support himself until he could continue his studies, and subsequently studied law at the University of Vienna. As a student he became involved in social democratic politics and participated in the first great May Day demonstration of 1893. His military service acquainted him with the great variety of nationalities in the Austro-Hungarian Empire and aroused his strong interest in the problem of nationality, on which some of his earliest works were written. His legal studies were primarily in the theory and sociology of law, and his book on the social functions of law (1904), which was a pioneering Marxist study in this field, has remained a classic. During the first world war and afterwards Renner came to be regarded as the leader of the more reformist right wing of the SPÖ in opposition to Otto Bauer who led the dominant left wing. From 1916, when he published a series of essays on 'problems of Marxism', Renner was particularly concerned with revising the Marxist theory of the state (to take account of massive state intervention in the economy) and of class (to deal with the question of the 'new middle classes', or what he termed the 'service class'). In 1918 he became the first Chancellor (later President) of the Austrian Republic, and in 1945 was again President of the second Republic. (See AUSTRO-MARXISM.)

Reading

Hannak, Jacques 1965: *Karl Renner und seine Zeit.*

Renner, Karl 1902: *Der Kampf der Österreichischen Nationen um der Staat.*

— 1904 (1949): *The Institutions of Private Law and their Social Functions.*

— 1916: 'Probleme des Marxismus'. In *Der Kampf*, vol. ix.
                                          TOM BOTTOMORE

rent. *See* landed property and rent.

reproduction

Whatever the social form of the production process, it has to be continuous, it must periodically repeat the same phases. A society can no more cease to produce than it can cease to consume. When viewed, therefore as a connected whole, and in the constant flux of its incessant renewal, every social process of production is at the same time a process of reproduction. (Marx, *Capital* I, ch. 23)

Reproduction therefore involves both production and the setting up of conditions whereby production can continue to take place. But the scope of those 'conditions under which' and their relation to the mode of production have given rise to substantial debate about the meaning of reproduction among Marxists in recent years. On the one hand, it has been claimed that processes which are necessary to the reproduction of capitalist production relations must be included in the economic base, and implicitly therefore form part of the mode of production itself. On the other hand, it has been argued that reproduction depends on processes which lie outside the mode of production and that it is their relative autonomy which makes the reproduction of any mode of production problematic, contingent and hence the possible object of class struggle.

Marx's exposition of simple and extended reproduction (see REPRODUCTION SCHEMA) tended to concentrate on the reproduction of the capital–labour relation itself, as the nexus of exploitation under capitalism. For since any mode of production must be capable of continued existence if it is to characterize an epoch of history, those conditions which allow production to take place must also allow for their reproduction. But the consideration of reproduction puts the relations of production in a different light. Thus even simple reproduction, in which all surplus value is consumed by the capitalist class and not accumulated, although it is just a continuous repetition of the production process allows some misleading characteristics of the single circuit of production to disappear and the full exploitative character of the relation between capital and the working class as a

whole to become apparent. For the continued extraction of surplus value, for which the repetition of the capitalist production process provides, ensures that, however a capital was initially obtained, it eventually consists entirely of accumulated surplus value. It is from this characteristic of capitalist reproduction that Marx drew the conclusion: 'Therefore the worker himself constantly produces objective wealth in the form of capital, an alien power that dominates and exploits him' (ibid.). While this statement is not strictly true for every individual worker, nor for every individual circuit of capital, it becomes true for the working class as a whole as soon as the reproduction process is considered.

But Marx is clear that not only does labour create capital but, as this passage continues: 'the capitalist just as constantly produces labour-power, in the form of a subjective source of wealth which is abstract, exists merely in the physical body of the worker, and is separated from its own means of objectification and realization; in short, the capitalist produces the worker as wage-labourer' (ibid.). Here it is the relation in which the wage labourer as seller of labour power confronts capital which is 'produced' by the capitalist. And this too is revealed by consideration of repeated circuits rather than a single circuit of production. For workers must spend the wages received at the end of one period of production to replace their now consumed labour power. They are therefore reproduced in the same position as before, separated from the means of production with only that 'subjective source of wealth', their labour power, to sell.

So putting the reproduction of capital and of labour power together: 'The capitalist process of production, therefore, seen as a total, connected process, i.e. a process of reproduction, produces not only commodities, not only surplus-value, but it also produces and reproduces the capital relation itself; on the one hand the capitalist, on the other the wage-labourer' (ibid.).

Other writings of Marx, and those of later Marxists, have extended the concept of reproduction to encompass processes outside that of production itself, which are seen as necessary to the continued existence of a mode of production. Marx gives an example of how, in order to ensure the reproduction of 'its' labour force, capital was prepared to use political means to prevent the emigration of skilled workers in times of high unemployment (see POPULATION). And in the Introduction to the *Grundrisse* he talks of the process of 'social reproduction', of which production is to be seen as only one moment. But this passage, which forms part of his methodological discussion of political economy, is sufficiently vague to leave unspecified *which* processes have to be reproduced in order that social reproduction takes place. And it is around this issue that debates have turned, both about the basic processes of a mode of production without whose reproduction it would cease to exist, and about which (possibly) other processes are necessary to carry out that reproduction successfully.

The distinction between these two types of processes can be seen as an elaboration of the classical Marxist distinction between BASE AND SUPERSTRUCTURE; here the 'superstructural' elements are those in practice necessary to the reproduction of, but not definitionally part of, the 'base'. Thus the superstructural elements could take different forms without changing the MODE OF·PRODUCTION, but such forms would be constrained by the need to ensure the reproduction of the basic processes. Thus, for example, ideological processes, such as those which justify the freedom of the individual to exchange and own property are necessary to the continuation of the capitalist mode of production, but are not part of its definition which depends on economic relations alone, and other ideologies e.g. those of corporatism, may at times take their place. It is easy to see how this view of reproduction has difficulty escaping the charge of functionalism for it reads as though modes of production exist only to reproduce themselves, and if they need to call upon the resources of other non-economic processes these will automatically perform their teleological duty (see Clarke *et al.* 1980; Edholm *et al.* 1977).

Balibar's formulation hardly escapes this charge, though it does encompass the possibility of change (Althusser and Balibar 1970). For him, there are three instances or practices, the economic, the ideological and the political, *all* of which have to be reproduced so that the structured totality which is the mode of production can be reproduced. This does allow for variation

and relative autonomy in how each level is reproduced, but the levels remain fixed and the possibility of change results from contradiction at the economic level. A situation may be overdetermined, that is involve contradictions at more than one level, but these must include the economic as determinant in the last instance if fundamental change is to result. Thus for Althusser and Balibar, reproduction and contradiction occur at different structural levels. The former results from the working of the whole mode of production, the latter can be pinpointed at the level of specific practices, of which the economic is crucial.

Following on from this, post-Althusserians critical of this concept of reproduction, replaced it first with the notion of conditions of existence under which given relations of production can operate (Hindess and Hirst 1977) and then demoted the relations of production from such a 'privileged' position within this schema, widening the area within which social reproduction takes place and refusing to give it any specific boundary (Friedman 1976; Cutler *et al.* 1977).

Feminists (see FEMINISM) have criticized the traditional Marxist view of reproduction for ignoring much of the process by which people and their labour power are reproduced, thus missing out a crucial component of social reproduction. This has taken place on two levels; first that of the reproduction of labour power both in a daily and a generational sense, and second that of human or biological reproduction, which the recognition of people as more than just potential suppliers of labour power distinguishes from the first. On the former, writings on DOMESTIC LABOUR have demonstrated how the transformation of the wage into labour power is not merely a process of consumption, for labour power does not result from the direct consumption of money but involves labour and the production of use values, which takes place under relations of production essential to the continued existence of capitalism but distinct from those of wage-labour for capital.

But the reproduction of labour power is also an intergenerational process and new human beings must be reproduced too. Under capitalism, where producers are separated from the means of production, the process of production of babies is separated from that of use values. The implications of this separation are the subject of debate as to whether the reproduction of people is inherently indeterminate under capitalism (O'Laughlin 1977), or a labour process with its own connected laws of motion involving relations of control of women as biological reproducers different from those to which they are subject as producers (Edholm *et al.* 1977, Meillassoux 1975).

Consideration of human reproduction *per se* has led some authors to suggest that any society must contain a historically specific mode of reproduction articulated with or parallel to its mode of production (e.g. Rubin (1975) talks about a 'political economy of sex'). Engels indeed suggests as much in his oft-quoted statement:

> According to the materialist conception, the determining factor in history is, in the last resort, the production and reproduction of immediate life. But this itself is of a twofold character. On the one hand, the production of the means of subsistence, of food, clothing and shelter and the tools requisite for it; on the other, the production of human beings themselves, the propagation of the species.
> (*Origin of the Family*, Preface to 1st edn)

but he failed to take his own prescription seriously and totally subordinated the forms of reproduction to those of production in his account of the development of family forms. Indeed, despite stated intentions to the contrary, both Marx and Engels appear to have taken human reproduction to be an essentially natural process that is not subject to conscious human agency (Himmelweit forthcoming).

Others would suggest that this separation is a mistake, a fetishism which naturalizes categories specific to the forms of reproduction under capitalism rather than being a transhistorical duality (Edholm *et al.* 1977). Since sexual difference turns upon different potential roles in human reproduction, the integration of an understanding of GENDER divisions, the social form through which sexual difference is expressed, with that of class divisions, to which production relations give rise, can only be achieved by recognizing the very separation between reproduction and production, between the production of human beings and the production of things, as itself a social form and thus subject to change (Himmelweit 1984).

Only on this basis could an analysis unifying the aims of feminist and socialist movements be achieved.

Reading

Althusser, L. and Balibar, É. 1970: *Reading 'Capital'*.

Clarke, S. *et al.* 1980: *One-Dimensional Marxism*.

Cutler, A. *et al.* 1977: *Marx's Capital and Capitalism Today*.

Edholm, F. *et al.* 1977: 'Conceptualising Women'.

Friedman, J. 1976: 'Marxist Theory and Systems of Total Reproduction'.

Himmelweit, S. 1984: 'The Real Dualism of Sex and Class'.

— forthcoming: 'Reproduction and the Materialist Conception of History: A Feminist Critique'. In T. Carver ed. *Cambridge Companions to Philosophy: Marx*.

Hindess, B. and Hirst, P. 1977: *Mode of Production and Social Formation*.

Meillassoux, C. 1975 (1981): *Maidens, Meal and Money: Capitalism and the domestic community*.

O'Laughlin, B. 1977: 'Production and Reproduction: Meillassoux's *Femmes, Greniers et Capitaux*'.

Rubin, G. 1975: 'The Traffic in Women'. In Reiter, ed. *Toward an Anthropology of Women*.

SUSAN HIMMELWEIT

reproduction schema In *Capital* II (chs. 18–21), Marx investigates the reproduction of the different parts of the aggregate social capital, which is not merely a reproduction of value magnitudes but at the same time also a *material* reproduction; the relation between the two reproductions is studied within the schema. Marx divides the social production into two departments: (1) Production of means of production; (2) Production of means of consumption. As a consequence, the movements of the social capital are analysed under the assumption that it consists of two capitals only. This necessary abstraction makes clear that, albeit they are an indispensable basis, the reproduction schema cannot be sufficient to analyse the interaction among the manifold individual capitals, this inquiry belonging to the theory of COMPETITION at a more concrete level of analysis. Marx classified reproduction into two types: *simple* and *extended* reproduction. Simple reproduction implies that the entire surplus value is unproductively consumed by capitalists (e.g. is totally spent to purchase consumption goods); extended reproduction means accumulation, where a given fraction of the total surplus value is employed to purchase additional capital, variable and constant, in order to increase the existing scale of production.

Marx bases his study of reproduction on a certain number of assumptions, not all of them strictly necessary: (1) constant and equal ORGANIC COMPOSITION OF CAPITAL (c/v) and rates of surplus value (s/v); (2) commodities are exchanged at their values; (3) constant productivity; (4) the capitalists dispose of unlimited reserves of labour power. Now, writing 1 and 2 as the indices of the two departments of production which respectively produce means of production and consumption goods, we have

$$c_1 + v_1 + s_1 = w_1 \text{ and } c_2 + v_2 + s_2 = w_2$$

with

$$c = c_1 + c_2, v = v_1 + v_2, s = s_1 + s_2$$

as the social aggregates.

In Paul Sweezy's words (1942) since S is entirely consumed rather than accumulated by capitalists in Simple Reproduction

the constant capital used up must be equal to the output of the producers' goods branch, and the combined consumption of capitalists and workers must be equal to the output of the consumers' goods branch. This means that

$$c_1 + c_2 = c_1 + v_1 + s_1$$
$$v_1 + s_1 + v_2 + s_2 = c_2 + v_2 + s_2$$

By eliminating c_1, from both sides of the first equation and $v_2 + s_2$ from both sides of the second equation, it will be seen that the two reduce to the following single equation:

$$c_2 = v_1 + s_1$$

This, then, may be called the basic condition of Simple Reproduction. It says simply that the value of the constant capital used up in the consumption goods branch must be equal to the value of the commodities consumed by the workers and capitalists engaged in producing means of production. If this condition is satisfied, the scale of production remains unchanged from one year to the next (pp. 76–77).

This equation expresses a condition that *must* be fulfilled in order to secure the reproduction of the total social capital on the same scale.

The situation becomes more complex when we deal with extended reproduction as we have now to insert into the formulas for the product of the two Departments the fraction of surplus value employed for capital accumulation ($\triangle c + \triangle v$). If we assume, as a first hypothesis, that *all* the surplus value is converted into capital (*maximum expanded reproduction*) then each Department uses its own surplus value entirely for its own accumulation, that is:

$$s_1 = \triangle c_1 + \triangle v_1, s_2 = \triangle c_2 + \triangle v_2$$

hence:

$$c_1 + v_1 + \triangle c_1 + \triangle v_1 = w_1$$
$$c_2 + v_2 + \triangle c_2 + \triangle v_2 = w_2$$

Since the two organic compositions c_1/v_1 and c_2/v_2 are assumed constant, the two ratios $\triangle c_1/\triangle v_1$ and $\triangle c_2/\triangle v_2$ must also be constant, so that constant proportions of the surplus value will be transformed into variable and constant capital. Let us posit these proportions as k_v and k_c respectively (one must obviously have $k_v + k_c = 1$). The two formulas now appear as follows:

$$c_1 + v_1 + k_c s_1 + k_v s_1 = w_1$$
$$c_2 + v_2 + k_c s_2 + k_v s_2 = w_2$$

What are now the new value magnitudes put on the market to be exchanged? Since the entire s is accumulated, Dept. 1 must sell the quantities v_1 and $k_v s_1$ whereas it consumes the quantities c_1 and $k_c s_1$ (all of these being means of production). Dept. 2 in turn must put on the market the magnitudes c_2 and $k_c s_2$ while consuming v_2 and $k_v s_2$, all of them being means of consumption. In this way we obtain the equation which expresses the relation between the Departments when expanded reproduction takes place at its maximum rate (that is, if capitalists invest all their profits):

$$v_1 + k_v s_1 = c_2 + k_c s_2$$

We have now to relax the hypothesis of a full accumulation of the surplus value, allowing the capitalists to consume a part of their own profits. The proportion of the surplus value consumed by capitalists must now have a place in the equation, in such a way that $(k_c + k_v) < 1$. The new equations are:

$$c_1 + v_1 + k_c s_1 + k_v s_1 + (1 - k_c - k_v) s_1 = w_1$$
$$c_2 + v_2 + k_c s_2 + k_v s_2 + (1 - k_c - k_v) s_2 = w_2$$

From the equations above it is easy to deduce the fundamental exchange relation of the enlarged reproduction:

$$v_1 + k_v s_1 + (1 - k_c - k_v) s_1 = c_2 + k_c s_2$$

which reduces to

$$v_1 + s_1 (1 - k_c) = c_2 + k_c s_2$$

Once the consumption of a part of the surplus value by capitalists is introduced, there is no further reason to assume equal ratios of accumulation, k_v and k_c, for the two Departments. Then we can differentiate k_c into k_{c1} and k_{c2}, and k_v into k_{v1} and k_{v2}. Thus the fundamental exchange relation becomes:

$$v_1 + s_1 (1 - k_{c1}) = c_2 + k_{c2} s_2$$

The above equation is relevant as it shows a major result of Marx's analysis of the reproduction process: reproduction itself is not compatible with an arbitrary choice of the two accumulation rates k_{c1} and k_{c2}. The two of them must be consistent with each other, or else the reproduction process will be obstructed.

The fundamental relation of expanded reproduction shows how the social aggregate capital *can* grow without any problem of market and effective demand. This possibility can be extended to cover the case of fixed capital, and even more importantly, it is also possible to introduce both increases in productivity and changes in organic composition of capital and rates of surplus value. With such changes all major variables become functions of time, which make the conditions for balance considerably stricter. (For the case of reproduction with fixed capital see Glombowski 1976.)

Some theorists hold that Marx's reproduction schema are somehow analogous to Keynes's theory of effective demand, since the latter too is founded upon the subdivison of the social output between I (capital goods) and C (consumption goods). But this is a purely superficial similarity which obscures deep differences. Keynes, concentrating on the demand side, does not investigate the conditions of reproduction, the conditions for balance between the two Departments, and he does not take into consideration the necessary reproduction of the consumed constant capital (following the tradition of Adam Smith). Lastly, it can be shown that neither Keynes's analysis of the state (where the

value appropriated by the state appears to originate outside the production process), nor his discussion of secular stagnation due to a decline in the propensity to consume, are compatible with Marx's analysis of reproduction and accumulation. (For a different view, see Tsuru 1968, and for a critique of this approach, Bettelheim 1948. See also KEYNES AND MARX.)

A discussion of the schema long engaged outstanding Marxist thinkers, among them Luxemburg, Hilferding, Bauer, Lenin, Grossman and Rosdolsky. The entire debate is accurately summarized by Rosdolsky (1980) who pointed out that reproduction schema are nothing but a *first approximation* to the concrete interaction of the single capitals, the scope of which is only to show the relationship between value and use value within the reproduction of capital. Nonetheless, Rosdolsky added the unjustified idea that it is impossible to introduce into the schema changes in productivity, organic composition and rate of surplus value.

Two of the most important contributions to the study of reproduction came from Luxemburg and Hilferding. Luxemburg (1913) put forward a twofold criticism of Marx's schema. First, she regarded as a mistake the lack, within the schema, of a third Department for the production of gold, the commodity which serves as money, which is neither a means of production nor a consumption good but a simple means of circulation. Hence, she proposed a new schema divided into three Departments, where Dept. 3 produces the quantity of gold which is yearly consumed for the circulation process. There is still a shortcoming however; the necessary exchanges cannot be carried on in this way since they need all the existing amount of gold, not only the quantity produced in the last year. The production and the consumption of gold form part of the so-called *faux frais* of capitalist production, and this is why Marx inserts gold production into Dept. 1, together with the other metals; gold considered as money has no direct role for the reproduction of the social capital. More interesting is Luxemburg's second critique, concerning effective demand. She remarks that in the numerical examples given by Marx the rate of accumulation of Dept. 2 seems to vary in an arbitrary way according to the necessities of accumulation of Dept. 1, with no possibility of seeing the origin of the *increasing demand* which allows the realization of the social surplus value. According to Luxemburg the schema *must* show this demand deficit; the additional effective demand must originate outside the schema, i.e. *outside the capitalist system*, so that capitalists are obliged to look continuously for new markets in the non-capitalist world. Yet she is unable to explain in turn the source of the exchange-value offered by the non-capitalist world against the commodities of the two Departments. By generalizing Marx's simple numerical examples it is easy to see that the growing demand originates inside the two Departments themselves, and this is independent of the smooth course of the reproduction process in practice.

Hilferding (1910) tried to employ the schema for an explanation of crisis phenomena. He argued that the critical point for capital reproduction is how to secure a balanced growth between the two sectors, which is actually realized only through a continuous process of price adjustments. This can be only temporary; since investments are much larger in Dept. 1, where the organic composition is usually higher, the entire process must end in periodical interruptions of accumulation in order to restore the violated balance conditions. What is unclear in Hilferding's position is the mechanism which would necessarily provoke an imbalance between the productions of Dept. 1 and Dept. 2 as a consequence of different amounts of accumulated capital.

Reading

Bettelheim, C. 1948: 'National Income, Saving and Investment in Keynes and Marx'.

Glombowski, J. 1976: 'Extended Balanced Reproduction and Fixed Capital'.

Hilferding, R. 1910 (*1981*): *Finance Capital*.

Luxemburg, R. 1913 (*1963*): *The Accumulation of Capital*.

Rosdolsky, R. 1968 (*1977*): *The Making of Marx's 'Capital'*.

Sweezy, Paul M. 1942: *The Theory of Capitalist Development*.

Tsuru, S. 1968: 'Keynes vs Marx: The Methodology of Aggregates'. In Horowitz, D. ed. *Marx and Modern Economics*.

PAOLO GIUSSANI

reserve army of labour   A pool of unemployed and partially employed labour is an inherent feature of capitalist society, and is created and reproduced directly by the accumulation of capital itself. Marx calls this pool the reserve army of labour, or industrial reserve army. The accumulation of capital means its growth. But it also means new, larger-scale, more mechanized methods of production which competition obliges capitalists to introduce. The growth of capital increases the demand for labour, but mechanization substitutes machinery for workers and thus reduces the demand for labour. The net demand for labour therefore depends on the relative strengths of these two effects, and it is precisely these relative strengths which vary so as to maintain the reserve army of labour. When the employment effect is stronger than the displacement effect for long enough to dry up the reserve army, the resulting shortages of labour and acceleration in wages will automatically strengthen displacement relative to employment; a rise in wages slows down the growth of capital and hence of employment, and together with the shortages of labour speeds up the pace of mechanization and hence of displacement. In this way the accumulation of capital automatically replenishes the reserve army. (*Capital* I, ch. 23; Mandel 1976, pp. 63–4.) Added to this is the import of labour from areas of high unemployment, and the mobility of capital to areas with low wages, both of which serve to re-establish the 'proper' relation between capital and a relatively superfluous population.

Whatever its historical boundaries, the capitalist system has always created and maintained a reserve army. Modern capitalism spans the whole globe, and so does its reserve army. The starving masses of the third world, the importation and subsequent expulsion of 'guest workers' by the industrialized countries, and the flight of capital to low wage regions, are simply manifestations of this fact.

Reading

Coontz, Sydney H. 1957: *Population Theories and the Economic Interpretation*.

Mandel, Ernest 1976: 'Introduction' to Karl Marx, *Capital* I.

ANWAR SHAIKH

revisionism Revisionism can be understood in a narrow or a wide sense. At its widest it is integral to Marxist theory and practice, predicated as that must be on a social ontology which has 'self creation through labour as the fundamental characteristic of being human' (Gould 1978, p. xiv), and on an epistemology which has the knowing subject in a dialectical relationship of analysis and action with the object known (see DIALECTICS; KNOWLEDGE, THEORY OF). A body of inherited truths, frozen beyond revision by the pedigree of its authorship, ought to be wholly incompatible with such a tradition of scholarship and political practice; and particularly so under capitalism, where that system's unique propensity to institutionalize perpetual change, and to create in the proletariat the agency of its own destruction, means that neither Marxist theory nor its associated political practice can afford to atrophy into a set of timeless axioms. It ought not to surprise us, therefore, that ever since 1883 the imperatives of a changing class structure and the ambiguous legacy of Marx himself have combined to make each major Marxist a revisionist by default. Lenin revised Marx. So did Luxemburg, Trotsky and Mao. Even Engels has been castigated as 'the first revisionist' by those who see in his interpretation of Marx's writings the theoretical roots of a non-revolutionary political degeneration (Elliott 1967; Levine 1975).

Yet this serves to remind us that revisionism is rarely understood in so wide and so positive a way. Instead, as later Marxists became adept at legitimizing their own innovations by denying them and tracing instead a direct line of descent for them from Marx's own writings, Marxism became canonized and revisionism gained a narrower, negative and shifting connotation. Before 1914, in the first general use of the term, revisionism became synonymous with 'those writers and political figures who, while starting from Marxist premises, came by degrees to call in question various elements of the doctrine, especially Marx's predictions as to the development of capitalism and the inevitability of socialist revolution' (Kolakowski 1978, vol. II, p. 98). After 1945, in contrast, revisionism became a term of abuse used by communist parties to criticize the practices of other communist parties and to denigrate critics of their own policy, programme or doctrines. It is important to differentiate these two phases of the revisionist controversy, not least because in the first the term was used to protect the revolutionary current in the European labour movement from the rising tide of conservatism, while in the second it has been mobilized so often to defend a different type of conservatism from critics keen to return to a more independent and even at times revolutionary path. And yet in each period the term was meant to carry the same sense: of a break with the 'truth' contained in 'scientific socialism' (Marx's own before 1917, Bolshevik orthodoxy thereafter) that carried with it the associated danger of a reformist political practice that could only reconstitute or consolidate capitalism (see REFORMISM).

It was certainly this danger of reformism that inspired Rosa Luxemburg to criticize Eduard Bernstein in the first major revisionist controversy, in the German Social Democratic Party (SPD) in the 1890s. The Marxism that Bernstein sought to revise was a highly deterministic one (see DETERMINISM) which argued the inevitability of capitalist crises, class polarization and socialist revolution. Bernstein challenged the philosophy underpinning these assertions, preferring a neo-Kantianism (see KANTIANISM AND NEO-KANTIANISM) that made socialism desirable without being inevitable. He challenged too the political strategy to which they gave rise, one that declined to pursue that parliamentary alliance with the liberal middle class and peasantry that he saw as crucial to the peaceful and gradual democratic transformation of capitalism. Against the predictions of the SPD he offered his famous alternative: that 'peasants do not sink; middle class does not disappear; crises do not grow ever larger; misery and serfdom do not increase', and argued instead that socialists should build a radical coalition on the more realistic premiss that 'there is increase in insecurity, dependence, social distance, social character of production, functional superfluity of property owners' (quoted in Gay 1952, p. 250). It was this revision of Marx's characterization of capitalism that was formally rejected by the SPD in 1903 but which in the end came to inspire the more moderate politics of the party in the Weimar Germany of the 1920s.

The subsequent use of the term has had a different focus and origin, serving mainly to discredit those who challenged the orthodoxy of

STALINISM. Tito's Yugoslavia was condemned as revisionist by the CPSU after 1948, and each side regularly condemned the other as revisionist during the long Sino-Soviet dispute from the late 1950s. Soviet leaders have regularly denounced as revisionist the repeated and courageous attempts of East European militants to humanize socialism there by moderating the political monopoly of the highly bureaucratized communist parties; and the attempts by certain Eurocommunists (see EUROCOMMUNISM) to find a third way to socialism in the advanced capitalist countries have been similarly condemned as revisionist by more orthodox comrades both in the West European communist parties and in Moscow.

Finally it should be noted that revisionism has also been a feature of the social democratic parties (see SOCIAL DEMOCRACY) that took the Bernsteinian route after 1917. Many of these parties reacted to prolonged capitalist prosperity after 1948 by removing elements of doctrine and programme that remained from their Marxist past (or in the British case, in the absence of such a past, from the socialist consensus of the Attlee period). A new generation of social democratic revisionists declared capitalism replaced by a mixed economy in which further nationalization was no longer necessary and where socialist parties were left only with the task of pursuing greater social equality within a Keynesian consensus. It has been the failure of that revisionism to cope with the return of capitalist crises in the 1970s that has prompted many left-wing social democrats to adopt radical policies that are close to certain of the positions taken by Eurocommunism; and in this way revisionism within the communist movement, and the failure of a very different revisionism within social democracy, are starting to erode the divisions within the West European socialist movement that was set in train by the original revisionist debate of the 1890s.

Reading

Bernstein, E. 1899 (1961): *Evolutionary Socialism*.

Crosland, A. 1956: *The Future of Socialism*.

Elliott, C. F. 1967: 'Quis Custodiet Sacra? Problems of Marxist Revisionism'.

Gay, P. 1952: *The Dilemma of Democratic Socialism: Eduard Bernstein's Challenge to Marx*.

Gould, C. C. 1978: *Marx's Social Ontology*.

Haseler, S. 1969: *The Gaitskellites: Revisionism in the British Labour Party*.

Kolakowski, L. 1978: *Main Currents of Marxism*.

Labedz, L. ed. 1962: *Revisionism*.

Levine, N. 1975: *The Tragic Deception: Marx contra Engels*.

DAVID COATES

revolution In the scheme of history first sketched by Marx and Engels in the *German Ideology*, the leading idea was that of a succession of eras each based on a MODE OF PRODUCTION; and revolution in its fullest sense meant a cataclysmic leap from one of these to the next. It would be brought about by a convergence of conflicts: between old institutions and new productive forces straining for freedom, and, less impersonally, between higher and lower classes within the old order, and between the former and a new class growing up to challenge it, until, at the level of socialist revolution, old exploited class and new dominant class are identical. Subsequently, it was only about revolutions in modern Europe, past, present and future, that Marx and Engels had time to think seriously. Marx had made a beginning in 1843, with a study of the English, French, and American revolutions (as indicated in his notebooks). All these were 'bourgeois revolutions' (though the American was national as well), led that is by ambitious sections of the middle-class and motivated at bottom by the need of new capitalist forces of production to expand.

Of all such attempts to ring out the old and ring in the new, Marx and Engels soon came to think of the Lutheran Reformation, and the Peasant War of 1524–25 in Germany which accompanied its first and boldest stage – and on which Engels wrote a book – as the earliest; though as an effort by burghers and peasants to break down the feudal ascendancy only very partially effective. Far more mature and successful was the rising of the 1640s in England. It would not have been pushed so far, however, Marx and Engels believed, if there had not been yeomen and urban plebeians to do most of the fighting for the rising bourgeoisie and bourgeoisified landowners; and this suggested what they came to consider a general rule, that all such movements of revolt had to be pushed well beyond the the point required by bourgeois interests proper, if the inevitable ebb of the tide was not to pass the point represented by a settlement like that of 1688 (Engels, introduction to English edition of *Socialism: Utopian and Scientific*).

Another general feature was that the new propertied class coming to the front, being able to gather support from the masses, could pose as, and even deem itself for the time being, the representative of the whole People against the old order. This was so above all in the great bourgeois revolution, that of 1789–94, during which the Jacobins, the most thoroughgoing revolutionary party, pushed things on from stage to stage with the backing, partly spontaneous and partly stirred up by them, of the Paris masses.

It was by some of the French liberals of the post-1815 generation that the French Revolution was first interpreted in class terms, as a transfer of power from aristocracy to bourgeoisie. Marx and Engels adopted this view when they were developing their theory of history, with which it fitted in well. The *Communist Manifesto* of 1848, however, included a brief forecast that, because of special conditions there, 'the bourgeois revolution in Germany will be but the prelude to the immediately following proletarian revolution.' In 1848–49, taking part on the left in the radical movement in Germany, Marx and Engels had an opportunity to see a bourgeois revolution from inside, and were disgusted by the spectacle of shuffling hesitation and weakness, ending in defeat; later they did much thinking and writing about it. They began by enlarging the idea, touched on in the *Manifesto*, of what came to be called 'permanent revolution'. It was expounded in a programmatic statement drawn up by them for the Communist League in March 1850. According to this, the next time revolution broke out the militant workers must organize themselves separately from the outset, compel the middle classes to carry out bourgeois-democratic reforms in full, and then advance at once to the further stage of seizing the lead from them and setting up working-class power and socialism (see Blackburn 1972, pp. 33ff.).

This somewhat fanciful scheme was soon dropped. Study of recent economic history convinced Marx that the European upheaval had been set off by the trade depression of 1847 and the mass discontent it stirred up, and that no new rebellion could have any chance until the next slump brought the masses into action again. In reality the bourgeoisie of Central and Eastern Europe, even more nervous of the workers behind them than of the governments facing them, never risked the experiment again, except half-heartedly in Russia in 1905. It was able to secure, if not political power, a position within the old framework enabling it to pursue industrial growth unhindered, and this was all that really mattered to it.

Engels tried (in 'The Role of Force in History') to fit this into the Marxist scheme, so far as Germany was concerned, by depicting Bismarck's unification as 'revolutionary' – an example of how flexibly he and Marx could use the term, another being Marx's dictum about the disruption of the Indian village by British pressure being the first 'social revolution' in the history of Asia ('The British Rule in India', 10 June 1853). But numerous problems have arisen over the concept of 'bourgeois revolution', impressively developed though this has been by Marxist scholarship in the past half century. In the English case it has still not proved possible to demonstrate incontrovertibly a collision between classes, and between economic systems represented by them. Even the French case of 1789, where the Marxist approach or something akin to it has had wider acceptance, remains highly controversial, though it has undeniably done more than any other to stimulate detailed research into an extraordinarily complex subject. Debate among historians in the bicentenary year 1989 showed a prevalent feeling that the theory of aristocracy challenged and overthrown by bourgeoisie was too simple and clear-cut, and even threw doubt on the existence of any such dissatisfied, ambitious class as the bourgeoisie postulated by Marxists.

Another kind of revolution, the communistic, had been afloat in a few minds for a long time, but could have no practical meaning, Marx always insisted, before the material conditions for it were present. Communism, that is, could only be a sequel to capitalism, which brought into being a new working class, one for the first time capable of wiping out all class divisions because it represented not an alternative form of property but alienation from all property. Its coming to power would be a moral as well as social transformation, since it would make a clean sweep of the past, empty humanity's Augean stables, and allov; it to make a fresh start (*German Ideology*, pt. 1, sect. 2C). Another early-formed conviction which Marx and Engels never abandoned was that the grand change could not take place in odd corners here and there, but must be the work of a decisive number of industrial nations acting at once (ibid. sect. IA).

From the defeat of the Paris workers' insurrection in June 1848 Marx drew the conclusion that this was only the start of a struggle as long-drawn as the Israelites' wanderings in the wilderness (*Class Struggles*, sect. 3) – later a favourite image with Stalin. In subsequent years Marx and Engels had to confess that in 1848 they were carried away by the impetuosity of youth, and that to expect the overthrow of capitalism when it was only in the first stage of its march across the continent was very premature. Power could not be won by a surprise attack of a few enthusiasts, a militant vanguard not backed by the energy of a whole class (Engels, introduction to 1895 edition of *Class Struggles*).

Engels came to see a possible exception to this axiom in Russia. By 1875 he was thinking of revolution there, hastened perhaps by war, as imminent ('Social Conditions in Russia'); and in 1885 he told a Russian correspondent that there if anywhere the Blanquist fantasy of society overturned by a band of conspirators might have some substance, because the whole structure of tsarism was so unstable that one resolute push might bring it down (letter to Vera Zasulich, 23 April). Elsewhere things would be slower, although in most cases the climax would be a trial of physical strength. Marx was willing to suppose that a few countries, England with its long political tradition foremost, might escape the final ordeal. Developments in England were disappointing, with the working class after the failure of Chartism retreating to non-political trade-unionism, and no sense of socialist 'mission' dawning. In France political spirit was livelier, but from soon after 1848 Marx understood that in a mainly agricultural country the limited working class could not come to power without the aid of the peasantry, whose deepening poverty he counted on to ensure this (*18th Brumaire*, sect. 7). In Russia it would

clearly be even more indispensable.

After 1870 Germany's rapid industrialization made it seem the country whose workers might take the lead. A strong socialist movement was soon under way, with increasing representation in the Reichstag. Engels was all the more impressed by its growth as an electoral force because he was also, as an expert on military matters, conscious that new weaponry was strengthening all governments in terms of physical power. Street fighting and barricades were things of the past, he wrote to Lafargue on 3 November 1892; in a combat with the army socialists were certain to come off worst, and he confessed that he did not yet see a clear solution to this difficulty. But this made it all the more necessary to involve the masses, to broaden the movement as widely as possible, and in Germany to carry it into the army's chief recruiting-grounds, such as East Prussia.

Engels underlined these warnings in a preface written in 1895 for a German edition of Marx's *Class Struggles*. He was, nevertheless, indignant at his text being mangled by its editors for fear of the censorship; it exposed him to misrepresentation as 'a peaceful worshipper of legality', he complained in a letter to Kautsky (1 April 1895). This did in fact very soon happen, when in 1898, three years after his death, Bernstein began putting forward the ideas which led to the 'Revisionist' controversy (see REVISIONISM). In this complex debate what Bernstein regarded as his main contention was that the alleged inevitable collapse of capitalism in the near future was only wishful thinking; but as generally understood the argument was about whether revolution in the old sense was still a practical possibility, or whether reliance must now be exclusively on constitutional methods.

In Russia there were no constitutional rights before the 1905 upheaval, and not many after. Lenin was bent on forging a party capable of preparing and then guiding a revolution; he was carrying to its furthest point the idea of revolution planned in advance, unlike all earlier ones. His party was too small and untried to make much of a mark in the mainly spontaneous outbreak of 1905, and this could not at best go beyond bourgeois-democratic limits, along with broad agrarian reform. But its failure showed up the irresoluteness of the weak Russian bourgeoisie just as 1848–49 had that of the

German. Hence the paradox that its revolution would have to be made for it, or even in spite of it, by the masses led b y the working class and its party. Such thinking led back easily to the more sweeping concept of 'permanent revolution' which had appealed to Marx and Engels in 1848–50. It was frequently discussed among Russian socialists, and was taken up most prominently by Trotsky.

When Europe in 1914 obediently took up arms at its rulers' command, Lenin tried to counter the charge that the International had been foolish to predict that war would mean revolutions. It had never guaranteed this, he wrote: not every revolutionary situation leads to revolution, which cannot come about of itself ('The Collapse of the Second International', *CW* 21, pp. 213–14). It could come about only when the masses were ready for revolt, and when in addition the higher classes were incapable of carrying on under the old order; these were objective conditions, independent of the will of parties and classes. In another war-time polemic, in March 1916, Lenin declared that socialist revolution could not be contemplated as a single swift blow: it would be a series of intensifying struggles on all fronts (*CW* 22, p. 143). But whereas not long since he had considered socialism in Russia too weak as yet to be ready for power, he came back from exile after the fall of the Tsar early in 1917 convinced that the war had altered everything; while the behaviour of the bourgeois provisional government convinced him that it could and must be swept away without delay.

No revolution, Trotsky wrote in his history (1932–3, appendix 2), can ever fully correspond with the intentions of its makers, but the October revolution did so more fully than any before it. In one very important respect it went astray. He and Lenin were reckoning on it to be the signal for revolt across Europe; for them as for Marx and Engels it was in the international arena that the outcome would be decided. But east and west were too far apart, and the socialists elsewhere showed little readiness to emulate the Bolsheviks, who were left feeling abandoned, alone in the breach. Controversy soon broke out, with Lenin and Kautsky the chief antagonists, as to whether this was a genuine socialist revolution or not. Lenin accused his critics of having abandoned Marxism for reformism.

Kautsky accused the Bolsheviks of keeping themselves in power by terrorism, under pretence of the DICTATORSHIP OF THE PROLETARIAT which Marx had deemed a necessity of any post-revolutionary transition. Marx and Engels's own views on terrorism, as distinct from this dictatorship, are indicated in a letter from Engels to Marx of 4 September 1870, about the Terror of 1793 as a regime of men themselves terrified, perpetrating cruelties mostly useless in order to bolster their own confidence.

A few attempted revolts elsewhere in Europe in the next few years were fiascos. Trotsky, in exile, clung to his theory and went on elaborating it, especially in *The Permanent Revolution*. He was chiefly concerned to emphasize its international aspect: socialist revolution could not be completed within national boundaries. It would be 'permanent' now in a further sense, going on and on until the whole world was socialist – a view which, a critic pointed out, ignored all the discontinuities of history (Claudin 1975, p. 78). Gramsci's meditations, in prison leisure, led him to opposite conclusions about what he termed 'the Jacobin/Forty-eightist formula' of permanent revolution. It had only seemed plausible at a time when the state was still rudimentary and society inchoate and fluid; since 1848, and still more since 1870–1, politics had been transformed by the growth of parliamentarism, trade-unionism, parties, bureaucracies (*1971*, pp. 179, 220, 243). He worked out a distinction, based on events in nineteenth-century Italy, between active risings like Mazzini's and 'passive revolution', with Cavour as its exponent and patient preparation as its method, bringing about through 'molecular change' in men's minds an altered composition of social forces. Perhaps the two were both necessary for Italy, he conjectured, and he saw the rest of Europe after 1848 as moving towards the 'passive' variant. He was writing of bourgeois-democratic, or bourgeois-national, revolution; after 1918, and more deliberately after 1945, European socialism may be said to have made a similar shift. In the West adherence to the goal of revolution has come in effect to mean belief in a thoroughgoing transformation of society, as opposed to any mere patching up of the old society by piecemeal bits of reform. In the USSR a slower drift in the same direction has been visible; by the early 1960s Soviet theory was ready to adopt the view that with socialism already established over much of the world it might come to power elsewhere by peaceful stages.

This thesis was being endorsed under pressure of the blood-and-thunder doctrines of Maoism (see MAO TSE-TUNG), competing with Moscow for leadership of the socialist camp, and re-asserting once more the international character of the struggle. In more recent years Peking has abandoned its ultra-revolutionary posture. But since the time, before 1914, when Lenin welcomed the prospect of revolutionary move-ments in the colonial world as reinforcements to those within Europe, armed revolt has been displaced from Europe to the third world. There it remains a burning question, because right-wing military rule with foreign backing, over a great part of Asia and Latin America, seems to leave no alternative. Socialism and national or agrarian feeling are frequently intertwined, but in many regions it is Marxism, or some adapta-tion of it, that has provided the guiding thread. (See also NATIONALISM; WAR.)

Reading

Bricianer, Serge 1978: *Pannekoek and the Workers' Councils.*

Blackburn, Robin ed. 1978: *Revolution and Class Stuggle: A Reader in Marxist Politics.*

Gramsci, Antonio 1929–35 (1971): *Selections from the Prison Notebooks.*

Hobsbawm, E. J. 1973: *Revolutionaries.*

Kautsky, Karl 1902: *The Social Revolution.*

Lenin, V. I. 1918b (1965): *The Proletarian Revolution and the Renegade Kautsky.*

Marek, Franz 1966: *Philosophy of World Revolution.*

Trotsky, Leon 1932–33 (1967): *History of the Russian Revolution.*

Woddis, J. 1972: *New Theories of Revolution.*

V. G. KIERNAN

Revolution Betrayed, The   *What is the Soviet Union and Where is it Going?* Written in 1936 in Norway, this was the last book Trotsky man-aged to complete; and it is regarded by many as his political testament. Over the years it has become one of the most influential books of this century. It contains a wealth of most original ideas; it also contains contradictions and highly

tentative statements, which allowed writers of widely divergent views to make adventitious use of it. In this highly complex work, Trotsky gives his definitive analysis of Soviet society and of the origins and history of Stalinism. He sets out to refute Stalin's claims about the achievement of socialism in the USSR by confronting the grim realities with the classical Marxist vision of socialism. Thus, he also effectively disclaims the moral responsibility of Marxism for Stalin's perversion of the Marxist idea.

The Revolution Betrayed contains a classical indictment of bureaucracy, which achieved its terrifying might in post-revolutionary Russia. This was due to the backwardness and poverty of the country where, amid glaring inequalities, the ruling group shielded its interests and privi-leges against the discontent of deprived masses. Here, incidentally, Trotsky inserts a warning that some remnants of such conflict would re-main even in the wealthiest of countries, since no proletarian revolution would be able im-mediately to reward labour 'according to needs'. This may come about when society attains undreamt of levels of production and a universal standard of education which would bridge the gap between manual and intellectual labour.

During the transition to socialism, the revolu-tionary state is socialist only in so far as it defends social property in the means of produc-tion, but retains its 'bourgeois' character so far as it presides over an unequal distribution of goods. This 'bourgeois' factor does not, however, constitute 'state capitalism'. 'The attempt to represent the Soviet bureaucracy as a class of "State capitalism" will obviously not withstand criticism' (p. 236). Periodically purged, harassed and dispersed by Stalin, it was unable to consolidate and acquire the homo-geneity characteristic of a class. It has privileges but does not own the means of production; moreover it cannot perpetuate itself by passing them to its descendants.

The chapter of the work most intensely de-bated has been the one in which Trotsky throws out bold prognostications as to the future of the Soviet Union. 'The means of production belong to the State. But the State, so to speak, "belongs" to the bureaucracy' (p. 236). If 'these relations should solidify and become the legal-ized norm, they would in the long run lead to complete liquidation of the social conquest of the proletarian revolution' (ibid.).

The bureaucracy – the command 'parasitic' strata – defends state property as the source of its power and income. 'In this aspect of its activity it still remains a weapon of proletarian dictatorship' (ibid.). Because the bureaucracy may be seen as defending state property, 'the workers fear lest, throwing out the bureaucracy, they will open the way for a capitalist restoration' (p. 269). On the other hand, says Trotsky further, the bureaucracy 'continues to preserve State property only to the extent that it fears the proletariat' (p. 238).

Trotsky abandons his previous expectations that the conflict may be resolved in a reformist manner, and opts, somewhat hesitatingly, for a revolutionary solution. In the last analysis, the question will be decided by 'a struggle of living social forces . . .' (p. 241), and Trotsky warns against adopting categorical formulas with regard to phenomena which don't have a finished character. Trotsky foresees that, not content with command and consumer privileges, the bureaucracy would seek to take public property into its own hands: the 'captains of industry' and managers of agriculture would acquire shares, bonds and stocks; they would also do away with the monopoly of Soviet trade (p. 240). A backslide of the transitional regime to capitalism is wholly possible (p. 241).

Trotsky certainly underrated the staying power of the Stalinist regime. Viewing the Second World War through the prism of the First, he expected it to be brought to an end by proletarian revolution *in the West*; only thus, he thought, could Stalinist Russia emerge victorious from the contest.

In one of his illuminating historical analogies, Trotsky deals with what Marxists hitherto took for granted: that a workers' state issued from a proletarian revolution could only be a proletarian democracy. Trotsky demonstrates that, like the bourgeois post-revolutionary order which had developed various political forms – constitutional, monarchical or autocratic – so the workers' state could exist in various political forms, from a bureaucratic absolutism to government by democratic Soviets.

As a theoretician, the author of *The Revolution Betrayed* enriches the Marxist legacy; as an analyst he is unsurpassed; in his polemical zeal he commits mistakes, but such is the quality of his mistakes that they do not detract from the unique seminal value of the work.

Reading

Trotsky, Leon 1937: *The Revolution Betrayed; What is the Soviet Union and Where is it Going?*

TAMARA DEUTSCHER

Ricardo and Marx   Marx regarded Ricardo as the greatest classical economist, and as his own point of departure, but at the same time he clearly differentiated his own theory from that of Ricardo. Although Ricardo posits as a general principle that relative prices are regulated by embodied labour time (which is his main scientific achievement) he does not make the crucial distinction between *abstract* (VALUE producing) labour and *concrete* (USE VALUE producing) labour, or between *socially necessary* labour (which determines the exact amount of labour time embodied in a given commodity) and *individual* labour. As a consequence, since the necessity and functions of money can only be explained by means of the category of value of a commodity (socially necessary quantity of abstract labour time), Ricardo does not understand what money really is. He considers money as a simple device for the circulation process, and ends by promulgating both Say's law (the necessary balance of supply and demand at a social level) and a mechanical form of the quantity theory of money (derived from David Hume) in which the price level is determined by the circulating quantity of money and not the other way round, as Marx argued.

Ricardo, being interested only in the quantitative determination of relative prices independently of their own substance (value), is unable to grasp the distinction between labour and labour power. Hence he does not explain profits through the surplus value produced by workers, and tries to make the production prices of single commodities agree directly with the amounts of labour time embodied in them, which is impossible. Marx points out that if one simply presupposes the existence of a uniform rate of profit, the two categories of commodity and price of production become inconsistent with each other. According to Marx, when we are at the simple level of abstraction in the analysis of a commodity, profit rate and capital must be still unknown and cannot be purely assumed, as Ricardo does. The result is that Ricardo is unable to show where the uniform rate of profit comes from, or to determine a way of calculating it.

Marx answers the same question by showing that profit is nothing but a redistribution of the total surplus value produced by the individual capitals, so that the rate of profit is calculated as the social surplus value over the sum of the social constant capital and the social variable capital. Nonetheless, even though Ricardo does not explain the differences between value and price of production, he ends by downplaying these differences as empirically minor, a theoretical gap which later led to a crisis in the Ricardian school (Mill, McCulloch) and eventually forced it to abandon altogether the connection between embodied labour time and prices (Torrens). Marx, however, notes that Ricardo is *empirically* correct in his proposition that intertemporal changes in relative prices are regulated by corresponding changes in values (*Theories of Surplus Value*, vol. II, ch. 10, par. A, pt. 5). Anwar Shaikh (1980) has shown how astonishingly accurate Ricardo's 93 per cent labour theory is for US data.

By applying the principle that relative prices are regulated by embodied labour time Ricardo was able to disprove an old and common idea, according to which increases in wages must cause increases in prices; on the contrary he showed that prices rise only for those commodities produced by capitals with an organic composition below the average, whereas they must fall for capitals of a higher composition, in such a way that, other things being equal, the sum of prices is unchanged while the mass and rate of profit have diminished.

This relevant result, however, leads Ricardo to concentrate exclusively upon the inverse relation between wages and profits, and produces great differences as far as his and Marx's analyses of ACCUMULATION are concerned. In the first place Ricardo tends to forget that constant capital, particularly *fixed capital*, also plays a crucial role in determining the rate of profit. He therefore tends to reduce the laws which govern the rate of profit to those which govern the rate of surplus value. This very same neglect also leads him to overlook the increasing relevance of fixed

capital (mechanization) in the production process in creating and maintaining a reserve army of unemployed labourers. Though Ricardo concedes that machinery *may* on occasion displace workers, he tends to argue that on the whole accumulation would absorb more workers than it 'set free'. Therefore he generally opposed attempts to help the poor, on the grounds that the money would be better directed to investment, which would on balance increase employment. Lastly, though Marx and Ricardo both insist that capitalist accumulation is characterized by a secularly FALLING RATE OF PROFIT, they treat it in opposite ways. According to Ricardo, increasing employment creates a corresponding increase in the demand for basic consumption goods, especially agricultural products. This makes it necessary to resort to the cultivation of new lands of lower productivity than the previously utilized ones, which according to Ricardo raises the share of ground rent in total surplus, and lowers the corresponding share of industrial profit. The growth of the system thus produces a secular fall in the rate of profit due to the declining productivity in goods which enter the workers' consumption, the *value* of labour power rises, and the rate of surplus value falls independently of the fact that a greater share of surplus value goes to ground rent. Secondly, Ricardo in any case fails to give adequate recognition to the effect that technical progress in agriculture can have in offsetting the resort to worse lands. Thus, Ricardo's expectation of a falling rate of profit was based on the niggardliness of nature, whereas for Marx the tendency of the profit rate to fall is due to the social relations that generate accumulation and technical progress. According to Marx, this should produce a generally rising rate of surplus value, but the overall rate of profit falls nevertheless because *the capitalist form of technical progress* necessarily generates an even faster rise in the organic composition of capital.

The next important difference has to do with the question of crises. Since Ricardo conceives money as a simple means of lubricating exchange, he tends to view exchange itself as a direct interchange of product versus product. In this case the production of a good (supply) means that its owner automatically possesses the means to barter it against other goods, so that – if one excepts local disturbances or accidental factors – *supply creates its own demand* (Say's law). Marx notes that this argument falls apart once money is introduced, because to produce something does not guarantee its sale for money, and to possess money does not imply its expenditure. Money is therefore the root of the *possibility* of crises, which Ricardo entirely fails to grasp. More importantly, whereas for Ricardo the secularly falling rate of profit leads only to eventual stagnation, in Marx this same mechanism is also the source of the *necessity* of periodic crises. (See ECONOMIC CRISES; MONEY.)

One last consideration arises about Ricardo's theory of rent. Ricardo's advance over Smith is that he considers rent as a pure transfer of wealth, instead of being itself a source of value. But Ricardo explains rent only by means of differential fertilities of land, and in this way he only explains *differential* rent and not *absolute* rent, which according to Marx is due to the barriers to capital investment created by the private ownership of land (see LANDED PROPERTY AND RENT).

The evaluation of Ricardo's work and its relation to Marx among Marxists is uneven. Authors such as Dobb and those in the neo-Ricardian tradition tend to minimize the differences between Marx and Ricardo, arguing that their theories of prices of production are virtually the same, and that both analyses ultimately rest upon the category of a *physical surplus*. At the opposite extreme writers such as Sweezy, Hilferding and Petry insist that Marx's and Ricardo's theories have totally different fields of application, in that Ricardo aims to determine the relative prices of commodities whereas Marx is *only* interested in the analysis of the *social relations* underlying the capitalist economy. This position seems weak, because if Marx's theory of value fails to unify the analysis of accumulation and the social relations *which rest upon it*, the concept of value is deprived of its *raison d'être* and therefore has no real place in the analysis of social relations. A more precise appreciation of Ricardo's political economy and the links it has with Marx's work can be found in the writings of Rubin and Rosdolsky, who both emphasize the decisive role of value for the whole of Marx's analysis.

Reading

Dobb, M. 1973: *Theories of Value and Distribution since Adam Smith*.

Hilferding, R. 1904 (*1949*): 'Böhm-Bawerk's Criticism of Marx'. In Sweezy ed, *Karl Marx and the Close of his System*.

Petry, F. 1916: *Der soziale Gehalt der Marxschen Werttheorie*.

Ricardo, D. 1817 (*1973*): *The Principles of Political Economy and Taxation*.

Rosdolsky, R. 1968 (*1977*): *The Making of Marx's 'Capital'*.

Rubin, I. I. 1979: *A History of Economic Thought*.

Shaikh, A. 1980b: *The Transformation from Marx to Sraffa*.

Sweezy, P. 1949: Preface to Hilferding's 'Böhm-Bawerk's Criticism of Marx'. In *Karl Marx and the Close of his System*.

PAOLO GIUSSANI

Robinson, Joan Violet   Born 31 October 1903, Camberley, Surrey; died 5 August 1983, Cambridge. Born into a tradition of dissent, Joan Robinson became a rebel *par excellence*. She went to St Paul's Girls School and in 1922 to Girton College, Cambridge, to read economics because she wanted to know why poverty in general and unemployment in particular occurred. She graduated in 1925, and was appointed to a university assistant lectureship in economics and politics in 1934. She became a university lecturer in 1937, a reader in 1949 and professor of economics in 1965. Her academic career was spent in Cambridge (with extensive travelling abroad). She was a key member of the 'circus' arguing out the *Treatise on Money* with Keynes in the 1930s and a leader of the Cambridge post-Keynesian economists in the postwar period.

Her first major contribution was *The Economics of Imperfect Competition* (1933), which she was later to repudiate. She saw this work at the time as a critique of the benefits of *laissez-faire* competitive capitalism, for it seemed to deny that in a slump the beneficial purging of the unfit in fact occurred.

Her subsequent contributions ranged across the whole spectrum of economic theory; here we focus on two areas. The first is a critique of the orthodox theory of value and distribution itself (for example, she effectively questioned the meaning of 'capital', which plays a key role in the dominant supply and demand theories). Increasingly her critique focused on what she perceived to be the method of orthodoxy, its procedure of comparing equilibrium positions in order to analyse processes following a disturbance. She identified the problem of path-dependent equilibria and the possibility of the non-existence of equilibrium itself, thus severely undermining conventional (and so-called neo-Ricardian) economic analysis. The economy has then to be analysed in terms of a process in historical time, instead of ignoring the essential properties of time in a way which has been common in economic analysis.

The second is her attempt to generalize Keynes's *General Theory* to the long period with a return to classical *cum* Marxian preoccupations with accumulation, distribution and growth in the light of the findings of, and insights gained from, the (true) Keynesian revolution. Her *magnum opus* was *The Accumulation of Capital* (1956). A further contribution was her extensive criticisms and developments of the theory of money and the rate of interest in the context of debates over liquidity preference versus loanable funds. She pointed out that in the analysis of the economy as a whole, it is not always possible to use the device of the representative individual. Macroeconomic outcomes reflect the balancing of forces associated with the behaviour of different individuals or groups with different power and expectations in uncertain situations.

Joan Robinson became interested in Marx in the mid-1930s. The main thing she took from him was a sense of history and of the importance of societies' institutions, their 'rules of the game'. She was always sceptical of the labour theory of value itself, asking why she needed to believe in it to explain that those who commanded finance and the means of production could push around those who had only their labour services to sell. She stereotyped many Marxists as Billy Graham Marxists, but she was a perceptive and sympathetic critic of Marx himself. Her own structures of thought increasingly came to reflect his influence, partly filtered through Kalecki's use of the reproduction schemas, first, independently to discover the principal propositions of the *General Theory*, and then to analyse the processes of cyclical growth of capitalist societies. Another Marxian element in her thought, her postwar discussions of the origin of the rate of profits, was much influenced by the arguments of Piero Sraffa's

introduction to volume I of the Ricardo volumes (1951) and his *Production of Commodities by Means of Commodities* (1960). So she used the labour theory of value after all, even though she did not believe in it.

Reading

Harcourt, G. C. 1982: 'Joan Robinson'. In Prue Kerr, ed. *The Social Science Imperialists*.

Kalecki, Michal 1971: *Selected Essays on the Dynamics of the Capitalist Economy 1933–1970*.

Robinson, Joan 1933 (1969): *The Economics of Imperfect Competition*.

— 1937 (1969): *Introduction to the Theory of Employment*.

— 1942 (1966): *An Essay on Marxian Economics*.

— 1951, 1960, 1965, 1973, 1979: *Collected Economic Papers*, 5 vols.

— 1956 (1969): *The Accumulation of Capital*.

Sraffa, Piero 1960: *The Production of Commodities by Means of Commodities*.

Sraffa, Piero, with the collaboration of M. H. Dobb eds. 1951: *The Work and Correspondence of David Ricardo*, vol. I.

G. C. HARCOURT

Roy, Manabendra Nath Born in Bengal about 1887; died 25 January 1954, Dehra Dun. Roy stands out as one of the first generation of Indian communists. Very early involved in the revolutionary movement in his native Bengal, he was first arrested in 1910. He left India in 1915, and made his first acquaintance with socialism in America. After the Bolshevik revolution he went to Russia, and in 1920 was sent to Tashkent to organize a training centre for Indian revolutionaries. He came into prominence that year at the second congress of the Communist International, where the colonial theses adopted were partly drafted by him, though modified by Lenin. Whereas Lenin was impressed by the fact of Asia being populated mainly by peasants, Roy was convinced that at any rate in India there was a rapidly growing working class, capable of taking the political lead. This went with an illusion of massive industrialization in progress, which led him to believe that the Indian bourgeoisie was satisfied with the opportunities it now had: communists must therefore have no truck with the middle-class national movement represented by the Congress party, led now by

Gandhi. Lenin favoured independent collaboration with it; but the question of whether or not there could or should be alliances between communists and 'national bourgeoisies' continued to be a controversial one in colonial countries down to the end.

Setting up a communist party in India proved a very slow and difficult process, and Roy could not easily keep in touch with developments, although he remained optimistic. His book published in 1922 elaborated his contention that British government and Indian bourgeoisie were moving closer, because the former, alarmed at mass unrest, wanted to win the latter round by concessions. Clinging to this theory, he came to be somewhat out of step with official Comintern thinking, but his standing was high enough for him to be in China as delegate during the crisis of 1927, when Soviet and Comintern guidance failed to rescue the young Chinese party from isolation and defeat. Next year at the sixth congress he restated his belief that India was turning into an industrial country, and depicted its agriculture too as on the verge of fundamental change. From this he inferred the likelihood of bigger political concessions to the bourgeoisie, leading towards decolonization, in a political as well as economic sense. On the industrial side, he was supported by most of the British representatives, and a heated debate took place. In the end both the economic and the political conclusions drawn by Roy were rejected. With this and his lack of success in China he was now out of favour, and in July 1929 he was expelled. In 1930 he returned to India, where he spent the years 1931 to 1936 in prison.

When the second world war came he supported the British government, on anti-fascist grounds; from then on he was drifting away from Marxism towards a kind of liberalism. Some of his earlier works remain of interest, although, largely self-taught, he was an unsystematic as well as copious writer. His book on materialism (1940) begins with the Greeks, and materialist strands in old Indian philosophy, and comes down to the problems of twentieth-century physics. It shows him critical in some respects of Marxist historical theory – 'Marx went too far' (p. 199n). His work on China includes an attempted interpretation of Chinese history, interesting if only as a pioneer study in a field which Chinese Marxists were only in the first stage of exploring. (See also NATIONALISM; REVOLUTION.)

Reading

Ghose, Sankar 1973: *Socialism, Democracy and Nationalism in India.*

Gupta, Sobhanlal Datta 1980: *Comintern, India and the Colonial Question, 1920–37.*

Haithcox, John P. 1971: *Communism and Nationalism in India: M. N. Roy and Comintern Policy, 1920–39.*

Roy, M. N. 1922: *India in Transition.*

— 1930s (1946): *Revolution and Counterrevolution in China.*

— 1934 (1940): *Materialism. An Outline of the History of Scientific Thought.*

V. G. KIERNAN

ruling class The term 'ruling class' conflates two notions which Marx and Engels themselves distinguished although they did not explicate them systematically. The first is that of an economically dominant class which by virtue of its economic position dominates and controls all aspects of social life. In the *German Ideology* (vol. I, sect. IA2) this is expressed as follows: 'The ideas of the ruling class are, in every age, the ruling ideas; i.e. the class which is the dominant *material* force in society is at the same time its dominant *intellectual* force. The class which has the means of material production at its disposal has control over the means of mental production.' The second notion is that the dominant class, in order to maintain and reproduce the existing mode of production and form of society, has necessarily to exercise state power, i.e. to *rule* politically. In the *Communist Manifesto*, Marx and Engels wrote that 'the bourgeoisie has at last, since the establishment of modern industry and the world market, conquered for itself, in the modern representative state, exclusive political sway. The executive of the modern state is but a committee for managing the common affairs of the whole bourgeoisie.'

Among later Marxists, Gramsci made the clearest and most explicit distinction between class domination of civil society, for which he employed the term hegemony, and political rule as such, or state power: 'What we can do, for the moment, is to fix two major superstructural "levels": the one that can be called "civil society", that is the ensemble of organisms commonly called "private", and that of "political society" or "the State". These two levels correspond on the one hand to the function of "hegemony" which the dominant group exercises throughout society and on the other hand to that of "direct domination" or command exercised through the State and "juridical" government' (*1971*, p. 12; see also the extended analysis in pt. II, sect. 2, 'State and civil society').

In recent years two main questions have preoccupied those who have tried to develop a more systematic Marxist political theory. One concerns the specific role of hegemony (i.e. the general cultural influence of ideology) in sustaining and reproducing class domination. Gramsci clearly recognized its importance, but it was above all the FRANKFURT SCHOOL thinkers who made it the principal explanation of the absence of revolutionary class consciousness and the continued subordination of the working class in the advanced capitalist societies. A 'dominant ideology' – the elements of which are not very precisely specified – ensures, it is argued, a 'pacification' of social conflict, a more or less total assimilation of the working class into the existing social order, and the exclusion from public discussion of any radical alternative conceptions of social life. This is evidently not what Marx and Engels thought the 'ruling ideas' could achieve; and the dominant ideology thesis has itself been criticized as departing from Marxism by its exaggeration of the influence of ideas, as against the 'dull compulsion of economic relations', political repression, and successful reformism (see Abercrombie et al. 1980).

The second question has to do with the relation between class domination and state power; and in recent studies (e.g. Poulantzas 1973, Miliband 1977) there has been a strong emphasis upon the 'relative autonomy' of the State. Class domination, it is argued, is not automatically translated into state power, and the state cannot properly be regarded simply as the instrument of a class. Other radical thinkers have gone farther in separating economic dominance from political rule, and Mills (1956), for example, preferred the term 'power elite' to 'ruling class' (see ELITE).

A further set of problems is posed by the identification and delineation of the ruling class

in particular historical forms of society. In the debate about the transition from feudalism to capitalism, Dobb raised a question about which class ruled in the European feudal societies between the late fourteenth and the seventeenth centuries (Hilton 1976), and similar questions can be put in other contexts. The exact lineaments of a dominant or ruling class are difficult to trace in ANCIENT SOCIETY or ASIATIC SOCIETY. In the case of capitalist societies it may be asked whether in the late twentieth century they are dominated by the bourgeoisie in exactly the same way as they were in the nineteenth; or whether the dominant class now comprises bourgeois, technocratic and bureaucratic elements (as may be implied by definitions of present-day capitalism as State monopoly capitalism), and at the same time stands in a different relation to subordinate classes and groups as a result of the increase in the countervailing power of working-class and other organizations. Finally, there is the question which is frequently raised concerning the emergence of a new, historically unique, ruling class in the present-day socialist societies (see CLASS; also Konrád and Szelényi 1979). These issues are at the centre of the current debates about Marxist political theory, and have elicited new attempts at theoretical clarification (see Poulantzas 1973, Therborn 1978) as well as a number of more empirical studies, especially of capitalist societies (Domhoff 1967, Miliband 1969, Scott 1991).

Reading
Abercrombie, N. et al. 1980: *The Dominant Ideology Thesis.*

Domhoff, G. William 1967: *Who Rules America?*

Konrád, George and Szelényi, Ivan, 1979: *The Intellectuals on the Road to Class Power.*

Miliband, Ralph 1977: *Marxism and Politics.*

Poulantzas, Nicos 1973: *Political Power and Social Classes.*

Scott, John 1991: *Who Rules Britain?*

Therborn, Göran 1978: *What Does the Ruling Class do When it Rules?*

TOM BOTTOMORE

rural class structure A major concern of Marxism in a number of contexts: transitions to capitalism, anti-imperialist struggles, transitions to socialism. It now receives less emphasis in developed countries where the agricultural labour force is small and capital is concentrated in agribusiness, but remains central to most Third World countries. The issues are both economic – the effects of rural class structures for the development (or stagnation) of the productive forces in agriculture, and for general accumulation and industrialization – and political: the relations of rural classes with other classes and the state, and class alliances. These issues are linked in the concept of the AGRARIAN QUESTION.

In the TRANSITION FROM FEUDALISM TO CAPITALISM the land question is central: overthrowing landed property and landlordism as obstacles to the development of agriculture and to social progress more generally. This preoccupied the Bolsheviks, Chinese and other Asian communists, and Marxists in southern Europe and Latin America – as well as, from their different viewpoints, anti-colonial nationalists, aspiring bourgeois modernizers and agrarian populists. Anti-feudal struggles can thus stimulate broad class alliances, especially in the context of the national question, comprising the working class, national bourgeois elements and different classes of peasants. This generated the Marxist concept of the worker–peasant alliance (symbolized in the hammer and sickle), as well as the potent populist slogan of 'land to the tiller'.

The land question in this sense was resolved either by revolutionary means, by bourgeois land reforms, or by the internal transformation of feudal property to capitalist farming. While land remains a burning issue in many areas of the Third World, arguably this now concerns forms of capitalist (rather than feudal) property, even when their labour regimes utilize debt bondage, share-cropping, or labour reserves of semi-proletarianized peasants.

A related question of even wider significance concerns the formation and reproduction of agrarian capital and wage labour. In The Development of Capitalism in Russia (1899) Lenin distinguished two principal 'paths': the Prussian path whereby landed property transforms itself into capitalist enterprise, proletarianizing a formerly dependent peasantry; and the American path whereby agrarian capital and

wage labour emerge from the class differentiation of family farmers (see PEASANTRY, PETTY COMMODITY PRODUCTION). Of course, paths of agrarian transition and their class coordinates are historically much more varied and complex (Byres 1990) with respect to the origins and forms of organization of agrarian capital, and to processes of peasant differentiation, historically marked in Third World formations by different experiences of COLONIALISM.

While most Marxists concur with Lenin's view of a general tendency to differentiation within capitalism, the mechanisms, extent and relative stability of rural class formation are always the outcome of specific historical conditions of competition and struggle among peasants, and between peasants and other social forces. On one hand, the semi-proletarianization of many 'peasants' throughout the Third World is evident; that is, their reproduction through wage labour combined with marginalized household farming, petty trade and non-agricultural petty commodity production. On the other hand, (rich) peasant accumulation may be inhibited by the exactions of rent, of merchant capital and usurer's capital (Bhaduri 1983), or of the state (notably in sub-Saharan Africa, Mamdani 1987), or by competition with more powerful capitals including international agribusiness.

A third type of question concerns the effects of rural class structures and the nature of peasantries for political struggles. Marxism is often considered intrinsically 'anti-peasant', not least by reference to Marx's writings on France, in which the nature of smallholder farming explained both the backwardness of agriculture and the inability of the peasantry to constitute a 'class for itself'. In The 18th Brumaire of Louis Bonaparte (1852), however, Marx distinguished the revolutionary peasant who 'strikes out beyond the condition of his social existence, the smallholding' and the conservative peasant who 'wants to consolidate this holding'.

By the late nineteenth century, with rapid industrialization and parliamentary democracy, Western European Marxists investigated which 'subdivisions of the rural population [can] be won over by the Social Democratic Party' (Engels, 'The Peasant Question in France and Germany', 1894–5), which also prompted the analysis of differences between the development of capitalism in agriculture and industry in

Kautsky's *The Agrarian Question* (1899). Similarly Lenin distinguished the two 'paths' (the Prussian and American, above) to identify which was more propitious for the development of bourgeois democracy, and hence freedom of action of the working class (the American path). With the formation of the Third International, consideration of rural class structure was further extended to the arena of anti-imperialist struggle, especially in Asia (see NATIONALISM).

From the 1920s to the 1950s, Mao Zedong produced a series of analyses of rural class structure in China in relation to anti-feudal struggle, national democratic struggle and socialist construction, including the remarkable *Report on an Investigation of the Peasant Movement in Hunan* (1927). In this work and others he attributed much greater dynamism than had the Bolsheviks to the role that poor peasants especially can take in struggles against the *ancien régime* and subsequently for socialism. This positive evaluation of peasant political capacity found a resonance in other Marxist analyses and programmes of national liberation elsewhere in Asia, in Africa, in Central and South America.

The record of attempts at socialist agrarian transition – whether in the USSR, China, Vietnam, Mozambique or Sandinista Nicaragua – remains highly problematic. In China in the 1980s the communes were disbanded in favour of a return to private production; the place of commodity production and markets within a socialist framework – a critical theme of Soviet agrarian debates in the 1920s, to which Lenin, Preobrazhensky, Bukharin and Kritsman made contributions of continuing relevance – is at the core of *perestroika* at the beginning of the 1990s. To what extent experiences of socialist agrarian transition in economically 'backward' countries have foundered on peasant affinities with private property and tendencies to class differentiation, and to what extent they manifest other contradictions of objective conditions, and of the theory and practice of imposed COLLECTIVIZATION and modernization and 'large is beautiful' (state farms), are questions of continuing investigation, debate and critique.

Marxist analysis also continues to be tested against complex rural class structures and dynamics of agrarian change in the contemporary Third World, including the development of capitalist relations of exploitation within apparently pre-capitalist, servile or customary forms of labour organization; the ability of rich peasants to control rural political organization and articulate the interests of 'farmers as a whole'; the class violence often inflicted by rich and middle peasants (as well as agrarian capital) on rural workers. Current Marxist work has also expanded its agenda to investigate the gender dimensions of rural class structures; the detailed workings of markets for rural labour, credit, inputs, and agricultural commodities; processes of semi-proletarianization and rural immiseration; technical and environmental change in the countryside; changes in the global political economy of capitalist agriculture; and, as noted, to re-examine inherited concepts of the project of socialist agrarian transition itself.

Reading

Benería, Lourdes ed. 1985: *Women and Development: The Sexual Division of Labour in Rural Societies.*

Bhaduri, Amit 1983: *The Economics of Backward Agriculture.*

Brass, Tom 1986: 'Unfree Labour and Capitalist Restructuring in the Agrarian Sector: Peru and India'.

Byres, T. J. 1990: 'The Agrarian Question and Differing Forms of Capitalist Agrarian Transition: An Essay with Reference to Asia'. In Jan Breman and Sudipto Mundle, eds. *Rural Transformation in Asia.*

de Janvry, Alain 1981: *The Agrarian Question and Reformism in Latin America.*

Levin, Richard and Neocosmos, Michael 1989: 'The Agrarian Question and Class Contradictions in South Africa: Some Theoretical Considerations'.

Lewin, Moshe 1968: *Russian Peasants and Soviet Power: A Study of Collectivisation.*

Mamdani, Mahmood 1987: 'Extreme but not Exceptional: Towards an Analysis of the Agrarian Question in Uganda'.

Patnaik, Utsa ed. 1990: *Agrarian Relations and Accumulation: The 'Mode of Production' Debate in India.*

Saith, Ashwani ed. 1985: *The Agrarian Question in Socialist Transition.*

HENRY BERNSTEIN

Russian commune   An ancient community of Russian peasants in which land was held inalienably by the *obshchina*, or commune and periodically redistributed in allotments to member households, generally according to the number of adult males in each. It was first popularized as the embryonic institution of an egalitarian decentralized socialist society by Alexander Herzen, and subsequently adopted by almost all the theorists of revolutionary POPULISM in Russia as the vehicle through which the moral and economic ravages of capitalism could be avoided and Russia's exceptional destiny to show the world the way to socialism could be achieved. The commune, they believed, had preserved the natural solidarity and socialist instincts of the Russian peasants. The federation of free communes would displace the authoritarian state and establish the basis for the fusion of ancestral Russian social institutions with contemporary Western socialist thought.

Prompted by Russian critics (Mikhailovsky and Zasulich), Marx conceded that it was at least possible that Russia might avoid the disruption of communal land-tenure and the worst abuses of capitalism. The commune, in his view, had an innate dualism: communal ownership of land on the one hand, private ownership of forces of production applied to it and of movable property on the other. It might, therefore, develop in either direction. The issue of the peasant commune led him to an important clarification of his conception of historical necessity. There was, he maintained in 1877, no abstractly necessary or ineluctable progression from primitive communal ownership to private (capitalist) ownership, and thence to socialism, applicable to all societies (see HISTORICAL MATERIALISM; STAGES OF DEVELOPMENT). He had not intended in *Capital* to construct 'a general historico-philosophical theory, the supreme virtue of which consists in being suprahistorical'. He also noted that the prospects for the commune depended very heavily on the policies of the Russian state. His general conclusion was that the socialist potential of the commune could be realized only if tsarism was overthrown and, further, if revolution in Russia 'becomes the signal for a proletarian revolution in the West so that both complement each other'. (Preface to Russian edition of the *Communist Manifesto*, 1882).

Marx's appraisal gave greater comfort to the voluntarist politics of the populists than to his Russian *émigré* supporters in the Emancipation of Labour Group led by Plekhanov, who by this time had already concluded that commodity production and social differentiation had so undermined the commune as to render it implausible as a springboard into socialism. The controversy between Marxists and populists over the vitality of the peasant commune continued throughout the 1880s and 1890s. The fullest rebuttal of the populist case was Lenin's *The Development of Capitalism*, but the argument was to reappear in a new form in the debates between Marxists and Socialist Revolutionaries in the first two decades of the twentieth century.

Reading

Blackstock, P. W. and Hoselitz, B. F. eds. 1952: *Marx and Engels: The Russian Menace to Europe.* (Contains texts and letters cited above.)

Herzen, A. 1852 (1956): 'The Russian People and Socialism'. In *Selected Philosophical Works*, pp. 470–502.

Lenin, V. I. 1899b (1960): *The Development of Capitalism in Russia.* See especially sect. XII of ch. II and sect. XI of ch. III.

Plekhanov G. V. 1885 (1961): *Our Differences.* In *Selected Philosophical Works*, vol. I. See esp. ch. III.

Venturi, F. 1960: *Roots of Revolution.*

NEIL HARDING

S

Sartre, Jean-Paul Born 21 June 1905, Paris; died 15 April 1980, Paris. Philosopher, novelist, playwright, critic, pamphleteer: probably the most influential and popular intellectual of modern times in his immediate impact on events. A supporter of many noble causes, he often came into conflict with established powers and institutions. Anxious not to allow his own institutionalization, he rejected all official honours, including membership of the French Academy, the Légion d'Honneur, and even the Nobel Prize. For several years a *compagnon de route* of the French Communist Party, he tried to influence its policies from the outside, until he quarrelled with the party first over Hungary, in 1956 (see *Le fantôme de Stalin*), then over Algeria, in 1963, and finally over the events of May 1968 which led to a complete break. After May 1968 he supported the Maoist and other *groupuscules*, advocating libertarian-anarchist political perspectives for the future. He died a rather lonely figure at a time when the 'new philosophers' were in vogue in France, but his funeral procession was followed by tens of thousands of people, and tributes came from all over the world for the causes he so passionately supported at the time of his active involvement in politics.

A graduate of the École Normale Supérieure, Sartre taught philosophy in the 1930s, starting to publish an original blend of philosophy and literature with *The Legend of Truth* and later *La Nausée* which received great critical acclaim. The power of literary evocation remained a prominent feature of all his writings, not only of the fictional ones, such as his novel cycle (the trilogy: *Roads to Freedom*, 1945–1949) and his gripping plays (*Huis clos*: 1945; *Dirty Hands*: 1948; *Lucifer and the Lord*: 1952; *Les séquestrés d'Altona*: 1960), but also of his biographies (*Baudelaire*: 1946; *Saint Genet*: 1952; the autobiographical *Words*:

1964, and *L'idiot de la famille: Gustave Flaubert de 1821 à 1857*: 1971), of his numerous critical essays (collected in the ten volumes of *Situations* between 1947 and 1976), and even of his most abstract philosophical works, from *The Transcendence of the Ego* (1936) to the *Critique of Dialectical Reason* (1960).

In his philosophical writings Sartre championed a popular and politically activist version of existentialism. Influenced by Descartes, Kant, Hegel, Husserl and Heidegger, he advocated a 'philosophy of freedom' in order to be able to insist on everyone's *total responsibility* for the 'whole of mankind'. In his early work entitled *Sketch for a Theory of the Emotions* he presented an anti-Freudian conception of consciousness and freedom, and he further developed the same position in the concept of 'bad faith' of his *Being and Nothingness*: a massive work on 'phenomenological ontology'. In the latter work he spelled out 'the *ontological solitude* of the For-itself' (p. 456), insisting that 'the Other is an *a priori* hypothesis with *no justification* save the unity which it permits to operate in our experience' (ibid. p. 277).

At the time of his political rapprochement with Marxism Sartre embarked on a project of 'making history intelligible' through a *Critique of Dialectical Reason* which was originally intended as a 'critique of historical reason'. However, since he retained the ontological solitude of *Being and Nothingness* as the foundation of his conception of history and anthropology, his intended 'Marxisant project' (Sartre's expression) turned out to be the greatest Kantian work of the twentieth century, confined to the investigation of the 'formal structures' of history' in their circularity, promising but never achieving the demonstration of 'the real problem of History . . . of its motive forces and of its non-circular direction' (p. 817) in a second volume.

Sartre's greatest impact was as a passionate moralist. In this sense, as well as in several others, his work recalls that of Voltaire in powerfully affecting the moral and intellectual preoccupations of his time.

Reading

Aron, Raymond 1973: *Histoire et dialectique de la violence*.

de Beauvoir, Simone 1947 (*1964*): *The Ethics of Ambiguity*.

Lukács, György 1948: *Existentialisme ou marxisme*.

Manser, Anthony 1966: *Sartre*.

Marcuse, Herbert 1948: 'Sartre's Existentialism'.

Merleau-Ponty, Maurice 1955 (*1973*): *Adventures of the Dialectic*.

Mészáros, István 1979: *The Work of Sartre*.

Sartre, Jean-Paul 1972: *Between Existentialism and Marxism*.

ISTVÁN MÉSZÁROS

science   Science figures in Marxism under two aspects: (α) as something that Marxism is, or claims to be; and (β) as something that it sets out to explain (and perhaps even change). Under (α) science is a value or norm; under (β) a topic of research and investigation. Under the first *intrinsic* aspect, Marxism involves or presupposes an epistemology (see KNOWLEDGE, THEORY OF); under the second *extrinsic* aspect, it constitutes an historical sociology. Because there are sciences other than Marxism, an adequate epistemology will exceed Marxism in its intrinsic bounds; but because there are social practices other than science, Marxism will be greater in extensive scope. Many of the problems associated with the concept of science in Marxism arise from the failure to reconcile and sustain both these aspects of science. Thus emphasis on (α) at the expense of (β) leads to *scientism*, the dislocation of science from the socio-historical realm and a consequent lack of historical reflexivity; while emphasis on (β) at the expense of (α) leads to historicism, the reduction of science to an expression of the historical process and a consequent judgemental relativism.

Both aspects are present in Marx: on the one hand, he regards himself as engaged in the construction of a science, and so presupposes some epistemological position; on the other he regards all science, including his own, as the product of, and a putative causal agent in, history. *Historically*, Marx was a *rationalist* in the sense that he viewed science as a progressive, potentially and actually liberating force, increasing man's power over nature and his own destiny. *Epistemically*, Marx was, or at least became, a *realist* in a sense close to that of modern scientific REALISM – in that he understood (i) the job of theory as the empirically-controlled retroduction of an adequate account of the structures producing the manifest phenomena of socio-economic life, often in opposition to their spontaneous mode of appearance; (ii) such structures to be ontologically irreducible to and normally out of phase with the phenomena they generate, so acknowledging the stratification and differentiation of reality; (iii) their adequate re-presentation in thought as dependent upon the critical transformation of pre-existing theories and conceptions, including those (in part) practically constitutive of the phenomena under study; (iv) recognition of the process of scientific knowledge as a practical, laborious activity (in the 'transitive dimension') as going hand-in-hand with recognition of the independent existence and transfactual activity of the objects of such knowledge (in the 'intransitive dimension') which remain 'outside the head, just as before' (*Grundrisse*, Introduction). For Marx there is no contradiction between the *historicity* of knowledge and the *reality* of their objects – rather they must be thought as two aspects of the unity of known objects.

The characteristic emphases of Marx's view of science – historical rationalism and epistemic realism – were maintained in the Engelsian Marxism which dominated the Second and Third Internationals, but became expressed in an increasingly vulgar form (for which, it must be said, Marx himself provided ample precedent). Thus a sheer Promethean technological triumphalism, decked out in an evolutionist or mechanistic-voluntaristic schema of history, and a vulgar or contemplative realism, in which thought was conceived as reflecting or copying reality, interpreted in terms of a monistic processual cosmology, prevailed. At least since Engels, Marxism had used the concept of dialectic to register the '*historicity*' of its subject matter and that of materialism to indicate the '*scientificity*' of its approach. What had been rather mechanically (and hypernaturalistically) conjoined in DIALECTICAL MATERIALISM, split in WESTERN MARXISM into antithetical dialectical (mainly anti-naturalist) and materialist (predominantly naturalist) currents – with the former displaying a tendency to historicism and epistemological idealism, and the latter a tendency to scientism and an epistemological materialism.

In the three main schools of dialectical Western Marxism, viz (i) the Hegelian historicism of Lukács, Korsch and Gramsci, (ii) the critical theory of Horkheimer, Adorno, Marcuse and Habermas and (iii) the humanism of Lefebvre, Sartre, Kosik, Petrović *et al.*, the stress successively shifts from science as a source of mystification to science as an agent of domination to science as *hermeneutically inappropriate* in the human world. (i) For Lukács, remarking that 'there is something highly problematic in the fact that capitalist society is predisposed to harmonize with scientific method' (*1971*, p. 7), science, breaking up wholes into fragmented (atomized) facts, is essentially an expression of the REIFICATION endemic to capitalist society; and HISTORICAL MATERIALISM is counterposed to science in being characterized by a totalizing method of its own. Similar themes prevail in Korsch and Gramsci. (ii) In the FRANKFURT SCHOOL tradition, science comes to be associated with an instrumental reason or interest, which is seen, at least in the social sphere, as a more or less directly repressive agency; counterposed to instrumental reason is an emancipatory, life-enhancing, or de-repressing reason or interest. (iii) Humanistic Marxism has been generally disposed to a more or less pronounced dualism, with the method of social inquiry regarded as distinctively interpretive or dialectical etc., in contrast to that of the natural sciences. Common to all three schools is a positivistic misconception of science (see POSITIVISM) and an emphasis on human practice, in the transitive dimension, at the expense of transfactual efficacy, in the intransitive dimension, leading to epistemic idealism, judgemental relativism, practical voluntarism and/or historical pessimism.

On the other hand, the leading figures of materialist Western Marxism, such as Althusser, Della Volpe and Colletti, have tended either to extrude science from the historical process (as in Althusserian 'theoreticism') or to scientize, hypernaturalistically rationalize, history (as in Della Volpe); while on the epistemic plane, there has been a tendency to revert to a philosophical position such as rationalism (Althusser), empiricism (Della Volpe), or Kantianism (Colletti), already practically transcended by Marx. This group does, however, possess the merit of recognizing that Marxism, at least as understood by Marx, whatever else it also is, claims to be a science, not as such a philosophy, world-view or practical art.

Appreciation of both the intrinsic and extrinsic aspects of science places the questions of Marxism's specific autonomy as a science, and relative autonomy as a practice, within the field of sciences and the social totality. More specifically, recognition of the epistemic aspect raises the familiar problems of ideology and of *naturalism*, i.e. of how social scientific, more especially Marxist, discourses and practices are differentiated from, on the one hand, ideological and, on the other, natural scientific discourses and practices – that is, the issue of the specific autonomy of Marxism as a scientific research programme. Recognition of the historical aspect raises a complex series of questions, concerning the location of the sciences generally, and Marxism in particular, within the topography of historical materialism, whose theoretical and practical importance it would be difficult to exaggerate. Thus, is science itself or merely its applications a productive force? If science is part of the superstructure (see BASE AND SUPERSTRUCTURE) how is its relative autonomy to be conceived? Is natural science perhaps a productive force but social science part of the superstructure destined to wither away under communism? Can there be a proletarian natural science, as Bogdanov and Gramsci (and Lysenko; see LYSENKOISM) believed, or merely a proletarian social science; or is the latter itself, as Hilferding claimed, a contradiction in terms? What is the relation between the development of scientific knowledge, in Marxism and in the sciences quite generally, and popular struggles for workers' control in scientific labour processes; and, most globally, between these and the great unfinished project of human emancipation? (See also DETERMINISM; DIALECTICS; MATERIALISM; TRUTH.)

Reading
Bhaskar, Roy 1978: *A Realist Theory of Science*.
Della Volpe, G. 1950 (*1980*): *Logic as a Positive Science*.
Habermas, Jürgen 1968b (*1971*): *Knowledge and Human Interests*.
Lecourt, D. 1977: *Proletarian Science?*
Lukács, Georg 1923 (*1971*): *History and Class Consciousness*.
Rose, H. and S. 1976: *The Political Economy of Science*.

ROY BHASKAR

scientific and technological revolution A term which has come to be widely used by social scientists in the USSR and Eastern Europe, apparently to refer to a new phase of history. Those who employ it insist that the scientific and technological revolution has to be seen in the context of the 'social relations specific to a given social system' (Richta 1977), and 'brought into correlation with the profound processes of social development underlying the mounting social revolution' (Fedoseyev 1977), but in fact their approach gives primacy to the forces of production as the motor of history, while treating the relations of production as largely derivative. In this conception, moreover, science is regarded as an unequivocally progressive force (once the distortions produced by capitalism have been eliminated) which will lead necessarily to communism. Marx's rich definition of social production as more than technical – as human, moral, political, and embracing modes of cooperation and organization – is reduced to merely technical labour power. On the other side, the scientific and technological revolution is seen as enhancing the contradictions in capitalist societies, and hence the possibility of revolutionary social change. Critics of this notion, however, regard it as only another form of technological determinism in Marxist thought, having affinities with ECONOMISM and with the evolutionist Marxism of the Second International, which ignores the dynamics of class struggle and seeks to depict 'the objective course of man's sociohistorical progress' (Arab-Ogly 1971, p. 379). (See also LABOUR PROCESS.)

Reading
Arab-Ogly, E. A. 1971: 'Scientific and Technological Revolution and Social Progress'. In Pospelow, P. M. *et al. Development of Revolutionary Theory by the CPSU*.
Clarke, Simon 1977: 'Marxism, Sociology and Poulantzas's Theory of the State'.
Corrigan, Philip, *et al*. 1978: *Socialist Construction and Marxist Theory: Bolshevism and Its Critique*.
Fedoseyev, P. 1977: 'Social Significance of the Scientific and Technological Revolution'. In International Sociological Association, *Scientific-Technological Revolution*.
Richta, R. 1977: 'The Scientific and Technological Revolution'. In ibid.
Young, Robert M. 1977: 'Science is Social Relations'.

ROBERT M. YOUNG

self-management In a restricted sense self-management refers to the direct involvement of workers in basic decision-making in individual enterprises. Means of production are socialized (owned by the workers' community or by the entire society). In smaller communities directly, in larger ones through their delegates in the workers' council, workers decide on basic issues of production and the distribution of income. Technical operative management is subordinated to them and controlled by them. In a more general sense self-management is a democratic form of organization of the whole economy, constituted by several levels of councils and assemblies. Central workers' councils in the enterprises send their delegates to higher-level bodies of the whole branch and of the entire economy. At each level the self-management body is the highest authority responsible for the development and implementation of policy, and coordination among relatively autonomous enterprises.

In the most general sense self-management is the basic structure of socialist society, in economy, politics and culture. In all domains of public life – education, culture, scientific research, health services, etc. – basic decision-making is in the hands of self-management councils and assemblies organized on both productive and territorial principles. In this sense it transcends the limits of the state. Members of the self-management bodies are freely elected, responsible to their electorate, recallable, rotatable, without any material privileges. This puts an end to the traditional state, to political bureaucracy as a ruling elite and to professional politics as a sphere of alienated power. The remaining professional experts and administrators are simply employees of self-management bodies, fully subordinated to them. Self-management involves a new socialist type of democracy. In contrast to parliamentary democracy it is not restricted to politics, but extends to the economy and culture; it emphasizes decentralization, direct participation and delegation of power for the purpose of a minimum of necessary coordination. Political parties lose their ruling function and oligarchical structure; their new role is to educate, express a variety of interests, formulate long-range programmes and seek mass support for them.

The earliest ideas on self-managed workers' associations were formulated by Utopian Socialists: Owen, Fourier, Buchez, Blanc, and the spiritual father of anarchism, Proudhon. As early as 'On the Jewish Question' Marx expressed the view that 'human emancipation will only be complete when the individual . . . has recognized and organized his own powers as *social* powers so that he no longer separates this social power from himself as a *political* power'. Working-class associations would have to replace the political administration of bourgeois society (*Poverty of Philosophy*). In *Capital* III (ch. 48) Marx explains the idea of freedom in the sphere of material production: 'the associated producers regulate their exchange with nature rationally' and 'under conditions most favourable to, and worthy of, their human nature'.

Anarchists (Bakunin, Kropotkin, Reclus, Malatesta) developed the idea of a federation of self-governing communities as the substitute for the state. Guild socialism contributed the idea of vertical workers' integration. Syndicalism advocated management by trade unions, an important alternative to the leadership claims of vanguard political parties. The proper role of independent trade unions seems to be, however, articulating interests and building the common will of workers rather than controlling self-management organs which alone must be responsible for decision-making. All socialist revolutionary upheavals, whether successful or not, from the Paris Commune to Polish *Soli-*

darity, more or less spontaneously created organs of self-management. Especially important are the practical experiences of Yugoslavia where initial forms of self-management (alongside a liberalized one-party political system) were created in the early 1950s. (See also COUNCILS.)

Reading

Cole, G. D. H. 1917 (1972): *Self-government in Industry*.

Gramsci, Antonio 1920: Articles in *Ordine Nuovo*.

— 1929–35 (1971): *Selections from the Prison Notebooks*.

Horvat, B. *et al.* 1975: *Self-governing Socialism*, vols I and II.

Korsch, Karl 1968: *Arbeitsrecht für Betriebsräte*.

Pannekoek, Antonie 1970: *Workers' Councils*.

Programme of the League of Communists of Yugoslavia, 1958.

Proudhon, Pierre Joseph 1970: *Selected Writings*.

Topham, A. J. and Coates, Ken 1968: *Industrial Democracy in Great Britain*.
MIHAILO MARKOVIC

serfdom Marx and Engels were well aware that compulsion, either by the landlord or by the state, was the necessary condition of serfdom, however that compulsion might be juridically legitimated. But their main interest was in the transfer of the surplus labour of the producer which serfdom was supposed to guarantee. For them, the essence of societies where serfdom was predominant was that the production of the subsistence needs of the vast majority (the peasants) was provided by the family labour of the household, the division of labour being determined by age and sex. Peasants had effective possession of their small landed resources, but were not proprietors. The proprietors normally gained their income by obliging the peasants to transfer their surplus labour on to the lord's demesne lands. The form of appropriation was open and visible, two or three out of six or seven days a week being done on the lord's land, the rest being devoted to the peasant holding. This contrasted with the concealed surplus value derived by the employer from the wage labourer in capitalist societies.

The conversion of labour rent into a rent in

kind or money from the peasant holding itself did not essentially change the relationship. Marx adds that owing to the force of custom, serf labour (or rent in money or kind) tended to become fixed, whereas family labour on the holding could vary in intensity and productivity, enabling peasant households to generate their own surplus and acquire property.

Some Marxist historians have been tempted to equate serfdom with labour rent and further to equate this form of surplus extraction with feudalism. This is an oversimplification, based on Marx's development of the labour theory of value in the context of the historical development of capitalism out of the European feudal economy. In fact serfdom, in the sense of the non-economic compulsion used by landlords (or states) to acquire peasant surplus, has been widespread throughout history. It can be identified from time to time in ancient China, in India, in Pharaonic Egypt, in classical antiquity and in modern eastern Europe as well as in the feudalism of medieval western Europe and Japan.

Nevertheless, serfdom in European feudal society is well documented and can be taken as reasonably typical of societies whose ruling classes derive their income from the surplus of peasant production. This well documented era also presents typical problems and complexities in that while unfree peasants from time to time constituted an important core of the peasant population, they were usually in a minority. The majority, as a consequence of varying historical circumstances, were of free legal status even if subjected to heavy demands for rent, tax and other payments to jurisdictional lords and the state. This suggests a *de facto* as well as a *de jure* serfdom, and indeed the one could, according to circumstances, develop into the other.

The main constituents of juridical serfdom were as follows. The servile family had no rights in public law against the lord. It was subject to the lord's jurisdiction in all matters concerning daily social and economic affairs. Lords also often had police jurisdiction, limited in varying degrees by the jurisdiction of public courts. Serfs were deprived of freedom of movement by being bound to their holding (*ascripticius glebae*), and by lords' control of servile marriages and of inheritances. The latter included a heavy death duty emphasizing the

lord's legal right to all the serf's chattels. Some effort was made to control the marketing of livestock, though market control was minimal if lords wanted serfs to go to market to get money for rent. If lords cultivated their own demesnes, further restrictions on freedom of movement were involved in forced labour and carrying services.

Free peasants might live under similar conditions, according to the local strength of landlord power. This would apply to the poor and middling peasants rather than to the rich freemen. They by no means escaped seigneurial jurisdiction and could be as much subject as the serfs to seigneurial monopolies (of the mill, the oven or the wine-press). Freedom of movement was easier, the main constraints being economic. They had more chance of enjoying low fixed rents for their hereditary holdings, though they might have to pay a high market price for additional land.

The fluctuations between freedom and serfdom were determined by various factors. If lords wanted forced labour on their estates they moved to enserf their free peasants. Such seems to have happened as early as the end of the tenth century in Catalonia and Languedoc, was reintroduced in thirteenth-century England and in central and eastern Europe from the sixteenth century onwards. Such factors as the desire to expand grain production for the market lay behind these moves. On the other hand if lords wanted to attract peasants to colonize new land they offered good terms of tenure as a bait. Much of east Germany and the western Slav lands saw a rise of free peasant communities for this reason in the central Middle Ages, before the later plunge into serfdom. Again, lords' need for cash, for instance in twelfth- and thirteenth-century France, made it possible for unfree peasants to buy free status, even for semi-free peasant communities to buy elements of self-government. In many countries unfree as well as free peasant communities developed collective resistance to lords which enabled them to keep rents at a fixed low level.

Oppressive as juridical serfdom could be, its very existence demonstrates that lords had to use non-economic means to guarantee their incomes. Peasant communities, servile or not, were not passive subjects of servile domination, as the history of peasant revolts shows.

Reading

See the reading for FEUDAL SOCIETY, also

Bloch, Marc 1975: *Slavery and Serfdom in the Middle Ages.*

Bonnassie, Pierre (forthcoming): *From Slavery to Feudalism.*

Hilton, R. H. 1969 (1982): *The Decline of Serfdom in Medieval England.*

de Sainte-Croix, G. 1981: *The Class Struggle in the Ancient Greek World.*

Smith, R. E. F. 1968: *The Enserfment of the Russian Peasantry.*

Société Jean Bodin 1959: *Le Servage.*

R. H. HILTON

slavery Labour under some kind of non-economic compulsion was the rule for most of history and is still a recurrent phenomenon (Kloosterboer 1960). Because the slave is the best known and most dramatic type of bondsman it has been widely believed that he was also the most common; hence the metaphorical use of 'slave', 'slavery', 'slavish', in non-labour contexts in western languages ever since ancient Greek. However, the fact is that, within world history as a whole, slaves have been greatly outnumbered by other, less total types of unfreedom (though exact numbers are rarely available). The slave was himself a privately owned commodity, denied in perpetuity ownership of the means of production, denied control over his labour or the products of his labour and over his own reproduction. This was not the case with the serf (see SERFDOM), the peon, the more or less tied peasant in ASIATIC SOCIETY, the Spartan helot and other varieties of bondsmen. An individual slaveowner could always give his slaves specific privileges, extending to manumission, the grant of freedom. But such actions in no way constituted a flaw in the definition, or a breakdown of the system of slavery, important though they were as an indicator of the precise way in which slavery functioned in any given society – most obviously in the contrast between the frequency of manumission in ancient Rome and its rarity in the United States.

There is no dispute over the fact that slaves are to some extent different from the others, but there is sharp disagreement as to whether or not stress on this distinction is mere peasantry. Schematically, the alternative is between viewing slavery as one species of the genus 'dependent (or involuntary) labour' and viewing slavery as the genus, the others as species. Retention of the slave/serf distinction even by those who reject further differentiation provides a clue to the answer, which, in Marxist terms, is embedded in the concepts of MODE OF PRODUCTION and SOCIAL FORMATION. Serfs were the appropriate form of labour under feudalism (see FEUDAL SOCIETY), slaves in ancient society, a major element in the social relations of production along with private property and commodity production.

Complications then set in. Firstly, within the Graeco-Roman world, not only was slavery insignificant in the extensive eastern regions, once part of the Persian empire, but it appears also to have been marginal in most of the northern and western provinces of the Roman Empire (see ANCIENT SOCIETY). There the dependent labour force was subject to varying, but lesser, degrees of unfreedom; for instance, they were normally not themselves commodities and they frequently owned at least the tools of production (Finley 1981, pt. II). In other words, the dependent labour existed and functioned within societies with different social relations of production (whether or not those societies were parts of a single political unit, notably the Roman Empire). The open question, with important theoretical implications, is then whether the relations of production were sufficiently different to preclude the inclusion of such societies within a single social formation in which the slave mode of production was dominant.

Secondly, analogous difficulties have emerged with the fairly recent interest in slavery in the simpler societies of Africa and Asia. The prevailing approach among anthropologists appears to be to get round the difficulties by removing from the definition of slavery its property aspect and the quality of kinless 'outsider' as a characteristic of the slave. Marxist anthropologists, however, have had to grapple with differences in the mode of production as well (see ANTHROPOLOGY). Thus, Meillassoux (1975) complains that there is no 'general theory which permits us to identify slavery' and that 'it is really not obvious that slavery is only a relationship of "production"'. And Maurice

Bloch (in Watson 1980) suggests that 'we should all retain the right to construct as many or as few modes of production as we like for the purposes at hand'.

A third complication arises from the indubitable existence of slave societies in the New World, notably in the American South, the Caribbean and Brazil (Padgug 1976). As Marx wrote in the *Grundrisse* (Penguin edn, p. 513): 'The fact that we now not only call the plantation owners in America capitalists, but that they *are* capitalists, is based on their existence as anomalies within a world market based on free labour.' That anomalous position is surely the key to the distinction that, whereas New World slavery was *abolished*, ancient slavery was not. American slavery came to an abrupt end through a constitutional amendment in 1865, to be replaced by free labour; Graeco-Roman slavery was replaced over a period of centuries, not by free labour but by another kind of dependent labour that ultimately evolved into serfdom in a process and at a tempo that are still much disputed (e.g. Dockès 1979). And it was never fully displaced: chattel slaves continued to exist in substantial numbers into the late Middle Ages though no longer as the dominant labour form (Verlinden 1955–77).

Such 'survival' is inherent in the conception of social formation. Slaves have been ubiquitous throughout most of human history, but as the dominant labour force only in the west in a few periods and regions. Likewise, free peasants working their own land and free independent craftsmen in the towns remained numerous in slave societies, especially in the ancient world in which they were normally essential for the successful operation of slave production (Garnsey 1980). The test of the dominance of a slave mode of production lies not in the numbers of the slaves but in their location, that is, in the extent to which the élite depended on them for their wealth.

Reading

Ampolo, C. and Pucci, G. eds. 1982: *Problemi della Schiavitù = Opus*, 1.1.

Dockès, P. 1979: *La libération mediévale*.

Finley, M. I. 1980: *Ancient Slavery and Modern Ideology*.

— 1982: *Economy and Society in Ancient Greece*.

Garlan, Y. 1982: *Les esclaves en Grèce ancienne*.

Garnsey, P. ed. 1980: 'Non-slave Labour in Graeco-Roman Antiquity'.

Kloosterboer, W. 1960: *Involuntary Labour after the Abolition of Slavery*.

Meillassoux, C. ed. 1975: *L'esclavage en Afrique précoloniale*.

Padgug, R. A. 1976: 'Problems in the Theory of Slavery and Slave Society'.

Verlinden, C. 1955–77: *L'esclavage dans l'Europe mediévale*.

Watson, J. L. ed. 1980: *Asian and African Systems of Slavery*.

(See also the reading list for ANCIENT SOCIETY; and, for extensive additional bibliography, Finley 1980.)

MOSES FINLEY

social democracy A term which has acquired various meanings over the past century and a half. In their earlier writings Marx and Engels regarded social democracy as 'a section of the Democratic or Republican Party more or less tinged with socialism' (Engels's note to the 1888 English edn of the *Communist Manifesto*, sect. IV), and they also referred, in the same sense, to 'democratic socialists'. In the *18th Brumaire* (sect. III) Marx described how, in opposition to the coalition of the bourgeoisie in France after the revolution of 1848, 'a coalition between petty bourgeois and workers had been formed, the so-called *social-democratic* party'. By the last decade of the nineteenth century, however, Marxist working-class parties had been created – notably in Germany and Austria – which called themselves Social Democratic parties, and Engels, though he expressed some objections, said that 'the word will pass muster' (foreword to his essays from the *Volksstaat* 1894). The reasons for choosing this name were partly no doubt to affirm a continuity with the revolutions of 1848, but still more to express the idea that these parties, engaged in fierce struggles for political democracy (for universal suffrage and for elected assemblies which would have real powers instead of being mere advisory bodies), had as their ultimate aim the extension of democracy to social life as a whole, and in particular to the organization of production. In this sense social democracy was contrasted with class domination, and was seen as bringing about a general social emancipation of the working class (which Marx in his early writings called 'human emancipation').

But as the social democratic parties, particularly in Germany and Austria, developed into mass parties, they faced a number of problems (Przeworski 1980). First, they had to decide whether to concentrate their struggle for socialism mainly, or even exclusively, upon the existing political institutions – that is to say, upon gaining a majority of seats in national, regional and local assemblies – or whether to engage at the same time (and to what extent) in 'extra-parliamentary' battles. This issue was most fully discussed in the controversies about the 'political mass strike' during the first decade of this century, in which Kautsky, Luxemburg, Hilferding and others took part (see STRIKES), and about the role of violence in the working-class struggle. The latter question became most acute after the Bolshevik seizure of power in 1917, and especially in the period of the rise of fascism; but most social democratic leaders accepted the view summed up by Bauer at the Linz Congress (1926) of the Austrian party (SPÖ) in the phrase 'defensive violence', which envisaged a resort to the mass strike and armed insurrection only as an extreme measure in response to bourgeois violence. The fact that the social democratic parties did concentrate their efforts upon electoral representation – and they were encouraged to do so by Engels in letters of the 1890s to Bebel, Kautsky, Viktor Adler and others – raised another issue, most sharply formulated by Michels (1911). Michels argued that as the social democratic parties developed into legal mass organizations there emerged a radical division between the members or supporters on one side, and the leaders and officials on the other, together with a progressive *embourgeoisement* of the latter, and that this tendency necessarily gave rise to reformist policies (see REFORMISM).

Two other features of social democratic politics were also thought by critics to encourage reformist tendencies. One was the need, in order to obtain an overall majority in a democratic system, to appeal to other social groups beyond the working class (and also, on occasion, to enter into coalitions with other parties), a need which became more pressing, according to some interpretations, with the growth in numbers of the middle class; and this

might involve making compromises about the ultimate aims of the socialist movement. A second important feature was that the social democratic parties devoted much of their effort to the achievement of partial reforms within capitalism, and although such a policy is by no means incompatible with the long-term aim of a complete transformation of capitalism and a transition to socialism – as Kautsky, the Austro-Marxists, and others consistently argued – the continual emphasis upon immediate reforms in everyday politics and in electoral campaigns may well come to overshadow this aim. Nevertheless, up to 1914 the social democratic parties continued to present themselves, and to be generally regarded, as revolutionary parties. It was the support which most of their leaders gave to their national governments during the first world war, and the victory of the Bolsheviks in Russia, which resulted in their being denounced as reformist, in the strong sense of not being socialist parties at all, by Lenin, by the Leninist communist parties and by the Communist International (see INTERNATIONALS). This denunciation reached a peak during the period of the rise of fascism in Germany, when the social democrats were described as 'social fascists' or in Stalin's phrase, 'the moderate wing of fascism'.

Since 1945 the meaning of social democracy has again changed in certain respects. Some parties which were formerly Marxist and affirmed their revolutionary aims, have explicitly renounced such goals and transformed themselves from working-class parties into 'people's parties' – notably the German party (SPD) at its Bad Godesberg conference in 1959 – while adopting policies which essentially try to achieve no more than a 'reformed capitalism' and a 'mixed economy'; and in Britain a new party, the Social Democratic Party, was created in the 1980s as a specifically non-socialist 'centre' party, although it proved unviable and merged with the established 'centre' party, the Liberals. On the other side, the West European communist parties have been moving towards a reconciliation with social democracy in its older sense, by emphasizing the importance of democracy and representative institutions as they already exist in Western Europe (see Carrillo 1977), abandoning the use of the term dictatorship of the proletariat, and criticizing in varying degrees the Leninist conception of a centralized vanguard party which will take power and then rule as the unique representative of the working class (see EURO-COMMUNISM).

Two aspects of social democracy in its late nineteenth-century sense deserve particular attention. One is the fact that in all capitalist countries social democratic parties have been the principal – and in terms of the achievement of substantial reforms the most successful – form of working-class political organization, while communist parties, and other groups claiming to be still more uncompromisingly revolutionary in their aims, have never succeeded in gaining the political support of more than a minority of the working class; in many cases such a small minority that these parties have become little more than political sects (although they have occasionally been influential in trade unions). The trend of development in the capitalist societies of the late twentieth century is to enhance this pre-eminence of social democratic politics still more, and any further movement towards socialism – which itself appears less certain than it did in Marx's and Engels's day – is therefore most likely to take place through electoral victories and a gradual accumulation of reforms, at least so long as capitalism avoids catastrophic economic crises or wars. The second important feature of social democracy is the consistent emphasis in its docrine upon the value of democracy as a political system. Engels himself, in his later years, generally supported this emphasis in his letters to social democratic leaders, and notably in his critical comments on the Erfurt Programme of the SPD (enclosed in a letter to Kautsky of 29 June 1891) in which he wrote: 'If one thing is certain it is that our Party and the working class can only come to power under the form of the democratic republic. This is even the specific form for the dictatorship of the proletariat'. In his comment on the name 'social democracy' cited earlier, though (*Volksstaat* foreword 1894), he still claimed that the ultimate political aim of communism was to overcome the state as such, and hence also democracy as one form of the state. There is undoubtedly some ambiguity in Engels's various pronouncements, but so far as the Marxists of the Second International were concerned there was a clear, and frequently reiterated, commitment to democracy not only as the process by which the working class would come to power, but as the substance of a socialist society. This was evident, in diverse ways, in the general outlook and particular writings of such different Marxists as Luxemburg, Kautsky and the Austro-Marxists. The latter perhaps chose the electoral road to socialism more firmly than any other group and refused to consider taking power without the clearly expressed support of a majority of voters; and one of them, Hilferding, confronting the fascist threat in Germany, made his principal aim the defence of Weimar democracy at a time when Thälmann and other communist party leaders were declaring that there was no essential difference between bourgeois democracy and fascist dictatorship.

Ever since 1917 the working-class movement, and Marxist thought, have been divided between social democracy and communism (i.e. Leninism, Bolshevism); a division which is seen by social democrats as one between democratic socialism and authoritarian or totalitarian socialism. In recent years, however, the difference in outlook has been somewhat attenuated by the development of the Eurocommunist movement, though it remains to be seen how far this will proceed. Two main problems face social democracy at the present time. One concerns not the possibility of attaining power – in the sense of forming a government – for several social democratic parties in Europe have done so for longer or shorter periods, but whether, having attained power in this sense they are able to accomplish a real socialist transformation of society; and indeed, whether that is what their electors actually want them to do. The second problem concerns the actual institutions of a democratic socialist society – how the economy, the political system, education, cultural life, etc. would be organized, or might be expected to develop – and this is still a matter of intense controversy among Marxists, including those who attempt to reform the existing socialist countries from within. (See SOCIALISM; COMMUNISM.)

Reading
Bauer, Otto 1920: *Bolschewismus oder Sozialdemokratie?*

Gay, Peter 1952: *The Dilemma of Democratic Socialism*.

Przeworski, Adam 1980: 'Social Democracy as a Historical Phenomenon'.

Praxis International, I, No. 1, 1981.

TOM BOTTOMORE

social formation   A term used rarely by Marx, who referred more frequently to SOCIETY. In the 1859 Preface he used the two terms interchangeably: after discussing the conditions in which bourgeois society, as the 'last antagonistic form of the social process of production', will disappear he concluded that 'with this social formation, therefore, the prehistory of human society comes to an end'. The term has become fashionable in the works of recent structuralist Marxists (see STRUCTURALISM), some of whom (e.g. Hindess and Hirst 1977) have contrasted the scientific concept 'social formation' with the ideological notion 'society', although the grounds on which this is done are not made clear. At all events, social formation, in actual usage, refers to two phenomena which are quite familiar to Marxists, and to sociologists of all persuasions – namely to *types of society* (e.g. feudal society, bourgeois or capitalist society), and to *particular societies* (e.g. France or Britain as a society) – and it does not appear that the mere introduction of a new term has brought any greater analytical rigour. A further development is to be seen in the use of the term 'social and economic (or socio-economic) formation', preferred by Godelier (1977) who says that it 'seems useful, above all, in the analysis of *concrete* historical realities' and employs it in a study of the Inca Empire in the sixteenth century. This term may have a certain value in so far as it expresses explicitly the idea present in the Marxist concept of society that economic and social elements are interrelated and articulated in a structure; but it still does not mention the ideological elements, and in short, like all concepts, it does not provide a comprehensive description.

Reading

Godelier, Maurice 1977: *Perspectives in Marxist Anthropology*, ch. 2.

Hindess, Barry and Hirst, Paul 1977: *Mode of Production and Social Formation*.

TOM BOTTOMORE

socialism   The modern socialist movement dates from the publication in 1848 of *The Communist Manifesto* by Marx and Engels. Its historical roots go back at least two hundred years earlier to the period of the English Civil War (1642–52) which produced a radical movement (the Diggers) with a brilliant spokesman in Gerrard Winstanley whose ideas corresponded in important respects to the principal tenets of socialism as we know them today. Other outstanding forerunners were Babeuf and his Conspiracy of the Equals during the French Revolution, the great English and French Utopians (Owen, Fourier, St. Simon; see UTOPIAN SOCIALISM) of the early nineteenth century, and the English Chartists of the 1830s and 1840s who first incorporated socialist ideas of democracy, equality, and collectivism into a large-scale working-class movement.

Unlike most of their predecessors, Marx and Engels saw socialism not as an ideal for which an attractive blueprint could be drawn up, but as the product of the laws of development of capitalism which the classical economists had been the first to discover and try to analyse. The form or forms which socialism might take would therefore only be revealed by an historical process which was still unfolding. Given this perspective, Marx and Engels quite logically refrained from any attempt to provide a detailed description, or even a definition, of socialism. To them it was first and foremost a negation of capitalism which would develop its own positive identity (communism) through a long revolutionary process in which the proletariat would remake society and in so doing remake itself.

Marx's most important text on the subject is the *Critique of the Gotha Programme* (1875) which was directed against the programme adopted by the congress at which the two branches of the German workers' movement (Lassalleans and Eisenachers) united to form the Socialist Workers Party, later renamed the Social Democratic Party of Germany. In his critique Marx distinguishes between two phases of communist society. The 'first phase' is the form of society which will immediately succeed capitalism. This phase will bear the marks of its origin: the workers as the new ruling class will need their own state (the DICTATORSHIP OF THE PROLETARIAT) to protect them against their enemies; people's mental and spiritual horizons will be coloured by bourgeois ideas and values; income, though no longer derived from the ownership of property, will have to be calculated according to work done rather than according to need. Nevertheless, society's productive forces will develop rapidly under this new order, and in the course of time the limits imposed by the capitalist past will be transcended. Society will then enter what Marx called 'the higher stage of communist society', under which the state will wither away, a totally different attitude to work will prevail, and society will be able to inscribe on its banner the motto 'from each according to his ability, to each according to his need'.

The *Critique of the Gotha Programme* was not published until 1891, eight years after Marx's death, and its key place in the body of Marxist doctrine was not established until Lenin made it a central focus of his enormously influential STATE AND REVOLUTION (1917), in which he stated that: 'what is usually called socialism was termed by Marx the "first" or lower phase of communist society', and this usage was thereafter recognized or adopted by practically all who regard themselves as Marxists. This explains why individuals or parties can without any inconsistency call themselves either socialist or communist, depending on whether they wish to emphasize the immediate or the ultimate goal of their revolutionary endeavours. It also explains why there is no anomaly in a party which calls itself communist governing a country it considers to be socialist.

In keeping with this theory the Soviet Union, as the society which emerged from the Russian Revolution, was officially designated socialist (the Union of Soviet *Socialist* Republics). In addition, all but one or two of the countries which, since 1917, have undergone revolutions involving profound structural change have adopted or accepted the socialist label. Including the Soviet Union these countries now comprise about 30 per cent of the world's land area and about 35 per cent of its population. In one sense, therefore, these countries can be treated

as 'really existing socialism' (Bahro 1978) and studied in the same way as any other historical formation like capitalism or feudalism.

For Marxists, however, this is not and could not be the end of the matter. For in their theory socialism is essentially a transitional stage on the road to communism. In analysing 'really existing socialist societies', therefore, it is necessary for Marxists to pose a very specific question: are these societies showing signs of moving in the direction of COMMUNISM, which for present purposes may be thought of as characterized by the elimination of classes and of certain very fundamental socio-economic differences among groups of individuals (manual and mental workers, city and country dwellers, industrial and agricultural producers, men and women, people of different races)? If they do show signs of moving in the direction of communism, they can be judged to be socialist in the sense of the Marxist theory. Otherwise they cannot be considered socialist in the Marxist meaning of the term.

So far answers to this question have tended to fall into four categories:

(1) Those that see 'really existing socialist' societies as conforming to the Marxist theory. This is the answer of the ruling parties in the Soviet Union and its close allies. According to official Soviet doctrine, the USSR is no longer characterized by antagonistic class or social conflicts (see CLASS CONFLICT). The population consists of two harmonious classes (workers and peasants) and one stratum (the intelligentsia), and is presided over by a 'state of all the people'. In place of class struggle as the driving force of history, the new socialist mode of production (labelled 'advanced socialism' in the Brezhnev era) is driven forward by the 'SCIENTIFIC AND TECHNOLOGICAL REVOLUTION' towards the ultimate goal of communism. (Giraud 1978).

(2) The second category of answers holds that Soviet-type societies remain socialist in their basic structure but that progress towards communism has been interrupted by the rise of a BUREAUCRACY which, owing to the underdeveloped state of the forces of production at the time of the revolution has been able to install itself in power and divert to its own uses a grossly disproportionate share of the social product. This bureaucracy, however, is not a

ruling class, and as the forces of production develop, its position will be weakened and it will eventually be overthrown by a second, purely political, revolution. After that, progress towards communism will be resumed. There are a number of versions of this theory, all stemming originally from the writings of Trotsky.

(3) The third category of answers holds that capitalism has been restored in the USSR and the other countries of 'really existing socialism' which acknowledge Moscow's leadership. The most prominent advocate of this view was the Communist Party of China (CPC) in the later years of the chairmanship of Mao Tse-tung. Mao believed that classes and class struggle must necessarily continue after the revolution, and that if the proletariat should fail to maintain its control over the ruling party and to pursue a consistent revolutionary line, the result would be the restoration of capitalism. The Maoists held that this had occurred in the USSR when Khrushchev came to power after Stalin's death. Others – most notably Bettelheim (1976, 1978) – argued that the capitalist restoration occurred in the 1920s and 1930s. After Mao's death the leadership of the CPC abandoned this position and reverted to one which appears to be increasingly close to the official Soviet doctrine summarized above under (1).

(4) The fourth category of answers is basically similar to the third but with one significant difference: it denies that capitalism has been restored in Soviet-type societies, arguing instead that these are class-exploitative societies of a new type. In the USSR itself the new ruling class formed itself in the course of intense struggles during the 1920s and 1930s. After the second world war the Soviet Union imposed similar structures on the countries liberated by the Red Army. Defining characteristics of this social formation are state ownership of the essential means of production, centralized economic planning, and the monopolization of political power through a communist party controlling a highly developed security apparatus. To those who hold this view, Soviet-type societies are obviously not in transition to communism and hence cannot be classified as socialist in the sense of the classical Marxist theory.

What emerges from the foregoing is that 'really existing socialism' is an extraordinarily complicated and controversial subject over which the views and theories of the world-wide Marxist movement are divided into various, often sharply conflicting, groups and subgroups. No resolution of these differences now seems to be in sight, though it remains possible that the course of history will alter the terms of the debate and perhaps lead eventually to something closer to a consensus than exists or seems possible under present circumstances. (See also CRISIS IN SOCIALIST SOCIETY; MARKET SOCIALISM.)

Reading

Bahro, Rudolf 1978: *The Alternative in Eastern Europe*.

Bettelheim, Charles 1976, 1978: *Class Struggles in the USSR*. Vols. I and II.

Giraud, Pierre-Noel 1978: 'L'Economie politique des régimes de type soviétique'.

Lenin, V. I. 1917c (1969): *State and Revolution*.

Mao Tse-tung 1977: *A Critique of Soviet Economics*.

Nuti, D. M. 1981: 'Socialism on Earth'.

Sweezy, Paul M. 1980: *Post-revolutionary Society*.

Trotsky, Leon 1937: *The Revolution Betrayed*.
                                          PAUL M. SWEEZY

socialization The concept has two different meanings, one in social anthropology and educational theory, the other in economics. To socialize a person in anthropological and educational terms means to create an environment in which he or she can learn a language, rules of conceptual thought, a segment of history of the community, practical habits necessary for survival and development, moral rules that regulate relationships with other members of the community. An individual is born with various potential dispositions characteristic of a human being. Without proper interaction with members of a social community at the appropriate stages of growth these dispositions would remain latent and would eventually fade away. Without actualizing his or her capacities for communication, reasoning, creative activity, cooperation in play and work, an individual would not develop into a human being. Moreover, many personal talents and hidden capacities would remain unrealized.

However, socialization also plays a restrictive, sometimes even crippling role. In transferring a specific culture to an individual, the community (the family, the school, the neighbourhood, the state), more often than not rigidly, heteronomously, imposes certain traditional ideas and norms on a young mind. The enormous spontaneity, curiosity and creativity of the child tend to be suppressed under the pressure of the *super-ego*. Beyond certain limits social repression, external or internalized, produces a 'little man' on a large scale, a weak, conformist personality who fears responsibility and ends up lending full support to authoritarian leaders and movements.

Socialization as an economic concept means the transformation of private property in the means of production into social property. *Abolition of private property* runs through all Marx's writings as a necessary, though not sufficient condition of communism. However the concept of private property has two meanings. One is private ownership of the means of production. The other is a general attitude to life characterized by the desire to *own* an object (or a person reduced to a thing) in order to be able to enjoy it, to appropriate it. The abolition of private property in this general philosophical sense involves an entirely different socialization of human individuals, characterized by a full development of creative capacities, of the *sense of being* rather than the *sense of having*.

Abolition of private ownership of the means of production may assume three different forms. One is *nationalization*, transferring all property rights from private firms to the state. In the countries of 'real socialism' socialization is largely reduced to nationalization. The state owns and manages the majority of enterprises (except in agriculture in some cases), plans the production and distributes the products. As a result a large political bureaucracy emerges which monopolizes both political and economic power. The economic system becomes overcentralized, leading to considerable suppression of initiative, waste and inefficency.

Another form of socialization involves transforming the means of production into group property. In agriculture, small-scale production and service cooperatives based on group property may be the most rational form of economic organization. The very nature of work in those areas favours small autonomous systems. This form of socialization is limited in so far as the cooperative may behave as a collective capitalist; hiring wage labourers, earning profit on the market, accumulating capital, producing a petty bourgeois class.

A third form of economic socialization most compatible with the aims of a classless society involves turning the means of production into the property of the entire society. Those means are then at the disposal of particular workers' communities which pay society a proportion of their total income for covering general social needs. They can decide freely about the distribution of the rest of the product. But they cannot alienate (sell, give to others, bequeath) those means of production. Socialization of this type presupposes SELF-MANAGEMENT as the form of social organization.

Reading
Korsch, Karl 1969: *Schriften zur Sozialisierung.*

Marković, Mihailo 1982: *Democratic Socialism, Theory and Practice*, ch. 5.

Nuti, Domenico Mario 1974: 'Socialism and Ownership'. In L. Kolakowski and S. Hampshire eds. *The Socialist Idea.*

                    MIHAILO MARKOVIĆ

socially necessary labour A concept concerned with the quantitative measurement of value. Marx writes in *Capital* I, ch. 1 that

> Socially necessary labour-time is the labour-time required to produce any use-value under the conditions of production normal for a given society and with the average degree of skill and intensity of labour prevalent in that society . . . What exclusively determines the magnitude of the value of any article is therefore the amount of labour socially necessary, or the labour-time socially necessary for its production.

Socially necessary labour is accordingly synonymous with ABSTRACT LABOUR, the substance of VALUE, and its measure is in units of time. The term invites a contrast with individual labour. Different firms in a particular branch of production will produce at varying degrees of technical efficiency, and not necessarily with the same technology of production.

Consequently, the individual labour time required to produce the commodity in each firm will differ. Yet the commodity will sell at the same price, no matter from which production process it emerges. Clearly, more efficient firms, in which individual labour time is less than socially necessary labour time, will realize more surplus value as profit per unit of output than less efficient firms, in which individual labour time is greater than socially necessary labour time. This difference between market value and individual value is behind the impulse continually to introduce new methods of production under capitalism, whereby each firm tries to reduce individual value by as much as possible in order to derive a competitive advantage over its rivals.

The labour time which proves to be socially necessary for the production of a commodity cannot be determined *a priori*, on the basis of some particular 'average' technique of production, as a quantity of embodied labour. This is for the same reason that value only appears in the form of exchange value as a sum of money; market value is the outcome of the process of COMPETITION, itself a consequence of the fact that it is only through market exchange that the social connections between the individual commodity producers are established under capitalism, and hence it is only in money that private labour takes the form of social labour.

There is sometimes confusion as to whether market value is determined by some sort of *averaging* process in the market, as the above remarks would imply, or whether it is determined by the individual labour time of the most efficient firm. The answer is both: the determination of value is not a static equilibrium state but a dynamic process in which no sooner has socially necessary labour time been established, than it is being altered by the bankruptcy of inefficient producers and by the innovations of more efficient ones. (See also VALUE AND PRICE; PRICE OF PRODUCTION AND THE TRANSFORMATION PROBLEM.)

Reading

Rubin, I. I. 1928 (*1973*): *Essays on Marx's Theory of Value*.

SIMON MOHUN

society Marx used the term 'society' (as do most sociologists) in three senses, which are contextually distinguished, to refer to distinct but related phenomena: (i) human society or 'socialized humanity' as such; (ii) historical types of society (e.g. feudal or capitalist society); and (iii) any particular society (e.g. ancient Rome or modern France).

What is distinctive in Marx's conception is, first, that it begins from the idea of human beings living in society, and does not involve an antithesis between individual and society which can be overcome only by supposing some kind of social contract, or alternatively, by regarding society as a supra-individual phenomenon. Thus, in the *Economic and Philosophical Manuscripts* (3rd MS), he writes: 'Even when I carry out *scientific* work . . . I perform a *social*, because *human*, act. It is not only the material of my activity – like the language itself which the thinker uses – which is given to me as a social product. My *own* existence *is* a social activity'. He continues by saying that we must avoid postulating 'society' as an abstraction confronting the individual, 'for the individual is a *social being*'. This aspect of Marx's conception was most fully developed later by Adler, who saw it, in neo-Kantian terms, as positing a transcendental condition for a science of society (Adler 1914).

A second feature of Marx's conception of human society in general is that it does not separate society from nature; on the contrary, human beings are treated as part of the natural world, which is the real basis of all their activities. The production and reproduction of material life, by labour and procreation, is thus both a natural and a social relationship (*EPM*). In this respect Marx's view differs profoundly from that which has been prevalent in much sociology, where society has often been treated as an autonomous phenomenon, and its relation to the natural world ignored, with the consequence that the study of economic processes and relationships has been largely excluded, and consigned to the sphere of a separate, specialized social science. It is for this reason that Korsch (1967) argued that Marx's 'materialistic science of society is not sociology, but political economy'.

Marx's general conception has a third distinguishing characteristic which connects it with his notion of 'types of society'; namely that it treats the relation between society and nature as a historically developing interchange, through human labour, which at the same time creates and transforms the social relationships among human beings (*Capital* I, ch. 5). This historical process (see HISTORICAL MATERIALISM) has two aspects, one being the development of productive forces (or technological advance), the other, the changing social division of labour which constitutes the social relations of production (see FORCES AND RELATIONS OF PRODUCTION) and above all class relations.

For Marx, therefore, it is the level of development of material powers of production, and the corresponding relations of production, which determine the character of distinct types of society; and in the 1859 *Preface* he designates the Asiatic, the ancient, the feudal and the modern bourgeois MODES OF PRODUCTION as 'progressive epochs in the economic formation of society'. The transition from one type of society to another occurs when the material forces of production come into conflict with the existing relations of production (see STAGES OF DEVELOPMENT), and this antagonistic relation takes the form of class conflict. Later Marxist scholars have been concerned with refining, extending and revising Marx's schematic presentation of the principal types of society. Thus on one side the concept of ASIATIC SOCIETY has been the object of considerable controversy, while on the other, the concept of TRIBAL SOCIETY has been more thoroughly analysed, as a result of the growth of Marxist anthropology, largely influenced in recent years by structuralism. At the same time, both the historical sequence of types of society and the precise nature of the transition from one to another (in particular the TRANSITION FROM FEUDALISM TO CAPITALISM), have been more closely examined on the basis of a far wider range of historical data.

Another major problem for Marxist analysis is posed by the present-day socialist societies (see CRISIS IN SOCIALIST SOCIETY; SOCIALISM). Here the main questions concern, first, the character of the social relations of production based upon collectivized forces of production – whether new class relations have emerged, in which there is a new dominant class constituted

by the party officials, the bureaucracy (Djilas 1957), the intellectuals (Konrád and Szelényi 1980) or some combination of these groups – and second, the nature of the state and political power in this type of society. More generally it can be asked to what extent the whole 'form of life' in these societies, as they actually exist, corresponds with Marx's idea of a 'society of associated producers' (socialism or communism). Only in the past few decades has a systematic and substantial Marxist analysis of this type of society begun to develop.

Finally, both Marx and Engels emphasized the need to engage in real historical study of particular societies, and followed this precept in their writings on England, France and Germany. Engels (letter to C. Schmidt, 5 August 1890) expressed their general view by saying that 'our conception of history is above all a guide to study . . . all history must be studied afresh'; while Marx (*Capital* III, ch. 47, sect. II) observed that an economic basis which is the same in its main characteristics can manifest 'infinite variations and gradations, owing to the effect of innumerable external circumstances, climatic and geographical influences, racial peculiarities, historical influences from the outside, etc.', and that such variations could only be grasped by investigating the 'empirically given conditions'. In fact, Marx's general conception of society, and his classification of the types of society, have shown their value above all in providing a framework for detailed historical and sociological studies of particular societies and conjunctures.

Reading

Adler, Max 1914: *Der soziologische Sinn der Lehre von Karl Marx.*
Godelier, Maurice 1977: *Perspectives in Marxist Anthropology,* ch. 3.
Korsch, Karl 1938 (1967): *Karl Marx.*

TOM BOTTOMORE

sociology Soon after Marx's death, in the period when sociology was becoming established as an academic discipline, there began a close, but often antagonistic, relationship between the Marxist theory of society and sociology which has continued to the present day. Undoubtedly Marxism was an important stimulus to the formation of sociology itself. Tönnies, in the preface to his influential book *Community and Association* (1887), acknowledged his indebtedness to Marx, whom he described as the discoverer of the capitalist mode of production, engaged in formulating the same idea about modern society that Tönnies himself was trying to express in new concepts. At the first international congress of sociology in 1894 scholars from several countries (among them Tönnies, and from Russia, Kovalevsky) contributed papers which discussed Marx's theory. This was also the time when the founding fathers of modern sociology – Max Weber and Émile Durkheim – were beginning to establish, in different ways, the principles and domain of the new discipline, to a considerable extent in critical opposition to Marxism (see CRITICS OF MARXISM). The relation of modern sociology to Marxist thought is most apparent in the case of Max Weber, the greater part of whose work bears directly upon Marxist problems, not only in his substantive studies of the origins and development of capitalism, and in his analyses of the state, class and status, the labour movement and socialism, but also in his methodological writings directed against historical materialism. Less intensely, Durkheim too was preoccupied with the Marxist theory: the *Année Sociologique* (which he founded and edited) in its early years paid serious attention, in book reviews, to the materialist conception of history. In 1895 Durkheim began a series of lectures on socialism which was intended to lead on to a comprehensive examination of Marxism (though it was abandoned before reaching that point), and in his last major work (1912) he took pains to distinguish his conception of the social functions of religion from the 'total social explanation' proposed by historical materialism.

By the end of the nineteenth century there was also a substantial independent Marxist contribution to sociology, including Kautsky's study of the French Revolution (1889); Mehring's *Die Lessing-Legende* (1893) which laid the foundations of a Marxist sociology of art and literature, and of the history of ideas; Sorel's critical examination of Durkheim's sociology in *Le Devenir social* (1895); and Grünberg's early studies of agrarian history

and the history of the labour movement. In Russia the diffusion of Marx's work gave rise to a strong Marxist current of thought in the social sciences, with Plekhanov as its major figure. Soon afterwards the first Marxist school of sociology emerged in the shape of AUSTRO-MARXISM, whose principal thinkers produced, over the next quarter of a century, major sociological studies of the development of capitalism, the class structure, law and the state, nationalities and nationalism.

The growth of Marxist sociology at this time took place almost entirely outside the universities (there were only two 'professorial Marxists', Grünberg and Labriola), and a considerable gulf therefore existed between Marxist thought, closely related to political movements and party organizations, and academic sociology. The situation could well be described, as it was later by Löwith (1932) in a study of Weber and Marx, as being such that, 'like our actual society, which it studies, social science is not unified but divided in two; bourgeois sociology and Marxism'. This view was reinforced after the Russian Revolution when Marxism became the doctrine of a workers' state encircled by capitalism. In 1921 Bukharin could still describe historical materialism as a 'system of sociology', and critically examine the work of such academic sociologists as Weber and Michels, but with the rise of Stalin sociology came to be officially categorized as 'bourgeois ideology', was excluded from academic and intellectual life, and replaced by historical materialism, expounded in an abstract and dogmatic form. This scheme of thought was then imposed upon the East European countries after 1945, and it also prevailed in China where sociology was abolished in universities and research institutes in 1952.

From the mid-1920s, therefore, Marxist sociology could only develop outside the USSR and in opposition to Bolshevik orthodoxy, and it became one important strand of thought in what has subsequently been called WESTERN MARXISM. But it was only one strand, for Western Marxism has been characterized by an extreme diversity of views. Thus on one side the Austro-Marxists pursued their sociological researches, while on the other Korsch, Lukács and Gramsci all rejected the idea of Marxism as sociology, and conceived it rather as a philosophy of history. Korsch (1923) described Marxism as 'the philosophy of the working class', 'the theoretical expression of the revolutionary movement of the proletariat', just as German idealist philosophy had been the expression of the revolutionary movement of the bourgeoisie. Lukács (1925), in a review of Bukharin's book on historical materialism, criticized his 'false methodology' and his 'conception of Marxism as a "General Sociology"', arguing that 'the dialectic can do without such independent substantive achievements [as those of sociology]; its realm is that of the historical process as a whole . . . the *totality* is the territory of the dialectic'. Similarly, Gramsci (1971) – also in a commentary on Bukharin – rejected sociology as 'evolutionist positivism' and presented Marxism as a philosophical world view, containing within itself 'all the fundamental elements needed to construct a total and integral conception of the world . . . and to become a total and integral civilization'. But the unsettled and fluctuating nature of Western Marxism is illustrated by the way in which Korsch (1938) subsequently revised his views, concluding that 'the main tendency of historical materialism is no longer "philosophical", but is that of an empirical scientific method' (p. 203).

The variability of Marxist attitudes to sociology also appears clearly in the work of the FRANKFURT SCHOOL. Though strongly influenced in its dominant ideas by Korsch and Lukács the School, and still more the Frankfurt Institute for Social Research which was its institutional basis, encompassed a wide variety of views (Held 1980). In its early years the Institute was directed by Grünberg, whose main interests lay in the field of social history and were close to sociology, and its members included sociologists, political scientists and economists, among them Franz Neumann whose *Behemoth* (1942) remains one of the most important Marxist studies of FASCISM. It was after 1945, and particularly in the 1960s, that the school came to be dominated by mainly philosophical thought, in the form of 'critical theory', directed against positivism in the social sciences, and of 'ideology-critique', which focused Marxist theory on the criticism of cultural phenomena, including science and technology treated as ideologies. But in its more recent development, notably in the work of HABERMAS and Offe, the orientation of critical theory has again changed, towards a greater concern with economic and political questions, in studies of the foundations of historical materialism as a theory of history, of the nature of capitalist crisis, and of the significance of the interventionist state in advanced capitalism. Since the 1960s another important new approach in Marxist sociology has developed under the influence of structuralism. Emerging primarily from the work of ALTHUSSER, but strongly affected by the general structuralist movement in linguistics and anthropology, Marxist structuralism has largely redirected attention away from historical problems and the idea of Marxism as a theory of history (which is rejected as historicism), towards the analysis of particular forms of society, and in particular capitalist society (though Godelier (1977) has brought the same approach to bear in the analysis of tribal society), as 'structures' in which economic, political, ideological and theoretical 'levels' or 'instances' are variously interrelated in a total system. Thus Poulantzas (1973, 1975) has analysed in structuralist terms the relation between social classes and political power, and the class position of the petty bourgeoisie or middle class in advanced capitalist societies. Even within the broad structuralist movement, however, there is considerable diversity, and one distinctive approach is that of Goldmann, whose 'genetic structuralism' combines historical and structuralist methods of analysis.

Since the mid 1950s, with the rapid decline in the intellectual influence of Stalinist (and more recently Leninist) orthodoxy, and the rise in the 1960s of a 'New Left', a notable revival of Marxist sociology has taken place, animated principally, in the West, by the ideas of critical theory and STRUCTURALISM, though as noted earlier there has also been a renewed interest in Austro-Marxism as a school of sociology. This revival has brought about a significant change in the position of Marxist theory in intellectual life as a whole; for whereas in the period from the 1890s to the 1940s Marxism existed primarily as a subculture in capitalist societies, closely related to political parties and studied mainly within party organizations (and after 1917 also as the official doctrine of a ruling party), it is now firmly established in academic life and constitutes an important element in the mainstream of sociological thought (as of anthropological and economic thought). One consequence of this change is that Marxist thinkers are now much more involved in the general controversies about the concepts and methods of the social sciences – Marxist and non-Marxist contributions to the debates about structuralism, positivism, the role of 'human agency' in social change, display many affinities as well as important differences – and about particular substantive issues, as for example in the analysis of political power, and of social classes, where Weberian conceptions are now taken more seriously, if not directly incorporated, in extensively revised Marxist schemas.

There has also been a revival in the socialist countries, where sociology was reinstated as an academic discipline in the years after 1953 in the USSR and Eastern Europe (earlier in Yugoslavia), and more recently (1979) in China. Here, however, the discipline has developed primarily in the form of social surveys and empirical studies in particular fields – such as education, welfare services, the family, industrial relations – which do not differ greatly from similar studies carried out by non-Marxist western sociologists. This preoccupation with policy research conforms with Lenin's early directive to the newly established Socialist Academy of Social Sciences to make 'a series of social investigations one of its primary tasks' (cited in Matthews 1978), and with Gramsci's view of the proper place of sociology, expressed in his criticism of Bukharin noted earlier, where he referred to its value as 'an empirical compilation of practical observations' which, in the form of statistics, would provide, for instance, a basis of planning. In most of these countries there has been little attempt (or opportunity) to develop Marxism as a sociological theory in a critical confrontation with other theories, and those who have undertaken such efforts, raising at the same time fundamental issues concerning the structure of existing socialist societies, have frequently been treated as dissidents and forced into exile (see, for example, Bahro 1978, Konrád and Szelényi 1979). The precise relation of sociological theory to historical materialism remains an acute problem, but this has not altogether prevented the borrowing and partial incorporation of elements from some non-Marxist western conceptions, such as functionalism or systems theory, or a considerable influence, in some countries, of earlier sociological orientations (e.g. conceptions of sociological theory strongly marked by positivism in Poland). In Yugoslavia the situation has been different and fundamental theoretical debates have taken place, frequently involving western Marxists (see Marković and Petrović 1979, and the contributions to the journal Praxis from 1964–74).

Marxism is now recognized as one of the major paradigms in sociology; but like other sociological systems today it is characterized by considerable internal diversity, and uncertainty, though perhaps retaining a greater coherence than many of its rivals. Its future development depends upon how successfully it can deal with a range of unresolved problems concerning the class structure, the role of classes and other social groups in bringing about social change, the relation between state and society, and between the individual and the collectivity; or in more general terms, can achieve 'a real analysis of the inherent nature of present-day capitalism' (as Lukács expressed it in 1970; see his prefatory note to Mészáros 1971), and also of present-day socialism. Progress in these respects will certainly involve further revision of some central theoretical conceptions, will be affected by more general currents of social thought and practice, and can scarcely hope to approach the goal of a more unified Marxist sociology without bridging the considerable gulf that still separates Western Marxism from Soviet Marxism.

Reading

Avineri, Shlomo 1968: *The Social and Political Thought of Karl Marx.*

Bottomore, T. 1975: *Marxist Sociology.*

Goldmann, Lucien 1970a: *Marxisme et sciences humaines.*

Gurvitch, Georges 1963: *La vocation actuelle de la sociologie*, ch. 12.

Korsch, Karl 1938 (1967): *Karl Marx.*

Löwith, Karl 1932 (1982): *Max Weber and Karl Marx.*

Matthews, Mervyn 1978: Introduction to *Soviet Sociology, 1964–75: A Bibliography.*

Osipov, G. V. and Rutkevich, M. N. 1978: 'Sociology in the USSR, 1965–1975'.

Schumpeter, J. A. 1976: *Capitalism, Socialism and Democracy*, ch. 2.

TOM BOTTOMORE

Sorel, Georges Born 2 November 1847, Cherbourg; died 28 August 1922, Boulogne-sur-Seine. Georges Sorel has traditionally been regarded as one of the most controversial figures in the history of Marxism. Such is the paradoxical nature of his thought that while he has been described as one of the most original of all Marxists it has also been suggested that he should be seen as a thinker of the right rather than of the left. What cannot be denied is that Sorel's thought went through a series of distinct phases in which his interpretation of Marxism and of what Marx had to say varied dramatically.

Sorel was educated at the École Polytechnique in Paris and until the age of forty-five was employed as a government engineer. His first writings began to appear in 1886 but it was not until 1893 (after his retirement) that he turned his attention to Marxism. Initially Sorel saw Marxism as a science and believed that Marx had discovered the laws that 'determined' the development of capitalism. He was, however, among the first to recognize the difficulties inherent in this position and from 1896 onwards began to develop his own highly original and idiosyncratic re-interpretation, according to which Marxism should be seen primarily as an ethical doctrine. Hence, in place of a predetermined economic collapse of capitalism, Sorel put forward the theory of a moral catastrophe facing bourgeois society.

In the first instance Sorel's reformulation of Marxism involved him in the attempt to elucidate a specifically working-class morality, support for working-class trade unions and cooperatives (which he believed capable of developing this morality), and also, like Bernstein, recommendation of the policies and practices of political reformism and democracy. Disillusionment with reformism and democracy followed rapidly and dramatically with the termination of the Dreyfus Affair, and after 1902 Sorel was to become the foremost theoretical exponent of revolutionary SYNDICALISM.

It was in his syndicalist writings, most notably *Reflections on Violence* (1906), that Sorel's earlier criticisms of Marxism as a deterministic science reached their logical conclusion. Taking the class war as the 'alpha and omega' of socialism, Sorel argued that the central tenets of Marxism should be seen as 'myths', as images capable of inspiring the working class to action. The most powerful of these 'myths', according to Sorel, was that of the general strike (see STRIKES) which, he believed, embodied in a vivid manner all the major features of Marxist doctrine. And it was to be through action, especially acts of VIOLENCE, that the working classes would simultaneously develop an ethic of sublimity and grandeur, destroy their bourgeois opponents, and, less obviously, establish the moral and economic foundations of socialism. In the process Western civilization would be saved from irredeemable decline. Not surprisingly, the syndicalist movement did not live up to Sorel's expectations and he withdrew his support for it in 1909. There followed a brief flirtation with the extra-parliamentary right, but Sorel's enthusiasm was rekindled shortly before his death by the new 'man of action', Lenin. He also cast an admiring glance at Mussolini.

Reading

Berlin, Isaiah 1979: 'Georges Sorel'. In *Against the Current: Essays in the History of Ideas*.

Jennings, Jeremy 1985: *Georges Sorel: The Character and Development of his Thought*.

— 1990: *Syndicalism in France: A History of Ideas*.

Roth, Jack J. 1980: *The Cult of Violence: Sorel and the Sorelians*.

Sand, S. 1984: *L'illusion du politique: Georges Sorel et le débat intellectuel 1900*.

Sorel, Georges 1906a (1969): *The Illusions of Progress*.

— 1906b (1972): *Reflections on Violence*.

— 1919 (1981): *Matériaux d'une théorie du prolétariat*.

— 1976: *From Georges Sorel: Essays in Socialism and Philosophy*.

Stanley, John L. 1982: *The Sociology of Virtue: The Political and Social Theories of Georges Sorel*.

Vernon, Richard 1978: *Commitment and Change: Georges Sorel and the Idea of Revolution*.

JEREMY JENNINGS

Soviet Marxism   Four distinct periods can be distinguished in Soviet Marxism up to the early 1980s: the Jacobin-ideological (the period of Lenin); the totalitarian manipulative (the period of Stalin); the reformist quest for the lost ideological dimension (the period of Khrushchev); and the conservative-iconographic (the period of Brezhnev).

Bolshevism brought to power elements of four theoretical heritages from which it extracted its own vintage of Marxism. The first was the Plekhanovian tradition of understanding Marx's (and Marxist) philosophy as DIALECTICAL MATERIALISM. This, in fact, meant the acceptance, albeit with some criticism, of the position of Engels (see MARXISM, DEVELOPMENT OF). Lenin, who was, and publicly called himself, Plekhanov's disciple in philosophy, introduced in his pre-revolutionary writings (the best-known being *Materialism and Empirio-criticism*) certain important modifications of Plekhanov's doctrine. Lenin went along happily with Plekhanov's rejection of the 'absolute' materialism of Engels, which meant attributing materiality to the whole universe in a philosophically naive and uncritical manner. Lenin's brand of materialism was based on his so-called 'epistemological' definition of matter which can be summed up in the following assertion: the concept of matter expresses nothing more than the objective reality which is given to us in sensation. This epistemological position would only have allowed for a phenomenalist formulation; i.e. for asserting the characteristic features of the phenomena as they appear to our knowledge (see KNOWLEDGE, THEORY OF). Instead, Lenin gave an essentialist twist to his conception when he treated the first and most important law of dialectics as reformulated by him – the unity and struggle of opposites – as an essential feature of reality itself.

Two further modifications introduced by Lenin into Plekhanov's conception, and into Marxist philosophy in general, were his type of atheism, and the tenet of two global trends ('two great camps') in philosophy. Both had antecedents in Marxism. But while for Marx religious belief as ALIENATION was an important socio-ontological aspect of the general problem of alienation, for Lenin it was primarily, if not exclusively, a socio-political issue.

The tenet of two global trends, materialism and idealism, in philosophy, had been invented by Engels who regarded them as individually selectible attitudes. With Lenin they became sociologically definable trends which inherently contained the later division of philosophy into a materialist form, carried by a socially progressive force, and an idealist form, carried by a reactionary one.

The second element was the sociological-economic dimension. Lenin himself, in his pre-revolutionary writings on the development of capitalism in Russia, on the theory of imperialism and the typology of revolutions, was a significant sociologist. However, the sociological aspect of the Bolshevik heritage was not greatly developed after the seizure of power, mainly because of the Jacobin self-delusions of the regime, although Bukharin (1921) expounded a conception of Marxism as a 'system of sociology' and examined critically some major works of Western sociology. Economic theory, however, was in full bloom. All the Bolshevik and leftist Menshevik leaders had been brought up in various schools of economic determinism and some of them (Bukharin, Bogdanov, and especially Preobrazhensky) were original thinkers in economic matters. After the seizure of power they all had to address theoretical economic problems of entirely unexpected dimensions. War Communism resulting from the civil war and foreign intervention presented the problem of the realization of a purely socialist model of production and distribution, while the New Economic Policy raised the problem of a mixed economy. Both implied the problem of the compatibility of the market with socialism and a planned economy. During the next 65 years of Soviet history there was never again a period of such vigour and originality in the theoretical discussion of economic, and to some extent social, issues. It took Stalin's crusades against the 'Leftist' and 'Rightist' opposition to stamp out this living spirit of Soviet Marxist (or *marxisant*) economic theory.

A further element of Soviet Marxism in the first period was a discussion of matters related to state power, violence and 'revolutionary law' (by Pashukanis, Stuchka, Krylenko and others). The dialogue was sincere and committed, but also restricted, for one major premiss, the principle of the dictatorship of the proletariat, in the sense given to it by the Bolshevik leaders, could not be radically or fully criticized, though the Workers' Opposition attempted to do so in the early years. The final dimension of Soviet Marxism in this period was its cultural theory, with Lunacharsky as its major representative (see ART).

In the following period Soviet Marxism assumed a radically different function. It was deployed in the service of charismatic legitimation and the charismatic leader, homogenizing society through the 'exclusively correct and scientific world-view' of Marxism-Leninism, and became purely instrumental. The first step was the introduction of the concept of Leninism, whose author, Stalin, established the framework of the 'new phase of Marxism' in his lectures on *Problems of Leninism* at the Sverdlovsk University of Moscow in 1924, and in his book, *Questions of Leninism* (1926). The lectures and the book enumerated the main tenets of Leninism as the Marxism of the new period: the general crisis of capitalism and the theory of imperialism, the party and its supporting organizations, the dictatorship of the proletariat, and so on – problems which Soviet political theory was obliged to address until recently.

The second phase was constituted by the destruction of two feuding groups, the mechanists and the Deborinists, whose theoretical dispute centred on the following issue. The mechanists (to whom Bukharin was also distantly related) denied the existence, or the relevance, of a separate Marxist philosophy, and regarded the natural sciences as the embodiment of a Marxist world-view. Deborin and his group, on the other hand, orthodox followers of Plekhanov, demanded the theoretical guidance of Marxist philosophy in all scientific research. The debate, which was carried on over a period of years (see Kolakowski 1978, vol. 3, ch. II; Wetter 1958, chs. VI–VIII), provided a good opportunity to establish the party's collective, and Stalin's personal, authority in theoretical questions. For the first time since 1917, a Central Committee session (25 January 1931) passed a resolution on purely theoretical matters, condemned both groups, dismissed scholars from their jobs and introduced new forms of administrative supervision over intellectual life.

The third major event was the publication of the *History of the CPSU(B)* (1938), which included a chapter on ' Dialectical and Historical Materialism'. The real author of the whole work was certainly not Stalin, as semi-official gossip had it; at best he played the role of supreme arbiter. However, it is correct to some extent to state that he was the author of the chapter on Marxist philosophy. The text listed three fundamental ontologico-epistemological features of philosophical materialism: 'the world is by its very nature material', 'matter is an objective reality existing outside and independent of the cognizing subject', 'philosophical materialism asserts that there are no unknowable things in the world'. It added four characteristics of dialectics: transformation of quantity into quality, the unity of opposites, the law of universal connections, and the law of universal mutability, the last two of which were innovations when compared with Engels, Plekhanov, and Lenin. From here, the text proceeds to treat historical materialism as the 'application' of dialectical materialism to social matters, briefly analysing such concepts as base and superstructure, modes and forces of production. Stalin clearly stated that dialectical and historical materialism thus described was the world-view of the communist party. However, Marcuse (1958) in a major study of Soviet Marxism in the Leninist, Stalinist and immediate post-Stalinist periods argued that it 'is not merely an ideology promulgated by the Kremlin in order to rationalize and justify its policies but expresses in various forms the realities of Soviet developments' (p. 9); and he went on to analyse in detail the principal theoretical tenets of Marxism in relation to Soviet practice.

In the main, the post-second world war history of Soviet Marxism up to Stalin's death consisted of purges and public reprobations, and the publication of two major texts by Stalin. In 1947, a version of a collective work on the *History of Western European Philosophy* was discussed in the Central Committee. The so-called 'Aleksandrov-discussion' (after the name of the general editor, G. F. Aleksandrov, director of the Philosophical Institute of the Soviet Academy of Sciences) served one major purpose. It was a public demonstration that the party, and Stalin himself, had not relaxed their ideological vigilance in an atmosphere of postwar hopes of a thaw. As such, it provided Zhdanov with the opportunity for an all-out attack against any signs of alleged or real attempts at liberalization in Soviet cultural life. The next representative discussion, the 1948 Michurin-debate over which Lysenko presided, rejected genetics as a bourgeois science on the basis of dialectical materialism (see LYSENKOISM). It was made crystal-clear that not even the natural sciences enjoyed immunity from ideological censorship.

Stalin's two texts, *Marxism and the Problems of Linguistics* (1950) and *Economic Problems of Socialism in the USSR* (1952), are extremely confused, and difficult to discuss from a theoretical standpoint; and more problematically this time, neither the aim in selecting these particular subjects, nor their sociological relevance, can easily be deciphered. The most likely interpretation is that Stalin wanted to defend his rule from two 'deviations'. On the one hand, he put an end to the obligatory principle of 'revolutionary leaps', and with it 'revolutions from above', and introduced instead the confused principle of a 'gradual leap' in 'nonantagonistic' Soviet society. He also rejected the economic principles of 'production for production's sake', and the demand for a direct exchange of products which would have eliminated even the remnants of the market. On the other hand, he further insisted on the necessity and possibility of a 'socialist world-market', and with it the hermetic separation of the Soviet Union and Eastern Europe from the capitalist world.

It was Khrushchev, not Stalin, who in fact put an end to the 'revolutions from above' and thereby introduced a new period in Soviet history, as well as in the history of Soviet Marxism. The main objective of Soviet Marxism in this period was to find the way back from mere propaganda to the functions of an attractive ideology. This happened with the characteristic inconsistency of the Khrushchev period, and comprised four main features. First, it involved not only the political but also the theoretical demotion of Stalin, at the XXth and XXIInd congresses of the CPSU. Second, a cult of Lenin, with the concomitant aim of the revival of 'Leninism', was initiated. Third, a measure of objectivity in research was demanded, of course combined with *partijnost* (party spirit),

which resulted in the publication of a number of more serious academic works, mainly from disciplines which had been touched upon in Khrushchev's criticism of Stalin, such as history and jurisprudence. Sociology was also re-established as an academic discipline at this time, and a good deal of empirical research has been undertaken in certain areas. It is noteworthy that much of this research differs little in method and approach from that in Western societies, and is not systematically related to Marxist theory. The main beneficiaries of the changes, however, were the natural sciences which, as a consequence also of the increased role of the military in Soviet society, gained almost complete freedom for scientific research. Finally, as Leninist fuel for their reformism, Khrushchev and his entourage revived Lenin's religious intolerance.

The fourth period of Soviet Marxism, the conservative iconographic era, was characterized by two main features. On the one hand, even nominal reforms were now abandoned. On the other hand, Marxism became iconographic in the sense that the content of 'Marxism-Leninism' in lectures and publications was now largely irrelevant, the major requirement being to pay respect to the existence and validity of its tenets. While Marxist-Leninist works were published in millions of copies, the society, and especially its ruling apparatus, became overwhelmingly pragmatic in outlook. Much of the political and ideological opposition which has become a more or less public factor in the last two decades, has turned its back on Marxism, though some critics (e.g. Roy and Zhores Medvedev) in the USSR as in Eastern Europe remain Marxists, while drawing upon forms of Marxist theory other than the official version (see MARXISM IN EASTERN EUROPE). Thus Soviet Marxism, treated as an empty formula by the rulers, ignored by a large part of the population (as is Christianity in the West), and rejected as an unimportant, if not outright dangerous, premiss by many in the opposition, traced a full circle of negative dialectics.

Reading

Blakeley, T. 1961: *Soviet Scholasticism*.

Bocheński, I. M. 1950: *Der sowjetrussische dialektische Materialismus*.

Chambre, H. 1974: *L'évolution du marxisme soviét-ique: théorie économique et droit.*
Chesnokov, D. I. 1969: *Historical Materialism.*
Glezerman, G. et al. 1959: *Historical Materialism.*
Jordan, Z. 1967: *The Evolution of Dialectical Materialism.*
Marcuse, H. 1958: *Soviet Marxism.*
Sheptulin, A. I. 1962: *Introduction to Marxist-Leninist Philosophy.*
Wetter, G. A. 1958: *Dialectical Materialism.*

FERENC FEHÉR

Postscript

Since the mid-1980s, as a consequence of the policies of *perestroika* and *glasnost*, the cultural context of Soviet Marxism has changed profoundly, in a cumulative process which has two principal features. First, Soviet scholars and intellectuals have been able to establish much closer contacts with, and have acquired a more thorough knowledge of, non-Marxist currents of thought in philosophy, the social sciences and the humanities. Secondly, against the background of this wider range of ideas, they can now examine in a more critical spirit some of the contentious issues in Marxist theory itself, investigate more thoroughly and realistically problems in the organization and functioning of Soviet society, and publish the results of their analyses and researches. Thus sociologists have begun to publish studies of a variety of social problems and to raise questions about social policies; economists have examined a range of issues concerning possible future forms of public and private ownership of productive resources, the development of markets in relation to new kinds of planning, and the improvement of economic management; and the growth of democratic debate accompanying the rise of new political movements has encouraged studies of public opinion, political attitudes and the structure of government. In philosophy, dialectical materialism seems no longer to hold undisputed sway, but is challenged or qualified by other philosophical conceptions, among them notably that of scientific realism.

The eventual outcome of these fundamental changes cannot yet be clearly foreseen, but a reorientation of Marxist thought in several directions seems inescapable. In the first place

Soviet Marxism will almost certainly shed the specific character imparted to it above all by Stalin, and will be increasingly reintegrated into a more general Marxist tradition, with all its diversity. This will also involve a thoroughgoing critical reappraisal of the history of Marxist thought, in which the contributions of different schools and thinkers will be more dispassionately examined. At the same time the role of Soviet Marxism as a state ideology will diminish, as has already happened in much of Eastern Europe, and this process will revive discussion of the general relationship between social theory and political practice, and more specifically the relation between Marxism as a theory of society and socialism as a doctrine, a movement or a form of society. Out of this there may emerge, in the best case, a fresh and invigorating style of Marxist analysis.

TOM BOTTOMORE

soviets. *See* councils.

Sraffa, Piero Born 5 August 1898, Turin; died 3 September 1983, Cambridge. A major, if enigmatic, figure in modern Marxism for two reasons: first, his relationship with Gramsci and the early Italian communist movement; second, the influence of his economic writings. As a student in 'Red Turin' in 1918–20 Sraffa contributed to Gramsci's journal *Ordine Nuovo*. By 1924, however, now a lecturer in Cagliari, he had become disenchanted with the communist party's leadership and its factions, and engaged in a significant exchange of correspondence on the subject with Gramsci just before the latter's leadership was consolidated. During Gramsci's subsequent incarceration Sraffa became his close friend, supporter and intellectual comrade.

In 1921 Sraffa visited Cambridge, initiating contacts with Keynes's circle which matured quickly to a point where he was a central member, and in 1927 became a Fellow of Trinity College where he carried out all his subsequent intellectual work. In 1926 he published a seminal article on price theory in the *Economic Journal*, 'The Laws of Returns Under Competitive Conditions', which was 'destined to produce the English branch of the theory of imperfect competition' (Schumpeter 1954, p. 1047) and set off a train of investigation culminating in the publication of *Production of Commodities by Means of Commodities* (1960). That book established Sraffa as a major figure in economic thought, for it provided the starting point of a vigorous school which set out to criticize the logical foundations of neo-classical economics, and to reconstruct those of Marxist economics, by posing an alternative theory of distribution based on class struggle over the level of wages and profits. The problems with which the school grapples can be traced back to Ricardo, and Sraffa's other intellectual monument is the definitive edition of Ricardo's *Collected Works* to which he devoted two decades of scholarship (see also RICARDO AND MARX).

Reading
Steedman, Ian 1977: *Marx after Sraffa.*
                                    LAURENCE HARRIS

stages of development Setting out to divide world history into stages, each with its own social-economic structure, and each following the other in some logical pattern, Marx and Engels inherited the thinking of the eighteenth century about four 'modes of subsistence' – hunting, pastoralism, agriculture, commerce – usually considered as forming a single sequence. Their own first outline, in *German Ideology* (vol. I, sect. I), was fairly simple, being restricted to European history: it singled out four eras, first the primitive communal or tribal, second the ancient or classical, based on slavery, third the feudal, and then the capitalist. In the preface to his *Critique of Political Economy* Marx seemed to take this series for granted, with the earliest epoch now dubbed 'Asiatic'. But his unpublished notes of the two previous years on pre-capitalist economic formations (in *Grundrisse*, pp. 471–514) show him groping into an evolutionary record which he realized to be far more complicated. He was seeking to identify all possible types of productive system, rather than to arrange them in order, or to explain how one had been supplanted by another. He did nevertheless put much weight on a quality of individual energy and initiative, a factor economic only at one or more removes, which evidently seemed to him part of the reason for Europe evolving and Asia failing to

do so beyond a certain point. He found two sources of it: the classic Mediterranean city, cradle of a civic life unknown to Asia, and a kind of ownership in early western Europe which he called 'Germanic', in contrast with the 'Slavonic' or eastern, with land he believed owned individually instead of communally. In the *Grundrisse* the example in which he showed most interest was that of Rome, winning mastery of a Mediterranean world dominated by armed competition for land. He saw a peasant folk transformed by over-population and resulting wars of conquest into an oligarchical slave economy. Why this simple Malthusian causation did not have similar consequences elsewhere, particularly in Asia, was a question he did not raise.

In *Anti-Dühring* (pt. 2, ch. 4) Engels derived slavery more directly from primitive life, out of which he saw it as the first step forward. Later, sharing Marx's enthusiasm for Morgan's study (1877) of the primitive clan, he drew on it to analyse the disintegration of 'gentile' or clan society, and the emergence of the state on its ruins, in Athens; he explained the mutation as being due to growing exchange of commodities, which were gaining the ascendancy over their makers, many of whom were plunged into debt as money came into circulation. Under this stimulus, with increasing division of labour and the rise of a merchant class, an 'upper stage' of barbarism arrived at the threshold of civilization (*Origin of the Family*, chs. 5, 9). Lafargue followed in his footsteps with a lively popularization of the theory, tracing history's successive eras from primitive communism to capitalism, whose mission was to lay the foundations for a new and more advanced communism. He thought of all societies as travelling the same road, just as all human beings pass from birth to death (1895, ch. 1).

Marx himself had repudiated with some warmth any belief in a fixed series, to be expected everywhere (draft letter to editor of *Otechestvenniye Zapiski*, November 1877); and near the close of his life he tentatively considered the possibility of a direct advance, given favourable European conditions, from the lingering primitive communism of the *mir* or Russian commune to modern socialism. Marxists after him and Engels were left with many puzzles. Plekhanov elaborated the European cycle, but described Asia as moving away from their common beginnings in a different direction, because of geographical and climatic circumstances which promoted state power founded on water-control. In 1931, however, the concept of a distinct 'Asiatic' mode (see ASIATIC SOCIETY) was rejected by Soviet scholars at the end of a searching review of the problems of periodization (Dirlik 1978, pp. 180–1, 196–8; Enteen 1978, pp. 165 ff.). With it could be banished the enigma of Asia's long immobility that Marx had tried to find reasons for. A mode of production, Stalin pronounced (1938) 'never stays at one point for a long time', and is always in a state of change and development in which the labouring masses are the chief motive force. The field was now open to the hypothesis of a single, universal pattern. This could be simplified by slavery ceasing to be regarded as a necessary part of it, which would leave nothing between clan and capitalist factory except feudalism. But the textbook edited by Kuusinen (1961) included slavery, and laid it down firmly that despite local variations 'all peoples travel what is basically the same path', because the development of production always 'obeys the same internal laws' (p. 153). Somewhat inconsistently, room was found for 'many periods of stagnation and retrogression', and the collapse of not a few civilizations (p. 245).

Another Soviet theorist, Glezerman, agreed that the laws of history cannot be abrogated and the order in which stages occur is unalterable, but he dwelt on the possibility of some stages, like slavery, being missed out, and thought the doctrine of an invariable series had done harm to the Second International by allowing it to be argued that imperialism was performing a needful task by forcing capitalism on to colonies (1960, pp. 202, 206). Lenin, it may be noted, derided any notion of China being able to jump to socialism without passing through a long preparatory era of capitalism ('Democracy and Narodism in China', July 1912). But WESTERN MARXISM has been inclined in recent years to think of more and more flexible and variable sequences. Thus Gordon Childe made much of cases of 'leapfrogging', like that of Europe learning metallurgy from the Near East without having to go through the preliminary steps leading up to it (see e.g.

1950; also ARCHAEOLOGY AND PREHISTORY), while Garaudy maintained that Marxism is stultified by being applied woodenly, and the 'five stages' taken as 'absolute and complete truth' for all mankind (1969, p. 46). Melotti in Italy is another who finds the unilinear scheme imperialistic, while at the same time he dismisses the postulate, derived in his opinion from Montesquieu, Hegel, and the classical British economists, of two separate and unequal lines of development, European and Asian (1972, pp. 46, 156). In their place he puts forward a complex diagram of five parallel but interacting lines, all stemming from the primitive commune (pp. 25–26).

With all this, the mechanics of change, and the question why change has seemed to follow diverse routes, or not to happen at all over very long epochs, have remained in many ways elusive. Much thought has been expended on the emergence of medieval feudalism not from a single predecessor but from an intricate combination of late Roman and barbarian. Marx and Engels wrote about capitalism arising from feudalism, that is from the peculiar European form of this, with its significant urban element; but even here, it has often been observed, they had not much to say about the process in detail, or about inner contradictions of feudalism to bring it on. Europe's transition from medieval to modern continues to be one of the most difficult and absorbing of all problems for Marxist historians (see TRANSITION FROM FEUDALISM TO CAPITALISM).

These now include many outside Europe, with points of view of their own to put forward. In India they have been coming to reject Marx's picture of long-drawn stagnation, in favour of a supposition (for which adequate evidence is so far lacking) that early forms at least of capitalism were sprouting when progress was cut short by British conquest (see MARXISM IN INDIA). For some Asian Marxists a universal sequence, far from being resented as a Western imposition, has had the attraction of representing a claim to equality with Europe. It was being discussed in China by 1930, and the idea of a separate 'Asiatic society' found little acceptance. Among the difficulties which have arisen has been that of discovering a slave era in ancient China corresponding with the Graeco-Roman. (See also HISTORICAL

MATERIALISM; MODE OF PRODUCTION; PRO-
GRESS.)

Reading

Dirlik, Arif 1978: *Revolution and History. The Origins of Marxist Historiography in China, 1919–1937.*

Enteen, George M. 1978: *The Soviet Scholar-Bureaucrat. M. N. Pokrovski and the Society of Marxist Historians.*

Evans, M. 1975: *Karl Marx.*

Glezerman, Grigory 1960: *The Laws of Social Development.*

Hilton, R. H. ed. 1976: *The Transition from Feudalism to Capitalism.*

Kuusinen, O. ed. 1961: *Fundamentals of Marxism-Leninism.*

Lafargue, Paul 1895 (1910): *The Evolution of Property from Savagery to Civilisation.*

Melotti, Umberto 1972 (1977): *Marx and the Third World.*

Plekhanov, G. V. 1895 (1945): *In Defence of Materialism. The Development of the Monist View of History.*

V. G. KIERNAN

Stalin (real name Dzhugashvili), Iosif Vissarionovich Born 21 December 1879, Gori, Georgia; died 5 March 1953, Kuntsevo, Moscow. Stalin was the son of a poor cobbler, and was almost the only top leader of the Soviet Communist Party who rose from the lower depths of tsarist society. He was educated at a theological seminary in Tbilisi, but was frequently punished for his revolutionary interests (which included reading such forbidden literature as Victor Hugo's novels); in 1899 he left or was expelled, and became a professional revolutionary. He advanced steadily in the Social-Democratic (Marxist socialist) movement, identifying himself with Lenin and Bolshevism as early as 1904, and was coopted to the Bolshevik central committee in 1912. From 1902 onwards his revolutionary activities frequently led to arrest, imprisonment, exile and escape; in 1913 he was exiled to the far north of Siberia, being released only after the Russian revolution of February/March 1917.

After the Bolshevik revolution of October/November 1917 and during the Civil War which followed it Stalin occupied many leading posts, and was elected to the party Politburo

as soon as it was established. In April 1922 he was appointed general secretary of the party, and after Lenin's death in January 1924 defeated the successive oppositions of Trotsky, Zinoviev and Bukharin; by the time of his fiftieth birthday in December 1929 he was the supreme leader of Soviet party and state. In the 1930s, he dominated the triumphs of industrialization and the horrors of famine and purges; in 1941–45 he was commander-in-chief of the bitter struggle against the Nazi invasion; after the war he was the only major wartime leader to remain uninterruptedly in office until his death.

Stalin was an outstanding tactician, and a ruthless and unscrupulous politician; he used his power both to destroy all who stood in his way and to transform agrarian Russia into an industrial super-power. For these dual qualities he was both feared and admired. He is often portrayed as a man of mediocre intellect who obtained his power purely by ruthless cunning. Trotsky described him as a 'stubborn empiricist', but this is an underestimation; the pervasive ideology designed by Stalin was of major importance in consolidating the Soviet regime.

Stalin's theoretical writings were lucid and oversimplified; this was an important element in their appeal. Already in 1906 he had written *Anarchism or Socialism?*, a polemic against Kropotkin which at the same time presented an account of dialectical and historical materialism; and the essay reappeared in revised form in 1938 as chapter four of *A History of the Communist Party of the Soviet Union (Bolsheviks): Short Course.* This exposition of the laws of society dominated Marxist thinking in many communist parties until Mao Tse-tung's writings *On Practice* and *On Contradiction* were publicized after Stalin's death. Stalin's second major theoretical work, *Marxism and the National Question*, written in 1912–13 with Lenin's participation, defended the establishment of a centralized Social-Democratic party for all the nationalities of the Russian Empire. In April 1924, Stalin's lectures *The Foundations of Leninism* boldly declared that Leninism was not merely a version of Marxism applicable to a peasant country; it was 'Marxism of the era of imperialism and the proletarian dictatorship', of world-wide validity. Stalin stressed the role of the party as the 'leading and organized detachment' of the working class, 'the embodiment of unity and will', which 'becomes strong by cleansing itself of opportunist elements'. The Leninist style in work combined 'Russian revolutionary sweep' with 'American efficiency'. These pronouncements were combined with the insistence (from the end of 1924 onwards) on Socialism in One Country: the construction of SOCIALISM could be completed in the Soviet Union without a socialist revolution elsewhere. In a further development of doctrine in 1928 he proclaimed that the class struggle would be intensified as the advance to socialism proceeded (see STALINISM).

This distinctively Stalinist ideology underpinned the drive for industrialization and collectivization, and the ruthlessness with which it was carried out. Thus the doctrine of the intensification of the class struggle provided the basis for proclaiming the necessity of 'eliminating the kulaks [rich peasants] as a class' in December 1929. In the course of the 1930s Stalin also ruled that the proletarian state could not wither away with the transition to socialism; it must be strengthened because of the capitalist encirclement. In the midst of the purges of 1936–38 he announced that socialism had been established in the USSR and that the absence of antagonistic contradictions within socialist society meant that all hostile actions and beliefs came from outside. Stalin effectively combined a quasi-Marxist class analysis with an appeal to Russian patriotism.

In 1950 and 1952, Stalin's pamphlets *Marxism and Linguistics* and *Economic Problems of Socialism in the USSR*, though largely within the established framework of Stalinist orthodoxy, curiously and tentatively launched the process of ideological destalinization, insisting on the importance of the 'clash of opinions' (!) within Marxism and admitting the possibility that the relations of production could lag behind the forces of production (see FORCES AND RELATIONS OF PRODUCTION) within socialist society. But no one in the world communist movement could question any of Stalin's ideas until after his death; and they were still influential in the Soviet Union, and elsewhere, thirty years later.

Reading

Alesandrov, G. F. *et al.* 1952: *Joseph Stalin: a Short Biography.*

Carr, E. H. 1958: 'Stalin'. In *Socialism in One Country, 1924–1926*, vol. 1.

Deutscher, I. 1949 *(1966)*: *Stalin.*

Ellis, J. and Davies, R. W. 1951: 'The Crisis in Soviet Linguistics'.

McNeal, R. H. ed. 1967: *Stalin's Works: an Annotated Bibliography.*

Rigby, T. H. ed. 1966: *Stalin.*

Souvarine, B. 1935 *(1939)*: *Stalin: a Critical Survey of Bolshevism.*

Stalin, J. V. 1901–34 *(1952–5)*: *Works*, vols. 1–13 (covering 1901–34).

— 1972: *The Essential Stalin: Major Theoretical Writings, 1905–52.*

Tucker, R. C. 1973: *Stalin as Revolutionary, 1879–1929: a Study in History and Personality.*

R. W. DAVIES

Stalinism mainly refers to the nature of the regime which existed in the Soviet Union under Stalin from the late 1920s, when he achieved supreme power, to his death in 1953. The term 'Stalinism' was not officially used in the Soviet Union during Stalin's lifetime; nor has it been officially used there since his death. But since the XXth Congress of the Communist Party of the Soviet Union in 1956, when Khrushchev denounced Stalin's crimes, the terms 'Stalinism' and 'Stalinist' have been given a loose and highly pejorative meaning, notably on the left, and are intended to denote dictatorial, arbitrary and repressive modes of conduct by left-wing individuals and regimes.

The first and most notable characteristic of Stalinism is the absolute power which Stalin wielded for a quarter of a century. Stalinism was obviously not the work of Stalin alone, and must be seen in the context of Russian history, the conditions in which the Bolshevik Revolution was made, and the problems which the Bolshevik regime confronted in the years preceding Stalin's achievement of absolute power (see BOLSHEVISM). But Stalin nevertheless played a crucial role in determining the particular character of the regime which bears his name. The 'cult of personality' which surrounded him, and which grew to utterly grotesque dimensions in the last years of his rule, is an accurate reflection of the extent of the power he wielded.

In its early phase, from 1929 to 1933, Stalinism represented what Stalin himself called a 'revolution from above', designed to lay the basis for the transformation of the Soviet Union into an industrialized country. One part of that 'revolution from above' was the 'collectivization' of Soviet agriculture, which brought the great majority of peasants into collective and state farms. This policy met with fierce resistance in the countryside and was carried out with ruthless determination and at terrible human and material cost. The other part of the Stalinist 'revolution from above' was an exceedingly ambitious programme of heavy industrialization, as proposed in the First Five Year Plan adopted in 1929 and pushed forward in the following years.

These policies could not have been put into practice without an extreme centralization of power, the suppression of dissent and the complete subordination of society in all its aspects to the dictates of the state. Tendencies in these directions were already well developed before Stalin's accession to supreme power: Stalinism enormously accentuated them. The Communist Party itself was turned into an obedient instrument of Stalin's will; and foreign communist parties were also required to follow and defend whatever policies were decided by Stalin and his lieutenants.

The first phase of the Stalinist revolution appeared to be over by 1934; after the turmoil of the previous years, the time seemed ripe for more measured forms of development and for a reduction in the state's power of arbitrary repression. Yet it was in the following years that the 'Great Terror' engulfed millions of Soviet citizens and saw the extermination of most major figures of the Bolshevik Revolution. The most spectacular feature of these years (in a macabre literal sense) was the succession of trials in which 'Old Bolsheviks' such as Bukharin, Zinoviev, Kamenev and many others confessed in open court to an extraordinary number of crimes, including complicity with Trotsky (exiled from the Soviet Union since 1929) and foreign intelligence services in plotting the overthrow of the Soviet regime, the restoration of capitalism and the dismemberment of the Soviet Union.

A unique feature of the repression, then and later, was the extent to which it affected all parts of the Soviet 'power elite', including its administrative, military, scientific, cultural and other cadres, not least the police and security apparatus itself. The Soviet elites were accorded considerable privileges by the regime: but the price they paid for these privileges was the constant danger of sudden arrest on false charges, deportation and death. The system made possible extraordinarily rapid advances in the bureaucratic hierarchies of Soviet society, because of the need to fill the vast number of posts rendered vacant by repression; but those who filled them were themselves equally vulnerable to repression. No regime in history has cast down with such murderous ferocity so many of those whom it had previously raised.

By 1939, however, much had been accomplished by way of economic and social development; and the visible achievements greatly helped to blur, at least abroad, the repressive and arbitrary side of the regime. So did such events as the promulgation of the Stalin Constitution of 1936 ('the most democratic Constitution in the world'). But perhaps most important of all in helping to blur the negative aspects of the regime was the threat of aggression posed by Nazi Germany and Fascist Italy, and the Soviet regime's opposition to FASCISM.

A 'Stalinized' Comintern (see COMMUNISM; INTERNATIONALS) had from 1928 until 1935 laid down policies for all communist parties which proclaimed that Social Democrats were 'Social Fascists' who must be viewed as the most dangerous enemies of the working class. This had greatly divided working-class movements everywhere and had contributed, in Germany, to the victory of Nazism. In 1934, however, the Soviet Union had joined the League of Nations and a new 'line' adopted by the Comintern in 1935 now proclaimed the need for 'Popular Fronts' in which Communists, Social Democrats, radicals, liberals and all other people of good will could join in the defence of democracy against fascism. In the following four years, marked by repeated fascist aggression, the Soviet Union appeared to many people to be the staunchest bulwark against fascism, almost the only one in fact, given the appeasement policies pursued by Britain and France.

This image was dealt a severe blow by the Nazi–Soviet Pact of non-aggression in August 1939; but this was soon forgotten when Hitler attacked the Soviet Union in June 1941. The heroic struggles of the Soviet armies and people made a decisive contribution to the Allied victory over fascism; and the war cost the Soviet Union some 20,000,000 lives and untold devastation. On the other hand, success in war also meant that Stalin's concern for the Soviet Union's security could be satisfied by the imposition of sympathetic regimes in contiguous countries. Eastern Poland and the Baltic states had already been annexed to the Soviet Union in 1939. Regimes acceptable to Stalin also came into being at the end of the war in Poland, Bulgaria, Hungary, Romania and East Germany. In due course, and in part at least under the impact of the Cold War, these regimes came to assume a wholly 'Stalinized' form.

Neither the ordeal of war nor victory brought any change to the nature of the Stalinist regime in the Soviet Union itself. On the contrary, the regime remained as repressive as ever and the labour camps now received new intakes of returned prisoners of war and workers repatriated from forced labour in Germany. The years following the war were also marked by further campaigns designed to impose Stalinist orthodoxy in all areas of intellectual and cultural life, with the wholesale persecution of intellectuals and others suspected of deviant thoughts: among those particularly affected were Jewish intellectuals, artists and others, who were denounced as 'rootless cosmopolitans'. It was only Stalin's death in March 1953 which prevented a further and massive extension of repression and terror.

In doctrinal terms, Stalinism was marked by the attempt to turn Marxism into an official state ideology, whose main tenets and prescriptions were authoritatively laid down by Stalin, and which therefore required total and unquestioning obedience. The most notable document in which this Stalinist orthodoxy found expression was the *History of the Communist Party of the Soviet Union (Bolsheviks)*, first published in 1938, and often reprinted, with suitable changes as circumstances demanded. At the time of publication, only the section on 'Dialectical and Historical Materialism' was attributed to Stalin, but it was said after the war that he was the

author of the whole book. At any rate, it provided an historical, philosophical and political compendium of official truth in the Stalin era. Stalin also intervened from time to time in a variety of theoretical areas, from history and economics to linguistics; and so did his lieutenants. His opinions and theirs were also binding on all Soviet citizens.

A number of tenets of Stalinism may be singled out. Perhaps the most important was the assertion that it was possible to build 'socialism in one country'; and this was counterposed to Trotsky's alleged adventurist internationalism. 'Socialism in one country' had strong nationalist connotations and enhanced what Lenin had earlier denounced as 'Great Russian chauvinism'. Another Stalinist tenet was that the state must be greatly strengthened before it could be expected to 'wither away', in accordance with Marxist doctrine. A third tenet of Stalinism, related to the second, was that the class struggle would grow in intensity as socialism advanced.

The question of the relationship of Stalinism to Marxism has been the subject of fierce controversy. The claim has often been made – both by Stalinists and by opponents of Marxism on the right – that Stalinism was a direct continuation or 'application' of Marxism. One of the main grounds on which this claim could seem to be sustained, was that Stalin maintained and extended the 'socialist' basis of the regime, that is to say the public ownership of the means of economic activity. This was also one of the main reasons for the difficulty which Marxist opponents of Stalinism experienced in explaining the nature of the regime, and in deciding whether it should be seen as a 'deformed workers' state', a form of 'state capitalism', or a regime of 'bureaucratic collectivism' (see TROTSKYISM). Against the view of Stalinism as a continuation or 'application' of Marxism, it may be said that Stalinism contravened the most fundamental propositions of Marxism at many points, and most of all in its total subordination of society to a tyrannical state.

Stalin's successors did not fundamentally transform the main structures of the regime which they inherited from him. But they did bring mass repression and terror to an end; and it is in this sense that Stalinism may be said to have come to a close with the death of Stalin.

Reading

Cliff, Tony 1964: *Russia: a Marxist Analysis*.

Cohen, Stephen F. 1974: *Bukharin and the Bolshevik Revolution*.

Deutscher, Isaac 1963: *The Prophet Outcast: Trotsky 1929–40*.

— 1949: *Stalin*.

Medvedev, Roy 1971: *Let History Judge*.

Nove, A. 1964: *Economic Rationality and Soviet Politics: or, Was Stalin Really Necessary?*

Shachtman, Max 1962: *The Bureaucratic Revolution: The Rise of the Stalinist State*.

Stalin, Joseph V. 1972: *The Essential Stalin: Major Theoretical Writings, 1905–1952*.

Trotsky, Leon 1937: *The Revolution Betrayed: What is the Soviet Union and Where is it Going?*

Tucker, Robert, C. 1977: *Stalinism*.

                                    RALPH MILIBAND

State, the A concept of crucial importance in Marxist thought, for Marxists regard the state as the institution beyond all others whose function it is to maintain and defend class domination and exploitation. The classical Marxist view is expressed in the famous formulation of Marx and Engels in the *Communist Manifesto*: 'The executive of the modern state is but a committee for managing the common affairs of the whole bourgeoisie.' This is a more complex statement than appears at first sight, but it is too summary and lends itself to over-simplification: however, it does represent the core proposition of Marxism on the subject of the state.

Marx himself never attempted a systematic analysis of the state. But his first lengthy piece of writing after his doctoral dissertation, namely *Critique of Hegel's Philosophy of the State* (1843), is in large part concerned with the state; and the subject occupies an important place in many of his works, notably in his historical writings, for instance in *Class Struggles* (1850), *18th Brumaire* (1852) and *Civil War in France* (1871). Engels too deals at length with the state in many of his writings, for instance in *Anti-Dühring* (1878) and in *Origin of the Family* (1894).

One of Lenin's most famous pamphlets, *State and Revolution*, written on the eve of the Bolshevik Revolution, was intended as a restatement of the Marxist theory of the state against what he took to be its corruption by Second International 'revisionism'; and others in the Marxist tradition have been concerned with the state – for instance members of the 'Austro-Marxist' school such as Max Adler and Otto Bauer (see AUSTRO-MARXISM) and, most notably, Gramsci. But it is only since the 1960s that the state has become a major field of investigation and debate within Marxism. This relative neglect may be attributed in part to the general impoverishment of Marxist thought produced by the predominance of Stalinism from the later 1920s to the late 1950s; and also to an over-'economistic' bias (see ECONOMISM) which tended to allocate a mainly derivative and 'superstructural' role to the state, and to see it, unproblematically, as the mere servant of dominant economic classes. Much of the recent work on the state has, on the contrary, been concerned to explore and explain its 'relative autonomy' and the complexities which attend its relationship to society.

In *The Philosophy of Right*, Hegel had sought to present the state as the embodiment of society's general interest, as standing above particular interests, and as being therefore able to overcome the division between CIVIL SOCIETY and the state and the split between the individual as private person and as citizen. Marx rejects these claims in his *Critique* on the ground that the state, in real life, does not stand for the general interest but defends the interests of property. In the *Critique*, Marx advances a mainly political remedy for this inability of the state to defend the general interest, namely the achievement of democracy. But he soon moved on to the view that much more than this was required and that 'political emancipation' alone could not bring about 'human emancipation'. This required a much more thorough reorganization of society, of which the main feature was the abolition of private property.

This view of the state as the instrument of a ruling class, so designated by virtue of its ownership and control of the means of production, remained fundamental throughout for Marx and Engels. The state, Engels said in the last book he wrote, is 'as a rule, the state of the most powerful, economically dominant class, which, through the medium of the state, becomes also the politically dominant class, and thus acquires new means of holding down and exploiting the oppressed class' (*Origin of the Family*, ch. 9). This, however, leaves open the question why and how the state, as an institution separate from the economically dominant class or classes, plays this role; and the question is particularly relevant in capitalist society, where the distance between the state and economic forces is usually quite marked.

Two different approaches have, in recent years, been used to provide an answer to this question. The first relies on a number of ideological and political factors: for instance, the pressures which economically dominant classes are able to exercise upon the state and in society; and the ideological congruence between these classes and those who hold power in the state. The second approach emphasizes the 'structural constraints' to which the state is subject in a capitalist society, and the fact that, irrespective of the ideological and political dispositions of those who are in charge of the state, its policies must ensure the accumulation and reproduction of capital. In the first approach, the state is the state of the capitalists; in the second, it is the state of capital. However, the two approaches are not exclusive but complementary.

Notwithstanding the differences between them, both approaches have in common a view of the state as subordinate to and constrained by forces and pressures external to itself: the state, in these perspectives, is indeed an agent or instrument, whose dynamic and impulse is supplied from outside. This leaves out of account a very large part of the Marxist view of the state, as conceived by Marx and Engels. For they attributed to the state a considerable degree of autonomy. This is particularly clear in relation to the phenomenon to which both Marx and Engels gave particular attention, namely dictatorial regimes such as the Bonapartist regime in France after Louis-Napoleon Bonaparte's *coup d'état* of 1852 (see BONAPARTISM). In *18th Brumaire*, Marx said that France seemed as a result of the *coup d'état* 'to have escaped the despotism of a class only to fall back beneath the despotism of an individual, and indeed beneath the authority of an individual without authority'. 'The struggle', he went on, 'seems to have reached the compromise that all classes fall on their knees, equally mute and equally impotent, before the rifle

butt' (sect. 7). Bonapartism, Marx also said in *The Civil War in France* nearly twenty years later, 'was the only form of government possible at a time when the bourgeoisie had already lost, and the working class had not yet acquired, the faculty of ruling the nation' (sect. 3); and Engels also noted in *Origin of the Family* that, 'by way of exception', 'periods occur in which the warring classes balance each other so nearly that the state power, as ostensible mediator, acquires, for the moment, a certain degree of independence of both' (ch. 9). The absolute monarchies of the seventeenth and eighteenth centuries, and the regimes of Napoleon I and Napoleon III, were examples of such periods, as was the rule of Bismarck in Germany: 'here', says Engels, 'capitalists and workers are balanced against each other and equally cheated for the benefit of the impoverished Prussian cabbage junkers' (ch. 9).

These formulations come very close to suggesting not only that the state enjoys a 'relative autonomy', but that it has made itself altogether independent of society, and that it rules over society as those who control the state think fit and without reference to any force in society external to the state. An early case in point is that of 'Oriental despotism' (see ASIATIC SOCIETY), to which Marx and Engels devoted much attention in the 1850s and 1860s; but it applies more generally. In fact, the 'Marxist theory of the state', far from turning the state into an agency or instrument subordinate to external forces, sees it much more as an institution in its own right, with its own interests and purposes. In *18th Brumaire*, Marx also speaks of the executive power of the Bonapartist state as an 'immense bureaucratic and military organization, an ingenious and broadly based state machinery, and an army of half a million officials alongside the actual army, which numbers a further half million'; and he goes on to describe this force as a 'frightful parasitic body, which surrounds the body of French society like a caul and stops up all its pores' (sect. 7). Such a 'state machinery' must be taken to have interests and purposes of its own.

This, however, does not contradict the notion of the state as concerned to serve the purposes and interests of the dominant class or classes: what is involved, in effect, is a *partner-*

ship between those who control the state, and those who own and control the means of economic activity. This is the notion which must be taken to underlie the concept of STATE MONOPOLY CAPITALISM, which is the description of present-day advanced capitalism used by 'official' communist writers. The description is vulnerable, in so far as it suggests a *merger* of the political and economic realms, whereas the real position is one of partnership, in which the political and economic realms retain a separate identity, and in which the state is able to act with considerable independence in maintaining and defending the social order of which the economically dominant class is the main beneficiary. This independence is implied even in the formulation from the *Communist Manifesto* which was quoted at the beginning, and which seems to turn the state into such a subordinate institution. For Marx and Engels speak here of 'the *common* affairs of the *whole* bourgeoisie': this clearly implies that the bourgeoisie is made up of different and particular elements; that it has many separate and specific interests as well as common ones; and that it is the state which must manage its common affairs. It cannot do so without a considerable measure of independence.

A major function of the state in its partnership with the economically dominant class is to regulate class conflict and to ensure the stability of the social order. The class rule which the state sanctions and defends assumes many different forms, from the 'democratic republic' to dictatorship; the form which class rule assumes is a matter of great importance to the working class. In a context of private ownership and appropriation, however, it remains class rule, whatever its form.

Before the first world war, Lenin, like Marx and Engels before him, had made a distinction between different forms of regime, to the point of referring to the United States and Britain, in contrast to tsarist Russia, as countries 'where complete political liberty exists' ('Inflammable Material in World Politics', 1908, CW 15, p. 186). With the first world war, Lenin no longer took such distinctions to be significant. In the preface to *State and Revolution*, dated August 1917, he said that the 'monstrous oppression of the working people by the state, which is merging more and more with the all-

powerful capitalist associations, is becoming increasingly monstrous. The advanced countries – we mean their hinterland – are becoming military convict prisons for the workers'. In the pamphlet itself, he insisted that, with the war, 'both Britain and America, the biggest and last representatives – in the whole world – of Anglo-Saxon "liberty", in the sense that they had no military cliques and bureaucracy, have completely sunk into the all-European filthy, bloody morass of bureaucratic-military institutions which subordinate everything to themselves and suppress everything' (CW 25, pp. 383, 415–16). Given the immense authority which Lenin's pronouncements came to enjoy in the world of Marxism as a result of the Bolshevik Revolution, his virtual obliteration of the distinction between 'bourgeois democracy' and other forms of capitalist rule (for instance FASCISM) may well have contributed to the baneful Marxist neglect of such distinctions in subsequent years.

Lenin's concern, in *State and Revolution* and elsewhere, was to combat the 'revisionist' notion that the bourgeois state might be reformed: it must be 'smashed'. This was the point which Marx himself had made in *18th Brumaire* ('all revolutions perfected this machine instead of smashing it'), and which he reiterated at the time of the Paris Commune ('the next attempt of the French Revolution will be no longer, as before, to transfer the bureaucratic-military machine from one hand to another, but to smash it, and this is the preliminary condition for every real people's revolution on the Continent' (letter to Kugelmann, 12 April 1871). The state would then be replaced by the DICTATORSHIP OF THE PROLETARIAT, in which there would occur what Lenin called 'a gigantic replacement of certain institutions by other institutions of a fundamentally different type . . . instead of the special institutions of a privileged minority (the privileged officialdom, the chiefs of the standing army) the majority itself can directly fulfil all these functions, and the more the functions of state power are performed by the people as a whole, the less need there is for the existence of this power' (*State and Revolution*, CW 25, pp. 419–20). This echoes faithfully the basic propositions of classical Marxism on the subject. In a famous passage of *Anti-Dühring* Engels had said: 'The first act by virtue of which the state really constitutes itself the representative of the whole of society – the taking possession of the means of production in the name of society – this is, at the same time, its last independent act as a state. State interference in social relations becomes, in one domain after another, superfluous, and then withers away of itself; the government of persons is replaced by the administration of things, and by the conduct of processes of production. The state is not "abolished". It *withers away*' (p. 385: italics in text). This, and many other references to the state in the writings of Marx and Engels, show the affinities of classical Marxism to ANARCHISM: the main difference between them, at least in regard to the state, is that classical Marxism rejected the anarchist notion that the state could be done away with on the very morrow of the revolution.

Classical Marxism and Leninism always stressed the coercive role of the state, almost to the exclusion of all else: the state is essentially the institution whereby a dominant and exploiting class imposes and defends its power and privileges against the class or classes which it dominates and exploits. One of Gramsci's major contributions to Marxist thought is his exploration of the fact that the domination of the ruling class is not only achieved by coercion but is also elicited by consent; and Gramsci also insisted that the state played a major role in the cultural and ideological fields and in the organization of consent (see HEGEMONY). This process of legitimation, in which both the state and many other institutions in society are engaged, has attracted considerable attention from Marxists in the last two decades. A question which has in this connection preoccupied a number of theorists in recent years is how far the state in capitalist-democratic regimes is able to cope with the task of eliciting consent in circumstances of crisis and contraction. On the one hand, the state in these regimes is required to meet a variety of popular expectations. On the other, it is also required to meet the needs and demands of capital. It is argued that the growing incompatibility of these requirements produces a 'crisis of legitimation' which is not readily resolved within the framework of capitalist-democratic regimes (see CRISIS IN CAPITALIST SOCIETY).

The establishment of the Soviet state was bound to offer a major conceptual challenge to the Marxist theory of the state; for here was a society in which the means of production had come under public ownership, and whose regime proclaimed its allegiance to Marxism. This raised the question of the nature of the state which had been brought into being. Any discussion of that question was, however, overshadowed by the experience of Stalinism and, as was to be expected, Stalinist thought on the state insisted on its paramount and enduring importance: far from 'withering away', the state must be reinforced as the prime motor in the construction of socialism, and also in order to deal with its many enemies at home and abroad. The 'revolution from above' of which Stalin spoke was made, he also said, 'on the initiative of the state'.

This state, Stalin also claimed, was a 'state of a new type', which represented the interests of the workers, the peasants and the intelligentsia – in other words, of the whole Soviet population. It was, in this sense, no longer a class state, seeking to maintain the power and privileges of a ruling class to the detriment of the vast majority; it was rather, in a phrase which came to be used under Khrushchev, a 'state of the whole people'.

This claim has been strongly contested by Marxist critics of the Soviet regime. Their own view of the Soviet state (and of the state in all Soviet-type regimes) has been greatly influenced by their judgement of the nature of Soviet-type societies. Those critics who viewed them as class societies also took the state in them to be the instrument of a 'new class', and, as such, not significantly different, in conceptual terms, from the state in other class societies. Those critics, on the other hand, who viewed Soviet-type societies as 'transitional' between capitalism and socialism, and who rejected the notion of a 'new class', spoke of the state in these societies as a 'deformed workers' state', under the control of a 'bureaucracy' avid for power and privilege, and which a workers' revolution would eventually dislodge (see CLASS; TROTSKY). This debate still proceeds; but there is at any rate no disagreement among its protagonists as to the immense power wielded by the state in these societies. Nor is this affected by the fact that the state itself is controlled by the party leaders (see CRISIS IN SOCIALIST SOCIETY).

Marxists concerned with the state in capitalist societies are also confronted by many different questions and problems: what is the precise nature and role of the state in advanced capitalist societies today? How does its class character manifest itself? How far can it be transformed into the instrument of the subordinate classes? How can it be prevented, in a future socialist society, from appropriating an undue measure of power; or, as Marx put it in the *Critique of the Gotha Programme*, how can the state in such a society be converted 'from an organ superimposed upon society into one completely subordinated to it?' These and many other unresolved questions about the state are certain to give it a major place in Marxist discussion for many years to come.

Reading

Beetham, D. ed. 1984: *Marxists in Face of Fascism*.

Draper, H. 1977: *Karl Marx's Theory of Revolution*, vol. 1: *State and Bureaucracy*.

Evans, P., Rueschmeyer, D. and Skocpol, T., eds. 1985: *Bringing the State Back In*.

Gramsci, A. 1929–35 (1971): *Selections from the Prison Notebooks*, ed. Quintin Hoare and Geoffrey Nowell Smith.

Jessop, B. 1982: *The Capitalist State: Marxist Theories and Methods*.

Lenin, V. 1917c (1969): *State and Revolution*.

McLennan, G. 1989: *Marxism, Pluralism and Beyond*.

Miliband, R. 1983: *Class Power and State Power*.

Parkin, F. 1979: *Marxism and Class Theory: A Bourgeois Critique*.

Poulantzas, N. 1973: *Political Power and Social Classes*.

Therborn, G. 1978: *What Does the Ruling Class Do When it Rules?*

Tucker, R. C., ed. 1977: *Stalinism*.

RALPH MILIBAND

State and Revolution Lenin wrote *State and Revolution* in the summer of 1917, while in hiding in Finland. The book represents the culmination of a reappraisal of the Marxist theory of the state which he had begun on the eve of the February Revolution, and which was greatly influenced both by 'Left Communists', notably Bukharin, and by the popular upsurge which followed the outbreak of revolution.

Until the beginning of 1917, Lenin had paid little attention to an idea first advanced by Marx in *The 18th Brumaire of Louis Bonaparte* (1852), and later emphasized in his *The Civil War in France* (1871), namely that 'the working class cannot simply lay hold of the ready-made state machinery, and wield it for its own purposes', and that the 'state machinery' must therefore be 'smashed', and replaced by an entirely new form of rule. Lenin now made this the main theme of *State and Revolution*.

In the *18th Brumaire*, Lenin noted, Marx had said that whereas all previous revolutions had 'perfected' the state machine, the point was to destroy it. This, said Lenin, was 'the chief and fundamental point in the Marxist theory of the state'. The old state would be replaced by a state of an entirely new type, which, in a phrase used by Engels in *Anti-Dühring* (1878), would immediately begin to 'wither away'.

Instead of the special institutions of a privileged minority (privileged officialdom, the chiefs of the standing army) the majority itself can directly fulfil all these functions, and the more the functions of state power are performed by the people as a whole, the less need there is for the existence of this power.

As for what remained of the state, Lenin followed faithfully Marx's depiction of the principles of the Paris Commune: all officials would be elected, be subject to recall at any time and their salary would be fixed at the level of workers' wages. Representative institutions would be retained, but the representatives would be closely and constantly controlled by their electors, and also subject to recall. In effect, the proletarian majority was intended not only to rule but actually to govern in a regime which amounted to the exercise of semi-direct popular power.

A very remarkable feature of *State and Revolution*, given the importance Lenin always attributed to the role of the party, is the quite subsidiary role it is allotted in this instance. The book has three references to the party, only one of which allows to the party the role of 'leader of all the working and exploited people in organising their social life without the bourgeoisie and against the bourgeoisie'. The emphasis throughout is on all but unmediated popular rule.

Lenin's endorsement of 'Left Communist' perspectives did not survive the Bolshevik seizure of power. By May 1918, he was denouncing 'Left Communists' in a series of articles entitled ' "Left-Wing" Childishness and Petty-Bourgeois Mentality', and insisting that socialism was 'inconceivable without planned state organisation which keeps tens of millions of people in the strictest observance of a unified standard in production and distribution'.

Nevertheless, Lenin never formally renounced the perspectives which had inspired *State and Revolution*; and it has endured as one of the major texts of Marxism. Many of its formulations are unrealistic and naïve: all the same, it expresses forcibly what is perhaps the strongest aspiration of classical Marxism – the creation of a society in which the state would be strictly subordinated to the rule and self-government of the people.

RALPH MILIBAND

state monopoly capitalism The most recent stage of capitalism, characterized by the rise of the state as a significant economic power directly concerned with the accumulation of capital (see PERIODIZATION OF CAPITALISM). In most analyses of this stage the state is linked in some way with one fraction of capital, monopoly capital represented by giant enterprises and large financial blocks. The existence of such a stage, distinct from MONOPOLY CAPITALISM, is controversial, but the idea has been an important theoretical foundation for the strategies of communist parties. The class nature of the modern capitalist state is seen to turn on monopoly capital being ranged against all other fractions and classes so that an anti-monopoly alliance comprising medium and small capitals, the working class, and middle strata can be built in the struggle for state power.

The concept of state monopoly capitalism ('stamocap') originated in Soviet and East European writing in the early 1950s, although several different strands emerged following Stalin's death (see Hardach and Karras 1975; Wirth 1972; and especially the comprehensive study by Jessop 1982). One strand emphasizes the instrumental agency of monopolies, which subordinate the state to their purposes in the struggle for profits within a moribund capitalism; an imperialism that is in general crisis. A second considers state monopoly capitalism a product of capital's innate laws: the development of the forces of production and the CENTRALIZATION AND CONCENTRATION OF CAPITAL produce a state which intervenes in the economy on the side of monopolies partly because of the contradiction between relations of production and the increasingly socialized productive forces, partly because of the importance of the monopolies for the whole economy, and partly because of the monopolies' need for state management of the business cycle.

Writers such as Zieschang in the German Democratic Republic give particular emphasis to the state's role in stabilizing capitalism by Keynesian policies towards accumulation, production, demand and the valorization of capital. Boccara (1976) and other French theorists place this view in a more general framework which sees economic crises as the outcome of overaccumulation, and the state's modern role as one which attempts to overcome crises by a fundamental devalorization of capital. Like Fine and Harris (1979) they place the origins of this stage in the 1930s, while Soviet writers who treat 'stamocap' in terms of a moribund imperialist capitalism locate its origins in the first world war and believe the concept originates in Lenin's writings of that period (although in fact he did not distinguish this as a separate stage from monopoly capitalism). Similarly, Baran and Sweezy (1966) reject the distinction, on the grounds that the state has always been significant for the capitalist economy, and Poulantzas (1975) argues that state monopoly capitalism is merely one phase within capitalism's second great stage, imperialism.

The manner in which, according to 'stamocap' theory, the state relates to capital is controversial. In Soviet writings an essential element is the idea of 'fusion' between the state and monopoly capital. According to Afanasyev (1974), for example, this stage involves a qualitatively new phenomenon: 'the growing coalescence of the monopolies and the bourgeois state, the emergence of state-monopoly management based on the fusion of state and monopoly power'. However, the idea of 'fusion' is not found in all concepts of state monopoly capitalism; Boccara (1976) and Fine and Harris (1979) reject it, while Herzog (1971) emphasizes the state's relative autonomy in the context of a 'contradictory separation in unity' (see also STATE).

Reading

Afanasyev, L. et al. 1974: The Political Economy of Capitalism.

Baran, Paul and Sweezy, Paul 1966: Monopoly Capital.

Boccara, Paul ed. 1969 (1976): Le Capitalisme monopoliste d'état.

Fine, Ben and Harris, Laurence 1979: Rereading 'Capital'.

Hardach, Gerd and Karras, Dieter 1975 (1978): A Short History of Socialist Economic Thought.

Herzog, Philippe 1971: 'Le rôle de l'état dans la société capitaliste actuelle'.

Jessop, Bob 1982: The Capitalist State.

Poulantzas, Nicos 1975: Classes in Contemporary Capitalism.

Wirth, Margaret 1972: Kapitalismustheorie in der DDR.

LAURENCE HARRIS

strikes Overtly rupturing workers' routine subordination to the employer within capitalist relations of production, in most countries throughout the nineteenth century (and often later) strikes were illegal acts and were thus at least implicitly a challenge to the state. Often they formed part of more general outbursts of working-class disaffection.

Strikes inspired early enthusiastic assessments of TRADE UNIONS by Marx and Engels. In *Condition of the Working Class* Engels argued that English strikes were usually defeated, but heralded 'the social war', and were 'the military school of the working-men in which they prepare themselves for the great struggle which cannot be avoided'. Marx argued in *Poverty of Philosophy* that isolated conflicts developed naturally into 'a veritable civil war', establishing the proletariat as 'a class for itself'. The same message appeared in the *Communist Manifesto*. Later, much of the practical work of the First International (see INTERNATIONALS), involved material support for strikers (whose numbers increased during

the economic crisis of the 1860s). But Marx recognized that strikes could be mere routinized engagements of relatively conservative unions for limited objectives. When he urged the unions in the International that they 'ought not to forget that they are fighting with effects, but not with the causes of those effects', the implication was that unionists *were* content to become 'exclusively absorbed in these unavoidable guerilla fights' (*Value, Price and Profit*).

A different perspective on strikes was developed by Bakunin and his supporters, embracing the idea of a General Strike (which can be traced back to Benbow's 1832 proposal for a 'Grand National Holiday'). In 1868 the International endorsed the strategy of such a strike to resist a declaration of war, much to Marx's displeasure. Subsequently the Bakuninites elaborated the principle of the revolutionary general strike, which was to become a central slogan of SYNDICALISM. The general strike was also an important issue for the social democracy of the Second International, though as a limited tactic, in particular to win or defend the extension of the franchise. The Belgian example of 1893 was followed in many countries of Europe, though the credibility of the political strike was undermined by the growing opposition of the German trade unions, and by the defeat suffered by Swedish labour in 1909. August 1914 destroyed any remaining illusions about the general strike against war.

The decline of the reformist general strike (to which 1926 in Britain was a confirmatory footnote) coincided with important advances in Marxist analysis. The revolutionary upsurge in Russia in 1905 inspired Luxemburg's pamphlet *The Mass Strike, the Political Party and the Trade Unions*. She emphasized the spontaneity of the movement: 'the living pulsebeat of the revolution and at the same time its most powerful driving wheel . . .'. Such spontaneous action, she argued, overturned the established routines of the unions, broke through reformist demarcations between politics and economics, and revealed the essential unity of the class struggle.

Lenin was also profoundly influenced by the events of 1905. In the 1890s he had echoed Marx and Engels in stressing the importance of strikes in enlarging class consciousness. But strikes unaccompanied by political organization and struggle could not overturn capitalist control and the power of the state: not even a general strike. This qualification became a central argument of *What Is To Be Done?*: 'class political consciousness can be brought to the workers only from without, that is, only from outside the economic struggle.' Yet he recognized that in 1905 'the movement in certain parts of the country has progressed in a few days from a mere strike to a tremendous revolutionary outbreak.' Like Luxemburg, he was to insist thereafter that the mass strike was linked dialectically to the growth of revolutionary consciousness.

After the October Revolution a new issue was posed: in a workers' state, would strikers be 'striking against themselves'? Lenin argued in 1921 that 'strikes in a state where the proletariat holds political power can be explained and justified only by the bureaucratic distortions of the proletarian state and by all sorts of survivals of the old capitalist system.' Under Stalin, while strikes were never formally prohibited, they were in practice suppressed as acts of indiscipline, absenteeism, or even 'counterrevolutionary sabotage'.

In the west, the early communist parties placed great emphasis on the role of strikes in the class struggle, particularly during the 'third period' (defined by the Communist International as a new phase of revolutionary upsurge in Europe from 1928 onwards). But with the turn to 'popular front' tactics in 1934 this emphasis was reduced, and after 1941, in the countries of Russia's co-belligerents, communist parties rabidly opposed strikes. Since the war, communist unions in many countries have resorted frequently to the national strike as a political demonstration (showing parallels with the Second International at the turn of the century). The main role of advocates of strikes to advance class struggle has meanwhile been assumed by Trotskyist and other groups to the left of 'official' communism.

Reading
Beecher, J. 1972: *STRIKE!*

Crook, W. H. 1931: *The General Strike.*

Hyman, R. 1972: *Strikes.*

Lenin, V. I. 1970: *On Trade Unions.*

Lozovsky, A. 1931: *The World Economic Crisis,*

Strike Struggles and the Tasks of the Revolutionary Trade Union Movement.

— 1935: *Marx and the Trade Unions.*

Luxemburg, R. 1970: *Rosa Luxemburg Speaks.*
RICHARD HYMAN

structuralism A method of inquiry – or in some formulations a more general philosophy of science which has affinities with REALISM and contests the positions of EMPIRICISM and POSITIVISM – which has made its way from linguistics into literary criticism and the sociology of literature, aesthetic theory, the social sciences, especially anthropology, and Marxism, though it has earlier antecedents in a variety of disciplines (see Piaget 1970). The principal feature of the structuralist method is that it takes as its object of investigation a 'system', that is, the reciprocal relations among a set of facts, rather than particular facts considered in isolation; its basic concepts according to Piaget are those of totality, self-regulation and transformation. In ANTHROPOLOGY, structuralism is particularly associated with the work of Lévi-Strauss and in this form it has had a strong influence upon recent Marxist anthropology (see especially Godelier 1977, pt. I). The main structuralist current in Marxist thought generally, however, has its source in the work of ALTHUSSER, even though he has tried to differentiate his view from what he calls the 'structuralist ideology'. According to Althusser (1969, 1970), Marx eliminated the human subject from social theory and constructed a 'new science' of the levels of human practice (economic, political, ideological and scientific) which are inscribed in the structure of a social totality. Hence Marxist theory is not 'humanist' or 'historical' (in a teleological sense) but is concerned essentially with the structural analysis of social totalities (e.g. MODE OF PRODUCTION, SOCIAL FORMATION); and the object of such analysis is to disclose the 'deep structure' which underlies and produces the directly observable phenomena of social life. Thus Godelier (1977), in his argument against empiricism and functionalism in anthropology, says that for Lévi-Strauss, as for Marx, 'structures are not directly visible or observable realities, but levels of reality which exist beyond man's visible relations and whose functioning constitutes the deeper logic of a social system' (p. 45). This idea of a real structure behind appearances has been influential not only in anthropology but also in Marxist political economy, where Marx's analysis of the commodity in *Capital* is seen as an exemplary instance of structuralist analysis, and in sociology, especially in the study of social classes and the state (Poulantzas 1973).

The relation of Marxist structuralism to historical studies has given rise to much controversy. Althusser (1970, p. 65) wrote that 'Marx regards contemporary society (and every other past form of society) both as a *result* and as a *society*', and that the problem of the result, 'i.e. of the historical production of a given mode of production, of a given social formation' has to be posed and solved, but in practice Althusser has paid little or no attention to historical changes. Godelier (1977, p. 6) also claims to take account of history, but argues that 'laws of change refer to constants because they reflect the structural properties of social relations. History, therefore, does not explain: it has to be explained'; and in another text (1972) he emphasizes (as did Marx) contradiction as a basic feature of social systems which engenders change, thereby introducing a specific and different element into the Marxist version of structuralism. But Godelier has not attempted to construct a theory of history in these terms. Some Marxist structuralists have developed their views to an extreme point and concluded: 'There is no real object "history"; the notion that there is a *real* history is the product of empiricism. The word "history" should be confined to designating the ideological non-subject constituted by philosophies of history and the practice of the writing of history' (Hindess and Hirst 1975, p. 317). In turn, this has provoked Marxist historians into a vigorous counter-criticism of the abstract sterility of this kind of structuralism (see especially Thompson 1978). But there have also been attempts to combine structuralist and historical approaches, notably in the 'genetic structuralism' of Goldmann (strongly influenced by Lukács and Piaget), who has formulated its basic principle thus: 'From this standpoint the structures which constitute human behaviour are not in reality universally given facts, but specific phenomena resulting from a past genesis and undergoing transformations which foreshadow a future

evolution' (1970, p. 21).

The rejection by Althusser and his followers of any causal influence of human agents, and the assertion of a rigorous structural determinism has also aroused criticism, notably in the dispute between Poulantzas and Miliband (in Blackburn ed. 1972) where the latter argues that this 'super-determinism', with its exclusive stress on 'objective relations', disregards and obscures very important differences between forms of the capitalist state which range from a democratic constitutional state to military dictatorships and fascism. More generally, structuralism stands in sharp opposition to the versions of Marxist theory expounded by Lukács, Gramsci and the FRANKFURT SCHOOL which stress the role of human consciousness and action in social life, and base their thought upon a conception of history in which the idea of progress is implicit. In a broad sense, therefore, structuralism has given fresh expression to the longstanding tension between two poles of Marxist thought, which is conceived at one extreme as a rigorous science of society, at the other as a humanist doctrine which, in Gramsci's words (1929-35 (1971)), contains in itself all the elements 'needed to give life to an integral practical organization of society, that is, to become a total integral civilization' (p. 462); and it has raised again all the fundamental questions about the determinism of Marx's theory.

Reading
Althusser, L. and Balibar, E. 1970: *Reading 'Capital'*.

Godelier, Maurice 1972: 'Structure and Contradiction in *Capital*'. In Robin Blackburn ed. *Ideology in Social Science.*

— 1977: *Perspectives in Marxist Anthropology.*

Goldmann, Lucien 1970a: 'Genèse et structure'. In *Marxisme et sciences humaines.*

Lévi-Strauss, Claude 1958: *Structural Anthropology.*

Piaget, Jean 1970: *Structuralism.*

Schaff, Adam 1974: *Structuralisme et Marxisme.*

Thompson, E. P. 1978: *The Poverty of Theory.*
                                    TOM BOTTOMORE

superstructure.   *See* base and superstructure.

surplus value   The extraction of surplus value is the specific way EXPLOITATION takes place under capitalism, the *differentia specifica* of the capitalist mode of production, in which the surplus takes the form of PROFIT, and exploitation results from the working class producing a net product which can be sold for more than they receive as wages. Thus profit and wages are the specific forms that surplus and necessary labour take when employed by capital. But profit and wages are both MONEY and thus an objectified form of labour only through a set of historically specific mediations in which the concept of surplus value is crucial.

Capitalist production is a form of, indeed the most generalized form of, COMMODITY production. Thus products are produced for sale as values, which are measured and realized in the form of price, that is, as quantities of money (see VALUE AND PRICE). The product belongs to the capitalist, who obtains surplus value from the difference between the value of the product and the value of the capital involved in the production process. The latter has two parts: constant capital, corresponding to the value laid out in means of production which is simply transferred to the product during the production process; and variable capital, which is used to employ workers, workers being paid the value of what they sell, their LABOUR POWER. Variable capital is so called because its quantity varies from the beginning to the end of the production process; what starts as the VALUE OF LABOUR POWER ends as the value produced by that labour power in action. Surplus value is the difference between the two, the value produced by the worker which is appropriated by the capitalist without equivalent given in exchange. There is no unfair exchange going on here; nevertheless the capitalist manages to appropriate the results of surplus unpaid labour.

This is possible because labour power is the commodity with the unique property of being able to create value. It is therefore the essential ingredient of capitalist production. Means of production are used up (consumed) in the production process, their use values are realized in the production process and will reappear in the product in a new form. Their value is simply transferred to the value of the product. Labour power is also consumed in the production process, but the consumption of labour-power is labour itself. Since, in commodity production,

the latter has the twin characteristics of being both useful and ABSTRACT LABOUR; so correspondingly the use value of labour power has also a dual character: that of being able to create use values (useful labour) and that of being able to create value (abstract labour). It is the latter which interests the capitalist. For the value produced when labour power is consumed is new value, and it is only in the expectation that this new value will be more than the value of their labour power that workers are employed. The working class consists of those who own nothing but their own labour power. Because workers have no other access to the means of production and have to sell something in order to live, they are forced to sell their labour power and cannot make use of its value-creating property themselves. So workers are exploited not by unequal exchange in the labour market, for they sell their labour power at its value, but through the class position of having to enter the capitalist production process wherein exploitation actually occurs. Although each individual wage labour contract is, like any other free exchange contract, not forced on either of the participants, workers are not free not to sell their labour power at all, since they have no other way to live. Thus this freedom, although real at the level of the individual wage contract, is in reality what Marx called the workers' two-fold freedom: the freedom to sell his or her labour power or the freedom to starve.

Marx's analysis of surplus value differs significantly from those of the early writers of classical political economy. The latter, particularly Ricardo, tended to see surplus value arising from an unfair exchange of labour for the wage between worker and capitalist. Workers were forced to sell their labour below its value; the surplus thus arose in exchange. But Marx's distinction between labour and labour power enabled him to show how, with no unfair exchange, labour power could be sold at its value and surplus value arise within production. Thus he showed that capitalist exploitation, like that in all previous modes of production, occurred in the process of production; that the establishment of fair exchange rates was not the end of exploitation; and that the position of exploiter and exploited were class positions defined by access to the means of production (rather than individual incomes being the result of individual negotiation of exchange contracts as neo-classical economics was later to claim).

Since values are quantities, the amounts of surplus value are quantities too. The amount of surplus value a worker produces is the difference between the value he or she produces and the value of his or her labour power. The former is determined by the conditions of the LABOUR PROCESS in which the particular worker is involved and by the market for its product. The latter is determined outside the individual labour process, by conditions on the labour market and the value of the goods the worker must consume. The law of value (see COMPETITION) will tend to ensure that the value produced by workers across different industries will be the same, and competition in the labour market will tend to ensure a uniform value of labour power at least for unskilled labour. Thus we can talk about a common rate of surplus value across an economy, where the rate of surplus value (sometimes called the rate of exploitation) is defined as the ratio:

$$s/v = \frac{\text{amount of surplus produced}}{\text{variable capital laid out}}$$

If skilled labour is seen as a multiple of unskilled, producing value proportionate to the extra pay received, the rate of surplus value will be constant across skilled labour too. (For discussion of whether this is a reasonable assumption see Roncaglia 1974; Rowthorn 1980; Tortajada 1977.)

Because the value the worker produces can be divided up in this way, so can the time the worker spends creating that value. Hence a similar division can be made of the working day, dividing it into two parts: necessary labour, in which time the worker is producing an equivalent of what he or she receives as wages, and surplus labour, in which time the worker is producing simply for the capitalist. By definition then these two parts are so divided that:

$$s/v = \frac{\text{surplus labour}}{\text{necessary labour}}$$

$$= \frac{\text{hours worker spends working for capitalist}}{\text{hours worker spends working for personal consumption}}$$

The history of capitalist production can be seen as the history of struggle over attempts by capital to increase, and attempts by the working class to resist increases in, the rate of surplus value. This has occurred in two main ways. The first, the extraction of absolute surplus value, involves raising the rate of surplus value by increasing the total value produced by each worker without changing the amount of necessary labour. This can be done by either an intensive or an extensive extension of the working day, either of which, however, not only meets with organized resistance from the working class, but also reaches physical limits as the health of the class, on which capital as a whole (if not the individual capitalist) depends, deteriorates from overlong hours, too high an intensity of labour and insufficient wages. Thus in Britain in 1847 we see working-class organizations, philanthropic capitalists, and the interests of large long-lasting as opposed to small capital, combining to get the Ten Hours Bill passed (*Capital* I, ch. 10, particularly sect. 6).

When the extraction of absolute surplus value reaches its limit, the alternative to increasing the total value produced by each worker is to divide the same quantity in proportions more favourable to capital, that is to take the same length of working day and redivide it so that more is available as surplus labour to be appropriated by capital. This requires necessary labour time to be reduced, that is, a fall in the value of labour power. This is the extraction of relative surplus value, which can take place in two ways. Either the quantity of use values the worker consumes, or the socially necessary labour time to produce the same quantity of use values, must be reduced. The former method encounters the same limits as does the extraction of absolute surplus value: resistance by the working class and deterioration in its physical condition. The latter method is that by which capitalism has become the most dynamic mode of production to date, continually changing its production methods and introducing technological improvements. For it is only by technical change that the socially necessary labour time in the production of particular goods can be reduced. Increased productivity resulting from new methods of production, in which dead labour in the form of machines takes the place of living labour, decreases the value of the individual goods produced. When this applies to those goods whose value is reflected in the value of labour power – that is, goods which form part of the workers' consumption – the value of labour power falls and a greater proportion of the working day can be devoted to surplus labour.

The extraction of relative surplus value results from sharing out among all capitals the benefits of increased productivity in the sectors producing goods consumed by workers. This sharing out is a consequence of the process of CIRCULATION and capitalist competition, whereby the extra profits of an innovating capitalist are gradually lost as the value of the product falls when the new techniques are adopted by competitors. If the innovation was in a wage goods producing industry, the benefit will be shared between all capitals in the form of a lowered value of labour power; if in the production of means of production which eventually feed into the production of workers' consumption goods the effect will be similarly felt since the value of wage goods will be similarly reduced. If, however, the innovation is in an industry which produces only for capitalist consumption, or one which produces means of production whose only use is in such a sector, the end result will be no change in the rate of surplus value, simply a reduced price for some luxury goods.

Thus the extraction of relative surplus value does not occur as a conscious process for capitalists, whose aim is to reduce their own individual costs in order to increase their own profits. Competition will ensure that they lose the immediate benefit they have gained over their rivals, with any gain that may result spreading among all capitals. Whether the ultimate result is the extraction of relative surplus value or not – that is, whether the product is the sort that could ever have any effect on the value of labour power – does not matter to the individual innovating capitalist. He is constrained by, and eventually loses all individual advantage to, the forces of competition in either case.

Much of the history of the development of capitalist economies can be examined in terms of the processes of extraction of absolute and relative surplus value (see e.g. Fine and Harris 1979, ch. 7; Himmelweit 1979). Although the

former is characteristic of earlier periods of capitalist development, the two go hand in hand, with technical change that allows for the extraction of relative surplus value, laying the basis for a renewed drive to extract absolute surplus value (see LABOUR PROCESS). Many processes can be analysed as a mixture of the extraction of both relative and absolute surplus value; for example, the entry of married women into paid employment has allowed both the extraction of relative surplus value, since their low wages represent a lower individual value for labour power, while this has at the same time laid the basis for the extraction of absolute surplus value as more value creating labour is being performed by the family as a whole without a corresponding rise in their costs of REPRODUCTION and thus in the quantity of necessary labour paid for by capital (see e.g. Beechey 1977).

Reading

Beechey, V. 1977: 'Some Notes on Female Wage Labour in Capitalist Production'.

Fine, B. and Harris, L. 1979: Rereading 'Capital'.

Himmelweit, S. 1979 : 'Growth and Reproduction'. In F. Green and P. Nore eds. Issues in Political Economy.

Roncaglia, A. 1974: 'The Reduction of Complex to Simple Labour'.

Rowthorn, R. 1980: Capitalism, Conflict and Inflation; Essays in Political Economy.

Tortajada, R. 1977: 'A Note on the Reduction of Complex Labour to Simple Labour'.

SUSAN HIMMELWEIT

surplus value and profit A capitalist advances MONEY to buy LABOUR POWER and means of production; after the workers have produced a new COMMODITY with the help of the means of production, the capitalist normally sells the produced commodity for more money than he advanced. Marx expressed this motion in the diagram M-C-M' (Money-Commodity-Money) where M', the money realized by the sale of the commodities, exceeds M, the money advanced. This additional money is the surplus value which, in this phenomenal form, corresponds to the conventional accounting category of gross margin (or gross profit); the excess of sales revenue over the direct cost of goods sold. For capital as a whole (but not individual capitals) Marx argued that total surplus value, defined in value terms, equals total profit, defined in terms of prices, even if the price of each commodity does not equal its value. The possibility of this equality holding simultaneously with other of Marx's axioms has been the subject of dispute in the context of the theory of PRICES OF PRODUCTION AND THE TRANSFORMATION PROBLEM.

The labour theory of value reveals that the source of surplus value in the system of capitalist production is unpaid labour of workers. On average a worker in a day (or hour, or any unit of labour time) produces a certain money VALUE, but the wage he receives is the equivalent of only a fraction of that value. Thus the worker is paid an equivalent for only a part of the working day, and the value produced in the other, unpaid part, is the surplus value. The form of the wage obscures this fact by making it seem that the worker is paid for every hour, but from the point of view of the labour theory of value a fraction of the labour is expended without the worker receiving an equivalent, and hence is unpaid. The EXPLOITATION of workers in a capitalist system of production is contrary to neither the mores nor the laws of capitalist society, which view the worker as an owner of a commodity, labour power, and protected as long as he can secure the full value of that commodity in exchange on the market. But even when workers are paid the full value of labour power, this value falls short of the value they produce, so that from a social point of view a part of their labour is appropriated by the capitalist class as surplus value.

Wages are spent by workers to reproduce themselves. The labour time for which the wage is an equivalent can be seen as the labour time necessary to produce the commodities required for the reproduction of the workers. If we abstract from the contribution to social reproduction of labour which is not mediated by commodity relations, such as family and household labour, or labour expended in non-commodity modes of production, the aggregate wage thus corresponds to the labour necessary to reproduce the producers themselves, and the surplus value to the surplus labour of the society. From the perspective of social REPRODUCTION we see surplus value as the specific form

surplus labour takes in capitalist society. The appropriation of surplus value by the capitalist class is thus a particular mode of appropriation of surplus labour; capitalist society rests like other class societies on the appropriation of the surplus labour of the society by a particular class. All societies capable of development produce a surplus, and thus expend surplus labour; in all class societies the surplus labour is appropriated by a class through some mechanism of exploitation; in capitalist society the specific form of exploitation is the appropriation of surplus value through the exploitation of wage labour.

The capitalist is forced to give up some part of the surplus value as rent to the owners of land (see LANDED PROPERTY AND RENT). The remaining part of his portion of total surplus value appears to the capitalist as profit. This profit in turn is paid out in part to others. The capitalist must pay the unproductive labour (see PRODUCTIVE AND UNPRODUCTIVE LABOUR) which does the work of supervising and policing production, and marketing the commodity. If the capitalist has borrowed money to finance production, some part of the surplus value must be paid as interest to the lender (see FINANCIAL CAPITAL AND INTEREST). What remains in the capitalist's pocket after these payments is called by Marx *profit of enterprise*. The state may tax this residual profit and claim a part of it.

In using conventional accounting measures of profit, it is essential to discover exactly what part of the flow of surplus value is included in the measure. Marx (*Capital* III, chs. 1–4, 21–24) normally uses the term 'profit' to mean the whole surplus value, since he abstracts in much of his analysis from rent, and from the further differentiation of profit into interest, commercial profit and so forth. In bourgeois economic theories the average rate of profit on capital invested is viewed as 'normal profit', or as 'interest', or as the 'factor cost of capital services'; and the term 'profit' or 'economic profit' is reserved for extraordinary profits due to monopoly or innovation. Normal profit in this sense is part of surplus value.

DUNCAN FOLEY

syndicalism Syndicalism is merely the English rendering of the French word for trade-unionism. *Syndicalisme révolutionnaire* commonly denoted the theories of Fernand Pelloutier (1867–1901), secretary of the Fédération des Bourses du Travail; and the principles of the Confédération Générale du Travail (CGT) after its merger with the Fédération in 1902. Syndicalist doctrine was never fully explicit or precise: the emphasis was on action rather than theory. Key themes were the need for rank-and-file initiative; the value of militancy (including sabotage); and the overthrow of capitalism and the state by purely industrial organization and struggle. Spontaneity and violence (involving the actions of a militant minority), together with the 'myth' of the revolutionary general strike, were propagated by SOREL, though his connection with syndicalist trade-union practice was neither close nor lasting. His writings particularly influenced the Italian left, some of whom – notably Mussolini – turned to fascism.

Before 1914, revolutionary syndicalism became the official position of important sections of the trade-union movement, mainly in countries with anarchist traditions (see ANARCHISM), a substantial artisan base, and little experience of institutionalized collective bargaining. As well as the CGT in France, notable examples were the Confederación Nacional de Trabajo in Spain and the Unione Sindicale Italiana. Syndicalists elsewhere opposed official union policies. In Britain the Industrial Syndicalist Education League was formed in 1910 by activists such as Mann, who rejected centralized collective bargaining and proclaimed the slogans of solidarity and direct action. In the United States the term syndicalism was rarely used, but the Industrial Workers of the World (IWW) displayed significant parallels with revolutionary syndicalism in Europe.

In much of Northern Europe, the dominant meaning of syndicalism was the rejection of the need for a socialist party. Parties were bureaucratic, corrupted with parliamentarism, prone to compromise with the bourgeois state; to destroy capitalism, the working class must concentrate on the industrial battlefield. Allied to such arguments was often a rejection of the goal of centralized state socialism. An intermediate position between such syndicalists and orthodox social democracy was the De Leonite tendency (expelled from the IWW in 1908) and

their British followers – notably Connolly – who urged the primacy of industrial struggle but defined some role for the revolutionary party.

The first major crisis for syndicalism was the outbreak of war, when many supporters abandoned their previous fervent anti-patriotism. Those who sustained an anti-war position provided many of the leaders of wartime industrial struggles, playing an important part within the council movements (see COUNCILS) in developing demands for workers' control of production. But revolution in Russia provoked a further crisis. As early as 1907, Lenin had attacked the parallels between syndicalism and the ECONOMISM which he had earlier denounced. BOLSHEVISM and syndicalism were manifestly incompatible; and many pre-war and wartime syndicalists demonstrated their commitment to the Bolshevik revolution by abandoning their anti-party doctrines. Some specific aims of the earlier movements – workplace organization, industrial unionism, direct action – were carried over into the new communist parties. But the underlying theories of socialism from below and workers' management – expressed in Russia itself by the Workers' Opposition – were systematically eradicated.

Those syndicalists who stayed aloof from (or broke with) the Comintern position tended to reject the Moscow model of the workers' state as well as the Leninist conception of the party (see LENINISM). Increasingly, anarcho-syndicalism became dominant within the remaining syndicalist organizations, which associated in a Syndicalist International in 1922. But with the systematic working-class defeats of the 1920s, syndicalism (at least outside Spain and Latin America) became displaced as a serious rival to socialist, communist and trade-union orthodoxies. It is possible to see continuities with syndicalist ideas in recent propaganda for workers' control and in rank-and-file oriented left groups. But 'syndicalism' itself remained almost solely a term of abuse.

Reading

Brown, G. 1977: *Sabotage.*
Cole, G. D. H. 1913: *The World of Labour.*
Dubofsky, M. 1969: *We Shall Be All: a History of the IWW.*

Holton, B. 1976: *British Syndicalism 1900–1914*.

Lewis, A. D. 1912: *Syndicalism and the General Strike*.

Payne, S. G. 1970: *The Spanish Revolution*.

Ridley, F. F. 1970: *Revolutionary Syndicalism in France*.

Roberts, D. D. 1979: *The Syndicalist Tradition and Italian Fascism*.

Westergard-Thorpe, W. 1978: 'Towards a Syndicalist International: the 1913 London Congress'. *International Review of Social History XXIII*.

Williams, G. A. 1975: *Proletarian Order*.

RICHARD HYMAN

T

technology It could be argued that Marxism is the socialist theory and practice of specifically technological societies. That is, if human labour transforming nature for collective human purposes is central to the Marxist conception of praxis, then technology is the product – artefacts which embody value and have use values. The Marxist analysis of production focuses on the LABOUR PROCESS in which raw materials are transformed by purposive human activity (labour), using the means of production to produce use values. This model can be extended from production to other spheres of human activity; to science and to the non-productive sector including the home. Marx stresses that it is technology, not nature, which is central: 'Nature builds no machines, no locomotives, railways, electric telegraphs, self-acting mules, etc. These are products of human industry; natural material transformed into organs of the human will over nature, or of human participation in nature. *They are organs of the human brain, created by the human hand*; the power of knowledge objectified' (*Grundrisse*, p. 706). What distinguishes humans from animals is that human creations are built first in the imagination; we are architects, not bees (*Capital* I, ch. 5). The history of technology is a history of the moving resolution of class forces. 'It would be possible to write a whole history of the inventions made since 1830, for the sole purpose of providing capital with weapons against working-class revolts. We would mention, above all, the self-acting mule, because it opened up a new epoch in the automatic system' (*Capital* I, ch. 15, sect. 5). On this model the history of manufacture – both processes and products – is the history of class relations. This, according to Marx, is the true anthropological nature, nature as it comes to be through human industry.

The capitalist revolution and the development from manufacture to machinofacture (see MACHINERY AND MACHINOFACTURE) in the industrial revolution, and on to Taylorism, Fordism, automation and robotics, are seen as the history of technology in the productive sphere. They provide the increasingly complex capital goods and the goods which make up technology in the sphere of consumption. Human activities have always been mediated through technologies and are becoming increasingly so in domestic life and in culture. Technology has, of course, also come to be seen as the criterion of developmental status in the Third World, and the measure of both military and domestic achievement in the first and second worlds.

Reading

Levidow, Les and Young, Robert M. eds. 1981: *Science, Technology and the Labour Process: Marxist Studies*, vol. I.

Lukács, Georg 1973: 'Technology and Social Relations'. In *Marxism and Human Liberation*.

Slater, Phil ed. 1980: *Outlines of a Critique of Technology*.

Young, Robert M. 1979: 'Science is a Labour Process'.

ROBERT M. YOUNG

totalitarianism A term, used infrequently by Marxists, which was first introduced by political scientists in the 1920s to describe the fascist regime in Italy, and was subsequently extended to include National Socialist Germany and the USSR (particularly in the Stalinist era; see STALINISM). It became firmly established in the vocabularies of Western political science and journalism during the Cold War period of the 1950s. One of the best known definitions (Friedrich 1969) lists six features which distinguish totalitarian regimes from other autocracies, and from democracies: a totalist ideology;

a single party committed to this ideology; a fully developed secret police; and three kinds of monopolistic control – of mass communications, of operational weapons, and of all organizations, including economic ones.

Two Marxists, however, did make a rigorous use of the concept. Neumann (1942) described the National Socialist regime in Germany as a 'totalitarian monopolistic economy' (see FASCISM), and analysed in detail the doctrine of the 'totalitarian state' as one 'pervading all spheres of public life' in Goebbels' words. Hilferding, in two of his last writings (1940, 1941) argued that the USSR was a 'totalitarian state economy' – rejecting the characterization of it as 'state capitalism' (a concept which, like Neumann, he thought could not withstand serious economic analysis) or as a system of bureaucratic rule (Trotsky) – and observed that the Bolsheviks 'created the first totalitarian state before that term was invented'. He then went on to propose a more comprehensive revision of Marx's theory of the STATE. The modern state, he claimed, having become independent, now subordinates social groups to its own purposes: 'history, that "best of all Marxists", has taught us that in spite of Engels' expectations, the "administration of things" may become an unlimited "domination over men" . . .' and thus lead to 'the subjection of the economy by the holders of state power'. Hilferding argued, finally, that 'the development of state power accompanies the development of the modern economy', and the state becomes a totalitarian state to the extent that it subordinates all historically significant social processes to its will. The analyses of Neumann and Hilferding have a continuing importance in the context of Marxist debates about the growth of the interventionist state in all modern societies.

Reading

Friedrich, Carl J. 1969: 'The Evolving Theory and Practice of Totalitarian Regimes'. In Friedrich et al., Totalitarianism in Perspective: Three Views.

Hilferding, Rudolf 1940: 'State Capitalism or Totalitarian State Economy'.

— 1941 (1954): Das historische Problem

Neumann, Franz 1942 (1944): Behemoth: The Structure and Practice of National Socialism.

TOM BOTTOMORE

totality In contrast to metaphysical and formalist conceptions which treat it as an abstract, timeless, hence '*inert* totality' in which the parts occupy a fixed position in an unchanging whole, the dialectical concept is a *dynamic* one, reflecting the comprehensive but historically shifting mediations and transformations of objective reality. As Lukács puts it:

> The materialist-dialectical conception of totality means first of all the concrete unity of interacting contradictions . . .; secondly, the systematic relativity of all totality both upwards and downwards (which means that all totality is made of totalities subordinated to it, and also that the totality in question is, at the same time, overdetermined by totalities of a higher complexity . . .) and thirdly, the historical relativity of all totality, namely that the totality-character of all totality is changing, disintegrating, confined to a determinate, concrete historical period. (1948, p. 12)

In Hegel's philosophy the concept of totality is central. As 'concrete totality', with its internal differentiations, it constitutes the beginning of progress and development (Hegel 1812, vol. II, p. 472). The result of development is the 'self-identical whole' (ibid. p. 480) which recovers the original immediacy in the form of 'transcended determinateness' through the 'system of totality' (ibid. p. 482). Hence

> the pure immediacy of Being, in which at first all determination appears to be extinct or omitted by abstraction, is the Idea which has reached its adequate self-equality through mediation – that is, through the transcendence of mediation. The method is the pure Notion which is related only to itself; it is therefore the simple self-relation which is Being. But now it is also Being fulfilled, the self-comprehending Notion, Being as the concrete and also thoroughly *intensive* totality. (Ibid. p. 485)

Thus the Hegelian concept of totality is both the organizing core of the dialectical *method* and the criterion of truth. The latter is strongly stressed by Lenin when he praises Hegel in these terms:

> The *totality* of all sides of the phenomenon, of reality and their (reciprocal) *relations* –

that is what *truth* is composed of. The *relations* (= transition = contradictions) of notions = the main content of logic, by which these concepts (and their relations, transitions, contradictions) are shown as reflections of the objective world. The dialectics of things produces the dialectics of ideas, and not vice versa. Hegel brilliantly divined the dialectics of things (phenomena, the world, nature) in the dialectics of concepts. (Lenin, 1916, p. 196)

Social totality in Marxist theory is a structured and historically determined overall complex. It exists in and through those manifold mediations and transitions through which its specific parts or complexes – i.e., the 'partial totalities' – are linked to each other in a constantly shifting and changing, dynamic set of interrelations and reciprocal determinations. The significance and limits of an action, measure, achievement, law, etc., cannot therefore be assessed except in relation to a dialectical grasp of the structure of totality. This in turn necessarily implies the dialectical comprehension of the manifold concrete mediations (see MEDIATION) which constitute the structure of a given social totality.

Marx's conception of HISTORICAL MATERIALISM theorizes social development from the totalizing vantage point of a 'world history' that arises from the objective determinations of material and inter-personal processes. 'The *social structure* and the state are continually evolving out of the *life-process of definite individuals*' (*German Ideology*, vol. I. sect. IA), even if alienated and reified objectivity may appear as totally independent of them. The comprehensive vantage point is itself a sociohistorical product. For 'human anatomy contains a key to the anatomy of the ape. The intimations of higher development . . . can be understood only after the higher development is already known. The bourgeois economy thus supplies the key to the ancient, etc.' (*Grundrisse*, Introduction). Thus world history becomes decipherable only when its totalizing interconnections *objectively* arise out of the conditions of capitalist development and competition which 'produced world history for the first time, insofar as it made all civilized nations and every individual member of them dependent for

the satisfaction of their wants on the *whole world*, thus destroying the former natural exclusiveness of separate nations' (*German Ideology*, vol. I, sect. IB1). Accordingly,

things have *now* come to such a pass that the individuals must appropriate the existing totality of productive forces, not only to achieve self-activity, but, also, merely to safeguard their very existence. This appropriation is first determined by the object to be appropriated, the productive forces, which have been developed to a *totality* and which only exist within a *universal intercourse*. . . . The appropriation of these forces is itself nothing more than the development of the individual capacities corresponding to the material instruments of production. The appropriation of a *totality of instruments of production* is, for this very reason, the development of a *totality of capacities* in the individuals themselves. This appropriation is further determined by the persons appropriating. Only the proletarians of the present day . . . are in a position to achieve a *complete* and no longer restricted *self-activity*, which consists in the appropriation of a totality of productive forces and in the development of a totality of capacities entailed by this.' (Ibid. sect. IB3)

In a fashion reminiscent of the last passage, Lukács (1923, p. 28) argues that 'The totality of the *object* can be posited only when the positing *subject* is itself a totality.' And in criticizing the 'individual standpoint' of bourgeois theory, he insists that 'it is not the predominance of economic motives in the interpretation of society which is the decisive difference between Marxism and bourgeois science, but rather the *point of view of totality*. The category of totality, the all-round, determining domination of the whole over the parts is the essence of the method which Marx took over from Hegel and, in an original manner, transformed into the basis of an entirely new science' (ibid. p. 27). Centred around the 'standpoint of totality', Lukács elaborates a most influential theory of IDEOLOGY and CLASS CONSCIOUSNESS. Later this Lukácsian *methodological* principle is turned by Karl Mannheim into the postulated sociological entity of the 'free-floating intellectuals' (*freischwebendes*

Intelligenz), with a 'need for *total orientation* and synthesis'. Thanks to the claimed fact that they 'subsume in themselves all those interests with which social life is permeated . . . the intellectuals are still able to arrive at a *total orientation* even when they have joined a party' (Mannheim 1929, pp. 140–3).

Marx's *Capital* culminates with vol. III: 'The Process of Capitalist Production *as a Whole*'. For it is only in terms of the necessary structural interrelationship between *total* social capital and the *totality* of labour that the tendencies and laws of capital's self-expansion and ultimate disintegration as unearthed by Marx acquire their real significance, while fully taking into account also the contrary tendencies and structural determinations which tend to displace capital's contradictions and thus prolong the period of its social/historical viability. Lenin, at a later historical stage of social confrontations, is particularly concerned with identifying the historically specific and necessarily changing, objective lever or *strategic* 'link of the chain' (Lenin 1922) through which the given social totality is most effectively controlled in the form of organized social/political action, provided that an adequate, conscious, collective agency is available for implementing the overall strategic conception.

By contrast, in Sartre 'totality' is a problematical concept, since *totalisation* as such is an inherently *individual* venture. Consequently 'it is important to realize that what we are dealing with here is not a *totality* but a *totalization*, that is to say, a multiplicity which *totalizes itself* in order to totalize the practical field from a certain perspective, and that its common action, through *each organic praxis*, is revealed to every common individual as a developing objectification' (Sartre, 1960, p. 492). In view of such determinations, 'structure' itself cannot be other than an adopted inertia, and the 'whole' is essentially a question of *interiorization*. For 'Structure is a specific relation of the terms of a reciprocal relation to the whole and to each other through the mediation of the whole. And the whole, as a developing totalization, exists *in everyone* in the form of a unity of the *interiorised multiplicity* and *nowhere else*' (ibid. p. 499).

Reading
Hegel, G. W. F. 1812 (*1929*): *The Science of Logic.*

Lenin, V. I. 1914–16 (*1961*): 'Conspectus of Hegel's *The Science of Logic*'.
— 1922: Notes for a Speech on March 27.
Lukács, György 1923 (*1971*): *History and Class Consciousness.*
— 1948: *A marxista filosófia feladatai az ui demokráciában.* (The Tasks of Marxist Philosophy in the New Democracy.)
Mannheim, Karl 1929 (*1936*): *Ideology and Utopia.*
Sartre, Jean-Paul 1960 (*1976*): *Critique of Dialectical Reason.*

ISTVÁN MÉSZÁROS

trade unions Combinations of workers in the same occupation or branch of industry have a considerable history, but trade unionism as a widespread movement is a product of the growth of capitalist wage-labour. Early trade unions were commonly regarded as subversive organizations, and state repression was frequent (unions in France faced illegality until 1884, in Germany until 1890). Outlaw status was in turn often associated with turbulent forms of social protest.

Marx and Engels analysed unions in greatest detail while strongly influenced by the radicalism of early British labour struggles. Engels devoted a chapter of *Condition of the Working Class* to 'Labour Movements' (focusing mainly on Lancashire cotton-factory workers), and also discussed unionism among coal-miners. Marx concluded *The Poverty of Philosophy* with an enthusiastic assessment of English union struggles; and this view of localized combinations generating an 'ever-expanding union of the workers' was reiterated in the *Communist Manifesto*. These early writings developed three main arguments. First, unions were a natural product of capitalist industry; workers were forced to combine as a defence against wage-cutting and labour-displacing machinery. Second, unions were *not* (as claimed by Proudhon, and later by Lassalle) ineffectual economically; they could prevent employers reducing the price of labour power below its value. But they could not raise wages above this level, and even their defensive power was eroded by the concentration of capital and recurrent economic crises (see Marx, *Wage-Labour and Capital*). Hence third, the limited efficacy of defensive economic action forced workers to organize increasingly on a class-wide basis, to raise political demands, and ultimately to engage in revolutionary class struggle. (British examples cited were the Ten Hours campaign of the cotton workers, the Chartist movement, and the National Association of United Trades of 1845.) Above all else experience in trade unions enlarged workers' self-confidence and class consciousness; 'as schools of war, the Unions are unexcelled' (Engels, op. cit.).

But the ambitious movements in Britain soon collapsed. The correspondence of Marx and Engels revealed their disillusion; unions had become the preserve of a LABOUR ARISTOCRACY, their leaders were corrupted by bourgeois politicians, and the whole working class had been bought off by the fruits of colonial exploitation. Yet in the 1860s Marx cooperated with the leaders of major British unions in the First International, seeing their participation as vital to its success. In *Value, Price and Profit* (1865) and in his draft resolution for the Geneva Congress the following year, he urged them to expand their objectives, and although any hope in this direction was soon disappointed Marx and Engels could still insist that the trade union was 'the real class organization of the proletariat', criticizing the Gotha programme for omitting any discussion of the question (Engels to Bebel, 18–28 March 1875).

There is a major tension in the experience and writings of Marx and Engels from the 1850s onwards, between a view of unions as institutions which had become legitimate and complacent, and a vision of a more radical potential and practice. Surprisingly, this tension was never confronted systematically or theoretically; *Capital* contains only a handful of passing references to trade unions (though political struggles to limit the working day are discussed in some detail).

Later, four broad perspectives on trade unionism may be distinguished. 'Pure-and-simple' trade unionism, associated particularly with the American Federation of Labor but also characteristic of most British unionism, tacitly or explicitly accepted capitalist production relations as the framework for union aims and methods. The same was true of Catholic unions, formed in Europe from the 1890s. Anarcho-syndicalist unionism was revolution-

ary in aspiration and saw militant class-conscious unions as the necessary and sufficient basis for the overthrow of capitalism (see SYNDICALISM). The dominant, and in practice increasingly reformist, position of the Second International was that trade unions and the social-democratic party had complementary but distinct spheres of competence. While national unions in much of Europe arose under social-democratic tutelage, after the turn of the century they largely established their autonomy. Finally there was a revolutionary Marxist viewpoint. Luxemburg, for example, saw trade union action as a 'labour of Sisyphus'; often dominated by bureaucratic officials, unions became preoccupied with narrow employment issues. Lenin's notion of 'trade union consciousness' identified similar tendencies. Both insisted on the need to fight for revolutionary strategy within the unions, to combat the demarcation between economics and politics; and for the social-democratic party to guide this intervention (see also STRIKES).

During the 1914–18 war the emergence across Europe of COUNCILS based on rank-and-file factory organization provided a new element in the party–union dialectic. Marxists such as Gramsci stressed the conservative and bureaucratic character of union organization, 'divorced from the masses', and counterposed the vitality, authenticity and revolutionary potential of factory councils. This experience was to enlarge the perspectives of anarcho-syndicalism, but also inspired non-Bolshevik Marxists with the model of 'council communism' (see PANNEKOEK). The Russian revolution was however the dominant influence on Marxist attitudes to trade unions in subsequent decades. Within Russia itself, controversy over the role of unions in a workers' state culminated in the 'Trade Union debate' of 1920–1. The Workers' Opposition pressed for the unions to take over the management of the economy, while Trotsky argued for them to become agencies of the state. Lenin's position was that trade unions should remain formally independent of the state but should function as a 'school of communism' within which party cadres would seek to exert decisive leadership. The logic of his definition of unions as 'transmission belts from the Communist Party to the masses' was rigorously applied by Stalin; after his victory within the party and the institution of the first five-year plan the leadership of the unions was purged, and they were transformed into agencies of the production drive. The Congress of Trade Unions which endorsed these changes in 1932 was not convened again until 1949. By then the Stalinist model of trade unionism had become the pattern for Eastern Europe.

For the communist parties of the West, intervention in trade union struggles was defined as a key area of action. To provide central leadership a Red International of Labour Unions (RILU) was formed in 1921 on the initiative of the Comintern. Factory organization was pursued as a counteracting force to the 'reactionary trade union bureaucracy'. The clandestine formation of party cells within unions and workplaces was a necessary element in this strategy. Hostility to the existing trade union leadership was sharpened during the period of 'class against class', with the formation of 'revolutionary trade union oppositions' and some breakaway unions, as well as the encouragement of factory committees including non-unionists. But with the commitment to the politics of the 'popular front', trade union perspectives changed radically; one indication was that the RILU (which had not held a congress since 1930) was formally disbanded in 1937. International unity was briefly achieved with the formation of the World Federation of Trade Unions (WFTU) in 1945, but in 1949 most Western unions seceded to form the International Confederation of Free Trade Unions (ICFTU) (the main exceptions being the communist unions in France and Italy).

Cold war divisions weakened in the 1980s as a result of differentiation within the ICFTU, moves towards deconfessionalization in the originally Catholic World Council of Labour, and the impact of EUROCOMMUNISM in the WFTU. Meanwhile Marxist theory has advanced little. Official communists have largely clung to the 'transmission belt' conception; other Marxists have tended either to write off the organized working class in the industrialized West as an agency of revolution, or to reiterate earlier strategies of 'rank-and-file' action.

Reading
Collins, H. and Abramsky, C. 1965: *Karl Marx and the British Labour Movement.*

Deutscher, I. 1950: *Soviet Trade Unions.*

Foster, W. Z. 1956: *Outline History of the World Trade Union Movement.*

Gramsci, A. 1977: *Selections from Political Writings 1910–1920.*

Hammond, T. T. 1957: *Lenin on Trade Unions and Revolution.*

Hyman, R. 1971: *Marxism and the Sociology of Trade Unionism.*

— 1980: 'Theory in Industrial Relations: Towards a Materialist Analysis'. In P. Boreham and G. Dow eds. *Work and Inequality,* vol. 2.

Lenin, V. I. 1970: *On Trade Unions.*

Lozovsky, A. 1935: *Marx and the Trade Unions.*

Luxemburg, R. 1970: *Rosa Luxemburg Speaks.*

Smart, D. A. 1978: *Pannekoek and Gorter's Marxism.*

RICHARD HYMAN

transformation problem.   *See* value and price.

transition from feudalism to capitalism   This was never a major preoccupation for Marx and Engels. It was nonetheless a problem addressed periodically in discussions of more central themes such as historical materialist method (see HISTORICAL MATERIALISM), the capitalist mode of production, or class conflict in history. Attention to 'transition' was therefore episodic, the main instances being (in chronological order) the suggestive sketches of the *German Ideology*, the bald propositions of the *Communist Manifesto*, the rich complexity of Marx's notes published as *Pre-Capitalist Economic Formations*, and the sustained discussions of PRIMITIVE ACCUMULATION and MERCHANT CAPITAL in *Capital*.

Two features of this work are especially noteworthy. First, exploration of the transition to capitalism ceases over time to be seen as deducible from some general formula of social change. This is evident in Marx's shift away from the prominent 1840s emphasis on 'productive force' determinism, sometimes portrayed as 'technological determinism' as in the celebrated aphorism 'the handmill gives you society with the feudal lord, the steam mill society with the industrial capitalist' (*Poverty of Philosophy*, ch. II, sect. 1). In *Pre-Capitalist Economic Formations*, by contrast, Marx's method involves the use of a set of formal concepts (e.g. mode of production, property, etc.) which are however applied in different ways to particular instances of social change. There is, in other words, no generic theory of transition.

Secondly, Marx's substantive interpretations of the transition from feudalism to capitalism remain ambivalent and far from unitary. Two broad perspectives are offered. The first, evident for example in the 1840s and 1850s, emphasizes the corrosive effect upon the feudal system of mercantile activity, the growth of the world market, and new expanding cities. Mercantile capitalism, within an autonomous urban sphere, provides the initial dynamic towards capitalism. The second variant, especially evident in *Capital*, centres on the 'producer' and the process whereby 'producer' becomes merchant and capitalist. This Marx calls 'the really revolutionary path'. Causal analysis is then directed to the preconditions which allow some producers to become capitalists, notably the separation of the vast majority of producers from ownership of the means of production and the creation of propertyless wagelabour. In *Capital*, Marx speaks of these variants as two ways to capitalist development, but opts for the latter as the really decisive characterization of transition. Mercantile activity may well turn products more and more into commodities (see COMMODITY), but it does not explain how and why labour power itself should become a commodity. Hence it cannot explain the transition. Causal primacy, therefore, does not lie within exchange relations, but rather within the social relations of production. In *Capital*, therefore, attention is directed less to the dynamic of the expanding world market or towns, and more to changes in property relations manifest through class struggle, as in Tudor England, whereby the peasantry lost its land and a landless proletariat was gradually created. Yet for all this Marx is more concerned to establish the structural preconditions for the emergence of capitalism, than the detailed causal mechanisms whereby these preconditions were realized.

The theoretical ambivalence and empirical inadequacies in Marx's account of transition help to explain why this issue remains a perennial topic of debate. In postwar and especially post-Stalinist Marxism, greater attention has been given to the analysis of the transition from feudalism to capitalism in Western Europe, than to the more controversial question whether this transition can be regarded as a universal stage of social evolution through which all societies must pass (see STAGES OF DEVELOPMENT). In the former framework, three largely divergent approaches have emerged since the celebrated exchange between Sweezy and Dobb in the early 1950s (see Dobb 1946; Hilton 1976).

The 'exchange relations' perspective (Sweezy 1976; Wallerstein 1974) defines capitalism in terms of production for profit through market exchange as contrasted with the nearsubsistence economy of feudalism. Capitalism emerges through forces such as trade and the international division of labour which are seen as 'external' to feudalism. But where do trade and the market originate if not within feudalism? And is their articulation within a system of production for profit through the market adequate to distinguish capitalism from other modes of production?

The 'property relations' perspective (Dobb 1946; Hilton 1973; Brenner 1976, 1977), in taking up these difficulties, aligns itself more with the Marx of *Capital* than of the *German Ideology*. Capitalism is now defined in terms of social relations of production founded on free wage-labour, and entailing a structural imperative to continuous capital accumulation. Feudalism in contrast is based on relations of personal dependence, mutual obligation and juridicallyenforced surplus extraction, within such institutions as SERFDOM and vassalage. Rather than the external 'Smithian' hidden hand dynamic implicit in Sweezy and Wallerstein (Brenner 1977), this approach sees feudalism broken down through internal contradictions. These are manifest in class conflict, which tends to destroy serfdom and create a move towards freer agrarian tenures. Over time there is produced a social structure based on capitalist farmers and landless labourers. Such views help to explain problems within the exchange relations perspective such as the lack of correlation between the demise of serfdom and the presence of market forces. Much more remains to be established, however, as to why class struggle between lords and serfs had different outcomes in different areas of Europe, and why serf freedom should have led in some places towards agrarian capitalism, in others to peasant agriculture (see FEUDAL SOCIETY; PEASANTRY).

Anderson's approach to the transition (1974a, 1974b) involves the synthesis of non-Marxist themes, such as neo-Malthusian demography, with more conventional Marxist emphases. In so far as he depends on Marxist resources he moves freely between the previous two perspectives. Anderson's belief that changes in social relations preceded the development of productive forces characteristic of capitalism aligns him with Dobb *et al.* Yet he rejects any simple evolutionary theory of change in which class struggle within feudalism plays a decisive role in bringing about the 'feudal crisis'. Like Sweezy and Wallerstein, he stresses the importance of towns and international trade. Urban cultural dynamism is not, however, left hanging in a sphere external to feudalism, but is seen as a legacy of the classical world of Greece and Rome. Here Anderson shares with Max Weber a notion of the importance of the classical inheritance for the making of capitalism. Anderson implicitly reads human history in terms of the emergence of a material order capable of universalizing the urban cultural and political legacy of classical slave-based societies. This contrasts with the Smithian view of man implicit in Sweezy and Wallerstein. It also recasts the traditional Marxist teleology according to which history unfolds as a result of humanity's striving to realize its essential powers of creative praxis through the mastery of nature and the overcoming of alienating social relations.

Reading
Anderson, P. 1974a: *Lineages of the Absolutist State.*
— 1974b: *Passages from Antiquity to Feudalism.*
Brenner, R. 1976: 'Agrarian Class Structure and Economic Development in Pre-Industrial Europe'.
— 1977: 'The Origins of Capitalist Development: a Critique of neo-Smithian Marxism'.
Dobb, M. 1946: *Studies in the Development of Capitalism.*
Hilton, R. 1973: *Bond Men Made Free.*
Hilton, R. ed. 1976: *The Transition from Feudalism to Capitalism.*
Holton, R. 1981: 'Marxist Theories of Social Change and the Transition from Feudalism to Capitalism'.

Sweezy, P. 1976: Essays reprinted in R. Hilton, ed. *op. cit.*
Wallerstein, I. 1974: *The Origins of the Modern World System.*

ROBERT J. HOLTON

transition to socialism   The Marxist concept of socialist revolution implies that there must be a period of transition from capitalism to socialism. In contrast to bourgeois revolution which is an overthrow of the political power of the aristocracy *at the end* of a long process of growth of the capitalist economy and bourgeois culture within the framework of feudal society, the seizure of political power from the bourgeoisie is, according to Marx, only 'the first episode' of the revolutionary transformation of capitalism into socialism. Marx (*Critique of the Gotha Programme*, sect. 3) distinguished between the *lower phase* of communism (a mixed society which still lacks its own foundations) and its *higher phase* (after the disappearance of the 'enslaving subordination of the individual to the division of labour' and of 'the antithesis between mental and physical labour', when such abundance would be attained that goods could be distributed to each 'according to his needs'). Most Marxists identify the lower phase as 'socialism' and the higher phase as 'communism'. In SOCIALISM there are still classes, occupational division of labour, elements of a market economy and of bourgeois right, exemplified in the principle of distribution of goods according to the amount of labour given to society.

The original programme of Marx and Engels, formulated in the *Communist Manifesto*, was quite flexible and construed the transition to COMMUNISM as a series of steps which eventually revolutionize the entire mode of production. The first step is 'winning the battle of democracy', 'raising the proletariat to the position of ruling class', 'seizing political power'. Marx is aware that political power is merely the organized power of one class for oppressing another, but in his view the proletariat 'is compelled by the force of circumstances' to use it in order to sweep away by force the old conditions of production, classes generally, and its own supremacy as a class. In order to specify the character of the workers' state Marx used the term 'DICTATORSHIP OF THE PROLETARIAT', which was controversial in his own time and is challenged by many democratic socialists today. Anarchists (especially Bakunin) objected that the idea would help to perpetuate the existence of an authoritarian state and of a tyrannical bureaucratic ruling elite. On the other hand, reformists (e.g. Bernstein) rejected the idea of a political revolution since they thought the very economic process of capitalism led spontaneously towards socialism.

The economic programme of transition expounded in the *Communist Manifesto* comprised measures meant 'to wrest *by degrees* all capital from the bourgeoisie', 'to centralize all instruments of production in the hands of the state' and 'to increase the total of productive forces as rapidly as possible'. Property in land and the right of inheritance would be abolished, property of all emigrants and rebels would be confiscated, other enterprises would only gradually pass into the hands of the State. The latter message was later forgotten. When the Bolsheviks came to power in 1917 they nationalized the whole economy (outside agriculture) at once and this lead was followed in other twentieth-century socialist revolutions. It is part of the official Marxist ideology in all countries of 'real socialism' that the establishment of a dictatorship of the proletariat, in a particular, highly centralized form, and nationalization of the means of production, are obligatory steps in the transition to socialism. Experience has amply shown that the new state created in this way invariably escapes any control by the working class and becomes an instrument of domination of the vanguard party. After a series of purges the revolutionary vanguard grows into a powerful bureaucracy which assumes more or less total control over all spheres of public life, politics, economy, and culture. Rigid administrative planning secures steady general growth but stifles initiative and innovation, and it has a particularly harmful effect on all those branches of the economy that need flexible, decentralized decision-making (agriculture, small-scale production, trade, services). Once the new centres of alienated power are established further development towards socialism fails to take place. The state with its coercive organs and professional apparatus tends to become stronger rather than 'wither

away'. The workers' councils (soviets) lose any significance. The expected free flourishing of culture does not materialize, and instead there is a spectacular quantitative growth of culture dominated by official ideology. The development of a 'wealth of needs' is largely replaced by the pursuit of material wealth.

This kind of society does not nearly approach the goal of the entire process of transition, which Marx described (in the *Communist Manifesto*) as 'an association in which the free development of each is the condition for the free development of all'. Such a goal requires different means and different stages of the transition process. Under the pressure of powerful social movements, and of the need to resolve various inner contradictions, some important reforms have been accomplished even within the framework of the old capitalist society (progressive taxation, nationalization of some key branches of the economy, workers' participation, planning, social welfare, socialized medicine, universal free education, free culture, humanization of work etc.) The political supremacy of radical socialist forces may take place near the end of this process rather than being its precondition. Once they prevail these forces will be able to turn the state into a self-governing rather than authoritarian structure. A professional army would be replaced by a non-professional, self-defence organization. Underprivileged social groups (women, oppressed nations or races) would acquire, first, equality of rights, then equality of condition. Means of production would be socialized and put under the control of self-managing bodies (see SOCIALIZATION). The market for capital and labour would disappear, workers' wages being replaced by a share in the net income of the working organization, corresponding with the amount, intensity and quality of their work. The market for commodities would remain an indicator of social needs for a long time, but more and more goods would lose the character of commodities, as they were produced in order to meet human needs and more or less subsidized by society (medical drugs, educational and cultural goods and services, dwellings, basic foodstuffs). To the extent that the basic needs of all individuals were met, the growth of material production would slow down. The increase in the productivity of labour would remain a lasting policy, but its purpose would no longer be the increase of material output but liberation from toil, reduction of working hours. Higher level cultural, spiritual, communal needs would grow in importance. Work would gradually lose its alienated character (see ALIENATION), with workers' participation in decision-making, the free choice among alternative technologies, and a reorganization of the process of production to emphasize autonomy and self-control of workers as well as a rational coordination among them. The principle of federalism would govern the social organization at all levels. In the socialization of individuals, preparation for work would lose its present-day primary importance, and also become much more flexible with a freer choice of work, and access to jobs regardless of sex, race, nationality or age. The division of labour would no longer be so rigidly professionalized and there would be greater opportunities for workers to change their working roles when additional knowledge and skill qualified them for new ones. Moreover, the most important activities would come to be those in which the individual's creative capacities find expression, whether in productive work or outside it.

Socialism is not a perfect society but only the optimal possibility of the present historical epoch. It does not resolve all human conflicts, and it will probably generate some new ones which are at present unforeseeable, but it puts an end to wasteful production for profit, to class domination and exploitation, and to oppression by the state.

Reading

Bernstein, Eduard 1899 (1961): *Evolutionary Socialism: A Criticism and Affirmation.*

Gorz, André 1967: *Strategy for Labor.*

Lenin, V. I. 1917c (1969): *State and Revolution.*

Marković, Mihailo 1974: *From Affluence to Praxis.*

Medvedev, Roy 1971: *Let History Judge: The Origins and Consequences of Stalinism.*

Stojanović, Svetozar 1973: *Between Ideals and Reality.*

MIHAILO MARKOVIĆ

tribal society Although Marx (especially in his notes on L. H. Morgan's *Ancient Society*; see Krader 1972) and Engels (in *Origin of the Family*) occasionally used the terms 'tribe' and 'tribal', they did not define or analyse 'tribal society' as a distinct type of society. Engels (ibid. ch. 1) attached particular importance to Morgan's attempt 'to introduce a definite order into the history of primitive man' through his conception of stages of prehistoric culture, passing from savagery to barbarism and thence to civilization, which Engels found entirely congruent with the materialist conception of history. Marx, in his notebooks of the period 1879–82 when he undertook more systematic ethnological studies (Krader 1972) was also mainly concerned with the historical development of early societies and commented not only on Morgan but also on the work of Maine, Lubbock, Kovalevsky and others. Thus both Marx and Engels were primarily interested in the emergence – within 'primitive society' in its various forms – of class divisions and the state.

In modern academic anthropology the term 'tribal' is as ambiguously viewed as is the term 'primitive'. Although Kroeber (1948) had initially challenged the concept of 'tribe' as the basis of the social formations of native North America, his objections went largely unnoticed until Fried (1966) launched a crusade against the use of the word with reference to indigenous societies generally. Both scholars pointed out that the tribe – as designated in metropolitan theory and practice – was an administrative unit forced upon otherwise varied and politically autonomous groups in a colonial context. Leacock (1983) adds that the 'tribe' as a hierarchically structured political group may also be an internal response to the necessity of defence against imperialist efforts to dominate a given area.

Recent Marxist studies have been concerned both with conceptual problems (Godelier 1973) and with historical and political reality. If, for example, we examine a politically hierarchical structure composed of formerly egalitarian indigenous groups who may also be involved in some kind of tributary relationship with the dominating elite (or if the people from whom that elite is drawn has itself been internally divided in a similar fashion), the term 'tribe' becomes innocuous, unless it is used in the context of a proto-state (to use Diamond's term 1983) – hence the term 'tribal state' employed by Service. On the other hand, if the designation 'tribe' is also applied to an egalitarian, classless, that is, primitive society, then the ambiguity of the category becomes evident. 'Egalitarian', it should be noted, does not indicate the absence of statuses, ranks or generational hierarchies, but only the absence of economic exploitation. Since the term 'tribe' also has associations with the term 'folk' and with other vague expressions such as 'traditional', or 'uncivilized', the image of a sectarian, ingrown, kin-bonded, and fiercely self-protective unit has grown out of the contacts between literate/high civilizations and non-literate, presumably less sophisticated and technologically 'inferior' cultures. These ethnocentric criteria tend to overshadow the division between tribal states and stateless tribal societies. But it should also be kept in mind that a stateless tribal society may owe its social bonding to a direct or indirect imperialist assault from the outside. Such a secondary construction should not be confused with the incipient tribal state.

The problems posed by the various meanings of 'tribe' are real but may be solved through redefinition, although Godelier (op. cit. pp. 93–6) argues that a more fundamental theoretical reconstruction is necessary, which would pay less attention to the 'forms' in which these societies appear, and would analyse more rigorously the action of different modes of production within them. 'Tribe' should not be used with reference to the various types of statist social formations that have emerged historically (Asiatic, ancient, feudal, capitalist, socialist) but there is no reason to abandon the term with reference to stateless, or primitive, societies. Hence, a horticulturally based primitive society in e.g. north-central Nigeria, composed of several villages recognizing a traditional relationship to each other based upon a shared name, a common language and culture, marital boundaries that are isomorphic with the boundaries of the village ensemble, and possibly recognizing supra-village religious authorities, meets the definition of 'tribe'. Such a society is classless, functions through designated kin or quasi-kin associations, has no civil structure and no civil authority. The constituent villages are autonomous but linked; just as they maintain an internal egalitarianism so they relate to other villages in a non-exploitative framework. Cooperative work groups, military

and/or hunting units may also cross-cut villages in a 'tribal' context. The cultural bonding evident within a 'tribe' may however exist in the absence of a determinate tribal structure, and may embrace a large number of local groups extending over a considerable area, as among the pre-contact Ibo-speaking peoples of eastern Nigeria. Such a group may be considered a primitive nationality; beyond a certain radius this shared cultural identity may not even be known by the people themselves, in the absence of political federation or far-flung ritual or trading connections.

A tribal society, then, is a primitive society in its fundamental characteristics. When the term 'tribe' is used as a substantive, even with reference to a direct or indirect 'secondary response' to imperialist incursion, it reflects a certain type of reciprocal affiliation among local groups. When 'tribal' is used as an adjective it may refer to a band (which is also a primitive society) or to an incipient state in which primitive characteristics are maintained, albeit transformed, in the local areas but where the external, exclusively civil affiliations are class and/or caste oriented. The Iroquois would exemplify a 'tribe', Dahomey a 'tribal state', and the Bushmen a 'tribal' band society. Marx himself appears to incorporate social formations of the tribal state type under the general rubric of the Asiatic mode of production. (See also PRIMITIVE COMMUNISM.)

Reading

Diamond, Stanley 1981: *In Search of the Primitive: A Critique of Civilization*.

— 1983: *Dahomey: Transition and Conflict in State Formation*.

Fried, Morton 1966: 'On the Concepts of "Tribe" and "Tribal Society"'.

Godelier, Maurice 1973 (1977): 'The concept of the "tribe"'. In *Perspectives in Marxist Anthropology*.

Krader, Lawrence ed. 1972: *The Ethnological Notebooks of Karl Marx*.

Kroeber, Alfred 1948: *Anthropology*.

Leacock, Eleanor 1983: 'Interpreting the Origins of Gender Inequality: Conceptual and Historical Problems'.

Service, Elman 1962: *Primitive Social Organization: An Evolutionary Perspective*.

STANLEY DIAMOND

Trotsky, Leon Born 7 November (26 October, old style) 1879, Yanovka, Ukraine; died 20 August 1940, Coyoacán, Mexico. Lev Davidovich Bronstein, pen-name 'Trotsky', a member of the Russian Social-Democratic Labour Party, was prominent in the Russian Revolutions of 1905 and October 1917, People's Commissar for Foreign Affairs, 1918, then for Military and Naval Affairs, 1918–25. From 1923 he led opposition movements against 'betrayal' of the revolution by the Soviet bureaucracy. Expelled from Russia in 1929 by Stalin, he formed the Fourth International (see INTERNATIONALS) abroad to oppose STALINISM. He criticized Comintern policy on fascism and social-democracy, and was assassinated by an agent of Stalin.

Trotsky's major contribution to Marxist thought was the theory of 'uneven and combined development', and the derived doctrine of 'permanent revolution'. A backward country overcomes its backwardness not by passing through the stages already traversed by advanced countries but by telescoping or even skipping them, which results in a combination of features of backwardness with features of an advanced stage of development, usually at the highest level available. This process is seen as typical of countries outside the advanced capitalist nucleus of Western Europe and North America. The practical political consequence is that since, normally, introduction of advanced industry takes place in a colonial or semi-colonial way (see COLONIALISM), the country affected will acquire a proletariat stronger than the native bourgeoisie. The latter being incapable, or afraid, of attempting to carry out a bourgeois revolution this task falls to the proletariat, leading the lower orders of the pre-capitalist sector in a revolution which proceeds immediately from abolition of feudal survivals (see FEUDAL SOCIETY) to taking steps in the direction of socialism. The expression 'permanent revolution' was borrowed from the Address of the General Council to the Communist League, 1850, by Marx and Engels.

The victorious proletariat must try to promote revolutions in other countries, especially advanced ones, since progress towards socialism cannot get far within the confines of a single country, especially one (like Russia) with substantial elements of pre-capitalist relations to overcome. The very circumstances facilitating revolution in such a country also hinder its socialist development. 'Permanent revolution' challenged the view that a prolonged period of capitalist development must follow an anti-feudal revolution, during which the bourgeoisie would rule, or else some combination of social forces (e.g., 'revolutionary-democratic dictatorship of proletariat and peasantry') acting as surrogate (see LENIN; LENINISM). Trotskyists claim that Lenin in April 1917 adopted Trotsky's concept and put it into practice in the October Revolution.

When Stalin propounded the doctrine of 'socialism in one country' Trotsky warned that this would lead to disastrous adventures within Russia (premature collectivization of agriculture) and conversion of the Communist International into a mere instrument of non-revolutionary Russian foreign policy. While Soviet Russia must develop industry and modernize society generally, such achievements were not to be identified with socialism. Socialism is not seen as merely industrialization plus an improved standard of living, but as a society with higher labour productivity and, based on this, a higher standard of living, than in capitalist society at its most advanced stage. This presupposes conquest of power by the proletariat on the 'commanding heights' of the world economy. Trotsky saw Russia's social order under Stalin as merely 'transitional' between capitalism and socialism, fated either to progress towards socialism (which would require revolutions in the advanced capitalist countries plus a supplementary political revolution in Russia) or to regress into capitalism. The ruling bureaucracy is seen not as a 'new class' but as a parasitic excrescence, and Soviet society not as 'state capitalism' but as a 'degenerated workers' state', in which nevertheless some fundamental gains of the October Revolution survived, so that in the event of war revolutionaries everywhere must defend the USSR.

Characteristic of Trotsky's thought is the rejection of false claims made for Marxism as a universal system, providing the key to every problem. He opposed charlatanism in the guise of Marxism in the sphere of 'military science', and combated attempts to subject scientific research, literature and art to direction in the name of Marxism, ridiculing the concept of 'proletarian culture'. He emphasized the role of non-rational factors in politics: 'In politics one must not think rationalistically, and least of all where the national question is concerned'. A cultured Marxist in the tradition of Marx and Engels themselves, he made many enemies among those whose Marxism, combining narrowness and ignorance with a propensity to make fantastic claims, was of the sort that caused Marx to say that he was 'not a Marxist'.

It may well be that, were Trotsky alive today, he would say he was 'not a Trotskyist', in view of the extreme fragmentation of the movement he founded, in which some groups could be said to take his name in vain. Nevertheless, since the 1960s, organizations calling themselves Trotskyist have in several countries acquired influence, and Trotsky's own writings have achieved circulations far greater than in his lifetime (see REVOLUTION BETRAYED; TROTSKYISM).

Since 1985, with Gorbachev and *glasnost*, it has become possible in the USSR to mention Trotsky without saying bad things about him, and even to indicate (if only implicitly) that his role was not always necessarily negative. Some of his less controversial writings (e.g. in praise of Lenin) have been published in the more advanced journals. Nevertheless, works continue to appear in which the story of the civil war and the building of the Red Army is told without so much as naming him.

Although it is now hinted that communists who opposed Stalin in the 1920s might have been correct, the trend favoured is Bukharin's Right Opposition, Trotsky's ideological opponents. When obliged by foreign questioners to talk about Trotsky, official spokesmen tend to dwell on the authoritarian Trotsky of 1920, presented as 'worse than Stalin', rather than the later advocate of greater democracy.

Much of Trotsky's criticism of Soviet society in the post-Lenin period must, in so far as it is known, seem to Soviet people an anticipation of the critique now being made by Gorbachev himself. But Trotsky's insistence that the needed changes could come about only through what he called a political revolution (making comparisons with 1830 and 1848 in France), and not through self-reform by the bureaucracy, makes his doctrine unacceptable in leading circles. In addition to which, Trotsky's

further insistence that solving Russia's economic and social problems must depend upon 'world revolution' clashes with the conciliatory line in foreign policy promoted by Gorbachev.

Reading

Broué, Pierre 1988: *Trotski.*

Day, Richard B. 1973: *Leon Trotsky and the Politics of Economic Isolation.*

Deutscher, Isaac 1954: *The Prophet Armed: Trotsky, 1879–1921.*

— 1959: *The Prophet Unarmed; Trotsky, 1921–1929.*

— 1963: *The Prophet Outcast: Trotsky, 1929–40.*

Gori, F. ed. 1982: *Pensiero e azione politica di Lev Trotsky.*

Knei-Paz, Baruch 1978: *The Social and Political Thought of Leon Trotsky.*

Sinclair, Louis 1972: *Leon Trotsky: A Bibliography.*

Trotsky, Leon 1932–3: *History of the Russian Revolution.*

— 1937 (1972): *The Revolution Betrayed.*

— 1962: *The Permanent Revolution and Results and Prospects.*

— 1963: *My Life.*

BRIAN PEARCE

Trotskyism Like every important school of thought, Trotskyism has been subjected to diverse interpretations, with different aspects coming to the fore in different historical circumstances. The cornerstone of Trotskyism has been and remains the theory of permanent revolution, originally formulated by Marx, which Trotsky reformulated in 1906, applied to Russia, and then elaborated further in 1928. Trotsky viewed the transition to socialism as a series of interconnected and interdependent social, political, and economic upheavals proceeding on various levels and in diverse social structures – feudal, underdeveloped, pre-industrial and capitalist – and occurring at different historical junctures. This 'combined and uneven development' would be driven by circumstances and by its own dynamics from its anti-feudal bourgeois phase to its anti-capitalist socialist phase; in the process it would transcend geographical and man-made boundaries and pass from its national to its international phase towards the establishment of a classless and stateless society on a global scale. Although revolution must *start* on a national basis (and may even condemn the revolutionary state to a period of isolation), this will inevitably constitute only the first act of the drama followed by the next one played in another part of the international arena. Internationalism – the second aspect of the permanency of the revolution – thus constitutes an indelible hallmark of Trotskyism.

The theory clashed most fiercely in the country of its origin with Stalin's theory of socialism in a single country, which for Trotskyism is a contradiction in terms, and was banished as the heresy of all heresies from the part of the world where the Soviet model of socialism prevailed. However, it remained alive outside that region, and although it had to contend with the growth of nationalism intrinsically hostile to it, has become a major component of a renascent socialist consciousness, especially since the 1960s.

The Fourth International (see INTERNATIONALS), set up by Trotsky in 1938, has not proved effective as an instrument to promote revolution, but it played a significant role as a stimulus to a world-wide debate on the basic tenets of Trotskyism and to the creation of numerous Trotskyist groups searching for a correct revolutionary strategy for the present time. The stalemate in the class struggle (see CLASS CONFLICT) in the advanced West and the awakening of national and social consciousness among peoples of Asia and Africa may be interpreted as a confirmation of the permanency of the revolution. The liberation movements in 'backward' countries raise anew the question as to who should be regarded as the main and decisive agent of the revolution: the industrial proletariat, as postulated by classical Marxism (and Trotskyism), or the peasantry, which, as was seen in China in 1948–9, brought the revolution from the countryside into the town (see MAO TSE-TUNG).

The establishment of a classless socialist society, according to Trotskyism, cannot come about otherwise than through a revolutionary break with the existing order. Trotskyism rejects the evolutionary parliamentary road of the ballot box as illusory; it takes for granted that the exploited classes will not be able to take power without a struggle against the property owning classes defending their economic dominance. The victory of the proletariat in such a class

struggle will, in the Trotskyist scheme of things, have to be safeguarded by the establishment of a 'proletarian dictatorship'. This concept, which with the experience of totalitarian regimes (see TOTALITARIANISM) has become overgrown with repulsive accretions, denoted to Trotsky (as to Marx and Engels) not a form of government but the social-political dominance of a class. Thus he described parliamentary democracies of the West as bourgeois dictatorships; that is, regimes which assured the propertied classes their dominance.

The DICTATORSHIP OF THE PROLETARIAT will be established through the seizure of power by the political party of the proletariat to which Trotsky assigned the leading role in the revolution. He warned, however, that such a party must beware of substituting itself for the proletariat or subjugating it once its task has been accomplished. Under the dictatorship of the proletariat, proletarian democracy will be secured through the effective control of the government by the Soviets (see COUNCILS) constituted by representatives of legal Soviet parties, freely elected by all toilers. Soviet parties, including pro-bourgeois elements, are those which respect the Constitution of the workers' state based on the socialist organization of production and distribution, and do not engage in violent attempts to overthrow it. In addition the sovereignty of the proletariat will be preserved through the placing of industry under workers' control and management at the point of production by means of Factory Committees. This association of producers will be complemented by the association of consumers controlling the distribution and pricing of consumer goods.

Trotsky's conception of a revolutionary party was not consistent and varied at different historical periods. Among present-day Trotskyists some groups subscribe fully to Trotsky's youthful (pre-1917) criticisms of Lenin's rigid centralist principles and see the party as a broad and loose organization. Others, while not rejecting completely Lenin's centralism, lay more stress on the democratic form of the party, referring to Trotsky's writings after 1923 and during his subsequent struggle against the bureaucratic dictatorship of the Stalinized Soviet party. Still others, a minority, adhere strictly to Leninist centralism and refer to Trotsky's most centralist phase of 1917–23.

The principle of pluralistic socialism and the belief in the necessity of workers' control is common to most groups which claim allegiance to Trotskyism; so also is their refusal to regard the Soviet Union as a socialist society. They are, however, divided in their definition of the nature of the Soviet Union. Two main currents of thought come to the fore: one maintains that the Soviet Union is still a workers' state though, as Trotsky had stated, it underwent a process of degeneration; the other maintains that nothing of a workers' state is left in the Soviet Union and that its regime is that of state capitalism. The third, less widespread, considers the Soviet bloc as a *sui generis* formation of a new type. These theoretical conceptions determine in large measure the character of Trotskyist opposition to the Soviet Union. The question is posed: will the Soviet Union shed its vestiges of Stalinism and enter on the road to socialism by way of gradual reforms from above, reforms for which the pressure will come from below; or will a violent upheaval from below be needed to achieve what Lenin, Trotsky, and the Bolsheviks set out to achieve in 1917? This question came to the fore after M. S. Gorbachev, the new leader, assumed power in February 1985 and embarked on a series of drastic reforms aiming at the radical liberalization and democratization of the regime. In this framework the censorship was abolished, Trotsky's writings were taken off the index and became accessible to students.

Whatever hopes may have been aroused among Western Trotskyists that Trotsky's ideas might be vindicated were, however, short-lived. It became clear that the new leadership's goal was not 'to achieve what Lenin, and Trotsky and the Bolsheviks set out to achieve in 1917'. What was the order of the day was not the internationalism of 'permanent revolution', the support of liberation movements, or the attainment of 'proletarian democracy' at home, as envisaged by Trotsky. By the end of the 1980s it became evident that in pursuing the reforms the new team looked rather towards the bourgeois West; from there it drew its inspiration and saw in the resort to market forces the model for reforms designed to pull Russia out of its economic stagnation and technological backwardness and put it on the road to the

twenty-first century. Some Trotskyists in the West (and not only they) may have recalled Trotsky's warning: the definition of the Soviet regime as 'transitional' from capitalism to socialism proved inadequate: in reality a backsliding to capitalism was wholly possible (*The Revolution Betrayed*, p. 241).

The new policy of 'openness' allowed outside observers an insight into the 'state of Trotskyism' inside the Soviet Union. As might have been foreseen, among the population at large there was very little awareness of Trotsky and his role. Curiously enough, it was as the most consistent and unrelenting adversary of Stalin that the interest in him was at first aroused. Some writers were using freely Trotsky's invective against Stalin, and even his attacks on bureaucracy, but showed no familiarity with his analysis of Stalinism.

Although the study of Trotsky was not encouraged in the academies, gradually intellectuals and historians took advantage of the opening of the archives to study the past. The decades of persecution and obloquy had, however, their effect: an unthinking hostility still persists among scholars who, in their work on Trotsky, concentrate on and even exploit those episodes where Trotsky was at his most disciplinarian and authoritarian. They do this all the more eagerly as they sense that Trotsky's revolutionary personality does not accord well with the political and social philosophy of the ruling hierarchy at the present historical juncture.

If among a small number of students, political activists and workers one might detect some affinity with Trotskyism, this is due more to their own independent intellectual searchings than to the direct influence of Trotsky and his theories. There is no organization or grouping which would explicitly and unreservedly proclaim its allegiance to 'Trotskyism'.

Anathemized, vilified and banished from his own country in the 1920s and 1930s, now, at the turn of the century Trotsky has not been welcomed by the official USSR; unlike other revolutionary victims of Stalin, he has not been 'rehabilitated'; his martyrdom has been acknowledged, but his honour has not been restored.

Reading

Cliff, T. 1974: *State Capitalism in Russia*.

Deutscher, I. 1954: *The Prophet Armed, Trotsky 1879–1921.*

— 1959: *The Prophet Unarmed, Trotsky 1921–1929.*

— 1963: *The Prophet Outcast, Trotsky 1929–40.*

Documents of the Fourth International (1973).

Löwy, M. 1981: *The Politics of Combined and Uneven Development.*

Mandel, E. 1979: *Revolutionary Marxism Today.*

Trotsky, L. 1932–3: *History of the Russian Revolution.*

— 1937 (1972): *The Revolution Betrayed.*

— 1962: *The Permanent Revolution* and *Results and Prospects.*

— 1973b: *The Transitional Programme for Socialist Revolution.*

TAMARA DEUTSCHER

truth In the writings of Marx and Engels (α) 'truth' normally *means* 'correspondence with reality', while (β) the *criterion* for evaluating truth-claims normally is, or involves, human practice; i.e. Marx and Engels subscribe to a classical (Aristotelian) concept, and a practicist criterion of truth.

'Correspondence' in the Marxist tradition has usually been interpreted under the metaphor of 'reflection' or some kindred notion. This notion enters Marxist epistemology at two levels. Marx talks of both (a) the immediate forms and (b) the inner or underlying essence of objects being '*reflected*', but whereas what is involved at (a) is an explanatory postulate or methodological starting-point, at (b) it is a norm of descriptive or scientific adequacy. Thus whereas at (a), Marx criticizes vulgar economy for merely reflecting 'the direct form of manifestation of essential relations' (letter to Engels, 27 June 1867), his concern at (b) is precisely with the production in thought of an adequate representation or 'reflection' of their inner connection – a task which involves theoretical work and conceptual transformation, not a simple passive replication of reality. Note that a 'reflection', as normally understood, is both (1) *of* something which exists independently of it and (2) *produced* in accordance with certain principles of projection or representative conventions. If (1) is the realist element, (2) is consistent with a practicist emphasis and the idea that there are

no unmediated representations of reality. However, if (1) is not to become epistemically otiose (as it tends to e.g. in Althusser), there must be some constraints on the representative process generated by the real object itself; for instance, that an experimental outcome, or the belief it motivates, is causally dependent upon the structure under investigation.

Marx and Engels talk of 'images' and 'copies', and Lenin of 'photographs', as well as 'reflections'. These metaphors readily encourage a collapse of the cognitive to the causal function of the metaphor, of case (b) to case (a), and of theories of knowledge and justification to theories of perception and explanation. REALISM presupposes the irreducibility of objects to knowledge, and it entails the socially produced and hence historically relative (but not judgementally relativist) character of such knowledge. But in orthodox Engelsian 'reflection theory' there is a tendency for truth to be reified and reflection to be interpreted in an explanatory-perceptual way, thus reverting to the problem-field of 'contemplative materialism' which Marx belaboured in the *Theses on Feuerbach* for neglecting the active role of human practice in constituting social life, including knowledge.

It is precisely this theme, together with the connected idea that the object of cognition is not absolutely independent of the cognitive process (as it may be presumed to be in the natural sciences) that forms the epistemological starting point for anti-reflectionist Western Marxist theories (see WESTERN MARXISM), in which truth is conceived as essentially the practical *expression* of a subject, rather than the theoretically adequate *representation* of an object. Thus on Lukács's *coherence* theory of truth, truth becomes a totality to be achieved in the realized identity (in proletarian self-consciousness) of subject and object in history; on Korsch's *pragmatic* theory, truths are the this-worldly manifestations of particular class-related needs and interests; on Gramsci's *consensus* theory, truth is an ideal asymptotically approached in history but only finally realized under communism after a practical consensus has been achieved. Such theories, and those later ones related to them, all tend to (i) judgemental relativism and (ii) (collective) voluntarism. Hence if the generic weakness of reflection-

TRUTH 551

ist and objective empiricist Marxist theories of truth is neglect of the socially produced and historical character of truth judgments, that of epistemically idealist Marxist theories is neglect of the independent existence and transfactual efficacy of the objects of such judgements.

Turning to *criteria* of truth (β), the impossibility of artificially establishing, and the unavailability of spontaneously occurring, closed systems in the socio-economic sphere (*Capital* I, Preface) means that criteria for the empirical assessment of theories cannot be predictive and so must be exclusively *explanatory*. Such a non-historicist but still empirical criterion differs from the undifferentiated empirical criterion of Della Volpe and positivistic Marxism (see POSITIVISM), the rationalist (but otherwise very different) criteria of Lukács and Althusser, the moral-practical criteria of humanistic theories from Gramsci to Habermas and subjective-pragmatic criteriologies from Korsch to Kolakowski. (See also DIALECTICS; KNOWLEDGE, THEORY OF; MATERIALISM.)

Reading

Bhaskar, Roy 1986: *Scientific Realism and Human Emancipation*.

Della Volpe, G. 1950 (*1980*): *Logic as a Positive Science*.

Gramsci, Antonio 1929–35 (*1971*): *Selections from the Prison Notebooks*.

Kolakowski, Leszek 1958 (*1968*): 'Karl Marx and the Classical Definition of Truth'.

Korsch, Karl 1923 (*1970*): *Marxism and Philosophy*.

ROY BHASKAR

U

underconsumption A situation where a shortfall of demand for consumption goods arises and persists due to systemic tendencies. It is advanced as a cause of periodic crises (see ECONOMIC CRISES) as well as of a chronic tendency towards overproduction and stagnation in capitalist economies.

Capitalism is a system subject to recurrent phases of booms and slumps, or trade cycles. These cycles are not the result of accidents or fortuitous circumstances, but constitute a part of the dynamics of capitalist accumulation. In *Capital* I (pt. VII, and in particular ch. 23 on 'The General Law of Capitalist Accumulation') Marx set out a model of the interrelations between the rate of accumulation, the rate of absorption of labour and the increase in labour productivity, and the resultant rate of change in real wages. By determining the rate and mass of profits, these variables determine the rate of future accumulation. In this sequence, accumulation is the primary motive force for the self-expansion of capital and in turn is fuelled by the reinvestment of profits which are a form of capital's self-expansion. The main antagonism in this sequence is between the mass of labour power available and the rate of accumulation which absorbs it. Rapid accumulation overruns labour supply and raises real wages. This would threaten the rate of profit in the absence of counteracting forces, such as a rise in the rate of relative surplus value (via a rise in labour productivity) or a rise in the rate of absolute surplus value (longer hours of work), or again an increase in labour supply from non-capitalist sectors (peasant agriculture, household industry, colonies or other foreign nations not yet fully capitalist). The response to a threat to the rate of profit would be the introduction of new methods which would displace labour and replenish the pool of unemployed.

This is a brief summary of Marx's argument in *Capital*. As a theory of cycles it leaves out two important dimensions of the capitalist accumulation problem: the role of money, especially of credit, in facilitating or hindering accumulation; and the realization problem, i.e. the need to sell the output that is produced in order to convert surplus value from its labour form via its commodity form to profit, its money form. Nowhere else in his subsequent or earlier work did Marx treat fully the problem of capitalist crisis in its whole complexity, albeit there are scattered remarks on these matters throughout his writings.

In the twenty years between Engels's death and the outbreak of the first world war there was an extensive discussion among European Marxists as to how a theory of crises could be developed out of the various disconnected parts of Marx's writings on the subject. This discussion took place against a historical background of vigorous capitalist expansion in new regions and new industries rather than any signs of an immediate breakdown of the system. There was already a movement towards REVISIONISM inaugurated by Bernstein which questioned the Marxian prognosis of a crisis-ridden capitalism.

A theory of crisis could, analytically speaking, be fashioned on the premiss of capitalism continuing without an economic breakdown, just as a breakdown could come from external political forces (e.g. a defeat in war leading to insurrection) independently of an economic crisis (see CRISIS IN CAPITALIST SOCIETY). In the discussions of 1895–1914, these two positions were not separated. A theory of crisis had not only to provide an explanation of how economic crises were endogenous (if not endemic) in capitalism, but an account of crises of *increasing severity* leading eventually to a breakdown of the capitalist system. Theories which were quite adequate to explain particular crises often failed to satisfy these additional requirements, and the debate, while it generated much of the finest writing in Marxism, remained inconclusive.

A central difficulty in any attempt to fashion a Marxist theory of crisis was the demonstration by Marx in *Capital* II (ch. 21) of the possibility of sustained crisis-free expansion under capitalism. The precise analytical purpose that this chapter serves in Marx's overall theory is still a matter of controversy, but the Scheme for Expanded Reproduction (see REPRODUCTION SCHEMA) gave an arithmetical example of sustained (balanced) growth in the two Departments, one making machine goods and the other wage goods. Marx showed that the mutual requirements of the two Departments for each other's products could sustain steady accumulation almost indefinitely. Subsequent writers such as Tugan-Baranowsky, Luxemburg, Bukharin, Lenin, and Bauer chose the scheme as a basic tool in their debate. The glaring contradiction between *Capital* I (ch. 23) and *Capital* II (ch. 21) became a major problem, and not entirely because of the revisionist attack. Marx's particular numerical example seemed to conjure away the realization problem, the problems of money or credit, and even of the falling rate of profit, by positing a balanced-*proportional*-expansion in the two Departments. It was for this reason that *disproportionality* became a major element for fashioning a Marxist theory of crisis (e.g. in Hilferding, *Finance Capital*, pt. IV).

It was in this context that underconsumption was put forward as a possible cause of the realization problem. The demand for wage goods – the output of Department II – could come only from the workers (except for a small amount from capitalists), but in their desire to shore up the rate of surplus value and expand the mass of profits capitalists must constantly try to arrest the tendency of real wages to rise. By restricting employment (maintaining a reserve army of labour) as well as real wages, the capitalists put a definite brake on the ability of Department II to sell its goods. The poverty of workers, so necessary in this view to keep up the rate of profit, boomerangs on the system by making it difficult to realize surplus value (convert it into money profits). This was the nub of the underconsumptionist argument.

There are a host of objections, theoretical as well as factual, to this simple argument. Let us follow the theoretical route first. It was argued that capitalists did not care what goods they produced and who bought them as long as they were sold; thus if the demand for capital goods could be sustained, the expansion of Department I could take up the slack and leave just enough room for Department II to sell its output. This after all was the essential message of Marx's scheme. But Luxemburg, often mistakenly labelled as underconsumptionist, questioned the basis for this expanding demand for machine goods. Obviously the demand for machine goods was not restrained either by workers' poverty or by the capacity of human beings to absorb consumption goods. There is however a straightforward constraint on the demand for machines; namely, the prospect of profits to be derived from their employment. Machines could make either machines or wage goods, but eventually all machines directly or indirectly make consumption goods, so if there was a brake on total demand for wage goods due to the need to stave off the pressure on profits, then buying machines could not be profitable for ever.

There are three escape routes from this argument, which do not totally negate the underconsumptionist view but modify its thrust. First, as Luxemburg pointed out, markets outside the capitalist sectors – pre-capitalist agriculture within the national economy or foreign countries whether formally colonies or not – exist to absorb some of the output, and thus the two-Department scheme does not describe the total economy. The need for capitalism to rely constantly on foreign markets to sustain accumulation was a major plank of the Russian Narodniks' critique of capitalism as a plant alien to Russian soil. Lenin used Marx's scheme to refute this variant of underconsumptionism in his 'On the So-Called "Market Question"'. The argument that trade is a 'vent for surplus' goes back to classical and even Mercantilist doctrine. In more recent years it has formed a part of the analysis of Japanese capitalism, with its constant need to export.

The second escape route is via expenditure on armaments. The argument here is that armament expenditure is not subject to a profit calculus and does not pose the problem of realization as the state does not have to sell these armaments. The state does however have to finance its purchases either from taxation or by borrowing. The debatable issue is whether the burden of taxation and debt servicing falls on a static mass of profits or whether by relieving the problem, the state guarantees sufficient extra profits to finance the armaments purchase. If the latter is the case then armaments or any other activities that generate employment without producing exchange values will solve the realization problem and stave off the underconsumptionist threat. This line of argument, according to which the state can fill the gap in total demand by its expenditure on armaments or ditch-digging, takes its most optimistic form after Keynes's work which, though in no way part of the debate within Marxism, addresses itself to a critique of classical political economy, especially of Say's Law (see KEYNES AND MARX). The happy union of a large mass of profits, full employment, and rising real wages brought about by a beneficent state, which dominated the perceptions of many writers in the 1950s and 1960s, has recently been soured by inflationary pressures. A conflict between the rate of profit and full employment has been unavoidable and a retreat from the Keynesian view is now quite widespread. Some Marxist writers have seen this as the political inability of the capitalist state to solve the underconsumption problem, even if they concede that a theoretical solution can be said to have been provided by Keynes.

A third escape route is via luxury consumption. Consumption by capitalists as well as by members of other groups neither proletarian nor capitalists – government officials, commercial and industrial white-collar workers, the clergy and the educational sector employees, self-employed professionals – is said to provide another source for total demand for consumer goods. The invention of new goods and the proliferation of different brands of the same basic good by advertising and product differentiation are part of this luxury consumption.

These three escape routes are variously advanced as counter-arguments to underconsumption, or as evidence of the problem and of the capitalist system's attempts to counter it. Thus, for example, in a modern statement of the problem, Baran and Sweezy (1966) put together various elements such as luxury consumption, wasteful public and private expenditure, armaments etc. as devices to absorb what they believe is a rising economic surplus. The empirical importance of these various elements is still, however, a matter of controversy. Real wages have risen along with rising productivity through much of the last hundred years in advanced capitalist countries, and while unemployment has varied it has no discernible trend. The experience of inflation in the period since the second world war can hardly be blamed on a shortfall in demand, though it could be laid at the door of strategies to bolster effective demand. It could be argued that if the threat to the rate of profit arising from high employment and working-class action through trade unions can be neutralized via methods of income (wage) policies, then the *technical* probability of underconsumption is not great. But the *political* limits to the ability of the state to ensure full employment and solve the realization problem without eroding profitability remain very real. The wage/profit antagonism caused by the interaction between accumulation and the demand for labour power relative to its supply would seem thus to be the more persistent antagonism, and underconsumptionist problems a secondary antagonism, notwithstanding the useful insights the theory offers into the working of capitalism.

Reading
Baran, P. and Sweezy, P. M. 1966: *Monopoly Capital*.
Bleaney, M. 1976: *Underconsumption Theories: A History and Critical Analysis*.
Brewer, A. 1980: *Marxist Theories of Imperialism*.
Lenin, V. 1. 1893a (1960): 'On the So-Called "Market Question"'.
Luxemburg, R. 1913: *The Accumulation of Capital*.
Mattick, P. 1969: *Marx and Keynes. The Limits of the Mixed Economy*.
O'Connor, J. 1973: *The Fiscal Crisis of the State*.
Sweezy, P. 1942: *The Theory of Capitalist Development*.

MEGHNAD DESAI

underdevelopment and development Although many of its notions are present in earlier Marxist debates on COLONIALISM and IMPERIALISM, Underdevelopment Theory first emerged in the

1950s as a critique of Keynesian and neo-classical approaches to the problems of economic development in post-colonial societies (see COLONIAL AND POST-COLONIAL SOCIETIES). Its major concepts, formulated by Paul Baran, were later extended by a number of authors, notably Celso Furtado and André Gunder Frank. The theory is founded on the notions of economic surplus, and the generation and absorption of this surplus within the capitalist economic system. Baran (1973) defines economic surplus as 'the difference between society's actual current output and its actual current consumption'. Surplus is either invested productively to increase output, used for speculation, invested outside the economy that produced it, or hoarded. Baran argues that industrial capitalist economies paradoxically generate an ever-increasing surplus, while at the same time failing to provide the consumption and investment outlets required for its absorption. This lack of effective demand is said to be met through a number of political and economic mechanisms: defence production, state expenditure, planned obsolescence, technological innovation, and (most important) through economic dominance of colonial and post-colonial societies which, by providing consumption and investment outlets, help to alleviate the potentially damaging effects of overproduction. In this way, however, the industrialized economies impose a particular form of development on post-colonial societies, in which the economic surplus produced is appropriated by foreign concerns and domestic elites to the detriment of the indigenous population. Whereas the problem for the industrialized economies is one of an overproduction of economic surplus, for post-colonial societies the problem thus lies in their lack of access to surplus for their own economic development.

Baran argues that in post-colonial societies development is largely confined to sectors producing and processing commodities for the industrialized economies or the indigenous elite, while those sectors producing basic commodities for domestic consumption (both productive and non-productive) stagnate, since the surplus produced in the former sectors is not invested in the domestic economy. The problem is thus not a lack of development, but an underdevelopment of the domestic economy;

an undermining of its potential for development due to the appropriation of an investable surplus which could generate and sustain its growth. Baran contrasts the supposedly typical way in which the surplus is now actually utilized with the way in which it could potentially be utilized if the domestic economy were not constrained by the distorting requirements of current surplus utilization. He posits a state of 'rational allocation' of the surplus, based on the present and future needs of the indigenous population. This allocation is based on: (i) a mobilization of potential surplus through an expropriation of foreign and domestic capitalists and landowners, and an elimination of the drain on current income resulting from excess consumption and capital removals abroad; (ii) the reallocation of unproductive labour; (iii) the planned development of domestic agriculture related to domestic industry based on a new mobilization of the surplus. Baran tries to show how, by changing current patterns of surplus utilization towards a planned rational allocation of the surplus based on domestic economic requirements, the pattern of underdevelopment imposed by the reproductive requirements of the industrialized economies can be overcome, and domestic development generated.

Baran's notions are generalized by Frank, who combines the concepts of surplus absorption and utilization with a model of the world economy based upon 'metropolitan' and 'satellite' economies. Industrial metropoles dominate underdeveloped satellites through an expropriation of their surpluses resulting from the imposition of an export-oriented capitalist development. This metropolitan–satellite model is also held to apply to relations between and within underdeveloped economies. For Frank, the alleviation of underdevelopment can only occur during periods of retreat or withdrawal by the industrial capitalist economies. Underdevelopment is always primarily the result of industrial capitalist penetration: 'Therefore, short of liberation from this capitalist structure or the dissolution of the world capitalist system as a whole, the capitalist satellite countries, regions, localities and sectors are condemned to underdevelopment' (Frank 1969).

The major tenet of Underdevelopment Theory, that the reproductive requirements of the industrial capitalist economies impose a sectorally uneven capitalist development which restricts the potential growth of the domestic economy, is shared both with DEPENDENCY THEORY and with the theories of peripheral capitalist and world systems expounded by Samir Amin and Immanuel Wallerstein. It also has its precursors in debates within Marxist theory and politics; from the writings of Marx and Engels on the Russian *mir*, to Lenin's critique of Narodnism and the intense debates on India and the colonial question in the Third International.

The main Marxist criticisms can be summarized as follows:

(i) That Underdevelopment Theory erroneously over-stresses the role of colonial and post-colonial economies in industrial capitalist development. Brenner (1977), for example, shows how the market and investment outlets provided by these economies have been of only minor significance in all phases of capitalist accumulation and industrialization. Such critics also stress the inadequacies of the theory's underconsumptionist tenets, emphasizing its focus on forms of distribution rather than on the structure of production which is held by Marxist theory ultimately to determine consumption, distribution and exchange in a capitalist economy.

(ii) That there is no one general form of capitalist development particular to the less developed economies of Asia, Africa and Latin America. Aside from its inclusion of economies whose similarities with industrialized economies are often heuristically more crucial than their shared features, Underdevelopment Theory has been rejected for its inadequacies in explaining the emergence of vigorous forms of national capitalist industrialization in less developed economies, particularly from the beginning of the 1970s. It is argued that the extensions of manufacturing industry and machine production into sectors producing for domestic consumption in both industry and agriculture in a number of less developed economies undermine the conclusion that sustained capitalist development is necessarily confined to a limited number of sectors by the requirements of industrial capitalist countries and the entrenched interests of comprador elites.

(iii) That Underdevelopment Theory estab-

lishes a false barrier between so-called domestic and export-oriented sectors, and that the development of the former need not necessarily undermine the potential for the development of the latter – indeed, it can impel its development. This is achieved through accumulations of capital being invested in indigenous industries, agricultural differentiation, the creation of a home market, the development of industries geared to this market, etc. The reference point for authors such as Warren (1980), who stress these points, is Lenin's criticism (1899) of the Russian Narodnik argument that capitalism was incapable of successfully developing a domestic market in a country characterized by a combination of capitalist and non-capitalist production and dominated by the reproductive requirements of the industrial capitalist economies.

(iv) That accepting the general validity of the Underdevelopment approach entails holding a number of secondary assumptions which severely restrict the analysis of both historical and contemporary aspects of less developed economies: namely, that feudal forms of production predated the various phases of capitalist entry into the economies of Africa, Asia and Latin America; that many of these economies were beginning a transition from feudalism to capitalism similar to that which occurred in Western Europe, and that the industrial capitalist impact distorted a path to industrialization which would have followed a trajectory similar to that of Western Europe; that capitalism can be defined as the pursuit of profit through the sale of commodities on the market, thereby failing to recognize as a continuing characteristic of less developed economies, the coexistence within them of capitalist and non-capitalist forms of production which both exhibit these features; that different phases of industrializing and industrial capitalist entry into non-capitalist economies are conflated in one all-embracing effect of overproduction – the search for market and investment outlets; that using the notions of surplus and surplus absorption leads to an economic reductionism in which political, cultural and social phenomena come to be analysed as means for, or barriers to, the realization of surplus, having no autonomous development; that the primary focus on nation states as the basic economic units leads to a neglect of international aspects of the world economy which can themselves determine national development. These latter criticisms focus on such issues as trans- and multi-national forms of ownership and control of production, the influence of the actions of internationally coordinated fractions of industrial and banking capital on nation states, and the equalization of rates of profit at a world economic level.

Reading

Baran, Paul 1957: *The Political Economy of Growth*.

Brenner, Robert 1977: 'The origins of capitalist development: a critique of neo-Smithian Marxism'.

Frank, André Gunder 1969: *Capitalism and Underdevelopment in Latin America*.

Furtado, Celso 1971: *Development and Underdevelopment*.

Laclau, Ernesto 1971: 'Feudalism and Capitalism in Latin America'.

Lenin, V. I. 1899b (*1960*): *The Development of Capitalism in Russia*.

Roxborough, Ian 1979: *Theories of Underdevelopment*.

Taylor, John G. 1979: *From Modernisation to Modes of Production*.

Warren, Bill 1980: *Imperialism: Pioneer of Capitalism*.

JOHN G. TAYLOR

unequal exchange An extremely influential theory in the 1970s first propounded by Emmanuel 1969 (1972) to explain uneven development on a world scale (see IMPERIALISM AND WORLD MARKET). The central element in the theory is the mechanism by which international exchange ratios are determined. In this analysis, capitalists in all countries are treated as having available to them the same technical production possibilities, regardless of the level of development of the productive forces in each country. This approach is similar to neo-classical trade theory, which makes the assumption of the same production function prevailing in each country. With the additional assumption that capital is perfectly mobile internationally, it follows that the production costs of the means of production will be the same in each country if we ignore circulating means of production.

On these assumptions unit costs will be lower in countries where the wage is lower unless a lower wage is associated with a correspondingly lower level of productiveness of labour. Emmanuel assumes that productiveness of labour does not vary as much as wage levels, so the generality of this theory is not affected by simply assuming equal productivity of labour in each country. If non-labour costs are the same across countries, and current (living) labour creates the same value per period of time, the rate of profit will be higher where wages are lower. Unequal exchange results through the movement of capital in search of the higher profit rates. Commodity prices rise in the high-wage country as capital flees (relatively), and commodity prices fall in the low-wage country. As a consequence of the equalization of the rate of profit through these price movements, international exchange occurs at rates which are not equal to the labour time embodied in commodities. In particular, the ratio of advanced country prices to backward country prices is greater than the ratio of the labour time in advanced country commodities to the labour time in backward country commodities, where 'advanced' and 'backward' are defined purely in terms of the wage level in each country. In this way, through exchange, advanced countries appropriate more labour time in exchange than they generate in production. A surplus is transferred from backward countries, reducing the rate of accumulation there for lack of a sufficient investable surplus.

This theory has been extensively criticized. On an empirical level it suggests that the main tendency would be for foreign investment to flow to backward countries, but this is not the case (see MULTINATIONAL CORPORATIONS). This aside, by stressing the equalization of the rate of profit the theory implicitly predicts that the worst that can happen is that the relative surplus will be the same in advanced and backward countries: i.e. at the worst, the surplus remaining in backward countries is sufficient to match the rate of accumulation of advanced countries.

A basic theoretical objection to Emmanuel's work from a Marxist viewpoint is that he fails to distinguish between use value and exchange value in his discussion of wages. Workers must consume a certain mass of use values in order to reproduce labour power currently and in future generations. This mass of use values constitutes the standard of living for a worker, and the standard of living for the working class varies enormously among countries. The wage tends to represent the exchange value of those use values (see WAGES). Given the mass of use values (the standard of living), the wage is determined by how efficiently the commodities which workers buy are produced. The greater the productivity of labour the lower the value of commodities, and the lower the exchange value. As capitalism develops, productivity rises, the value of commodities falls, and the wage which must be paid to cover a given mass of use values (a given standard of living) also falls. Marx called this process the raising of *relative* surplus value. Since it is in the developed capitalist countries that labour productivity is higher it is not obvious that a high standard of living of workers in such countries implies that the exchange value of the commodities making up that standard of living is also higher than in backward countries. It appears that it cannot be established theoretically that the appearance of things (differences in living standards) necessarily implies differences in the exchange value of labour power, and no general conclusion can be drawn about the rate of profit in advanced countries compared to backward countries (Bettelheim 1972). Criticisms from the standpoint of neoclassical economics have also proved quite devastating.

Recent writings have demonstrated that unequal exchange is internally contradictory (Dore and Weeks 1979); one can grant all of its assumptions and show that no transfer of surplus occurs within the model. It should be recalled that the unequal exchange argument assumes that the elements of constant capital (machinery, intermediate commodities, raw materials) are internationally traded. This is a necessary assumption for the theory to reach its conclusion of surplus transfer, which is held to occur, as we saw, because profit rates are higher in underdeveloped countries in the absence of trade. According to the theory, trade equalizes profit rates, and this effects the transfer of profits to developed capitalist countries. If profit rates were not higher in underdeveloped countries, no transfer of profits would take place, or the transfer would be in the other

direction. If the elements of constant capital are not internationally traded, then one must accept the possibility that these elements are cheaper in the developed countries, either because the same machinery and current inputs are cheaper or because more advanced techniques are used (with lower costs) which are not available in underdeveloped countries. Hence, if these elements are not internationally traded (available to all producers at a common price) it cannot be logically concluded that profit rates will be higher in underdeveloped countries, a conclusion which is the keystone of unequal exchange theory.

Further, Amin (1977) has demonstrated, in an apparent defence of unequal exchange, that the theory requires that articles of mass consumption must also be internationally traded. This assumption is necessary to meet Bettelheim's criticism (see above); for if such articles are not internationally traded the possibility cannot be excluded that the rate of exploitation is lower in underdeveloped countries despite their lower standard of living. This is the contradictory relationship between the value of labour power and the use values that make up the standard of living. International trade in basic consumption commodities seems to resolve this problem for the theory of unequal exchange.

However, unequal exchange is impossible for traded commodities. It requires the rate of profit to equalize across countries, while free trade requires that the price of a traded commodity be the same across countries. Thus the process which equalizes profit rates (and transfers surplus) also equalizes prices. But it is logically impossible for both profit rates and prices to equalize if labour costs are lower in the underdeveloped country (given that non-labour costs must be the same). If profit rates equalize, then the price of a given commodity must be higher in the developed country, which contradicts the *necessary* assumption that the commodities are internationally traded. If prices equalize, consistent with the trade assumption, then the rate of profit must be higher in the underdeveloped country where labour costs are lower, and no transfer of surplus occurs. Thus the rate of profit can only equalize for non-traded commodities, or for commodities produced exclusively in one country. Such commodities comprise a small proportion of total world production and thus the theory, even on its own terms, is reduced at best to a minor logical curiosity.

Reading

Amin, Samir 1973b (1977): 'The End of a Debate'. In *Imperialism and Unequal Development*.

Bettelheim, C. 1972: 'Theoretical Comments'. In A. Emmanuel ed. *Unequal Exchange*.

de Janvry, A. and Kramer, F. 1971: 'The Limits of Unequal Exchange'.

Dore, Elizabeth and Weeks, John 1979: 'International Exchange and the Causes of Backwardness'.

Emmanuel, A. 1969 (1972): *Unequal Exchange: A Study of the Imperialism of Trade*.

JOHN WEEKS

uneven development In the most general sense of the word, uneven development means that societies, countries, nations, develop at an uneven pace, so that in certain cases those which start with a lead over others can increase that lead, while in other cases, due to the same difference in rhythm of development, those left behind can catch up and overtake those which enjoyed an initial advantage. In order to be meaningful, therefore, the notion of 'uneven development' must include, in each specific case, the main driving force(s) determining these differences in pace of development.

Under capitalism, it is mainly the possibility of overtaking competitors in the use of up-to-date production techniques and/or labour organization, i.e. enjoying a higher productivity of labour, which determines the rhythm of development both of firms and of nations. *Cumulative growth* becomes possible once a certain threshold of accumulation of capital, industrialization, technical training of workers, engineers, and scientists, etc. is passed. Hence, the first countries going through the industrial revolution in the late eighteenth and early nineteenth centuries gained decisive advantages compared with those which entered later on the same road, thereby increasing the difference in level of development, which was initially small. On the other hand, given that periodically there are real breakthroughs of new techniques, countries which come somewhat later into the development of large-scale industry, but which

already have the basic preconditions for cumulative growth, can overtake those which were predominant on the world market before them. They do that essentially by acquiring a more up-to-date technical profile than those who already operated on a large-scale industrial basis twenty or thirty years earlier, and for that very reason have much older plant side-by-side with that which is more up-to-date. In addition, these relative latecomers can move with greater ease into new branches of industry. That is one of the reasons why Germany and the USA could overtake Britain and France as the main industrial producers at the end of the nineteenth century, and why Japan and West Germany are catching up with the USA today.

Trotsky extended the concept of uneven development (widely used by Marx and Lenin) to encompass a more complex phenomenon, that of *uneven and combined development*. While relatively backward countries under *laissez-faire capitalism* by and large went through stages of development similar to those the more advanced ones had passed through a few decades before, this was no longer true under *imperialism*. Instead of organic growth, most less-developed countries experienced a combined 'development of development and of underdevelopment'. Their economies appeared as a combination of a 'modern sector' (very often foreign-dominated, or developed by the state, or a combination of both), and a 'traditional sector' (either primitive, as in agriculture, or dominated by pre-capitalist or merchant capitalist ruling classes). As a result of this peculiar combination there was no cumulative growth, the backwardness of agriculture determined a limitation of the internal market which put a brake upon the pace of industrialization, and a significant part of accumulated money capital was diverted away from industry into real estate speculation, usury and hoarding. (See also UNDERDEVELOPMENT AND DEVELOPMENT.)

Reading

Lenin, V. I. 1916 (1964): 'Imperialism, the Highest Stage of Capitalism'.

Trotsky, Leon 1932: *History of the Russian Revolution*, vol. I, Preface.

ERNEST MANDEL

unproductive labour   *See* productive and unproductive labour.

urbanization   Marx and Engels frequently allude to the significance of urbanization in the history and transformation of different modes of production. 'The antagonism between town and country begins with the transition from barbarism to civilization', they wrote in the *German Ideology* (vol. I, pt. IB2) 'and runs through the whole history of civilisation to the present day.' It was the 'foundation' of the division of labour and class distinctions, while 'the existence of the town implies the necessity of administration, police, taxes, etc., in short of . . . politics in general'. Engels's remarkable study of Manchester and surrounding towns in *Condition of the Working Class* provided the raw material, furthermore, for much of the initial analysis of the dynamics of capitalism and its impact upon working people. And the *Communist Manifesto* dwells at length on the economic and political consequences of the vast concentration of productive forces and of the proletariat in large urban centres.

Yet in spite of its evident theoretical, political and historical importance (under capitalism, for example, increasing proportions of the world's population have poured into urban centres and occupations and been exposed thereby to a distinctively urban politics and culture) the study of urbanization has not been in the forefront of Marxist concern. This neglect is all the more surprising since the urban basis of many revolutionary movements (from 1848 through the Paris Commune to the ghetto uprisings of the 1960s in the United States and the urban social movements which contributed so strongly to events of May 1968 in Paris) is undeniable. Furthermore, the importance of class alliances across the urban–rural contradiction (between, for example, an urban proletariat and a rural peasantry) had to be recognized, particularly in the Third World, as the basis for revolutionary strategy (examples abound in the writings of Gramsci and Mao Tse-tung). And how to overcome the urban–rural contradiction (as Marx and Engels urged) in the transition to socialism became a pressing issue in the Soviet Union, China, Cuba, Tanzania, etc.

Spurred on by events, Marxists turned to a direct analysis of urban issues in the 1960s. They sought to understand the economic and political meaning of urban, community-based social movements and their relation to work-based movements – the traditional focus of attention. The relations between production and social reproduction came under intense scrutiny as the city was variously studied as the locus of production, of realization (effective demand through consumption, sometimes conspicuous), of the reproduction of labour power (in which the family and community institutions, supported by physical and social infrastructures – housing, health care, education, cultural life – played a key role, backed by the local state). The city was also studied as a built environment to facilitate production, exchange and consumption, as a form of social organization of space (for production and reproduction), and as a specific manifestation of the division of labour and function under capitalism (finance capital versus production, etc.). The overall conception which emerged was urbanization as the contradictory unity of all these aspects of capitalism. Old questions, such as the historical role of the urban–rural contradiction, have been reopened in Third World, advanced capitalist and socialist contexts. New perspectives have been opened up on the quality of urban life, the relations between community and class, the role of the local state, the functioning of land markets, urban fiscal problems and social distress, the ideology of the country and the city, and, above all, on the tense and challenging relation between community-based and work-based struggles.

Reading
Anderson, J. 1975: *The Political Economy of Urbanism: an Introduction and Bibliography.*

Castells, M. 1977: *The Urban Question.*

Dear, M. and Scott, A. eds. 1981: *Urbanization and Urban Planning in Capitalist Societies.*

Harvey, D. 1973: *Social Justice and the City.*

Lefebvre, H. 1972: *Le Droit et la ville: suivi de Espace et politique.*

Merrington, J. 1975: 'Town and Country in the Transition to Capitalism'.

Roberts, B. 1978: *Cities of Peasants: The Political Economy of Urbanization in the Third World.*

Williams, R. 1973: *The Country and the City.*

DAVID HARVEY

use value Since the COMMODITY is a product which is exchanged, it appears as the union of two different aspects: its usefulness to some agent, which is what permits the commodity to enter into EXCHANGE at all; and its power to command certain quantities of other commodities in exchange. The first aspect the classical political economists called *use value*, the second, *exchange value*.

Marx emphasizes the fact that while use value is a necessary condition for a product to enter into exchange and hence to have an exchange value (no one will exchange a product useful to someone for a product of no use to anyone) the use value of the commodity bears no systematic quantitative relation to its exchange value, which is a reflection of the conditions of the commodity's production. He further argues that the proper object of study of political economy is the laws governing the production and movement of exchange value, or to put it more rigorously, the laws governing VALUE, the inherent property of the commodities which appears as exchange value (*Capital* I, ch. 1).

The use value of commodities in general is thus not a major focus of Marx's investigations. But it is important to recognize that use value differentiates itself as a concept in human consciousness as a result of the development of the commodity form of production. Without commodity exchange the usefulness of products in general is a fact self-evident and thus invisible to producers and users. Only with the emergence of commodity relations do the opposition of usefulness and exchangeability and the resulting contradictions and puzzles of commodity-organized life become an object of speculation and investigation. It is also important to recognize that the specific usefulness of products depends on the social relations and development of forces of production in any given society. Structural steel has no use value for nomadic cattle-herders.

Use value plays a critical role in Marx's analysis of the contradictions arising from the emergence of LABOUR POWER as a commodity. The use value of labour power is its ability to produce new value by being turned into labour in production. Thus the use value of labour power derives from the development of commodity relations, value and money. The contra-diction between use value and exchange value inherent in the commodity form, when it appears in labour power viewed as a commodity, is the source of the major social contradiction of capitalist production, the class division between workers and capitalists.

Reading

Rosdolsky, Roman 1968 (1977): *The Making of Marx's 'Capital'*, ch. 3.

DUNCAN FOLEY

utopian socialism The term generally used to describe the first stage in the history of socialism, the period between the Napoleonic Wars and the Revolutions of 1848. It is associated in particular with three thinkers from whom the main currents of pre-Marxist socialist thought are generally considered to have sprung: Claude Henri de Rouvroy, Comte de Saint Simon (1760–1825), François-Charles Fourier (1772–1837) and Robert Owen (1771–1858).

The grouping together of these thinkers as 'utopians', like the term 'socialist' itself, first became common in the late 1830s, both in England and France. But it was the Marxist use of the term 'utopian socialism' which most heavily influenced the subsequent picture of the 'socialism' of this period. This was delineated in the critique of 'Critical-Utopian Socialism' in the *Communist Manifesto* where it was associated with 'the early undeveloped period . . . of the struggle between proletariat and bourgeoisie', and entrenched in subsequent socialist historiography from the time of Engels's *Socialism: Utopian and Scientific*. What was designated 'utopian', according to this approach, was the imagination of the possibility of total social transformation involving the elimination of individualism, competition and the sway of private property, without a recognition of the necessity of class struggle and the revolutionary role of the proletariat in accomplishing the transition.

But this treatment of pre-1848 socialism as a Marxism *manqué* misses some of its central characteristics. The harnessing of 'socialism' to the specific interests of the working class was a product of the particular political conditions in England and France in the 1830s. The distinctive features of Owenism, Saint-Simonianism and Fourierism predated this conjunction. Some of the hallmarks of what came to be identified with a socialist position during this period can be discerned from a comparison of the first systematic works of the three founding thinkers – Saint-Simon's *Letters from an Inhabitant of Geneva* (1802), Fourier's *Theory of the Four Movements* (1808) and Robert Owen's *New View of Society* (1812–16).

What is immediately most apparent is the dissimilarity of starting-point in England and France. While the thought of both Saint-Simon and Fourier started out from reactions against Enlightenment theories of human nature which were held responsible for the disastrous course of the French Revolution, Owen's theory in contrast represented a continuation of Enlightenment themes. In particular, Fourier and Saint-Simon started out from (very different) theories of innate psychological types and conceived reform as the construction of social arrangements which would enable the harmonious interaction of these types. Owen, on the other hand, believed man's character to be formed by external circumstances. Therefore, the reform of society involved the creation of circumstances which would associate the pursuit of happiness with harmony and cooperation in place of competition and conflict. These differences of approach to character and circumstances formed the core of disagreements between the followers of different tendencies when they began to compete with each other from the late 1820s.

Nevertheless, beneath these differences are some common presuppositions distinctive of pre-Marxist socialist thought. First, all three theories start from the ambition to construct a new science of human nature. Secondly, they focus on the moral/ideological sphere as the determining basis of all other aspects of human behaviour. Thirdly, the ambition is to make this sphere the object of an exact science which will resolve the problem of social harmony. Fourthly, each identifies pre-existing moral, religious and political *theory* (not class or state practices) as the principal obstacle to the actualization of the newly discovered laws of harmony. Fifthly, no distinction is made between physical and social sciences. Each had the ambition to be the Newton of the human/social sphere. These similarities demarcate

what is relatively constant in the many variants and hybrids of 'socialism' which sprang up between the 1820s and 1840s.

In England Owen became famous both because of his management of the New Lanark textile mills which, he claimed, were a practical vindication of his theory, and because of his proposal to cure post-war unemployment through the construction of communities based upon his principles. His attempt to convince the ruling political establishment of the value of his scheme failed, not least because of its explicit clash with the assumptions of established Christianity. Thereafter Owen went to America to validate his principles through the establishment of the New Harmony community. In his absence, some of his ideas were taken up by working-class radicals interested, not so much in communities as in cooperative production and exchange as an alternative to competition (see COOPERATIVE ASSOCIATION). In the early 1830s several hundred cooperatives were set up and analogous attempts were made to establish labour exchanges and general unions of producers. These culminated in the unsuccessful Grand National Consolidated Trade Union of 1834. After the failure of these schemes, Owenites reverted to community experiment (at Queenswood) and the battle of their 'rational religion' against orthodox Christianity.

In France, Saint-Simon's ideas, particularly those of his last work, *The New Christianity* (1825) were taken up by the science and engineering students of the Paris École Polytechnique. Led by Saint-Amand Bazard (1791–1832) and Prosper Enfantin (1796–1864), this group in 1829 published *The Doctrine of Saint-Simon*, a work of immense importance in spreading Saint-Simonian ideas across the intelligentsias of Europe. After 1829 the group dispersed. The impact of Fourierism followed the break-up of the Saint Simonian school, but many of its ideas, particularly on sexuality, had already been absorbed by its leaders. The main body of Saint-Simonians under Enfantin founded an ill-fated and short-lived Saint-Simonian church and community in Menilmontant in 1832. Some of those who had split off, notably Philippe Buchez (1796–1865) and Pierre Leroux (1791–1871) after the July Revolution introduced modified forms of Saint

Simonianism into workers' circles – the first explicit attempts to connect the doctrine, now called 'socialism' to the specific aspirations of the proletariat.

Reading

Beecher, J. and Bienvenu, R. eds. 1972: *The Utopian Vision of Charles Fourier.*

Droz, J. ed. 1972: *Histoire générale du socialisme.*

Duveau, Georges 1961: *'Sociologie de l'Utopie' et autres essais.*

Fourier, Charles 1808 (*1968*): *La théorie des quatres mouvements.*

Harrison, J. F. C. 1969: *Robert Owen and the Owenites in Britain and America.*

Iggers, G. C. ed. 1829 (*1958*): *Doctrine of Saint-Simon, An Exposition, First Year.*

Johnson, C. 1974: *Icarian Communism in France: Cabet and the Icarians, 1839–1851.*

Lichtheim, George 1969: *The Origins of Socialism.*

Owen, Robert 1812–16 (*1969*): *Report to the County of Lanark: A New View of Society.*

GARETH STEDMAN JONES

V

value   Marx's concept of value is arguably the most controversial in the corpus of his thought. It is universally condemned by non-Marxists as the source of major logical errors, whatever other insights Marx might be allowed to have had (Böhm-Bawerk 1896 is still the *locus classicus*), and is also the subject of considerable controversy among Marxists. Of the latter, some conceive value to be redundant to the analysis of the concrete economic phenomena of capitalism, and therefore superfluous to the basic Marxist analysis of EXPLOITATION; whereas others conceive it to be the foundation of any successful understanding of MONEY, CAPITAL and the dynamics of capitalism, so that the Marxist analysis of capitalism falls apart without it. (For the former, see Steedman 1977; for the latter, see Hilferding 1904, Rubin 1928, Rosdolsky 1968; and for a representative sample of widely differing views from both sides, Steedman *et al.* 1981.)

For Marx the value of a COMMODITY expresses the particular historical form that the social character of labour has under capitalism, as the expenditure of social LABOUR POWER. Value is not a technical relation but a social relation between people which assumes a particular material form under capitalism, and hence appears as a property of that form. This suggests first, that the generalization of the commodity form of human labour is quite specific to capitalism, and that value as a concept of analysis is similarly so specific. Secondly, it suggests that value is not just a concept with a mental existence; it has a real existence, value relations being the particular form taken by capitalist social relations. Since this form is the commodity, this determines the starting-point of Marx's analysis. In one of his last writings on political economy, he summarized his procedure as follows:

I do not proceed on the basis of 'concepts', hence also not from the 'value-concept' . . . What I proceed from is the simplest social form in which the product of labour in contemporary society manifests itself, and this as 'commodity'. That is what I analyse, and first of all to be sure in the *form in which it appears*. Now I find at this point that it is, on the one hand, in its natural form a *thing of use-value*, alias *use-value*, and on the other hand that it is *bearer of exchange-value*, and is itself an exchange-value from this point of view. Through further analysis of the latter I discovered that exchange-value is only an 'appearance-form', an independent mode of manifestation of the *value* which is contained in the commodity, and then I approach the analysis of this value. ('Notes on Adolph Wagner', 1880) (See USE VALUE.)

Since a commodity is anything produced for the purpose of EXCHANGE, a commodity has 'exchange-value', defined as the quantitative proportion in which use values of one kind exchange for use values of another kind. Commodities are thus both use values and exchange values. But this is a misleading statement. Exchange values are always contingent with respect to time, place and circumstance, and a commodity has as many different exchange values as different commodities with which it exchanges; hence each commodity with which it exchanges must be equal in some sense, and therefore there is something which renders all commodities which exchange with each other equal. Exchange value, that is, is the form of appearance of something distinguishable from it. This common element of identical magnitude cannot be anything to do with the physical or natural properties of the commodities in question, because of their heterogeneity. In the process of exchange something homogeneous is expressed, and the only common property which all commodities have is that they are products of labour. Thus the process of exchange renders all the different types of labour producing commodities homogeneous: the homogeneous labour which produces commodities is called ABSTRACT LABOUR. Value is then defined as the objectification or materialization of abstract labour, and the form of appearance of value is the exchange value of a commodity. A commodity is accordingly not a use value and an exchange value, but a use value and a value.

From Böhm-Bawerk onwards critics have interpreted this argument from the first few pages of *Capital* I as Marx's attempt to prove that value exists, and, typically, this alleged proof is found wanting on the grounds that there are other properties common to all commodities which Marx ignores. For example all commodities which are exchanged are scarce relative to the demand for them (if they were not, things would be freely given, not exchanged), and hence the common property sought by Marx is to be found in psychology, in the motives people have for demanding and supplying commodities. (This is the route taken by bourgeois economics.) Such an argument is irresistible from the perspective of positivism, or empiricism, but fails to account for Marx's position in a quite different philosophical tradition; Marx does not provide a formal proof of the existence of value by arriving at some (arbitrary) abstract property common to our experience of all the heterogeneous commodities that exist. On the contrary, he analyses the typical relation between people that actually exists in bourgeois society – the exchange of one commodity for another – because, first, the categories of political economy are a necessary reflection of particular relations of production, and hence second, it is through a critical examination of these categories and the forms they take that the content of bourgeois relations is developed and revealed. A formal, non-dialectical analysis will always miss Marx's analysis of value because it will have no intrinsic connection with the concrete relationships involved. Marx himself remarked to Kugelmann (letter of 11 July, 1868) that:

even if there were no chapter on 'value' in my book, the analysis of the real relationships which I give would contain the proof and demonstration of the real value relation. All that palaver about the necessity of proving the concept of value comes from complete ignorance both of the subject dealt with and of scientific method.

Having arrived at a definition of value as the objectification of abstract labour, Marx proceeds to consider its measure. Value is measured by measuring the abstract labour, in units of time, which is on average necessary to produce the commodity in question (see SOCIALLY NECESSARY LABOUR). Consequently, when that labour time is shortened, as by a productivity increase which is generalized across all producers, the value of the commodity falls. Thus the value of a commodity varies directly with the quantity of abstract labour objectified in it, and inversely with the productivity of the concrete labour producing it. Following this brief consideration of value independently of its form of appearance, Marx proceeds to show how exchange value is the necessary form of appearance of value. This analysis has been much neglected until comparatively recently; after all, to use exchange value to derive value, and then to use value to derive exchange value seems to indicate a certain circularity of argument. But this is again to adopt the approach of formal logic, and this is not adequate to capturing the significance of questions of essence and appearance, or content and form. Rubin comments on this point:

One cannot forget that on the question of the relation between content and form, Marx took the standpoint of Hegel and not of Kant. Kant treated form as something external in relation to the content, and as something which adheres to the content from the outside. From the standpoint of Hegel's philosophy, the content is not in itself something to which form adheres from the outside. Rather, through its development, the content itself gives birth to the form which is already latent in the content. Form necessarily grows from the content itself. (1928, p. 117)

Indeed, one of Marx's major criticisms of his predecessors in political economy, particularly

Smith and Ricardo, is their neglect of the form of value, their treatment of it as something external to the nature of the commodity, and hence their failure to understand why it is that labour is expressed in value and why the measure of value (socially necessary labour time) is expressed in sums of money. Marx suggests that the reason for this mistake is that the value form of the product of labour, the most abstract and at the same time the most universal form of capitalism, is treated not as the product of capitalist relations of production but as the eternal, natural form of social production. Value and its magnitude are thereby divorced from specific relations of production, and analysis is rendered formal rather than dialectical (see RICARDO AND MARX). Only by showing how value is necessarily expressed as exchange value is it possible to understand how value is expressed as sums of money, how the value form implies the money form. Marx's theory of value is thus simultaneously his theory of money.

As commodities, then, products of labour have simultaneously a natural form and a value form. But the latter only appears when one commodity exchanges for another. Value is not something intrinsic to a single commodity, considered apart from its exchange for another, but rather reflects a DIVISION OF LABOUR of independent commodity producers, the social nature of whose labour is only revealed in the act of exchange. Value therefore has a purely social reality, and its form can only appear in the social relation between commodity and commodity. So consider what Marx calls the 'simple, isolated or accidental form of value' in which x units of commodity A exchange for y units of commodity B. Since commodity A expresses its value in commodity B, its value is expressed in relative terms, and commodity A is in the 'relative form of value'. By contrast, commodity B is the material in which the value of commodity A is expressed, and hence commodity B is the 'equivalent form of value'. Relative and equivalent forms always both belong to any expression of value, and they are obviously mutually exclusive in such an expression.

Consider first the relative form of value. Commodity B is the material embodiment of commodity A's value, but commodities are not simply quantities of embodied labour, because this does not give them a form of value different from their natural form. The value of commodity A, as embodied labour, has to have an objective existence different from commodity A itself; so the physical form of commodity B becomes the value form of commodity A. It is only the expression of equivalence between different sorts of commodities which reveals the specific character of value-creating labour, because it is the process of exchange itself which reduces all the different kinds of labour embodied in the different kinds of commodities exchanged to their common quality of being labour in general. Further, since the value of commodity A is expressed in the use value of commodity B, there is the possibility that changes in the magnitude of the value of commodity A are not necessarily reflected in changes in the magnitude of relative value, and vice versa. (The development of this potentiality lies at the core of Marx's theory of ECONOMIC CRISES.)

Secondly, consider the equivalent form of value. Marx proceeds to identify what he calls the three 'peculiarities' of the equivalent form. First, use value becomes the form of appearance of value: commodity B expresses the value of commodity A, and does not express its own value at all; the material body of commodity B is thus the objectification of abstract labour. Hence, secondly, the concrete labour which produces commodity B becomes the form of appearance of abstract labour. This means that the concrete labour which produces commodity B, despite being the private labour of private individuals, is immediately identical with other kinds of labour. Hence thirdly, private labour takes the form of directly social labour. These three peculiarities, that use value appears as value, concrete labour as abstract labour, and private labour as social labour, are crucial for understanding Marx's theory of value. While a commodity is both a use value and a value, it only appears in this dual role when its value possesses a form of appearance independent of and distinct from its use value form. This independent form of expression is exchange value. The nature of value leads to its independent expression as exchange value, and, within the exchange relation, the natural form of commodity A counts only as a use value whereas the natural form of commodity B counts only as the form of value. In this manner, the internal opposition between use value and value within the commodity is externalized.

Marx then develops the simple form of value into the 'total or expanded form of value', by noting that commodity A not only exchanges with commodity B, but also with commodities C, D, E etc.; it is a matter of indifference which commodity is in the equivalent form. Commodity A is then revealed as standing in a social relation with the whole world of commodities; every other commodity appears as a physical object possessing value, particular forms of realization of human labour in general. Consequently, and quite contrary to modern bourgeois economics, it is not commodity exchange which regulates the magnitude of value, but rather the magnitude of the value of commodities which regulates the proportion in which they exchange. However, the series of representations of the value of commodity A is effectively limitless, and different from the relative form of value of any other commodity; and since there are innumerable equivalent forms all concrete labours appear as abstract labour, with no single, unified appearance of human labour in general.

This is easily rectified by inverting the total or expanded form of value, to derive the 'general form of value': if commodity A expresses its value in innumerable other commodities, then all of these express their value in commodity A. One single commodity is set apart to represent the values of all commodities, differentiating each commodity from its own use value and from all other use values, thereby expressing what is common to all commodities. This commodity is called the 'universal equivalent', and its natural form is the form assumed in common by the values of all commodities, the visible representation of all labour, what Marx calls 'the social expression of the world of commodities'. The particular commodity whose natural form serves as the value form of all other commodities becomes the money commodity in the 'money form of value', and this completes the separation of the expression of the value of a commodity from the commodity itself. The value of a commodity has no expression except as exchange value, and exchange value is only expressed in terms

of money. Value is never expressed in terms of its substance, abstract labour, nor in terms of its measure, socially necessary labour time. The only form in which value appears, and the only form in which it can appear is in terms of the money commodity and its quantitative measure. As Marx wrote to Engels (2 April 1858), 'From the contradiction between the general character of value and its material existence in a particular commodity etc. . . . arises the category of money.' In his earlier drafts on value and money, Marx notes in parentheses: 'It will be necessary later, before this question is dropped, to correct the idealist manner of the presentation, which makes it seem as if it were merely a matter of conceptual determinations and of the dialectic of these concepts. Above all in the case of the phrase: product (or activity) becomes commodity; commodity, exchange-value; exchange-value, money' (*Grundrisse*, 'The Chapter on Money'.) Economic categories are reflections of human activity, and Marx parallels his logical derivations with a historical derivation of the same categories. He emphasizes that the historical development of the commodity form of the product of labour coincides with the development of the value form, and in general he always compares the results of his logical analysis with the results of real historical development. But he emphasizes in his Postface to the 2nd edn of *Capital* I, that there is a major difference between investigative work and its presentation. The method of inquiry

has to appropriate the material in detail, to analyse its different forms of development and to track down their inner connection. Only after this work has been done can the real movement be appropriately presented. If this is done successfully, if the life of the subject-matter is now reflected back in the ideas, then it may appear as if we have before us an *a priori* construction.

Marx took great trouble over his presentation of value and the value form. Following criticism by Engels of the page-proofs of *Capital* I, Marx wrote an appendix to the first chapter which in the second and following editions of *Capital* was reworked into the first chapter. This appendix to the first edition is the clearest exposition of Marx's theory of the form of value (see Marx, 'The Value Form'). And while Marx recognized that his exposition was difficult, he considered that his analysis of the value form could not be dropped: 'the matter is too decisive for the whole book' (letter to Engels, 22 June 1867). And it is not 'an *a priori* construction', 'a matter of conceptual determinations and of the dialectic of these concepts'. The abstraction which considers the commodity form as the value form is a real one (Colletti 1972, pp. 76–92), since the process of exchange is the real process whereby products of labour are commensurated under capitalism. This means that there can be no *a priori* determination of value, because it is only the process of exchange which renders production social, establishes connections between independent commodity producers, and ensures that the value realized in exchange is the form of appearance of that labour, and only that labour, which is socially necessary to the production of the commodity in question. The value of a commodity can only be expressed after its production, in the use value of another commodity, which, in developed capitalism, is money, the universal equivalent of value. Once Marx has demonstrated this, he can proceed to explore the elaboration of the 'law of value' (the determination of the magnitude of value by socially necessary labour time) in terms of the supremacy of money and money relations, by developing the category of capital and its ACCUMULATION and ultimately exploring those phenomena which on the surface of capitalism appear to contradict the law of value. (See PRICE OF PRODUCTION AND THE TRANSFORMATION PROBLEM; SURPLUS VALUE AND PROFIT.) And, in parallel, in the supremacy of money and money relations he also has a basis for exploring how social relations of production are inverted in capitalism, and how this inversion is reflected in consciousness. (See COMMODITY FETISHISM; FETISHISM.)

Reading

Böhm-Bawerk, Eugen von 1896 (*1949*): *Karl Marx and the Close of his System*, ed. Paul M. Sweezy.

Colletti, Lucio 1968 (*1972*): *From Rousseau to Lenin.*

Hilferding, Rudolf 1904 (*1949*): *Böhm-Bawerk's Criticism of Marx.*

Rosdolsky, Roman 1968 (*1977*): *The Making of Marx's 'Capital'.*

Rubin, I. I. 1928 (*1973*): *Essays on Marx's Theory of Value.*

Steedman, Ian et al. 1981: *The Value Controversy.*

SIMON MOHUN

value and price In order for the individual labour time objectified in a COMMODITY to have a universal character as ABSTRACT LABOUR one particular commodity must take the form of objectified, universal labour time. The contradiction between the general character of the commodity as VALUE and its particular character as USE VALUE is only resolved by being itself objectified; the process of EXCHANGE materially separates the commodity's exchange value from the commodity itself so that all commodities as use values confront the MONEY commodity as the form in which they express their values. Consequently, Marx defines price as the money form of value, the expression of the value of the commodity in units of the money commodity (e.g. gold).

The money commodity then, as well as functioning as a measure of value must also function as a standard of price. While it can only function as a measure of value because it is itself a product of labour, and hence potentially variable in value, as a standard of price stability of measurement is obviously important. Why then might prices fluctuate? Either because commodity values have changed, the value of money remaining constant, or because the value of money changes, the values of commodities remaining constant, or through some combination of such changes. But this assumes that prices always measure values accurately, and that is by no means the case. Value is measured by SOCIALLY NECESSARY LABOUR TIME, and this is always, conceptually, a precise measure. But it can only appear as the exchange ratio between the commodity in question and the money commodity in a particular exchange; with two independent commodities involved, this exchange ratio can express both the magnitude of the value of the commodity and a greater or lesser amount of money for which it can be sold in the particular circumstances of the exchange. Hence price and magnitude of value can easily differ; and Marx comments: 'This is not a defect, but, on the contrary, it makes this form the adequate one for a mode of production whose laws can only assert themselves as blindly operating averages between constant irregularities' (*Capital* I, ch. 3).

The price of a commodity represents its ideal value form, an equation with the money commodity in the imagination; but in order for this value form to be realized an exchange must occur. In this sense the price form implies both the exchangeability of commodities for money and the necessity of such exchanges, and the analysis of such exchanges provides Marx with the basis for the development of the concept of CAPITAL. It is a common misinterpretation to consider *Capital* I as being about values and *Capital* III as being concerned with prices; on the contrary, the price form is developed at the beginning of vol. I. Marx then uses it in a manner appropriate to the development of the dynamics of the capitalist mode of production from the perspective of what all capitals have in common. Differentiation of capitals via the process of competition requires a further development of the price form into price of production and market price, but this COMPETITION is only analysed after a developed analysis of capitalist PRODUCTION and hence is explored fully in vol. III. (See also PRICE OF PRODUCTION AND THE TRANSFORMATION PROBLEM; SURPLUS VALUE AND PROFIT.)

SIMON MOHUN

value composition of capital. *See* organic composition of capital.

value of labour power 'The value of labour power is determined, as in the case of every other commodity, by the labour-time necessary for the production, and consequently also the reproduction, of this specific article' (*Capital* I, ch. 6). But this seemingly innocuous, certainly consistent statement of how the value of that peculiar commodity, LABOUR POWER is determined, hides a number of problems, some of which were recognized by Marx, some of which have provoked controversy only in more recent times.

First, Marx recognized that the set of use values a worker requires in order that his or her labour power be replenished is not just a physical subsistence minimum. While physical needs

can vary according to type of labour performed and may be affected by climatic or other geographical factors, these variations are dwarfed by those due to social differences. The needs of the working class 'depend therefore to a great extent on the level of civilization attained by a country; in particular they depend on the conditions in which, and consequently on the habits and expectations with which, the class of free workers has been formed' (ibid.). Thus in contrast with Ricardo and Malthus, who regarded the extent to which wages allowed for more than the bare minimum subsistence level as due only to favourable conditions of excess demand for labour – labour's value, around which its market price, the wage, fluctuated being for them physically and thus naturally determined – Marx saw a 'historical and moral element' entering into the determination of labour power's value itself, around which wages would fluctuate according to the demand for and supply of labour power.

This leads on to another problem which Marx does not seem to have considered, but which has come to the fore in the recent 'domestic labour debate' (see DOMESTIC LABOUR): that not all labour time necessary for the production and reproduction of labour power enters into its value. For a substantial part of necessary labour is not consumed in the form of commodities, but directly produces use values consumed in the home, without ever being valued in the market. This labour is housework. If such labour did enter into the value of labour power then this would always be more than the value of the commodities needed for the replenishment of labour power. Various attempts have been made to explain why the worker might be paid such a 'surplus' wage, most seeing it as some sort of transferred payment for a housewife (see e.g. Seccombe 1974), but all these have foundered on the unreality of adding like to non-like, labour not subject to the law of value to commodity producing labour which is so subject (see Gardiner *et al.* 1975). Exchange across the boundaries between commodity and non-commodity producing labour makes the latter indistinguishable from the former and fails to recognize the specific and different relations of production involved in each. Hence Marx's definition needs to be modified as follows:

'The value of labour-power is determined, as in the case of every other commodity, by the *commodity producing* labour-time necessary for the production, and consequently also the reproduction, etc. . . .' All other labour that enters may well be just as necessary, but must be considered as part of the historical and moral element which forms the background against which the worker's commodity needs are established. Of course, this different role in the determination of the value of labour power does not apply only to housework but to all other necessary non-commodity producing labour. Labour in circulation – in advertising, for example – does not enter into the value of labour power, though it forms part of the background against which the latter is determined.

Another problem which Marx did recognize was that labour-power needs to be reproduced in two entirely different ways. First, each worker needs to have his or her own labour power reproduced on a day-to-day basis. Second, the worker is mortal and needs eventually to be replaced by another younger worker in order that capitalism can continue to exist. Hence the labour time included in the value of labour power must include that which is necessary to provide for the new generation. However, this is not entirely straightforward, for the replacement of workers does not go on at an individual level, but within families (see FAMILY). Thus it would be more consistent to talk about the value of a family's labour power, as the unit in which labour power is reproduced. But this then begins to lose touch with the reality of the wage-labour system, in which wages are paid to individual workers who sell their individual labour power. The two only become the same when the family contains only one wage earner, the ideal of the Victorian bourgeoisie perhaps, but one for which the working class needed to fight; an ideal which was never universal and certainly not an inbuilt necessity of capitalist production (Humphreys 1977; Barrett and McIntosh 1980; Curtis 1980).

In particular, this would appear to leave the value of female labour power indeterminate, but in reality the indeterminacy applies to the value of the labour power of all members of all households. For working-class households consist of a variable number of wage-earning members and the contribution that individual members need to make will depend on the earning power of other members, just as the jobs that each can take will depend on their domestic commitments. Instead of seeing the (commodity producing) labour-time necessary to reproduce the family as determining directly the value of labour power, it may be better to see the former as determining the average level of household income, with struggle, involving not only the working-class and their capitalist employers but also the state, affecting the form in which this income is received. For most households this will be as wages to one or more members of the household, supplemented or reduced by state benefits or taxation, which may take some account of the variation in household composition (de Brunhoff 1978).

Marx seems to have recognized this when he wrote his list of 'all the factors that determine changes in the amount of the value of labour-power; the price and the extent of the prime necessities of life in their natural and historical development, the cost of training the workers, the part played by the labour of women and children, the productivity of labour, and its extensive and intensive magnitude' (*Capital* I, ch. 22), but he never attempted a full analysis of the problems in the determination of its value caused by the unusual nature of the commodity, labour power. It is produced, if produced be the right word, outside capitalist production, by a unit which consists of others than those who sell it. It therefore differs from any other commodity, if commodity be the right word, in that its exchange value is certainly not the sole aim, or even an aim at all, of its producers. Labour power and the worker are inseparable; and if that is a problem for capital it is also one for the understanding of the working-class family and the role of the value of labour power in its reproduction.

Another issue concerns the reduction of skilled to simple labour. Marx argued that skilled labour should be seen as a simple multiple of unskilled (simple) labour:

Simple average labour, it is true, varies in character in different countries and at different cultural epochs, but in a particular society it is given. More complex labour counts only as *intensified*, or rather *multiplied* simple labour, so that a smaller quantity of complex labour is considered equal to a larger quantity of simple labour. Experience shows that this reduction is constantly being made. (*Capital*, ch. 1, sect. 2)

But this concerns the value produced by skilled labour, not the value of skilled labour power itself, which was determined, like that of simple labour, by the costs of its reproduction, which in the case of skilled labour would take account of the cost and time spent on training. There has been some debate in recent years as to whether the values of differently skilled labour-powers can be determined independently of the values they produce – in which case rates of exploitation would vary – or whether there is a real social process that brings them into line (Itoh 1988, p. 163; Himmelweit 1984). The issues involved are very similar to those that arise in the debate over UNEQUAL EXCHANGE.

Reading

Barrett, M. and McIntosh, M. 1980: 'The Family Wage'.

Curtis, Bruce 1980: 'Capital, State and the Origins of the Working-Class Household.' In Bonnie Fox ed. *Hidden in the Household.*

de Brunhoff, S. 1978: *The State, Capital and Economic Policy.*

Gardiner, J., Himmelweit, S. and Mackintosh, M. 1975: 'Women's Domestic Labour'.

Himmelweit, Susan 1984b: 'Value Relations and Divisions within the Working Class'.

Humphreys, J. 1977: 'Class Struggle and the Persistence of the Working Class Family'.

Itoh, Makoto 1988: *The Basic Theory of Capitalism.*

Seccombe, W. 1974: 'The Housewife and her Labour under Capitalism'.

SUSAN HIMMELWEIT

Veblen, Thorstein Bunde Born 30 July 1857, Manitowas County, Wisconsin; died 3 August 1929, near Menlo Park, California. The son of Norwegian immigrants settled in a farming community which resisted 'Americanization', Veblen studied at Carleton College in Minnesota, Johns Hopkins University and Yale University, where he completed his doctorate in philosophy in 1884. But he was unable to obtain a teaching post (largely because of his religious scepticism and other eccentricities)

and returned to his father's farm, spending much of the next seven years reading widely in the social sciences. In 1891, to improve his prospects of employment, he enrolled as a graduate student in economics at Cornell University and then accompanied his supervisor to the new University of Chicago, where he eventually began his teaching career.

Veblen's relation to Marxism and socialism is unclear and has been interpreted in various ways, but it is evident that he read widely in the socialist literature during the 1880s, and in the following decade he reviewed numerous books on socialism and historical materialism, including Marx's *Poverty of Philosophy.* In an early essay (1891) he examined more generally some aspects of socialist theory, outlining the ideas of economic emulation and conspicuous display in the struggle for social esteem that were subsequently elaborated in *The Theory of the Leisure Class* (1899), but also emphasizing the dominant influence of private property in this process, and the possibility of a new form of society in which productive resources would be nationalized and emulation might 'find exercise in other, perhaps nobler and socially more serviceable, activities'. Two later essays (1906–7) were devoted to the economic theory of Marx and his followers and here Veblen demonstrated his wide knowledge of Marxist writing, but his approach was largely critical, particularly of what he regarded as the Hegelian, teleological foundation of Marx's thought, to which he opposed a causal conception of economic evolution derived from DARWINISM. From this 'scientific standpoint' he drew attention to difficulties in the materialist conception of history and the theory of value, emphasizing the psychological and cultural elements in the formation of social attitudes and noting in particular the strength of nationalism and its influence on the socialist movement in Germany. Nevertheless, he argued that Marx's 'work must be construed from such a point of view and in terms of such elements [of modern science] as will enable his results to stand substantially sound and convincing' (p. 437), though it is not easy to see in what way Veblen's own work, with its emphasis on the contrast between 'business' and 'industry' rather than on the development of capitalism, actually followed such a course.

Few later commentators have attributed much importance to the affinities between Veblen's thought and Marxism. Sweezy (1952), however, argued that 'Marxism was one of the decisive factors shaping his thought', that his interpretation of history was a form of economic determinism, that he gave a crucial place to the development of private property in the transformation of early societies, that class and class conflict are central concepts in his writings, and that, like Marx, he saw the accumulation of capital as being an end in itself in societies based on private property. After pointing to other affinities, Sweezy concluded that Veblen 'was the channel through which essentially Marxian ideas reached and influenced intellectual circles which were too prejudiced or too timid to judge Marx on his scientific merits'.

Reading

Dorfman, Joseph 1935: *Thorstein Veblen and His America*.

Sweezy, Paul M. 1952: 'The Influence of Marxism on Thorstein Veblen'. In Donald Drew Egbert and Stow Persons, eds. *Socialism and American Life*, vol. 1.

Veblen, Thorstein 1891: 'Some Neglected Points in the Theory of Socialism'.

— 1899 (1953): *The Theory of the Leisure Class: An Economic Study of Institutions*.

— 1904: *The Theory of Business Enterprise*.

— 1906–7: 'The Socialist Economics of Karl Marx and his Followers'.

— 1919 (1961): *The Place of Science in Modern Civilization and Other Essays*.

— 1921: *The Engineers and the Price System*.

— 1923 (1945): *Absentee Ownership and Business Enterprise in Recent Times: The Case of America*.

TOM BOTTOMORE

violence The question of whether extensive violence would have to be used to effect a socialist tranformation is a perennial one in relating means to ends in the Marxist tradition, and has long been one of the principal issues dividing that tradition. It has a changing historical setting. The mystique of radical change being attainable only through violent conflict originated in the French Revolution of 1789. It was perpetuated in the socialist tradition by Babeuf and Blanqui (see BLANQUISM) and given renewed cogency in the European revolutions of 1848. The general failure of these revolutions to secure the franchise to the working class and the apparent worsening of its living standards led many, Marx included, to the view that there were no means other than revolutionary violence to accomplish the emancipation of labour. The search for a peaceful transformation of capitalism was, he concluded, characteristic of utopian socialism. Occasionally (as in his Hague speech, September 1872), Marx acknowledged that in those countries where bureaucracy and standing army did not dominate the state 'the workers may attain their goal by peaceful means', but 'in most continental countries the lever of the revolution will have to be force'.

The gradual extension of the franchise, the startling success of the German Social Democratic Party in mobilizing working-class support, together with the increased efficiency, discipline and firepower of modern armies, led Engels (1895 Introduction to *The Class Struggles in France*) to conclude that 'a real victory of an insurrection over the military in street fighting . . . is one of the rarest exceptions'. He counselled caution and the patient building up of support; the movement was 'thriving far better on legal methods than on illegal methods and overthrow'. The principal Marxist parties of the Second International whilst retaining an abstract rhetoric of revolution made no preparations for it. Part of the strength of Bernstein's case was that the revolutionary theory of the movement bore little relation to its reformist practice.

The Russian party, acting in conditions of illegality and absence of democratic structures alone preserved a commitment to organizing mass political strikes which would culminate in armed conflict, and came near to success in 1905. The success of the Bolshevik revolution in October 1917 generated renewed controversy about the role of violence and led to a split in the international movement. SOCIAL DEMOCRACY argued that capitalist democracies were amenable to peaceful socialist transformation which, in any case, could only be meaningful and enduring on the basis of majority support. Communists maintained that the imperialist state was bound to foreclose on democratic liberties as soon as private ownership of the means of production was seriously threatened. The experience of European fascism confirmed them in their view that the imperialist state was essentially an instrument of violence. Through the Communist International the Russian experience was universalized and the DIC-TATORSHIP OF THE PROLETARIAT, signifying the unrestricted use of force by one class against another, was held to be the sole form of the transition to socialism. It was further maintained that the dialectical opposition of hostile class forces within society, which could only resolve their contradictory interests (or antagonistic contradictions) through violent struggle and civil war, was now replicated on a world scale in the confrontation of the armed camps of socialism and capitalism. It was this structure of ideas that became associated with the Stalin era.

Khrushchev contended that since the Soviet Union had eliminated antagonistic social groups the state need no longer be a coercive dictatorship. On the international plane he maintained that the balance of forces between socialism and capitalism had so altered in favour of the former that it could triumph through competition and peaceful coexistence. He further observed that the qualitative growth in the destructive power of atomic weapons dictated this as the only feasible course. At this point the leaders of the People's Republic of China felt their interests threatened, and Mao Tse-tung's experience as guerrilla leader in decades of civil war accorded ill with the new formulation. Many Marxists believed that the struggle for national liberation and socialism in South-East Asia and Latin America entailed armed conflict. Mao's ideas of protracted war in which popular support and commitment, generated by the guerrillas in their base areas, is the decisive factor, rather than sophisticated weaponry, commanded international attention in their successful application in Vietnam. Régis Debray and Che Guevara extended the importance of the guerrilla foci in creating the pre-conditions for revolution in Latin America.

The issue of violence also has an epistemological setting that stems from differences within Marxism about how individuals and classes come to understand their world. In general, Marxists who wish to decry the role of violence lay emphasis upon history as a law-governed process working with an inner necessity towards the breakdown of capitalism. Men, being creatures of reason, can comprehend, articulate and publicize these laws of historical development and demonstrate the reasonableness and superiority of socialism. They further argue that unlike anarchism Marxism set out to restructure rather than destroy the productive system created by capitalism, and that the constructive tasks of managing a modern economy and of inaugurating a more harmonious social solidarity are quite at odds with the arbitrariness of mass violence and the habits it instils. In short the ends of socialism could not be realized through violent means. On the other side, with an equal claim to orthodoxy, are those who argue that man knows his world only by acting upon it. In history, groups and classes come to a consciousness of themselves only by confronting other groups, and the most heightened form of this activity – the terminal point of the class struggle (see CLASS CONFLICT) – is the violent confrontation of civil war. Violence itself can become a creative force insofar as it reveals the class bias and violent nature of the state and serves to accelerate the development of class consciousness and organization. Lenin and Luxemburg were influential in developing the theory of a progression in which the economic polarities of society revealed themselves in antagonistic political groupings which, in turn, became the organizational foci for civil war.

The relative popularity and currency of these rival interpretations depends very much upon the degree of stability, prosperity and security of Marxist parties and regimes, their distance in time from revolutionary activity and the efficacy of non-violent avenues of attaining their goals. (See also SOREL.)

Reading
Bernstein, E. 1899 (1961): *Evolutionary Socialism*.
Black, C. E. and Thornton, T. P. 1964: *Communism and Revolution. The Strategic Uses of Political Violence*.
Friedrich, C. J. ed. 1966: 'Revolution'.
Girling, J. L. S. 1969: *People's War*.
Guevara, E. (Che) 1967: *Guerilla Warfare*.
Kautsky, K. 1920: *Terrorism and Communism*.
Luxemburg, R. 1906 (1925): *The Mass Strike, the Political Party and the Trade Unions*.

Trotsky, L. 1920 *(1961): Terrorism and Communism.*
NEIL HARDING

vulgar economics An epithet chosen by Marx to characterize post-Ricardian economics. The word has since been used as a portmanteau expression by Marxist writers to cover both post-Ricardian classical economics and neo-classical economics. Vulgar economics refers in particular to writings which concentrate on an analysis of surface phenomena, e.g. demand and supply, to the neglect of structural value relations, and also analysis which is reluctant to inquire into economic relations in a disinterested scientific manner, and especially afraid to probe into the class relations underlying commodity transactions. The latter aspect makes vulgar economics *apologetic*; i.e. it is more interested in defending and rationalizing the interests of the bourgeoisie, even at the cost of scientific impartiality.

The *locus classicus* of Marx's definition of vulgar economics is his Preface to the 2nd German edn of *Capital* I. In the course of characterizing the underdevelopment of economics in Germany, Marx periodizes the growth of political economy in England in its scientific and vulgar phases, linking it to the development of class struggle. Political economy which remains 'within the bounds of the bourgeois horizon' looks upon capitalism as 'the absolute final form of social production instead of a passing historical phase of its evolution'. In such a case, political economy can be a science only in so far as the class struggle is latent or merely sporadic. Thus if modern industry is in its infancy and if the capital/labour struggle is subordinate to other struggles, e.g. that of the bourgeoisie against feudalism, then the scientific pursuit is still possible. Ricardo (see RICARDO AND MARX) is described as the last great representative of English political economy since in his work the antagonism of class interests is central.

The period between 1820 and 1830, according to Marx, was the last decade of scientific activity, consisting of popularizing and extending Ricardo's theory, and of unprejudiced polemic against bourgeois interpretations of Ricardo's theory. Marx is referring here to the school of Ricardian socialists and the early attacks on Ricardo's theory in the Political Economy Club. The year 1830 marks the decisive dividing line. By then, according to Marx, the bourgeoisie had conquered political power in France and England, and once in power it no longer needed political economy as a critical weapon in its struggle against the old feudal order. Also class struggle now assumed a more explicit form. 'It sounded the knell of scientific bourgeois economy. It was thenceforth no longer a question whether this theorem or that was true, but whether it was useful to capital or harmful, expedient or inexpedient, politically dangerous or not.' Despite this, political economy was used as a critical weapon in the Anti-Corn Law struggle. With the repeal of the Corn Laws, vulgar economy lost its residual critical power.

Marx's periodization has been accepted by subsequent Marxist historians of political economy (e.g. Rubin 1979), but has not been critically examined. The extent to which a precise date, 1830, can be established as the time when the bourgeoisie captured power is one issue. It is also questionable whether the infancy of modern industry cited as a permissive factor in the possibility of scientific political economy in the 1820s could be said to have ended with that decade. An uncritical acceptance of the label and the periodization may also be said to have led to a failure to differentiate among subsequent (vulgar) economists by Marxists.

Reading
Blaug, Mark 1958: *Ricardian Economics.*
Rubin, I. I. 1979: *A History of Economic Thought.*
MEGHNAD DESAI

W

---

wages Wages are the monetary form in which workers are paid for the sale of their LABOUR POWER. Their level is the price of labour power, and like other prices this fluctuates around its VALUE, according to the particular situation of demand and supply, in this case in the labour market. Unlike other commodities, however, labour power is not produced under capitalist relations of production, and the value of labour power therefore undergoes no transformation into a price of production as the price around which, for other commodities, the market price fluctuates (see PRICE OF PRODUCTION AND THE TRANSFORMATION PROBLEM). The value of labour power, in that sense, remains untransformed.

The most important point Marx makes about the wage-form is its deceptive nature. Because a day's wage is paid only after a whole day's work, it appears that it is payment for that day's labour. That was how the classical political economists conceived the wage, and it left them with no explanation of how the capitalist manages to extract a profit from the workers' labour, unless he underpays them. For them, therefore, profits arose from UNEQUAL EXCHANGE on the labour market (see SURPLUS VALUE). For Marx, however, this was not an adequate analysis of the problem. Profit was the capitalist mode of production's form of surplus, and like the surplus in any other mode was the result of production. Unequal exchange could not produce, only possibly redistribute, the surplus. The specific way the surplus was extracted in the capitalist mode of production had to be explained on the basis of production by wage labour, the specific capitalist form that labour took, not by an unequal exchange of labour for the wage. The wage form itself had to be analysed, and shown to be illusory, to hide behind itself the mechanism of EXPLOITATION, a mechanism which could not therefore depend on quanti-

tative variations in the amount of money that constituted the wage.

The illusory character of the wage follows from the fact that the condition under which it is paid is the agreement to perform a certain quantity of labour, while what is really being bought and sold is a worker's labour power. This is paid for at its value, and its value must be less than that which the worker could create in one day, otherwise no profit would be made. So while it appears that a worker is being paid for a day's labour, in reality he or she is being paid for his or her labour power, the value of which is only equal to that of the product of part of the day's labour; thus he or she is only in effect being paid for a part of the day's labour, the portion Marx called necessary labour. The remainder of the time he or she is creating a surplus which the capitalist appropriates and this portion of the day is surplus labour. Like other illusory appearances of capitalist production (see COMMODITY FETISHISM) the wage form is also real. It *is* the case that workers receive a day's wages only if they provide a day's labour, and any who stopped after having done the hours of necessary labour, claiming that was all they had been paid to do, would have their wages reduced in proportion. The wage form is illusory in the sense of hiding the exploitation that goes on underneath it, not in the sense of being unreal. It is a real and necessary appearance of the underlying mode of surplus extraction of capitalism.

Marx's analysis has implications for his consideration of the particular ways in which wages can be paid. Wage rates paid by time – hourly rates, for example – are determined by the length of the working day. Since the VALUE OF LABOUR POWER – the amount required to replenish the worker's labour power – is paid for a full day's labour, the hourly rate is just that amount divided by the number of hours worked. Thus the hourly rate is inversely related to the hours worked, and the poorly paid are those who must work longest. The payment of overtime, or even the payment of higher rates for overtime does not alter the basic method of determination of wage rates. Overtime itself may become part of the normal working day, the relative rates of pay for the basic and overtime hours reflecting this, so that the worker is forced to do overtime to recover the value of his or her labour power. Rates of pay for casual labour may be determined in a similar way, even though this by no means guarantees the reproduction of the worker's labour power when the required quantity of employment is not forthcoming. It is interesting to note that Marx thought that these bad practices of low hourly rates, obligatory overtime, and casual labour would disappear with the legal limitation of the working day. He does not seem to have reckoned with the family and the state as alternative forms through which a worker's labour power might be replenished, leaving capital free to continue these superexploitative practices (see e.g. de Brunhoff 1978).

Marx did not consider piece rates to be fundamentally different from hourly wages. Although the worker appears to be paid for the labour performed, measured by the quantity produced, in reality the rate per item is determined by spreading the value of labour power over the quantity that a worker can produce in a working day. Thus a general increase in productivity lowers the rate of pay rather than increasing the amount with which a worker goes home. This makes clear that what the worker sells is his or her labour power, and the capitalist uses it in the most profitable way, so that the benefits of increased productivity, the extraction of relative surplus value, accrue to, and are seen as the product of, capital rather than the worker.

This fundamental point about the process of capitalist development – namely, that the growth of wages cannot keep pace with the growth of productivity – comes out most clearly when Marx considers national differences in wages. In this context he argues that although the level of wages may be higher in absolute terms in more advanced capitalist countries the value of labour power will be lower than in less developed nations. This is because the purpose of capitalist accumulation is the extraction of more and more surplus value, and ultimately this must take the form of the extraction of relative surplus value through a lowering of the value of labour power. Thus, although wages rise both through time and in the movement from less to more developed capitalist economies, this is not in proportion to the relative increase in productivity, and workers become more exploited as the value of their labour power falls.

Reading

de Brunoff, S. 1976: *The State, Capital and Economic Policy.*
Geras, N. 1971: 'Essence and appearance: aspects of fetishism in Marx's *Capital*'.

SUSAN HIMMELWEIT

war   Marx and Engels grew up just after the quarter-century of the Revolutionary and Napoleonic wars, in a long interval of European peace from 1815 to 1854 which might well have predisposed them to think of war as not the most important of human activities. They were moreover progressive middle-class youths growing up under an uncongenial government, the Prussian military monarchy. The approach to history which they began working out in the 1840s took as its bedrock methods of economic production, and discounted by comparison the wars, conquest, violence which chroniclers hitherto had taken as their staple. In the *German Ideology* they admitted the frequency of conflict, but belittled its significance by saying that conquerors had to adapt themselves to the productive system they found, as did the barbarians overrunning the Roman empire, adopting with it also the languages and religion of the conquered (pt I, sect. 2).

In 1848 however they and their friends of the Communist League pined for a 'revolutionary war' against Russia. It was a strategy founded on the precedent of the French Revolutionary armies marching across Europe – which, they might have recalled, did as much to disgust Europe with progress as to revolutionize it. From this time to the end of their lives questions concerning war forced themselves on the attention of the two men. They developed divergent but complementary interests, Marx in the more theoretical issues, Engels in the methods and technical evolution of warfare. He had served a short compulsory spell in the Prussian artillery, and took part in the abortive rising of 1849 in south-west Germany. A letter of 1851 (to Weydemeyer, 19 June) shows him planning a broad range of military studies, with the very practical motive of qualifying himself to supply guidance next time insurrection flared up. He contributed numerous articles on military topics to Marx's running commentaries on current events, and these and other writings earned him a reputation as an expert.

On the relation between economics and war in modern times Marx and Engels expressed various views, never drawn together into a regular pattern. In the *German Ideology* (pt I, sect. 2) and elsewhere they recognized that the early period of capitalism, down to about 1800, with merchant capital in the lead, had been marked by many wars, with the scramble for colonies sharpening trade competition. But the newer industrial capitalism seems to have appeared to them in a different light. It must be regretted that they never returned to an early intuition which found its way into *The Holy Family* (ch. 6, sect. 3). According to this Napoleon, obsessed with battle and glory for their own sake, was not fostering the French bourgeoisie by opening markets for it, as latter-day Marxism has been apt to assume, but on the contrary was dragging it away from its true path of industry-building. In 1849 Marx extended this pacific conception of modern capitalism to the financial oligarchy, saying that it was always for peace because fighting depressed the stock market (*Class Struggles*, sect. 1). In an article of June 1853 he held that nothing would bring about the rumoured war except an economic crisis, which might provoke it, seemingly, more for political than for strictly economic reasons ('Revolution in China and Europe').

Europe was then on the brink of the Crimean War of 1854–6, the first of its new round of conflicts, and one in which Marx took a passionate interest. When war broke out he was well aware of a blend of economic motives on the Allied side, such as concern for eastern markets, with political: Napoleon III's need for glory to brighten his ill-gotten crown, Palmer-

ston wanting to sidetrack the demand for parliamentary reform. To condemn war as a curse inflicted by governments on their peoples (*Eastern Question*, no. 108) was in one way the natural tendency of Marx's thinking. On the other hand he and Engels, like Lenin after them, were always firmly opposed to pacifism; and their overriding thought now was of the intervention by the tsar, 'the policeman of Europe', which helped to ensure the defeat of the revolutions of 1848–49. A successful war against Nicholas I would liberate Russia and reopen the way to progress in Europe; all the more if a conventional set-to of governments could be transformed into a truly revolutionary war of peoples and principles. They were disgusted therefore at the contest being pressed far less resolutely than they felt it could and ought to be. Engels deplored the incompetence of commanders, the decay of the 'art of war'; Marx feared that the struggle would be allowed to peter out, and shook his head over 'the present tame race of men' (*Eastern Question*, nos. 88, 104), as if he thought civilization condemned by its failure, under the spell of industrial prosperity, to fight in earnest. Detestation of mill-owners helped to mingle abuse of Cobdenism with his grumblings about the sham war.

From the vision, or mirage, of the 'revolutionary war' it was a come-down to the limited approval that could be given to the struggles which followed, down to 1870. They were to be classed by Marxism as 'bourgeois-progressive', or wars of national liberation. Socialists could not have a directing part in them, but would support whichever side might hold out more favourable prospects for the working class. Among them was the American civil war, which Marx and Engels followed closely, with an ardent wish for Northern victory. Engels as military observer was disagreeably impressed by the fighting spirit and skill of the South, Marx was more alive to underlying factors that told in favour of the North.

By the time of the Austro-Prussian war of 1866 the First International was in existence, and a resolution, not inspired by Marx and Engels, censured the breach of peace as a quarrel of rulers in which the workers should be neutral. But this and the Franco-Prussian war of 1870 brought about the unification of Germany, following that of Italy; and while Marx and Engels thought it deeply regrettable that Germany was being united from above, by Bismarck and the Prussian army, instead of by its people, they nevertheless welcomed the change as facilitating economic expansion and thereby hastening the growth of the working class. They were inclined to think the 1870 war the result of provocation by Napoleon III – always much hated by them – and so on the German side defensive; but they called on German socialists to oppose annexations and work for reconciliation with French workers.

Events, and further studies, were compelling them to reconsider some of their original views on the place of war in history. Curiously it was Engels who was the less willing to give it a more prominent place. Marx was obliged when wrestling with riddles of early history in about 1857 (his notes on them, in the *Grundrisse*, pp. 471–514, do not seem to have been read by his friend) to acknowledge war, in some areas at least, as a fundamental factor. Competition for land, he wrote, must have made fighting one of the prime tasks of all primitive agrarian communities. In Greece it was the grand collective function, and the city developed as its focal point of organization. War and conquest were equally an integral part of Roman life, in the long run subverting the republic by fostering slavery and inequality. Engels, by contrast, repeated in *Anti-Dühring* one of the leading tenets of the *German Ideology* by deriding any notion of history being essentially the exercise of force. To the chapters devoted in this work to 'The Force Theory' he planned ten years later a lengthy supplement, illustrating his thesis from German history since mid-century. He sought to demonstrate that Bismarck had unwittingly done the bourgeois revolution's work for it, by sweeping away the medley of petty German states, and that the regime he set up was only a temporary price to pay. Western Europe had now taken the shape of a few large national states, among whom the international harmony essential for the progress of the labour movement could be looked for ('The Role of Force in History', sect. 1). The work was left unfinished; perhaps Engels lost confidence in his argument.

It had some affinity with another line of thinking which for a good many years Marx and Engels and some of their disciples like Lafargue found persuasive. Happenings of 1848–9, and then their picture of the Crimean War as mere shadow-boxing, led them to conclude that modern armies were really no more than gendarmeries, maintained to keep their own people under control. After 1848 the middle classes, Marx wrote, in terror of the workers turned to governments and soldiers for protection. 'This is the secret of the standing armies of Europe, which otherwise will be incomprehensible to the future historian' ('Revolution in Spain' (1856)). He was commenting on a Spanish counter-revolution, and his words were applicable to the Spanish army through most of the nineteenth century and all the twentieth century. It was moreover in the habit of meddling in politics on its own account. Here was another menace that Marx took into account, particularly after 1851 when Louis Napoleon was able to make use of French generals, a good many of them formed in the brutal school of Algerian conquest, to carry out his *coup d'état* and secure the throne.

Marx understood that armies could have some popular appeal, not only to chauvinism but, for solider reasons, to those whom they provided with employment. In France the peasants had the strongest liking for war and glory, he wrote, because army recruiting relieved over-population in the countryside (*18th Brumaire*, sect. 7). But from 1848 onward he and Engels were advocating abolition of regular armies and their replacement, not by middle-class militias on the model of the National Guard in France, but by a more democratic 'arming of the people'. Very likely when Engels threw himself enthusiastically into the Volunteer movement in the 1860s he was thinking of it as a step in this direction. In Germany and elsewhere socialist parties took up the demand. Instead governments expanded their regular armies on the basis of universal conscription. Either way, Engels – like Lenin – indulged the hope that the governments were giving the masses a training in arms which eventually the masses would use to overthrow them (*Anti-Dühring*, pt. 2, ch. 3).

In the meantime he was increasingly disturbed by the hypertrophy of armies, their growth almost into an estate of the realm. Armed forces had become an end in themselves, he wrote in *Anti-Dühring* (pt. 2, ch. 3), while the nation was reduced to a mere appendage with no function but to provide for them. In his later years he was more and more preoccupied by the danger of war. There could be no thought of a 'revolutionary war' now, and none was needed when socialist parties were growing and seemed capable of taking power before long by themselves; while a conflict fought with the fearsome new weapons of destruction would be a terrible setback to socialism, and to civilization. In a very long letter to Lafargue (25 October 1886) about the Balkan crisis and the incendiary forces at work – among them the ambitious French general Boulanger – he argued that if war came its real purpose would be to forestall social revolt. 'Therefore I am for "peace at any price" . . .'. In 1891 he had something different to say: Germany must be prepared to defend itself against an attack by Russia and France, now allies (letter to Bebel, 29 September). His words were quoted in 1914, and he was overlooking the difficulty for the man in the street of knowing which side in such a case was the aggressor. Very near the end he hugged the too hopeful thought that new weaponry was making the perils of war more incalculable than any government would dare to risk, and that the coalitions between which the continent was divided might be expected to fade away (letter to Lafargue, 22 January 1895). Amid the press of events and the mounting intricacy of international relations his impressions were evidently fluctuating; his logic is not always easy to follow, and no single point of view emerges clearly.

His successors inherited this deepening perplexity. As 1914 approached the conferences held by the Second International, most of whose leading circles were of Marxist or semi-Marxist persuasion, were dominated by the war peril. In 1905 the French socialist Jaurès made two forecasts about the outcome of a European war which were both to prove correct: it might touch off revolution, as ruling classes would do well to remember, but it might also usher in an epoch of national hatreds, reaction, dictatorship (Pease 1916, p. 126). Kautsky, after Engels's death the International's leading theoretician, as a historian could cheer himself with the reflection that petrified social systems have been more often

shaken to pieces by war than by revolution; but he realized as Engels had done that fear of revolution might induce an insecure regime to gamble on war as a way out. In more sanguine moods he hoped that the shadow of revolt would have the opposite effect of frightening governments away from drawing the sword. For thirty years, he wrote in The Road to Power (1909, pp. 149, 154), this was what had deterred them from a war which otherwise would have come long since. But he could not contemplate the future without gloomy misgivings. Each ruling class accused its neighbours of plotting against it, feuds were being fanned into hysteria; imperialist expansion made certain a further piling up of arms, and it would go on to the point of exhaustion and explosion. Nothing could halt the slide except total, revolutionary change.

Militarism, Karl Liebknecht wrote in the book which earned him eighteen months in jail, is a phenomenon 'so complicated, multiform, many-sided' as to be very hard to dissect. Military men and capitalists had no friendly feelings for one another, he thought, though each accepted the other as a necessary nuisance; financially the army was an old man of the sea, in spite of most of the burden being placed on the workers (1907, pp. 9, 41, 48–52). Such an appraisal cannot be called a straightforward assertion that the cause of war lies in capitalism. And no such assertion can be found in or deduced from Capital. But since that work was written capitalism had spread over Europe and North America, and in recent decades its structure had been altering, the concentration of financial power growing rapidly. In the years before 1914 it came to seem increasingly natural to blame it for the drive to war, all the more because its own spokesmen were so clamorously positive that trade follows the gun, and that nations must join in the struggle for existence or go under. In 1912 the Basle congress of the International resolved that if the working classes failed to avert the catastrophe they should endeavour to bring hostilities to a halt, and make use of the resulting crisis to overthrow capitalism; for workmen to slaughter one another for the benefit of private profit would be criminal.

When 1914 came the International was hopelessly split, as socialism has been ever since. Lenin counted this division among capitalism's principal gains from the war. In the manifesto which he drafted for the party committee in October 1914 Lenin made room for a complexity of causes: the piling up of armaments, the sharpening struggle for markets, dynastic interests of the old monarchies, and the wish to distract and divide the workers, whose answer must be to turn war into civil war ('The War and Russian Social-Democracy'). There are no 'pure' phenomena in history, only mixtures, he pointed out in a long polemic against right-wing socialists in the summer of 1915. Serbia's national rights were one ingredient in the cauldron, but a very minor one. In essence, all governments had been preparing this war; all were guilty; it was futile to ask which struck the first blow, and it was dishonest to repeat now what Marx and Engels had said about the 'progressive' wars of a different era (*The Collapse of the Second International*).

It can of course be said that the Bolsheviks had more to hope for from a defeat of their country than any other socialist party, because they were too weak to have a chance of power in any other way for a long time to come. However, as the war went on Lenin laid the blame for it more and more exclusively on capitalism, also weaker in Russia than anywhere else. Capitalist guilt was the theme running through his *Imperialism*, and Bukharin's *Imperialism and World Economy* drew parallel conclusions; both works, however, were heavily indebted to Hilferding's *Finance Capital*. At its first congress, in March 1919, the new Communist International formally confirmed the diagnosis of the Great War as an explosion of the contradictions of capitalism and the anarchy of a world economy governed by it. Russia was now experiencing strife of another kind, civil war combined with foreign intervention. Lenin drew some political conclusions from it in a Report to the 7th All-Russian Congress of Soviets (5 December 1919). 'War is not only a continuation of politics, it is the epitome of politics'; he believed that the struggle was giving workers and peasants caught up in it more rapid political education than anything else could have done. At its close Trotsky, builder of the Red Army, pointed to some military lessons. They were of a practical common-

sense sort. War could neither be reduced to a science with eternal laws, as traditionalists supposed, nor be guided, any more than a game of chess, by precepts derived from Marxism, as some young enthusiasts fancied (1971, pp. 113 ff.).

Very soon after 1918 communists were warning of the peril of another world war. Since the experience of 1941–45, with its incalculable losses to Russia, Marxists (other than Chinese) have laid very great stress on prevention of war, as mankind's most urgent need. In a formal declaration in 1961, really a disclaimer of Maoist adventurism and talk of war as inevitable, the other communist parties asserted (not altogether accurately) that Marxism had never regarded war as the path to revolution. Meanwhile historical study of war and society has been pushed on actively, though much still remains for debate. Marxists have made valuable contributions to an understanding of the Second World War; they have underlined the share of responsibility of German big business, which has been obscured by Western treatment of the struggle as simply against Hitler, or Nazism. But it cannot really be said that there is a comprehensive doctrine of the causes of war which can claim the title of Marxist, though there is a Leninist doctrine concerning the wars of this century. Among diverse hypotheses, that of Engels in his last years, of war being likeliest to break out through over-accumulation of armaments, may seem the one with most relevance today.

Fresh thinking has been made necessary by the wars of colonial liberation of the past half-century. Marxists have been able to give far more unmixed approval to these than Marx and Engels could give to nation-building wars of their day inside Europe; and indeed colonial risings have been very extensively organized and led by communists. Engels wrote frequently on overseas campaigns of his time, chiefly on the Indian Mutiny and the second China war (1856–60); he wrote in a spirit highly critical of imperialism, but with an expectation of its proving in an unintended sense revolutionary, by destroying fossilized old regimes. His estimate of the fighting ability of Indians, Persians, Chinese, ill-organized and ill-led as they were, was usually very low. In Trotsky's writings and speeches during the civil war there is an uncompromising rejection of guerrilla tactics, as anarchic and useless. Later experience was to show that guerrilla fighting guided by a firm political leadership can be highly effective; but men like Mao and General Giap believed in going on as quickly as possible to the creation of regular armies, with guerrillas as auxiliaries. Over wide areas the wars of colonial liberation have been completed; a new turn was given to the question of the causes of war by the invasion in 1979 of communist Vietnam by communist China. (See also NATIONALISM.)

Reading

Carr, E. H. 1950–3 (1966): *The Bolshevik Revolution 1917–1923*, vol. 3, Note E: 'The Marxist Attitude to War'.

Chaloner, W. H. and Henderson, W. O. eds. 1959: *Engels as Military Critic*.

Cole, G. D. H. 1889–1914 (1956): *A History of Socialist Thought*, vol. 3.

Giap, General Vo Nguyen 1964: *Dien Bien Phu*.

Guevara, E. (Che) 1967: *Guerrilla Warfare*.

Liebknecht, Karl 1907 (1973): *Militarism and Anti-Militarism*.

Mao Tse-tung 1961–77: *Selected Works*, vols. 1, 2.

Pease, Margaret 1916: *Jean Jaurès, Socialist and Humanitarian*.

Trotsky, Leon 1971a: *Military Writings*.

V. G. KIERNAN

Western Marxism In the 1920s a philosophical and political Marxism originating in Central and Western Europe challenged SOVIET MARXISM which was codifying the gains of the Russian Revolution. Subsequently labelled 'Western Marxism', it shifted the emphases of Marxism from political economy and the state to culture, philosophy and art. The Western Marxists, never more than a loose collection of individuals and currents, included Gramsci in Italy, Lukács and Korsch in central Europe, while from the 1930s the FRANKFURT SCHOOL played an essential role in maintaining this style of thought. After world war II, Goldmann and the circles around *Les Temps Modernes* (Sartre, Merleau-Ponty) and *Arguments* (Lefebvre) constituted a French Western Marxism (see Kelly 1982). Under the influence of Lukács,

Gramsci and the Frankfurt School, new generations of Western Marxism emerged, especially in Germany, Italy and the United States. In a broader sense, of course, there have been many other influential forms of Marxist thought in Western Europe which rejected the Soviet version of Marx's theory, among them AUSTRO-MARXISM and 'Dutch' Marxism (PANNEKOEK).

The Russian Revolution conferred an immense prestige on Leninism and Soviet Marxism, hence the first Western Marxists claimed, and believed, that they worked within a Leninist framework. When Lukács and Korsch published in 1923 their fundamental texts *History and Class Consciousness* and *Marxism and Philosophy*, they were loyal theorists of the Communist Party. However, the Marxists of the Third International responded with hostility to their work, and the German Communist Party eventually expelled Korsch, while Lukács practised a series of 'self-criticisms' in which he distanced himself from his early views. Nevertheless, the exact relationship between Western Marxism as a whole and conventional Leninism remains hotly disputed. Complex and involuted paths marked the relationship of many Western Marxists, including Gramsci, Lukács and Sartre, to the Communist Party.

Western Marxism assumed a philosophical shape, but politics laced the philosophizing. The opposition which it generated did not derive solely from metaphysical differences; its philosophical orientation implied, and sometimes stated, principles of political organization that conflicted with Leninism. The Western Marxists gravitated less towards the vanguard party than towards COUNCILS and other forms of self-management. Their theories and principles were also stamped with the consequences of a particular historical fact, namely the uniform defeat of the West European revolutions in the twentieth century, and Western Marxism may be considered in part a philosophical meditation on these defeats.

The Western Marxists reread Marx with particular attention to the categories of culture, class consciousness and subjectivity. They broke sharply with the conventional Marxist authorities from Kautsky to Bukharin and Stalin who outlined Marxism as a materialist theory formulating laws of development. In Marx's own writings they were drawn less to the analyses of 'objective' structures – imperialism or accumulation – than to those of 'subjective' structures – commodity fetishism, alienation or ideology.

The status of Marxism as a science regularly troubled the Western Marxists. Basic texts of the Second International and Soviet Marxism championed Marxism as a universal science of history and nature. To the Western Marxists, these definitions were close to positivism, the reduction of a social theory to a natural science; and a positivist approach undermined the critical categories of subjectivity and class consciousness, which were foreign to pure nature. Both Lukács (1925) and Gramsci (1929–35) criticized Bukharin's *Historical Materialism* for similar reasons; namely, that it reduced Marxism to a scientific sociology. All the Western Marxists agreed that Marxism required a theory of culture and consciousness; and in order to accentuate these dimensions they confined Marxism to social and historical reality. Marxism, for them, was not a general science but a theory of society.

In their efforts to rescue Marxism from positivism and crude materialism the Western Marxists argued that Marx did not simply offer an improved theory of political economy. Marxism was primarily a critique. In his most utopian formulations – and many Western Marxists shared a utopian impulse – Lukács viewed Marxism as committed to the abolition of political economy or to emancipation from the rule of the economy. The categories of political economy themselves expressed an economic domination that Marxism sought to subvert.

Korsch recalled that Marx subtitled all his major works 'critique'. Marxism was not exhausted by the discovery of new laws of social development; critique also required an intellectual engagement with bourgeois consciousness and culture. Vulgar Marxists mistakenly believed that Marxism meant the death of philosophy, but according to the Western Marxists, it preserved the truths of philosophy until their revolutionary transformation into reality. Marx outlined the essential role of philosophy in a favourite text of the Western Marxists, 'Contribution to the Critique of Hegel's Philosophy of Right. Introduction', where he asserted that the proletariat was the heart of emancipation, but philosophy was its head. Both were essential: 'Philosophy cannot realize itself without the transcendence of the proletariat, and the proletariat cannot transcend itself without the realization of philosophy.' Marx's early writings – his encounters with Hegel, the Young Hegelians and Feuerbach – revealed the philosophical core of Marxism, and they breathed a utopian and libertarian spirit that was more subdued in his later writings. In this sense Western Marxism is almost synonymous with a return to the early Marx.

The texts of the young Marx offered a correction to the widespread presentation of Marxism as an anti-philosophical materialism. Marxism was materialist, but it was clear from Marx's criticism of Feuerbach, which turned exactly on this point, that he did not advocate a simple or passive materialism. Feuerbach had failed to incorporate the philosophical truths of German idealism into his outlook, and since he was unable to conceptualize the critical role of thought and philosophy, quietism pervaded his materialism. Marx hardly provided an apology for philosophy; he forcefully reiterated that the point was to transform, not simply understand, the world. Yet he did validate the philosophical enterprise. Over a century later, Adorno in the first sentence of his *Negative Dialectics* alluded to Marx's critique of Feuerbach as justifying philosophy: 'Philosophy, which once seemed obsolete, lives on because the moment to realize it was missed.'

The vocabulary and concepts of Western Marxism were resonant with Hegel, and almost without exception its thinkers were schooled in German idealism. The return to the Hegelian sources of Marxism marked the whole tradition, producing works such as Lukács's *The Young Hegel*, Kojève's *Introduction to the Reading of Hegel* and Marcuse's *Reason and Revolution*. In fact, Western Marxism only emerged where a Hegelian tradition remained alive or had been established. In Central Europe Wilhelm Dilthey revived Hegelian studies; in Italy the Hegelianism of Betrando Spaventa, Giovanni Gentile and Benedetto Croce nourished Gramsci; and before the emergence of French Western Marxism, Kojève, Jean Hyppolite and Jean Wahl introduced Hegel to a French public. Its distinct Hegelian hue set Western Marxism (in the sense with which we are concerned here) off from other forms of West European Marxism such as Austro-Marxism, which drew upon neo-Kantianism, and the structural Marxism of Althusser which sought to purge Marxism of Hegelian concepts.

If the return to the Hegelian roots of Marxism seemed benign, it spilled into more controversial areas in the evaluation of Engels and the dialectics of nature. For orthodox Marxists Marx and Engels both founded historical materialism, and it was idle to separate their distinct contributions. After Marx's death, Engels published a series of works, which gained popularity as one of the official versions of Marxism, in which he argued that dialectics was simply 'the science of the general laws of motion' valid in both nature and society (*Anti-Dühring*, ch. 13). This principle proved congenial to orthodox Marxism since it confirmed DIALECTICS as a universal and scientific law, but the Western Marxists dissented, and Lukács in *History and Class Consciousness* criticized Engels for distorting Marx. By extending dialectics to nature the dimensions unique to history – subjectivity and consciousness – were eclipsed. 'The crucial determinants of dialectics – the interaction of subject and object, the unity of theory and practice, the historical changes . . . are absent from our knowledge of nature.' Lukács was the most prominent, but not the first, critic to accuse Engels of misunderstanding Marx; several Italian Hegelians (Croce and Gentile) and French socialists (Charles Andler and Sorel) had preceded him. However, the question for the Western Marxists was not so much Engels himself, although this remained a volatile issue, as the dialectics of nature which he legitimated. Soviet Marxism committed itself to a dialectic of nature; the Western Marxists discarded it. In their view physical and chemical matter was not dialectical; moreover the dialectic of nature shifted attention away from the proper terrain of Marxism, which is the cultural and historical structure of society.

The Western Marxists used every concept they could extract from the Marxist tradition to confront the formation and deformation of social consciousness; indeed, an engagement with the intellectual and material forces of bourgeois culture defined their project. They believed that this culture possessed a life and reality which could not be dismissed as simple

mystification; and they agreed that the more conventional Marxist schemes of material base and ideological superstructure had to be given up (see BASE AND SUPERSTRUCTURE), since such schemes failed to do justice to either the truth or the obdurate quality of the dominant culture. In order to explain and undo bourgeois culture they rediscovered or invented the concepts of false consciousness, reification and cultural hegemony, which regularly appeared in the titles of their works (Lukács 1923; Guterman and Lefebvre 1936; Gabel 1975). Several consequences flowed from this orientation. First, the Western Marxists, from Gramsci to Marcuse, elevated intellectuals to a pivotal role. Intellectuals were more than lackeys of the ruling class; Marxism itself required an intellectual credibility and the support of intellectuals, and so had to remain abreast of bourgeois culture. The Western Marxists undertook a wide variety of cultural studies, which ranged over literature, music and art. They also, increasingly, subjected to scrutiny popular, mass and commercial culture; since in their view mass culture constituted bourgeois society as much as did the labour process – perhaps more so. Some of them, especially the Frankfurt School, turned to psychoanalytic theory (see PSYCHOANALYSIS) for similar reasons; it was not only a cutting edge of bourgeois culture, but also promised to illuminate how the individual imbibed culture.

The philosophical and theoretical formulations of Western Marxism merged into political formulations that challenged LENINISM. The philosophical concepts of subjectivity, consciousness and self-activity could be translated into such political organizations as workers' or factory councils, which seemed more faithful political expressions of the Western Marxist commitments than did the vanguard party. They became the object of a sustained interest and qualified defence, which had affinities with the Marxism of the *Praxis* group of Yugoslav philosophers and sociologists. On this more political terrain, Western Marxism also intersected with the great heresy that beset Leninism in the 1920s, 'left' communism. With some justification, critics regularly accuse Western Marxists of 'leftism', and 'left' communists undoubtedly expressed, more forcefully though in a less philosophical manner, similar political principles. They began with the same concern about the impact of bourgeois culture, and drew the conclusion that Leninism failed to confront the reality of cultural domination. This weakness was due to its origins in Russia, where the bourgeoisie and bourgeois culture were not politically powerful; hence Leninism as a political form was not designed to contest widespread and quasi-democratic cultural domination. On the basis of these principles the 'left' communists advocated worker and factory councils as the proper proletarian vehicle for emancipation. Cultural emancipation could not be commanded from above, since the hierarchical organization replicates the cultural dependency which already paralyses the proletariat; whereas in autonomous working-class groups the subjective and objective moments of emancipation converge. On this issue the 'left' communists, who included the Dutch School (Pannekoek, Gorter) and also possibly Luxemburg, converged with Lukács, Korsch and other Western Marxists.

Critics have argued that Western Marxism constitutes an abandonment of classical Marxism by its neglect of political economy and its departure from materialism; and they discover in the texts of the Western Marxists idealism and a remoteness from the prosaic realities of party life. Yet it must not be forgotten that Marx too was often distant from daily politics. Moreover, the Stalinization of the working-class movement, and fascism, which forced many Western Marxists into exile, were hardly conducive to practical politics by undogmatic Marxists. In any event, the Western Marxists produced a compelling literature, often in fields ignored by others; and this literature was provoked by the weaknesses of the classical tradition they are sometimes accused of deserting.

Reading

Adorno, Theodor 1966 (1973): Negative Dialectics.

Anderson, Perry 1976: Considerations on Western Marxism.

Arato, Andrew and Breines, Paul 1979: The Young Lukács and the Origins of Western Marxism.

Gabel, Joseph 1975: False Consciousness: An Essay on Reification.

Gramsci, A. 1929–35 (1971): 'Critical Notes on an Attempt at Popular Sociology'. In Selections from the Prison Notebooks.

Guterman, Norman and Lefebvre, Henri 1936: La Conscience mystifiée.

Jacoby, Russell 1981: Dialectic of Defeat: Contours of Western Marxism.

Kelly, Michael 1982: Modern French Marxism.

Korsch, Karl 1923 (1970): Marxism and Philosophy.

Lukács, G. 1923 (1971): History and Class Consciousness.

— 1925 (1966): 'Technological and Social Relations'.
                                    RUSSELL JACOBY

Williams, Raymond Born 31 August 1921 in the Welsh border village of Pandy; died 26 January 1988, Saffron Walden. Born into a rural working-class family, Williams was educated at Trinity College, Cambridge; he later reflected on this difficult social transition, and found a powerful geographical metaphor for it, in his first novel, *Border Country* (published in 1960). As a student, Williams was briefly a member of the Communist Party; in the postwar period he was a founder of the British 'New Left', editing its *May Day Manifesto* in 1967, and was later active in many socialist, Welsh nationalist and ecological political projects. He was an adult education tutor from 1946 to 1961, when he became lecturer in English (later Professor of Drama) at Cambridge University, retiring in 1983.

Images of Williams's intellectual trajectory remain dominated by what we might term its 'English' phase, of which *Culture and Society* (1958) and *The English Novel from Dickens to Lawrence* (published in 1970) are the highpoints. Here he works within and against the literary-critical tradition of Matthew Arnold, T. S. Eliot and F. R. Leavis, aligning himself with this tradition against the cultural reductivism of the British Marxism of the 1930s, but against its literary and social elitism, nostalgia and pessimism, insisting that 'culture is ordinary', residing in exchange and extension of values and meanings between working people in their everyday interactions or 'whole way of life'. *Culture and Society* seeks to recover the radical-conservative English critique of industrial capitalism from Edmund Burke on, and to transform it into a resource for what Williams saw as the morally impoverished British Left of the late fifties. During this phase Williams's aesthetic predilections are determinedly 'realist' in a familiar Lukácsian sense.

However, before *Culture and Society*, there had already appeared *Drama from Ibsen to Eliot* (1952), *Preface to Film* (in 1954) and *Drama in Performance* (in 1954), which promised a European rather than 'English', modernistic rather than realist, intellectual project. In *Preface to Film* (with Michael Orrom) Williams first formulated his most distinctive concept in cultural analysis – the 'structure of feeling' as the barely articulable emergence of new experience and forms beyond the official definitions of preformed social ideology. This theoretical impulse received its first full expression in *The Long Revolution* (1961), which seeks to deconstruct the opposition between 'high' culture and 'ordinary' experience, refuses the Marxist model of the determination of culture by the economic in favour of a model of the mutual interaction of all social levels, and offers a pioneering set of studies of the social history of education, reading and the press. It was the founding text of the discipline that has come to be termed 'cultural studies'.

Critics of Williams's early work argued that it was too neutrally descriptive, too 'anthropological' to catch the substance of sharply class-divided societies; 'whole way of struggle' was E. P. Thompson's famous emendation. Similarly, though the model of the mutual interaction of systems or levels has its moment of truth as a protest against 'vulgar' reductivism, it led to a merely 'circular' or 'organic' or 'expressive' version of the social totality. Yet even as these criticisms were being made, Williams's work was moving decisively beyond them. 'Struggle', certainly, rather than whole ways of life was a major theme of *The Country and the City* (1973), and the attempt to integrate ecology and socialist economics preoccupied Williams increasingly through the 1970s and 1980s. His formal rapprochement with the Marxist tradition he had abandoned in the late 1930s was made with *Marxism and Literature* (1977), which shows his continuing engagement throughout the 1970s with many imported continental Marxisms (Lukács, Goldmann, Benjamin, Althusser). He now defined his own position as 'cultural materialism':

a theory of culture as a (social and material) productive process and of specific practices, of 'arts', as social uses of material means of production (from language as material 'practical consciousness' to the specific technologies of writing and forms of writing, through to mechanical and electronic communications systems).

The themes of 'place' and 'bonding' are broached in *Towards 2000* (1983) and in his last, extraordinary novel, *People of the Black Mountains* (1989–90). With this last redirection of a remarkably fertile career, Britain's foremost twentieth-century cultural theorist, having passed through both realist and modernist phases, broached some of the major themes of *post*modernism (see MODERNISM AND POSTMODERNISM), of the reassertion of space, geography, heterogeneity in social theory, which continue to preoccupy us today.

Reading

Eagleton, Terry 1976: *Criticism and Ideology.*

— ed. 1989: *Raymond Williams: Critical Perspectives.*

Williams, Raymond 1958: *Culture and Society.*

— 1961: *The Long Revolution.*

— 1973: *The Country and the City.*

— 1977: *Marxism and Literature.*

— 1980: *Problems in Materialism and Culture.*

— 1983: *Towards 2000.*

— 1989–90: *People of the Black Mountains*, 2 vols.

TONY PINKNEY

working class For Marx and Engels the working class, engaged in a struggle with the bourgeoisie, was the political force which would accomplish the destruction of capitalism and a transition to socialism – 'the class to which the future belongs' (Marx, Preface to the *Enquête Ouvrière* 1880). In the *Communist Manifesto* they outlined the process of its formation:

The proletariat goes through various stages of development. With its birth begins its struggle with the bourgeoisie. At first the contest is carried on by individual labourers, then by the workpeople of a factory, then by the operatives of one trade, in one locality. ... But with the development of industry the proletariat not only increases in number; it becomes concentrated in greater masses, its strength grows . . . the workers begin to form combinations.

Ultimately, the local struggles become centralized, with the help of modern means of communication 'into one national struggle between classes'. During the second half of the nineteenth century the growth of WORKING-CLASS MOVEMENTS conformed broadly with the expectations of Marx and Engels, though the creation of distinct party organizations was relatively slow except in Germany and Austria where, by the end of the century, large and powerful Marxist parties existed. Then, however, the first doubts about the revolutionary role of the working class began to be expressed, notably by Bernstein, who contested the idea of an increasing polarization of classes and a revolutionary confrontation, and advocated a policy of more gradual and peaceful transition to socialism. From this time the working-class movement was clearly divided between reformist (see REFORMISM) and revolutionary wings, though there were also various intermediate positions, one of which was taken by the Austrian party (SPÖ) led by the Austro-Marxists (see AUSTRO-MARXISM); and the division was more starkly emphasized after the Russian Revolution, with the creation of communist parties and the Third (Communist) International as rivals of the old Social-Democratic parties and the Second International (see COMMUNISM; INTERNATIONALS; LENINISM).

The argument between reformists and revolutionaries has continued until the present time, but it has not been, and cannot be, simply a debate about first principles. It has to be concerned with the real social situation and political outlook of the working class in the developed capitalist countries; and in this respect two broad problems have emerged. The first centres upon the fact that nowhere has more than a minority of the working class (in some countries, e.g. Britain, USA, a very small minority) ever developed a revolutionary CLASS CONSCIOUSNESS, and that a socialist consciousness of any kind has never become profoundly rooted in the whole class. On the other hand, the socialist revolutions of this century, led for the most part by communist parties, have

occurred in peasant societies, not in those of advanced capitalism. Marxists have responded to this situation in a variety of ways. Lenin argued generally, though not on every particular occasion, that the working class could not by itself attain a revolutionary consciousness, which must be brought to it from the outside by a party of dedicated Marxist revolutionaries, and the same view was expounded in more theoretical terms by Lukács (1923). Other Marxists, and particularly Luxemburg, criticized Lenin's doctrine as tending to substitute the party for the class, and to lead to a party dictatorship over the class. But the idea of bringing revolutionary consciousness from the outside confronts another kind of difficulty when, over a relatively long period, it becomes apparent that in most capitalist countries revolutionary parties, and in particular Leninist parties, have not succeeded in gaining the support of more than a very small part of the working class. This situation, in turn, has led Leninists and others to attribute the reformism of working-class movements to the growing influence of a LABOUR ARISTOCRACY; but more recently this notion has tended to merge with the idea of a gradual *embourgeoisement* of large sections of the working class and to generate more pessimistic assessments of its historical mission. Such pessimism has been most fully expressed by Marxists associated with the FRANKFURT SCHOOL, whose recognition of the non-revolutionary character of the Western working class led them to depreciate radically the role of the working class and to look elsewhere for the revolutionary forces in modern society – especially during the upheavals of the late 1960s – among students, youth, exploited ethnic groups, and the peasant masses of the Third World.

There is also, however, a broad system of Marxist thought which interprets the development of working-class politics in the twentieth century (in a manner which occupies the middle ground between the two preceding positions) as a more gradual conquest of power through successive reforms – a 'slow revolution' in Otto Bauer's phrase – as a result of which there occurs a progressive socialization of the economy within capitalism and ultimately the construction of a democratic socialist form of society. This conception, however, runs into the second problem referred to above; namely, the question of whether the working class is steadily and inexorably declining as a proportion of the total population in the advanced capitalist countries. On this subject, bound up with the question of the growth of the MIDDLE CLASS, there is now a vigorous debate between those who see a 'proletarianization' of sections of the middle class (Braverman 1974) or the emergence of a 'new working class' (Mallet 1975) embracing what have usually been regarded as middle-class occupations; and those who regard the middle class as a distinctive, and growing, category defined by the character of its labour – mental and supervisory – or by its market situation and social status, and who therefore see any advance towards socialism as depending upon an alliance between the working class and large sections of the middle class. On either of these interpretations, however, any continuation of the 'march into socialism' (Schumpeter) is regarded as being crucially dependent upon the organized working class, which remains the most powerful political force for radical change.

Reading

Adler, Max 1933 (*1978*): 'Metamorphosis of the Working Class?' In Bottomore and Goode eds. *Austro-Marxism.*

Braverman, Harry 1974: *Labor and Monopoly Capital.*

Mallet, Serge 1975: *The New Working Class.*

Mann, Michael 1973: *Consciousness and Action among the Western Working Class.*

Przeworski, Adam 1977: 'Proletariat into a Class: The Process of Class Formation from Karl Kautsky's *The Class Struggle* to Recent Controversies'.

Wright, E. O. 1985: *Classes.*

TOM BOTTOMORE

working-class movements To say that working-class movements are fundamental to Marxist thought is to risk understatement. Marxists have had much to say about the chronology and the typology of working-class movements. But more fundamental than such opinions about working-class movements, there is a sense in which Marxist thought itself has been constructed from, even determined by, such movements.

This should not surprise historical materialists. What distinguishes historical materialism from other bodies of thought is its sense of its own subordination to actually existing (and changing) movements in history, intelligible (and changeable) in class ways. Class movement precedes any science of its development: such science, to the extent that it becomes historically significant, is articulated through class movement. A key finding of historical materialism, expressed in *Capital* I, ch. 24, is that working-class movement is part and parcel of the laws of motion of capitalism:

> Along with the constant decrease in the number of capitalist magnates, who usurp and monopolize all the advantages of this process of transformation, the mass of misery, oppression, slavery, degradation and exploitation grows; but with this there also grows the revolt of the working class, a class constantly increasing in numbers, and trained, united and organized by the very mechanism of the capitalist process of production. The monopoly of capital becomes a fetter upon the mode of production which has flourished alongside and under it. The centralization of the means of production and the socialization of labour reach a point at which they become incompatible with their capitalist integument. This integument is burst asunder. The knell of capitalist private property sounds. The expropriators are expropriated.

And from working-class movement theories adequate to the task of changing the world proceeded. Hence the way in which the revolt of the Silesian weavers, the Chartists, the revolutions of 1848 and their aftermath, the Fenian movement, the development of English trade unions, 'cooperative factories of the labourers themselves', the Paris Commune, and the experiences of the first workers' parties, particularly the German Social Democratic Party, each provided crucibles for fashioning the thought which gradually became known, first of all by its opponents, as 'Marxist'.

Four moments in the relationship between working-class movements and Marxist thought have been particularly important for the development of the latter. There was, first, the moment of its inception as historical materialism in the mid 1840s. Here the experience of working-class conditions and political associations in Manchester digested by Engels between 1842 and 1844 and conveyed to Marx thereafter, was crucial. Emphasis on production rather than on competition, on the specifically capitalist features of modern industry, on the state as the oppressive instrument of private property, and on communism as a real class-movement rather than a philosophical idea, came through 'the social movement' into socialist thought and not vice-versa. From the moment in the 1840s when class became a latent – and potentially a manifest – mass movement for itself, contradiction (in Marxist thought) became a material phenomenon rooted in the labour processes of capitalism rather than in abstraction or in nature. Internal to capitalist development were things (relations) external to it. For the quarter-century following the *Communist Manifesto* the key political questions for historical materialist analysis of working-class movements became: (i) to what extent could working-class movements use democratic bourgeois revolutions to go beyond them in the interests of the majority? (ii) where and how was 'the political economy of labour', 'social production controlled by social foresight', encroaching upon that of capital? (iii) to what extent could unions of working people – whether trades, cooperative, or political – form *'centres of organisation* of the working class, as the medieval municipalities and communes did for the middle class (*Bürgertum*)' (Marx, 'Briefing for Delegates' [to the Geneva Congress of the IWMA] 1867, sect. 6)? (iv) where were the contradictions, negative and positive, which were enabling new modes to become visible 'as forms of transition from the capitalist mode of production to the associated one' (*Capital* III, ch. 27)? (v) how could the real possibility of sectional struggles becoming general ones get expressed rather than repressed?

A second crucial moment was that of the PARIS COMMUNE of 1871. The effect on Marxist thought of this 'practical experience . . . where the proletariat for the first time held political power for two whole months' (Marx and Engels, *Communist Manifesto*, Preface to 2nd German edn 1872), can be traced through the drafts and text of *The Civil War in France*. It led to what some analysts have seen as 'a

revolution in Marx's thought'. The Commune provided a critique in practice of bourgeois separations of the political from the economic; it suggested the replacement rather than the capture of state power as the goal of working-class movements; and it swept away the 'whole deception' that workers could not run the world because there was something inevitable or natural about the existing political division of labour. It led Marx and Engels to revise some of the centralizing emphases of the *Manifesto* period.

A third new moment in the interaction between working-class movements and Marxist thought was of longer duration. It began with the creation, particularly in Germany, of mass working-class political parties. During the 1880s and 1890s Marxism became for the first time influential within significant labour movements. During the Second International period the opportunities for and constraints upon large-scale, working-class political organization became the stuff of Marxist political thinking (see INTERNATIONALS). Its main preoccupations, and the day-to-day debates within the working-class movements affiliated to the International were such matters as: how to celebrate May Day; the role of trade unions, STRIKES and general strikes in the emancipation of labour; participation in bourgeois assemblies and governments; the role of reforms as stepping stones or as inhibitions on revolution, and the extent to which capitalism could ride its contradictions through reform; the nature (constraints and opportunities) of nationalism, imperialism, intranational and international WAR; the extent to which conscious organization along new lines was necessary for the labour movement to get over the limiting effects of spontaneity; the divisions in capitalism between the economic and the political, and iron laws of organizational ossification (see Michels 1911; ELITE). Such debates were the daily diet of working-class movements during the later nineteenth and early twentieth centuries. They provided the lines of fracture along which these movements split into 'revisionists' and 'revolutionaries', 'scientific' socialists and 'ethical' socialists, 'syndicalists' and 'social democrats'.

During the period following the fourth crucial moment in the interaction between working-class movements and Marxist thought – the Bolshevik Revolution of 1917 and its containment elsewhere in Europe in the turbulent years till 1921 – such debates continued. But they took place in a context transformed by these events, and they assumed permanent *organizational* divisions congealed in communist parties, social democratic or labour parties and predominantly unpolitical trade-union movements. Marxist thought on working-class movements developed into dogma within post-revolutionary 'socialist' regimes. Within Western capitalist societies it developed into attempted explanations of why the thought and the movement had been severed, through imperialism, incorporation, successful reformism, repression, cultural hegemony and the like. During the period from the early 1920s to the late 1960s the main and tragic relationship between Marxist thought and working-class movements – at least from a political point of view – has been one of distance, even conflict. History did not go the way most Second International Marxists before 1914 thought that it would, and the unfinished task for Marxist thought has been to explain why.

The orthodoxy within Marxist thought on the development of working-class movements was fixed quite early through Engels's British experience in the 1840s, remained in place throughout his lifetime, and has been fairly constant since. It is that individualized protest gives way to local or sectional struggles. These are at first either narrowly economic or narrowly political and do not explicitly challenge emerging capitalist definitions of those categories. They are also at first relatively unorganized, and only slowly turn into formal organizations with constitutional structures, rationalized procedures and internal divisions of labour. When they do so, goal displacements away from class ends towards the interests of particular social layers, occupational groupings, national and sub-national entities all too easily take place. None the less, the development of the contradictions of capitalism is such that a stage of 'one national struggle between classes' succeeds these local and sectional contests. This assumes a coordinated political shape, contesting for power at the level of the state. Inexorably, although with set-backs and delays, the different wings of the labour movement – political and industrial –

come together to turn it into a class movement in the fullest sense. Uneven development at the intranational level has its parallel at the international level. But there too, Marxist thought has it, it will be overcome: in the words of the *Communist Manifesto*: 'in place of the old bourgeois society, with its classes and class antagonisms, we shall have an association, in which the free development of each is the condition for the free development of all'. Leading sectors will lead, but all in the end will catch up. Development will be uneven but it will also be combined.

Such orthodoxies are well known. But they have not always helped in the unfinished task referred to above, and in recent years they have been challenged within Marxist thought itself. Three directions of work may be mentioned. Labour historians have tried to get back behind dominant communist and social democratic forms of working-class movement in the twentieth century to see the rationality, effectiveness and creativity of so-called 'primitive' and 'utopian' forms of movement (see UTOPIAN SOCIALISM), and to see them as more than forerunners. Feminists have tried to get back behind the dominant male composition of working-class movements and dominant male versions of their history, to discover the way in which half the human race has been hidden from history, even from its own active and creative past (see FEMINISM). Gender is now being treated as a variable independent from, but related to, class. And practitioners of the emerging discipline of 'cultural studies' have tried to get back behind dominant versions of what constitutes 'production' in order to put Marxist thought on the LABOUR PROCESS back not only into 'economic' production but into cultural and political production too. In these three complementary ways the notion of vanguard sectors in the development of working-class movements is being criticized, and less evolutionary views on the development of working-class movements are being proposed. Creative thinking on the problem of agency from a working-class point of view is being resumed – thinking which to some extent had been made otiose by the mid-nineteenth-century equation of working-class movements with the movement of history.

Reading

Blackburn, Robin ed. 1978: *Revolution and Class Struggle: a Reader in Marxist Politics.*

Braunthal, Julius 1961–71 (1966–80): *History of the International*, vols. I–III.

Caute, D. 1966: *The Left in Europe since 1789.*

Cole, G. D. H. 1889–1914: *A History of Socialist Thought*, vols. I–V.

Hobsbawm, Eric J. *et al.* eds. 1978–82: *History of Marxism*, vols. I–IV.

Kuczynski, J. 1967: *The Rise of the Working Class.*

Rowbotham, S. 1973: *Hidden from History.*

Stedman Jones, G. 1977: *Engels and the Genesis of Marxism.*

Thompson, E. P. 1963: *The Making of the English Working Class.*

Williams, R. 1979: *Politics and Letters.*

STEPHEN YEO

world-system   The idea of a world-system was there and not there at the same time, from the beginning, in Marxist thought. In retrospect, what we can say is that Marx violated his own methodological injunctions by not being *sufficiently* historically specific, particularly in *Capital*. This being the case, his writings have lent themselves to ambiguous, even contrary, interpretations concerning the concept of a world-system, a term (it should be noted) neither Marx nor Engels ever used.

In the more abstract discussions of capitalism in *Capital*, the geographical boundaries to which the analysis applies are obscure. The opening sentence indicates that Marx will be talking of 'those societies in which the capitalist mode of production prevails', and the implication (common to most nineteenth-century thinkers) is that the boundaries of a 'society' are normally those of a 'state'. It is also implied, therefore, that there are some 'societies' in which capitalism prevails and others in which it does not.

Yet, of course, there are other passages with a different geography. The first paragraph of volume I, part 2, chapter 4 contains the oft-quoted phrase: 'The modern history of capital dates from the creation in the sixteenth century of a world-embracing commerce and a world-embracing market.' Here, too, there is lacking a clear specification of what exactly is meant by 'world'.

The third volume contains some even stronger statements about a world-system: Marx calls 'competition on the world market . . . the basis and the vital element of capitalist production' (III, pt. I, ch. 6, sect. 2). He makes 'the creation of the world-market' one of the 'three cardinal facts of capitalist production', on a par with the 'concentration of means of production in a few hands' and the 'organization of labour itself into social labour' (III, pt. 3, ch. 15, sect. 14). And perhaps most strongly of all he summarizes his views by reasserting that 'production for the world market and the transformation of the output into commodities, and thus into money, [are] the prerequisite and condition of capitalist production' (III, pt. 6, ch. 47, sect. 1). Earlier, in the *Grundrisse*, Marx had asserted: 'The tendency to create the *world market* is directly given in the concept of capital itself' (Notebook 4).

There is, however, no concrete analysis of how the 'world market' operates in *Capital*. This was presumably to be treated in the probably never written sixth volume, according to the original plan, which was described as 'Volume on the world market and crises'. In any case, do the various references to a 'world-market' imply the view that there is a 'capitalist world-system'? We have no direct answer. A careful reading, however, of *The Class Struggles in France* and the *18th Brumaire* does none the less suggest such an interpretation. Marx repeatedly explains the different concrete political actions of the British and French bourgeoisies by the fact that they played different roles in the world market. Explaining the constraints on France's industrial bourgeoisie in 1848–50, Marx wrote:

> The industrial bourgeoisie can only rule where modern industry shapes all property relations with itself, and industry can only win this power when it has conquered the world market, for national bounds are not wide enough for its development. (*Selected Works*, II, pp. 203–4)

Despite these and other arguments in the corpus of Marx, Marxist parties, as they became established in the Second and Third Internationals, were national parties, and to all intents and purposes pursued their class analyses within a purely national context. The concept of the world market, *a fortiori* anything resembling a world-system, was treated as largely epiphenomenal, and certainly not as one of the 'three cardinal facts of capitalist production'. This seemed to be true of most of the representatives of all the varying versions of Marxism then extant.

It is not that the 'international' dimension was ignored. After all, internationals were founded. And in the wake of the colonial expansion of the last third of the nineteenth century, 'imperialism' became an object of analysis – of course, most notably by Lenin. Lenin's discussion of imperialism should be viewed as part of a large awareness of and debate about world 'structures' or a world-system. This discussion certainly included Hilferding's *Finance Capital*, Rosa Luxemburg's *The Accumulation of Capital*, Kautsky in various writings, and Bukharin's *Imperialism and World Economy*, for which Lenin wrote a laudatory introduction. The last work is the closest to seeing capitalism as a world-system, at least in more recent times. 'Just as every individual enterprise is part of the "national" economy, so every one of these "national economies" is included in the system of world economy' (Bukharin 1917–18, ch. 1, p. 17). Indeed Bukharin puts forth an early version of a core–periphery analysis:

> Entire countries appear today as 'towns', namely, the industrial countries, whereas entire agrarian territories appear to be 'country'. International division of labour coincides here with the division of labour between the two largest branches of social production as a whole, between industry and agriculture, thus appearing as the so-called 'general division of labour'. (p. 22)

This whole discussion ended soon thereafter, primarily because the Communist Party of the Soviet Union decided on the pursuit of 'socialism in one country' and the Stalin–Trotsky struggle closed the open debate of the previous twenty years. The codification of a stage theory of modes of production situated both political and intellectual analysis squarely within the framework of national states/societies/social formations which were taken as givens rather

than as phenomena to be historically explained.

It was the reality of world political developments after the Second World War – US hegemony, the growing role of transnational corporations, the creation of a 'socialist bloc', the Sino–Soviet split, and the emergence of a 'Third World' collective presence in the political arena – which forced back on the Marxist agenda the issue of capitalism as a 'world-system'. Those Marxists who began to analyse capitalism in this way – such as Paul Baran and Samir Amin – came to be labelled by others who disagreed as 'neo-Marxists'. The heart of the debate today hinges on the so-called internal/external, factor distinction. For some, class struggle 'internal' to the state/society social formation is primary, and 'external' factors (such as 'world trade') are secondary, and are phenomena of the 'sphere of circulation', ontologically subordinate to the 'sphere of production'. For others, not only has a trans-state division of labour marked capitalism from its earliest history, but it is integral to the very mode of functioning of capitalism. In this view, the modern states are themselves an institutional product, and an evolving one, of a capitalist mode of production. There are, of course, many Marxists who seek to pursue a 'compromise' path between these two positions.

This fundamental debate is played out in a series of subdebates: whether 'feudal' forms/social formations still persist in parts of the world; whether the socialist countries are socialist, state capitalist, or some third difficult-to-name phenomenon; whether surplus value is obtained only through wage labour, or can be acquired through other forms of labour as well; whether the strategic priorities of the world socialist struggle lie in the so-called developed countries, in the Third World, or in both.

The debate within Marxism has led to a new 'reading' of Marx's writings – a popular exercise for many these days. The essential problem is that the current debate hinges around issues which, for various reasons – ignorance, uncertainty, prudence – Marx left unresolved or at least ambiguous in his writings.

I. WALLERSTEIN

Y

Young Hegelians The Young or Left Hegelians were the radical disciples of Hegel who formed a rather amorphous school in Germany during the late 1830s and early 1840s. At first, they were exclusively preoccupied with religious questions as this was the only area where relatively free debate was possible. Genuine political arguments among the Young Hegelians were not possible until 1840 when the accession of Frederick William IV and the attendant relaxation of press censorship opened newspapers for a short time to their propaganda. The reimposition of government control some three years later spelt the end of the movement.

In origin, the Young Hegelians were a philosophical school and their approach to religion and politics was always intellectual. Their philosophy is best called a speculative rationalism. To their romantic and idealistic elements they added the sharp critical tendencies of the *Aufklärung* and an admiration for the principles of the French Revolution. They believed in reason as a continually unfolding process and considered it their task to be its heralds. Like Hegel, they believed that the process would achieve an ultimate unity, but they tended to consider that it would be preceded by an ultimate division. This meant that some of their writings had a very apocalyptic ring, for they thought it their duty to force divisions by their criticism to a final rupture, and thus hasten their resolution.

The Young Hegelians had considerable influence on the formation of the ideas of the early Marx. From the most prominent of the Young Hegelians, Bruno Bauer, Marx took his incisive criticism of religion which served as a model for his early analysis of politics and economics. From FEUERBACH, he took over a radical humanism which involved a systematic transformation of Hegel's philosophy and a rejection of the supremacy of Hegel's Idea. Stirner, the supreme egoist and most negative of all the Young Hegelians, compelled Marx to go beyond the somewhat static humanism of Feuerbach. Finally, Hess, the first propagator of communist ideas in Germany, pioneered the application of radical ideas in economics. By the mid-1840s, however, Marx had moved towards a materialist conception of history which involved the trenchant criticism of the Young Hegelians contained in the *German Ideology*.

Reading
McLellan, David 1969: *The Young Hegelians and Karl Marx*.

DAVID MCLELLAN

Bibliography

I The Writings of Marx and Engels cited in the Dictionary

The following abbreviations are used:

MEGA   Karl Marx/Friedrich Engels. *Historisch-Kritische Gesamtausgabe*. Part and vol. indicated thus: I,1. (Vol. 1 is in two half vols.; thus I,1/1 and I,1/2)

NRZ   *Neue Rheinische Zeitung* (Cologne 1848–1849)

NRZ-Revue *Neue Rheinische Zeitung. Politisch-ökonomische Revue* (London/Hamburg 1850)

NYDT   *New York Daily Tribune*

For a comprehensive bibliography see Maximilien Rubel, *Bibliographie des œuvres de Karl Marx* (with an appendix listing the writings of Engels). Paris: Marcel Rivière, 1960.

A Marx

1843 *Critique of Hegel's Philosophy of the State.* First published in *MEGA* I, 1/1 (1927). Title has been variously trans. into English; e.g. *Critique of Hegel's Philosophy of Right, Critique of Hegel's Doctrine of the State.*

1844 'On the Jewish Question', *Deutsch-Französische Jahrbücher* ed. Arnold Ruge and Karl Marx. Paris.
'Critique of Hegel's Philosophy of Right. Introduction', *Deutsch-Französische Jahrbücher*.
Economic and Philosophical Manuscripts. First published in *MEGA* I,3.

1845 *Theses on Feuerbach*. First published by Engels as an appendix to his *Ludwig Feuerbach and the End of Classical German Philosophy* (1888).

1847 *The Poverty of Philosophy*. Paris: A. Franck; Brussels: C. G. Vogeler.

1850 *The Class Struggles in France*. A series of three articles in *NRZ-Revue*, March/April, afterwards collected by Engels in a book with this title. New edn Berlin 1895 with preface by Engels and a fourth article by Marx and Engels jointly.

1852 *The 18th Brumaire of Louis Bonaparte*. First published in the journal founded in New York, by J. Weydemeyer, *Die Revolution*. Second edn with a foreword by Marx, Hamburg: Meissner, 1869.

1853 'Capital Punishment'. *NYDT*, 18 February.
'Revolution in China and Europe'. *NYDT*, 14 June.
'The British Rule in India'. *NYDT*, 25 June.
'War in Burma'. *NYDT*, 30 July.

'The Future Results of British Rule in India'. *NYDT*, 8 August.

1854 'The Decay of Religious Authority'. *NYDT*, 24 October. Unsigned leading article attributed to Marx by Rubel in his *Bibliographie* (1960), and also included by Eleanor Marx in *The Eastern Question* (see Part D).

1856 'Revolution in Spain'. *NYDT*, 8 and 18 August. (See also *Revolution in Spain* 1939, in Part D below.)

1857–8 *Grundrisse der Kritik der politischen Ökonomie*. First published 1939–41 (2 vols), Moscow: Foreign Languages Publishing House (new edn in 1 vol., Berlin: Dietz, 1953). The 'Introduction' had previously been published by Kautsky in *Die Neue Zeit*, XXI, 1 (1903). English trans., with a foreword, by Martin Nicolaus, *Grundrisse*, Harmondsworth: Penguin Books in association with *New Left Review*, 1973. One section previously trans. in Eric Hobsbawm, *Pre-Capitalist Economic Formations*, London: Lawrence & Wishart, 1964.

1859 *A Contribution to the Critique of Political Economy*, Berlin: Franz Duncker.
'Population, Crime and Pauperism'. *NYDT*, 16 September.

1864 'Inaugural Address of the Working Men's International Association'. London: *The Bee-Hive* Newspaper Office.

1865 *Value, Price and Profit*. First published by Eleanor Marx Aveling. London: Swan Sonnenschein 1898. Republished under the title *Wages, Price and Profit*. Moscow: Foreign Languages Publishing House 1952.

1867   'Briefing for the Delegates of the Provisional General Council on Particular Questions'. *The International Courier*, 20 February and 13 March.

Capital, Vol. I. Hamburg: Otto Meissner. The first edn contained an appendix to ch. 1, 'The Value Form', absorbed into the chapter in later editions. This appendix has been republished separately in English in *Capital and Class*, 4 (Spring 1978).

1861–1879   Manuscripts of later volumes of *Capital* and related economic writings, which were published as follows:
(i) *Capital*, Vol. II, edited by Engels, Hamburg: Otto Meissner, 1885.
(ii) *Capital*, Vol. III, edited by Engels. Hamburg: Otto Meissner, 1894.
(iii) *Theories of Surplus Value*, edited by Karl Kautsky. Stuttgart: J.H.W. Dietz Nachf., Vols. I and II, 1905; Vol. III, 1910.
(iv) A chapter entitled 'Results of the Immediate Process of Production' which Marx indicated on the manuscript as Chapter 6 of the first volume of *Capital*, though it was not finally included there. First published in *Arkhiv Marxa i Engelsa*, II. Moscow, 1933.
The best account of the whole range of these manuscripts, and of their publication, will be found in Maximilien Rubel's edition of Marx's economic writings (2 vols., 1965, 1968; see Part D below).

1871   *The Civil War in France*. Published anonymously as an Address of the General Council of the International Working Men's Association. London: Edward Truelove. See also the earlier drafts of the address, first published in *Arkhiv Marxa i Engelsa*, III. Moscow, 1934.

1872   Speech on the Hague Congress [of the IWMA]. Published in *La Liberté*, no. 37, 15 September.

1874–5   'Conspectus of Bakunin's book *Statism and Anarchy*'. Published in *Werke*, vol. 18, 1962.

1875   *Critique of the Gotha Programme*. First published by Engels, with a prefatory note, in *Die Neue Zeit*, IX,1 (1891).

1877   Letter on the future development of society in Russia written to the editor of *Otechesvenniye Zapisky* (N.K. Mikhailovsky) but not sent. First published by Vera Zasulich in *Vestnik Narodnoi Voli* (Geneva), May 1884.

1880   'Notes on Adolph Wagner'. First published in a Russian translation in *Arkhiv Marxa i Engelsa*, I. Moscow, 1930. English trans. with commentary in Terrell Carver, ed., *Karl Marx: Texts on Method*. Oxford: Basil Blackwell, 1975.

'Preface' to a proposed *enquête ouvrière*. *Revue socialiste* (Saint-Cloud), no. 4, 20 April.

B   Engels

1844   'Outlines of a Critique of Political Economy', *Deutsch-Französische Jahrbücher* (Paris).
'The Condition of England'. Two essays in *Vorwärts* (Paris), 31 August–11 September and 18 September–19 October.

1845   *The Condition of the Working Class in England*. Leipzig: Otto Wigand.
'Two Speeches at Elberfeld' (8 and 15 February), *Rheinische Jahrbücher zur gesellschaftlichen Reform* (Darmstadt), I.
'The Festival of Nations in London', *Rheinische Jahrbücher zur gesellschaftlichen Reform*, II (1846). Part appeared earlier in *The Northern Star*, 27 September 1845.

1847   *Principles of Communism*. First published by Eduard Bernstein in *Vorwärts* (Berlin) 1914.

1851–52   *Revolution and Counter-Revolution in Germany*. Twenty articles in *NYDT*, 25 October 1851–22 December 1852, signed by Marx. Collected in a volume by Eleanor Marx Aveling (1896) who attributed them to Marx.

1873   'On Authority', *Almanacco Repubblicano per l'anno 1874* (Lodi).

1871–75   Articles in *Der Volksstaat*, collected and published under the title *Internationales aus dem Volksstaat*. Berlin: 1894. Includes the articles 'Social Conditions in Russia' (with an afterword) and 'The Programme of the Blanquist Commune Refugees'.

1876   'The Part Played by Labour in the Transition from Ape to Man'. Unfinished MS. First published in *Die Neue Zeit*, XIV, 1895–1896.

1877–78   *Herr Eugen Dühring's Revolution in Science (Anti-Dühring)*. First published as articles in *Vorwärts* (Leipzig) between January 1877 and July 1878, then as a book, Leipzig, 1878.

1880   *Socialism: Utopian and Scientific*. Three chapters from *Anti-Dühring* revised to form a short book, and translated by Paul Lafargue. For the English edn (1892) Engels wrote a new introduction.

1878–82   *Dialectics of Nature*. First published in *Marx–Engels Archiv*, II, 1927. New edn with additional MSS. in *MEGA* (Special volume) 1935.

1882   'Bruno Bauer and Early Christianity', *Sozialdemokrat*, 4 and 11 May.

1883   Speech at the Graveside of Karl Marx, *Sozialdemokrat* (Zurich), 22 March.

1884   *Origin of the Family, Private Property and the State*. Stuttgart: Dietz, 1884 (rev. 4th edn 1894); 1972 edition, introduced by E.B. Leacock, New York: International; 1985 edition introduced by Michèle Barrett and containing references to various modern discussions and critiques, Harmondsworth: Penguin.

1885 'On the History of the Communist League', *Sozialdemokrat* (nos. 46–48), 12, 19 and 26 November. Also as the introduction to the 3rd German edn (1885) of Marx's pamphlet, *Revelations Concerning the Trial of the Communists in Cologne*.

1886 *Ludwig Feuerbach and the End of Classical German Philosophy*, in *Die Neue Zeit*, IV. Republished as a book with a new preface 1888.

1887–88 'The Role of Force in History'. First published in *Die Neue Zeit*, XIV, 1895–1896.

1894–5 'The Peasant Question in France and Germany', in *Die Neue Zeit*, XIII: 10. In Marx and Engels 1951: *Selected Works*, vol. 2 Moscow: Foreign Language Publishing House.

C Marx and Engels

1845 *The Holy Family*. Frankfurt am Main: Literarische Anstalt (J. Rütten).

1845–1846 *German Ideology*. First published in full in *MEGA*, I,5 (1932).

1848 *Manifesto of the Communist Party*. London. Three anonymous editions were published in 1848 (two with J.E. Burghard as printer, one with R. Hirschfeld as printer). The names of Marx and Engels as authors first appeared in the Leipzig edn of 1872, when the title was also changed to *Communist Manifesto*.

1875 'For Poland', *Der Volksstaat* (34), 24 March.

D Collections (cited or used)

1897 *The Eastern Question*. A collection of Marx's articles on the Crimean War (1853–1856), edited by Eleanor Marx Aveling and Edward Aveling. London: S. Sonnenschein.

1927–1935 Karl Marx/Friedrich Engels. *Historisch-kritische Gesamtausgabe. Werke/Schriften/Briefe. (MEGA)*. (The most scholarly edition of Marx's and Engels's writings in the original language of composition, initiated by D. Riazanov and brought to an abrupt halt after 12 volumes had been published, following Riazanov's 'disappearance' in 1931 as an early victim of Stalinism. The individual volumes were published in different places (Frankfurt am Main, Berlin, Vienna, Moscow) by various publishers). Publication of a 'new MEGA' with an elaborate critical apparatus, began in 1975; by 1990, 47 of the planned 130 volumes had appeared. *Karl Marx/Friedrich Engels Gesamtausgabe* (Berlin: Dietz Verlag).

1939 *Revolution in Spain*. A collection of articles (of the 1850s) by Marx and Engels, from *NYDT*, *Putnam's Magazine* and the *New American Cyclopaedia*. New York: International Publishers.

1957 Marx and Engels, *On Religion*. Moscow: Foreign Languages Publishing House.

1957–67 Karl Marx, Friedrich Engels, *Werke*. Berlin: Dietz Verlag.

1959 Marx, *The First Indian War of Independence, 1857–1859*. Moscow: Foreign Languages Publishing House. (A collection of Marx's articles in the *NYDT*).

1965, 1968 Marx, *Oeuvres: Économie*, Vols. I and II, edited with a comprehensive introduction and notes by Maximilien Rubel. Paris: Gallimard (Bibliothèque de la Pléiade). (An admirable collection of Marx's economic writings, including excerpts from notebooks and letters.)

1968 *Karl Marx on Colonialism and Modernisation*, edited with an introduction by Shlomo Avineri. Garden City, N.Y.: Doubleday. (Mainly articles from the *NYDT*, but also excepts from other writings and letters of both Marx and Engels.)

1968 *Marx und Engels über Kunst und Literatur*. 2 vols. edited by Manfred Kliem. Frankfurt am Main: Europäische Verlagsanstalt. (The most comprehensive collection available.)

1972 Marx, Engels, Lenin *Anarchism and Anarcho-syndicalism*. Moscow: Progress.

The Ethnological Notebooks of Karl Marx, edited by L. Krader. Netherlands: Van Gorcum. (Contains Marx's original notes.)

1973 Marx and Engels, *On Literature and Art*, edited by L. Baxandall and S. Morawski. New York: International General. (A collection of major texts and references.)

1974 *Marx-Engels über Sprache, Stil und Übersetzung* edited by H. Ruscinski and B. Retzlaff Kress. Berlin: Dietz.

1975 Marx and Engels, *Collected Works*. English translation which will eventually comprise 50 volumes. Moscow: Progress Publishers; London: Lawrence and Wishart; New York: International Publishers. (The introductions and notes to the early volumes embody a very orthodox Bolshevik view.)

Marx, *Early Writings*, introduced by Lucio Colletti. Harmondsworth: Penguin.

Marx and Engels, *Materiales para la Historia de América Latina. Cuadernos de Pasado y Presente*, no. 30 (Mexico City).

II   All Other Works Cited

(*Note*:   The convention 1920 (*1970*) indicates a work first published in 1920 but most readily accessible in a translation or edition of 1970, to which the publication details refer.)

Abalkin, L. 1988: Obnovlenye sotsialisticheskoy sobstvennosti (Renewal of Socialist Ownership). *Ekonomicheskaya Gazieta* 45 (Moscow).

Abdel-Malek, Anouar 1969: *Idéologie et renaissance nationale: L'Égypte moderne.* Paris: Éditions Anthropos.

Abercrombie, Nicholas, Hill, Stephen and Turner, Bryan S. 1980: *The Dominant Ideology Thesis.* London and Boston: Allen & Unwin.

Abercrombie, Nicholas and Urry, John 1983: *Capital, Labour and the Middle Classes.* London: Allen & Unwin.

Adams, R. McC. 1966: *Evolution of Urban Society.* Chicago: Aldina; London: Weidenfeld & Nicolson.

Adler, Max 1904: *Kausalität und Teleologie im Streite um die Wissenschaft.* Vienna: Wiener Volksbuchhandlung.

—— 1904–27 (*1978*): Selections on 'The Theory and Method of Marxism'. In Bottomore and Goode, eds., *Austro-Marxism.*

—— 1914: *Der soziologische Sinn der Lehre von Karl Marx.* Leipzig: C.L. Hirschfeld. Partly trans. in Bottomore and Goode, eds., *Austro-Marxism.*

—— 1919: *Demokratie und Rätesystem.* Vienna: Wiener Volksbuchhandlung.

—— 1922: *Die Staatsauffassung des Marxismus. Ein Beitrag zur Unterscheidung von soziologischer und juristischer Methode.* Vienna: Wiener Volksbuchhandlung.

—— 1925: *Kant und der Marxismus.* Berlin: E. Laub'sche Verlagsbuchhandlung.

—— 1930, 1932 (*1964*): *Soziologie des Marxismus*, 3 vols. New edn with previously unpub. 3rd vol. Vienna: Europa Verlag.

—— 1933 (*1978*): Metamorphosis of the Working Class. *Der Kampf* 26. Trans. in Bottomore and Goode, eds., *Austro-Marxism.*

—— 1967: *Démocratie et conseils ouvriers*, ed. Yvon Bourdet. Paris: François Maspero.

Adorno, Theodor W. 1946: Social Science and Sociological Tendencies in Psychoanalysis. Unpublished paper. German version in Max Horkheimer and Theodor W. Adorno, eds, *Sociologica II: Reden und Vorträge.* Frankfurt: Europäische Verlagsanstalt (1962).

—— 1949 (*1973*): *Philosophy of Modern Music.* New York: Seabury.

—— 1951 (*1974*): *Minima Moralia.* London: New Left.

—— 1955a (*1967*): *Prisms.* London: Neville Spearman.

—— 1955b (*1967, 1968*): Sociology and Psychology. *New Left Review* 46 and 47.

—— 1964 (*1975*): The Culture Industry Reconsidered. *New German Critique* 6.

—— 1966 (*1973*): *Negative Dialectics.* New York: Seabury; London: Routledge & Kegan Paul.

—— 1970–: *Gesammelte Schriften.* 23 vols. Frankfurt: Suhrkamp.

—— (*1982*): *Against Epistemology: Studies in Husserl and the Phenomenological Antinomies*, trans. Willis Domingo. Oxford: Basil Blackwell; Cambridge, Mass.: MIT.

Adorno, Theodor and Horkheimer, Max 1947 (*1973*): *Dialectic of Enlightenment.* New York. Herder & Herder; London: Allen Lane (1978).

Adorno, Theodor *et al.* 1950: *The Authoritarian Personality.* New York: Harper & Row.

Afanasyeu, L. *et al.* 1974: *The Political Economy of Capitalism.* Moscow: Progress.

Aglietta, Michael 1979: *A Theory of Capitalist Regulation: The US Experience.* London: New Left.

Aguilar, L.E. 1968: *Marxism in Latin America.* New York: Knopf.

Agulhon, M. *et al.* 1986: *Blanqui et les blanquistes.* Actes du Colloque Blanqui. Paris: SEDES.

Alavi, Hamza 1972: The State in Post-colonial Societies. *New Left Review* 74.

—— 1975: India and the Colonial Mode of Production. In Miliband and Saville, eds, *The Socialist Register*, no. 12.

Alavi, Hamza and Shanin, T., eds. 1982: *Introduction to the Sociology of the Developing Societies.* London: Macmillan; New York: Monthly Review Press.

Alavi, Hamza *et al.* 1982: *Capitalism and Colonial Production.* London: Croom Helm.

Albritton, Robert 1986: *A Japanese Reconstruction of Marxist Theory.* London: Macmillan.

Alesandrov, G.F. *et al.* 1952: *Joseph Stalin: a Short Biography.* Moscow: Foreign Languages Publishing House.

Allen, Chris 1989: *Benin.* London: Macmillan.

Althusser, L. 1965 (*1969*): *For Marx.* London: Allen Lane; New York: Pantheon.

—— 1971: *Lenin and Philosophy and other Essays.* London: New Left; New York: Monthly Review Press (1972).

—— 1976: *Essays in Self-Criticism.* London: New Left; Atlantic Highlands, N.J.: Humanities.

Althusser, L. and Balibar, É. 1970: *Reading 'Capital'.* London: New Left; New York: Pantheon (1971).

Amin, Samir 1973a (1976): *Unequal Development.* New York: Monthly Review Press; Brighton: Harvester.

—— 1973b (1977): *Imperialism and Unequal Development.* New York: Monthly Review Press; Brighton: Harvester.

—— 1974: *Accumulation on a World Scale.* Sussex: Harvester.

Ampolo, C. and Pucci, G., eds. 1982: *Problemi della schiavitù. Opus* 1.1.

Anderson, J. 1975: *The Political Economy of Urbanism: an Introduction and Bibliography.* London: Architectural Association.

Anderson, Perry 1974a: *Lineages of the Absolutist State.* London: New Left; New York: distr. Schocken.

—— 1974b: *Passages from Antiquity to Feudalism.* London: New Left; New York: distr. Schocken.

—— 1976: *Considerations on Western Marxism.* London: New Left; New York: distr. Schocken.

—— 1976–7: The Antinomies of Antonio Gramsci. *New Left Review* 100.

—— 1980: *Arguments Within English Marxism.* London: Verso Editions New Left; New York: distr. Schocken.

Andreski, S., ed. 1974: *The Essential Comte.* London: Croom Helm; New York: Barnes & Noble.

Anuchin, V. 1977: *Theoretical Problems of Geography.* Columbus OH: Ohio State University Press.

Anweiler, Oskar 1958 (1974): *The Soviets: The Russian Workers, Peasants and Soldiers Councils.* New York: Pantheon.

Apple, M.W. 1979: *Ideology and Curriculum.* London: Routledge & Kegan Paul.

Apter, David and Joll, James, eds. 1971: *Anarchism Today.* London: Macmillan; Garden City, N.Y.: Doubleday.

Arato, Andrew 1972: Lukács's Theory of Reification. *Telos* 11.

—— 1973–74: Re-examining the Second International. *Telos* 18.

Arato, Andrew and Breines, Paul 1979: *The Young Lukács and the Origins of Western Marxism.* New York: Seabury; London: Pluto.

Arato, Andrew and Gebhardt, E. eds. 1978: *The Essential Frankfurt School Reader.* Oxford: Basil Blackwell.

Archetti, Eduardo P. 1981: *Campesino y Estructuras Agrarias en América Latina.* Quito: CEPLAES.

Aricó, José 1980 (1983): *Marx y América Latina.* Mexico City: Alianza.

Aristotle 1954: *The Nicomachean Ethics,* ed. W.D. Ross. London: Oxford University Press.

Armstrong, Philip and Glyn, Andrew 1980: The law of the falling rate of profit and oligopoly. *Cambridge Journal of Economics* 3.1.

Arneson, Richard J. 1981: What's Wrong with Exploitation? *Ethics* 91.

Aron, Raymond 1973 (1975): *Dialectics of Violence.* Oxford: Basil Blackwell; New York: Harper & Row.

Arthur, C.J. 1986: *Dialectics of Labour: Marx and his Relation to Hegel.* Oxford: Basil Blackwell.

—— 1986: Marx and Engels: *The German Ideology.* In G. Vesey, ed. *Philosophers Ancient and Modern.* Cambridge: Cambridge University Press.

Artisikhovskii, V.A. 1973: Archaeology. *Great Soviet Encyclopedia.* Trans. of 3rd edn, vol. 2.

Arvon, Henri 1973: *Marxist Esthetics.* Ithaca and London: Cornell University Press.

Ascher, A. 1972: *Pavel Axelrod and the Development of Menshevism.* Cambridge, Mass. and London: Harvard University Press.

—— ed. 1976: *The Mensheviks in the Russian Revolution.* London: Thames & Hudson; Ithaca, N.Y.: Cornell University Press.

Ashton, Basil, Hill, Kenneth, Piazza, Alan and Zeitz, Robin 1984: Famine in China. *Population and Development Review,* 1.4.

Ashton, E. 1976: *A Social and Economic History of the Near East in the Middle Ages.* London: Collins.

Aston, T.H. and Philpin, C.H.E. eds. 1985: *The Brenner Debate.* Cambridge: Cambridge University Press.

Aumont, Jacques 1987: *Montage Eisenstein.* London: British Film Institute; Bloomington: Indiana University Press.

Avineri, S., 1968: *The Social and Political Thought of Karl Marx.* Cambridge and New York: Cambridge University Press.

—— ed. 1968: *Karl Marx on Colonialism and Modernization: his despatches and other writings on China, India, Mexico, the Middle East and North Africa.* Garden City, New York: Doubleday Anchor.

—— 1972: *Hegel's Theory of the Modern State.* Cambridge University Press.

Ayer, A.J. 1936 (1946): *Language, Truth and Logic.* London: Gollancz; New York: Dover.

Bagchi, A.K. 1982: *The Political Economy of Underdevelopment.* Cambridge: Cambridge University Press.

Bahro, Rudolf 1978: *The Alternative in Eastern Europe.* (Trans. of *Die Alternative.* Frankfurt: Europäische Verlagsantalt, 1977.) London: New Left; New York: distr. Schocken.

—— 1980: *Elemente einer neuen Politik zum Verhaltnis von Ökologie und Sozialismus.* Berlin: Olle & Wolter.

Bailey, Anne M. and Llobera, Josep R. 1981: *The Asiatic Mode of Production.* London: Routledge & Kegan Paul.

Bailey, F.G. 1963: *Politics and Social Change: Orissa in 1959.* Berkeley and Los Angeles: University of California Press.

Balibar, Étienne 1970: The Basic Concepts of Historical Materialism. In Althusser and Balibar, *Reading 'Capital'*.

—— 1977: *On the Dictatorship of the Proletariat*. London: New Left; New York: distr. Schocken.

Ball, M. 1977: Differential Rent and the Role of Landed Property. *International Journal of Urban and Regional Research* 48.

—— 1980: On Marx's Theory of Agricultural Rent: a reply to Ben Fine. *Economy and Society* 9.3.

Ball, T. 1979: Marx and Darwin: A Reconsideration. *Political Theory* 7.

Banaji, J. 1977: Modes of Production in a Materialist Conception of History. *Capital and Class* No. 2.

Banks, Olive 1981: *Faces of Feminism*. Oxford: Martin Robertson; New York: St Martins.

Baran, Paul 1957: *The Political Economy of Growth*. New York: Monthly Review Press; London: Penguin (1973).

Baran, Paul and Sweezy, Paul 1966: *Monopoly Capitalism*. New York: Monthly Review Press; London: Penguin.

Barnet, Richard J. and Müller, Ronald E. 1974: *Global Reach: the power of the multinational corporations*. New York: Simon & Schuster, London: Cape (1975).

Baron, S.H. 1962: Between Marx and Lenin: George Plekhanov. In L. Labedz, ed., *Revisionism*.

—— 1963: *Plekhanov: The Father of Russian Marxism*. London: Routledge & Kegan Paul; Stanford, Calif.: Stanford University Press.

Barone 1908 (*1935*): Il Ministerio della Produzione nella Stato Collectivista (Ministry of Production in a Collectivist State). In English in F.A. von Hayek, ed. 1935: *Collectivist Economic Planning*. London.

Barratt-Brown, M. 1974: *The Economics of Imperialism*. London: Penguin.

Barrett, Michèle 1988: *Women's Oppression Today*, 2nd edn. London: Verso.

Barrett, M. and McIntosh, M. 1980: The Family Wage, *Capital and Class* No. 11.

—— 1991: *The Anti-social Family*. London: Verso.

Barrett, Michèle *et al.*, eds. 1979: *Ideology and Cultural Production*. London: Croom Helm; New York: St Martin's.

Barth, Hans 1945: *Wahrheit und Ideologie*. Zurich: Manesse Verlag.

Bartra, Roger 1974: *Estructura Agraria y Clases Sociales en Mexico*. Mexico: Ediciones Era.

Barun De, *et al.* eds. 1976: *Essays in Honour of Professor S. C. Sarkar*. New Delhi: People's Publishing House.

Basso, Lelio 1969 (*1975*): *Rosa Luxemburg*. London: André Deutsch; New York: Praeger.

Bauer, Bruno 1843a: Die Fähigkeit der heutigen Juden und Christen frei zu werden. In Herwegh, G (Hrg) *Einundzwanzig Bogen aus der Schweiz*. Zurich

and Winterhur: Verlag des Literarischen comptoirs.

—— 1843b: *Die Judenfrage*. Braunschweig: Verlag Friedrich Otto.

Bauer, Otto 1907 (*1924*): *Die Nationalitätenfrage und die Sozialdemokratie*. Vienna: Wiener Volksbuchhandlung, 2nd enlarged edn with new preface, 1924.

—— 1909–10: Review of *Finance Capital. Der Kampf* 3, 391–7.

—— 1919: *Der Weg zum Sozialismus*. Vienna: Wiener Volksbuchhandlung.

—— 1920: *Bolschewismus oder Sozialdemokratie?* Vienna: Wiener Volksbuchhandlung.

—— 1923 (*1970*): *Die Österreichische Revolution*. Vienna: Wiener Volksbuchhandlung. Abridged Eng. version 1925, *The Austrian Revolution* trans. H.J. Stenning. London: L. Parsons; New York: Burt Franklin.

—— 1927: *Was ist Austro-Marxismus?* Arbeiter-Zeitung (Vienna), 3 November. Eng. trans. in Bottomore and Goode, eds., *Austro-Marxism*.

—— 1931: *Kapitalismus und Sozialismus nach dem Weltkrieg*. Vol. I. *Rationalisierung oder Fehlrationalisierung*. Vienna: Wiener Volksbuchhandlung.

—— 1936: *Der Faschismus*. In *Zwischen zwei Weltkriegen? Die Krise der Weltwirtschaft, der Demokratie und des Sozialismus*. Bratislava: Eugen Prager Verlag. The essay on fascism partly trans. in Bottomore and Goode, *Austro-Marxism*.

—— 1961: *Eine Auswahl aus seinem Lebenswerk*. Vienna: Wiener Volksbuchhandlung.

—— 1968: *Otto Bauer et la révolution*, ed. Yvon Bourdet. Paris: Études et Documentation Internationales.

Baxandall, Lee 1968: *Marxism and Aesthetics: A Selective Annotated Bibliography*. New York: Humanities.

—— ed. 1972: *Radical Perspectives in the Arts*. London: Penguin.

Bazin, André 1967, 1971: *What is Cinema?* (2 vols) Berkeley: University of California Press.

Bebel, August 1879 (*1886*): *Woman and Socialism*. New York: H.W. Lovell.

Beckford, L.G. 1972: *Resistant Poverty: Underdevelopment in Plantation Economies of the Third World*. New York: Oxford University Press.

Beecher, J. and Bienvenu, R. eds. 1972: *The Utopian Vision of Charles Fourier*. London: Cape; Boston: Beacon.

Beechey, V. 1977: Some Notes on Female Wage Labour in Capitalist Production. *Capital and Class* No. 3.

Beetham, David 1981: Michels and his critics. *European Journal of Sociology* 32.1.

—— ed. 1984: *Marxists in face of Fascism*. Manchester: Manchester University Press.

Beidelman, Thomas O. ed. 1971: *The Translation of Culture: Essays in Honor of E.E. Evans Pritchard*.

London: Tavistock; Totowa, N.J.; Barnes & Noble.

Benería, Lourdes ed. 1985: *Women and Development: The Sexual Divison of Labour in Rural Societies.* New York: Praeger.

Benjamin, Walter 1968 *(1973)*: *Illuminations* (with an introduction by Hannah Arendt). New York: Harcourt, Brace & World; London: Collins/ Fontana (1973).

—— 1972: *Gesammelte Schriften.* Frankfurt: Suhrkamp.

—— 1977: *Origin of German Tragic Drama.* Frankfurt: Suhrkamp.

—— 1977: *Understanding Brecht.* Frankfurt: Suhrkamp.

—— 1979: *One-Way Street and Other Writings.* London: New Left.

Bennett, Tony 1979: *Formalism and Marxism.* London & New York: Methuen.

Bentley, Eric 1981: *The Brecht Commentaries 1943–1980.* New York: Grove; London: Methuen.

Benton, T. 1977: *Philosophical Foundations of the Three Sociologies.* London and Boston: Routledge & Kegan Paul.

Berdyaev, N.A. 1937: *The Origin of Russian Communism.* London: Bles; New York: Scribner.

Berg, M., ed. 1979: *Technology and Toil in Nineteenth-Century Britain.* London: CSE Books.

Bergmann, Theodor and Schäfer, Gert eds, 1989: *'Liebling der Partei': Nikolai Bucharin.* Papers from international Bukharin symposium, Wuppertal, 1988. Hamburg: VSA-Verlag.

Berle, A.A. and Means, G.C. 1932: *The Modern Corporation and Private Property.* New York: Macmillan.

Berlin, Isaiah 1969: *Four Essays on Liberty.* London and New York: Oxford University Press.

—— 1979: Georges Sorel. In *Against the Current: Essays in the History of Ideas.* pp. 296–332. London: Hogarth; New York: Viking Press (1980).

Berlinguer, Enrico 1982: *After Poland: Towards a New Internationalism.* Nottingham: Spokesman.

Bernal, J.D. 1939 (1967): *The Social Function of Science.* Cambridge, Mass. and London: MIT Press.

—— 1954 (1969): *Science in History,* London: Watts.

Bernstein, Eduard 1891a (1969): *Ferdinand Lassalle as a Social Reformer.* London: S. Sonnenschein; New York: C. Scribner. Repr.: New York & London: Greenwood.

—— 1891b: *Gesellschaftlichen und Privateigentum.* Berlin: Vorwärts.

—— 1895 (1980): *Cromwell and Communism. Socialism and Democracy in the Great English Revolution.* Nottingham: Spokesman.

—— 1899 (1961): *Die Voraussetzungen des Sozialismus und die Aufgaben der Sozialdemokratie.*

Stuttgart: Dietz. (Eng. trans., with omissions, *Evolutionary Socialism* 1909. London: I.L.P.; New York: Huebsch. Reprinted 1961 New York: Schocken.)

Bernstein, Henry 1979: African Peasantries: A Theoretical Framework. *Journal of Peasant Studies* 6.4.

Bernstein, Richard 1971: *Praxis and Action: Contemporary Philosophies of Human Activity.* Philadelphia: University of Pennsylvania Press.

Bernstein, R.J. 1985: *Habermas and Modernity.* Cambridge: Polity.

Bernstein, Samuel 1970 (1971): *Auguste Blanqui and the Art of Insurrection.* London: Lawrence & Wishart; Brooklyn Heights, N.Y.: Beckman.

Besemeres, John F. 1980: *Socialist Population Policies: The Political Implications of Demographic Trends in the USSR and Eastern Europe.* White Plains, N.Y.: M.E. Sharpe.

Best, Michael and Connolly, William 1976: *The Politicized Economy.* Lexington, Mass.: D.C. Heath.

Béteille, André 1965: *Caste, Class and Power: Changing Patterns of Stratification in a Tanjore Village.* Berkeley and Los Angeles: University of California Press.

Bettelheim, C. 1948: National Income, Saving and Investment in Keynes and Marx. *Revue d'économie politique.*

—— 1968: *India Independent.* New York: Monthly Review Press.

—— 1972: Theoretical Comments. In A. Emmanuel ed., *Unequal Exchange.*

—— 1974, 1976 (1978): *Class Struggles in the USSR.* Vols. I & II. New York: Monthly Review Press.

Bhaduri, Amit 1983: *The Economics of Backward Agriculture.* London: Academic.

Bhaskar, Roy 1978: *A Realist Theory of Science.* Brighton: Harvester; Atlantic Highlands, N.J.: Humanities.

—— 1979: *The Possibility of Naturalism.* Brighton: Harvester; Atlantic Highlands, N.J.: Humanities.

—— 1986: *Scientific Realism and Human Emancipation.* London: Verso.

Billig, M. 1982: *Ideology and Social Psychology.* Oxford: Basil Blackwell; New York: St Martin's.

Bisztray, George 1978: *Marxist Models of Literary Realism.* New York: Columbia University Press.

Black, C.E. and Thornton, T.P. 1964: *Communism and Revolution. The Strategic Uses of Political Violence.* Princeton: Princeton University Press.

Blackburn, Robin ed. 1972: *Ideology in Social Science.* London: Fontana; New York: Pantheon.

—— ed. 1978: *Revolution and Class Struggle: A Reader in Marxist Politics.* Brighton: Harvester; Atlantic Highlands, N.J.: Humanities.

Blackstock, P.W. and Hoselitz, B.F., eds. 1952: *Marx and Engels: The Russian Menace to Europe.* Glencoe, Illinois: Free Press; London: Allen & Unwin (1953).

Blakely, T. 1961: *Soviet Scholasticism*. Dordrecht: Reidel.

Blanqui, Louis-Auguste 1977: *Oeuvres Complètes*, vol. 1, *Écrits sur la révolution*. Paris: Galilée.

Blaug, Mark 1958: *Ricardian Economics*. New Haven: Yale University Press.

Bleaney, M. 1976: *Underconsumption Theories: A History and Critical Analysis*. London: Lawrence & Wishart; New York: International Publisher.

Bleicher, J. 1980: *Contemporary Hermeneutics*. London and Boston: Routledge & Kegan Paul.

Bloch, Ernst 1918 (*1971*): *Geist der Utopie*. Frankfurt am Main: Suhrkamp.

—— 1921 (*1969*): *Thomas Münzer als Theologe der Revolution*. Frankfurt am Main: Suhrkamp.

—— 1954–9 (*1969*): *Das Prinzip Hoffnung*. Frankfurt am Main: Suhrkamp.

—— 1967: *Gesamtausgabe*. 16 vols. Frankfurt am Main: Suhrkamp.

—— 1971: *On Karl Marx*. New York: Herder & Herder.

Bloch, Ernst et al. 1977: *Aesthetics and Politics*. London: New Left Books; New York: distr. Schocken.

Bloch, Marc (*1961*): *Feudal Society*. London: Routledge & Kegan Paul; Chicago: University of Chicago Press.

—— 1975: *Slavery and Serfdom in the Middle Ages*. Berkeley and London: University of California Press.

Bloch, Maurice 1975: *Marxist Analyses and Social Anthropology*. London: Malaby; New York: Wiley.

Blomström, Magnus and Hettne, Björn 1984: *Development Theory in Transition. The Dependency Debate and Beyond: Third World Responses*. London: Zed.

Bloom, S.F. 1941: *The World of Nations: a Study of the National Implications of the World of Karl Marx*. New York: Columbia University Press.

Bloomfield, J., ed. 1977: *Papers on Class, Hegemony and Party*. London: Lawrence & Wishart.

Blumenberg, Werner 1960: *Karl Kautskys literarisches Werk. Eine bibliographische Übersicht*. The Hague: Mouton.

Boccara, Paul, ed. 1969 (*1976*): *Le Capitalisme monopoliste d'État*. 2nd edn. Paris: Éditions sociales.

Bocheński, I.M. 1950: *Der sowjetrussische dialektische Materialismus*. Berne-Munich: A. Francke.

Boff, L. 1985: *Church, Charism and Power*. London: SCM.

Boff, L. and Boff, C. 1987: *Introducing Liberation Theology*. Tunbridge Wells: Burns & Oates.

Böhm-Bawerk, Eugen von 1896 (*1949*): *Karl Marx and the Close of his System*, ed. Paul M. Sweezy. New York: Augustus M. Kelley; London: Merlin (1975).

Bois, G. 1976: *Crise du Féodalisme*. Paris: Éditions d'études en science sociales.

Bonger, Willem A. 1905 (*1916*): *Criminality and Economic Conditions*. Boston: Little Brown.

Bonino, J. 1983: *Towards a Christian Political Ethics*. London: SCM.

Bonnassie, Pierre (forthcoming): *From Slavery to Feudalism*.

Bornstein, Stephen et al. 1982: *The State in Capitalist Europe*. London: Allen & Unwin.

Bortkiewicz, L. von 1907 (*1949*): Zur Berichtigung der grundlegenden theoretischen Konstruktion von Marx im dritten Band des 'Kapitals'. Trans. in Sweezy, ed. 1949.

—— 1952: Value and Price in the Marxian System. *International Economic Papers*.

Bottomore, Tom 1966: *Elites and Society*. London & New York: Penguin.

—— 1973 (*1979*): *Karl Marx*. Oxford: Basil Blackwell; Englewood Cliffs, N.J.: Prentice Hall.

—— 1975: *Marxist Sociology*. London: Macmillan; New York: Holmes & Meier.

—— ed. 1988: *Interpretations of Marx*. Oxford: Basil Blackwell.

—— 1990: *The Socialist Economy: Theory and Practice*. Hemel Hempstead: Harvester and Wheatsheaf.

—— 1991: *Classes in Modern Society*. 2nd edn. London: Unwin Hyman.

Bottomore, Tom and Brym, Robert J. eds. 1989: *The Capitalist Class: An International Study*. Hemel Hempstead: Harvester Wheatsheaf.

Bottomore, Thomas B. and Goode, Patrick, eds. 1978: *Austro-Marxism*. Oxford and New York: Oxford University Press.

Bourdet, Yvon 1967: Introduction. In Max Adler, *Democratie et conseils ouvriers*. Paris: François Maspero.

Bourdieu, Pierre 1979: *La Distinction*. Paris: Minuit.

—— and Passeron, Jean-Claude 1970 (*1977*): *Reproduction in Education, Society and Culture*. London and Beverley Hills: Sage.

Bourguina, Anna 1968: *Russian Social Democracy: The Menshevik Movement: a Bibliography*. Stanford: Hoover Institution.

Bowles, S. 1981: Technical Change and the Profit Rate. *Cambridge Journal of Economics* 5.2.

Bowles, S. and Gintis, H. 1976: *Schooling in Capitalist America*. London: Routledge & Kegan Paul; New York: Basic Books.

—— 1990: Contested Exchange: New Micro-foundations for the Political Economy of Capitalism. *Politics and Society* 18.2.

Boyer, Robert 1986: *La théorie de la régulation: une analyse critique*. Paris: La Découverte. English trans., New York: Columbia University Press (1989).

Bradley, I. and Howard M., eds. 1982: *Classical and Marxian Political Economy*. London: Macmillan; New York: St Martin's.

Brady, Thomas A. 1978: *Ruling Class, Regime and Reformation in Strasbourg, 1520–1555*. Leiden: Brill.

Brass, Tom 1986: Unfree Labour and Capitalist Restructuring in the Agrarian Sector: Peru and India. *Journal of Peasant Studies* 14.

Braunthal, Julius 1961–71 (1966–80): *History of the Internationals*. Vols. 1–2 London: Nelson; New York: Praeger. Vol. 3 London: Gollancz; Boulder, Colo.: Westview Press.

—— 1961: *Otto Bauer: Eine Auswahl aus seinem Lebenswerk*. Vienna: Wiener Volksbuchhandlung.

Braverman, Harry 1974: *Labor and Monopoly Capital: The Degradation of Work in the Twentieth Century*. New York: Monthly Review Press.

Brecher, J. 1972: *STRIKE!* San Francisco: Straight Arrow.

Brecht, Bertolt 1961: *Plays*. Ed. Eric Bentley. New York: Grove; London: Methuen.

—— 1964: *Brecht on Theater*. Ed. John Willett. New York: Hill & Wang.

—— 1971: *Collected Plays*. Ed. Ralph Mannheim and John Willett. New York: Random House, Vintage; London: Methuen.

—— 1976: *Poems 1913–1956*. Ed. John Willett and Ralph Mannheim. New York: Random House, Vintage; London: Methuen.

Breines, Paul, ed. 1970: *Critical Interruptions: New Left Perspectives on Herbert Marcuse*. New York: Herder & Herder.

Brenkert, George G. 1983: *Marx's Ethics of Freedom*. London: Routledge & Kegan Paul.

Brenner, Robert 1976: Agrarian Class Structure and Economic Development in Preindustrial Europe. *Past and Present* 70.

—— 1977: The Origins of Capitalist Development: A Critique of Neo-Smithian Marxism. *New Left Review* 104 (July–Aug).

Breugel, Irene 1979: Women as a Reserve Army of Labour. *Feminist Review* 3.

Brewer, Anthony 1980: *Marxist Theories of Imperialism: A Critical Survey*. London and Boston: Routledge & Kegan Paul.

Bricianer, Serge 1978: *Pannekoek and the Workers' Councils*. St Louis, Missouri: Telos.

Broue, Pierre 1988: *Trotski*. Paris: Fayard.

Brovkin, Vladimir N. 1987: *The Mensheviks after October: Socialist Opposition and the Rise of the Bolshevik Dictatorship*. Ithaca: Cornell University Press.

Brown, G. 1977: *Sabotage*. Nottingham: Spokesman.

Brown, L.B., ed. 1981: *Psychology in Contemporary China*. Oxford and New York: Pergamon.

Brus, Wlodzimierz 1961 (1972): *The Market in a Socialist Economy*, London and Boston: Routledge & Kegan Paul.

—— 1973: *The Economics and Politics of Socialism*. London and Boston: Routledge & Kegan Paul.

—— 1975: *Socialist Ownership and Political Systems*. London and Boston: Routledge & Kegan Paul.

—— 1979: East European Economic Reforms: What Happened to Them? *Soviet Studies* 31.2.

Brus, Wlodzimierz and Laski, Kazimierz 1989: *From Marx to the Market: Socialism in Search of an Economic System*. Oxford: Clarendon.

Buchanan, Allen E. 1982: *Marx and Justice: The Radical Critique of Liberalism*. London: Methuen; Totowa, NJ: Rowman & Littlefield.

—— 1985: *Ethics, Efficiency, and the Market*. Oxford: Clarendon.

Buci-Glucksmann, C. 1979: *Gramsci and the State*. London: Lawrence & Wishart.

Buck-Morss, Susan 1977: *The Origin of Negative Dialectics*. Brighton: Harvester; New York: Free Press.

Buhle, Paul 1987: *Marxism in the USA*. London: Verso.

Bukharin, Nikolai I. 1917–18 (1972): *Imperialism and World Economy*. London: Merlin; New York: Monthly Review Press (1973).

—— 1919 (1927): *Economic Theory of the Leisure Class*. London: Martin Lawrence; New York: International Publishers.

—— 1920 (1971): *Economics of the Transformation Period*. New York: Bergman.

—— 1921 (1925): *Historical Materialism: A System of Sociology*. New York: International Publishers; London: Allen & Unwin (1926). (New edn 1969 Ann Arbor: University of Michigan Press.)

—— (1972): Imperialism and the accumulation of capital. In Luxemburg and Bukharin, *Imperialism*.

Bukharin, N.I. 1982: *Selected Writings on the State and the Transition to Socialism*, ed. Richard B. Day. New York: M.E. Sharpe.

Bukharin, Nikolai, with Preobrazhensky, E.A. 1919 (1969): *ABC of Communism*. London and Baltimore: Penguin.

Bukharin, Nikolai, et al. 1931 (1971): *Science at the Crossroads*. London: Frank Cass.

Bullock, Chris and Peck, David 1980: *Guide to Marxist Literary Criticism*. Bloomington: Indiana University Press.

Burkett, Paul 1983: Value and Crisis: Essays on Marxian Economics in Japan. A Review. *Review of Radical Political Economics*.

Burnham, James 1943: *The Managerial Revolution*. London: Putnam; New York: John Day.

Burns, A.F. 1969: *The Business Cycle in a Changing World*. New York: Columbia University Press.

Byres, T.J. 1986: The Agrarian Question and Differentiation of the Peasantry. In Atiur Rahman, ed. *Peasants and Classes: A Study in Differentiation in Bangladesh*. London and New Jersey: Zed.

—— 1991: The Agrarian Question and Differing Forms of Capitalist Agrarian Transition: An Essay with Reference to Asia. In J.C. Breman and S. Mundle, eds. *Rural Transformation in Asia*. Delhi: Oxford University Press.

Byres, T.J. and Mukhia, H. eds 1985: *Feudalism and Non-European Societies*. London: Frank Cass.

Cabral, Amilcar 1969: *Revolution in Guinea: An African People's Struggle*. London: Stage 1; New York: Monthly Review Press (1970).

—— 1980: *Unity and Struggle: Selected Writings*. London: Heinemann.

Cain, Maureen and Hunt, Alan, eds. 1979: *Marx and Engels on Law*. London and New York: Academic Press.

Callinicos, Alex 1976: *Althusser's Marxism*. London: Pluto.

Capogrossi, Luigi, Giardina, Andrea and Schiavone, Aldo, eds. 1978: *Analisi marxista e società antiche*. Rome: Editori Riuniti, Istituto Gramsci.

Carchedi, Guglielmo 1977: *On the Economic Identification of Social Classes*. London and Boston: Routledge & Kegan Paul.

Cardoso, F.H. and Faletto, E. 1969 (1979): *Dependency and Development in Latin America*. Berkeley: University of California Press.

Carlebach, Julius 1978: *Karl Marx and the Radical Critique of Judaism*. London and Boston: Routledge & Kegan Paul.

Carr, Edward H. 1937: *Michael Bakunin*. London: Macmillan. Repr. New York: Octagon Books (1975).

—— 1950–3 (1966): *The Bolshevik Revolution 1917–1923*. London: Penguin; New York: Macmillan.

—— 1958: *Stalin: (vol. 1 of Socialism in one Country, 1924–1926)*. London and New York: Macmillan.

Carrère d'Encausse, Hélène 1978: *L'Empire éclaté. La révolte des nations en URSS*. Paris: Flammarion.

—— and Schram, Stuart R. 1965 (1969): *Marxism and Asia*. London: Allen Lane.

Carrillo, Santiago 1977: *Eurocommunism and the State*. London: Lawrence & Wishart; Westport, Conn.: Lawrence Hill (1978).

Carsten, Francis L. 1967: *The Rise of Fascism*. London: Batsford; Berkeley: University of California Press.

Carter, Alan B. 1988: *Marx: A Radical Critique*. Hemel Hempstead: Harvester Wheatsheaf.

Carver, Terrell 1981: *Engels*. Oxford and New York: Oxford University Press.

—— 1982: The 'Guiding Threads' of Marx and Darwin. *Political Theory* 10.

—— 1983: *Marx and Engels: The Intellectual Relationship*. Brighton: Harvester.

—— 1985: Engels's Feminism. *History of Political Thought* 6.

—— ed. (forthcoming): *Cambridge Companions to Philosophy: Marx*. New York: Cambridge University Press.

Castells, M. 1972 (1977): *The Urban Question*. Lon-

don: Edward Arnold; Cambridge, Mass.: MIT.

Caudwell, Christopher 1965: *The Concept of Freedom*. London: Lawrence & Wishart.

Caute, D. 1966: *The Left in Europe since 1789*. London: Weidenfeld & Nicolson.

Centre d'Études et de recherches marxistes 1974: *Sur le Féodalisme*. Paris: Éditions Sociales.

Cerutti, Furio, Claussen, Detlev, Krahl, Hans-Jürgen, Negt, Oskar and Schmidt, Alfred 1971: *Geschichte und Klassenbewusstsein Heute*. Amsterdam: Verlag de Munter.

Chaloner, William H. and Henderson, William O., eds. 1959: *Engels as Military Critic*. Manchester: Manchester University Press; Westport, Conn.: Greenwood (1976).

Chambre, H. 1974: *L'évolution du marxisme soviétique: théorie économique et droit*. Paris: Seuil.

Chandra, Bipan 1983: *Indian Left: Critical Appraisals*. Delhi: Vikas Publishing House.

Chandra, N.K. 1988: *The Retarded Economies*. Bombay: Oxford University Press.

Chattopadhyaya, Debiprasad 1959: *Lokayata: A Study in Ancient Indian Materialism*. Delhi: People's Publishing House.

—— 1969 (1980): *Indian Atheism: A Marxist Approach*. New Delhi: People's Publishing House.

—— 1976: Social Function of Indian Idealism. In Barun De *et al.*, eds., *Essays in Honour of Professor S.C. Sarkar*.

Chesneaux, Jean *et al.* 1972 (1977): *China from the 1911 Revolution to Liberation*. Sussex: Harvester.

Chesnokov, D.I. 1969: *Historical Materialism*. Moscow.

Childe, V. Gordon 1936: *Man Makes Himself*. London: C.A. Watts; New York: Oxford University Press (1939).

—— 1942 (1954): *What Happened in History*. London: Penguin; New York: Penguin (1966).

—— 1947: *History*. London: Cobbett.

—— 1950: *Prehistoric Migrations in Europe*. London: Routledge & Kegan Paul; Cambridge, Mass.: Harvard University Press.

—— 1951: *Social Evolution*. New York: Schuman; London: Watts.

Chlebowczyk, Jozef 1980: *On Small and Young Nations in Europe: Nation-forming Processes in Ethnic Borderlands in East-Central Europe*. Wroclaw: Polish Historical Society.

Christie, Ian and Elliott, David 1988: *Eisenstein at Ninety*. Oxford: Museum of Modern Art.

Cieszkowski, A. 1838: *Prolegomena zur Historiosophie*. Berlin: Veit.

Clark, Joseph 1981: Marx and the Jews: Another View. *Dissent*.

Clarke, Dean H. 1978: Marxism, Justice and the Justice Model. *Contemporary Crises* 2, 27–62.

Clarke, J., Critcher, C. and Johnson, R. eds. 1979: *Working-Class Culture: Studies in History and*

Theory. London: Hutchinson.

Clarke, Simon 1977: Marxism, Sociology and Poulantzas's Theory of the State. *Capital and Class* 2.

—— 1980: Althusserian Marxism. In *One-Dimensional Marxism.*

Clarke, Simon and Ginsberg, N. 1976: The Political Economy of Housing. *Kapitalistate* Summer 4/5.

Clarke, Simon *et al.* 1980: *One-Dimensional Marxism.* London: Allison & Busby; New York: distr. Schocken.

Clarkson, S. 1979: *The Soviet Theory of Development.* London: Macmillan; Toronto and Buffalo: University of Toronto Press.

Claudin, Fernando 1972 (1975): *The Communist Movement: From Comintern to Cominform.* London: Penguin; New York: Monthly Review Press.

—— 1979: *Eurocommunism and Socialism.* London: New Left.

Cliff, Tony 1964: *Russia: A Marxist Analysis.* London: International Socialism.

—— 1974: *State Capitalism in Russia.* London: Pluto.

—— 1975–79: *Lenin* 4 vols. London: Pluto.

Clifton, James 1977: Competition and the Evolution of the Capitalist Mode of Production. *Cambridge Journal of Economics* 1.2.

Coakley, Jerry 1982: Finance Capital. *Capital and Class.*

Cohen, Arthur A. 1964: *The Communism of Mao Tse-Tung.* Chicago and London: University of Chicago Press.

Cohen, Gerald A. 1978: *Karl Marx's Theory of History: A Defence.* Oxford: Clarendon; Princeton: Princeton University Press.

—— 1983: Review of *Karl Marx* by Allen W. Wood. *Mind* 92.

—— 1983: The Structure of Proletarian Unfreedom. *Philosophy and Public Affairs* 12.1.

Cohen, Marshall, Nagel, Thomas and Scanlon, Thomas, eds. 1980: *Marx, Justice and History.* Princeton: Princeton University Press.

Cohen, Stephen F. 1974: *Bukharin and the Bolshevik Revolution: A Political Biography 1888–1938.* London: Wildwood House; New York: Knopf.

Cole, G.D.H. 1889–1914 (1956): *A History of Socialist Thought.* 5 vols. London: Macmillan; New York: St Martins.

—— 1913: *The World of Labour.* London: Bell. (Repr. 1973 Brighton: Harvester; New York: Barnes & Noble).

—— 1917 (1972): *Self-government in Industry.* London: Bell. (Repr. 1971: London: Hutchinson; New York: Arno.)

Coleman, Stephen 1990: *Daniel de Leon.* Manchester: Manchester University Press.

Coleman, S. and O'Sullivan, P. 1990: *William Morris and News from Nowhere.* Hartland, Devon: Green Books.

Colletti, Lucio 1968 (1972): *From Rousseau to Lenin.* London: New Left; New York: Monthly Review Press.

—— 1969 (1973): *Marxism and Hegel.* London: New Left; New York: distr. Schocken (1979).

—— 1975a: Introduction to Karl Marx, *Early Writings.* London: Penguin; New York: Vintage.

—— 1975b: Marxism and the Dialectic. *New Left Review* 93.

Collins, Henry and Abramsky, Chimen 1965: *Karl Marx and the British Labour Movement: Years of the First International.* London: Macmillan; New York: St Martin's.

Communist Party (of Great Britain) 1957: *The Report of the Commission on Inner Party Democracy,* majority and minority reports. London: Communist Party.

Concilium, 189 Special Column, 1987, pp. 1–133. Edinburgh: T. and T. Clark.

Cone, J. 1969: *Black Theology and Black Power.* New York: Seabury.

Congregation for the Doctrine of the Faith 1984: *Instruction on Certain Aspects of the Theology of Liberation.* Rome: Vatican Press.

Coontz, Sydney H. 1957: *Population Theories and the Economic Interpretation.* London: Routledge & Kegan Paul; New York: Humanities.

Cornforth, Maurice ed. 1978: *Rebels and Their Causes.* London: Lawrence & Wishart.

Corrigan, Philip, Ramsay, Harvie and Sayer, Derek 1978: *Socialist Construction and Marxist Theory: Bolshevism and Its Critique.* New York and London: Macmillan.

Cowling, K. 1982: *Monopoly Capitalism.* London: Macmillan; New York: Halsted.

Cox, Oliver Cromwell 1948 (1970): *Caste, Class and Race.* New York and London: Monthly Review Press.

Cox, Terry and Littlejohn, Gary eds. 1984: *Kritsman and the Agrarian Marxists.* London: Frank Cass.

Crook, W.H. 1931: *The General Strike.* Chapel Hill: North Carolina University Press.

Crosland, A. 1956: *The Future of Socialism.* London: Jonathan Cape; New York: Macmillan (1957).

Cueva, Agustín 1976: Problems and Perspectives of Dependency Theory. *Latin American Perspectives* 3.4.

Cummins, Ian 1980: *Marx, Engels and National Movements.* London: Croom Helm; New York: St Martin's Press.

Curtis, Bruce 1980: Capital, State and the Origins of the Working-Class Household. In Bonnie Fox, ed. *Hidden in the Household.* Toronto: Women's Press.

Cutler, A. et al. 1977: *Marx's 'Capital' and Capitalism Today.* London and Boston: Routledge & Kegan Paul.

Dalla Costa, M., ed. 1973: *The Power of Women and the Subversion of the Community*. 2nd edn. Bristol: Falling Wall.

Daniel, G. 1976: *A Hundred and Fifty Years of Archaeology*. Cambridge, Mass.: Harvard University Press; London: Duckworth.

—— ed. 1981: *Towards a History of Archaeology*. London: Thames & Hudson; New York: Norton.

Davidoff, Leonore and Hall, Catherine 1986: *Family Fortunes: Men and Women of the English Middle Class, 1780–1850*. London: Hutchinson.

Davidson, A. 1977: *Antonio Gramsci: Towards an Intellectual Biography*. London: Merlin; Atlantic Highlands, N.J.: Humanities.

Davidson, Basil 1967: *Which Way Africa? The Search for a New Society*. Revised edn. London and Baltimore: Penguin.

Davies, R.W. 1989: *Soviet History in the Gorbachev Revolution*. London: Macmillan.

Davis, Horace Bancroft 1967: *Nationalism and Socialism: Marxist and Labour Theories of Nationalism to 1917*. New York and London: Monthly Review Press.

Day, R.B. 1973: *Leon Trotsky and the Politics of Economic Isolation*. Cambridge and New York: Cambridge University Press.

—— 1975: Preobrazhensky and the Theory of the Transition Period. *Soviet Studies* 8, 2 April.

Dear, M. and Scott, A., eds. 1981: *Urbanization and Urban Planning in Capitalist Societies*. London and New York: Methuen.

de Beauvoir, Simone 1947 (1964): *The Ethics of Ambiguity*. New York: Citadel.

Deborin, A.M. 1923: *Ludwig Feuerbach: Personality and Weltanschauung*. (In Russian.) Moscow: 'Materialist' Publishing House.

de Brunoff, Suzanne 1973 (1976): *Marx on Money*. New York: Urizen; London: Pluto.

—— 1976 (1978): *The State, Capital and Economic Policy*. London: Pluto.

de Giovanni, B. *et al.* 1977: *Egemonia, Stato, partito in Gramsci*. Rome: Editori Riuniti.

Degras, Jane ed. 1956–65 (1971): *The Communist International 1919–1943: Documents*. 3 vols. London: Oxford University Press.

de Janvry, Alain 1981: *The Agrarian Question and Reformism in Latin America*. Baltimore and London: Johns Hopkins University Press.

de Janvry, A. and Kramer, F. 1971: The Limits of Unequal Exchange. *Review of Radical Political Economics*. 11.4.

De Leon, Daniel 1931: *Industrial Unionism: Selected Editorials by Daniel de Leon*. New York: New York Labor News.

—— 1952: *Socialist Landmarks: Four Addresses*. New York: New York Labor News.

Della Volpe, G. 1950 (1980): *Logic as a Positive Science*. London: New Left; New York: distr. Schocken.

—— 1964 (1978): *Rousseau and Marx*. London: Lawrence & Wishart; Atlantic Highlands, N.J.: Humanities.

Delphy, C. 1977: *The Main Enemy*. London: Women's Research and Resources Centre.

Demetz, Peter 1967: *Marx, Engels and the Poets: Origins of Marxist Literary Criticism*. Chicago and London: University of Chicago Press.

Desai, Meghnad 1979: *Marxian Economics*. 2nd edn. Oxford: Basil Blackwell; Totowa, N.J.: Rowman & Littlefield.

de Ste Croix, G.E.M. 1981: *The Class Struggle in the Ancient Greek World*. London: Duckworth; Ithaca, N.Y.: Cornell University Press (1982).

Deutscher, Isaac 1949 (1967): *Stalin: A Political Biography*. 2nd edn. London and New York: Oxford University Press.

—— 1950: *Soviet Trade Unions*. London: Royal Institute of International Affairs.

—— 1954: *The Prophet Armed: Trotsky, 1879–1921*. London and New York: Oxford University Press.

—— 1955 (1969): *'Heretics and Renegades', and other essays*. London: Cape; Indianapolis: Bobbs-Merrill.

—— 1959: *The Prophet Unarmed: Trotsky, 1921–1929*. London and New York: Oxford University Press.

—— 1963: *The Prophet Outcast: Trotsky, 1929–40*. London and New York: Oxford University Press.

—— 1964a (1966): *Ironies of History*. London: Oxford University Press.

—— 1964b (1971): On Internationals and Internationalism. In *Marxism in our Time*.

—— 1967: *The Unfinished Revolution*. Galaxy Books; New York: Oxford University Press.

—— 1968: *The Non-Jewish Jew*. Devon: Merlin.

—— 1972: *Marxism in our Time*. London: Cape; Berkeley, Calif.: Ramparts Press.

Devine, Pat 1988: *Democracy and Economic Planning: The Political Economy of a Self-Governing Society*. Cambridge: Polity.

Dews, P. ed. 1986: *Autonomy and Solidarity: Interviews with Jürgen Habermas*. London: Verso.

Diamond, Stanley 1972: Anthropology in Question. In *Reinventing Anthropology*, ed. Dell Hymes. New York: Pantheon.

—— ed. 1979: *Toward a Marxist Anthropology*. The Hague: Mouton.

—— 1981: *In Search of the Primitive: A Critique of Civilization*. New Brunswick, N.J.: Transaction.

—— 1983: *Dahomey: Transition and Conflict in State Formation*. South Hadley, Mass.: J.E. Bergin.

Dickinson, 1933: Price Formation in a Socialist Community. *Economic Journal*, June.

Dietzgen, Josef 1906: *Philosophical Essays*. Chicago: Charles Kerr.

—— 1906: *The Positive Outcome of Philosophy*. Chicago: Charles Kerr.

Dirlik, Arif 1978: *Revolution and History: The Origins of Marxist Historiography in China 1919–1937*. Berkeley and London: University of California Press.

Djilas, M. 1957: *The New Class*. London: Thames & Hudson; New York: Praeger.

Dmitriev, V.K. 1964 (*1974*): *Economic Essays on Value Competition and Utility*. Cambridge and New York: Cambridge University Press.

Dobb, M.H. 1925: *Capitalist Enterprise and Social Progress*. London: Routledge & Kegan Paul; Westport, Conn.: Hyperion (1980).

—— 1928: *Wages*. Cambridge: Cambridge University Press. (Revised edn 1946 Cambridge: Cambridge University Press; New York: Pitman.)

—— 1937: *Political Economy and Capitalism*. London: Routledge & Kegan Paul; Westport, Conn.: Greenwood (1972).

—— 1946 (*1963*): *Studies in the Development of Capitalism*. London: Routledge & Kegan Paul; New York: International Publishers.

—— 1955: *On Economic Theory and Socialism*. London: Routledge & Kegan Paul.

—— 1960: *An Essay on Economic Growth and Planning*. London: Routledge & Kegan Paul.

—— 1969: *Welfare Economics and the Economics of Socialism*. London: Cambridge University Press.

—— 1970: *Socialist Planning: Some Problems*. London: Lawrence & Wishart.

—— 1973: *Theories of Value and Distribution since Adam Smith*. Cambridge and New York: Cambridge University Press.

—— 1974: Some Historical Reflections on Planning and the Market. In C. Abramsky, ed. *Essays in Honour of E.H. Carr*. London: Macmillan.

Dockès, Pierre 1979: *La Libération médiévale*. Paris: Flammarion. (Trans. as: *Medieval slavery and liberation*. London: Methuen; Chicago: University of Chicago Press (1982).)

Documents of the First International, vols. 1–5. 1963–68: London: Lawrence & Wishart.

Documents of the Fourth International: The Formative Years (1933–1940) 1973: New York: Pathfinder.

Dolgoff, Sam, ed. 1971: *Bakunin on Anarchy*. New York: Vintage.

Domhoff, G. William 1967: *Who Rules America?* Englewood Cliffs, N.J.: Prentice Hall.

Dommanget, Maurice 1957: *Les idées politiques et sociales d'Auguste Blanqui*. Paris: Rivière.

Dore, Elizabeth and Weeks, John 1977: Class Alliances and Class Struggle in Peru. *Latin American Perspectives* 4.3.

—— 1979a: International Exchange and the Causes of Backwardness. *Latin American Perspectives* 4.2.

—— 1979b: International Exchange and the Causes of Backwardness. *Latin American Perspectives* 6.2.

Dorfman, Joseph 1935: *Thorstein Veblen and his America*. New York: Viking. (Revised eds publ. Augustus M. Kelley.)

Dos Santos, T. 1970: The Structure of Dependency. *American Economic Review* 60.21.

Draper, Hal 1962: Marx and the Dictatorship of the Proletariat. *Cahiers de l'Institut de Science Économique Appliquée* 129.

—— 1977 (*1986*): *Karl Marx's Theory of Revolution*. 3 vols. New York and London: Monthly Review Press.

Droz, J., ed. 1972: *Histoire générale du socialisme*. Paris: Presses Universitaires de France.

Drucker, P. 1976: *The Unseen Revolution. How Pension Fund Socialism Came to America*. New York: Harper & Row.

Dubiel, Helmut 1978: *Wissenschaftsorganisation und politische Erfahrung*. Frankfurt: Suhrkamp.

Dubofsky, M. 1969: *We Shall be All: A History of The IWW*. Chicago: Quadrangle.

Duby, Georges 1973 (*1974*): *The Early Growth of the European Economy: Warriors and Peasants*. London: Weidenfeld & Nicolson; Ithaca, N.Y.: Cornell University Press.

—— 1986: *The Three Orders: Feudal Society Imagined*. London and Chicago: University of Chicago Press.

Dumenil, G. 1980: *De la valeur aux prix de production*. Paris: Economica.

Dumont, Louis 1967 (*1970*): *Homo Hierarchicus: The Caste System and its Implications*. London: Weidenfeld & Nicolson; Chicago: University of Chicago Press.

Dunayevskaya, Raya 1964: *Marxism and Freedom from 1776 until Today*. 2nd edn. New York: Twayne.

Duncan, C. 1983: Under the Cloud of Capital: History versus Theory. *Science and Society* 47.3.

Dunn, John 1970 (*1989*): *Modern Revolutions: An Introduction to the Analysis of a Political Phenomenon*. Cambridge: Cambridge University Press.

Dupriez, Léon 1947: *Des mouvements économiques généraux*. 2 vols. Louvain.

Durkheim, Émile 1912 (*1915*): *The Elementary Forms of the Religious Life*. London: Allen & Unwin; New York: Macmillan.

Dutt, R. Palme 1940: *India Today*. London: Gollancz.

—— 1964: *The Internationale*. London: Lawrence & Wishart.

Duveau, Georges 1961: *Sociologie de l'Utopie et autres essais*. Paris: Presses Universitaires de France.

Eagleton, Terry 1976a: *Criticism and Ideology: A Study in Marxist Literary Theory*. London: New Left; Atlantic Highlands, N.J.: Humanities.

—— 1976b: *Marxism and Literary Criticism*. London: Methuen; Berkeley: University of California Press.

—— 1981: *Walter Benjamin or, Towards a Revolutionary Criticism*. London: New Left; New York: distr. Schocken.

Eagleton, Terry, ed. 1989: *Raymond Williams: Critical Perspectives*. Cambridge: Polity.

Edel, M. 1976: Marx's Theory of Rent: Urban Applications. *Kapitalistate* Summer 4/5.

Edholm, F., Harris, O. and Young, K. 1977: Conceptualising Women. *Critique of Anthropology* 9/10.

Edwards, Stewart, ed. 1969: *Selected Writings of Pierre-Joseph Proudhon*. London: Macmillan; Garden City, N.Y.: Anchor.

Eisenstein, Sergei 1942: *The Film Sense*. New York: Harcourt Brace Jovanovich; London: Faber (1943).

—— 1949: *Film Form: Essays in Film Theory*. New York: Harcourt Brace Jovanovich; London: Dennis Dobson (1951).

—— 1968: *Film Essays and a Lecture*. London: Dobson; New York: Praeger (1970).

—— 1970: *Notes of a Film Director*. New York: Dover.

—— 1985: *Immoral Memories: An Autobiography*. Boston: Hughton Mifflin; London: Peter Owen.

—— 1987: *Nonindifferent Nature*, trans. Herbert Marshall. Cambridge: Cambridge University Press.

—— 1988: *Selected Works, I: Writings, 1922–34*, ed. Richard Taylor, London: British Film Institute; Bloomington: Indiana University Press.

—— 1991: *Selected Works, 2: Towards a Theory of Montage*, ed. Michael Glenny and Richard Taylor. London: British Film Institute; Bloomington: Indiana University Press.

Eisenstein, Zillah ed. 1979: *Capitalist Patriarchy and the Case for Socialist Feminism*. New York: Monthly Review Press.

Elger, Tony 1979: Valorization and 'Deskilling': A Critique of Braverman. *Capital and Class* 7.

Elliott, C.F. 1967: Quis Custodiet Sacra? Problems of Marxist Revisionism. *Journal of the History of Ideas* 28.

Elliot, Gregory 1987: *Althusser: The Detour of Theory*. New York and London: Verso.

Elliott, John E. 1981: *Marx and Engels on Economics, Politics and Society*. Santa Monica: Goodyear.

Ellis, John, ed. 1977: *Screen Reader I: Cinema/Ideology/Politics*. London: Society for Education in Film and Television.

Ellis, J. and Davies, R.W. 1951: The Crisis in Soviet Linguistics. *Soviet Studies* II.

Ellis, M.H. 1987: *Towards a Jewish Theology of Liberation*. New York, Maryknoll: Orbis.

Ellman, M. 1989: *Socialist Planning*. Cambridge: Cambridge University Press.

Elson, Diane, ed. 1979: *Value: The Representation of Labour in Capitalism: Essays*. London: CSE Books; Atlantic Highlands, N.J.: Humanities.

Elster, Jon 1985: *Making Sense of Marx*. Cambridge: Cambridge University Press.

Emmanuel, Arghiri 1969 (1972): *Unequal Exchange: A Study of the Imperialism of Trade*. London: New Left; New York: Monthly Review Press.

Ennew, Judith, Hirst, Paul and Tribe, Keith 1977: 'Peasantry' as an Economic Category. *Journal of Peasant Studies* 4.4.

Enteen, George M. 1978: *The Soviet Scholar-Bureaucrat. M.N. Pokrovski and the Society of Marxist Historians*. University Park: Pennsylvania State Press.

Erard, Z. and Zygier, G.M. 1978: *La Pologne: une société en dissidence*. Paris: Maspero.

Erlich, Alexander 1960: *The Soviet Industrialization Debate 1924–1928*. Cambridge, Mass.: Harvard University Press; London: Oxford University Press.

Ettinger, Elzbieta 1987: *Rosa Luxemburg: A Life*. London: Harrap.

Evans, Michael 1975: *Karl Marx*. London: Allen & Unwin; Bloomington: Indiana University Press.

Evans, P., Rueschmeyer, D. and Skocpol, T. eds. 1985: *Bringing the State Back In*. Cambridge: Cambridge University Press.

Ewen, Frederic 1967: *Bertolt Brecht*. New York: Citadel; London: Calder & Boyars (1970).

Fabian Society 1986: *Market Socialism: Whose Choice? A Debate*. Fabian Society Pamphlet 516, London.

Fanon, Frantz 1961 (1967): *The Wretched of the Earth*. Harmondsworth: Penguin.

Farr, James 1987: Marx and Positivism. In T. Ball and J. Farr, eds. *After Marx*. Cambridge: Cambridge University Press.

Faulkner, Peter 1980: *Against the Age: An Introduction to William Morris*. London: Allen & Unwin.

Favory, F. 1981: Validité des concepts marxistes pour une théorie des sociétés de l'Antiquité: le modèle impérial romain. *Klio* 63.

Fee, T. 1976: Domestic Labour: An Analysis of Housework and its Relation to the Production Process. *Review of Radical Political Economy* 8.2.

Feher, F., Heller, A. and Markus, G. 1983: *Dictatorship over Needs*. Oxford: Basil Blackwell; New York: St Martin's.

Femia, Joseph V. 1981: *Gramsci's Political Thought: Hegemony, Consciousness and the Revolutionary Process*. Oxford and New York: Oxford University Press.

Ferge, Zsuzsa 1979: *A Society in the Making*. London: Penguin; White Plains, N.Y.: M.E. Sharpe.

Festschrift für Carl Grünberg zum 70. Geburtstag 1932. Leipzig: C.L. Hirschfeld.

Fetscher, Iring 1967 (1970): Karl Marx and Marxism. New York.

—— 1982: Fortschrittsglaube und Ökologie im Denken von Marx und Engels. In *Vom Wohlfahrtsstaat zur neuen Lebensqualität*. Cologne.

Feuerbach, Ludwig 1841 (1957): *The Essence of*

Christianity. Translated by Marian Evans (George Eliot). Reprinted New York: Harper & Row.

—— 1843 *(1966): Principles of the Philosophy of the Future.* Translated and with an introduction by Manfred H. Vogel. Indianapolis: Bobbs Merrill.

—— 1851a *(1873): The Essence of Religion.* Translated by Alexander Loos. New York: A.K. Butts.

—— 1851b *(1967): Lectures on the Essence of Religion.* Translated by Ralph Manheim. New York: Harper & Row.

—— 1967: *The Essence of Faith according to Luther.* Translated by Melvin Cherno. New York: Harper & Row.

Filtzer, Donald A. 1978: Preobrazhensky and the Problem of Soviet Transition. *Critique* 9. Spring/Summer.

Fine, Ben 1975: *Marx's 'Capital'.* London: Macmillan; Atlantic Highlands, N.J.: Humanities.

—— 1979: On Marx's Theory of Agricultural Rent. *Economy and Society* 8.3.

—— 1980a: *Economic Theory and Ideology.* London: Edward Arnold; New York: Holmes & Meier.

—— 1980b: On Marx's Theory of Agricultural Rent: A Rejoinder. *Economy and Society* 9.3.

—— 1982: *Theories of the Capitalist Economy.* London: Edward Arnold; New York: Holmes & Meier.

Fine, Ben and Harris, Laurence 1976: Controversial Issues in Marxist Economic Theory. In Miliband and Saville, eds, *Socialist Register.*

—— 1979: *Rereading 'Capital'.* London: Macmillan; New York: Columbia University Press.

Finley, Moses 1973: *The Ancient Economy.* London: Chatto & Windus; Berkeley: University of California Press.

—— 1980: *Ancient Slavery and Modern Ideology.* London: Chatto & Windus; New York: Viking.

Fiori, Giuseppe 1965 (1970): *Antonio Gramsci: Life of a Revolutionary.* London: New Left; New York: Dutton (1971).

Firestone, Shulamith 1970: *The Dialectic of Sex.* New York: Morrow; London: Cape (1971). Repr. London: Women's Press (1979).

Firth, Raymond 1972: *The Sceptical Anthropologist? Social Anthropology and Marxist Views on Society.* London: Oxford University Press. From *Proceedings of the British Academy,* vol. LVIII.

Fishman, William J. 1970: *The Insurrectionists.* London: Methuen; Totowa, N.J.: Barnes & Noble.

Fisk, Milton 1979: Dialectic and Ontology. In J. Mepham and D.H. Ruben, eds, *Issues in Marxist Philosophy,* vol. 1.

—— 1981: Determination and Dialectic. *Critique* 13.

Fitch, Robert and Oppenheimer, Mary 1970: Who Rules the Corporations? *Socialist Review* 1.4 pp. 73–108.

Foley, D. 1982: The Value of Money, the Value of Labor-power and the Marxian Transformation Problem. *Review of Radical Political Economy* 14.2.

Fondazione Istituto Gramsci 1990: *Bibliografia gramsciana.*

Footman, David 1946: *The Primrose Path: A Life of Ferdinand Lassalle.* London: Cresset; New York: Greenwood (1969) (Under the title *Ferdinand Lassalle, Romantic Revolutionary.*)

Foster, John 1974: *Class Struggle and the Industrial Revolution.* London: Weidenfeld & Nicolson; New York: St Martin's.

Foster, W.Z. 1956: *Outline History of the World Trade Union Movement.* New York: International Publishers.

Fourier, Charles 1808 *(1968): La théorie des quatres mouvements.* Oeuvres de Charles Fourier, vol. 1. Paris. Éditions Anthropos.

Fox, Bonnie ed. 1980: *Hidden in the Household: Women's Domestic Labour under Capitalism.* Toronto: Women's Press.

Frank, André Gunder 1966: The Development of Underdevelopment. *Monthly Review* 18.4.

—— 1967: *Capitalism and Underdevelopment in Latin America: Historical Studies of Chile and Brazil.* New York and London: Monthly Review Press.

Frankel, Jonathan 1969: *Vladimir Akimov on the Dilemma of Russian Marxism 1895–1903.* Cambridge: Cambridge University Press.

—— 1981: *Prophecy and Politics: Socialism, Nationalism and the Russian Jews.* Cambridge: Cambridge University Press.

Freire, Paolo 1970: *Pedagogy of the Oppressed.* New York: Herder & Herder; London: Sheed & Ward and Penguin (1972).

Freud, Sigmund 1927: The Future of an Illusion. *Standard Edition of the Complete Psychological Works of Sigmund Freud* vol. 21. London: Hogarth; New York: Norton.

—— 1930: Civilisation and its Discontents. *Standard Edition* vol. 21. London: Hogarth; New York: Norton.

—— 1932: New Introductory Lectures on Psycho-Analysis. *Standard Edition* vol. 22. London: Hogarth; New York: Norton.

Fried, Morton 1966: On the Concepts of 'Tribe' and 'Tribal Society'. *Transactions of the New York Academy of Sciences* series III, 28.

—— 1967: *The Evolution of Political Society.* New York: Random House.

Friedman, Andrew 1977: *Industry and Labour.* London: Macmillan; Atlantic Highlands, N.J.: Humanities.

Friedman, J. 1976: Marxist Theory and Systems of Total Reproduction. *Critique of Anthropology* No. 7.

Friedmann, Georges 1936: *La crise du progrès.* Paris: Gallimard.

Friedmann, Harriet 1980: Household Production and the National Economy: Concepts for the Analysis of Agrarian Formations. *Journal of Peasant Studies* 7.

Friedrich, C.J., ed. 1966: Revolution. *Nomos* no. VIII. New York: Atherton.

Friedrich, C.J., Curtis, Michael and Barber, Benjamin R. 1969: *Totalitarianism in Perspective. Three Views*. New York: Praeger; London: Pall Mall.

Frölich, Paul 1939 (1972): *Rosa Luxemburg*. London: Pluto; New York: Monthly Review Press.

Fromm, Erich 1942: *Fear of Freedom*. London: Routledge & Kegan Paul. American edn: *Escape from Freedom*. New York: Farrar and Rinehart (1941).

—— 1955: *The Sane Society*. New York: Rinehart; London: Routledge & Kegan Paul (1956).

—— 1961: *Marx's Concept of Man*. New York: Frederick Ungar.

—— ed. 1965: *Socialist Humanism*. New York: Doubleday; London: Allen Lane (1967).

—— 1971: *The Crisis of Psychoanalysis: Essays on Freud, Marx and Social Psychology*. London: Jonathan Cape; New York: Holt, Rinehart & Winston.

—— 1973: *The Anatomy of Human Destructiveness*. New York: Holt, Rinehart & Winston.

Fuegi, John 1972: *The Essential Brecht*. Los Angeles: Hennessy & Ingalls.

Funk, Rainer 1983: *Erich Fromm*. Reinbek bei Hamburg: Rowohlt Taschenbuch.

Furtado, Celso 1971: *Development and Underdevelopment*. Berkeley: University of California Press.

Fuwa, Tetsuzo 1982: *Stalin and Great Power Chauvinism*. Tokyo: Japan Press Service.

Gabel, Joseph 1962 (1975): *False Consciousness: An Essay on Reification*. Oxford: Basil Blackwell.

Galbraith, J.K. 1967: *The New Industrial State*. London: Hamish Hamilton; Boston: Houghton Mifflin.

Gandy, D. Ross 1979: *Marx and History: From Primitive Society to the Communist Future*. Austin and London: University of Texas Press.

Garaudy, Roger 1970: *Marxism and the Twentieth Century*. London: Collins; New York: Scribner.

Gardiner, J. 1975: *Women's Domestic Labour. New Left Review*.

Gardiner, J., Himmelweit S. and Mackintosh, M. 1975: Women's Domestic Labour. *Bulletin of the Conference of Socialist Economists* 4.2.

Garegnani, P. 1978: Notes on Consumption, Investment and Effective Demand: A reply to Joan Robinson. *Cambridge Economic Journal* 3, 184–5.

Garlan, Y. 1982: *Les Esclaves en Grèce ancienne*. Paris: Maspero.

Garnsey, P., ed. 1980: Non-Slave Labour in Graeco-Roman Antiquity. *Proceedings of the Cambridge Philosophical Society*, Sup. 6.

Gay, Peter 1952: *The Dilemma of Democratic Socialism: Eduard Bernstein's Challenge to Marx*. New York: Columbia University Press; London: Oxford University Press.

Gellner, Ernest 1981: *Muslim Society*. Cambridge: Cambridge University Press.

—— 1987: How did Mankind Acquire its Essence? Or The Palaeolithic October. In W. Outhwaite and M. Mulkay, eds. *Social Theory and Social Criticism*. Oxford: Basil Blackwell.

Geras, Norman 1971: Essence and Appearance: Aspects of Fetishism in Marx's Capital. *New Left Review* 65.

—— 1972: Althusser's Marxism: An Account and Assessment. *New Left Review* 71.

—— 1976: *The Legacy of Rosa Luxemburg*. London: New Left; New York: distr. Schocken.

—— 1985: The Controversy about Marx and Justice. *New Left Review* 150.

Geremek, B. 1968: *Le Salariat dans l'artisanat parisien aux XIIIe–XIVe siècles*. The Hague: Mouton.

Gerratana, Valentino 1977: Althusser and Stalinism. *New Left Review* 101–2.

Gerth, H. and Mills, C. Wright, eds. 1947: *From Max Weber*. London: Routledge & Kegan Paul; New York: Oxford University Press.

Getzler, Israel 1967a: *Martov: A Political Biography of a Russian Social Democrat*. Cambridge and New York: Cambridge University Press.

—— 1967b: The Mensheviks. *Problems of Communism* 6.

—— 1980: Martov e i menscevichi prima e dopo la rivoluzione. *Storia del Marxismo*, III. Torino: Einaudi.

Geuss, Raymond 1982: *The Idea of a Critical Theory*. Cambridge and New York: Cambridge University Press.

Ghose, Sankar 1973: *Socialism, Democracy and Nationalism in India*. Bombay: Allied Publishers.

Giap, General Vo Nguyen 1964: *Dien Bien Phu* (revised edn). Hanoi: Foreign Languages Publishing House.

Giardina, A. 1981: Lavoro e storia sociale: antagonismi e alleanze dall'ellenismo al tardo antico. *Opus* 1.

Gibbon, Peter and Neocosmos, Michael 1985: Some Problems in the Political Economy of 'African Socialism'. In Henry Bernstein and Bonnie K. Campbell, eds. *Contradictions of Accumulation in Africa: Studies in Economy and State*. Beverly Hills: Sage.

Giddens, Anthony 1973: *The Class Structure of the Advanced Societies*. London: Hutchinson; New York: Harper & Row.

—— ed. 1974: *Positivism and Sociology*. London: Heinemann.

—— 1985: *The Nation-State and Violence*. London: Macmillan.

Gilman, A. 1981: The Development of Social Stratification in Bronze Age Europe, *Current Anthropology* 22.

Giraud, Pierre-Noel 1978: L'Économie Politique des régimes de type Soviétique. Le Monde Diplomatique (August).

Girault, Jacques 1970: Paul Lafargue: textes choisies. Paris: Éditions Sociales.

Girling, J.L.S. 1969: People's War. London: Allen & Unwin; New York: Praeger.

Girvan, N. 1973: The Development of Dependency Economics in the Caribbean and Latin America: Review and Comparison. Social and Economic Studies 22.1.

Glezerman, G. et al. 1959: Historical Materialism. Moscow: 1959.

—— 1960: The Laws of Social Development. Eng. trans. of revised edn. Moscow: Foreign Languages Publishing House.

Glombowski, J. 1976: Extended Balanced Reproduction and Fixed Capital. Mehrwert 2.

Glucksmann, André 1972: A Ventriloquist Structuralism. New Left Review 72.

Godelier, Maurice 1966 (1972): Rationality and Irrationality in Economics. London: New Left; New York: Monthly Review Press.

—— 1973 (1977): Perspectives in Marxist Anthropology. Cambridge: Cambridge University Press.

Goldmann, Lucien 1948 (1971): Immanuel Kant. London: New Left; New York: distr. Schocken.

—— 1952 and 1966 (1969): The Human Sciences and Philosophy. London: Cape.

—— 1956 (1967): The Hidden God. London and Boston: Routledge & Kegan Paul.

—— 1958: Recherches dialectiques. Paris: Gallimard.

—— 1964 (1975): Towards a Sociology of the Novel. London: Tavistock.

—— 1970a: Marxisme et sciences humaines. Paris: Gallimard.

—— 1970b: Stuctures mentales et création culturelle. Paris: Editions Anthropos.

—— 1971 (1976): Cultural Creation in Modern Society. St Louis, Missouri: Telos; Oxford: Basil Blackwell (1977).

—— 1977: Lukács and Heidegger. London and Boston: Routledge & Kegan Paul.

—— 1981: Method in the Sociology of Literature. Oxford: Basil Blackwell: Washington: Telos.

Goldsmith, Maurice 1980: Sage: A Life of J.D. Bernal. London: Hutchinson.

Goldsmith, Maurice and McKay, A.L. 1966: The Science of Science. London: Penguin; New York: Simon & Schuster.

Golubović, Z. and Stojanović, S. 1986: The Crisis of the Yugoslav System. (Crises in Soviet-type Systems, no. 14).

Goode, Patrick 1979: Karl Korsch. London: Macmillan.

Gorbachev, Mikhail 1987: Perestroika: New Thinking for Our Country and the World. London: Collins.

—— 1988: Report to the Nineteenth All-Union Conference of the CPSU. Moscow: Novosti.

Gordon, D., et al. 1982: Four Ways to Change the Corporations. The Nation 15 May.

Gordon, R. 1971: A Rare Event. Survey of Current Business 51.7, pt. II.

Gori, F. ed. 1982: Pensiero e azione politica di Lev Trotsky (Follonica colloquium). Florence: Leo S. Olschki Editore.

Gorz, André 1967: Strategy for Labor. Boston: Beacon.

Gottschalch, Wilfried 1962: Strukturveränderungen der Gesellschaft und politisches Handeln in der Lehre von Rudolf Hilferding. Berlin: Duncker & Humblot.

Gough, I. 1972: Marx's Theory of Productive and Unproductive Labour. New Left Review 76.

—— 1973: On Productive and Unproductive Labour: A Reply. Bulletin of the Conference of Socialist Economists II.7.

Gough, I. and Harrison, J. 1975: Unproductive Labour and Housework Again. Bulletin of the Conference of Socialist Economists 4.1.

Gough, Kathleen 1971: Nuer Kinship: A Reexamination. In Beidelman, ed., The Translation of Culture: Essays in Honor of E.E. Evans-Pritchard.

—— 1975: The Origin of the Family. In Reiter, ed., Toward an Anthropology of Women.

Goulbourne, Harry 1979: Politics and State in the Third World. London: Macmillan.

Gould, C.C. 1978: Marx's Social Ontology. Cambridge, Mass. and London: MIT Press.

Graham, Loren R. 1973: Science and Philosophy in the Soviet Union. New York: Knopf; London: Allen Lane.

Gramsci, Antonio 1920: Articles in Ordine Nuovo. London: Lawrence & Wishart; New York: International Publishers.

—— 1929–35 (1971): Selections from the Prison Notebooks, ed. Quintin Hoare and Geoffrey Nowell Smith. London: Lawrence & Wishart; New York: International Publishers.

—— 1949: Note sul Machiavelli sulla politica e sullo Stato moderno. Turin: Einaudi.

—— 1957: 'The Modern Prince' and Other Writings. London: Lawrence & Wishart; New York: International Publishers.

—— 1973: L'alternativa pedagogica. Florence: La Nuova Italia.

—— 1975: Quaderni del Carcere I–IV. Turin: Einaudi. (A complete critical edition of all versions of his notes in prison.)

—— 1977: Selections from Political Writings 1910–1920. London: Lawrence & Wishart; New York: International Publishers.

—— 1978: Selections from Political Writings 1921–1926. London: Lawrence and Wishart.

—— 1985: Selections from Cultural Writings. London: Lawrence & Wishart.

—— 1990: *Bibliografia gramsciana*. Fondazione Istituto Gramsci.

Green, F. and Nore, P., eds. 1979: *Issues in Political Economy*. London: Macmillan; Atlantic Highlands; N.J.: Humanities.

Green, S. 1981: *Prehistorian: A Biography of V. Gordon Childe*. Wiltshire: Moonraker.

Greenberg, David F., ed. 1981: *Crime and Capitalism: Readings in Marxist Criminology*. Palo Alto, Calif.: Mayfield.

Gregory, D. 1978: *Ideology, Science and Human Geography*. London: Hutchinson; New York: St Martin's.

Gregory, P.R. and Stuart, R.C. 1981: *Soviet Economic Structure and Performance*. 2nd edn. New York: Harper & Row.

Grünberg, Carl ed. 1910–1930: *Archiv für die Geschichte des Sozialismus und der Arbeiterbewegung*. 15 vols. Leipzig: C.L. Hirschfeld. *Indexband* zur: Akademische Druck- und Verlaganstalt, Graz/Limmet Verlag, 1973.

Guback, Thomas 1969: *The International Film Industry*. Bloomington: Indiana University Press.

Guérin, Daniel 1970: *Anarchism*. New York: Monthly Review Press.

Guevara, E. (Che) 1967: *Guerrilla Warfare*. New York and London: Monthly Review Press.

Guha, Amalendu 1982: *The Indian National Question: A Conceptual Frame*. Occasional Paper 45. Calcutta: Centre for the Study of Social Sciences.

Gupta S. Datta (1980): *Comintern, India and the Colonial Question 1920–37*. Calcutta: K.P. Bagchi.

Gurland, A.R.L. 1941: Technological Trends and Economic Structure under National Socialism. *Studies in Philosophy and Social Science* 9.

Gurvitch, Georges 1963: *La vocation actuelle de la sociologie*. Paris: Presses Universitaires de France.

Guterman, Norman and Lefebvre, Henri 1936: *La Conscience mystifiée*. Paris: Gallimard.

Gutierrez, G. 1973: *A Theology of Liberation: History, Politics and Salvation*. New York, Maryknoll: Orbis.

Habermas, Jürgen 1962: (1989): *Structural Transformation of the Public Sphere*. Cambridge: Polity.

—— 1963 (1974): *Theory and Practice*. London: Heinemann; Boston, Mass.: Beacon.

—— 1967 (1988): *On the Logic of the Social Sciences*. Cambridge: Polity.

—— 1968a (1970): *Toward a Rational Society*. London: Heinemann; Boston, Mass.: Beacon.

—— 1968b (1971): *Knowledge and Human Interests*. London: Heinemann; Boston, Mass.: Beacon.

—— 1968c: *Technologie und Wissenschaft als Ideologie*. Frankfurt: Suhrkamp.

—— 1971: *Philosophisch-politische Profile*. Frankfurt: Suhrkamp.

—— 1973 (1976): *Legitimation Crisis*. London: Heinemann; Boston, Mass.: Beacon.

—— 1976 (1979): *Communication and the Evolution of Society*. London: Heinemann; Boston, Mass.: Beacon.

—— 1981 (1984): *The Theory of Communicative Action*, vol. 1. London: Heinemann.

—— 1981 (1988): *The Theory of Communicative Action*, vol. 2, Cambridge: Polity.

—— 1985 (1989): *The Philosophical Discourse of Modernity*. Cambridge: Polity.

—— ed. 1968: *Antworten auf Herbert Marcuse*. Frankfurt: Suhrkamp.

—— et al. 1961: *Student und Politik: eine Soziologische Untersuchung zum politischen Bewusstsein Frankfurter Studenten*. Neuwied: Luchterhand.

Haight, R. 1985: *An Alternative Vision: An Interpretation of Liberation Theology*. Mahwah, N.J.: Paulist Press.

Habib, Irfan 1963: *The Agrarian System of Mughal India*. London: Asia Publishing House.

Haimson, L.H. 1955: *The Russian Marxists and the Origins of Bolshevism*. Cambridge, Mass.: Harvard University Press; London: Oxford University Press.

—— ed. 1974 (1976): *The Mensheviks: From the Revolution of 1917 to the Outbreak of the Second World War*. Chicago and London: University of Chicago Press.

Haithcox, John P. 1971: *Communism and Nationalism in India: M.N. Roy and Comintern Policy 1920–39*. Princeton, N.J.: Princeton University Press; Bombay: Oxford University Press.

Hall, Stuart 1977: Rethinking the Base and Superstructure Metaphor. In J. Bloomfield, ed., *Class, Hegemony and Party*.

—— 1990: Cultural Studies: Two Paradigms. *Media, Culture and Society* 3. Reprinted in Tony Bennett et al., eds, *Culture, Ideology and Social Process*. London: Batsford.

Hall, Stuart et al. 1978: *Policing the Crisis: Mugging, the State, and Law and Order*. London: Macmillan; New York: Holmes & Meier.

Hammond, T.T. 1957: *Lenin on Trade Unions and Revolution*. New York: Columbia University Press; London: Oxford University Press.

Hannack, Jacques 1965: *Karl Renner und seine Zeit*. Vienna: Europa Verlag.

Harcourt, G.C. 1982: Joan Robinson. In Prue Kerr, ed. *The Social Science Imperialists*. London: Routledge & Kegan Paul.

Hardach, Gerd and Karras, Dieter 1975 (1978): *A Short History of Socialist Economic Thought*. London: Edward Arnold: New York: St Martin's.

Harding, N. 1977 (1982): *Lenin's Political Thought*. 2 vols. in one. London: Macmillan; New York: St Martin's.

Harman, C. 1980: Theories of Crisis. *International Socialism* 2.9, 45–80.

Harnecker, Marta 1969: *Los Conceptos Elementales del Materialismo Historico.* Mexico City: Siglo Veintiuno Editores.

Harrington, M. 1972: *Socialism.* New York: Saturday Review Press.

—— 1979: The Democratic Socialist Organizing Committee and the Left. *Socialist Review.*

Harris, Laurence 1976: On Interest, Credit and Capital. *Economy and Society* 5.2.

Harrison, John F.C. 1969: *Robert Owen and the Owenites in Britain and America.* London: Routledge & Kegan Paul; New York: Scribner (under the title *Quest for the New Moral World).*

—— 1973: Political Economy of Housework. *Bulletin of the Conference of Socialist Economists* 3.1.

Harrison, Mark 1977: Resource Allocation and Agrarian Class Formation: The Problem of Social Mobility among Russian Peasant Households, 1880–1930. *Journal of Peasant Studies* 4.2.

Harstick, Hans-Peter, ed. 1977: *Karl Marx über Formen vorkapitalischer Produktion.* Frankfurt am Main and New York: Campus Verlag.

Hartmann, Heidi 1979: The Unhappy Marriage of Marxism and Feminism: Towards a More Progressive Union. *Capital and Class* 8. Also in Lydia Sargent, ed. *The Unhappy Marriage of Marxism and Feminism.* Boston: South End Press; London: Pluto (1981).

Harvey, David W. 1973: *Social Justice and the City.* London: Edward Arnold; Baltimore: John Hopkins University Press.

—— 1982: *The Limits to Capital.* Oxford: Basil Blackwell; Chicago: University of Chicago Press.

—— 1989: *The Condition of Postmodernity: An Enquiry into the Origins of Cultural Change.* Oxford: Basil Blackwell.

Haseler, S. 1969: *The Gaitskellites: Revisionism in the British Labour Party.* London: Macmillan.

Haupt, G., Lowy, M. and Weill, C., eds. 1974: *Les Marxistes et la question nationale, 1848–1914.* Paris: Maspero.

Haupt, G. and Marie, J.J. 1974: *Makers of the Russian Revolution.* London: George Allen & Unwin; Ithaca, N.Y.: Cornell University Press.

Havemann, Robert 1980: *Morgen die Industriegesellschaft am Scheidewege, Kritik und reale Utopie.*

Hay, Douglas, Linebaugh, Peter, Rule, John G., Thompson, E.P. and Winslow, Cal 1975: *Albion's Fatal Tree: Crime and Society in Eighteenth-Century England.* London: Allen Lane; New York: Pantheon.

Hayek, F.A. von, ed. 1935: *Collectivist Economic Planning.* London.

Hazard, John N., 1969: *Communists and their law: a Search for the Common Core of the Legal Systems of the Marxian Socialist States.* Chicago: University of Chicago Press.

Hegedüs, A., *et al.* 1974 *(1976): Die Neue Linke in Ungarn.* 2 vols. Berlin: Merve.

—— 1976: *Socialism and Bureaucracy.* London: Allison & Busby; New York: St Martin's.

Hegel, G.W.F. 1807 *(1931): The Phenomenology of Mind.* London and New York: Allen & Unwin; New York: Humanities (1946).

—— 1812–16 *(1929): Science of Logic.* Vol. 2. London: Allen & Unwin; New York: Macmillan.

—— 1821 *(1942): Philosophy of Right.* Oxford: Oxford University Press.

—— 1830–1 *(1956): The Philosophy of History.* New York: Dover.

Heidegger, M. 1927 *(1967): Being and Time.* Oxford: Basil Blackwell; New York: Norton.

Heilbroner, R.L. 1980: *Marxism: For and Against.* New York: W.W. Norton.

Heimann, E. 1932: *Sozialistische Wirtschafts- und Arbeitsordnung* (Socialist Economic and Labour Order). Potsdam.

Heinen, H., ed. 1980: *Die Geschichte des Altertums im Spiegel der sowjetischen Forschung.* Darmstadt: Wissenschaftliche Buchgesellschaft.

Heintel, Peter 1967: *System und Idologie: Der Austromarxismus im Spiegel der Philosophie Max Adlers.* Munich: Verlag R. Oldenbourg.

Heitman, Sidney 1969: *Nikolai I. Bukharin: A Bibliography with Annotations.* Stanford: Hoover Institution.

Held, David 1980: *Introduction to Critical Theory: Horkheimer to Habermas.* London: Hutchinson; Berkeley: University of California Press.

—— 1989: *Political Thory and the Modern State.* Cambridge: Polity.

Heller, Agnes 1976: *The Theory of Need in Marx.* London: Allison & Busby; New York: St Martin's.

—— ed. 1983: *Lukács Revalued.* Oxford: Basil Blackwell; New York: Columbia University Press.

Henderson, W.O. 1976: *The Life of Friedrich Engels.* 2 vols. London: Frank Cass.

Herzen, A. 1852 *(1956):* The Russian People and Socialism. In *Selected Philosophical Works* pp. 470–502. Moscow: Foreign Languages Publishing House.

Herzog, Philippe 1971: Le rôle de l'état dans la société capitaliste actuelle. *Économie et politique* 200–201.

Hess, Moses 1843 *(1921):* Philosophie der Tat. In T. Zlocisti, *Moses Hess – Sozialistische Aufsätze.* Berlin: Weltverlag.

Hettne, Björn 1990: *Development Theory and the Three Worlds.* London: Longman.

Hexter, J.H. 1961: *Reappraisals in History.* Evanston, Ill.: Northwestern University Press; London: Longman.

Hibbin, S. ed. 1978: *Politics, Ideology and the State.* London: Lawrence & Wishart.

Hilferding, Rudolf 1904 *(1949): Böhm-Bawerk's Criticism of Marx.* Ed. P. Sweezy, New York; Augustus Kelly; London Merlin (1975).

—— 1910 (1981): *Finance Capital*. London and Boston: Routledge & Kegan Paul.

—— 1915: Arbeitsgemeinschaft der Klassen. *Der Kampf* 8.

—— 1924: Probleme der Zeit. *Die Gesellschaft* 1.1.

—— 1940: State capitalism or totalitarian state economy? *Socialist Courier*, New York. Repr. *Modern Review* 1 (1947).

—— 1941 (1954): *Das historische Problem*. Unfinished study first published in *Zeitschrift für Politik* n.s. 1.

Hill, Christopher 1964: *Society and Puritanism in Pre-Revolutionary England*. London: Secker & Warburg: New York: distr. Schocken.

—— 1972: *The World Turned Upside Down*. London: Maurice Temple Smith.

Hilton, R.H. 1969 (1982): *The Decline of Serfdom in Medieval England*. London: Macmillan; New York: St Martin's.

—— 1973: *Bond Men Made Free*. London: Temple Smith; New York: Viking.

—— ed. 1976: *The Transition from Feudalism to Capitalism*. London: New Left; New York: distr. Schocken.

—— 1978: A Crisis of Feudalism. *Past and Present* 80.

—— 1984: *Class Conflict and the Crisis of Feudalism*. London: Hambledon.

Himmelweit, S. 1974: The Continuing Saga of the Falling Rate of Profit – A Reply to Mario Cogoy. *Bulletin of the Conference of Socialist Economists* II.9.

—— 1984a: The Real Dualism of Sex and Class. *Review of Radical Political Economics* 16.1.

—— 1984b: Value Relations and Divisions Within the Working Class. *Science and Society* 48.3.

Hindess, Barry and Hirst, Paul Q. 1975: *Pre-Capitalist Modes of Production*. London and Boston: Routledge & Kegan Paul.

—— 1977: *Mode of Production and Social Formation: An Autocritique*. London: Macmillan; Atlantic Highlands, N.J.: Humanities.

Hirsch, Helmut 1980: *Marx und Moses, Karl Marx zur 'Judenfrage' und zu Juden*. Frankfurt a.M., Bern, Cirencester/U.K: Peter D. Lang.

Hobbes, Thomas 1651: *Leviathan*. London: Printed for Andrew Crooke.

Hobsbawm, Eric 1962: *The Age of Revolution, 1789–1848*. London: Weidenfeld & Nicolson.

—— 1964a: *Labouring Men*. London: Weidenfeld & Nicolson; New York: Basic Books.

—— 1964b: Introduction to Karl Marx, *Pre-Capitalist Economic Formations*. London: Lawrence & Wishart; New York: International Publishers.

—— 1968: *Industry and Empire*. London: Weidenfeld & Nicolson; New York: Pantheon.

—— 1973: *Revolutionaries*. London: Weidenfeld & Nicolson; New York: Pantheon.

—— 1975: *The Age of Capital, 1848–1875*. London:

Weidenfeld & Nicolson.

—— ed. 1977: *The Italian Road to Socialism*. Interview with Giorgio Napolitano. London: Journeyman Press; Westport, Conn.: Lawrence Hill.

—— 1978: The Historians Group of the Communist Party. In Maurice Cornforth, ed. *Rebels and Their Causes*. London: Lawrence & Wishart.

—— 1987: *The Age of Empire, 1875–1914*. London: Weidenfeld & Nicolson; New York: Pantheon.

Hobsbawm, Eric and Rudé, George 1969: *Captain Swing*. London: Lawrence & Wishart.

Hobsbawm, Eric et al., eds 1978–82 (1980–): *The History of Marxism*. Brighton: Harvester; Bloomington: Indiana University Press. (Trans. of *Storia del Marxismo*. Turin: Einaudi.)

Hodgkin, Dorothy 1980: J.D. Bernal. *Biographical Memoirs of the Fellows of the Royal Society* 26.

Hodgkin, Thomas 1981: *Vietnam: the Revolutionary Path*. London: Macmillan; New York: St Martin's.

Hodgson, G. 1974: The Theory of the Falling Rate of Profit. *New Left Review* 84.

—— 1975: *Trotsky and Fatalistic Marxism*. Nottingham: Spokesman.

—— 1977: *Socialism and Parliamentary Democracy*. Nottingham: Spokesman.

Hodgson, Marshall G.S. 1974: *The Venture of Islam*. 3 vols. Chicago and London: University of Chicago Press.

Holton, B. 1976: *British Syndicalism 1900–1914*. London: Pluto.

Holton, R. 1981: Marxist Theories of Social Change and the Transition from Feudalism to Capitalism. *Theory and Society* 10.6.

Honjo, Eijiro 1935 (1965): *The Social and Economic History of Japan*. New York: Russell & Russell.

Horkheimer, Max 1939: Die Juden und Europa. *Zeitschrift für Sozialforschung* 8.

—— 1947 (1974): *Eclipse of Reason*. New York: Oxford University Press. Repr. New York: Seabury.

—— 1968 (1972): *Critical Theory*. New York: Herder & Herder. (This volume includes 'Art and Mass Culture', 'Authority and the Family' and 'Traditional and Critical Theory'.)

—— 1974: *Notizen 1950 bis 1969 und Dämmerung*. Zurich: Oprecht und Helbling.

Horkheimer, Max and Adorno, Theodor W. 1947 (1973): *Dialectic of Enlightenment*. Trans. John Cumming. London: Allen Lane; New York: Seabury.

Horkheimer, Max, Fromm, Erich and Marcuse, Herbert 1936: *Studien über Autorität und Familie*. Paris: Félix Alcan.

Horowitz, D. ed. 1968: *Marx and Modern Economics*. London: MacGibbon & Kee; New York: Modern Reader Paperbacks.

—— ed. 1971: *Isaac Deutscher: The Man and his Work*. London: Macdonald.

Horowitz, Irving L. ed. 1970: *Masses in Latin America*. New York: Oxford University Press.

Horvat, Branko 1982: *The Political Economy of Socialism*. Oxford: Martin Robertson.

Horvat, B., Supek, R. and Marković, M. 1975: *Self-governing Socialism*. 2 vols. White Plains, N.Y.: International Arts and Sciences Press.

Houtart, François and Lemercinier, Geneviève 1980: *The Great Asiatic Religions and their Social Functions*. Louvain: Université Catholique.

Howard, Dick, ed. 1971: *Selected Political Writings of Rosa Luxemburg*. New York and London: Monthly Review Press.

Hsiung, James Chieh 1970: *Ideology and Practice. The Evolution of Chinese Communism*. New York: Praeger.

Hudson, Wayne, 1982: *The Marxist Philosophy of Ernst Bloch*. New York: St Martin's; London: Macmillan.

Hughes, H.S. 1959: *Consciousness and Society*. London: MacGibbon & Kee; New York: Knopf.

Humphrey, Richard 1951: *Georges Sorel: Prophet Without Honor*. Cambridge, Mass.: Harvard University Press.

Humphreys, J. 1977: Class Struggle and the Persistence of the Working Class Family. *Cambridge Journal of Economics* 1.3.

Hunt, Alan, ed. 1980: *Marxism and Democracy*. London: Lawrence & Wishart; Atlantic Highlands, N.J.: Humanities.

Hunt, E. and Schwartz, J., eds. 1972: *A Critique of Economic Theory*. London: Penguin.

Hunt, Richard N. 1974: *The Political Ideas of Marx and Engels*. London: Macmillan; Pittsburgh: University of Pittsburgh Press.

Hussain, Athar and Tribe, Keith 1981: *Marxism and the Agrarian Question*. 2 vols. London: Macmillan; Atlantic Highlands, N.J.: Humanities.

Hutcheon, Linda 1988: *A Poetics of Postmodernism: History, Theory, Fiction*. New York and London: Routledge.

Huxley, Julian 1949: *Soviet Genetics and World Science: Lysenko and the Meaning of Heredity*. London: Chatto & Windus; New York: Schuman.

Hyman, R. 1971: *Marxism and the Sociology of Trade Unionism*. London: Pluto.

—— 1972: *Strikes*. London: Fontana; New York: Watts Franklin.

—— 1980: Theory in Industrial Relations: Towards a Materialist Analysis. In P. Boreham and G. Dow, eds., *Work and Inequality* vol. 2. Melbourne: Macmillan.

Hyppolite, Jean 1955 (1969): *Studies on Marx and Hegel*. London: Heinemann; New York: Basic.

Iggers, G.C., ed. 1829 (1958): *Doctrine of Saint Simon, An Exposition, First Year*. Boston: Beacon.

Indexband zu Archiv für die Geschichte des Sozialismus und der Arbeiterbewegung 1973. Graz: Akademische Druck- u. Verlagsanstatt.

Inglehart, Ronald 1977: *The Silent Revolution: Changing Values and Political Styles among Western Publics*. Princeton: Princeton University Press.

Ingram, D. 1987: *Habermas and the Dialectic of Reason*. New Haven: Yale University Press.

International Sociological Association 1977: *Scientific-Technological Revolution: Social Aspects*. London and Beverley Hills: Calif.: Sage.

Ionescu, G. and Gellner, E., eds. 1969: *Populism*. London: Weidenfeld & Nicolson; New York: St Martin's.

Israel, Joachim 1972: *Der Begriff Entfremdung*. Reinbek bei Hamburg: Rowohlt.

Itoh, Makoto 1980: *Value and Crisis, Essays on Marxian Economics in Japan*. London: Pluto; New York: Monthly Review Press.

—— 1988: *The Basic Theory of Capitalism*. London: Macmillan.

Jackson, J. Hampden 1943: *Jean Jaurès, his Life and Work*. London: Allen & Unwin.

Jacoby, Russell 1971: Towards a Critique of Automatic Marxism: The Politics of Philosophy from Lukács to the Frankfurt School. *Telos* 10.

—— 1974: Marxism and the Critical School. *Theory and Society* 1.

—— 1975: The politics of crisis theory. *Telos* 23.

—— 1981: *Dialectic of Defeat: Contours of Western Marxism*. Cambridge and New York: Cambridge University Press.

Jameson, Fredric 1971: *Marxism and Form: Twentieth-Century Dialectical Theories of Literature*. Princeton, NJ and London: Princeton University Press.

—— 1984: Postmodernism, or the Cultural Logic of Late Capitalism. *New Left Review* 146 (July/August).

Jaurès, Jean 1898–1902 (1922–4): *Histoire Socialiste*, ed. Albert Mathiez. Paris: Librarie de l'humanité.

—— 1899: *Le socialisme et l'enseignment*. Paris: G. Bellais.

—— 1901: *Études socialistes*. Paris: Cahiers de la quinzaine.

—— 1910: *L'Armée nouvelle*. Paris: Rouff.

Jaworskyj, M., ed. 1967: *Soviet Political Thought: An Anthology*. Baltimore and London: Johns Hopkins University Press.

Jay, Martin 1973: *The Dialectical Imagination: A History of the Frankfurt School and the Institute of Social Research 1923–1950*. Boston: Little Brown.

Jennings, Jeremy 1985: *Georges Sorel: The Character and Development of his Thought*. London: Macmillan.

—— 1990: *Syndicalism in France: A History of Ideas*. London: Macmillan.

Jessop, Bob 1982: *The Capitalist State*. Oxford:

Martin Robertson; New York: New York University Press.

—— 1985: *Nicos Poulantzas: Marxist Theory and Political Strategy*. London: Macmillan.

Jha, D.N. 1976: Temple and Merchants in South India c.A.D. 900–A.D. 1300. In Barun De, *op. cit.*

Jocteau, G.C. 1975: *Leggere Gramsci: Una guida alle interpretazioni*. Milan: Feltrinelli.

Johnson, C. 1974: *Icarian Communism in France: Cabet and the Icarians, 1839–1851*. Ithaca, N.Y.: Cornell University Press.

Johnson, Richard 1979: Culture and the Historians. In J. Clarke, C. Critcher and R. Johnson, eds. *Working-Class Culture: Studies in History and Theory*. London: Hutchinson.

Johnson, Richard *et al.* eds. 1982: *Making Histories: Studies in History-Writing and Politics*. London: Hutchinson.

Johnson, R.J., ed. 1986: *The Dictionary of Human Geography*. 2nd edn, Oxford: Basil Blackwell.

Johnstone, Monty 1967: Marx and Engels and the Concept of the Party. *Socialist Register* 4.

—— 1970: Socialism, Democracy and the One-party System. *Marxism Today*, Aug., Sept., Nov.

—— 1980: Uno strumento politico di tipo nuovo; il partito leninista d'avanguardia. In E.J. Hobsbawm *et al.*, eds. *Storia del Marxismo*, III/1.

—— 1983: Marx, Blanqui and Majority Rule. *Socialist Register*.

Johnstone, Monty *et al.* 1979: Conflicts between Socialist Countries. *Marxism Today* August.

Joll, James 1955 (1975): *The Second International 1889–1914*. London and Boston: Routledge & Kegan Paul.

Joravsky, David 1961: *Soviet Marxism and Natural Science 1917–1932*. London: Routledge & Kegan Paul; New York: Columbia University Press.

—— 1970: *The Lysenko Affair*. Cambridge, Mass.: Harvard University Press.

—— 1977: The Mechanical Spirit: the Stalinist marriage of Pavlov to Marx. *Theory and Society* 4.

Jordan, Z.A. 1967: *The Evolution of Dialectical Materialism*. London: Macmillan; New York: St Martin's.

Josephson, Eric and Josephson, Mary, eds. 1962: *Man Alone: Alienation in Modern Society*. New York: Doubleday.

Journal of Peasant Studies, from 1973 onwards (vol. 1, no. 1).

Kahn, J. and Llobera, J.R. 1981: *The Anthropology of Pre-capitalist Societies*. Atlantic Highlands, N.J.: Humanities.

Kalecki, Michał, 1954: *Theory of Economic Dynamics*. London: Allen & Unwin; New York: Rinehart.

—— 1971: *Selected Essays on the Dynamics of the Capitalist Economy 1933–1970*. Cambridge and New York: Cambridge University Press.

—— 1972: *Selected Essays on the Economic Growth of the Socialist and the Mixed Economy*. Cambridge: Cambridge University Press.

—— 1976: *Essays on Developing Economies*. Brighton: Harvester.

—— 1986: *Selected Essays on Economic Planning*. Cambridge: Cambridge University Press.

—— (forthcoming): *Collected Works*. Oxford: Oxford University Press.

Kamenka, Eugene 1969: *Marxism and Ethics*. London: Macmillan; New York: St Martin's.

—— 1970: *The Philosophy of Ludwig Feuerbach*. London: Routledge & Kegan Paul; New York: Praeger.

Kamenka, Eugene and Tay, Alice Erh-Soon 1978: Socialism, Anarchism and Law. In Eugene Kamenka, Robert Brown and Alice Erh-Soon Tay, eds., *Law and Society: The Crisis in Legal Ideals*. London: Edward Arnold; New York: St Martin's.

Kangrga, Milan 1967: Das Problem der Entfremdung in Marx' Werk. *Praxis* 1.

—— 1968: Was ist Verdinglichung? *Praxis* 1–2.

Kann, R.A. 1950: *The Multinational Empire: Nationalism and National Reform in the Habsburg Monarchy, 1848–1918*. New York: University of Columbia Press.

Kant, Immanuel 1781 (1964): *Critique of Pure Reason*. London: Macmillan; New York: St Martin's.

Katz, N. and Kemnitzer, D.S. 1979: *New Directions in Political Economy: An Approach from Anthropology*, ed. Leons and Rothstein. Westport, Conn. and London: Greenwood.

Kautsky, Karl 1887 (1912): *Karl Marx: Ökonomische Lehren*. Berlin: Dietz.

—— 1890 (1910): *The Class Struggle*. Chicago: C.H. Kerr.

—— 1899a (1988): *The Agrarian Question*, trans. Pete Burgess. London: Zwan.

—— 1899b: *Bernstein und das sozialdemokratische Programm: Eine Antikritik*. Stuttgart: Dietz.

—— 1920 (1916): *The Social Revolution*. Chicago: Charles H. Kerr.

—— 1906 (1918): *Ethics and the Materialist Conception of History*. Chicago: Charles H. Kerr.

—— 1908 (1925): *Foundations of Christianity: A Study of Christian Origins*. London: Orbach & Chambers; New York: International Publishers.

—— 1909: *The Road to Power*. Trans. A.M. Simon. Chicago: S.A. Bloch.

—— 1911: Finanzkapital und Krisen. *Die Neue Zeit* 39.

—— 1914: *Der politische Massenstreik*. Berlin: Buchhandlung Vorwärts.

—— 1918 (1919): *The Dictatorship of the Proletariat*. Ann Arbor: University of Michigan Press; Manchester: National Labour Press.

—— 1920: *Terrorism and Communism*. Manchester: National Labour Press; Westport, Conn.: Hyperion (1973).

—— 1922: *Die proletarische Revolution und ihr Programm* (The Proletarian Revolution and its Programme). Stuttgart and Berlin.

—— 1927 (1988): *The Materialist Conception of History*, ed. John H. Kautsky. New Haven: Yale University Press.

—— 1983: *Selected Political Writings*. London: Macmillan.

Kay, Cristóbal 1989: *Latin American Theories of Development and Underdevelopment*. London and New York: Routledge.

Kay, G. 1975: *Development and Underdevelopment: A Marxist Analysis*. London: Macmillan; New York: St Martin's.

Kaye, Harvey 1984: *The British Marxist Historians: An Introductory Analysis*. Cambridge: Polity; New York: Basil Blackwell.

—— 1988a: George Rudé, Social Historian. In George Rudé, *The Face of the Crowd: Selected Essays of George Rudé*, ed. Harvey Kaye. London: Harvester Wheatsheaf; Atlantic Highlands, NJ: Humanities.

—— 1988b: V.G. Kiernan, Seeing Things Historically. In V.G. Kiernan, *History, Classes and Nation-States: Selected Writings of V.G. Kiernan*, ed. Harvey Kaye. Cambridge: Polity; New York: Basil Blackwell.

—— 1990: E.P. Thompson, the British Marxist Historical Tradition and the Contemporary Crisis. In Harvey Kaye and Keith McClelland, eds. *E.P. Thompson: Critical Perspectives*. Cambridge: Policy; Philadelphia: Temple.

Kaye, Harvey and McClelland, Keith eds. 1990: *E.P. Thompson: Critical Perspectives*. Cambridge: Polity: Philadelphia: Temple.

Keane, J. ed. 1988a: *Civil Society and The State*. London: Verso.

—— 1988b: *Democracy and Civil Society*. London: Verso.

Keep, J.L.H. 1963: *The Rise of Social Democracy in Russia*. Oxford: Oxford University Press.

Kelly, Alfred 1981: *The Descent of Darwin: The Popularization of Darwinism in Germany 1860–1914*. Chapel Hill, N.C.: University of North Carolina Press.

Kelly, Michael 1982: *Modern French Marxism*. Oxford: Basil Blackwell; Baltimore: Johns Hopkins University Press.

Kemp, T. 1967: *Theories of Imperialism*. London: Dobson.

Kidron, M. and Segal, R. 1981: *The State of the World Atlas*. London: Pluto; New York: Simon & Schuster.

Kiernan, V.G. 1972: *The Lords of Human Kind*. London: Weidenfeld & Nicolson.

—— 1974: *Marxism and Imperialism*. London: Edward Arnold: New York: St Martin's.

—— 1980: *State and Society in Europe, 1550–1650*.

Oxford: Basil Blackwell.

—— 1982: *European Empires from Conquest to Collapse, 1815–1960*. London: Fontana; New York: Pantheon.

—— 1988a: *The Duel in European History*. Oxford: Oxford University Press.

—— 1988b: *History, Classes and Nation-States: Selected Writings of V.G. Kiernan*, ed. Harvey Kaye. Cambridge: Polity; New York: Basil Blackwell.

Kim, Soo Haeng 1982: The Theory of Crisis. A Critical Appraisal of some Japanese and European Reformulations. Unpublished PhD dissertation. University of London.

Kindersley, R. 1962: *The First Russian Revisionists. A Study of Legal Marxism in Russia*. Oxford: Oxford University Press.

Kitching, G. 1982: *Development and Underdevelopment in Historical Perspective*. New York: Methuen.

Klejn, L.S. 1977: A Panorama of Theoretical Archaeology. *Current Anthropology* 18.

Kliem, Manfred, ed. 1968: *Marx und Engels über Kunst und Literatur*. 2 vols. Frankfurt am Main: Europäische Verlagsanstalt.

Klingender, Francis D. 1947 (1968): *Art and the Industrial Revolution*. London: Adams & Dart; New York: A.M. Kelley.

Kloosterboer, W. 1960: *Involuntary Labour after the Abolition of Slavery*. Leiden: E.J. Brill.

Klugman, James 1970: Lenin's Approach to the Question of Nationalism and Internationalism. *Marxism Today* January–February.

Knei-Paz, B. 1978: *The Social and Political Thought of Leon Trotsky*. Oxford and New York: Oxford University Press.

Kojève, A. 1947: *Introduction à la lecture de Hegel*. Paris: Gallimard.

Kolakowski, Leszek 1958 (1969): Karl Marx and the Classical Definition of Truth. In *Marxism and Beyond*. London: Pall Mall.

—— 1960: *Der Mensch ohne Alternative. Über die Richtigkeit der Maxime 'Der Zweck heiligt die Mittel'*. Munich: Piper.

—— 1968: *Toward a Marxist Humanism*. New York: Grove.

—— 1978: *Main Currents of Marxism*. 3 vols. Oxford and New York: Oxford University Press.

Kolakowski, L. and Hampshire, S. eds. 1974: *The Socialist Idea: A Reappraisal*. London: Weidenfeld & Nicolson.

Kollontai, Alexandra 1977: *Selected Writings*. London: Allison & Busby; Westport, Conn.: Lawrence Hill.

Komintern und Revolutionäre Partei: Auswahl von Dokumenten und Materialien 1919–1943, 1986. Berlin: Dietz Verlag.

Kondratiev, N.D. 1926: Die Langen Wellen der Konjunktur. *Archiv für Sozialwissenschaft und Realpolitik*, vol. 56. Tübingen.

Konrád, George and Szelényi, Ivan 1979: *The Intellectuals on the Road to Class Power*. New York: Harcourt Brace Jovanovitch; Brighton: Harvester.

Kornai, J. 1986: The Hungarian Reform Process: Vision, Hopes and Reality. *Journal of Economic Literature*, Dec.

Korner, S. 1955: *Kant*. London and Baltimore: Penguin.

Korsch, Karl 1922 (1968): *Arbeitsrecht für Betriebsräte*. Berlin: Vereinigung Internationaler Verlagsanstalten.

—— 1923 (1970): *Marxism and Philosophy*. London: New Left; New York: distr. Schocken.

—— 1929: *Die materialistische Geschichtsauffassung*. Leipzig: C.L. Hirschfeld.

—— 1938 (1967): *Karl Marx*. London: Chapman & Hall; New York: Wiley. Revised German edn. Frankfurt: Europäische Verlagsanstalt.

—— 1950 (1965): Zehn Thesen über Marxismus heute. *Alternative* 41.

—— 1969: *Schriften zur Sozialisierung*. Frankfurt: Europäische Verlagsanstalt.

Kosambi, D.D. 1944: Caste and Class in India. *Science and Society* 8.3.

—— 1956 (1975): *An Introduction to the Study of Indian History*. Bombay: Popular Prakashan.

—— 1962: *Myth and Reality: Studies in the Formation of Indian Culture*. Bombay: Popular Prakashan.

Koshimura, Shinzaburo 1975: *Theory of Capital Reproduction and Accumulation*. Kitchener, Ontario: DPG Publishing.

Kosik, Karl 1963 (1976): *Dialectics of the Concrete*. Dordrecht and Boston: Reidel.

Kotz, David 1978: *Bank Control of Large Corporations in the United States*. University of California Press.

Krader, Lawrence, ed. 1972: *The Ethnological Notebooks of Karl Marx*. Assen: Van Gorcum.

—— 1975: *The Asiatic Mode of Production*. Assen: Van Gorcum.

Kreissig, H. 1982: *Geschichte des Hellenismus*. Berlin: Akademie Verlag.

Kroeber, Alfred 1948: *Anthropology*. New York: Harcourt Brace Jovanovitch.

—— ed. 1953: *Anthropology Today: An Encyclopaedic Inventory*. Chicago: University of Chicago Press.

Kropotkin, P.A. 1970: *Selected Writings on Anarchism and Revolution*. Cambridge, Mass. and London: MIT Press.

Kuchenbuch, L. and Michael, B., eds. 1977: *Feudalismus-Materialen zur Theorie und Geschichte*. Frankfurt: M. Ullstein.

Kuczynski, J. 1967: *The Rise of the Working Class*. London: Weidenfeld & Nicolson; New York: McGraw Hill.

Kuhn, Thomas S. 1970: *The Structure of Scientific Revolutions*. 2nd edn. Chicago and London: University of Chicago Press.

Kühne, Karl 1979: *Economics and Marxism*. 2 vols. London: Macmillan; New York: St Martin's.

Kula, Witold 1962 (1976): *Economic Theory of the Feudal System*. London: New Left; New York: distr. Schocken.

Kunzli, Arnold 1966: *Karl Marx – Eine Psychographie*. Vienna: Europa Verlag.

Kurotaki, Masaaki 1984: *Zur Todesursache Rudolf Hilferdings*. Sendai: Beiträge der Miyagi-Gakui Frauenhochschule.

Kuusinen, O., ed. 1961: *Fundamentals of Marxism-Leninism*. London: Lawrence & Wishart.

Labedz, L., ed. 1962: *Revisionism*. London: Allen & Unwin; New York: Praeger.

Labriola, Antonio 1895, 1896 (1904): *Essays on the Materialist Conception of History*. Chicago: C.H. Kerr.

—— 1898 (1907): *Socialism and Philosophy*. Chicago: C.H. Kerr.

Laclau, E. 1971 (1977): Feudalism and Capitalism in Latin America. *New Left Review* 67. (Reprinted in *Politics and Ideology in Marxist Thought*.)

—— 1977: *Politics and Ideology in Marxist Thought*. London: New Left; New York: distr. Schocken.

Laclau, E. and Mouffe, C. 1985: *Hegemony and Socialist Strategy*. London: Verso.

Lafargue, Paul 1883 (1907): *The Right to be Lazy*. Repr. 1975. Chicago: Charles H. Kerr.

—— 1895 (1910): *Origine et évolution de la propriété*. Eng. edn: *The Evolution of Property from Savagery to Civilisation*. Chicago: Charles H. Kerr. (Originally pub. as series under the name Fergus in the *Nouvelle Revue* (Paris).)

—— (1959–60): *Frederick Engels, Paul and Laura Lafargue. Correspondence*. 3 vols. Moscow: Foreign Languages Publishing House.

Laing, David 1978: *The Marxist Theory of Art*. Brighton: Harvester; Atlantic Highlands, N.J.: Humanities.

Lall, S. 1975: Is Dependence a Useful Concept in Analysing Underdevelopment? *World Development* 11.

Landauer, C. 1931: *Planwirtschaft und Verkehrswirtschaft* (Planned Economy and Exchange Economy). Munich and Leipzig.

Lane, D. 1984: *Foundations for a Social Theology*. Dublin: Gill and Macmillan.

Lane, D.S. 1981: *Leninism: A Sociological Interpretation*. Cambridge and New York: Cambridge University Press.

Lane, David 1969 (1975): *The Roots of Russian Communism*. Assen: Van Gorcum.

Lange, Oskar 1936–7 (1964): On the Economic Theory of a Socialist Economy. In O. Lange and F. Taylor, *On the Economic Theory of Socialism*, ed. B. Lippincott. New York, Toronto and London: McGraw Hill.

—— 1963: *Political Economy*. Oxford: Pergamon.

—— 1970: *Papers on Economics and Sociology*. Oxford: Pergamon.

—— 1973–86: *Dziela* (Works), vols. 1–8. Warsaw: Panstwowe Wydawnictwo Ekonomiczne.

Lange, Oskar and Taylor, Fred M. 1938 *(1964)*: *On the Economic Theory of Socialism*, ed. and intro. Benjamin E. Lippincott. New York, Toronto and London: McGraw Hill.

Lange, Peter and Maurizio, Vannicelli 1981: *Eurocommunism: A Case Book*. London and Boston: Allen & Unwin.

Langevin, Paul 1950: *La pensée et l'action*. Paris: Éditeurs français réunis.

Larrain, Jorge 1979: *The Concept of Ideology*. London: Hutchinson; Athens: University of Georgia Press.

—— 1983: *Marxism and Ideology*. London: Macmillan.

—— 1989: *Theories of Development*. Cambridge: Polity; Cambridge, Mass.: Basil Blackwell.

Lavoie, Don 1985: *Rivalry and Central Planning: The Socialist Calculation Debate Reconsidered*. Cambridge: Cambridge University Press.

Leacock, E.B. 1972: 'Introduction' to Engels, *The Origin of the Family*. New York: International Publishers.

—— 1981: Marxism and Anthropology. In Bertell Ollman and Edward Vernoff, eds., *The Left Academy*. New York and London: McGraw Hill.

—— 1982: *Myths of Male Dominance*. New York: Monthly Review.

—— 1983: Interpreting the Origins of Gender Inequality: Conceptual and Historical Problems. *Dialectical Anthropology* 7.4.

Lebowitz, Michael 1988: Is 'Analytical Marxism' Marxism? *Science and Society* 52.2.

Lecourt, D. 1977: *Proletarian Science? The Case of Lysenko*. London: New Left; New York: distr. Schocken.

Lefebvre, H. 1939 *(1968)*: *Dialectical Materialism*. London: Cape.

—— 1965: *Métaphilosophie prolégomènes*. Paris: Éditions de Minuit.

—— 1972: *Le Droit et la ville; Espace et politique*. Paris: Anthropos.

Leff, Gordon 1969: *History and Social Theory*. London: Merlin.

Lehning, Arthur, ed. 1973: *Michael Bakunin: Selected Writings*. London: Cape; New York: Grove.

Leiss, William 1974: *The Domination of Nature*. New York: George Braziller.

Leith, J.A., ed. 1978: *Images of the Commune*. Montreal and London: McGill-Queen's University Press.

Lekas, Padelis 1988: *Marx on Classical Antiquity*. Brighton: Wheatsheaf.

Lenin, V.I. [Where possible references are to the *Collected Works* in 45 vols. Moscow: Foreign Languages Publishing House, 1960–63; Progress Publishers, 1964–70.]

—— 1893a *(1960)*: On the So-called 'Market Question'. *CW* 1.

—— 1893b *(1960)*: What the 'Friends of the People' are and how they fight the Social-Democrats. *CW* 1.

—— 1894 *(1960)*: The Economic Content of Narodism. *CW* 1.

—— 1895–1916 *(1961)*: Philosophical Notebooks. *CW* 38.

—— 1897 *(1960)*: A Characterization of Economic Romanticism. *CW* 2.

—— 1899a *(1960)*: Apropos of the Profession de Foi. *CW* 4.

—— 1899b *(1960)*: The Development of Capitalism in Russia: The Process of the Formation of a Home Market for Larger-Scale Industry. *CW* 3.

—— 1899c *(1960)*: Retrograde Trend in Russian Social-Democracy. *CW* 4.

—— 1901 *(1961)*: A Talk with Defenders of Economism. *Iskra* 12 (December). *CW* 5.

—— 1902 *(1961)*: What is to be Done? (pamphlet). *CW* 5.

—— 1905 *(1967)*: *On Literature and Art*. Moscow: Progress.

—— 1907 *(1962)*: The Agrarian Programme of Social Democracy in the First Russian Revolution. *CW* 13.

—— 1908 *(1962)*: Materialism and Empirio-Criticism. *CW* 14.

—— 1908 *(1963)*: Inflammable Material in World Politics. *CW* 15.

—— 1909 *(1963)*: The Attitude of the Workers' Party Towards Religion. *CW* 15.

—— 1912 *(1963)*: Democracy and Narodism in China. *CW* 18.

—— 1913a *(1963)*: The Question of Ministry of Education Policy. *CW* 19.

—— 1913b *(1963)*: The Working Class and Neo-Malthusianism. *CW* 19.

—— 1914a *(1964)*: The Position and tasks of the Socialist International. *CW* 28.

—— 1914b *(1964)*: The War and Russian Social-Democracy. *CW* 21.

—— 1915 *(1964)*: The Collapse of the Second International. *CW* 21.

—— 1914–16 *(1961)*: Conspectus of Hegel's Book *The Science of Logic*. *CW* 38.

—— 1916 *(1964)*: Imperialism: the Highest Stage of Capitalism. *CW* 22.

—— 1917a *(1964)*: Report on the Present Situation and the Attitude Towards the Provisional Government. *CW* 24.

—— 1917b *(1964)*: Can the Bolsheviks Retain State Power? *CW* 26.

—— 1917c *(1969)*: State and Revolution. *CW* 25.

—— 1918a *(1965)*: The Immediate Tasks of the Soviet Government. *CW* 27.

—— 1918b (1965): The Proletarian Revolution and the Renegade Kautsky. CW 28.

—— 1919 (1965): Report to the 7th All-Russian Congress of Soviets. CW 30.

—— 1919 (1965): Speech delivered at the First Congress of Agricultural Communes and Agricultural Artels. CW 30.

—— 1920a (1966): 'Left Wing' Communism – An Infantile Disorder. CW 31.

—— 1920b (1966): On Polytechnical Education. Notes on Theses by Nadezhda Konstantinovna. CW 36.

—— 1920c (1966): Speech at 3rd Komsomol Congress, 2 October 1920. CW 31.

—— 1920d (1966): The Tasks of the Youth Leagues. CW 31.

—— 1922. Notes for a Speech on March 27.

—— 1923 (1966): On Cooperation. CW 33.

—— 1962: The National-Liberation Movement in the East. Moscow: Foreign Languages Publishing House.

—— 1970: On the National Question and Proletarian Internationalism. Moscow: Progress.

—— 1970: On Trade Unions. Moscow: Progress.

Lenin, V.I. and Gorky, M. 1973: Letters, Reminiscences, Articles. Moscow: Progress.

Lerner, A. 1934: Economic Theory and Socialist Economy. Review of Economic Studies 2.

—— 1936: A Note on Socialist Economics. Review of Economic Studies 4.

—— 1937: Statics and Dynamics in Socialist Economics. Economic Journal.

Leser, Norbert 1968: Zwischen Reformismus und Bolschewismus. Der Austromarxismus als Theorie und Praxis. Vienna: Europa Verlag.

Lévi-Strauss, Claude 1958 (1963): Structural Anthropology. New York and London: Basic Books.

Levidow, Les and Young, Robert M., eds. 1981: Science, Technology and the Labour Process: Marxist Studies. London: CSE Books; Atlantic Highlands, N.J.: Humanities.

Levin, Richard and Neocosmos, Michael 1989: The Agrarian Question and Class Contradictions in South Africa: Some Theoretical Considerations. Journal of Peasant Studies 16.

Levine, A. and Wright, E.O. 1980: Rationality and Class Struggle. New Left Review 123.

Levine, N. 1975: The Tragic Deception: Marx contra Engels. Santa Barbara: Clio.

Lévy, Louis, ed. 1947: Anthologie de Jean Jaurès. Paris: Calman Lévy; London: Penguin.

Lewin, Moshe 1967 (1969): Lenin's Last Struggle. London: Faber & Faber; New York: Pantheon.

—— 1968: Russian Peasants and Soviet Power: A Study of Collectivisation. London: Allen & Unwin.

—— 1975: Political Undercurrents in Soviet Economic Debates: From Bukharin to the Modern Reformers. London: Pluto; Princeton, N.J.: Princeton University Press.

Lewis, Arthur D. 1912: Syndicalism and the General Strike. London: Unwin; Boston, Mass.: Small, Maynard.

Lewontin, Richard and Levins, Richard 1976: The Problem of Lysenkoism. In H. and S. Rose, eds. The Radicalisation of Science. London: Macmillan.

Leyda, Jay and Voynow, Zina 1982: Eisenstein at Work. New York: Pantheon; London: Methuen (1985).

Lichtheim, George 1961: Marxism: An Historical and Critical Study. London: Routledge & Kegan Paul; New York: Praeger.

—— 1969: The Origins of Socialism. London: Weidenfeld & Nicolson; New York: Praeger.

—— 1971: From Marx to Hegel and other Essays. London: Orbach & Chambers; New York: Herder & Herder.

Liebknecht, Karl 1907 (1973): Militarism and Anti-Militarism. Cambridge: Rivers.

Liebman, Marcel 1973 (1975): Leninism under Lenin. London: Cape.

Lifshitz, Mikhail 1933 (1973): The Philosophy of Art of Karl Marx. New York: Critics Group; repub. London: Pluto.

Lindberg, L.N., ed. 1975: Stress and Contradiction in Modern Capitalism: Public Policy and the Theory of the State. Lexington, Mass.: Lexington.

Lindenberg, D. 1972: L'Internationale communiste et l'école de classe. Paris: François Maspero.

Lipietz, Alain 1982: The So-Called Transformation Problem Revisited. Journal of Economic Theory 26.1.

—— 1983: Le monde enchanté: De la valeur à la crise inflationniste. Paris: La Découverte. English trans., London: Verso (1985).

—— 1985: Mirages et miracles: Problèmes de l'industrialisation dans le Tiers Monde. Paris: La Découverte. English trans., London: Verso (1986).

Lipset, S.M. 1960: Political Man. New York: Doubleday; London: Heinemann.

Lipowski, A. 1988: Mechanizm rynkowy w gospodarce polskiej (The Market Mechanism in the Polish Economy). Warsaw: PWN.

Liss, Sheldon B. 1984: Marxist Thought in Latin America. Berkeley: University of California Press.

Lobkowicz, Nicholas 1967: Theory and Practice: History of a Concept from Aristotle to Marx. Notre Dame, Ill. and London: University of Notre Dame Press.

Locke, John 1690 (1975): Essay Concerning Human Understanding, ed. P.H. Nidditch. Oxford and New York: Oxford University Press.

Loren, Graham 1973: Science and Philosophy in the Soviet Union. ch. 6. New York: Knopf; London: Allen Lane.

Lorenzo, J.L. 1981: Archaeology South of the Rio Grande. *World Archaeology* 13.3.

Lowie, Robert H. 1929: *The Origin of the State*. New York: Harcourt.

Lowit, T. 1962: Marx et le mouvement coopératif. *Cahiers de l'Institut de science économique appliquée* series 129, 'Études de Marxologie'.

Löwith, Karl 1932 (1982): *Max Weber and Karl Marx*. London and Boston: Allen & Unwin.

—— 1941 (1964): *From Hegel to Nietzsche: The Revolution in Nineteenth-Century Thought*. London: Constable; New York: Holt, Rinehart & Winston.

Löwy, Michael 1973: *The Marxism of Che Guevara: Philosophy, Economics and Revolutionary Warfare*. New York: Monthly Review Press.

—— 1980: *Le Marxisme en Amérique Latine de 1909 à nos jours*. Paris: François Maspero. English edn. New York: Monthly Review Press.

—— 1981: *The Politics of Combined and Uneven Development*. London: New Left; New York: distr. Schocken.

Lozovsky, A. 1931: *The World Economic Crisis, Strike Struggles and the Tasks of the Revolutionary Trade Union Movement*. Moscow: State Publishers.

—— 1935: *Marx and the Trade Unions*. London: Martin Lawrence; New York: International Publishers.

Lukács, G. 1910 (1974): *The Soul and The Forms*. London: Merlin; Cambridge, Mass.: MIT Press.

—— 1911: *History of the Development of Modern Drama*. London: Merlin.

—— 1913: *Aesthetic Culture*. (In Hungarian.) Budapest: Athenaum.

—— 1916 (1971): *The Theory of the Novel*. London: Merlin; Cambridge, Mass.: MIT Press.

—— 1920 (1970): The Old Culture and the New Culture. *Telos* 5.

—— 1923 (1971): *History and Class Consciousness*. London: Merlin; Cambridge, Mass.: MIT.

—— 1924 (1970): *Lenin: A Study on the Unity of his Thought*. London: New Left; New York: distr. Schocken.

—— 1925 (1966): Technology and Social Relations. *New Left Review* 39.

—— 1937 (1962): *The Historical Novel*. London: Merlin; Boston: Beacon.

—— 1938 (1975): *The Young Hegel*. London: Merlin; Cambridge, Mass.: MIT Press.

—— 1948: Existentialisme ou marxisme. Paris: Nagel.

—— 1948: *The Tasks of Marxist Philosophy in the New Democracy*. (In Hungarian.) Budapest: Székesfővárosi Irodalmr Intézet.

—— 1949: *Literature and Democracy*. Bratislava.

—— 1963: *Die Eigenart des Ästhetischen*. Neuwied am Rhein, Berlin. Spandau: Luchterhand.

—— 1964a: *Essays on Thomas Mann*. London: Merlin; New York: Grosset & Dunlap.

—— 1964b: *Realism in our Time: Literature and the Class Struggle*. New York: Harper & Row.

—— 1968: *Goethe and his Age*. London: Merlin.

—— 1972a: *Political Writings 1919–1929*. London: New Left.

—— 1972b: *Studies in European Realism*. London: Merlin.

—— 1974a: *Heidelberger Ästhetik (1916–18)*. Darmstadt: Luchterhand.

—— 1974b: *Heidelberger Philosophie der Kunst*. Darmstadt: Luchterhand.

Lukes, Steven 1973: *Individualism*. Oxford: Basil Blackwell; New York: Harper & Row.

—— 1985: *Marxism and Morality*. Oxford: Oxford University Press.

Lunn, Eugene 1985: *Marxism and Modernism: An Historical Study of Lukács, Brecht, Benjamin, and Adorno*. London: Verso.

Luxemburg, Rosa 1899 (1937): *Reform or Revolution*. New York: Three Arrows.

—— 1905 (1972): *Socialism and the Churches*. London: Merlin.

—— 1906 (1925): *The Mass Strike, the Political Party and the Trade Unions*. Detroit: Marxian Educational Society.

—— 1913 (1963): *The Accumulation of Capital*. London: Routledge & Kegan Paul; New Haven: Yale University Press.

—— 1922 (1961): *The Russian Revolution*. Ann Arbor: University of Michigan Press.

—— 1954: *What is Economics?* New York: Pioneer; London: Merlin.

—— 1970: *Rosa Luxemburg Speaks*, ed. Mary-Alice Waters, New York: Pathfinder.

—— 1972: *Selected Political Writings*, ed. Robert Looker. London: Cape; New York: Grove.

—— 1976: *The National Question: Selected Writings of Rosa Luxemburg*, ed. Horace B. Davis. New York and London: Monthly Review Press.

Luxemburg, Rosa and Bukharin, Nikolai 1972: *Imperialism and the Accumulation of Capital*. London: Allen Lane; New York: Monthly Review Press.

Lyotard, Jean-François 1979 (1984): *The Postmodern Condition: A Report on Knowledge*. Manchester: Manchester University Press.

McCarthy, Thomas 1978: *The Critical Theory of Jürgen Habermas*. London: Hutchinson; Cambridge, Mass.: MIT Press.

Macintyre, Stuart 1974: Joseph Dietzgen and British Working-class Education. *Bulletin of the Society for the Study of Labour History* 29.

—— 1980: *A Proletarian Science: Marxism in Britain 1917–1933*. Cambridge: Cambridge University Press.

Mackail, J.W. 1899: *The Life of William Morris*.

Maclean, B. 1981: Kozo Uno's Principles of Political Economy. *Science and Society* 45.2.

McLeish, J. 1975: *Soviet Psychology: History, Theory and Content*. London and New York: Methuen.

McLellan, David 1969: *The Young Hegelians and Karl Marx*. London: Macmillan.

—— 1973: *Marx's Grundrisse*. St Albans: Paladin.

—— 1974: *Karl Marx: His Life and Thought*. London: Macmillan; New York: Harper & Row.

—— 1977: *Engels*. London: Collins; New York: Viking.

—— 1987: *Marxism and Religion*. London: Macmillan.

McLennan, G. 1989: *Marxism, Pluralism and Beyond*. Cambridge: Polity.

McMurtry, John 1978: *The Structure of Marx's World-View*. Princeton: Princeton University Press.

McNeal, R.H., ed. 1967: *Stalin's Works: an Annotated Bibliography*. Stanford: Hoover Institution.

McNeal, Robert H. (general ed.) 1974: *Resolutions and Decisions of the Communist Party of the Soviet Union*, vols. 1–4. Toronto: University of Toronto Press.

Macpherson, C.B. 1962: *The Political Theory of Possessive Individualism*. Oxford and New York: Oxford University Press.

Magdoff, Harry 1978: *Imperialism: From the Colonial Age to the Present*. New York: Monthly Review Press.

Maguire, John M. 1978: *Marx's Theory of Politics*. Cambridge and New York: Cambridge University Press.

Mallet, Serge 1975: *The New Working Class*. Nottingham: Spokesman.

Malos, E., ed. 1980: *The Politics of Housework*. Nottingham: Allison & Busby; New York: distr. Schocken.

Mamdani, Mahmood 1987: Extreme but not Exceptional: Towards an Analysis of the Agrarian Question in Uganda. *Journal of Peasant Studies* 14.2.

Manacorda, M.A. 1966: *Marx e la pedagogia moderna*. Rome: Editori Riuniti.

Mandel, Ernest 1971 (1977): *The Formation of the Economic Thought of Karl Marx*. New York: Monthly Review Press.

—— 1972 (1978): *Late Capitalism*. London: Verso.

—— 1976: 'Introduction' to Karl Marx. *Capital I*. London: Penguin; New York: Vintage.

—— 1978: *From Stalinism to Eurocommunism*. London: New Left; New York: distr. Schocken.

—— 1979: *Revolutionary Marxism Today*. London: New Left; New York: distr. Schocken.

—— 1980: *Long Waves of Capitalist Development*. Cambridge: Cambridge University Press.

Mangoni, L. 1987: La genesi delle categorie storico-politiche nei Quaderni del carcere. *Studi storici* 3.

Mann, Michael 1973: *Consciousness and Action among the Western Working Class*. London: Macmillan; Atlantic Highlands, N.J.: Humanities.

Mannheim, Karl 1929 (1936): *Ideology and Utopia*. London: Routledge & Kegan Paul; New York: Harcourt Brace.

Manser, Anthony 1966: *Sartre: A Philosophic Study*. Oxford and New York: Oxford University Press.

Mao Tse-tung (Mao Zedong) 1927: *Report on an Investigation of the Peasant Movement in Hunan*. In *Selected Works*, vol. 1. Peking: Foreign Languages Press.

—— 1937a (1967): *On Contradiction*. Selected Readings. Peking: Foreign Languages Press.

—— 1937b: *On Practice*. New York: International Publishers.

—— 1955 (1971): On the Question of Agricultural Cooperation. In *Selected Works*. Peking: Foreign Languages Press.

—— 1961–77: *Selected Works*. 5 vols. Peking: Foreign Languages Press.

—— 1974: *Miscellany of Mao Tse-tung Thought* (1949–68). Arlington, Virginia: Joint Publications Research Service (JPRS-61269).

—— 1977: *A Critique of Soviet Economics*. New York: Monthly Review Press.

Marchais, Georges 1973: *Le Défi démocratique*. Paris: Grasset.

Marcus, S. 1974: *Engels, Manchester and the Working Class*. New York: Random House; London: Weidenfeld & Nicolson.

Marcuse, Herbert 1928 (1969): Contribution to a Phenomenology of Historical Materialism. *Telos* 4.

—— 1932 (1983): *From Luther to Popper: Studies in Critical Philosophy*. London: Verso.

—— 1941 (1955): *Reason and Revolution: Hegel and the Rise of Social Theory*. New York: Oxford University Press.

—— 1948: Sartre's Existentialism. *Philosophical and Phenomenological Research* 4.

—— 1955 (1966): *Eros and Civilization: A Philosophical Inquiry into Freud*. Boston: Beacon.

—— 1958 (1964): *Soviet Marxism*. Boston: Beacon.

—— 1964 (1968): *One-Dimensional Man*. London: Routledge & Kegan Paul; Boston: Beacon.

—— 1968: *Negations: Essays in Critical Theory*. Boston: Beacon.

—— 1978: *The Aesthetic Dimension*. Boston: Beacon.

Marek, Franz 1966 (1969): *Philosophy of World Revolution*. Revised edn. London: Lawrence & Wishart; New York: International Publishers.

Marglin, S. 1974–5: What do bosses do? The Origins and Functions of Hierarchy in Capitalist Production. Part 1. *Review of Radical Political Economy* 6.2, summer 1974; Part II ibid. 7.1, spring 1975.

Mariátegui, José Carlos 1928 (1971): *Seven Interpretive Essays on Peruvian Reality*. Austin: University of Texas Press.

Marini, Ruy Mauro 1972 (1973): *Dialéctica de la dependencia*. Mexico: Ediciones Era.

Marković, Mihailo 1974: *The Contemporary Marx*. Nottingham: Spokesman.

—— 1974: *From Affluence to Praxis: Philosophy and Social Criticism*. Ann Arbor: University of Michigan Press.

—— 1982: *Democratic Socialism: Theory and Practice*. Brighton: Harvester; New York: St Martin's.

Marković, Mihailo and Petrović, Gajo, eds. 1969: *Praxis: Yugoslav Essays in the Philosophy and Methodology of the Social Sciences*. Dordrecht: D. Reidel.

Martinez-Alier, Juan 1987: *Ecological Economics*. Oxford: Basil Blackwell.

Martov, Julius 1938: *The State and the Socialist Revolution*. New York: International Review.

Martov, Y.O. and Dan, F.I. 1926: *Geschichte der russischen Sozialdemokratie*. Berlin: J.H.W. Dietz Nachfolger.

Marx and Morality 1981: Supplementary vol. of *Canadian Journal of Philosophy* 7.

März, Eduard 1968: Introduction to *Finance Capital*. Frankfurt: Europäische Verlagsanstalt.

Mashkin, M.N. 1981: *Frantsuzkie sotsialisti i demokrati i kolonial'nii vopros 1830–1871* (French socialists and democrats and the colonial question). Moscow: Izdatel'stvo 'Nauka'.

Mason, Philip 1970: *Patterns of Domination*. Oxford and New York: Oxford University Press.

Masson, V.M. 1980: U istokov teoreticheskoi misli sovetskoi arkheologii. (On the Sources of the Theoretical Concepts of Soviet Archaeology). *Kratkie Socbsheheniya* 163.

Matthews, Mervyn 1978: *Soviet Sociology 1964–75: A Bibliography*. New York: Praeger.

Mattick, P. 1969 (1971): *Marx and Keynes: The Limits of the Mixed Economy*. London: Merlin.

Medvedev, Roy 1971: *Let History Judge*. New York: Alfred A. Knopf; London: Macmillan.

Medvedev, Zhores A. 1969: *The Rise and Fall of T.D. Lysenko*. New York and London: Columbia University Press.

Meek, Ronald L., ed. 1953: *Marx and Engels on Malthus*. London: Lawrence & Wishart; Berkeley, Calif.: Ramparts Press (1971).

—— 1967: *'Economics and Ideology' and Other Essays*. London: Chapman & Hall.

Mehring, Franz 1893: *Die Lessing-Legende*. Stuttgart: J.H.W. Dietz. Abridged Eng. trans. New York: Critics Group Press (1938).

—— 1897–98: *Geschichte der deutschen Sozialdemokratie*. Stuttgart: J.H.W. Dietz.

—— 1918 (1936): *Karl Marx*. London: John Lane; New York: Covici, Friede.

Meier, Paul 1972 (1978): *William Morris: The Marxist Dreamer*. 2 vols.

Meillassoux, Claude 1964: *Anthropologie économique des Gouro de Côte d'Ivoire: de l'économie d'autosubsistance à l'agriculture commerciale*. Paris: Mouton.

—— ed. 1975: *L'esclavage en Afrique précoloniale*. Paris: Maspero.

—— 1975 (1981): *Maidens, Meal and Money: Capitalism and the domestic community*. Cambridge and New York: Cambridge University Press.

Melotti, Umberto 1972 (1977): *Marx and the Third World*. London: Macmillan; Atlantic Highlands, N.J.: Humanities.

Mendel, A.P. 1961: *Dilemmas of Progress in Tsarist Russia: Legal Marxism and Legal Populism*. Cambridge, Mass. and London: Harvard University Press.

Menschikow, Stanislaw 1989: *Lange Wellen in der Wirtschaft*. Frankfurt: Institut für Marxistische Studien und Forschungen.

Mepham, John and Ruben, David-Hillel, eds. 1979: *Issues in Marxist Philosophy*. Brighton: Harvester; Atlantic Highlands, N.J.: Humanities.

Merleau-Ponty, Maurice 1947 (1969): *Humanism and Terror*. Trans. John O'Neill. Boston: Beacon.

—— 1955 (1973): *Adventures of the Dialectic*. London: Heinemann.

Merrington, J. 1975: Town and Country in the Transition to Capitalism. *New Left Review* 93.

Mészáros, István 1970: *Marx's Theory of Alienation*. London: Merlin. Repr. 1972. New York and London: Harper & Row.

—— ed. 1971: *Aspects of History and Class Consciousness*. London: Routledge & Kegan Paul; New York: Herder & Herder.

—— 1972: *Lukács's Concept of Dialectic*. London: Merlin.

—— 1979: *The Work of Sartre*. Brighton: Harvester.

Metz, J-B. 1968: The Church's Social Function in the Light of Political Theology. *Concilium* 6.4.

—— 1969: *Theology of the World*. New York: Herder & Herder.

Meyer, A.G. 1957: *Leninism*. New York: Praeger.

Michels, R. 1911 (1959): *Political Parties*. New York: Dover.

Miliband, Ralph 1969: *The State in Capitalist Society*. London: Weidenfeld & Nicolson; New York: Basic Books.

—— 1970: The Capitalist State: Reply to Poulantzas. *New Left Review* 59, pp. 53–60.

—— 1977: *Marxism and Politics*. Oxford and New York: Oxford University Press.

—— 1980: Military Interventions and Socialist Internationalism. *Socialist Register* 17.

—— 1983: *Class Power and State Power*. London: Verso.

Miller, David 1984: *Anarchism*. London: J.M. Dent.

Millett, Kate 1971: *Sexual Politics*. Garden City, N.Y.: Doubleday; London: Hart Davis.

Mills, C. Wright 1951: *White Collar.* New York: Oxford University Press.
—— 1956: *The Power Elite.* New York: Oxford University Press.
—— 1960 (1963): *Power, Politics and People: The Collected Papers of C. Wright Mills,* ed. I.L. Horowitz. New York: Oxford University Press.
—— 1962: *The Marxists.* New York: Dell.
Minns, Richard 1980: *Pension Funds and British Capitalism.* London: Heinemann.
Mises, L. von 1920 (1935): Economic Calculation in a Socialist Community. In F.A. von Hayek, ed., *Collectivist Economic Planning.* London.
Mitchell, Juliet 1974: *Psychoanalysis and Feminism.* London: Penguin.
Mitchell, Juliet and Oakley, A. 1976: *The Rights and Wrongs of Women.* London: Penguin.
Mitra, A. 1977: *Terms of Trade and Class Relations.* London: Frank Cass.
Mlynar, Zdenek (director) 1982–9: *Crises in Soviet-type Systems,* nos. 1–16.
Molnar, E. 1967: *La Politique d'Alliances du Marxisme* (1848–1889). Budapest: Akademiei Kiado.
Molyneux, John 1978: *Marxism and the Party.* London: Pluto.
Molyneux, M. 1979: Beyond the Domestic Labour Debate. *New Left Review* 16.
—— 1981: Socialist Societies Old and New: Progress towards Women's Emancipation. *Feminist Review* 8.
A Monograph of Christian Jewish Relations 21.1, Spring 1988.
Moore, Stanley 1980: *Marx on the Choice between Socialism and Communism.* Cambridge, Mass. and London: Harvard University Press.
Moorhouse, H.F. 1978: The Marxist Theory of the Labour Aristocracy. *Social History* 3.1.
Morawski, Stefan 1974: *Inquiries into the Fundamentals of Aesthetics.* Cambridge, Mass. and London: MIT Press.
Morgan, Lewis Henry 1877 (1974): *Ancient Society.* New York: Henry Holt.
—— 1881 (1965): *Houses and House-life of the American Aborigines.* Chicago and London: University of Chicago Press.
Morgan, R. 1965: *The German Social Democrats and the First International 1864–1872.* Cambridge: Cambridge University Press.
Morishima, Michio 1973: *Marx's Economics.* Cambridge and New York: Cambridge University Press.
—— 1974: Marx in the Light of Modern Economic Theory. *Econometrica.*
Morris, William 1910–15: *Collected Works.* 24 vols.
—— 1936: *William Morris: Artist, Writer, Socialist.* 2 vols. Oxford: Basil Blackwell.
—— 1962 (1984): *William Morris, Selected Writings and Designs,* ed. Asa Briggs. New edn. Harmondsworth: Penguin.

—— 1968 (1974): *Three Works by William Morris: News from Nowhere, The Pilgrims of Hope, A Dream of John Ball,* ed. A.L. Morton. London: Lawrence & Wishart.
—— 1970: *News from Nowhere,* ed. James Redmond. London: Routledge.
—— 1973 (1984): *Political Writings of William Morris,* ed. A.L. Morton. London: Lawrence & Wishart.
—— 1984–7: *The Collected Letters of William Morris,* ed. Norman Kelvin. Vol. 1: *1848–80* (1984); vol. 2: part A, *1881–4,* part B, *1885–8* (1987); vol. 3 in prep. Princeton: Princeton University Press.
Morton, A.L. 1938: *A People's History of England.* London: Gollancz.
Mosca, Gaetano 1896 (1939): *The Ruling Class.* New York: McGraw Hill.
Mosetic, G. 1987: *Die Gesellschaftstheorie des Austromarxismus.* Darmstadt: Wissenschaftliche Buchgesellschaft.
Mouffe, C., ed. 1979: *Gramsci and Marxist Theory.* London and Boston: Routledge & Kegan Paul.
Mousnier, Roland 1969 (1973): *Social Hierarchies.* London: Croom Helm; New York: distr. Schocken.
Müller, Hans 1967: *Ursprung und Geschichte des Wortes 'Sozialismus' und seiner Verwandten.* Hanover: J.H.W. Dietz.
Müller-Doohm, Stefan 1990: Media Research as Symbol Analysis. In Michael Charlton and Ben Bachmair, eds. *Media Communication in Everyday Life,* vol. 9. Munich: K.G. Saur.
Munk, Erika 1972: *Brecht: A Collection of Critical Pieces.* New York: Bantam.
Murray, R. 1977: Value and Theory of Rent. *Capital and Class* 3.
Nagai, Yonosuke and Iriye Akira, eds. 1977: *The Origins of the Cold War in Asia.* Tokyo: University of Tokyo Press.
Naïr, Sami 1981: Goldmann's Legacy. *Telos* 46.
Nairn, Tom 1977: *The Break-up of Britain: Crisis and Neo-Nationalism.* London: New Left; New York: distr. Schocken.
Namboodripad, E.M.S. 1952: *The National Question in Kerala.* Bombay: People's Publishing House.
—— 1966: *Economics and Politics of India's Socialist Pattern.* New Delhi: People's Publishing House.
Narkiewicz, Olga A. 1981: *Marxism and the Reality of Power 1919–1980.* London: Croom Helm; New York: St Martin's.
Negt, Oskar, ed. 1970: *Aktualität und Folge der Philosophie Hegels.* Frankfurt am Main: Suhrkamp.
Nehru, Jawaharlal 1936: *An Autobiography.* London: John Lane.
Nettl, J.P. 1966: *Rosa Luxemburg.* 2 vols. London: Oxford University Press.
Neumann, Franz 1942: *Behemoth: The Structure and Practice of National Socialism.* 2nd edn with appendix 1944. New York: Oxford University Press.

Neurath, O. 1973: *Empiricism and Sociology*, ed. Marie Neurath and Robert S. Cohen. Dordrecht and Boston: Reidel.

Nichols, Theo 1980: *Capital and Labour: Studies in the Capitalist Labour Process*. London: Fontana.

Nicolaus, Martin 1967: Proletariat and Middle Class in Marx. *Studies on the Left 7*.

Nielsen, K. and Patten, S.C., eds. 1981: Marx and Morality. *Canadian Journal of Philosophy*, suppl. vol. 7.

Nimni, Ephraim 1991: *Marxism and Nationalism*. London: Pluto Press.

Nolan, Peter 1988: *The Political Economy of Collective Farms*. Cambridge: Polity.

Norman, Dorothy, ed. 1965: *Nehru, the First Sixty Years*. London: Bodley Head; New York: John Day.

Norman, R. and Sayers, S. 1980: *Hegel, Marx and Dialectic*. Brighton: Harvester; Atlantic Highlands, N.J.: Humanities.

Nove, A. 1964: *Economic Rationality and Soviet Politics: or, Was Stalin Really Necessary?* London: Allen & Unwin; New York: Praeger.

—— 1983: *The Economics of Feasible Socialism*. London: Allen and Unwin.

Nun, José 1969: Superpoblación relativa, ejército industrial de reserva y masa marginal. *Revista Latinoamericana de Sociología 5.2*.

Nuti, D.M. 1981: Socialism on Earth. *Cambridge Journal of Economics 5*.

—— 1988: Perestroika: Transition from Central Planning to Market Socialism. *Economic Policy 7*.

O'Connor, James 1973: *The Fiscal Crisis of the State*. New York: St Martin's.

Offe, Claus 1972a: *Strukturprobleme des kapitalistischen Staates*. Frankfurt: Suhrkamp.

—— 1972b: Political Authority and Class Structures: An Analysis of Late Capitalist Societies. *International Journal of Sociology 2.1*.

—— 1980: The Separation of Form and Content in Liberal Democratic Politics. *Studies in Political Economy 3*.

Ogurtsov, A.P.: Alienation. In *Soviet Encyclopaedia of Philosophy*.

Ojzerman, T.I. 1962: *Formirovanije Filozofii Marxisma*. Moscow.

Okishio, Nubuo 1961: Technical Change and the Rate of Profit. *Kobe University Economic Review*.

—— 1963: A Mathematical Note on Marxian Theory. *Weltwirtschaftliches Archiv 91*.

—— 1977: Notes on Technical Progress and Capitalist Society. *Cambridge Journal of Economics 1.1*.

O'Laughlin, B. 1977: Production and Reproduction: Meillassoux's *Femmes, Greniers et Capitaux*. *Critique of Anthropology 8*.

O'Leary, Brendan 1989: *The Asiatic Mode of Production*. Oxford: Basil Blackwell.

Ollman, Bertell 1971 (1976): *Alienation: Marx's Conception of Man in Capitalist Society*. 2nd edn. Cambridge and New York: Cambridge University Press.

O'Malley, Joseph 1970: Editorial Introduction to Karl Marx, *Critique of Hegel's Philosophy of Right*. Cambridge: Cambridge University Press.

Omredt, Gail 1976: *Cultural Revolt in a Colonial Society: The Non-Brahmin Movement in Western India, 1873–1930*. Bombay: Scientific Socialist Education Trust.

Oncken, Hermann 1920: *Lassalle: Eine politische Biographie*. 3rd edn. Stuttgart and Berlin: Deutsche Verlagsanstalt.

Orleans, L.A., ed. 1980: *Science in Contemporary China*. Stanford: Stanford University Press.

Osiatynski, Jerzy 1988: *Michal Kalecki on a Socialist Economy*. London: Macmillan.

Osipov, G.V. and Rutkevich, M.N. 1978: Sociology in the USSR 1965–1975. *Current Sociology 26.2*.

Ossowski, Stanislaw 1957 (1963): *Class Structure in the Social Consciousness*. London: Routledge & Kegan Paul; New York: Free Press of Glencoe.

Outhwaite, W. 1975: *Understanding Social Life*. London: Allen & Unwin; New York: Holmes & Meier.

Owen, Robert 1812–16 (1969): *Report to the County of Lanark: A New View of Society*, ed. V. Gatrell. London: Penguin.

Pachter, Henry 1979: Marx and the Jews. *Dissent* Fall.

Padgug, R.A. 1976: Problems in the Theory of Slavery and Slave Society. *Science and Society 40*.

Palma, G. 1978: Dependency: A Formal Theory of Underdevelopment or a Methodology for the Analysis of Concrete Situations of Underdevelopment. *World Development 6. 7–8*.

Pane, Luigi dal 1935: *Antonio Labriola: La vita e il pensiero*. Rome: Edizioni Roma. Repr.: Bologna: Forni (1968).

Panitch, L. 1977: The Development of Corporatism in Liberal Democracies. *Comparative Political Studies 10*.

Pannekoek, Antonie 1909 (1912): *Marxism and Darwinism*. Chicago: Charles H. Kerr.

—— 1938 (1948): *Lenin as Philosopher*. New York: New Essays. London: Merlin (1975).

—— 1951 (1961): *A History of Astronomy*. London: Allen & Unwin; New York: Interscience Publishers.

—— 1970: *Workers' Councils*. Somerville, Ma.: Kont & Branch.

Parkin, Frank 1979: *Marxism and Class Theory: A Bourgeois Critique*. London: Tavistock.

Parkinson, G.H.R. ed. 1970: *Georg Lukács: The Man, his Work and his Ideas*. London: Weidenfeld & Nicolson.

Parti Communiste Français (PCF) 1976: *Le Socialisme pour la France*. Paris: Éditions Sociales.

Pashukanis, E.B. 1979: *Selected Writings on Marxism and Law*. Translated by Peter B. Maggs with an introduction by Piers Beirne and Robert Sharlet. London and New York: Academic Press.

Past and Present 1978, 1979, 1982: Symposium on Agrarian Class Structure and Economic Development in Western Europe.

Patnaik, Utsa 1976: Class Differentiation within the Peasantry: An Approach to Analysis of Indian Agriculture. *Economic and Political Weekly* 11. 39, Sept.

—— 1987: *Peasant Class Differentiation: A Study in Method with Reference to Haryana*. Delhi: Oxford University Press.

—— ed. 1989: *Agrarian Relations and Accumulation: The Mode of Production Debate*. Bombay: Oxford University Press for the Sameeksha Trust.

Pavlov, I.P. 1932 (*1958*): *Experimental Psychology and Other Essays*. London: Peter Owen; New York: Philosophical Library.

Payne, S.G. 1970: *The Spanish Revolution*. London: Weidenfeld & Nicolson; New York: Norton.

Pearce, Frank 1976: *Crimes of the Powerful: Marxism, Crime and Deviance*. London: Pluto.

Pease, Margaret 1916: *Jean Jaurès, Socialist and Humanitarian*. London: Headley; New York: Huebsch (1917).

Peet, R. 1977: *Radical Geography*. London and New York: Methuen.

Pennock, J.R. and Chapman, J.W. eds. 1978: *Anarchism*. New York: New York University Press.

Perlo, V. 1966: Capital Output Ratios in Manufacturing. *Quarterly Review of Economics and Business* 8.3.

Peterson, Arnold 1941: *Daniel de Leon: Socialist Architect*. New York: New York Labor News.

Petrović, Gajo 1967: *Marx in the Mid-Twentieth Century*. Garden City, N.Y.: Doubleday.

—— 1971: *Philosophie und Revolution*. Reinbek bei Hamburg: Rowohlt.

Petry, F. 1916: *Der soziale Gehalt der Marxschen Werttheorie*. Jena: Fischer.

Phillips, Paul 1981: *Marx and Engels on Law and Laws*. Oxford: Martin Robertson. New York: Barnes & Noble.

Piaget, Jean 1970: *Structuralism*. London: Routledge & Kegan Paul.

Pinkus, Theo ed. 1974: *Conversations with Lukács*. London: Merlin.

Pipes, R. 1970: *Struve*. 2 vols. Vol. 1. *Liberal on the Left*. Cambridge, Mass.: Harvard University Press.

Plamenatz, John 1975: *Karl Marx's Philosophy of Man*. Oxford and New York: Oxford University Press.

Plekhanov, G.V. 1885 (*1961*): *Our Differences*. In *Selected Philosophical Works* vol. 1.

—— 1895 (*1945*): *In Defence of Materialism. The Development of the Monist View of History*. London: Lawrence & Wishart; New York: International Publishers (1972).

—— 1898 (*1940*): *The Role of the Individual in History*. London: Lawrence & Wishart; New York: International Publishers.

—— 1908 (*1969*): *Fundamental Problems of Marxism*. London: Lawrence & Wishart; New York: International Publishers.

—— 1908–10 (*1973*): *Materialismus Militans*. Moscow: Progress; London: Lawrence & Wishart (1974).

—— 1912 (*1953*): *Art and Social Life*. London: Lawrence & Wishart.

—— 1961–81: *Selected Philosophical Works*. 5 vols. London: Lawrence & Wishart; Chicago: distr. Imported Publications. (Includes several of the above works.)

—— 1974: *The Development of the Monist View of History*. London: Lawrence & Wishart.

Plotke, D. 1977: Marxist political thought and the problem of revisionism. *Socialist Revolution* 7(6).

Poggi, Gianfranco 1978: *The Development of the Modern State*. London: Hutchinson; Stanford: Stanford University Press.

Pollock, Frederick 1975: *Stadien des Kapitalismus*, ed. with intro. by Helmut Dubiel. Munich: C.H. Beck.

Pomeroy, William J. 1970: *American Neo-colonialism: Its Emergence in the Philippines and Asia*. New York: International Publishers.

Ponzio, Augosto 1973: *Produzione linguistica e ideologia sociale. Per una teoria marxista del linguaggio e della communicazione*. Bari: De Donato.

Popper, Karl 1957: *The Poverty of Historicism*. London: Routledge & Kegan Paul.

Porshnev, Boris 1948 (*1963*): *Les soulèvements populaires en France*. Paris: S.E.V.P.E.N.

Porter, Cathy 1980: *Alexandra Kollontai: A Biography*. London: Virago.

Pospelow, P.M., *et al.* 1971: *Development of Revolutionary Theory by the CPSU*. Moscow: Progress.

Poster, Mark 1978: *Critical Theory of the Family*. London: Pluto; New York: Seabury.

Poulantzas, Nicos 1968 (*1973*): *Political Power and Social Classes*. London: New Left; New York: distr. Schocken.

—— 1969: The Problem of the Capitalist State. *New Left Review* 58, pp. 67–78.

—— 1970 (*1974*): *Fascism and Dictatorship*. London: New Left; New York: distr. Schocken.

—— 1974 (*1975*): *Classes in Contemporary Capitalism*. London: New Left; New York: distr. Schocken.

—— 1975 (*1976*): *Crisis of the Dictatorships*. 2nd edn. London: Verso.

—— 1978: *State, Power, Socialism*. London: New Left; New York: distr. Schocken.

Prawer, S.S. 1976: *Karl Marx and World Literature*. Oxford and New York: Oxford University Press.

Preobrazhensky, Evgeny A. 1922 (*1973*): *From NEP to Socialism*. London: New Park.

—— 1926 (1965): *The New Economics*. Trans. Brian Pearce, Oxford: Oxford University Press.

—— 1980: *The Crisis of Soviet Industrialization*. Selected Essays, ed. Donald A. Filzer. London: Macmillan; White Plains, N.Y.: M.E. Sharpe.

Programme of the League of Communists of Yugoslavia 1958. Belgrade.

Pronin, A. 1940: *India*. Moscow.

Proudhon, Pierre-Joseph 1970: *Selected Writings*. London: Macmillan; Garden City, N.Y.: Anchor.

Przeworski, Adam 1977: Proletariat into a Class: The Process of Class Formation from Karl Kautsky's *The Class Struggle* to Recent Controversies. *Politics and Society* 7.4.

—— 1980: Social democracy as a historical phenomenon. *New Left Review* 122.

Praxis International 1.1. 1981: Symposium on Socialism and Democracy.

Quaini, Massimo 1974 (*1982*): *Geography and Marxism*. Oxford: Basil Blackwell. Totowa, N.J.: Barnes & Noble.

Quijano, Aníbal 1974: The Marginal Pole of the Economy and the Marginalised Labour Force. *Economy and Society* 3.4.

Quinney, Richard (1977): *Class, State and Crime*. New York and London: Longman.

Radical Science Journal Collective 1981: Science, Technology, Medicine and the Socialist Movement. *Radical Science Journal* 2.

Radice, Hugo ed. 1975: *International Firms and Modern Imperialism*. London and Baltimore: Penguin.

Rahman, Atiur 1986: *Peasants and Classes: A Study in Differentiation in Bangladesh*. London and New Jersey: Zed Books.

Rahmani, L. 1973: *Soviet Psychology: Philosophical, Theoretical and Experimental Issues*. New York: International Universities Press.

Rakovski, M. 1978: *Toward an East European Marxism*. London: Allison & Busby; New York: St Martin's.

Ranadive, B.T. 1982: *Caste, Class and Property Relations*. Delhi: National Book Centre.

Raphael, Max 1933 (*1980*): *Proudhon, Marx, Picasso: Three Studies in the Sociology of Art*. London: Lawrence & Wishart; Atlantic Highlands, N.J.: Humanities.

Rapp, R. 1978: Family and class in contemporary America: Notes toward an understanding of ideology. *Science and Society* 42.3.

Rappoport, Charles 1915: *Jean Jaurès: l'homme, le penseur, le socialiste*. Paris: L'Emancipatrice.

Razeto Migliaro, L. and Misuraca, P. 1978: *Sociologia e marxismo nella critica di Gramsci*. Bari: De Donato.

Redclift, Nanneke and Mingione, Enzo, eds. 1985: *Beyond Employment, Household, Gender and Subsistence*. Oxford: Basil Blackwell.

Ree, Jonathan 1984: *Proletarian Philosophies: Problems in Socialist Culture in Britain, 1900–1940*. Oxford: Clarendon.

Reich, W. 1942 (*1975*): *The Mass Psychology of Fascism*. London: Penguin; New York: Farrar, Strauss and Giroux.

—— 1945: *The Sexual Revolution*. New York: Orgone Institute; London: Vision (1961).

Reiter, R., ed. 1975: *Toward an Anthropology of Women*. New York and London: Monthly Review Press.

Renner, Karl 1902: *Der Kampf der Österreichischen Nationen um der Staat*. Leipzig and Vienna: Franz Deutike.

—— 1904 (*1949*): *The Institutions of Private Law and their Social Functions*. Translated by Agnes Schwartzschild. Ed. with introduction and notes by Otto Kahn-Freund. London: Routledge & Kegan Paul.

—— 1916: Probleme des Marxismus. In *Der Kampf* vol. ix.

—— 1953a: *Wandlungen der modernen Gesellschaft*. Vienna: Wiener Volksbuchhandlung.

—— 1953b (*1978*): The Service Class. In Bottomore and Goode, eds., *Austro-Marxism*. (A trans. from one chapter of *Wandlungen*.)

Rex, John 1982: *Race Relations in Sociological Theory*. New revised edn. London and Boston: Routledge & Kegan Paul.

Rey, P.-P. 1973: *Les Alliances de Classes*. Paris: Maspero.

—— 1975: The Lineage Mode of Production. *Critique of Anthropology* 3 (Spring) 17–79.

Rhodes, R. ed. 1970: *Imperialism and Underdevelopment: a Reader*. New York: Monthly Review Press.

Ricardo, D. 1817 (*1973*): *The Principles of Political Economy and Taxation*. London: J.M. Dent; New York: E.P. Dutton.

Ridley, F.F. 1970: *Revolutionary Syndicalism in France*. Cambridge and New York: Cambridge University Press.

Riedel, Manfred 1974: *System und Geschichte*. Frankfurt am Main: Suhrkamp.

Rigby, H. 1979: *Lenin's Government Sovnarkom 1917–1922*. Cambridge and New York: Cambridge University Press.

Rigby, T.H. ed. 1966: *Stalin*. Englewood Cliffs, N.J.: Prentice-Hall.

Riley, Denise 1981: Left Critiques of the Family. In *Women in Society* ed. Cambridge Women's Studies Group. London: Virago.

Roberts, B. 1978: *Cities of Peasants: The Political Economy of Urbanization in the Third World*. London: Edward Arnold; Beverley Hills: Sage.

Roberts, D.D. 1979: *The Syndicalist Tradition and Italian Fascism*. Manchester: Manchester University Press; Chapel Hill: University of North Carolina Press.

Roberts, Julian 1982: *Walter Benjamin*. London: Macmillan; Atlantic Highlands, N.J.: Humanities.

Robertson, Roland 1972: *The Sociological Interpretation of Religion*. Oxford: Basil Blackwell; New York: distr. Schocken.

Robinson, Joan 1933 (1969): *The Economics of Imperfect Competition*. London: Macmillan.

—— 1937 (1969): *Introduction to the Theory of Employment*. London: Macmillan.

—— 1942: *An Essay on Marxian Economics*. London: Macmillan; New York: St Martin's.

—— 1951–79: *Collected Economic Papers*. 5 vols. Oxford: Basil Blackwell.

—— 1956 (1969): *The Accumulation of Capital*. London: Macmillan.

Robinson, Paul 1969: *The Sexual Radicals*. London: Temple Smith; New York: Harper & Row (under the title *The Freudian Left*).

Roderick, R. 1986: *Habermas and the Foundations of Critical Theory*. London: Macmillan.

Rodinson, Maxime 1971: *Mohammad*. London: Allen Lane.

—— 1974: *Islam and Capitalism*. London: Allen Lane.

—— 1979: *Marxism and the Muslim World*. London: Allen Lane.

Rodney, Walter 1972: *How Europe Underdeveloped Africa*. London: Bogle-l'Ouverture.

Roemer, John E. 1979: Continuing Controversy on the Falling Rate of Profit: Fixed Capital and Other Issues. *Cambridge Journal of Economics* 3(4).

—— 1982: *A General Theory of Exploitation and Class*. Cambridge: Harvard University Press.

—— ed. 1986: *Analytical Marxism*. Cambridge: Cambridge University Press.

—— 1988: *Free to Lose: An Introduction to Marxist Economic Philosophy*. London: Radius.

Roff, W.R. ed. 1987: *Islam and the Political Economy of Meaning: Comparative Studies of Muslim Discourse*. Berkeley and Los Angeles: University of California Press.

Roncaglia, A. 1974: The Reduction of Complex to Simple Labour. *Bulletin of the Conference of Socialist Economists* III.9.

Rosas, Paul 1943: Caste and Class in India. *Science and Society* 7.2.

Rosdolsky, Roman 1968 (1977): *The Making of Marx's 'Capital'*. London: Pluto; Atlantic Highlands, N.J.: Humanities.

Rose, Gillian 1978: *The Melancholy Science*. London: Macmillan; New York: Columbia University Press.

Rose, H. and S. 1976: *The Political Economy of Science*. London: Macmillan; Boston, Mass.: G.K. Hall (1980).

Ross, George 1982: *Workers and Communists in France*. Berkeley, Calif.: University of California Press.

Rossi-Landi, Ferruccio 1968: Per un uso marxiano di Wittgenstein. In *Il linguaggio come lavoro e mer-*

cato. Milan: Bompiani.

—— 1975: *Linguistics and Economics*. The Hague and Paris: Mouton.

Rostow, W.W. 1960: *The Stages of Economic Growth*. Cambridge: Cambridge University Press.

—— ed. 1963: *The Economics of Take Off into Sustained Growth*. International Economic Association. London: Macmillan; New York: St Martin's.

Roszak, Theodore 1970: *The Making of a Counter Culture*. London: Faber.

Roth, Jack J. 1980: *The Cult of Violence: Sorel and the Sorelians*. Berkeley and Los Angeles: University of California Press.

Rougerie, J., ed. 1871 (1972): *Jalons pour une histoire de la commune de Paris*. Amsterdam: International Institute of Social History.

Routley, Richard and Meyer, Robert K. 1976: Dialectical Logic, Classical Logic, and the Consistency of the World. *Studies in Soviet Thought* 16.

Rowbotham, Sheila 1973: *Hidden from History*. London: Pluto; New York: Pantheon (1975).

—— 1974: *Women, Resistance and Revolution*. London: Penguin; New York: Pantheon.

Rowthorn, R. 1980: *Capitalism, Conflict and Inflation; essays in Political Economy*. London: Lawrence & Wishart; Atlantic Highlands, N.J.: Humanities.

Roxborough, Ian 1979: *Theories of Underdevelopment*. London: Macmillan; Atlantic Highlands, N.J.: Humanities.

Roy, M.N. 1922: *India in Transition*. Geneva: J.B. Target.

—— 1930s (1946): *Revolution and Counterrevolution in China*. Calcutta: Renaissance.

—— 1934 (1940): *Materialism: An Outline of the History of Scientific Thought*. Calcutta: Renaissance.

Rubel, Maximilien 1948: *Pages choisies pour une éthique socialiste*. Paris: Marcel Rivière.

—— 1960: *Karl Marx devant le Bonapartisme*. The Hague and Paris: Mouton.

—— 1980: *Marx: Life and Works*. London: Macmillan; New York: Facts on File.

—— 1981: *Rubel on Karl Marx: Five Essays*, ed. Joseph O'Malley and Keith Algozin. Cambridge and New York: Cambridge University Press.

Ruben, David-Hillel 1977: *Marxism and Materialism*. Brighton: Harvester; Atlantic Highlands, N.J.: Humanities.

Rubery, Jill 1978: Structured Labour Markets. Workers' Organization and Low Pay. *Cambridge Journal of Economics* 2.1.

Rubin, G. 1975: The Traffic in Women. In R. Reiter, ed., *Toward an Anthropology of Women*. New York: Monthly Review Press.

Rubin, Isaak I. 1928 (1972): *Essays on Marx's Theory of Value*. Montreal: Black Rose; Detroit: Black & Red.

—— 1979: *A History of Economic Thought*. London: Ink Links; Atlantic Highlands, N.J.: Humanities.

Rudé, George 1964: *The Crowd in History, 1730–1848*. New York: Wiley; London: Lawrence & Wishart.

—— 1980: *Ideology and Popular Protest*. London: Lawrence & Wishart; New York: Pantheon.

—— 1988: *The Face of the Crowd: Selected Essays of George Rudé*, ed. Harvey Kaye. London: Harvester Wheatsheaf; Atlantic Highlands, N.J.: Humanities.

Rudebeck, Lars 1983: *On the Class Basis of the National-Liberation Movement of Guinea-Bissau*. Uppsala: AKUT.

Runciman, W.G., ed. 1978: *Max Weber: Selections in Translation*. Cambridge and New York: Cambridge University Press.

Rusche, Georg and Kirchheimer, Otto 1939: *Punishment and Social Structure*. New York: Columbia University Press.

Ryan, Cheyney C. 1980: Socialist Justice and the Right to the Labour Product. *Political Theory* 8.

Ryazanov, David B. 1928: Zur Frage des Verhältnisses von Marx zu Blanqui. *Unter dem Banner des Marxismus* 2.

Safonov, V. 1951: *Land in Bloom*. Moscow: Foreign Languages Press.

Sahlins, Marshall 1976: *Culture and Practical Reason*. Chicago and London: University of Chicago Press.

Said, Edward W. 1978: *Orientalism*. London: Routledge & Kegan Paul.

Saith, Ashwani ed. 1985: *The Agrarian Question in Socialist Transitions*. London: Frank Cass.

Salvadori, M. 1979: *Karl Kautsky and the Socialist Revolution*. London: New Left; New York: distr. Schocken.

Samuel, Raphael, ed. 1977: *The Workshop of the World: Steam Power and Hand Technology in mid-Victorian Britain. History Workshop* 3.

—— 1980: The British Marxist Historians I. *New Left Review* 120.

—— ed. 1981: *People's History and Socialist Theory*. London and Boston: Routledge & Kegan Paul.

Sand, S. 1984: *L'Illusion du politique: Georges Sorel et le débat intellectuel 1900*. Paris: Découverte.

Sankrityayana, Rahul 1942 (1947): *Volga se Ganga (From Volga to Ganga* (Ganges), trans. from Hindi by V.G. Kiernan.) Bombay: People's Publishing House.

Sartre, Jean-Paul 1943 (1969): *Being and Nothingness*.

—— 1948: *Portrait of the Anti-Semite*. London: Secker & Warburg; New York: distr. Schocken.

—— 1960 (1976): *Critique of Dialectical Reason*. London: New Left; New York: distr. Schocken.

—— 1962: *Literary and Philosophical Essays*. New York: Collier.

—— 1963: *The Problem of Method*. London: Methuen; New York: Knopf.

—— 1972: *Between Existentialism and Marxism*. London: New Left.

Sassoon, Anne Showstack 1980 (1987): *Gramsci's Politics*. London: Croom Helm; New York: St Martin's.

—— ed. 1982: *Approaches to Gramsci*. London: Writers and Readers Publishing Cooperative.

Saville, John 1987: *1848: The British State and the Chartist Movement*. Cambridge: Cambridge University Press.

Saville, John *et al*. eds. 1954: *Democracy and the Labour Movement*. London: Lawrence & Wishart.

Sawyer, Malcolm 1985: *The Economics of Michal Kalecki*. London: Macmillan.

Sayer, D. 1979: *Marx's Method*. Brighton: Harvester; Atlantic Highlands, N.J.: Humanities.

Sayers, Janet, Evans, Mary and Redclift, Nanneke eds. 1987: *Engels Revisited*. London and New York: Tavistock.

Schacht, Richard 1970: *Alienation*. Garden City, N.Y.: Doubleday.

Schaff, Adam 1963: *A Philosophy of Man*. New York: Monthly Review Press.

—— 1974: *Structuralisme et Marxisme*. Paris: Éditions Anthropos.

—— 1980: *Alienation as a Social Phenomenon*. Oxford and New York: Pergamon.

Schiller, Herbert 1976: *Communication and Cultural Domination*. White Plains, N.Y.: International Arts and Sciences Press.

Schmidt, Alfred 1962 (1971): *The Concept of Nature in Marx*. London: New Left.

—— 1974: *Zur Idee der kritischen Theorie: Elemente der Philosophie Max Horkheimers*. Munich: Carl Hanser.

Schmied-Kowarzik, W. 1981: *Die Dialektik der gesellschaftlichen Praxis*. Freiburg and Munich: Verlag Karl Alber.

Schmitter, P.C. 1977: Modes of Interest, Intermediation and Models of Societal Change in Western Europe. *Comparative Political Studies* 10.

Schoeps, Karl H. 1977: *Bertolt Brecht*. New York: Frederick Ungar.

Scholem, Gershom 1982: *Walter Benjamin: History of a Friendship*. London: Faber.

Schram, Stuart R. 1969: *The Political Thought of Mao Tse-tung*. (Revised edn.) New York: Praeger.

—— ed. 1974: *Mao Tse-tung Unrehearsed*. London: Penguin.

—— 1977: The Marxist. In Dick Wilson, ed., *Mao Tse-tung in the Scales of History*.

Schulkind, Eugene 1972: *The Paris Commune: The View from the Left*. London: Cape; New York: Grove House.

Schumpeter, J.A. 1919 (1951): The Sociology of Imperialisms. In Paul Sweezy, ed. *Imperialism and Social Classes*. New York: Augustus M. Kelley.

—— 1939: *Business Cycles*, 2 vols. New York.

—— 1976: *Capitalism, Socialism and Democracy.* 5th edn. London: Allen & Unwin; New York: Harper & Row.

Scientific-Technological Revolution: Social Aspects 1977. London and Beverly Hills: Sage.

Schwarz, Bill 1982: The People in History: The Communist Party Historians' Group, 1946–56. In Richard Johnson *et al.*, eds. *Making Histories: Studies in History-Writing and Politics.*

Scott, Alison MacEwen ed. 1986: *Rethinking Petty Commodity Production. Social Analysis* 20, special issue series.

Scott, John 1979: *Corporations, Classes and Capitalism.* London: Hutchinson; New York: St Martin's.

—— 1991: *Who Rules Britain?* Cambridge: Polity.

Seddon, D., ed. 1978: *Relations of Production: Marxist Approaches to Economic Anthropology.* London: Frank Cass.

Seeman, M. 1971: The Urban Alienations: Some Dubious Themes from Marx to Marcuse. *Journal of Personality and Social Psychology* 19.2.

Segundo, J-L. 1973: *The Community Called Church.* Maryknoll, N.Y.: Orbis.

Sekine, Thomas 1975: Uno-Riron: a Japanese Contribution to Marxian Political Economy. *Journal of Economic Literature* 13.3.

—— 1984: *The Dialectic of Capital*, vol. 1. Tokyo: Yushindo.

Selden, M. 1982 (*1988*): Cooperation and Conflict. In *The Political Economy of Chinese Socialism.* New York: M.E. Sharpe.

Seliger, Martin 1977: *The Marxist Conception of Ideology.* Cambridge and New York: Cambridge University Press.

Selucky, Radoslav 1979: *Marxism, Socialism, Freedom.* London: Macmillan; New York: St Martin's.

Seretan, L.G. 1979: *Daniel de Leon: The Odyssey of an American Marxist.* Cambridge, Mass.: Harvard University Press.

Service, Elman 1962: *Primitive Social Organisation: An Evolutionary Perspective.* New York: Random House.

Seton, F. 1957: The Transformation Problem. *Review of Economic Studies* 24.

Sève, L. 1974 (*1978*): *Man in Marxist Theory and the Psychology of Personality.* Brighton: Harvester; Atlantic Highlands, N.J.: Humanities.

Shachtman, Max 1962: *The Bureaucratic Revolution: The Rise of the Stalinist State.* New York: Donald Press.

Shaikh, A. 1978a: *U.S. Capitalism in Crisis.* Union for Radical Political Economics.

—— 1978b: Political Economy and Capitalism: Notes on Dobb's Theory of Crisis. *Cambridge Journal of Economics* 242–7.

—— 1980a: Marxian Competition versus Perfect Competition. *Cambridge Journal of Economics* 4.

—— 1980b: *The Transformation from Marx to Sraffa.* Mimeo.

—— 1982: Neo-Ricardian Economics: A Wealth of Algebra, A Poverty of Theory. *Review of Radical Political Economy* 14.2.

Sharma, R.S. 1959: *Aspects of Political Ideas in Ancient India.* New Delhi: Motilal Banarsidas.

—— 1965: *Indian Feudalism c.300–1200.* Calcutta: University of Calcutta.

—— 1966: *Light on Early Indian Society and Economy.* Bombay: Manaktalas.

—— 1976: Forms of Property in the Early Portions of the Rg Veda. In Barun De, *et al.*, eds *Essays in Honour of Professor S.C. Sarkar.* New Delhi: People's Publishing House.

Shaw, William H. 1978: *Marx's Theory of History.* London: Hutchinson; Stanford: Stanford University Press.

Sheptulin, A.I. 1962: *Introduction to Marxist-Leninist Philosophy.* Moscow.

Sher, Gerson S. 1977: *Praxis: Marxist Criticism and Dissent in Socialist Yugoslavia.* Bloomington and London: Indiana University Press.

Shonfield, A. 1965: *Modern Capitalism.* London: Oxford University Press.

Shroyer, Trent 1973: *The Critique of Domination.* New York: George Brazillev.

Shub, D. 1948: *Lenin.* Garden City, N.Y.: Doubleday; London: Penguin (1966).

Silberner, Edmund 1962: *Sozialisten zur Judenfrage.* Berlin: Colloquium Verlag. (The chapter on Marx, originally published as 'Was Marx an Anti-Semite?' in *Historia Judaica* 11 (1949).)

Silnitsky, F., *et al.* eds. 1979: *Communism and Eastern Europe.* New York: Karz.

Simons, H.J. and Simons, R.E. 1969: *Class and Colour in South Africa 1850–1950.* London: Penguin.

Sinclair, Louis 1972: *Leon Trotsky: A Bibliography.* Stanford, Calif.: Hoover Bibliographical Services.

Skocpol, Theda 1979: *States and Social Revolutions.* Cambridge and New York: Cambridge University Press.

Slater, Phil, ed. 1980: *Outlines of a Critique of Technology.* London: Ink Links; Atlantic Highlands, N.J.: Humanities.

Smart, D.A. 1978: *Pannekoek and Gorter's Marxism.* London: Pluto.

Smith, Joan, Evers, Hans-Dieter and Wallerstein, Immanuel, eds. 1984: *Households and the World Economy.* Beverly Hills: Sage.

Smith, R.E.F. 1968: *The Enserfment of the Russian Peasantry.* Cambridge and New York: Cambridge University Press.

Sobolev, A.I., *et al.* 1971: *Outline History of the Communist International.* Moscow: Progress.

Sobrino, J. 1978: *Spirituality of Liberation.* Maryknoll, NY: Orbis.

Société Jean Bodin 1959: *Le Servage.* 2nd edn. Brussels: Éditions de la Librarie encyclopédique.

Sohn-Rethel, Alfred 1978: *Intellectual and Manual Labor*. London: Macmillan; Atlantic Highlands, N.J.: Humanities.

Sombart, Werner 1906 (*1976*): *Why is there no Socialism in the United States?* London: Macmillan; White Plains, N.Y.: International Arts and Sciences Press.

Sorel, Georges 1906 (*1969*): *The Illusions of Progress*. Berkeley, Los Angeles and London: University of California Press.

—— 1906 (*1972*): *Reflections on Violence*. New York: Macmillan.

—— 1919 (*1981*): *Matériaux d'une théorie du prolétariat*. Paris and Geneva: Slatkine.

—— 1976: *From Georges Sorel: Essays in Socialism and Philosophy*. New York and London: Oxford University Press.

Souvarine, B. 1935 (*1938*): *Stalin: A Critical Survey of Bolshevism*. London: Secker & Warburg; New York: Alliance Book Corp.

Sowell, T. 1960: Marx's 'Increasing Misery' Doctrine. *American Economic Review* March.

Spence, Jonathan D. 1982: *The Gate of Heavenly Peace: The Chinese and their Revolution, 1895–1980*. London: Faber & Faber.

Spitzer, Alan B. 1957: *Revolutionary Theories of Louis-Auguste Blanqui*. New York and London: Columbia University Press.

Springborg, Patricia 1981: *The Problem of Human Needs and the Critique of Civilisation*. London: Allen & Unwin.

Sraffa, Piero 1960: *The Production of Commodities by Means of Commodities*. Cambridge: Cambridge University Press.

Sraffa, Piero, with the collaboration of M.H. Dobb, eds. 1951: *The Work and Correspondence of David Ricardo*. Cambridge: Cambridge University Press.

Srinivas, M.N., *et al.* 1959: Caste: A Trend Report and Bibliography. *Current Sociology* 8.3.

Stack, C. 1974: *All Our Kin*. New York: Harper & Row.

Stalin, Joseph V. 1901–34 (*1952–5*): *Works* vols. 1–13. London: Lawrence & Wishart.

—— 1913 (*1936*): Marxism and the National Question. In *Marxism and the National and Colonial Question*. London: Lawrence and Wishart; New York: International Publishers.

—— 1924a: The Foundations of Leninism. Repr. in *The Essential Stalin*, ed. B. Franklin.

—— 1924b (*1945*): *Problems of Leninism*. Moscow: Foreign Languages Publishing House.

—— 1925–7 (*1975*): *On Chinese Revolution*. Calcutta: Suren Dutt.

—— 1928 (*1953*): On the Grain Front. In *Problems of Leninism*. Moscow: Foreign Languages.

—— 1938: *Dialectical and Historical Materialism*. New York: International Publishers; London:

Lawrence & Wishart (1940).

—— 1940: *Leninism*. London: Allen & Unwin.

—— 1950: Marxism in Linguistics. Supplement to *New Times* 26, 28 June.

—— 1952: *Economic Problems of Socialism in the USSR*. New York: International Publishers.

—— 1972: *The Essential Stalin: Major Theoretical Writings, 1905–1952*. Ed. Bruce Franklin. Garden City, N.Y.: Anchor.

Stanley, John L. 1982: *The Sociology of Virtue: The Political and Social Theories of Georges Sorel*. Berkeley: University of California Press.

Starr, John Bryan 1979: *Continuing the Revolution. The Political Thought of Mao*. Princeton, N.J. and London: Princeton University Press.

Stedman Jones, G. 1973: Engels and the End of Classical German Philosophy. *New Left Review* 79.

—— 1977: Engels and the Genesis of Marxism. *New Left Review* 106.

Stedman Jones, G. *et al.* 1977: *Western Marxism: A Critical Reader*.

Steedman, Ian 1977: *Marx after Sraffa*. London: New Left; New York: distr. Schocken.

Steedman, Ian, Sweezy, Paul, *et al.* 1981: *The Value Controversy*. London: New Left and Verso; New York: distr. Schocken.

Steenson, Gary P. 1979: *Karl Kautsky 1854–1938*. Pittsburgh: University of Pittsburgh Press.

Steindl, Josef 1952: *Maturity and Stagnation in American Capitalism*. Oxford: Basil Blackwell; New York: Monthly Review Press.

Stojanović, Svetozar 1973: *Between Ideals and Reality: A Critique of Socialism and its Future*. New York and Oxford: Oxford University Press.

Stolz, Georges 1938: *Paul Lafargue: théoricien militant du socialisme*. Paris: Éditions Nouveau Promethée.

Stone, Lawrence 1965: *The Crisis of the Aristocracy*. Oxford and New York: Oxford University Press.

Struve, P.B., 1933–1935: My Contacts and Conflicts with Lenin (2 parts). *Slavonic Review* 12 and 13.

Subaltern Studies 1982– : ed. Ranajit Guha. Delhi: Oxford University Press.

Suh Kwang-sun, D. 1983: A Biographical Sketch of an Asian Theology. In *Minjung Theology: People as the Subjects of History*, ed. Commission on Theological Concerns of the Christian Conference of Asia. Maryknoll, NY: Orbis.

Sunkel, Osvaldo 1969: National Development Policy and External Dependence in Latin America. *Journal of Development Studies* 6.1.

Sunkel, Osvaldo and Paz, Pedro 1970: *El subdesarrollo latinoamericano y la teoria del desarrollo*. Mexico: Siglio XXI.

Sweezy, Paul 1946: *The Theory of Capitalist Development*. New York and London: Monthly Review Press.

—— ed. 1949: 'Karl Marx and the Close of his System',

by Eugen von Böhm-Bawerk, and 'Böhm-Bawerk's Criticism of Marx' by Rudolf Hilferding. New York: Augustus M. Kelley; London: Merlin (1972).

—— 1952: The Influence of Marxism on Thorstein Veblen. In Donald Drew Egbert and Stow Persons, eds. *Socialism and American Life*, vol. 1. Princeton: Princeton University Press.

—— 1976: Essay reprinted in R. Hilton, ed., *The Transition from Feudalism to Capitalism*.

—— 1980: *Post-Revolutionary Society*. New York: Monthly Review Press.

—— *Monthly Review Press* 32.5.

Syrè, L. 1984: *Isaac Deutscher – Marxist Publizist Historiker: Sein Leben und Werk 1907–1967*. Hamburg: Junius Verlag.

Szentes, Tamas 1973: *The Political Economy of Underdevelopment*. Budapest: Akademiai Kiado.

Tardos, M. 1986: The Conditions of Developing a Regulated Market. *Acta Oeconomica* 36. 1–2 (Budapest).

Taylor, F. 1929 (1948): The Guidance of Production in a Socialist State. In O. Lange and F. Taylor, *On the Economic Theory of Socialism*, ed. B. Lippincott. New York, Toronto and London: McGraw Hill.

Taylor, Ian 1975: *Critical Criminology*. London and Boston: Routledge & Kegan Paul.

Taylor, Ian, Walton, Paul and Young, Jock 1973: *The New Criminology: For a Social Theory of Deviance*. New York: Harper & Row; London: Routledge & Kegan Paul.

Taylor, John G. 1979: *From Modernisation to Modes of Production*. London and New York: Macmillan; Atlantic Highlands, N.J.: Humanities.

Terray, Emmanuel 1969 (1972): *Marxism and 'Primitive Societies'*. New York: Monthly Review Press.

—— 1975: Classes and class-consciousness in the Abron Kingdom of Gyaman. In M. Bloch, ed., *Marxist Analyses and Social Anthropology*.

Tersen, Bruhat Dantry 1970: *La Commune de 1871*. 2nd edn. Paris: Éditions sociales.

Thapar, Romila 1966: *A History of India* Vol. I. London and Baltimore: Penguin.

Therborn, Göran 1978: *What does the Ruling Class do when it Rules?* London: New Left; New York: distr. Schocken.

Thomas, Paul 1980: *Karl Marx and the Anarchists*. London and Boston: Routledge & Kegan Paul.

Thompson, E.P. 1955 (1976): *William Morris: Romantic to Revolutionary*. 2nd edn, shortened with postscript.

—— 1963: *The Making of the English Working Class*. London: Gollancz; New York: Pantheon.

—— 1975: *Whigs and Hunters: The Origin of the Black Act*. New York: Pantheon.

—— 1978a: *The Poverty of Theory*. London: Merlin; New York: Monthly Review Press.

—— 1978b: Eighteenth-century English Society: Class Struggle without Class? *Social History* 3.

Thompson, John 1981: *Critical Hermeneutics*. Cambridge and New York: Cambridge University Press.

—— 1990: *Ideology and Modern Culture*. Cambridge: Polity.

Thompson, John and Held, David, eds. 1982: *Habermas: Critical Debates*. London: Macmillan; Cambridge, Mass.: MIT Press.

Thomson, George 1941: *Aeschylus and Athens: A Study in the Social Origins of the Drama*. London: Lawrence & Wishart; New York: International Publishers (1950).

—— 1949: *An Essay on Religion*. London: Lawrence & Wishart, Repr. 1954.

Thorner, Daniel 1966: Marx on India and the Asiatic Mode of Production. *Contributions to Indian Sociology* 9.

Thorner, Daniel et al., eds. 1966: *The Theory of the Peasant Economy*. Homewood, Illinois: Richard D. Irwin.

Tilly, Louise A. and Tilly, Charles, eds. 1981: *Class Conflict and Collective Action*. Beverly Hills and London: Sage.

Timpanaro, S. 1976: *On Materialism*. London: New Left; New York: distr. Schocken.

Tökei, F. 1979: *Essays on the Asiatic Mode of Production*. Budapest: Akademische Verlag.

Tönnies, Ferdinand 1887 (1955): *Community and Association*. London: Routledge & Kegan Paul; East Lancing, Michigan: State University Press (1957).

Topham, A.J. and Coates, Ken 1968: *Industrial Democracy in Great Britain*. London: MacGibbon & Kee.

Torr, Dona, ed. 1940: *Marxism, Nationality and War*. London: Lawrence & Wishart.

—— 1956: *Tom Mann and His Times*. London: Lawrence & Wishart.

Tortajada, R. 1977: A Note on Reduction of Complex Labour to Simple Labour. *Capital and Class* 1.

Toynbee, Arnold 1934–61: *A Study of History*. 12 vols. Oxford and New York: Oxford University Press.

Trigger, B.G. 1980: *Gordon Childe: Revolutions in Archaeology*. London: Thames & Hudson.

Trotsky, Leon D. 1904 (1980): *Our Political Tasks*. London: New Park.

—— 1920 (1961): *Terrorism and Communism*. Ann Arbor: University of Michigan Press.

—— 1932–3: *History of the Russian Revolution*. London: Victor Gollancz. Repr. 1967 Sphere. Ann Arbor: University of Michigan Press.

—— 1937: *The Revolution Betrayed: What is the Soviet Union and Where is it Going?* London: Faber (trans. Max Eastman); London: New Park (1957); New York: Pathfinder (1972).

—— 1962: *The Permanent Revolution and Results and Prospects*. New York: Pioneer; London: New Park.

—— 1963: *My Life*. New York: Grosset & Dunlap.
—— 1971a: *Military Writings*. New York: Pathfinder.
—— 1971b: *The Struggle against Fascism in Germany*. New York: Pathfinder.
—— 1973a: *Problems of Everyday Life and Other Writings on Culture and Science*. New York: Moned.
—— 1973b: *The Transitional Programme for Socialist Revolution*, with introductory essays by J. Hansen and G. Novack. New York: Pathfinder.

Trotsky, Leon, Dewey, John and Novack, George (1969): *Their Morals and Ours: Marxist versus Liberal Views on Morality*. 4th edn. New York: Pathfinder.

Tucker, D.F.B. 1980: *Marxism and Individualism*. Oxford: Basil Blackwell. New York: St Martin's.

Tucker, Robert C. 1973: *Stalin as Revolutionary, 1879–1929: a Study in History and Personality*. New York: Norton.
—— 1977: *Stalinism*. New York: W.W. Norton.

Tudor, H. and Tudor, J.M. eds. 1988: *Marxism and Social Democracy: The Revisionist Debate 1896–1898*. Cambridge: Cambridge University Press.

Tugan-Baranowsky, M.I. 1908: *Der moderne Sozialismus in seiner geschichtlichen Entwicklung*. Dresden: Böhmert.

Turner, Bryan S. 1974: *Weber and Islam: A Critical Study*. London: Routledge & Kegan Paul.
—— 1978: *Marx and the End of Orientalism*. London: Allen and Unwin.

Tuzmuhamedov, R. 1973: *How the National Question was Solved in Soviet Central Asia*. Moscow: Progress.

Ulam, A.B. 1965: *Lenin and the Bolsheviks*. London: Collins; New York: Macmillan (under the title *The Bolsheviks*).

Uno, Kozo 1964 (1980): *Principles of Political Economy: Theory of a Purely Capitalist Society*. Trans. Thomas Sekine. Brighton: Harvester; Atlantic Highlands, N.J.: Humanities.

Urlanis, B.T. 1941: *The Growth of Population in Europe*. (In Russian). Moscow.

Vajda, M. 1981: *The State and Socialism*. London: Allison & Busby; New York: St Martin's.

Van Den Berghe, Pierre 1978: *Race and Racism: A Comparative Perspective*. New York: Wiley.

Varga, Eugene 1948: *Changes in the Economy of Capitalism Resulting from the Second World War* (mimeo). Washington.

Vázquez, Adolfo Sanches 1973: *Art and Society: Essays in Marxist Aesthetics*. London: Merlin; New York: Monthly Review Press.

Veblen, Thorstein 1891 (1961): Some Neglected Points in the Theory of Socialism. *Annals of the American Academy of Political and Social Science*, Nov. Reprinted in T. Veblen, *The Place of Science in Modern Civilisation and Other Essays*. New York: Russell & Russell.

—— 1899 (1953): *The Theory of the Leisure Class: An Economic Study of Institutions*. New York: New American Library.
—— 1904: *The Theory of Business Enterprise*. New York: Scribner.
—— 1906–7 (1961): The Socialist Economics of Karl Marx and his Followers. *Quarterly Journal of Economics*, Aug. 1906, Feb. 1907. Reprinted in T. Veblen, *The Place of Science in Modern Civilisation and Other Essays*. New York: Russell & Russell.
—— 1919 (1961): *The Place of Science in Modern Civilisation and Other Essays*. New York: Russell & Russell.
—— 1921: *The Engineers and the Price System*. New York: Huebsch.
—— 1923 (1945): *Absentee Ownership and Business Enterprise in Recent Times: The Case of America*. New York: Viking.

Veliz, Claudio, ed., 1965: *Obstacles to Change in Latin America*. Oxford and New York: Oxford University Press.

Venable, Vernon 1946 (1966): *Human Nature: The Marxian View*. Cleveland, Ohio: Meridian; London: Denis Dobson (1946).

Venturi, F. 1960: *Roots of Revolution*. London: Weidenfeld & Nicolson; New York: Knopf.

Verlinden, C. 1955–77: *L'esclavage dans l'Europe médiévale*, 2 vols. University of Ghent.

Vernon, Richard 1978: *Commitment and Change: Georges Sorel and the Idea of Revolution*. Toronto and Buffalo: University of Toronto Press.

Vertov, Dziga 1984: *Kino-Eye: The Writings of Dziga Vertov*, ed. and intro. Annette Michelson. Berkeley: University of California Press.

Vico, Giambattista 1744 (1968): *The New Science*. Ithaca and London: Cornell University Press.

Volker, Klaus 1975: *Brecht Chronicle*. New York: Seabury.

Vološinov, V.N. 1973: *Marxism and the Philosophy of Language*. New York and London: Seminar Press.

von Stein, Lorenz 1842 (1964): *The Social Movement in France*. Totowa, N.J.: Bedminster Press.

Vranicki, Predrag 1972, 1974: *Geschichte des Marxismus*. 2 vols. Frankfurt am Main: Suhrkamp.

Vygotsky, L.S. 1934 (1986): *Thought and Language*. Cambridge, Mass.: MIT Press.

Wagner, Adolph 1879: *Allgemeine oder theoretische Volkswirthschaftslehre, Erster Teil, Grundlegung*. Leipzig and Heidelberg: C.F. Winter'sche Verlagshandlung.

Walicki, A. 1969: *The Controversy over Capitalism*. Oxford: Clarendon Press.
—— 1980: Marx, Engels and the Polish Question. *Dialectics and Humanism* (Warsaw), No. 1, pp. 5–32.

Walker, P. ed. 1980: *Between Capital and Labour*. London: Harvester.

Waller, Michael 1981: *Democratic Centralism: An*

Historical Commentary. Manchester: Manchester University Press.

Wallerstein, Immanuel 1974: *The Modern World-Economy.* Cambridge: Cambridge University Press.

—— 1982: Fernand Braudel, Historian, *homme de la conjoncture. Radical History Review* 26, pp. 105–19.

Walras, L. 1954: *Elements of Pure Economics.* Homewood, Ill.: Irwin.

Ware, Robert and Neilsen, Kai eds. 1989: Analyzing Marxism. *Canadian Journal of Philosophy* 15, suppl. vol.

Warren, B. 1973: Imperialism and Capitalist Industrialization. *New Left Review* 81 (Sept./Oct.).

—— 1980: *Imperialism: Pioneer of Capitalism.* London: New Left; New York: distr. Schocken.

Warren, Mark 1987: The Marx–Darwin Question: Implications for the Critical Aspects of Marx's Social Theory. *International Sociology* 2.

Wartofsky, Marx W. 1977: *Feuerbach.* Cambridge and New York: Cambridge University Press.

Watkinson, Ray 1966 (*1990*): *William Morris as Designer.* London: Trefoil.

Watson, J.L. ed. 1980: *Asian and African Systems of Slavery.* Oxford: Basil Blackwell; Berkeley: University of California Press.

Webb, Sidney and Beatrice 1920: *Industrial Democracy.* London and New York: Longman.

Weber, Max 1904 (*1976*): *The Protestant Ethic and the Spirit of Capitalism.* London: Allen & Unwin.

—— 1918 (*1970*): 'Socialism'. In J.E.T. Eldridge ed., *Max Weber: The Interpretation of Social Reality.* London: Michael Joseph.

—— 1921 (*1968*): *Economy and Society.* 3 vols. New York: Bedminster.

Weeks, John 1981a: *Capital and Exploitation.* Princeton: Princeton University Press; London: Edward Arnold.

—— 1981b: The Differences between dependency theory and Marxian theory and why they matter. *Latin American Perspectives.*

Weimann, Robert 1976: *Structure and Society in Literary History.* Charlottesville: University Press of Virginia.

Weiner, Richard 1981: *Cultural Marxism and Political Sociology.* Beverly Hills and London: Sage.

Wellmer, Albrecht 1974: *Critical Theory of Society.* New York: Seabury.

—— 1988: Critique of Marx's Positivism. In Bottomore, ed., *Interpretations of Marx.*

Welskopf, E.C. 1957: *Der Produktionsverhältnisse im alten Orient und in der griechischrömischen Antike.* Berlin: Akademie-Verlag.

Wersky, Gary 1978: *The Visible College.* London: Allen Lane; New York: Holt Rinehart & Winston.

Wertsch, J.V., ed. 1981: *The Concept of Activity in Soviet Psychology.* Armonte, N.Y.: M.E. Sharpe.

Weselowski, W. 1979: *Classes, Strata and Power.* London and Boston: Routledge & Kegan Paul.

Westergard-Thorpe, W. 1978: Towards a Syndicalist International: the 1913 London Congress. *International Review of Social History* 23.

Wetter, Gustav A. 1952 (*1958*): *Dialectical Materialism: A Historical and Systematic Survey of Philosophy in the Soviet Union.* London: Routledge & Kegan Paul; New York: Praeger.

White, Leslie A. 1959: *The Evolution of Culture.* New York: McGraw Hill.

White, S.K. 1988: *The Recent Work of Jürgen Habermas: Reason, Justice and Modernity.* Cambridge: Cambridge University Press.

Wielenga, Bastiaan 1976: *Marxist Views on India in Historical Perspective.* Madras: Christian Literature Society.

Willett, John 1968: *Theatre of Bertolt Brecht.* 3rd rev. edn. New York: New Directions.

—— 1978: *The New Sobriety 1917–1933: Art and Politics in the Weimar Period.* London: Thames & Hudson; New York: Pantheon.

Williams, Christopher, ed. 1980: *Realism and the Cinema: A Reader.* London: Routledge & Kegan Paul.

Williams, G.A. 1975: *Proletarian Order.* London: Pluto.

Williams, Raymond 1958: *Culture and Society: 1780–1950.* London: Chatto & Windus.

—— 1961: *The Long Revolution.* London: Chatto & Windus.

—— 1971: Literature and Society: In Memory of Lucien Goldmann. *New Left Review* 67.

—— 1973: *The Country and the City.* London: Chatto & Windus; New York: Oxford University Press.

—— 1974: *Television: Technology and Cultural Form.* London: Fontana/Collins.

—— 1976: *Keywords.* London: Fontana; New York: Oxford University Press.

—— 1977: *Marxism and Literature.* Oxford and New York: Oxford University Press.

—— 1979: *Politics and Letters.* London: New Left; New York: distr. Schocken.

—— 1980: *Problems in Materialism and Culture: Selected Essays.* London: New Left (Verso Edns); New York: distr. Schocken.

—— 1981: *Culture.* Glasgow: Fontana.

—— 1983: *Towards 2000.* London: Chatto & Windus.

—— 1989: *The Politics of Modernism: Against the New Conformists,* ed. Tony Pinkney. London: Verso.

—— 1989–90: *People of the Black Mountains.* 2 vols. London: Chatto & Windus.

Wilson, Dick 1977: *Mao Tse-tung in the Scales of History.* Cambridge and New York: Cambridge University Press.

Winkler, H.A., ed. 1974: *Organisierter Kapitalismus: Voraussetzungen und Anfänge.* Göttingen: Vandenhoeck & Ruprecht.

Wirth, Margaret 1972: *Kapitalismustheorie in der DDR*. Frankfurt am Main: Suhrkamp.

Wittfogel, Karl A. 1957: *Oriental Despotism: A Comparative Study of Total Power*. New Haven: Yale University Press.

Witt-Hansen, J. 1960: *Historical Materialism: The Method, the Theories*. Copenhagen: Munksgaard.

Woddis, J. 1972: *New Theories of Revolution*. London: Lawrence & Wishart; New York: International Publishers.

Wolf, E.R. 1957: Closed corporate communities in Mesoamerica and Central Java. *Southwestern Journal of Anthropology* 13.1, 1–18.

Wolf, Eric R. 1971: *Peasant Wars of the Twentieth Century*. London: Faber & Faber.

Wolf, Dieter 1979: *Hegel und Marx. Zur Bewegungsstruktur des absoluten Geistes und des Kapitals*.

Wolfe, B.D. 1956 (1966): *Three Who Made a Revolution*. London: Penguin; Boston: Beacon (1959).

Wolin, Richard 1982: *Walter Benjamin: An Aesthetic of Redemption*. New York: Columbia University Press.

Womack, Brantly 1982: *The Foundations of Mao Zedong's Political Thought*. Honolulu: Hawaii University Press.

Wood, Allen 1972: The Marxian Critique of Justice. *Philosophy and Public Affairs* 1.

—— 1981: *Karl Marx*. London and Boston: Routledge & Kegan Paul.

Woodcock, George 1956: *Pierre-Joseph Proudhon*. London: Routledge & Kegan Paul; New York: Macmillan.

—— 1963 (1986): *Anarchism*. London: Penguin; Cleveland: Meridian.

World Socialist System and Anti-Communism 1972. Moscow: Progress.

Wright, Erik Olin 1978: *Class, Crisis and the State*. London: New Left; New York: distr. Schocken.

Yaffe, D. 1976: Hodgson and Activist Reformism. *Revolutionary Communist*.

Young, Gary 1978: Justice and Capitalist Production: Marx and Bourgeois Ideology. *Canadian Journal of Philosophy* 8.

Young, Robert M. 1977: Science *is* Social Relations. *Radical Science Journal* 5.

—— 1978: Getting Started on Lysenkoism. *Radical Science Journal* 6/7.

—— 1979: Science is a Labour Process. *Science for People* 43/44.

Zelený, Jindřich, 1980: *The Logic of Marx*. Trans. Terrell Carver. Oxford: Basil Blackwell; New York: Rowman & Littlefield.

Zenushkina, L. 1975: *Soviet Nationalities Policy and Bourgeois Historians*. Moscow: Progress.

Zirkle, Conway 1949: *Death of a Science in Russia*. Philadelphia: University of Pennsylvania Press.

Zubaida, Sami, ed. 1970: *Race and Racialism*. London: Tavistock; Totowa, N.J.: Barnes & Noble.

Index

Note: Headwords and page references to entries on a subject are in bold type. References to Marx, Engels, and major countries have been largely omitted. Most text entries contain cross-references in capital letters to other entries: these have not been included in the Index.